Mass Media Law

17th Edition

Mass Media Law

17th Edition

Don R. Pember
University of Washington

Clay Calvert
University of Florida

McGraw Hill

Connect
Learn
Succeed™

Published by McGraw-Hill, an imprint of The McGraw-Hill Companies, Inc., 1221 Avenue of the
Americas, New York, NY 10020. Copyright © 2011. All rights reserved. No part of this publication may
be reproduced or distributed in any form or by any means, or stored in a database or retrieval system,
without the prior written consent of The McGraw-Hill Companies, Inc., including, but not limited to, in
any network or other electronic storage or transmission, or broadcast for distance learning.

This book is printed on acid-free paper.

1 2 3 4 5 6 7 8 9 0 DOC / DOC 0

ISBN-13: 978-0-07-351197-9
MHID: 0-07-351197-8

Vice President, Editorial: *Michael Ryan*
Sponsoring Editor: *Katie Stevens*
Managing Editor: *Meghan Campbell*
Developmental Editor: *Craig Leonard*
Marketing Manager: *Pamela Cooper*
Production Editor: *Brett Coker*
Production Service: *Deepti Narwat Agarwal, Glyph International*
Manuscript Editor: *Sharon O'Donnell*
Designer: *Ashley Bedell*
Manager, Photo Research: *Brian J. Pecko*
Production Supervisor: *Louis Swaim*
Media Project Manager: *Thomas Brierly*
Composition: *10/12 Times Roman by Glyph International*
Printing: *45# New Era Matte Plus by R. R. Donnelley & Sons*

Cover: Columns and pediment, Dade County courthouse, Florida, USA. © Dennie Cody/ Getty Images/ Taxi

Members of the international media gather at the gates of the High Court. © Ian Waldie/ Getty Images/ Reportage

The Internet addresses listed in the text were accurate at the time of publication. The inclusion of a
Web site does not indicate an endorsement by the authors or McGraw-Hill, and McGraw-Hill does not
guarantee the accuracy of the information presented at these sites.

www.mhhe.com

CONTENTS

6 Libel: Defenses and Damages _____ 205

7 Invasion of Privacy:
Appropriation and Intrusion _____ 241

8 Invasion of Privacy: Publication of Private Information and False Light ——————— 277

9 Gathering Information: Records and Meetings ——————— 303

PREFACE

Consider this new edition to be like a well-stocked restaurant buffet, loaded with items. You can pick and choose lots of different topics and subjects to read and study, while simultaneously opting not to address some others. Rather than attempting during one semester or term to cover the entire book, you might select particular ideas on which to devote more attention and depth. For instance, one of the authors of this book devotes an entire class period to the topic "Real-Life Violence: Blaming Movies, Video Games and Books" (Chapter 2), another lecture focuses solely on "Censorship of Expression in Public High Schools" (Chapter 3) and one class period covers FCC regulation in "Obscene, Indecent and Profane Material" (Chapter 16). All three topics are lively, interesting and important to students. Simultaneously, that same author does not cover material in other chapters and units of the book. In brief, don't feel, either as an instructor or student, that you must rush through the entire book; study some areas in depth, particularly those that are most relevant to your interests and needs.

This edition is packed with new material—cases, statutes and examples—across all chapters. Media law is constantly changing, with new issues and controversies cropping up daily. We have done our best to capture those developments here.

Even the foundational chapter—Chapter 1—includes new content on overruling precedent, with an updated example and a numbered list of reasons why courts are most likely to overrule precedent. It also now addresses how state constitutions can give more speech rights to citizens than the U.S. Constitution, as well as providing all-new material on federal magistrate judges and updated information on federal courts.

Chapter 2 provides new examples and devotes more attention to "community censorship" (including corporate self-censorship—think Wal-Mart not selling Green Day's latest CD "21st Century Breakdown"), which can be just as powerful today as government censorship. Chapter 2 also introduces the "symbolic speech doctrine," which is used by courts for deciding when conduct (for example, burning a flag) rises to the level of speech for First Amendment purposes. New examples of controversial political speech and the right to criticize the government are covered in Chapter 2, as well as new issues involving prior restraints of speech on the Internet.

Chapter 3, devoted to contemporary First Amendment problems, includes new material in nearly all of its many units, including censorship during wartime; free speech in public high schools and universities; book banning; hate speech and fighting words; campaign finance reform; and net neutrality. Chapter 3 is one of those chapters where you might decide to cover some niche areas but not others.

Libel and privacy law (Chapters 4, 5, 6, 7 and 8) have remained relatively stable over the past two years, but there has been no shortage of new cases, many of which are included here. Perhaps the most interesting and ominous development in libel is the growth of "libel tourism"—American celebrities and public figures suing American media companies in countries other than the United States. The Internet broke down international barriers in many ways, including legal ones, and much of what is published and broadcast in the United States today finds its way overseas. Because British libel laws protect plaintiffs far more than laws in the United States where the First Amendment helps shield media defendants, many more cases of libel are being filed in the United Kingdom, based on material originally published in the United States and designed for domestic consumption.

Important new issues in Chapter 9 are FOIA reform and whether President Barack Obama will make good on his promise of greater government transparency and openness to information. Chapter 9 also includes new and/or revised material on FERPA, HIPAA and the Privacy Act.

An emerging area of law covered in Chapter 10 in which a great deal has transpired in the past two years is anonymous speech posted on the Internet. One only needs to think about the erstwhile Web site JuicyCampus.com and the offensive comments that were posted there anonymously to realize the importance of this issue. In addition, since the last edition of the book, four states—Texas, Maine, Hawaii and Utah—have added shield laws to protect journalists from revealing information in court, and the Free Flow of Information Act of 2009 was pending in Congress that would create a federal shield law.

Two developments in the free press–fair trial area, addressed in Chapter 11, are worth noting. First, the seemingly never-ending issue of the use of military commissions to try suspected terrorists, and the ancillary issue of whether these tribunals would be accessible to the public and the press, remain open matters. While some speculated that President Obama would abandon these tribunals in favor of open hearings in federal courts, at this point he has chosen to keep at least a modified version of the commissions in use. Who knows whether they will be open or closed to the public.

The growing use of electronic equipment in courtrooms also is highlighted in this edition in Chapter 12. These topics range from bloggers reporting directly from courtrooms during trials and the webcasting of civil trials held in federal courtrooms to the use of personal communication texting devices by jurors to communicate with others outside the courtroom during a trial and seek information not introduced at trial about a case.

Chapter 13 is replete with information on the federal government's crackdown on sexually explicit speech, including the 2008 obscenity conviction of adult producer Paul Little. It also covers the new and timely issue of "sexting"—when minors become their own child pornographers by taking and texting sexually explicit images of themselves to other minors as a high-tech form of flirting or invitation to sex.

There have been many developments in the copyright area in the past 24 months, including some widely publicized cases (e.g., the J.K. Rowling/Harry Potter Lexicon trial and the Shepard Fairey/AP case involving the Obama HOPE poster). As the recession drains revenue from mass media companies, many are becoming more aggressive, attacking others who use their creations without paying the tab. The Associated Press is clamping down on other Web content providers who republish its material without permission or pay. Viacom continues its billion-dollar lawsuit against YouTube for transmitting copyrighted matter, and video production companies like film and television studios are mounting new attacks to stop the illegal streaming of TV shows and films. Copyright issues also arose during the 2008 political campaign as candidates, including John McCain, used copyrighted music in campaign ads without permission.

Finally, Chapters 15 and 16 discuss new developments in the areas of advertising and telecommunications regulation. For instance, Chapter 16 covers the U.S. Supreme Court's 2009 decision in *FCC* v. *Fox Television Stations, Inc.* affecting the Federal Communications Commission's ability to regulate broadcast indecency.

You will notice there is not a separate chapter devoted to speech on the Internet. That is because Internet-based regulations of expression cut across nearly all of the substantive areas of media law covered in the book, from libel and privacy to obscenity and advertising. Icons are placed in the margins next to Web-centric discussions, such as Chapter 3's section called "The First Amendment and the Information Superhighway." This preface also includes a list of such material.

As this book went to press, two important Supreme Court cases were pending on which you should keep a close eye: *Citizens United* v. *Federal Election Commission* and *United States* v. *Stevens*.

Oral argument in *Citizens United* occurred in September 2009. The high court's decision in this case will impact the future of the Bipartisan Campaign Reform Act of 2002 and, in particular, federal regulations limiting ads funded by corporations and unions that target political candidates (see Chapter 3, "The First Amendment and Election Campaigns"). The speech at issue in *Citizens United* is a full-length documentary critical of Hillary Rodham Clinton called "Hillary: The Movie" that the Federal Elections Commission considered to be the equivalent of a campaign ad attacking Clinton while she was seeking to be the Democratic presidential candidate in 2008.

In *Stevens*, the high court will consider the constitutionality of a federal statute banning the sale of movies and other images depicting animal cruelty unless the content has serious religious, political, scientific, educational, journalistic, historical or artistic value. The law was designed to stop people from profiting from the unlawful torturing and killing of animals, but it also raises First Amendment concerns because it targets speech products (movies and magazines) rather than the underlying illegal conduct. If the court upholds the law, it will be carving out another area of speech that, like fighting words and obscenity, is not protected by the First Amendment.

Many hands are needed to produce a book. Don R. Pember would like to single out three people for special recognition. Thanks to my co-author Clay Calvert who graciously picked up the slack when I had some medical issues. Thanks to editor Craig Leonard, who listens patiently to complaints from a curmudgeonly author. And special thanks and a nomination for sainthood to my wife Diann, who helped me get through both the trauma and inconvenience of a badly broken leg.

Clay Calvert thanks his co-author, Don R. Pember, for imparting his sage advice and wisdom about both writing and media law over the past four editions of the textbook. He also thanks both Don and Craig Leonard for guiding him through the publishing process. Professor Calvert also thanks the cadre of undergraduates who reviewed drafts of many of the changes in his chapters. Those individuals are Bryanna Hahn, Andrew McGill and Alexandra Petri. Finally, he thanks the University of Florida and Dean John Wright for relieving him from winter driving duties in Pennsylvania—something for which a California boy never was made.

IMPORTANT NEW, EXPANDED OR UPDATED MATERIAL

The following are merely highlights of new, expanded or updated material. Other new and revised content appears in this edition that is not listed below.

Overruling precedent: New example and list of factors, pages 4–5

Article III judges and federal magistrate judges, page 22

Sonia Sotomayor: The newest high court justice, page 24

WEB MATERIAL

CHAPTER 1

The American Legal System

Before studying mass media law, a student must first have a general background in the law and the judicial system. In the United States, as in most societies, law is a basic part of existence, as necessary for the survival of civilization as are economic systems, political systems, mass communication systems, cultural achievement and the family.

This chapter has two purposes: to acquaint readers with the law and to outline the legal system in the United States. While this is not designed to be a comprehensive course in law and the judicial system, it does provide sufficient introduction to understand the remaining 15 chapters.

The chapter opens with a discussion of the law, giving consideration to the most important sources of the law in the United States, and moves on to the judicial system, including both the federal and state court systems. A summary of judicial review and a brief outline of how both criminal and civil lawsuits are started and proceed through the courts are included in the discussion of the judicial system.

> **FIVE SOURCES OF LAW**
>
> 1. Common law
> 2. Equity law
> 3. Statutory law
> 4. Constitutional law
> 5. Executive orders and administrative rules

SOURCES OF THE LAW

There are many definitions of law. Some people say law is any social norm or any organized method of settling disputes. Most writers insist it is a bit more complex, that some system of sanctions is required for a genuine legal system. John Austin, a 19th-century English jurist, defined law as definite rules of human conduct with appropriate sanctions for their enforcement. He added that both the rules and the sanctions must be prescribed by duly constituted human authority.[1] Roscoe Pound, an American legal scholar, suggested that law is social engineering—the attempt to order the way people behave. For the purposes of this book, it is helpful to consider law to be a set of rules that attempt to guide human conduct and a set of formal, governmental sanctions that are applied when those rules are violated.

What is the source of American law? There are several major sources of the law in the United States: the Constitution; the common law; the law of equity; the statutory law; and the rulings of various executives, such as the president and mayors and governors, and administrative bodies and agencies. Historically, we trace American law to Great Britain. As colonizers of much of the North American continent, the British supplied Americans with an outline for both a legal system and a judicial system. In fact, because of the many similarities between British and American law, many people consider the Anglo-American legal system to be a single entity. Today, our federal Constitution is the supreme law of the land. Yet when each of these sources of law is considered separately, it is more useful to begin with the earliest source of Anglo-American law, the common law.

COMMON LAW

Common law,* which developed in England during the 200 years after the Norman Conquest in the 11th century, is one of the great legacies of the British people to colonial America. During those two centuries, the crude mosaic of Anglo-Saxon customs was replaced by a single system of law worked out by jurists and judges. The system of law became common throughout England; it became common law. It was also called common law to distinguish it from the ecclesiastical (church) law prevalent at the time. Initially, the customs of the people were used by the king's courts as the foundation of the law, disputes were resolved according to community custom, and governmental sanction was applied to enforce the resolution. As such, common law was, and still is, considered "discovered law."

---

* Terms that are in boldfaced type are defined in the glossary.
1. Abraham, *Judicial Process.*

As legal problems became more complex and as the law began to be professionally administered (the first lawyers appeared during this era, and eventually professional judges), it became clear that common law reflected not so much the custom of the land as the custom of the court—or more properly, the custom of judges. While judges continued to look to the past to discover how other courts decided a case when given similar facts (precedent is discussed in a moment), many times judges were forced to create the law themselves. Common law thus sometimes is known as judge-made law.

Common law thus sometimes is known as judge-made law.

Common law is an inductive system in which a legal rule is arrived at after consideration of many cases. (In a deductive system of law, which is common in many other nations, the rules are expounded first and then the court decides the legal situation under the existing rule.) Colonial America was a land of new problems for British and other settlers. The old law frequently did not work. But common law easily accommodated the new environment. The ability of common law to adapt to change is directly responsible for its longevity.

Fundamental to common law is the concept that judges should look to the past and follow court precedents.* The Latin expression for the concept is this: "Stare decisis et non quieta movere" (to stand by past decisions and not disturb things at rest). **Stare decisis** is the key phrase: Let the decision stand. A judge should resolve current problems in the same manner as similar problems were resolved in the past. Put differently, a judge will look to a prior case opinion to guide his or her analysis and decision in a current case. Following precedent is beneficial as it builds predictability and consistency into the law—which in turn fosters judicial legitimacy. Courts may be perceived as more legitimate in the public's eye if they are predictable and consistent in their decision-making process.

Stare decisis is the key phrase: Let the decision stand.

The Role of Precedent

At first glance one would think that the law never changes in a system that continually looks to the past. What if the first few rulings in a line of cases were bad decisions? Are the courts saddled with bad law forever? Fortunately, the law does not operate quite in this way. While following **precedent** is desired (many people say that certainty in the law is more important than justice), it is not always the proper way to proceed. To protect the integrity of common law, judges developed means of coping with bad law and new situations in which the application of old law would result in injustice.

Imagine that the newspaper in your hometown publishes a picture and story about a 12-year-old girl who gave birth to a 7-pound son in a local hospital. The mother and father do not like the publicity and sue the newspaper for invasion of privacy. The attorney for the parents finds a precedent, *Barber* v. *Time,*[2] in which a Missouri court ruled that to photograph a patient in a hospital room against her will and then to publish that picture in a newsmagazine is an **invasion of privacy.**

Does the existence of this precedent mean that the young couple will automatically win this lawsuit? Must the court follow and adopt the *Barber* decision? The answer to both questions is no. For one thing, there may be other cases in which courts have ruled that publishing such a picture

---

* Appellate courts (see page 14) often render decisions that decide only the particular case and do not establish binding precedent. Courts refer to these as "unpublished decisions." In some parts of the country it is even unlawful for a lawyer to mention these onetime rulings in legal papers submitted in later cases.
2. 159 S.W. 2d 291 (1942).

> **FOUR OPTIONS FOR HANDLING PRECEDENT**
>
> 1. Accept/Follow
> 2. Modify/Update
> 3. Distinguish
> 4. Overrule

is not an invasion of privacy. In fact, in 1956 in the case of *Meetze* v. *AP*[3] a South Carolina court made such a ruling. But for the moment assume that *Barber* v. *Time* is the only precedent. Is the court bound by this precedent? No. The court has several options concerning the 1942 decision.

First, it can *accept* the precedent as law and rule that the newspaper has invaded the privacy of the couple by publishing the picture and story about the birth of their child. When a court accepts a prior court ruling as precedent, it is adopting it and following it for guidance. Second, the court can *modify,* or change, the 1942 precedent by arguing that *Barber* v. *Time* was decided nearly 70 years ago when people were more sensitive about going to a hospital, since a stay there was often considered to reflect badly on a patient. Today hospitalization is no longer a sensitive matter to most people. Therefore, a rule of law restricting the publication of a picture of a hospital patient is unrealistic, unless the picture is in bad taste or needlessly embarrasses the patient. Then the publication may be an invasion of privacy. In our imaginary case, then, the decision turns on what kind of picture and story the newspaper published: a pleasant picture that flattered the couple or one that mocked and embarrassed them? If the court rules in this manner, it *modifies* the 1942 precedent, making it correspond to what the judge perceives to be contemporary sensibilities.

As a third option the court can decide that *Barber* v. *Time* provides an important precedent for a plaintiff hospitalized because of an unusual disease—as Dorothy Barber was—but that in the case before the court, the plaintiff was hospitalized to give birth to a baby, a different situation: Giving birth is a voluntary status; catching a disease is not. Because the two cases present different problems, they are really different cases. Hence, the *Barber* v. *Time* precedent does not apply. This practice is called *distinguishing the precedent from the current case,* a very common action. In brief, a court can distinguish a prior case (and therefore choose not to accept it and not to follow it) because it involves either different facts or different issues from the current case.

Finally, the court can *overrule* the precedent. When a court overrules precedent, it declares the prior decision wrong and thus no longer the law. Courts generally overrule prior opinions as bad law only when there are changes in:

1. factual knowledge and circumstances;
2. social mores and values; and/or
3. judges/justices on the court.

---

3. 95 S.E. 2d 606 (1956).

For instance, in 2003 the U.S. Supreme Court in *Lawrence* v. *Texas*[4] overruled its 1986 opinion called *Bowers* v. *Hardwick*[5] that had upheld a Georgia anti-sodomy statute prohibiting certain sexual acts between consenting gay adults. By 2003, American society increasingly accepted homosexuality (evidenced then by both the dwindling number of states that prohibited the conduct referenced in *Bowers* and by at least two Supreme Court rulings subsequent to *Bowers* but before *Lawrence* that were favorable to gay rights and thus eroded *Bowers'* strength). There also was growing recognition that consenting adults, regardless of sexual orientation, should possess the constitutional, personal liberty to engage in private sexual conduct of their choosing. Furthermore, six of the nine justices on the Supreme Court had changed from 1986 to 2003. Thus, 17 years after *Bowers* was decided, there were changes in social values, legal sentiment and the court's composition. The Supreme Court in *Lawrence* therefore struck down a Texas anti-sodomy statute similar to the Georgia one it had upheld in *Bowers*. It thus overruled *Bowers*. Justice Kennedy noted that although "the doctrine of stare decisis is essential to the respect accorded to the judgments of the court and to the stability of the law," it "is not, however, an inexorable command." In the hypothetical case involving the 12-year-old girl who gave birth, the only courts that can overrule the Missouri Supreme Court's opinion in *Barber* v. *Time* are the Missouri Supreme Court and the U.S. Supreme Court.

Obviously, the preceding discussion oversimplifies the judicial process. Rarely is a court confronted with only a single precedent. And whether or not precedent is binding on a court is often an issue. For example, decisions by the Supreme Court of the United States regarding the U.S. Constitution and federal laws are binding on all federal and state courts. Decisions by the U.S. Court of Appeals on federal matters are binding only on other lower federal and state courts in that circuit or region. (See pages 22–23 for a discussion of the circuits.) The supreme court of any state is the final authority on the meaning of the constitution and laws of that state, and its rulings on these matters are binding on all state and *federal* courts in that state. Matters are more complicated when federal courts interpret state laws. State courts can accept or reject these interpretations in most instances. Because mass media law is so heavily affected by the First Amendment, state judges frequently look outside their borders to precedents developed by the federal courts. A state court ruling on a question involving the First Amendment guarantees of freedom of speech and freedom of the press will be substantially guided by federal court precedents on the same subject.

Lawyers and law professors often debate how important precedent really is when a court makes a decision. Some have suggested the "hunch theory" of jurisprudence: A judge decides a case based on instinct or a feeling of what is right and wrong and then seeks out precedents to support the decision.

Finding Common-Law Cases

Common law is not specifically written down someplace for all to see and use. It is instead contained in hundreds of thousands of decisions handed down by courts over the centuries. Many attempts have been made to summarize the law. Sir Edward Coke compiled and analyzed the precedents of common law in the early 17th century. Sir William Blackstone later

4. 539 U.S. 558 (2003).
5. 478 U.S. 186 (1986).

FIGURE 1.1

Reading a case citation.

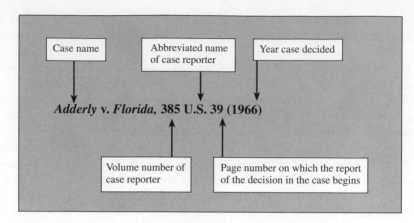

expanded Coke's work in the monumental "Commentaries on the Law of England." More recently, in such works as the massive "Restatement of the Law, Second, of Torts," the task was again undertaken, but on a narrower scale.

Courts began to record their decisions centuries ago. The modern concept of fully reporting written decisions of all courts probably began in 1785 with the publication of the first British Term Reports.

While scholars and lawyers still uncover common law using the case-by-case method, it is fairly easy today to locate the appropriate cases through a simple system of citation. The cases of a single court (such as the U.S. Supreme Court or the federal district courts) are collected in a single **case reporter** (such as the "United States Reports" or the "Federal Supplement"). The cases are collected chronologically and fill many volumes. Each case collected has its individual **citation,** or identification number, which reflects the name of the reporter in which the case can be found, the volume of that reporter, and the page on which the case begins (Figure 1.1). For example, the citation for the decision in *Adderly* v. *Florida* (a freedom-of-speech case) is 385 U.S. 39 (1966). The letters in the middle (U.S.) indicate that the case is in the "United States Reports," the official government reporter for cases decided by the Supreme Court of the United States. The number 385 refers to the specific volume of the "United States Reports" in which the case is found. The second number (39) gives the page on which the case appears. Finally, 1966 provides the year in which the case was decided. So, *Adderly* v. *Florida* can be found on page 39 of volume 385 of the "United States Reports."

The computer age affected the legal community in many ways. Court opinions are now available via a variety of online services. For instance, two legal databases attorneys often use and that frequently are available free to students at colleges and universities are LexisNexis and Westlaw. These databases provide access to court opinions, statutory law (see pages 8–9) and law journal articles. In many jurisdictions, lawyers are permitted to file documents electronically with the court.

If you have the correct citation, you can easily find any case you seek. Locating all citations of the cases apropos to a particular problem—such as a libel suit—is a different matter and is a technique taught in law schools. A great many legal encyclopedias, digests, compilations of common law, books and articles are used by lawyers to track down the names and citations of the appropriate cases.

> **TYPICAL REMEDIES IN EQUITY LAW**
>
> 1. Temporary restraining order (TRO)
> 2. Preliminary injunction
> 3. Permanent injunction

EQUITY LAW

Equity is another kind of judge-made law. The distinction today between common law and equity law has blurred. The cases are heard by the same judges in the same courtrooms. Differences in procedures and remedies are all that is left to distinguish these two categories of the law. Separate consideration of common law and equity leads to a better understanding of both, however. Equity was originally a supplement to the common law and developed side by side with common law.

The rules and procedures under equity are far more flexible than those under common law. Equity really begins where common law leaves off. Equity suits are never tried before a jury. Rulings come in the form of **judicial decrees,** not in judgments of yes or no. Decisions in equity are (and were) discretionary on the part of judges. And despite the fact that precedents are also relied upon in the law of equity, judges are free to do what they think is right and fair in a specific case.

Equity provides another advantage for troubled litigants—the restraining order. While the typical remedy in a civil lawsuit in common law is **damages** (money), equity allows a judge to issue orders that can either be preventive (prohibiting a party from engaging in a potential behavior it is considering) or remedial (compelling a party to stop doing something it currently is doing). Individuals who can demonstrate that they are in peril or are about to suffer a serious irremediable wrong can usually gain a legal writ such as an injunction or a restraining order to stop someone from doing something. Generally, a court issues a temporary restraining order until it can hear arguments from both parties in the dispute and decide whether an injunction should be made permanent. For instance, Verne Troyer, the diminutive actor who played Mini Me in the "Austin Powers" movies, obtained a temporary restraining order (TRO) in June 2008 that stopped the TMZ celebrity Web site and its related television show from posting and broadcasting a 25-second clip from a sex tape Troyer made with a former girlfriend, Ranae Shrider. Troyer claimed the tape was his property that was stolen from his residence and that its display would cause irreparable harm to his reputation and privacy. Later, however, when Shrider signed a legal declaration stating that she both owned the tape and had given TMZ permission to post and broadcast snippets from it, the judge allowed TMZ to use the material.

Ultimately, a party seeks an equitable remedy (a restraining order or injunction) if there is a real threat of a direct, immediate and irreparable injury for which monetary damages won't provide sufficient compensation. For instance, when Louisiana adopted a law in 2006 prohibiting the sale of violent video games to minors, the video game industry successfully sought and won a preliminary injunction that stopped and prohibited Louisiana from enforcing the law. In determining whether such an equitable remedy should be granted, the federal judge in *Entertainment Software Association* v. *Foti*[6] balanced the First Amendment speech rights of both video game creators or developers and players with the interests Louisiana claimed the statute served (preventing physical and psychological harm to minors). Reasoning that the "loss of constitutionally protected freedoms in and of itself constitutes irreparable harm" and that "it is undoubtedly in the public interest to protect First Amendment liberties," the judge found that the injury to free speech rights outweighed the alleged harms caused by violent video games and he granted the equitable remedy of a preliminary injunction.

STATUTORY LAW

While common law sometimes is referred to as discovered or judge-made law, the third great source of laws in the United States today is created by elected legislative bodies at the local, state and federal levels and is known as statutory law. In the beginning of our nation, legislation did not play a very significant role in the legal system. Certainly many laws were passed, but the bulk of our legal rules were developed from common law and equity law. After 1825 statutory law began to play an important role in our legal system, and it was between 1850 and 1900 that a greater percentage of law began to come from legislative acts than from common-law court decisions.

Several important characteristics of statutory law can best be understood by contrasting them with common law. First, **statutes** tend to deal with problems affecting society or large groups of people, in contrast to common law, which usually deals with smaller, individual problems. (Some common-law rulings affect large groups of people, but this occurrence is rare.) It should also be noted in this connection the importance of not confusing common law with constitutional law. Certainly when judges interpret a constitution, they make policy that affects us all. However, it should be kept in mind that a constitution is a legislative document voted on by the people and is not discovered law or judge-made law.

Second, statutory law can anticipate problems, and common law cannot. For example, a state legislature can pass a statute that prohibits publication of the school records of a student without prior consent of the student. Under common law the problem cannot be resolved until a student's record has been published in a newspaper or transmitted over the Internet and the student brings action against the publisher to recover damages for the injury incurred.

The criminal laws in the United States are all statutory laws.

Third, the criminal laws in the United States are all statutory laws—common-law crimes no longer exist in this country and have not since 1812. Common-law rules are not precise enough to provide the kind of notice needed to protect a criminal defendant's right to due process of law.

Fourth, statutory law is collected in codes and law books, instead of in reports as is common law. When a bill is adopted by the legislative branch and approved by the executive branch, it becomes law and is integrated into the proper section of a municipal code, a state code or whatever. However, this does not mean that some very important statutory law cannot be found in the case reporters.

Passage of a law is rarely the final word. Courts become involved in determining what that law means. Although a properly constructed statute sometimes needs little interpretation by the

6. 451 F. Supp. 2d 823 (M.D. La. 2006).

courts, judges are frequently called upon to rule on the exact meaning of ambiguous phrases and words. The resulting process of judicial interpretation is called **statutory construction** and is very important. Even the simplest kind of statement often needs interpretation. For example, a statute that declares "*it is illegal to distribute a violent video game to minors* [emphasis added]" is fraught with ambiguities that a court must construe and resolve in order to determine if it violates the First Amendment speech rights of video game creators and players (see pages 59–61 regarding regulation of video games). What type of content, for instance, falls within the meaning of the word "violent" as it is used in this statute? How young must a person be in order to be considered a "minor" under the law? Does the term "distribute" mean to sell a video game, to rent a video game or to give it away for free? Finally, because games are played in arcades, on computers and via consoles, just what precisely is a "video" game under the statute?

Usually a legislature tries to leave a trail to help a judge find out what the law means. When judges rule on the meaning of a statute, they are supposed to determine what the legislature meant when it passed the law (the legislative intent), not what they think the law should mean. Minutes of committee hearings in which the law was discussed, legislative staff reports and reports of debate on the floor can all be used to determine legislative intent. Therefore, when lawyers deal with statutes, they frequently search the case reporters to find out how the courts interpreted a law in which they are interested.

CONSTITUTIONAL LAW

Great Britain lacks a written **constitution.** The United States, in contrast, has a written constitution, and it is an important source of our law. In fact, there are many constitutions in this country: the federal Constitution, state constitutions, city charters and so forth. All these documents accomplish the same ends. First, they provide the plan for the establishment and organization of the government. Next, they outline the duties, responsibilities and powers of the various elements of government. Finally, they usually guarantee certain basic rights to the people, such as freedom of speech and freedom to peaceably assemble.

Legislative bodies may enact statutes rather easily by a majority vote. It is far more difficult to adopt or change a constitution. State constitutions are approved or changed by a direct vote of the people. It is even more difficult to change the federal Constitution. An amendment may be proposed by a vote of two-thirds of the members of both the U.S. House of Representatives and the Senate. Alternatively, two-thirds of the state legislatures can call for a constitutional convention for proposing amendments. Once proposed, amendments must be approved either by three-fourths of the state legislatures or by three-fourths of the constitutional conventions called in all the states. Congress decides which method of ratification or approval is to be used. Because the people have an unusually direct voice in the approval and change of a constitution, constitutions are considered the most important source of U.S. law.

One Supreme Court justice described a constitution as a kind of yardstick against which all the other actions of government must be measured to determine whether the actions are permissible. The U.S. Constitution is the supreme law of the land. Any law or other constitution that conflicts with the U.S. Constitution is unenforceable. A state constitution plays the same role for a state: A statute passed by the Michigan legislature and signed by the governor of that state is clearly unenforceable if it conflicts with the Michigan Constitution. And so it goes for all levels of constitutions.

The U.S. Constitution is the supreme law of the land.

Constitutions tend to be short and, at the federal level and in most states, infrequently amended. Consequently, changes in the language of a constitution are uncommon. But a considerable amount of constitutional law is nevertheless developed by the courts, which are asked to determine the meaning of provisions in the documents and to decide whether other laws or government actions violate constitutional provisions. Hence, the case reporters are repositories for the constitutional law that governs the nation.

Twenty-seven amendments are appended to the U.S. Constitution. The first 10 are known as the Bill of Rights and provide a guarantee of certain basic human rights to all citizens. Included are freedom of speech and press, rights you will understand more fully in future chapters.

The federal Constitution and the 50 state constitutions are very important when considering mass media law problems. All 51 of these charters contain provisions, in one form or another, that guarantee freedom of speech and freedom of the press.

The scope of protection for speech and press afforded by any given state constitution thus may be broader than that bestowed by the First Amendment.

Importantly, state constitutions can give more and greater rights to their citizens than are provided under the U.S. Constitution; they cannot, however, reduce or roll back rights given by the federal Constitution. The scope of protection for speech and press afforded by any given state constitution thus may be broader than that bestowed by the First Amendment to the U.S. Constitution. For instance, whereas obscene speech is not protected by the First Amendment (see Chapter 13), the Oregon Supreme Court held in 1987 that obscene expression is protected in that state under Article I, Section 8 of the Oregon Constitution.[7] A lawyer challenging a state statute that allegedly restricts any form of speech therefore is wise to argue before a court that the statute in question violates either or both the First Amendment and the relevant state's constitutional provision protecting expression. Consequently, any government action that affects in any way the freedom of individuals or mass media to speak or publish or broadcast must be measured against the constitutional guarantees of freedom of expression. There are several reasons why a law limiting speaking or publishing might be declared unconstitutional. The law might be a direct restriction on speech or press that is protected by the First Amendment. For example, an order by a Nebraska judge that prohibited the press from publishing certain information about a pending murder trial was considered a direct restriction on freedom of the press (see *Nebraska Press Association* v. *Stuart,*[8] Chapter 11). A criminal obscenity statute or another kind of criminal law might be declared unconstitutional because it is too vague. Under the **void for vagueness doctrine,** a law will be declared unconstitutional and struck down if a person of reasonable and ordinary intelligence would not be able to tell, from looking at its terms, what speech is allowed and what speech is prohibited. Put differently, people of ordinary intelligence should not have to guess at a statute's meaning. Vague laws are problematic because they

▮ don't provide fair notice of what speech is permitted; and
▮ can be enforced unfairly and discriminatorily because they give too much discretion (due to the vague terms) to those who enforce them (police and judges).

7. *Oregon* v. *Henry*, 302 Ore. 510 (1987). Article I, Section 8 of the Oregon Constitution provides that "no law shall be passed restraining the free expression of opinion, or restricting the right to speak, write, or print freely on any subject whatever; but every person shall be responsible for the abuse of this right." A 1996 ballot measure, drafted in part in response to the *Henry* opinion and that would have amended Article I, Section 8 so as not to protect obscenity, narrowly failed when put before Oregon voters.
8. 427 U.S. 539 (1976).

An Indianapolis pornography ordinance that made it a crime to publish pornographic material was declared void, at least in part, because the law's definition of pornography was not specific enough. The law defined pornography as including depictions of subordination of women." It is almost impossible to settle in one's own mind upon a single meaning or understanding of that term, noted Judge Sarah Barker (see *American Booksellers Association* v. *Hudnut,*[9] Chapter 13).

A statute might also be declared to be unconstitutional because it violates what is known as the **overbreadth doctrine.** A law is overbroad if it does not aim specifically at evils within the allowable area of government control but sweeps within its ambit other activities that constitute an exercise of protected expression. Struthers, Ohio, an industrial community where many people worked at night and slept during the day, passed an ordinance that forbade knocking on the door or ringing the doorbell at a residence in order to deliver a handbill. The Supreme Court ruled that the ordinance was overbroad. The city's objective could be obtained by passing an ordinance making it an offense for any person to ring a doorbell of a householder who had, through a sign or some other means, indicated he or she did not wish to be disturbed, the court noted. As written, however, the law prohibited individuals from distributing handbills to all people—to those who wanted to see and read them as well as those who did not (see *Martin* v. *City of Struthers,*[10] Chapter 3). So there are many reasons why a court might declare a law to be an unconstitutional infringement upon the freedom of speech and press.

EXECUTIVE ORDERS AND ADMINISTRATIVE RULES

The final source of American law has two streams. First are orders issued by elected officers of government, often called executive orders. Second are rules generated by the administrative agencies of government, at the federal, state and local levels.

Government executives—the U.S. president, governors, mayors, county executives, village presidents—all have more or less power to issue rules of law, sometimes referred to as executive orders or declarations. This power is normally defined by the constitution or the charter that establishes the office, and it varies widely from city to city or state to state. In some instances the individual has fairly broad powers; in others the power is sharply confined. President George W. Bush issued numerous executive orders related to the nation's war on terror. Such declarations are possible so long as they are properly within the delegated powers held by the executive. An order from an executive who exceeds his or her power can be overturned by the legislature (the mayor's order can be changed or vacated by the city council, for example) or by a court.

For instance, the U.S. Supreme Court in 2008 in *Medellin* v. *Texas*[11] rebuked President Bush when it held he lacked the power to unilaterally adopt a ruling by the International Court of Justice that would have ordered Texas to grant a new hearing to a Mexican citizen convicted of murder and held on death row in that state. Bush had issued a memorandum that would have trumped state domestic law (the law of Texas) by ordering states to adopt the ICJ ruling (the ruling held that Texas violated a provision of an international treaty by failing to notify the defendant that he had

9. 598 F. Supp. 1316 (1985).
10. 319 U.S. 141 (1943).
11. 128 S. Ct. 1346 (2008).

the right under the treaty to contact the consulate of Mexico after his arrest). The Supreme Court, however, concluded that Bush did not possess authority to transform ICJ judgments, based on an international treaty, into law without prior U.S. congressional authority. In reaching its decision, the high court reflected on key notions of separation of powers between the judicial, legislative and executive branches of government. It observed that presidential authority to act in any matter "must stem either from an act of Congress or from the Constitution itself" and that, in this instance, "the responsibility for transforming an international obligation arising from a non-self-executing treaty into domestic law falls to Congress." In brief, Bush overstepped his authority by trying to make domestic law, thus rendering his memorandum nugatory.

A more substantial part of U.S. law is generated by myriad administrative agencies that exist in the nation today, agencies that first began to develop in the latter part of the 19th century. By that time in the country's history, Congress was being asked to resolve questions going far beyond such matters as budgets, wars, treaties and the like. Technology created new kinds of problems for Congress to resolve. Many such issues were complex and required specialized knowledge and expertise that the representatives and senators lacked and could not easily acquire, had they wanted to. Specialized federal administrative agencies were therefore created to deal with these problems.

Hundreds of such agencies now exist at both federal and state levels. Each agency undertakes to deal with a specific set of problems too technical or too large for the legislative branch to handle. Perhaps the most relevant **administrative agency** for purposes of media law, along with the Federal Trade Commission (FTC; see Chapter 15), is the Federal Communications Commission (FCC), created by Congress in 1934. Its task is to regulate broadcasting and other telecommunication in the United States, a job that Congress has attempted only sporadically. Its members must be citizens of the United States and are appointed by the president. The single stipulation is that at any one time no more than three of the five individuals on the commission can be from the same political party. The Senate must confirm the appointments.

Congress has sketched the framework for the regulation of broadcasting in the Federal Communications Act of 1934 and subsequent amendments to this statute. This legislation is used by the FCC as its basic regulatory guidelines. But the agency generates much law on its own as it interprets the congressional mandates, and uses its considerable authority to generate rules and regulations. Recently the FCC has exerted its authority over broadcast content, cracking down on indecency on the airwaves (see Chapter 16). As rapper Eminem famously sang, "the FCC won't let me be or let me be me."

But courts have limited power to review decisions made by administrative agencies.

People dissatisfied with an action by an agency can attempt to have it modified by asking the legislative body that created and funds the agency—Congress, for example, when considering the FCC—to change or overturn the action. In the 1980s when the FTC made several aggressive pro-consumer rulings, Congress voided these actions because members disagreed with the extent of the rulings. More commonly the actions of an agency will be challenged in the courts. But courts have limited power to review decisions made by administrative agencies and can overturn such a ruling in only these limited circumstances:

1. If the original act that established the commission or agency is unconstitutional.
2. If the commission or agency exceeds its authority.
3. If the commission or agency violates its own rules.
4. If there is no evidentiary basis whatsoever to support the ruling.

The reason for these limitations is simple: These agencies were created to bring expert knowledge to bear on complex problems, and the entire purpose for their creation would be defeated if judges with no special expertise in a given area could reverse an agency ruling merely because they had a different solution to a problem.

The case reporters contain some law created by the administrative agencies, but the reports that these agencies themselves publish contain much more such law. Today, you can look up recent opinions and rulings of both the FCC and FTC at their respective Web sites, located at http://www.fcc.gov and http://www.ftc.gov.

There are other sources of American law but the sources just discussed—common law, law of equity, statutory law, constitutional law, executive orders and rules and regulations by administrative agencies—are the most important and are of most concern in this book. First Amendment problems fall under the purview of constitutional law. Libel and invasion of privacy are matters generally dealt with by common law and equity law. Obscenity laws in this country are statutory provisions (although this fact is frequently obscured by the hundreds of court cases in which judges attempt to define the meaning of obscenity). And of course the regulation of broadcasting and advertising falls primarily under the jurisdiction of administrative agencies.

SUMMARY

There are several important sources of American law. Common law is the oldest source of our law, having developed in England more than 700 years ago. Fundamental to common law is the concept that judges should look to the past and follow earlier court rulings, called precedents. Stare decisis (let the decision stand) is a key concept. But judges have developed the means to change or adapt common law by modifying, distinguishing or overruling precedent case law. Common law is not written in a law book but is collected in volumes that contain the reports of legal decisions. Each case is given its own legal identity through a system of numbered citations.

Equity law is the second source of American law. The rules and procedures of equity are far more flexible than those of common law and permit a judge (equity cases are never heard before a jury) to fashion a solution to unique or unusual problems. A court is permitted under equity law to restrain an individual or a corporation or even a government from taking an action. Under common law a court can attempt to compensate the injured party only for the damage that results from the action.

A great volume of law is generated by legislative bodies. This legislation, called statutory law, is the third important source of American law. All criminal laws are statutes. Statutes usually deal with problems that affect great numbers of people, and statutes can anticipate problems, whereas common law cannot. Statutes are collected in codes or statute books. Courts become involved when they are called on to interpret the meaning of the words and phrases contained in a statute.

Constitutions, the fourth source of law, take precedence over all other American law. The U.S. Constitution is the supreme law of the land. Other laws, whether they spring from common law, equity, legislative bodies or administrative agencies, cannot conflict with the provisions of the Constitution. Courts interpret the meaning of the provisions of our constitutions (one federal and 50 state constitutions) and through this process often make these seemingly rigid legal prescriptions adaptable to contemporary problems.

Executives (presidents and governors) can issue orders that carry the force of law. And there are thousands of administrative agencies, boards and commissions in the nation that produce rules and regulations. This administrative law usually deals with technical and complicated matters requiring levels of expertise that members of traditional legislative bodies do not normally possess. Members of these agencies and commissions are usually appointed by presidents or by governors or mayors, and the agencies are supervised and funded by legislative bodies. Their tasks are narrowly defined and their rulings, while they carry the force of law, can always be appealed.

THE JUDICIAL SYSTEM

This section introduces the court system in the United States. Since the judicial branch of our three-part government is the field on which most of the battles involving communications law are fought, an understanding of the judicial system is essential.

It is technically improper to talk about the American judicial system. There are 52 different judicial systems in the United States, one for the federal government and one for each of the 50 states, plus the District of Columbia. While each system is somewhat different from the others, the similarities among the 52 systems are much more important than the differences. Each of the systems is divided into two distinct sets of courts—trial courts and appellate courts. Each judicial system is established by a constitution, federal or state. In each system the courts act as the third branch of a triumvirate of government: a legislative branch, which makes the law; an executive branch, which enforces the law; and a judicial branch, which interprets the law.

FACTS VERSUS THE LAW

The facts are what happened. The law is what should be done because of the facts.

Common to all judicial systems is the distinction between trial courts and appellate courts. Each level of court has its own function: Basically, **trial courts** are fact-finding courts and **appellate courts** are law-reviewing courts. Trial courts are the courts of first instance, the place where nearly all cases begin. Juries sit in trial courts, but never in appellate courts. Trial courts are empowered to consider both the facts and the law in a case. Appellate courts normally consider only the law. The difference between facts and law is significant. The facts are what happened. The law is what should be done because of the facts.

The difference between facts and law can be emphasized by looking at an imaginary libel suit that might result if the River City Sentinel published a story about costs at the Sandridge Hospital, a privately owned medical facility.

Ineffective Medications Given to Ill, Injured
SANDRIDGE HOSPITAL OVERCHARGING
PATIENTS ON PHARMACY COSTS

Scores of patients at the Sandridge Hospital have been given ineffective medications, a three-week investigation at the hospital has revealed. In addition, many of those patients were overcharged for the medicine they received.

The Sentinel has learned that many of the prescription drugs sold to patients at the hospital had been kept beyond the manufacturer's recommended storage period.

Many drugs stored in the pharmacy (as late as Friday) had expiration dates as old as six months ago. Drug manufacturers have told the Sentinel that medication used beyond the expiration date, which is stamped clearly on most packages, may not have the potency or curative effects that fresher pharmaceuticals have.

Hospital representatives deny giving patients any of the expired drugs, but sources at the hospital say it is impossible for administrators to guarantee that none of the dated drugs were sold to patients.

In addition, the investigation by the Sentinel revealed that patients who were sold medications manufactured by Chaos Pharmaceuticals were charged on the basis of 2009 price lists despite the fact that the company lowered prices significantly in 2010.

The Sandridge Hospital sues the newspaper for libel. When the case gets to court, the first thing that must be done is to establish what the facts are—what happened. The hospital and the newspaper each will present evidence, witnesses and arguments to support its version of the facts. Several issues have to be resolved. In addition to the general questions of whether the story has been published and whether the hospital has been identified in the story, the hospital will have to supply evidence that its reputation has been injured, that the story is false and that the newspaper staff has been extremely careless or negligent in the publication of the report. The newspaper will seek to defend itself by attempting to document the story or raise the defense that the report was privileged in some way. Or the newspaper may argue that even if the story is mistaken, it was the result of an innocent error; the newspaper staff was not negligent when it wrote and published the story.

All this testimony and evidence establishes the factual record—what actually took place at the hospital and in preparation of the story. When there is conflicting evidence, the jury decides whom to believe (in the absence of a jury, the judge makes the decision). Suppose the hospital is able to prove by documents that pharmacists in fact had removed the dated medicine from their shelves and stored it to return to the manufacturers. Further, the hospital can show that while it did accidentally overcharge some patients for Chaos products, it quickly refunded the excess charge to these patients. Finally, attorneys for the hospital demonstrate that the story was prepared by an untrained stringer for the newspaper who used but a single source—a pharmacist who had been fired by Sandridge for using drugs while on the job—to prepare the story and failed to relate to readers the substance of the evidence (which the reporter had when the story was published) presented by the hospital in court. In such a case, a court would likely rule that the hospital had carried its burden of proof and that no legitimate defense exists for the newspaper. Therefore, the hospital wins the suit. If the newspaper is unhappy with the verdict, it can appeal.

In an appeal, the appellate court does not establish a new factual record. No more testimony is taken. No more witnesses are called. The factual record established by the jury or judge at the trial stands. The appellate court has the power in some kinds of cases (libel suits that involve constitutional issues, for example) to examine whether the trial court properly considered the facts in the case. But normally it is the task of the appellate court to determine whether the law has been applied properly in light of the facts established at the trial. Perhaps

The appellate court does not establish a new factual record. No more testimony is taken.

the appellate court might rule that even with the documentary evidence the hospital presented in court, this evidence failed to prove that the news story was false. Perhaps the judge erred in allowing certain testimony into evidence or refused to allow a certain witness to testify. Nevertheless, in reaching an opinion the appellate court considers only the law; the factual record established at the trial stands.

What if new evidence is found or a previously unknown witness comes forth to testify? If the appellate court believes that the new evidence is important, it can order a new trial. However, the court itself does not hear the evidence. These facts are developed at a new trial.

There are other differences between the roles and procedures of trial and appellate courts. Juries are never used by appellate courts; a jury may be used in a trial court proceeding. The judge normally sits alone at a trial; appeals are heard by a panel of judges, usually three or more. Cases always begin at the trial level and then proceed to the appellate level. Although the appellate courts appear to have the last word in a legal dispute, that is not always the case. Usually cases are returned to the trial court for resolution with instructions from the appeals court to the trial judge to decide the case, keeping this or that factor in mind. This is called remanding the case to the trial court. In such a case the trial judge can often do what he or she wants.

In the discussion that follows, the federal court system and its methods of operating are considered first, and then some general observations about state court systems are given, based on the discussion of the federal system.

THE FEDERAL COURT SYSTEM

Congress has the authority to abolish every federal court in the land, save the Supreme Court of the United States. The U.S. Constitution calls for but a single federal court, the Supreme Court. Article III, Section 1 states: "The judicial power of the United States shall be vested in one Supreme Court." The Constitution also gives Congress the right to establish inferior courts if it deems these courts to be necessary. And Congress has, of course, established a fairly complex system of courts to complement the Supreme Court.

The jurisdiction of the federal courts is also outlined in Article III of the Constitution. The jurisdiction of a court is its legal right to exercise its authority. Briefly, federal courts can hear the following cases:

1. Cases that arise under the U.S. Constitution, U.S. law and U.S. treaties
2. Cases that involve ambassadors and ministers, duly accredited, of foreign countries
3. Cases that involve admiralty and maritime law
4. Cases that involve controversies when the United States is a party to the suit
5. Cases that involve controversies between two or more states
6. Cases that involve controversies between a state and a citizen of another state (remember that the 11th Amendment to the Constitution requires that a state give its permission before it can be sued)
7. Cases that involve controversies between citizens of different states

While special federal courts have jurisdiction that goes beyond this broad outline, these are the circumstances in which a federal court may normally exercise its authority. Of the seven categories, Categories 1 and 7 account for most of the cases tried in federal court. For example, disputes that involve violations of the myriad federal laws and disputes that involve constitutional rights such as the First Amendment are heard in federal courts. Also, disputes between citizens of different states—what is known as a diversity of citizenship matter—are heard in federal courts. It is very common, for example, for libel suits and invasion-of-privacy suits against publishing companies to start in federal courts rather than in state courts. If a citizen of Arizona is libeled by the Los Angeles Times, the case will very likely be tried in a federal court in the state of Arizona rather than in a state court in either Arizona or California. Arizona law will be applied. The case will most often be heard where the legal wrong, in this case the injury to reputation by libel, occurs. Congress has limited federal trial courts to hearing only those diversity cases in which the damages sought exceeded $75,000.

The Supreme Court

The Supreme Court of the United States is the oldest federal court, having been in operation since 1789. The Constitution does not establish the number of justices who sit on the high court. That task is left to Congress. Since 1869 the Supreme Court has comprised the chief justice of the United States and eight associate justices. (Note the title: not chief justice of the Supreme Court, but chief justice of the United States.)

Since 1869 the Supreme Court has comprised the chief justice of the United States and eight associate justices.

The Supreme Court exercises both original and appellate jurisdictions. Under its **original jurisdiction,** which is established in the Constitution, the Supreme Court is the first court to hear a case and acts much like a trial court. Sometimes the justices will hold a hearing to ascertain the facts; more commonly they will appoint what is called a special master to discern the facts and make recommendations. For example, the Supreme Court in 2008 exercised the original jurisdiction it holds in lawsuits brought by one state against another state (see category 5 of federal court jurisdiction) in a dispute between New Jersey and Delaware over control of a portion of the Delaware River that flows between them.[12] The high court, in ruling in favor of Delaware's ability to stop New Jersey from developing a heavy industrial-use pier that would jut out more than 2,000 feet from the New Jersey side of the river, adopted in principal part the recommendation of a special master it had appointed.

The primary task of the Supreme Court is as an appellate tribunal, hearing cases already decided by lower federal and state courts of last resort. The appellate jurisdiction of the Supreme Court is established by Congress, not by the Constitution. A case will come before the Supreme Court of the United States for review in one of two principal ways: on a direct appeal or by way of a writ of certiorari. The certification process is a third way for a case to get to the high court, but this process is rarely used today.

In some instances a litigant has an apparent right, guaranteed by federal statute, to appeal a case to the Supreme Court. This is called **direct appeal.** For example, if a federal appeals court declares that a state statute violates the U.S. Constitution or conflicts with a federal law, the state has a right to appeal this decision to the Supreme Court. But this is only an apparent right, because since 1928 the Supreme Court has had the right to reject such an appeal "for want of a substantial federal question." This is another way of the court saying, "We think this is a trivial matter." Almost 90 percent of all appeals that come to the Supreme Court via the direct appeal process are rejected.

12. *New Jersey v. Delaware*, 128 S. Ct. 1410 (2008).

The much more common way for a case to reach the nation's high court is via a **writ of certiorari.** No one has the right to such a writ. It is a discretionary order issued by the court when it feels that an important legal question has been raised. Litigants using both the federal court system and the various state court systems can seek a writ of certiorari. The most important requirement that must be met before the court will even consider issuing a writ is that a petitioner first exhaust all other legal remedies. Although there are a few exceptions, this generally means that if a case begins in a federal district court (the trial level court) the **petitioner** must first seek a review by a U.S. Court of Appeals before bidding for a writ of certiorari. The writ can be sought if the Court of Appeals refuses to hear the case or sustains the verdict against the petitioner. All other legal remedies have then been exhausted. In state court systems every legal appeal possible must be made within the state before seeking a review by the U.S. Supreme Court. This usually means going through a trial court, an intermediate appeals court, and finally the state supreme court.

When the Supreme Court grants a writ of certiorari, it is ordering the lower court to send the records to the high court for review. Any litigant can petition the court to grant a writ, and the high court usually receives about 5,000 such requests each year. Each request is considered by the entire nine-member court. If four justices think the petition has merit, the writ will be granted. This is called the **rule of four.** But the court rejects the vast majority of petitions it receives. Recently only 75 to 85 cases a year have been accepted. In fact, during its 2007–08 term, the Supreme Court issued only 67 signed opinions. The number, however, increased during the 2008–09 term. Workload is the key factor. Certain important issues must be decided each term, and the justices do not have the time to consider thoroughly most cases for which an appeal is sought. Term after term, suggestions to reduce the court's workload are made, but most are not popular with Congress or the people in the nation. All citizens believe that they should have the right to appeal to the Supreme Court, even if the appeal will probably be rejected, even if the court may never hear the case.

One final point needs to be made. The Supreme Court of the United States is not as interested in making certain that justice has been served as it is in making certain that the law is developing properly. A petitioner seeking redress through the high court may have a completely valid argument that a lower court has ignored an important precedent in ruling against him or her. But if the law on this point has been established, the Supreme Court is very likely to reject the petition and instead use this time to examine and decide a new or emerging legal issue.

LEARNING MORE ABOUT THE U.S. SUPREME COURT

To find out more about the United States Supreme Court, ranging from its history to biographies of the current justices to its docket and recent opinions, you can visit the high court's official Web site at http://www.supremecourtus.gov and peruse its many links. In addition, the Legal Information Institute at Cornell University Law School has an excellent online database at http://www.law.cornell.edu/supct that features a wealth of information about the high court, its justices and its decisions.

Hearing a Case   The operation of the Supreme Court is unique in many ways, but by gaining an understanding of how the high court does its business, a reader will also gain an understanding of how most appellate courts function.

Once the Supreme Court agrees to hear a case the heaviest burden falls upon the attorneys for the competing parties. The oral argument—the presentation made by the attorneys to the members of the court—will be scheduled. The parties (their attorneys) are expected to submit what are called **legal briefs**—their written legal arguments—for the members of the court to study before the oral hearing. The party that has taken the appeal to the Supreme Court—the **appellant**—must provide the high court with a complete record of the lower-court proceedings: the transcripts from the trial, the rulings by the lower courts and other relevant material.

Arguing a matter all the way to the Supreme Court takes a long time, often as long as five years (sometimes longer) from initiation of the suit until the court gives its ruling. James Hill brought suit in New York in 1953 against Time, Inc. for invasion of privacy. The U.S. Supreme Court made the final ruling in the case in 1967 (*Time, Inc.* v. *Hill*).[13] Even at that the matter would not have ended had Hill decided to go back to trial, which the Supreme Court said he must do if he wanted to collect damages. He chose not to.

After the nine justices study the briefs (or at least the summaries provided by their law clerks), the **oral argument** is held. For a generation schooled on television dramas like "Law and Order," oral argument before the Supreme Court (or indeed before any appellate court) must seem strange. For one thing, the attorneys are strictly limited as to how much they may say. Each side is given a brief amount of time, usually no more than 30 minutes to an hour, to present its arguments. In important cases, "friends of the court" (**amici curiae**) are allowed to present briefs and to participate for 30 minutes in the oral arguments. For example, the American Civil Liberties Union often seeks the friend status in important civil rights cases. Likewise, the Reporters Committee for Freedom of the Press (http://www.rcfp.org) may file a friend-of-the-court brief in cases affecting journalists' rights, even though it is not a party in the cases.

Deciding a Case   After oral argument (which is given in open court with visitors welcome), the members of the high court move behind closed doors to undertake their deliberations. No one is allowed in the discussion room except members of the court itself—no clerks, no bailiffs, no secretaries. The discussion, which often is held several days after the arguments are completed, is opened by the chief justice. Discussion time is limited, and by being the first speaker the chief justice is in a position to set the agenda, so to speak, for each case—to raise what he or she thinks are the key issues. Next to speak is the justice with the most seniority, and after him or her, the next most senior justice. The court will have many items or cases to dispose of during one conference or discussion day; consequently, brevity is valued. Each justice has just a few moments to state his or her thoughts on the matter. After discussion a tentative vote is taken and recorded by each justice in a small, hinged, lockable docket book. In the voting procedure the junior justice votes first; the chief justice, last.

---

13. 385 U.S. 374 (1967).

TYPES OF SUPREME COURT OPINIONS

1. Opinion of the court (majority opinion)
2. Concurring opinion
3. Dissenting opinion (minority opinion)
4. Plurality opinion
5. Per curiam opinion (unsigned opinion)
6. Memorandum order

Under the United States legal system, which is based so heavily on the concept of court participation in developing and interpreting the law, a simple yes-or-no answer to any legal question is hardly sufficient. More important than the vote, for the law if not for the **litigant,** are the reasons for the decision. Therefore the Supreme Court and all courts that deal with questions of law prepare what are called **opinions,** in which the reasons, or rationale, for the decision are given. One of the justices voting in the majority is asked to write what is called the **court's opinion.** If the chief justice is in the majority, he or she selects the author of the opinion. If not, the senior associate justice in the majority makes the assignment. Self-selection is always an option.

Opinion writing is a difficult task. Getting five or six or seven people to agree to yes or no is one thing; getting them to agree on why they say yes or no is something else. The opinion must therefore be carefully constructed. After it is drafted, it is circulated among all court members, who make suggestions or even draft their own opinions. The opinion writer may incorporate as many of these ideas as possible into the opinion to retain its majority backing. Although all this is done in secret, historians have learned that rarely do court opinions reflect solely the work of the writer. They are more often a conglomeration of paragraphs and pages and sentences from the opinions of several justices.

A justice who writes a concurring opinion may agree with the outcome of the decision, but does so for reasons different from those expressed in the majority opinion.

A justice in agreement with the majority who cannot be convinced to join in backing the court's opinion has the option of writing what is called a **concurring opinion.** A justice who writes a concurring opinion may agree with the outcome of the decision, but does so for reasons different from those expressed in the majority opinion. Or the concurring justice may want to emphasize a specific point not addressed in the majority opinion.

Justices who disagree with the majority can also write an opinion, either individually or as a group, called a **dissenting opinion.** Dissenting opinions are very important. Sometimes, after the court has made a decision, it becomes clear that the decision was not the proper one. The issue is often litigated again by other parties who use the arguments in the dissenting opinion as the basis for a legal claim. If enough time passes, if the composition of the court changes sufficiently or if the court members change their minds, the high court can swing to the views of the original dissenters.

An opinion in which five justices cannot agree on a single majority opinion—there is no opinion of the court—but that is joined by more justices than any other opinion in the case is known as a **plurality opinion.** For instance, imagine that four justices agree with a particular outcome in a case for reason A. Two other justices may also agree with that same outcome, but for reason B, while three other justices do not agree with the outcome at all. In this split of 4-2-3 among the justices, the four-justice opinion constitutes the plurality.

Finally, it is possible for a justice to concur with the majority in part and to dissent in part as well. That is, the justice may agree with some of the things the majority says but disagree with other aspects of the ruling. Such splits thwart the orderly development of the law. They often leave lawyers and other interested parties at a loss when trying to predict how the court might respond in the next similar case that comes along.

The Supreme Court can dispose of a case in two other ways. A **per curiam** (by the court) **opinion** can be prepared. This is an unsigned opinion drafted by one or more members of the majority and published as the court's opinion. Per curiam opinions are not common, but neither are they rare.

Finally, the high court can dispose of a case with a **memorandum order**—that is, it just announces the vote without giving an opinion. Or the order cites an earlier Supreme Court decision as the reason for affirming or reversing a lower-court ruling. In cases with little legal importance and in cases in which the issues were really resolved earlier, the court saves a good deal of time by just announcing its decision.

One final matter in regard to voting remains for consideration: What happens in case of a tie vote? When all nine members of the court are present, a tie vote is technically impossible. However, if there is a vacancy on the court, only eight justices hear a case. Even when the court is full, a particular justice may disqualify himself or herself from hearing a case. When a vote ends in a tie, the decision of the lower court is affirmed. No opinion is written. It is as if the Supreme Court had never heard the case.

During the circulation of an opinion, justices have the opportunity to change their vote. The number and membership in the majority may shift. It is not impossible for the majority to become the minority if one of the dissenters writes a particularly powerful dissent that attracts support from members originally opposed to his or her opinion. This event is probably very rare. Nevertheless, a vote of the court is not final until it is announced on decision day, or opinion day. The authors of the various opinions—court opinions, concurrences and dissents—publicly read or summarize their views. Printed copies of these documents are handed out to the parties involved and to the press, and are quickly available online.

Courts have no real way to enforce decisions and must depend on other government agencies for enforcement of their rulings. The job normally falls to the executive branch. If perchance the president decides not to enforce a Supreme Court ruling, no legal force exists to compel the president to do so. If former President Nixon, for example, had chosen to refuse to turn over the infamous Watergate tapes after the court ruled against his arguments of executive privilege, no other agency could have forced him to give up those tapes.

At the same time, there is one force that usually works to see that court decisions are carried out: It is that vague force called public opinion or what political scientists call "legitimacy." Most people believe in the judicial process; they have faith that what the courts do is probably right. This does not mean that they always agree with court decisions, but they do agree that the proper way to settle disputes is through the judicial process. Jurists help engender this spirit or philosophy by acting in a temperate manner. The Supreme Court, for example, has developed means that permit it to avoid having to answer highly controversial questions in which an unpopular decision could weaken its perceived legitimacy. The justices

People believe in the judicial process; they have faith that what the courts do is probably right.

21

might call the dispute a political question, a **nonjusticiable matter,** or they may refuse to hear a case on other grounds. When the members of the court sense that the public is ready to accept a ruling, they may take on a controversial issue. School desegregation is a good example. In 1954 the Supreme Court ruled in *Brown* v. *Board of Education*[14] that segregated public schools violated the U.S. Constitution. The foundation for this ruling had been laid by a decade of less momentous desegregation decisions and executive actions. By 1954 the nation was prepared for the ruling, and it was generally accepted, even in many parts of the South. The legitimacy of a court's decisions, then, often rests upon prudent use of the judicial power.

Other Federal Courts

The Supreme Court of the United States is the most visible, perhaps the most glamorous (if that word is appropriate), of the federal courts. But it is not the only federal court nor even the busiest. There are two lower echelons of federal courts, plus various special courts, within the federal system. These special courts, such as the U.S. Court of Military Appeals, U.S. Tax Court, and so forth, were created by Congress to handle special kinds of problems.

Most federal cases begin and end in one of the 94 U.S. District Courts located across the nation, in Puerto Rico and in various U.S. territories. In 2009, the district courts were staffed with 678 authorized judgeships (at any moment, however, there are more than a dozen vacant judgeships), a figure that Congress can vote to increase or decrease. In addition to these authorized U.S. District Court judges (known as "Article III" judges), there are more than 450 federal magistrate judges. Federal magistrate judges are appointed for eight-year terms by a federal district court to handle some matters (initial proceedings in criminal cases, for instance) and certain cases delegated to them by the district court judges or with the consent of the parties (magistrate judges cannot, however, preside over felony criminal trials).

District courts are the trial courts of the federal court system, hearing both civil and criminal matters. Each state has at least one federal district court, with more populous states divided into two or more districts, leading to the total of 94 U.S. judicial districts. Pennsylvania, for instance, has three districts (western, middle and eastern), as does Florida (northern, middle and southern). The district courts are busy; in March 2008, they had a total of about 270,000 pending civil cases and approximately 70,000 criminal cases.

At the intermediate appellate level in the federal judiciary there are 13 circuits of the U.S. Courts of Appeals, with 179 authorized judgeships in 2009. As of March 2008, there were about 51,000 total cases in the U.S. Courts of Appeals. These courts were created by the Federal Judiciary Act of 1789. Until 1948 these courts were called Circuit Courts of Appeal, a reflection of the early years of the republic when the justices of the Supreme Court "rode the circuit" and presided at the courts-of-appeal hearings. While the title Circuit Courts of Appeal is officially gone, the nation is still divided into 11 numbered circuits, each of which is served by one court (see Figure 1.2).

The 12th and 13th circuits are unnumbered. One is the Court of Appeals for the District of Columbia. This is a very busy court because it hears most of the appeals from decisions made by federal administrative agencies. The 13th is the Court of Appeals for the Federal

---

14. 347 U.S. 483 (1954).

4th Circuit: Maryland, North Carolina, South Carolina, Virginia and West Virginia
5th Circuit: Mississippi, Louisiana and Texas
6th Circuit: Kentucky, Michigan, Ohio and Tennessee
7th Circuit: Illinois, Indiana and Wisconsin
8th Circuit: Arkansas, Iowa, Minnesota, Missouri, Nebraska, North Dakota and South Dakota
9th Circuit: Alaska, Arizona, California, Hawaii, Idaho, Montana, Nevada, Oregon, Washington, Guam and Northern Mariana Islands
10th Circuit: Colorado, Kansas, New Mexico, Oklahoma, Utah and Wyoming
11th Circuit: Alabama, Florida, Georgia and the Canal Zone

1st Circuit: Maine, Massachusetts, New Hampshire, Rhode Island and Puerto Rico
2nd Circuit: Connecticut, New York and Vermont
3rd Circuit: Delaware, New Jersey, Pennsylvania and Virgin Islands

FIGURE 1.2

Circuits 1 through 11 comprise the 50 states and the multiple U.S. territories.

Circuit, a court created by Congress in 1982 to handle special kinds of appeals. This court is specially empowered to hear appeals from patent and trademark decisions of U.S. District Courts and other federal agencies such as the Board of Patent Appeals. It also hears appeals from rulings by the U.S. Claims Court, the U.S. Court of International Trade, the U.S. International Trade Commission, the Merit Systems Protection Board and from a handful of other special kinds of rulings. Congress established this court to try to develop a uniform, reliable and predictable body of law in each of these very special fields.

The 12 regional federal courts of appeal (the 11 numbered circuits, plus the District of Columbia circuit) hear appeals from the federal district courts located within them, as well as appeals from decisions of federal administrative agencies. The courts are the last stop for 95 percent of all cases in the federal system. The number of appellate judges in each circuit varies, depending upon geographic size and caseload. The 9th U.S. Circuit Court of Appeals, which sweeps up nine western states as well as the Territory of Guam and the Commonwealth of the Northern Mariana Islands, is the largest and busiest circuit; in 2008, it was staffed by 28 authorized judges as well as more than 20 senior judges (retired federal judges who maintain reduced caseloads) and it had more than 16,500 pending cases. There occasionally are moves to break up the 9th Circuit, which is perceived as too large (and too liberal by some conservatives). Typically, a panel of three judges will hear a case. In unusual cases, a larger panel of judges, usually 11, will hear the appeal. When this happens the court is said to be **sitting en**

banc. A litigant who loses an appeal heard by a three-judge panel can ask for a rehearing by the entire court. This request is not often granted.

Federal Judges

All federal judges, other than magistrate judges, are appointed for life terms under Article III of the U.S. Constitution by the president, with the advice and consent of the Senate. The only way a federal judge can be removed is by **impeachment.** Eleven federal judges have been impeached: Seven were found guilty by the Senate, and the other four were acquitted. Impeachment and trial is a long process and one rarely undertaken.

Political affiliation plays a distinct part in the appointment of federal judges. Democratic presidents usually appoint Democratic judges, and Republican presidents appoint Republican judges. Nevertheless, it is expected that nominees to the federal bench be competent jurists. This is especially true for appointees to the Courts of Appeals and to the Supreme Court. The Senate must confirm all appointments to the federal courts, a normally perfunctory act in the case of lower-court judges. More careful scrutiny is given nominees to the appellate courts.

The appointment process now is of great public interest, as the current justices appear in many people's eyes to be narrowly divided along ideological and political lines. After the departure of Sandra Day O'Connor in 2005, Associate Justice Anthony Kennedy became the pivotal swing vote on the nation's high court that parties arguing before it hoped to capture. In fact, while John Roberts is the official chief justice, many people nonetheless referred in 2009 to the Supreme Court as "the Kennedy Court."

The president appoints the members of the high court with the "advice and consent" of the U.S. Senate. When the White House and the Senate are both in the hands of the same party, Republicans or Democrats, this appointment process will usually proceed smoothly. But when the White House and Senate are not controlled by the same party, bitter fights over future justices can occur, with a president sometimes struggling or even failing to gain the advice and consent of the Senate over a given appointee. In 2009, President Obama's nominee, Sonia Sotomayor, was approved by the Senate in a 68 to 31 vote that split largely between party lines, as most Republicans voted against the third woman ever to serve on the nation's highest court.

Presidents and senators alike have discovered that the individual who is nominated is not always the one who spends the remainder of his or her lifetime on the court. Justices and judges appointed to the bench for life sometimes change. Perhaps they are affected by their colleagues. Or maybe it is because they are largely removed from the pressures faced by others in public life. For whatever reasons, men and women appointed to the bench sometimes drastically modify their philosophy. For instance, current Associate Justice Kennedy was appointed by Republican President Ronald Reagan in 1988, but now has alienated cultural conservatives by writing decisions that struck down a Texas anti-sodomy statute and that declared unconstitutional a law against virtual child pornography (see pages 480–482).

THE STATE COURT SYSTEM

The constitution of each of the 50 states either establishes a court system in that state or authorizes the legislature to do so. The court system in each of the 50 states is somewhat different from the court system in all the other states. There are, however, more similarities than differences among the 50 states.

The trial courts (or court) are the base of each judicial system. At the lowest level are usually what are called courts of limited jurisdiction. Some of these courts have special functions, such as a traffic court, which is set up to hear cases involving violations of the motor-vehicle code. Some of these courts are limited to hearing cases of relative unimportance, such as trials of persons charged with misdemeanors, or minor crimes, or civil suits in which the damages sought fall below $1,000. The court may be a municipal court set up to hear cases involving violations of the city code. Whatever the court, the judges in these courts have limited jurisdiction and deal with a limited category of problems.

Above the lower-level courts normally exist trial courts of general jurisdiction similar to the federal district courts. These courts are sometimes county courts and sometimes state courts, but whichever they are, they handle nearly all criminal and civil matters. They are primarily courts of original jurisdiction; that is, they are the first courts to hear a case. However, on occasion they act as a kind of appellate court when the decisions of the courts of limited jurisdiction are challenged. When that happens, the case is retried in the trial court—the court does not simply review the law. This proceeding is called hearing a case **de novo.**

A **jury** is most likely to be found in the trial court of general jurisdiction. It is also the court in which most civil suits for libel and invasion of privacy are commenced (provided the state court has jurisdiction), in which prosecution for violating state obscenity laws starts, and in which many other media-related matters begin.

Above this court may be one or two levels of appellate courts. Every state has a supreme court, although some states do not call it that. In New York, for example, it is called the Court of Appeals, but it is the high court in the state, the court of last resort.* Formerly, a supreme court was the only appellate court in most states. As legal business increased and the number of appeals mounted, the need for an intermediate appellate court became evident. Therefore, in nearly all states there is an intermediate court, usually called the court of appeals. This is the court where most appeals end. In some states it is a single court with three or more judges. More often, numerous divisions within the appellate court serve various geographic regions, each division having three or more judges. Since every litigant is normally guaranteed at least one appeal, this intermediate court takes much of the pressure off the high court of the state. Rarely do individuals appeal beyond the intermediate level.

State courts of appeals tend to operate in much the same fashion as the U.S. Courts of Appeals, with cases being heard by small groups of judges, usually three at a time.

Cases not involving federal questions go no further than the high court in a state, usually called the supreme court. This court—usually a seven- or nine-member body—is the final authority regarding the construction of state laws and interpretation of the state constitution. Not even the Supreme Court of the United States can tell a state supreme court what that state's constitution means.

State court judges are frequently elected. Normally the process is nonpartisan, but because they are elected and must stand for re-election periodically, state court judges are generally a bit more politically active than their federal counterparts. Nearly half the states in the nation use a kind of compromise system that includes both appointment and election. The

Not even the Supreme Court of the United States can tell a state supreme court what that state's constitution means.

*To further confuse matters, the trial court of general jurisdiction in New York is called the Supreme Court. This is a fact with which avid "Law & Order" fans should already be readily familiar.

compromise is designed to minimize political influence and initially select qualified candidates but still retain an element of popular control. The plans are named after the states that pioneered them, the **California Plan** and the **Missouri Plan.**

JUDICIAL REVIEW

One of the most important powers of courts (and at one time one of the most controversial) is the power of **judicial review**—that is, the right of any court to declare any law or official governmental action invalid because it violates a constitutional provision. We usually think of this right in terms of the U.S. Constitution. However, a state court can declare an act of its legislature to be invalid because the act conflicts with a provision of the state constitution. Theoretically, any court can exercise this power. The Circuit Court of Lapeer County, Mich., can rule that the Environmental Protection Act of 1972 is unconstitutional because it deprives citizens of their property without due process of law, something guaranteed by the Fifth Amendment to the federal Constitution. But this action isn't likely to happen, because a higher court would quickly overturn such a ruling. In fact, it is rather unusual for any court—even the U.S. Supreme Court—to invalidate a state or federal law on grounds that it violates the Constitution. Judicial review is therefore not a power that the courts use excessively. A judicial maxim states: When a court has a choice of two or more ways in which to interpret a statute, the court should always interpret the statute in such a way that it is constitutional.

Judicial review is extremely important when matters concerning regulations of the mass media are considered. Because the First Amendment prohibits laws that abridge freedom of the press and freedom of speech, each new measure passed by Congress, by state legislatures and even by city councils and township boards must be measured by the yardstick of the First Amendment. Courts have the right, in fact have the duty, to nullify laws and executive actions and administrative rulings that do not meet the standards of the First Amendment. While many lawyers and legal scholars rarely consider constitutional principles in their work and rarely seek judicial review of a statute, attorneys who represent newspapers, magazines, broadcasting stations and motion-picture theaters constantly deal with constitutional issues, primarily those of the First Amendment. The remainder of this book will illustrate the obvious fact that judicial review, a concept at the very heart of American democracy, plays an important role in maintaining the freedom of the American press, even though the power is not explicitly included in the Constitution.

SUMMARY

There are 52 different judicial systems in the nation: one federal system, one for the District of Columbia and one for each of the 50 states. Courts within each of these systems are divided into two general classes—trial courts and appellate courts. In any lawsuit both the facts and the law must be considered. The facts or the factual record is an account of what happened to prompt the dispute. The law is what should be done to resolve the dispute. Trial courts determine the facts in the case; then the judge applies the law. Appellate courts, using the factual record established by the trial court, determine whether the law was properly applied by the lower court and whether proper judicial procedures were followed. Trial courts exercise original jurisdiction almost exclusively; that is, they are the first courts to hear a case. Trial courts have very little discretion over which cases they will and will not hear. Appellate courts exercise appellate jurisdiction almost exclusively; that is, they review the work done by the lower courts when decisions are appealed. Whereas the intermediate appellate courts (i.e., courts of appeals; the appellate division) have limited discretion in the selection of cases, the high courts (supreme courts) in the states and the nation generally have the power to select the cases they wish to review.

Federal courts include the Supreme Court of the United States, the U.S. Courts of Appeals, the U.S. District Courts and several specialized tribunals. These courts have jurisdiction in all cases that involve the U.S. Constitution, U.S. law and U.S. treaties; in disputes between citizens of different states; and in several less important instances. In each state there are trial-level courts and a court of last resort, usually called the supreme court. In about half the states there are intermediate appellate courts as well. State courts generally have jurisdiction in all disputes between citizens of their state that involve the state constitution or state law.

Judicial review is the power of a court to declare a statute, regulation or executive action to be a violation of the Constitution and thus invalid. Because the First Amendment to the U.S. Constitution guarantees the rights of freedom of speech and press, all government actions that relate to the communication of ideas and information face potential scrutiny by courts to determine their validity.

LAWSUITS

The final topic is lawsuits. To the layperson, and even those who work in the legal system, the United States appears to be awash in lawsuits. The notion that there appears to be a lawsuit around every corner in every city can probably be blamed on the increased attention the press has given legal matters. Courts are fairly easy to cover and stories about lawsuits are commonly published and broadcast.

This is not to say that we are not a highly litigious people. The backlogs in the courts are evidence of this. Going to court today is no longer a novelty but a common business or personal practice for a growing number of Americans. And too many of these lawsuits involve silly or trivial legal claims. In the end, the public pays a substantial price for all this litigation, through higher federal and state taxes to build and maintain courthouses and money to pay the salaries of those who work in the judiciary, and through higher insurance costs on everything from automobiles to protection from libel suits.

The material that follows is a simplified description of how a lawsuit proceeds. The picture is stripped of a great deal of the procedural activity that so often lengthens the lawsuit and keeps attorneys busy.

The party who commences a civil action is called the **plaintiff,** the person who brings the suit. The party against whom the suit is brought is called the **defendant.** In a libel suit the person who has been libeled is the plaintiff and is the one who starts the suit against the defendant—the newspaper, the magazine, the television station or whatever. A civil suit is usually a dispute between two private parties. The government offers its good offices—the courts—to settle the matter. A government can bring a civil suit such as an antitrust action against someone, and an individual can bring a civil action against the government. But normally a civil suit is between private parties. (In a criminal action, the government always initiates the action.)

To start a civil suit the plaintiff first picks the proper court, one that has jurisdiction in the case. Then the plaintiff files a **civil complaint** with the court clerk. This complaint, or **pleading,** is a statement of the charges against the defendant and the remedy that is sought, typically money damages. The complaint will also include:

1. A statement of the relevant facts upon which the plaintiff is suing
2. The legal theory or theories (known as causes of action) upon which the plaintiff is suing (libel, for instance, is a cause of action or legal theory)
3. A request for a remedy or relief (typically, the plaintiff requests monetary damages in a civil lawsuit, although equitable relief also can be sought in some instances)

The plaintiff also summons the defendant to appear in court to answer these charges. While the plaintiff may later amend his or her pleadings in the case, usually the initial complaint is the only pleading filed. After the complaint is filed, a hearing is scheduled by the court.

If the defendant fails to answer the charges, he or she normally loses the suit by default. Usually, however, the defendant will answer the summons and prepare his or her own set of pleadings, which constitute an answer to the plaintiff's charges. If there is little disagreement at this point about the facts—what happened—and that a wrong has been committed, the plaintiff and the defendant might settle their differences out of court. The defendant might say, "I guess I did libel you in this article, and I really don't have a very good defense. You asked for $100,000 in damages; would you settle for $50,000 and keep this out of court?" The plaintiff might very well answer yes, because a court trial is costly and takes a long time, and the plaintiff can also end up losing the case. Smart lawyers try to keep their clients out of court and settle matters in somebody's office.

Smart lawyers try to keep their clients out of court and settle matters in somebody's office.

If there is disagreement, the case is likely to continue. One common response to a complaint is for the defendant to file in court and to serve the plaintiff with an **answer.** An answer typically denies most of the facts and all of the allegations in the complaint; it may also assert various defenses to the plaintiff's complaint. Another typical move for the defendant to make at this point is to file a motion to dismiss, or a **demurrer.** In such a motion the defendant says this to the court: "I admit that I did everything the plaintiff says I did. On June 5, 2010, I did publish an article in which she was called a socialist. But, Your Honor, it is not libelous to call someone a socialist." The plea made then is that even if everything the plaintiff asserts is true, the defendant did nothing that was legally wrong. The law cannot help the plaintiff. The court might grant the motion, in which case the plaintiff can appeal. Or the court might refuse to grant the motion, in which case the defendant can appeal. If the motion to dismiss is ultimately rejected by all the courts up and down the line, a trial is then held. It is fair play for the defendant at that time to dispute the plaintiff's statement of the facts; in other words to deny, for example, that his newspaper published the article containing the alleged libel.

Before the trial is held, the judge may schedule a conference between both parties in an effort to settle the matter or to narrow the issues so that the trial can be shorter and less costly. If the effort to settle the dispute fails, the trial goes forward. If the facts are agreed upon by both sides and the question is merely one of law, a judge hears the case without a jury. There are no witnesses and no testimony; only legal arguments are brought before the court. If the facts are disputed, the case can be tried before either a jury or, again, only a judge. Note that both sides must waive the right to a jury trial. In this event, the judge becomes both the fact finder and the lawgiver. Now, suppose that the case is heard by a jury. After all the testimony is given, all the evidence is presented, and all the arguments are made, the judge instructs the jury in the law. Instructions are often long and complex, despite attempts by judges to simplify them. **Judicial instructions** guide the jury in determining guilt or innocence if certain facts are found to be true. The judge will say that if the jury finds that *X* is true and *Y* is true and *Z* is true, then it must find for the plaintiff, but if the jury finds that *X* is not true, but that *R* is true, then it must find for the defendant.

After deliberation the jury presents its **verdict,** the action by the jury. The judge then announces the **judgment of the court.** This is the decision of the court. The judge is not always bound by the jury verdict. If he or she feels that the jury verdict is unfair or unreasonable, the judge can reverse it and rule for the other party. This rarely happens.

If either party is unhappy with the decision, an appeal can be taken. At that time the legal designations may change. The person seeking the appeal becomes the *appellant,* or petitioner. The other party becomes the **appellee,** or **respondent.** The name of the party initiating the action is usually listed first in the name of the case. For example: Smith sues Jones for libel. The case name is *Smith* v. *Jones.* Jones loses and takes an appeal. At that point in most jurisdictions Jones becomes the party initiating the action and the case becomes *Jones* v. *Smith.* This change in designations often confuses novices in their attempt to trace a case from trial to final appeal. If Jones wins the appeal and Smith decides to appeal to a higher court, the case again becomes *Smith* v. *Jones.* In more and more jurisdictions today, however, the case name remains the same throughout the appeal process. This is an effort by the judiciary to relieve some of the confusion wrought by this constant shifting of party names within the case name. In California, for example, the case of *Smith* v. *Jones* remains *Smith* v. *Jones* through the entire life of that case.

The end result of a successful civil suit is usually the awarding of money damages. Sometimes the amount of damages is guided by the law, as in a suit for infringement of copyright in which the law provides that a losing defendant pay the plaintiff the amount of money he or she might have made if the infringement had not occurred, or at least a set number of dollars. But most of the time the damages are determined by how much the plaintiff seeks, how much the plaintiff can prove he or she lost and how much the jury thinks the plaintiff deserves. It is not a very scientific means of determining the dollar amount.

A **criminal prosecution,** or **criminal action,** is like a civil suit in many ways. The procedures are more formal, elaborate and involve the machinery of the state to a greater extent. The state brings the charges, usually through the county or state prosecutor. The defendant can be apprehended either before or after the charges are brought. In the federal system people must be **indicted** by a **grand jury,** a panel of 16 to 23 citizens, before they can be charged with a serious crime. But most states do not use grand juries in that fashion, and the law provides that it is sufficient that the prosecutor issue an **information,** a formal accusation. After being charged, the defendant is arraigned. An **arraignment** is the formal reading of the charge. It is at the arraignment that the defendant makes a formal plea of guilty or not guilty. If the plea is guilty, the judge gives the verdict of the court and passes sentence, but usually not immediately, for presentencing reports and other procedures must be undertaken. If the plea is not guilty, a trial is scheduled.

Some state judicial systems have an intermediate step called a preliminary hearing or preliminary examination. The preliminary hearing is held in a court below the trial court, such as a municipal court, and the state has the responsibility of presenting enough evidence to convince the court—only a judge—that a crime has been committed and that there is sufficient evidence to believe that the defendant might possibly be involved. Today it is also not uncommon that **pretrial hearings** on a variety of matters precede the trial.

In both a civil suit and a criminal case, the result of the trial is not enforced until the final appeal is exhausted. That is, a money judgment is not paid in civil suits until defendants exhaust all their appeals. The same is true in a criminal case. Imprisonment or payment of a fine is not always required until the final appeal. If the defendant is dangerous or if there is some question that the defendant might not surrender when the final appeal is completed, bail can be required. Bail is money given to the court to ensure appearance in court.

SUMMARY

There are two basic kinds of lawsuits—civil suits and criminal prosecutions or actions. A civil suit is normally a dispute between two private parties in which the government offers its good offices (the courts) to resolve the dispute. The person who initiates the civil suit is called the plaintiff; the person at whom the suit is aimed is called the defendant. A plaintiff who wins a civil suit is normally awarded money damages.

A criminal case is normally an action in which the state brings charges against a private individual, who is called the defendant. A defendant who loses a criminal case can be assessed a fine, jailed or, in extreme cases, executed. A jury can be used in both civil and criminal cases. The jury becomes the fact finder and renders a verdict in a case. But the judge issues the judgment in the case. In a civil suit a judge can reject any jury verdict and rule in exactly the opposite fashion, finding for either plaintiff or defendant if the judge feels the jury has made a serious error in judgment. Either side can appeal the judgment of the court. In a criminal case the judge can take the case away from the jury and order a dismissal, but nothing can be done about an acquittal, even an incredible acquittal. While a guilty defendant may appeal the judgment, the state is prohibited from appealing an acquittal.

As stated at the outset, this chapter provides only a glimpse of both our legal system and our judicial system. It is not a substitute for a political science course in the legal process.

The United States legal and judicial systems are old and tradition-bound, but they have worked fairly well for more than two centuries. In the final analysis the job of both the law and the men and women who administer it is to balance the competing interests of society. How this balancing act is undertaken comprises the remainder of this book. The process is not always easy, but it is usually interesting.

BIBLIOGRAPHY

Abraham, Henry J. *The Judicial Process.* 7th ed. New York: Oxford University Press, 1998.
_____. *The Judiciary: The Supreme Court in the Government Process.* 3rd ed. Boston: Allyn & Bacon, 1973.
Cohn, Bob. "The Lawsuit Cha-Cha." *Newsweek,* 26 August 1991, 58.
Franklin, Marc A. *The Dynamics of American Law.* Mineola, N.Y.: Foundation Press, 1969.
Pound, Roscoe. *The Development of the Constitutional Guarantees of Liberty.* New Haven: Yale University Press, 1957.
Rembar, Charles. *The Law of the Land.* New York: Simon & Schuster, 1980.
Roche, John P. *Courts and Rights.* 2nd ed. New York: Random House, 1966.

CHAPTER 2

The First Amendment

THE MEANING OF FREEDOM

The First Amendment is the wellspring for nearly all U.S. laws on freedom of speech and press. The amendment, adopted in 1791 as part of the Bill of Rights, is only 45 words. But court decisions during the past two-plus centuries added substantial meaning to this basic outline. This chapter explores the evolution of freedom of expression, outlines the adoption of the First Amendment, and examines the development of some elements of the fundamental meaning of freedom of speech and press.

HISTORICAL DEVELOPMENT

Freedom of expression is not exclusively an American idea. It can be traced back to Socrates and Plato. The concept developed more fully during the past 400 years. The modern history of freedom of the press began in England during the 16th and 17th centuries as printing developed. Today the most indelible embodiment of the concept is the First Amendment to the U.S. Constitution, forged in the last half of the 18th century by individuals who built upon their memory of earlier experiences and unchanged in its wording today. To understand the meaning of freedom of the press and speech, it is necessary to understand the meaning of censorship, for viewed from a negative position freedom of expression can be simply defined as the absence of censorship or a freedom from government control.

FREEDOM OF THE PRESS IN ENGLAND

When William Caxton set up the first British printing press in 1476, his printing pursuits were restricted only by his imagination and ability. There were no laws governing what he could not print—he was completely free. For more than five centuries, the British and Americans have attempted to regain the freedom that Caxton enjoyed, for shortly after he started publishing, the British Crown began to regulate printing presses in England. Printing developed during a period of religious struggle in Europe, and it soon became an important tool in that struggle. Printing presses made communication with hundreds of people fairly easy and thus gave considerable power to small groups or individuals who owned or could use a press.

The British government realized that unrestricted publication and printing could dilute its power. Information is a potent tool in any society, and those who control the flow and content of information exercise considerable power. The printing press broke the Crown's monopoly of the flow of information, and therefore control of printing was essential.

Between 1476 and 1776 the British used several means to limit or restrict the press in England. **Seditious libel** laws were used to punish those who criticized the government or the Crown, and it did not matter whether the criticism was truthful or not. The press also suffered under **licensing** or **prior restraint** laws, which required printers to obtain prior approval from the government or the church before printing their handbills, pamphlets or newspapers. Printers were often required to deposit with the government large sums of money called **bonds.** This money was forfeited if material appeared that the government felt should not have been published. And the printer was forced to post another bond before printing could be resumed. The British also granted special patents and monopolies to certain printers in exchange for their cooperation in printing only acceptable works and in helping the Crown ferret out other printers who broke the publication laws.

British control of the press during these 300 years was generally successful, but did not go unchallenged. As ideas about democracy spread throughout Europe, it became harder and harder for the government to limit freedom of expression. The power of the printing press in spreading ideas quickly to masses of people greatly helped foster the democratic spirit. Although British law regulated American printers as well during the colonial era, regulation of the press in North America was never as successful as it was in Great Britain.

As ideas about democracy spread throughout Europe, it became harder and harder for the government to limit freedom of expression.

FREEDOM OF THE PRESS IN COLONIAL AMERICA

There were laws in the United States restricting freedom of the press for almost 30 years before the first newspaper was published. As early as 1662, statutes in Massachusetts made it a crime to publish anything without first getting prior approval from the government, 28 years before Benjamin Harris published the first—and last—edition of Publick Occurrences. The second and all subsequent issues were banned because Harris had failed to get permission to publish the first edition, which contained material construed to be criticism of British policy in the colonies, as well as a report that scandalized the Massachusetts clergy because it said the French king took immoral liberties with a married woman (not his wife).

Despite this inauspicious beginning, American colonists had a much easier time getting their views into print (and staying out of jail) than did their counterparts in England. There was censorship, but American juries were reluctant to convict printers prosecuted by the colonial authorities. The colonial governments were less efficient than the government in England. Also, the British had only limited control over the administration of government in many of the colonies.

The British attempted to use licensing, taxes and sedition laws to control American printers and publishers. Licensing, which ended in England in 1695, lasted until the mid-1720s in the American colonies. Benjamin Franklin's older brother James was jailed in 1722 for failing to get prior government approval for publishing his New England Courant. The unpopular government move failed to daunt the older Franklin, and licensing eventually ended in the colonies as well. The taxes levied against the press, most of which were genuine attempts to raise revenues, were nevertheless seen as censorship by American printers and resulted in growing hostility toward Parliament and the Crown. Most publishers refused to buy the tax stamps, and there was little retribution by the British.

The most famous case of government censorship in the American colonies was the seditious libel trial of immigrant printer John Peter Zenger, who found himself involved in a vicious political battle between leading colonial politicians in New York. Zenger published the New York Weekly Journal, a newspaper sponsored by Lewis Morris and James Alexander, political opponents of the unpopular colonial governor, William Cosby. Zenger was jailed in November 1734 after his newspaper published several stinging attacks on Cosby, who surmised that by jailing the printer—one of only two working in New York—he could silence his critics. There is little doubt that Zenger was guilty under 18th-century British sedition law. But his attorneys, including the renowned criminal lawyer Andrew Hamilton, were able to convince the jury that no man should be imprisoned or fined for publishing criticism of the government that was both truthful and fair. Jurors simply ignored the law and acquitted the German printer. It was an early example of what today is called **jury nullification**—the power of a jury in a criminal case to ignore (and thereby to "nullify") a law and to return a verdict (typically a not guilty verdict) according to its conscience. While certainly controversial and relatively rare, jury nullification can be seen as an essential part of the legislative process because a law that is repeatedly nullified by juries probably should be revised or discarded by the legislative body that created it.

The verdict in the Zenger case was a great political triumph but did nothing to change the law of seditious libel. In other words, the case did not set an important legal precedent. But the revolt of the American jurors did force colonial authorities to reconsider the use of

The most famous case of government censorship in the American colonies was the seditious libel trial of immigrant printer John Peter Zenger.

The trial of John Peter Zenger in New York in 1734. The printer was defended by attorney Andrew Hamilton and the acquittal of the printer put the British Crown on notice that American jurors were not inclined to convict those who criticized British officials.

Source: © Bettmann/CORBIS

sedition law as a means of controlling the press. Although a few sedition prosecutions were initiated after 1735, there is no record of a successful prosecution in the colonial courts after the Zenger case. The case received widespread publicity both in North America and in England, and the outcome of the trial played an important role in galvanizing public sentiment against this kind of government censorship.

The Zenger trial today is part of American journalism mythology, but it doesn't represent the end of British attempts to control the press in the American colonies. Rather than haul printers and editors before jurors hostile to the state, the government instead hauled them before colonial legislatures and assemblies hostile to journalists. The charge was not sedition, but breach of parliamentary privilege or contempt of the assembly. There was no distinct separation of powers then, and the legislative body could order printers to appear, question, convict and punish them. Printers and publishers were thus still being jailed and fined for publications previously considered seditious. Only the means of exacting this punishment had changed.

Despite these potent sanctions occasionally levied against publishers and printers, the press of this era was remarkably robust. Researchers who have painstakingly read the newspapers, pamphlets and handbills produced in the last half of the 18th century are struck by the seeming lack of concern for government censorship. Historian Leonard Levy notes in his book "Emergence of a Free Press" the seeming paradox uncovered by scholars who seek to understand the meaning of freedom of expression during that era.[1] "To one [a scholar] whose prime

1. Levy, *Emergence of a Free Press.*

concern was law and theory, a legacy of suppression [of the press] came into focus; to one who looks at newspaper judgments on public men and measures, the revolutionary controversy spurred an expanding legacy of liberty," he wrote. What Levy suggests is that while the law and legal pronouncements from jurists and legislatures suggest a fairly rigid control of the press, in fact journalists and other publishers tended to ignore the law and suffered little retribution.

But the appearance of such freedom can be deceptive, as political scientist John Roche points out in his book "Shadow and Substance,"[2] for the community often exerted tremendous, and sometimes extralegal, pressure on anyone who expressed an unpopular idea. The belief of many people that freedom was the hallmark of society in America ignores history, Roche argues. In colonial America the people simply did not understand that freedom of thought and expression meant freedom for the other person also, particularly for the person with hated ideas. Roche points out that colonial America was an open society dotted with closed enclaves—villages and towns and cities—in which citizens generally shared similar beliefs about religion and government and so forth. Citizens could hold any belief they chose and could espouse that belief, but personal safety depended on the people in a community agreeing with a speaker or writer. If they didn't, the speaker then kept quiet—an early example of self-censorship or what scholars today call a "chilling effect" on speech—or moved to another enclave where the people shared those ideas. While there was much diversity of thought in the colonies, there was often little diversity of belief within individual towns and cities, according to Roche.

The belief of many people that freedom was the hallmark of society in America ignores history.

The propaganda war that preceded the Revolution is a classic example of the situation. In Boston, the patriots argued vigorously for the right to print what they wanted in their newspapers, even criticism of the government. Freedom of expression was their right, a God-given right, a natural right, a right of all British subjects. Many people, however, did not favor revolution or even separation from England. Yet it was extremely difficult for them to publish such pro-British sentiments in many American cities after 1770. Printers who published such ideas in newspapers and handbills did so at their peril. In cities like Boston the printers were attacked, their shops were wrecked and their papers were destroyed. Freedom of the press was a concept with limited utility in many communities for colonists who opposed revolution once the patriots had moved the populace to their side.

Community Censorship, Then and Now

The plight of the pro-British printer in Boston in the 1770s is not a unique chapter in American history. Today such community censorship still exists—and in some instances is growing.

Community censorship does not mean censorship or punishment imposed by the government, but rather the silencing of speech by private people or business entities, often as a result of pressure exerted by political activists, public interest groups and economic stakeholders. It amounts to self-censorship, not government censorship. For instance, a radio station in Anchorage, Alaska, suspended two disc jockeys in 2008 for making sexually offensive, on-air remarks about native Alaskan women. The suspension was not the result of government action (the Federal Communications Commission, for instance, did not order it); it was a corporate decision made after the station received complaints from listeners and others. More famously, when Don Imus left the airwaves in April 2007 after his "nappy-headed hos" comment about Rutgers' female basketball

2. Roche, *Shadow and Substance.*

players, it was the result of a determination by officials at CBS Radio and MSNBC after receiving complaints from the likes of Al Sharpton and the NAACP and after businesses pulled advertisements from the Imus program. The FCC did not fire Don Imus. But just as it was political pressure and advertising concerns that drove Imus from the airwaves, it was economic-marketplace forces (he remained popular in many quarters) that brought him back, just eight months later, to 77 WABC in New York City to host a nationally syndicated show.

Community censorship occurred in 2008 when rapper Nas (Nasir Jones) released a CD called "Untitled." Originally, it was to be titled "Nigger," but loud complaints about that controversial moniker were made by Sharpton, Jesse Jackson and the NAACP, among others (several black recording artists, in contrast, defended Nas and his proposed title). There also was economic concern that large retail stores would not stock the CD if it carried the original title. Nas got some revenge when he rapped on the CD about the community censorship, proclaiming "I'm hog-tied, the corporate side blocking y'all from going to stores and buying it." Corporate censorship in music was also present in 2009 when Wal-Mart chose not to sell Green Day's CD "21st Century Breakdown," with the mega-retailer citing its policy against selling CDs with parental advisory stickers.

Book publisher Random House engaged in self-censorship in 2008 when it cancelled publication of "The Jewel of Medina" by author Sherry Jones because some Muslims found the book offensive and the publisher feared it "would become a new 'Satanic Verses,' the Salman Rushdie novel of 1988 that led to death threats, riots and the murder of the book's Japanese translator, among other horrors."[3] Random House also feared the historical-fiction book, which deals with a young wife of the prophet Muhammad, would place its own employees' lives in jeopardy. Perhaps not surprisingly, the North American publishing rights for the tome were later picked up by Beaufort Books, the same company that published O.J. Simpson's "If I Did It" book after it was dropped by ReganBooks in 2006 after public outrage. It seems that community censorship plays a significant role in silencing controversial books at some major publishing houses. After Gibson Square publishers in London picked up the European rights to "The Jewel of Medina," its headquarters were deliberately set on fire in September 2008. Unlike Random House, however, Gibson Square stood firm in its resolve to publish the book.

YouTube voluntarily altered its community guidelines in 2008 to prohibit the posting of certain violent-themed videos—including those showing sniper attacks and videos that train terrorists—that could incite violent acts or dangerous activities involving a risk of serious physical harm or death. The move came in response to political pressure about the prevalence on YouTube of videos allegedly produced by radical extremist groups and terrorist organizations.

Sexual content is another typical target of community censorship. For instance, movie producer Kevin Smith had difficulty placing ads in newspapers and on television for his 2008 movie "Zack and Miri Make a Porno" starring Seth Rogen. The word "porno" in the provocative title was simply too objectionable for some companies.

It is important to understand that the First Amendment does not protect against community censorship. It protects only against censorship by government officials and government entities. Students at some universities have attempted to block the appearances of right-wing speakers with whom they disagree. For instance, in 2006 hundreds of students at the left-leaning New

---

3. Nomani, "You Still Can't Write About Muhammad."

School in New York City called for that university's president to rescind an invitation to Republican U.S. Senator John McCain to be its commencement speaker. Although McCain ultimately was allowed to speak, he was heckled repeatedly. But such instances of nongovernmental community censorship also run in the opposite political direction, as when The New York Times' Chris Hedges, "a war correspondent who sharply criticized the war in Iraq, had to cut his speech short after he was repeatedly interrupted by boos and his microphone was unplugged twice" during a commencement address at Rockford College in Illinois.[4] This is an example of what attorneys sometimes call a **heckler's veto**—when a crowd or audience's reaction to a speech or message is allowed to control and silence that speech or message. In August 2009, some of the raucous town-hall meetings hosted by U.S. senators and representatives to address health-care legislation nearly turned into such heckler's veto situations. In an ideal world, of course, speakers from *both* the right and the left would be allowed to speak freely on college campuses in order to expose students to competing viewpoints. But community censorship is not just a problem on college campuses; it was famously present when radio stations, in response to outraged conservatives, stopped playing songs by the Dixie Chicks, a Dallas-based country music trio, in early 2003 after lead singer Natalie Maines told an audience in London, England, that "we're ashamed the President of the United States is from Texas."[5]

In many of these instances the general public finds little cause for concern about such censorship. Public malaise about such conditions is dangerous. No individual's freedom is secure unless the freedom of all is ensured. This last point—that the freedom of speech must be ensured for *all* people, not simply those on one side of the political spectrum—is critical. As Nadine Strossen, president of the American Civil Liberties Union, told one of the authors of this textbook, "the notion of neutrality is key. You cannot have freedom of speech only for ideas that you like and people that you like."[6] Those who would engage in community censorship because they don't like what someone has to say would be wise to remember this principle of viewpoint neutrality embodied in the freedom of speech.

SUMMARY

Freedom of the press, part of the great Anglo-American legal tradition, is a right that has been won only through many hard-fought battles. The British discovered the power of the press in the early 16th century and devised numerous schemes to restrict publication. Criticism of the government, called seditious libel, was outlawed. Licensing or prior censorship was also common. In addition, the Crown for many years used an elaborate system of patents and monopolies to control printing in England.

While under British law for more than 100 years, American colonists enjoyed somewhat more freedom of expression than did their counterparts in England. Censorship laws existed before the first printing press arrived in North America, but they were enforced erratically or not at all. Licensing ended in the colonies in the 1720s. There were several trials for sedition in the colonies, but the acquittal of John Peter Zenger in 1735 by a recalcitrant jury ended

4. Young, "The Tyranny of Hecklers."
5. Parks, "Chicks Face 'Landslide.'"
6. Richards and Calvert, "Nadine Strossen and Freedom of Expression," 202.

that threat. Colonial legislatures and assemblies then attempted to punish dissident printers by using their contempt power. By the time the American colonists began to build their own governments in the 1770s and 1780s, they had the history of a 300-year struggle for freedom of expression on which to build.

THE FIRST AMENDMENT

In 1781, even before the end of the Revolutionary War, the new nation adopted its first constitution, the Articles of Confederation. The Articles provided for a loose-knit confederation of the 13 colonies, or states, in which the central or federal government had little power. The Articles reflected the spirit of the Declaration of Independence, adopted five years earlier, which ranked the rights of individuals in the society higher than the needs of a government to organize and operate a cohesive community. The Articles of Confederation did not contain a guarantee of freedom of expression. In fact, it had no bill of rights of any kind. The individuals who drafted this constitution did not believe such guarantees were necessary. Guarantees of freedom of expression were already a part of the constitutions of most of the 13 states.

But the system of government created by the Articles of Confederation did not work very well. In the hot summer of 1787, 12 of the 13 states sent a total of 55 delegates to Philadelphia to revise or amend the Articles, to make fundamental changes in the structure of the government.

THE NEW CONSTITUTION

It was a remarkable group of men; perhaps no such group has gathered before or since. The members were merchants, planters and professionals. None were full-time politicians. These men were members of the economic, social and intellectual aristocracy of their states. They shared a common education centered on history, political philosophy and science. Some spent months preparing for the meeting—studying the governments of past nations. Whereas some members came to modify the Articles of Confederation, many others knew that a new constitution was needed. In the end that is what they produced, a new governmental charter. The charter was far different from the Articles in that it gave vast powers to a central government. The states remained supreme in some matters, but in other matters they relinquished their sovereignty to the new federal government.

No official record of the convention was kept. The delegates deliberated behind closed doors as they drafted the new charter. However, some personal records remain. We know, for example, that inclusion of a bill of rights was not discussed until the last days of the convention. The Constitution was drafted in such a way as not to infringe on state bills of rights. When the meeting was in its final week, George Mason of Virginia indicated his desire that "the plan be prefaced with a Bill of Rights. . . . It would give great quiet to the people," he said, "and with the aid of the state declarations, a bill might be prepared in a few hours." Few joined Mason's call. Only one delegate, Roger Sherman of Connecticut, spoke against the suggestion. He said he favored protecting the rights of the people when it was necessary, but in this case there was no need. "The state declarations of rights are not repealed by this Constitution; and being in force are sufficient." The states, voting as units, unanimously opposed Mason's plan. While the Virginian later attempted to add a bill of rights in a piecemeal fashion, the Constitution emerged from the convention and was placed before the people for ratification without a bill of rights.

The new Constitution was not without opposition. The struggle for its adoption was hard fought. The failure to include a bill of rights in the document was a telling complaint raised against the new document. Even Thomas Jefferson, who was in France, lamented, in a letter to his friend James Madison, the lack of a guarantee of political rights in the charter. When the states finally voted on the new Constitution, it was approved, but only after supporters in several states had promised to petition the First Congress to add a bill of rights.

James Madison was elected from Virginia to the House of Representatives, defeating James Monroe only after promising his constituents to work in the First Congress toward adoption of a declaration of human rights. When Congress convened, Madison worked to keep his promise. He first proposed that the new legislature incorporate a bill of rights into the body of the Constitution, but the idea was later dropped. That the Congress would adopt the declaration was not a foregone conclusion. There was much opposition, but after several months, 12 amendments were finally approved by both houses and sent to the states for ratification. Madison's original amendment dealing with freedom of expression states: "The people shall not be deprived or abridged of their right to speak, to write or to publish their sentiments and freedom of the press, as one of the great bulwarks of liberty, shall be inviolable." Congressional committees changed the wording several times, and the section guaranteeing freedom of expression was merged with the amendment guaranteeing freedom of religion and freedom of assembly. The final version is the one we know today:

> *Congress shall make no law respecting an establishment of religion, or prohibiting the free exercise thereof; or abridging the freedom of speech, or of the press; or the right of the people peaceably to assemble, and to petition the Government for a redress of grievances.*

The concept of the "first freedom" is discussed often. Historical myth tells us that because the amendment occurs first in the Bill of Rights it was considered the most important right. In fact, in the Bill of Rights presented to the states for ratification, the amendment was listed third. Amendments 1 and 2 were defeated and did not become part of the Constitution.

Passage of Amendments 3 through 12 did not occur without struggle. Not until two years after being transmitted to the states for approval did a sufficient number of states adopt the amendments for them to become part of the Constitution. Connecticut, Georgia and Massachusetts did not ratify the Bill of Rights until 1941, a kind of token gesture on the 150th anniversary of its constitutional adoption. In 1791 approval by these states was not needed, since only three-fourths of the former colonies needed to agree to the measures.

Historical myth tells us that because the amendment occurs first in the Bill of Rights it was considered the most important right.

FREEDOM OF EXPRESSION IN THE 18TH CENTURY

What did the First Amendment mean to the people who supported its ratification? Technically, the definition of freedom of the press approved by the nation when the First Amendment was ratified in 1791 is what is guaranteed today. To enlarge or narrow that definition requires another vote of the people, a constitutional amendment. This notion is referred to today as "original intent" of the Constitution; that is, if we knew the meaning intended by the framers of the First Amendment, then we would know what it means today.

Most people today consider this notion misguided. The nation has changed dramatically in 219 years. Television, radio, film and the Internet did not exist in 1791. Does this mean that the guarantees of the First Amendment should not apply to these mass media? Of course not. Our Constitution has survived more than two centuries because the Supreme Court of the United States, our final arbiter on the meaning of the Constitution, has helped adapt it to changing times.

Still, it is important that we respect the document that was adopted more than two centuries ago. If we stray too far from its original meaning, the document may become meaningless; there will be no rules of government. The Constitution will mean only what those in power say it means. Thus the judicial philosophy of historicism, despite what law professor Rodney Smolla correctly calls "the obstinate illusiveness of original intent in the free speech area,"[7] remains an important consideration for some judges and justices. For instance, Justice Clarence Thomas on the U.S. Supreme Court often uses historicism/originalism. "The experience of the framers will never give us precise answers to modern conflicts," Smolla writes, "but it will give us a sense of how deeply free speech was cherished, at least as an abstract value."[8]

What was the legal or judicial definition of the First Amendment in 1791? Surprisingly, that is not an easy question to answer. The records of the period carry mixed messages. There was no authoritative definition of freedom of the press and freedom of speech rendered by a body like the Supreme Court. And even the words used by people of that era may have meant something different than they mean in the 21st century. Most everyone agrees that freedom of expression meant at least the right to be free from prior restraint or licensing. Sir William Blackstone, a British legal scholar, published a major summary of common law between 1765 and 1769. In "Commentaries on the Law of England," Blackstone defined freedom of expression as "laying no previous restraints upon publication." Today we call this no prior censorship. Many scholars argue that freedom of expression surely meant more than simply no prior censorship, that it also protected people from punishment *after publication* or, as First Amendment scholars might put it, from subsequent punishments. In other words, the First Amendment also precluded prosecutions for seditious libel. After all, they argue, one of the reasons for the American Revolution was to rid the nation of the hated British sedition laws.

Most everyone agrees that freedom of expression meant at least the right to be free from prior restraint or licensing.

The truth is that we probably don't know what freedom of the press meant to American citizens in the 1790s. The written residue of the period reveals only a partial story. It's very likely that it meant something a little different to different people, just as it does today. Even those individuals who drafted the Bill of Rights probably held somewhat different views on the meaning of the First Amendment.

WHAT IS "SPEECH" ANYWAY?

The word "speech" in the First Amendment sometimes (but not always) encompasses and includes *conduct*, not simply what we might think of as *pure speech*, such as the written, printed or spoken word or image. Under the **symbolic speech doctrine,** courts treat conduct, such as burning a flag in political protest at a rally, as speech if two elements—one focusing on the actor, the other on the audience—are satisfied:

---

7. Smolla, *Free Speech in an Open Society,* 28.
8. Ibid., 39.

1. *Actor:* The person engaging in the conduct must intend to convey a particular or specific message with his or her conduct.
2. *Audience:* There must be a great likelihood, under the surrounding circumstances in which the conduct takes place, that some people who witness it will reasonably understand the particular message that was intended by the actor.

Under the two-part symbolic speech doctrine, burning an American flag in one's own backyard, when no one else is around and in an effort to stay warm during a snowstorm, does not constitute speech. On the other hand, the U.S. Supreme Court has recognized that burning the flag outside of a political convention in the midst of a protest or rally may be speech. The court has held that nude dancing in a strip club is a form of symbolic speech (see Chapter 13); there's an intent to convey an erotic, sexual message and there is a clear likelihood (judging by the tips, if nothing else) that the message will be understood as intended. An Oregon judge even held in 2008 that nude bicycle riding constitutes speech, at least when it takes place during the annual "World Naked Bike Ride" and is designed to protest against the use of cars and gasoline and to draw attention to oil dependency.

FREEDOM OF EXPRESSION TODAY

If we are not certain what the First Amendment meant in 1791, do we know what it means today? More or less. The First Amendment means today what the Supreme Court of the United States says it means.

The First Amendment means today what the Supreme Court of the United States says it means.

The Supreme Court is a collection of nine justices, not a single individual. Consequently, at any given time there can be nine different definitions of freedom of expression. This has never happened—at least not on important issues. What has happened is that groups of justices have subscribed to various theoretical positions regarding the meaning of the First Amendment. These ideas on the meaning of the First Amendment help justices shape their vote on a question regarding freedom of expression. These ideas have changed during the past 90 years, from the point at which the First Amendment first came under serious scrutiny by the Supreme Court.

Legal theories are sometimes difficult to handle. Judge Learned Hand, the most important judge *never* to have served on the U.S. Supreme Court, referred to the propagation of legal theory as "shoveling smoke." With such cautions in mind, here are seven important First Amendment theories or strategies to help judges develop a practical definition of freedom of expression.

SEVEN FIRST AMENDMENT THEORIES

1. Absolutist theory
2. Ad hoc balancing theory
3. Preferred position balancing theory

> 4. Meiklejohnian theory
> 5. Marketplace of ideas theory
> 6. Access theory
> 7. Self-realization theory

Absolutist Theory. Some argue that the First Amendment presents an absolute or complete barrier to government censorship. When the First Amendment declares that "no law" shall abridge freedom of expression, the framers of the Constitution meant *no law*. This is the essence of the **absolutist theory.** The government cannot censor the press for any reason. There are no exceptions, no caveats, no qualifications.

A majority of the Supreme Court never has adopted an absolutist position.

Few have subscribed to this notion wholeheartedly. A majority of the Supreme Court *never* has adopted an absolutist position. In fact, as this book later illustrates, the Supreme Court has held that several types of speech fall outside the scope of First Amendment protection and thus can be abridged without violating the freedoms of speech or press. As Justice Anthony Kennedy wrote in 2002, "[t]he freedom of speech has its limits; it does not embrace certain categories of speech, including defamation, incitement, obscenity, and pornography produced with real children."[9] Other categories of speech also fall outside the ambit of First Amendment protection, including fighting words (see pages 121–125) and true threats of violence.[10]

Ad Hoc Balancing Theory. Freedom of speech and press are two of a number of important human rights we value in this nation. These rights often conflict. When conflict occurs, it is the responsibility of the court to balance the freedom of expression with other values. For example, the government must maintain the military to protect the security of the nation. To function, the military must maintain secrecy about many of its weapons, plans and movements. Imagine that the press seeks to publish information about a secret weapons system. The right to freedom of expression must be balanced with the need for secrecy in the military.

This theory is called *ad hoc* balancing because the scales are erected anew in every case; the meaning of the freedom of expression is determined solely on a case-by-case basis. Freedom of the press might outweigh the need for the government to keep secret the design of its new rifle, but the need for secrecy about a new fighter plane might take precedence over freedom of expression.

Ad hoc balancing is really not a theory; it is a strategy. Developing a definition of freedom of expression on a case-by-case basis leads to uncertainty. Under ad hoc balancing we will never know what the First Amendment means except as it relates to a specific, narrow problem (e.g., the right to publish information about a new army rifle). If citizens cannot reasonably predict whether a particular kind of expression might be protected or prohibited, they will have the tendency to play it safe and keep silent. This is known as a "chilling effect" on speech. This will limit the rights of expression of all persons. Also, ad hoc balancing relies too heavily in its final determination on the personal biases of the judge or justices who decide a

---

9. *Ashcroft* v. *Free Speech Coalition*, 535 U.S. 234, 245–46 (2002).
10. *Watts* v. *U. S.*, 394 U.S. 705, 708 (1969).

case. Ad hoc balancing is rarely invoked as a strategy these days except by judges unfamiliar with First Amendment law.

Preferred Position Balancing Theory. The Supreme Court has held in numerous rulings that some constitutional freedoms, principally those guaranteed by the First Amendment, are fundamental to a free society and consequently are entitled to more judicial protection than other constitutional values are.[11] Freedom of expression is essential to permit the operation of the political process and to permit citizens to protest when government infringes on their constitutionally protected prerogatives. The Fourth Amendment guarantee of freedom from illegal search and seizure surely has diminished value if citizens who suffer from such unconstitutional searches cannot protest such actions. Freedom of expression does not trump all other rights. Courts, for example, have attempted to balance the rights of free speech and press with the constitutionally guaranteed right of a fair trial. On the other hand, courts have consistently ruled that freedom of expression takes precedence over the right to personal privacy and the right to reputation, neither of which is explicitly guaranteed by the Bill of Rights.

Giving freedom of expression a preferred position *presumes* that government action that limits free speech and free press to protect other interests is usually unconstitutional. This presumption forces the government to bear the burden of proof in any legal action challenging the censorship. The city, county, state or federal government must prove to the court that its censorship is, in fact, justified and is not a violation of the First Amendment. Were it not for this presumption, the persons whose expression was limited would be forced to convince a court that they had a constitutional right to speak or publish. This difference sounds minor, but in a lawsuit this presumption means a great deal.

While this theory retains some of the negative features of ad hoc balancing, by tilting the scales in favor of freedom of expression, it adds somewhat more certainty to our definition of freedom of expression. By basing this balancing strategy on a philosophical foundation (the maintenance of all rights is dependent on free exercise of speech and press), it becomes easier to build a case in favor of the broad interpretation of freedom of expression under the First Amendment.

Meiklejohnian Theory. Philosopher and educator Alexander Meiklejohn presented a rather complex set of ideas about freedom of expression in the late 1940s.[12] Meiklejohn argued that freedom of expression is a means to an end. That end is successful self-government or, as Meiklejohn put it, "the voting of wise decisions." Freedom of speech and press are protected in the Constitution so that our system of democracy can function, and that is the only reason they are protected. Expression that relates to the self-governing process must be protected absolutely by the First Amendment. There can be no government interference with such expression. Expression that does not relate to the self-governing process is not protected absolutely by the First Amendment. The value or worth of such speech must be balanced by the courts against other rights and values. Meiklejohnian theory thus represents a hierarchical approach to First Amendment theory, with political speech placed at the top of this hierarchy.

Critics of this theory argue that it is not always clear whether expression pertains to self-government (public speech) or to other interests (private speech). Although not providing the

Expression that relates to the self-governing process must be protected absolutely by the First Amendment.

---

11. See *U.S.* v. *Carolene Products,* 304 U.S. 144 (1938); and *Palko* v. *Connecticut,* 302 U.S. 319 (1937). See also *Abrams* v. *U. S.*, 250 U.S. 616 (1919).
12. Meiklejohn, *Free Speech.*

specific definition sought by critics, Meiklejohn argued that a broad range of speech is essential to successful self-government. He included speech-related education (history, political science, geography, etc.), science, literature and many other topics. This theory has been embraced by some members of the Supreme Court of the United States, most notably former justice William Brennan. American libel law was radically changed when Brennan led the Supreme Court to give First Amendment protection to people who have defamed government officials or others who attempt to lead public policy, a purely Meiklejohnian approach to the problem.

Marketplace of Ideas Theory. The marketplace of ideas theory embodies what First Amendment scholar Daniel Farber calls "the truth-seeking rationale for free expression."[13] Although the theory can be traced back to the work of John Milton and John Stuart Mill, it was U.S. Supreme Court Justice Oliver Wendell Holmes Jr. who introduced the marketplace rationale for protecting speech to First Amendment case law more than 90 years ago. In his dissent in *Abrams* v. *United States,*[14] Holmes famously wrote:

> But when men have realized that time has upset many fighting faiths, they may come to believe even more than they believe the very foundations of their own conduct that the ultimate good desired is better reached by free trade in ideas—that the best test of truth is the power of the thought to get itself accepted in the competition of the market, and that truth is the only ground upon which their wishes safely can be carried out.[15]

Today, the economics-based marketplace metaphor "consistently dominates the Supreme Court's discussion of freedom of speech."[16] For instance, in writing for a unanimous Supreme Court in 2003 in *Virginia* v. *Hicks,* Justice Antonin Scalia described how overbroad laws—laws that are drafted so broadly that they punish a substantial amount of protected free speech along with unprotected speech—are unconstitutional because they harm "society as a whole, which is deprived of an *uninhibited marketplace of ideas.*"[17]

The marketplace theory, however, is often criticized by scholars. Common condemnations are that much shoddy speech, such as hate speech (see pages 121–125), circulates in the marketplace of ideas despite its lack of value and that access to the marketplace is *not* equal for everyone. In particular, those having the most economic resources (today, large conglomerates such as Viacom, News Corp. and Clear Channel) are able to own and to control the mass media and, in turn, to dominate the marketplace of ideas. Nonetheless, professor Martin Redish observes that "over the years, it has not been uncommon for scholars or jurists to analogize the right of free expression to a marketplace in which contrasting ideas compete for acceptance among a consuming public."[18] The premise of this idealistically free and fair competition of ideas is that truth will be discovered or, at the very least, conceptions of the truth will be tested and challenged.[19]

The premise of this idealistically free and fair competition of ideas is that truth will be discovered.

---

13. Farber, *The First Amendment,* 4.
14. 250 U.S. 616 (1919).
15. 250 U.S. 616, 630 (Holmes, J., dissenting).
16. Baker, *Human Liberty,* 7.
17. 539 U.S. 113, 119 (2003).
18. Redish and Kaludis, "The Right of Expressive Access," 1083.
19. Chemerinsky, *Constitutional Law,* 753.

Access Theory. A.J. Liebling wrote that freedom of the press belongs to the man who owns one. What the iconoclast meant was that a constitutional guarantee of freedom of expression had little meaning if a citizen did not have the economic means to exercise this right. Owners of magazines, newspapers and broadcasting stations could take advantage of the promises of the First Amendment, whereas the average person lacked this ability. Put differently, access to the metaphorical marketplace of ideas is *not* equal for all, but is skewed in favor of those with the most economic resources. What Liebling wrote is true today, although the evolution of the Internet has at least given millions more Americans the opportunity to share their ideas as "bloggers" with a wider audience than was accessible in the past. Still, the audience for the vast majority of Web sites is small in comparison with the number of people reached by a television network, national magazine or even a metropolitan newspaper.

In the mid-1960s some legal scholars, most notably professor Jerome Barron, former dean of the National Law Center at George Washington University, argued that the promise of the First Amendment was unfulfilled for most Americans because they lacked the means to exercise their right to freedom of the press.[20] To make the guarantees of the First Amendment meaningful, newspapers, magazines and broadcasting stations should open their pages and studios to the ideas and opinions of their readers and listeners and viewers. If the press will not do this voluntarily, the obligation falls upon the government to force such access to the press. The access theory thus can be seen as a remedy to correct some of the flaws of the marketplace of ideas theory described earlier.

The Supreme Court unanimously rejected the access theory in 1974 in *Miami Herald* v. *Tornillo*.[21] Chief Justice Warren Burger, writing for the court, said that the choice of material to go into a newspaper and the decisions made as to content and treatment of public issues and public officials are decisions that must be made by the editors. The First Amendment does not give the government the right to force a newspaper to publish the views or ideas of a citizen. The *Tornillo* case sounded the legal death knell for this access theory for print media.

At the same time that federal courts were rejecting the access theory as it applied to the printed press, many courts were embracing these notions to justify the regulation of American radio and television. In 1969 the Supreme Court ruled in *Red Lion Broadcasting* v. *FCC*[22] that "[i]t is the right of the public to receive suitable access to social, political, esthetic, moral, and other ideas and experiences, which is crucial here." The apparent contradiction in accepting the access theory for broadcast media but rejecting its application to the printed press was based on what many broadcasters regarded as an ill-conceived notion of differences in the two media forms. There could be an unlimited number of voices in the printed press, it was argued, but technological limits in the electromagnetic broadcast spectrum controlled the number of radio and television stations that could broadcast, and the government was required to protect the public interest in the case of the latter. The flaw in this assumption, the broadcasters argued, was that it failed to take into account 20th-century (and now 21st-century) economic limits that sharply curtailed the number of printing presses.

Self-Realization/Self-Fulfillment Theory. While the primary goal of Meiklejohnian theory is successful self-government and the main objective of the marketplace theory is discovery

The access theory thus can be seen as a remedy to correct some of the flaws of the marketplace of ideas theory.

---

20. Barron, "Access to the Press."
21. 418 U.S. 241 (1974).
22. 395 U.S. 367 (1969).

Speech is important to an individual regardless of its impact on politics or its benefit to society at large.

of the truth, it may be that speech is important to an individual *regardless* of its impact on politics or its benefit to society at large. For instance, transcribing one's thoughts in a private diary or a personal journal can be beneficial to the writer, even though no one else ever will (at least the writer hopes!) read them. Speech, in other words, can be inherently valuable to a person regardless of its effect on others—it can be an end in itself. An individual who wears a shirt with the name of his or her favorite political candidate on it may not change anyone else's vote or influence discovery of the truth, yet the shirt-wearer is realizing and expressing his or her own identity through speech.

SUMMARY

The nation's first constitution, the Articles of Confederation, did not contain a guarantee of freedom of speech and press, but nearly all state constitutions provided for a guarantee of such rights. Citizens insisted that a written declaration of rights be included in the Constitution of 1787, and a guarantee of freedom of expression was a part of the Bill of Rights that was added to the national charter in 1791.

There is a debate over the meaning of the First Amendment when it was drafted and approved in the late 18th century. Some people argue that it was intended to block both prior censorship and prosecution for seditious libel. Others argue that it was intended to prohibit only prior censorship. We will never know what the guarantee of free expression meant to the people who drafted it, but it is a good bet they had a variety of interpretations of the First Amendment.

The meaning of the First Amendment today is largely determined by the Supreme Court of the United States. Jurists use legal theories to guide them in determining the meaning of the constitutional guarantee that "Congress shall make no law abridging freedom of speech or of the press." Seven such theories are (1) absolutist theory, (2) ad hoc balancing theory, (3) preferred position balancing theory, (4) Meiklejohnian theory, (5) marketplace of ideas theory, (6) access theory and (7) self-realization theory.

THE MEANING OF FREEDOM

The struggle since 1791 to define the meaning of freedom of expression has involved a variety of issues. Three topics are at the heart of this struggle: the power of the state to limit criticism or published attacks on the government; the power of the state to use taxation to censor the press; and the power of the government to forbid the publication of ideas or information it believes to be harmful. Each of these classic battles will be considered in the remainder of this chapter.

SEDITIOUS LIBEL AND THE RIGHT TO CRITICIZE THE GOVERNMENT

The essence of a democracy is participation by citizens in the process of government. This participation involves selecting leaders through the electoral process. Popular participation also includes examination of government and public officials to determine their fitness for serving the people. Discussion, criticism and suggestion all play a part in the orderly transition of governments and elected leaders. The right to speak and print, then, is inherent in a nation governed by popularly elected rulers.

The right to criticize and oppose the government is central to our political philosophy in the United States. The Supreme Court has ruled, for example, that the First Amendment protects both the right to burn the American flag as a form of political protest[23] and the right to wear a jacket with the words "Fuck the Draft" in a public courthouse during the Vietnam War.[24] But even today it is not always possible to criticize the government or to advocate political change without suffering government reprisals. During the war in Iraq, for instance, a peace activist named Dan Frazier began selling an anti-war T-shirt carrying the large, boldfaced words "BUSH LIED" and "THEY DIED" emblazoned on top of the names (each printed in tiny font) of every U.S. soldier killed in Iraq. He advertised the T-shirt on his Web site, with the ad showing part of the shirt and revealing the names of actual deceased soldiers. Five states soon passed laws that either criminalized the use of dead soldiers' names on a commercial product without the permission of immediate relatives or created civil remedies allowing relatives to sue Frazier for the wrongful appropriation of the names of their deceased loved ones. In 2008, however, a federal judge in Arizona ruled that Frazier could sell his T-shirts despite a criminal law in that state prohibiting the use of the names of dead soldiers in ads for the sale of goods (in this case, T-shirts for sale) without permission of relatives.[25] Judge Neil V. Wake reasoned that the shirts constitute "core political speech fully protected by the First Amendment, notwithstanding the fact that [Frazier] offers them for sale." He added that "superimposing 'BUSH LIED—THEY DIED' over the names of fallen soldiers obviously critiques the initiation and administration of the war in Iraq, among the most debated issues in current American politics." Judge Wake concluded that Arizona did not have sufficient grounds to "criminalize Frazier's decision to honestly display his T-shirts to his customers" on his Web site.

In 2006, the federal government launched the first treason case since World War II, targeting California-born Adam Gadahn. The case was based largely on five propaganda videos for Al Qaeda calling for the death of Americans in which Gadahn allegedly appeared and/or translated the words (i.e., he did the voiceovers) of Osama bin Laden's terrorist network. In one video Gadahn called on U.S. citizens to "escape from the unbelieving army and join the winning side," while in another he referred to the events of Sept. 11, 2001, as "the blessed raids on New York and Washington." In early 2008, Gadahn surfaced on another Internet-posted video, this one showing him tearing up his American passport, ranting against President Bush and calling for Bush to be met "with bombs" during a then upcoming visit to the Middle East. In November 2008, an Al Qaeda videotape calling then President Elect Barack Obama a "house negro" was thought to have involved Gadahn's work. By October 2009, however, he still had evaded capture,

---

23. *Texas* v. *Johnson,* 491 U.S. 397 (1989).
24. *Cohen* v. *California,* 403 U.S. 15 (1971).
25. *Frazier* v. *Boomsma,* 2008 U.S. Dist. LEXIS 63896 (D. Ariz. Aug. 20, 2008). The law at issue, Arizona Revised Statute Section 13-3726, provided that "a person shall not knowingly use the name, portrait or picture of a deceased soldier for the purpose of advertising for the sale of any goods, wares or merchandise or for the solicitation of patronage for any business without having obtained prior consent to the use by the soldier or by the soldier's spouse, immediate family member, trustee if the soldier is a minor or legally designated representative."

and the Rewards for Justice program, sponsored by the U.S. State Department, was offering a $1 million reward for information leading to Gadahn's arrest for treason and providing material support to Al Qaeda. The case pitted the First Amendment right of speech against the U.S. Constitution's seldom-used treason provision (Art. III, Sect. 3), which states that "treason against the United States, shall consist only in levying war against them, or in adhering to their enemies, giving them aid and comfort." As this chapter later describes in its discussion of *Brandenburg* v. *Ohio*, the abstract advocacy of violence is protected by the First Amendment while the direct incitement of imminent lawless action that is likely to occur is not protected (see page 54). Ultimately, Gadahn's treason prosecution indicated that there are limits in the United States on how far people may go in their political speech against the government.

**CRITICAL DATES IN THE HISTORY OF SEDITION LAW
IN THE UNITED STATES**

1735	Acquittal of John Peter Zenger
1791	Adoption of First Amendment
1798	Alien and Sedition Acts of 1798
1917	Espionage Act
1918	Sedition Act
1919	Clear and present danger test enunciated
1927	Brandeis sedition test in *Whitney* v. *California*
1940	Smith Act adopted
1951	Smith Act ruled constitutional
1957	Scope of Smith Act greatly narrowed
1969	*Brandenburg* v. *Ohio* substantially curbs sedition prosecutions

---

ALIEN AND SEDITION ACTS

The United States wasn't even 10 years old when its resolve in protecting free expression was first tested. Intense rivalry between President John Adams' Federalist party and Thomas Jefferson's Republican or Jeffersonian party, coupled with the fear that the growing violence in the French Revolution might spread to this country, led to the adoption by the Federalist-dominated Congress of a series of highly repressive measures known as the **Alien and Sedition Acts of 1798.**[26] The sedition law forbade false, scandalous and malicious publications against the U.S. government, Congress and the president. The new law also punished persons who sought to stir up sedition or urged resistance to federal laws. Punishment was a fine of as much as $2,000 and a jail term of up to two years. This latter statute was aimed at the Jeffersonian political newspapers, many of which were relentless in attacks on President Adams and his government.

26. Smith, *Freedom's Fetters.*

There were 15 prosecutions under this law. Among those prosecuted were editors of eight Jeffersonian newspapers, including some of the leading papers in the nation. Imagine the federal government bringing sedition charges today against the editors of The New York Times, Washington Post and Chicago Tribune. Also prosecuted was a Republican member of Congress. The so-called seditious libel that was the basis for the criminal charges was usually petty and hardly threatened our admittedly youthful government. But Federalist judges heard most of the cases and convictions were common.

Far from inhibiting dissent, the laws succeeded only in provoking dissension among many of President Adams' supporters. Many argue that Adams lost his bid for re-election in 1800 largely because of public dissatisfaction with his attempt to muzzle his critics. The constitutionality of the laws was never tested before the full Supreme Court, but three members of the court heard Sedition Act cases while they were on the circuit. The constitutionality of the provisions was sustained by these justices. The Sedition Act expired in 1801 and newly elected President Thomas Jefferson pardoned all people convicted under it, while Congress eventually repaid most of the fines. This was the nation's first peacetime sedition law and it left such a bad taste that another peacetime sedition law was not passed until 1940.

Most historians of freedom of expression in the United States focus on two eras in the 19th century during which censorship was not uncommon: the abolitionist period and the Civil War. A wide range of government actions, especially in the South, were aimed at shutting down the abolitionist press in the years between 1830 and 1860. And both the U.S. government and the Confederate States government censored the press during the Civil War. But in his book "Free Speech in Its Forgotten Years" author David M. Rabban argues that there were also extensive censorship efforts in the latter half of the 19th century against radical labor unionists, anarchists, birth control advocates and other so-called freethinkers. And there was little meaningful public debate about such activities. "In the decades before World War I," Rabban wrote, "Americans generally needed to experience repression of views they shared before formulating a theory of free speech that extended to ideas they opposed."[27]

The issue of political dissent did not enter the national debate again until the end of the 1800s, when hundreds of thousands of Americans began to understand that democracy and capitalism were not going to bring them the prosperity promised as an American birthright. Thousands were attracted to radical political movements such as socialism and anarchism, movements that were considered by most in the mainstream to be foreign to the United States. Revolution arose as a specter in the minds of millions of Americans. Hundreds of laws were passed by states and cities across the nation to try to limit this kind of political dissent. War broke out in Europe in 1914; the United States joined the conflict three years later. This pushed the nation over the edge and anything that remained of our national tolerance toward political dissent and criticism of the government and economic system vanished. At both the state and the federal level, government struck out at those who sought to criticize or suggest radical change.

27. Rabban, *Free Speech.*

SEDITION IN WORLD WAR I

*Suppression of
freedom of expression
reached a higher level
during World War I
than at any other time
in our history.*

Suppression of freedom of expression reached a higher level during World War I than at any other time in our history.[28] Government prosecutions during the Vietnam War, for example, were minor compared with government action between 1918 and 1920. Vigilante groups were active as well, persecuting when the government failed to prosecute.

Two federal laws were passed to deal with persons who opposed the war and U.S. participation in it. In 1917 the **Espionage Act** was approved by Congress and signed by President Woodrow Wilson. The measure dealt primarily with espionage problems, but some parts were aimed expressly at dissent and opposition to the war. The law provided that it was a crime to willfully convey a false report with the intent to interfere with the war effort. It was a crime to cause or attempt to cause insubordination, disloyalty, mutiny or refusal of duty in the armed forces. It also was a crime to willfully obstruct the recruiting or enlistment service of the United States. Punishment was a fine of not more than $10,000 or a jail term of not more than 20 years. The law also provided that material violating the law could not be mailed.

In 1918 the **Sedition Act,** an amendment to the Espionage Act, was passed, making it a crime to attempt to obstruct the recruiting service. It was criminal to utter or print or write or publish disloyal or profane language that was intended to cause contempt of, or scorn for, the federal government, the Constitution, the flag or the uniform of the armed forces. Penalties for violation of the law were imprisonment for as long as 20 years or a fine of $10,000 or both. Approximately 2,000 people were prosecuted under these espionage and sedition laws, and nearly 900 were convicted.

In addition the U.S. Post Office Department censored thousands of newspapers, books and pamphlets. Some publications lost their right to the government-subsidized second-class mailing rates and were forced to use the costly first-class rates or find other means of distribution. Entire issues of magazines were held up and never delivered, on the grounds that they violated the law (or what the postmaster general believed to be the law). Finally, the states were not content with allowing the federal government to deal with dissenters, and most adopted sedition statutes, laws against **criminal syndicalism,** laws that prohibited the display of a red flag or a black flag, and so forth.

Political repression in the United States did not end with the termination of fighting in Europe. The government was still suspicious of the millions of European immigrants in the nation and frightened by the organized political efforts of socialist and communist groups. As the Depression hit the nation, first in the farm belt in the 1920s, and then in the rest of the nation by the next decade, labor unrest mushroomed. Hundreds of so-called agitators were arrested and charged under state and federal laws. Demonstrations were broken up; aliens were detained and threatened with deportation.

But what about the First Amendment? What happened to freedom of expression? The constitutional guarantees of freedom of speech and press were of limited value during this era. The legal meaning of freedom of expression had developed little in the preceding 125 years. There had been few cases and almost no important rulings before 1920. The words of the First Amendment—"Congress shall make no law"—are not nearly as important as the meaning attached to them. And that meaning was only then beginning to develop through court rulings

---

28. See Peterson and Fite, *Opponents of War.*

that resulted from the thousands of prosecutions for sedition and other such crimes between 1917 and the mid-1930s.

THE SMITH ACT

Congress adopted the nation's second peacetime sedition law in 1940 when it ratified the **Smith Act,** a measure making it a crime to advocate the violent overthrow of the government, to conspire to advocate the violent overthrow of the government, to organize a group that advocated the violent overthrow of the government, or to be a member of a group that advocated the violent overthrow of the government.[29] The law was aimed directly at the Communist Party of the United States. While a small group of Trotskyites (members of the Socialist Workers Party) were prosecuted and convicted under the Smith Act in 1943, no Communist was indicted under the law until 1948 when many of the nation's top Communist Party leaders were charged with advocating the violent overthrow of the government. All were convicted after a nine-month trial and their appeals were denied. In a 7-2 ruling in 1951, the Supreme Court of the United States rejected the defendants' arguments that the Smith Act violated the First Amendment.[30]

Government prosecutions persisted during the early 1950s. But then, in a surprising reversal of its earlier position, the Supreme Court in 1957 overturned the convictions of West Coast Communist Party leaders.[31] Justice John Marshall Harlan wrote for the 5-2 majority that government evidence showed that the defendants had advocated the violent overthrow of the government but only as an abstract doctrine, and this was not sufficient to sustain a conviction. Instead there must be evidence that proves the defendants advocated actual *action* aimed at the forcible overthrow of the government. This added burden of proof levied against the government prosecutors made it extremely difficult to use the Smith Act against the Communists, and prosecutions dwindled. The number of prosecutions diminished for other reasons as well, however. The times had changed. The Cold War was not as intense. Americans looked at the Soviet Union and the Communists with a bit less fear. In fact, political scientist John Roche has remarked with only a slight wink that it was the dues paid to the party by FBI undercover agents that kept the organization economically solvent in the mid-to-late 1950s.

With the practical demise of the Smith Act, sedition has not been a serious threat against dissent for more than 45 years. No sedition cases were filed against Vietnam War protesters, and the last time the Supreme Court heard an appeal in a sedition case was in 1969 when it overturned the conviction of a Ku Klux Klan leader (*Brandenburg* v. *Ohio*).[32] The federal government has filed sedition charges several times in recent years against alleged white supremacists, neo-Nazis and others on the fringe of the right wing. Whereas juries have been willing to convict such individuals of bombing, bank robbery and even racketeering, the defendants have been acquitted of sedition. The federal government had greater success in the 1990s using a Civil War–era sedition statute to prosecute Muslim militants who bombed the World Trade Center in New York City in 1993. Sheikh Omar Abdel Rahman and nine

---

29. Pember, "The Smith Act," 1.
30. *Dennis* v. *U.S.,* 341 U.S. 494 (1951).
31. *Yates* v. *U.S.,* 354 U.S. 298 (1957).
32. 395 U.S. 444 (1969).

of his followers were found guilty of violating a 140-year-old law that makes it a crime to "conspire to overthrow, or put down, or to destroy by force the Government of the United States." Although the government could not prove that Abdel Rahman actually participated in the bombing, federal prosecutors argued that his exhortations to his followers amounted to directing a violent conspiracy. The sheikh's attorneys argued that his pronouncements were protected by the First Amendment. In August 1999 the 2nd U.S. Circuit Court of Appeals disagreed, noting that the Bill of Rights does not protect an individual who uses a public speech to commit crimes. Abdel Rahman's speeches were not simply the expression of ideas; "in some instances they constituted the crime of conspiracy to wage war against the United States," the court ruled. "Words of this nature," the three-judge panel wrote, "ones that instruct, solicit, or persuade others to commit crimes of violence—violate the law and may be properly prosecuted regardless of whether they are uttered in private, or in a public place."[33] In the wake of the terror attacks on Sept. 11, 2001, federal prosecutors in New York said they were looking into the possibility that the attacks included a seditious conspiracy to levy war against the United States. This accusation means that individuals suspected of playing a part in the attacks could be charged under the same seditious conspiracy statute that was used against the previously convicted Trade Center bombers. No such charges were filed. Also, the USA Patriot Act, which was passed as a part of the anti-terrorism bill adopted in 2001, defines terrorism as any "attempt to intimidate or coerce a civilian population" or change "the policy of the government by intimidation or coercion." Some civil libertarians argue that this defini-tion could include some kinds of political dissent and that it closely resembles what tradition-ally has been called sedition.

Another controversial section of the Patriot Act that pits free speech against the war on terror makes it a crime to provide "expert advice or assistance" to terrorists. In 2004, a fed-eral jury acquitted a Saudi-born computer doctoral student at the University of Moscow, Sami Omar Al-Hussayen, of charges under this provision that he spread terrorism by "designing websites and posting messages on the Internet to recruit and raise funds for terrorist missions in Chechnya and Israel. His attorneys argued that he was being prosecuted for expressing views protected by the First Amendment."[34] Georgetown University law professor David Cole remarked after the verdict that it was a "case where the government sought to criminalize pure speech and was resoundingly defeated."

The Espionage Act of 1917 (see page 50) was resuscitated in 2006 when a federal judge allowed charges to proceed under it against two former lobbyists for the American Israel Public Affairs Committee—known by the acronym AIPAC—who allegedly obtained classified U.S. defense information and then communicated it to both Israeli officials and journalists.[35] The defendants in *United States* v. *Rosen*, neither of whom was either a govern-ment employee or a spy, contested the constitutionality of the Espionage Act on, among other things, free speech grounds. Judge T.S. Ellis III noted that their "First Amendment challenge exposes the inherent tension between the government transparency so essential to a demo-cratic society and the government's equally compelling need to protect from disclosure infor-mation that could be used by those who wish this nation harm." Although the judge rejected

---

33. *U.S.* v. *Rahman,* 189 F. 3d 88 (1999).
34. Schmitt, "Acquittal in Internet Terrorism Case."
35. *U.S.* v. *Rosen*, 445 F. Supp. 2d 602 (E.D. Va. 2006).

the government's argument that "for a categorical rule that Espionage Act prosecutions are immune from First Amendment scrutiny," he nonetheless stressed the government was seeking to punish the disclosure of information which could threaten national security. Ellis concluded "the Constitution permits the government to prosecute . . . [a person] for the disclosure of information relating to the national defense when that person knew that the information is the type which could be used to threaten the nation's security, and that person acted in bad faith, *i.e.,* with reason to believe the disclosure could harm the United States or aid a foreign government." Although upholding the Espionage Act and allowing the case to continue, Ellis suggested Congress revisit the aging act's provisions to ensure they reflect "contemporary views about the appropriate balance between our nation's security and our citizens' ability to engage in public debate about the United States' conduct." By the start of 2009, *United States* v. *Rosen* had yet to go to trial after being postponed more than a half-dozen times. In February 2009, a federal appellate court ruled the defendant AIPAC lobbyists, Steven Rosen and Keith Weissman, could present as part of their defense certain classified documents pursuant to the Classified Information Procedures Act. The move was a blow to the government's case, and in May 2009 federal prosecutors gave up and asked the judge to dismiss the case, citing the inevitable disclosure of classified information that would occur at trial. The case had been closely watched by journalists because the government was attempting to punish lobbyists (Rosen and Weissman) for leaking classified U.S. information not just to the Israeli government, but also to American reporters at major newspapers such as the Washington Post.

DEFINING THE LIMITS OF FREEDOM OF EXPRESSION

The first time the Supreme Court of the United States seriously considered whether a prosecution for sedition violated the First Amendment was in 1919. The Philadelphia Socialist Party authorized Charles Schenck, the general secretary of the organization, to publish 15,000 leaflets protesting against U.S. involvement in World War I. The pamphlet described the war as a cold-blooded and ruthless adventure propagated in the interest of the chosen few of Wall Street and urged young men to resist the draft. Schenck and other party members were arrested, tried and convicted for violating the Espionage Act (see page 50). The case was appealed to the Supreme Court, with the Socialists asserting that they had been denied their First Amendment rights of freedom of speech and press. Justice Oliver Wendell Holmes penned the court's opinion and rejected the First Amendment argument. In ordinary times, he said, such pamphlets might have been harmless and protected by the First Amendment. "But the character of every act depends upon the circumstances in which it is done. . . . The question in every case is whether the words used, are used in such circumstances and are of such a nature as to create a clear and present danger that they will bring about the substantive evils that Congress has a right to prevent. It is a question of proximity and degree."[36]

How can prosecutions for sedition be reconciled with freedom of expression? According to the Holmes test, Congress has the right to outlaw certain kinds of conduct that might be harmful to the nation. In some instances words, through speeches or pamphlets, can push

"The question in every case is whether the words used . . . create a clear and present danger that they will bring about the substantive evils that Congress has a right to prevent."

36. *Schenck* v. *U.S.,* 249 U.S. 47 (1919).

people to undertake acts that violate the laws passed by Congress. In such cases publishers or speakers can be punished without infringing on their First Amendment freedoms. How close must the connection be between the advocacy of the speaker or publisher and the forbidden conduct? Holmes said that the words must create a "clear" (unmistakable? certain?) and "present" (immediate? close?) danger.

In rejecting Schenck's appeal, the high court ruled that these 15,000 seemingly innocuous pamphlets posed a real threat to the legitimate right of Congress to successfully conduct the war. To many American liberals this notion seemed farfetched, and Holmes was publicly criticized for the ruling. But the magic words "clear and present danger" stuck like glue on American sedition law. Holmes changed his mind about his test in less than six months and broke with the majority of the high court to outline a somewhat more liberal definition of freedom of expression in a ruling on the Sedition Act in the fall of 1919.[37] But the majority of the court continued to use the Holmes test to reject First Amendment appeals.

Justice Louis Brandeis attempted to fashion a more useful application of the clear and present danger test in 1927, but his definition of "clear and present danger" was confined to a concurring opinion in the case of *Whitney* v. *California*.[38] The state of California prosecuted Anita Whitney, a 64-year-old philanthropist. She was charged with violating the state's Criminal Syndicalism Act after she attended a meeting of the Communist Labor Party. She was not an active member in the party and during the convention had worked against proposals made by others that the party dedicate itself to gaining power through revolution and general strikes in which workers would seize power by violent means. But the state contended that the Communist Labor Party was formed to teach criminal syndicalism, and as a member to the party she participated in the crime. After her conviction she appealed to the Supreme Court.

Justice Edward Sanford wrote the court's opinion and ruled that California had not violated Whitney's First Amendment rights. The jurist said it was inappropriate to even apply the clear and present danger test. He noted that in *Schenck* and other cases, the statutes under which prosecution occurred forbade specific actions, such as interference with the draft. The clear and present danger test was then used to judge whether the words used by the defendant presented a clear and present danger that the forbidden action might occur. In this case, Sanford noted, the California law forbade specific words—the advocacy of violence to bring about political change. The Holmes test was therefore inapplicable. In addition, the law was neither unreasonable nor unwarranted.

Justice Brandeis concurred, but only because the constitutional issue of freedom of expression had not been raised sufficiently at the trial to make it an issue in the appeal. (If a legal issue is not raised during a trial it is often impossible for an appellate court to later consider the matter.) Brandeis disagreed sharply with the majority regarding the limits of free expression. In doing so he added flesh and bones to Holmes' clear and present danger test. Looking to *Schenck*, the justice noted that the court had agreed there must be a clear and

37. *Abrams* v. *U.S.,* 250 U.S. 616 (1919).
38. 274 U.S. 357 (1927).

*Justice Louis Brandeis,
author of an important
concurring opinion in
Whitney v.* California *and
other First Amendment
rulings.*

imminent danger of a substantive evil that the state has the right to prevent before an interference with speech is allowed. He described what he believed to be the requisite danger:

> To justify suppression of free speech there must be reasonable ground to
> fear that serious evil will result if free speech is practiced. There must be
> reasonable ground to believe that the danger apprehended is imminent.
> There must be reasonable ground to believe that the evil to be prevented is
> a serious one. Every denunciation of existing law tends in some measure
> to increase the probability that there will be violation of it. Condonation
> of a breach enhances the probability. Expressions of approval add to the
> probability. Propagation of the criminal state of mind by teaching syndical-
> ism increases it. Advocacy of law-breaking heightens it further. But even
> advocacy of violation, however reprehensible morally, is not a justification
> for denying free speech where the advocacy falls short of incitement, and
> there is nothing to indicate that the advocacy would be immediately acted
> on. The wide difference between advocacy and incitement, between prepa-
> ration and attempt, between assembling and conspiracy, must be borne in
> mind. In order to support a finding of clear and present danger it must be
> shown either that immediate serious violence was to be expected or was
> advocated, or that the past conduct furnished reason to believe that such
> advocacy was then contemplated.[39]

Brandeis concluded that if there is time to expose through discussion the falsehoods and fal-
lacies, to avert the evil by the process of education, the remedy to be applied is more speech,
not enforced silence. Put differently, Brandeis believed that counterspeech is the ideal, self-
help remedy (i.e., adding more speech to the marketplace of ideas in order to counterargue),
not censorship.

39. *Whitney* v. *California,* 274 U.S. 357 (1927).

The next major ruling in which the high court attempted to reconcile sedition law and the First Amendment came in 1951 in the case of *Dennis* v. *U.S.*[40] Eleven Communist Party members had been convicted of advocating the violent overthrow of the government, a violation of the Smith Act. The defendants raised the clear and present danger test as a barrier to their convictions; the actions of a small band of Communists surely did not constitute a clear and present danger to the nation, they argued. Chief Justice Vinson, who wrote the opinion for the court, used a variation of the clear and present danger test enunciated by Holmes in the *Schenck* case. He called it a clear and probable danger test. Surely the Congress has a right to prevent the overthrow of the government, Vinson said. How likely is it that the words spoken or written by the defendants would lead even to an attempted overthrow? "In each case [courts] must ask whether the gravity of the 'evil' discounted by its improbability, justifies such invasion of free speech as is necessary to avoid the danger," Vinson wrote, quoting a lower-court opinion written by Judge Learned Hand.

The test went only slightly beyond the original Holmes test, and the court ruled that the defendants' First Amendment rights had not been violated. If the Brandeis test from *Whitney* had been applied, however, it is likely the convictions would have gone out the window.

It has been more than 40 years since the Supreme Court heard the case of *Brandenburg* v. *Ohio* (see page 48) and made its last and probably best attempt to resolve the apparent contradiction between sedition law and freedom of expression. A leader of the Ku Klux Klan was prosecuted and convicted of violating an Ohio sedition law for stating: "We're not a revengent [revengeful] organization, but if our President, our Congress, our Supreme Court, continues to suppress the white Caucasian race, it's possible there might have to be some revengeance [revenge] taken." In reversing the conviction, the high court said the law must distinguish between the abstract advocacy of ideas and the incitement to unlawful conduct. "The constitutional guarantees of free speech and free press do not permit a state to forbid or proscribe advocacy of the use of force or of law violation except *where such advocacy is directed to inciting or producing imminent lawless action and is likely to incite or produce such actions [emphasis added]*."[41]

This test, which represents the current version of Justice Holmes' old clear and present danger standard, can be broken down into four components. First, the word "directed" represents an intent requirement on the part of the speaker: Did the speaker actually intend for his or her words to incite lawless action? Second, the word "imminent" indicates that the time between the speech in question and the lawless action must be very close or proximate. Third, the conduct itself must be "lawless action," requiring that there be a criminal statute forbidding or punishing the underlying action that is allegedly advocated. Finally, the word "likely" represents a probability requirement—that the lawless action must be substantially likely to occur and not merely a speculative result of the speech. All four of these elements must be proven before the speech can be considered outside the scope of First Amendment protection.

The legal theory behind the law of sedition was outlined previously; if someone publishes something that incites another person to do something illegal, the publisher of the incitement can be punished. While charges of sedition are rarely filed today, it is not uncommon for private persons to sue the mass media on the grounds that something that was published or recorded or exhibited incited a third person to commit an illegal act. These cases are similar to sedition prosecutions in many ways, and the constitutional shield developed by the courts that protects the mass media against convictions for sedition is applied in these cases as well.

"The constitutional guarantees of free speech and free press do not permit a state to forbid or proscribe advocacy of the use of force or of law violation except where such advocacy is directed to inciting or producing imminent lawless action and is likely to incite or produce such actions."

40. 341 U.S. 494 (1951).
41. 395 U.S. 444 (1969).

Real-Life Violence: Blaming Movies, Video Games and Books

In 2009, when 17-year-old Kyle Shaw was arrested in connection with the bombing of a Starbucks in Manhattan, he supposedly was inspired by the movie "Fight Club." Should the producers of that movie be held civilly liable to Starbucks for damages caused by the bombing if, in fact, Shaw really did it and was inspired by Brad Pitt's character, Tyler Durden, in the movie?

Courts are frequently asked to rule in wrongful death, negligence and product liability lawsuits whether a media artifact like a film or recording played some part in inciting the actual perpetrator of the crime to commit illegal acts. To determine liability in such cases, courts often use the *Brandenburg* test for incitement to violence outlined earlier in this chapter. For example, in 2002 the 6th U.S. Court of Appeals ruled that the producers of the film "The Basketball Diaries," the makers of several video games and some Internet content providers were not liable in a lawsuit brought by the parents of students who were killed and wounded when teenager Michael Carneal went on a shooting rampage in the lobby of Heath High School in Paducah, Ky. The plaintiffs argued, among other things, that Carneal had watched the film, which depicts a student daydreaming about killing a teacher and several classmates. "We find it is simply too far a leap from shooting characters on a video screen (an activity undertaken by millions) to shooting people in a classroom (an activity undertaken by a handful, at most) for Carneal's activities to have been reasonably foreseeable to the manufacturers of the media Carneal played and viewed," the court ruled. The material in this case falls far short of the standard required by *Brandenburg,* the judges added.[42] Why did they reach this conclusion? First and foremost, the movie was not "directed" to cause violence. As the appellate court wrote in *James* v. *Meow Media,* "while the defendants in this case may not have exercised exquisite care regarding the persuasive power of the violent material that they disseminated, they certainly did not 'intend' to produce violent actions by the consumers, as is required by the *Brandenburg* test."[43] In addition, the appellate court reasoned that "it is a long leap from the proposition that Carneal's actions were foreseeable to the *Brandenburg* requirement that the violent content was 'likely' to cause Carneal to behave this way."[44]

In 2001 a Louisiana trial court dismissed a lawsuit against Warner Brothers and other defendants brought by plaintiffs who claimed that a robbery and shooting at a convenience store was the result of the thieves' attempting to mimic characters in the film "Natural Born Killers."[45] Cases like those just outlined are typical of the way the courts have handled claims that the mass media have incited a criminal act by a reader or a viewer. It is very difficult for a plaintiff ever to prove the intent ("directed") prong of the *Brandenburg* test against the media. The media simply don't intend for violence to occur as a result of viewing, playing or reading their products. Rather, the typical intent is to entertain and to make a profit! But of course, there are exceptions to the rule.

In 1996 the families of Mildred and Trevor Horn and Janice Saunders filed a wrongful death suit against Paladin Enterprises and its president, Peter Lund. The company published a book titled "Hit Man: A Technical Manual for Independent Contractors." Lawrence Horn hired

42. *James* v. *Meow Media Inc.,* 300 F. 3d 683 (2002).
43. Ibid., 698.
44. Ibid., 699.
45. *Delgado* v. *American Multi-Cinema Inc.,* 85 Cal. Rptr. 2d 838 (1999); and *Byers* v. *Edmondson,* 29 M.L.R. 1991 (2001). See also *Pahler* v. *Slayer,* 29 M.L.R. 2627 (2001).

Leonardo Dicaprio, right, and James Madio, in a scene from "The Basketball Diaries," which was the focus of a lawsuit in 2002.

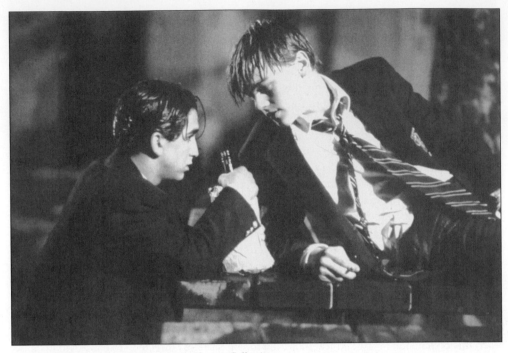

Source: © New Line Cinema Courtesy The Everett Collection

James Perry to kill his ex-wife, their 8-year-old quadriplegic son and the son's nurse to gain access to the proceeds of a medical malpractice settlement. Both Perry and Horn were arrested and convicted of the murders; Perry was sentenced to death, Horn to life in prison. The plaintiffs contended that Perry used the Paladin publication as an instruction manual for the killings. A U.S. District Court in Maryland ruled in August 1996 that the book was protected by the First Amendment. "However loathsome one characterizes the publication, 'Hit Man' simply does not fall within the parameters of any recognized exceptions to the First Amendment principles of freedom of speech." The book failed to cross the line between permissible advocacy and impermissible incitation to crime or violence, Judge Williams wrote.[46]

Fifteen months later the 4th U.S. Circuit Court of Appeals reversed the lower-court ruling. The defendant had agreed to a stipulation in the case that stated Paladin provided its assistance to Perry with both the knowledge and the intent that the book would immediately be used by criminals and would-be criminals in the solicitation, planning and commission of murder and murder for hire. The court said the book was not an example of abstract advocacy but a form of aiding and abetting a crime. The book "methodically and comprehensively prepares and steels its audience to specific criminal conduct through exhaustively detailed instructions on planning, commission and concealment of criminal conduct," the panel ruled. There is no First Amendment protection for such a publication. The court noted that this case was unique and should not be

---

46. *Rice* v. *Paladin Enterprises Inc.,* 940 F. Supp. 836 (1996).

read as expanding the potential liability of publishers and broadcasters when third parties copy or mimic a crime or other act contained in a news report or a film or a television program.[47] An appeal to the U.S. Supreme Court was denied and the case was returned to the U.S. District Court for trial. In May 1999 Paladin Press settled the case out of court. In spite of this case, the stringent requirements of the *Brandenburg* test make it difficult, bordering on impossible, for a plaintiff to win a lawsuit that alleges a play or book or song or movie was responsible for causing someone's illegal acts. The case law is highly one-sided in this regard.[48]

"TO CATCH A PREDATOR": MEDIA LIABILITY FOR SUICIDE?

In 2006, Louis William Conradt Jr. took his own life, just as police were about to arrest him at home for allegedly soliciting sex from a minor on the Internet. In fact, there was no minor but rather a decoy that was part of a sting orchestrated by the TV show "NBC Dateline," along with a group called Perverted Justice, as part of the show's sensationalistic "To Catch a Predator" series. But when Conradt never went to the "sting" house to meet the supposed minor, NBC took its cameras and crew to Conradt's residence, along with a SWAT team and local police in Murphy, Texas, who had an arrest warrant. Apparently unable to face the humiliation and public spectacle, Conradt killed himself. His sister, Patricia Conradt, sued for more than $100 million, alleging that "NBC Dateline" was responsible for her brother's death. In 2008, in *Conradt* v. *NBC Universal*, 536 F. Supp. 2d 380 (S.D. N.Y. 2008), Judge Denny Chin refused to dismiss the lawsuit, reasoning that if the allegations in Patricia Conradt's amended complaint were true, "a reasonable jury could find that NBC crossed the line from responsible journalism to irresponsible and reckless intrusion into law enforcement" and that "NBC created a substantial risk of suicide or other harm." He added that the complaint stated facts sufficient to render plausible the claims the suicide was foreseeable and that "NBC acted with deliberate indifference and in a manner that would shock one's conscience." Rather than going to trial, NBC settled the case for an undisclosed sum. The dispute suggests that journalists should take caution when they stage news and, in the process, cross the line separating news reporting from news making.

Due to the success of "Grand Theft Auto," "Mortal Kombat" and "Resident Evil," video games depicting violent images and storylines are under scrutiny today by lawmakers who believe the games cause real-life violence and/or psychologically harm kids who play them. School shootings often are blamed on games ("Doom" was blamed, in part, for the tragedy at Columbine in 1999). Several states (California, Illinois, Louisiana, Michigan, Minnesota, Oklahoma and Washington) and municipalities (St. Louis County, Mo., and Indianapolis, Ind.) recently adopted statutes that attempted to limit minors' access to violent video games

---

47. *Rice* v. *Paladin Enterprises Inc.*, 128 F. 3d 233 (1997).
48. See *Herceg* v. *Hustler*, 814 F. 2d 1017 (1987).

by either prohibiting their sale or rental to minors or by fining kids who buy them.[49] All of these laws, however, were enjoined as unconstitutional by federal courts, thus stopping their enforcement. Here's why.

First, because video games have stories and plots, they are considered speech products and receive First Amendment protection. Thus, in order to justify regulation of them based upon their content (here, violent content), the **strict scrutiny** standard of judicial review must be satisfied. In particular, a state or municipality must prove both it has a compelling interest (an interest of the highest order) that justifies the games' regulation, and that the regulation restricts no more speech than absolutely necessary to serve that allegedly compelling interest (the law is narrowly tailored). By 2009, all courts that considered the issue found the social science evidence offered by the states and municipalities named previously to be lacking and insufficient to prove that playing violent video games either causes minors to commit violence or harms them psychologically. In other words, social science evidence failed to demonstrate a compelling interest. Second, laws targeting video games often are declared unconstitutional because they fail to clearly define "violence." As noted earlier (see page 9), a statute will be declared unconstitutional under the void for vagueness doctrine if people of reasonable and ordinary intelligence cannot discern, from looking at its terms, what speech is allowed and what speech is prohibited. Some states have used vague terms like "inappropriate violence" and "ultra-violent video games" in their laws. The Washington case discussed next illustrates some of these points.

In 2004, a federal court issued an order[50] striking down, on First Amendment grounds, a Washington state law that restricted minors' access to video games containing "realistic or photographic-like depictions of aggressive conflict in which the player kills, injures, or otherwise causes physical harm to a human form in the game who is depicted, by dress or other recognizable symbols, as a public law enforcement officer."[51] The decision was anything but surprising. It followed in the footsteps of opinions issued by two federal appellate courts that held unconstitutional similar legislation regulating minors' access to fictional images of violence in video games.

---

49. Statutes restricting minors' access to violent video games have been enjoined by federal district courts in *Entertainment Software Ass'n* v. *Blagojevich*, 404 F. Supp. 2d 1051 (N.D. Ill. 2005) (issuing a permanent injunction against Illinois' law); *Entertainment Software Ass'n* v. *Foti*, 451 F. Supp. 2d 823 (M.D. La. 2006) (issuing a preliminary injunction against Louisiana's law); *Entertainment Software Ass'n* v. *Granholm*, 426 F. Supp. 2d 646 (E.D. Mich. 2006) (issuing a permanent injunction against Michigan's law); *Entertainment Merchants Ass'n* v. *Henry*, 2007 U.S. Dist. LEXIS 69139 (W.D. Okla. Sept. 17, 2007) (issuing a permanent injunction against Oklahoma's law); and *Video Software Dealers Ass'n* v. *Maleng*, 325 F. Supp. 2d 1180 (W.D. Wash. 2004) (issuing a permanent injunction against Washington's law). Similar statutes have been enjoined by federal appellate courts in *American Amusement Machine Ass'n* v. *Kendrick*, 244 F. 3d 572 (7th Cir. 2001), cert. den., 534 U.S. 994 (2001) (affirming a permanent injunction against an Indianapolis, Ind., ordinance); *Entertainment Software Ass'n* v. *Swanson*, 519 F. 3d 768 (8th Cir. 2008) (affirming a permanent injunction against Minnesota's law); *Interactive Digital Software Ass'n* v. *St. Louis County*, 329 F. 3d 954 (8th Cir. 2003) (reversing a district court's opinion and issuing a permanent injunction against a St. Louis County, Mo., ordinance); and *Video Software Dealers Ass'n.* v. *Schwarzenegger*, 556 F. 3d 950 (9th Cir. 2009) (affirming a permanent injunction against California's video game statute).
50. *Video Software Dealers Ass'n* v. *Maleng,* 325 F. Supp. 2d 1180 (W.D. Wash. 2004).
51. Washington Revised Code § 9.91.180 (2004).

In striking down Washington's law, Judge Robert S. Lasnik articulated a list of flaws that fatally plagued the statute.

- The current state of social science research was seriously lacking and failed to provide substantial evidence to support "the Legislature's belief that video games cause violence." In particular, the judge wrote that "neither causation nor an increase in real-life aggression is proven by these studies."
- The Washington law was "both over-inclusive and under-inclusive" in its attempt to single out "just one type of violence" for regulation, namely game-related aggression toward law enforcement officers. As Judge Lasnik reasoned, the law "sweeps too broadly in that it would restrict access to games that reflect heroic struggles against corrupt regimes" or "involve accidental injuries to officers," while it simultaneously "is too narrow in that it will have no effect on the many other channels through which violent representations are presented to children."
- The law's limitations on game-related violence "impact more constitutionally protected speech than is necessary to achieve the identified ends and are not the least restrictive alternative available." The judge observed that regulation was "not limited to the ultra-violent or the patently offensive and is far broader than what would be necessary to keep filth like Grand Theft Auto III and Postal II out of the hands of children."
- The law was "unconstitutionally vague." Judge Lasnik pointed out that attorneys for Washington state were unable, during oral argument, to answer the seemingly simple question of whether a firefighter would be a "public law enforcement officer" as that term is used in the statute.

It seems unlikely that anti-access video game legislation will ever survive judicial scrutiny. Nonetheless, attacking video games is a politically popular move—what politician doesn't want to stop violence?—so more unconstitutional legislation is likely to be produced.

Taxpayers, however, pay a high price for such political shenanigans. By 2009, courts had ordered the states and municipalities with unconstitutional video game laws to pay the Entertainment Software Association, a trade group for the gaming industry, nearly $2 million in legal fees and expenses it had incurred in successfully fighting the statutes. When the 9th U.S. Circuit Court of Appeals struck down California's video game statute in *Video Software Dealers Association* v. *Schwarzenegger* in February 2009, the cash-strapped Golden State had already spent more than $280,000 defending its fatally flawed law. Nonetheless, in May 2009 California Attorney General Jerry Brown petitioned the U.S. Supreme Court for a writ of certiorari to hear and to reverse the 9th Circuit's decision earlier that year declaring California's violent video game statute unconstitutional. As Grover Norquist, president of Americans for Tax Reform, stated in July 2008 when New York Gov. David Paterson signed into law a violent video game bill, "It's moral preening. The bill is unconstitutional and has been found that way in other states. And when the inevitable lawsuit comes, the state pays for everybody's legal expenses."[52]

A widely publicized case involving the application of the *Brandenburg* test involved Web postings by anti-abortion activists that branded doctors who performed abortions as

It seems unlikely that anti-access video game legislation will ever survive judicial scrutiny.

52. *Associated Press*, "NY Law Seeks to Restrict Violent Video Games."

"baby butchers." The postings were prepared by the American Coalition of Life Activists. They included dossiers—so-called Nuremberg files (a reference to the war crimes trials held after the Second World War)—on abortion rights supporters, including doctors, clinic employees, politicians and judges. The group said the files could be used to conduct Nuremberg-like war crime trials in "perfectly legal courts once the tide of this nation's opinion turns against the wanton slaughter of God's children." On the site the names of murdered abortion supporters were struck through and the names of those wounded were grayed out. A Planned Parenthood affiliate in Oregon sued, claiming that the material constituted threats against the persons named. A jury agreed and awarded more than $100 million in actual and punitive damages. A panel of the 9th U.S. Court of Appeals overturned this verdict in 2001. The court said the postings may have made it more likely that third parties would commit violent acts against the physicians, but they did not constitute a direct threat from the anti-abortion activists against the doctors.[53] The plaintiffs petitioned for a rehearing by the court and 14 months later, in a 6-5 vote, the court changed its ruling, declaring that there was no First Amendment protection for the Web postings. "While advocating violence is protected," wrote Judge Pamela Ann Rymer, "threatening a person with violence is not." She noted that three abortion providers had been murdered after similar "wanted posters" had circulated regarding them. By the time the posters at issue were published, the poster format had acquired currency as a death threat for abortion providers, she added. The postings connote something they do not literally say, Judge Rymer wrote, yet both the actor and the recipient get the message.[54] The Supreme Court denied a petition to review the case.[55]

Inflammatory anti-abortion content on the Internet remains controversial. In 2007, a federal judge in Philadelphia issued a permanent injunction stopping John Dunkle, a self-described anti-abortionist from Reading, Pennsylvania, from operating a Web page and blog that the federal government claimed encouraged others to use deadly force against specific reproductive-health clinic physicians, including shooting one doctor in the head.[56] For instance, Dunkle's page stated, "While it does not sound good to say go shoot her between the eyes, it sounds even worse to say let her alone." Judge Thomas Golden found that the online material constituted a threat of violence prohibited under the federal Freedom of Access to Clinic Entrances Act (known as the FACE Act) and was not protected by the First Amendment.

The Gitlow *Ruling and the Incorporation Doctrine*

The First Amendment provides that "Congress" shall make no law abridging the freedoms of speech and press. Read literally, this language ("Congress") indicates the amendment prohibits actions by only the U.S. Congress; the First Amendment's terms say nothing about actions by state or local governments. Thus it would seem the First Amendment does not prevent or prohibit state or local government officials or entities from abridging or restricting people's speech and press rights.

---

53. *Planned Parenthood at Columbia/Willamette, Inc.* v. *American Coalition of Life Activists,* 244 F. 3d 1007 (2001).
54. *Planned Parenthood of the Columbia/Willamette, Inc.* v. *American Coalition of Life Activists,* 290 F. 3d 1058 (2002).
55. 539 U.S. 958 (2003).
56. Order, *Keisler* v. *Dunkle,* Case No. 07-3577 (E.D. Pa. Nov. 8, 2007).

That indeed was the case until a 1925 U.S. Supreme Court opinion called *Gitlow* v. *New York*[57] in which, for the first time, the nation's high court held that the term "Congress" in the First Amendment was not so narrowly limited in scope to the U.S. Congress or actions by the federal government. The case involved the prosecution, under a New York state criminal anarchy law, of a socialist named Benjamin Gitlow for printing a document called "The Left Wing Manifesto." Initially it appeared the First Amendment was irrelevant because it was a New York state law under which Gitlow was prosecuted, not an act of Congress.

But the U.S. Supreme Court concluded differently, writing that "we may and do assume that freedom of speech and of the press—which are protected by the First Amendment from abridgment by Congress—are among the fundamental personal rights and 'liberties' protected by the due process clause of the Fourteenth Amendment from impairment by the States." What the high court did in *Gitlow*, in brief, was to link the First Amendment with the 14th Amendment and, in particular, with the due process clause of the 14th Amendment, which provides that "*no state*" shall "deprive any person of life, *liberty*, or property, without due process of law [emphasis added]." Notice that the 14th Amendment dictates what states cannot do; it restricts the power of states. The *Gitlow* court then, essentially, read into (incorporated into) the 14th Amendment's term "liberty" the freedoms of speech and press explicitly found in the First Amendment.

The importance of the ruling in *Gitlow* is that the high court acknowledged that the Bill of Rights places limitations on the actions of states and local governments as well as on the federal government. *Gitlow* states that freedom of speech is protected by the 14th Amendment. This is known as the incorporation doctrine: The free speech and free press clauses of the First Amendment have been "incorporated" through the 14th Amendment due process clause as fundamental liberties to apply to state and local government entities and officials, not just to "Congress." Today, most rights in the Bill of Rights are protected via the 14th Amendment from interference by states and cities as well as the federal government. The importance of the *Gitlow* case cannot be underestimated. It marked the beginning of attainment of a full measure of civil liberties for the citizens of the nation.

SUMMARY

Within eight years of the passage of the First Amendment, the nation adopted its first (and most wide-ranging) sedition laws, the Alien and Sedition Acts of 1798. Many leading political editors and politicians were prosecuted under the laws, which made it a crime to criticize both the president and the national government. While the Supreme Court never heard arguments regarding the constitutionality of the laws, several justices presided at sedition act trials and refused to sustain a constitutional objection to the laws. The public hated the measures. John Adams was voted out of office in 1800 and was replaced by his political opponent and target of the sedition laws, Thomas Jefferson. The laws left such a bad taste that the federal government did not pass another sedition law until World War I, 117 years later.

Sedition prosecutions in the period from 1915 to 1925 were the most vicious in the nation's history as war protesters, socialists, anarchists and other political dissidents became

57. 268 U.S. 652 (1925).

the target of government repression. It was during this era that the Supreme Court began to interpret the meaning of the First Amendment. In a series of rulings stemming from the World War I cases, the high court fashioned what is known as the clear and present danger test to measure state and federal laws and protests and other expressions against the First Amendment. In 1925 the court ruled that the guarantees of freedom of speech apply to actions taken by all governments, that freedom of speech under the First Amendment protects individuals from censorship by all levels of government, not just from actions by the federal government. This pronouncement in *Gitlow* v. *New York* opened the door to a much broader protection of freedom of expression in the nation.

The Supreme Court made its last important attempt to reconcile the First Amendment and the law of sedition in 1969 when it ruled in *Brandenburg* v. *Ohio* that advocacy of unlawful conduct is protected by the Constitution unless it is directed toward inciting or producing imminent lawless action and is likely to incite or produce such action.

TAXATION AND THE PRESS

Does it violate the First Amendment protection of a free press for state and federal government entities to tax newspapers and other press outlets? No. News organizations are subject to ordinary taxes that apply generally to everyone and/or to all businesses. On the other hand, taxes that specifically target and single out the press for application, as well as taxes that discriminate against some members of a particular branch of the press but not others (i.e., taxing only newspapers with circulations over 100,000, but not those under 100,000) are generally unconstitutional.[58] In addition, taxes that discriminate against the content of a publication are generally unconstitutional. As constitutional law scholar Erwin Chemerinsky writes, the U.S. Supreme Court has "emphasized that any differential taxation of the press—either of the press as opposed to others in society or at particular parts of the press—risked chilling reporting."[59]

But in a 1991 case, *Leathers* v. *Medlock*, the high court held that Arkansas did not violate the First Amendment when it extended a generally applicable sales tax to cable television

---

58. See *Grosjean* v. *American Press Co.,* 297 U.S. 233 (1936), which held unconstitutional a Louisiana license tax on the gross receipts of advertising published in newspapers, magazines and periodicals with circulation of more than 20,000 copies per week, and reasoned that the tax is "measured alone by the extent of the circulation of the publication in which the advertisements are carried, with the plain purpose of penalizing the publishers and curtailing the circulation of a selected group of newspapers"; and *Minneapolis Star & Tribune Co.* v. *Minnesota Commissioner of Revenue*, 460 U.S. 575 (1983), which addressed "the question of a State's power to impose a special tax on the press and, by enacting exemptions, to limit its effect to only a few newspapers," and concluded that a Minnesota use tax on ink and paper that exempted the first $100,000 worth of paper and ink consumed in any calendar year "violates the First Amendment not only because it singles out the press, but also because it targets a small group of newspapers. The effect of the $100,000 exemption enacted in 1974 is that only a handful of publishers pay any tax at all, and even fewer pay any significant amount of tax."
59. Chemerinsky, *Constitutional Law*, 1124.

services, while exempting print media from the tax.[60] The court upheld the law because it found it was a tax of general applicability that did not target the content of mass media communications, noting that "it applies to receipts from the sale of all tangible personal property and a broad range of services, unless within a group of specific exemptions." The court concluded:

> The Arkansas Legislature has chosen simply to exclude or exempt certain media from a generally applicable tax. Nothing about that choice has ever suggested an interest in censoring the expressive activities of cable television. Nor does anything in this record indicate that Arkansas' broad-based, content-neutral sales tax is likely to stifle the free exchange of ideas. We conclude that the State's extension of its generally applicable sales tax to cable television services alone, or to cable and satellite services, while exempting the print media, does not violate the First Amendment.

Importantly, the Supreme Court in *Leathers* cited favorably its own "rule that selective taxation of the press through the narrow targeting of individual members offends the First Amendment," and it emphasized that "differential taxation of First Amendment speakers is constitutionally suspect when it threatens to suppress the expression of particular ideas or viewpoints. Absent a compelling justification, the government may not exercise its taxing power to single out the press."

SUMMARY

Governments have traditionally used taxation as a means of controlling the press. The First Amendment has posed a substantial barrier to such efforts by governments in the United States. Newspapers, broadcasting stations and other mass media must pay the same taxes imposed on other businesses. But taxes levied only against the press that tend to inhibit circulation or impose other kinds of restraints are unconstitutional. Also, taxes levied against mass media based solely on the content of the particular medium are generally regarded as unconstitutional.

PRIOR RESTRAINT

The great compiler of the British law, William Blackstone, defined freedom of the press in the 1760s as freedom from "previous restraint," or prior restraint. Regardless of the difference of opinion on whether the First Amendment is intended to protect political criticism or to protect the press from unfair taxation, most agree the guarantees of free speech and press were intended to bar the government from exercising prior restraint. Despite the weight of such authority, the media in the United States in the 2000s still face instances of prepublication censorship.

Prior restraint comes in many different forms. Most obvious are instances in which the government insists on giving prior approval before something may be published or broadcast, or simply bans the publication or broadcast of specific kinds of material. There are examples

Prior restraint comes in many different forms.

60. 499 U.S. 439 (1991).

of these varieties in this chapter and the next. Similar kinds of prior restraint occur when the courts forbid the publication of certain kinds of material before a trial (see Chapters 11 and 12) or when a court issues an order forbidding the publication of material that might constitute an invasion of privacy (Chapters 7 and 8).

In terms of nongovernmental efforts to restrain allegedly libelous statements (see Chapters 4, 5 and 6 regarding libel), the traditional principle in U.S. law is that courts will not issue an injunction stopping the publication of an allegedly libelous statement before it occurs. Thus, if you believe a newspaper next week is going to print something false about you that will harm your reputation, you will not be able to obtain a prior restraint from a court stopping in advance its publication. The preferred remedy in American libel law, instead, is to allow the allegedly libelous statement to be published and then to sue for monetary damages. In other words, a subsequent punishment of speech is the traditional remedy. Once a statement has been judicially determined after a trial to be false and libelous, however, then some courts have allowed an injunction prohibiting the defendant in the case from repeating the same statement that has been held to be libelous.[61]

Although courts sometimes can issue prior restraints stopping publication by private parties of trade secrets and other intellectual property that is stolen, the publication of such information on the Internet, even if only for a brief moment, may make any order prohibiting its future publication ineffective. On the Internet, even if a court shuts down a specific Web site or orders the information on it removed, there may be mirror sites in different countries (and thus outside an American court's jurisdiction) that still exist or the information may already have been downloaded and/or reposted by others. This happened in 2008 in *Bank Julius Baer & Co. Ltd.* v. *WikiLeaks*, in which a federal judge dissolved a prior restraint he initially had issued targeting a Web site that published proprietary and confidential information allegedly leaked and posted by whistle-blowers.[62] As U.S. District Court Judge Jeffrey S. White wrote in what has become known as the *WikiLeaks* case, "there is evidence in the record that the cat is out the bag," noting that mirror sites existed around the world and that the information in question thus "was readily accessible online." This reasoning illustrates a key point about prior restraints: Courts generally will not grant them unless they will be effective in preventing the alleged harm or injury.

Prior restraints also occur when a federal, state or local ordinance requires individuals or groups to first obtain a permit before engaging in protected speech like holding a rally, picket or march. As described later in Chapter 3, however, such ordinances are permissible in some cases if they meet the requirements of content-neutral time, place and manner restriction.

But there are subtler forms of prior restraint as well. For example, many states have laws aimed at discouraging convicted criminals from profiting from their crimes by making money from books or films that detail their exploits (see pages 118–119). These are called Son of Sam laws because the first state statute enacted was aimed at stopping a notorious New York serial murderer, David Berkowitz, nicknamed the Son of Sam, from earning money by selling an account of his rampage. Such laws are permissible, but broadly worded statutes have been ruled to be a prior restraint because they may stop the convicted felon from expressing his or

61. *Balboa Island Village Inn, Inc.* v. *Lemen*, 40 Cal. 4th 1141 (2007).
62. *Bank Julius Baer & Co. Ltd.* v. *WikiLeaks,* 535 F. Supp. 2d 980 (N.D. Cal. 2008).

her views on a variety of subjects. And some courts have considered laws that limit how or how much a political candidate can spend during an election campaign to be prior censorship as well (see pages 126–128). The discussion in this chapter focuses on the most blatant kind of prior restraint, direct government restrictions on expression.

Before studying some key prior restraint cases involving the government, some rules are important to understand:

1. Prior restraints on speech by the government are presumptively unconstitutional. The burden falls on the government to prove in court that a prior restraint is justified.

2. The government's burden is high, with courts often requiring it to prove there is a compelling interest or an interest of the highest order justifying the restraint.

3. The scope of any prior restraint (how broadly the restraint is drafted and how much speech is restrained) must be very narrow, so as not to stop publication of any more speech than actually is necessary to effectively serve the government's allegedly compelling interests.

4. Speech that falls outside the scope of First Amendment protection (obscenity, child pornography and false advertising, for instance) can be restrained by the government, but only after a judicial proceeding in which a court has determined that the speech indeed is not protected. Thus, if a particular issue of a sexually explicit magazine like Hustler has been found by a court to be obscene (see Chapter 13), then all future sales of the exact same issue may be restrained in the area within that court's jurisdiction.

NEAR v. *MINNESOTA*

The Supreme Court did not directly consider the constitutionality of prior restraint until more than a decade after it had decided its first major sedition case. In 1931, in *Near* v. *Minnesota*,[63] the high court struck an important blow for freedom of expression.

City and county officials in Minneapolis, Minn., brought a legal action against Jay M. Near and Howard Guilford, publishers of the Saturday Press, a small weekly newspaper. Near and Guilford were self-proclaimed reformers whose ostensible purpose was to clean up city and county government in Minneapolis. In their attacks on corruption in city government, they used language that was far from temperate and defamed some of the town's leading government officials. Near and Guilford charged that Jewish gangsters were in control of gambling, bootlegging and racketeering in the city and that city government and its law enforcement agencies did not perform their duties energetically. They repeated these charges over and over in a highly inflammatory manner.[64]

Minnesota had a statute that empowered a court to declare any obscene, lewd, lascivious, malicious, scandalous or defamatory publication a public nuisance. When such a publication was deemed a public nuisance, the court issued an injunction against future publication or distribution. Violation of the injunction resulted in punishment for contempt of court.

---

63. 283 U.S. 697 (1931).
64. Friendly, *Minnesota Rag.*

In 1927 county attorney Floyd Olson initiated an action against the Saturday Press. A district court declared the newspaper a public nuisance and "perpetually enjoined" publication of the Saturday Press. The only way either Near or Guilford would be able to publish the newspaper again was to convince the court that their newspaper would remain free of objectionable material. In 1928 the Minnesota Supreme Court upheld the constitutionality of the law, declaring that under its broad police power the state can regulate public nuisances, including defamatory and scandalous newspapers.

The case then went to the U.S. Supreme Court, which reversed the ruling by the state Supreme Court. The nuisance statute was declared unconstitutional. Chief Justice Charles Evans Hughes wrote the opinion for the court in the 5-4 ruling, saying that the statute in question was not designed to redress wrongs to individuals attacked by the newspaper.[65] Instead, the statute was directed at suppressing the Saturday Press once and for all. The object of the law, Hughes wrote, was not punishment but censorship—not only of a single issue, but also of all future issues—which is not consistent with the traditional concept of freedom of the press. That is, the statute constituted prior restraint, and prior restraint is clearly a violation of the First Amendment.

The object of the law, Hughes wrote, was not punishment but censorship—not only of a single issue, but also of all future issues—which is not consistent with the traditional concept of freedom of the press.

One maxim in the law holds that when a judge writes an opinion for a court, he or she should stick to the problem at hand and not wander off and talk about matters that do not really concern the specific issue before the court. Such remarks are considered **dicta,** or words that do not really apply to the case. These words, these dicta, are never considered an important part of the ruling in the case. Chief Justice Hughes' opinion in *Near* v. *Minnesota* contains a good deal of dicta.

In this case Hughes wrote that the prior restraint of the Saturday Press was unconstitutional, but in some circumstances, he added, prior restraint might be permissible. In what kinds of circumstances? The government can constitutionally stop publication of obscenity, material that incites people to acts of violence, and certain kinds of materials during wartime. (It is entirely probable that the chief justice was forced to make these qualifying statements in order to hold his slim five-person majority in the ruling.) Hughes admitted, on the other hand, that defining freedom of the press as only the freedom from prior restraint is equally wrong, for in many cases punishment after publication (i.e., subsequent punishment) imposes effective censorship upon the freedom of expression.

Near v. *Minnesota* stands for the proposition that under American law prior censorship is permitted only in very unusual circumstances; it is the exception, not the rule. Courts have reinforced this interpretation many times since 1931. Despite this considerable litigation, there remains an incomplete understanding of the kinds of circumstances in which prior restraint might be acceptable under the First Amendment, as the following cases illustrate.

PENTAGON PAPERS CASE

Another important, well-known Supreme Court ruling on prior restraints came in 1971 and addressed the federal government's ability to stop publication of stolen, classified information that it contended jeopardized national security during the war in Vietnam. This is the famous

---

65. *Near* v. *Minnesota,* 283 U.S. 697 (1931).

Pentagon Papers decision.[66] The case began in the summer of 1971 when The New York Times, followed by the Washington Post and a handful of other newspapers, began publishing a series of articles based on pilfered copies of a top secret 47-volume government study officially titled "History of the United States Decision-Making Process on Vietnam Policy." The day after the initial article on the so-called Pentagon Papers appeared, Attorney General John Mitchell asked The New York Times to stop publication of the material. When The Times' publisher refused, the government went to court to get an injunction to force the newspaper to stop the series. A temporary restraining order was granted as the case wound its way to the Supreme Court. The government also sought to impose a similar injunction on the Washington Post after it began to publish reports based on the same material.

At first the government argued that the publication of this material violated federal espionage statutes. When that assertion did not satisfy the lower federal courts, the government argued that the president had inherent power under his constitutional mandate to conduct foreign affairs to protect the national security, which includes the right to classify documents secret and top secret. Publication of this material by the newspapers was unauthorized disclosure of such material and should be stopped. This argument did not satisfy the courts either, and by the time the case came before the Supreme Court, the government argument was that publication of these papers might result in irreparable harm to the nation and its ability to conduct foreign affairs. The Times and the Post made two arguments. First, they said that the classification system is a sham, that people in the government declassify documents almost at will when they want to sway public opinion or influence a reporter's story. Second, the press argued that an injunction against the continued publication of this material violated the First Amendment. Interestingly, the newspapers did not argue that under all circumstances prior restraint is in conflict with the First Amendment. Defense attorney Alexander Bickel argued that under some circumstances prior restraint is acceptable—for example, when the publication of a document has a direct link with a grave event that is immediate and visible. Apparently, both newspapers decided a victory in that immediate case was far more important than to establish a definitive, long-lasting constitutional principle. They therefore concentrated on winning the case, acknowledging that in future cases prior restraint might be permissible.[67]

On June 30 the high court ruled 6-3 in favor of The New York Times and the Washington Post and refused to block the publication of the Pentagon Papers. But the ruling was hardly the kind that strengthened the First Amendment. In a very short per curiam opinion, the majority said that in a case involving the prior restraint of a publication, the government bears a heavy burden to justify such a restraint. In this case the government failed to show the court why such a restraint should be imposed on the two newspapers.[68] In other words, the government failed to justify its request for the permanent restraining order.

The decision in the case rested on the preferred position First Amendment theory or doctrine (see page 43). The ban on publication was *presumed* to be an unconstitutional infringement on the First Amendment. The government had to prove that the ban was needed to protect the nation in some manner. If such evidence could be adduced, the court would strike the balance in favor of the government and uphold the ban on the publication of the articles. But in this case the government simply failed to show why its request for an injunction was

66. *New York Times* v. *U.S.,* 403 U.S. 713 (1971).
67. Pember, "The Pentagon Papers," 403.
68. *New York Times* v. *U.S.,* 403 U.S. 713 (1971).

What many people initially called the case of the century ended in a First Amendment fizzle.

vital to the national interest. Consequently, the high court denied the government's request for a ban on the publication of the Pentagon Papers on the grounds that such a prohibition was a violation of the First Amendment. The court did not say that in all similar cases an injunction would violate the First Amendment. It merely said that the government had not shown why the injunction was needed, why it was not a violation of the freedom of the press.

What many people initially called the case of the century ended in a First Amendment fizzle. The press won the day; the Pentagon Papers were published. But a majority of the court had not ruled that such prior restraint was unconstitutional—only that the government had failed to meet the heavy burden of showing such restraint was necessary in this case.

PROGRESSIVE MAGAZINE CASE

In a rare case in which national security concerns were found by a federal court to merit a prior restraint, a federal judge in 1979 in *United States* v. *Progressive*[69] issued a preliminary injunction stopping publication of a magazine article that specified "with particularity the three key concepts necessary to construct a hydrogen weapon." The judge determined the article included information "not found in the public realm" and that its publication "would likely cause a direct, immediate and irreparable injury to this nation."

The decision, however, is of little precedential value, as it was the opinion of only one federal district court judge, not an appellate court. Before the decision worked its way up the appellate court ladder, a newspaper in Wisconsin published the same information, thus rendering moot the case against the publishers of the Progressive magazine. We will never know if the prior restraint would have been sustained by an appellate court.

COME ON AND TAKE A FREE RIDE: RESTRAINING INFORMATION ABOUT SECURITY FLAWS WITH BOSTON'S TRANSIT SYSTEM

Government entities today still try to stop publication of information that could provide a recipe for others to break the law or cause harm. In 2008 the Massachusetts Bay Transportation Agency (MBTA) obtained from a federal judge a 10-day temporary restraining order (see page 7 discussing temporary restraining orders) that prevented a trio of Massachusetts Institute of Technology undergraduates from presenting an academic paper at DEFCON, a huge computer-security and hackers' convention. The paper, titled "Anatomy of a Subway Hack," allegedly revealed security flaws and vulnerabilities with Boston's mass transit fare-payment system that would allow people to obtain free rides and thus defraud the system. After the convention, however, a different federal judge lifted the prior restraint and rejected the MBTA's efforts to obtain a longer injunction, thus allowing the students to speak publicly about their findings. Judge George O'Toole found little likelihood the MBTA would ultimately prevail, in light of the First Amendment concerns about protecting dissemination of truthful information. It was a case of shooting the messenger, as the MBTA itself admitted there were some flaws with its automated fare-payment system.

---

69. 486 F. Supp. 5 (W.D. Wisc. 1979).

UNITED STATES v. *BELL*

Prior restraint speech cases need not always involve national security interests (the Pentagon Papers case and *United States* v. *Progressive*) or vociferous attacks against public officials (*Near* v. *Minnesota*). Indeed, in some instances the government may seek a prior restraint against an individual in order to stop the dissemination of false or fraudulent speech that subverts federal laws. That happened in 2005 when a federal appellate court in *United States* v. *Bell*[70] upheld a permanent injunction barring Thurston Paul Bell from promoting and selling unlawful tax advice. Bell, as the court put it, was a "professional tax protester who ran a business and a Web site selling bogus strategies to clients endeavoring to avoid paying taxes." Bell's Web site, the court wrote, "invited visitors to violate the tax code, and sold them materials instructing them how to do so." The federal government sought and won a district court injunction stopping Bell from engaging in false, deceptive or misleading commercial speech relating to any "abusive tax shelter, plan or arrangement that incites taxpayers to attempt to violate the internal revenue laws or unlawfully evade the assessment or collection of their federal tax liabilities or unlawfully claim improper tax refunds."

The 3rd U.S. Circuit Court of Appeals in *Bell* began its analysis by noting that "permanent injunctions like the one here are 'classic examples of prior restraints' on speech." The appellate court then cited the Pentagon Papers case described earlier in this chapter for the proposition that "prior restraints are generally presumed unconstitutional." But the appellate court then wrote, citing *Near* v. *Minnesota*, that prior restraints "may be permissible depending on the type of speech at issue."

In this case, the appellate court determined that the general principle of First Amendment law that prior restraints bear a heavy presumption against their constitutional validity "does not apply to restrictions on unprotected speech, including false or unlawful commercial speech" (see Chapter 15 regarding commercial speech). The court thus affirmed the injunction restraining Bell's false commercial speech. The outcome suggests that when speech falls completely outside the scope of the First Amendment protection of speech, a government-requested restraint against its dissemination may be permissible.

SUMMARY

While virtually all American legal scholars agree that the adoption of the First Amendment in 1791 was designed to abolish prior restraint in this nation, prior restraint still exists. A reason it still exists is the 1931 Supreme Court ruling in *Near* v. *Minnesota* in which Chief Justice Charles Evans Hughes ruled that although prior restraint is unacceptable in most instances, there are times when it must be tolerated if the republic is to survive. Protecting the security of the nation is one of those instances cited by Hughes. In the past quarter century in two important cases, the press has been stopped from publishing material the courts believed to be too sensitive. Although the Supreme Court finally permitted The New York Times and the Washington Post to publish the so-called Pentagon Papers, the newspapers were blocked for two weeks from printing this material. And in the end the high court merely ruled that

70. 414 F. 3d 474 (3d Cir. 2005).

the government had failed to make its case, not that the newspapers had a First Amendment right under any circumstance to publish this history of the Vietnam War. Eight years later the Progressive magazine was enjoined from publishing an article about thermonuclear weapons. Only the publication of the same material by a small newspaper in Wisconsin thwarted the government's efforts to permanently stop publication of this article in the Progressive.

BIBLIOGRAPHY

Alexander, James. *A Brief Narrative on the Case and Trial of John Peter Zenger.* Edited by Stanley N. Katz. Cambridge: Harvard University Press, 1963.

Associated Press. "NY Law Seeks to Restrict Violent Video Games." 22 July 2008.

Baker, C. Edwin. *Human Liberty and Freedom of Speech.* New York: Oxford University Press, 1989.

Barron, Jerome. "Access to the Press—A New First Amendment Right." *Harvard Law Review* 80 (1967): 1641.

Brooke, James. "Lawsuit Tests Legal Power of Words." *The New York Times,* 14 February 1996, A12.

Carelli, Richard. "High Court Allows 'Killers' Lawsuit." *Seattle Post-Intelligencer,* 9 September 1998, A3.

Chafee, Zechariah. *Free Speech in the United States.* Cambridge: Harvard University Press, 1941.

Chemerinsky, Erwin. *Constitutional Law: Principles and Policies.* 2nd ed. New York: Aspen, 2002.

Farber, Daniel A. *The First Amendment.* 2nd ed. New York: Foundation Press, 2003.

Friendly, Fred. *Minnesota Rag.* New York: Random House, 1981.

Gupta, Rani. "Reporters or Spies?" *The News Media and the Law,* Fall 2006, 4.

Herman, Ken. "Suit Alleges Protesters Are Muzzled at Bush Events." *Atlanta Journal-Constitution,* 21 October 2004, 10A.

Levy, Leonard. *Emergence of a Free Press.* New York: Oxford University Press, 1985.

Meiklejohn, Alexander. *Free Speech and Its Relation to Self-Government.* New York: Harper & Brothers, 1948.

Nomani, Asra. "You Still Can't Write About Muhammad." *Wall Street Journal*, 6 August 2008, A15.

Parks, Louis B. "Chicks Face 'Landslide' of Anger after Remark." *Houston Chronicle,* 15 March 2003, A1.

Pember, Don R. "The Pentagon Papers: More Questions Than Answers." *Journalism Quarterly* 48 (1971): 403.

———. "The Smith Act as a Restraint on the Press." *Journalism Monographs* 10 (1969): 1.

Peterson, H.C., and Gilbert Fite. *Opponents of War, 1917–1918.* Seattle: University of Washington Press, 1957.

Rabban, David M. *Free Speech in Its Forgotten Years.* Cambridge, United Kingdom: Cambridge University Press, 1997.

Redish, Martin H., and Kirk J. Kaludis. "The Right of Expressive Access in First Amendment Theory." *Northwestern University Law Review* 93 (1999): 1083.

Richards, Robert D., and Clay Calvert. "Nadine Strossen and Freedom of Expression." *George Mason University Civil Rights Law Journal* 13 (2003): 185.

Roche, John P. *Shadow and Substance.* New York: Macmillan, 1964.

Rutland, Robert. *The Birth of the Bill of Rights.* Chapel Hill: University of North Carolina Press, 1955.

Schechter, Harold. "A Movie Made Me Do It." *The New York Times,* 3 December 1995, A17.

Schmitt, Richard B. "Acquittal in Internet Terrorism Case Is a Defeat for Patriot Act." *Los Angeles Times,* 11 June 2004, A20.

Siebert, Fredrick. *Freedom of the Press in England, 1476–1776.* Urbana: University of Illinois Press, 1952.

Smith, James M. *Freedom's Fetters.* Ithaca, N.Y.: Cornell University Press, 1956.

Smith, Jeffrey A. "Prior Restraint: Original Intentions and Modern Interpretations." *William and Mary Law Review* 28 (1987): 439.

Smolla, Rodney. *Free Speech in an Open Society.* New York: Knopf, 1992.

Weiser, Benjamin. "Appellate Court Backs Convictions in '93 Terror Plot." *The New York Times,* 17 August 1999, A1.

Young, Cathy. "The Tyranny of Hecklers." *The Boston Globe,* 2 June 2003, A13.

CHAPTER 3

The First Amendment

CONTEMPORARY PROBLEMS

While First Amendment battles over sedition and taxation have been fought and won, other important issues related to free expression continue to be debated. Most prior restraints are unconstitutional. The use of prior restraint to protect the national security, however, continues to be regarded differently. Similarly, school authorities may censor school newspapers, magazines and yearbooks without always running afoul of the First Amendment. In addition, prior restraint is part of an entire class of government regulations called time, place and manner rules that frequently win judicial approval. Governments at all levels face the dilemma of what to do about so-called hate speech, given the constitutional guarantees of freedom of expression. These are some of the issues in this chapter.

PRIOR RESTRAINT DURING WARTIME

War reporting is difficult and deadly. By August 2009, more than 135 journalists from around the world had been killed in Iraq since fighting began there in March 2003, according to the Committee to Protect Journalists.[1] Two journalists for the Associated Press were injured in August 2009 when a bomb exploded underneath the U.S. military vehicle in which they were riding in Afghanistan. A New York Times reporter was kidnapped by the Taliban and held hostage in Afghanistan for seven months before he escaped in June 2009. What's more, the government itself can hinder reporting. For instance, in 2008 a veteran Associated Press television camera-person, Ahmed Nouri Raziak, was arrested by U.S. military officials in Iraq and held in detention for at least six months for what the government called "imperative reasons of security," but without specifying the allegations.[2] More shockingly, AP photographer Bilal Hussein was released from U.S. military custody in April 2008 after spending more than two years in prison in Iraq for alleged links to insurgents and possession of bomb-making materials.[3] After Iraqi judges dismissed the case against him and U.S. officials declared he was no longer a security threat, Hussein reiterated his long-held claim of innocence, and AP President and Chief Executive Officer Tom Curley proclaimed Hussein's release "a great relief to us."[4] Curley knows well the troubles of wartime reporting, as 11 of the AP's journalists in Iraq have been detained for more than 24 hours since 2003. During a speech at the University of Kansas in February 2009, shortly after Barack Obama became president, Curley summed up the need for change when he proclaimed "now is the time to re-negotiate the rules of engagement between the military and the media. Now is the time to insist that the First Amendment does apply to the battlefield. Now is the time to resist the propaganda the Pentagon produces and live up to our obligation to question authority and thereby help protect our democracy."[5]

1. Data about journalists killed while covering Iraq and other wars can be found on the Committee to Protect Journalists' Web site at http://www.cpj.org.
2. *Associated Press*, "Review Board Orders AP Journalist Held."
3. *Associated Press*, "AP Photographer Freed by US After 2 Years in Custody."
4. Ibid.
5. *Associated Press*, "AP CEO Urges Better Press Access to Military Ops."

Censorship of the press during wartime is not uncommon. There was censorship in every war in which the United States was involved, beginning with the Civil War. Censorship in both World War I and World War II was extensive. For example, the American people did not know the full extent of damage to the U.S. Pacific Fleet in the wake of the bombing of Pearl Harbor on December 7, 1941, until after the war. During World War II reporters had few limits on where they could go or with whom they could talk, but all news reports were screened by military censors before they were allowed to be published or broadcast. The press accepted some kind of censorship as a given—something normal in time of war. Such a belief in the normalcy of wartime censorship was reasonable in light of the U.S. Supreme Court's statement in *Schenck* v. *United States* in 1919 that "when a nation is at war many things that might be said in time of peace are such a hindrance to its effort that their utterance will not be endured so long as men fight and that no Court could regard them as protected by any constitutional right."[6]

In addition to *Schenck*'s words, recall from Chapter 2 that the Supreme Court in *Near* v. *Minnesota* suggested more than 75 years ago that prior restraints are permissible on some material during wartime. The court in *Near* wrote that "[n]o one would question but that a government might prevent actual obstruction to its recruiting service or the publication of the sailing dates of transports or the number and location of troops." But today, as professor Jeffery A. Smith observed, "the constitutional questions raised by government restraints on wartime reporting remain far from settled" such that there is "perplexity over press freedom in wartime."[7]

This section provides an overview of various modes and examples of censorship during wartime, particularly in recent years with the protracted war on terror sweeping up battles in Iraq and Afghanistan. Entire books are devoted to wartime censorship, and students should seek them out for details.[8] With that caveat, four common modes of censorship are identified and discussed here.

MODES OF CENSORSHIP DURING WARTIME

1. Denial of access to locations
2. Denial of access to documents and photographs
3. Punishment for publishing national security information
4. Self-censorship by the news media

ACCESS TO LOCATIONS

To accurately report on the realities of wartime fighting, the press needs access to the places where fighting occurs. During the war in Vietnam, American reporters could pretty much go where there wanted, talk to whomever they met and report on most military matters; they enjoyed a freedom to report that their colleagues in earlier wars had not experienced. When

---

6. 249 U.S. 47, 52 (1919).
7. Smith, *War and Press Freedom*, 27.
8. See Smith, *War and Press Freedom;* and Stone, *Perilous Times: Free Speech in Wartime.*

the United States failed to win the conflict in Southeast Asia, many military leaders blamed press reports, footage and photographs for turning public sentiment against the war. It thus was inevitable that such relatively unfettered access would not occur again if the government could prevent it.

Indeed, the situation proved radically different deep into the Iraq War. As The New York Times wrote in July 2008:

> If the conflict in Vietnam was notable for open access given to journalists—too much, many critics said, as the war played out nightly in bloody newscasts—the Iraq war may mark an opposite extreme: after five years and more than 4,000 American combat deaths, searches and interviews turned up fewer than a half-dozen graphic photographs of dead American soldiers.[9]

In Iraq, the Department of Defense used a system called "embedding" in which members of the press were allowed to accompany military units directly into battle and to report on what they saw, subject to limited restrictions and ground rules. Such access was a positive change from both the tightly controlled press briefings and the pooling system used in 1990–91 during the Persian Gulf War when the United States attacked Iraq after Saddam Hussein's troops invaded neighboring Kuwait. Under the pooling system, journalists had to travel in groups with the military; if they ventured outside the pools, they risked capture by the enemy, as happened with a CBS news team. As Jeffery Smith writes, the pooling system allowed fewer "than 200 reporters, photographers and technicians to cover over half a million Americans in armed forces" and it "created strong resentments and quickly collapsed under combat conditions."[10]

While many people feel the embedding system—which allows for immediacy of information and up-close reporting but which may sacrifice objectivity as journalists identify with the soldiers they live with—is an improvement over pooling, does the law require reporters to have such access? In 2004, a federal appellate court held in *Flynt* v. *Rumsfeld* that "there is no constitutionally based right for the media to embed with U.S. military forces in combat."[11] In this case, the publisher of Hustler magazine, Larry Flynt, asserted that there is "a First Amendment right for legitimate press representatives to travel with the military, and to be accommodated and otherwise facilitated by the military in their reporting efforts during combat, subject only to reasonable security and safety restrictions." The U.S. Court of Appeals for the District of Columbia, however, held that "[t]here is nothing we have found in the Constitution, American history or our case law to support this claim," and the Supreme Court declined to hear the case.[12] Thus the future ability of journalists to be embedded with U.S. troops is subject to the discretion and control of the military.

This was not the first time that Flynt had sued seeking access. In 1983, the United States invaded the tiny island nation of Grenada and a total news blackout of the military action was

---

9. Kamber and Arango, "4,000 U.S. Deaths, and a Handful of Images."
10. Smith, *War and Press Freedom,* 194.
11. 355 F. 3d 697 (D.C. Cir. 2004).
12. *Flynt* v. *Rumsfeld*, 543 U.S. 925 (2004).

© *Mario Tama/Getty Images*

In Iraq, reporters who were embedded were usually close to the coalition troops they covered. This journalist was attached to the Irish Guard's 7th Armored Brigade in fighting around Basra.

imposed during the initial phases of the fighting. Flynt sued Caspar W. Weinberger, the secretary of defense, seeking a court order preventing enforcement of the blackout.[13] Unfortunately, by the time the case was heard, the issue was moot—the case was no longer live, as the press ban had been lifted.

Other courts have similarly declined to squarely address questions of access to battlefields, as a federal judge in 1991 in *Nation Magazine* v. *U.S. Department of Defense*[14] was asked to consider, in the context of the Persian Gulf War, whether the First Amendment provides the press with "a right to gather and report news that involves United States military operations" and whether the pooling regulations noted above "are an unconstitutional limitation on access to observe events as they occur." By the time district court heard the case, the war was over, and Judge Leonard B. Sand dodged the issue, writing that "prudence dictates that we leave the definition of the exact parameters of press access to military operations

13. *Flynt* v. *Weinberger*, 762 F. 2d 134 (D.C. Cir. 1985).
14. 762 F. Supp. 1558 (S.D. N.Y. 1991).

abroad for a later date when a full record is available, in the unfortunate event that there is another military operation."

War zones are not, of course, the only physical locations to which the press would like access during times of war. For instance, the press has unsuccessfully sought access during the war on terror to detainees at Guantanamo Bay, Cuba. As professor David Anderson observed in 2006:

> While the press was not completely excluded from the detention facilities at Guantanamo, severe restrictions on access precluded first-hand reporting on the prisoners and the interrogation methods. As a result, information about the identities or treatment of the prisoners has come not from independent press reporting, but from official reports, lawyers for the few prisoners who were represented by counsel, and statements of prisoners after their release. Reporters were never allowed to speak with prisoners, and those who tried to do so were expelled.[15]

The Defense Department also prohibited press access to Dover Air Force Base in Delaware—the place where coffins carrying soldiers killed overseas arrive back in the United States. As Karen Meredith, the mother of a soldier killed in Iraq, put it, "it's just one more way this administration restricts the public's access to images and information—to hide its failures and mistakes and the true cost of its war in American lives."[16] In 1993, a group of professional journalistic photographers and other representatives of the news media unsuccessfully challenged this ban, first imposed in 1991, on First Amendment grounds in a case called *JB Pictures, Inc.* v. *Department of Defense*.[17] Reasoning that "the government need not open up all sources of information to everyone" and observing that "no member of the public has access to the hangar," the district court held that "the First Amendment does not give plaintiffs a right of access to the hangar at Dover Air Force Base. As no First Amendment rights are implicated, plaintiffs' complaint must be dismissed." A federal appellate court in 1996 upheld this decision and the policy, remarking that "the Dover policy does not impede acquisition of basic facts, the raw material of a story" and commenting that "we do not think the government hypersensitive in thinking that the bereaved may be upset at public display of the caskets of their loved ones."[18]

In February 2009, Defense Secretary Robert Gates agreed to review and reconsider the ban on photojournalists taking pictures of flag-draped coffins of dead U.S. soldiers at Dover Air Force Base. The move came after two U.S. senators, John Kerry and Frank Lautenberg, sent a letter to President Barack Obama asking him to lift the 18-year-old prohibition in a manner that would strike a better balance between the privacy rights of grieving families and the public's right to know. Gates ultimately changed the policy that same month to allow news photographers at the base to document the return of fallen troops' caskets from Iraq, provided that the families of those who died agreed to the photographers' presence. In April 2009, the relatives of Air Force Staff Sgt. Phillip Myers, who was killed in Afghanistan, became the first family to grant permission to the press to attend the arrival

15. Anderson, "Freedom of the Press in Wartime," 61.
16. Meredith, "Military's Ban on Coffin Photos Hurts Families."
17. 21 M.L.R. 1564 (D.D.C. 1993).
18. *JB Pictures, Inc.* v. *Department of Defense*, 86 F. 3d 236 (D.C. Cir. 1996).

of a loved one's casket at Dover. The Associated Press reported that by the end of April 2009, 14 of 19 families asked had given permission for media coverage of the ceremonies marking the arrival of the caskets on American soil.

Access to military funerals was still a hot issue in 2008. That's when the public affairs director of Arlington National Cemetery, Gina Gray, was fired for allegedly challenging an army policy keeping the media 50 yards away from burial ceremonies for soldiers killed in Iraq, even if the families had granted journalists permission to be closer. The 50-yard distance is such that media photographers' views are blocked and statements made at the services are inaudible at the publicly funded cemetery. The government denied Gray was fired for challenging the rule. Although ostensibly enacted in the name of protecting family privacy during a time of grief, the 50-yard buffer can be viewed more skeptically as an effort to hide the grim reality of death caused by the war from the media and, by extension, the public. Later in 2008 the Army adopted a new policy giving more power to mourning families in terms of controlling media access (both visual and audio) and allowing for the presence of a wireless microphone, if a family requests it, to be worn by the main speaker at Arlington burials so that the media can hear the eulogy.

Other locations during the war on terror to which the press wants access include courts where trials and proceedings of terrorism suspects and foreign detainees occur. Access sometimes is denied by the use of **secret dockets** in which court records about the mere existence of a case are kept secret by removing them from the public docket where one typically locates a case. For instance, names may be replaced by a caption such as *Sealed* v. *Sealed,* or the number assigned to the case may be removed altogether. At a communications law convention in New York in November 2008, the head of the Reporters Committee for Freedom of the Press, Lucy Dalglish, called the proliferation of secret docket cases (including many civil and criminal cases not related to the war in Iraq) "an epidemic" and "an absolute mess." To address the problem and in response to a long-sealed case within its jurisdiction, the 3rd U.S. Circuit Court of Appeals issued a notice that same month pledging it would no longer seal dockets. But the problem persists at the state level too. As the Albuquerque Journal reported in 2008 regarding secret dockets in New Mexico:

Access sometimes is denied by the use of secret dockets.

> State judges seal hundreds of cases each year. The sealing orders don't just prevent the public from looking at what's inside files. They wipe out all references to the cases in courthouse records available to the public. It's as if the cases never existed. Call it secret justice.[19]

A secret or private docketing system thus leads to secret trials because a reporter will never know that the case exists in the first place. A real-life example illustrates this point. In 2004, the U.S. Supreme Court gave "a green light for the government to conduct certain federal court cases in total secrecy"[20] in *M.K.B.* v. *Warden*[21] when it declined to hear the challenge of a man from Algeria named Mohamed K. Bellahouel who was secretly jailed in Florida as part of a federal terrorism investigation after the attacks of Sept. 11, 2001. The case of Bellahouel, who worked as a server at a Florida restaurant where two of the suspects in the Sept. 11 attacks allegedly ate, was kept off the public record completely and was discovered only after a clerical error. The high court's refusal to hear the case showed that it would not, in some instances, "second-guess lower court decisions

19. Cole, "Cases Involving Top Lawyer Sealed."
20. Richey, "Supreme Court Decision May Limit Access to Terror Cases."
21. 540 U.S. 1213 (2004).

to keep secret all documents and proceedings in terrorism cases."[22] In 2008, the Supreme Court again declined to consider the issue of secret docket cases when it denied a petition for a writ of certiorari in a federal employment discrimination case that was sealed for more than seven years.[23] The refusal to hear the case came despite the fact that 29 media organizations had joined together in filing a friend-of-the-court brief urging the high court to take it.

Access to some trials . . . during wartime may disappear completely when the federal government successfully asserts the state secrets privilege.

Finally, access to some trials and proceedings during wartime may disappear completely when the federal government successfully asserts the **state secrets privilege.** This happened in 2006 when a federal judge in *El-Masri* v. *Tenet*[24] dismissed the claim of a man who sued the CIA and its then director, George Tenet, based upon the alleged detention, interrogation and torture of the plaintiff at what he claimed was a classified, CIA-operated prison facility known as the "Salt Pit" near Kabul, Afghanistan. The government moved to dismiss the case, asserting that state secrets privilege, which allows the government to block a lawsuit if any information disclosed during it would adversely affect national security. As discussed by the federal district court in *El-Masri*, the privilege arises from the "president's constitutional authority over the conduct of this country's diplomatic and military affairs," and it "must be formally asserted by the head of the executive branch agency with responsibility for, and control over, the state secrets involved." Judge T.S. Ellis III observed that a court must accept the assertion of the privilege whenever the court's independent inquiry discloses a "reasonable danger that compulsion of the evidence will expose military matters which, in the interest of national security, should not be divulged." Finding this to be the situation in *El-Masri*, Judge Ellis then dismissed the case against Tenet and the CIA because he next determined that the claims could not be fairly litigated without disclosing state secrets protected by the privilege. In reaching this conclusion, the judge noted that "any answer to the [plaintiff's] complaint would potentially disclose information protected by the privilege," thus refuting "El-Masri's argument that special procedures short of dismissal [of the case] would be adequate to protect the government's validly asserted privilege."

In 2007, a federal appellate court affirmed the ruling by Judge Ellis in *El-Masri*.[25] In holding that Judge Ellis had correctly applied the state secrets privilege, the appellate court made it clear that the privilege

> is governed primarily by two standards. First, evidence is privileged pursuant to the state secrets doctrine if, under all the circumstances of the case, there is a reasonable danger that its disclosure will expose military (or diplomatic or intelligence) matters which, in the interest of national security, should not be divulged. . . . Second, a proceeding in which the state secrets privilege is successfully interposed must be dismissed if the circumstances make clear that privileged information will be so central to the litigation that any attempt to proceed will threaten that information's disclosure.

In 2008, the U.S. Senate Judiciary Committee issued a report finding that "courts have largely acquiesced" to the assertion of the state secrets privilege during the administration of President George W. Bush and that "a strong public perception has emerged that sees the privilege as a tool for Executive abuse."[26] Indeed, a group called OpenTheGovernment.org

22. Denniston, "High Court Declines to Rule on Secrecy."
23. *New York Law Publishing Company* v. *Doe*, 129 S. Ct. 576 (2008).
24. 437 F. Supp. 2d 530 (E.D. Va. 2006).
25. *El-Masri* v. *U.S.*, 479 F. 3d 296 (4th Cir. 2007).
26. *State Secrets Protection Act*, Report 110-442 (Aug. 1, 2008), available online at http://www.fas.org/sgp/congress/2008/srep110-442.pdf.

reported in 2008 that "between 1953 and 1976, the federal government invoked the 'state secrets' privilege only six times. Between 1977 and 2000, administrations invoked the privilege 59 reported times (a rate of 2.46 times per year). Since 2001, the state secrets privilege has been invoked at least 45 times, a rate of 6.42 times each year."[27] The state secrets privilege can easily be abused; U.S. District Judge Royce Lamberth, for instance, ruled in 2009 that CIA officials committed fraud by wrongly invoking it to shut down a lawsuit filed by a former Drug Enforcement Agency official, Richard A. Horn, who claimed the CIA had illegally bugged and wiretapped his residence.

ACCESS TO DOCUMENTS AND PHOTOGRAPHS

Another censorship issue during wartime relates to press access to government documents and photographs. As Chapter 9 makes clear, the Freedom of Information Act (FOIA)[28] creates a presumptive right of access to records kept by federal government agencies, yet one of the nine exemptions from FOIA is for records that could jeopardize national security. The government uses the national security exemption, as well as other exemptions, to keep secret documents about wartime information. Details about the presidential classification of information for national security information are found on the National Archives and Records Administration Web site at http://www.archives.gov/isoo.

Another FOIA exemption sometimes used to protect wartime information from disclosure relates to "records or information compiled for law enforcement purposes." Other exemptions also are used to stanch the flow of records to the public relating to the war on terror. As attorney and FOIA expert Stephen Gidiere wrote on the 40th anniversary of FOIA in 2006, "the executive branch made 14.2 million new decisions to classify information as secret" in 2005, nearly double the figure from 1998 and largely attributable "to the Iraq and Afghanistan wars and increased military and intelligence operations since 9/11."[29] Professor Geoffrey R. Stone of the University of Chicago observes that "excessive secrecy has been a consistent feature of the Bush administration," including "its refusal to disclose the names of those it detained after Sept. 11 and its narrowing of the Freedom of Information Act."[30]

FOIA, however, is a very useful tool for learning about wartime information if no exemption is used by the government or if a requestor successfully challenges the government's assertion of an exemption. For instance, the ACLU in 2008 obtained from the Department of Justice a five-year-old memorandum authored by John Yoo, then a deputy with that department's Office of Legal Counsel, regarding domestic and international legal standards governing military interrogations of alien unlawful combatants held outside the United States.[31] Yoo's memo garnered massive media attention, as it concluded that the Fifth Amendment

27. *Secrecy Report Card 2008*, 20. OpenTheGovernment noted in its report that the "numbers of orders during the George W. Bush administration vary according to the counting methods used" and "in some cases, the assertion in the reported case at trial and in a reported opinion on appeal, if there is one, for the same case are counted as two assertions." Ibid.
28. 5 U.S.C. § 552 (2007).
29. Gidiere, "Checks, Balances and FOIA's 40th Anniversary."
30. Stone, *Perilous Times*, 557.
31. Yoo's memorandum is posted on the ACLU's Web site at http://www.aclu.org/pdfs/safefree/yoo_army_torture_memo.pdf.

right against self-incrimination and the Eighth Amendment prohibition against cruel and unusual punishment did not apply to alien enemy combatants held abroad. It also seemed to authorize torturous interrogations, as Yoo wrote:

> If a government defendant were to harm an enemy combatant during an interrogation in a manner that might arguably violate a criminal prohibition, he would be doing so in order to prevent further attacks on the United States by the al Qaeda terrorist network. In that case, we believe that he could argue that the executive branch's constitutional authority to protect the nation from attack justified his actions.

Not all FOIA requests relating to the war on terror, however, are successful. For instance, in 2009 the 2nd U.S. Circuit Court of Appeals held that FOIA privacy Exemption 7(c) (see page 337 regarding Exemption 7) protected from disclosure the names and other identifying information of detainees held at Guantanamo Bay and contained in Department of Defense records documenting allegations of abuse of detainees committed by both military personnel and other detainees.[32] Although the Department of Defense produced the abuse records in question to the Associated Press upon a FOIA request, it redacted (blacked out) from them all identifying information of the detainees involved (both the detainee victims and detainee abusers), asserting that it did so to protect their personal privacy. The appellate court held that the privacy interests of the detainees outweighed the public interest in obtaining the identifying information about them. It noted that the victims of abuse "are entitled to some protection of personal information that would be revealed if their names were associated with the incidents of abuse. The disclosure of their names could certainly subject them to embarrassment and humiliation." With regard to the detainees who were alleged to have abused other detainees, the court wrote that "these alleged abusers have a significant privacy interest in keeping their identities undisclosed. It is likely that identifying them could subject them to embarrassment and humiliation."

In April 2004, the Department of Defense tightened its policy preventing the release of photographs of coffins or funerals of American soldiers killed in Iraq, citing privacy concerns.[33] That occurred after the U.S. Air Force granted—much to the government's chagrin—the FOIA request by Russ Kick for "all photographs taken after February 2003 of caskets containing the remains of U.S. military personnel at Dover Air Force Base in Delaware."[34] He displayed the photographs, 73 of which turned out to be of the deceased Columbia space shuttle astronauts, for the world to see on his Web site, The Memory Hole.[35]

In 2008, a federal appellate court affirmed a lower-court decision compelling the Department of Defense to turn over to the ACLU infamous images from the war in Iraq—21 photos depicting abusive treatment of detainees by U.S. soldiers in Iraq and Afghanistan, including some taken at Abu Ghraib prison.[36] In ordering the release of the photos after an ACLU FOIA request, the 2nd U.S. Circuit Court of Appeals rejected the government's argument that FOIA Exemption 7(f) prevented their release (see page 337 regarding Exemption 7). That exemption

---

32. *Associated Press* v. *Department of Defense*, 554 F. 3d 274 (2d Cir. 2009).
33. Schorr, "Why Hide Flag-Draped Coffins?"
34. Smith, "Coffins and Now Chaos."
35. The Memory Hole Web site at http://www.thememoryhole.org/war/coffin_photos/dover.
36. *American Civil Liberties Union* v. *Department of Defense*, 543 F. 3d 59 (2d Cir. 2008).

authorizes the withholding of records "compiled for law enforcement purposes" where disclosure "could reasonably be expected to endanger the life or physical safety of any individual." According to the government, release of the Abu Ghraib photos could reasonably be expected to endanger the life or physical safety of U.S. troops, coalition forces and civilians in Iraq and Afghanistan. In 2009, President Obama, to the shock of many liberals, decided to fight the release of the photos all the way to the U.S. Supreme Court. Obama's argument that release of the photos would jeopardize American lives by inflaming anti-U.S. sentiment was filed by the Justice Department with the high court in August 2009.

In late 2008, the Associated Press faced a new problem with photos obtained from the U.S. Army–digital alteration and manipulation of the images. In particular, the AP issued a "photo elimination" notice and banned the use of two images, each depicting a soldier killed in Iraq, that appeared to be identical other than the faces, names and ranks of the two soldiers. As one newspaper article put it, "their poses, body types, placement in front of a U.S. flag and their camouflage uniforms, down to the creases, were identical."[37]

Sometimes access to documents is completely denied. In 2006, for example, a federal court in *Los Angeles Times Communications* v. *Department of the Army*[38] upheld the government's refusal to grant a FOIA request by a newspaper for the names of American private security contractors involved in serious shooting incidents in Iraq. In this case, the government successfully asserted two other FOIA exemptions—Exemption 2 that shields from disclosure matters that related solely to the internal rules and practices of an agency (see page 331 regarding Exemption 2), and Exemption 7(f) for records compiled for law enforcement purposes that "could reasonably be expected to endanger the life or physical safety of any individual" (see page 337 regarding Exemption 7).

In addition to various FOIA exemptions, the federal government also uses the **Classified Information Procedures Act (CIPA)**[39] during the ongoing war on terror. Enacted in 1980, CIPA details procedures for courts to consider when the government argues that classified information could be publicly disclosed during a criminal prosecution that might jeopardize national security (including both national defense and foreign relations) and thus the information should be sealed from public access. As attorneys Natalie Spears and Gregory Naron wrote in 2006, "as the government continues to prosecute more terrorism-related cases, the occasions for the executive branch to invoke CIPA are likewise increasing."[40]

PUNISHMENT FOR PUBLISHING NATIONAL SECURITY INFORMATION

In addition to government efforts to stop publication of information by denying the press access to both physical locations and documents or photographs, there remains today the slight possibility that the government could punish the press for publishing information that exposes national security secrets. Put differently, in addition to prior restraints on wartime speech, subsequent punishments may be possible as well. Recall from Chapter 2 that the federal government in 2006 in *United States* v. *Rosen* used the Espionage Act of 1917, which

37. Richter, "Army Post Spokesman Says Photo of Slain Soldier Was Digitally Altered."
38. 442 F. Supp. 2d 880 (C.D. Cal. 2006).
39. 18 U.S.C. App. 3 (2007).
40. Spears and Naron, "CIPA and the Right of Access."

protects national defense information, to go after two lobbyists who allegedly disclosed information that could jeopardize national security (see pages 52–53). In addition, 2006 saw the government open a treason case (see page 47). While neither case was against a journalist, Tim Rutten of the Los Angeles Times wrote in May 2006 that, after Washington Post reporter Dana Priest wrote a Pulitzer Prize–winning story exposing the existence of secret Central Intelligence Agency prison camps in Eastern Europe, "a chorus of intensely partisan Republican commentators [has] been demanding that reporters who write stories based on leaks of classified information be prosecuted under the Espionage Act of 1917."[41] In July 2006, the editors of The New York Times and Los Angeles Times jointly wrote and published a commentary after their papers, along with the Wall Street Journal, exposed the Bush administration's program of secretly monitoring international banking transactions.[42] The two editors wrote, "Our reports—like earlier press disclosures of secret measures to combat terrorism—revived an emotional national debate, featuring angry calls of 'treason' and proposals that journalists be jailed along with much genuine concern and confusion about the role of the press in times like these." In a separate commentary, the associate editor of the Washington Post, Robert G. Kaiser, wrote in 2006 that "the Bush administration has been publicly toying with the idea of using the Espionage Act . . . to prosecute journalists for disclosing classified information."[43]

While no treason or espionage charges have yet to be filed against journalists for such reporting on the war on terrorism, the mere threat of such actions may have a chilling effect on the reporting of future stories involving national security interests. Self-censorship, in other words, may occur during wartime as some members of the press fear government reprisals for reporting information.

SELF-CENSORSHIP BY THE NEWS MEDIA

As noted, self-censorship may occur because some members of the media worry about government retaliation under espionage laws. It may also occur, however, because the media simply feel a sense of duty not to reveal some information that could jeopardize U.S. soldiers. In the same commentary in which the editors of The New York Times and Los Angeles Times noted calls for treason against journalists, they wrote:

> Each of us, in the past few years, has had the experience of withholding or delaying articles when the administration convinced us that the risk of publication outweighed the benefits. Probably the most discussed instance was The New York Times's decision to hold its article on telephone eavesdropping for more than a year, until editors felt that further reporting had whittled away the administration's case for secrecy. . . . In April, the Los Angeles Times withheld information about American espionage and surveillance activities in Afghanistan discovered on computer drives purchased by reporters in an Afghan bazaar.

Self-censorship of war-related information also may occur because some members of the press decide either not to offend viewers or readers or not to give coverage that could

---

41. Rutten, "Regarding Media."
42. Baquet and Keller, "When Do We Publish a Secret?"
43. Kaiser, "Public Secrets."

hurt public support for American war efforts. A vivid example of such self-censorship came in April 2004 when the Sinclair Broadcast Group "ordered its ABC affiliates to preempt Ted Koppel's 'Nightline: The Fallen' Roll Call Tribute to U.S. Military Killed in Iraq."[44] Sinclair is "known for including conservative commentary in its news and for its almost exclusively Republican political contributions."[45]

Finally, self-censorship by the news media may occur simply because (1) journalists perceive the public as losing interest in war coverage (known as "war fatigue"); (2) other major stories (a presidential election, a sagging economy) compete for time and space; and (3) the cost of keeping correspondents abroad is steep. As the American Journalism Review reported in June 2008, "for long stretches over the past 12 months, Iraq virtually disappeared from the front pages of the nation's newspapers and from the nightly network newscasts. The American press and the American people had lost interest in the war."[46]

SUMMARY

The U.S. Supreme Court suggested in both *Schenck* and *Near* that censorship is permissible in some instances during wartime. Four modes of censorship against the press during wartime are (1) denial of access to locations; (2) denial of access to documents and photographs; (3) punishment for publishing national security information; and (4) self-censorship by the news media.

THE FIRST AMENDMENT IN SCHOOLS

Censorship of school newspapers and magazines is a serious First Amendment issue in America today. Consider the following instances of apparent censorship of public school student newspapers in 2008 and 2009, each reported by the Student Press Law Center in its online "News Flashes"[47] database:

- The principal of Grover Cleveland High School in the Los Angeles Unified School District confiscated copies of the "V-Day" (a movement to stop violence against females) issue of the student paper because it had the word "vagina" in a front-page headline (the headline read "Have a Happy Vagina Day!") and included a medical diagram of a vagina.
- The principal of Eureka High School in California confiscated about 400 copies of an issue of the student paper because it included, in the context of a profile of a student-artist, a black-and-white, fantasy-style drawing by the student-artist that included nude female figures.
- An article called "Are Suspensions Necessary?" was withheld by the principal Loy Norrix High School in Kalamazoo, Mich. Editors of the student paper, The Knight Life, believed it was held back because it criticized the school's use of out-of-school suspensions, but the principal claimed it was due to factual inaccuracies. Eventually it was published after revisions were made at the principal's request.

44. Jensen, "Sinclair Broadcast Group."
45. Jensen, "Sinclair Broadcast Group."
46. Ricchiardi, "Whatever Happened to Iraq?"
47. Visit the SPLC's Web site at http://www.splc.org.

Not only does such censorship deprive students and others of information they should rightfully see, but when practiced in the schools, censorship can take on the aura of being good policy, the right thing for the government to do. School, after all, is where students are taught the difference between right and wrong, where students learn about the freedoms Americans enjoy under their Constitution.

CENSORSHIP OF EXPRESSION IN PUBLIC HIGH SCHOOLS

For centuries, students were presumed to have few constitutional rights. They were regarded as second-class people and were told it was better to be seen and not heard. Parents were, and still are, given wide latitude in controlling the behavior of their offspring, and when these young people moved into schools or other public institutions, the government had the right to exercise a kind of parental control over them: in loco parentis, in the place of a parent. During the social upheaval of the 1960s and 1970s, students began to assert their constitutional rights, and in several important decisions the federal courts acknowledged these claims. In 1969, in the case of *Tinker* v. *Des Moines,* the Supreme Court ruled that students in the public schools do not shed at the schoolhouse gate their constitutional rights to freedom of speech or expression.

During the social upheaval of the 1960s and 1970s, students began to assert their constitutional rights, and in several important decisions the federal courts acknowledged these claims.

On December 16, 1966, Christopher Eckhardt, 16, and Mary Beth Tinker, 13, went to school wearing homemade black armbands, complete with peace signs, to protest the war in Vietnam. Mary Beth's brother John, 15, wore a similar armband the following day. All three were suspended from school after they refused requests by school officials to remove the armbands. School administrators said they feared that wearing the armbands might provoke violence among the students, most of whom supported the war in Vietnam. The students appealed to the courts to overturn their suspensions. Three years later Justice Abe Fortas, writing for the Supreme Court, said that students have a First Amendment right to express their opinions on even controversial subjects like the war in Vietnam if they do so "without materially and substantially interfering with the requirements of appropriate discipline in the operation of the school and without colliding with the rights of others."[48] In ruling in favor of the Tinker children and Christopher Eckhardt, the Supreme Court added that an "undifferentiated fear or apprehension of disturbance is not enough to overcome the right to freedom of expression" in public schools. Judge Fortas wrote that, in this case, the "record does not demonstrate any facts which might reasonably have led school authorities [in Des Moines] to forecast substantial disruption of or material interference with school activities, and no disturbances or disorders on the school premises in fact occurred."

The *Tinker* standard played a very important role in the 2003 federal district court opinion in *Barber* v. *Dearborn Public Schools.*[49] The case arose from a dispute in Dearborn, Mich. That city boasts, the court noted, "the largest concentration of Arabs anywhere in the world outside of the Middle East" and "approximately 31.4% of Dearborn High's students are Arab." Many of these residents reportedly fled Iraq to escape the regime of the now captured former dictator, Saddam Hussein. It was in this environment on Feb. 17, 2003—just before the launch of the U.S. military offensive in Iraq—that Bretton Barber, then a high school junior,

48. *Tinker* v. *Des Moines School District,* 393 U.S. 503 (1969).
49. 286 F. Supp. 2d 847 (E.D. Mich. 2003).

© Reuters/CORBIS

Bretton Barber wears the T-shirt that landed him in trouble with administrators at Dearborn High School. A federal judge ruled that he had a First Amendment right to wear the shirt to school.

wore a T-shirt labeling President George W. Bush an "International Terrorist" in order "to express his feelings about President Bush's foreign policies and the imminent war in Iraq." Barber went through the first three class periods of the day without having anyone mention the shirt. It was during the lunch period, however, that one student (and one student only) complained to an assistant principal about Barber's political fashion statement. That student was upset because he had a relative in the military being sent to Iraq and at least one of his family members served in each of the country's prior wars. Barber soon was asked to remove the T-shirt—he was wearing a different shirt underneath it—or turn it inside out. Refusing to take either option, Barber called his father and went home from school that day. Shortly thereafter, he filed a federal lawsuit against the school district.

Judge Patrick J. Duggan faced the issue of whether the school violated Barber's First Amendment right to free speech and political expression when it prohibited him from wearing the anti-Bush T-shirt. He first held that Barber's case was controlled by the U.S. Supreme Court's 1969 opinion in *Tinker* v. *Des Moines Independent Community School District* that upheld the right of students to wear black armbands to school to protest the Vietnam War. Duggan thus decided that Barber's case was not guided by the high court's more recent decisions in either the sexually offensive, captive-audience expression case of *Bethel School District* v. *Fraser*[50] (see pages 96–97) or the school-sponsored newspaper case of *Hazelwood School District* v. *Kuhlmeier*[51] (see pages 91–95). Barber's situation, in brief, was much more factually similar to *Tinker* than it was to either *Bethel* or *Hazelwood,* thus allowing the judge to distinguish the latter two cases.

Applying the *Tinker* precedent, Judge Duggan reasoned that the school officials' "decision to ban Barber's shirt only can withstand constitutional scrutiny if they show that the T-shirt caused a substantial disruption of or material interference with school activities or created more than an unsubstantiated fear or apprehension of such a disruption or interference." The judge found that only one student and one teacher had expressed negative opinions about the shirt and that there was "no evidence that the T-shirt created any disturbance or disruption in Barber's morning classes, in the hallway between classes or between Barber's third hour class and his lunch period, or during the first twenty-five minutes of the lunch period."

As for the school officials' argument that the continued wearing of the shirt might cause trouble in the future, given the ethnic composition of the student body and the imminence of war, Judge Duggan found that "even if the majority or a large number of Dearborn High's Arab students are Iraqi, nothing in the present record suggests that these students were or would be offended by Barber's shirt which conveys a view about President Bush. More importantly, there is nothing in the record before this Court to indicate that those students, or any students at Dearborn High, might respond to the T-shirt in a way that would disrupt or interfere with the school environment." He added that "it is improper and most likely detrimental to our society for government officials, particularly school officials, to assume that members of a particular ethnic group will have monolithic views on a subject and will be unable to control those views."

Comparing the situation in Barber's case with the Vietnam War protest scenario at issue in the *Tinker* case, Judge Duggan wrote: "[C]learly the tension between students who support and those who oppose President Bush's decision to invade Iraq is no greater than the tension that existed during the United States' involvement in Vietnam between supporters of the war and war-protesters." The judge added that "students benefit when school officials provide an environment where they can openly express their diverging viewpoints and when they learn to tolerate the opinions of others." Judge Duggan thus ruled in favor of Bretton Barber.

Think censorship like that in *Barber* v. *Dearborn Public Schools* is rare or isolated? Think again. In September 2008, shortly before the presidential election that year, a fifth-grader at a public school near Denver was suspended for wearing a T-shirt with the message "Obama Is a Terrorist's Best Friend." The school claimed it was not engaging in viewpoint-based censorship but rather was quashing the shirt because it might cause a disruption. Without actual evidence of a material and substantial (in other words, not a minor or fleeting) disruption, however, such censorship clearly is unconstitutional under the logic of both *Tinker* and Judge Duggan's ruling in *Barber*. The 5th U.S. Circuit Court of Appeals recently heard a case involving a Texas high school student suspended for wearing a shirt with an innocuous

---

50. 478 U.S. 675 (1986).
51. 484 U.S. 260 (1988).

political message—"John Edwards '08" (a reference to an erstwhile Democratic presidential candidate). Paul "Pete" Palmer was suspended because his school's dress code barred all nonschool messages, political or otherwise, on shirts. Exceptions were made for small logos on shirts and principal-approved shirts promoting school clubs, organizations and teams. The appellate court in *Palmer* v. *Waxahachie Independent School District* ruled in August 2009 against the student, concluding the shirt policy was a permissible content-neutral regulation on speech (see pages 110–111) that served the school's interests behind it of providing a safer, more orderly learning environment and encouraging professional dress. The court added that the policy did not prevent all messages, as students could wear buttons.

The legacy of *Tinker* has largely failed to live up to Justice Fortas' bold language in the case. Although *Tinker*'s material-and-substantial interference or disruption standard remains good law and has never been overruled, many lower courts attempt to factually distinguish *Tinker* in student-speech cases to avoid applying its precedent. It is a major problem for students' speech rights that has grown worse after the tragedy at Columbine High School in Littleton, Colo., in 1999. Judges today are extremely sensitive to the legacy of Columbine and other school shootings and, in turn, give great deference to school administrators and principals and are loathe to question their judgment about when speech might reasonably lead to a substantial and material disruption of the educational process or interference with the rights of other students.

While the *Tinker* standard applies today in cases involving student speech that happens to occur on school grounds and that is neither school sponsored nor sexually lewd, vulgar or profane, a very different legal standard applies when the speech is sponsored by the school, such as a school newspaper that is part of the curriculum. The standard in this latter situation was created by the Supreme Court in 1988 in a case called *Hazelwood School District* v. *Kuhlmeier*[52] and it is discussed next.

The Hazelwood *Case*

In 1983 the principal at Hazelwood East High School near St. Louis censored the school newspaper by completely removing two pages. The pages contained articles about teen pregnancy and the impact of parents' divorce on children. The articles on pregnancy included personal interviews with three Hazelwood students (whose names were not used) about how they were affected by their unwanted pregnancies. There was also information about birth control in the story. The story on divorce quoted students—again not identified—about the problems they had suffered when their mothers and fathers had split up. The censorship of the articles was defended on the grounds of privacy and editorial balance. School officials said they were concerned that the identity of the three girls who agreed to anonymously discuss their pregnancies might nevertheless become known. School officials said they acted to protect the privacy of students and parents in the story on divorce as well. In addition, the principal said the latter story was unbalanced, giving the views of only the students. In 1988 the Supreme Court ruled that the censorship was permissible under the First Amendment.[53]

---

52. 484 U.S. 260 (1988).
53. *Hazelwood School District* v. *Kuhlmeier,* 484 U.S. 260 (1988).

It is important to note that this ruling involved censorship of a high school newspaper that was published as a part of the school curriculum. The court strongly suggested the ruling would not necessarily apply to a high school paper published as an extracurricular activity where any student might contribute stories. Justice Byron White, author of the court's opinion, noted specifically in a footnote that the court did not at that time have to decide whether its ruling might also be applied to school-sponsored college and university newspapers.

The Supreme Court refused to apply the *Tinker* standard by distinguishing the *Hazelwood* case from the earlier ruling. The *Tinker* ruling, Justice White said in the 5-3 decision, deals with the right of educators to silence a student's personal expression that happens to occur on school property. *Hazelwood* concerns the authority of educators over school-sponsored publications. "Educators are entitled to exercise greater control over this second form of student expression to assure that participants learn whatever lessons the activity is designed to teach, that readers or listeners are not exposed to material that may be inappropriate for their level of maturity, and that the views of individual speakers are not erroneously attributed to the school," he wrote. Educators do not offend the First Amendment by exercising editorial control over the style and content of student speech in school-sponsored publications as long as their actions are reasonably related to "legitimate pedagogical concerns." This means school officials could censor out material they found "ungrammatical, poorly written, inadequately researched, biased or prejudiced, vulgar or profane, or unsuitable for immature audiences." Justice White stressed at one point in the ruling that the education of the nation's youth is primarily the responsibility of parents, teachers and state and local school officials, not federal judges. Only when the decision to censor has "no valid educational purpose" is the First Amendment directly and sharply involved.

In the years since the *Hazelwood* ruling censorship of the student press has escalated. Each year the Student Press Law Center, a clearinghouse and legal advocate for student First Amendment fights, reports hundreds of calls from student-journalists seeking help with censorship problems.

It is not only stories about sexual behavior or violence that can provoke school administrators to censor student publications. School officials frequently seek to block the publication of stories that will make school administrators or teachers appear to be foolish or incompetent or lacking judgment. For example, the principal at a high school near Chicago censored an article about four school administrators who had spent $5,600 on trips to meetings when the district faced a serious budget crisis. The article included material about potential impropriety in the way the funds were spent. The principal ordered the names of the administrators taken out of the article.[54] Other reports of censorship are reported almost weekly in newspapers and magazines.

There are only a few rare instances in which courts have held that school administrators have gone too far and violated the rights of student-journalists under *Hazelwood*'s expansive "legitimate pedagogical concerns" standard. One such case of a First Amendment violation involved the censorship of an article in the Utica High School Arrow in Utica, Mich. The student-authored article in question reported on a lawsuit filed against the Utica Community Schools (UCS) by two local residents, Joanne and Rey Frances, who lived next door

Educators do not offend the First Amendment by exercising editorial control over the style and content of student speech in school-sponsored publications as long as their actions are reasonably related to "legitimate pedagogical concerns."

---

54. "Suspension of Student"; and "Students Censored."

to the UCS bus depot. The Frances' lawsuit claimed injuries and illnesses allegedly caused by breathing in the diesel fumes emitted by the UCS's idling buses each school day. A local newspaper had already covered the story about the lawsuit before student Katherine "Katy" Dean researched and wrote an article about the situation for her school newspaper, the Arrow. The Arrow is an officially sponsored publication of the UCS and, as part of the high school's curriculum for which students receive credit and grades, operates under the direction of a faculty adviser. The faculty adviser, however, does not regulate the subjects covered by students, but instead merely provides advice on which stories to run. She also reviews, criticizes and checks the grammar contained in articles. The Arrow's staff of student journalists controls the content of the monthly paper, is responsible for major editorial decisions without significant administrative intervention and typically does not submit its content to school administrators for prepublication review.

The article written by Dean was balanced and accurate, and it correctly reported that school district officials declined to comment on the lawsuit. One day before the article was scheduled to go to press, however, UCS administrators ordered that it be removed from the Arrow, citing so-called journalistic defects and "inaccuracies" (for instance, the UCS administration did not like the fact that Dean's article accurately attributed scientific data to a story in USA Today—apparently it was not a credible source in the minds of the school officials—and the fact that a draft of the story used pseudonyms for the Frances' real names). The American Civil Liberties Union filed a lawsuit on behalf of Dean, claiming the censorship violated Dean's First Amendment rights under *Hazelwood*.[55]

In 2004 U.S. District Court Judge Arthur Tarnow applied the *Hazelwood* legitimate-pedagogical-concerns standard and ruled in favor of Dean and against the school. The judge called the school's censorship and suppression of the article "unconstitutional," adding that the school's "explanation that the article was deleted for legitimate educational purposes such as bias and factual inaccuracy is wholly lacking in credibility in light of the evidence in the record."[56] Judge Tarnow distinguished the Arrow's article about the lawsuit from the censored content in the *Hazelwood* case that dealt with teen pregnancy and divorce. He observed that Katy Dean's article about the bus-fumes lawsuit did not raise any privacy concerns since a local paper had already addressed the lawsuit, and it did not contain any sexual "frank talk" and thus could not reasonably be perceived as being unsuitable for immature audiences. Beyond such critical distinctions, Judge Tarnow found the article to be fair and balanced, noting that Dean's story "sets forth the conflicting viewpoints on the health effects of diesel fumes, and concludes that the link between diesel fumes and cancer is not fully established." Finally Tarnow noted that the story contained no serious grammatical errors and that "Dean's article properly and accurately attributes its quotations to their sources. The article qualifies any statement made by its sources. The article does not present the author's own conclusions on unknown facts." Judge Tarnow thus concluded that "Katy Dean had a right to publish an article concerning the Frances' side of the lawsuit so long as it accurately reported the Frances' side of the lawsuit."

In addition to holding that the school's actions against Dean violated the *Hazelwood* standard, Judge Tarnow ruled that the censorship of her article violated the more general but

55. *Dean v. Utica Community Schools,* 345 F. Supp. 2d 799 (E.D. Mich. 2004).
56. *Associated Press,* "Utica Schools."

important First Amendment rule against **viewpoint-based discrimination.** In support of this holding, Judge Tarnow noted that the UCS attorney "conceded that Dean's article would not have been removed from the Arrow if it had explicitly taken the district's side with respect to the Frances' lawsuit against UCS." This is the essence of viewpoint-based discrimination: The government (in this case, the school district) restricts and restrains one side of a debate but not the other. For instance, it would violate the rule against viewpoint-based discrimination if a public school only allowed pro-choice views on the topic of abortion to be printed in the school newspaper while it simultaneously prohibited and censored pro-life views. More simply put, the government should remain neutral in the marketplace of ideas (see pages 44–45) and not favor one side of a debate over the other. By acknowledging that the school would have allowed Katy Dean to print an article that favored the UCS's position in the lawsuit filed against it by the Franceses, the UCS attorney essentially admitted the viewpoint-based discrimination that drove it to censor Dean's story.

The case of *Dean* v. *Utica Community Schools* should stand as a stark reminder to overzealous and censorious high school administrators that there are limits, even under the *Hazelwood* legitimate-pedagogical-concern standard, to censorship of the student press.

High school journalism remains vigorous in many schools. And the legislatures in a handful of states, including California, Colorado, Arkansas, Iowa, Massachusetts, Oregon and Kansas, have passed statutes granting student-journalists in those states a fuller measure of freedom of expression than was granted by the Supreme Court in *Hazelwood*. For instance, Oregon's anti-*Hazelwood* statute, enacted in 2007, provides that student-journalists "have the right to exercise freedom of speech and of the press in school-sponsored media, whether or not the media are supported financially by the school or by use of school facilities or are produced in conjunction with a high school class" and that "student journalists are responsible for determining the news, opinion and feature content of school-sponsored media," subject only to the substantial-and-material disruption limitations articulated by the U.S. Supreme Court in *Tinker* (rather than to the *Hazelwood* standard) and general rules of libel and privacy laws.[57]

California's anti-*Hazelwood* statute was used in late 2008. That's when a lawsuit was filed against Fallbrook Union High School District and Principal Rod King contending, in part, that the censorship and removal from the student newspaper, the Tomahawk, of both an article regarding the contract buy-out of a former superintendent and an editorial critiquing the Bush Administration's abstinence-only policy for sex education violated the statute.[58] California's anti-*Hazelwood* statute bans the prior restraint of articles in public school papers unless the content is "obscene, libelous or slanderous" or would cause "substantial disruption of the orderly operation of the school."[59] The incident at Fallbrook also was troubling because the principal canceled the journalism class, thus terminating publication of the Tomahawk as a curricular activity, and removed the newspaper's faculty adviser. Importantly, California in late 2008 amended its anti-*Hazelwood* statute to prohibit retaliation, such as dismissal or reassignment, against high school newspaper advisers for protecting the statutory and First Amendment rights of student-journalists and editors.

---

57. Oregon Revised Statutes § 336.477 (2009).

58. Complaint, *Ariosta* v. *Fallbrook Union High School District*, Case No. 3:2008CV02421 (Superior Ct., San Diego County, Cal. 2008).

59. California Education Code § 48907 (2009).

The question, In what ways can a high school newspaper be censored? cannot be answered until two other questions are. First, is the newspaper published at a public or private high school? Constitutional protections have substantially less meaning at private schools. The First Amendment is not considered an impediment at private high schools or private colleges and universities. A newspaper at a private school can be censored in just about any way imaginable. There is, however, one minor exception to this general rule. In particular, California has a statute known as the "Leonard Law" that applies First Amendment standards to private, secular high schools and to secondary schools; these private schools, in other words, are forbidden from violating students' First Amendment rights.[60] Although California is the only state to have such a law extending First Amendment rights to private school students, there is nothing to prevent legislative bodies in other states from drafting and approving similar legislation in the future.

The next question to ask when focusing on public schools is, What kind of newspaper is it? Three kinds of publications are possible:

- A school-sponsored newspaper, generally defined as a paper that uses the school's name and resources, has a faculty adviser and serves as a tool to teach knowledge or skills. Typically this kind of newspaper is produced as part of a journalism class.
- An unsupervised or student-controlled newspaper produced on the school's campus as an extracurricular activity.
- A student newspaper produced and distributed off campus.

The *Hazelwood* ruling spoke only to the first kind of newspaper. This type of paper can be most heavily censored. Most authorities agree that school officials have less power to censor the second kind of publication, and no power to censor the third kind of newspaper, unless students attempt to distribute it on campus. School administrators can ban the on-campus distribution of material produced elsewhere, and this authority provides them with a kind of informal censorship power if students seek to circulate the material on school property.

STUDENT SPEECH RIGHTS ON THE WEB: THE ISSUE THE SUPREME COURT MUST ADDRESS

When students use their home computers, outside school and on their own time, to post Internet content that ridicules their teachers, administrators or classmates, can schools punish them without violating the First Amendment right of free speech? As of early 2010, the U.S. Supreme Court had not ruled on this issue, and lower courts were split on whether schools should have jurisdiction over such off-campus-created student expression. Only one thing appears fairly clear today: If a student who creates the off-campus, Internet-posted speech later downloads it at school and shows it to other

---

60. California Education Code § 48950 (providing in relevant part that "school districts operating one or more high schools and private secondary schools shall not make or enforce any rule subjecting any high school pupil to disciplinary sanctions solely on the basis of conduct that is speech or other communication that, when engaged in outside of the campus, is protected from governmental restriction by the First Amendment to the United States Constitution").

students while on campus, then the school has jurisdiction and the *Tinker* standard typically applies. But some courts have held that schools can punish student-authors even if they never download the speech in school.

In 2008, the 2nd U.S. Circuit Court of Appeals held in *Doninger* v. *Niehoff*, 527 F. 3d 41 (2d Cir. 2008), that if it is "reasonably foreseeable" that off-campus speech posted on the Internet will come to the attention of school authorities and that its posting creates "a foreseeable risk of substantial disruption to the work and discipline of the school," then the student-author can be punished under the *Tinker* standard. The appellate court in *Doninger* used this rationale to punish a student for posting, while off campus, a blog entry on livejournal.com that called school administrators "douchebags" and urged fellow students to write administrators to complain about a scheduling controversy over a battle-of-the-bands "Jamfest" concert.

A federal court in Pennsylvania in 2008 upheld the suspension of a girl who created, while off campus, a fake MySpace profile of her principal that suggested, in crude and crass terms, he was a pedophile and sex addict. *J.S.* v. *Blue Mountain School District*, 2008 U.S. Dist. LEXIS 72685 [M.D. Pa. Sept. 11, 2008]. Despite finding that "a substantial disruption so as to fall under *Tinker* did not occur," U.S. District Judge James M. Munley held that the school was justified in punishing the girl "because the lewd and vulgar off-campus speech had an effect on-campus." The only effect of the Web site, however, "was a general 'buzz' in the school with quite a few people knowing about it." The bottom line is that more and more school-speech cases today center on Internet-posted content that was created off campus, and the Supreme Court must hear a case in this area very shortly.

The Bethel *Case*

In addition to the tests created in the *Tinker* and *Hazelwood* rulings, the U.S. Supreme Court prior to 2007 had considered the speech rights of public high school students in one other case. In particular, the court held in 1986 in *Bethel School District* v. *Fraser*[61] that officials at Bethel High School in Pierce County, Wash., did not violate the free speech rights of student Matthew Fraser when they suspended him for making a sexually suggestive speech nominating a classmate for student government at an assembly packed with 600 students. Although he did not use profanity, the sexual innuendos were clear to some students in the audience who "hooted and yelled" (other students, conversely, were "bewildered and embarrassed") when Fraser said:

> Jeff Kuhlman is a man who takes his point and pounds it in. If necessary, he'll take an issue and nail it to the wall. He doesn't attack things in spurts—he drives hard, pushing and pushing until finally—he succeeds. Jeff is a man who will go to the very end—even the climax, for each and every one of you.

61. 478 U.S. 675 (1986).

In rejecting Fraser's First Amendment argument, the majority of the Supreme Court refused to apply the *Tinker* substantial-and-material-disruption standard, noting what it called a "marked distinction between the political 'message' of the armbands in *Tinker* and the sexual content" of Fraser's talk, as well as the fact that the speech in *Tinker* was "passive expression" (it was an armband) while Fraser's speech was actively spoken to a captive audience of students gathered for the assembly. Having thus distinguished *Tinker*, the court in *Fraser* held that schools can punish students who use "offensively lewd and indecent speech" that is "unrelated to any political viewpoint" because

- such expression "would undermine the school's basic educational mission";
- "it is a highly appropriate function of public school education to prohibit the use of vulgar and offensive terms in public discourse"; and
- society has an interest "in teaching students the boundaries of socially appropriate behavior."

In addition to these rationales for allowing the school's punishment of Matthew Fraser, the majority reasoned that "by glorifying male sexuality, and in its verbal content, the speech was acutely insulting to teenage girl students."

The bottom line is that, prior to 2007, there was a trilogy of Supreme Court cases (*Tinker*, *Hazelwood* and *Bethel*), each with its own rules and guidelines, that public schools may use to squelch the speech rights of students. They are summarized in the following box.

THREE KEY SCHOOL-SPEECH CASES PRIOR TO 2007

1. ***Tinker:*** School officials may regulate speech that they reasonably believe will materially and substantially disrupt or interfere with classwork, educational activities and/or discipline.

2. ***Hazelwood:*** Schools may regulate speech that is school sponsored and/or that is part of the school curriculum, so long as the censorship is reasonably related to legitimate pedagogical (i.e., teaching and learning) concerns.

3. ***Bethel:*** Schools may regulate sexually offensive speech that is lewd, vulgar or indecent (they also can regulate obscene speech since it is without any First Amendment [see Chapter 13]; *Fraser*'s language about speech that "would undermine the school's basic educational mission" also is used successfully by some schools to ban images and ads for drugs, tobacco and alcohol).

In reality, many student-speech cases do not fit squarely into any of the three Supreme Court precedents described in the box. For instance, a case may be a hybrid of political content and drug-related imagery (a T-shirt showing a pot leaf and the accompanying message, "Vote Yes on Proposition 42: Legalize Marijuana"). Lower courts in these situations are forced to try to find the precedent that comes the closest, factually speaking, to the issue at hand.

The Morse *Case*

In 2007, the U.S. Supreme Court heard a student-speech case called *Morse* v. *Frederick*. In this dispute, known as the "Bong Hits 4 Jesus" case, the 9th U.S. Circuit Court of Appeals ruled in 2006 that the First Amendment protected a student's right to unfurl, while standing on a sidewalk across the street from his high school as an Olympic torch relay passed by, a banner emblazoned with that drug-related catchphrase.[62] The students at Juneau-Douglas High School in Alaska had school permission to be on the sidewalk during the relay and were under teacher supervision at the time. While student Joseph Frederick claimed the "Bong Hits 4 Jesus" language was meaningless, funny and done in order to get on television, Principal Deborah Morse did not find it amusing and considered it a pro-drug message in conflict with the school's "basic educational mission to promote a healthy, drug-free life style." Frederick's banner was taken down and he was suspended for 10 days.

In ruling for Frederick, the 9th Circuit applied the *Tinker* standard. Noting there was no substantial and material disruption of educational activities caused by Frederick's banner, the 9th Circuit focused on the fact that the school conceded the banner "was censored only because it conflicted with the school's 'mission' of discouraging drug use." This justification was not sufficient under *Tinker* to stop its display, the 9th Circuit ruled. Importantly, the appellate court rejected the school's argument that the *Bethel* precedent should control the case since the message was "offensive" to the school's educational mission. The 9th Circuit interpreted *Bethel* far more narrowly, holding *Bethel* was not "an invitation to censor and punish any speech that offends school authorities," but instead only allows schools to stop "vulgar, obscene, lewd or sexual speech that, especially with adolescents, readily promotes disruption and diversion from the educational curriculum."

The school petitioned the U.S. Supreme Court to hear the case and to reverse the 9th Circuit's opinion, and the high court granted the petition. The school was represented by Ken Starr, the former independent counsel who investigated Bill Clinton's affair with Monica Lewinsky. Starr asked the nation's high court to consider the following question:

> *Whether the First Amendment allows public schools to prohibit students from displaying messages promoting the use of illegal substances at school-sponsored, faculty-supervised events.*

The Supreme Court ruled in June 2007, holding that the First Amendment rights of Joseph Frederick were not violated. Writing for a five-member majority of the court, Chief Justice John Roberts explained that "schools may take steps to safeguard those entrusted to their care from speech that can reasonably be regarded as encouraging illegal drug use. We conclude that the school officials in this case did not violate the First Amendment by confiscating the pro-drug banner and suspending the student responsible for it." Roberts rejected the idea that the banner constituted political speech, writing that "this is plainly not a case about political debate over the criminalization of drug use or possession."[63] The long-term impact of this decision in *Morse* remains to be seen, but the ruling itself was very narrow and limited. It is important to note that the court in *Morse* did not overrule *Tinker*, *Hazelwood* or *Bethel*; those decisions remain intact. The *Morse* opinion is limited in scope to nonpolitical speech that advocates or celebrates the use of illegal drugs.

62. *Frederick* v. *Morse*, 439 F. 3d 1114 (9th Cir. 2006).
63. *Morse* v. *Frederick*, 127 S. Ct. 2618 (2007).

Unfortunately for advocates of student-speech rights, some courts are stretching the Supreme Court's ruling in *Morse* far beyond its narrow facts about nonpolitical speech advocating illegal drug use. Just six months after the *Morse* decision, the 5th U.S. Circuit Court of Appeals interpreted *Morse* to stand for a broad, pro-censorship principle—that "speech advocating a harm that is demonstrably grave and that derives that gravity from the 'special danger' to the physical safety of students arising from the school environment is unprotected."[64] The 5th Circuit held in *Ponce* v. *Socorro Independent School District* that a "*Morse* analysis is appropriate"—rather than the traditional and more rigorous substantial-and-material disruption standard from the high court's ruling in *Tinker*—when the student speech at issue "threatens a Columbine-style attack on a school." As the 5th Circuit wrote in holding that *Morse* can be used to squelch and punish not just speech that advocates illegal drug use, but also student speech that threatens mass violence:

> If school administrators are permitted to prohibit student speech that advocates illegal drug use because "illegal drug use presents a grave and in many ways unique threat to the physical safety of students" . . . then it defies logical extrapolation to hold school administrators to a stricter standard with respect to speech that gravely and uniquely threatens violence, including massive deaths, to the school population as a whole.

The 5th Circuit is not alone in holding that *Morse* supports suppression of student speech threatening violence. The 11th U.S. Circuit Court of Appeals held in *Boim* v. *Fulton County School District*, a case centering on a notebook entry in which the student-author described killing her math teacher, that the *Morse* rationale for stopping speech advocating illegal drug use "applies equally, if not more strongly, to speech reasonably construed as a threat of school violence."[65] Why is this important? It means that courts like those in *Ponce* and *Boim* can sidestep a *Tinker* analysis when trying to justify censorship and punishment of student speech that references violent conduct and, instead, simply say that *Morse* justifies its censorship outright because violent-themed speech might lead to actual violence against students, just like the illegal drug use allegedly advocated by Joseph Frederick's banner in *Morse* could lead to physical harm. Whether other courts similarly stretch *Morse* beyond its rather unique facts about drug use remains to be seen.

CENSORSHIP OF COLLEGE NEWSPAPERS

The Supreme Court in *Hazelwood* did not decide whether its "reasonably related to legitimate pedagogical concerns" test applied to college newspapers. In fact, it wrote, "We need not now decide whether the same degree of deference is appropriate with respect to school-sponsored expressive activities at the college and university level." Since then, two federal appellate court decisions have addressed censorship by university officials of student-run publications:

- *Kincaid* v. *Gibson*[66]
- *Hosty* v. *Carter*[67]

64. *Ponce* v. *Socorro Independent School District*, 508 F. 3d 765, 770 (5th Cir. 2007).
65. 494 F. 3d 978, 984 (11th Cir. 2007).
66. 236 F. 3d 342 (6th Cir. 2001).
67. 412 F. 3d 731 (7th Cir. 2005), cert. den., 126 S. Ct. 1330 (2006).

The first case suggests that the federal courts are reluctant to expand the censorial powers of college administrators via *Hazelwood*. In 2001 the 6th U.S. Court of Appeals ruled that when administrators at Kentucky State University refused to permit the distribution of the school's yearbook because they didn't approve of its content and the color of its cover, they violated the First Amendment rights of the students at the school. But the 10-3 ruling was based largely on the fact that the creation of the yearbook was not a classroom activity in which students are assigned a grade. The yearbook was a designated public forum (see pages 114–117) created by the university to exist in an atmosphere of free and responsible discussion and intellectual exploration, the court said. What the school officials did was clearly censorship. "There is little if any difference between hiding from public view the words and pictures students use to portray their college experience, and forcing students to publish a state-sponsored script. In either case, the government alters student expression by obliterating it," Judge R. Guy Cole wrote. But in reality, the court had merely distinguished the production of the yearbook from the classroom-generated newspaper in *Hazelwood*.

A more disturbing, disappointing and important federal appellate court decision affecting the college press was handed down in 2005 in *Hosty* v. *Carter*. The *Hosty* case centered on demands by university administrators in 2000 for prior review and approval—a classic prior restraint on speech, in other words—of the Innovator, the student-run newspaper at Governors State University, located south of Chicago, Ill. The Innovator had previously published articles under the byline of student Margaret Hosty that were critical of a school official, sparking the confrontation.

A major issue in the resulting lawsuit was whether the legitimate-pedagogical-concerns standard articulated by the U.S. Supreme Court in the *Hazelwood* case for controlling the censorship of school-sponsored, high school newspapers that are part of the curriculum is also applicable to college newspapers.

In *Hosty,* the student-journalist plaintiffs argued that *Hazelwood*'s legitimate-pedagogical-concerns standard was never made applicable to the college press, and they contended that university administrators cannot ever insist that student newspapers be submitted for review and approval. But by a 7-4 vote, the U.S. 7th Circuit Court of Appeals rejected these contentions and rebuffed the idea that there is a bright-line difference between high school and college newspapers. The 7th Circuit wrote that the Supreme Court's footnote in *Hazelwood* "does not even hint at the possibility of an on/off switch: high school papers reviewable, college papers not reviewable." It added that "whether *some* review is possible depends on the answer to the public-forum question, which does not (automatically) vary with the speakers' age." The key in *Hosty,* then, was whether the student newspaper constituted a public forum. Whether a particular physical venue or location constitutes a public forum for purposes of First Amendment speech protection is discussed later in this chapter (see pages 114–117). Writing for the seven-judge majority in *Hosty,* Judge Frank Easterbrook articulated a rule that "speech at a non-public forum, and underwritten at public expense, may be open to reasonable regulation even at the college level."

Thus, for the majority of the 7th Circuit, "*Hazelwood*'s first question therefore remains our principal question as well: was the reporter a speaker in a public forum (no censorship allowed?) or did the University either create a non-public forum or publish the paper itself (a closed forum where content may be supervised)?" This meant that the appellate court had to examine the status of the particular student newspaper at issue in *Hosty,* namely the Innovator, to determine whether or not it was a public forum. The court noted that if the Innovator "operated in a public forum, the University could not vet its contents." The appellate court, unfortunately, held that it was not possible on the record in front of it to determine what kind of forum Governors State University had established with the Innovator. The court did, however, provide some guidance on this for the future, noting among other things that

- while "being part of the curriculum may be a *sufficient* condition of a non-public forum, it is not a *necessary* condition. Extracurricular activities may be outside any public forum . . . without also falling outside all university governance [emphasis added]." In other words, just because a college newspaper is an extracurricular activity and not part of the curriculum does not mean that it necessarily escapes all university control or regulation; and

- "a school may declare the pages of the student newspaper open for expression and thus disable itself from engaging in viewpoint or content discrimination while the terms on which the forum operates remain unaltered."

Another important factor in the public forum determination of a university newspaper is whether the university underwrote and subsidized the newspaper without any strings attached or, conversely, whether it "hedge[d] the funding with controls that left the University itself as the newspaper's publisher."

What does all of this mean for college newspapers? First, it's important to remember that the decision is binding in only the three states that comprise the 7th Circuit Court of Appeals—Illinois, Indiana and Wisconsin (see page 23 for a map of the federal appellate court circuits). Second, many college newspapers, such as the Alligator at the University of Florida, are independent of the universities that their student-journalists attend and are not directly funded by the university. In an official press release on the *Hosty* decision, Mark Goodman, former executive director of the Student Press Law Center that had filed a friend-of-the-court brief in the case, stated:

> As a practical matter, most college student newspapers are going to be considered designated public forums and entitled to the strongest First Amendment protection because that's the way they've been operating for decades. But this decision gives college administrators ammunition to argue that many traditionally independent student activities are subject to school censorship.

In 2006, California became the first state to pass so-called anti-*Hosty* legislation after the U.S. Supreme Court refused earlier that year to hear the *Hosty* case. California's new law prohibits state public university officials from making and enforcing rules "subjecting any student to disciplinary sanction solely on the basis of conduct that is speech or other communication that, when engaged in outside a campus of those institutions, is protected from governmental restriction by the First Amendment."[68] In brief, the law prohibits prior restraints and censorship by university administrators (officials, for instance, in the University of California and California State University systems) of public college and university newspapers. This, in turn, means that the *Hazelwood* rule cannot apply to the public collegiate press in California;

---

68. California Education Code § 66301. Illinois adopted similar law in 2007.

instead, college newspapers in the Golden State must be treated like real-world professional newspapers such as the Los Angeles Times and San Francisco Chronicle.

In 2007, Illinois followed California's lead and adopted the College Campus Press Act, which provides that student newspapers and other student media outlets at state-sponsored institutions of higher learning (including, importantly, Governors State University where *Hosty* arose) are public forums for expression by student-journalists and, in turn, are immune from prior review by university officials. By transforming all student media outlets at public colleges and universities in Illinois into public forums exempt from prior restraints by administrators, the College Campus Press Act renders the *Hosty* opinion nugatory (inconsequential) in Illinois and leaves it relevant now only in the other 7th Circuit states of Indiana and Wisconsin.

Problems for College Journalists

What kinds of censorship problems affect the college press? Getting access to information is one problem. Student-journalists often have difficulty gaining access to reports on faculty performance, student government meetings and school disciplinary hearings. It is not uncommon for a college to reject the criminal prosecution of a student apprehended for a minor crime, and instead punish the student through a disciplinary proceeding. The criminal trial would be open to the public and the press; disciplinary hearings are routinely closed. Hence, no bad publicity for the school. Campus administrators have even attempted to bar all reporters from access to university police reports, citing the Family Educational Rights and Privacy Act (FERPA; see pages 355–356), which limits the public access to most student records. School officials have argued—unsuccessfully—that crime reports that name students as victims, perpetrators or even witnesses are educational records and hence inaccessible under this law. If the press can't see the official police reports, stories about the incident generally won't be written. The courts have rejected this interpretation of the law.[69]

For instance, in 2008 the attorney general of North Dakota issued an opinion rebuking the University of North Dakota for failing to provide a newspaper with student disciplinary records related to alleged incidents of anti-Semitic behavior on campus.[70] The opinion made it clear that FERPA does not prohibit the release of student disciplinary records that redact (black out) the names of the students involved and other personally identifiable information about them. In this case, the university failed to consider whether personal identifiable information could be removed and redacted from the requested records; instead, it simply refused to turn over the documents. The attorney general concluded that

> FERPA does not prohibit the release of disciplinary proceeding records if an educational institution can adequately remove all personally identifiable information from those records. The University of North Dakota violated the [North Dakota] open records law when it incorrectly responded that FERPA prevented the release of all disciplinary proceeding records and because it failed to consider whether the requested records could be released after removing all personally identifiable information.

69. See *Student Press Law Center* v. *Alexander,* 778 F. Supp. 1227 (1991); and *Ohio ex rel The Miami Student* v. *Miami University,* 79 Ohio St. 3d 168 (1997).
70. Open Records And Meetings Opinion, No. 2008-O-27 (N.D. Attorney General Dec. 1, 2008), available online at http://www.ag.nd.gov/documents/2008-O-27.pdf.

In 2008, staff members of the Progress, the student newspaper at Eastern Kentucky University, obtained a letter from the Kentucky attorney general's office agreeing with the newspaper that the university's police department was unnecessarily and excessively redacting some information from police incident reports. The university's police department had justified its redacting under the guise of protecting privacy. The state attorney's general office, however, found the police were misusing a privacy exemption under the Kentucky Open Records Act.

Under a federal law called the Clery Act (named for a Lehigh University student raped and killed in her dorm in 1986), all colleges and universities that participate in federal student-aid programs are required to give timely warnings of campus crimes that represent a threat to the safety of students and/or employees and to make public their campus security policies. The law also mandates that colleges and universities collect data and statistics on a number of specific crimes and then report that information to the campus community on an annual basis. These data obviously can help student-journalists in reporting on problems on their campuses. One major problem with the law is that it does not define what constitutes a timely warning. In light of shooting tragedies in recent years at Virginia Tech and Northern Illinois University, such warnings are of obvious importance. Due in part to these terrible events, the Clery Act was amended in August 2008 to require campus authorities "to immediately notify the campus community upon the confirmation of a significant emergency or dangerous situation involving an immediate threat to the health or safety of students or staff occurring on the campus." Violating the Clery Act, which is enforced by the Department of Education, can prove expensive. In 2008, Eastern Michigan University agreed to pay a record-setting $350,000 fine for multiple violations of the Clery Act that were exposed after the murder of a student in a campus residence hall in December 2006.

Some newspapers that have published advertising for alcohol, tobacco or other products regarded as harmful by some members of society, or that have published ads supporting controversial ideas or promoting certain speakers or books, have been the focus of censorship attempts. News stories, editorials, letters to the editor and columns that focus on racial, ethnic, gender and even political issues are often the target of protests and sometimes attempts at censorship. These matters especially provoke campus actions, not only by administrators but by students as well. The theft of all the issues of a single edition of a newspaper by those who disagree with the material published in the paper is a problem on some campuses.* About 30 to 40 such thefts occur each year, according to Mark Goodman, former executive director of the Student Press Law Center (SPLC). Campus police usually claim they are powerless to pursue the thieves, since, because the student newspapers are free, no law has been broken.

And therein lies the problem of quite literally stealing "free" speech: How can one steal something if it is free? In fact, only three states—California, Colorado and Maryland—have statutes specifically aimed to penalize the theft of free newspapers. California's law, which took effect in 2007, provides that a person can be fined $250 on a first offense for taking more

---

*Such problems are not confined to college campuses. In the midst of a heated election in a community in southern Maryland, several sheriff's deputies bought out, with the encouragement and support of the sheriff, all the copies of a weekly newspaper that published material critical of the sheriff, who was a candidate for re-election. The deputies paid for the papers, and conducted the buyout off duty. But the 4th U.S. Court of Appeals nevertheless ruled the action was a civil rights violation, calling the activity a classic example of the kind of suppression of political criticism that the First Amendment was intended to prohibit. *Rossignol* v. *Voorhaar,* 315 F. 3d 516 (2003).

than 25 copies of a free or complimentary newspaper if done so with the intent to "deprive others of the opportunity to read or enjoy the newspaper."[71]

Because only three states have statutes targeting the theft of free newspapers, incidents of newspaper theft on college campuses are rampant today. The SPLC tracks and describes the incidents from a link on its Web site at http://www.splc.org/newspapertheft.asp and provides a helpful "Newspaper Theft Checklist" of strategies and advice for college newspaper journalists at http://www.splc.org/theftchecklist.asp. The SPLC reported more than 20 incidents in 2008 of apparent thefts of college newspapers, including the removal and disappearance of

- more than half of the 9,000 copies of an issue of the Oregon State University student paper, the Daily Barometer, that identified in a front-page article six students arrested in connection with an alleged drug-trafficking ring.
- more than 8,000 copies of an issue of the Daily News at Ball State University in Indiana that included an article regarding the arrest of a player on the women's soccer team. It was third theft of the Daily News in 18 months.
- about 900 copies of an issue of the Campus Carrier, the student paper at Berry College in Georgia, that included a column castigating the college's cheerleaders for an alleged lack of enthusiasm during basketball games. The SPLC reported that copies were taken by some members of the cheerleading squad.

In 2009, the SPLC reported that 300 copies of the student newspaper at the Massachusetts Institute of Technology were trashed by, ironically, two campus police officers who apparently were upset over a story about an MIT police officer who had been arrested on drug-related charges. About 4,000 copies of the student paper at Middle Tennessee State University were stolen in 2009. The stolen issue featured a story about police halting a boxing match and underage drinking at a specific fraternity.

Sometimes university administrators harass student media organizations by refusing to return calls or give interviews. That happened in 2008 when officials at Quinnipiac University, a private institution in Connecticut, issued a gag order preventing administrators, staff, coaches and athletes from talking with reporters from the Quad News, a new and independent online student newspaper.[72] What's more, Quinnipiac President John L. Lahey threatened to ban the Quinnipiac student chapter of the Society of Professional Journalists (SPJ) if the chapter supported the Quad News. Although the First Amendment does not apply at Quinnipiac because it is a private university, the incidents and actions of university administrators were so troubling that The New York Times inveighed against them in an editorial.[73] Due in part to that editorial, Quinnipiac officials in November 2008 withdrew the threat to ban the SPJ chapter.

Finally, attempts to censor college newspapers indirectly, by reducing or even ending their funding, have generally failed. In 1983 the 8th U.S. Court of Appeals handed down an important ruling that still represents the state of the law,[74] 25 years later. The case began in the late 1970s when the University of Minnesota Daily published a year-end edition containing content that, according to one university faculty member, offended Third World students,

---

71. California Penal Code § 490.7 (2009).

72. The Quad News can be found online at http://www.quadnews.net.

73. Editorial, "Curbing Speech at Quinnipiac."

74. *Stanley* v. *McGrath,* 719 F. 2d 279 (1983).

blacks, Jews, feminists, gays, lesbians and Christians.[75] In the wake of complaints from students and off-campus readers, the university regents embarked on a plan to cut the funding for the newspaper. The plan was to allow students to decide whether or not to contribute $2 each semester to fund the newspaper. The $2 fee had automatically gone to the newspaper in the past. Two university review committees advised the regents the plan was a bad idea, but it was adopted nevertheless. Before the vote many of the regents publicly stated they favored the plan because students should not be forced to support a newspaper that was "sacrilegious and vulgar."

A lawsuit followed the decision, and the appellate court ruled the move by the regents violated the First Amendment. A reduction in or even the elimination of fees is certainly permissible, the court said, so long as it is not done for the wrong reasons. But there was ample evidence in this case, the court said, that the reduction was enacted to punish the newspaper. As such it was an attempt at censorship. The court cited the negative comments about the newspaper by the regents during consideration of the plan, as well as the fact that the change was not made at other University of Minnesota campuses (which are governed by the same board of regents), only the Twin Cities campus, home of the offending newspaper, as evidence of the punitive nature of the new policy. "Reducing the revenues available to the newspaper is therefore forbidden by the First Amendment," the court concluded.[76]

Such funding-cutback controversies, however, continue today for college newspapers. For instance, a 2008 federal lawsuit filed by editors of The Inkwell, the student paper at Armstrong Atlantic State University (AASU) in Savannah, Ga:, contended that the Student Government Association (SGA) at this public university cut the paper's 2008–09 budget by nearly $15,000 in retaliation for reporting and editorializing critical of the administration. The complaint in *Mensing* v. *Armstrong Atlantic State University* asserted that the actions were "motivated wholly or in substantial part by the disagreement of AASU officials with the content and viewpoint of the Inkwell newspaper" and "were taken for the express purpose of infringing, interfering with, punishing and retaliating against plaintiffs for their exercise of First Amendment rights." Ultimately, the parties settled when the SGA agreed to restore the budget and to pay $7,500 in legal fees. In a separate incident, the SGA at the University of West Georgia in Carrollton passed a bill in 2009 designed to cut funding to the student newspaper, The West Georgian, after it ran a satirical column making fun of fraternities and titled "Join a Frat with Buck Futter, Jr."

Alcohol Advertisements and the College Press

In 1996, Pennsylvania adopted a law known as Act 199. The law prohibited the paid dissemination of alcoholic beverage advertising in college newspapers.[77] After Act 199 became law, the Pennsylvania Liquor Control Board issued an advisory notice clarifying how the law applied to universities and the collegiate press. The notice stated:

> Advertisements which indicate the availability and/or price of alcoholic beverages may not be contained in publications published by, for and in behalf of any educational institutions. Universities are considered educational institutions under this section. Thus, an advertisement in a college newspaper or a college football program announcing beverages would not be permissible.

75. Gillmor, "The Fragile First."
76. *Stanley* v. *McGrath,* 719 F. 2d 279 (1983).
77. 47 Pennsylvania Statutes Annotated § 4-498 (2004).

What does this statement mean? Under this law, an advertisement paid for by a local bar in State College, Pa., and placed in the student newspaper at the Pennsylvania State University, the Daily Collegian, that described the availability and/or price of beer at the bar during happy hours would not be permissible. The student newspaper at the University of Pittsburgh, the Pitt News, decided to challenge the law on First Amendment grounds because the Pitt News, like the Daily Collegian, had received a substantial portion of its advertising revenue from alcoholic beverage ads prior to the enactment of Act 199. But in 1998 alone, the Pitt News lost $17,000 in advertising revenue because of the law.

Pennsylvania, in contrast, argued that the law was necessary to curb both underage drinking (although many college students and all faculty are of at least the legal drinking age of 21) and binge drinking/alcohol abuse. The theory on the latter interest apparently was that if students didn't know where the cheap beer was being served because they couldn't find advertisements for it in college newspapers, then they wouldn't drink as much.

In July 2004, however, the U.S. Court of Appeals for the 3rd Circuit held in a case called *Pitt News* v. *Pappert* that Act 199 violated the First Amendment rights of the Pitt News and, by implication, other college newspapers in Pennsylvania.[78] The appellate court ruled that the law was "an impermissible restriction on commercial speech" (see Chapter 15) and that it was presumptively unconstitutional because it targeted a too narrow segment of the media—newspapers affiliated with colleges and universities—and thus conflicted with U.S. Supreme Court precedent on taxation of the press (see pages 64–65). The appellate court observed that Pennsylvania "has not pointed to any evidence that eliminating ads in this narrow sector [of the media] will do any good. Even if Pitt students do not see alcoholic beverage ads in the Pitt News, they will still be exposed to a torrent of beer ads on television and the radio, and they will still see alcoholic beverage ads in other publications, including the other free weekly Pittsburgh papers that are displayed on campus together with the Pitt News." The appellate court added that "in contending that underage and abusive drinking will fall if alcoholic beverage ads are eliminated from just those media affiliated with educational institutions, the Commonwealth relies on nothing more than 'speculation' and 'conjecture.'" The court suggested that rather than restricting the First Amendment speech and press rights of college newspapers, the "most direct way to combat underage and abusive drinking by college students is the enforcement of the alcoholic beverage control laws on college campuses."

The same issue later arose when the ACLU sued in federal court in Richmond, Va., on behalf of Collegiate Times and the Cavalier Daily, the student-run papers at Virginia Tech and the University of Virginia, respectively, challenging Virginia Alcohol Beverage Control regulations prohibiting all advertisements for beer, wine and mixed beverages in "college student publications" unless made in reference to a dining establishment.[79] The Virginia statute, like the Pennsylvania one at issue in *Pitt News* v. *Pappert*, was declared unconstitutional on First Amendment grounds. In June 2008, a federal district court issued a permanent injunction prohibiting Virginia from enforcing it.[80] Although the court agreed with Virginia that there was a

78. *Pitt News* v. *Pappert*, 379 F. 3d 96 (2004).

79. Complaint, *Educational Media Co. at Va. Tech* v. *Swecker* (E.D. Va. filed June 8, 2006).

80. Order, *Educational Media Co.* v. *Swecker*, Case No. 3:06CV396 (E.D. Va. June 19, 2008). The same judge earlier in 2008 had granted summary judgment in favor of the student newspapers. *Educational Media Co.* v. *Swecker*, 2008 U.S. Dist. LEXIS 45590 (E.D. Va. Mar. 31, 2008).

substantial interest in reducing underage and excessive drinking in college, it found, as did the appellate court in *Pitt News*, "that any suggestion that the regulation materially advanced the governmental interest was speculative."

BOOK BANNING

Jon Stewart, the quick-witted and acerbic host of Comedy Central's popular fake-news program, "The Daily Show," earned a dubious accolade in 2005 when his best-selling book "America (The Book): A Citizen's Guide to Democracy Inaction" was briefly banned from the Jackson-George Regional Library System in Mississippi. What provoked the ban? A digitally altered image of Supreme Court justices' faces superimposed on naked bodies. The director of the library system told a reporter for the Associated Press, "I've been a librarian for 40 years and this is the only book I've objected to so strongly that I wouldn't allow it to circulate. We're not an adult bookstore." The library board eventually rescinded its ban and put the book, which Wal-Mart stores refused to stock because of the satirical image, back on the shelves of its eight libraries. While the brief-lived ban suggests a humor-challenged library system in southern Mississippi that couldn't handle the naked truth, book banning is no laughing matter. In fact, it is all too common.

The American Library Association, which in 2008 received more than 500 reports of efforts to abolish materials from school curricula and library bookshelves, reported that the most challenged book that year was "And Tango Makes Three." The children's book, which also was the most frequently challenged book in 2007, is based on a true story about two male penguins that together care for and hatch an orphaned egg. Trouble for "And Tango Makes Three" continued in 2008, when it was removed from elementary school libraries in Loudoun County, Va., for allegedly promoting what an upset parent complained was a homosexual agenda. Other 2008 controversies in the United States involving books and school libraries and/or curricula centered on tomes including, among others, "One Flew Over the Cuckoo's Nest" (a dispute in the town of Mexico, Mo., over its inclusion in advanced-level high school English classes) and "The Kite Runner" (a dispute over whether to prohibit its inclusion as reading for a high school English honors class in Morganton, N.C). In October 2008, Mark Bowden's book "Black Hawk Down," which describes the 1993 U.S. military operation in Mogadishu, Somalia, that left more than a dozen American soldiers dead, was banned by a high school in Raceland, La., due to complaints about profanity. Sometimes, however, there is good news, as in December 2008 when the school board in Coeur dAlene, Idaho, voted to restore 26 books to an approved list from which teachers could assign novels for students in grades six through 12. The restored books, about which some parents had complained due to profanity and the topics addressed, include American classics such as "Death of a Salesman," "The Grapes of Wrath" and "The Great Gatsby."

Public libraries also continue to engage in censorship; for instance, the library board in Nampa, Idaho, voted in June 2008 to remove the sex-education books "The New Joy of Sex" and "The Joy of Gay Sex" from open shelves and to make them available only upon request. Nampa library officials later reversed their decision after receiving a letter from the ACLU threatening a lawsuit. More recently, these books were also the subject of censorship in February 2009. That's when minors' access to four sex-themed tomes—"The Joy of Sex," "The Joy of Gay Sex," "The Lesbian Kama Sutra" and "Sex for Busy People: The Art of the Quickie for Lovers on the Go"—was limited in the public libraries of Topeka, Kan., after a complaint was received from a group called Kansans for Common Sense Policy suggesting the books were harmful to minors. In a victory for free expression, however, the Topeka and Shawnee County Public Library board reversed itself in April 2009 and allowed those four books to remain available to anyone with a library card, including minors.

When it comes to removing books from public school libraries, the only U.S. Supreme Court opinion on point is an aging 1982 case called *Board of Education* v. *Pico*.[81] Unfortunately, there was no majority opinion in *Pico* (there were seven separate opinions) as the court addressed the issue of whether a school board could constitutionally remove from a public school library books by the likes of Kurt Vonnegut and Langston Hughes that it characterized as "Anti-American, Anti-Christian, Anti-Sem[i]tic, and just plain filthy." There was, however, a plurality opinion (see pages 20–21) holding that "local school boards may not remove books from school library shelves simply because they dislike the ideas contained in those books and seek by their removal to 'prescribe what shall be orthodox in politics, nationalism, religion, or other matters of opinion.'" The plurality opinion noted that school boards

> rightly possess significant discretion to determine the content of their school libraries. But that discretion may not be exercised in a narrowly partisan or political manner. If a Democratic school board, motivated by party affiliation, ordered the removal of all books written by or in favor of Republicans, few would doubt that the order violated the constitutional rights of the students denied access to those books. . . . Our Constitution does not permit the official suppression of ideas. Thus whether [the school board's] removal of books from their school libraries denied [students'] their First Amendment rights depends upon the motivation behind [the school board's] actions.

In contrast to unconstitutional justifications for removing books from school libraries based upon dislike of the ideas and political viewpoints in them, the plurality wrote that it would be okay to remove books if done so "based solely upon the 'educational suitability' of the books in question" or if the books were "pervasively vulgar." The court thus suggested that motivation of a school board in removing a book is key in determining whether its removal violates the First Amendment rights of minors to access the ideas in the book.

The guidelines from *Pico* were applied in 2006 by a federal court in Florida in *ACLU of Florida* v. *Miami-Dade County School Board*.[82] The dispute centered not on pervasive vulgarity, but on the removal from school libraries of particular books, targeting kids from 4 to 8 years old, about Cuba and life in that island nation. The school removed the books after a parent complained they were "untruthful" and portrayed "a life in Cuba that does not exist." As U.S. District Court Judge Alan S. Gold wrote, the "heart of the argument is that the Cuba books omit the harsh truth about totalitarian life in Communist Cuba."

81. 457 U.S. 853 (1982).
82. 439 F. Supp. 2d 1242 (S.D. Fla. 2006).

In ruling against the school board and in ordering it to immediately replace the Cuba books, the judge wrote that "[s]ignificant weight must be given to the board's failure to consider, much less adopt, the recommendations of the two previous committees, and that of the school superintendent, to leave the Cuba books on the library shelves because they were educationally suitable." Recall that in *Pico* the Supreme Court wrote that school boards could legitimately remove books from libraries if they did so based upon concerns about "educational suitability." This case, however, was different, as Judge Gold reasoned:

> The majority of the Miami-Dade County School Board members intended by their removal of the books to deny schoolchildren access to ideas or points-of-view with which the school officials disagreed, and that this intent was the decisive factor in their removal decision. In so acting, the School Board abused its discretion in a manner that violated the transcendent imperatives of the First Amendment.

In 2009, however, the 11th U.S. Circuit Court of Appeals reversed Judge Gold's opinion with a split 2-1 decision and, in so doing, it allowed the school board to remove the contested book, "Vamos a Cuba," from its libraries.[83] The two-judge majority initially noted there was no majority opinion in the Supreme Court's *Pico* ruling and thus it observed that "the question of what standard applies to school library book removal decisions is unresolved" and "we have no need to resolve it here." But in ruling in favor of the school board, the 11th Circuit majority adopted the school board's position that its motive for removing the book was not based on any improper political reasons or the book's political viewpoint, but rather was due to legitimate pedagogical concerns (akin to *Hazelwood*, page 90) about factual inaccuracies and critical omissions. The majority wrote that "whatever else it prohibits, the First Amendment does not forbid a school board from removing a book because it contains factual inaccuracies, whether they be of commission or omission. There is no constitutional right to have books containing misstatements of objective facts shelved in a school library." This was the situation with "Vamos a Cuba," the majority found:

> The book did not tell the truth. It made life in Cuba under Castro appear more favorable than every expert who testified for either side at the hearing knows it to be, more favorable than the State Department knows it to be, more favorable than the district court knows it to be, and more favorable than we know it to be. Once you find, as we have, that the book presents a false picture of life in Cuba, one that misleadingly fails to mention the deprivations and hardships the people there endure, the argument that the [school] board acted for ideological reasons collapses on itself.

There was a strenuous dissent by Judge Charles R. Wilson, who wrote that "the school board's claim that 'Vamos a Cuba' is grossly inaccurate is simply a pretense for viewpoint suppression, rather than the genuine reason for its removal. The record supports the district court's determination that the book was not removed for a legitimate pedagogical reason." The ACLU vowed to appeal the decision.

---

83. *ACLU of Florida* v. *Miami-Dade County School Board*, 2009 U.S. App. LEXIS 2253 (11th Cir. Feb. 5, 2009).

SUMMARY

Three Supreme Court decisions—*Tinker*, *Hazelwood* and *Bethel*—guide the free-expression rights of public high school students, each providing different justifications and standards for censorship in specific circumstances. School officials have abused *Hazelwood*'s "reasonably related to legitimate pedagogical concerns" standard when it comes to censoring student newspapers produced as part of the school curriculum. A new problem not addressed in these three cases is school censorship of speech created by students off campus, on their own computers and posted on the World Wide Web. The impact of the court's 2007 ruling in *Morse* remains to be seen, but the scope of the *Morse* ruling is very narrow.

Two federal appellate court cases—*Kincaid* and *Hosty*—address censorship of college newspapers. Another problem college papers face today is theft by disgruntled students. Alcohol ads pose an additional issue for some college newspapers, as some states have attempted to regulate them.

Book banning and removal from public school libraries is a problem today.

TIME, PLACE AND MANNER RESTRICTIONS

Most attempts by the government to use prior censorship are based on the content of the material it seeks to censor. National security interests may be at stake, or a school official might fear that a news story in a student newspaper deals with a subject too mature for high school students. But the government can also base its attempts at prior censorship on other factors—specifically, the time, the place or the manner of the communication. There would certainly be few content-based objections to an individual presenting a speech on how to grow mushrooms. But the government (as well as citizens) would surely object if the speaker wanted to give the speech while standing in the middle of Main Street, or on a sidewalk at 2 a.m. in a residential neighborhood. These are called **time, place and manner restrictions or rules.**

But the government can also base its attempts at prior censorship on other factors—specifically, the time, the place or the manner of the communication.

Such rules generate no serious First Amendment problems so long as they meet a set of criteria the courts have developed. This set of criteria is sometimes referred to as the **intermediate scrutiny** standard of judicial review.

1. **The rule must be neutral as to content, or what the courts call content neutral, both on its face and in the manner in which it is applied.** A rule that is content neutral is applied the same way to all communications, regardless of what is said or printed. In other words, a law cannot permit the distribution of flyers promoting the construction of a new stadium, but restrict persons from handing out material in favor of tearing down a viaduct. A viable time, place and manner rule must be content neutral. In 2000 the Supreme Court ruled that a Colorado law that made it unlawful for any person within 100 feet of the entrance to a health care facility to approach within 8 feet of another person to pass out a handbill or a leaflet, display a sign or engage in "oral protest, education or counseling" was content neutral. The statute prohibited unwanted approaches to all medical facilities in the state, *regardless* of the message the speaker was attempting to communicate, the court said.[84]

84. *Hill* v. *Colorado*, 530 U.S. 703 (2000).

A Gladstone, Mo., ordinance that prohibited property owners from placing political signs on their property more than 30 days before an election was ruled to be content based, not content neutral. The law singled out political speech for special regulation, but did not regulate for-sale signs or other such displays, the court said.[85] And the 9th U.S. Court of Appeals ruled that a Las Vegas ordinance that banned the distribution of commercial leaflets along Las Vegas Boulevard, commonly known as Las Vegas Strip, was not content neutral because it didn't apply to persons handing out other kinds of leaflets as well.[86] An ordinance like this that is not content neutral is considered a content-based law and is subject to the much more rigorous **strict scrutiny** standard of judicial review that requires the government to prove a compelling interest—not simply a substantial interest—and that the statute restricts no more speech than is absolutely necessary to serve the allegedly compelling interest (see page 60).

Sometimes a law will appear to be content neutral but is not because it gives far too much discretion to the officials who are assigned to administer it. For instance, in 2008 the 9th U.S. Circuit Court of Appeals held that a Seattle parade-permit law that allowed the police chief there to decide whether marchers had to use sidewalks instead of streets for their parades was unconstitutional.[87] In this case, a group of marchers (the plaintiff) wanted to use the streets, but were ordered by the police to use the sidewalks because there allegedly were too few marchers, even though Seattle did not include a minimum numbers requirement in all—or even most—parade permits as a condition of allowing marchers to utilize the streets. The appellate court reasoned that "the ordinance by its terms gives the chief of police unbridled discretion to force marchers off the streets and onto the sidewalks, unchecked by any requirement to explain the reasons for doing so or to provide some forum for appealing the chief's decision. We therefore hold that the parade ordinance is facially unconstitutional." It added that the "danger of abuse is acutely presented in this case, where the speech the [plaintiff] seeks to engage in—protesting police brutality—is directly critical of the governmental body that administers Seattle's permit scheme."

2. **The law must not constitute a complete ban on a kind of communication.** There must be ample alternative means of accomplishing this communication. In the 1980s several states sought to ban the polling of voters outside voting booths. The polling was conducted by the news media for several reasons, including an attempt to find out what kinds of people (age, political affiliation, occupation, etc.) voted for which candidates. Many of these statutes were struck down at least in part, the courts ruled, because the press could not ask these questions at any other place or in any other manner and expect to get the same data. There is no assurance, for example, that people responding to such questions in a telephone survey had voted for anyone. The ban on exit polling, then, constituted a complete ban on the kinds of questions reporters sought to ask.

---

85. *Whitton* v. *Gladstone,* 354 F. 3d 1400 (1995).
86. *S.O.C.* v. *Clark County, Nevada,* 152 F. 3d 1136 (1998).
87. *Seattle Affiliate of Oct. 22nd Coalition to Stop Police Brutality, Repression & Criminalization of a Generation* v. *City of Seattle,* 2008 WL 5192062 (9th Cir. Dec. 12, 2008).

GUIDELINES FOR TIME, PLACE AND MANNER RESTRICTIONS

1. Rules must be content neutral.
2. Rules must not constitute a complete ban on communication.
3. Rules must be justified by a substantial state interest.
4. Rules must be narrowly tailored.

---

3. **The state must articulate a substantial interest to justify this restraint on speech.** A ban against using loudspeakers to communicate a political message after 10 p.m. could surely be justified on the grounds that most people are trying to sleep at that time. A ban against passing out literature and soliciting money in the passageways between an airport terminal and the boarding ramps could also be justified by the state, which wants to keep these busy areas clear for passengers hurrying to board airplanes.[88] But attempts by the government to ban distribution of handbills on city streets because many people throw them away and cause a litter problem are typically rejected.[89] The state interest in keeping the streets clean can be accomplished by an anti-litter law. At times communities have attempted to raise aesthetic reasons to justify limiting or banning newspaper boxes. Some courts refuse to allow these concerns alone to justify limits on First Amendment freedoms, usually noting that many other common objects on the streets (telephone poles, trash cans, fire hydrants, street signs) are also eyesores.[90] Other courts have ruled that aesthetic considerations can be included in a community's justification for limits.[91] If the community can demonstrate a strong rationale for its aesthetic concerns, even a total ban on the placement of racks in a specific area might be acceptable. In 1996 the 1st U.S. Court of Appeals permitted the city of Boston to completely ban news racks from the public streets of a historic district of the city, where the architectural commission was trying to restore the area to what it looked like hundreds of years earlier.[92]

In addition to asserting a substantial interest, the state is required to bring evidence to court to prove its case. Southwest Texas State University in San Marcos attempted to restrict the distribution of a small community newspaper on its campus. It told the 5th U.S. Circuit Court of Appeals that it sought such restrictions in order to preserve the academic environment and the security of the

---

88. See, for example, *International Society for Krishna Consciousness* v. *Wolke,* 453 F. Supp. 869 (1978).
89. *Schneider* v. *New Jersey,* 308 U.S. 147 (1939); and *Miller* v. *Laramie,* 880 P. 2d 594 (1994).
90. See *Providence Journal* v. *Newport,* 665 F. Supp. 107 (1987); and *Multimedia Publishing Co. of South Carolina, Inc.* v. *Greenville-Spartanburg Airport District,* 991 F. 2d 154 (1993).
91. See *Gold Coast Publications, Inc.* v. *Corrigan,* 42 F. 3d 1336 (1995); and *Honolulu Weekly Inc.* v. *Harris,* 298 F. 3d 1037 (2002).
92. *Globe Newspaper Company* v. *Beacon Hill Architectural Commission,* 100 F. 3d 175 (1996).

campus, protect privacy on campus, control traffic, preserve the appearance of the campus, prevent fraud and deception and eliminate unnecessary expenses. These were all laudable goals, but the court said the university presented no evidence to support the notion that restricting the sale of these newspapers to a few vending machines or direct delivery to subscribers on campus would accomplish these goals. "[T]he burden is on the defendants [university] to show affirmatively that their restriction is narrowly tailored to protect the identified interests. Defendants failed to carry this burden," the court ruled.[93] And in 2002 a U.S. District Court ruled that the city of Calistoga, Calif., would have to produce evidence to show how its new limits on the number of news racks in the city was arrived at, and how they would advance the goal of enhancing pedestrian safety and the flow of traffic on the streets and sidewalks.[94]

4. **The law must be narrowly tailored so that it furthers the state interest that justifies it, but does not restrain more expression than is actually required to further this interest.** "A regulation is narrowly tailored when it does not burden substantially more speech than is necessary to further the government's legitimate interests."[95] Officials in the city of Sylvania, Ga., believed they had a litter problem. The Penny-Saver, a weekly free newspaper, was thrown on the lawn or driveway of each residence in the city. Oftentimes residents just left the paper where it fell. These unclaimed papers were unsightly and sometimes wound up on the street or in the gutter. The city adopted an ordinance that made it illegal to distribute free, printed material in yards, on driveways or on porches. The publisher of the Penny-Saver sued, claiming the new law was a violation of the First Amendment. The Georgia Supreme Court agreed, rejecting the city's argument that this was a proper time, place and manner rule. The ordinance was certainly content neutral, but it was not narrowly tailored. The law blocked the distribution of the Penny-Saver but also barred political candidates from leaving literature on doorsteps, stopped many religious solicitors who hand out material and blocked scores of others from passing out pamphlets door-to-door. In addition, the court ruled, the problem could be solved in other ways that do not offend the First Amendment. The city could require either the Penny-Saver publisher or the city residents to retrieve the unclaimed papers or could punish the publisher for papers that end up in the ditch or on the street.[96]

A law can be declared invalid if it fails to pass any of these four criteria. The manner in which courts apply the intermediate scrutiny test—how rigorously they employ it, how much deference they grant to asserted legislative interests and even whether they choose to use a different test—often depends on the nature of the specific location where the law in question applies.

93. *Hays County Guardian* v. *Supple,* 969 F. 2d 111 (1992).
94. *Napa Valley Publishing Co.* v. *Calistoga,* 225 F. Supp. 1176 (2002).
95. *Ward* v. *Rock Against Racism,* 491 U.S. 781 (1989).
96. *Statesboro Publishing Company* v. *City of Sylvania,* 516 S.E. 2d 296 (1999); see also *Houston Chronicle* v. *Houston,* 630 S.W. 2d 444 (1982); and *Denver Publishing Co.* v. *Aurora,* 896 P. 2d 306 (1995).

FORUM ANALYSIS

Courts have identified four kinds of forums:

Traditional Public Forum: Traditional public forums are public places that have by long tradition been devoted to assembly and speeches, places like street corners, public parks, public sidewalks or a plaza in front of city hall. The highest level of First Amendment protection is given to expression occurring in traditional public forums.

Designated Public Forum: Designated public forums are places created by the government to be used for expressive activities, among other things. A city-owned auditorium, a fairgrounds, a community meeting hall and even a student newspaper intended to be open for use by all students are examples of designated public forums. It is clear today that "the government must have an affirmative intent to create a public forum in order for a designated public forum to arise."[97] Intent may be determined by three factors:

1. Explicit expressions of intent
2. Actual policy and history of practice in using the property
3. Natural compatibility of the property with the expressive activity

For instance, in 2006 a federal appellate court in *Bowman* v. *White*[98] held that three specific areas on the University of Arkansas at Fayetteville campus were designated public forums: the Union Mall (an outdoor area in the center of campus near the library composed of grassy mounds surrounded by sidewalks and walkways, benches and potted trees and plants); the Peace Fountain (a metallic tower structure, also located in the center of the campus, with a fountain at the base); and an area outside a major campus dining hall. In concluding these areas were designated public forums, the court reasoned that

> [the] tradition of free expression within specific parts of universities, the University's practice of permitting speech at these locations, and the University's past practice of permitting both University Entities and Non-University Entities to speak at these locations on campus demonstrate that the University deliberately fosters an environment that permits speech.

Although a government entity is not required either to create or to maintain indefinitely a designated public forum (i.e., a designated public forum can be closed if the government wishes to do so), once it creates a designated public forum and chooses to keep it open, it "is bound by the same rules that govern traditional forums."[99] This means that a time, place and manner regulation in both a traditional public forum and a designated public forum must survive and pass the four-part intermediate scrutiny standard just described,[100] whereas a content-based restriction must pass the more stringent strict scrutiny standard of review (see page 60) and thus is more likely to be held invalid and unconstitutional.

97. *Ridley* v. *Massachusetts Bay Transportation Authority*, 390 F. 3d 65 (1st Cir. 2004).
98. 444 F. 3d 967 (8th Cir. 2006). See also *Hays County Guardian* v. *Supple*, 969 F. 2d 111, 117 (5th Cir. 1992), which found certain outdoor areas at Southwest Texas State University to be a designated public forum, designated for the speech of students.
99. Weaver and Lively, *Understanding the First Amendment*, 118.
100. See *Wells* v. *City and County of Denver*, 257 F. 3d 1132, 1147 (10th Cir. 2001), which wrote that"a content-neutral restriction in a traditional or designated public forum is subject to review as a regulation on the time, place, and manner of speech."

Public Property That Is Not a Public Forum: Some kinds of public property not considered to be public forums are obvious—prisons and military bases, for example. The Supreme Court has stated that a nonpublic forum consists of "[p]ublic property which is not by tradition or designation a forum for public communication."[101] Law professors Russell Weaver and Donald Lively observe that courts have identified a number of places as nonpublic forums including:

- Postal service mailboxes
- Utility poles
- Airport terminals
- Political candidate debates on public television[102]

In (and on) such places and venues, the government has much greater power to regulate and restrict speech, and thus "regulation of speech in a nonpublic forum is subject to less demanding judicial scrutiny."[103] Regulations on speech activities in nonpublic forums will be upheld and allowed as long as they are reasonable and viewpoint neutral (see page 94 discussing viewpoint-based discrimination and page 37 discussing viewpoint neutrality). The latter requirement entails "not just that a government refrain from explicit viewpoint discrimination, but also that it provide adequate safeguards to protect against the improper exclusion of viewpoints."[104]

For instance, in 2006 a federal appellate court in *Center for Bio-Ethical Reform* v. *City and County of Honolulu*[105] held that the airspace over the beaches of Honolulu was a nonpublic forum. As visitors to the Jersey Shore and beaches of California and Florida know, small planes often fly above beaches, towing banners behind them advertising everything from restaurants and bars to political candidates and television shows. Thus there is a link between such airspaces and the First Amendment protection of free speech. But Honolulu, concerned about preserving the area's visual beauty and preventing "potentially dangerous aerial distractions for its coastal vehicle traffic," has an ordinance prohibiting such banner-towing flights above its beaches. This law was challenged by the Center for Bio-Ethical Reform, which an appellate court described as "a pro-life/anti-abortion advocacy group that hires airplanes to tow aerial banners over heavily populated areas. These banners are typically 100 feet long and display graphic photographs of aborted fetuses."

So how did the appellate court conclude the airspace above Honolulu's beaches was a nonpublic forum? First, the court reasoned that the airspace was not a traditional public forum because "it is not among those places that have immemorially been held in trust for the use of the public and, time out of mind, have been used for purposes of assembly, communicating thoughts between citizens, and discussing public questions." Second, the court found that the airspace was not a designated public forum because, in fact, a local ordinance "explicitly prohibits using Honolulu's airspace as a forum for expressive conduct and neither party cites

---

101. *Perry Education Association* v. *Perry Local Educators' Association*, 460 U.S. 37, 46 (1983).
102. Weaver and Lively, *Understanding the First Amendment*, 120.
103. *Faith Center Church Evangelistic Ministries* v. *Glover*, 462 F. 3d 1194, 1203 (9th Cir. 2006).
104. *Child Evangelism Fellowship of Maryland* v. *Montgomery County Public Schools*, 457 F. 3d 376, 384 (4th Cir. 2006).
105. 448 F. 3d 1101 (9th Cir. 2006), cert. den., 127 S. Ct. 730 (2006).

a single example where expressive activity was sanctioned to occur in Honolulu's airspace. Further, Honolulu's airspace is not naturally compatible with expressive activity."

Having determined the above-beach airspace was neither a traditional public forum nor a designated public forum, the appellate court thus considered the space to be a nonpublic forum and it next examined whether the ordinance was "(1) reasonable in light of the purpose served by the forum and (2) viewpoint neutral." As for the first step, the appellate court held:

> The ordinance fulfills several legitimate needs, including preserving the economically vital scenic beauty of Honolulu and minimizing traffic safety hazards for motorists and pedestrians. Although both of these goals are surely legitimate, preservation of the visual beauty of Honolulu's coastal and scenic areas is of paramount importance.

The appellate court then found the ordinance was viewpoint neutral and upheld the law. In reaching its conclusion on viewpoint neutrality, the court emphasized:

> The ordinance prohibits the "display in any manner or for any purpose whatsoever any sign or advertising device" by an "aircraft or other self-propelled or buoyant airborne object." The ordinance says nothing about the content of the signs or the views expressed. In contrast to the laws at issue in other sign cases, the ordinance makes no distinction between commercial signs and other displays.

Private Property: Owners of private property, which includes everything from a backyard patio to a giant shopping mall, are free to regulate who uses their property for expressive activity. There are no First Amendment guarantees of freedom of expression on private property.

The problem of dealing with distribution of materials at privately owned shopping centers has been a troubling one. In 1968, in *Amalgamated Food Employees Local 590* v. *Logan Valley Plaza,*[106] the Supreme Court ruled that the shopping center was the functional equivalent of a town's business district and permitted informational picketing by persons who had a grievance against one of the stores in the shopping center. Four years later in *Lloyd Corp.* v. *Tanner,*[107] the court ruled that a shopping center can prohibit the distribution of handbills on its property when the action is unrelated to the shopping center operation. Protesters against nuclear power, for example, could not use the shopping center as a forum. People protesting against the policies of one of the stores in the center, however, could use the center to distribute materials.

In 1976 the Supreme Court recognized the distinctions it had drawn between the rules in the *Logan Valley* case and the rules in the *Lloyd Corp.* case for what they were—restrictions based on content. The distribution of messages of one kind was permitted, while the distribution of messages about something else was banned. In *Hudgens* v. *NLRB,*[108] the high court ruled that if, in fact, the shopping center is the functional equivalent of a municipal street, then restrictions based on content cannot stand. But rather than open the shopping center to the distribution of all kinds of material, *Logan Valley* was overruled, and the court announced that "only when . . . property has taken all the attributes of a town" can property be treated as public. Distribution of materials at private shopping centers can be prohibited.

---

106. 391 U.S. 308 (1968).
107. 407 U.S. 551 (1972).
108. 424 U.S. 507 (1976).

Just because the First Amendment does not include within its protection of freedom of expression the right to circulate material at a privately owned shopping center does not mean that such distribution might not be protected by legislation or by a state constitution. That is exactly what happened in California. In 1974 in the city of Campbell, Calif., a group of high school students took a card table, some leaflets and unsigned petition forms to the popular Pruneyard Shopping Center. The students were angered by a recent anti-Israel U.N. resolution and sought to hand out literature and collect signatures for a petition to send to the president and Congress. The shopping center did not allow anyone to hand out literature, speak or gather petition signatures, and the students were quickly chased off the property by a security guard. The students filed suit in court, and in 1979 the California Supreme Court ruled that the rights of freedom of speech and petitioning are protected under the California Constitution, even in private shopping centers, as long as they are "reasonably exercised."[109] The shopping center owners appealed the ruling to the U.S. Supreme Court, arguing that the high court's ruling in *Lloyd Corp.* v. *Tanner* prohibited the states from going further in the protection of personal liberties than the federal government. But six of the nine justices disagreed, ruling that a state is free to adopt in its own constitution individual liberties more expansive than those conferred by the federal Constitution.[110]

A state is free to adopt in its own constitution individual liberties more expansive than those conferred by the federal Constitution.

Courts in many states (Washington, Colorado, New Jersey, Oregon, New York and others) have interpreted their state constitutions as providing broader free speech and press rights than those provided by the First Amendment to the U.S. Constitution. This trend becomes particularly noticeable when the federal courts narrow the meaning of the First Amendment.

SUMMARY

The prior restraint of expression is permissible under what are known as time, place and manner regulations. That is, the government can impose reasonable regulations about when, where and how individuals or groups may communicate with other people. In order to be constitutional, time, place and manner restraints must meet certain criteria:

1. The regulation must be content neutral; that is, application of the rule should not depend on the content of the communication.

2. The regulation must serve a substantial governmental interest, and the government must justify the rule by explicitly demonstrating this interest.

3. There cannot be total prohibition of the communication. The speakers or publishers must have reasonable alternative means of presenting their ideas or information to the public.

4. The rules cannot be broader than they need to be to serve the governmental interest. For example, the government cannot stop the distribution of literature on all public streets if it only seeks to stop the problem of congestion on public streets that carry heavy traffic.

---

109. *Robins* v. *Pruneyard Shopping Center,* 592 P. 2d 341 (1979).
110. *Pruneyard Shopping Center* v. *Robins,* 447 U.S. 74 (1980).

OTHER PRIOR RESTRAINTS

Major issues regarding prior restraint have been outlined in the previous pages. Yet each year other instances of prior restraint are challenged in the courts, and frequently the Supreme Court is called on to resolve the issue. Here is a brief outline of some of these issues.

SON OF SAM LAWS

Americans have always been interested in crime and criminals. But in recent decades our desire to know more about this sordid side of contemporary life has spawned books and television programs about killers, rapists, robbers, hijackers and their victims. Indeed, it is often jokingly said of those accused of high-profile crimes that when they are captured they are more eager to contact an agent than a defense attorney. Efforts have been made by government to stop felons from receiving money that might be earned by selling stories about their crimes. Many civil libertarians say this is a prior censorship. The laws in question, which have been adopted in one form or another by about 40 states and the federal government, are called "Son of Sam" laws after a serial killer in New York who was dubbed that name by the press. Before the Son of Sam (David Berkowitz) was caught, reports circulated that the press was offering to pay for the rights to his story. The New York legislature responded to those reports by passing a law that permits the state to seize and hold for five years all the money earned by an individual from the sale of his or her story of crime. The money is supposed to be used to compensate the victims of the crimes caused by the felon. The criminal/author collects what is left in the fund after five years.

Two separate challenges to the New York law were mounted in the late 1980s and early 1990s. Simon & Schuster contested the law when it was applied against the best-selling book "Wiseguys" (the basis for the film "GoodFellas"). Career mobster Henry Hill was paid for cooperating with the book's author, Nicholas Pileggi. Macmillan Publishing Co. also challenged the validity of the law when New York sought to seize the proceeds of Jean Harris' autobiography, "Stranger in Two Worlds," because some of the material in the work was based on her trial for the murder of her lover, diet doctor Herman Tarnower.

The statute was upheld in both federal and state courts. The 2nd U.S. Circuit Court of Appeals ruled in *Simon & Schuster* v. *Fischetti*[111] that the purpose of the law was not to suppress speech but to ensure that a criminal did not profit from the exploitation of his or her crime, and that the victims of the crime are compensated for their suffering. A compelling state interest is served, and the fact that this imposes an incidental burden on the press is not sufficient to rule the law a violation of freedom of expression.

But in late 1991 the U.S. Supreme Court disagreed and in an 8-0 decision ruled that the Son of Sam law was a content-based regulation that violated the First Amendment.[112] "The statute plainly imposes a financial disincentive only on a particular form of content," wrote Justice Sandra Day O'Connor. In order for such a law to pass constitutional muster,

---

111. 916 F. 2d 777 (1990).
112. *Simon & Schuster, Inc.* v. *New York Crime Victims Board,* 502 U.S. 105 (1991); see also *Bouchard* v. *Price,* 694 A. 2d 670 (1998) and *Keenan* v. *Superior Court,* 40 P. 3d 718 (2002) in which courts in Rhode Island and California struck down similar laws.

the state must show that it is necessary to serve a compelling state interest and that the law is narrowly constructed to achieve that end. The members of the high court agreed that the state has a compelling interest in ensuring that criminals do not profit from their crimes, but this law goes far beyond that goal; it is not narrowly drawn. The statute applies to works on any subject provided they express the author's thoughts or recollections about his or her crime, however tangentially or incidentally, Justice O'Connor noted. The statute could just as easily be applied to "The Autobiography of Malcolm X" or Thoreau's "Civil Disobedience" or the "Confessions of St. Augustine," she added. While Justice O'Connor specifically noted that this ruling was not necessarily aimed at similar laws in other states because they might be different, the decision has forced substantial changes in most of the existing laws. In Massachusetts, however, the Supreme Judicial Court of that commonwealth approved a probationary scheme that had clear earmarks of a Son of Sam law. Katherine Power, a 1970s radical who participated in a bank robbery in which a police officer was killed, pleaded guilty to her crimes and a trial court ordered the defendant to serve 20 years' probation. Attached to the probation sentence was a provision that Power could not in any way profit from the sale of her story to the news media during those 20 years. Power appealed the provision, citing the First Amendment and the Supreme Court ruling in *Simon & Schuster.* The Massachusetts high court rejected this appeal, arguing that a specific condition of probation (which frequently restricts a probationer's fundamental rights) is not the same as a Son of Sam law, which is a statute of general applicability.[113] So, are Son of Sam laws constitutional? They certainly can be, but most of the current laws are not narrowly tailored in such a way as to pass muster. Because the laws are content-based statutes, the state has to first demonstrate that a compelling state interest is at stake and then prove that the law does not bar more speech than is necessary to further that interest.

Although courts are likely to find that two different compelling interests justify these laws (compensating victims of crimes and preventing criminal profiteering), they also are likely to declare the laws not narrowly tailored because most Son of Sam laws regulate more speech than is necessary to serve these twin interests. For instance, in 2004, the Supreme Court of Nevada in *Seres* v. *Lerner* struck down that state's law that allowed felony victims to recover from the felon any monetary proceeds the felon might generate from published materials substantially related to the offense.[114] The high court of Nevada held the law unconstitutional because it "allows recovery of proceeds from works that include expression both related and unrelated to the crime, imposing a disincentive to engage in public discourse and non-exploitative discussion of it." A nonexploitative discussion might include such things as the writer (the felon) warning about the consequences of crime, describing life behind bars and urging others not to commit the same acts.

PRIOR RESTRAINT AND PROTESTS

Two 1994 decisions by the Supreme Court focus on the prior restraint of those seeking to demonstrate or protest. In June the Supreme Court unanimously ruled that cities may not bar residents from posting signs on their own property. Margaret Gilleo had challenged the Ladue, Mo., ordinance by posting an 8-by-11-inch sign in a window of her house protesting the Persian Gulf

113. *Massachusetts* v. *Power,* 420 Mass. 410 (1995).
114. 102 P. 3d 91 (Nev. 2004).

War. The lower courts ruled that the ban on residential signs was flawed because the city did not ban signs on commercial property; the law favored one kind of speech over another. But the Supreme Court struck down the ordinance in a broader fashion, ruling that the posting of signs on residential property is "a venerable means of communication that is both unique and important. A special respect for individual liberty in the home has long been part of our culture and law," wrote Justice John Paul Stevens. "Most Americans would be understandably dismayed, given that tradition, to learn that it was illegal to display from their window an 8-by-11-inch sign expressing their political views," he added.[115]

In another ruling involving the right to protest, the high court upheld a Florida state court injunction that established a 36-foot buffer zone between an abortion clinic in Melbourne, Fla., and anti-abortion protesters.[116] The buffer zone, or ban on picketing, was designed to keep protesters away from the entrance to the clinic, the parking lot, and the public right-of-way. Chief Justice Rehnquist, who wrote the 6-3 ruling, said the ban "burdens no more speech than is necessary to accomplish the governmental interest at stake." The court did strike down, however, a 300-foot buffer zone within which protesters could not make uninvited approaches to patients and employees, as well as a buffer zone the same size around the houses of clinic doctors and staff members. The chief justice said a smaller zone or restriction on the size and duration of demonstrations would be constitutional.*

In 1995 the Supreme Court struck down an Ohio law (and for all intents and purposes laws in almost every other state in the nation) that prohibited the distribution of anonymous election campaign literature. Margaret McIntyre had circulated leaflets opposing an upcoming school levy, but failed to include her name and address on the campaign literature as required by law. She was fined $100. The state argued the statute was needed to identify those responsible for fraud, false advertising and libel, but seven members of the high court said the law was an unconstitutional limitation on political expression. "Under our constitution, anonymous pamphleteering is not a pernicious, fraudulent practice, but an honorable tradition of advocacy and of dissent," wrote Justice John Paul Stevens for the majority. "Anonymity is a shield from the tyranny of the majority." Stevens said anonymity might in fact shield fraudulent conduct, but our society "accords greater weight to the value of free speech than to the dangers of its misuse."[117]

SUMMARY

A wide variety of legal issues relate to prior restraint. In recent years the Supreme Court of the United States has voided a statute aimed at denying criminals the right to earn profits from books or films about their crimes and voided a city ordinance that barred residents from putting signs on their front lawns or in their windows. At the same time, the high court has permitted limited restrictions aimed at those seeking to protest abortion at a clinic in Florida.

*In 2003 the Supreme Court refused to permit two abortion clinics and the National Organization for Women to use the federal Racketeer Influenced and Corrupt Organizations Act (RICO; see pages 484–485 for a discussion of this law) when they sued anti-abortion activists who disrupted and blockaded abortion clinics in Chicago in the 1990s. The high court said the protests did not constitute extortion, a crime that might make the RICO law applicable. *Scheidler* v. *National Organization for Women,* 537 U.S. 393 (2003). The court implied that it was inappropriate to use the federal racketeering law as a weapon against political protests.
115. *City of Ladue* v. *Gilleo,* 512 U.S. 43 (1994).
116. *Madsen* v. *Women's Health Center,* 512 U.S. 753 (1994).
117. *McIntyre* v. *Ohio Elections Commission,* 514 U.S. 334 (1995).

HATE SPEECH/FIGHTING WORDS

Hate speech—words written or spoken that attack individuals or groups because of their race, ethnic background, religion, gender or sexual orientation—is a controversial but not altogether uncommon aspect of contemporary American life. Few people openly acknowledge a value in such speech, but there is a considerable debate over what to do about it. How do you balance the need to protect the sensibilities of members of the community with the right to speak and publish freely, a right guaranteed by the First Amendment?

The Supreme Court endeavored to balance these issues more than 65 years ago when it ruled that those who print such invective in newspapers or broadcast them on the radio or paint them on walls or fences are generally protected by the Constitution, but those who utter the same words in a face-to-face confrontation do not enjoy similar protection. The case involved a man named Chaplinsky, who was a member of the Jehovah's Witness religious sect. Face-to-face proselytization or confrontation is a part of the religious practice of the members of this sect. Chaplinsky attracted a hostile crowd as he attempted to distribute religious pamphlets in Rochester, N.H. When a city marshal intervened, Chaplinsky called the officer a "God-damned racketeer" and a "damned fascist." The Jehovah's Witness was tried and convicted of violating a state law that forbids offensive or derisive speech or name-calling in public. The Supreme Court affirmed the conviction by a 9-0 vote. In his opinion for the court Justice Frank Murphy outlined what has become known as the **fighting words doctrine**:

> There are certain well-defined and narrowly limited classes of speech, the prevention and punishment of which have never been thought to raise any constitutional problems. These include . . . fighting words—those which by their very utterance inflict injury or tend to incite an immediate breach of the peace. It has been well observed that such utterances are no essential part of any exposition of ideas, and are of such slight social value as a step to the truth that any benefit that may be derived from them is clearly outweighed by the social interest in order and morality.[118]

"There are certain well-defined and narrowly limited classes of speech, the prevention and punishment of which have never been thought to raise any constitutional problems."

Fighting words may be prohibited, then, so long as the statutes are carefully drawn and do not permit the application of the law to protected speech. Also, the fighting words must be used in a personal, face-to-face encounter—a true verbal assault. The Supreme Court emphasized this latter point in 1972 when it ruled that laws prohibiting fighting words be limited to words "that have a direct tendency to cause acts of violence by the person to whom, individually, the remark is addressed."[119] It is important to note that the high court has given the state permission to restrict so-called fighting words because their utterance could result in a breach of the peace, a fight, a riot; not because they insult or offend or harm the person at whom they are aimed.

The legal principle that speech cannot be censored merely because it offends or annoys is illustrated by the Supreme Court of Oregon's 2008 ruling in *Oregon* v. *Johnson*.[120] In a road-rage scenario, the defendant had made "extremely rude gestures" and "shouted various obscene and racist epithets" at two women who had pulled in front of him while stuck in rush-hour traffic. As the court put it, "the car had a rainbow decal on the rear, which

---

118. *Chaplinsky* v. *New Hampshire,* 315 U.S. 568 (1942).
119. *Gooding* v. *Wilson,* 405 U.S. 518 (1972).
120. 191 P. 3d 665 (Ore. 2008).

caused [the] defendant to assume that the women were lesbians." The defendant was prosecuted under a state law that made it a crime to harass or annoy another person by "publicly insulting such other person by abusive words or gestures in a manner intended and likely to provoke a violent response." There was no requirement, however, under the statute that any possible violence that might ensue be imminent (see page 56 regarding the imminence requirement under *Brandenburg*). In holding that the law violated the state's constitutional provision protecting expression because it lacked an imminence or immediacy requirement, the Oregon high court wrote:

> Harassment and annoyance are among common reactions to seeing or hearing gestures or words that one finds unpleasant. Words or gestures that cause only that kind of reaction, however, cannot be prohibited in a free society, even if the words or gestures occur publicly and are insulting, abusive, or both. Stated another way, [Oregon] constitutionally may protect a hearer or viewer from exposure to a reasonable fear of immediate harm due to certain types of expression, but it cannot criminally punish all harassing or annoying expression.

In a 2008 opinion called *South Dakota* v. *Suhn*, the Supreme Court of that state protected the speech of Marcus J. Suhn. Suhn had yelled, while standing on a crowded sidewalk as the bars closed at 2:00 a.m. in the town of Brookings, a string of epithets and expletives at police officers in a patrol car as they drove by.[121] In concluding that the speech did not constitute fighting words, the court reasoned that "just because someone may have been offended, annoyed, or even angered by Suhn's words does not make them fighting words. As offensive or abusive as Suhn's invective to the police may have been, when addressed to the ordinary citizen, Suhn's words were not inherently likely to provoke violent reaction." In tossing out Suhn's disorderly conduct conviction, the high court of South Dakota added that the "crowd merely responded with facial expressions of disbelief."

Very few types of speech . . . fall completely outside the scope of First Amendment protection.

Another key point here is that legislators must be very precise when they try to carve out statutory exceptions for categories of speech they believe should not be protected by the First Amendment. Very few types of speech, in fact, fall completely outside the scope of First Amendment protection, according to the U.S. Supreme Court; unprotected categories include (1) child pornography involving real minors, as well as obscenity (see Chapter 13); (2) fighting words under *Chaplinsky*, described here; (3) incitement to violence under *Brandenburg* v. *Ohio* (see Chapter 2); (4) certain types of libelous statements (see Chapters 4, 5 and 6); and (5) advertising that is false, misleading or about an unlawful product or service (see Chapter 15). In an interesting potential development of a new category of unprotected expression, the U.S. Supreme Court in 2009 agreed to hear a case called *United States* v. *Stevens* involving a challenge, based on First Amendment speech grounds, to a federal law outlawing the knowing creation, distribution and possession of images depicting animal cruelty. In other words, videos of illegal dog fights or cock fights would be treated like illegal child pornography. Thus, just because an anti-religious message ("religion is but myth and superstition") posted at Christmastime may offend some

---

121. *South Dakota* v. *Suhn*, 2008 WL 5413753 (S.D. Dec. 30, 2008). According to the court, Suhn yelled "Fucking cop, piece of shit. You fucking cops suck. Cops are a bunch of fucking assholes."

people and even be considered hateful by religious believers, it does not mean that the message is unprotected.[122]

Hate speech is one thing, but what about symbolic acts that attempt to communicate the same kinds of messages, burning a cross on someone's lawn, for example? The Supreme Court faced this question in 1992 when it struck down a St. Paul, Minn., ordinance that forbade the display of a burning cross or a Nazi swastika or any writing or picture that "arouses the anger, alarm or resentment in others on the basis of race, color, creed, religion or gender." Minnesota courts had approved the law, saying the phrase "arouses anger, alarm or resentment in others" was another way of saying "fighting words." But the statute violated the First Amendment, the high court said, because it was content based—that is, it only applied to fighting words that insult or provoke violence on the basis of race, color, creed or gender. What about fighting words used to express hostility toward someone because of their political affiliation, or their membership in a union or the place where they were born? Justice Antonin Scalia asked. The city has chosen to punish the use of certain kinds of fighting words, but not others, he said. The majority of the court agreed that cross burning was a reprehensible act, but contended there were other laws that could be used to stop such terroristic threats that did not implicate the First Amendment, such as trespass or criminal damage to property. Eleven years later the high court revisited the issue in a case involving Virginia's law against cross burning and ruled that a state could proscribe cross burning without infringing on First Amendment freedoms, so long as the state made it a crime to burn a cross *with the purpose to intimidate the victim.* The intimidation factor is the key, Justice Sandra Day O'Connor wrote. The state would have to prove that the cross burner intended to intimidate the victim; the threat could not be inferred simply because a cross was burned on the victim's lawn.[123]

The online postings of hate groups also generate controversies. For instance, in July 2009 a federal judge held that the anti-Semitic, anti-gay Web postings of William White on his Overthrow.com site were protected by the First Amendment even though they were directed at (and provided detailed information about the address and whereabouts of) the foreperson of a jury that had convicted white supremacist Matthew Hale of soliciting the murder of a federal judge. Should the speech be stopped because it might cause others to track down the foreperson and harm him? The answer, the court said, was no. In ruling in favor of White's speech rights, District Judge Lynn Adelman wrote in *United States* v. *White* that "although the posts may be reasonably read as criticizing [the foreperson's] vote to convict Hale, nowhere in them does defendant expressly advocate that [the foreperson] be harmed." Judge Adelman added that White's posts about the foreperson "are disturbing because of the possibility that others might respond to them, but the cases hold that the government may not, consistent with the First Amendment, criminalize general calls to action."

The efforts to control hate speech in the past three decades have focused particularly on public schools and universities. More than 300 colleges promulgated speech codes in the 1980s and early 1990s, but after several court rulings against such policies, most school policies were either abandoned or simply unenforced.[124] The courts tended to follow the principles

---

122. This scenario took place in 2008 when a group called Freedom From Religion Foundation posted such a sign near a nativity scene in the Capitol Rotunda area in Washington state, provoking the ire of conservative commentators such as Bill O'Reilly.
123. *Virginia* v. *Black,* 538 U.S. 343 (2003); see also Greenhouse, "Justices Allow Bans."
124. See, for example, *John Doe* v. *University of Michigan,* 721 F. Supp. 852 (1989); and *UWM Post* v. *Board of Regents of the University of Wisconsin,* 774 F. Supp. 1163 (1991).

from *Chaplinsky* and *Gooding* that limit prosecution of such hate speech to face-to-face encounters that could result in physical injury or provoke violent acts.

A policy drafted by the school board in State College, Pa., was declared unconstitutional by a federal appeals court because it was vague and overbroad and would punish students for "simple acts of teasing and name calling." A lawsuit against the policy was filed on behalf of two students who said they feared they would be punished if they expressed their religious belief that homosexuality is a sin. The district defined harassment as verbal or physical conduct based on race, sex, national origin, sexual orientation or other personal characteristics that has the effect of creating an intimidating or hostile environment. Examples of such harassment included jokes, name-calling, graffiti and innuendo as well as making fun of a student's clothing, social skills or surname. The appeals court agreed that preventing actual discrimination in school was a legitimate, even compelling, government interest. But the school district's policy was simply overbroad, prohibiting a substantial amount of speech that would not constitute actionable harassment under either federal or state law.[125] The government cannot prohibit invectives or epithets that simply injure someone's feelings or are merely rude or discourteous. The Pennsylvania ruling mirrors other similar decisions throughout the nation that pose a real dilemma for school administrators and legislators who are seeking to reduce the verbal aggressiveness common on many school yards.

The government cannot prohibit invectives or epithets that simply injure someone's feelings or are merely rude or discourteous.

At the college level, the difference between unprotected harassment and protected expression that merely offends was clarified by the Office of Civil Rights (OCR) of the U.S. Department of Education in a July 28, 2003, memorandum. That memorandum provides that harassment

> must include something beyond the mere expression of views, words, symbols or thoughts that some person finds offensive. Under OCR's standard, the conduct must also be considered sufficiently serious to deny or limit a student's ability to participate in or benefit from the educational program. Thus, OCR's standards require the conduct be evaluated from the perspective of a reasonable person in the alleged victim's position, considering all the circumstances, including the alleged victim's age.

This statement is important because many public universities today have policies that, although they are no longer called or referred to as speech codes, nonetheless restrict students' expressive rights. A Philadelphia-based organization called the Foundation for Individual Rights in Education (FIRE) aggressively challenges such policies while it simultaneously defends college students' rights of free speech. FIRE keeps tabs on these policies online at http://www.speechcodes.org and encourages students to come forward with instances of campus censorship.

University speech codes are still litigated today and, almost inevitably, are declared unconstitutional. For example, in 2007 a federal magistrate issued an injunction stopping California State University campuses from enforcing a policy that required all students to be "civil to one another."[126] The policy was challenged by members of the College Republicans at San Francisco State University who faced disciplinary charges for acts of incivility after they stepped on makeshift Hezbollah and Hamas flags at an anti-terrorism rally. Magistrate Wayne Brazil, finding that the civility rule was unconstitutionally vague (see page 10 regarding the

---

125. *Saxe* v. *State College Area School District*, 240 F. 3d 200 (2001).
126. Egelko, "CSU's Civility Rule Violates First Amendment."

void for vagueness doctrine), remarked during oral argument: "It might be fine for the university to say, 'Hey, we hope you folks are civil to one another,' but it's not fine for the university to say, 'If you're not civil, whatever that means, we're going to punish you.'" He added that "the First Amendment permits disrespectful and totally emotional discourse or communication." In March 2008, California State University settled the case when it agreed to amend the civility policy, as well as another rule that had too broadly defined sexual harassment as any "unwelcome conduct which emphasizes another person's sexuality," and to pay more than $41,000 in legal fees incurred by the College Republicans.[127]

In August 2008, the 3rd U.S. Circuit Court of Appeals held that Temple University's sexual harassment policy (notice it was not called a speech code) was unconstitutionally overbroad in the scope of the speech it restricted (see page 11 regarding the overbreadth doctrine).[128] In ruling against Temple, the appellate court in *DeJohn* v. *Temple University* observed that "overbroad harassment policies can suppress or even chill core protected speech, and are susceptible to selective application amounting to content-based or viewpoint discrimination." In language incredibly favorable to the First Amendment freedom of speech, the court wrote that "discussion by adult students in a college classroom should not be restricted." Importantly, the court distinguished between high schools and colleges when it comes to restricting speech, writing "that Temple's administrators are granted *less leeway* in regulating student speech than are public elementary or high school administrators." Temple's policy was flawed, in part, because it punished individuals for the intent of their speech, even if the speech caused no harm. As the court wrote, "under the language of Temple's policy, a student who sets out to interfere with another student's work, educational performance, or status, or to create a hostile environment would be subject to sanctions *regardless* of whether these motives and actions had their intended effect [emphasis added]." Such a focus on motive rather than actual effect was impermissible. The 3rd Circuit also concluded the policy's use of the words "hostile" "offensive" and "gender-motivated" made it so broad and subjective that it "could conceivably be applied to cover any speech of a gender-motivated nature, the content of which offends someone."

SUMMARY

Hate speech is not a new problem in America, but for the first time in many years the courts have been called in to determine just how far the state may go in limiting what people say and write about other people when their language is abusive or includes racial, ethnic or religious invective. In the early 1940s the Supreme Court ruled that so-called fighting words could be prohibited, but these words have come to mean face-to-face invective or insults that are likely to result in a violent response on the part of the victim. The high court voided a St. Paul, Minn., ordinance that punished such abusive speech because, the court said, the law did not ban all fighting words, merely some kinds of fighting words (i.e., racial or religious invective) that the community believed were improper. The decision in this case has sharply limited attempts by state universities and colleges and public schools to use speech codes to discourage hate speech or other politically incorrect comments or publications.

127. Egelko, "Settlement Ends Rules on Civility for CSU Students."
128. *DeJohn* v. *Temple University*, 537 F. 3d 301 (3d Cir. 2008).

THE FIRST AMENDMENT AND ELECTION CAMPAIGNS

The First Amendment is clearly implicated in any election campaign. Candidates give speeches, publish advertising, hand out leaflets, and undertake a variety of other activities that clearly fall within the ambit of constitutional protection. But since the mid-1970s the First Amendment and political campaigns have intersected in another way as well. Attempts by Congress and other legislative bodies to regulate the flow of money in political campaigns have been consistently challenged as infringing on the right of freedom of expression.

Campaign reform laws tend to fall into one of two categories: those that limit how much candidates and their supporters can spend on the election, and those that limit how much money people can contribute to candidates and political parties. The courts have tended to find more serious First Amendment problems with the laws that limit spending than the laws that limit contributions, although this is not always the case.

A Supreme Court opinion on point is a 2006 decision, *Randall* v. *Sorrell*.[129] At issue was a Vermont campaign-finance statute limiting both the amounts that candidates for state office could spend on their campaigns (expenditure limitations) and the amounts that individuals, organizations and political parties could contribute to those campaigns (contribution limitations). For instance, a candidate for governor could spend no more than $300,000 during a two-year general election cycle, while a candidate for lieutenant governor could spend an even lower maximum of $100,000 (under the statute, the figures could be adjusted upward slightly for inflation). Vermont also had the most strict campaign contribution limits in the nation, including a $400 cap that any single individual could contribute to the campaign of a candidate for statewide office (governor, lieutenant governor, etc.) during a two-year general election cycle and a $200 cap for contributions to state legislators.

In 2006, the nation's high court declared both the expenditure and contribution limits in Vermont "inconsistent with the First Amendment." It noted that "well-established precedent makes clear that the expenditure limits violate the First Amendment." The precedent referred to was the 1976 decision in *Buckley* v. *Valeo*[130] in which the court first adopted, in the context of the Federal Election Campaign Act of 1971, the dichotomy between expenditure limits and contribution limits. In *Buckley*, the court upheld a $1,000 per election limit on individual contributions and reasoned that contribution limits are permissible in order to prevent "corruption and the appearance of corruption."[131] The court in *Buckley*, however, held that this same interest was not sufficient to justify limits on expenditures by candidates and, instead, reasoned that expenditure caps are not permissible because they "necessarily reduce the quantity of expression by restricting the number of issues discussed, the depth of their exploration, and the size of the audience reached."

As for Vermont's contribution limits, a majority of the justices found they were "well below the limits this court upheld in *Buckley*," noting that "in terms of real dollars (i.e., adjusting for inflation), [Vermont's limit] on individual contributions to a campaign for governor is

---

129. 548 U.S. 230 (2006).
130. 424 U.S. 1 (1976).
131. Subsequent to *Buckley*, the court also upheld a $1,075 limit on contributions to candidates for Missouri state auditor in *Nixon* v. *Shrink Missouri Government PAC*, 528 U.S. 377 (2000).

slightly more than one-twentieth of the limit on contributions to campaigns for federal office before the Court in *Buckley*." The court concluded in *Randall* that Vermont's contribution limits were simply "too restrictive," threatened "to inhibit effective advocacy by those who seek election, particularly challengers," and imposed burdens on the First Amendment right of expression that were "disproportionately severe" to advancing the goals of preventing actual corruption and the appearance of corruption. The court, however, did not identify a precise dollar amount limitation that would be permissible on contributions.

The bottom line from Supreme Court decisions stretching from *Buckley* through *Randall* is that expenditure limits imposed on candidates violate free expression rights of candidates for public office, while contribution limits imposed on donors are permissible unless, as was the case in *Randall*, they become so restrictive and limiting that they prevent more expression than is needed to serve the interests of preventing corruption and its appearance. The decision in *Randall* was seen by some as "a defeat for liberal reformers who wanted to lessen the impact of money in politics."[132] Both cases, however, involved splintered decisions among the justices, suggesting that the still-valid dichotomy between expenditure limits (not permissible) and contributions (permissible if not too low) is tenuous and may change if the court's composition shifts significantly. In fact, only three justices in *Randall* firmly endorsed the continued use of the *Buckley* dichotomy.

Other recent issues affecting the intersection of money, speech and politics involve challenges to the Bipartisan Campaign Reform Act (BCRA) of 2002 that, among other things, makes it a federal crime for any corporation to broadcast, shortly before an election, any ads that name a federal candidate for elected office and that target the electorate. Although the Supreme Court in 2003 upheld this provision to the extent it regulates express advocacy or its functional equivalent that constitutes an appeal to vote for or against a specific candidate, a 2007 decision by the high court made it clear that issue advocacy ads that do not constitute such express advocacy for or against a candidate are permissible and do not fall within the reach of the BCRA. In particular, the Supreme Court in *Federal Election Commission* v. *Wisconsin Right to Life, Inc.* adopted a murky dichotomy for corporate speech between

- *issue advocacy* (speech about public policy matters and legislative issues like abortion rights, same-sex marriage and gun control), which is fully protected by the First Amendment from regulation by the BCRA; and
- *campaign advocacy* (speech for or against a specific candidate for federal office), which is not protected by the First Amendment from BCRA regulation, regardless of whether it is express advocacy or its functional equivalent.[133] The court held that "an ad is the functional equivalent of express advocacy only if the ad is susceptible of no reasonable interpretation other than as an appeal to vote for or against a specific candidate."

In 2008, the Supreme Court in *Davis* v. *Federal Election Commission* struck down as unconstitutional a portion of the BCRA called the Millionaire's Amendment.[134] The provision stated that if a candidate for the U.S. House of Representatives spent more than $350,000 of

---

132. Savage, "Kennedy Moves Front and Center."
133. 127 S. Ct. 2652 (2007).
134. 128 S. Ct. 2759 (2008).

his or her own personal funds running for office, then that candidate's opponent was exempt from the normal, strict limits on contributions that can be received from individual donors (the 2008 contribution cap on a donor to a candidate for Congress was $2,300 during a two-year election cycle) and could instead receive three times the normal amount. The self-financing candidate (the one spending more than $350,000), however, was still subject to the normal limits on donor contributions. In brief, if a wealthy candidate spent too much of his or her own money (more than $350,000), then his or her opponent was cut a break from the normal contribution limits while the wealthy candidate was not. In declaring that the Millionaire's Amendment impermissibly burdened the First Amendment right of a wealthy, self-financing candidate "to spend his own money for campaign speech" by imposing asymmetrical contribution limits, Samuel Alito wrote for the five-justice majority that "we have never upheld the constitutionality of a law that imposes different contribution limits for candidates who are competing against each other." The majority rejected the idea that leveling the playing field for candidates of different wealth justified the provision.

In September 2009 the U.S. Supreme Court heard oral argument in *Citizens United* v. *Federal Election Commission*. The case centers on the Bipartisan Campaign Reform Act of 2002 and, in particular, on whether a 2008 documentary called "Hillary: The Movie" that was paid for by nonprofit, conservative-oriented Citizens United was subject to the act's restrictions. The high court had yet to rule when this textbook went to press. The decision could have a huge impact on the future of government restrictions on corporate-funded speech activities and expenditures that either oppose or support political candidates.

SUMMARY

Efforts to reform the expensive American electoral process seem to be gaining momentum in the early part of the 21st century, but under the Constitution there is only so much that the law can do. The Supreme Court has ruled that while it is permissible to place a limit on how much money one person or business can donate to a campaign, it may be a violation of the First Amendment to place a limit on how much a candidate may spend. Because the presentation of campaign messages via the mass media is so much a part of the current electoral process and because sending such messages costs money, campaign spending is tied closely to freedom of speech and press and is protected by the First Amendment, the court has ruled.

THE FIRST AMENDMENT AND THE INFORMATION SUPERHIGHWAY

The First Amendment was drafted and approved in the late 18th century, a time when newspapers, magazines, books and handbills comprised the press that was intended to be protected by the constitutional provision. As each new mass medium has emerged—radio, motion pictures, over-the-air television, cable television and so forth—the courts have had to define the scope of First Amendment protection appropriate to that medium. And so it is with the Internet, computer-mediated communication. The next 13 chapters of this text contain references to laws regarding libel, invasion of privacy, access to information, obscenity, copyright and advertising, and they contain references to how these laws are being applied to computer-mediated communication. These emerging rules have in no small part been dictated by decisions by the federal courts that speak to the general question of the application of the First Amendment to the Internet. The next few pages focus on this general question.

How the government regulates a message communicated by any medium is generally determined by the content of that particular message. A plea to burn down city hall and kill the mayor is sedition; a call to vote the mayor out of office is not. Calling Mary Smith a thief is libelous; calling Mary Smith a good student is not. The law is applied, then, based on what the message says. But in some instances the regulation of a message is based on more than the content of the message; it is also influenced by the kind of medium through which the message is transmitted. As some have stated, there is a medium-specific First Amendment jurisprudence in the United States, meaning that the scope and amount of protection that speech receives will be influenced by the nature of the medium on which it is conveyed.

At least four categories of traditional communications media were in common use when the Internet first burst onto the scene, and even today each is regulated somewhat differently by the law. The printed press—newspapers, magazines, books and pamphlets—enjoys the greatest freedom of all mass media from government regulation. The over-the-air broadcast media—television and radio—enjoy the least amount of freedom from government censorship. Cable television is somewhere between these two, enjoying more freedom than broadcasting but somewhat less than the printed press. Few limits are placed on the messages transmitted via the telephone, and those that are must be very narrowly drawn.[135] There are some ifs, ands or buts in this simple outline, but it is an accurate summary of the hierarchy of mass media when measured by First Amendment freedom.

Why is the printed press allotted the most protection by the First Amendment? There are no physical limits on the number of newspapers and magazines or handbills that can be published. (Economic limits are another matter, but one not considered by the courts in this context.) Since the founding of the Republic in 1789, the printed press has traditionally been free. The receiver must generally take an active role in purchasing a book or a magazine or newspaper. Young people must have the economic wherewithal to buy a newspaper or magazine, and then have the literacy skills to read it.

It is just as obvious why broadcast media have fared the poorest in First Amendment protection. There is an actual physical limit on the number of radio and television channels that exist. All but a very few are in use. Since not everyone who wants such a channel can have one, it is up to the government to select who gets these scarce broadcast frequencies and to make certain those who use the frequencies serve the interests of all listeners and viewers. Because of spectrum scarcity and other reasons, broadcasting has been regulated nearly since its inception. It has no tradition of freedom. All the receiver must do to listen to the radio or watch television is to flick a switch. Even children who don't know how to read can do this; radio and television are easily accessible to kids.

Cable television and telephones fit somewhere in between. There is potentially an unlimited capacity for messages to be transmitted by each medium. Both have been historically

135. *Sable Communications* v. *FCC,* 492 U.S. 115 (1989).

regulated, but not to the extent that broadcasting has been regulated. Although a receiver can watch a cable television channel as easily as he or she can watch an over-the-air channel, the receiver must take a far more active role by subscribing to a cable system. Although this action may seem like a trivial distinction, the courts have made much of it. Judges have presumed that the people who subscribe to cable television should know what they will receive. Federal law mandates that cable television companies provide safeguards (called cable locks) for parents who want to shield their children from violent or erotic programming.* Such screening technology is only now coming into use for over-the-air television. The use of a telephone also requires a more active role by the receiver than simply switching on a radio or television set.

Where do computer-mediated communication systems fit into this hierarchy? In June 1997 the Supreme Court ruled in a 7-2 decision that communication via the Internet deserves the highest level of First Amendment protection, protection comparable to that given to newspapers, magazines and books.[136] (The dissenters on the court agreed with this portion of the ruling.) The high court made this decision as it ruled that the central provisions of the 1996 Communications Decency Act that restricted the transmission of indecent material over the Internet violated the U.S. Constitution. Recognizing that each medium of communication may present its own constitutional problems, Justice John Paul Stevens wrote that the members of the high court could find no basis in past decisions for "qualifying the level of First Amendment scrutiny that should be applied to this medium [the Internet]."

The court rejected the notion prevalent among those in Congress who voted for the Communications Decency Act that communication via the Internet should be treated in the same manner as communication via over-the-air radio and television. The court said that the scarcity of frequencies that had long justified the regulation of broadcasting did not apply in the case of the Internet, which, it said, can hardly be considered a "scarce" expressive commodity.

The importance of this ruling cannot be overestimated. Not only did the court strike down a restrictive federal law that was certain to retard the growth of computer-mediated communication, it ruled that any other governmental agency that seeks to regulate communication via the information superhighway must treat this medium in the same manner it would treat a newspaper or a book.

NET NEUTRALITY

The potential of the Internet as "vast democratic fora" and a "new marketplace of ideas"—terms used by Justice Stevens to describe it back in 1997 in *Reno* v. *ACLU*—is seriously jeopardized by the possibility that the companies controlling broadband access to the Internet will block, degrade and otherwise discriminate against some types of Internet content, services and applications. Put differently, the danger exists today that those who provide on-ramps to the Internet will harm the open and nondiscriminatory nature of the medium. Interest groups such as Public Knowledge[137] thus advocate the concept of *net neutrality*, a relatively abstract

*But in *U.S.* v. *Playboy Entertainment Group, Inc.,* 529 U.S. 803 (2000), the Supreme Court suggested that cable television enjoys the full protection of the First Amendment. This notion has yet to be fleshed out by the court.

136. *Reno* v. *American Civil Liberties Union,* 521 U.S. 844 (1997).

137. The organization describes itself as a Washington, D.C.–based "advocacy group working to defend your rights in the emerging digital culture." See http://www.publicknowledge.org.

term suggesting that Internet service providers should treat all traffic and content similarly and that they should not charge more money for or block access to faster services. More simply put, as the San Francisco Chronicle described it, net neutrality is "the idea that traffic on the Internet should flow as democratically as possible."[138]

Net neutrality raises important First Amendment issues for all Internet users, including the right to receive speech (including a diversity of ideas) and the right to access information. The statutes and regulations adopted by Congress and the Federal Communications Commission today will largely determine whether net neutrality becomes a reality or whether the Internet will someday be treated more like cable, where the cable system provider charges different rates for different content and services. As media merge (possibly changing the nature of the medium-specific First Amendment jurisprudence adopted by the Supreme Court) and as cable operators and phone companies compete for control over the on-ramps to the Internet, the First Amendment rights of all citizens are placed in the balance.

The issue of network neutrality heated up among lawmakers in 2008 when legislation called the Internet Freedom Preservation Act was proposed in Congress and when the FCC held hearings to investigate allegations that Comcast, a major opponent of government action mandating network neutrality, was restricting and interfering with Internet access to the flow of content, such as video clips, songs and software files, on a file-sharing service called Bit-Torrent.[139] Such a discriminatory practice by a service provider like Comcast, which provides broadband Internet access over cable lines, that targets the use of a particular peer-to-peer application is precisely what advocates of network neutrality fear.

In August 2008, the FCC ruled by a 3-2 vote that Comcast had unduly interfered with Internet users' right to access lawful Internet content and to use the applications of their choice.[140] The FCC ordered Comcast to disclose details about its discriminatory network management practices and to submit a plan showing how it would stop such practices by the end of 2008. The order, a huge victory for network neutrality advocates, signaled the FCC's willingness to police Internet disputes regarding discriminatory network management practices and consumer access to lawful content. In particular, the FCC made it clear that it was going to enforce as law four policy principles it adopted in 2005. Those principles provide that Internet consumers are entitled to

1. access the lawful Internet content of their choice;
2. run applications and use services of their choice, subject to the needs of law enforcement;
3. connect their choice of legal devices that do not harm the network; and
4. compete among network providers, application and service providers and content providers.

138. Abate and Kopytoff, "Are Internet Toll Roads Ahead?"

139. Kang, "FCC Head Says Action Possible on Web Limits"; *Associated Press*, "FCC Poised to Punish Comcast for Traffic Blocking."

140. *In re Formal Complaint of Free Press and Public Knowledge Against Comcast Corporation for Secretly Degrading Peer-to-Peer Applications*, Memorandum Opinion and Order, File No. EB-08-IH-1518 (Aug. 20, 2008).

Comcast, however, announced shortly after the FCC's ruling that it would cap the amount of download volume of its heaviest consumers who, perhaps not so coincidentally, are those who use peer-to-peer, file-sharing services. Comcast also appealed the FCC's precedent-setting order in September 2008, taking its case to the U.S. Circuit Court of Appeals for the District of Columbia.

BIBLIOGRAPHY

Abate, Tom, and Verne Kopytoff. "Are Internet Toll Roads Ahead?" *San Francisco Chronicle*, 7 February 2006, C1.

Anderson, David A. "Freedom of the Press in Wartime." *University of Colorado Law Review* 77 (2006): 49.

Associated Press. "AP CEO Urges Better Press Access to Military Ops." 7 February 2009.

———. "AP Photographer Freed by US After 2 Years in Custody." 16 April 2008.

———. "FCC Poised to Punish Comcast for Traffic Blocking." 26 July 2008.

———. "Review Board Orders AP Journalist Held." 8 July 2008.

——— "Shippensburg Agrees to Drop Speech Code Rules." 25 February 2004.

———. "UNC Students Sue Over Newspaper Funding Cuts." 15 July 2004.

———. "U.S. Judge Says Utica Schools Illegally Censored Prep Paper." 13 October 2004.

Baquet, Dean, and Bill Keller. "When Do We Publish a Secret?" *Los Angeles Times*, 1 July 2006, B19.

Blumenthal, Ralph, and Jim Rutenberg. "Journalists Are Assigned to Accompany U.S. Troops." *The New York Times,* 18 February 2003, A12.

Boot, William. "Covering the Gulf War: The Press Stands Alone." *Columbia Journalism Review,* March/April 1991.

Bruni, Frank. "Dueling Perspectives: Two Views of Reality Vying on the Airwaves." *The New York Times,* 18 April 1999, A11.

Burnett, John. "Embedded/Unembedded II." *Columbia Journalism Review,* May/June 2003, 43.

Cole, Thomas J. "Cases Involving Top Lawyer Sealed." *Albuquerque Journal*, 22 October 2008, A1.

Cranberg, Gilbert. "The Gulf of Credibility." *Columbia Journalism Review,* March/April 1988, 19.

DeFalco, Beth. "Body Piercing Photo Causes Friction Between Administration, Student Press." *Associated Press,* 20 November 2004.

Delgado, Richard. "Words That Wound: A Tort Action for Racial Insults, Epithets, and Name Calling." *Harvard Civil Rights—Civil Liberties Law Review* 17 (1982): 133.

Denniston, Lyle. "High Court Declines to Rule on Secrecy in Terror Case." *The Boston Globe*, 24 February 2004, A2.

———. "Son of Sam Law vs. First Amendment." *Washington Journalism Review*, May 1991, 56.

Editorial, "Curbing Speech at Quinnipiac." *The New York Times*, 29 October 2008, A30.

Edmonson, George. "Suit Seeks Military Coffin Photos." *Atlanta Journal-Constitution,* 5 October 2004, 7A.

Egelko, Bob. "CSU's Civility Rule Violates First Amendment." *San Francisco Chronicle*, 8 November 2007, B3.

———. "Settlement Ends Rules on Civility for CSU Students." *San Francisco Chronicle*, 8 March 2008, B1.

Estrada, Naldy, and Julio Robles. "All the News That's Fit to Print and Won't Upset the Faculty." *Los Angeles Times,* 7 July 2003, California Metro 11.

Galloway, Angela. "Political Spending Unchecked." *Seattle Post-Intelligencer,* 28 July 2000, A1.

Garofoli, Joe. "Flag-Draped Coffin Photos Released." *San Francisco Chronicle,* 29 April 2005, A10.

Gidiere, Stephen. "Checks, Balances and FOIA's 40th Anniversary." *USA Today*, 5 July 2006, 11A.

Greenhouse, Linda. "Court Strikes Down Curb on Visits by Jehovah's Witnesses." *The New York Times,* 18 June 2003, A12.

———. "Justices Allow Bans on Cross Burnings Intended as Threats." *The New York Times,* 8 April 2003, A1.

———. "Justices, in a 5-to-4 Decision, Back Campaign Finance Law That Curbs Contributions." *The New York Times,* 11 December 2003, A1.

Hentoff, Nat. *Free Speech for Me—But Not for Thee: How the American Left and Right Relentlessly Censor Each Other.* New York: HarperCollins, 1992.

Jacobs, Matthew J. "Assessing the Constitutionality of Press Restrictions in the Persian Gulf War." *Stanford Law Review* 44 (1992): 674.

Jensen, Elizabeth. "Sinclair Broadcast Group Thrusts Itself into the News." *Los Angeles Times,* 8 May 2004, E14.

Kaiser, Robert G. "Public Secrets." *Washington Post*, 11 June 2006, B1.

Kamber, Michael, and Tim Arango. "4,000 U.S. Deaths, and a Handful of Images." *The New York Times*, 26 July 2008, A1.

Kang, Cecilia. "FCC Head Says Action Possible on Web Limits." *Washington Post*, 26 February 2008, D1.

Lewis, Neil A., and Richard A. Oppel Jr. "U.S. Court Issues Discordant Ruling on Campaign Law." *The New York Times,* 3 May 2003, A1.

Lewis, Richard. "College Newspapers Stolen Over Reparations Ad." *The Seattle Times,* 18 March 2001, A5.

Lively, Donald. "The Information Superhighway: A First Amendment Roadmap." *Boston College Law Review* 35 (1994): 1066.

MacArthur, John R. *Second Front: Censorship and Propaganda in the Gulf War.* New York: Hill and Wang, 1992.

MacCormack, Zeke. "No Snow: Texas School Bans Book." *Seattle Post-Intelligencer,* 10 September 1999, A1.

Meredith, Karen. "Military's Ban on Coffin Photos Hurts Families." *Buffalo News*, 24 March 2005, A8.

"The Message Is the Medium: The First Amendment on the Information Superhighway." *Harvard Law Review* 107 (1994): 1062.

Paulk, Crystal. "Campus Crime Real Despite What You Read." *Quill,* September 1997, 48.

Preston, Julia. "Judge Says U.S. Must Release Prison Photos." *The New York Times,* 27 May 2005, A10.

Ricchiardi, Sherry. "Whatever Happened to Iraq?" *American Journalism Review*, June/July 2008, 20.

Richey, Warren. "Supreme Court Decision May Limit Access to Terror Cases." *Christian Science Monitor*, 24 February 2004, 4.

Richter, Bob. "Army Post Spokesman Says Photo of Slain Soldier Was Digitally Altered." *San Antonio Express-News*, 20 September 2008, 2A.

Riskin, Cynthia. "Communications Students Support Some Speech, Press Censorship." *The Washington Newspaper,* January/February 1994.

Rutten, Tim. "Regarding Media; A Nasty Turn in Criticism of Press." *Los Angeles Times*, 6 May 2006, E1.

Salamon, Julie. "New Tools for Reporters Make Images Instant, but Coverage No Simpler." *The New York Times,* 6 April 2003, B13.

Savage, David G. "Kennedy Moves Front and Center on Court." *Los Angeles Times*, 2 July 2006.

"School Censorship on Rise, Civil Liberties Group Says." *Seattle Post-Intelligencer,* 29 August 1991.

Schorr, Daniel. "Why Hide Flag-Draped Coffins?" *Christian Science Monitor*, 30 April 2004, 9.

Secrecy Report Card 2008. Washington, D.C.: OpenTheGovernment.org, 2008.

Sharkey, Jacqueline. "The Shallow End of the Pool." *American Journalism Review,* December 1994, 43.

Smith, Jeffery A. *War and Press Freedom: The Problem of Prerogative Power*. New York: Oxford University Press, 1999.

Smith, Lynn. "Coffins and Now Chaos." *Los Angeles Times*, 26 April 2004, E1.

Spears, Natalie, and Gregory Naron. "CIPA and the Right of Access to Judicial Proceedings." *Communications Lawyer*, Fall 2006, 1.

Sterngold, James. "For Artistic Freedom, It's Not the Worst of Times." *The New York Times,* 20 September 1998, section 2, p. 1.

Stone, Geoffrey R. *Perilous Times: Free Speech in Wartime*. New York: W.W. Norton, 2004.

"Students Censored, but Issue Lives On." *The New York Times,* 7 September 1997, A9.

"Suspension of Student for Poem of Violence Upheld." *Seattle Post-Intelligencer,* 21 July 2001, B2.

Tenhoff, Greg C. "Censoring the Public University Student Press." *Southern California Law Review* 64 (1991): 511.

Thompson, Mark. "The Brief Ineffective Life of the Pentagon's Media Pool." *Columbia Journalism Review,* March/April 2002, 66.

Vaina, David. "The Vanishing Embedded Reporter in Iraq." *Project for Excellence in Journalism*, 26 October 2006, http://www.journalism.org/node/2596.

Weaver, Russell L., and Donald E. Lively. *Understanding the First Amendment*. Newark, N.J.: LexisNexis.

White, Josh. "Government Authenticates Photos From Abu Ghraib." *Washington Post*, 11 April 2006, A16.

Wilgoren, Jodi. "Don't Give Us Little Wizards, The Anti-Potter Parents Cry." *The New York Times,* 1 November 1999, A1.

Zeller, Tom. "Unfit: Harry Potter and Potty Humor." *The New York Times,* 15 June 2003, B2.

Zernike, Kate. "Free-Speech Ruling Voids School District's Harassment Policy." *The New York Times,* 16 February 2001, A11.

CHAPTER 4

Libel

ESTABLISHING A CASE

The law of libel is centuries old. Its roots in this country spring directly from the British common law. Throughout most of this nation's history the states were left to fashion their own libel laws. But since the mid-1960s the U.S. Supreme Court has "federalized" basic elements of defamation law, obligating the states to keep their rules and regulations within boundaries defined by the First Amendment. This development has transformed what was a fairly simple aspect of American law into a legal thicket akin to a blackberry patch. In this first of three chapters about defamation some basic dimensions of this common tort action are characterized and the requirements that have been placed on the plaintiff to establish a cause of action for libel are outlined.

THE LIBEL LANDSCAPE

Defamation, or libel, is what lawyers call a **tort,** or a civil wrong. It is undoubtedly the most common legal problem faced by people who work in the mass media, and often the most troublesome. Allegations of libel are the basis of about two-thirds of all legal complaints filed against mass media defendants in any given year. In simple terms, **libel** is the publication or broadcast of any statement that

- injures someone's reputation or
- lowers that person's esteem in the community.

Anyone who speaks or publishes (including material on the Internet) or broadcasts anything can become the target of a defamation action. Libel can lurk in a news story or editorial, press release, company newsletter, advertising copy, letters to the editor, comments made in an Internet chatroom or in a Web log or even statements made orally at a public gathering.[1] The mainstream mass media face the vast majority of libel suits, and that is why most of the cases cited in the three subsequent chapters tend to involve lawsuits against newspapers, radio and television stations, magazines and books and the growing number of information-oriented sites on the Internet. But the editors of company magazines and corporate public information specialists need to be cautious as well. The law, as it is applied to companies like CBS or The New York Times, applies just as well to other mediated forms of communication. However, the public press, such as newspapers and broadcast stations, enjoy some First Amendment protections in libel suits that may not accrue to defamation published in a company newsletter or a press release.

Libel suits are as troublesome for the press as they are common. While any lawsuit against any person or business creates problems, there are some special aspects to libel law that seem to make these problems even worse.

- The protracted nature of many libel cases, plus the high cost of defending against such suits, can result in a heavy financial burden for the defendant.
- Plaintiffs often make outrageous damage claims and at times even win enormous damage awards.
- Libel law is especially complicated and often confusing, to the point that sometimes jurors and even judges don't understand the law and make erroneous decisions.
- Some plaintiffs file frivolous libel lawsuits to try to silence their critics in the press and the public.

Let's examine each of these factors briefly.

TIME AND MONEY

All lawsuits take time to resolve. Some libel suits take a very long time. The Knight-Ridder Company settled a libel suit in 1996 brought by a former Philadelphia prosecuting attorney. The case began 23 years earlier. Consumers Union, the publisher of Consumer Reports, settled a libel suit in 2004 that had been brought by the Suzuki Motor Corporation. The case

---

1. See, for example, *Troy Group, Inc.* v. *Tilson*, 364 F. Supp. 2d 1149 (2005) for a suit based on an e-mail; and *600 West 115th Street Corp.* v. *von Gotfeld*, 80 N.Y. 2d 130 (1992) for a case based on a comment made at a public meeting.

began in 1996.[2] Although these cases aren't necessarily typical, protracted litigation is always a threat in a defamation action because of the complex nature of libel law. And while the case goes on, the defense lawyers remain on the job, racking up billable hours.

Successfully defending a newspaper or broadcasting network in a libel suit requires the work of talented attorneys. Defending a libel suit is far more complicated than writing a will or seeking damages for an automobile accident. Hourly fees of hundreds of dollars are not unusual. Book publisher Simon & Schuster and author James B. Stewart were sued in the 1990s by an attorney who claimed he was defamed in Stewart's book "Den of Thieves," an account of Wall Street figures who participated in the corporate takeover madness of the late 1980s. By the time the lawsuit was dismissed in 1999, the defendants had spent more than $1 million defending themselves.[3] The Washington Post spent $1.3 million in the mid-1980s defending itself in a libel suit brought by the then president of the Mobil Oil Company for a story it had published about the executive's son. The Post won the case after a trial and appeal.[4] Author Stewart told a reporter that after he was sued for "Den of Thieves" he felt as if someone was trying to punish or harass him. "It is unpleasant, time-consuming and distracting. Its [the lawsuit] existence has clouded my credit rating and made it difficult for me to get a mortgage. I am sure it has intimidated other journalists and publishers," he said.

DAMAGES SOUGHT AND WON

Plaintiffs sometimes claim exaggerated damage and seek extraordinary sums. In 1994 Phillip Morris Co. sought $10 billion (that's right, billion) in damages in a libel action against ABC. The Church of Scientology once sued Time Warner for $416 million because it described the church as a global racket.[5] Damage claims this high are never awarded. Phillip Morris settled for a televised apology and $3 million. But the lawsuits have to be defended. And damage awards are often very high. In June of 2007 the Boston Herald paid $3.4 million to a Massachusetts judge who won a libel suit over articles contending that he had made insensitive remarks about a teenage rape victim. Within a two-week period in early 2005 two libel judgments of more than $2 million were levied against two Boston newspapers. In 2006 a jury awarded an Illinois Supreme Court justice $7 million in libel damages. In many instances the trial judge or an appellate court will lower these amounts. In Illinois, for example, the trial judge lowered the award to $4 million. The MLRC reported in 2007 that between 1980 and 2006, in the 223 cases the libel plaintiffs won, the average jury award of $2.85 million was reduced to an average of $560,000 after post-verdict motions and appeals—still a healthy sum.[6]

2. Hakim, "Suzuki Resolves a Dispute."
3. Carvajal, "Libel Wrangle Over Miliken Book." The Appellate Division of the New York Supreme Court granted Simon & Schuster's motion for a summary judgment on Sept. 27, 1999, and dismissed the lawsuit. See *Armstrong* v. *Simon & Schuster*, 27 M.L.R. 2289 (1999).
4. *Tavoulareas* v. *The Washington Post Co.*, 817 F. 2d 726 (1987). See also Brill, "1982: Behind the Verdict," 31.
5. *Church of Scientology International* v. *Time Warner Inc.*, 903 F. Supp. 637 (1995). The case brought by the church was ultimately dismissed in July 1996. Time Warner settled a parallel libel suit based on the same 1991 article brought by church member Michael Bayback in November 1996.
6. See MLRC 2005 Report on Trials and Damages. 2005 Issue 1, February 2005. See also *Ayash* v. *Dana-Farber Cancer Institute*, 443 Mass. 367 (2005); Liptak, "A Judge at the Plaintiff's Table Tips the Scales"; Belluck, "Boston Herald Is Ordered to Pay"; *Bohl* v. *Hesperia Resorter*, SCV55068052; and Seelye, "Jury Finds That Columnist Acted with Malice."

THE LIBEL PUZZLE

Libel law is among the most tangled areas of American law. It is filled with many poorly defined amorphous concepts. Although it is based on traditional common law, it is infused with statutory and constitutional elements. The vast majority of American judges will never hear a libel case, no matter how many years they sit on the bench. And most lawyers have never considered the topic since two or three days of lectures in a torts class in law school. Jurors—laypeople who have little or no experience with any aspect of the law—are usually even more in the dark. Mistakes are often made at trials; wrong decisions are handed down. Errors can be corrected on appeal—and usually are. But this takes time and costs money for the defendant newspaper or broadcasting station.

Lawyers who represent the press usually follow the same strategy: First, try to have the case dismissed before it goes to trial. Failing that, offer to settle the case. Most of the time this can save money. (The cost of settling a case can often be much lower than the legal costs involved in a trial.) A settlement before a trial also makes sense because, according to MLRC research, the odds are better than 50-50 that the press will lose the case if it goes before a jury. Why? Well, some libel plaintiffs have actually been wronged and deserve to win their case. But there are other reasons as well.

- As noted, the law is complex and errors are sometimes made by jurors and judges.
- Important libel defenses are anchored in the First Amendment, an abstract concept to many people. A juror can often see damage to a person's reputation much more clearly than the theoretical value inherent in freedom of the press.
- The mass media today are not held in high regard by a great many people in the nation. A lot of people don't like the press. There is a lot of bad news out there today and people—not just Americans—have always had a tendency to want to shoot the messenger. A libel trial can provide an opportunity for a juror to express his or her frustrations with the press by awarding damages to a libel plaintiff. Attorney Thomas D. Yannucci, who represents libel plaintiffs, called the jury box the mass media's Achilles' heel. "If you take it to the jury, the ordinary citizen begins [the trial] thinking the media is unfair."[7]

So going to trial is not a good strategy most of the time.

THE LAWSUIT AS A WEAPON

Most libel suits are filed because a person believes that his or her reputation has been damaged by published comments. But in recent years some plaintiffs have filed a libel action for another reason: to stop others from criticizing them. In other words, the lawsuit is used as a weapon to threaten or harass the speaker or publisher. Imagine this scenario. A large land development company asks the county to rezone a parcel of land so it can build a shopping mall. People who live adjacent to the property oppose the development and speak out against it at a public hearing. One homeowner accuses the developer of putting its financial interests ahead of the community good. "This same company has destroyed neighborhoods in other

---

7. Moscov, "Truth, Justice and the American Tort," 22.

parts of the state," the homeowner says. "What they propose to do is a crime against the people who live here," she adds.

The developer brings a libel suit against the woman, claiming she accused the company of criminal behavior. The developer has little or no interest in winning a judgment against the woman; it really doesn't want to win a judgment against its critic. It wants to stop her and her neighbors from trying to block the rezone. A lawsuit can be a powerful tool for censorship. These lawsuits send the message, "It will cost you a lot of headaches, time and money if you criticize us."

These kinds of lawsuits are called Strategic Lawsuits Against Public Participation, or SLAPP suits. More and more have been filed in the past two decades. They have become so common that at least 20 states have passed what are called anti-SLAPP laws that are designed to impede these harassment libel suits.* California has what is perhaps the broadest law. The statute states:

> A cause of action against a person arising from any act of that person in furtherance of the person's right of petition or free speech under the United States or California constitution in connection with a public issue shall be subject to a special motion to strike, unless the court determines that the plaintiff has established that there is a probability that the plaintiff will prevail on the claim.[8]

The statute requires a trial court to undertake a two-step process to decide whether the challenged lawsuit is a SLAPP. First, the court decides whether the defendant has made a showing that the libel action arises from the protected activity outlined in the law; was the defendant using free speech rights to comment on a public issue? Then the court determines whether the plaintiff has stated a legally sufficient claim; that is, has the plaintiff brought forth enough evidence to show that he or she has a probability of winning the case? If the defendant establishes the first element and the plaintiff fails to establish the second, the lawsuit must be stricken under the statute.[†]

Looking at the hypothetical case discussed previously, the woman who spoke out at the meeting was clearly using her free speech rights to comment on a public issue. And it is highly unlikely that the developer could bring forth enough evidence to establish a case for libel. The suit would be stricken or dismissed. When the case is dismissed the plaintiff must pay the defendant's legal costs. In 2002 the California Supreme Court issued a series of rulings that the lower courts should construe the statute broadly and be aggressive in controlling these harassment suits.[9] The California statute also applies to material published or broadcast by the

---

*California, Delaware, Florida, Georgia, Indiana, Louisiana, Maine, Massachusetts, Minnesota, Nebraska, Nevada, New Mexico, New York, Oklahoma, Oregon, Pennsylvania, Rhode Island, Tennessee, Utah and Washington. The Colorado Supreme Court has ruled that protections similar to those in SLAPP statutes are contained in the state's common law. *Protect Our Mountain Environment* v. *District Court*, 677 P. 2d 136 (1984).

†See, for example, *Simpson-Strong-Tie Co.* v. *Gore* 36 M.L.R. 1833 (2008), where the California Court of Appeals dismissed a lawsuit by a manufacturer of galvanized screws against an attorney after the lawyer claimed in a newspaper ad that the screws might be defective. The court ruled that the ad could not be understood to convey a false assertion of fact, and there was no possibility the plaintiff could prevail.

8. *California Code of Civil Procedure*, § 425.16(b)(1).

9. See, for example, *Equilon Enterprise, LCC* v. *Consumer Cause, Inc.*, 29 Cal. 4th 53 (2002). But the California statute was slightly modified in 2003 to give business and financial institutions a broader right to sue for libel by limiting the scope of the anti-SLAPP statute. See California Code of Civil Procedure, § 425.17(c). See also Pring, "SLAPPs"; Pring and Canan, "Strategic Lawsuits"; and Dill, "Libel Law Doesn't Work."

mass media, and while it was initiated to block libel actions, it has been applied to lawsuits for invasion of privacy as well.[10]

Not all state statutes are as broad as the California law, but most accomplish the same goals. Most legal authorities agree that someone who has been injured because of a libelous publication deserves the opportunity to convince a jury that he or she has been harmed and should be compensated. But they also agree that suits initiated to harass or silence critics work against the interests of the public debate that is integral to a democratic form of government.

RESOLVING THE PROBLEM

Going to court in a libel action is rarely a happy experience for any of the participants.

Going to court in a libel action is rarely a happy experience for any of the participants. Plaintiffs are rarely gratified. Lawyers' fees can take as much as 50 percent of their winnings. The typical case takes four years to litigate, four years during which their lives are disrupted. Two-thirds of the plaintiffs questioned by researchers in the massive Iowa Libel Research Project said they were dissatisfied with their litigation experience.[11]

The press isn't happy either. Defense costs and damage awards cut into revenues. Reporters and editors are immobilized for long periods of time. Publicity about the lawsuit only reinforces the negative attitudes many people have about the news media. Even the public suffers in the end. Tax dollars subsidize the cost of litigation. Lawsuits often result in a more cautious press that may, to avoid the threat of lawsuits, deny readers and viewers important information.

An important question to ask is this: Are there better ways to resolve legitimate disputes between a mass medium and an injured party? Is going to court, or even threatening to go to court, the only solution? Newspapers, broadcasting stations, magazines and others often have been reluctant to publish or broadcast corrections, retractions or apologies. Few people like to admit they were wrong, especially in a public forum. But three-fourths of the plaintiffs interviewed for the Iowa Libel Research Project just discussed said they would not have filed a lawsuit if the news medium had published or broadcast a correction or retraction. The publication of such corrections has become more common in the past two decades. Undoubtedly this has helped defuse many disputes that might otherwise have ended up in court.

Laws have been adopted in about 30 states that reward the press for publishing a correction or retraction. These laws also make it harder for those who claim to have been defamed to win damages in a lawsuit if they fail to ask for a correction or retraction. These so-called retraction statutes are discussed in greater depth on pages 234–235.

Proposals that states provide some kind of arbitration system to resolve issues of libel have also been advanced, but most have been met with little enthusiasm, despite the success of a few small or experimental programs. No large-scale effort has been mounted. Most lawyers and many in the press don't find the arbitration notion an attractive alternative.[12] For the time,

---

10. *Savala* v. *Freedom Communications Inc.*, 34 M.L.R. 2241 (2006). In 2008 the Georgia Supreme Court applied the state's anti-SLAPP statute to a mass media defendant, when a television station was sued for reporting that a company was under investigation by the state. See *Boxcar Development Corp.* v. *New World Communications*, 36 M.L.R. 1784 (2008). A Massachusetts Superior Court made a similar ruling in 2009, *Joyce* v. *Slager* 37 M.L.R. 1820 (2009).
11. Bezanson, Cranberg, and Soloski, *Libel Law and the Press.*
12. See Dill, "Libel Law Doesn't Work."

most libel cases will continue to find their way into the court system. And that process is the focus of the remainder of this chapter and Chapters 5 and 6 as well.

SUMMARY

Libel is the most common and often the most troublesome problem faced by people who work in the mass media. It usually takes a great deal of money to successfully defend a libel suit. Damage claims are sometimes outrageous, and occasionally damage awards are extremely high and have little to do with the harm caused by the defamation. The law is very complicated, and mistakes made by judges and juries have to be rectified by lengthy and costly appeals. Some plaintiffs attempt to use the law to harass or punish defendants rather than simply repair a damaged reputation, but many states have attempted to block these so-called SLAPP suits with legislation. Researchers have demonstrated that most libel plaintiffs are unhappy about their experiences in litigation and would not sue if the mass medium simply corrected or retracted the libelous statement. More ambitious schemes to resolve the libel problem have generally met with opposition or indifference from the press and from organizations of trial lawyers.

LAW OF DEFAMATION

The law of defamation is ancient; its roots can be traced back several centuries. Initially, the law was an attempt by government to establish a forum for persons involved in a dispute brought about by an insult or by what we today call a defamatory remark. One man called another a robber and a villain. The injured party sought to avenge his damaged reputation. A fight or duel of some kind was the only means of gaining vengeance before the development of libel law. It was obvious that fights and duels were not satisfactory ways to settle such disputes, so government offered to help solve these problems. Slowly the law of defamation evolved.

In other parts of the world, different schemes are used to accomplish similar ends. In continental Europe libel suits are less common. When a newspaper defames a person, that person has the right—under law—to strike back, using the columns of the same newspaper to tell his or her side of the story. This right is called the right of reply, and it exists in the United States in a far less advanced form, as is noted near the end of Chapter 6.

Parts of the law of libel do not concern those who work in mass communications. For example, elements of libel deal with allegations contained in private communications, a letter from one person to another, a job recommendation from a former employer to a prospective employer. The material in this chapter focuses on public communications—material that is published or broadcast via the mass media, using that term in its broadest sense to include advertising, company magazines, trade association newsletters, press releases, the Internet and so on. Similarly, because newspapers, broadcasting stations, magazines and the like tend to focus on material considered to be of public concern, courts often treat them differently from nonmedia defendants. Unless otherwise stated, it can be presumed the discussion in this text focuses on the rights and responsibilities of media defendants.

Additionally, it must be remembered that libel law is essentially state law. It is possible to describe the dimensions of the law in broad terms that transcend state boundaries, and that is what this text attempts to do. But important variations exist in the law from state to state, as will be demonstrated in the next chapter in the discussion of fault requirements. It is important for students to focus on the specific elements of the law in their states after gaining an understanding of the general boundaries of the law.

The law of defamation includes both libel (written defamation) and **slander** (oral defamation). One hundred and fifty years ago these two kinds of defamation were treated differently by the courts. Written defamation was considered a more serious offense because it lasted longer, was more widely circulated and was planned or more purposeful (as opposed to a spoken comment made in the heat of anger). Therefore the law treated libel more harshly. The coming of radio, television, film and other forms of electronic media in which spoken communication could be recorded and retained, circulated as widely or more widely than a newspaper or handbill, and was often written down in a script before it was spoken, forced changes in the law. While the law in some states still distinguishes between libel and slander, in most states the two are treated alike.[13] A more meaningful distinction today is between published communication, which includes printed matter, radio, television, film, the Internet and so on, and purely spoken, interpersonal conversation. All published communication is treated today as libel.

ELEMENTS OF LIBEL

There are many definitions of defamation, and they are all about the same. In their book "Libel," Phelps and Hamilton include this definition:

> Defamation is a communication which exposes a person to hatred, ridicule, or contempt, lowers him in the esteem of his fellows, causes him to be shunned, or injures him in his business or calling.[14]

The "Restatement of the Law of Torts," a compilation by the American Law Institute of what it thinks common law says, defines libel this way:

> [Libel is] a communication which has the tendency to so harm the reputation of another as to lower him in the estimation of the community or to deter third persons from associating with him.[15]

Defamation is any communication that holds a person up to contempt, hatred, ridicule or scorn.

Here is another definition: Defamation is any communication that holds a person up to contempt, hatred, ridicule or scorn.

Each of the preceding definitions reveals common and important elements of defamation:

1. **Defamation is a communication that damages the reputation of a person, but not necessarily the individual's character.** Your character is what you are; your reputation is what people think you are. Reputation is what the law protects. Pleading a loss of self-esteem is not sufficient to win damages in a libel suit.

---

13. See, for example, *Grotti* v. *Belo Corp.*, 34 M.L.R. 1969 (2006).
14. Phelps and Hamilton, *Libel.*
15. American Law Institute, *Restatement of the Law of Torts.*

2. **To be actionable defamation, the words must actually damage a reputation. There must be proof offered that the individual's reputation was harmed.** The plaintiff must bring evidence before the court that the allegedly libelous communication lowered his or her reputation among the people in the community. If the plaintiff fails to convince the judge and/or jury that there has been harm, no damages can be recovered. It should be noted in passing, however, that proof of damage, especially to something as amorphous as a reputation, is often an elusive task. And at times jurors are willing to assume there has been damage to reputation, based on the barest of evidence, especially if the plaintiff is a respected or well-known person.

   Defendants will frequently argue that the allegedly libelous communication has caused little or no harm to reputation and therefore no damages, or only a small amount of compensation, should be awarded. In the past three decades the argument has even been made—and it has been accepted by the courts—that a particular plaintiff has such a poor reputation that nothing anyone could say or write about this person could harm the reputation further. These people are said to be "libel-proof." Perhaps the most widely publicized libel-proof plaintiff is the physician Dr. Jack Kevorkian. The Michigan doctor received great notoriety for assisting patients who sought to end their lives because they were terminally ill. Dr. Kevorkian was castigated by many other physicians who called him a "reckless instrument of death" and a doctor who "engages in criminal practice." But those who support so-called assisted suicide regarded Dr. Kevorkian as a hero. When the doctor sued the American Medical Association and others for libel the Michigan Court of Appeals ruled that he was libel-proof. His reputation, the court said, is such "that the effect of more people calling him either a murderer or a saint is de minimis [of very little significance]."[16] In those instances where an allegedly libelous statement "cannot realistically cause impairment of reputation because the persons reputation is already so low . . . the claim should be dismissed," the court added.

   The most common variety of libel-proof plaintiffs tend to be convicted criminals. For example, an Alabama trial court ruled that David L. Williams—who had been convicted seven different times for forgery, burglary and larceny, and was sentenced to prison as a habitual felony offender—was libel-proof for purposes of defamation.[17]

3. **At least a significant minority of the community must believe that the plaintiff's reputation has been damaged, but the minority must not be an unrepresentative minority.** This is an important dimension of the law because it protects the communicator from being successfully sued for publishing something about an individual that appears innocent, but in fact is offensive to only a small

---

16. *Kevorkian* v. *American Medical Association*, 602 N.W. 2d 233 (1999).
17. *Williams* v. *Fox Television Stations Inc.*, 34 M.L.R. 1168 (2005). See also *Lamb* v. *Rizzo*, 31 M.L.R. 2513 (2003), aff'd 381 F. 3d 1133 (2004). See also *Thomas* v. *Telegraph Pub. Co.*, 35 M.L.R. 1769 (2007) where the New Hampshire Supreme Court ruled that the plaintiff would be regarded as libel proof only if his or her criminal activities had been widely reported to the public.

number of unrepresentative people. Imagine that a newspaper reports that Amanda Black was seen playing with a cat in a local park. The story is wrong; it was another woman who was playing with the cat. Black sues. She argues that she is a member of a group that believes cats are manifestations of Satan, and women who play with them are witches. The story in the newspaper suggests she is a witch, she argues, and her reputation has been damaged in the minds of the other people in the group.

Would a representative member of the community, say the average person, think less of Black because of the news report? No. And how could the newspaper editor know that it would be libelous to report that a woman was seen playing with a cat? He or she couldn't know. So the words must harm the plaintiff in the eyes of people in the community who represent what might be called average or mainstream thinking.

For example, describing someone as an "informant" has resulted in libel actions. A convict in a penitentiary once sued a television station for describing him as an alleged FBI informer. He argued the allegation lowered his reputation among fellow prisoners. More recently an investigative reporter/private investigator sued a newspaper for calling him an informer. He said he regarded himself as a whistle-blower. Both plaintiffs lost. In the first case the court ruled that prisoners in a penitentiary were not representative members of the community. What they thought of the prisoner didn't matter, as far as the libel action was concerned.[18] In the second case the court ruled that while informers are not always held in high esteem and law violators might shun such a person, the average person in the community would not. "To hold otherwise would be contrary to the public interest, in that it would penalize the law abiding citizen and give comfort to the law violator," the court ruled.[19] In both instances, then, the plaintiff's reputation may have been harmed, but not in the eyes of the right-thinking, representative people in the community.

Any living person can bring a civil action for libel. A dead person can't sue; that's obvious. Common law bars suits by the relatives of someone who has died in behalf of the deceased. Note, however, that if a living person is defamed, brings suit and then dies before the matter is settled by the court, it is possible in some states that have what are called **survival statutes** for relatives to continue to pursue the lawsuit.[20] A business corporation can sue for libel. So can a nonprofit corporation, if it can show that it has lost public support and contributions because of the defamation. There is a division in judicial opinion about whether unincorporated associations like labor unions and political action groups can sue for libel. Some court rulings say no; others say yes. Find out what the law is in your state. Cities, counties, agencies of government and governments in general cannot bring a civil libel suit. This question was decided years ago and is settled law.[21]

One important key to understanding any lawsuit is to understand the concept of the burden of proof. Which party must prove what? While this point sounds like a trivial matter to

---

18. *Saunders* v. *WHYY-TV*, 382 A. 2d 257 (1978).
19. *Clawson* v. *St. Louis Post-Dispatch LLC*, 32 M.L.R. 2008 (2004), aff'd 34 M.L.R. 2217 (2006).
20. See *MacDonald* v. *Time*, 554 F. Supp. 1053 (1983); *Canino* v. *New York News*, 475 A. 2d 528 (1984); and *Coppinger* v. *Schantag,* 34 M.L.R. 1141 (2006).
21. *City of Chicago* v. *Tribune Publishing Co.*, 139 N.E. 2d 86 (1923).

many laypeople, it is a very significant element in a lawsuit. Remember, under our adversarial legal system, the court does nothing but evaluate and analyze the material that is brought before it by the adversaries. Judges and juries don't go out and look for evidence themselves. So the matter of who must bring the evidence before the court is a critical one. If a plaintiff, for example, is required to prove a specific element in a case and fails to bring sufficient evidence before the court to convince the judge or jury, the plaintiff loses the case.

In a libel case the plaintiff bears the initial burden of proof. He or she must establish five separate elements of the case in order to have any chance of winning.

> **TO WIN A LIBEL SUIT A PLAINTIFF MUST PROVE:**
>
> 1. The libel was published.
> 2. Words were of and concerning plaintiff.
> 3. Material is defamatory.
> 4. Material is false.
> 5. Defendant was at fault.

Each of the five elements in this box is outlined in detail shortly. Items 4 and 5 are probably required only if the plaintiff is suing a mass media defendant. These elements are fairly recent additions to the law of libel, and the courts have not yet fully resolved the question of how far they should be extended.[22] Since this book is about mass media law, it is written with the assumption that plaintiffs will generally have to prove the falsity of the matter. The fifth element, proof of fault, is also presumed to be a requirement to be met by the plaintiff for purposes of this discussion. Fault will be discussed in Chapter 5.

PUBLICATION

Before the law recognizes a statement or comment as a civil libel, the statement must be published. Under the law, **publication** means that one person, in addition to the source of the libel and the person who is defamed, sees or hears the defamatory material. Just one person is all it takes. But isn't this a contradiction to what was written on page 143 that a significant number of persons must believe that the plaintiff's reputation has been harmed before he or she can collect damages? Here it is stated that only a single person must see or hear the libel for publication to take place. Two different concepts are being discussed. The first is publication. The plaintiff has to show that at least one other person saw the libelous material or the court will not allow the lawsuit to proceed. No publication, no lawsuit. Assume the plaintiff can show all five elements needed—publication, identification, defamation, falsity and fault—and the publisher of the libel fails to raise a workable defense. The plaintiff wins the case. Then comes the assessment of damages. At this point the plaintiff must show that the false statement that was published lowered his or her reputation among a significant number of the right-thinking

---

22. See *Columbia Sussex* v. *Hay*, 627 S.W. 2d 270 (1981); *Mutafis* v. *Erie Insurance Exchange*, 775 F. 2d 593 (1985); and *Philadelphia Newspapers* v. *Hepps*, 475 U.S. 767 (1986).

people in the community. If the plaintiff cannot show this, the victory is a moral one at best. No damages will be awarded. It is even possible that the court might rule that the words are not defamatory if they don't lower the plaintiff's reputation in the eyes of a significant number of persons.

The question of publication is largely academic when the mass media are sued. If something is in a newspaper or on television or transmitted over the Internet, the court will presume that a third party has seen or heard the matter.[23]

Republication of a libel can also result in a successful lawsuit. Author and courtroom observer Dominick Dunne was sued when, during an appearance on a radio program, he repeated allegations he said he had heard from a third party that implicated a U.S. congressman in the disappearance of a legislative intern named Chandra Levy. When Congressman Gary Condit sued, Dunne said that he was only repeating what others had told him—he did not initiate the charge, but said he thought the charges might be true—and argued that he was protected by the First Amendment. A federal district court disagreed and rejected the motion for a summary judgment, noting that republication of false facts threatens the target's reputation as much as does the original publication. "The First Amendment does not absolutely protect a speaker who republishes false assertions of fact, then disclaims any awareness of the actual truth of the republication, then 'theorizes' that the defamatory implication of the republication is true."[24] After his motion was denied Dunne settled the lawsuit.

Some people mistakenly believe that attributing a libel to a third party will shield them from a lawsuit, but this is one of the great myths of American journalism.

Some people mistakenly believe that attributing a libel to a third party will shield them from a lawsuit, but this is one of the great myths of American journalism. For example, most good reporters know that it is libelous to label someone a murderer. But a remarkably high percentage of professionals erroneously believe you can label someone a murderer, as long as you attribute the statement to a third party. "Jones killed his wife" is obviously defamatory. So is "Jones killed his wife, according to neighbor Ned Block." The newspaper or broadcasting station has simply republished Block's original libel of Jones. (Because the reporter apparently quoted a source for the allegation of murder, the plaintiff might find it more difficult to prove the required fault element. And that could doom Mr. Jones' libel suit. But it doesn't change the fact that the allegation—attributed or not—is the republication of a libel.) Because of the republication rule, nearly everyone in the chain of production of a news story is technically liable in a lawsuit.

Publishers and Vendors

A long-standing exception to the republication rule is the notion that news vendors, bookstores, libraries and others who actually distribute the finished printed product cannot be held responsible for republishing the defamation unless the defendant can show that these people or institutions knew the printed matter contained a defamation, or should have had reason to know. This concept is called **scienter,** or guilty knowledge, and is fundamental in many areas of the law. For example, the Tennessee Court of Appeals ruled that a shop owner was not liable when he allowed a publisher to place a free newspaper that contained allegedly defamatory

---

23. *Hornby* v. *Hunter*, 385 S.W. 2d 473 (1964).
24. *Condit* v. *Dunne*, 317 F. Supp. 2d 344 (2004).

content on a counter next to other free newspapers that anyone could pick up and take home.[25] The shop owner was a vendor, not a publisher. Similarly, network-affiliated television stations are not responsible for defamatory content in the programming they transmit for the networks. They too are regarded as vendors. These same rules have been applied to Internet publishers as well. A federal court in Maine ruled in 2008 that an Internet-based print-on-demand service was not liable for the defamatory content in a manuscript it printed because it neither knew nor had reason to know the contents of the book. BookSurge printed the manuscript for a customer, but provided no editorial service and did not review the contents. " One who only delivers or transmits defamatory matter published by a third party is subject to liability, but only if he knows or has reason to know of its defamatory contents," the court said.[26]

Libel on the Internet

The great bulk of the law of libel that is outlined in this chapter and the next two applies to defamation that is transmitted via the Internet. Courts regard communication on the World Wide Web the same way they regard material published in newspapers, magazines or books. Two issues have arisen, however, that have forced the courts and Congress to consider the relationship between libel and the Internet. The first has to do with the status of online service providers (OSPs) in the transmission of a libel; the second has to do with jurisdiction, a subject that will be discussed in Chapter 6.

There are many contexts in which a libel might be published on the Internet. A defamatory message might be sent to every person who logs on to an OSP's computers. Libelous material might be contained in a database that is viewed or downloaded by a user. Defamation might be posted on a bulletin board generally accessible to some or all of the OSP's customers. A libelous remark might be made during an online real-time discussion among users connected to an OSP. Or defamation might be contained in a message sent to an e-mail addressee.

If the OSP is the author or originator of the libelous message, it will be regarded as a publisher of the material in a libel suit and be treated as a newspaper publisher is treated. It is liable for the defamatory publication and can be sued for libel.

More commonly, however, the OSP merely transmits what another party has posted on the system as an e-mail or a message on a bulletin board or on a Web site. In this case the system operator will be regarded as a vendor or distributor rather than a publisher. This was an issue that courts debated in a series of rulings in the early 1990s. Then Congress settled the matter in 1996 when it adopted the Communications Decency Act (CDA). Section 230 of the federal law states: "No provider . . . of an interactive computer service shall be treated as the publisher or speaker of any information provided by another information content provider."[27] The purpose of the provision is to protect providers for letting content flow through, or for distributing content they did not create. As the number of lawsuits arising from Web publications continues to increase, Section 230 of the 1996 law has become an increasingly valuable tool for online service providers. Here are some examples:

---

25. *Piper* v. *Mize*, 31 M.L.R. 1833 (2003).
26. *Sandler* v. *Calcagni*, 36 M.L.R. 2286 (2008).
27. 47 U.S.C. § 230(C)(1).

■ A federal court ruled in 1998 that America Online was shielded from a libel suit brought by an aide to President Bill Clinton based on comments made in an online political gossip column transmitted but not created by AOL.[28]

■ Section 230 immunized Internet-book vendor Amazon.com from liability when it was sued by an author for including readers' comments on its Web site that were critical of the author's work.[29]

■ A U.S. District Court in South Dakota ruled that a shop that rents the use of Internet-accessible computers to customers is protected by the federal law.[30]

■ A Web site operator who refused to remove allegedly defamatory matter from its site, even after the author of the material asked that it be removed, was immune from liability. The plaintiff argued that by refusing to remove the material, the Web site operator had adopted the content of the message as its own. The federal court disagreed.[31]

■ The 5th U.S. Court of Appeals ruled in 2008 that the CDA immunized MySpace Inc., a social networking site, from liability when claims were made that it was negligent in not protecting underage users from online sexual predators. The court ruled that the Web publisher enjoys immunity for both the transmission of the third-party content, and the consequences of the content.[32]

If the Web site operator encourages a third party to submit content that is unlawful, it is possible for the operator to lose immunity. The 9th U.S. Court of Appeals ruled that when a roommate-matching Web site required users to answer questions about housing preferences that allegedly violated anti-discrimination provisions of federal and state law, it lost the immunity that protected it from lawsuits. It was clear in this case that the Web site directly participated in developing the content that violated the law, the court said. If a site operator encourages illegal content, or designs a Web site that requires users to input illegal content, immunity will be lost.[33]

While courts continue to interpret the full meaning of the protection provided to online service providers by the CDA, new questions are raised. For example, does Section 230 immunize interactive service providers from the legal consequences of transmitting allegedly false advertising provided by third parties? In 2008 Subway, the sandwich vendor, sued competitor Quiznos for a series of ads that were transmitted both online and on a few cable channels. Subway claimed the ads were false and depicted its brand in a derogatory way. The ads were created by members of the public at the behest of Quiznos as part of a contest. People were invited to submit homemade commercials that attacked Subway.

28. *Blumenthal* v. *Drudge*, 992 F. Supp. 44 (1998).

29. *Schneider* v. *Amazon.com Inc.*, 31 P. 3d 37 (2001).

30. *Patent Wizard Inc.* v. *Kinkos, Inc.*, 29 M.L.R. 2530 (2001). See also *Universal Communications Systems Inc.* v. *Lycos Inc.*, 35 M.L.R. 1417 (2007), where the U.S. Court of Appeals ruled that the defendant, which operates a financial message board, was an online service provider for purposes of the law.

31. *Globe Royalties Ltd.* v. *Xcentric Ventures LLC*, 544 F. Supp. 929 (2008). See also *Barnes* v. *Yahoo! Inc.*, 37 M.L.R. 1705 (2009), where the U.S. 9th Circuit Court of Appeals ruled the CDA shielded Yahoo! from a claim that it negligently failed to remove content posted by a third party on an online message board.

32. *Doe* v. *MySpace Inc.*, 36 M.L.R. 1737 (2008).

33. *Fair Housing Council of San Fernando Valley* v. *Roommates.com*, 36 M.L.R. 1545 (2008).

When sued, Quiznos argued that the ads had been created by third parties and hence, the company was immune from suit under provisions of Section 230 of the CDA. Quiznos merely transmitted the allegedly false content, the company said. As this chapter was being written, the courts had not yet resolved the issue.[34]

As applied to libel suits, the bottom line is simply this: An online service provider is immune from a defamation suit for transmitting defamatory matter created by a third party, unless the Web site operator has in some way encouraged the creation of the illegal content, or has designed the Web site in such a way that requires users who wish to post material to input illegal content.

While U.S. law appears to be effective in protecting the OSPs from libel suits initiated in the United States, it is unlikely to protect the OSPs from lawsuits filed in other countries. British law, for example, does not protect online service providers who simply act as distributors of a defamatory message that has been posted on the Web by a third party. British courts have traditionally been friendlier to libel claimants than U.S. courts, and recently London has gained the reputation as the libel capital of the world, according to a report by Eric Pfanner, published in The New York Times in 2009. Saudis, Russians, Ukrainians and even Hollywood celebrities have gone to London to seek redress over stories that were originally published in the United States, but distributed globally. The stories were distributed both in traditional media and online. New York and Illinois have passed laws that block enforcement of British libel judgments in the United States.[35] But the issue is far from resolved. The basic points to remember are these: At this time only U.S. law provides protection for OSPs regarding the content they simply distribute as opposed to originate. And the Internet, as a global medium, reaches nations with laws fundamentally different from those in the United States.

IDENTIFICATION

The second element in a libel suit is **identification:** The injured party must show the court that the allegedly defamatory statement is "of and concerning him, her, or it." Failing to do this, the plaintiff will lose the suit. Author William Peter Blatty, who wrote "The Exorcist" and other popular thrillers, once sued The New York Times for libel because the newspaper did not include one of the author's books on its best-selling book list. By not including the work, Blatty argued, this defamed him; it lowered his reputation. But the California Supreme Court dismissed the case. How could Blatty complain of libel for not being identified? the court asked. The plaintiff must establish that the defamatory remarks are "of and concerning" him, and if Blatty wasn't included on the list, there were no remarks at all of and concerning him.[36] This suit was surely an odd one, but it makes the point: The plaintiff must be identified. Not every reader or viewer needs to know to whom the libel refers. But certainly more than one or two people must be able to recognize the plaintiff as the subject of the derogatory remark. Libel authorities disagree on how many people must be able to identify the subject of the remark. But remember, to win damages the plaintiff must prove that his or her reputation has been lowered in the eyes of a

---

34. Story, "Can a Sandwich Be Slandered?"
35. Pfanner, "A Fight to Protect."
36. *Blatty* v. *The New York Times*, 728 P. 2d 1177 (1986).

significant minority of the members of the community. If only a handful of people can recognize the plaintiff, it is doubtful that he or she can prove sufficient harm to win damages.

Identification can occur in several ways. A plaintiff may be explicitly named. Or the defendant can use a similar name that suggests the plaintiff's actual name. The producers of the television show "Hard Copy" were sued for using the name Sweepstakes Clearing House when they aired a story on sweepstakes scams. Sweepstakes Clearing House is a made-up name, but there is a company called Sweepstakes Clearinghouse and its owners sued. The Texas Court of Appeals reversed the summary judgment granted the defendant and ruled that a publication is "of and concerning" the plaintiff if persons who knew or were acquainted with the plaintiff believed that the libelous material referred to the plaintiff.[37] The individual can be described, for example, as the host of the quiz show "Jeopardy" or the city's superintendent of public works. A picture or a drawing, even without a caption, can be sufficient if the likeness is recognizable. Even descriptive circumstances can sometimes point the finger at someone. In 1991 a young woman, after attending a party, was abducted as she was standing outside a house near the University of Pennsylvania campus. She said she was raped by her abductor. A local television station reported the attack, including comments by a police officer who cast some doubts on the victim's story. The young woman claimed these comments defamed her. The station did not use the victim's name, but described her as a female Bryn Mawr student (Bryn Mawr is a small college near the University of Pennsylvania that enrolls less than 1,500 undergraduates) who had been raped on a certain day, that she lived in a dorm at Bryn Mawr, that she drove a Nissan, and that she had attended a party at the University of Pennsylvania shortly before her abduction. The station claimed that broadcasting these facts did not constitute identification. But a U.S. District Court disagreed, noting the small school environment at Bryn Mawr. "In this type of environment, it would not be surprising if some people could identify the plaintiff from the information supplied in the broadcast."[38] In fact, the plaintiff presented affidavits from students attesting to the fact that the story of her rape had spread rapidly across campus after the broadcast. The Illinois Supreme Court held the publishers of Seventeen magazine liable for publishing a short story labeled fiction that described as a slut a girl identified only as Bryson. The author of the story, Lucy Logsdon, a native of southern Illinois, wrote a first-person narrative that recounts a conflict she said she had with a high school classmate. The classmate in the short story bore a slight physical resemblance to the plaintiff, Kimberly Bryson, who had attended high school with Logsdon. The court said that third persons familiar with both the plaintiff and the defendant would understand that the story was referring to the plaintiff despite the fiction label.[39]

It is possible for the plaintiff to put two or more stories together to establish identification. Police arrested eight people in Brookline, Mass., in connection with drug smuggling. One of the people arrested was identified as a former employee of Haim's Deli in Brookline. Police said gang members at times met at the deli. An area radio station mistakenly reported: "The owner of a Brookline deli and seven other people are arrested in connection with an international cocaine ring." Haim Eyal, the owner of Haim's Deli, sued for libel. The radio station attempted to defeat

---

37. *Allied Marketing Group Inc.* v. *Paramount Pictures Corp.*, 111 S.W. 3d 168 (2003).
38. *Weinstein* v. *Bullock*, 827 F. Supp. 1193 (1994).
39. *Bryson* v. *News America Publications Inc.*, 672 N.E. 2d 1207 (1996).

the suit by arguing that its report did not include the name of the delicatessen and that there were scores of delis in Brookline. Therefore, it had not identified Eyal. But the Massachusetts Supreme Judicial Court ruled that because nearly all other news stories about the incident had mentioned Haim's Deli, listeners to the erroneous radio report would know which deli was involved and would think Haim Eyal was arrested as a gang member.[40]

If a libelous statement does not make an explicit identification, then the plaintiff must somehow prove that the defamatory words refer to him or her. There have been a handful of cases in which plaintiffs have sued for libel, arguing that they have been fictionally portrayed in a novel. This is generally difficult for a plaintiff to prove, but it can be accomplished. The U.S. Court of Appeals for the 2nd Circuit ruled in 1980 that an identification might be established if "a reasonable reader rationally suspects that the protagonist is in fact the plaintiff, notwithstanding the author's and publisher's assurances that the work is fiction." To do this, the court said, the plaintiff must show that the fictional work "designates the plaintiff in such a way as to let those who knew her understand that she was the person meant. It is not necessary that all the world should understand the libel; it is sufficient if those who knew the plaintiff can make out that she is the person meant."[41] A New York trial court was faced with a so-called libel-in-fiction case in 2008 when an attorney sued the producer of the popular television series "Law and Order" for telecasting an ostensibly fictional episode about a Brooklyn judge who was accused of accepting bribes from an attorney. There had been a widely publicized case in New York City in which a judge was accused of taking bribes from a divorce lawyer. Both the fictional TV lawyer and the real-life lawyer were about the same age and bore a physical resemblance to one another. The producers of the TV show petitioned the court to dismiss the case, but the court rejected the request. Given the context in which the TV show was presented, and the extensive media coverage of the actual scandal, "there is a reasonable likelihood that the ordinary viewer, unacquainted with Batra [the real-life lawyer] personally, could understand Patel's [the TV lawyer] corruption to be the truth about Batra," the court said.[42] Please note, it is rare for a plaintiff to win a libel-in-fiction lawsuit.

Journalists face somewhat of a conundrum today regarding identification. Traditionally, reporters have been taught to include full identification when writing or talking about someone: John Smith, 36, of 1234 Boone Street, a carpenter. This information will separate this John Smith from any other person with the same name. But the issue of privacy is of great concern today, and many people don't want their ages or addresses in the newspaper or broadcast on television. Some news organizations now permit less than complete identification in sensitive situations. The reporter should always get complete identification for the subject of a news story, if only to confirm that he or she is writing about the correct person. Newspaper or broadcast station policy will determine how much of this information is used.

The reporter should always get complete identification for the subject of a news story, if only to confirm that he or she is writing about the correct person.

Group Identification

Can an individual who is not specifically identified in a libelous communication successfully prove identification by arguing that he or she is a member of a group or organization that was

40. *Eyal* v. *Helen Broadcasting Corp.*, 583 N.E. 2d 228 (1991).
41. *Geisler* v. *Petrocelli*, 616 F. 2d 636 (1980).
42. *Batra* v. *Wolf*, 36 M.L.R. 1592 (2008).

named in the communication? For example, the newspaper reports that the Okemos police are crooks. Cathy Mitchell is an Okemos police officer. Has she been identified?

The "Restatement of the Law of Torts" says this:

> One who publishes defamatory matter concerning a group or class of persons is subject to liability to an individual member of it, but only if (a) the group or class is so small that the matter can be reasonably understood to refer to the individual, or (b) the circumstances of publication give rise to the conclusion that there is a particular reference to him.[43]

The first consideration is the size of the group. The courts have not come up with a magic number in this regard. If the group is very small, the plaintiff usually has little difficulty convincing a court that identification has occurred. If the editor of a company's employee newsletter asserts that the three-person employee benefit board is incompetent, each member could claim identification. On the other hand, if the group is very big it is improbable that a suit will stand. In a 2002 "60 Minutes" broadcast the CBS network included a report on multimillion-dollar verdicts against corporations rendered by juries in rural Mississippi, including Jefferson County. There were comments made by people interviewed that jurors were "paying back these Yankee corporations or businesses for them being disenfranchised." The jurors were mad and held resentment, the interviewees said. One even suggested that the jurors benefited by receiving money under the table after their verdicts. Several former Jefferson County jurors sued, claiming that the defamatory statements were clearly "directed toward" and "of and concerning" them. The U.S. District Court judge disagreed, noting that none of the plaintiffs were named. The court said the segment referred to juries in rural, impoverished places like Jefferson County. But "no connection can be shown between the plaintiffs and the allegedly defamatory statement other than the fact that the plaintiffs served as jurors in Jefferson County." There were far too many people who had been jurors one time or another in that county.[44] The 2007 feature film "American Gangster," which starred Denzel Washington and Russell Crowe, was based on a true story involving a New York heroin dealer named Frank Lucas and corruption in New York law enforcement agencies. At the end of the film there was a legend or note: Frank Lucas' "collaboration [with law enforcement] led to the conviction of three quarters of New York City's Drug Enforcement Agency." Three of the 400 present or former agents employed in the drug enforcement agency sued for libel, but the court rejected the lawsuit, saying that the plaintiffs could not demonstrate that the statement was of and concerning them. The group of agents was simply too large.[45]

Courts will look at the circumstances as well as the number in the group. A police undercover agent reported to the owner of a paper mill in Maine that employee Harry Hudson had been drinking on the job. The agent was assigned to the mill to look for illegal drug use. A dozen workers at the mill were ultimately fired, 11 for illegal drug use, and Hudson for drinking on the job. A local television station subsequently reported that 12 workers had been terminated at the mill for involvement with illegal drugs. No names were given, but the mill was

43. American Law Institute, *Restatement of the Law of Torts.*
44. *Berry* v. *Safer*, 32 M.L.R. 2057 (2004). See also *Gales* v. *CBS*, 32 M.L.R. 2067 (2004), aff'd 124 Fed. Appx. 275 (2005).
45. *Diaz* v. *NBC Universal Inc.*, 536 F. Supp. 2d 337 (2008).

identified. Hudson sued and argued that it was common knowledge in the small community who the 12 workers were—and as such he had been erroneously identified as an illegal drug user. The station sought to have the suit dismissed, but the Maine Supreme Court refused, ruling that it was a jury question whether or not the broadcast had identified Hudson.[46] Courts have ruled that groups of 29 teachers,[47] 30 firefighters[48] and 21 police officers[49] were all too large to permit identification.

But caution is urged on reporters who describe even a very large group in a defamatory manner. Care is especially appropriate if only a small number of the defamed group live in the community. If the charge is made that all astrologers are frauds and there is only one astrologer in the community, the remark can be dangerous. The plaintiff could convince a sympathetic jury that the comment was aimed at him, and that he has been severely harmed by the remark.

DEFAMATION

The third element in the plaintiff's case focuses on the words themselves. There are two kinds of defamatory words. The first kind consists of words that are libelous on their face, words that obviously can damage the reputation of any person. Words like "thief," "cheat" and "traitor" are libelous per se—there is no question that they are defamatory.

The second kind of words are innocent on their face and become defamatory only if the reader or viewer knows other facts. To say that Duane Arnold married Jennifer Carter appears safe enough. But if the reader knows that Arnold is already married to another woman, the statement accuses Arnold of bigamy. And that is a libelous accusation.

The distinction between these two kinds of words was once more important than it is now. At one time plaintiffs had to prove they were specifically harmed by the words in the second category, usually called "libel per quod." Damage was presumed from the words in the first category, usually called "libel per se." All plaintiffs today must prove they were damaged by the publication of the libel. Still, in many jurisdictions, courts have erected significant barriers that make it more difficult for persons who sue for libel per quod to win their case than persons who sue for words that are clearly defamatory on their face.

The law does not contain a list of words that are defamatory. In each case a court must examine the particular words or phrase or paragraph and decide whether these words lower the individual's reputation among a significant number of so-called right-thinking people in the community. Sometimes a precedent or many precedents will exist. Numerous cases, for example, establish that stating a woman is unchaste is libelous. But sometimes precedents aren't always that useful. Times change; the meanings of words change. Describing someone as a slacker today might be unkind, but hardly libelous. But during World War I the term "slacker" was used to identify a draft dodger and was certainly defamatory. Author Oscar Hijuelos used these phrases in his novel "The Mambo Kings Play Songs of Love": "Gloria huddled at a table drinking daiquiris." She touched the "skin and gnarly hair" of the Mambo

46. *Hudson v. Guy Gannett Broadcasting*, 521 A. 2d 714 (1987).
47. *O'Brien v. Williamson Daily News*, 735 F. Supp. 218 (1990).
48. *Olive v. New York Post*, 16 M.L.R. 2397 (1989).
49. *Arcand v. Evening Call*, 567 F. 2d 1163 (1987).

King before saying to him, "Come on, ya big lug, why don't you kiss me?" Eighty years ago such a description of a woman's behavior might in fact harm her reputation. But in 1991, a U.S. District Court ruled that "reporting that a person has requested a kiss or [was] sipping a daiquiri, true or not, simply does not subject [a person] to the scorn of the average reader."[50]

At a libel trial a judge and jury are supposed to consider the words in light of their ordinary meaning unless the evidence is persuasive that the defendant meant something else when the statement was published. As a general rule, the judge will decide as a matter of law whether particular words are capable of conveying a defamatory meaning. The court will ask whether a reasonable person would regard this as a defamatory comment.

The Rhode Island Supreme Court ruled in 2002 that a cartoon in the Sunday comics section of the Providence Journal was not capable of a defamatory meaning. Two workmen, one wearing a shirt that said Budget Pest Control, were shown standing in front of a blazing house. The one wearing the shirt was holding a gas can and grinning maniacally. The other worker was telling a distraught woman, "Easy now, ma'am. This is Billy Bob's first day on the job and them carpenter ants can be real stubborn." The court asked the question, would ordinary readers have reasonably understood the cartoon to be making a defamatory comment about the plaintiff, Budget Termite & Pest Control? The court said no. The comment carried an exaggerated comic tone and was published on the comics page. These factors would suggest a humorous idea, not a statement of fact. The court also noted that the name Budget Pest Control was almost a generic label and the plaintiff really couldn't connect its business with the cartoon.[51] Peter Damon was an Army reservist who lost his arms while fighting in Iraq. He was interviewed on NBC television and told reporter Brian Williams "the pain is like my hands are being crushed in a vice." Medication, he said, made the pain more tolerable. Damon added that despite his injuries and the injuries to others, he and other wounded servicemen and women were not anti-war; they stood behind the war effort. Filmmaker Michael Moore used a portion of Damon's remarks about his pain in his anti-war film, "Farenheit 9/11." He did not, however, include the comments about Damon's support of the war.

Damon sued, arguing that by including any of his comments in the film, it falsely portrayed him as endorsing Moore's attack on the war and President Bush. The 1st U.S. Court of Appeals rejected this argument, ruling that there was no way that a reasonable viewer could construe Damon's limited remarks about his injuries as supporting Moore's attack on the war and the president.[52]

If the judge rules that the words *are capable* of a defamatory meaning, the fact finder— the jury, if there is one, or the judge—then must determine whether the words *in fact convey* a defamatory meaning. For example, when the superintendent of the sewer department for the small town of Abington, Mass., was terminated because he allegedly used town computers for personal business, he sued the local newspaper for stories about his firing. Town officials said they found pictures of nude and scantily clad women and other sexually suggestive subject matter on the computers. The newspaper reported that "pornography" was found on the computers. The Massachusetts Court of Appeals ruled that, as a matter of law, charges that the

---

50. Cohen, "Use of Real Name."
51. *Budget Termite & Pest Control* v. *Bousquet*, 811 A. 2d 1169 (2002).
52. *Damon* v. *Moore* 520 F. 3d 98 (2008).

plaintiff had stored "pornography" on the town computers would be defamatory. But it said a jury would have to decide whether the images stored on the computers were really "pornography," as that term is commonly understood.[53]

Innuendo as opposed to a flat assertion can be defamatory. Read the following actual news item from the Boston Record:

> The Veterans Hospital here suspected that 39-year-old George M. Perry of North Truro, whose death is being probed by federal and state authorities, was suffering from chronic arsenic poisoning.
>
> State police said the body of Perry, and of his brother, Arthur, who is buried near him, would probably be exhumed from St. Peter's Cemetery in Provincetown.
>
> George Perry died in the VA hospital last June 9, forty-eight hours after his tenth admission there. . . . His brother, who lived in Connecticut and spent two days here during George's funeral, died approximately a month later. About two months later, in September, George's mother-in-law, seventy-four-year-old Mrs. Mary F. Mott, who had come to live with her daughter, died too. Her remains were cremated.

While the story lacked a good deal in journalistic clarity, it didn't take a terribly insightful reader to understand what the reporter was trying to suggest. Mrs. Perry murdered her husband, her brother-in-law, and her mother. The insinuations are that Arthur died after visiting the plaintiff's home and that the mother had "died too." Isn't it too bad that her remains were cremated? This story cost the Hearst Corporation, publishers of the Boston Record, $25,000.[54]

A libel suit cannot be based on an isolated phrase wrenched out of context. The article as a whole must be considered. A story about baseball's legendary base stealer, Ricky Henderson, might contain the sentence "Henderson might be the best thief of all time," referring to his prowess as a base-stealer. Henderson cannot sue on the basis of that single sentence. The story itself makes it clear the kind of thievery the writer is discussing. Nevertheless, a libelous remark in a headline—even though it is cleared up in the story that follows—may be the basis for a libel suit.

One week after O.J. Simpson was acquitted of the criminal charge of murdering his wife and her companion the National Examiner carried a headline on its cover, "Cops Think Kato Did It—He fears they will want him for perjury, pals say." The story appeared on page 17 and carried the headline, "Kato Kaelin. . . . Cops Think He Did It." The story said the police were trying to prove that when Kaelin testified at Simpson's trial, he lied under oath, that he committed perjury. In his libel suit Kaelin argued that the headlines for the story suggested he was a suspect in the murders. Attorneys for the National Examiner said no, that was not what was intended. The word "it" meant perjury. Judges on the 9th U.S. Circuit Court of Appeals ruled that under California law the meaning of the publication must be measured by the effect it would have on the mind of the average reader, and in this case it was highly likely that an average, reasonable reader might conclude that the word "it" referred to murder.[55] Kaelin and the Examiner settled this suit in October 1999.

---

53. *Howell* v. *Enterprise Publishing Co.*, 893 N.E. 2d 1270 (2008).
54. *Perry* v. *Hearst Corp.*, 334 F. 2d 800 (1964).
55. *Kaelin* v. *Globe Communications Corp.*, 162 F. 3d 1036 (1998).

The Indiana Supreme Court was confronted with a situation in which a restaurant owner argued that a newspaper headline defamed his establishment. The court adopted the rule that if a headline fairly indicates the substance of an otherwise accurate article, the headline is not defamatory. In this case a county health inspector reported that there was evidence of roaches and rodents in the restaurant. The headline in the Ft. Wayne Journal Gazette stated: "Health board shuts doors of Bandido's. Inspectors find rats, roaches at local eatery." The state high court ruled that the headline was not an accurate indication of the article, because it contained the word "rats," and the story only referred to "rodents." Every rat is a rodent, the court ruled, but not every rodent is a rat.[56]

Factual assertions can obviously be the basis of a libel suit. Can a statement of opinion be defamatory? Well, that depends. If the question is, Can an opinion lower someone's reputation? which is the definition of defamation, the answer is yes, an opinion can be defamatory. But if the question is, Can a defamatory opinion be the basis for a libel suit? The answer is probably no. American courts have ruled on numerous occasions that pure opinion is protected by the First Amendment.[57] A plaintiff cannot successfully sue for libel based on a statement that is pure opinion. Why? Because pure opinion cannot be proved to be true or false—it is simply an opinion. For example, "I think Brenda Baylor is a stupid jerk." Even though this comment might lower Brenda's reputation in the eyes of the community, how can you prove or disprove that someone is a stupid jerk? Without proof of falsity, the libel suit fails. So pure opinion is not a problem. But unfortunately, courts frequently have a devil of a time determining what is and what is not pure opinion. Clearly, an opinion statement that contains a false fact can be libelous because of the false fact. "I think Brenda Baylor is a stupid jerk. You know, she scored only 150 on her SAT test." The second sentence is a factual assertion and if it is false, it could surely support a claim of libel. But other kinds of statements are not so clear. "Emissions from the Acme Smelter are harming the environment." Is that a statement of fact or an opinion? Some people might believe that any emission from a smokestack harms the environment. But Acme might be in full compliance with Environmental Protection Agency rules and will argue its emissions are safe. So it depends. This topic is explored more fully on pages 223–229. Suffice to say for this discussion, opinion statements can harm a person's reputation and are therefore defamatory. But if such statements are free of false and libelous facts, they cannot sustain a defamation lawsuit.

Although there is no space in this book for a catalog of defamatory words, an outline of the most common categories of problem words, words to which writers and editors need to pay special attention, is feasible.

Crime

Imputations of criminal behavior are responsible for a great many libel suits. Saying someone has done something illegal—from jaywalking to murder—is libelous. The use of the word "alleged" in these cases is often of little help. The meaning of the word "alleged" is "to be declared or asserted to be as described." An alleged murderer is someone who has been declared or asserted to be a murderer. But by whom? If the state has charged Jones with murder, the state has alleged that he is a murderer. If that is the case, a reporter should say so:

---

56. *Journal-Gazette Company* v. *Bandido's Inc.*, 712 N.E. 2d 446 (1999).
57. See, for example, *Milkovich* v. *Lorain Journal Co.*, 110 S. Ct. 2695 (1991).

"Jones, who has been charged with murder" rather than simply, "the alleged murderer Jones." But if Jones is merely being questioned in connection with the murder, he is not an alleged murderer, he is an alleged suspect. To call him an alleged murderer is inaccurate and libelous. The best guide for the reporter is this: Report what you know to be true. If Jones is being questioned as a suspect, say that. If police consider him a suspect, say that. Take the word "alleged" and put it in the circular file next to your desk.

Sexual References

Statements that a woman is unchaste, is sleeping with a man to whom she is not married, has been raped, or is just promiscuous can be defamatory. A 2003 issue of Boston Magazine carried a story titled "The Mating Habits of the Suburban High School Teenager." The thrust of the article was that teenagers in the Boston area have become more sexually promiscuous in the last decade. The article was illustrated with a photograph of Stacey Stanton and four other teenagers. In small type on the first page of the article was the following disclaimer:

> The photos on these pages are from an award-winning five-year project on teen sexuality taken by photo journalist Dan Habib. The individuals pictured are unrelated to the people or events described in this story. The names of the teenagers interviewed for this story have been changed.

Stanton sued for libel, alleging that by juxtaposing her photo and the text in the article, the magazine insinuated that she was engaged in the promiscuous behavior described in the article. The trial court ruled against the plaintiff, saying that the disclaimer negated this interpretation. But the 1st U.S. Court of Appeals reversed this ruling, saying that the type in the disclaimer was so small that it might be overlooked by readers, or a reader might just look at the first sentence, describing where the photos came from, and ignore the second and third sentences. The lawsuit was allowed to proceed. And a U.S. District Court ruled in 2006 that allegations that a woman was using her position in the media to meet and engage in sexual relations with powerful and prestigious men to advance her career and social status was defamatory.[58]

The law traditionally has been less protective of men in this regard, but there are indications that this might be changing. A young male model sued the publishers of gay and lesbian publications for including his photo in advertising for "Lust," a collection of photographs of naked, sexually aroused men engaged in explicit sex acts. The defendant was alone in the photo and was clothed from the waist down, but he argued that the use of the photo in advertising for such a publication suggests that he is sexually promiscuous. The defendants tried to argue that even if the use of the photo did imply sexual promiscuity, this was not a defamatory statement when made about a man rather than a woman. The Appellate Division of the New York Supreme Court disagreed, stating that "the notion that while the imputation of sexual immorality to a woman is defamatory per se, but is not so with respect to a man, has no place in modern jurisprudence. Such a distinction, having its basis in gender-based classification— would violate constitutional precepts."[59]

---

58. *Stanton* v. *Metro Corp.*, 438 F. 3d 119 (2006); and *Benz* v. *Washington Newspaper Publishing Co. LLC*, 34 M.L.R. 2368 (2006).
59. *Rejent* v. *Liberation Publications, Inc.*, 197 A.D. 2d 240 (1994).

Comments about other kinds of sexual behavior are also sensitive, but as Americans seem to be developing a more open mind regarding sexual behavior, the law is changing. Twenty-five years ago any allegation that a man was gay or a woman was a lesbian was defamatory per se.[60] There are surely courts that would still abide by that rule today. But many courts have taken a different position. A federal court in Massachusetts ruled in mid-2004 that an accusation that an individual is gay no longer imputes criminal conduct and, therefore, cannot be the basis for a claim of libel per se. The plaintiff in the case argued that some people in the community believe that homosexuals are less reputable than heterosexuals and cited laws against gay marriage to support his case. The court rejected this argument, noting that in the past, statements misidentifying whites as blacks were also considered defamatory, but not so today.[61]

Personal Habits

Material about the personal habits of an individual need to be carefully screened. To raise questions about an individual's honesty, integrity or financial responsibility can be dangerous. Comments about consumption of alcohol or drugs can also cause problems. Libel law has traditionally protected people from false assertions that they have a contagious disease. Such an allegation can cause friends and acquaintances to shun the supposed victim because they don't want to be infected by the disease themselves. This is not a common libel problem today. But it is a problem to suggest that someone suffers from a medical condition that implies, for example, sexual promiscuity or unsavory behavior on the part of the victim. The Nebraska Supreme Court in 1990 sustained a jury award of $23,350 to a Springfield, Neb., man who was falsely accused of having AIDS. This was a slander suit; it resulted when a prominent woman in a small town began spreading rumors about the plaintiff.[62] Finally, comments about an individual's personal religious faith ("She doesn't live up to the teachings of her church"), patriotism or political activities have also generated libel actions.

Ridicule

A person can be libeled by ridicule. Not all humorous stories about someone are necessarily defamatory; only those in which the subject of the story is made to appear "uncommonly foolish" tend to be dangerous. Newspapers are commonly victimized by false obituaries. At times the "deceased" has brought a libel suit in response to such a publication, but the courts have consistently ruled that to say someone has died is not defamatory; it does not lower that person's reputation. But once a New England newspaper ridiculed a man by saying he was so thrifty that he built his own casket and dug his own grave. This story made the man appear to be foolish or unnatural.[63]

---

60. *Gray* v. *Press Communications LLC*, 775 A. 2d 678 (2001).
61. *Albright* v. *Morton*, 321 F. Supp. 2d 130 (2004). See also *Donovan* v. *Fiumara*, 114 N.C. App. 524 (1994); *Miles* v. *National Enquirer*, 38 F. Supp. 2d 1226 (1999); and *Amrak Productions Inc.* v. *Morton,* 33 M.L.R. 1891 (2005).
62. Robbins, "A Rumor of AIDS."
63. *Powers* v. *Durgin-Snow Publishing Co.*, 144 A. 2d 294 (1958).

Business Reputation

Libel law probably goes furthest in protecting people in their business and occupations. Any comment that injures people's ability to conduct a business, harms them in their job or makes it more difficult for them to pursue their occupation is generally defamatory. And businesspeople are generally more likely to sue. They tend to be more acquainted with law and more comfortable initiating a legal suit. There are some interesting quirks in libel law as it relates to comments about the way an individual does business. To report that a businessperson or professional person has made an error is not always defamatory. Business and professional people are not expected to be perfect. Everyone makes a mistake now and then. A story, for example, that suggests a physician has misdiagnosed a case or that a real estate developer has botched a deal may not be considered defamatory under what is called the **single mistake rule.** The community would not think less of a doctor or businessperson who made a single error, the reasoning goes. Hence, the statement is not defamatory. Stories that suggest a pattern of incompetence, that go beyond asserting a single error, are defamatory, however.[64] The single mistake rule should not be used as an excuse for sloppy reporting, but it can come in handy if an error is inadvertently made.

Corporations that believe their credit has been damaged or their reputation has been harmed can do exactly what an individual plaintiff can do and sue for this injury. The list of kinds of defamatory accusations is long. Assertions that a company is involved in illegal business or that it fails to pay its bills on time or that it deliberately manufactures unsafe products or that it is trying to break a union are all libelous. The law, however, does not hold a public business responsible for the bad behavior of its customers. The owners of a bar in Ohio sued a local newspaper for headlines calling an assault in a municipal parking lot adjacent to the bar a "bar beating," an "assault at bar." But the stories explained where the attack took place, and did not accuse the plaintiffs of any wrongdoing, the court ruled.[65] A suggestion that the proprietor of a public business encourages rowdy behavior, or tolerates fighting, or permits drug deals to be made is a different matter. In these cases the story does reflect on the behavior of the owner and would be libelous.

Criticism of a Product

Criticism of a product falls into a different legal category, called "disparagement of property." Such criticism is often called **trade libel,** but it is not really libel at all. What is the difference between libeling a business and disparaging a product?

Criticism of a product falls into a different legal category, called "disparagement of property."

- ▮ Trade libel, or product disparagement, focuses on the product itself. "Viking Runabout automobiles continually stall during a rainstorm." That is an attack on the product.
- ▮ A libel of a business tends to focus on the alleged failings of the people who operate the business. "Viking Runabout automobiles continually stall during a rainstorm. The manufacturer, in order to save a few dollars, did not shield the electrical system properly and water leaks in at alarming levels, causing a short circuit." This is an attack on the company as well as the product.

64. *Bowes* v. *Magna Concepts, Inc.*, 561 N.Y.S. 2d 16 (1990); see also *Sermidi* v. *Battistotti*, 27 M.L.R. 2523 (1999).
65. *BMT Management LLC* v. *Sandusky Newspapers Inc.*, 37 M.L.R. 1954 (2009).

To win a trade libel suit the plaintiff must prove three things.

1. The plaintiff must show that the statements made about the products are false. This can be difficult. Organizations that test products and then publish their results tend to be very careful in the way they present their findings. Rather than report that the Viking Runabouts stall in a rainstorm, the story will usually say the Viking Runabout that was tested stalled. Viking may be able to prove that most of its Runabouts run properly; it is difficult to dispute that one car, the one tested, failed to run correctly.

2. The plaintiff must show specific monetary loss because of the false comments about the product. Courts insist on fairly precise dollars-and-cents losses from canceled orders, for example, or a drop in sales.

3. The plaintiff must show that the false comments about the product were motivated either by ill will and bad feelings, or by what the law calls actual malice. Actual malice, which is defined more completely on pages 191–196, means that the defendant knew that the statements about the product were false, or exhibited reckless disregard for the truth in making the comments.

This is a difficult challenge for the plaintiff. Even proving that the statements were false is not always easy. For example, in 1989 the television program "60 Minutes" suggested that apples grown in Washington state were unsafe because they had been treated with a chemical called Alar, which some scientists contend causes an increased risk of cancer, especially to children. Farmers in the state sued CBS and others for $100 million, alleging among other things product disparagement, or trade libel. But the case came to an abrupt ending four years later when a U.S. District Court granted the network's motion for a summary judgment, ruling that the plaintiffs in the case could not possibly prove that the statements were false. The apple growers contended that three statements made in the broadcast were false.

1. Daminozide (the active ingredient in Alar) is the most potent cancer-causing agent in our food supply.

2. Daminozide poses an imminent hazard and unacceptable cancer risk.

3. Daminozide is most harmful to children.

Judge Nielsen said that there was substantial debate within the scientific community about the potential harm caused by daminozide. CBS presented evidence that the Environmental Protection Agency considers daminozide to be among the most carcinogenic synthetic pesticides and that ingesting a carcinogen at any time could create the hazard of suffering a cancer in the future. But, the judge said, researchers have sharp differences of opinion regarding the potential harm that daminozide might cause to children. If science is seemingly in disagreement about the danger posed by this chemical, Judge Nielsen said, how did the plaintiffs think they were going to prove that these allegations were false?[66] The 9th U.S. Circuit Court of Appeals upheld this decision in 1995.[67]

---

66. *Auvil* v. *CBS "60 Minutes,"* 836 F. Supp. 740 (1993).
67. *Auvil* v. *CBS "60 Minutes,"* 67 F. 3d 816 (1995).

Banks, Insurance Companies and Vegetables

Many states have adopted statutes aimed at protecting the reputations of specific kinds of businesses. Banks and insurance companies in many jurisdictions are shielded by special statutes designed to protect them from attacks on their fiscal integrity. If successful, such an attack could turn customers against these businesses and destroy them quite easily. In recent years many states have adopted statutes that outlaw publication of intentional lies about the fruits and vegetables grown in the state. These so-called veggie hate laws are aimed at preventing the kind of damage suffered by Washington apple growers because of the Alar controversy noted earlier. These laws generally give farmers and growers a cause of action to sue anyone who makes a statement about the health risks of a particular food product that is not based on "verifiable fact or scientific or other reliable evidence." Some of these laws also shift the burden of proving truth or falsity from the plaintiff to the defendant. Although such laws as these seem odd, they nevertheless exist and could result in legal woes for the careless journalist.

Talk show producer and host Oprah Winfrey was sued in 1998 by Texas cattle ranchers under that state's False Disparagement of Perishable Food Products Act. A guest on Winfrey's talk show had alleged that thousands of head of U.S. cattle were infected with bovine spongiform encephalopathy, the so-called mad cow disease, prompting the talk show host to declare that she was giving up eating hamburgers. Cattle prices dropped precipitously after the broadcast, and the ranchers sought millions of dollars in damages. Experts who viewed the case as the first important test of the constitutionality of the veggie hate laws were disappointed when U.S. District Judge Mary Lou Robinson ruled that the case could not proceed under the Texas law because the plaintiffs had not proved that cattle are "perishable food" as defined by the statute, or that "knowingly false" statements had been made, a requirement under the Texas law.[68] The 5th U.S. Circuit Court of Appeals affirmed the lower-court decision, but solely on the grounds that no knowingly false statements had been made about the cattle.[69]

FALSITY

The fourth requirement the plaintiff must meet to sustain a libel suit is proof of falsity. But as previously noted, not every plaintiff must meet this requirement.

The world of libel plaintiffs is divided into two groups, public people and private people. A public person is a government official, an elected officer, someone who is leading a public crusade, a prominent entertainer, a visible religious or business leader. A private person is someone who is not a public person. As you will soon see, the law makes it far more difficult for a public person, as opposed to a private person, to win a libel suit.

In every instance a public-person plaintiff must prove that the libelous remarks are not truthful. But the Supreme Court has ruled that a private-person plaintiff must prove the falsity of the libelous statements only when the subject of the statement is a matter of public concern.[70] What is a matter of public concern? The Supreme Court has not given a definition but, in another case, noted that whether a statement dealt with a matter of public concern must

---

68. *Texas Beef Group* v. *Winfrey*, 11 F. Supp. 2d 858 (1998).
69. *Texas Beef Group* v. *Winfrey*, 201 F. 3d 680 (2000).
70. *Philadelphia Newspapers, Inc.* v. *Hepps*, 475 U.S. 767 (1986).

be determined on the basis of the statement's "content, form and context."[71] Not a very clear definition.

Over time, courts will flesh out the definition of a "matter of public concern." This issue has simply not arisen often enough in the past 25 years for the courts to provide much meaningful insight on it. Most authorities will argue that when a solid definition emerges, it will be one that is broadly based and include most of what is published in mainstream newspapers and magazines, and what is aired on television or radio or what is carried on the Internet. It could be argued that when the editor at a publication or broadcasting station, which is aiming to attract and please a large, diverse audience, selects an item to report, that in itself is evidence that the content of the item is a matter of public concern. But no court has yet gone this far.

Most plaintiffs, then, must prove that the defamatory material is false. In those few instances when a private person sues for a story that is not a matter of public concern, the defendant must prove that the material is truthful. How does one prove falsity or truth?

The first rule of proving truth or falsity is that the evidence presented in court must go to the heart of the libelous charge.

The first rule of proving truth or falsity is that the evidence presented in court must go to the heart of the libelous charge. The proof must be direct and explicit. If there is conflicting evidence, the fact finder—the judge or the jury—will decide who is telling the truth. Every word of a defamatory charge need not be truthful, only the part that carries the gist or the sting of the libel.

In other words, isolate the words in the story or report that cause the harm to the reputation. Are these words true or false? Imagine that ace radio reporter Hardley Wright tells his listeners that Mavis Martin was arrested on Sunday evening when she was apprehended driving a stolen Toyota Camry on Marshall Street. The true story is that Martin was arrested Saturday night while driving a stolen Honda Accord on Baker Avenue. Is that story true or false as far as the libel case is concerned? It's true. The libelous words, the words that harm the reputation, are those that say Martin was arrested for driving a stolen car. Everything else is wrong, but the libelous sting was correctly reported.

An author wrote a book in which she recounted events in her stepsister's life. She wrote that while the girl was hitchhiking to California she got picked up and then was raped by the driver. Actually the girl was raped while in high school when she was living in a house with two men she had met at a party. The sting was the rape allegation and that was true, despite the other errors.[72] A television station in Mississippi reported that a man was arrested in connection with a theft ring. Police had charged him only with receiving stolen property. He sued, arguing that the television report made it sound as though he had organized the theft ring or that he was distributing stolen goods. The federal court disagreed. The libelous sting in the story was that he was arrested in connection with a theft ring—and that was true.[73] Plaintiffs often try to get courts to read more into a story than there is in order to prove falsity. A doctor in Texas argued that when a television station reported she was being investigated because of allegations that she took a patient off life support without informing the family, it was charging her with murdering a patient. (Taking someone off life support in this situation is a violation of state law, but is not considered murder.) But the court disagreed that the story accused the plaintiff of intentionally murdering patients.

71. *Dun & Bradstreet* v. *Greenmoss*, 472 U.S. 749 (1985).
72. *Wingard* v. *Hall*, 34 M.L.R. 1537 (2006).
73. *Green* v. *Media General Operations*, 34 M.L.R. 1898 (2006).

What the TV station reported was true.[74] Finally, the Michigan Court of Appeals overturned a lower-court ruling that favored a former congresswoman who claimed she was misquoted in a newspaper story. The former legislator said in an interview that she didn't believe all white people were intolerant. "That's why I love the individuals, but I don't like the race." The news report quoted the plaintiff as saying "I hate the race." The trial court agreed that the word "hate" meant something different from the words "don't like." But the appellate court disagreed, saying the words had about the same meaning. The libelous sting was true.[75]

Courts give libel defendants considerable leeway when evaluating the truth or falsity of a statement. But not all errors will be tolerated. At times even what might be regarded as a detail will result in a verdict for the plaintiff if it can be proved to be false. A firefighter in Des Moines, Iowa, was fired because, fire officials said, he had failed to pass a written emergency medical technician exam, a requirement to hold the job. The fire chief told reporters that the man had a reading problem. Despite undergoing tutoring at taxpayers' expense, he was still capable of reading at only the third-grade level. The defendants in the press asked that the case be dismissed because it was substantially true. But the court refused, and the Iowa Supreme Court affirmed this decision. There were two errors in the story, perhaps only details, but they carried a libelous sting. First, the firefighter had himself paid a substantial portion of the cost of the tutoring. More important, tests showed he read at a level comparable with the lower one-third of community college students, not a third-grader. The story was not substantially true.[76]

Reporters must also remember that a jury in a libel suit will determine the truth or falsity of a story based on what the story said, not what the reporter meant. ABC was sued by the maker of a garbage recycling machine. Lundell Manufacturing sold the $3 million machine to a county in Georgia. After using the machine for a year or so, some people in the county said that the new machine had not solved the garbage problem. An ABC "World News Tonight" story included these comments:

> In this south Georgia county of tobacco farms and pecan groves taxpayers
> are angry that they are stuck with a three million dollar debt for this gar-
> bage recycling machine that they never approved and does not work.

Network attorneys argued that the reporter meant that the machine does not work in the larger sense, that it doesn't solve the county's garbage problem. But a jury agreed with the plaintiff instead and said that they interpreted the comment to mean that the garbage recycling machine did not work, that it was defective. In 1996 the 8th U.S. Circuit Court of Appeals upheld the more than $1 million jury award and ruled that a jury could conclude that the network's statement about the machine was false.[77]

How does the court evaluate the truth of the charge? The jury does this with guidance from the judge. The jurors are presented with both the libelous untruthful statement about the plaintiff and the truth about the plaintiff. The untruthful statement will leave a certain impression about the plaintiff in the jurors' minds. Does learning the truthful statement change that impression? For example, a television station refers to Hal Jones as a wife beater. Jurors gain an impression of Jones based on that statement. In truth, Jones struck his wife only once, during an argument,

---

74. *Grotti* v. *Belo Corp.*, 34 M.L.R. 1969 (2006).

75. *Collins* v. *Detroit Free Press*, 627 N.W. 2d 5 (2001).

76. *Jones* v. *Palmer Communications, Inc.*, 440 N.W. 2d 884 (1989).

77. *Lundell Manufacturing Co.* v. *ABC Inc.*, 98 F. 3d 351 (1996).

after she threw a coffee pot at him. Does the truth leave a different impression of Jones in the jurors' minds? One court said that "a workable test of truth is whether the libel as published would have a different effect on the mind of the reader from that which the pleaded truth would have produced."[78]

Even if a story contains nothing but truthful statements it still might be regarded as false if important facts are left out and the story leaves a false impression.

Even if a story contains nothing but truthful statements it still might be regarded as false if important facts are left out and the story leaves a false impression. Some courts have called this defamation by implication. A South Carolina driver accidentally struck and injured the police chief of Eastover, S.C. She pleaded guilty to driving too fast for road conditions. A year later the police chief died and in two stories the newspaper repeated the account of the traffic accident, adding that the woman would not face additional charges despite the chief's death. Everything in both stories was true, but the newspaper did not report that the police chief died from cancer. Readers could easily conclude that he had died from injuries sustained in the accident, and this would be false, the South Carolina Court of Appeals concluded.[79] In 2007 the Iowa Supreme Court said that defamation by implication was recognized in that state. However, a year earlier the Ohio Court of Appeals ruled false innuendo emanating from accurate statements—defamation by implication—was not actionable under Ohio libel law.[80]

One more point should be stressed about truth and falsity. Correctly quoting someone or accurately reporting what someone else has said does not necessarily constitute publishing a truthful statement. Imagine that John Smith tells a reporter that the police chief changes arrest records of certain prisoners to simplify their getting bail and winning acquittal. This charge, attributed to John Smith, is contained in the reporter's story, which is subsequently published. The police chief sues for libel. It is not sufficient for the reporter to prove merely that the statement in the story was an accurate account of what Smith said. Even if the reporter's story contained an exact duplicate of Smith's charge, truth can be sustained only by proving the substance of the charge, that the police chief has altered arrest records. It is the truth of the libelous charge that is at issue, not merely the accuracy of the quote in the story. Accuracy, then, is not always the same thing as truth.

The initial burden in the libel suit rests with the plaintiff, who must prove five important elements: that the defamation was published, that it was of and concerning the plaintiff, that the words were defamatory, that the allegations were false and that the defendant was at fault in causing this legal harm. The first four elements have been discussed in this chapter. Proving fault, the most complicated of the five elements, is the subject of Chapter 5.

SUMMARY

A plaintiff in a libel suit must first prove that the defamatory material was published; that is, that one additional person besides the plaintiff and the defendant has seen the material. The plaintiff must next show that the libel is of and concerning him or her. An individual can be identified for purposes of a libel suit by a name, nickname, photograph or even through a report

78. *Fleckstein* v. *Friedman*, 195 N.E. 537 (1934).
79. *Richardson* v. *State-Record Co.*, 499 S.E. 2d 822 (1998).
80. *Stevens* v. *Iowa Newspapers Inc.*, 35 M.L.R. 1385 (2007); and *Stohlman* v. *WJW-TV, Inc.*, 35 M.L.R. 1103 (2006).

of circumstances. Statements made about a very large group of people cannot be used as the basis for a libel suit for a single member of that group. However, if the group is smaller, individual members of the group may be able to sue for comments made about the entire group. The plaintiff must also prove that the words in the offensive statement are defamatory, that they lower his or her reputation. The most common kinds of defamatory statements contain allegations about criminal acts or sexual impropriety, include comments about personal habits or characteristics, or reflect on the plaintiff's patriotism, political beliefs or competence and qualifications in a business or occupation. Corporations or other businesses can be defamed, and the manufacturer of a product can sue, with great difficulty, for product disparagement. In lawsuits against the mass media the plaintiff normally must prove that the damaging statements are false. The evidence presented in court must go to the heart of the libelous charge; the gist or sting of the libel must be false. Minor errors, unless they relate directly to the gist of the libel, will not usually result in a finding of falsity. The test of falsity is whether the proven truth leaves a different impression of the plaintiff in the minds of the jury than the impression created by the defamatory falsehood.

BIBLIOGRAPHY

American Law Institute. *Restatement of the Law of Torts*. 2nd ed. Philadelphia: American Law Institute, 1975.

Ashley, Paul. *Say It Safely*. 5th ed. Seattle: University of Washington Press, 1976.

Belluck, Pam. "Boston Herald Is Ordered to Pay Judge $2 Million for Libel." *The New York Times*, 19 February 2005, A8.

Bezanson, Randall P., Gilbert Cranberg, and John Soloski. *Libel Law and the Press*. New York: The Free Press, 1987.

Carvajal, Doreen. "Libel Wrangle Over Miliken Book Drags On." *The New York Times*, 28 June 1999, C1.

Cohen, Roger. "Suit Over Novel's Use of Real Name Is Dismissed." *The New York Times*, 19 July 1991.

Dill, Barbara. "Libel Law Doesn't Work, But Can It Be Fixed?" In *At What Price? Libel Law and Freedom of the Press*, by Martin London and Barbara Dill. New York: Twentieth Century Fund Press, 1993.

Hakim, Danny. "Suzuki Resolves a Dispute with a Consumer Magazine." *The New York Times*, 9 June 2004, C6.

Libel Law: A Report of the Libel Reform Project. Washington, D.C.: The Annenberg Washington Program, 1988.

Liptak, Adam. "A Judge at the Plaintiff's Table Tips the Scales. *The New York Times*, 25 June 2007, A12.

Media Law Resource Center. MLRC 2005 Report on Trials and Damages. Bulletin 2005 No. 1 (February 2005).

Moscov, Jim. "Truth, Justice and the American Tort." *Editor & Publisher*, 27 November 2000, p. 16.

Pfanner, Eric. "A Fight to Protect Americans From British Libel Law." *The New York Times,* 25 May 2009, B3.

Phelps, Robert, and Douglas Hamilton. *Libel.* New York: Macmillan, 1966.

Pring, George. "SLAPPs: Strategic Lawsuits Against Public Participation." *Pace Environmental Law Review*, Fall 1989, 8.

———, and Penelope Canan. "Strategic Lawsuits Against Public Participation." *Social Problems* 35 (1988): 506.

Prosser, William L. *Handbook of the Law of Torts.* St. Paul: West Publishing, 1963.

Robbins, William. "A Rumor of AIDS, a Slander Suit." *The New York Times*, 23 July 1990.

Seelye, Katherine. "Jury Finds That Columnist Acted with Malice and Awards Judge $7 Million." *The New York Times,* 15 November 2006, A18.

Smolla, Rodney A. "Dun & Bradstreet, Hepps, and Liberty Lobby: A New Analytic Primer on the Future Course of Defamation." *Georgetown Law Journal* 75 (1987): 1519.

Story, Louise. "Can a Sandwich Be Slandered? "*The New York Times*, 29 January 2008, C1.

Yankwich, Leon R. *It's Libel or Contempt If You Print It.* Los Angeles: Parker & Sons Publications, 1950.

CHAPTER 5

Libel

PROOF OF FAULT

In 1964, for the first time, the U.S. Supreme Court ruled that a libel plaintiff was required to show that a defendant had been at fault when the defamatory material was published. Until that time, civil libel law had been governed by what is known as the doctrine of strict liability. Under this doctrine a libel defendant was responsible for harming a plaintiff regardless of how cautious and careful he or she had been in preparing and publishing or broadcasting the story. This ruling changed the face of libel law. What had been a relatively simple tort became a complex legal morass when it was infused with First Amendment considerations. This chapter outlines the two basic considerations relevant to fault:

   Who is the plaintiff?

   How was the story or material processed or prepared?

NEW YORK TIMES v. SULLIVAN

A difficult and often violent struggle for civil rights was taking place in much of the Deep South in the late 1950s and early 1960s. Blacks, often accompanied by white civil rights workers, used various acts of nonviolent civil disobedience to challenge a wide range of voting, accommodation and education laws that had left them as second-class citizens. Network television news was still in its early adolescence in this era; NBC and CBS carried only 15 minutes of news each night. The story of the civil rights movement was carried throughout the nation via a handful of prestigious and frequently liberal newspapers, especially The New York Times. Segregationist leaders in the South hated these newspapers, which each day carried stories and pictures of another peaceful civil rights protest that had been met with violence or some other illegal act by city, county or state officials or by angry southern citizens.

On March 29, 1960, the Times carried a full-page editorial-advertisement titled "Heed Their Rising Voices." The ad was placed by an ad hoc coalition of civil rights leaders called the "Committee to Defend Martin Luther King and the Struggle for Freedom in the South." The text of the ad leveled charges against public officials in the South who, the committee contended, had used violence and illegal tactics to try to quell the peaceful civil rights struggle. The basic thrust of the charges contained in the advertisement was true; but the ad was filled with small, factual errors.* Several public officials in Alabama brought suit against the newspaper. The first case to go to trial was one brought by Montgomery, Ala., police commissioner L.B. Sullivan, who sought $500,000 in damages for false and defamatory statements about the conduct of the Montgomery police department.† Sullivan was never named in the ad but contended that comments about the behavior of the police reflected on him. A trial court ruled on behalf of Sullivan, and his $500,000 damage award was upheld by the Alabama Supreme Court. This was despite the fact that only 35 copies of the offending issue of The New York Times were circulated in Montgomery County.

The U.S. Supreme Court unanimously reversed the decision, ruling that Sullivan could not recover damages in this case unless he proved that The New York Times published the false and defamatory advertisement knowing it was false, or that the paper exhibited reckless disregard for the truth when it printed the material.[1] That is, the Montgomery police commissioner had to show that the newspaper had actually lied when it printed the ad (knowledge of falsity), or that the persons who published the ad (both the members of the committee and the members of the newspaper's staff) had been extraordinarily careless by not examining the charges made in the statement much more carefully (reckless disregard for the truth). Justice William Brennan labeled these two elements "actual malice"; proof of knowledge of falsity or proof of reckless disregard for the truth was proof of actual malice. The language in the court's opinion extended the ruling in this case to all people whom the court called **public officials.** All public officials

---

*For example, the ad claimed that when students at Alabama State College staged a protest, armed police "ringed" the campus. Police were at the protest, but they did not ring the campus. When students refused to register for classes as a protest, the dining hall was padlocked, the ad claimed. In fact, only a small number of students without valid meal tickets were turned away from the dining hall.
†Compared with the multimillion-dollar damage awards sought today, $500,000 doesn't sound like much. But it was a staggering amount half a century ago.
1. *New York Times Co.* v. *Sullivan*, 376 U.S. 254 (1964).

Associate Justice William Brennan, the author of the Supreme Court decision in New York Times *v.* Sullivan *in 1964 and many other notable First Amendment rulings.*

© AP/Wide World Photos

who sought to win a libel suit based on defamatory allegations about how they did their jobs or whether they were fit to hold those jobs henceforth would have to prove actual malice. Before examining the various elements in this new libel standard, let's look briefly at the rationale Brennan and his colleagues used to support this fundamental change in the law.

THE RATIONALE FOR THE RULING

■ **Stripped of its civil libel cover, this case was clearly one of seditious libel.** A government official was criticized for the way he handled his public office. The newspaper was punished for publishing this criticism. The issues that generated the court ruling and the penalty for the newspaper were really not much different from what occurred in prosecutions under the Alien and Sedition Acts of 1798 and the Espionage and Sedition Acts of 1917 and 1918. Rulings by the Supreme Court had sharply limited the government's power to use seditious libel to punish those who criticize it (see pages 53–56). What Sullivan and his co-plaintiffs were attempting to do was to resurrect sedition law via a civil libel action.

■ **The nation has a profound and long-standing national commitment to the principle that debate on public issues should be uninhibited, robust and wide**

open. Debate on public issues is a fundamental part of the democratic process. All citizens are encouraged to take part in this debate. In the heat of any discussion it is inevitable that erroneous statements will be made by the participants. Many people will be fearful of taking part in the debate if they think they might be sued for libel if they make a misstatement that harms someone's reputation. Whatever is added to the field of libel, wrote Justice Brennan, is taken away from the field of free debate. Freedom of expression, Brennan noted, needs breathing space to survive.[2]

Freedom of expression, Brennan noted, needs breathing space to survive.

■ **When public officials like Sullivan take a government post, they must expect that their work will be closely scrutinized and even criticized by the people they serve.** Officers of government have ample means to rebut this criticism. They usually have easy access to the press to deny allegations made against them, to give their side of the story, and to even verbally attack their critics. This kind of speech is also a part of the important debate within a democracy. Police commissioner Sullivan could have easily talked to reporters in Montgomery if he sought to publish the truth. Instead he chose to punish The New York Times.

The actual malice rule imposed on the law of libel by the Supreme Court was already a part of the law in a handful of states prior to the 1964 ruling in *New York Times* v. *Sullivan*. In the wake of the *Sullivan* decision, all state and federal courts had to follow this rule. By the end of the decade, the Supreme Court had extended the actual malice rule to people called **public figures.** People outside government frequently try to lead public debate on important issues. These people should not be any more immune to criticism and complaints than government officials, the court rationalized.[3] Public figures would also have to prove actual malice in order to sustain a successful libel suit. Finally, in 1974, the high court added the final element to the libel fault rule when it declared that even private persons, persons who are not part of government or who have not tried to influence public opinion, must prove that the mass medium was at fault when the libel was published or broadcast.[4] The state courts were given some freedom in this ruling to determine just what kind of fault the private party suing a mass medium must prove. Under the First Amendment the private-person plaintiff at least must prove that the mass media defendant failed to exercise reasonable care in preparing and transmitting the story, or was negligent, the high court said. But a state could ask that these plaintiffs prove even more to sustain their libel suits, the court added. The issue of the level of fault that the plaintiff must prove will be discussed in the second half of this chapter (see pages 188–201).*

Several words have been used in the past few pages that beg for fuller explanation. Who is a public official? Who is a public figure? How do you define negligence? How do you define actual malice? The next section of this chapter attempts to add flesh to these bones, to make these legal concepts come more alive. Before moving to that, let's briefly summarize the fault rules to this point.

---

*In 2006 Britain's highest court, the Law Lords, ruled that journalists in that nation have added protections in libel actions brought by public figures, as long as their reporting is responsible and in the public interest. This was the first time a European nation adopted a *Sullivan*-like libel rule.

2. *New York Times Co.* v. *Sullivan*, 376 U.S. 254 (1964).

3. *Curtis Publishing Co.* v. *Butts*, 388 U.S. 130 (1967).

4. *Gertz* v. *Robert Welch, Inc.*, 418 U.S. 323 (1974).

1. Private persons who sue the media for defamation must at least prove that the material was published through negligence. Negligence is defined in the law as the failure to exercise reasonable care.

2. Individuals who have been deemed to be public persons for purposes of a libel suit against a mass medium have to prove that the defendant exhibited actual malice when the material was published. Actual malice is defined in the law as publishing with the knowledge that the libelous assertion is false, or with reckless disregard for whether it is true or false.

PUBLIC PERSONS VERSUS PRIVATE PERSONS

All libel plaintiffs who sue the mass media must prove that the defendant in the case was at fault, that the publication or broadcast of the libelous material was not simply the result of an innocent error. Public officials and public figures have to prove a higher level of fault than do private individuals. But who are public officials and public figures in the eyes of the law? Before exploring this issue a brief caution is warranted. One of the problems in the law of libel is that courts have taken perfectly good words that most of us use daily and have attached a slightly different meaning to these words. Students need to exercise caution because of this. Most of us could probably agree on a general definition of a public figure, for example. But in libel law these words mean something different. What we need to remember is the legal definition of these words, not the common everyday definition.

WHO IS A PUBLIC OFFICIAL?

Two questions must be asked to determine whether a libel plaintiff should be considered a public official:

1. Who is this plaintiff—what kind of government job does he or she have? What is the **job description?**
2. What was the allegedly libelous story about? What is the **nature of the story?**

We will consider these questions separately.

Job Description

The kind of government job a person holds is one key to determining who is and who is not a public official for purposes of libel law. Let's start with three general rules:

1. Any person who is elected to public office, to even the most lowly public office, qualifies as a public official.
2. Individuals who are appointed to or hired for government jobs *may qualify* as public persons in a libel action. It depends on the nature of the job.
3. But not everyone who works for the government will be regarded as a public official.

Determining if a nonelected government employee should be considered a public official in a libel action is often troublesome for the courts. What lawyers like to call a bright-line rule doesn't exist. (When courts consistently rule the same way on a legal question lawyers often say a bright-line rule has been established. If, for example, in every instance the courts rule that a school teacher or a public works supervisor is a public official, this would be considered a bright-line rule.) Nevertheless, the Supreme Court has provided some useful guidance for the lower courts.

The Supreme Court has said:

> It is clear that the "public official" designation applies at the very least to those among the hierarchy of government employees **who have or appear to have to the public a substantial responsibility for or control over the conduct of governmental affairs** [emphasis added].[5]

Justice Brennan added that when a position in government has such apparent importance that the public has an independent interest in the qualifications and performance of the person who holds it, beyond the general public interest in the qualifications and performance of all government employees, the person in that position qualifies as a public official. While Brennan's remarks are fairly clear, let's try to translate a bit. Citizens are concerned that everyone who works for the government—from the clerk at the welfare office to the crossing guard outside the school to the person who reads the water meter—does his or her job efficiently and correctly. But some government employees have jobs that have responsibilities that go far beyond the responsibilities of the average government employee: people like the head of the city's welfare department, the individual in charge of school safety programs and the supervisor of the city water department. We have a special interest in their qualifications and how well they do their jobs. These people are likely to be counted as public officials.

Here are some examples of cases in which the public official designation has been an issue.

- A timber management and contracting officer in the Eldorado National Forest in California was deemed to be a public official by a U.S. Court of Appeals. ABC News had called the plaintiff a "bureaucrat who got away with a $25 million mistake" after he was accused of making serious errors in awarding 16 contracts for the sale of timber on federal lands. The appellate court said that his role in management of the sale of U.S. resources clearly marked him as one who had substantial responsibility for the administration of government matters.[6]

- The curator of marine mammals at the Minnesota Zoo was not a public official for the purposes of a libel suit based on reports that he had been negligent in the care of a Beluga whale that had become ill and had to be moved to another aquatic facility. The sick whale's plight was widely publicized in the Twin Cities, but the Minnesota appellate court ruled that even though there was an important public controversy, the curator simply did not have the substantial responsibility for the conduct of government affairs needed to designate him a public official. The Supreme Court had previously said the person must hold a position that invites public scrutiny of the person holding it, entirely apart from the scrutiny and discussion of the particular controversy that gave rise to the defamation. The public became interested in how the curator did his job only after the controversy regarding the whale began, the court said.[7]

---

5. *Rosenblatt* v. *Baer*, 383 U.S. 75 (1966).

6. *Baumback* v. *American Broadcasting Cos.*, 26 M.L.R. 2138 (1998).

7. *McDevitt* v. *Tilson*, 453 N.W. 2d 53 (1990).

- The Ohio Court of Appeals ruled that the chief of the criminal section of a city law department was a public official because of his responsibilities and the importance of his position in the eyes of the public.[8]

- A junior state social worker was ruled to be a public official because her job carried with it "duties and responsibilities affecting the lives, liberty, money or property of a citizen that may enhance or disrupt his enjoyment of life."[9] The rationale of looking at how certain government employees deal daily with the welfare or safety of people in the community has also been used to support a public official designation for many public school teachers and police officers.[10]

- In Washington state the administrator of a motor pool for a small county was declared to be a public official because he had the power to spend county funds without his supervisors' approval.[11]

- The secretary and chief examiner of the Public Safety Civil Service Commission in Seattle was a public official, a federal court ruled, because she supervised other employees, managed the application process for people seeking employment with both the police and fire departments, and supervised the testing process for all these applicants.[12]

- The city manager of a small Texas town was ruled to be a public official. "In his capacity as city manager, Sparks [the plaintiff] . . . wielded substantial responsibility for or control over the conduct of public affairs," the court said.[13]

The context in which the defamation occurs is often important. A planner with a state geological survey office might not normally hold a position that invites public scrutiny. But if this person is appointed by the governor to conduct a study of the feasibility of constructing a hazardous waste dump site near the state capital, this special assignment brings with it closer public scrutiny. In such a case a person who was not a public official might suddenly become one in terms of libel law.

To summarize, it is impossible to provide a nice, neat list of the kinds of jobs that elevate nonelected government employees to the status of public official. But some of the criteria to look for include the following:

- The level of responsibility the individual has. In other words, how important is the job?

- The kind of responsibility the person has. Police officers, teachers and social workers may be lower-level employees, but the way they do their jobs can have an important and immediate impact on people's lives.

- Does the individual have the authority to spend public money independently, without supervision?

---

8. *Scaccia* v. *Dayton Newspapers Inc.*, 30 M.L.R. 1172 (2001).
9. *Press* v. *Verran*, 589 S.W. 2d 435 (1978).
10. See, for example, *Soke* v. *The Plain Dealer*, 69 Ohio St. 3d 395 (1994); and *Clark* v. *Clark*, 21 M.L.R. 1650 (1993).
11. *Clawson* v. *Longview Publishing Co.*, 589 P. 2d 1223 (1979).
12. *Harris* v. *City of Seattle*, 315 F. Supp. 2d 1105 (2004).
13. *Sparks* v. *Reneau Publishing Inc.*, 35 M.L.R. 2185 (2007).

■ What is the nature of the person's job? The head of a task force to reorganize city employee health benefits and the head of the city's anti-terrorism task force might supervise the same number of workers, earn the same salary and be at the same city management level. But it is likely that the public will take a far greater interest in the qualifications of the anti-terrorism task force supervisor and the way she does her job than in the qualifications and competency of the person heading the employee benefits task force.

The Nature of the Story

Who the person is—the kind of job he or she holds—is an important criterion. But it is only half the test. Equally important is the nature of the story. What was the defamatory content about? Whether proof of actual malice will be required depends upon the focus of the libelous statement. If the statement concerns (1) *the manner in which the plaintiff conducts himself or herself in office—in other words, the way he or she does the job*—or (2) *the plaintiff's general fitness to hold that job*, then the plaintiff carries the burden of proving actual malice.

The first criterion relates to the plaintiff's official duties and focuses on matters directly related to public responsibilities. For example, in the Seattle Civil Service Commission case noted earlier, the allegations against the chief examiner focused on a trip she took to Las Vegas to attend a black public administrators conference. The television station said she spent little time in seminars and workshops during the trip, but considerable time at the gaming tables. The court ruled that the strong nexus between her position and the alleged false statements meant that the story directly related to the way she conducted herself on the job.[14]

But remember that public officials have private lives and not everything a government employee does in public necessarily relates to his or her official conduct. Dr. Lazelle Michaelis was the coroner of Otter Tail County, Minn., a position of substantial responsibility. She was also a private physician employed by a medical association. Because of her expertise in pathology she occasionally, as a favor, performed autopsies for the coroner in neighboring Becker County. A controversy developed when Michaelis concluded that the death of a young woman in Becker County was a suicide. Claiming her reputation was damaged by the publicity, she sued CBS broadcasting station WCCO for libel. The station argued that because Michaelis was the coroner in Otter Tail County she was a public official, obligated to prove actual malice. The court disagreed, saying that when Michaelis performed the autopsy in Becker County she was acting as a private doctor; she was paid by the medical association for which she worked. Her position in Otter Tail County had no relevance in this case.[15]

The second element in this test—the plaintiff's general fitness to hold office—is much broader and can even relate to a public official's private life or personal habits. For example, the fact that the fire chief's personal financial affairs are in considerable disarray probably doesn't have much to do with how well she performs her job as fire chief. But a city treasurer who has problems with personal finances could be a different story. This might suggest the treasurer is not fit to manage the city's financial affairs. The decision whether a particular allegation reflects on a public official's fitness to hold the job will necessarily be a subjective one. And it is complicated

14. *Harris* v. *City of Seattle*, 315 F. Supp. 2d 1223 (2004).
15. *Michaelis* v. *CBS, Inc.*, 119 F. 3d 697 (1997).

by the fact that courts, in making this determination, seem to use an elastic standard that relates to the importance of the plaintiff's job. It seems that almost anything about the personal life of the president of the United States is considered a measure of his or her fitness to hold that office. But the courts are unwilling to say the same thing about lower government officials. And the lower you go on the totem pole of public officeholders, the more the courts seem willing to rule that stories about private life have little to do with being a public official for purposes of a libel suit. It is incumbent on any journalist preparing a story on a public official's private life to demonstrate within the story just how these revelations affect the government officer's official responsibilities. This, in itself, could thwart a lawsuit.

ALL-PURPOSE PUBLIC FIGURES

Individuals deemed to be public figures must also prove actual malice when suing for libel. The Supreme Court has said that there are two kinds of public figures: all-purpose public figures and limited-purpose public figures. It was Justice Lewis Powell who established these twin categories in his opinion in *Gertz* v. *Welch*.[16] He identified all-purpose public figures as those persons who "occupy positions of such pervasive power and influence that they are deemed public figures for all purposes."

While Justice Powell's description of an all-purpose public figure sounds simple enough, this is a category of libel plaintiffs that most courts have had difficulty identifying. Do the criteria relate to power or fame? Sometimes the powerful have little public recognition. Name the presidents of the 10 largest U.S. corporations—powerful individuals, but hardly widely known. For example, in the late 1980s, federal judges refused to classify William Tavoulareas, the president of Mobil Oil, one of the nation's largest companies, as a public figure, saying that such a person must be so well known that his or her name is a household word (see page 137). On the other hand, the famous often have little real power. People like Paris Hilton or Adam Sandler come to mind. So who is an all-purpose public figure?

Entertainers Johnny Carson[17] and Wayne Newton[18] were both declared to be all-purpose public figures, largely because they were so famous. But so was conservative writer and editor William Buckley,[19] who was certainly well known to his conservative readers and followers, but was hardly a household name. But these are old cases. Surprisingly, perhaps, there haven't been a lot of other similar cases since. In the past decade or so, it is typically the plaintiff himself or herself who agrees to the designation as an all-purpose public figure.[20] Why would a plaintiff agree to such a designation since it certainly makes it more difficult to win a libel action? Most likely they want to exaggerate their prominence in the public eye to support a higher damage claim. Then again, a lot of celebrities, sports stars and others have very large egos that need constant care and feeding.

But there is more than one way to look at the all-purpose public figure question. Some people might have the pervasive power and influence Justice Powell talked about on a national level;

16. 418 U.S. 323 (1974).
17. *Carson* v. *Allied News*, 529 F. 2d 206 (1976).
18. *Newton* v. *NBC*, 677 F. Supp. 1066 (1985).
19. *Buckley* v. *Litell*, 539 F. 2d 882 (1976).
20. See *Masson* v. *New Yorker Magazine, Inc.*, 881 F. 2d 1452 (1989), for example.

everyone, everywhere knows about them. But others may enjoy such power and influence strictly on a local level. Everyone in a specific town or region or state knows about them. These people can be deemed all-purpose public figures as well. Consider the woman who lives in a community of 6,500 people. She was formerly the mayor, has served on the school board in the past and has been a perennial choice for president of the parent-teacher association. She is the president of the largest real estate company in town, is a director on the board of the local bank and owns the local pharmacy and dry cleaners. She is active in numerous service clubs, is a leader in various civic projects and is instantly recognizable on the street by the town's residents. Her family founded the town 150 years earlier. If she is libeled in a community newspaper whose circulation remains almost exclusively in the community, it could be argued persuasively that this woman is an all-purpose public figure in the community. (See *Steere* v. *Cupp*,[21] in which the Kansas Supreme Court ruled such an individual was a total, or all-purpose, public figure.) In 1982, the Montana Supreme Court ruled that investment and commodity advisor Larry Williams was an all-purpose public figure for his libel suit based on a state Democratic Party press release that erroneously charged that he had been under federal indictment for political dirty tricks. The court listed the following activities by Williams, which convinced the judges that he was an all-purpose public figure for the purposes of a libel suit based on the circulation of defamatory allegations in Montana: He published an investment advisory service; he wrote three books on stocks; he was the subject of an article in Forbes magazine and another article in The Wall Street Journal; he frequently gave speeches and ran unsuccessfully for the U.S. Senate; he was chair of the Republican Party in Montana; and he was an active member of the National Taxpayers Union.[22]

But some courts have rejected the notion that because someone is well known in a community this automatically makes him or her an all-purpose public figure. A television reporter in Utah sued the station where she had worked for making false statements about why she was fired. The station argued she was an all-purpose public figure. She had reported stories for the station for three years, done promotional spots and appeared at special events for the station. One could speculate that a large percentage of people in the community could recognize the plaintiff, Holly Wayment. At least that is what the trial court surmised. But the Utah Supreme Court rejected the ruling that she was an all-purpose public figure. There was no evidence presented that she wielded any particular social or political influence or even proof that the news show on which she appeared was widely watched. "If we accept these facts as sufficient evidence of general fame in the local community, any reporter would qualify as an all-purpose public figure," the court said.[23]

What if the defamatory material circulates outside the local community, as well, to people who may not be familiar with the plaintiff? This question arose in 1985 in a libel suit by business executive George Martin against the Chariho Times in Rhode Island. Martin was clearly well known in the village of Shannock, where he owned and had developed a considerable amount of property over a period of 15 years. The Times was widely read by the 300 residents of the village, and a trial court ruled that Martin was a local all-purpose public figure. On appeal Martin argued that the newspaper had 3,000 subscribers, a far larger readership than just among the village residents by whom he was so well known. The Rhode Island Supreme Court, noting that Martin's fame had spread beyond the Shannock village limits, agreed with the lower court

21. 602 P. 2d 1267 (1979).
22. *Williams* v. *Pasma*, 565 P. 2d 212 (1982).
23. *Wayment* v. *Clear Channel Broadcasting*, 116 P. 3d 271 (2005).

and added that "very few individuals will be known to all subscribers or purchasers of any publication."[24] Wally Butts and Major General Edwin Walker were not known to all subscribers of the Saturday Evening Post, yet were declared to be public figures by the Supreme Court,[25] the Rhode Island justice noted, recalling that famous 1967 decision (see pages 193–196). "It is sufficient to attain a public figure status that the plaintiff should have been known to a substantial portion of the publication's readership," the court ruled.[26] And Martin met this test.

LIMITED-PURPOSE PUBLIC FIGURES

Individuals in the second category of public figures outlined by Justice Powell in the *Gertz* decision are called limited-purpose public figures. "More commonly," he said, "those classed as public figures have thrust themselves to the forefront of particular public controversies in order to influence the resolution of the issues involved."[27] This kind of libel plaintiff is regarded as a public person for a discrete part of his or her life, usually because of something this person has done to try to influence public opinion on a public issue. Between 1974 and 1979 the Supreme Court made four attempts to try to flesh out the definition of a limited-purpose public figure. From these four decisions three elements of a definition emerged. These elements form a base upon which other courts have erected their own definitions of limited-purpose public figures. Here are the elements:

"More commonly, those classed as public figures have thrust themselves to the forefront of particular public controversies in order to influence the resolution of the issues involved."

- **A public controversy must exist before the publication or broadcast of the libelous matter. The outcome of this controversy must have an impact on individuals beyond those directly involved in the dispute. In other words, it must be a public controversy.**
- **The plaintiff must have voluntarily participated in this controversy. The press cannot generate a controversy and then pull the plaintiff into the fray.**
- **The plaintiff must take a role in trying to influence public opinion regarding the controversy. He or she cannot take a distinctly secondary role in the matter. One measure of the plaintiff's ability to exercise such influence is whether or not he or she has access to the mass media to accomplish this feat.**

Now let's look briefly at the four rulings to see how these elements emerged.

In the first case the plaintiff was Elmer Gertz, a well-known civil rights attorney. A police officer shot and killed a young man and a serious controversy erupted in Chicago as authorities tried to determine what had happened. The officer was ultimately tried and convicted of murder. Gertz was retained by the family of the dead man to bring a civil action against the officer and the city. He played no part in the criminal investigation that resulted in the trial and conviction of the police officer. An extreme right-wing organization called the John Birch Society made outrageous charges against Gertz in a publication and he sued for libel. Was he a limited-purpose public figure?

The Supreme Court said no. Justice Lewis Powell wrote, "It is preferable to reduce the public figure question . . . by looking to the nature and extent of an individual's participation

24. *Martin* v. *Wilson Publishing*, 497 A. 2d 322 (1985).
25. *Curtis Publishing Co.* v. *Butts*, 388 U.S. 130 (1967).
26. *Martin* v. *Wilson Publishing*, 497 A. 2d 322 (1985).
27. *Gertz* v. *Welch*, 418 U.S. 323 (1974).

in the particular controversy giving rise to the defamation." The controversy was about the murder of an innocent man by a police officer, and his subsequent trial and conviction. Gertz was at the periphery of this controversy, and he made no attempt to influence public opinion in this matter. He had a limited role as an attorney who represented the family in their attempt to win damages because of the death.[28]

The plaintiff in the second case was a young Florida socialite named Mary Alice Firestone. She and her husband, Russell Firestone, a member of the Firestone tire family, sued each other for divorce. She contended she was libeled by Time magazine when it inadvertently labeled her an adulteress in a short article in the magazine. Mary Alice Firestone was widely known in the community as a member of the elite Palm Beach Society, an active member of the so-called sporting set. The divorce was messy with charges and countercharges tossed out in court and in the press. And Mary Alice Firestone was aggressive in meeting with reporters on an almost daily basis to give her side of the story. When she sued, attorneys for Time argued this certainly made her a public figure. The Supreme Court disagreed.

The kind of controversy generated by the divorce was not the kind of public controversy the justices had in mind. Mary Alice Firestone did not assume any *"role of especial prominence"* in the affairs of society, other than Palm Beach society, Justice William Rehnquist wrote. And she did not volunteer to participate in the controversy that resulted from the divorce action. She was forced by law to go to court to dissolve her marriage.[29]

In 1979 the high court decided two more cases. Ilya Wolston was the prototype of the private citizen. Unfortunately, he was the nephew of Myra and Jack Soble, two well-publicized American communists who were arrested during the Red Scare of the 1950s and charged with spying. The government cast a broad net to find any other spies among the Sobles' friends and relatives and Wolston got snagged. He lived in Washington, D.C. at the time, and after he was interviewed by the FBI he was ordered on several occasions to testify before a federal grand jury in New York. He grew weary of the harassment and after several grand jury appearances ignored a subpoena. He was held in contempt of court and was sentenced to three years' probation. Fifteen news stories were published about Wolston and his grand jury appearances and one nonappearance. But after all the investigation, the government failed to discover any information that linked Wolston to communist activities.

Fifteen years later a book published by the Reader's Digest identified Wolston as a Soviet agent. When he sued for libel the publisher argued that because he was called to testify before a grand jury, because he was held in contempt of court and because this episode was reported in the press, Wolston was a limited-purpose public figure. The Supreme Court disagreed. Wolston did not voluntarily inject himself into any controversy; he was pulled in as the government pursued him because of his relationship with the Sobles. In the mid-1950s there was a legitimate public controversy over Soviet espionage in the United States, but Wolston had little if anything to do with that controversy. He just happened to be related to two people who turned out to be Soviet spies. Finally, he made no effort to influence public opinion about any controversy.[30]

In the final case, the high court decided that the research director of a public mental health hospital in Michigan was not a limited-purpose public figure. The plaintiff had applied for and received about $500,000 in federal grants to conduct research on animal aggression. Each

28. Ibid.
29. *Time, Inc.* v. *Firestone*, 424 U.S. 448 (1976).
30. *Wolston* v. *Reader's Digest*, 443 U.S. 157 (1979).

month, William Proxmire, a United States senator from Wisconsin who some regarded as the "fiscal conscience" of the Senate, awarded a federal agency or a federal official what he called "The Golden Fleece" award, because Proxmire believed he or she or it wasted taxpayer money. Proxmire regarded Hutchinson's research as inconsequential if not silly and gave a Golden Fleece award to the agencies that had been funding his studies for the previous seven years and made derogatory comments about Hutchinson as well. The researcher sued for libel.

Proxmire argued that Hutchinson was a limited-purpose public figure. What was the controversy? A general concern about how taxpayers' money is spent. And he voluntarily injected himself into this controversy when he sought research grants from the government, the defendant argued. Chief Justice Warren Burger and seven other members of the high court disagreed. Hutchinson played no part in the broad general controversy over how tax dollars are spent. He did not try to influence public opinion about this matter—all he did was apply for research grants to sustain his work. Simply taking public money to undertake research is not enough to make a person like Hutchinson into a public figure.[31]

From these four cases emerge the three aforementioned criteria. A couple of observations are warranted before moving on. In this quartet of decisions the high court really didn't tell us who was a limited-purpose public figure—only who wasn't. A ruling in which the plaintiff was deemed to be a limited-purpose public figure would help, but the high court has not handed down another decision on this question in the past 30 years. It seems as though the justices are content to let the lower federal courts and state courts fine-tune the elements of the definition. And that is what has happened.[32] Comparing the three guidelines from the Supreme Court to decisions by the lower court reveals that the Supreme Court's definition of a limited-purpose public figure is somewhat conservative. That is, a plaintiff who might not meet the definition of a limited-purpose public figure enunciated by the Supreme Court in the 1970s might in fact be regarded as a limited-purpose public figure today by a lower court. While the lower courts have not strayed significantly from the high court's definition, lower courts seem to be somewhat more liberal in defining what is a public controversy, and the role played by the plaintiff in the controversy. A look at some lower-court rulings will illuminate these points.

LOWER-COURT RULINGS

Deciding who is and who is not a limited-purpose public figure is one of the most subjective decisions courts must make in applying the law of libel. It is not surprising then that, despite the guidance from the Supreme Court, differences in this definition exist among the lower courts. The tests emerging from the lower courts surely reflect the language of the high court rulings, but often four or five rather than three criteria are applied. In Washington state, for example, the test requires the judge to answer five questions:

- Did the plaintiff have access to the media?
- What was the nature of the plaintiff's role in the controversy?
- Were the defamatory comments germane to the controversy?
- Did the controversy exist before the defamation was published?
- Was the plaintiff still a public figure at the time of defamation?

---

31. *Hutchinson* v. *Proxmire*, 443 U.S. 111 (1979).
32. See Stonecipher and Sneed, "Survey of the Professional Person," 328.

The 4th U.S. Circuit Court of Appeals uses this test:

▮ Did a controversy exist prior to the publication of the defamatory matter?
▮ Did the plaintiff voluntarily assume a role of special prominence in the controversy?
▮ Did the plaintiff seek to influence resolution of the controversy?
▮ Does the plaintiff have access to effective channels of communication?
▮ Did the plaintiff retain the public-figure status at the time of the alleged defamation?[33]

While these two tests and tests used by other courts vary from the test forged by the U.S. Supreme Court, they nevertheless retain the basic elements: A limited-purpose public figure voluntarily becomes involved in a pre-existing public controversy with both the hope and the means (media access) to help resolve that controversy. A few lower courts have viewed the "voluntary participation" element of the criteria in a more liberal fashion. The Pennsylvania Supreme Court noted in 2007 that "some courts have held that a controversy may be created by a plaintiff's own activities."[34] A criminal rarely seeks to attract attention; yet some courts have said that by committing a criminal act an individual can legitimately expect to draw the kind of public attention that fosters a definition of a public figure. But there is disagreement among the courts as well. In March 1998 a U.S. District Court in Connecticut ruled that the wife of a physician who had continuing legal problems was a public figure. The doctor, on probation for five years because of charges of incompetence, was arrested and charged with 20 counts of fraud. "Despite the fact that plaintiff has not sought a public role, she has been thrust into the role of a public figure by virtue of her marriage to Dr. Zupnik—who clearly is a public figure."[35] Three months later the Appellate Division of the New York Supreme Court ruled that the ex-husband of prominent television celebrity Joan Lunden was not a public figure simply because he was married for many years to the co-host of ABC's "Good Morning America." The Globe tabloid had suggested that prior to the divorce, while the couple was separated, Lunden's husband had an affair with a prostitute. "Plaintiff is not famous in his own right and his marriage to Lunden certainly did not bestow upon him the sort of fame that is necessary to be considered a general public figure."[36] The two cases present almost identical circumstances, yet the courts reached contrary decisions. What follows is a sampling of lower-court rulings that demonstrate both the consistencies and inconsistencies in the law.

The Nature of the Controversy

The kind of controversy that generated the libel is an obviously important factor in determining whether a plaintiff is a limited-purpose public figure.

The kind of controversy that generated the libel is an obviously important factor in determining whether a plaintiff is a limited-purpose public figure. In 1994 in a decision that echoed earlier Supreme Court rulings, the 4th U.S. Circuit Court of Appeals declared that "a public controversy is a dispute that in fact has received public attention because its ramifications will be felt

33. See *Clardy* v. *The Cowles Pub. Co.*, 912 P. 2d 1078 (1996); and *Carr* v. *Forbes,* 259 F. 3d 273 (2001).
34. *American Future Systems Inc.* v. *Better Business Bureau of Eastern Pennsylvania*, 923 A. 2d 389 (2007).
35. *Zupnik* v. *Associated Press Inc.*, 26 M.L.R. 2084 (1998); see also *Scaccia* v. *Dayton Newspapers Inc.*, 170 ch 10 App 3d 471 (2007).
36. *Krauss* v. *Globe International Inc.*, 674 N.Y.S. 2d 662 (1998).

by persons who are not direct participants."[37] This is the same standard applied by the Georgia Supreme Court when it ruled that a group of plastic surgeons who were involved in a fight with other physicians over what kinds of medical specialists were qualified to perform plastic surgery were not public figures. This was a dispute that affected only members of the medical community, not the general public.[38] A black woman, Linda Lewis, was arrested for shoplifting at a J.C. Penney store. She and her husband then filed a lawsuit against the retailer, claiming she had been beaten when store personnel detained her. After the lawsuit was filed a national civil rights organization became involved in the dispute, raising the specter of a boycott of Penney stores. Public meetings were held and the plaintiff in the lawsuit against the store spoke at these meetings. Weeks later a television station broadcast erroneous information about Lewis and she sued for libel. The TV station contended she was a public figure; she argued she was not. The Colorado Court of Appeals said it saw two controversies in this case. The first was the lawsuit by Lewis against the department store. She was not a public figure in regard to this dispute; simply a private citizen going to court to try to redress what she thought was a legal wrong. But Lewis then injected herself into the second controversy, the public protests against the Penney company. She spoke at public gatherings where the possible boycott of the retailer was discussed. She became a limited-purpose public figure at that point, the court said.[39]

Many courts have repeatedly ruled that the mass media cannot generate a controversy and then, when a libel suit is filed, label the people they pulled into that controversy as public figures. A radio station in Brunswick, Ga., tried this ploy recently after it broadcast rumors that a local musician had murdered his girlfriend, who was the mother of his child. Travis Riddle had achieved a small degree of notoriety in Brunswick. He performed at local rap concerts, appeared once in a segment on MTV, self-produced a CD that sold fairly well in the area and was the subject of at least one newspaper article. But testimony revealed most of the staff at the radio station had never heard of him prior to the lawsuit. One of the DJs at the station began receiving calls one day accusing Riddle of murder and aired some of these callers. Riddle, who at the time was working as a banquet server in Atlanta, sued for libel. The station claimed he was a public figure.

The Georgia Court of Appeals asked the question, What was the controversy in this case? The accusations of murder generated a controversy, the defendant argued. But Riddle was never named as a suspect in a murder investigation. In fact, there was no murder. His girlfriend had merely disappeared for a few days. Her disappearance might have been newsworthy, but it was never publicized. But even then, if this generated a controversy, it was an issue that affected only her family and friends. This would not have been a public controversy. A jury awarded Riddle $100,000.[40]

The Plaintiff's Role

Once a court has ruled that a legitimate controversy existed it must then determine what role the plaintiff played in the controversy. This is a more difficult question. Was the plaintiff actually involved in the controversy that gave rise to the defamation? Or was he or she simply on the

---

37. *Foretich v. Capital Cities/ABC, Inc.*, 37 F. 3d 1541 (1994).
38. *Georgia Society of Plastic Surgeons v. Anderson*, 363 S.E. 2d 710 (1987).
39. *Lewis v. McGraw-Hill Broadcasting Co., Inc.*, 832 P. 2d 1118 (1992).
40. *Riddle v. Golden Isle Broadcasting LLC*, 621 S.E. 2d 822 (2005); 36 M.L.R. 2084 (2008).

periphery? Was the participation voluntary or was the plaintiff drawn into the controversy by the mass media? Because no two cases are exactly alike, and because the answers to the questions raised above often involve subjective judgments, it is not surprising to find contradictory rulings among the courts in cases in which the facts seem somewhat similar. But this should stand as a warning to those who think the law is made up of a set of specific rules that are applied in exactly the same fashion in every case. This rarely happens, and perhaps never will, unless the human judges and jurors are replaced by computers. Let's look at a few cases to explore how various courts have dealt with the matter of the role of the plaintiff in the controversy.

A real controversy has simmered in the United States for the past 20 years as more and more women have joined the American armed forces. A sharp difference of opinion still exists on the role women should play in combat. One of the last bastions of male exclusivity was the job of combat pilot for the U.S. Navy. Carey D. Lohrenz was one of the first two women who became Navy combat pilots. She was at the top of her class during basic flight training, won the right to train in jet aircraft and, after Congress changed the law barring women from flying combat jets, was assigned as an F-14 pilot on a Navy aircraft carrier. This controversy heated up after the change in U.S. policy, and then it escalated even more when the other female combat pilot died when her aircraft malfunctioned as she attempted a carrier landing. At this point some people began attacking both the idea of allowing women to fly high-performance combat aircraft and Lohrenz herself, saying she was incompetent and unqualified. She sued for libel.

Was she a public figure? The defense argued that because of the controversy over whether women should be allowed to fly fighter aircraft, Lohrenz, a female combat pilot, surely was a public figure for purposes of this issue. But Lohrenz's attorney argued that she had not taken any part in this controversy—she simply trained as a naval aviator, chose to fly jets and accepted her assignment as a combat pilot when the opportunity presented itself. She certainly did not publicly participate in the debate over the wisdom of this change in policy.

The U.S. Court of Appeals sided with the defense. The court ruled that when Lohrenz *chose* to become a Navy aviator and when she *chose* to accept the assignment as an F-14 pilot, she should have realized she was becoming embroiled in the controversy over the role to be played by women in combat. She attained a special prominence in the dispute when she suited up to fly a Navy warplane. "A central role in the controversy came with the territory," the court said.[41]

In 1999 a Georgia court ruled that Richard Jewell was a public figure for purposes of his libel suit against Cox Enterprises Inc., publisher of the Atlanta Constitution and the Atlanta Journal. Jewell, a former deputy sheriff, is the man who discovered a bomb in a knapsack in a park during the 1996 Summer Olympic Games in Atlanta and then herded spectators out of the area before the device exploded. One person was killed, 11 others were injured. Jewell was regarded as a hero at first, and then law enforcement officers focused their attention on him as a suspect in the bombing. After the incident Jewell gave about a dozen interviews to local and national media about his role in clearing people out of the area after he discovered the bomb and about park security in general. He sued the Atlanta newspapers for comments published while he was regarded as a prime suspect in the bombing. He was later cleared. The court ruled that Jewell was a public person because he voluntarily stepped into the controversy by giving the interviews to the press. He was not at the time defending himself from

41. *Lohrenz* v. *Donnelly*, 350 F. 3d 1272 (2003). The Supreme Court refused in 2004 to review this decision.

accusations. "It is beyond argument," the court ruled, "that plaintiff did not reject any role in the debate, was a prominent figure in the coverage of the controversy, and, whatever his reticence regarding his media appearances, encountered them voluntarily."[42]

Michael Starr, the owner of several broadcast stations, became embroiled in a controversy when he shut down one of his radio stations. A local newspaper wrote stories concerning the removal of the station from the airwaves. Starr responded to the criticism regarding the closure of the station in a press release, and then sued the newspaper for libel. The Louisiana Court of Appeals ruled that to the extent that the newspaper article at issue discussed Starr in his capacity as an owner and operator of the station, and addressed the issues directly related to the ownership and management of the station, he was a public figure for that limited issue. He had thrust himself into the controversy when he issued the press release.[43]

But other courts have demanded more active participation by the plaintiff before applying the public-figure designation. A controversy arose in a small community in western Kentucky when a radiologist was fired at a regional medical center following complaints from former patients and a doctor who worked at the same facility. Extensive publicity accompanied the doctor's termination, and ultimately he sued the local newspaper for libel, among other things. The newspaper argued that because of the controversy in the community, and the attending publicity, the physician was a limited-purpose public figure. But a federal court disagreed, ruling that the radiologist had not injected himself into the controversy. He was pulled into the fray when he was terminated, the court said. Also, he did not act in a manner designed to attain publicity; nor did he have unusual access to the media.[44]

Contradictory decisions like these are often confusing, even to lawyers who specialize in libel law. They are evidence of two things: first, that the law of libel is still evolving, as it has during the past several centuries; and second, as noted in Chapter 4, that libel is still basically state law. While the constitutionalization of the tort has added some consistency to the development of the libel law, state judges still have considerable room to shape their own law.

BUSINESSES AS PUBLIC FIGURES

Businesses and corporations can sue for libel; they can also be classified as public figures for purposes of a libel suit. Surely if a business attempts to lead public opinion during a controversy over an important public issue, it could be categorized as a limited-purpose public figure. For example, General Motors could be classified as a limited-purpose public figure if it was libeled as it attempted to lead public opinion against government-imposed automobile emission standards. But businesses have been regarded as public figures based on other criteria as well, criteria hammered out over the past two decades. Some of the standards used to determine whether a business is a public figure include the following:

Businesses and corporations can sue for libel; they can also be classified as public figures for purposes of a libel suit.

■ **Whether a business has used a highly unusual advertising or promotional campaign to draw attention to itself.**

42. *Jewell* v. *Cox Enterprises Inc.,* 27 M.L.R. 2370 (1999), aff'd *Atlanta Journal-Constitution* v. *Jewell,* Ga. Ct. App., 29 M.L.R. 2537 (2001). In 2005 Eric E. Rudolph, who had bombed abortion clinics and a gay bar, admitted the Olympic bombing as well. Richard Jewell died on August 29, 2007.
43. *Starr* v. *Boudreaux,* 978 So. 2d 384 (2007).
44. *Trover* v. *Paxton Medical Group,* 36 M.L.R. 1241 (2007).

- **The notoriety of the business to the average person in the area where the business has a presence.**
- **Whether a business is regulated by the government.**
- **Whether the libelous comment about the business focuses on a matter of public concern.**
- **Frequency and intensity of media scrutiny of the business.**

Not all courts agree that these criteria are applicable. Here are some cases that offer guidelines in the application of these standards.

The Ohio Court of Appeals ruled in 2006 that two adult entertainment clubs that featured nude or partially nude dancing were public figures. The court said the clubs had been in the news for 10 years due to licensing matters and opposition from people in the area during zoning hearings.[45] A U.S. District Court ruled in 1981 that the Bose Corporation, which was suing Consumer Reports, was a limited-purpose public figure because the audio equipment manufacturer had advertised its new 901 speakers in a highly unconventional manner that precipitated a public discussion on the merits of the product. The company intentionally emphasized the unconventional design of the product in its advertising and publicity.[46]

But normal advertising will not generally establish the level of notoriety required to turn a business into a public figure. A spirited, but typical, comparative advertising campaign between U.S. Healthcare Inc. and Blue Cross in Pennsylvania did not propel either company into the public-figure status, according to the 3rd U.S. Circuit Court of Appeals.[47] Similarly, extensive advertising and promotion by entrepreneur Thomas Jadwin of a double tax-exempt, no-load bond mutual fund he had developed did not make him a public figure. Soliciting media attention for such an offering is normal, the Minnesota Supreme Court ruled.[48] But the Nevada Supreme Court recently ruled that because a restaurant actively seeks out public patronage, it should usually be considered a public figure, at least for purposes of comments on the food.[49]

A nursing home in Rhode Island was declared to be a public figure by the state's high court because it was regulated by the government and because there was considerable public concern about the conditions at such facilities.[50] The Ohio Court of Appeals ruled in 1997 that despite the novelty at that time of interactive computer systems, advertising on the Internet is not unusual enough to turn a software company into a public figure in a libel suit.[51] In 1984 a U.S. District Court in Kansas ruled that the Beech Aircraft Company was a public figure for the purposes of a libel suit against Aviation Consumer magazine, which had published a story about Beech aircraft involved in accidents. The court said that "the defamatory statements relate to part of Beech's business that is federally regulated and arose in the context of a federal investigation." By entering into a regulated activity like the manufacture of aircraft,

---

45. *Total Exposure.com, Ltd.* v. *Miami Valley Broadcasting Corp.*, 34 M.L.R. 1880 (2006).
46. *Bose Corp.* v. *Consumers Union of the United States, Inc.*, 508 F. Supp. 1249 (1981), rev'd 629 F. 2d 189 (1982), aff'd 446 U.S. 485 (1984).
47. *U.S. Healthcare, Inc.* v. *Blue Cross of Greater Philadelphia*, 898 F. 2d 914 (1990).
48. *Jadwin* v. *Minneapolis Star*, 367 N.W. 2d 476 (1985).
49. *Pegasus* v. *Reno Newspapers Inc.*, 57 P. 3d 82 (2002).
50. *Harris Nursing Home Inc.* v. *Narragansett Television Inc.*, 24 M.L.R 1671 (1995).
51. *Worldnet Software Co.* v. *Gannett Satellite Information Network, Inc.*, 25 M.L.R. 2331 (1997).

the company, in essence, invited public scrutiny, the court said.[52] And in 1988 the U.S. Court of Appeals for the 11th Circuit ruled that two men who owned jai alai frontons in Florida were public figures in their libel suit brought against ABC. The court ruled the pair had put themselves in the public eye by becoming involved in a heavily regulated industry.[53] In 1995 the New Jersey Supreme Court said it would not consider an ordinary business to be a public figure unless the business was concerned with matters of public health and safety or was subject to substantial government regulation. The court added, however, that it would also regard as a public figure a business accused of consumer fraud when the allegations, if true, would constitute a violation of New Jersey's Consumer Fraud Act. In this case a lawn mower repair business was accused of cheating its customers. The state Supreme Court affirmed a lower-court ruling that the plaintiff business would have to prove actual malice to win its libel suit.[54] Other courts have rejected the government-regulation criteria, however. The Supreme Court of Oregon did not even consider the rationale that a regulated business is a public figure when it ruled that the Bank of Oregon was not a public figure for purposes of a lawsuit against the Willamette Week newspaper. "There simply is no public controversy into which plaintiffs arguably thrust themselves. Merely opening one's doors to the public, offering stock for public sale, advertising, etc., even if considered a thrusting of one's self into matters of public interest, is not sufficient to establish a public figure," the court ruled.[55]

Two court rulings in the 1990s, including one by the 5th U.S. Circuit Court of Appeals, have provided additional criteria that might be applied when determining whether a business is a public figure for purposes of a libel suit. In *Snead* v. *Redland Aggregates, Ltd.*, the Court of Appeals ruled that the notoriety of a business to the average person in the relevant geographical area (the area in which the libel is circulated), the public prominence of the business because it manufactures widely known consumer goods, and the frequency and intensity of media scrutiny of the business are all factors that need to be considered when a court makes a determination about the public-figure status of a business.[56] Also to be considered, the court said, is whether the libelous speech involves a matter of public or private concern. In this case the court ruled that a British firm that quarried sand, gravel and crushed stone was not a public figure. And a U.S. District Court in Pennsylvania ruled that a business's relative access to the media and the manner in which the risk of defamation came upon the business (i.e., the context of the dispute that generated the libel) must be considered when deciding whether a business was a public figure or not.[57] While the criteria in both these decisions lack precision, these rulings indicate that some courts seem willing to consider the public figure status of businesses in a broader light.

As noted by the 5th U.S. Circuit Court of Appeals in the *Snead* decision, generalizations that have some value when determining the public or private status of an individual don't work well when applied to a business. Most courts seem more comfortable approaching the

---

52. *Beech Aircraft* v. *National Aviation Underwriters*, 11 M.L.R. 1401 (1984).

53. *Silvester* v. *ABC*, 839 F. 2d 1491 (1988).

54. *Turf Lawnmower Repair, Inc.* v. *Bergen Record*, 655 A. 2d 417 (1995). See also *LL NJ Inc.* v. *NBC Subsidiary (WCAU-TV)* L.P, 36 M.L.R. 1746 (2008).

55. *Bank of Oregon* v. *Independent News*, 963 P. 2d 35 (1985).

56. 998 F. 2d 1325 (1993).

57. *Rust Evader Corp.* v. *Plain Dealer Publishing Co.*, 21 M.L.R. 2189 (1993).

problem on a case-by-case basis. The lack of clear standards is an important reason journalists should be cautious when communicating about businesses, even those that have a high visibility in the community.

PUBLIC PERSONS OVER TIME

If someone is a public person (public official or public figure) today, will he or she still be regarded as a public figure 20 years from now? Yes, but only in regard to the issues or matters that generated the public-person status today. If Foster Pierson is a public figure today because he is at the forefront of a fight against a gun control initiative on the ballot in Indiana, he will still be regarded as a public figure in any story published or broadcast 20 years from now regarding this initiative battle. Similarly, a woman who retires to private life after being mayor of Houston will still be regarded as a public person if she sues for libel for a story published 25 years from now that focuses on her conduct while she was mayor.

The 10th U.S. Court of Appeals ruled in 2002 that the former associate deputy director of the Federal Bureau of Investigation was a public person for the purposes of a libel suit based on a book about the Oklahoma City bombing in 1995. Oliver Revell was retired from the FBI when the book was published, but the court ruled that this was immaterial. That

> the person defamed no longer holds the same position does not by itself strip him of this status as a public official for constitutional purposes. If the defamatory remarks relate to his conduct while he was a public official and the manner in which he performed his responsibilities is still a matter of public interest, he remains a public official within the meaning of *New York Times*.[58]

A U.S. District Court ruled that a U.S. Secret Service agent who saved the life of President Gerald Ford in 1975 must still be regarded as a public person for purposes of a libel suit based on a story broadcast in 1992 about the attempted assassination.[59] Two attempts were made on Ford's life in September 1975. Agent Larry Buendorf deflected the arm of assailant Lynette "Squeaky" Fromme on Sept. 5, 1975, and saved the life of President Ford while he was visiting Sacramento, Calif. Two weeks later a private citizen, Oliver Sipple, pushed away the arm of assailant Sara Jane Moore as she attempted to shoot the president when he was in San Francisco. This second incident became a major issue in the Bay Area when newspaper columnist Herb Caen speculated in print that the White House had not thanked Sipple for his heroic act because he was a homosexual. Sipple was gay, but sued the newspaper for invasion of privacy.[60] (See page 280 for more on this case.) Researchers at National Public Radio got the two incidents mixed up and commentator Daniel Schorr, in a report on how the press tramples on the privacy of public people, said it was revealed after he saved the president's life that agent Buendorf was a homosexual. The court ruled that Buendorf would have to prove actual malice to win his libel suit, something he was unable to do.[61] But in 1997 the Arkansas

---

58. *Revell* v. *Hoffman*, 309 F. 3d 1228 (2002). See also *Newsom* v. *Henry*, 443 So. 2d 817 (1984); and *Contemporary Mission* v. *New York Times*, 665 F. Supp. 248 (1987), 842 F. 2d 612 (1988).
59. *Buendorf* v. *National Public Radio, Inc.*, 822 F. Supp. 6 (1993).
60. *Sipple* v. *Chronicle Publishing Co.*, 154 Cal. App. 3d 1040 (1984).
61. *Buendorf* v. *National Public Radio, Inc.*, 822 F. Supp. 6 (1993).

Supreme Court ruled that J. Michael Fitzhugh, a former federal prosecutor, was not a public person for purposes of a libel action he brought against the Arkansas Democrat-Gazette. The newspaper published a story that federal prosecutor Robert Fiske Jr. was about to initiate the first prosecution in the Whitewater investigation. Two men, Charles Matthews and Eugene Fitzhugh, were the defendants in the case. The newspaper ran what it thought were pictures of the pair. The Matthews photo was correct, but the Democrat-Gazette mistakenly published a photo of J. Michael Fitzhugh instead of a picture of Eugene Fitzhugh. The newspaper argued that because the plaintiff had been a federal prosecutor for eight years—clearly a public official during those years—he surely should be considered a public person for the purposes of this lawsuit. The court disagreed, ruling that while J. Michael Fitzhugh was and still is a public person for any story relating to his work as a federal prosecutor, he was not a public person for stories about matters outside that realm, including the Whitewater investigation. The simple error cost the newspaper $50,000 in damages.[62]

PRIVATE PERSONS

In a libel action, if the plaintiff does not meet the definition of a public official, an all-purpose public figure, or a limited-purpose public figure, the court will regard the individual as a private person. This designation means the plaintiff will not be required to prove that the defendant lied or exhibited reckless disregard for the truth in publishing the libel. The plaintiff in most jurisdictions will have to demonstrate only that the defendant failed to exercise reasonable care in preparing and publishing the defamatory material. There are, however, a few exceptions to this rule. A few states, including California,[63] Colorado,[64] Indiana,[65] Alaska[66] and New York,[67] have decided that plaintiffs who are considered private persons must prove a higher degree of fault than simple negligence when they sue a mass medium for libel based on a story about a matter of public interest. In some states these plaintiffs must prove gross negligence or gross irresponsibility; in others these private-person plaintiffs must prove actual malice. Gross negligence is a higher degree of fault than simple negligence, but a lesser degree of fault than actual malice. To find out the rule in your state, locate the most recent state supreme court ruling on libel. Within the text of this decision there is very likely to be a reference to the level of fault required by private-person plaintiffs.

Under the fault requirement all individuals who sue a mass medium for libel must prove that the defendant was somehow at fault in publishing the defamatory material, that the publication (or broadcast) did not result from an innocent error.

SUMMARY

62. *Little Rock Newspapers* v. *Fitzhugh*, 954 S.W. 2d 187 (1997).
63. *Rollenhagen* v. *City of Orange*, 172 Cal. Rptr. 49 (1981).
64. *Walker* v. *Colorado Springs Sun, Inc.*, 538 P. 2d 450 (1975).
65. *AAFCO Heating and Air Conditioning Co.* v. *Northwest Publications, Inc.*, 321 N.E. 2d 580 (1974).
66. *Gay* v. *Williams*, 486 F. Supp. 12 (1979).
67. *Chapadeau* v. *Utica Observer-Dispatch, Inc.*, 341 N.E. 2d 569 (1975).

What the courts call a public person must normally prove that the defendant acted with actual malice in publishing the libel; that is, the defendant knew the material was false but still published it or exhibited reckless disregard for the truth. What the courts define as private persons must prove at least that the defendant acted negligently, that is, in such a way as to create an unreasonable risk of harm. The courts have ruled that there are three kinds of public persons:

I. *Public officials:* Individuals who work for a government in a position of authority, who have substantial control over the conduct of governmental affairs, and whose position in government invites independent public scrutiny beyond the general public interest in the qualifications and performance of all government employees. Libelous comments must focus on the plaintiff's official conduct (the manner in which the plaintiff conducts his or her job) or on the plaintiff's general fitness to hold public office.

II. *All-purpose public figures:* People who occupy persuasive power and influence in the nation or in a community, who are usually exposed to constant media attention.

III. *Limited-purpose public figures:* Individuals who voluntarily inject themselves into an important public controversy in order to influence public opinion regarding the resolution of that controversy. The key elements are these:

  a. Public controversy, the resolution of which must affect more people than simply the participants. The outcome must have an impact on people in a community.

  b. Plaintiffs who voluntarily thrust themselves into this controversy. An individual who has been drawn involuntarily into a controversy created by someone else (such as the press) will not usually be considered a limited-purpose public figure.

  c. Plaintiffs who attempt to influence the outcome of the controversy, to shape public opinion on the subject. This implies that a plaintiff has some access to the mass media to participate in the public discussion surrounding the controversy.

Using a variety of criteria, courts have ruled that businesses can be deemed public figures in a libel suit. Individuals who become public persons remain public persons throughout their lives with regard to stories published or broadcast that relate to incidents or events that occurred while they were public persons.

THE MEANING OF FAULT

> Negligence = Failure to exercise reasonable care
> Actual malice = Knowledge of falsity or reckless disregard for the truth

NEGLIGENCE

"Negligence" is a term that has been commonly used in tort law for centuries, but has been applied to libel law only since 1974. In simple terms, **negligence** implies the failure to exercise ordinary care. In deciding whether to adopt the negligence or the stricter actual malice fault requirements, state courts are providing their own definitions of the standard. Washington state adopted a "reasonable care" standard. Defendants are considered negligent if they do not exercise reasonable care in determining whether a statement is false or will create a false impression.[68] The Tennessee Supreme Court has adopted a "reasonably prudent person test": What would a reasonably prudent person have done or not have done in the same circumstance? Would a reasonably prudent reporter have checked the truth of a story more fully? Would such a reporter have waited a day or so to get more information? Would a reasonably prudent reporter have worked harder in trying to reach the plaintiff before publishing the charges?[69] In Arizona negligence has been defined as conduct that creates unreasonable risk of harm. "It is the failure to use that amount of care which a reasonably prudent person would use under like circumstances," the Arizona Supreme Court ruled.[70]

Some of the more common reasons a defendant might be found negligent are these:

- **Reliance on an untrustworthy source**
- **Not reading or misreading pertinent documents**
- **Failure to check with an obvious source, perhaps the subject of the story**
- **Carelessness in editing and news handling**

The question the court will always ask is, **Did the reporter make a good faith effort to determine the truth or falsity of the matter?** Here are some cases that illuminate these criteria.

Did the reporter make a good faith effort to determine the truth or falsity of the matter?

Courts will often scrutinize the source of the reporter's story when deciding whether or not there was negligence. After a reporter relied on a source whom police described as being an unreliable informant, and even the reporter admitted in court that he had found some of his source's information to be incorrect, the Massachusetts Supreme Judicial Court ruled that a jury might find negligence in such a case.[71] But a superior court in New Jersey ruled in 2003 that when a criminal suspect was misidentified in a news story there was no negligence, because the reporter had gotten the wrong name from both the police and an assistant prosecutor.[72] And the courts have consistently ruled that a newspaper or broadcast station is not negligent when it relies on reports received from the Associated Press, Reuters or other legitimate news services.[73]

Reportorial techniques are often scrutinized when a plaintiff asserts that a news medium has been negligent. But courts do not expect superhuman efforts from journalists, only general competence. The San Antonio Express-News was sued for libel when it inadvertently ran the wrong picture with a story it published on a woman convicted of prostitution, selling a child into prostitution and drug-related offenses. The plaintiff, who had the same name as the woman described in the Express-News story, had also been convicted of selling a child into prostitution, but was clearly not the woman described in the newspaper. Was there negligence in this case?

---

68. *Taskett v. King Broadcasting Co.*, 546 P. 2d 81 (1976).
69. *Memphis Publishing Co. v. Nichols*, 569 S.W. 2d 412 (1978).
70. *Peagler v. Phoenix Newspapers*, 547 P. 2d 1074 (1976).
71. *Jones v. Taibbi*, 512 N.E. 2d 260 (1987).
72. *Yeager v. Daily Record*, 32 M.L.R. 1667 (2003).
73. *Appleby v. Daily Hampshire*, 395 Mass. 2 (1985); *McKinney v. Avery Journal, Inc.*, 393 S.E. 2d 295 (1990); and *Cole v. Star Tribune*, 26 M.L.R. 2415 (1998).

The reporter had seven years of experience covering the courthouse and had spent six months researching the series of articles on the Texas Department of Correction's parole system. She had submitted a request to the county sheriff's office for a mug shot of the woman who was the subject of the story. The request included the woman's name, date of birth and Department of Corrections identification number. The sheriff's office gave her the wrong photo. The plaintiff insisted that the reporter failed to verify that she had the correct photo, that the reporter should have checked with the woman's mother to make certain the correct photo was being used. The court disagreed. "The issue was not what Fox [the reporter] could have done to avoid the mistake. It is whether she acted reasonably; that is, as a reasonable reporter under similar circumstances would have acted." The court said there was no negligence in this case.[74]

The South Carolina Supreme Court ruled that the failure of a reporter to examine a public judicial record when writing about a criminal case could be negligence. The plaintiff in the case had been arrested with four other men and charged with pirating stereo audiotapes. Two months later four of the men arrested pleaded guilty to the charges, but the charges were dismissed against the plaintiff. The newspaper published a story saying that the plaintiff had also pleaded guilty to the charges. The reporter had gotten his information about the case in a telephone conversation with the prosecuting attorney. The attorney testified that he had given the reporter the correct information. Six days elapsed between the dismissal of charges and the erroneous story. The South Carolina high court concluded that the correct information was available to the reporter in the court records and that he could have looked at this material before publishing the story. He instead chose to rely on a telephone conversation and in doing so got the story fouled up. The jury could readily conclude that the reporter was negligent, the court ruled.[75]

Finally, the Virginia Supreme Court ruled that when a newspaper published a very negative story about a local teacher, based largely on complaints from parents who called the newspaper, it exhibited negligence. Parents were quoted in the article as saying the teacher was erratic, disorganized, forgetful, unfair and demeaning to students. The reporter who wrote the story talked to a couple of students, the principal and two of the teacher's colleagues, but got little information. As such, the story was very one-sided. The court said that the reporter could have contacted many more students to try to verify the accusations since there was no deadline pressure. It was obvious, the court ruled, that the parents who contacted the reporter bore the teacher ill will. This should have pushed the reporter to do a more thorough job.[76]

The editorial process itself may be examined when a plaintiff seeks to prove negligence. And carelessness in the way that editors handle news copy can result in a finding of fault. In 1985 the editors at USA Today planned to run a special feature commemorating the 10th anniversary of the capture of Saigon by the North Vietnamese, the end of the Vietnam War. For the feature roundup, the editors wanted a short story from each state. An editor in Virginia called the paper's stringer in Vermont and asked him for a contribution. The stringer, Ron Wyman, talked with an acquaintance, Jeffrey Kassel, a clinical psychologist at a Veterans Administration hospital, and asked if he had any ideas for a short story. The thrust of Kassel's remarks was the notion that many American soldiers who fought in Vietnam felt as if they

---

74. *Garza* v. *The Hearst Corporation,* 23 M.L.R. 1733 (1995). See also *Martinez* v. *WTVG Inc.,* 35 M.L.R. 2176 (2007).
75. *Jones* v. *Sun Publishing,* 292 S.E. 2d 23 (1982).
76. *Richmond Newspapers* v. *Lipscomb,* 362 S.E. 2d 32 (1987).

were victims, forced to fight in a war they didn't want. As Wyman was leaving, Kassel noted that he had recently seen an article in another newspaper that said that former Vietnamese soldiers were amused by the idea that their painful experiences in the war might leave them with "post-traumatic stress disorder," the scourge of many U.S. veterans. Wyman put his notes together and read them over the telephone to his editor in Virginia. She in turn routed the notes to another editor who wrote the final story, which quoted Kassel as saying, "We've become a nation of handwringers. . . . It's amusing that vets feel they are the victims when the Vietnamese had the napalm and bombs dropped on them."[77] This, of course, was not what Kassel had said. USA Today had attributed to the psychologist the observations in the newspaper article he noted to reporter Wyman. Testimony at the trial revealed that no one ever called Kassel before publication to check the quote, no editor checked with Wyman after the story was written, and the individual who wrote that short story never even checked with the editor who had transcribed Wyman's notes over the telephone. The 1st U.S. Circuit Court of Appeals ruled that a jury might certainly construe this behavior as negligent.[78]

The definition of the term "negligence" will undoubtedly vary from state to state and possibly from judge to judge within a state. It is going to be some time before any kind of broad, consistently applied guidelines emerge. It is unlikely the Supreme Court will be of any help in this matter as it appears to be the intention of the court to leave the matter to the states.

ACTUAL MALICE

Defining actual malice is somewhat easier than defining who is and who is not a public figure or public official but it still presents judges with problems. In *New York Times Co.* v. *Sullivan*,[79] Justice Brennan defined **actual malice** as "knowledge of falsity or reckless disregard of whether the material was false or not." The two parts of this definition should be considered separately.

Knowledge of Falsity

"Knowledge of falsity" is a fancy way of saying "lie." If the defendant lied and the plaintiff can prove it, actual malice has then been shown. In 1969 Barry Goldwater was able to convince a federal court that Ralph Ginzburg published known falsehoods about him during the 1964 presidential campaign in a "psychobiography" carried in Ginzburg's Fact magazine. Ginzburg sent questionnaires to hundreds of psychiatrists, asking them to analyze Goldwater's mental condition. Ginzburg published only those responses that agreed with the magazine's predisposition that Goldwater was mentally ill and changed the responses on other questionnaires to reflect this point of view. Proof of this conduct, plus other evidence, led the court to conclude that Ginzburg had published the defamatory material with knowledge of its falsity.[80]

"Knowledge of falsity" is a fancy way of saying "lie."

Quotations are a part of most news stories, and they can pose an interesting problem for a court when libel is alleged. Two kinds of quotes might appear in a story. Statements that are enclosed within quote marks are called direct quotes and are supposed to represent an exact

---

77. *Kassel* v. *Gannett Co., Inc.,* 875 F. 2d 935 (1989).
78. Ibid.
79. 376 U.S. 254 (1964).
80. *Goldwater* v. *Ginzburg*, 414 F. 2d 324 (1969).

(or as close as possible) copy of what the subject said. But reporters also use what are called indirect quotes. These represent the substance of what the subject said, but not necessarily his or her exact words. Imagine that Sen. Maria Fernandez tells a reporter "We need to increase the size of the U.S. Army."

Direct quote: "We need to increase the size of the U.S. Army," Sen. Maria Fernandez said.

Indirect quote: Sen. Maria Fernandez said she believed the nation needs a larger army.

A legal question that can arise is this: If a journalist changes the words that were uttered by a subject, but still puts them inside quote marks, implying this is exactly what the subject said, can these be used as evidence of knowledge of falsity, actual malice? The Supreme Court confronted this question almost 20 years ago when a psychoanalyst named Jeffrey Masson sued New Yorker magazine and writer Janet Malcolm. Malcolm had interviewed Masson for more than 40 hours and wrote a long article about him, an article that was later republished as a book. Masson objected to many of the comments attributed to him as direct quotes, claiming that Malcolm had changed his words, that she had fabricated the statements. The quoted statements made him look foolish, he said, and he sued for defamation. Masson stipulated that he was a public figure, so he had to prove actual malice. He argued that changing his words in the direct quotes was evidence of knowledge of falsity.

A lower court agreed with the psychoanalyst, but the Supreme Court reversed this decision in a 7-2 ruling. The court ruled that readers do presume that words contained within quotation marks are a verbatim reproduction of what the subject said. Nevertheless, Justice Anthony Kennedy wrote, to demand that the press meet such a high standard is unrealistic. "If every alteration [of a quote] constituted the falsity required to prove actual malice, the practice of journalism, which the First Amendment is designed to protect, would require a radical change. . . . We conclude that a deliberate alteration of the words uttered by a plaintiff does not equate with knowledge of falsity . . . unless the alteration results in a *material change* [emphasis added] in the meaning conveyed by the statement."[81] The case was sent back for a trial in a lower court, but Masson was unable to convince a jury that Malcolm had knowledge of falsity when she wrote the story, and lost the case. An appellate court affirmed this verdict.

Reporters should strive to make certain direct quotes contain good copy of what a subject said, despite the leeway granted by the high court. But anyone who has worked as a journalist for even a short time knows it is often a real challenge to write down a speaker's exact words. People can talk a lot faster than a reporter can write. Indirect quotes are a useful substitute.

In a similar vein the Texas Supreme Court in 2005 ruled that it is not evidence of knowledge of falsity simply to show that a headline on a news story paraphrases the remarks of a speaker and is not a verbatim recitation of what the speaker said. The court said two questions must be answered: Would a reasonable reader believe these were the actual words of the speaker? And did the paraphrased comment alter the meaning of what the speaker actually said? If a reasonable reader would understand that this was a paraphrase or interpretation of what the speaker said, and not a recitation of the exact remark attributed to him or her, there can be no finding of actual malice.

---

81. *Masson* v. *The New Yorker, Inc.*, 111 S. Ct. 2419 (1991).

Reckless Disregard for the Truth

Reckless disregard for the truth is a bit more difficult to define. In 1964 the Supreme Court said that reckless disregard could be shown by proving that the defendant had "a high degree of awareness of [the] probable falsity" of the defamatory material when it was published.[82] Four years later the Supreme Court said that in order to show reckless disregard for the truth, the plaintiff must bring forth "sufficient evidence to permit the conclusion that the defendant in fact entertained serious doubts as to the truth of his publication."[83] Proof that the defendant failed to investigate a charge that later turns out to be false is not in and of itself sufficient evidence to prove actual malice.

Proof that the defendant failed to investigate a charge that later turns out to be false is not in and of itself sufficient evidence to prove actual malice.

KNOWLEDGE OF FALSITY

A high degree of awareness of the probable falsity of the defamatory
material when it was published

or

Sufficient evidence to permit the conclusion that the defendant in fact entertained
serious doubts as to the truth of the publication

These definitions of reckless disregard are certainly useful in a theoretical sense. It is surely possible to envision a reporter or editor entertaining serious doubts about the truth of an allegation and publishing it anyway. However, neither of these definitions is terribly helpful in a practical sense. As Judge Kozinski of the 9th U.S. Circuit Court of Appeals wrote in his decision in a case involving the National Enquirer and Clint Eastwood, "As we have yet to see a defendant who admits to entertaining serious subjective doubt about the authenticity of an article it published, we must be guided by circumstantial evidence."[84] Six years later the Georgia Court of Appeals ruled that "Absent an admission by the defendant that he knew his material was false or that he doubted its truth, a public figure [or public official] must rely upon circumstantial evidence to prove his case."[85] Fortunately there is language in a 1967 Supreme Court ruling that has been extremely helpful to both jurists and journalists in charting a course by using such evidence. The ruling involved two cases, *Curtis Publishing Co.* v. *Butts* and *AP* v. *Walker.*[86] Justice John Marshall Harlan outlined a test in his opinion to evaluate the conduct of both defendants in these libel cases. It is important to note that Justice Harlan never called the criteria he outlined a test for reckless disregard for the truth. He said he was attempting to establish a test to see whether the defendants in the two cases had seriously departed from the standards of responsible reporting. A few courts have rejected the Harlan criteria as a test for

---

82. *Garrison* v. *Louisiana*, 379 U.S. 64 (1964).
83. *St. Amant* v. *Thompson*, 390 U.S. 727 (1968).
84. *Eastwood* v. *National Enquirer Inc.*, 123 F. 3d 1249 (1997).
85. *Lake Park Post, Inc.* v. *Farmer*, 264 Ga. App. 299 (2003).
86. 388 U.S. 130 (1967).

actual malice.[87] But far more courts have used the three elements of Harlan's test as a basis for their own definition of reckless disregard for the truth.

The two cases that generated these criteria came before the Supreme Court at about the same time and were joined and decided as one case. In the first case, Wally Butts, the athletic director at the University of Georgia, brought suit against the Saturday Evening Post for an article it published alleging that Butts and University of Alabama football coach Paul "Bear" Bryant had conspired prior to the annual Georgia-Alabama football game to "fix" the contest. The Post obtained its information from a man who said that while making a telephone call, he had accidentally overheard a phone conversation between Butts and Bryant. George Burnett, who had a criminal record, told the Post editors that he had taken careful notes. The story was based on Burnett's recollection of what was said.

In the other case, Major General (retired) Edwin Walker, a political conservative and segregationist from Texas, brought suit against the Associated Press and a score of publications and broadcasting stations for publishing the charge that he led a mob of white citizens against federal marshals who were attempting to preserve order at the University of Mississippi in September of 1962, during the crisis over the enrollment of a black man, James Meredith. Walker was on campus during the disturbances, but did not lead a mob. The AP report was filed by a young AP correspondent on the scene.

The court ruled that in the *Butts* case the Post had exhibited highly unreasonable conduct in publishing the story but that in the *Walker* case no such evidence was present. Again, it is important to note that although Justice Harlan did not call the conduct reckless disregard at the time, most authorities accept these cases as good indicators of what the court means by reckless disregard. Look at the details of each case.

In the *Butts* case, the story was not what would be called a hot news item. It was published months after the game occurred. The magazine had ample time to check the report. The source of the story was not a trained reporter, but a layman who happened to be on probation on a bad-check charge. The Post made no attempt to investigate the story further, to screen the game films to see if either team had made changes in accord with what Bryant and Butts supposedly discussed. None of the many people supposedly with Burnett when he magically overheard this conversation were questioned by the Post. The magazine did little, then, to check the story, despite evidence presented at the trial that one or two of the editors acknowledged that Burnett's story needed careful examination. Finally, both Butts and Bryant had strong reputations for integrity. There had never even been hints of this kind of behavior in the past.

In the *Walker* case, different circumstances were present. For the AP editor back in the office who was responsible for getting the story on the wires, it was breaking news, a story that should be sent out immediately. The information was provided in the "heat of battle" by a young, but trained, reporter who in the past had given every indication of being trustworthy. All but one of the dispatches from the correspondent said the same thing: Walker led the mob. So there was internal consistency. Finally, when General Walker's previous actions and statements are considered, the story that he led a mob at Ole Miss was not terribly out of line with his prior behavior. There was nothing in the story to cause AP editors to suspect that it might be in error.

87. See, for example, *Clyburn* v. *News World Communications*, 903 F. 2d 29 (1990).

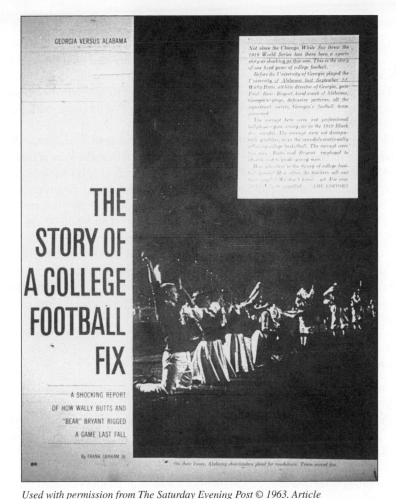

The Saturday Evening Post alleged that Wally Butts and Paul "Bear" Bryant conspired to fix the Georgia-Alabama football game during the 1962 college football season. Publication of this article ultimately resulted in the famous Curtis Publishing Co. v. Butts *ruling in 1967.*

Used with permission from The Saturday Evening Post © 1963. Article originally appeared in the March 23, 1963, issue of The Saturday Evening Post. Photo © Atlanta Journal Constitution

A story that on its face sounds improbable (e.g., the mob was being led by a prominent religious leader) should be viewed by editors like a flashing red light, suggesting that further investigation is needed. When all these are sorted out, three key factors emerge:

1. Was the publication of the story urgent? Was it hot or breaking news? Or was there sufficient time to more fully check the facts in the story?

2. How reliable was the source of the story? Should the reporter have trusted the news source? Was the source a trained journalist? Should the editor have trusted the reporter?

3. Was the story probable? Or was the story so unlikely that it cried out for further examination?

These elements form the base of most judicial definitions of reckless disregard for the truth. Two additional burdens face the plaintiff seeking to prove actual malice.

■ **The plaintiff must prove actual malice with "clear and convincing" evidence.**[88] Normally in a civil lawsuit the plaintiff must prove his or her allegations with a "preponderance of the evidence," which means that the plaintiff has more evidence than the defendant. "Clear and convincing" means that there can be little or no dispute about the evidence.

■ **The Supreme Court has instructed appellate courts to re-examine the evidence in the case to determine that the record "establishes actual malice with convincing clarity."**[89] Typically an appellate court is bound to accept the evidentiary findings of the trial court (see pages 14–16). But if the First Amendment defense applies in a libel case, the appellate court is mandated to take a close look and make certain the evidence supports the finding of malice. Allotting the appellate court such evidentiary power not only gives the defendant a second chance to win the case on the basis of the facts, but it also forces trial court judges to take extra pains when examining the facts, knowing that their work will likely be closely scrutinized in the future. The following overview of court rulings on actual malice will help illuminate both the criteria for such a finding and these two defense advantages.

Applying the Actual Malice Standard

Courts use a variety of means to try to determine whether or not the defendant acted with reckless disregard for the truth. Since, as noted earlier, few defendants admit to entertaining serious doubts about the truth of something they have published, circumstantial evidence becomes an important element in many cases. And different courts use different tests. The South Carolina Supreme Court ruled in 2005 that if a plaintiff could show there was an extreme departure from the standards of investigation and reporting ordinarily adhered to by reasonable publishers, this would be satisfactory proof of a reckless disregard for the truth. Tom Anderson lost an election for a seat in the state House of Representatives in 1996, but ran again the following fall in a special election. When queried, Anderson told a reporter for the Augusta Chronicle that during the previous campaign he had been called out to work in North Carolina as an appraiser for several insurance companies in the wake of hurricanes Bertha and Fran. He also worked for the National Flood Insurance Program.

The reporter contended Anderson told him he was called away to serve in the National Guard, and wrote two stories containing that statement. Anderson said he never saw the stories, and so made no effort to correct this mistake. Months later a different reporter from the same newspaper called Anderson and asked him if he was going to withdraw from the race for the House. Why would I do that? Anderson asked. Because, the reporter said, it was proved that he had lied about serving with the Guard. Anderson denied telling anyone he served in the National Guard. He sent documents to the newspaper supporting his claim of working as an insurance

88. *Gertz* v. *Robert Welch, Inc.*, 418 U.S. 323 (1974).
89. *Bose Corporation* v. *Consumers Union of the United States, Inc.*, 446 U.S. 485 (1984).

appraiser during the campaign. The newspaper published a third story, making the same claim (with Anderson's denial) and then published an editorial attacking Anderson, saying he had lied about serving in the National Guard, and that he had dishonored himself and the Guard with his fabrication. Anderson sued for libel. Was there evidence of actual malice by the newspaper?

The court said the record was replete with circumstantial evidence of bad faith on the part of the paper. Anderson had told the second reporter he had been in North Carolina working for the National Flood Program, not in the Guard. The information contained in the documents Anderson sent the newspaper directly contradicted the initial newspaper reports. A nearby newspaper had published material containing Anderson's insistence that he had been in North Carolina during the campaign. These facts, the court said, known to the Chronicle before it published the editorial, could lead a reasonable jury to infer that the newspaper had obvious reasons to doubt the reporter's recollection that Anderson told him he had been called to service in the National Guard. A lower court had dismissed the case because there was no evidence of actual malice. The state Supreme Court reversed this ruling and sent the case back for a jury trial.[90]

But in a somewhat similar case, the Virginia Supreme Court came to a contrary conclusion. A political candidate sued the Virginia Pilot newspaper for publishing what he described as erroneous and libelous material in 2003. He argued that the newspaper had acted with actual malice because five years earlier, in 1998, it had published stories that contained the correct information. The fact that the newspaper had published the correct information in 1998 was proof that the editors knew the truth when they published the erroneous stories in 2003. But the court disagreed. "The mere presence of news stories in a newspaper's files containing information that contradicts an allegedly defamatory statement by a news organization is insufficient to establish actual malice," the court said.[91]

In sorting out claims of actual malice, courts often are forced to delve deeply into the reporting process. Sports Illustrated published an article on fixed boxing matches. The article cited a match between Randall "Tex" Cobb and Paul "Sonny" Barch, which was promoted by Rick Parker, as an example of a fixed fight. A senior editor at the magazine had gotten a call from Barch in which he alleged the fix. He told the editor that he had given sworn testimony to the Florida State Athletic Commission (FSAC) regarding the fight. Barch said that he and Cobb had agreed that Barch would take a dive in the first round. He also said that he and Cobb and Parker had all used cocaine before the match. The editor assigned an experienced reporter to check out the story. She had worked for both the magazine and The Wall Street Journal, but she was not a boxing expert. The magazine took the following steps to check out the story:

- ∎ The reporter talked at length with an official at the FSAC who confirmed Barch's story.
- ∎ She talked with promoter Parker's ex-business partner who confirmed the allegations.
- ∎ Barch was a last-minute substitute in the fight, so the reporter interviewed the original opponent, who said he was replaced on the fight card at the last minute under phony circumstances.
- ∎ The reporter also talked with Barch and with Parker.

90. *Anderson* v. *Augusta Chronicle*, 619 S.E. 2d 428 (2005).
91. *Jackson* v. *Hartig*, 645 S.E. 2d 303 (2007).

- Cobb was a reluctant interview subject, but the reporter finally talked with him on the telephone. He denied the whole story.
- Several reporters, including some who regularly covered boxing, watched a tape of the fight.

But the magazine did not do the following:

- No one at Sports Illustrated talked with the referee for the fight or the ringside judges.
- No one reviewed the sworn testimony that Barch said he gave to the FSAC.
- No outside boxing experts were consulted.
- No one other than Barch was ever consulted about whether Cobb had been a knowing participant in the scheme.

A trial court awarded Cobb almost $10 million in damages, but the 6th U.S. Court of Appeals reversed the judgment, ruling that there was not clear and convincing proof that the magazine's editors or reporters entertained serious doubts about the truth or falsity of the story. The court agreed that the investigation could have been more comprehensive, noting that someone should have interviewed the referee and the judges. But the court ruled that while failure to take additional steps might not have been prudent, and could be considered negligence, this did not amount to actual malice.[92]

The law does not require the complete verification of a story, especially a breaking story.

The law does not require the complete verification of a story, especially a breaking story. Two cases make this point. In 2003 the New York Post carried a short rewrite of a story carried on the Los Angeles Times wire service. The story suggested that rock music personality Ozzy Osborne's former doctor had overprescribed various drugs during the time Ozzy was featured in a reality TV series, and these left him "stoned" most of the time during the TV series. The L.A. Times story accurately stated the state medical board "moved to revoke" the doctor's license. However, the Post story, headlined "Ozzy's RX doc's license pulled," said the board had revoked his license.[93] The physician had a well-known detoxification practice, and had been in movies and on TV. He was a public person and would have to prove actual malice. At the trial the reporter said he did not recall writing that the license had been revoked, and thought the error might have occurred during editing. The editors testified they had no knowledge of how the mistake got into the story, that they did not investigate the claim because they thought it came from the Times story. It was not normal practice to check the facts in wire stories, they said.[94] The New York Court of Appeals ruled that it could find no evidence that suggested with convincing clarity the Post had committed actual malice and ruled in favor of the newspaper.[95]

In 1996 the District of Columbia U.S. Circuit Court of Appeals ruled that evidence that a book publisher failed to completely verify defamatory allegations written by an author whose credibility had been frequently questioned was not sufficient to demonstrate that the publisher had in fact entertained serious doubts about the truth of these allegations. The book

---

92. *Cobb* v. *Time Inc.*, 278 F. 3d 629 (2002). Many courts have ruled that the failure of the defendant to investigate libelous allegations prior to publishing is not, in and of itself, evidence of actual malice. See, for example, *Paterson* v. *Little Brown and Co.*, 35 M.L.R. 2153 (2007).
93. *Kipper* v. *NYP Holding Co.*, 37 M.L.R. 1673 (2009).
94. Ibid.
95. Ibid.

in question is "Profits of War" by Ari Ben-Menashe, a man, the publisher acknowledged, whose credibility was often suspect. But Ben-Menashe was relied on as a credible source by many writers and television producers. The book contained allegations that Robert C. McFarlane, a former national security advisor, was really an Israeli agent who facilitated spying by the Israelis on the United States. Many of Ben-Menashe's allegations about McFarlane were proved to be false four months after the book was published when a congressional task force released a report on many topics related to relations between the United States and Middle Eastern nations. At the time the book was published, however, much of the evidence contained in the task force report had not yet been made public.

McFarlane argued that because Ben-Menashe's credibility was dubious at best, the book publisher had a duty to verify every one of his defamatory assertions. The court disagreed with that argument. "When the source of potentially libelous material is questionable . . . the investigatory efforts of the publisher are important only to the extent that they serve as evidence that it did not publish the material in reckless disregard for the truth," the judges said. The publisher does not have to corroborate every allegation, the court said. In this case the publisher did attempt to verify all the defamatory statements but was unable to find evidence to substantiate many of the charges. At the same time no contradictory evidence was uncovered either. "To hold that a publisher who relies upon a questionable source must not only investigate the allegations but actually corroborate them . . . would be to turn the inquiry away from the publisher's state of mind and to inquire instead whether the publisher satisfied an objective standard of care," the court ruled. The plaintiff had failed to demonstrate actual malice.[96]

Reporters and editors who attempt to rebut a charge of reckless disregard for the truth by using information they claim came from confidential sources need to be very careful. In some instances a court will simply block the efforts by the defense to even introduce such material. A federal court in Washington, D.C., recently ruled that The New York Times could not use such information in defending itself from a lawsuit by Dr. Stephen J. Hatfill, a germ warfare specialist who once worked for the Army. Hatfill asserted that a column by Nicholas D. Kristof suggested he was responsible for the deadly anthrax mailings in 2001. Kristof claimed he had five sources for the allegations, but refused to identify them. Three of those sources ultimately gave Kristof permission to reveal their identities, but two remain confidential. Judge Liam O'Grady ruled that information from these sources could not be introduced at trial to substantiate the allegations in the column.[97]* (See pages 382–383 and 387–390 for more on the problem of using confidential sources to defend a libel suit.)

One evolving issue related to actual malice is the matter of the defendant's motivation for publishing the defamatory material. Before the ruling in *New York Times* v. *Sullivan* the term "malice" was related to the question, Why did the defendant make these defamatory charges? Was it simply to inform the public of a problem or a concern, or were the charges published because the defendant didn't like the plaintiff or was angry with the plaintiff? In other words, was the publication fostered by ill will, spite or malice? The actual malice standard outlined

*In January 2007 the U.S. District Court granted the newspaper's motion for a summary judgment, ruling that Hatfill had failed to show evidence of actual malice. *Hatfill* v. *New York Times Co.*, 35 M.L.R. 1391 (2007); aff'd. 36 M.L.R. 1897 (2008).
96. *McFarlane* v. *Sheridan Square Press Inc.*, 91 F. 3d 1501 (1996).
97. Lewis, "Judge's Ruling Bars The Times."

by the Supreme Court in 1964 doesn't address why something was published or broadcast, but focuses instead on the defendant's behavior or belief that the matter is truthful. The high court called this actual malice, to distinguish it from traditional or common-law malice.

The Supreme Court has ruled on at least two occasions that a showing of ill will or spite by a plaintiff is not sufficient to prove actual malice.[98] But state courts in Kentucky[99] and Washington[100] have ruled that evidence of ill will and spite can be used as evidence of actual malice in some circumstances. The 2nd U.S. Circuit Court of Appeals ruled in 2001 a reporter's bias against an organization could be relevant to show a purposeful avoidance of the truth (actual malice) if it were coupled with evidence of an extreme departure from standard investigative techniques.[101] But even those courts willing to hear such evidence have set a fairly high standard for the plaintiff to meet. A recent case from South Carolina demonstrates this point.

A newspaper in a small South Carolina town ran a column in which it simply printed questions and comments from readers who submitted them by letter or telephone. One comment included in the column was a telephone message that questioned why the police chief had not stopped drug dealers in the community from selling their wares and questioned whether the chief was being paid by the dealers to allow their business to continue. The chief sued for libel and won at trial. The state's high court had to evaluate the evidence that the material was published with actual malice; the police chief is a public official and the comments related to his official duties. The plaintiff argued that the editor of the paper had failed to investigate or verify the information left on the telephone message. The phone message that was the supposed basis for the item was erased by someone at the newspaper. Four years earlier the paper's editor had been arrested for manufacturing marijuana. He pleaded guilty. And the chief said the editor had been rude to his wife on a recent occasion. Mere failure to investigate a charge is not evidence of actual malice, the plaintiff acknowledged. But the last three elements, the chief said, surely showed that the item in the newspaper was published with ill will and spite. The court ruled that while the defendant's motivation may bear some relation to the inquiry into actual malice, the courts must be careful not to place too much reliance on it. It is irrelevant in this case, the court said. Even if the editor's conviction on a drug charge and his rudeness do show some ill will toward the chief, these factors fall far short of the clear and convincing evidence required to prove that he had a high degree of awareness of the falsity of the charges.[102] The question of what motivates a broadcaster or editor to carry a story is a developing issue, and journalists need to remember that it is best to keep personal feelings out of the stories they prepare.

SUMMARY

In a lawsuit against a mass medium, a private person must prove that the defendant was at least negligent in publishing the defamatory matter. Negligence has been defined as the failure to exercise reasonable care or as acting in such a way as to create a substantial risk of harm. In some states, in certain cases private persons will be required to prove more than

98. See *Harte-Hanks Communications Inc.* v. *Connaughton*, 109 S. Ct. 2678 (1989); and *Beckley Newspapers* v. *Hanks*, 389 U.S. 81 (1967). See also *Johnson* v. *E.W. Scripps Co.*, 31 M.L.R. 1503 (2003).
99. *Ball* v. *E.W. Scripps Co.*, 801 S.W. 2d 684 (1990).
100. *Herron* v. *King Broadcasting Co.*, 746 P. 2d 295 (1987).
101. *Church of Scientology International* v. *Behar*, 238 F. 3d 168 (2001).
102. *Elder* v. *Gaffney Ledger*, 533 S.E. 2d 899 (2000).

simple negligence. They may be required to prove gross negligence, which is a standard that implies a greater degree of carelessness on the part of the defendant. An individual who has been declared to be a public person for the purposes of a libel suit must prove actual malice. Actual malice is defined as knowledge of falsity or reckless disregard of the truth. Transmitting a story with the knowledge of its falsity means that the publishers of the story knew it was not true but still communicated it to the public. To prove reckless disregard for the truth, the plaintiff must show that the publisher of the defamation had a "high degree of awareness of the probable falsity of the material" when it was published or that the publisher in fact "entertained serious doubts about the truth of the material" before it was published. The courts have established a set of three criteria to help determine whether material was published with reckless disregard for the truth. The jurists tend to look at these factors:

1. Whether there was time to investigate the story or whether the material had to be published quickly
2. Whether the source of the information appeared to be reliable and trustworthy
3. Whether the story itself sounded probable or farfetched

If the item was hot news, if the source was a trained journalist and if the information in the story sounded probable, there can be no finding of reckless disregard. However, if there was plenty of time to investigate, if the source of the material was questionable or if the information in the story sounded completely improbable, courts are more likely to permit a finding of reckless disregard for the truth.

INTENTIONAL INFLICTION OF EMOTIONAL DISTRESS

The tort, intentional infliction of emotional distress (IIED), first appeared in the late 19th century, but was not recognized by the "Restatement of the Law of Torts," the highly regarded synthesis of tort law published by the American Law Institute, until 1948. As noted by a federal judge in 2008, the tort was created for a limited purpose to allow recovery in those rare instances in which a defendant intentionally inflicts severe emotional distress in a manner so unusual that the victim has no other recognized theory of redress.[103] In 1965 the "Restatement" provided for the first time a definition of the tort, which has four parts:

▪ **The defendant's conduct was intentional or reckless.**
▪ **The defendant's conduct was extreme and outrageous.**
▪ **The defendant's conduct caused the plaintiff emotional distress.**
▪ **The emotional distress was severe.**[104]

103. *Conradt* v. *NBC Universal Inc.*, 536 F. Supp. 2d 380 (2008).
104. American Law Institute, *Restatement of the Law of Torts.*

In practice, courts focus on a single criterion—whether the defendant acted outrageously, according to an article by Susan Kirkpatrick in the Northwestern University Law Review.[105] Or as one court put it, the defendant's conduct went beyond all possible bounds of decency and was regarded as atrocious and utterly intolerable in a civilized community.*

What does this tort have to do with libel law? Some plaintiffs who feel blocked in their attempts to sue for libel by the First Amendment defenses erected since 1964 have sought to use IIED as an alternate legal remedy. The most notable case emerged in the 1980s. The lawsuit was prompted when Hustler magazine published a parody of a series of widely circulated ads for Campari liquor. The real Campari ads featured interviews with celebrities who discussed the first time they tasted the liquor. The printed advertisements had fairly strong sexual overtones as the subjects talked about their "first time." The Hustler parody was a fictitious interview with the Rev. Jerry Falwell, an evangelical preacher who in the 1980s led a conservative political action group called The Moral Majority. Falwell described his first sexual experience as an incestuous encounter with his mother. Falwell was also characterized by the parody as a drunkard. There was a small disclaimer at the bottom of the parody, and it was listed in the table of contents as fiction.

Falwell sued the magazine for libel, invasion of privacy and intentional infliction of emotional distress. The trial judge dismissed the invasion of privacy claim, but sent the other two to the jury. Jurors rejected the libel claim on the grounds that the parody was so far-fetched, no person could possibly believe that it described actual facts about Falwell. The jury did award the Baptist preacher $200,000 in damages for emotional distress.

Hustler appealed the ruling, but a unanimous three-judge panel of the U.S. Court of Appeals for the 4th Circuit upheld the damage award, noting that all the proof that was needed in such a case was that the item was sufficiently outrageous as to cause emotional harm and that it was published intentionally.[106] While most journalists did not condone the Hustler style of parody, they nevertheless viewed the decision as a serious threat to freedom of expression. The sturdy First Amendment barrier built up to protect the mass media from libel suits brought by persons in the public eye was neatly circumvented by Falwell in this case. Because of his presence as a spokesperson for the conservative religious right in this nation, Falwell would likely be considered a public figure in a libel action and be forced to prove actual malice before he could collect damages. In this suit he did not even have to show negligence. Nor did the broad First Amendment protection that is granted to statements of opinion apply outside the law of libel. In the future, individuals suing for satire or parody could avoid having to surmount the constitutional barriers in libel law by instead filing an action for intentional infliction of emotional distress.

Hustler appealed to the Supreme Court and in 1988, in a unanimous ruling, the high court reversed the appellate court ruling. Chief Justice Rehnquist, noting that most people would see the Hustler parody as gross and repugnant, nevertheless rejected Falwell's argument that because he was seeking damages for severe emotional distress rather than reputational harm, a standard different from that applied in libel should apply. "Were we to hold

---

* Courts usually apply an objective standard to determine whether the plaintiff has proved this element, but in cases where reasonable people may differ, a jury will be asked to make this determination. See *Moreno* v. *Hartford Sentinel, Inc.*, 37 M.L.R. 1496 (2009).

105. Kirkpatrick, "Intentional Infliction of Emotional Distress," 993.

106. *Falwell* v. *Flynt*, 797 F. 2d 1270 (1986).

otherwise," the chief justice wrote, "there can be little doubt that political cartoonists and satirists would be subjected to damages awarded without any showing that their work falsely defamed its subject." Rehnquist added:

> The appeal of the political cartoon or caricature is often based on exploration of unfortunate physical traits or politically embarrassing events—an exploration often calculated to injure the feelings of the subject of the portrayal. The art of the cartoonist is often not reasoned or evenhanded, but slashing and one-sided.[107]

Falwell contended it was making a mockery of serious political cartoons to compare them to the Hustler parody, which was truly outrageous. The law should protect even public figures from such outrageous caricatures. Rehnquist disagreed, noting the outrageousness standard of liability would not work.

> "Outrageousness" in the area of political and social discourse has an inherent subjectiveness about it which would allow a jury to impose liability on the basis of jurors' tastes and views or perhaps on the basis of their dislike of a particular expression.[108]

The court ruled that in order for a public figure or public official to win an emotional distress claim, it would be necessary to prove three things:

1. That the parody or satire amounted to statement of fact, not an opinion.
2. That it was a false statement of fact.
3. That the person who drew the cartoon or wrote the article knew it was false, or exhibited reckless disregard for the truth or falsity of the material. In other words, proof of actual malice is necessary.

Typical of many of the IIED cases that have been filed is a lawsuit from Florida that was being litigated as this chapter was prepared. The 2-year-old child of a woman named Melinda Duckett was reported missing. CNN's Nancy Grace, a former prosecutor, interviewed Duckett by telephone for use on her nightly cable broadcast. During the interview Grace verbally attacked Duckett, intimating that she had killed her own child. Just before the interview was aired on CNN, Duckett killed herself. CNN telecast the interview anyway, and rebroadcast it several times thereafter. The family sued for IIED/wrongful death. It claimed the interview was solicited by Grace under false pretenses, and was used merely to increase the ratings of the cable show. The federal court denied CNN's motion to dismiss the case, noting that the plaintiffs had correctly alleged all the needed elements of an IIED action. A trial would be needed. The judge noted that there had been very few IIED cases in Florida where damages had been awarded and affirmed, but added that courts have tended to find that conduct that would normally be merely insulting or careless can become "outrageous" if it follows the death of a family member.[109]

---

107. *Hustler Magazine* v. *Falwell*, 108 S. Ct. 876 (1988).
108. Ibid.
109. *Estate of Duckett* v. *Cable News Network*, LLLP, 36 M.L.R. 2210 (2008).

SUMMARY The intentional infliction of emotional distress is a new tort and punishes a wide range of conduct, including the publication or broadcast of material that is outrageous and causes severe emotional distress. Courts have made it extremely difficult for plaintiffs to win such suits by placing a substantial burden of proof on the injured party. The Supreme Court added to this burden in 1988 when it ruled that public-person plaintiffs would have to show actual malice as well to win their lawsuits.

BIBLIOGRAPHY

American Law Institute. *Restatement of the Law of Torts*. 2nd ed. Philadelphia: American Law Institute, 1975.

Ashley, Paul. *Say It Safely*. 5th ed. Seattle: University of Washington Press, 1976.

Barron, Jerome, and C. Thomas Dienes. *Handbook of Free Speech and Free Press*. Boston: Little, Brown, 1979.

Kirkpatrick, Susan. "*Falwell* v. *Flynt:* Intentional Infliction of Emotional Distress as a Threat to Free Speech." *Northwestern University Law Review* 81 (1987): 993.

Lewis, Anthony. *Make No Law*. New York: Random House, 1991.

Lewis, Neil A. "Judge's Ruling Bars The Times From Using Sources' Information in Defense Against Suit." *The New York Times,* 17 November 2006, A12.

Prosser, William L. *Handbook of the Law of Torts*. St Paul: West Publishing, 1963.

Smolla, Rodney A. *Suing the Press*. New York: Oxford University Press, 1986.

———. "Dun & Bradstreet, Hepps, and Liberty Lobby: A New Analytic Primer on the Future Course of Defamation." *Georgetown Law Journal* 75 (1987): 1519.

Stonecipher, Harry, and Don Sneed. "A Survey of the Professional Person as Libel Plaintiff." *Arkansas Law Review* 46 (1993): 303.

CHAPTER 6

Libel

DEFENSES AND DAMAGES

Libel defenses are hundreds of years old. Most of them grew out of common law, but today many defenses are contained in state statutes as well. Before the mid-1960s when the Supreme Court began to add substantial new First Amendment burdens upon libel plaintiffs, defenses were the primary means of warding off a defamation lawsuit. Most plaintiffs today lose because they can't meet the required burden of proof; but defenses remain a viable and important part of the law. Not only can a libel defense protect a defendant from a successful suit, it also can stop a plaintiff's case quickly, saving the publication or broadcasting outlet both time and money. Citing an appropriate defense, a defendant can ask a judge to dismiss a case even before a hearing is held. Such a dismissal is called a summary judgment. The judge may issue such a ruling if he or she does not think the plaintiff can prove what is required, as outlined in Chapters 4 and 5, or believes the defendant had a legal right (a defense) to publish or broadcast the defamatory material. Libel defenses are the primary subject of this chapter. Following this material is a brief outline of both civil libel damages and criminal libel.

SUMMARY JUDGMENT/STATUTE OF LIMITATIONS

The **summary judgment** is undoubtedly one of the best friends the mass media libel defendant has. About three-fourths of media requests for a summary judgment are granted by the courts. If the defendant's request for such a judgment is granted by the court, the case ends without a trial. Trials cost a lot of money and the press has not established a good track record for winning cases sent to a jury. Here is a brief outline of what happens in the summary judgment procedure.

After the plaintiffs have made their initial written allegations to the court, but before the trial begins, the defendants can argue that the lawsuit should be dismissed either because the plaintiff has failed to establish what is necessary to sustain the libel suit (publication, identification, defamation, falsity, and the requisite level of fault) or because there is a legal defense that blocks a successful lawsuit. As it considers this motion by the defense, the court is obligated to look at the plaintiff's allegation in the most favorable possible way. And if there is any dispute regarding facts (which would be settled at a subsequent trial), it must be for now resolved in favor of the plaintiff. If, having considered these factors, the court determines that a reasonable juror, acting reasonably, could not find for the plaintiff, then the motion for summary judgment will be granted.[1] (Please note that the plaintiff can also ask for a summary judgment, arguing there is no possible way a juror could find for the defendant.)

Here's a hypothetical example of how the summary judgment works. Imagine that Laura Parker, the editor of a small newsletter, the Iowa Consumer News, publishes a story that accuses Argot Farms, a giant corporate grain producer, of selling corn to cereal makers that has been labeled as adulterated and unfit for human consumption by the U.S. Department of Agriculture. For many years Argot has portrayed itself in television advertising as an environmentally friendly and responsible corporation. "Healthy food for healthy families" is the corporate slogan. Argot sues for libel, claiming that the story is false. Parker asks the court for a summary judgment and makes two arguments to support her request:

1. The story is true and therefore the case should be dismissed.
2. Argot Farms, because of its heavy television advertising, is a public figure. Therefore it must have proof of actual malice to win its case. It has made no allegations regarding actual malice, only charges of simple negligence on Parker's part.

---

1. See, for example, *Nader* v. *DeToledano,* 408 A. 2d 31 (1979).

Argot Farms asks the court to deny the motion for a summary judgment and makes the following three arguments:

1. It is not a public figure, simply a business trying to win customers through normal advertising. Therefore it must only show negligence.
2. The story is false.
3. Parker got the information for her story from an unreliable source.

In ruling on Parker's motion for a summary judgment the court must assume that the facts, as stated by Argot Farms, are true; that is, that the story is false, and that Parker got the information from an unreliable source. If the case later goes to trial, both these "facts" will be examined through the presentation of evidence.

Based on the record as presented by the plaintiff, the judge can

1. agree with Parker that Argot Farms is a public figure and, since there is not even an allegation of actual malice, grant the summary judgment; or
2. agree with Argot Farms that it is not a public figure and, based on the assumptions that the story is false and there is evidence of negligence, refuse to grant the motion for a summary judgment.

The loser in either case can appeal the ruling. The appellate court will reconsider the matter. Is Argot a public figure? Do the company's allegations present sufficient evidence of negligence or actual malice? If the appellate court agrees with the trial court, it will sustain the summary judgment. The case will end unless Argot appeals to an even higher court. But the appellate court may reverse the lower-court ruling, finding that the company is not a public figure and must prove only negligence or that it is a public figure but there is sufficient suggestion of actual malice in its allegations to go to trial. The case will then return to the lower court for a trial, unless Parker takes a subsequent appeal. When the case goes to trial, Argot and Parker must present evidence to support their allegations. The assumption that the plaintiff's allegations are true is no longer valid.[*]

The Supreme Court has given both trial and appellate courts wide latitude in granting summary judgments in libel cases, especially in suits brought by public persons. In 1986 the justices said that federal courts must grant a summary judgment in favor of the media defendants in cases involving actual malice unless the plaintiffs can demonstrate that they will be able to offer a jury clear and convincing evidence of actual malice.[2] Some trial judges had been hesitant about granting summary judgments because they believed that proof of actual malice calls the defendant's state of mind into question, which is a matter better considered at trial. But judges who force a trial even in the face of a weak libel claim are playing into the hands of those litigants who like to use the law to harass the press. Federal Judge Stanley Sarokin explained the importance of a summary judgment to the press in a 1985 ruling:

> Possibly the giants of the industry have both the finances and the stamina to run the risk in such situations [the threat of a libel suit]. But the independent will of smaller magazines, newspapers, television and radio stations undoubtedly bends with the spectre of a libel action looming. Even if convinced of

The Supreme Court has given both trial and appellate courts wide latitude in granting summary judgments in libel cases.

[*]This is a simplistic outline of how a motion for summary judgment may be treated by the courts and not a detailed explanation of how a libel suit may proceed.
2. *Anderson* v. *Liberty Lobby,* 477 U.S. 242 (1986).

their ultimate success on the merits, the costs of vindication may soon be too great for such media defendants to print or publish that which may entail any risk of a court action. If that is the result, it is a sorry state of affairs for the media, and, more important, for the country. Therefore, probably more than any other type of case, summary judgments in libel actions should be readily available and granted where appropriate.[3]

STATUTE OF LIMITATIONS

For nearly all crimes and most civil actions, there is a **statute of limitations.** Courts do not like stale legal claims. They have plenty of fresh ones to keep them busy. Prosecution for most crimes except homicide and kidnapping must be started within a specified period of time. For example, in many states if prosecution is not started within seven years after an armed robbery is committed, the robber cannot be brought to trial. He or she is home free. (However, the robber can still be prosecuted for failing to pay income tax on money taken from a bank, but that is another story.)

The duration of the statute of limitations for libel actions differs from state to state, varying from one to three years (Figure 6.1).[*] In most states the duration is one or two years; this means the libel suit must be started within one or two years following the date of publication of the offending material. Courts have had to decide what is the date of publication for the various mass media. The consensus is as follows:

- **Newspapers:** The date of publication for newspapers is the date that appears on the newspaper.
- **Radio and television:** The date of publication is the date on which the material is broadcast or telecast.
- **Magazines:** The date of publication is the date on which the magazine is distributed to a substantial portion of the public, regardless of the date printed on the cover of the magazine.[4] (The date printed on the cover rarely coincides with the date the magazine is distributed; for example, the October issue of a magazine is usually distributed in September or even August.)
- **Internet:** The date of publication is the date the material is posted on the Web.

What if one or a few copies of the offending material are redistributed or republished after the initial publication date? If the material is altered or revised before it is republished, the statute of limitations is restarted.[5] But if it is the same edition (on December 5, 2009, someone buys

---

[*]Most courts that have considered the question have ruled the statute of limitations for libel actions applies as well to invasion-of-privacy suits. See, for example, *Christoff* v. *Nestle USA Inc.*, 152 Cal. App. 4th 1439 (2007); attd. 37 M.L.R. 2089 (2009) *Pierce* v. *Clarion Ledger,* 34 M.L.R. 1275 (2006); and *Chaker* v. *Crogan,* 33 M.L.R. 2569 (2005).

3. *Schiavone Construction* v. *Time,* 619 F. Supp. 684 (1985).

4. *Printon Inc.* v. *McGraw-Hill Inc.*, 35 F. Supp. 2d 1325 (1998). See also *MacDonald* v. *Time,* 554 F. Supp. 1053 (1983); *Wildmon* v. *Hustler,* 508 F. Supp. 87 (1980); *Bradford* v. *American Media Operations, Inc.,* 882 F. Supp. 1508 (1995); and *Williamson* v. *New Times Inc.,* 980 S.W. 2d 706 (1998).

5. *Firth* v. *New York,* 747 N.Y.S. 2d 69 (2002); *Van Buskirk* v. *New York Times,* 325 F. 3d 87 (2003); *Mitan* v. *Davis,* W.D. Ky., Civil Action No. 3:00 CV-841-5, 2/3/03; *McCandliss* v. *Cox Enterprises Inc.,* 593 S.E. 2d 856 (2004); and *Traditional Cat Ass'n* v. *Gilbreath,* Cal. Ct. App. No. D041421, 5/6/04. In some states, if the offending material is republished in a different edition of a newspaper, or is posted by the newspaper on its Web site, this constitutes a separate publication. See *Rivera* v. *NYP Holdings Inc.,* 35 M.L.R. 2127 (2007). And some states have not adopted the single publication rule. See *Taub* v. *McClatchy Newspapers Inc.*, 35 M.L.R. 2179 (2007), for example.

MAP SHOWING DURATION OF STATUTE OF LIMITATIONS IN LIBEL ACTIONS

☐ = One year

☐ = Two years

■ = Three years

FIGURE 6.1

Plaintiffs must file libel suits before the statute of limitations expires. This chart indicates the duration of this filing period in the 50 states.

a copy of the May 3, 2008, Centralia Post), the single publication rule comes into play. This rule, which most states have adopted, says that the entire edition of a newspaper or magazine or Web posting is a single publication and isolated republication of the material months or years later does not constitute republication, which would restart the statute of limitations. However, the rebroadcast of defamatory material on radio or television is generally considered a new publication, since it is intended to reach a new audience, and therefore generates a new opportunity for injury.[6]

Jurisdiction

Is it possible for a plaintiff who has not filed a libel suit within the statute of limitations in his or her home state to file an action in another state that has a longer statute of limitations? The answer is yes, so long as the libel has been circulated in this other state. The Supreme Court clarified this question in two 1984 rulings, *Keeton* v. *Hustler*[7] and *Calder* v. *Jones.*[8] Kathy Keeton, a resident of New York, sued Hustler magazine, an Ohio corporation, for libel in the state of New Hampshire. Hustler challenged the action, arguing that the suit should be

6. *Lehman* v. *Discovery Communications Inc.,* 32 M.L.R. 2377 (2004).
7. 465 U.S. 770 (1984).
8. 465 U.S. 783 (1984).

brought in New York or Ohio but not New Hampshire, which had a six-year statute of limitations. (The statute of limitations is now three years in New Hampshire.) Only about 15,000 copies of the 1-million-plus circulation of the magazine were sold in New Hampshire, the defendant argued. A court of appeals ruled that the plaintiff had too tenuous a contact with New Hampshire to permit the assertion of personal jurisdiction in that state, but the Supreme Court unanimously reversed the ruling. Hustler's regular circulation of magazines in New Hampshire is sufficient to support an assertion of jurisdiction in a libel action, Justice William Rehnquist wrote. "False statements of fact harm both the subject of the falsehood and the readers of the statement: New Hampshire may rightly employ its libel laws to discourage the deception of its citizens," the justice continued. The state may extend its concern to the injury that in-state libel causes to a nonresident as well, he added.[9]

The same day, the high court ruled that California courts could assume jurisdiction in a case brought by a California resident against the authors of a story that was written and published in a newspaper in Florida but circulated in California. Shirley Jones sued two journalists for an article they wrote and edited in Florida and that was then published in the National Enquirer. At that time the Enquirer had a national circulation of about 5 million and distributed about 600,000 copies each week in California. A trial court ruled that Jones could certainly sue the publishers of the Enquirer in California, but not the reporters. Requiring journalists to appear in remote jurisdictions to answer for the contents of articles on which they worked could have a chilling impact on the First Amendment rights of reporters and editors, the court said. But again a unanimous Supreme Court disagreed, with Justice Rehnquist noting that the article was about a California resident who works in California. Material for the article was drawn from California sources and the brunt of the harm to both the career and the personal reputation of the plaintiff will be suffered in California where the Enquirer has a huge circulation. In other words, the primary negative effect of the libel will be in California, he added. "An individual injured in California need not go to Florida to seek redress from persons who, though remaining in Florida, knowingly cause the injury in California," Rehnquist wrote. The justice said that the potential chill on protected First Amendment activity stemming from libel actions is already taken into account in the constitutional limitations on the substantive law governing such suits. "To reinforce those concerns at the jurisdictional level would be a form of double counting," he said.[10]

Jurisdiction and the Internet

These two Supreme Court rulings stand for the proposition that publishers may be sued in any jurisdiction in which they distribute even a relatively small portion of their publication—even if the plaintiff does not reside in that jurisdiction. How does this principle apply to communication on the Internet? Any message contained on any Web site is conceivably accessible in any state in the nation. Can the Web site operator or publisher of the allegedly defamatory material be sued in any or every jurisdiction? Is evidence that the message was received and downloaded by residents of the jurisdiction sufficient to begin a lawsuit in that jurisdiction? Or must there be stronger ties to the jurisdiction? These are questions that have yet to be

9. *Keeton* v. *Hustler,* 465 U.S. 770 (1984).
10. *Calder* v. *Jones,* 465 U.S. 783 (1984).

completely answered. The Supreme Court of the United States has passed on reviewing at least three cases that involve this jurisdiction question.[11] The lower courts seem to be more or less following one of two strategies: one that fairly broadly applies the so-called effects test from the *Calder* case, or one that applies the *Calder* test much more narrowly. Remember in *Calder* the Supreme Court ruled that California courts could exercise jurisdiction over journalists who resided in Florida because the article concerned California activities of a California resident and was published in a national publication that had a large circulation in California.[12] The lower courts that read this test broadly are ruling that a court in Montana, for example, can exercise jurisdiction only if there is evidence that the out-of-state Internet publisher was aware that the material could cause harm in Montana, that the material was aimed at the residents of Montana, and that the out-of-state publisher had some contact with someone or something in Montana. In one recent case articles were posted on the Web site of a Connecticut newspaper that allegedly defamed a Virginia resident. The 4th U.S. Court of Appeals ruled that the Virginia courts could not exercise jurisdiction in the matter because there was no evidence that the newspaper aimed the content of the site at Virginia residents. The article had to do with a Virginia prison warden and allegations that he had permitted guards to abuse inmates in the Virginia prison who had been relocated there from Connecticut. The court said the article was directed toward Connecticut residents, and the lawsuit should be filed in that state.[13] The 5th U.S. Court of Appeals made a similar ruling in 2002 when it held a Massachusetts resident and the operator of a New York Web site could not be sued in a Texas court simply because the plaintiff lived in Texas, and would suffer damage to his reputation in that state. The key is the geographic focus of the article, not the location of the harm inflicted, the court said. The article contained no references to Texas, no references to any of the plaintiff's activities in Texas, and was not directed at Texas readers. The story was about an FBI official who was accused of covering up a possible advance warning of the 1988 bombing of Pan Am flight 103. This activity occurred when the plaintiff lived outside of Texas. He moved to Texas when he left the Bureau.[14]

But a federal court in Louisiana ruled that a court in a distant state or forum could exercise jurisdiction if the brunt of the harm felt by the plaintiff was in that forum. Questions about whether the material was about activities in that state or whether it was directed to readers in that state were not material, the court said.[15] Check to see how the courts in your state have ruled on this question.

One final point: Courts in Australia and Great Britain, among others, have asserted jurisdiction in cases involving allegedly defamatory Internet messages that originated in the United States. The High Court of Australia ruled that because the plaintiff lived in Australia,

11. *Als Scan Inc.* v. *Digital Services Consultants Inc.*, U.S. No. 02-483, cert. den. 1/13/03; *Griffs* v. *Luban,* U.S. No. 02-754, cert. den. 3/10/03; and *Young* v. *New Haven Advocate,* 315 F. 3d 256 (2002).
12. 465 U.S. 783 (1984).
13. *Young* v. *New Haven Advocate,* 315 F. 3d 256 (2002). In May 2003 the Supreme Court declined to review this decision.
14. *Revell* v. *Lidov,* 317 F. 3d 467 (2002). See also *Novak* v. *Benn,* 32 M.L.R. 2259 (2004); *Jackson* v. *California Newspapers Partnership,* 406 F. Supp. 2d 893 (2005); and *Shirlington Limousine and Transportation Inc.* v. *San Diego Union-Tribune* 36 M.L.R. 2201 (2008).
15. *Planet Beach Franchising Corp.* v. *C3ubit Inc., d/b/a Tantoday,* E.D. La. No. Civ. A. 02-1859, 8/12/02.

and because the harm from the allegedly defamatory message did not occur until it was downloaded in Australia, the courts there could exercise jurisdiction.[16] The British case involved a U.S. resident, boxing promoter Don King, who the court said had many friends and acquaintances in England. The court ruled that the publication of an Internet posting takes place when it is downloaded. Please note that when a court in a foreign nation asserts jurisdiction in a libel case, the many important First Amendment protections that apply in a case tried in the United States rarely protect a defendant tried outside this country.

SUMMARY

A libel suit must be started before the statute of limitations expires. Each state determines how long this period will be. In all states it is one, two or three years. A libel suit started after the expiration of the statute of limitations will be dismissed. Jurisdiction questions in Internet-based libel suits are still being sorted out by the courts, but usually are based upon where the content of the message was aimed, where the harm was caused and where the message was downloaded.

TRUTH

The First Amendment provides defendants in libel suits considerable protection. The defendant in a lawsuit filed against a newspaper or other mass medium is well defended by the constitutional fault requirements placed on the plaintiff. But there were defenses for libel even before the ruling in *New York Times* v. *Sullivan.*[17] These emerged through common law and via statutes in many states. Truth, privileged communication, fair comment, consent and right of reply all work to protect the libel defendant—no matter who he or she might be. The applicability of each of these defenses in a particular case is determined by the facts in the case: what the story is about, how the information was gained and the manner in which it was published.

Traditionally, truth has been regarded as an important libel defense that completely protected defendants in lawsuits for defamation. To use this defense, the defendant was required to prove the truth of the libelous allegations he or she published. Truth is still a defense in a libel action, but it has lost much of its importance in light of recent rulings that require most libel plaintiffs to carry the burden of proving a defamatory allegation to be false when the story focuses on a matter of public concern. In those few instances when a private-person plaintiff sues for a libelous statement that does not focus on something of public concern and therefore does not have to show the falsity of the matter as a part of proving negligence, the libel defendant can escape liability in the case by showing that the defamatory matter is true. But the defendant carries the burden of proof; truth becomes a defense. The same rules apply to proving truth that apply to proving falsity, only they are reversed. The defendant must show that the allegations are substantially true. Extraneous errors will not destroy the defense. See pages 161–164 to refresh your memory on these matters.

16. *King* v. *Lewis,* High Court of Justice, Queen's Bench Division, No. [2004] EWHC, 168 (QB), 2/6/04.
17. 376 U.S. 254 (1964).

PRIVILEGED COMMUNICATIONS

The people of the United States have traditionally valued robust debate as one means of discovering the truths essential to building consensus. The law takes pains to protect this debate, making sure that speakers are not unduly punished for speaking their minds. Article 1, Section 6 of the federal Constitution provides that members of Congress are immune from suits based on their remarks on the floor of either house. This protection is called a privilege. The statement in question is referred to as a privileged communication.

ABSOLUTE PRIVILEGE

Today this privilege, sometimes called the privilege of the participant, attaches to a wide variety of communications and speakers. Anyone speaking in a legislative forum—members of Congress, senators, state representatives, city council members and so forth—enjoys this privilege. In 2005 appellate courts in Colorado and Illinois ruled that the privilege applied to statements made during meetings of a county hospital board and a city council zoning committee, respectively.[18] Even the statements of witnesses at legislative hearings are privileged. But the comments must be made in the legislative forum. The Supreme Court ruled in 1979 that while a speech by a senator on the floor of the Senate would be wholly immune from a libel action, newsletters and press releases about the speech issued by the senator's office would not be protected by the privilege. Only speech that is "essential to the deliberations of the Senate" is protected, and neither newsletters to constituents nor press releases are parts of the deliberative process.[19]

> *Today, privilege attaches to a wide variety of communications and speakers.*

Similarly, the privilege attaches to communications and documents made in judicial forums—courtrooms, grand jury rooms and so forth. Judges, lawyers, witnesses, defendants, plaintiffs and all other individuals are protected so long as the remark is uttered during the official portions of the hearing or trial and the statement or document is in some way relevant to the proceeding. An attorney in Pennsylvania filed a complaint in a lawsuit and then faxed a copy of this complaint to a reporter. He was sued for libel by the person named in the complaint, who argued that when he sent the complaint to the journalist, he was publishing its defamatory allegations. The attorney argued that since the complaint was a privileged judicial document, which it is, his act of sending the complaint was also privileged. The Supreme Court of Pennsylvania disagreed, ruling that sending the document to a reporter was an extra-judicial act and was not relevant in any way to the legal proceedings.[20] A question that arises after this ruling is this: What if the attorney had merely told the reporter about the lawsuit that had been filed, and suggested he or she look at the complaint? Would that act be protected? Most likely.

Finally, people who work in the administrative and executive branches of government enjoy the privilege as well. Official communications including reports, policy statements, even press conferences, presented by presidents, governors, mayors, department heads and others are protected. The Supreme Court of the United States ruled in 1959 that the privilege

---

18. *Wilson* v. *Meyer,* 34 M.L.R. 1906 (2005); and *Stevens* v. *Porr* 34 M.L.R. 1086 (2005).
19. *Hutchinson* v. *Proxmire,* 443 U.S. 111 (1979). Proxmire was sued when he attacked a Michigan man in a press release critical of wasteful government spending.
20. *Bochetto* v. *Gibson,* 32 M.L.R. 2474 (2004).

applies to any publication by government officials that is in line with the discharge of their official duties.[21] This case involved a press release issued by an official explaining why two federal workers were fired. The New York Court of Appeals echoed this ruling 20 years later when it said that a press release issued by an assistant attorney general concerning the investigation of a possible fund-raising scam was protected by the privilege.[22] The difference in the manner in which the courts treated the press releases by Sen. William Proxmire in a case noted previously (see pages 178–179) and the two cases just cited stems from the different roots of the privilege. The congressional privilege stems directly from the U.S. Constitution and is limited by constitutional language that focuses on the deliberative process and lawmaking. Proxmire's remarks fell outside these boundaries. The common law and/or state statutes are the sources of all other parts of the privilege, and courts have construed this protection quite liberally.

The privilege just discussed is an **absolute privilege.** The speaker cannot be sued for defamation on the basis of such a remark. A similar kind of privilege applies also to certain kinds of private communications. Discussions between an employer and an employee are privileged; the report of a credit rating is privileged; a personnel recommendation by an employer about an employee is privileged. These kinds of private communications remain privileged so long as they are not disseminated beyond the sphere of those who need to know.

QUALIFIED PRIVILEGE

What is called **qualified privilege** goes far beyond the absolute immunity granted to speakers at public and official meetings and the conditional immunity granted to certain types of private communications. Under the qualified privilege, sometimes called the privilege of the reporter, an individual may report what happens at an official governmental proceeding or transmit the substance of an official government report or statement and remain immune from libel even if the publication of the material defames someone. This is how the privilege is outlined in the "Restatement of the Law of Torts":

> The publication of defamatory matter concerning another in a report of any official proceeding or any meeting open to the public which deals with matters of public concern is conditionally privileged if the report is accurate and complete, or a fair abridgment of what has occurred.[23]

Actually, this definition of the privilege in the "Restatement" is a bit conservative, as courts continually extend the protection of qualified privilege to reports of more diverse kinds of government activity. This qualified privilege is sometimes called the privilege of the reporter, as opposed to the absolute immunity noted previously, which is often referred to as the privilege of the participant. The use of the term "reporter" signifies anyone who reports on what has happened, as opposed to the journalistic meaning of the term, a newspaper or television reporter.

21. *Barr* v. *Mateo,* 353 U.S. 171 (1959).
22. *Gautsche* v. *New York,* 415 N.Y.S. 2d 280 (1979).
23. American Law Institute, *Restatement of the Law of Torts.*

> ## CRITERIA FOR APPLICATION OF QUALIFIED PRIVILEGE
> ▮ Report of a privileged proceeding or document
> ▮ A fair and accurate summary published or broadcast as a report

At the start it is important to note that qualified privilege is a conditional privilege; that is, the privilege works as a libel defense only if certain conditions are met. First, the privilege applies only to reports of certain kinds of meetings, hearings, proceedings, reports and statements. Second, the law requires that these reports be a fair and accurate or truthful summary of what took place at the meeting or what was said in the report. In the past there was a third condition—that the report containing the defamatory charges was published or broadcast in order to inform the people, not simply to hurt the plaintiff. It is generally considered today that this third condition no longer applies; the defendant's motivation for publishing or broadcasting the material is irrelevant.[24] Similarly, the privilege is not lost even though there are allegations of actual malice against the reporter. The "Restatement of the Law of Torts" states: "The privilege exists even though the publisher himself does not believe the defamatory words he reports to be true, and even when he knows them to be false."[25] Most state courts follow this rule.[26]

The defendant bears the burden of proving that the privilege applies to the libelous material. The court will determine whether the particular occasion (meeting, proceeding, report) is privileged. The jury will determine whether the defendant's report of the occasion is a fair and accurate report.

Before going into the details relating to the application of this defense, let's look at a brief hypothetical example. During a meeting of the Mayberry City Council, Councilman Floyd Lawson, while discussing an increase in the garbage rates for city residents, says this: "Allied Garbage Co., which supposedly gives us a good rate to pick up the trash, is run by a bunch of crooks who are intent on cheating this city and all its citizens. I mean, I read it in the newspaper. These guys are a part of organized crime." Because of the protection of the absolute privilege, the owners of Allied Garbage cannot sue Lawson. When the reporter who attended the meeting includes this comment in her story, the newspaper also is shielded from a lawsuit so long as the story is a fair and accurate summary of what Lawson said: "Councilman Floyd Lawson charged last night during a city council meeting that the owners of Allied Garbage Co. are a part of organized crime and are cheating the city."

Let's first examine the kinds of occasions that courts have found to be covered by the privilege.

24. See *Schiavone Construction* v. *Time,* 569 F. Supp. 614 (1983).
25. American Law Institute, *Restatement of the Law of Torts.*
26. See *Solaia Technology LLC* v. *Specialty Publishing Co.,* 34 M.L.R. 1997 (2006), for example. But see also *Freedom Communications Inc.* v. *Sotelo,* 34 M.L.R. 2207 (2006), where the Texas Court of Appeals said that actual malice would rebut the privilege.

Legislative Proceedings

The privilege applies to what occurs during meetings of legislative bodies, from the U.S. Congress down to the lowly village council meeting. But courts have ruled that only what is said during the official portion of the meeting is included within the protective ambit of the defense. A Pennsylvania superior court recently ruled that the privilege did not apply to a newspaper report of comments made by citizens while a township board of supervisors meeting was in recess.[27] The privilege also applies to the reports of committee meetings of such organizations as well as to stories about petitions, complaints and other communications received by these bodies. The only requirement that must be met with regard to this aspect of the privilege is that the official body, such as a city council, must officially receive the complaint or petition before the privilege applies. If the Citizens for Cleaner Streets bring to a city council meeting a petition charging the street superintendent with incompetence and various and sundry blunders in his or her job, publication of these charges is privileged as soon as the city council officially accepts the petition. Nothing has to be done with the document. It must merely be accepted. But if copies of the petition are circulated to citizens attending the meeting and never officially presented to the city council, the privilege may or may not apply, depending on how willing a judge is to apply a broad reading of the protection. The privilege usually applies to stories about the news conferences of members of a legislative body following a session, to stories about what was said during a closed meeting by the body, and to stories about what was said during an informal gathering of legislators before or after the regular session, especially if what is said or what occurs during these kinds of events is of great public interest.

Judicial Proceedings

The privilege of the reporter also applies to actions that take place in judicial forums: testimony and depositions of witnesses, arguments of attorneys, pronouncements of judges and so forth. Stories about trials, decisions, jury verdicts, court opinions, judicial orders and decrees and grand jury indictments are all protected by the privilege. A New York trial court ruled in 2002 that reports of attorney disciplinary hearings were protected by the privilege because the hearings are quasi-judicial. A woman's charge of marital rape made in open court against her husband was regarded as privileged when it was published in a local newspaper.[28] Probably the most difficult problem a reporter on the court beat has to face is what to do when a lawsuit is initially filed. Under our legal system a lawsuit is started when a person files a complaint with a court clerk and serves a summons on the defendant. The complaint is filled with charges, most of which are libelous. Can a reporter use that complaint as the basis for a story?

Traditionally states have followed one of two rules on this question. In some states a complaint that has been filed is not considered privileged until some kind of judicial action has been taken.[29] For example, a New Jersey appellate court ruled that material contained

---

27. *DeMary* v. *Latrobe Printing and Publishing Co.,* 28 M.L.R. 1337 (2000).

28. *Wong* v. *World Journal,* 31 M.L.R. 1214 (2002); and *Tonnessen* v. *Denver Publishing Co.,* 3 P. 3d 959 (2000).

29. See *Amway Corp.* v. *Procter and Gamble Co.,* 31 M.L.R. 2441 (2003), for example.

in a complaint filed in a bankruptcy proceeding was not privileged. The court said the fair report privilege doesn't cover preliminary proceedings—such as a complaint—until judicial action is taken.[30] The scheduling of an appearance by the litigants may be sufficient. This rule, which requires a judge to become involved in the matter before the complaint is privileged, is designed to protect an innocent party from being smeared in a news report written about a lawsuit that has been filed but then quickly withdrawn. Advocates of this system argue that it is much more difficult to withdraw such a lawsuit after a judge has gotten involved in the proceeding. Those who oppose this rule say the idea is a good one but it is out-of-date. Libel expert Bruce Sanford contends that "courts now recognize that the old rule can be easily circumvented by anyone determined to defame; judicial action may be obtained simply by filing a procedural motion."[31] Consequently, more and more states today follow the rule that the complaint becomes privileged as soon as it has been filed with the court and a docket number has been assigned or the defendant has been issued a summons.[32] Two cautionary notes are important. A reporter should never take a lawyer's word that the lawsuit has been filed. The announcement may be a hoax to get publicity favorable to a client. A call to the courthouse is always in order. Also, ignore what the lawyer says about the case when he or she proclaims that the legal action has been filed. Normally, only comments or material contained in the formal judicial proceedings or court documents are protected by privilege. The Iowa Supreme Court ruled that comments made to a reporter by an attorney after the lawyer had filed the complaint initiating the lawsuit were not protected by privilege.[33]

Stories about those parts of the judicial process that are closed to the public may or may not be protected by the privilege. For example, court sessions for juveniles and divorce proceedings are frequently closed to protect the privacy of the individuals involved.[34] Some states regard these closures as important public policy and attempt to discourage publicity about such proceedings by denying the mass media the opportunity to apply the privilege if a lawsuit should result from press coverage. But this rule is changing. The 9th U.S. Circuit Court of Appeals has ruled that under California law, the press enjoyed the privilege to publish reports of proceedings in a family court that excluded the general public during its hearings.[35] And a broad reading of U.S. Supreme Court rulings in certain privacy lawsuits that were generated because of press reports of court hearings suggests that the First Amendment may place substantial limits on libel plaintiffs as well as those who are suing because of a report of a closed legal proceeding.[36]

Executive Actions

Reports of the statements and proceedings conducted by mayors, department heads and other people in the administrative and executive branches of government are generally privileged.

---

30. *Salzano* v. *North Jersey Media Group Inc.,* 36 M.L.R. 2569 (2008).
31. Sanford, *Libel and Privacy.*
32. See *Clapp* v. *Olympic View Publishing Co., LLC,* 136 Wn. App. 1045 (2007), for example.
33. *Kennedy* v. *Zimmerman,* 601 N.W. 2d 61 (1999).
34. But see *Riemers* v. *Grand Forks Herald,* 32 M.L.R. 2381 (2004) for a ruling by the North Dakota Supreme Court that reports of divorce proceedings are protected by the privilege.
35. *Dorsey* v. *National Enquirer, Inc.,* 973 F. 2d 1431 (1992).
36. See *Cox Broadcasting Co.* v. *Cohn,* 420 U.S. 469 (1975); and *Florida Star* v. *B.J.F.,* 109 S. Ct. 2603 (1989).

The best guideline is that the privilege is confined to stories about actions or statements that are official in nature, the kinds of things that are substantially "acts of state." By law, administrators are required to prepare certain reports and to hold certain hearings, and the privilege certainly covers stories on these activities. Although not required by law, other actions are unmistakably part of the job. Reports on these activities are often protected as well. For example, a federal court ruled that a report of an investigation by a state consumer protection board was privileged. The plaintiff argued that the defendant newspaper never saw a copy of the report, but got its story from a press release issued by the board. The court said that didn't matter, as long as the story was a fair and true summary of the board's findings, as described in the press release.[37] But the Massachusetts Supreme Judicial Court refused to extend the privilege to remarks made by a police chief about an internal investigation into whether one of his officers was working part time at a second job while he was supposed to be on duty. "The conditional privilege to publish defamatory material is designed to allow public officials to speak freely on matters of public importance in the exercise of their official duties," the court said.[38] But it was not an official duty of the chief to report to the press on an internal departmental investigation. The New York Supreme Court ruled that reports of investigations by an environmental agency are privileged.[39] Even stories based on confidential government documents that focused on possible government misconduct were declared to be privileged under Massachusetts law.[40] Finally, a Nevada court ruled that defamatory remarks contained in an official press release issued by the Bureau of Land Management, a federal agency, were privileged.[41]

> *"The conditional privilege to publish defamatory material is designed to allow public officials to speak freely on matters of public importance in the exercise of their official duties."*

Reports of police activities also fall under the heading of executive actions. It is fairly well settled that a report that a person has been arrested and charged with a crime is privileged. Official statements made by police about an investigation are privileged in many instances. The Texas Court of Appeals ruled in 2006 that a news story based on a press release from the police department was protected by the privilege.[42] The U.S. Court of Appeals for the 2nd Circuit ruled that public statements made by the head of the New York City office of the FBI about an FBI search of law offices in Brooklyn were privileged. CNN had quoted the FBI agent as describing the offices as the headquarters for a dangerous left-wing group that sought to topple the U.S. government.[43] The U.S. Court of Appeals for the 3rd Circuit ruled that information obtained legally by Time magazine from FBI investigatory documents is also protected by a qualified privilege.[44] Courts in Ohio and Florida ruled recently that even stories based on inaccurate official police reports are protected by the fair report privilege. "It is inevitable that on occasion the media will publish information from government sources that turns out to be inaccurate," a Florida judge wrote. "While this might be irritating to the

---

37. *Testmasters Educational Services Inc.* v. *NYP Holdings Inc.*, 603 F. Supp. 584 (2009).
38. *Draghetti* v. *Chimielewski,* 416 Mass. 808 (1994).
39. *Quarcini* v. *Niagara Falls Gazette,* 13 M.L.R. 2340 (1987).
40. *Ingerere* v. *ABC,* 11 M.L.R. 1227 (1984).
41. *Mortensen* v. *Gannett Co.,* 24 M.L.R. 1190 (1995).
42. *Freedom Communications Inc.* v. *Sotelo,* 34 M.L.R. 2207 (2006).
43. *Foster* v. *Turner Broadcasting,* 844 F. 2d 955 (1988).
44. *Medico* v. *Time,* 634 F. 2d 134 (1981).

subjects of the newspaper or television reports, this is a small price to pay for the benefits the public receives from the privilege," the court added. And in 2009 the Arkansas Supreme Court ruled that witness statements contained in case reports were protected by the privilege even though these statements should not have been released. "There is nothing to suggest that the privilege is lost because the newspaper failed to investigate whether or not it was supposed to have access to that portion of the report," the court said.[45]

Caution needs to be exercised here, however. The privilege surely does not apply to every statement made by every police officer on every topic. The Idaho Supreme Court refused to apply the privilege to statements that were made privately to a reporter by a police officer. The court said these statements went beyond the official police reports, which are clearly privileged documents.[46] Another note of caution. Some American courts have refused to allow the privilege defense when the document that contained the defamatory statement was not generated in the United States. In 2001 the Nevada Supreme Court refused to extend the privilege to portions of a book based on a confidential report from British police. This kind of report is generally not available to the public, the court said, and does not qualify as an official act or proceeding. Four years later a U.S. District Court refused to allow the privilege defense to protect allegations that two Russians were involved in corrupt and criminal conduct. The court said, "the privilege is unavailable to defendants in this case because it does not extend to official reports of the actions of a foreign government."[47]

The privilege is not confined to those instances of reporting official government proceedings. The Washington Supreme Court ruled that the reporting of the charges on recall petitions is privileged.[48] A federal court in Idaho ruled that the privilege applied to a story about a meeting called by citizens to protest the actions of a judge. It clearly was not an official meeting but concerned important public business, the conduct of a public official. The court said, "There is a general doctrine that what is said at a public meeting, at which any person of the community or communities involved might have attended and heard and seen for himself, is conditionally privileged for publication."[49]

The "Restatement of the Law of Torts" says that reports of what occurs at meetings open to the public at which matters of public concern are discussed are privileged.[50] Paul Ashley, libel authority and author of "Say It Safely," wrote that the privilege probably applies to a public meeting even though admission is charged, so long as everyone is free to pay the price. "By supplying them with information about public events," Ashley wrote, "the publisher is acting as the 'eyes and ears' of people who did not attend."[51] In such a circumstance, the report of a public meeting, the key element undoubtedly is the subject of debate. Was it of public concern? Was it of limited public concern? Was it a purely private matter?

45. *Martinez* v. *WTVG Inc.*, 36 M.L.R. 1791 (2008); *Vaillcourt* v. *Media General Operations Inc.*, 36 M.L.R. 1543 (2007); and *Whiteside* v. *Russellville Newspapers Inc.*, 375 Ark. 245 (2009).
46. *Wiemer* v. *Rankin,* 790 P. 2d 347 (1990).
47. *Wynn* v. *Smith,* 16 P. 3d 424 (2001); and *OAO Alfa Bank* v. *Center for Public Integrity,* D.D.C., No. 00-2208 (JDB), 9/27/05.
48. *Herron* v. *Tribune Publishing Co.,* 736 P. 2d 249 (1987).
49. *Borg* v. *Borg,* 231 F. 2d 788 (1956).
50. American Law Institute, *Restatement of the Law of Torts.*
51. Ashley, *Say It Safely.*

NEUTRAL REPORTAGE

In 1977 the 2nd U.S. Court of Appeals created a new variety of qualified privilege called **neutral reportage.**[52] In a nutshell this privilege says that when the press reports newsworthy but defamatory allegations made by a responsible and prominent source, these reports are privileged, even if the reporter believed the allegations were false when he or she included them in the story. Very few other courts have joined the 2nd Circuit in accepting this privilege.[53] Most other courts that have been confronted with the defense have rejected it, most recently the Pennsylvania Supreme Court.[54] These courts have argued that neutral reportage is incompatible with previous Supreme Court rulings such as *Gertz* v. *Robert Welch Inc.,* that it is unnecessary because of other high-court rulings, or that there is simply no basis in the law to support the defense. Neutral reportage is simply not a viable defense in most jurisdictions. The courts that have accepted this defense seem to agree that it has four distinct elements.

- **The defamatory allegations must be newsworthy charges that create or are associated with a public controversy.**
- **The charges must be made by a responsible and prominent source.**
- **The charges must be reported accurately and neutrally.**
- **The charges must be about a public official or public figure.**[55]

ABUSE OF PRIVILEGE

A court will ask whether the story is a fair and accurate or true report of what took place or what is contained in the record.

Whether qualified privilege applies to a particular story is the first part of the test. Next, a court will ask whether the story is a fair and accurate or true report of what took place or what is contained in the record.

- Fair means balanced. The story should be complete and include all sides of a contentious dispute. If at a public meeting speakers both attack and defend Conrad Nagel, the story should reflect both the attack and the defense. If a court record contains both positive and negative references about the subject, the news account should contain both kinds of references as well. If a reporter writes a story about a lawsuit that has been filed against a local doctor, the story should also contain the doctor's response to the charges. There has to be balance; that is the key.
- An accurate or true report means that the story should honestly reflect what is in the record, or what was said. The story doesn't have to be a verbatim account of what was said. The Connecticut Court of Appeals recently ruled, "It is not necessary that it be exact in every immaterial detail or that it conform to the

---

52. *Edwards* v. *National Audubon Society, Inc.,* 556 F. 2d 113 (1977), cert. den. 434 U.S. 1002 (1977).
53. See *Price* v. *Viking Penguin, Inc.,* 881 F. 2d 1426 (1989); and *Schwartz* v. *Salt Lake City Tribune* (2005).
54. See, for example, *Dickey* v. *Columbia Broadcasting System, Inc.,* 583 F. 2d 1221 (1978); *Young* v. *The Morning Journal,* 76 Ohio St. 3d 627 (1996); *Norton* v. *Glenn,* 797 A. 2d 294 (2002); aff'd Nos. 18 & 19 MAP 2003, 10/20/04; and *Bennett* v. *Columbia University,* 34 M.L.R. 2202 (2006).
55. See *Khawar* v. *Globe International Inc.,* 46 Cal. App. 4th 22 (1996); aff'd 79 Cal. Rptr. 2d 178 (1998).

precision demanded in technical or scientific reporting."[56] And the California Court of Appeals noted, "The privilege applies unless the differences between the facts and the manner in which they are described are of such a substantial character that they produce a different effect on the readers."[57] The story must be an accurate summary of the statement or document. If the original statement or document contains erroneous material, it will not affect the privilege.

But stories that contain even seemingly small errors can lose the privilege, if the errors are such that they change the impact of the report in the minds of the average reader. In 1988 Glamour magazine printed a story about a widely publicized child custody case. The writer used a variety of sources for the story, including some depositions filed during the custody battle. These are privileged documents. A deposition from a clinical psychologist who had talked with the father in this case, Eric Foretich, discussed the death of his infant sister. The psychologist said that Foretich "was making funeral arrangements, selecting burial plots, you know, seeing the dead infant, things of that sort. . . . He spoke about his dead infant sister and being given this child to hold as his mother is running screaming through the house." The story in Glamour, however, contained these phrases: "When he [Foretich] was in his teens, a sister died shortly after birth. Eric's mother handed him the dead infant, and he arranged for the funeral."

A U.S. District Court in the District of Columbia said the magazine's statement was not a fair and accurate summary of the material in the deposition. The description of Eric's mother in the deposition suggests a woman who was distraught, distressed by grief. The description of her in the magazine shows a cold, uncaring woman.[58]

Other kinds of errors are not as important. A New Jersey newspaper was sued when it reported that a police officer was having sex with a woman at police headquarters. The source of the story was a letter read at a township council meeting by a county prosecutor. The occasion was privileged, the plaintiff agreed, but the story was in error. The official record said the sexual encounter took place in the Municipal Building, not the police station. The police station is in the Municipal Building, the court noted, and the slight error was not material.[59] A Spokane, Wash., newspaper was sued after it reported that a businessman had lost a $250,000 judgment in a suit brought against him by Microsoft. The software maker accused T. James Le of selling counterfeit copies of Microsoft software. There were a couple of minor inaccuracies in the story, which was based on a privileged court file. One statement was false. The story said that Le had sold counterfeit copies of Office Pro and Windows 95 in December of 1998. Actually, he sold only copies of Windows 95 in December of 1998. But the Washington Court of Appeals ruled that the error was insubstantial. "Viewed in context with the entire story, the challenged passage is substantially accurate and fair as a matter of law," the court said.[60]

56. *Burton* v. *American Lawyer Media Inc.,* 847 A. 2d 1115 (2004).

57. *Colt* v. *Freedom Communications Inc.,* 109 Cal. App. 4th 1551 (2003).

58. *Foretich* v. *Advance Magazine Publishers, Inc.,* 18 M.L.R. 2280 (1991); see also *Kaminsky* v. *Spring Publishing Corp.,* 880 N.Y.S. 2d 873 (2009), where a New York Supreme Court ruled that a newspaper story that said a member of a credit union board had committed fraud, when the actual report it quoted said only that the person "may have" committed fraud, was not an accurate report, and was not privileged.

59. *Rabbitt* v. *Gannett Satellite Information Network Inc.,* 32 M.L.R. 1410 (2003).

60. *Alpine Industries Computers Inc.* v. *Cowles Publishing Co.,* 57 P. 3d 1178 (2002).

The story should also be in the form of a report. If defendants fail to make it clear that they are reporting something that was said at a public meeting or repeating something that is contained in the public record, the privilege may be lost. The law says the reader should be aware that the story is a report of what happened at a public meeting or at an official hearing or is taken from the official record. These facts should be noted in the lead and in the headline if possible, as noted in the following boxed example.

AT CITY COUNCIL SESSION: MAYOR BLASTS CONTRACTOR WITH CHARGES OF FRAUD

Mayor John Smith during a city council meeting today charged the Acme Construction Company with fraudulent dealings.

The U.S. Court of Appeals for the District of Columbia Circuit ruled that qualified privilege did not apply to a magazine summary of statements contained in an official report from the National Transportation Safety Board. The report is an official record; it is clearly covered by the reporter's privilege. But the summary in the magazine gave readers no clue that the statements constituted a summary of an official document. "The challenged [defamatory] assertion is simply offered as historical fact without any particular indication of its source," the court said. The reader was left with the impression that the author of the article reached the conclusion contained in the defamatory allegations based on his own research.[61]

One last point needs to be made. Traditionally, under the common law, if even a fair and true report was published not to inform the public but because the publisher wanted to hurt the target of the defamation, the privilege could be lost. Courts called this intent to harm the plaintiff common-law malice because the publisher had a malicious intent. In most states today, even if the plaintiff is able to prove common-law malice, the privilege will still protect the publisher. But this protection is not the law everywhere. The Minnesota Court of Appeals decided in June 1999 that proof of common-law malice can defeat the privilege in that state.[62] Be forewarned.

SUMMARY

The publication of defamatory material in a report of a public meeting, legislative proceeding or legal proceeding or in a story that reflects the content of an official government report is conditionally privileged. The privilege extends to the meetings of all public bodies, to all aspects of the legal process, to reports and statements issued by members of the executive branch of government and even to nonofficial meetings of the public in which matters of public concern are discussed. Such reports cannot be the basis for a successful libel suit as long as the report presents a fair (balanced) and accurate (truthful) account of what took place at the meeting or what is contained in the record.

---

61. *Dameron* v. *Washingtonian,* 779 F. 2d 736 (1985); see also *Trover* v. *Kluger*, 37 M.L.R. 1165 (2008).
62. *Moreno* v. *Crookston Times Printing Co.,* 594 N.W. 2d 555 (1999).

PROTECTION OF OPINION

The law has traditionally shielded statements of opinion from suits for defamation. Opinion is a basic part of mass media in the 21st century, with art, music, film and television reviews; political commentary; news analysis; editorials, and even advertising. Opinion-filled exchanges, often heated and exaggerated, are part of the basic political and social discourse in the United States. For several centuries a common-law defense, called fair comment and criticism, was the shield used to protect opinion statements from libel suits. In the past 40 years, however, two other defenses have been added, and there is some question whether the common-law protection afforded to opinion statements by the fair comment defense is needed or viable. In the following pages we examine all three of these potential defenses.

The law has traditionally shielded statements of opinion from suits for defamation.

RHETORICAL HYPERBOLE

In the late 1960s, a real estate developer had engaged in negotiations with a local city council for a zoning variance on some land he owned. At the same time the developer was also negotiating with the same city council regarding another parcel of land that the city wanted him to buy. The local newspaper published articles on the bargaining and said that some people had characterized the developer's negotiating positions as "blackmail." The libel suit that followed ultimately found its way to the U.S. Supreme Court. The high court rejected the plaintiff's notion that readers would believe the developer had committed the actual crime of blackmail. The court said the stories gave readers all the background needed to understand the negotiations. "Even the most careless reader must have perceived that the word was no more than rhetorical hyperbole, a vigorous epithet used by those who considered the [developer's] negotiating position extremely unreasonable."[63]

Four years later the high court rendered a similar ruling in a case involving a dispute among postal workers. The National Association of Letter Carriers was trying to organize workers at a post office in Virginia. The monthly union newsletter included the names of those who had not yet joined the union under the heading "List of Scabs." To emphasize their point, the editors of the newsletter published a definition of a scab written years ago by American author Jack London. London said, among other things, that a scab carries a tumor of rotten principles where others have a heart, and is a traitor to his God, his country, his family and his class. A postal worker sued, claiming he was not a traitor. The high court cited the earlier decision in *Greenbelt* and said it was impossible to believe that any readers would have understood the newsletter to be charging the plaintiff with the criminal offense of treason. It was rhetorical hyperbole—lusty, imaginative expression.[64]

Opinion statements, then, may be defended as being unbelievable rhetoric. Here are some examples of the kinds of statements courts have ruled are rhetorical hyperbole:

Opinion statements, then, may be defended as being unbelievable rhetoric.

∎ Statements were made in a Detroit newspaper that former major league ballplayer Cecil Fielder had an "unstoppable gambling compulsion," and that he was hard up financially.[65]

---

63. *Greenbelt Publishing Ass'n, Inc.* v. *Bresler,* 398 U.S. 6 (1970).
64. *Old Dominion Branch No. 496, National Association of Letter Carriers* v. *Austin,* 94 S. Ct. 2770 (1974); see also *Delaney* v. *International Union UAW Local 94,* 32 M.L.R. 1454 (2004).
65. *Fielder* v. *Greater Detroit News Media Inc.,* 35 M.L.R. 1380 (2006).

■ A talk-show host stated that a woman, who ran an unlicensed and understaffed day-care center in her home, was no better than a murderer. Authorities found a 3-month-old baby dead in a crib at the woman's home and she had been convicted of endangering the welfare of a child and making false statements to police.[66]

■ Comments were made by a talk-show host that U.S. government contractors at the infamous Abu Ghraib prison in Iraq were "hired killers" and "mercenaries" who could kill without being held to account.[67]

■ Charges were made by a New York City council member that a DJ was a "sick, racist pedophile, a child predator," and a "lunatic" who must be put behind bars and "should be terminated from the face of the earth."[68]

Rhetorical hyperbole is protected, then, because the language is so expansive that the reader or listener knows it is only an opinion, that it is not an assertion of fact. The tone of the language is normally the key. But in cases of satire or parody, the writer or broadcaster must be certain that a reasonable reader will in fact realize that the assertions are not meant to be taken as statements of fact. And this can be a close call sometimes. In 2002 a Texas appellate court was faced with a difficult case after a Dallas alternative weekly newspaper published what was purported to be a news story but was actually a fictional satirical piece. A seventh grader in the small town of Ponder, Texas, had been held in juvenile detention for five days after he read a Halloween story to his classmates that was laced with references to drugs and violence. Local authorities said the story amounted to a threat of violence and punished the boy. A reporter for the Dallas Observer apparently thought the punishment was nonsense and wrote a satirical fictional story about the same Ponder judge and prosecutor. The satire said authorities locked up a first-grade girl for preparing a report on Maurice Sendak's "Where the Wild Things Are," a popular children's book. The story described the 6-year-old as being shackled in court and quoted the prosecutor as saying he had not yet decided whether to try the child as an adult. The story mentioned the earlier case, but everything else was pure fiction. It was published under a "News" heading in the newspaper. Some readers apparently thought the story was factual and many complaints were filed against the two public officials. The judge and prosecutor sued for libel. The newspaper sought a summary judgment, arguing that the column was rhetorical hyperbole. The trial court rejected the motion and an appellate court affirmed the refusal. The court said the story had to be viewed in the light of several years of media attention to violence in the schools, and the earlier real incident that occurred in Ponder, which involved two of the public officials quoted in the satirical column.[69] The Texas Supreme Court reversed and granted the summary judgment, ruling that reasonable readers would not understand the story as stating actual facts. There were clues within the column that the column was fiction, the court said, noting that the judge was quoted as calling for "panic and overreaction." The story also quoted former Texas Gov. George W. Bush as stating that Maurice Sendak's book "clearly has deviant sexual overtones," and that "zero tolerance means just that. We won't

66. *Anslow* v. *Gach,* 32 M.L.R. 2438 (2003).
67. *Caci Premier Technology Inc.* v. *Rhodes*, 36 M.L.R. 2121 (2008).
68. *Torain* v. *Liu*, 479 Fed. Appx. 46 (2008).
69. *New Times Inc.* v. *Isaacks,* 91 S.W. 3d 844 (2002).

tolerate anything." The court said the article did have a superficial degree of plausibility, but that is the hallmark of satire.[70] The paper won in the end, but it took about five years and undoubtedly cost a considerable sum. Satirists need to be careful.

THE FIRST AMENDMENT

The Supreme Court ruled in 1991 that a statement of "pure opinion" on a matter of public concern is protected by the First Amendment.[71] A libel action based on such a statement cannot succeed. Courts across America have adopted this principle as a fundamental rule of libel law. There has been substantially less agreement, however, on how to identify a statement of "pure opinion." Chief Justice Rehnquist, the author of the 1991 ruling, said a statement of pure opinion is a statement that is incapable of being proved true or false. Pure opinion, Rehnquist said, does not assert or even imply a provably false fact.

The Supreme Court decision flowed from a case in which an Ohio sports columnist wrote that a high school wrestling coach and a school superintendent "lied" during a hearing in which they argued for the reinstatement of the wrestling team, which had been disqualified from participating in the state wrestling tournament. It's hard to know what writer Ted Diadiun really meant when he wrote his column, but after a libel suit was filed against the newspaper, the sportswriter argued that he was simply stating his opinion that the coach and the school superintendent had not been honest when they testified at the hearing.

The case meandered through state and federal courts for nearly 15 years before the Supreme Court ultimately ruled in 1991 that Diadiun's statement was an assertion of a fact, not simply an opinion. Rehnquist said the columnist would not have helped his case had he written "In my opinion, Milkovich [the coach] lied" or "I think Milkovich lied." He is still asserting a fact. He is telling readers, the chief justice said, that "I know something that leads me to believe that this man lied under oath." And this is the assertion of a fact, nothing more, nothing less. The newspaper ultimately paid $116,000 in damages to the plaintiffs. More important, perhaps, the publication spent close to a half million dollars defending itself.

It is unusual for lower courts to reject outright a principle of law enunciated by the Supreme Court, but that is what has happened in this case. The majority of lower courts in the United States that since 1991 have decided cases involving statements of opinion have indicated a dissatisfaction with the *Milkovich* standard. The consensus seems to be that defining an opinion statement using the single criterion of proving a statement true or false is far too conservative, that it would deny First Amendment protection to statements that an author intended to be opinion and that a reader or viewer would assume was opinion.

Many courts have gravitated to a different test for determining whether a remark is intended as an assertion of fact or a statement of opinion. This test includes the criterion outlined by the high court—can the statement be proved true or false—but requires the court to look at other dimensions of the published comment as well.

70. *New Times Inc.* v. *Isaacks,* 32 M.L.R. 2480 (2004).
71. *Milkovich* v. *Lorain Journal Co.,* 110 S. Ct. 2695 (1991).

The **Ollman** *Test*

In 1984 the U.S. Court of Appeals for the District of Columbia Circuit outlined a four-part test to determine whether a statement should be regarded as the assertion of a fact or as simply the speaker's or writer's opinion. The test, which emerged from the case of *Ollman* v. *Evans,*[72] is known as the *Ollman* test for obvious reasons. Here are the four elements:

- **Can the statement be proved true or false?** This is the basic test from *Milkovich.*
- **What is the common or ordinary meaning of the words?** Some words that appear to be factual assertions are more often used as statements of opinion. If you call someone a turkey, you don't really mean to suggest that the person has feathers and says gobble-gobble. Calling someone a moron doesn't normally mean that his or her IQ score is way below average.
- **What is the journalistic context of the remark?** Newspaper readers expect to find factual assertions in news stories on the front page. They don't expect to find facts in editorial columns, they expect to find opinions. NBC news anchor Brian Williams gives us the news; Rush Limbaugh gives us his opinions, no matter how he happens to word the statements.
- **What is the social context of the remark?** Certain kinds of speech are common to certain kinds of political or social settings. The audience attending a lecture by an eminent scientist on the need to vaccinate young children is expecting to hear facts. In a debate between two candidates for the legislature, the audience is prepared to hear opinion. Labor disputes, political meetings, protest rallies and other such settings usually generate high-spirited and free-wheeling commentary. People don't usually expect to hear factual assertions.

***OLLMAN* TEST**

1. Can the statement be proved true or false?
2. What is the common or ordinary meaning of the words?
3. What is the journalistic context of the remark?
4. What is the social context of the remark?

Free Speech and Chimpanzees

The first important court to reject the single-criterion *Milkovich* test was the New York Court of Appeals, the high court in that state. The case, *Immuno, A.G.* v. *Moor-Jankowski,*[73] involved a scholarly scientific journal. The journal published a letter from a researcher who asserted that a plan by an Austrian pharmaceutical company to establish a laboratory in Sierra Leone that would use chimpanzees for research on hepatitis was simply a ploy to avoid the

---

72. 750 F. 2d 970 (1984).
73. 77 N.Y. 2d 235 (1991).

restrictions in place in western Europe and North America that prohibit the importation of the primates, which are regarded as an endangered species. The researcher, Dr. Shirley McGreal, further asserted that the plan could cause serious harm to the chimpanzee population in the region. The comments were published in a letter to the editor and were prefaced by an editorial note that identified McGreal as an animal rights advocate and stated that the company, Immuno, A.G., regarded the charges as inaccurate and reckless. The state high court said the letter was protected opinion. Under the single-criterion *Milkovich* standard some of the statements would likely be regarded as factual assertions. But Chief Judge Judith Kaye rejected the single-criterion test, calling it a "hypertechnical" test that paid no attention to contextual matters. The defamatory matter was published in a letter to the editor, a forum where readers expect to find opinion statements. The page carried a warning that the views expressed in the letters were those of the letter writers. Judge Kaye noted that the readers of this journal were highly specialized researchers who were aware of the ongoing debate over the use of primates in medical research. The statements were protected, the court ruled, under the free press provisions of the New York state constitution.[74]

Since this ruling, numerous courts have followed the lead of the New York high court and applied the broader *Immuno* test to determine whether a statement is pure opinion or an assertion of fact. Most recently the New York Court of Appeals reversed a judgment against a newspaper columnist in a libel suit brought by the city attorney in a small New York town. The columnist had written that the attorney was a political hatchet man, one of the powers behind the throne, someone who pulled the strings of city government, and could be leading the town to destruction. The column also outlined the role played by the plaintiff 35 years earlier in a contentious dispute involving the local school board. A jury awarded the attorney $90,000 in damages, but the state high court reversed, saying the comments were opinion. Viewed within the context of the article as a whole, a reasonable reader would conclude that the statements of issue were opinion, not factual assertions. There were several clues, the court said, including the fact that the column was published on an opinion page, that there was an editor's note saying the article was an expression of opinion, and the entire tenor of the column. The statement "leading the town to destruction" could only be regarded as an opinion, the court ruled.[75] Both a U.S. District Court and the 9th U.S. Circuit Court of Appeals have ruled that a statement published in a New York Post column about the late Johnnie Cochran, one of O.J. Simpson's attorneys, was protected by the First Amendment. The columnist called Cochran a "legal scoundrel" who "will say or do just about anything to win, typically at the expense of the truth." The trial court ruled that the tenor of the column and the context of the statements dictated the readers would view the remarks as opinion, not allegations of fact. The appellate court agreed.[76] And the 1st U.S. Circuit Court of Appeals ruled that statements in a biography of Robert K. Gray that said the former Republican politician and public relations practitioner had faked his closeness to Ronald Reagan and other senior administration officials were protected opinions. "This is just the kind of subjective judgment that is only minimally about

---

74. *Immuno, A.G.* v. *Moor-Jankowski*, 77 N.Y. 2d 235 (1991).
75. *Mann* v. *Abel*, 885 N.E. 2d 884 (2008). See also *Bonanni* v. *Hearst Communications Inc.*, N.Y. App. Div. No. 505007, 7/29/09.
76. *Cochran* v. *NYP Holdings Inc.*, 27 M.L.R. 1108 (1998), aff'd 210 F. 3d 1036 (2000).

'what happened,' but expresses instead a vague and subjective characterization of what happened," the court said.[77] Again, context was a key.

But care must be exercised. In some instances what is regarded as an opinion statement also contains facts. The pure opinion defense will not protect false facts contained in an opinion statement. A federal court in Georgia ruled that statements that a popular Atlanta radio personality who had left his job under mutual agreement with the station was pathetic, was a hack and a retard, were opinion statements. But the statement that he had been fired from his job was factual comment, and his libel suit against the plaintiffs could proceed.[78] In other instances the courts have ruled that some statements of opinion suggest the author has knowledge of defamatory facts, and these statements of what courts call mixed facts and opinion might fall outside the First Amendment protection given to pure opinion. And when an executive told the New York Post that he had fired an employee because "she had a lousy work ethic," and that "she was the highest paid person in the company who did the least amount of work," he was suggesting he knew certain facts, unknown to the audience, that supported his opinion, facts that are detrimental (and hence defamatory) to the person about whom he is speaking, the New York Supreme Court ruled.[79]

The Nevada Supreme Court ruled that just because a factual statement is contained in a restaurant review, a typical vehicle for opinion, doesn't mean it can't be considered a statement of fact. The reviewer suggested in her article that she thought a Mexican-American restaurant was using packaged or canned ingredients in its dishes. The reviewer wrote that after tasting her meal, "I was beginning to realize all of this [food] came out of some sort of package." She later noted that she saw a can of pinto beans sitting on a counter in the kitchen. The newspaper argued that every statement in the review should be regarded as protected opinion. But the court disagreed. The statement "this food came out of some sort of package" should be considered opinion, given the context—a restaurant review—and the opinion-laden tenor of the article. But the statement about the canned beans was an assertion of fact and, if untrue, could be regarded as defamatory. The restaurant owner denied using packaged products in the food but admitted he kept a can of pinto beans on the premises in case he ran out of fresh beans. So the appellate court affirmed the newspaper's motion for a summary judgment.[80]

Leaving out facts in a story can also be a problem when the defendant attempts to assert the opinion defense. It could give readers an impression of the plaintiff that was unintended by the opinion writer. A case in point was decided several years ago in Rhode Island.

A man picketing and protesting the dismissal of an employee at a YMCA branch collapsed. The president of the branch was a physician who was conducting a board meeting while protesters marched outside. When he was informed that a picketer had collapsed, he offered his assistance. He was told his help was not needed because an aid unit was expected momentarily.

77. *Gray* v. *St. Martin's Press, Inc.*, 221 F. 3d 243 (2000). See also *Moldea* v. *New York Times Co.*, 22 F. 3d 310 (1994); *Dworkin* v. *L.F.P., Inc.*, 839 P. 2d 903 (1992); *Maynard* v. *The Daily Gazette Co.*, 447 S.E. 2d 293 (1994); *Keohane* v. *Stewart*, 882 P. 2d 1285 (1994); *Stolz* v. *KSFM 102 FM*, 30 Cal. App. 4th 195 (1995); *Vail* v. *The Plain Dealer Publishing Co.*, 72 Ohio St. 3d 279 (1995); *Portington* v. *Bugliosi*, 56 F. 3d 1147 (1995); and *Biospherics, Inc.* v. *Forbes, Inc.*, 26 M.L.R. 2164 (1998).
78. *NoWitness LLC* v. *Cumulus Media Partners LLC*, 35 M.L.R. 2537 (2007).
79. *Pepler* v. *Rugged Land LLC*, 34 M.L.R. 1796 (2006).
80. *Pegasus* v. *Reno Newspapers Inc.*, 57 P. 3d 82 (2002).

When the protester died the story received widespread publicity. The press reports included criticism of the doctor for not aiding the stricken man. All the stories left out the fact that the physician had offered to help the victim. The doctor sued and argued that the stories made him appear to be indifferent, uncaring and even callous. The defendants argued that the defamatory criticisms were opinions. A jury agreed with the plaintiff, noting that by leaving out the essential fact that the doctor had offered to help, the stories implied something that was untruthful.[81] The absence of this information turned protected opinion statements into defamatory factual allegations.

FAIR COMMENT AND CRITICISM

Fair comment is a common-law defense that protects the publication of statements of opinion. It has worked satisfactorily for several centuries. But like many other elements in the law of libel, fair comment has been seriously affected by the application of First Amendment protections to libel law. With the emergence of the First Amendment privilege for statements of opinion that has been outlined in the previous section, most lawyers say it makes more sense to rely on the power of the Constitution to protect their clients as opposed to using a workable, but less powerful, common-law defense. Hence, the status of the fair comment defense is in a kind of legal limbo right now.[82] The hundreds of fair comment precedents remain on the books as good law, but no one seems to cite them anymore.

The use of a fair comment defense requires the court to apply a three-part test:

1. **Is the comment an opinion statement?** Courts have traditionally used a single-criterion test to answer this question: Can the statement be proved true or false?

2. **Does the defamatory comment focus on a subject of legitimate public interest?** The courts have defined legitimate public interest very broadly to include everything from cultural artifacts to religion to medicine to advertising.

3. **Is there a factual basis for the comment?** The third requirement of the three-part test is critical, for it is grounded in the legal rationale for the defense: the notion that both our democratic system of government and our culture are enhanced by the free exchange of ideas and opinions. Under this defense the facts may be outlined in the article or broadcast that contains the opinion, or, if the facts regarding a situation are so widely known, it is not necessary that they be spelled out anew for readers or viewers. For example, the comment that "O.J. Simpson is a sleazebag" would not need to be accompanied by a recitation of the facts surrounding his criminal and civil trials for the murder of his wife. Those facts are already widely known.

The defendant who is sued for defamatory opinion, then, may attempt to defeat the lawsuit using any or all of the three strategies just outlined. The defendant can argue that the defamatory statements are so broad, so exaggerated, that no one would regard them as factual assertions; that they are rhetorical hyperbole. The defendant may also argue that the statement is a pure opinion and protected by the Constitution. Finally, the defendant can argue that the common-law defense of fair comment provides a shield against a lawsuit.

81. *Healy v. New England Newspapers,* 520 A. 2d 147 (1987).
82. But see *Magnusson v. New York Times Co.,* 32 M.L.R. 2496 (2004), where the Oklahoma Supreme Court ruled the fair comment defense was applicable in a lawsuit brought against a TV station by a physician.

> ## TIPS ON AVOIDING A LIBEL SUIT BASED ON STATEMENTS OF OPINION
>
> Journalists can take steps to avoid such a lawsuit in the first place. Mass media attorney David Utevsky suggests the following:
>
> ■ When stating an opinion, try to make certain it is understood as such. But remember the words "in my opinion" don't change a statement of fact into protected opinion.
> ■ Don't rely on journalistic context to protect you. Just because the libel appears in a review or a column or a commentary does not mean a court will regard it as opinion.
> ■ Clearly state and summarize the facts on which your opinion is based. Ask yourself whether you believe a court could find that these facts support your opinion about the matter.
> ■ Make certain the facts are true. If there is a dispute about the fact, refer to both sides of the dispute when stating your opinion.

SUMMARY

Statements of opinion are often immune to a successful libel action. The courts have said that rhetorical hyperbole—broad, exaggerated comments about someone or something—are obviously not assertions of fact and cannot stand as the basis for a successful libel suit. The Constitution also protects statements of opinion, but only pure opinion, according to the Supreme Court. Opinion statements that imply the assertion of falsehoods are not protected. The Supreme Court has ruled that the test to determine whether a statement is opinion or not is whether the statement may be proved false. Other courts have applied somewhat broader tests for opinion that focus on the ordinary meaning of the words and the journalistic and social context of the statement in addition to whether the statement can be proved to be false. Finally, opinion is protected by the common-law defense of fair comment.

DEFENSES AND DAMAGES

The privilege of the reporter and the defenses for opinion are not the only means at hand to thwart a libel suit. At least two other common-law defenses exist: **consent** and **right of reply.** Like fair comment, these defenses are old. Both have been used on occasion in the past with substantial success. Yet they are not universally accepted, and only rarely have they been applied in a libel suit in the last 40 years. Let's briefly examine each.

CONSENT

Many legal authorities agree that an individual cannot sue for libel if he or she consented to the publication of the defamatory material.[83] Imagine that Mary Jones, a reporter for the

---

83. Phelps and Hamilton, *Libel;* and Sanford, *Libel and Privacy.*

River City Sentinel, hears rumors that John Smith is a leader of organized crime. Jones visits Smith and tells him that she has heard these rumors. Then Jones asks Smith if he cares if the rumors are published in the newspaper. Smith says it is OK with him, and Jones writes and publishes the story. In this instance Smith consented to publication of the defamation. Now this event is not too likely to happen, is it? Cases of this kind of express consent are extremely rare. Courts insist that the plaintiff either knew or had a good reason to know the full extent of the defamatory statement in advance of its publication before consent can be said to exist.

But there is another kind of consent that some courts have recognized. It is called indirect or implied consent. A plaintiff can give this kind of consent in at least a couple of ways. Courts have ruled that when an individual comments on a defamatory charge and this response is published with the charge, the injured party has given indirect consent to publish the libel.[84] The logic to this argument is simple: If the response is printed, the charge must be printed as well or the story won't make any sense. Courts have also ruled that if the plaintiff has told others of the defamatory charges against him or her, this amounts to implied consent to publication elsewhere.[85] Implied consent is constructed on sound legal theory, but only a handful of courts have accepted this theory. Nevertheless, getting a comment from an individual you are about to libel is a very good idea. Giving the subject of the story a chance to reply might reveal mistakes in the story, mistakes that can be corrected before publication or broadcast. It is the fair and equitable thing to do as well.

Implied consent is constructed on sound legal theory, but only a handful of courts have accepted this theory.

RIGHT OF REPLY

Right of reply is another secondary defense. Like consent, it has not been commonly applied in recent years. Right of reply is sometimes called "the self-defense." If an individual has been defamed, he or she may answer the defamation with a libelous communication and not be subject to a successful libel suit. The only limitation here is that the reply must approximate the original defamation in magnitude. Self-defense has this same limitation. The response cannot greatly exceed the provocation. The court will not accept a claim of self-defense if you shoot and kill someone who threw a spitwad at you.

As applied in libel law, if Joseph Adieu libels Kerry O'Shea, O'Shea has the right to respond. And if the response is defamatory, the right of reply defense will block a successful libel suit by Adieu. But scenarios like this are rare today; it is much more likely that O'Shea will forgo a reply, and simply sue Adieu. How the does right of reply defense protect the mass media, since newspapers and broadcasting stations rarely attack someone who has attacked them? Some libel authorities have argued that if the press acts as a conduit for comments carried by a party in a dispute, it can use the right of reply in defense of a lawsuit.[86] In other words, imagine Adieu libels O'Shea in a public speech. The local newspaper carries O'Shea's libelous reply in its letters to the editor column. Adieu then sues the newspaper for publishing the libel. The publication can argue the right of reply defense protects it.[87]

---

84. See *Pulverman* v. *A.S. Abell Co.,* 228 F. 2d 797 (1956), for example.
85. *Pressley* v. *Continental Can Co.,* 250 S.E. 2d 676 (1978).
86. See Phelps and Hamilton, *Libel.*
87. See *Fowler* v. *New York Herald,* 172 N.Y.S. 423 (1918).

In "Cases and Materials on Torts," law professors Charles Gregory and Harry Kalven wrote:

> The boundaries of this privilege are not clearly established and it gives rise to questions amusingly reminiscent of those raised in connection with self-defense: How vigorous must the plaintiff's original aggression have been? Must the original attack itself have been defamatory? What if it [the original attack] is true or privileged? How much verbal force can the defendant use in reply? Can he defend third parties?[88]

Questions like these continue to reduce the true effectiveness of the defense of right of reply.

DAMAGES

When a plaintiff sues for libel, in most instances he or she is seeking money damages as compensation for the alleged wrongdoing. In rare instances the plaintiff may seek to have the defendant cease circulating the allegedly libelous matter. In even rarer instances a judge might agree to enjoin the circulation of the material, possibly before a trial is held to determine whether the matter is defamatory. For example, a family court judge presiding at a divorce hearing in Vermont ordered a husband to stop posting items on his blog about his wife and his failing marriage. Many First Amendment attorneys argued that this constituted a prior restraint on speech.

As noted, in most libel cases, money damages are the issue at hand.[89] If the court gets to the point in a libel suit of assessing damages, it is obvious that the plaintiff has met all requirements, including proving fault, and that none of the defenses just outlined have worked. How damages are assessed is not an essential piece of information for a journalist to carry, yet some feeling for the subject is useful. Libel law operates with four kinds of damages today. In each instance, before any damages can be awarded, the plaintiff must prove one thing or another to the court.

Actual Damages

The most common libel damages are called actual damages, or damages for actual injury.

The most common libel damages are called **actual damages,** or damages for actual injury. Plaintiffs must bring evidence to the court to show that because of the publication of the defamation they have suffered actual harm, which might include impairment of reputation or standing in the community, monetary loss, personal humiliation, or mental suffering and anguish.[90] Some of these concepts are pretty nebulous. How can mental suffering or anguish be proved in court and then measured in dollar amounts? As such, the awarding of even so-called actual damages is rarely a precise process. The plaintiff will ask for an amount that may or may not bear any relationship to the actual harm inflicted, and the court—usually the jury—will award what it thinks the plaintiff deserves, often regardless of the amount of damage inflicted. If the amount is too high the trial judge or an appellate court will frequently modify the amount of

---

88. Gregory and Kalven, *Cases and Materials on Torts.*
89. Goodnough, "Blog Takes Failed Marriage."
90. See Justice Lewis Powell's opinion in *Gertz* v. *Robert Welch, Inc.,* 4118 U.S. 323 (1974).

money awarded. The gross imprecision in awarding damages puts considerable pressure on both parties, but especially the defendant, to settle the case without going to trial.

Special Damages

Special damages are specific items of pecuniary loss caused by published defamatory statements. Special damages must be established in precise terms, much more precise terms than those for the actual damages just outlined. If a plaintiff can prove that he or she lost $23,567.19 because of the libel, that amount is then what the plaintiff can ask for and what will likely be awarded if he or she can convince the jury of the validity of the case. Special damages represent a specific monetary, and only monetary, loss as the result of the libel. Most plaintiffs do not seek special damages. However, in some cases special damages are all that can be sought. In trade libel, for example, the only award a plaintiff can get is special damages.

Presumed Damages

Presumed damages are damages that a plaintiff can get without proof of injury or harm. A public-person plaintiff or a private-person plaintiff suing for a libelous statement that focuses on a matter of public concern can only be awarded presumed damages (sometimes called general or compensatory) damages on a showing of actual malice, knowledge of falsity or reckless disregard of the truth. However, a private person suing on the basis of a libelous statement that focuses on a private matter and not a public concern need only show negligence to collect presumed damages.[91]

Punitive Damages

Lawyers frequently call **punitive damages,** or exemplary damages, the "smart money." Punitive damage awards are usually very large. The other kinds of damages just discussed are designed to compensate the plaintiff for injury. Punitive damages are designed to punish defendants for misconduct and to warn other persons not to act in a similar manner.

A public-person plaintiff or a private-person plaintiff suing for a libelous statement that focuses on a matter of public concern can only win punitive damages on a showing of actual malice, knowledge of falsity or reckless disregard for the truth. A private person suing for libel based on remarks made about a private matter, and not a public concern, can win punitive damages on a showing of negligence.

Punitive damages are the most onerous aspect of any libel suit, and many persons think they are grossly unfair. Punitive damages have been barred in Louisiana, Massachusetts, Nebraska, New Hampshire, Oregon and Washington and have been limited in Colorado, Florida, Georgia, Kansas, Montana, Mississippi, North Dakota and Virginia.[92] Legislatures in other states, such as Alabama, Illinois and Indiana, have considered placing some kind of limits on punitive damages. Few, if any, legal authorities will argue that punitive damages ought to be completely abolished. They do in some instances serve a purpose. A business that consciously

---

91. *Dun & Bradstreet* v. *Greenmoss Builders,* 472 U.S. 479 (1985).
92. Dill, "Libel Law Doesn't Work."

and aggressively sells harmful or dangerous products must be punished, most legal experts will argue. A publisher who consistently prints gross lies that shred the reputations of innocent people should suffer serious consequences. But the gargantuan size of some punitive damage awards, amounts that bear no resemblance whatsoever to the harm inflicted, has led many attorneys to argue that such awards violate the Eighth Amendment to the U.S. Constitution, which forbids the levying of excessive fines. The Supreme Court has never fully agreed with this argument but in recent years has attempted, albeit subtly, to put the brakes on the imposition of excessive punitive awards. In 1991, the high court ruled that the methods used by the courts to assess punitive damages are not "so inherently unfair as to be per se unconstitutional." But, Justice Harry Blackmun wrote for the court, "the general concerns of reasonableness and adequate guidance from the court when the case is tried to a jury properly enter into the constitutional calculus."[93] Five years later the high court overturned as "grossly excessive" an award of $2 million to an Alabama man who sued BMW for selling him, as a new car, an automobile that had been refinished to correct minor paint damage incurred in shipping. Again, the court declined to provide a specific test that should be applied at trial to guide the assessment of punitive damage awards, but offered three guideposts that could be used: the degree of reprehensibility of the defendant's conduct, the ratio between punitive and actual damages, and a comparison between the punitive damage award and any criminal or civil fines that could be levied by the state for similar conduct.[94] In 2001 the high court again spoke to the problem, warning lower appellate courts that they must give "searching scrutiny" to whether a jury's punitive damage award is excessive.[95] In 2003 the high court made its sharpest attack on punitive damages when it overturned an award of $145 million that a Utah jury had given a couple who had sued State Farm insurance company. The lawsuit focused on the insurer's refusal to settle a claim and other related matters. Justice Anthony Kennedy, writing for the six-person majority, said that the wealth of a defendant cannot justify an otherwise unconstitutional punitive damage award. The couple had been awarded $1 million in compensatory damages, the remaining $144 million as punitive damages. Kennedy said the ratio of 145 to 1 resulted in a damage award that was "neither reasonable nor proportionate to the wrong committed." He called the award irrational and arbitrary and suggested it was based less on the harm caused by the defendants and more on the fact that State Farm was a wealthy defendant. He said the state courts had used the case as a platform to expose and punish the insurer for its perceived deficiencies throughout the country.[96] Whether rulings like these that talk in rather abstract terms about "reasonable" ratios between compensatory damage and punitive awards will reduce egregious awards handed out in state and lower federal courts remains to be seen.

RETRACTION STATUTES

The phrase "I demand a retraction" is common in the folklore of libel.

The phrase "I demand a retraction" is common in the folklore of libel. What is a **retraction?** A retraction is both an apology and an effort to set the record straight. Let's say you blow one as an editor. You report that Jane Adams was arrested for shoplifting, and you are

---

93. *Pacific Mutual Life Insurance Co.* v. *Haslip,* 111 S. Ct. 1032 (1991).
94. Greenhouse, "Justices Reject Punitive Award," A1.
95. Greenhouse, "Punitive Damages."
96. *State Farm* v. *Campbell,* 538 U.S. 408 (2003); and Greenhouse, "Justices Limit."

wrong. In your retraction you first tell readers or viewers that Jane Adams was not arrested for shoplifting, that you made a mistake. Then you might also apologize for the embarrassment caused Adams. You might even say some nice things about her. At common law a prompt and honest retraction is usually relevant to the question of whether the plaintiff's reputation was actually harmed. After all, you are attempting to reconstruct that part of her reputation that you tore down just the day before. She might have difficulty proving actual harm.

RETRACTION STATUTE FROM STATE OF OREGON

A typical retraction statute looks much like this one from the state of Oregon. Publishers and broadcasters who meet the letter of such laws can substantially reduce the amount of damages a plaintiff can win in a libel suit.

30.165 Publication of correction or retraction upon demand.

1. The demand for correction or retraction shall be in writing, signed by the defamed person or the attorney of the person and be delivered to the publisher of the defamatory statement, either personally or by registered mail at the publisher's place of business or residence within 20 days after the defamed person receives actual knowledge of the defamatory statement. The demand shall specify which statements are false and defamatory and request that they be corrected or retracted. The demand may also refer to the sources from which the true facts may be ascertained with accuracy.

2. The publisher of the defamatory statement shall have not more than two weeks after receipt of the demand for correction or retraction in which to investigate the demand; and, after making such investigation, the publisher shall publish the correction or retraction in:

   (a) The first issue thereafter published, in the case of newspapers, magazines or other printed periodicals.

   (b) The first broadcast or telecast thereafter made, in the case of radio or television stations.

   (c) The first public exhibition thereafter made, in the case of motion picture theaters.

3. The correction or retraction shall consist of a statement by the publisher substantially to the effect that the defamatory statements previously made are not factually supported and that the publisher regrets the original publication thereof.

4. The correction or retraction shall be published in substantially as conspicuous a manner as the defamatory statement. [1955 c.365 § 3]

Thirty-three states have some kind of retraction law, according to libel authority Bruce Sanford.[97] Some of these laws are very comprehensive; others provide extremely limited protection. The Washington state law, for example, relates only to the liability of editors and others who process the news, and most persons who work in the media in Washington don't even regard the law as a retraction statute.[98] Under a typical retraction statute, a plaintiff must give the publisher an opportunity to retract the libel before a suit may be started. If the publisher promptly honors the request for a retraction and retracts the libelous material in a place in the newspaper as prominent as the place in which the libel originally appeared, the retraction will reduce, and in some instances cancel, any damage judgment the plaintiff might later seek in a lawsuit. Failure to ask for a retraction or failure to ask for a retraction in the way prescribed by the statute can result in a dismissal of the libel complaint.[99]

In at least two states, retraction statutes adopted by the legislature have been ruled unconstitutional. In both Arizona[100] and Montana,[101] the state high courts have ruled that the state constitution gives citizens the right to sue for injury to person, property or character. The retraction statute diminishes that right and is hence unconstitutional, the courts ruled.

A court in at least one state applied a retraction statute to libel published on the Internet. The Georgia Supreme Court ruled in 2002 that the state's law, which applies only to punitive damages, not the right to sue, is applicable to publications occurring on the Internet. Both the trial court and the state court of appeals had ruled it did not apply to Internet publications, that it applied only to publications in the traditional media. In this case the plaintiff had failed to ask for a retraction and therefore was denied the opportunity to seek punitive damages.[102]

SUMMARY   Secondary defenses, consent and right of reply, exist and may in rare instances aid a libel defendant. To collect damages in a libel suit, plaintiffs must demonstrate to the court that there was actual harm to their reputations. These are called actual damages. If plaintiffs can demonstrate specific items of monetary loss, special damages may be awarded. Plaintiffs may also seek to win punitive damages. In many states, a timely retraction of the libel can reduce damages significantly and even lessen the likelihood of a libel suit. These rules are governed by state laws called retraction statutes.

CRIMINAL LIBEL

Criminal libel has been a part of the law of defamation for as long as the law has existed. It is a close cousin to seditious libel and civil libel. Chapters 4, 5 and the better part of this chapter have dealt with civil libel, one person suing another for defamation. **Criminal libel** is founded on the theory that sometimes it is appropriate for the state to act on behalf of the party injured

---

97. Sanford, *Libel and Privacy.*
98. Washington Revised Code Annotated § 9:58.040 (1977).
99. *Milsap* v. *Stanford,* 139 F. 3d 902 (1998).
100. *Boswell* v. *Phoenix Newspapers,* 730 P. 2d 186 (1986).
101. *Madison* v. *Yunker,* 589 P. 2d 126 (1978).
102. *Mathis* v. *Cannon,* 573 S.E. 2d 376 (2002).

by the libel and bring criminal charges against the defendant. Criminal libel has been justified traditionally with the argument that if the state fails to act, the injured party or parties may take violent action against the libeler to compensate for the damage they have suffered. The state has a substantial interest in preventing this violence from occurring.

Today, criminal libel law remains as kind of a relic of the past. But it is a relic that won't seem to go away. Only about 16 states and two U.S. possessions still have criminal libel statutes on the books.[*] In 2008 an appellate court in Washington state declared its statute unconstitutional.[103] And there have been fewer than 100 criminal libel cases in the past 45 years. But seemingly every year one or two cases pop up. In 2008 two Wisconsin high school students were charged with criminal libel after assembling and posting a nude photo collage of a female classmate. And a Colorado man was charged with criminal libel for allegedly doctoring photos of a woman to show her in a compromising position.

These cases are unusual because most criminal libel prosecutions are generated for political reasons, according to a study by the Media Law Resource Center. Law enforcement officers and elected public officials are the most frequent complainants in these prosecutions. For example, in August of 2005 a 32-year-old Farmington, N.M., man was found guilty of criminal libel because he circulated a petition asking the local police department to investigate one of its officers, and picketed the police station with signs calling the officer "dirty" and "liar." The city attorney who prosecuted the case told the local newspaper that he was extremely thankful that "we live in a country with free speech, but certain kinds of speech are not free." The man, Juan Mata, had previously filed a civil rights lawsuit against the city and five police officers alleging police brutality. The state's criminal libel statute had been declared unconstitutional 13 years earlier by a state appellate court.[104]

Authorities in most states are unwilling to take on someone else's troubles and prosecute for criminal libel so long as a civil remedy is available. A prosecutor will generally gain very little public support by taking such an action. In an age when people are murdered, robbed, raped and assaulted with alarming frequency, most voters would rather see government officers arrest and prosecute real criminals. Years ago in New York, a judge stated this proposition very well.

> The theory, in simplest terms, is that when an individual is libeled, he has an adequate remedy in a civil suit for damages. The public suffers no injury. Vindication for the individual and adequate compensation for the injury done him may be obtained as well in the civil courts. Thus the rule has always been that the remedy of criminal prosecution should only be sought where the wrong is of so flagrant a character as to make a criminal prosecution necessary on public grounds.[105]

Criminal libel differs from civil libel in several important respects. First of all, it is possible to criminally libel the dead. The state can use a criminal libel statute to prosecute an individual for damaging the reputation of someone who is deceased. In

---

[*]Colorado, Florida, Idaho, Kansas, Louisiana, Michigan, Minnesota, Montana, New Hampshire, New Mexico, North Carolina, North Dakota, Oklahoma, Utah, Virginia and Wisconsin.

103. *Parmelee* v. *O'Neal*, 36 M.L.R. 1863 (2008).
104. Mayeux, "Jury Finds Mata Guilty."
105. *People* v. *Quill,* 177 N.Y. 2d 380 (1958).

some states criminal libel is tied to causing or potentially causing a breach of the peace. This charge used to be quite common. If a publication, speech or handbill so provoked the readers or listeners that violence became possible or did in fact occur, criminal libel charges might result. In 1966 the U.S. Supreme Court undermined most of the "breach of the peace" statutes as well as the actions of those states that brought criminal libel actions under the common law. The case was *Ashton* v. *Kentucky*[106] and involved a mining dispute in Hazard, Ky. An agitator was arrested for circulating a pamphlet that contained articles attacking the chief of police, the sheriff and a newspaper editor, among others. At the criminal libel trial, the judge defined the offense as "any writing calculated to create a disturbance of the peace, corrupt public morals or lead to any act, which when done, is indictable."

The Supreme Court reversed the conviction. Writing for a unanimous court, Justice William O. Douglas said the crime, as defined by the trial court, was too general and indefinite. It left the standard of responsibility—whether something is illegal or not—wide open to the discretion of the judge. Also, Douglas noted, the crime is determined not by the character of the person's words, not by what that person says or writes, but rather by the boiling point of those who listen to or read those words. The law makes someone a criminal simply because his or her neighbors have no self-control and cannot refrain from violence. This decision was an important factor, but only one factor, in the passing of "breach of the peace" as an aspect of criminal libel. It is extremely rare for such a case to occur today.

The Supreme Court has heard one criminal libel case since the *New York Times* v. *Sullivan*[107] ruling. The court ruled in *Garrison* v. *Louisiana*[108] that when the defamation of a public official is the basis for a criminal libel suit, the state has to prove actual malice on the part of the defendant—that is, knowledge of falsity, reckless disregard for the truth or falsity of the matter. Justice Brennan wrote that the reasons that persuaded the court to rule that the First Amendment protected criticism of public officials in a civil libel suit apply with equal force in a criminal libel suit. "The constitutional guarantees of freedom of expression compel application of the same standard to the criminal remedy," he added. The Supreme Court has never answered the question of whether the actual malice rule applies to cases involving the criminal libel of private persons. Nevertheless, this ruling was a potent blow against criminal libel. Most of the state criminal libel laws that still exist fail to meet even the minimum constitutional requirements sent out by the high court in 1966.*

This ruling was a potent blow against criminal libel.

---

*In 2004 a U.S. District Court in California struck down on First Amendment grounds a state law that made it a crime to make a false accusation against a police officer. This wasn't technically a criminal libel law, but it had many elements common to such laws. *Hamilton* v. *City of San Bernardino,* 32 M.L.R. 2594 (2004). The 9th U.S. Court of Appeals made a similar ruling on this law in 2005. See *Chaker* v. *Crogan,* 33 M.L.R. 2569 (2005). The California Supreme Court had two years earlier upheld the same statute. *People* v. *Stanistreet,* 58 P. 3d 465 (2002).

106. 384 U.S. 195 (1966).
107. 376 U.S. 254 (1964); see also *Ivey* v. *State,* 29 M.L.R. 2089 (2001).
108. 379 U.S. 64 (1964).

BIBLIOGRAPHY

American Law Institute. *Restatement of the Law of Torts.* 2nd ed. Philadelphia: American Law Institute, 1975.

Ashley, Paul. *Say It Safely.* 5th ed. Seattle: University of Washington Press, 1976.

"Criminalizing Speech About Reputation: The Legacy of Criminal Libel in the U.S. After *Sullivan* and *Garrison.*" *Media Law Resource Center Bulletin*, 2003, No. 1.

"Developments in Criminal Defamation Law Since 2002." *Media Law Resource Center Bulletin,* 2004, No. 4, Pt. 2.

Dill, Barbara. "Libel Law Doesn't Work, But Can It Be Fixed?" In *At What Price? Libel Law and Freedom of the Press,* by Martin London and Barbara Dill. New York: The Twentieth Century Fund Press, 1993.

Goodnough, Abby. "Blog Takes Failed Marriage Into Fight Over Free Speech." *The New York Times*, 10 January 2008, A8.

Greenhouse, Linda. "For First Time Justices Reject Punitive Award." *The New York Times,* 21 May 1996, A1.

———. "Justices Limit Punitive Damages—Victory for Tort Reform." *The New York Times,* 8 April 2003, A16.

———. "Punitive Damages Must Get a Searching Review on Appeal, Justices Rule." *The New York Times,* 15 May 2001, A18.

Gregory, Charles O., and Harry Kalven. *Cases and Materials on Torts.* 2nd ed. Boston: Little, Brown, 1969.

McGraw, David. "The Right to Republish Libel: Neutral Reportage and the Reasonable Reader." *Akron Law Review* 25 (1991): 335.

Phelps, Robert, and Douglas Hamilton. *Libel.* New York: Macmillan, 1966.

Pogrebin, Robin. "Publication Date Open to Dispute in Internet Age." *The New York Times,* 3 November 1997, C1.

Prosser, William L. *Handbook of the Law of Torts.* St. Paul: West Publishing, 1963.

Sanford, Bruce W. *Libel and Privacy.* 2nd ed. Englewood Cliffs, N.J.: Prentice-Hall Law & Business, 1993.

CHAPTER 7

Invasion of Privacy

APPROPRIATION AND INTRUSION

Invasion of privacy is a multifaceted tort that is designed to redress a variety of grievances. These include the commercial exploitation of an individual's name or likeness, the intrusion on what might be called our private domains, the revelation of intimate information about someone, and the libel-like publication of embarrassing false information about a person. After an initial exploration of the broader dimensions of the right to privacy, we will explore these four discrete legal areas in this chapter and in Chapter 8.

INVASION OF PRIVACY

The right to privacy is a rapidly diminishing commodity in the United States. As much as die-hard civil libertarians try to sustain Americans' right to be left alone, they are being overwhelmed by the actions of government, businesses, and an increasingly uncaring public. Since the terrorist attacks on Sept. 11, 2001, federal and state governments have shifted into high gear passing legislation to protect the nation from subsequent attacks, but that places a very low premium on an individual's personal privacy. National security interests trump the right of individuals to protect their private lives, it is argued. And most Americans seem to buy into this philosophy. Private business, long involved in mining data about its customers and potential customers, has pitched in to help. The emphasis on data gathering has created what some have called a "security-industrial complex," reminiscent of the military-industrial complex President Dwight D. Eisenhower warned the nation against when he left office almost 60 years ago. And when corporations aren't gathering information for the government, they are collecting increasing amounts of personal information about the behavior of customers.

If an individual is willing to make sacrifices it is possible to retain a largely private life. Living in a cabin in the mountains or desert, without utilities, credit cards, insurance, bank accounts, medical services and so on, would go a long way in protecting a man or woman's right to be left alone. But most Americans aren't willing to do this. In fact, a growing number of citizens—largely the younger generations—are not only willing to, but delight in sharing personal information and photographs on the growing number of social networking sites (see Facebook, Flickr) that have been generated by the growth of the Internet. Anyone can get access to the material on these sites and use the images and information for any number of unintended purposes.* As cartoonist Walt Kelly wrote generations ago in his popular comic strip "Pogo," "We have met the enemy and it is us!"

While most Americans seem willing to part with large chunks of their private lives for a variety of reasons, they are still sensitive when others take advantage of them. The mass media have become a popular target of this anger—for good reason.

In recent years many mass media organizations and the people who work for them have given new meaning to the concept of the intrusive or prying reporter. The "anything goes" attitude of not most, but too many in the journalism business has angered not only the objects of this aggressive reporting but thoughtful members of the audience as well. This is where this text intersects with the right to privacy, for over the past century state legislatures and courts have fashioned legal rights that permit people who believe they have been injured to sue the mass media for infringing on their rights of privacy. The law is ragged in many ways because it is young and still developing, unlike libel law, which has existed for several centuries. And today, while concerns over the right to privacy range far beyond the behavior of the mass media, it is interesting to note that it was the intrusive newspaper reporting of the late 19th century that is the likely genesis of the law that exists today.

---

*Young people especially need to be aware that embarrassing, incriminating and provocative photos, perhaps taken in a moment of revelry at a party, are not private once they are posted online. Potential employers, college admission officers and others can easily find them.

THE GROWTH OF PRIVACY LAWS

Most rights that Americans believe to be basic are guaranteed by the U.S. Constitution and contained in the Bill of Rights. But a guarantee of a right to privacy is not to be found in this document. In fact, the word "privacy" is not even contained in the Constitution. Privacy, or at least the concept of privacy as we know it today, was not on the minds of many Americans in the largely rural America of the 17th and 18th centuries. The U.S. Supreme Court ruled in the past century that the protection of the right to privacy is at the core of several amendments contained in the Bill of Rights, but this notion was generated by 20th-century legal thinking and cannot necessarily be attributed to the nation's founders.*

It wasn't until the end of the 19th century that the need for a right to privacy became a public issue. Of course the nation had changed dramatically. America was rapidly becoming an urban nation. The streets of many cities were clogged with poor immigrants or first-generation Americans. Big city daily newspapers used a variety of sensational schemes to attract these potential readers. Editors often played out the lives of the "rich and famous" on the pages of their newspapers, permitting their readers to vicariously enjoy wealth, status and celebrity.

It was this kind of journalism that apparently pushed two Boston lawyers, Samuel D. Warren and Louis D. Brandeis, to use the pages of the Harvard Law Review to propose a legally recognized right to privacy. Warren, the scion of a prominent Boston family, urged his friend (and future Supreme Court justice) Brandeis to help him write the piece, "The Right to Privacy."[1] The article appeared in 1890 and can be legitimately regarded as the fountain from which the modern law of privacy has flowed.

The pair argued, "Instantaneous photographs and newspaper enterprise have invaded the sacred precincts of private and domestic life; and numerous mechanical devices threaten to make good the prediction that 'what is whispered in the closet shall be proclaimed from the house-tops.'" Warren and Brandeis said they were offended by the gossip in the press, which they said had overstepped in every direction the obvious bounds of propriety and decency:

> To satisfy a prurient taste the details of sexual relations are spread broad-cast in the columns of the daily papers. To occupy the indolent, column upon column is filled with idle gossip, which can only be procured by intrusion upon the domestic circle. . . .
>
> The common law has always recognized a man's house as his castle, impregnable, often, even to its own officers engaged in the execution of its commands. Shall the courts thus close the front entrance to constituted authority, and open wide the back door to idle or prurient curiosity?[2]

*In 1965 the Supreme Court ruled in *Griswold* v. *Connecticut,* 381 U.S. 479, that something like a right to privacy was implicit in the Bill of Rights. In that case and others the high court has decided that the First Amendment's guarantee of freedom of association, the Third Amendment's limits on the government's power to quarter soldiers in private homes during peacetime, the protection from unreasonable search and seizure in the Fourth Amendment and the protection against self-incrimination in the Fifth Amendment all speak indirectly, at least, to protection of the right of privacy. This constitutional right to privacy has been cited several times by the high court since 1965, including the *Roe* v. *Wade* abortion ruling in 1973 and the decision in *Lawrence* v. *Texas* in 2003 that declared the Texas anti-sodomy law to be unconstitutional.

1. Warren and Brandeis, "The Right to Privacy," 220.
2. Warren and Brandeis, "The Right to Privacy," 220.

To stop this illicit behavior, the two young lawyers proposed that the courts recognize the legal right of privacy; that is, citizens should be able to go to court to stop such unwarranted intrusions and also secure money damages for the hardship they suffered from such prying and from publication of private material about them.

It was 13 years from the time the Warren and Brandeis article was first published until the first state recognized the law of privacy. The state of New York adopted a law that prohibited the commercial exploitation of an individual and called it a right to privacy. Interestingly, the right this new statute sought to safeguard was not even mentioned in the famous Harvard Law Review article.

The law of privacy grew slowly and sporadically over the next 95 years.

The law of privacy grew slowly and sporadically over the next 95 years. All but three states today recognize some kind of legal right to privacy. North Dakota has thus far refused to recognize the tort, and there have been no reported privacy cases in either Vermont or Wyoming.[3] Other states have rejected one or more of the four torts that constitute the modern right to privacy.* And until the European Convention on Human Rights became a part of the law in western Europe, nations like England and France didn't recognize the invasion-of-privacy tort.†

Privacy law is far more idiosyncratic from state to state than is libel law. In other words, it is somewhat easier to make generalizations about libel law that reflect the law in every state or in most states than it is to make these generalizations about the law of privacy. Part of the problem is that some states have protected the right to privacy through statutes, and these often are very particular. The New York statute, for example, is quite explicit about how the right to privacy is protected in that state, and some aspects of the law common in most states are not a part of the New York law.

Today the law of privacy encompasses protection for at least four separate legal wrongs. Three of these have absolutely nothing to do with the law as outlined in 1890 by Warren and Brandeis.

FOUR AREAS OF PRIVACY LAW

1. Appropriation of name or likeness for trade purposes
2. Intrusion upon an individual's solitude
3. Publication of private information about an individual
4. Publishing material that puts an individual in a false light

---

The first kind of invasion of privacy is called **appropriation** and is defined as taking a person's name, picture, photograph or likeness and using it for commercial gain without permission. Appropriation is technically the only right of privacy guaranteed in some of the states that have privacy statutes. The laws are limited to outlawing this one kind of behavior. But as

---

*Several states have rejected the false-light invasion-of-privacy tort, for example, because it is too much like libel. See *Jews for Jesus Inc.* v. *Rapp*, 36 M.L.R. 2540 (2008), for example.
†In 2006 the Irish government was considering enacting a privacy law that included provisions that mirrored elements in U.S. laws regarding appropriation, intrusion and private facts. See Crampton, "Oops, Did It Again."
3. Sanford, *Libel and Privacy.*

a matter of fact, judicial construction of these laws has allowed them to encompass some of the other aspects of invasion of privacy as well.

Intrusion is the second type of invasion of privacy, an area of the law growing rapidly today, and is what most people think of when invasion of privacy is mentioned. Intrusion upon the solitude and into the private life of a person is prohibited.

The third arm of the law prohibits **publication of private information**—truthful private information—about a person. What is truthful private information? Gossip, substance of private conversations and details of a private tragedy or illness have all been used as the basis of a suit.

Finally, the publication of material that places a person in a **false light** is the fourth category of the law of privacy. This category is an outgrowth of the first area of the law, appropriation, and doesn't at first glance seem like an invasion of privacy at all, but it is regarded as such by the law.

The tremendous growth of communication via interactive computer systems (i.e., the Internet) has generated substantial challenges in the application of the law of privacy. The relative ease of access and use of these systems has resulted in numerous privacy problems. While research indicates many Internet users remain skittish about the safety and security of this communication channel, many users plow on ahead, oblivious to serious privacy problems. In many ways the Internet is just like any other mass communication system. And all four elements of the law of privacy are applicable in the lawsuits that result from claims of invasion of privacy via interactive computer systems. Practically, however, most problems fall under two of the privacy subtorts—intrusion and publication of private information. It is not difficult for outsiders to collect data from Internet users, with and without their knowledge. This can be categorized as intrusion. Similarly, these data can then be published in a variety of ways and for a variety of purposes. This can be regarded as the publication of private information. We will explore these Internet-related problems in this chapter and in Chapter 8.

A few caveats or warnings are appropriate before each of the four aspects of privacy law is detailed. First, only people enjoy protection for their right to privacy. Corporations, labor unions, associations and so forth can protect their reputations through libel law, but they do not have a right to privacy.* (Other laws protect businesses against unfair commercial exploitation.)

The right to privacy is most easily understood if each of the four areas of the law is considered as a discrete unit. Don't try to apply the defenses that may be applicable in appropriation to publication of private information. They don't work.

There is much about the law of privacy that defies logic. Why is putting someone in a false light considered an invasion of privacy, for example? Challenging the logic of the law serves little purpose and usually makes learning the law more difficult.

The law of privacy is young—about 120 years old if you start with the Warren and Brandeis proposal. There are a lot of legal questions that haven't been answered, or at least answered satisfactorily. Bad court decisions are abundant. Trial judges rarely see invasion-of-privacy cases; most lawyers are equally distant from the law. If you mix those two elements together, it is not uncommon for courts to render wrong-headed decisions. A trial court in Louisiana once ruled that a house had a right to privacy, for example.

---

*See *Felsher* v. *University of Evansville,* 755 N.E. 2d 589 (2001), for example.

Finally, it is worthwhile to raise the issues of ethics and morality. The following pages provide for journalists, photographers and advertising and public relations practitioners a kind of road map of how to stay within the law. But these roads aren't necessarily the ones that should be followed at all times. Today, more than ever, many readers and viewers are asking the mass media to exercise restraint in certain areas, restraint that often falls well within the boundaries of what is legal. Journalists would do well to ponder these requests. Publish and be damned is still an appropriate response in some situations. But more often a thoughtful journalist will take a different tack.

APPROPRIATION

It is illegal to appropriate an individual's name or likeness for commercial or trade purposes without consent.

Appropriation is the oldest of the four privacy torts. Until recently it was the most comprehensible. Appropriation protects an individual's name or likeness from commercial exploitation. Two of the earliest privacy cases on record are good examples of how the appropriation tort is supposed to protect an individual from commercial exploitation. In 1902 young Abigail Roberson of Albany, N.Y., awoke one morning to find her picture all over town on posters advertising Franklin Mills Flour. Twenty-five thousand copies of the advertisement had been placed in stores, warehouses, saloons and other public places. Roberson said she felt embarrassed and humiliated, that she suffered greatly from this commercial exploitation and she therefore sued for invasion of privacy. But she lost her case, and the state's high court ruled that

> an examination of the authorities leads us to the conclusion that the so-called "right of privacy" has not yet found an abiding place in our jurisprudence, and, as we view it, the doctrine cannot now be incorporated without doing violence to settled principles of law by which the profession and the public have long been guided.[4]

Following this decision a great controversy arose in New York, led by newspapers and magazines, many of whom expressed outrage at the way the court had treated Roberson. The controversy settled on the state legislature, which during the following year, 1903, adopted the nation's first privacy law. The statute was very narrow; that is, it prohibited a very specific kind of conduct. Use of an individual's name or likeness without the individual's consent for advertising or trade purposes was made a minor crime. In addition to the criminal penalty, the statute allowed the injured party to seek both an injunction to stop the use of the name or picture and money damages.

Two years later Georgia became the first state to recognize the right of privacy through the common law. Paolo Pavesich, an Atlanta artist, discovered that a life insurance company had used his photograph in newspaper advertisements. Pavesich's photograph was used in a before-and-after advertisement to illustrate a contented, successful man who had bought sufficient life insurance. A testimonial statement was also ascribed to the artist. He sued for $25,000 and won his case before the Georgia Supreme Court, which ruled that

4. *Roberson* v. *Rochester Folding Box Co.,* 171 N.Y. 538 (1902).

the form and features of the plaintiff are his own. The defendant insurance company and its agents had no more authority to display them in public for the purpose of advertising the business . . . than they would have had to compel the plaintiff to place himself upon exhibition for this purpose.[5]

RIGHT OF PUBLICITY

The appropriation tort actually encompasses two slightly different legal causes of action. One is the right to privacy; the other is called the **right of publicity.** The differences between these two sound legalistic, but they are actually quite important.

- Traditionally, the right-to-privacy dimension of appropriation was designed to protect an individual from the *emotional damage* that can occur when a name or likeness is used for a commercial or trade purpose. Imagine how embarrassed Abigail Roberson felt the morning she awoke to find her picture on all those advertising posters. The right to publicity, on the other hand, is an attempt to remunerate individuals for the *economic harm* suffered when their name or picture is used for advertising or trade purposes, and they are not compensated for it. The proposition is a simple one: An individual's name or likeness has monetary value, and using it without permission is akin to theft. But the difference between emotional harm and economic harm is sometimes easier to state than to apply.[6]

- The second distinction between the right of privacy and the right of publicity often helps resolve this question. Because the right of publicity protects a property right—the economic value in a name or likeness—only someone whose name or likeness has a commercial value can successfully allege a violation of his or her right of publicity. An average person—Jane Doe, for example—would likely be embarrassed to find her picture on a box of Wheaties. But it would be extremely difficult for Doe to argue in court that General Mills was actually promoting its cereal this way because kids all over America want to eat what Jane Doe eats. But kids may want to eat the same cereal that Derek Jeter or Venus Williams eats. The names and pictures of these professional athletes have commercial value and would enhance the value of the cereal (or the cereal box) in the eyes of consumers.[*] Simply put, only well-known people have a legally recognized economic value in their names or likenesses, and except in unusual cases, they are the only ones who can sue for damage to their right to publicity. The average person can only assert emotional damage in a right of privacy suit.

- Finally, something that has an economic value, like a house or a painting or a ring, can usually be passed on to an heir when the owner dies. Something of emotional value, like a reputation or mental health, is gone when its owner passes on.

---

[*]In the summer of 2009 lawyers for the former UCLA basketball star Ed O'Bannon filed a class-action lawsuit against the NCAA, arguing that the former college athletes should be compensated when the association sold the rights to their images and names for advertisements, video games and clothing.

5. *Pavesich* v. *New England Mutual Life Insurance Co.,* 122 Ga. 190 (1905).

6. See *Villalovos* v. *Sundance Associates Inc.,* 31 M.L.R. 1274 (2003), for example.

Consequently, it is possible in some states for a celebrity or sports star or some other well-known person who has died to pass on the property right in his or her name to his or her heirs. The heirs can sue for violation of the deceased's right to publicity. Lawyers say that the right of publicity is descendible. For the rest of the people, their right to privacy dies when they do.

As noted, the right to privacy is over 100 years old. But the right to publicity is only half that old, and it has been only in recent years that substantial case law has been generated.[7] The increase in right to publicity litigation has been fueled in large part by the tremendous growth in the cult of celebrity in the United States, the so-called celebrification of the nation. Today stories and pictures about entertainers, musicians, sports stars and others overflow on television and radio, in magazines and newspapers and on tens of thousands of Web sites. The public fascination with these personalities has inflated their egos and has often resulted in exaggerated efforts to protect the value in their names and images. Attorney Mark S. Lee recently remarked that the right of publicity is the most "intuitive of intellectual property rights," but it also has the greatest statutory confusion. States that recognize the right do so differently, and some states categorically reject it.[*]

Today there are probably as many right-to-publicity cases being litigated as right-to-privacy lawsuits. In the following discussion of the appropriation tort, the two—right of publicity and right of privacy—will be intermingled. The law is basically the same; only the damage asserted by the plaintiff in the lawsuit is different.

USE OF NAME OR LIKENESS

Courts have spent considerable time attempting to define what is or is not an illegal use of a name or likeness. In the 1970s and 1980s, most courts seemed to take a very expansive view of the concept of use. But beginning in the 1990s, some appellate courts began to narrow this definition. A summary of cases will illustrate this trend.

Everybody knows what a name is, and it is therefore unnecessary to dwell on that term. It should be noted, however, that stage names, pen names, pseudonyms and so forth count the same as real names in the eyes of the law. If the name of actor-musician Snoop Dogg is used in an advertisement for pizza without his permission, the suit cannot be defended on the basis that because Snoop Dogg's real name is Calvin Broadus, his "name" was not appropriated illegally. Only the names of people are protected under appropriation. The names of businesses, corporations, schools and other "things" are not protected under the law. However, the use of a trade name like Kodak or Crest can create other serious legal problems (see Chapter 14).

What is a likeness? A photograph of an individual is obviously a likeness; but not just a photo of a person's face. A New York court ruled it was up to a jury to decide if a photograph in a cosmetics advertisement of the back of a woman bathing in a stream could be identified as a likeness of the plaintiff, who had been secretly photographed.[8] On the other hand, a federal

---

[*]Only about one-half the states recognize the right to publicity. Pennsylvania most recently recognized this right in a 2007 case involving a jockey who rode the winning horse in the 2005 Preakness Stakes and later found his photo adorning bags of horse feed. *Rose* v. *Triple Crown Nutrition Inc.,* 35 M.L.R. 1545 (2007).

7. *Haelan Laboratories, Inc.* v. *Topps Chewing Gum,* 202 F. 2d 866 (1953).

8. *Cohen* v. *Herbal Concepts,* 473 N.Y.S. 2d 426 (1989).

court ruled that the picture of a baby who was photographed as she was carried by a firefighter away from the bombed Murrah Federal Building in Oklahoma City in 1995 was not identifiable and therefore could be used for commercial purposes.[9] A likeness can also be a sketch or a drawing. A federal court once ruled that a sketch of a black man sitting in a boxing ring was a likeness of former heavyweight champion Muhammad Ali.[10]

Protecting a voice might also be encompassed in a law protecting a name or likeness. In 2008 the 3rd U.S. Court of Appeals refused to dismiss a lawsuit by the son of John Facenda who sued N.F.L. Films for using his father's distinctive baritone voice in a commercial vehicle promoting the release of the video game "Madden N.F.L. 06." For years Facenda had been the voice of N.F.L. Films, a popular series of video summaries of the National Football League games. But he had never agreed to have his voice used in a commercial for the video game. The defendants used 13 seconds of his commentary from the N.F.L. Films series in the promotional TV video to underscore the degree to which the Madden video game authentically recreated the N.F.L. experience. The court said Facenda's voice had commercial value, that the N.F.L. used it for commercial purposes and that he had never consented to such a use. The case would have to go to trial.[11]

Celebrities have argued—with some success—that the protection of their likeness extends to depictions of characters they played in movies or on television. An actor named George McFarland, who as a child in the 1930s played a character called Spanky in a series of short comedies known as the "Our Gang" comedies (and later as "The Little Rascals" when they were shown on television), sued the owner of a restaurant called Spanky McFarland's. The eating establishment was filled with memorabilia from the film series. A federal appeals court ruled that it was clearly a triable issue of fact as to whether the actor had become so identified with the character that the use of the name in a commercial venture would invoke McFarland's own image.[12] The 9th U.S. Court of Appeals reached the same conclusion when George Wendt and John Ratzenberger sued a restaurant chain for installing animatronic robots that looked like Norm Peterson and Cliff Clavin, characters played by Wendt and Ratzenberger on the long-running TV series "Cheers." The court said a performer does not lose the right to control the commercial exploitation of his or her likeness merely by portraying a fictional character in a motion picture or television series.[13] In 2009 Woody Allen agreed to a $5 million settlement in his lawsuit against American Apparel, a trendy clothing company known for its racy advertising. The apparel company used a frame from the film "Annie Hall," which depicted Allen as a Hasidic Jew, on billboards in Los Angeles and New York, and on its Web site. Allen had sought a $10 million judgment.[14] But not all courts have followed this path. In 2008 a federal court in New York ruled that the state statute did not "extend to fictitious characters adopted or created by celebrities."[15]

Other celebrities have argued—again, sometimes successfully—that their right to publicity was violated when a business used someone who looked like or sounded like the celebrity in its advertisements. The Christian Dior company was sued successfully by Jacqueline

9. Queary, "Mother Denied Say."

10. *Ali* v. *Playgirl,* 447 F. Supp. 723 (1978).

11. *Facenda* v. *N.F.L. Films,* 36 M.L.R. 2473 (2008).

12. *McFarland* v. *Miller,* 14 F. 3d 912 (1994).

13. *Wendt* v. *Host International,* 125 F. 3d 800 (1997).

14. Hughes, "Woody Allen Settles."

15. *Burck d/b/a The Naked Cowboy* v. *Mars., Inc.,* No. 08 Cir. 1330 (S.D.N.Y., June 23, 2008).

Kennedy Onassis when it used an actress named Barbara Reynolds in an advertisement. When appropriately dressed and coifed, Reynolds bore an uncanny resemblance to Onassis. That was the point of using her in the ad, to fool readers. A New York court ruled that this was the use of the former first lady's likeness. Other performers have had similar success in pursuing such lawsuits.[16]

Bette Midler successfully sued the Ford Motor Company when it hired a singer who sounded almost exactly like Midler to sing one of Midler's hit songs for a soundtrack in a television advertisement. A federal appeals court ruled, "The singer manifests herself in the song. To impersonate her voice is to pirate her identity." Not every voice impersonation would necessarily be actionable, the court said. But when the distinctive voice of a widely known professional singer is deliberately imitated, this can amount to an appropriation.[17] Other performers have filed similar actions against advertisers. Will a disclaimer protect an advertiser from an appropriation suit when a look-alike model or sound-alike singer is used? Yes, if the disclaimer is prominent. Small type at the bottom of a full-page ad will not do the trick; nor will an audio disclaimer camouflaged by music or noise in a radio or television spot.

A high-water mark (or low-water mark, depending on your point of view) in the battle by celebrities against advertisers came in 1992 when television personality Vanna White successfully sued electronics manufacturer Samsung when it published a newspaper and magazine advertisement that depicted a robot, reminiscent of C3PO of "Star Wars" fame, wearing a blond wig, evening dress and jewelry, standing next to a video board similar to the one used on "Wheel of Fortune." The ad was supposedly saying that Samsung electronic products would still be state of the art long after White had been replaced by an android. A federal court ruled that this photo was a use of White's image, and constituted an actionable appropriation.[18]

The tide favoring celebrities seems to have turned somewhat in the wake of the *White* ruling, which was widely criticized. In some important cases defense attorneys were successful in raising First Amendment issues and the courts were asked to balance the protection for freedom of expression with the protection of a celebrity's image. The 10th U.S. Court of Appeals blocked an attempt by the Major League Players Association to stop the distribution of a set of satirical baseball cards that made fun of many well-known players. The court said even though the cards used caricatures of the players, and the sale of the items was a commercial enterprise, the cards were parodies or social commentary protected by the First Amendment. "While not core political speech . . . this type of commentary on an important social institution constitutes protected expression," the court said.[19] More recently a federal court ruled that the use of Major League baseball players' names in online fantasy baseball leagues did not amount to making commercial use of a player's identity.[20]

In an important ruling in 2001 the California Supreme Court fashioned a useful test for determining when the use of a celebrity's likeness constitutes an infringement on the right of publicity, and when it is protected free expression. The test has been cited favorably by other courts.

---

16. *Onassis* v. *Christian Dior,* 472 N.Y.S. 2d 254 (1984).

17. *Midler* v. *Ford Motor Co.,* 849 F. 2d 460 (1988).

18. *White* v. *Samsung Electronics America, Inc.,* 971 F. 2d 1395 (1992); rehearing den. 989 F. 2d 1512 (1992).

19. *Cardtoons* v. *Major League Baseball Players Association,* 95 F. 3d 959 (1996).

20. *C.B.C. Distribution and Marketing Inc.* v. *Major League Baseball Advanced Media L.P.,* 34 M.L.R. 2287 (2006). The Supreme Court refused to hear an appeal of this ruling. U.S. No. 07-1099 (2008).

An artist named Gary Saderup created a charcoal drawing of the Three Stooges comedy team. Making a single drawing is not a problem since the law exempts single and original works of fine art from the purview of the California statute. But Saderup went on to create lithographic prints and T-shirts that also contained the drawing and was sued by Comedy III Inc., a company that owns the rights to the Stooges. Justices on the California high court noted immediately the First Amendment implications in the issue. "Because celebrities take on public meaning, the appropriation of their likenesses may have important uses in uninhibited debate on public issues, particularly debates about culture and values," the court noted. The creative appropriation of celebrity images can be an important avenue of individual expression, the justices added. The importance of celebrities in society means that the right to publicity has the potential of censoring significant expression by suppressing alternative versions of celebrity images that are "iconoclastic, irrelevant, or otherwise attempt to redefine the celebrity's image." There must be a test, then, that takes these values into account, the justices went on. The court focused on what is called the transformative elements in the reproduction. If the reproduction is simply a literal translation of the celebrity's image, then the First Amendment concerns are surely minimal. But it is a different matter if the user has added other elements to the image, has transformed the image into a parody, used the name in a song, lampooned the prominent person, or in some way used the celebrity's likeness as a vehicle for the expression of opinion or ideas. Then the rights of free expression take precedence over the right of the celebrity to protect his or her right to publicity. In this case, the court said, Saderup used a literal depiction of the Stooges for commercial gain without adding significant expression beyond his trespass on the right to publicity. He was guilty of violating the law.[21]

The creative appropriation of celebrity images can be an important avenue of individual expression.

The 6th U.S. Court of Appeals, citing both the *Cardtoons* and *Saderup* decisions, ruled in 2003 that artist Rick Rush did not violate Tiger Woods' right to publicity when he painted a picture of the golfer commemorating his 1997 Master's golf tournament victory. The picture featured Woods in the foreground and six other golfing greats in the background. Rush produced 250 limited edition serigraphs, which he sold for $700 each, and 5,000 smaller lithographs, which were priced at $15 each. He was sued by ETW Corporation, which holds the exclusive marketing rights to Woods, for trademark infringement and violation of the golfer's right to publicity. (The court held a person's image or likeness cannot function as a trademark. See Chapter 14 for more on trademark law.) As for the right to publicity, the court said Rush's work was creative and transformative, and this made it worthy of First Amendment protection. The substantial creative content in the work outweighed any adverse effect on ETW's market.[22]

The only important *contrary* ruling involving a celebrity since the *Saderup* case was a decision in the summer of 2006 by the Missouri Court of Appeals upholding a $15 million verdict against comic book artist Todd McFarlane. McFarlane created a Spawn comic book character named Anthony Twistelli in 1992. McFarlane changed the name of the character to Tony Twist and later told fans the character was modeled after National Hockey League

21. *Comedy III Inc.* v. *Gary Saderup Inc.*, 21 P. 3d 797 (2001). The Supreme Court of the United States refused to hear an appeal of this ruling. See also *Kirby* v. *Sega of America Inc.*, 50 Cal. Rptr. 3d 607 (2006), where the California Court of Appeals used the transformative test to reject the claim of a woman who argued her likeness had been appropriated in a video game.

22. *ETW Corp.* v. *Jireh Publishing Inc.*, 332 F. 3d 915 (2003). See also Chambers, "Case of Art, Icons and Law."

© *Columbia/The Kobal Collection*

player Tony Twist. Twist sued for appropriation. After nearly 10 years of litigation the appellate court rejected free speech arguments and adopted what it called a "predominant-use" test. Speech with a predominant artistic purpose is protected, while speech with a predominant commercial purpose is not. This is a highly subjective test that had never been used by another court. The burden falls on the judge to decide what is art and what is commerce. McFarlane argued that when he first used Twist's name, he was a relatively unknown player in Canada, and therefore use of the name had no commercial benefit. The court disagreed. It was enough that McFarlane intended to create the impression that the hockey player was associated with the comic book, the court said.[23] McFarlane said he planned to appeal the ruling, since the judgment pushed his company into bankruptcy.

ADVERTISING AND TRADE PURPOSES

What are advertising and trade purposes? While minor differences exist among the states—especially among the states with statutes—a general guideline can be set down: Advertising or trade purposes are commercial uses; that is, someone makes money from the use. Here are examples of the kinds of actions that may be regarded as a commercial use:

23. *Doe* v. *McFarlane,* 34 M.L.R. 2057 (2006).

1. **Use of a person's name or photograph in an *advertisement* on television, on radio, in newspapers, in magazines, on the Internet, on posters, on billboards and so forth. Rapper 50 Cent sued a Philadelphia car dealer for $1 million in 2005 for using his name in an ad for a Dodge Magnum. The ads used the Slogan, "Just Like 50 Says."**

2. **Display of a person's photograph in the window of a photographer's shop to show potential customers the quality of work done by the studio.**

3. **A testimonial falsely suggesting that an individual eats the cereal or drives the automobile in question.**

4. **Use of an individual's name or likeness in a banner ad or some other commercial message on a Web site.**

5. **The use of someone's likeness or identity in a commercial entertainment vehicle like a feature film, a television situation comedy or a novel.**

Numerous court cases document liability outlined in these uses. For example, in 1992 the former wife of National Football League Hall of Fame running back John Riggins decided to sell the house the two had lived in, a home she had won as part of the divorce settlement. As a real estate agent she created a brochure that used John Riggins' name in several spots to advertise the house. The Virginia Supreme Court ruled that this was a commercial purpose and sustained the award of more than $50,000 to the former NFL star.[24] Sometimes the use is more oblique. After Third Coast Entertainment Inc. obtained an option on the film rights of an unauthorized biography of Priscilla Presley, the wife of Elvis Presley and a celebrity in her own right, the company attempted to generate interest in the possible video production by suggesting that Presley would work with them on preparing a film. Press releases included headlines that said Presley had been offered a consultant role on the film, something that wasn't true. The suggestion of her willingness to participate in the production certainly enhanced the potential value of the project, since the film would have been difficult if not impossible to produce without her cooperation. The California Court of Appeals said this was a commercial use of her name without her consent. Truthful use of a celebrity's name in advertising that is merely an adjunct to a legitimate film or book, and promotes only the work itself, is protected, the court ruled. In this case, the use was merely an attempt to generate publicity for Third Coast Entertainment and its efforts to promote the project.[25]

The kinds of uses outlined in Example 5 pose the most complicated legal problems because of the varied circumstances involved. And courts often have difficulty sorting through these circumstances to arrive at consistent decisions. What if a producer just happens to pick the name of a real person for use in a television program? Michael Costanza sued Jerry Seinfeld and others for use of the name Costanza in the successful situation comedy. But the fictional character was named George and the plaintiff's full name or photo was never associated with the show. The similarity of the plaintiff's last name and the fictional character did

---

24. *Town & Country Properties, Inc.* v. *Riggins,* 457 S.E. 2d 356 (1995). In 2008 former NBA star Larry Bird sued the couple that bought his former home in French Lick, Ind., and used his name to promote the property as a bed and breakfast.
25. *Presley* v. *Grant,* 31 M.L.R. 1385 (2002).

not amount to an illegal appropriation, the New York court ruled.[26] A Michigan case presented a far more complicated problem. NBC aired a docudrama depicting the story of the popular singing group, the Temptations. The estate of David Ruffin, the lead singer in the group from 1964 to 1968, sued, claiming that by depicting Ruffin in the film the producers had appropriated his identity and violated the right to publicity. The U.S. District Court ruled against Ruffin's heir, stating that the depiction of a person's life even in an entertainment film is not a violation of the right to publicity. The term "likeness" does not include general incidents from a person's life, the court said. The narrative of an individual's life standing alone lacks the value of a name or likeness that the appropriation tort protects.[27] And in 2005 the Florida Supreme Court ruled that the state's commercial misappropriation statute did not apply to a motion picture or any other use that does not "directly" promote a product or service. The children of two of the crew members of the Andrea Gail, the fishing boat that was lost during "The Perfect Storm," sued Time Warner for using the names of the men in the feature film of the same name without permission. The fact that the motion picture was created for profit did not warrant defining the term "commercial purpose" in the statute to include a motion picture, the court said.[28] But caution should be exercised in such cases as a cause of action for false-light privacy might be generated because the events included in the film have been fictionalized in some manner (see pages 294–296).

NEWS AND INFORMATION EXCEPTION

What about this argument? A newspaper runs a photograph of John Smith on the front page after his car rolled over several times during a high-speed police pursuit. Smith sues for invasion of privacy, arguing that his picture on the front page of the newspaper attracted readers to the paper, resulted in the sale of newspapers, and therefore was used for commercial or trade purposes.

More than 100 years ago New York courts first rejected this argument, ruling that the law was intended to punish commercial use not the dissemination of information.[29] And since that ruling other courts have consistently rejected this claim. The U.S. Supreme Court has ruled that the fact that newspapers and books and magazines are sold for profit does not deny them the protection of liberty of expression.[30]

Asking 15 different judges what is news or what is information could very likely result in getting 15 different answers. This is especially true today when much of what passes for news is really provided as entertainment. A New Jersey appellate judge recently noted this problem when he wrote, "It is neither feasible nor desirable to make a distinction between news for information and news for entertainment in determining the extent to which the publication is privileged." This was a case where several individuals who had been admitted to an emergency room at a hospital were videotaped for a television program, "Trauma: Life in

---

26. *Costanza* v. *Seinfeld,* 719 N.Y.S. 2d 29 (2001).
27. *Ruffin-Steinbeck* v. *de Passe,* 82 F. Supp. 2d 723 (2000), aff'd 267 F. 3d 457 (2001).
28. *Tyne* v. *Time Warner Entertainment Co.,* 901 S. 2d 802 (2005); 33 M.L.R. 2318 (2005).
29. *Moser* v. *Press Publishing Co.,* 109 N.Y.S. 963 (1908); *Jeffries* v. *New York Evening Journal,* 124 N.Y.S. 780 (1910).
30. *Time, Inc.* v. *Hill,* 385 U.S. 374 (1967).

the ER," which was telecast on The Learning Channel. (The fact that all had signed consent forms before the taping seriously undercut their cases, which they lost.) Nevertheless, the court ruled the production was privileged: It was not a commercial use.[31] The producers of the film "Borat: Cultural Learnings of America for Make Benefit Glorious Nation of Kazakhstan" were sued at least twice by people in scenes in New York City where Borat interacts with them in an attempt to learn about American culture. In one scene, as the fictional Middle Eastern TV personality Borat extends his hand and introduces himself to a passerby, the person runs away in terror, screaming "Get away; what are you doing?" The court said the use of the New Yorker's image was newsworthy. The film showing "bizarre and offensive reactions" of Americans carries a social message and clearly addresses a matter of public interest.[32]

A California Court of Appeals recently dismissed a lawsuit by a man who complained about the broadcast of an episode of the television show "Cops" in which he was filmed talking to Los Angeles County Sheriff's deputies after he was assaulted by someone from whom he was trying to buy drugs. Police didn't detain him, but the conversation was aired many times in the program. (His face was obscured, but his voice was not altered.) The court ruled that the law exempts news broadcasts, and other public affairs programming, and this use fell under that exemption.[33] In another case a 14-year-old Florida girl posed for a series of pictures that she believed would appear in Young and Modern, a magazine aimed at teenage girls. The photos appeared in a 1995 edition of the publication, but not exactly in the context the young model expected. They illustrated a regularly published column called Love Crisis. In this edition a 14-year-old letter writer told the columnist she had gotten drunk at a party and had sex with three different boys. What should I do? she asked. Don't do it again, the advice columnist replied, and be sure to get tested for both sexually transmitted diseases and pregnancy. The column was headlined, "I got trashed and had sex with three guys," and three photos of the plaintiff were used to illustrate the letter. She alleged the photos were published for commercial purposes, but the New York Court of Appeals disagreed. The article was newsworthy, the court said. It was not an advertisement in disguise. The fact that a publication may have used the photos primarily to enhance the value of the magazine by increasing its circulation did not mean that the photos were used for purposes of trade.[34]

The "Cops" show and the teen magazine are just two examples of the merger in contemporary mass media of news and entertainment. An even greater problem in privacy law is the convergence of information and marketing. The close association between advertising and the content of publications or television programs raises real questions about whether a particular use should be considered an exemption to the general prohibition against a commercial use. Two recent cases make the point.

Actor Dustin Hoffman sued Los Angeles Magazine in 1999 for using his photo in a fashion feature called Grand Illusions. Using computer imaging technology, the magazine combined still photos of actresses and actors (both living and dead) with photos of contemporary models wearing the latest fashions by many designers who were advertisers in the magazine. But the photo feature was not an advertisement; it was editorial copy. Hoffman's

31. *Castro* v. *NYT Television,* 32 M.L.R. 2555 (2004).
32. *Lemerond* v. *Twentieth Century Fox Film Corp.*, 36 M.L.R. 1743 (2008).
33. *Ingerson* v. *Twentieth Century Fox Film Corp.*, 31 M.L.R. 1289 (2003).
34. *Messenger* v. *Gruner + Jahr Printing and Publishing,* 94 N.Y. 2d 436 (2000).

picture was taken from a publicity still used to publicize the film "Tootsie," in which the actor is made up like a woman. Hoffman's face and head were attached to the body of a female model and the new photo appeared over this caption: "Dustin Hoffman isn't a drag in a butter-colored silk gown by Richard Tyler and Ralph Lauren heels." A trial court ruled that the use of the photo was for commercial purposes, but the 9th U.S. Circuit Court of Appeals disagreed. "Viewed in context the article as a whole is a combination of fashion photography, humor, and visual and verbal editorial content on classic films and famous actors. Any commercial aspects are 'inextricably entwined' with expressive elements and so they cannot be separated out 'from the fully protected whole,'" the court ruled.[35]

About the same time the *Hoffman* case was decided, the same U.S. Court of Appeals was faced with a somewhat similar fact situation. In this case the plaintiff's likeness was used in a 250-page Abercrombie & Fitch quarterly clothing catalog. Each issue of the retailer's catalog has a theme and contains information as well as product descriptions. The issue in question focused on the sport of surfing and included stories about famous California surfing venues and other similar material. The plaintiff's photo had been taken in 1965 and was printed adjacent to a page offering T-shirts for sale, shirts similar to the ones worn by surfers in the 1960s. In this case the court said the catalog at issue was a sales catalog and was published to sell Abercrombie & Fitch merchandise. This was unlike the feature article that was the genesis of the *Hoffman* lawsuit. The court didn't categorize the use of the photo as "commercial speech," but said it was far more commercial than the use of Hoffman's photo in Los Angeles Magazine. The publishers of the magazine had done nothing to try to connect the photo to the information articles in the catalog. The court called the use "window dressing" that would not justify the application of the information exemption under the law.[36]

OTHER EXCEPTIONS

The right to publish or broadcast an individual's name or likeness for news and information purposes is a broad exception to the appropriation rule. Other courts have found other exceptions as well, but this is where the law of privacy gets a little dicey. Not all courts view the same actions as exceptions to the appropriation rule. The doctrine of incidental use, for example, is recognized in many jurisdictions and permits a fleeting or brief use of an individual's name or likeness in some kinds of commercial creations. "The doctrine of incidental use was developed," one court ruled, "to address concerns that penalizing every unauthorized use, no matter how insignificant or fleeting, of a person's name or likeness would impose undue burdens on expressive activity."[37] When Amazon.com showed the cover of a book it was selling online, the model who had posed for the cover photo sued for appropriation. The 11th U.S. Court of Appeals ruled that the online seller merely displayed the book cover in an effort to replicate the experience of a physical bookstore. "It is clear that Amazon's use of book cover images is not an endorsement or promotion of any product or service, but is merely incidental

The doctrine of incidental use, for example, is recognized in many jurisdictions and permits a fleeting or brief use of an individual's name or likeness in some kinds of commercial creations.

---

35. *Hoffman* v. *Capital Cities/ABC Inc.,* 33 F. Supp. 2d 867 (1999), rev'd 255 F. 3d 1180 (2001).

36. *Downing* v. *Abercrombie & Fitch,* 265 F. 3d 994 (2001).

37. *Preston* v. *Martin Bregman Productions, Inc.,* 765 F. Supp. 116 (1991). See also *University of Notre Dame* v. *20th Century Fox,* 22 App. Div. 2d 452, 15 N.Y.S. 2d 907 (1962).

to, and customary for, the business of Internet book sales," the court said.[38] Plaintiff Evelyn Candelaria appeared for three to four seconds in the documentary film "Super Size Me," an attack on fast-food eating habits. She doesn't say anything in a scene that discusses the nutritional content of McDonald's offerings and the availability of this information to the public. A court ruled her appearance was incidental.[39] But the use of legendary pilot Chuck Yeager's name in a press release touting the introduction of a new mobile phone service by Cingular might not be merely incidental, a federal court in California ruled, rejecting a motion to dismiss. The press release said, "Nearly 60 years ago the legendary test pilot Chuck Yeager broke the sound barrier and achieved MACH 1. Today, Cingular is breaking another kind of barrier with our MACH 1 and MACH 2 mobile command centers."[40]

Booth *Rule*

The *Booth* rule is closely related to the incidental use doctrine; in fact, some courts refer to it as part of that doctrine. The rule has developed slowly over the past 45 years and today provides fairly broad protection to the mass media in most states if an individual's name or likeness is used in advertising for a particular information medium. In other words, the use of a person's name or likeness in an advertisement *for* a magazine or a newspaper or a television program is usually not regarded as an appropriation if the photograph or name has been or will be a part of the medium's news or information content.

The controversy that sparked this rule involved Academy Award–winning actress Shirley Booth.[*] She was photographed in Jamaica, and the picture was published in a feature story in Holiday, a popular travel magazine. Holiday then used the same picture to advertise the magazine itself. The full-page advertisement told readers that the picture was typical of the material appearing in Holiday magazine and urged people to advertise in the periodical or subscribe to Holiday. Booth did not object to her photograph in the feature story, only to its use in the subsequent advertisement. The courts, however, refused to call the use an invasion of privacy. The New York Supreme Court ruled that the maintenance of freedom of expression depends in no small part on the economic support of the press by advertisers and subscribers. And to win such support a publication or broadcasting station must be able to promote itself. Since the picture in this case was first used in an information story, its subsequent use in a promotion for the magazine was really only incidental to its original use and was merely to show the quality and content of the magazine. The picture was not used to sell spaghetti or used cars. Hence the use did not constitute an invasion of privacy.[41]

Originally it was believed that the *Booth* rule protected only the *republication* or *rebroadcast* of material previously used in the medium. Some courts still follow this rule, whereas other courts have enunciated a broader protection. For example, a U.S. District Court ruled that it is permissible for a newspaper or magazine to use previously published material in a television advertisement for the publication.[42] That is, a name or likeness that appeared

---

[*]Booth won an Oscar as Best Actress in 1952 for her role in the film "Come Back Little Sheba."

38. *Almeida* v. *Amazon.com Inc.,* 34 M.L.R. 2118 (2006).
39. *Candelaria* v. *Spurlock,* 36 M.L.R. 2150 (2008).
40. *Yeager* v. *Cingular Wireless LLC,* 36 M.L.R. 2396 (2008).
41. *Booth* v. *Curtis Publishing Co.,* 11 N.Y.S. 2d 907 (1962).
42. *Friedan* v. *Friedan,* 414 F. Supp. 77 (1976).

in a newspaper story can be *republished* in a television advertisement for that newspaper. In 1995 the New York Supreme Court ruled that the use of radio personality Howard Stern's photo without his permission in advertisements for an online service was not an invasion of privacy under this incidental republication rule. After Stern announced he was a candidate for the job of governor of New York, the Delphi online service set up a bulletin board for debates on his political candidacy. It used an outlandish photo of Stern (which he had earlier posed for) showing him with bare buttocks. The picture appeared in ads in New York Magazine and the New York Post with the caption, "Should this man be the next governor of New York?" Readers were invited to debate the issue on the bulletin board. Stern argued that Delphi wasn't a news or information medium like a newspaper or magazine and shouldn't be allowed to raise the incidental republication exception. The court disagreed, stating that the online service is analogous to news vendors, bookstores, letters to the editor and other news disseminators.[43] No one yet knows just how far the courts will go in extending the *Booth* rule. The tendency, however, seems to be to expand the protection rather than restrict it.

Clearly the use of a name or photo to promote a medium cannot be an explicit or even implied endorsement of the medium. Cher won a lawsuit against Forum magazine after it used her photo to promote an edition of the publication. The advertisements clearly implied that the actress-singer endorsed Forum, which was not true. That issue of the magazine did contain an interview with Cher, but the court ruled that the advertisements went far beyond establishing the news content and quality of the publication for potential readers.[44]

Finally, the use of an individual's name or likeness in a political advertisement is not regarded as an appropriation. A campaign advertisement that says "Vote for Jones, not Smith" would not give Smith a legal right to sue for appropriation. The use of an individual's name or likeness in an issue-oriented advertisement such as "Save the Whales" or "Stop Racism" likewise would not sustain an appropriation lawsuit. A federal court ruled in 2006 that the use of two plaintiffs' pictures in an advertisement attacking the American Association of Retired Persons' supposed support of gay marriage was not an appropriation because it was not a commercial use, and addressed an issue of public concern.[45] What about the use of a name or likeness in an advertisement or promotion for a nonprofit organization like the YMCA or the Red Cross? Many such groups put out brochures or pamphlets to stimulate donations to further their community work. Would the unauthorized use of the picture of a child swimming in the pool at the YMCA sustain a lawsuit? That is unlikely, but the 6th U.S. Circuit Court of Appeals did uphold a small damage award to a child whose picture was used without permission in a direct mail solicitation by a Kentucky religious order. The Little Sisters of the Assumption Order included the photo with a letter that was sent to 125,000 homes asking for donations for the poor. The appellate court affirmed the lower court award of $100 in damages for appropriation.[46] The New York Supreme Court came to a similar conclusion in 1995 when it found that the use of an individual's photo on a solicitation by a nonprofit corporation, the Community Service Society of New York, was an advertisement under the terms of the New York privacy statute. The defendant had used the plaintiff's picture in its newsletter aimed at

---

43. *Stern* v. *Delphi Internet Services Corp.,* 626 N.Y.S. 2d 694 (1995).
44. *Cher* v. *Forum International,* 692 F. 2d 634 (1982).
45. *Raymen* v. *United Senior Association Inc.,* 409 F. Supp. 2d 15 (2006).
46. *Bowling* v. *The Missionary Servants of the Most Holy Trinity,* 972 F. 2d 346 (1992).

soliciting funds for needy New Yorkers.[47] These two cases stand alone at present, but suggest that caution should be exercised by any organization, commercial or otherwise, that seeks to use the names and faces of real people in fund-raising efforts. The simplest solution to the problem is to get consent from these people.

CONSENT AS A DEFENSE

The law prohibits only the unauthorized use of a name or likeness for commercial or trade purposes. States with privacy statutes usually require that written authorization or consent be given before the use. The rule in the states that follow the common law is less specific with regard to the need for written consent. But in any legal action the defendant is going to have to prove that he or she had consent to use the name or photograph. Written consent is usually uncontestable and will stand as a solid defense against an appropriation claim, even if the plaintiff argues that he or she didn't really understand what he or she was signing. When a photographer took pictures of professional tennis player Anastasia Myskina, the athlete signed a consent form, or release, permitting Conde Nast publishers to include the photos in the 2002 sports issue of GQ magazine. But she sued the magazine for invasion of privacy, claiming that the magazine appropriated her likeness when it used the photos in ways she did not approve of or anticipate. In its defense the magazine raised the matter of the consent form she had signed. She said she misunderstood the document she signed; English was not her first language. A federal court said her assertion—even if true—was irrelevant. When a party signs a contract, which a release is, she is bound by the terms of the contract, whether or not she understood it, whether or not she read it.[48] Attempts to convince a court that oral consent was given can be met by the plaintiff's denial, and then the fact finder will have to decide who is telling the truth. Also, oral consent can be withdrawn up to the moment of publication or broadcast.

The consent issue is most easily resolved if the subject has signed a model release similar to the one printed on page 260. But such legal documents are not always required to establish consent. Two rulings make this point. Sam and Joseph Schifano sued the Greene County Greyhound Park, a dog racing track, for including their photo in an advertising brochure for the facility. The plaintiffs, who visited the park often, were photographed while they sat with several other persons in what is called The Winner's Circle, a section of the park that can be reserved by interested groups of spectators. There was no written consent for the use of their picture, but there was ample evidence that park officials had told the plaintiffs why they were taking the photos and gave them a chance to leave if they did not want to be in the picture. "Plaintiffs, neither by objecting nor moving, when those options were made available by park employees, consented to having their photograph taken at the Park," the Alabama Supreme Court ruled in 1993.[49]

A year later the 9th U.S. Circuit Court of Appeals handed down a similar ruling in a lawsuit involving a popular television situation comedy called "Evening Shade." Country music songwriter and performer Wood Newton sued the producers of the program because the lead character in the show, played by Burt Reynolds, was also named Wood Newton. The creator of the program, Linda Bloodworth-Thomason, grew up in the same town as the

The law prohibits only the unauthorized use of a name or likeness for commercial or trade purposes.

47. *Vinales* v. *Community Service Society of New York, Inc.,* 23 M.L.R. 1638 (1995).
48. *Myskina* v. *Conde Nast Publications Inc.,* 33 M.L.R. 2199 (2005).
49. *Schifano* v. *Greene County Greyhound Park, Inc.,* 624 So. 178 (1993).

real Wood Newton, and there are some similarities between the real and fictional characters. Newton never signed a release for the use of his name, but when the program was first telecast he sent a letter to the producers that said, "I want you to know that I'm flattered that you are using my name, everyone who I've talked to thinks it's exciting and so do I." The lawsuit was filed many months later, after the producers of the program had rejected music that Newton had written and submitted for use on the program. "Although Newton never uttered the words 'I consent,' it is obvious that he did consent," the court ruled.[50]

MODEL RELEASE OR CONSENT FORM USED BY A PHOTOGRAPHER

For and in consideration of my engagement as a model/subject by (insert photographer's name), hereafter referred to as the photographer, on terms or fee hereinafter stated, I hereby give the photographer, his/her legal representatives, and assigns, those for whom the photographer is acting, and those acting with his/her permission, or his/her employees, the right and permission to copyright and/or use, reuse, and/or publish, and republish photographic pictures or portraits of me, or in which I may be distorted in character, or form, in conjunction with my own or a fictitious name, on reproductions thereof in color, or black and white made through any media by the photographer at his/her studio or elsewhere, for any purpose whatsoever; including the use of any printed matter in conjunction therewith.

I hereby waive any right to inspect or approve the finished photograph or advertising copy of printed matter that may be used in conjunction therewith or to the eventual use that it might be applied.

I hereby release, discharge and agree to save harmless the photographer, his/her representatives, assigns, employees or any person or persons, corporation or corporations, acting under his/her permission or authority, or any person, persons, corporation or corporations, for whom he/she might be acting, including any firm publishing and/or distributing the finished product, in whole or in part, from and against any liability as a result of any distortion, blurring, or alteration, optical illusion, or use in composite form, either intentionally or otherwise, that may occur or be produced in the taking, or processing or reproduction of the finished product, its publication or distribution of the same, even should the same subject me to ridicule, scandal, reproach, scorn, or indignity.

When Consent Might Not Work

There are times when even written consent might not work as a defense, and the media must be aware of such situations:

1. **Consent given today may not be valid in the distant future, especially if it is gratuitous oral consent.** Consent given via a written contract will normally hold

---

50. *Newton* v. *Thomason,* 22 F. 3d 1455 (1994). But express oral or written consent is required under some state right-of-publicity statutes. See, for example, *Bosley* v. *Wildwet T. Com,* 310 F. Supp. 2d 914 (2004), rev'd on other grounds, 32 M.L.R. 1641 (2004).

up over time. But there have been instances in which courts have ruled that oral consent became invalid over time, especially if the notoriety of the person who gave the consent has increased. Imagine if Harry Carson took a picture of the kids in a local garage band, Hideous Shellfish, playing Acme guitars and bass. He says he will try to sell the photo to the instrument maker and the band members orally agree. But nothing comes of the deal. Fast-forward to five years later. The band has sold five million CDs. Acme now buys the picture and uses it in an advertising slogan, "Hideous Shellfish plays Acme instruments." The band sues; Harry and Acme say the group gave consent five years ago. The court very likely could rule the consent is no longer valid. Harry and Acme should have gotten reauthorization before using the photo in the ad. Written consent very likely would have held up.[51]

2. **Some people cannot give consent.** Who can't give consent? Here is a short list.

   ■ People who are under age cannot give consent. In most states a person must be 18 to enter into a legally binding agreement. There are many cases in which teenage girls who insist they are 18 have signed consent forms permitting photographers to use their pictures, for whatever reason. When they disapprove of the use and sue, they reveal that they were only 16 when they signed the forms. Courts usually demand to see evidence that the teenager was believable when he or she lied, and ask the defendant to show proof that he or she attempted to verify the age.
   ■ People who are mentally ill are very often unable to give consent.[52]
   ■ People incarcerated in prisons sometimes cannot give consent.

   It is up to the defendant to be certain that the individual who signs the consent form is in fact able to legally give his or her consent. Simply showing the judge a signed consent statement will rarely carry the day in court.

3. **Consent to use a particular photograph may be lost if the photograph is substantially altered.** Years ago a popular American fashion model signed a standard release form after a photo session giving the photographer and anyone else who came to own the pictures the right to use them in any way they chose. She gave up her right to approve of any use. The photo ended up in the hands of an advertiser that retouched it and created a rather salacious tableau. The model sued; the advertisers argued she had given consent for any use. A New York court agreed she had abandoned her rights to control the use of the original pictures, but the picture that appeared in the ad was not one of those taken by the photographer. The original photo had been substantially altered. The broad consent did not work to protect the defendants.[53] This case was decided 50 years ago when it took some work to retouch a photo. Nowadays anyone with a home computer and any one of a handful of software programs can substantially alter any photo in the blink of an eye. But just because it is easy, doesn't make it legal. Magazine editors and the providers of content for the Web must take special care. A signed consent will protect the

---

51. See *McAndrews* v. *Roy*, 131 So. 2d 256 (1961); and *Welch* v. *Mr. Christmas Tree*, 57 N.Y. 2d 143 (1982).
52. *Delan* v. *CBS*, 445 N.Y.S. 2d 898 (1981).
53. *Russell* v. *Marboro Books*, 183 N.Y.S. 2d 8 (1959).

use of only the original photo with slight retouching, not wholesale modification of the particular subject in the picture or the setting in which the subject has been photographed.[54]

LIFE AFTER DEATH

The right to privacy is a personal right that dies with the individual. But the right to publicity may live on after death. The word "may" is essential because there is inconsistency in the law in the states that have faced this question. And the question remains unanswered in many jurisdictions. State courts have handed down a mixed bag of rulings.[55] The legislatures in several states have passed statutes guaranteeing to heirs the right to protect the commercial exploitation of dead public figures for as long as 50 years.[*] And in at least one state, New York, the notion that an heir should be able to control such publicity has been flatly rejected. So where a particular lawsuit is tried is usually critical to the outcome.

The use of dead celebrities to sell products is a growing phenomenon. Viewers of the Super Bowl telecast in 1997 saw Fred Astaire, who died in 1987, dancing with a Dirt Devil vacuum cleaner. James Dean sells Levi's jeans and Converse shoes; Steve McQueen promotes Ford Mustangs. Forbes magazine reported that in 2005, 13 dead celebrities earned $247 million through licensing deals. Nirvana's Kurt Cobain topped the list, with Elvis Presley close behind. There are major American companies that do nothing but license the likenesses of dead celebrities. Advertisers who seek to associate their products with images of dead celebrities must be wary of the law in this area, which is generally unsettled in most states. It is usually worth the money and the effort to pay for the licensing rights rather than risk a lawsuit, which can be costly even if it is successfully defended.

New challenges in this area of privacy law will continue to emerge in the coming years as computer technology makes it possible to bring the images of creatures, aliens, starships and even dead celebrities to the motion picture and television screen. Using technologies pioneered by individuals like George Lucas and others, it is possible to create entire commercials and even feature films that contain the images of celebrities long since departed from this earth, images that look as real as photographs of living, breathing people. There is no doubt that the individuals who are charged with crafting the law in this realm will have to be as creative as the men and women who have generated this remarkable technology.

SUMMARY   Appropriation of a person's name or likeness for commercial or trade purposes without permission is an invasion of privacy and may be a violation of a person's right to publicity. Use of an individual's photograph, a sketch of the person, a nickname or a stage name are all considered use of a name or likeness. However, the publication of news and information in magazines, books,

---

[*]California, Florida, Indiana, Kentucky, Nebraska, Oklahoma, Tennessee, Utah and Virginia are among the states that have statutes that speak to this matter in some way.

54. See, for example, *Dittner* v. *Troma,* 6 M.L.R. 1991 (1980).

55. See, for example, *Reeves* v. *United Artists,* 572 F. Supp. 1231 (1983); *Lugosi* v. *Universal,* 160 Cal. App. 3d 323 (1979); *Acme* v. *Kuperstock,* 711 F. 2d 1538 (1983); and *The Martin Luther King Center* v. *American Heritage Products,* 296 S.E. 2d 697 (1982).

The 1968 film "Bullitt" featured one of the great motion picture car chases as Lt. Frank Bullitt, played by Steve McQueen, driving a Ford Mustang, chased two killers through the streets of San Francisco. Ford used McQueen's images from the film to market the sporty automobile.

© Warner Brothers/Kobal Collection

newspapers and news broadcasts is not considered a trade purpose, even though the mass medium may make a profit from such publication. Consequently, people who are named or pictured in news stories or other such material cannot sue for appropriation. Also, a news medium may republish or rebroadcast news items or photographs already carried as news stories in advertising for the mass medium to establish the quality or kind of material carried by the medium.

Anyone who seeks to use the name or likeness of an individual for commercial or trade purposes should gain written consent from that person. Even written consent may be invalid as a defense in an invasion-of-privacy suit if the consent was given many years before publication, if the person from whom the consent was gained cannot legally give consent or if the photograph or other material that is used is substantially altered.

Courts have also recognized what is known as the right to publicity. Right-to-publicity actions are most often instituted by well-known people who believe the unauthorized use of their name or likeness has deprived them of an opportunity to reap financial gain by selling this right to the user. In some states the right to publicity can be passed on to heirs like any other piece of property, which means that an individual's estate can control the use of his or her name and likeness after the person's death.

INTRUSION

It is illegal to intrude, physically or otherwise, upon the seclusion or solitude of an individual.

When people hear the phrase "invasion of privacy," the intrusion tort is what frequently comes to mind. Cameras with telephoto lenses, hidden microphones, snooping through records—all of these are associated with intrusion. Intrusion has a lot in common with both civil and criminal trespass. It is not unusual for a plaintiff to sue for both trespass and intrusion in the same lawsuit. But the causes of action are different: Not every intrusion is a trespass, and vice versa. Trespass is usually defined as the intentional and unauthorized entry onto land or property occupied or possessed by another. An illegal intrusion may be accomplished without physical entry onto private property. It could be done by taking a photo of someone who is in a private and secluded location, for example. The law governing the two legal actions is different as well. Intrusion is the focus of this section; trespass and other laws that regulate the use of hidden microphones or video cameras will be outlined in the section on news gathering in Chapter 9.

The intrusion tort differs from the other three invasion-of-privacy torts in a very important way: Intrusion cases focus exclusively on how information is assembled. The act of gathering the material constitutes the intrusion. In appropriation, publication of private facts and false-light invasion of privacy, publication of the material generates the legal wrong. How the information was gathered is much less important, if not totally immaterial.

The most important legal element in an intrusion case is what the courts call "a reasonable expectation of privacy." This is a subjective determination in many cases. But if a court rules that a plaintiff did not enjoy a reasonable expectation of privacy when the defendant gathered or attempted to gather the information at issue, the intrusion suit will fail.

INTRUSION AND THE PRESS

An illegal intrusion can occur in myriad ways. Eavesdropping to overhear a conversation could be an intrusion. Gathering personal information from an individual's private records could also be an intrusion. The use of a telephoto lens on a camera to photograph a subject might violate the law as well. *The court will ask in every case in which an intrusion is alleged whether the subject of the intrusion "enjoyed a reasonable expectation of privacy" when the information was collected.* This issue is the key to determining whether an invasion of privacy took place. A reporter who sits at a table in a restaurant and eavesdrops on the conversation at the next table is not committing an intrusion. If other diners can hear the conversation, the speakers did not enjoy a reasonable expectation of privacy.[56] If, however, the reporter hides in a closet in the subject's office and listens to a conversation, this would be an intrusion. Two people talking in a private office have a reasonable expectation of privacy. Courts are just beginning to sort out when an Internet user can expect to enjoy a reasonable expectation of privacy, and the decisions have not been favorable to those who think the Web should be a secure haven. At least two lower courts have ruled that the user of an online service who participated in a chat room conversation and sent e-mail messages to other chat room participants did not have a reasonable expectation of privacy with regard to the content of these messages.[57] A federal court in Massachusetts ruled in 2002 that two employees of an insurance company

---

56. See *Simtel Communications* v. *National Broadcasting Company Inc.,* 84 Cal. Rptr. 2d 329 (1999).
57. See *U.S.* v. *Charbonneau,* DC, S. Ohio, CR-2-97-83, 9/30/97; and *Pennsylvania* v. *Proetto,* Pa. Super. Ct. No. 1076 EDA 2000, 3/28/01.

did not enjoy a reasonable expectation of privacy in the content of the sexually explicit e-mail messages they sent and received at work.[58] A U.S. District Court in Maine ruled that a student lacked a reasonable expectation of privacy in files on a shared-usage university computer.[59] And the 1st U.S. Court of Appeals ruled that if e-mail messages were stored for even a millisecond on the computers of an Internet service provider that transmitted them, federal wiretap laws were not violated if employees of the provider read the messages. A company called Interloc Inc., a literary clearinghouse, made copies of the messages its subscribers sent to competitor Amazon.com. Interloc's customers were dealers in rare and out-of-print books, and while Amazon did not offer its customers out-of-print and rare books, it did help customers track down such books. The court ruled that while the wiretap law prohibits eavesdropping on messages that are not stored, it does not protect stored messages.[60]

While many questions regarding intrusion and online communications have been answered, many others have not. For example, courts have yet to rule on whether an Internet user who is sending or receiving material through a wireless connection—so-called wi-fi—enjoys a reasonable expectation of privacy. And while courts are generally in agreement that personal e-mails sent or received on a company computer are not shielded from company officials, there has been no determination whether e-mails sent on a company computer by using a personal e-mail account, such as one provided by Yahoo!, are also open to scrutiny by company officials.[61]

NO PRIVACY IN PUBLIC

What occurs in public is generally not regarded as being private. This sounds like a simple rule, and in some ways it is. If a man is photographed while dancing a jig on a street corner, he can't argue that he is in a private setting. On the other hand, what occurs between a man and wife in a bedroom is certainly private. But determining what is public and what is private in situations between these two extremes often gives judges and juries difficulty. The Utah Supreme Court recently ruled that whether a reasonable expectation of privacy existed "depends on the exact nature of the conduct and all the surrounding circumstances."[62] The court is saying, in simple terms, it all depends. And often it is left to a jury to decide. But recent case law can provide guidance.

- The California Court of Appeals ruled in 2006 that it was not an intrusion into a private place when a photographer standing in a public park took a picture of a crime victim.[63]
- A federal appeals court ruled that a woman who was photographed talking with a TV producer as she stood at the front door of her home did not enjoy a reasonable expectation of privacy. The court noted she was standing in plain sight of anyone passing on the street.[64]

58. *Garrity* v. *John Hancock Mutual Life Insurance Co.,* D. Mass., No. 00-12143-RWZ, 5/7/02.
59. *U.S.* v. *Bunnell,* D. Me., Crim. No. 0213-B-S, 5/10/02.
60. Jewell, "Setback Seen for E-Mail Privacy."
61. Glater, "Open Secrets."
62. *Jensen* v. *Sawyers,* 33 M.L.R. 2578 (2005).
63. *Savala* v. *Freedom Communications Inc.,* 34 M.L.R. 2241 (2006).
64. *Deteresa* v. *American Broadcasting Co. Inc.,* 121 F. 3d 460 (1997).

■ Many courts have ruled that it is unreasonable to expect privacy in public settings where people gather. The Iowa Supreme Court ruled that someone sitting in a public dining room in a restaurant could not have a reasonable expectation of privacy. If the person was in a private dining room, such an expectation may exist. Similarly, the 10th U.S. Court of Appeals ruled it was not an intrusion when a photographer snapped a picture of the body of an Oklahoma National Guardsman killed in Iraq at an open casket funeral attended by 1,200 people, including the state's governor.[65]

But determining whether or not there is a reasonable expectation of privacy in the workplace often causes problems for the courts. ABC sent a reporter to work as a telephone psychic at a telemarketing company in California. While there the reporter secretly photographed and tape-recorded conversations with several co-workers. The network was sued for intrusion, among other things. ABC argued that there was no legitimate expectation of privacy in the office setting because workers shared small, three-walled cubicles. Conversations could be heard by other employees. The California Supreme Court disagreed with the network, ruling that

> in an office or other workplace to which the general public does not have unfettered access employees may enjoy a limited, but legitimate expectation that their conversations and other interactions will not be secretly videotaped by undercover television reporters, even though their conversations may not have been completely private.[66]

ABC suffered another setback in 2004 when its motion for a summary judgment was denied in an intrusion case in which one of its reporter/producers had secretly taped conversations at a workshop given for aspiring actors and actresses by casting directors. By paying a fee to attend the workshops the performers got to meet and talk with casting directors, the people who play an important role in employing actors and actresses who appear in movies and on television. The workshops were a controversial issue in California and the network did a segment on it for a "20/20" broadcast. The reporter taped not only the actual presentations during the workshop but also private conversations among the performers during breaks. Some of the performers sued. In California all parties must agree to the recording of a conversation unless it takes place at a public gathering. ABC asked that the case be dismissed, claiming the conversations took place in public spaces. The U.S. District Court ruled that even though some of their conversations could have been overheard by other students, the plaintiffs still had a reasonable expectation of privacy. They could not have expected as they talked among themselves in the corners or against the walls of the classroom, much less in the restrooms, that a reporter was covertly recording their conversations. This was not a public place.[67]

In one of the most unusual cases on record the California Supreme Court recently ruled that a lawsuit for intrusion could proceed based on the theory that a writer falsely misrepresented

---

65. *Stressman* v. *American Blackhawk Broadcasting Co.,* 416 N.W. 2d 685 (1987); and *Showler* v. *Harper's Magazine,* 35 M.L.R. 1577 (2007).

66. *Sanders* v. *American Broadcasting Companies,* 978 P. 2d 67 (1999). Sanders received a settlement of more than $900,000 from ABC.

67. *Turnbell* v. *American Broadcasting Companies,* 32 M.L.R. 2442 (2004). However, the plaintiff lost the case at trial.

herself in order to get information about the plaintiff from a third party. Nicole Taus argued that Elizabeth Loftus, a psychologist who specializes in memory issues, misrepresented herself in order to get information from the plaintiff's former foster mother for an article she was writing on repressed memory recovery techniques, a strategy often used to recover the memory of someone alleging sexual abuse as a child. The court said a claim of improper intrusion would not stand if a relative or close friend of a plaintiff voluntarily disclosed personal information about the person. But, the court said, "it does not necessarily follow that no violation of a person's reasonable expectation of privacy occurs when a third party . . . obtains access to personal information by improper and unanticipated means." Loftus' conduct in the present case could reasonably be found by a jury to violate Taus' reasonable expectation of privacy.[68]

Finally, another California ruling demonstrates how carefully judges will sometimes look at a situation to judge the extent of a potential intrusion. A car containing four members of the Shulman family accidentally left Interstate 10, tumbled down an embankment and came to rest upside down in a drainage ditch. Rescue apparatus arrived at the scene, including a Mercy Air helicopter with a medic and a flight nurse. Also on board was a camera operator who worked for a television production company. The photographer was accumulating footage for a television program called "On Scene: Emergency Response." Nurse Laura Carnahan was wearing a microphone that supplied the audio stream for the video. As rescue workers cut Ruth Shulman out of the car, she was comforted by Carnahan. The conversation was recorded as the photographer videotaped the rescue. Shulman was placed in the rescue helicopter, and during the flight to the hospital more video and audio material was gathered. Shulman, who ended up a paraplegic because of her injuries, sued for invasion of privacy, both intrusion and publication of private facts. The California courts dismissed the private facts claim, noting that there was tremendous public interest in what happened in this case. But the California Supreme Court said a jury could certainly find a valid intrusion claim with regard to the video and audio recordings of Shulman while she was in the rescue helicopter on the way to the hospital. But she had no reasonable expectation of privacy while she was being removed from the vehicle, which was located along a public highway.[69]

Courts will almost always reject the argument that photographing someone in a truly public place is an invasion of privacy. But sometimes there is a fine line between taking a photograph, and harassing the subject of that photograph. More than 30 years ago the courts barred a photographer from coming within 10 yards of Jacqueline Kennedy Onassis and her children because he was, the judges decided, harassing the family with his incessant picture taking.[70] In 1996 a court in Pennsylvania issued a similar order to protect a family in the state from the intense scrutiny of reporters trying to prepare a story for the television program "Inside Story."[71] Paparazzi have been a problem in California and New York for many years. These aggressive photographers dog celebrities in hopes of getting a picture they can sell to the growing number of tabloid newspapers and magazines that focus on celebrities and the entertainment business. Paparazzi photos can fetch a lot of money. A photo of the late Princess

68. *Taus* v. *Loftus,* 151 P. 3d 1185 (2007). Loftus ultimately settled the case.
69. *Shulman* v. *Group W. Productions Inc.,* 955 P. 2d 469 (1998). The case was subsequently settled out of court. See also *Chavez* v. *City of Oakland,* 37 M.L.R. 1905 (2009), where a U.S. District Court ruled, "the press has no First Amendment right to an accident or crime scene it the general public is excluded."
70. *Gallela* v. *Onassis,* 487 F. 2d 986 (1973), 533 F. Supp. 1076 (1982).
71. *Wolfson* v. *Lewis,* 924 F. Supp. 1413 (1996).

Diana and Dodi al-Fayed reportedly sold for more than $3 million. Pictures of some celebrities have become so valuable—and hard to get in a normal fashion—that paparazzi ram the vehicles carrying the objects of their hunt to force the performers to leave their cars or SUVs to deal with the accident. Once they are in the open, the photographers go to work.

California has been especially aggressive in dealing with this problem. A state statute creates tort liability for physical and "constructive" invasions of privacy through photographing, videotaping or recording a person engaged in "personal or familial activity." While this law limits so-called in your face photography, it also sharply limits the use of visual (telephoto lens) or auditory enhancement devices (microphones that can pick up conversations from great distances). The law triples the damages celebrities can win from paparazzi if they are assaulted while the photos are being taken and denies the photographers any profits from the sale of pictures taken during the photographic melees.[72]

Critics of this law claim it could interfere with legitimate news gathering, and argue that it treats the paparazzi differently than other California citizens. Others note that the law is vague. Aren't ordinary eyeglasses visual enhancement devices? The law is evidence that the patience of many is wearing thin in the wake of the often-intrusive behavior of a small number of aggressive photographers. The Los Angeles city council has in the past considered adopting an ordinance creating a personal safety zone between the photographers and their subject.[73] Nothing had come of this as of late 2009.

THE USE OF HIDDEN RECORDING DEVICES

The miniaturization of video and audio equipment has made it possible for anyone, including reporters, to secretly record conversations, confrontations, meetings and other happenings. Can such recording constitute an intrusion, an invasion of privacy? It is not easy to answer this question definitively.

In 1971 a U.S. Court of Appeals in California ruled that such surreptitious recording could constitute an illegal intrusion. The case was an odd one. Two reporters for Life magazine agreed to cooperate with Los Angeles police who sought to arrest a man who was practicing medicine without a license. Posing as man and wife, the pair went to the "doctor's" home where he conducted his practice. While A.A. Dietemann examined the woman, the man secretly photographed the procedure. At the same time the conversation was secretly recorded. Police arrested Dietemann several weeks later, and following his apprehension the magazine published a story with a transcript of the recorded conversation and some of the photos taken in his home. The appellate court sustained his suit for intrusion, ruling that a homeowner should not "be required to take the risk that what is heard or seen [in his or her home] will be transmitted by photography or recording . . . to the public at large."[74] Other courts have not followed this precedent, although none of the subsequent cases involved recording or photography in a private home.

For example, in 1975 Arlyn Cassidy and several other Chicago police officers were acting as undercover agents, investigating massage parlors in the city. The owner of one massage parlor where police previously had made arrests believed he was being harassed by the officers

---

72. California Civil Code § 1708.8; and "Schwarzenegger Signs Law."
73. Steinhauer, "Los Angeles Proposes."
74. *Dietemann* v. *Time, Inc.,* 499 F. 2d 245 (1971).

and invited a television news camera crew to come in and secretly film an encounter between an undercover agent and a model at the parlor. The camera was set up behind a two-way mirror and was filming when officer Cassidy came in, paid $30 for deluxe lingerie modeling, and subsequently arrested the girl for solicitation. Three other agents came into the room at about the same time the television news crew burst through another door, filming as they left the building. The officers sued the station for intrusion, using the *Dietemann* case as precedent.

But an Illinois appellate court ruled in favor of the journalists, distinguishing the *Dietemann* case in some important ways. First, Cassidy and the other plaintiffs were public officers acting in the line of duty as the filming took place. Second, the film crew was not in a private home but in a public business. And third, the crew was on hand at the invitation of the operator of the premises. "In our opinion," the court ruled, "no right of privacy against intrusion can be said to exist with reference to the gathering and dissemination of news concerning discharge of public duties."[75]

A Kentucky circuit court ruled that it was not an intrusion when a young woman, at the instigation of a newspaper, secretly recorded a conversation she had with an attorney in the attorney's office. After the newspaper published a transcript of the conversation, during which attorney John T. McCall proposed an unethical fee arrangement with the woman, the lawyer sued for intrusion. Again, the court distinguished *Dietemann,* noting that the woman was in McCall's office at his invitation. "A lawyer, an officer of the court, discussing a public court with a potential client, is not in seclusion within the meaning of the law," the court ruled.[76] A Kentucky appellate court subsequently upheld this ruling.[77]

"A lawyer, an officer of the court, discussing a public court with a potential client, is not in seclusion within the meaning of the law."

Finally, a U.S. District Court in Illinois in 1994 rejected an intrusion claim made against ABC News after it had secretly photographed and recorded eye examinations at an ophthalmology clinic. The owners of the clinic sued. The court ruled that the plaintiffs in the case had alleged no damage from the recording, other than that it had been broadcast. The court also rejected the claim that the recording violated the doctor-patient privilege. That privilege, the court said, belongs to the patient, not the doctor. If the doctor had filmed the examination, it would have been a violation of this privilege and likely an intrusion. But when the patients authorized the recording (they were working for the network), no legal wrong occurred.

The 5th U.S. Circuit Court of Appeals upheld this ruling in early 1995. The appellate court specifically rejected the plaintiff's arguments that the 1971 *Dietemann* ruling should control in this situation. The court said Dietemann was operating out of his home, not a public place of business like the ophthalmology clinic. And Dietemann did no advertising whereas the eye clinic actively solicited the public to visit the facility.[78] Cases like those cited here have chipped away at the substance of the *Dietemann* ruling.

The use of hidden cameras or concealed microphones generates controversy among journalists as well as among the public. In some states 319–320 laws regulate the use of these reporting tactics. But whether such reporting techniques are illegal or not, they are regarded by many people as sneaky, intrusive and unethical. A journalist who uses such means without

75. *Cassidy* v. *ABC,* 377 N.E. 2d 126 (1978).

76. *McCall* v. *Courier-Journal,* 4 M.L.R. 2337 (1979).

77. *McCall* v. *Courier-Journal,* 6 M.L.R. 1112 (1980).

78. *Desnick* v. *Capital Cities/ABC, Inc.,* 851 F. Supp. 303 (1994), aff'd *Desnick* v. *American Broadcasting Companies, Inc.,* 44 F. 3d 1345 (1995).

careful consideration of risks undermining the public trust in his or her work and in the craft in general. In 1992 the Society of Professional Journalists and the Poynter Institute for Media Studies drafted guidelines for the use of hidden cameras. These guidelines, outlined in American Journalism Review,[79] state that hidden cameras should be used only

- when the information is of profound importance.
- when all other alternatives for obtaining the same information have been exhausted.*
- when the individuals involved and their news organizations apply—through outstanding quality of work as well as the commitment of time and funding—the excellence needed to pursue the story fully.
- when the harm prevented by the information revealed through deception outweighs any harm caused by the act of deception.
- when the journalists involved have conducted a meaningful, collaborative and deliberative decision to justify deception.

The guidelines say that winning a prize, beating the competition, getting a story cheaply, doing it because others have done it or doing it because the subjects of the story are unethical are not sufficient reasons to justify the use of hidden cameras.

INTRUSION AND THE PUBLICATION OF INFORMATION OBTAINED ILLEGALLY

Gathering information through illegal intrusions is not the way journalists typically behave. But using information gathered illegally by others is another matter altogether, and while not a common practice, it does occur. Can a newspaper or broadcasting station or Web site operator be successfully sued for publishing or broadcasting material obtained via an illegal intrusion by a third party? The Supreme Court, echoing some older lower-court decisions, recently said no when asked this question.[80] But it was a qualified no at best. The case involved the broadcast of an audiotape recording of a cell phone conversation between two officials of a teachers' union. Not-so-veiled threats were made during the conversation against local school board members. The conversation was illegally intercepted and taped by unknown persons and then distributed to the local press. The two union officials brought suit under the federal wiretap statute, which makes it a violation for anyone to disclose the contents of an illegally intercepted communication. In the 6-3 ruling, the high court acknowledged that the case presented a tough choice between protecting the free flow of information in society and the individual's right to privacy and the protection of private speech. Justice John Paul Stevens noted that the framers of the Constitution "surely did not foresee the advances in science that produced the conversation, the interception or the conflict" that generated the case. But while the majority of the court ruled that there was no liability in this case for broadcasting the tape, the justices said they did so only because the broadcasters in the case had played no part in

---

*In the *Turnbell* case noted on page 266, ABC admitted in court it could have done the story without the secret recording.

79. Lissit, "Gotcha," 17.

80. *Bartnicki* v. *Vopper,* 121 S. Ct. 1753 (2001).

intercepting or obtaining the taped conversation, and because of the public significance—not simply the newsworthiness—of the content of the conversation. Concurring justices Stephen Breyer and Sandra Day O'Connor made clear that had the facts been even slightly different, their decision could have gone the other way. Longtime New York Times Supreme Court reporter Linda Greenhouse accurately characterized the ruling as "a cautionary tale for the nation's newsrooms."[81]

Previous rulings had focused on cases in which a right-to-privacy intrusion claim was made. In three separate rulings, two by U.S. Courts of Appeals[82] and a third by a Maryland state court,[83] judges found that no liability for intrusion could be assessed against the publisher of that material so long as it had been obtained innocently. In the Maryland case several former and current members of the University of Maryland basketball team sued the Washington Evening Star for publishing an article that revealed portions of their academic records. Somebody gave the newspaper the information. There was no evidence presented that the reporters had either personally inspected the records or asked someone else to do it. Consequently, no suit could be maintained by the athletes on the intrusion theory.*

Remember, none of the rulings just cited protects a journalist who actually makes the illegal intrusion by pilfering documents or intercepting telephone conversations. And in some instances, as noted by the high court in the *Bartnicki* case, even the obvious newsworthiness of a story might be insufficient to shield a news medium that publishes the contents of illegally obtained material in direct violation of statutes such as the federal wiretap laws. Beyond just the law, ethical considerations abound as well and must be factored into the equation. Journalists whose decision to publish or broadcast is based on their often self-serving declaration of "serving the public good" will not always prevail in the 21st century.

SUMMARY

Intruding on an individual's solitude, or intrusion, can be an invasion of privacy. The legal wrong occurs as soon as the information about the individual is illegally collected. Subsequent publication of the material is not needed to establish a cause of action, and defending an intrusion by arguing that in publishing the information the defendant was serving the public interest rarely succeeds. The plaintiff carries the burden of convincing the court that when the intrusion occurred, he or she enjoyed a reasonable expectation of privacy. The general rule

*In 1996 a Florida couple used a police radio scanner to eavesdrop on a conference call conversation among members of the Republican congressional leadership, who were discussing an ethics investigation about to take place. The couple recorded the conversation and gave a copy of the tape to Rep. James McDermott, D-Wash., who sent copies to the fellow members of the Ethics Committee and played the tape for reporters. One of the people whose conversations were recorded sued McDermott under the federal wiretap statute. The U.S. Court of Appeals for the District of Columbia ruled in 2006 that the First Amendment did not shield the congressman from liability under the law for disclosing the conversation to newspapers because he knew who intercepted it and that it had been illegally intercepted. The same court sitting en banc affirmed this decision in May 2007. *Boehner* v. *McDermott,* 441 F. 3d 1010 (2006); *Boehner* v. *McDermott,* 35 M.L.R. 1705 (2007); and the Supreme Court refused to hear an appeal from the ruling.

81. Linda Greenhouse, "Court Says Press Isn't Liable."
82. *Liberty Lobby* v. *Pearson,* 390 F. 2d 489 (1968); and *Pearson* v. *Dodd,* 410 F. 2d 701 (1969).
83. *Bilney* v. *Evening Star,* 406 A. 2d (1979).

is that there can be no such expectation if the plaintiff was in a public place. Public streets, restaurants, even areas in private businesses normally accessible to the public are not places where an individual can reasonably expect to find privacy. The use of hidden cameras and microphones frequently prompts intrusion suits and the courts have viewed such intrusions in various ways, depending on where the information was gathered. But in some jurisdictions the use of such devices is barred by other laws. The subsequent publication or broadcast of material obtained through an intrusion by a third party (i.e., not the publisher or broadcaster) has not been regarded as a violation of privacy law.

INTRUSION AND THE INTERNET

The explosive growth of interactive computer systems has generated a revolution in communication worldwide. For most Americans today, using e-mail and the Internet is as common as communicating by telephone or U.S. mail. Users pull mounds of data out of the systems; users pour mounds of data into the systems. With all these data floating through these electronic canals, it is no wonder that privacy problems have arisen almost as rapidly as the Internet has grown. Computers are not like locked files, or secure telephone lines, or even desk drawers. In too many situations they present an open door to those who seek to uncover whatever it is the user has stored in the machine or is attempting to communicate via the system. Whereas 10 years ago this was probably news to most Internet users, today it must be regarded as common knowledge.[84] Careful computer users try to increase the odds in their favor by adopting security measures. Many users, however, simply push ahead with fingers crossed, hoping they won't have problems.

Since the mid-20th century most Americans have been of two minds about their privacy. On one hand they aggressively demand protection for their personal information. But on the other, they willingly give away personal information simply to enjoy the benefits of modern society. The law even recognized this in a perverse kind of way. A legal doctrine has developed, applicable in most jurisdictions, called the assumption of risk analysis. Under this doctrine an individual loses a privacy interest in personal information that is voluntarily made accessible to another person or is otherwise placed in the flow of commerce. The courts have said there can be no expectation of privacy when a customer fills out an application for a bank loan or applies for a credit card, dials a telephone number* or even puts out the trash on the edge of the driveway.[85]

Most people are aware that they are giving up personal information when they apply for a credit card or fill out a government form or are admitted to a hospital. However, fewer people are aware that when they use the Internet for communicating with businesses or government, for shopping, or for simply communicating with friends, they risk giving access to

---

*It is illegal to intercept a telephone conversation, but the numbers dialed by phone users are much more legally accessible.

84. See Fixmer, "New Way to Travel"; and Stellin, "Consumers' Views Split."
85. Stuckey, *Internet and Online Law.*

personal information to others who are not connected to the people with whom they are communicating. Huge data banks that were once contained on paper and stored in file cabinets have been moved to computers, accessible both legally and illegally to others. Unauthorized individuals are frequently hacking into these data banks, as the news media regularly report. And the problems are getting worse as more sophisticated software is developed to track personal and business computer use, and other daily activities.[86]

Access to government-held records has never been easier in some cases. In many communities citizens have expressed anger when they realized that with the click of a mouse their neighbors could gain access to personal and often embarrassing information about them: state tax liens, arrest warrants, bond postings, documents posted in divorce cases and other official records.[87] A man in California used data he obtained electronically to track down a person he later killed. (The California law permitting access to the data the killer used was changed.) Supporters of open government applaud the new electronic access to public records; privacy advocates recognize this information must remain open to public view, but say they are concerned about the easy access to such material.

LEGISLATIVE ACTION

The government—especially the Congress—has done very little to combat the problem of data theft from Internet users. Governments in other Western nations have worked to at least reduce the problem. These nations have comprehensive national privacy laws and offices of data protection, usually led by a privacy commissioner. Most European nations begin with the idea that data protection is a human right, and should be regulated by comprehensive principles that apply to both business and government. While American businesses are given relatively free rein to collect and sell information, European companies need consent from individual Internet users before undertaking such practices.[88] Why is there such a disparity among nations that have so many other laws in common? American business has fiercely fought any attempts by the federal government to adopt laws that would restrict its ability to gather and then disperse (e.g., sell) personal information. It waged this fight with the support of both the Clinton and Bush administrations. Most American businesses believe that self-regulation—not laws—will solve the problem. But it hasn't. Consequently the passage of data protection laws is on the rise, both in the United States and abroad, Edouard Goodman of Identity Theft 911 told an American Bar Association Forum in February 2009. Individual states are stepping in to fill the void left by the failure of the federal government to act. Forty-four states now have some sort of data protection law, Goodman noted.

Some laws already exist that focus directly on protecting privacy on the Internet and other contemporary communication devices like mobile telephones. But most of these are not rigorously enforced. More than 20 years ago Congress amended existing statutes that regulated wiretapping so it applied to many more kinds of electronic communication, including

---

86. See, for example, the discussion of the emerging field called "collective intelligence" which gathers data from phones, GPS units, tags in office ID badges and merges it with data gathered from Web surfing, credit cards, and so on in Markoff, "You're Leaving a Digital Trail."
87. Lee, "Dirty Laundry."
88. Dash, "Europe Zips Lips."

communication via the Internet. The Electronic Communications Privacy Act, or ECPA, has many provisions.[89] The law makes it illegal, for example, to intentionally intercept a cellular telephone conversation or disclose or air the communication with knowledge or reason to believe that the call was intercepted illegally. The law forbids the manufacturers and importers of radio scanners from making or selling scanners that can intercept communications on frequencies used for cellular telephones. Scanners that are sold should not be easily modified to enable them to intercept such communications, but most authorities agree that it is fairly easy for someone with a rudimentary training in radio electronics to make such modifications. The 1986 statute also prohibits the intentional interception of online communication and outlaws such practices as keystroke monitoring, tapping a data line and rerouting electronic communication to provide contemporaneous acquisition. It is also illegal under the ECPA to use or disclose the contents of any electronic communication if the user or discloser knew or had reason to know that the information was obtained through an illegal interception. This means it is illegal to use any device to read other users' private messages and to divulge the contents of another person's electronic mail. The online system provider cannot read the contents of users' e-mail, but the law does not apply to employers. The statute also prohibits "hacking," or gaining unauthorized access to other users' files or documents.

Two other important laws have been adopted during the past decade. In 1994 Congress adopted the Drivers' License Protection Act, which barred state departments of motor vehicles from disclosing personal information about individuals that is contained in driver's license records, information including photos, names, addresses, telephone numbers and the like. This data is used by many nongovernment entities, like the press, and many state governments do a lucrative business in selling this information to all sorts of businesses that market goods and services to drivers and automobile owners. Several states challenged the law, claiming that it violated the 10th Amendment to the U.S. Constitution because it forced state officials to perform a federal task—the protection of personal privacy. State officials said this federal mandate exceeded Congress' authority under the commerce clause and encroached on state authority. In January 2000 the Supreme Court ruled unanimously that the law did not violate the 10th Amendment. The court said the statute regulated states as owners of databases containing information that is an article of interstate commerce; it did not compel states to enact any laws or commandeer their officials to assist in administering federal programs.[90]

Frequent targets for surreptitious data gathering on the Internet are Web sites aimed at younger children. Using contests, games, chat rooms, message boards and other diversions, site operators (often food makers and toy manufacturers) attempt to collect personal information from children, including names, addresses, e-mail addresses, telephone numbers and even Social Security numbers. Under pressure, Congress responded to this problem by adopting the Children's Online Privacy Protection Act in 1998. This law authorized the FTC to regulate Internet sites that collect personal information from users under the age of 13. The law was implemented by the federal regulators and requires site operators to inform users that information is being collected, limits the kind of information that can be collected and provides a means for parents to review or even delete personal information that is being collected. Adopting the law

---

89. See Stuckey, *Internet and Online Law.*
90. *Reno* v. *Condon,* 120 S. Ct. 666 (2000).

is one thing; making it work is another. In the wake of its adoption a study done at the University of Pennsylvania revealed that only about 50 percent of the children's Web sites that collect information were following the rules. (See Chapter 15 for more on this law.)

The collection of data via the Internet about people who use the system could in many instances qualify as an illegal intrusion. The problem, however, is that the user usually doesn't know the data has been collected. What happens to the data that is gathered by cookies and intercepted e-mail and other means? It is often sold or released to the public for other purposes. These problems will be explored when publication of private facts is discussed in Chapter 8.

SUMMARY

The surreptitious collection of data from Internet users is a serious problem. Personal data flow freely through these electronic channels, and gathering this information is a common task performed by both honest and not-so-honest entrepreneurs and even the government. Laws dating back as far as the 1980s regulate some of this behavior, but Congress has resisted adopting stringent rules because businesses have argued self-regulation is a better solution. Congress has, however, adopted the Drivers' License Protection Act and the Children's Online Privacy Protection Act in an attempt to control some of the more egregious problems.

BIBLIOGRAPHY

Chambers, Marcia. "Case of Art, Icons and Law, with Woods in the Middle." *The New York Times,* 3 July 2002, C13.

"College Report Finds That Most Kids' Web Sites Fall Short of COPPA Requirements." *Electronic Commerce & Law Report,* 11 April 2001, 375.

Crampton, Thomas. "Oops, Did It Again. An Irish Bill Seeks to Protect Personal Privacy." *The New York Times,* 2 October 2006, C6.

Dash, Eric. "Europe Zips Lips; U.S. Sells ZIPs." *The New York Times,* 7 August 2005, Sec. 4, p. 9.1.

Fixmer, Rob. "New Way to Travel the Web While Leaving Fewer Footprints." *The New York Times,* 16 August 1999, C5.

Glater, Jonathan D., "Open Secrets." *The New York Times,* 27 June 2008, C1.

Greenhouse, Linda. "Court Says Press Isn't Liable for Use of Ill-Gotten Tapes." *The New York Times,* 22 May 2001, A14.

Hughes, C.J. "Woody Allen Settles Lawsuit for Big Money and Little Angst." *The New York Times,* 19 May 2009, A20.

Jewell, Mark. "Setback Seen for E-Mail Privacy." *Seattle Post-Intelligencer,* 2 July 2004, C2.

Kuczynski, Alex. "Dustin Hoffman Wins Suit on Photo Alteration." *The New York Times,* 23 January 1999, A30.

Labaton, Stephen. "White House and Agency Split on Internet Privacy." *The New York Times,* 23 May 2000, C1.

Lee, Jennifer S. "Dirty Laundry, Online for All to See." *The New York Times,* 5 September 2002, E1.

Lissit, Robert. "Gotcha." *American Journalism Review,* March 1995, 17.

Lohr, Steve. "Industry Group to Offer Standards for Privacy on Internet." *The New York Times,* 26 May 1997, C3.

Markoff, John. "You're Leaving a Digital Trail. Should You Care?" *The New York Times*, 30 November 2008, B1.

Pember, Don R. "The Burgeoning Scope of Access Privacy and the Portent for a Free Press." *Iowa Law Review* 64 (1979): 1155.

———. *Privacy and the Press.* Seattle: University of Washington Press, 1972.

Prosser, William L. "Privacy." *California Law Review* 48 (1960): 383.

Queary, Paul. "Mother Denied Say Over Baby's Photo." *The Seattle Times,* 19 January 1997, A8.

Sanford, Bruce W. *Libel and Privacy.* 2nd ed. Englewood Cliffs, N.J.: Prentice-Hall Law and Business, 1993.

"Schwarzenegger Signs Law Aimed at Paparrazi Wallet." *The New York Times,* 2 October 2005, 17.

"Senator Raises Privacy as Federal Web Site Issue." *The New York Times,* 17 April 2001, C3.

Steinhauer, Jennifer. "Los Angeles Proposes Restraints on Paparazzi." *The New York Times*, 1 August 2008, A12.

Stellin, Susan. "Consumers' Views Split on Internet Privacy." *The New York Times,* 21 August 2000, C3.

Stuckey, Kent. *Internet and Online Law.* New York: Law Journal Seminars-Press, 1996.

Warren, Samuel D., and Louis D. Brandeis. "The Right to Privacy." *Harvard Law Review* 4 (1890): 220.

Weinraub, Bernard. "2 Paparazzi Convicted of Stalking Celebrities." *The New York Times,* 4 February 1998, A36.

Invasion of Privacy

PUBLICATION OF PRIVATE INFORMATION AND FALSE LIGHT

Giving publicity to private facts about someone's life is what provoked legal scholars Samuel D. Warren and Louis D. Brandeis to propose in 1890 that the law should protect an individual's right to privacy. Some label this gossipmongering, others describe it as legitimate journalism. Whatever it is called, it has become the stock-in-trade of a growing number of American periodicals and television programs. And the law, as you will see in the next section of this text, has been largely ineffective in stopping it. We also explore in this chapter the strangest of the privacy torts, false-light invasion of privacy.

PUBLICITY ABOUT PRIVATE FACTS

It is illegal to publicize private information about a person if the matter that is publicized

a. **would be highly offensive to a reasonable person, and**

b. **is not of legitimate public concern or interest.**

"Keyhole journalism" is what press critics in the late 19th century called it. The snooping, prying, gossipy, scandal-driven reporting that many of us today have come to take for granted in both the print and electronic media was just emerging at the end of the 19th century. A lot of people believed it was offensive and wanted it stopped. Attorneys Samuel Warren and Louis Brandeis even proposed a legal solution, a right of privacy, enforceable in a court of law.[1] But American courts have been less than enthusiastic in their support for such ideas. Of all the four tort actions encompassed by the right to privacy, this one, a cause of action based on giving publicity to private facts, has gained the least acceptance from the judiciary. The courts in many states have not yet recognized or have refused to recognize this tort. The North Carolina Supreme Court, in refusing to recognize the tort action, called it "constitutionally suspect."[2] What makes this tort constitutionally suspect in the eyes of many judges and legal scholars is that it punishes the press, or whomever, for publishing truthful information that has been legally obtained. Making the press liable in such instances seems to run against basic American First Amendment tenets and a substantial body of case law. So although the courts in about 80 percent of U.S. jurisdictions are willing to hear arguments in such a case, plaintiffs rarely win these arguments. More than one legal scholar has argued that few would suffer if this entire tort area of privacy simply disappeared. University of Chicago law professor Harry Kalven wrote more than 40 years ago that the size and strength of the defenses in a private facts lawsuit raise the question of whether it is a viable tort remedy. "The mountain, I suggest, has brought forth a pretty small mouse," he said.[3]

But the courts and legal scholars may be out of step with public opinion on this question.

But the courts and legal scholars may be out of step with public opinion on this question. There seems to be a growing sensitivity among many Americans regarding the protection of personal privacy. Many people in the United States expressed a belief that press revelations about President Bill Clinton's private life were simply out of place on the front pages of American newspapers. A majority of people surveyed by researchers at Middle Tennessee State University in the early 1990s told the researchers that they believed the press deserves less than the full protection of the First Amendment when journalists delve into the past lives of public figures or report the sexual activities of people in the public eye. Congress took action in 1996 to protect the privacy of health care records when it adopted the Health Insurance Portability and Accountability Act (HIPAA). Provisions in the law make it much harder for the press to get even routine information from health care providers about patients in their care. When a nightclub burned down in West Warwick, R.I., in 2003, killing 100 people, reporters who contacted hospitals about the status of the injured patrons were usually rebuffed by hospital officials, even though the law had not yet gone into effect. And in 2005 the Louisiana Court of Appeals ruled that the 1996 federal statute even applied to information on 911 emergency tapes because the communications officers give callers medical advice and make medical assessments.[4] Some observers regard it as ironic that at the same time Americans seem to be growing concerned about protecting their own and others' private lives, the television programs, magazines, newspapers and blogs that focus on such material seem to be thriving as never before.

The law clearly favors the press when the mass media are sued for publishing private facts. But reporters need to be careful. This may be an area in which journalists need to ask

---

1. Warren and Brandeis, "The Right to Privacy," 220.
2. *Hall* v. *Post,* 15 M.L.R. 2329 (1988).
3. Kalven, "Privacy in Tort Law," 326.
4. *Hill* v. *East Baton Rouge Department of Emergency Services,* 925 So. 2d 17 (2005).

themselves some tough questions before pushing the law to its outer limits. What is legal may not always be what is right, either on an ethical/moral scale or in the eyes of readers and viewers. There are times when it is absolutely essential for the journalist to have the protection to publish what many would regard as offensive and embarrassing private information. But the routine publication of this kind of information may someday seriously dilute this valuable protection. (See pages 284–289 for a discussion of legitimate public concern.)*

It is easiest to understand this aspect of the law by taking the tort apart and looking at each element separately (see boxed text). The plaintiff in a private facts case carries the burden of proving each element. Failure to convince the court of any one of these three parts of the law means the lawsuit is doomed.

PUBLICITY TO PRIVATE FACTS

1. There must be publicity to private facts about an individual.
2. The revelation of this material must be offensive to a reasonable person.
3. The material is not of legitimate public concern.

PUBLICITY

The words "publicity" and "publication" mean different things in privacy law than they do in libel law. In defamation, "publication" means to communicate the material to a single third party. The word "publicity" in privacy law implies far more. It means that the material is communicated to the public at large or to a great number of people, making it certain that the facts will shortly become public knowledge.[5] This kind of publicity can usually be presumed when a story is published in a newspaper or broadcast over radio and television, or contained on a Web site, a chat room or an electronic bulletin board.

PRIVATE FACTS

Before an invasion-of-privacy suit can be successful, the plaintiff must demonstrate that the material publicized was indeed private. What happens in public is considered public information. When the Associated Press reported the identity of the victim of a sexual assault who testified at the sentencing hearing of the molester, the young man sued for invasion of privacy. The name was not in the court records and had not been made public before the hearing. But the

---

*European courts have been reluctant to embrace American privacy law, but in 2008 a British court ruled that a tabloid newspaper had invaded the privacy of a motor-racing official when it reported he had participated in a sadomasochistic orgy with a Nazi theme. Whether this signaled a change in at least British judicial philosophy remains to be seen. See Burns, "British Judge Rules Tabloid."

5. See *Lowe* v. *Hearst Communications Inc.*, 34 M.L.R. 1823 (2006). But in 2009 the Minnesota Court of Appeals ruled that simply posting private information on the Internet is enough to allow an invasion of privacy claim, no matter now many people see it. See http://www.rcfp.org/newsitems/index.php?i=10857.

testimony was given in open court. The 4th U.S. Court of Appeals ruled in favor of the news-gathering agency, saying "we cannot understand how the voluntary disclosure of information in an unrestricted, open courtroom setting could be anything but a matter of public interest."[6] One of two young women who were photographed while attending a rock concert at the Big Cypress Indian Reservation in Florida sued when her picture—showing her exposed breasts adorned with tattoos or body paint—was published in Stuff magazine with the caption "Their Parents Must Be Proud." She argued that because the picture was taken on privately owned land at a concert open only to ticket holders it was a private affair. The Florida Circuit Court disagreed, noting that as a matter of law and common sense, a rock concert is a public event.[7]

The California Supreme Court ruled in 2004 against a plaintiff who sued the Discovery cable channel for the broadcast of a documentary on a criminal trial that had taken place 10 years earlier. The defendant argued he had lived an obscure but lawful life since being released from prison. Friends and associates had no knowledge of his past deeds. But the information was in public court documents, the court noted, and ruled that it could not be considered private, no matter how much time had passed.[8] And a federal court in Oklahoma dismissed a privacy action brought against a magazine when it published a photo taken at the open casket funeral of a man who had died fighting in Iraq. "The photograph was a truthful and accurate depiction of the image that any member of the public who attended the funeral saw or could have seen," the court said. The 10th U.S. Court of Appeals affirmed this ruling in 2007.[9]

If a large segment of the public is already aware of supposedly intimate or personal information, it is not private. Oliver Sipple, who deflected a gun held by a woman who tried to assassinate President Gerald Ford, sued the San Francisco Chronicle after a columnist noted that the fact that Sipple was a homosexual was probably the reason Ford had never thanked his benefactor for his heroic act. But Sipple's suit failed, in part at least, because his sexual orientation was hardly a secret in San Francisco. A California Court of Appeals noted that Sipple routinely frequented gay bars, marched in parades with other homosexuals, and openly worked for the election of homosexual political candidates, and that many gay publications had reported stories about his activities in the homosexual community. That he was a homosexual was not a private fact, the court ruled.[10]

Information contained in documents and files that are considered public records—that is, open to public inspection—is generally not regarded as private. What if no person has ever inspected the file, but then its contents are published? It is still not regarded as private. The Idaho Statesman in Boise was sued when it published a photo of a handwritten statement that was given to the police in 1955 during the investigation of a sex scandal. The individual who gave the statement was charged and convicted, but the statement implicated other people who were never charged in the case. The document was never part of a criminal proceeding and never made it into a public court record, but was kept for 40 years in a public criminal case file that was stored in the court clerk's office. It was discovered and published in 1995 in an article about the earlier scandal during a debate on a public initiative to limit the rights of gays

---

6. *Doe 2* v. *Associated Press*, 331 F. 3d 417 (2003).
7. *Mayhall* v. *Dennis Stuff Inc.*, 31 M.L.R. 1567 (2002).
8. *Gates* v. *Discovery Communications Inc.*, 101 P. 3d 552 (2004).
9. *Showler* v. *Harper's Magazine Foundation*, 34 M.L.R. 2524 (2006); 35 M.L.R. 1577 (2007).
10. *Sipple* v. *Chronicle Publishing Co.*, 154 Cal. App. 3d 1040 (1984).

in Idaho. An individual who was linked to a homosexual relationship (but never charged with a crime) in the original 40-year-old document sued for invasion of privacy. The Idaho Court of Appeals said the publication was protected because it was a part of an official criminal court file. Quoting an opinion by Justice Warren Burger from 1975, the Idaho court noted, "A responsible press is an undoubtedly desirable goal, but press responsibility is not mandated by the Constitution and like many other virtues it cannot be legislated." After two hearings the Idaho Supreme Court affirmed the lower court rulings, saying the newspaper could not be held liable for accurately reporting what was contained in a court record open to the public.[11]

If an individual tells a reporter something about himself or herself that others don't know, is that information still private? No, but what if the reporter promised not to reveal the name of the person who revealed the information? This question has arisen in a case in Washington state where four high school students have sued the school district for invasion of privacy (among other things) because the student newspaper published detailed stories about their sex lives. The students said when they discussed the subject with the student reporters they were promised anonymity. The school district maintains that the students actually agreed to have their names included in the story. Courts have generally followed the standard that a person's consent is valid, so long as the person has the legal capacity to give it—regardless of age. The key is, does the individual understand the consequences of revealing the information? according to attorneys at the Student Press Law Center. Written consent would have resolved this case quickly, as noted on pages 259–260. Without it, a judge or jury will be asked to decide who is telling the truth.[12]

Naming Rape Victims

One of the most controversial issues in the private facts realm of privacy law concerns the publication of the name of a victim of a sexual assault. Two questions arise: *Can* the name or identity be legally published? And, *should* the name or identity be published? The law is clear on this matter; the ethical issue is more complicated.

Since the mid-1970s courts have consistently ruled that if the victim's name is part of a public document or proceeding, or if the press obtains it in another legal manner, it can be published without incurring liability. At one time four states—Florida, Georgia, South Carolina and Wisconsin—had statutes barring the publication of such material. But these laws have either been voided by the courts,[13] or have fallen into disuse. In 1975 the Supreme Court ruled that a privacy action against a Georgia broadcasting station for publishing the name of a rape victim could not succeed because the victim's identity had been included in public court documents. "We are reluctant to embark on a course that would make public records generally available to the media, but forbid their publication if offensive to the sensibilities of the supposed reasonable man," Justice Byron White wrote. "Such a rule would make it very difficult for the press to inform their readers about the public business and yet stay within the law," he added.[14] Fourteen years later the court reiterated this decision when it ruled that a privacy

11. *Uranga* v. *Federated Publications Inc.*, 28 M.L.R. 2265 (2000), aff'd 67 P. 3d 29 (2003).
12. Shukousky, "High School Students Sue."
13. *Florida* v. *Globe Communications Corp.*, 622 So. 2d 1066 (1993), aff'd 648 So. 2d 110 (1994); and *Dye* v. *Wallace*, 553 S.E. 2d 561 (2001).
14. *Cox Broadcasting* v. *Cohn*, 420 U.S. 469 (1975).

action could not proceed against a newspaper that inadvertently published a sexual assault victim's name it had obtained from a document that was not a public record. The document had been mistakenly given to the reporter by a police officer, and the publication violated the newspaper's own policy against publishing such information. "The fact that state officials are not required to disclose such reports does not make it unlawful for a newspaper to receive them when furnished by the government," wrote Justice Thurgood Marshall. But the justice noted that the court's ruling was a limited one. "We hold only that where a newspaper publishes truthful information which it has lawfully obtained, punishment may be imposed, if at all, only when narrowly tailored to a state interest of the highest order."[15] Since this 1989 decision lower courts have consistently followed this course.[16] The chances, then, of the victim of a sexual assault successfully suing a newspaper or broadcast station or blogger for revealing his or her name are extremely remote, if not impossible.

As a matter of fact, most publications and broadcasting stations do not routinely publicize the name of the victim of a sexual assault.

But should the name be published? As a matter of fact, most publications and broadcasting stations do not routinely publicize the name of the victim of a sexual assault.[17] What was once a common practice even 50 years ago has been largely abandoned. But some media outlets do publish this material. Critics of this practice raise three arguments:

- Someone who is sexually assaulted becomes a victim three times: the first during the assault; the second during the interrogation by often unsympathetic police, prosecutors and defense lawyers during the investigation and the public trial; and the third when the identity is published and broadcast in the press, revealing the details of the attack to neighbors, friends, co-workers and others.
- Society often judges the rape victim to be as guilty as the rapist, and this can stigmatize the victim for many years.
- Because of the first two factors, victims who realize that their identities will be revealed frequently fail to report the crime, especially if the rape has been committed by an acquaintance. The rapist is not punished and may go on to attack another victim.

The validity of the arguments is difficult to dispute. But some journalists will publish or broadcast the victim's name regardless of the consequences. They argue that it is important for society to know the names of all crime victims. Publishing the name of a victim adds credibility to a news story, makes the story more meaningful to readers or viewers. Others argue that when the press fails to publish the name of a rape victim it is treating this victim differently from the victim of a simple assault or a robbery. This reinforces the notion that rape victims are at least partly responsible for their fate, or that they are "damaged goods." "Now is the time for us to understand that keeping the hunted under wraps merely establishes her as an outcast and implies that her chances for normal social relations are doomed forevermore," said Karen DeCrow, former president of the National Organization for Women. "Pull off the veil of shame. Print the name," she added. Geneva Overholser, former editor of the Des Moines Register, argues that by not printing the name, the press is reinforcing the idea

15. *Florida Star* v. *B.J.F.,* 109 S. Ct. 2603 (1989).
16. See, for example, *Macon Telegraph Publishing Co.* v. *Tatum,* 436 S.E. 2d 655 (1993); and *Star Telegram Inc.* v. *Doe,* 23 M.L.R. 2492 (1995).
17. Marcus and McMahon, "Limiting Disclosure," 1019.

that rape is a different kind of attack, not a crime of brutal violence. She said that this "sour blight of prejudice is best subjected to strong sunlight."[18] Some newspapers are trying to reach a compromise on this matter by not printing the victim's name unless she or he consents to the use. Victims who fear the publicity are protected; using the names of those who don't mind undermines the myth noted by DeCrow.

OFFENSIVE MATERIAL

If the determination has been made that private facts about a person's life have been published, a court must then ask two subsequent questions:

1. Would the publication of the material offend a reasonable person?
2. Was the published material of legitimate public interest or concern?

Judges and juries are often faced with the dilemma of deciding whether the revelation of important, but offensive or embarrassing, information is an invasion of privacy. The law on this question is pretty clear: If the material is of legitimate public concern, it doesn't matter how offensive or embarrassing the revelation is. There was no invasion of privacy. For the past 100 years courts have been extremely reluctant to fashion narrow limits on the kinds of information people need to receive. Time and time again judges have ruled that it is not only the responsibility of the press to bring important public information to the public, but also that it is the job of editors and reporters, not the courts, to decide what is and what isn't important. If there is any legitimate public interest at all in the material, the press will usually win the case, regardless of how embarrassing revelation of the material might be. This notion is more fully discussed on pages 284–289.

It is the job of editors and reporters, not the courts, to decide what is and what isn't important.

Remember, the revelation of the material must be offensive to a reasonable person, not someone who is overly sensitive. Peggy Jo Fry sued the Ionia (Mich.) Sentinel-Standard for invasion of privacy when it reported that her husband and another woman had died in a fire that destroyed a cottage near Lake Michigan. The story mentioned that Ted Fry had been seen with Rita Hill at a tavern prior to the fire and related details about Fry's wife and children. The court ruled that these details were simply not highly offensive to a reasonable person.[19] Another Michigan woman sued Knight-Ridder Newspapers after the Miami Herald published a story about the murder of her daughter. The plaintiff in the case was mentioned incidentally in the story. It was noted that four of her six children were deaf and that she was a hardworking woman who had great faith in her daughter's ability to succeed in life. The court said such information is not offensive.[20]

But judges are human beings with feelings and sensitivities, and though they will most often bend over backward to support the right of the press to publish truthful information, once in a while a case comes along that presents what the court believes are outrageous circumstances that cry out for some punishment of the newspaper or broadcasting station. Two out-of-the-ordinary cases are cited here as a warning that there are exceptions to what even the experts regard as the hard-and-fast rules in the law of privacy.

18. Marcus and McMahon, "Limiting Disclosure," 1019.
19. *Fry* v. *Ionia Sentinel-Standard,* 300 N.W. 2d 687 (1980).
20. *Andren* v. *Knight-Ridder Newspapers,* 10 M.L.R. 2109 (1984).

Many years ago a woman with a rather unusual medical disorder—she ate constantly, but still lost weight—was admitted to a hospital. Journalists were tipped off and descended on her room, pushed past the closed door and took pictures against the patient's will. Time magazine ran a story about the patient, Dorothy Barber, and in it referred to her, in inimitable Time style, as "the starving glutton." Barber sued and won her case. The judge said the hospital is one place people should be able to go for privacy.[21] More than the patient's expectation of privacy in a hospital room influenced the ruling, because there are several decisions in which persons in hospitals have been considered to be the subject of legitimate concern and did not therefore enjoy the right to privacy. The story about the unusual disorder was surely offensive, almost mocking. The disorder was not contagious, and the implications for the general public were minimal. The Time story seemed to focus on Barber almost as if she were a freak, and in doing so the revelation of this information was highly offensive to any reasonable person, the court ruled.

The South Carolina Supreme Court affirmed a jury verdict against a newspaper that, in publishing a story about teenage pregnancies, had identified a young man—a minor—as the father of an illegitimate child. The teenage mother of the baby had given the reporter the father's name. The reporter talked to the young man, who understood that the newspaper was doing a survey on teenage pregnancy. He said he was never told that his name might be used in the story. The newspaper argued that the information—including the boy's name—was of great public interest. The state Supreme Court said that was a jury question, and a jury ruled that it was not of great public interest[22] and that its publication was highly offensive.

LEGITIMATE PUBLIC CONCERN

The previous rulings are not typical of the results of most private facts cases. Yes, there are instances when a court will rule that private facts have been published, and that the revelation of these facts is offensive to a reasonable person. More often than not, however, a judge or an appellate tribunal will rule that a legitimate public interest in the subject matter or the plaintiff outweighs any embarrassment the publication might have caused. Public interest trumps offensiveness. And during the past 100 years public interest has been broadly defined. Most judges set the public interest bar fairly low and focus not on what people *should* be interested in reading or hearing, but on what readers and listeners actually find interesting. The relatively narrow definition of public concern fashioned by the courts in applying the *New York Times* v. *Sullivan* libel rule (see pages 177–179) has not been applied in privacy rulings. A 70-year-old case, still often cited by jurists, set the standard in this regard.

In 1937 New Yorker magazine published a story about a child prodigy who had failed to fulfill the promise many had predicted for him. (See the following box.) The prodigy, then nearly 40, sued for invasion of privacy. A federal appeals court ruled that while the story might have embarrassed the man, the public enjoyed reading about the problems, misfortunes and troubles of their neighbors and members of the community. "When such are the mores of the community, it could be unwise for a court to bar their expression in the newspapers, books, and magazines of the day," wrote Judge Charles Clark.[23] Since that time courts have ruled

21. *Barber* v. *Time,* 159 S.W. 2d 291 (1942).
22. *Hawkins* v. *Multimedia,* 344 S.E. 2d 145 (1986).
23. *Sidis* v. *F-R Publishing Co.,* 113 F. 2d 806 (1940).

that there was public interest or legitimate public concern in stories about how two lawyers used extramarital affairs they arranged in a blackmail scheme[24]; in news reports that revealed the names of two undercover police officers who were charged with, but later cleared of, sexual assault[25]; in the sterilization of an 18-year-old girl[26]; in a young man being treated for substance abuse at a hospital[27]; in a 12-year-old giving birth to a child[28]; and in the personal activities of a body surfer.[29] A New York court ruled that even a television report celebrating a warm spring day that featured video of a man and a woman walking hand in hand on Madison Avenue had legitimate public interest. The couple objected to the story because he was married to another woman, and she was engaged to be married to another man. The court said that the film explored the prevailing attitudes on romance when it showed people behaving in this fashion, a subject that was newsworthy.[30]

But the newsworthiness argument will not always carry the day. The 11th U.S. Circuit Court of Appeals ruled in 2009 that when Hustler magazine published the 20-year-old nude photos of a female professional wrestler who had been murdered by her husband—also a professional wrestler—the newsworthiness defense did not shield the publication from a privacy lawsuit brought by her mother under Georgia state law. Attorneys for Hustler argued that because the photos accompanied a short biographical piece about the woman, they were newsworthy. The court agreed that the story was protected because it was newsworthy. The court also ruled that the pictures standing alone were not protected; they were offensive and not newsworthy. The question was, did including the short biography with the pictures insulate the photos from a lawsuit? The court said no. The publication of the brief biographical story did not "ratchet otherwise personal protected photographs into the newsworthiness exception," the judges ruled.[31]

Let's explore some often-asked questions about legitimate public concern, or what the courts sometimes call newsworthiness.

The following are excerpts from an article written by Jared L. Manley (a pen name for noted writer James Thurber) about William James Sidis. The piece was published in New Yorker on August 14, 1937, and provoked one of the nation's most celebrated invasion-of-privacy lawsuits (*Sidis* v. *F-R Publishing Co.*).

"Where Are They Now?" "April Fool!"
"One snowy January evening in 1910 about a hundred professors and advanced students of mathematics from Harvard University gathered in a lecture hall in Cambridge, Massachusetts, to listen to a speaker by the name of William James Sidis. He had never addressed an audience before, and he was abashed and a little awkward

---

24. *Lowe* v. *Hearst Communications Inc.*, 487 F. 3d 246 (2007).
25. *Alvarado* v. *KOB-TV*, 493 F. 3d 1210 (2007).
26. *Howard* v. *Des Moines Register*, 283 N.W. 2d 789 (1979).
27. *Carter* v. *Superior Court of San Diego County*, 30 M.L.R. 1193 (2002).
28. *Meetze* v. *AP*, 95 S.E. 2d 606 (1956).
29. *Virgil* v. *Time, Inc.*, 527 F. 2d 1122 (1975).
30. *DeGregario* v. *CBS*, 43 N.Y.S. 2d 922 (1984).
31. *Toffoloni* v. *LFP Publishing Group LLC*, 37 M.L.R. 1897 (2009).

at the start. His listeners had to attend closely, for he spoke in a small voice that did not carry well, and he punctuated his talk with nervous, shrill laughter. . . . The speaker wore black velvet knickers. He was eleven years old. . . . When it was all over, the distinguished Professor Daniel F. Comstock of Massachusetts Institute of Technology was moved to predict to reporters, who had listened in profound bewilderment, that young Sidis would grow up to be a great mathematician, a famous leader in the world of science."

(The next section of the article explains how Sidis, as a small child, had become a kind of guinea pig for his psychologist father, who used experimental techniques to educate his son when he was little more than a baby. Manley goes on to describe Sidis' education, his extreme efforts to hide from the spotlight of publicity, his series of mundane jobs and his rejection of a career in science or mathematics.)

"William James Sidis lives today, at the age of thirty-nine, in a hall bedroom of Boston's shabby south end. . . . He seems to get a great and ironic enjoyment out of leading a life of wandering irresponsibility after a childhood of scrupulous regimentation. . . . Sidis is employed now, as usual, as a clerk in a business house. He said that he never stays in one office long because his employers or fellow-workers soon find out that he is the famous boy wonder, and he can't tolerate a position after that. 'The very sight of a mathematical formula makes me physically ill,' he said."

(Manley relates that Sidis has become a passionate collector of streetcar transfers, that he enjoys the study of certain aspects of the history of Native Americans and that he is writing a treatise on floods.)

"His visitor [Manley] was emboldened, at last, to bring up the prediction, made by Professor Comstock . . . back in 1910, that the little boy who lectured that year on the fourth dimension to a gathering of learned men would grow up to be a great mathematician, a famous leader in the world of science. 'It's strange,' said William James Sidis, with a grin, 'but you know, I was born on April Fool's Day.'"

Does the manner in which the story is presented have an impact on whether it has legitimate public interest? In spite of the *Barber* case previously cited, sensational treatment of a story does not usually remove the protection of newsworthiness. The parents of two young children who had suffocated in an abandoned refrigerator said the sensational way the story was presented was as objectionable as the story itself. However, the court ruled that the manner in which the article was written was not relevant to whether the article was protected by the constitutional guarantees of free speech and free press—which, by the way, it was.[32] In another case a Boston newspaper published a horrible picture of an automobile accident in which the bloodied and battered body of one of the victims was clearly visible and identifiable, and the court rejected the plaintiff's claim. The Massachusetts Supreme Court noted, "Many things which are distressing or may be lacking in propriety or good taste are not actionable."[33] A woman told

---

32. *Costlow* v. *Cuismano,* 311 N.Y.S. 2d 92 (1970).
33. *Kelley* v. *Post Publishing Co.,* 327 Mass. 275 (1951).

police she was raped by her husband while she was unconscious and did not know it had happened until she found a videotape of the incident. She gave the tape to police, who promised it would be kept confidential and used only for law enforcement purposes. The tape nevertheless found its way to a TV station, which broadcast segments of it when the husband was arrested for other, alleged sexual assaults. The woman sued for publication of private facts. But the courts rejected her lawsuit, ruling the video was related to a matter of legitimate public concern—the prosecution of her husband. The court said the sensitive nature of the video did not make it any less newsworthy.[34]

Does the law of privacy protect what are called involuntary public figures, people who are pushed into the public spotlight through no fault of their own? While the so-called involuntary public person receives enhanced protection in libel law (see pages 177–183), this protection does not normally apply in privacy actions. Eighty years ago the Kentucky Supreme Court ruled that although the right of privacy protected the right of a person to live his or her life in seclusion, without being subject to undesired publicity, there are times "when one, whether willing or not, becomes an actor in an occurrence of public or general interest." At this point, the court noted, the individual loses much of his or her right to privacy.[35] A Kansas court ruled that a television report about a young man who had been arrested on suspicion of burglary, but who was released later when police admitted they had arrested the wrong man, was not an invasion of privacy. The court ruled that the plaintiff was involved in a noteworthy event, and the public had a right to be informed about the event. "This was true even though his involvement therein was purely involuntary and against his will," the court said.[36] And in 1978 an Illinois court ruled that a story that reported the death of a boy from an apparent drug overdose and recounted details of his life was not an invasion of privacy. He had become an involuntary public figure because of his actions within the drug culture in the community. "It is not necessary for an individual to actively seek publicity in order to be found in the public eye," the court ruled.[37] These cases are consistent with how the law is applied in most instances.

Do people who are closely associated with or related to public persons also lose elements of their right to privacy? Although there have not been a lot of court decisions based on this question, the current answer seems to be yes. People whose lives intersect with famous, infamous or other newsworthy individuals also lose some of their privacy. A story published in a Utah newspaper in 1997 said hikers had found the body of a man near a dirt trail. Police said the death looked "like one of those autoerotic things." When murder charges were subsequently filed the story was widely reported. Family members sued saying that the reports contained information that reflected upon intimate details of the marital relationship. The 10th U.S. Court of Appeals affirmed the dismissal of the complaint saying that while it was almost impossible to define the limits of the right to privacy, it did not block the revelation of information of a spouse's behavior that reflected on the marital relationship. "Any other conclusion would stretch the right to privacy beyond any reasonable limits," the court said.[38] A New York court came to a

34. *Anderson* v. *Suiters*, 499 F. 3d 1228 (2007).
35. *Jones* v. *Herald Post Co.*, 18 S.W. 2d 972 (1929).
36. *Williams* v. *KCMO Broadcasting Co.*, 472 S.W. 1d (1971).
37. *Beresky* v. *Teschner*, 381 N.E. 2d 979 (1978).
38. *Livsey* v. *Salt Lake County*, 275 F. 3d 952 (2002).

similar conclusion nine years earlier. The plaintiff's husband had secretly committed the plaintiff to a private psychiatric facility. Few of her friends and relatives knew of the commitment. Another patient at the facility, Hedda Nussbaum, had been in the national news for many months as the adoptive mother of a 6-year-old girl who had died from child abuse. A photographer secretly snapped a photo of Nussbaum while the plaintiff Pamela Howell was standing next to her. Howell was not identified in the photo that was published in a New York newspaper. She sued for invasion of privacy but lost. The court said the Nussbaum story still had considerable public interest and the only way Howell could win was to demonstrate that her photo bore no real relationship to the article and photo. But the court said she could not do this. She was in the wrong place at the wrong time, but this did not create liability.[39]

How far into a private life can the press go when discussing a newsworthy person? Are there limits? Courts began to enunciate guidelines for the press in cases decided in the last quarter of the 20th century. While these limits are narrow, they are nevertheless real. Two important cases illustrate this point.

In the early 1970s Sports Illustrated published a long article on a body surfer named Mike Virgil. At the time, body surfing was a relatively unknown sport outside the fraternity of surfers in Southern California and at other beaches. Reporter Curry Kirkpatrick asked Virgil why he seemed so willing to risk life and limb in a sport many regarded as extremely dangerous. Virgil replied that he lived his life pretty much as he practiced his sport and outlined some of his personal traits that most would regard as reckless, if not stupid (e.g., he would extinguish burning cigarettes with his mouth, dive headfirst down flights of stairs and eat live insects). When the story appeared, Virgil sued. He agreed that his public life was fair game for the press, but the embarrassing aspects of his private life should not have been reported. The court disagreed. The appellate court ruled that the line between private and public information "is to be drawn when the publicity ceases to be the giving of information to which the public is entitled, and becomes morbid and sensational prying into the private life *for its own sake* [emphasis added]."[40] When a lower court applied this standard it ruled "any person reading the article would conclude that the personal facts concerning the individual were revealed in a legitimate journalistic attempt to explain his extremely daring and dangerous style of body surfing." In other words, if the magazine had published a story that described this weird man who lived in California who ate bugs and dived down stairs, it very likely would have been an invasion of privacy. But the personal details were added to a story to try to explain Virgil's public life. Although they were embarrassing, they provided important context to the story of his public persona.

The Iowa Supreme Court made a similar ruling four years later when it rejected a claim of invasion of privacy made by a woman who had been named by the Des Moines Register as a victim of forced sterilization at a county medical facility. The newspaper published a series of stories about the appalling conditions at the facility, and cited the case of the plaintiff as an example of the malpractice that had taken place. The newspaper named her. When the story was published she was older and told the court that none of even her closest friends knew of this episode in her life.

39. *Howell* v. *New York Post Co.,* 612 N.E. 2d 699 (1993).
40. *Virgil* v. *Time Inc.,* 527 F. 2d 1122 (1975).

The court applied a Virgil-like rationale in its ruling, noting that the girl's name was not prominent in the story and that the newspaper had not pried into the girl's life simply to shock or outrage the community. The facts were presented to demonstrate to the community the kind of unethical, even illegal, activities taking place at the facility. Was it necessary to use the name? Could the story have been told by referring to a Jane Doe? Perhaps, the court said. But the use of the name lent specificity and credibility to the report and was an effective means of accomplishing the intended news function.[41]

What courts often look for in these kinds of cases, then, is a nexus between the admittedly private and embarrassing information and the newsworthy subject of the story. How far the press can go in reporting the private life of public persons often depends not only on what was said—how private the information is—but also on why the material was used. When an individual's public life is explained, many parts of that person's private life are of legitimate public concern.

FACTORS SOME COURTS TAKE INTO ACCOUNT IN DETERMINING LEGITIMATE PUBLIC CONCERN

- How much public interest or importance is there in the material?
- How deeply does publication of these facts intrude into an individual's privacy?
- How public or private is the individual who is the focus of the story?
- Is there a nexus between the information about the private life and the public life?

ETHICS AND PRIVACY

Journalists have to remember that liability in a private facts case is usually determined by a judge or jury asking questions about some fairly elastic concepts. Was the material offensive to a reasonable person? Was the material of legitimate public concern? The law in this area is not carved in stone and could change as public sentiments change. If nothing else, in the long term, decisions by judges and juries usually reflect public opinion. And this is why people who work in the mass media need to begin to ask more questions as well—especially, what are the ethical implications of revealing this personal information?

Journalism is in many ways a tough business. Many reporters and editors spend a lot of time, too much time it sometimes seems, reporting the sordid or tragic side of life. It is easy to become desensitized, to become immune to the anguish such reporting can cause. There are often hard choices to be made. Several years ago distinguished editor John Seigenthaler related to a television audience what takes place each day when the editors at a newspaper decide what stories and photos should go on the front page. He said he recalled one such meeting

---

41. *Howard v. Des Moines Register,* 283 N.W. 2d 789 (1979).

where the staff had to decide what picture to put on page one: a photo of a tragic automobile accident or a photo of a field full of spring flowers. He said they chose the picture of the flowers, but then reminded his audience that life is not just a field of flowers. There are many darker matters that must be reported.

When it comes to privacy, good editors agree that the feelings and sensibilities of the subject of the story should always be considered. But, at the same time, these feelings and sensibilities should never be used as a reason to deny to the public information that has legitimate public concern. The last three words are the key: *legitimate public concern*. The decision on whether to publish or broadcast a story will always be a judgment call that must be made carefully and thoughtfully. Too many journalists are reluctant to make this call. Instead, they declare that their job is to simply report the news, to pass along whatever they discover. Journalists are not supposed to make judgments, they argue. Some people call this the sewer pipe school of journalism: What goes in one end of a sewer pipe comes out the other end with little change. But today people in the mass media, and even members of their audience, know that journalists make judgments every day of the week. What stories should be covered? Who should be quoted? How should the story be played? Journalism is not now nor ever has been a purely objective activity.

It is worth noting that the ethics code of the Society of Professional Journalists (SPJ), an organization of reporters and editors, reminds reporters to "recognize that gathering and reporting information may cause harm and discomfort. Pursuit of the news is not a license for arrogance." The SPJ's ethics code also instructs journalists to "show good taste. Avoid pandering to lurid curiosity." Such ethical considerations are clearly relevant when considering whether to publish private facts.[42]

The courts and the public will continue to support the endeavors of the press in privacy actions so long as there is some assurance that journalists are willing to ask the question, Is there legitimate public concern in this story? At present, this is primarily an ethical issue. But if journalism is pursued with the kind of reckless abandon that is common today at a few media outlets, it could one day become a defining legal question as well. We must constantly remember the words of the great U.S. jurist Learned Hand. Liberty rests in the hearts and minds of the people, Hand wrote. When it dies there, no court or constitution can revive it.

RECOUNTING THE PAST

If an individual is in the public eye, revelations about his or her private life are normally fair game for the press. As noted, courts have erected an almost impenetrable defense that blocks such lawsuits. However, lawsuits by individuals who were once in the public eye, but have retreated to a quiet life of solitude out of the public spotlight, are fairly common. These litigants usually argue that the passing of time dims the public spotlight and that a person stripped of a right to privacy because of his or her notoriety regains at least some of that protection after an indeterminate period of time.

There are at least two kinds of cases that usually occur. The first is the simplest to describe: a news story or book or TV documentary that simply recounts the past. In other

---

42. Available online at http://www.spj.org/ethics.asp.

words, history. "On this day in 1990 Mary Beth Ellroy was convicted of killing her two-week-old baby and sentenced to 15 years in prison." These kinds of lawsuits are never successful. Typical is a decision by the New Jersey Supreme Court in a case involving a book that recounted a crime spree that occurred eight years earlier. Joseph Kallinger and his son were apprehended by police in 1975 after their criminal rampage that included killing, robbing and raping. In 1983 a professor of criminal justice at City University of New York published a book about Kallinger's life and crimes. One of Kallinger's victims sued, arguing that replaying this tragedy in public print was traumatic and disturbing and would be highly offensive. The court agreed with that assessment but ruled that the case failed because the facts revealed were not private but public, and "even if they were private, they are of legitimate concern to the public."[43] The lapse of time did nothing to insulate the plaintiff from such publicity. The facts were taken from the public trial record in the case, and the court noted that the Supreme Court ruling in *Cox* v. *Cohn*[44] was not limited to contemporaneous events.

The second kind of story is a bit more problematic. A report that film star Sid Feldman was accused in 1995 by his former wife of possessing child pornography is again retelling history. But the added sentence, "Today, Feldman is selling real estate in Dade County, Florida," pushes the report beyond history. Some courts have ruled that such "Where are they now" kinds of stories are permissible, so long as the report was not designed to purposely embarrass or humiliate the plaintiff.[45] But other judges are less tolerant of such publicity and will sometimes ask the question, What is the purpose of tying Feldman's current job with these accusations from the past?[46] To defend such a suit, the press needs a good answer. If Feldman were running for public office, if he ran a popular photographic studio that specialized in taking pictures of youngsters, if he were arrested today for possessing child pornography—all of these would supply the rationale for tying the past to the present. But simply reporting that he is selling real estate might not convince the court that such a story should be immune from suit.

Perhaps the most important question any journalist can ask when preparing to publish a story is, why? Why is this information being published? If there is a good reason, most judges will bend over backward to protect the press. But without a good reason, the legal terrain can get a lot more complicated.

PRIVATE FACTS ON THE INTERNET

In Chapter 7 the problem of gathering personal information via the Internet was explored as an intrusion. Disclosing personal information gathered through such an intrusion, or simply publishing private facts on the Internet, falls under the publication-of-private-facts area of privacy law. The law will apply in exactly the same way as it would if the information were published in a newspaper. Were private facts publicized, facts that would be offensive to a reasonable person, that are not of legitimate concern or public interest? But it is worth briefly mentioning other kinds of publication-of-private-facts issues that have arisen.

---

43. *Romaine* v. *Kallinger,* 537 A. 2d 284 (1988).
44. 420 U.S. 469 (1975).
45. See *Kent* v. *Pittsburgh Press,* 349 F. Supp. 622 (1972); *Sidis* v. *F-R Publishing Co.,* 113 F. 2d 806 (1940); and *Bernstein* v. *NBC,* 232 F. 2d 369 (1955).
46. See, for example, *Hall* v. *Post,* 355 S.E. 2d 816 (1987).

The collection of personal data is an important task for both government and business, and was going on for decades, long before the Internet was even a glint in someone's eye. But in the past, data about individuals were usually stored in folders or files and were not easy or inexpensive to share with others. "Today, with commercial databases, networks, and CD-ROMS, you can match data sets with a few keystrokes and literally surf through people's lives," noted Leslie L. Byrnes, a White House consumer affairs adviser.[47] Not many years ago, LexisNexis P-Trak databases promised purchasers access to the names and addresses of 300 million people. Some personal entries included a good deal more, such as birth dates, telephone numbers, prior addresses and even Social Security numbers, which are the primary registration numbers that key Americans to their bank accounts, insurance policies, medical records, and scores of credit card companies. For a short time even the federal government made citizens' Social Security numbers available when it put the Social Security system online.

There is no shortage of people in government and private business who regard the disclosure of such data as a threat to personal privacy. There is a distinct shortage, however, of people within these same venues who think government should do something about the problem. Most civic and business leaders regard the free flow of personal data as something that can be controlled through self-regulation and stricter internal business and government practices. The Federal Trade Commission has been an exception to this general rule, and in the past has moved against some of the more egregious offenders. (See pages 564–567 in Chapter 15 for examples.)

Each session of Congress seems to generate new attempts to adopt laws to protect personal privacy. There were promises made by members of the House of Representatives that a comprehensive Internet privacy law that would pre-empt all state laws would be adopted in 2002. But it never happened. Debate continues in each legislative session, but proponents of such a law face considerable opposition from powerful interests in the business community. In the past officials in the executive branch of government, who proclaim they are sensitive to the needs of business, also opposed such legislation. The position of the Obama administration on this issue had not been revealed as this was being written. There was pressure on the government to adopt some kind of law at the end of the 1990s in order to facilitate U.S. compliance with the broad privacy protections contained in the European Data Protection Directive that was adopted by member nations of the European Union in 1995. Failure to comply with the provisions of this directive would have limited American businesses and industries from operating in nations belonging to the European Union, which includes almost all the nations of Europe. But agreements were ultimately reached that permitted American commercial enterprises to continue to operate in Europe without the adoption of privacy legislation in the United States. All the American businesses had to do was to promise they would abide by certain privacy guidelines that were a part of the European Data Privacy Directive. Even then, many businesses failed to follow the guidelines but continued to operate abroad.

SUMMARY   It is an invasion of privacy to publicize private information about another person's life if the publication of this information would be embarrassing to a reasonable person and the information is not of legitimate public interest or concern. To publicize means to communicate

47. "White House Consumer Advisor Sees Role for Encryption in Privacy Protection," 2 E.L.P.R. 156 (1997).

the information to a large number of people. There is no liability for giving further publicity to information that is already considered public. The press is free, for example, to report even embarrassing and sensitive matters contained in public records. The information that is publicized must be considered offensive to a reasonable person; the law does not protect hypersensitive individuals.

Courts use many strategies to determine whether information has legitimate public concern. Stories that are of great interest have legitimate public concern. Stories about both voluntary and involuntary public figures are normally considered of legitimate public concern. When private information is published or broadcast, it is important that a connection exists between the revelation of the embarrassing private information and the newsworthy aspects of the story. Embarrassing details about a person's private life cannot be publicized simply to amuse or titillate audiences. News stories that recount past events—including embarrassing details of an individual's life—are normally protected from successful privacy suits. However, courts will usually insist on a good reason for relating these embarrassing past events to an individual's current life or work. There is no complete resolution of issues relating to the use of personal data gathered via the Internet.

FALSE-LIGHT INVASION OF PRIVACY

It is illegal to publicize material that places an individual in a false light if

a. **the false light in which the individual was placed would be offensive to a reasonable person, and**
b. **the publisher of the material was at fault when the publication was made.**

This fourth tort in the invasion-of-privacy quartet has engendered the most disputes within the law. What in the world does this have to do with invasion of privacy? Many state courts have refused to recognize this variety of invasion of privacy. In 1998 the Minnesota Supreme Court recognized a cause of action for appropriation, private facts and intrusion, but rejected the false-light tort. Four years later the Colorado Supreme Court also refused to recognize false-light invasion of privacy. Both courts said the cause of action was largely coextensive with libel and didn't see the need to embrace both torts.[48] And in 2008 the Florida Supreme Court ruled that state did not recognize the false-light tort for the same reason.[49]

The courts' logic is sound to a point—libel and false-light privacy are similar in some ways. At the base both involve the publication of something derogatory about the plaintiff. The practical difference between the two is that the nasty words published about the plaintiff don't have to actually be strong enough to harm a reputation to qualify for a false-light action. In other words, the plaintiff doesn't have to show the court that his reputation was harmed, only that something false was published and that this caused him to suffer embarrassment or

48. *Lake* v. *Wal-Mart Stores Inc.*, 582 N.W. 2d 231 (1998); and *Denver Publishing* v. *Bueno*, 54 P. 3d 893 (2002).
49. *Jews for Jesus Inc.* v. *Rapp*, 36 M.L.R. 2540 (2008); and *Anderson* v. *Gannett*, 36 M.L.R. 2553 (2008).

humiliation. But in a libel action, the plaintiff is going to have to prove harm to his or her reputation. The false-light tort was generated more than 75 years ago by judges who were trying to find a remedy for plaintiffs who alleged harm, but whose problems did not meet the specific requirements of existing privacy law. In the first recorded case a woman sued when she was pictured for six seconds selling bread on the streets of New York in a so-called documentary about the city. Because the main players in the film were actors, who had been given lines to speak, the court ruled the film was fiction or entertainment, not news, despite the fact there was no plot to the picture. (Yes, this sounds like appropriation, but the court didn't see it that way.) The false-light tort grew from that case.[50]

There are three important elements in the tort. The plaintiff must first prove that the specific allegations are false. The same rules that apply in a libel action when truth or falsity is at issue apply (see pages 161–164). The key is whether or not the words that carry the sting, that cause humiliation or embarrassment, are substantially true. Errors in details don't matter much. For example, Deangelo Bailey sued rapper Marshall Bruce Mathers III (better known as Eminem) for false-light invasion of privacy because of the lyrics in the 1999 song "Brain Damage." The supposedly autobiographical song described how Mathers was bullied when he was in school, how Bailey banged his head against a urinal, broke his nose, soaked his clothes in blood and so on. Bailey argued that there was no proof of these specific allegations, but the court said the sting in the song lyrics was that Bailey was a bully—and he had admitted that he picked on Mathers when they were younger. This amounted to substantial truth. Case dismissed.[51]

The plaintiff must also prove that the false statements are offensive to a reasonable person, and that the defendant was at fault in publishing this material. The definition of fault in privacy law is the same one that is applied in libel law (see pages 188–200). A false-light case can develop from a simple error made by the publisher, but there are other ways such cases arise as well. Here is a summary of the more common kinds of cases.

FALSE-LIGHT PRIVACY

1. Publication of material must put an individual in a false light.
2. The false light would be offensive to a reasonable person.
3. The publisher of the material was at fault.

FICTIONALIZATION

Fictionalization is really the purposeful distortion of the truth, usually for dramatic purposes. Some of the earliest false-light cases involved radio and television dramatizations of actual news events. Because they did not know exactly what happened, and because real life is generally boring, script writers often changed these events to increase the drama. False-light suits were often a

---

50. *Blumenthal* v. *Picture Classics,* 235 App. Div. 570 (1931); aff'd 261 N.Y. 504 (1933).
51. *Bailey* v. *Mathers,* 33 M.L.R. 2053 (2005).

consequence of this creativity.[52] Television programming and motion pictures are filled these days with stories that supposedly represent events that really happened. Television producers even have a name for these kinds of programs—docudramas. These kinds of productions pose risks for their creators because of libel and false-light invasion-of-privacy suits. The simple way to avoid these problems is for a television or motion picture company to buy the rights to the story from the real people they plan to portray. By signing a standard contract (and accepting a few dollars in payment), the real-life characters in the story forfeit their right to sue if they are unhappy with how they are portrayed. Individuals who refuse to sign such an agreement are simply written out of the story; they don't exist as far as the video story is concerned. (And you always thought these presentations were accurate and truthful.) More and more, production companies try to avoid involving the real characters in the story and simply advertise their productions as being "based on a true story." This is shorthand for a more honest statement—"most of this story is fiction."

It was not uncommon years ago for reporters and editors at many magazines and some newspapers to try to dramatize their stories a bit by adding what they suggested was real-life dialogue or maybe some additional "facts" to their news reports.[53] Today, most of this kind of journalism is confined to supermarket tabloid newspapers, or what most would call sleazy magazines. This kind of journalism has prompted more than its share of libel and false-light privacy claims. And some of the antics that prompt these lawsuits are hard to believe. A 96-year-old Arkansas resident sued the Sun tabloid newspaper for using her photo to illustrate a totally fabricated story about a 101-year-old female newspaper carrier who had to give up her route because she was pregnant. Plaintiff Nellie Mitchell's photo had been published 10 years earlier in another tabloid owned by the same company in a true story about the Mountain Home, Ark., woman. But the editors at the Sun needed a picture to illustrate their phony story and simply used Mitchell's, undoubtedly thinking she was dead. A U.S. District Court jury awarded the elderly woman $1.5 million in damages.[54] The simple rule for writers who want to be dramatists is this: If you change the facts, change the names and don't use photos of real people.

Real names often appear in novels, feature films, TV shows or even advertisements. Oftentimes individuals will sue (normally unsuccessfully) under appropriation when this occurs (see pages 253–254.) But false-light cases can result as well. In such actions the decision usually rests on whether just the name was taken, or whether the identity was taken as well. The New York Times, an advertising agency and the United Negro College Fund were recently sued for false-light invasion of privacy by Lawrence Botts Jr., a well-educated white man who complained that he and his family had been put in a false light by an ad carried in the newspaper for the educational charity. The ad depicts a fictional black man who has turned to alcohol and "wasted" his mind because he could not afford a college education. The man's name in the ad was Larry Botts. The 3rd U.S. Court of Appeals rejected the suit, saying the name in the ad was simply a John Doe, "a generic place holder for the prototypical underprivileged black youth."[55]

The differences between taking just a name and taking an identity can be subtle, but they are easy to grasp. Look at these hypothetical situations. Let's say that author Nora Roberts

52. See, for example, *Strickler* v. *NBC,* 167 F. Supp. 68 (1958).
53. See *Acquino* v. *Bulletin Co.,* 190 Pa. Super. 528 (1959), for example.
54. *Peoples Bank & Trust Co. of Mountain Home* v. *Globe International, Inc.*, 786 F. Supp. 791 (1992). See also *Varnish* v. *Best Medium*, 405 F. 2d 608 (1968).
55. *Botts* v. *New York Times Co.,* 106 Fed. Appx. 109 (2004).

writes a novel about a popular actress who has AIDS. In the book, the actress' best friend is a short, chubby nurse named Julia Roberts. The writer has taken actress Julia Roberts' name, but not her identity. But if, in the novel, an actress who has AIDS is named Julia Roberts, if she is rather tall and thin, if she won an Academy Award, if she is married to a cinematographer named Daniel Moder and so on, then the writer has taken the identity as well as the name. How many characteristics must be the same before plaintiffs can claim their identity was taken and they were placed in a false light? Courts decide this question on a case-by-case basis.

Novels and feature films often carry a disclaimer: "This is a work of fiction. All the characters and events portrayed are fictitious. Any resemblance to real people and events is purely coincidental." Will this ward off a false-light suit? No. Although the statement has minimal value in showing the intent of the author or publisher or producer, the rule is simple: You cannot escape liability for committing a legal wrong by announcing that you are not liable. If you put a large sign on the top of your car that said "Stay out of my way. I am a very bad driver and if I hit someone, it is not my fault," this would not relieve you from any liability if you caused an accident. Similarly, the disclaimer that a book is a work of fiction and the characters are fictitious will not prevent a successful privacy suit if the author has obviously appropriated someone's identity and put him or her in a false light.

OTHER FALSEHOODS

Misuse of photographs, both still and video, is a common problem.

False-light privacy suits based on fictionalization are not too common today. False-light lawsuits more typically involve simple editing or writing errors, or errors in judgment. Misuse of photographs, both still and video, is a common problem. The Saturday Evening Post was plagued by such lawsuits in the 1940s and 1950s. For example, the magazine once published a picture of a little girl who was brushed by a speeding car in an intersection and lay crying in the street. The girl was the victim of a motorist who ignored a red traffic light, but in the magazine the editors implied that she had caused the accident herself by darting into the street between parked cars. The editors simply needed a picture to illustrate a story on pedestrian carelessness and plucked this one out of the files. The picture was totally unrelated to the story, except that both were about people being hit by cars. Eleanor Sue Leverton sued the Post and won. Judge Herbert F. Goodrich ruled that the picture was clearly newsworthy in connection with Eleanor's original accident.

> But the sum total of all this is that this particular plaintiff, the legitimate subject for publicity for one particular accident, now becomes a pictorial, frightful example of pedestrian carelessness. This, we think, exceeds the bounds of privilege.[56]

WJLA-TV in the nation's capital was sued in a case that graphically demonstrates how a broadcasting station or publication can and cannot use unrelated pictures to illustrate a story. The station broadcast a story on a new medical treatment for genital herpes. Unfortunately, TV news directors believe all news reports need to be illustrated with pictures because viewers won't sit still for talking heads. But stories about medical matters usually offer few opportunities for visuals. The report on herpes appeared on both the 6 p.m. and 11 p.m. newscasts.

---

56. *Leverton* v. *Curtis Publishing Co.,* 192 F. 2d 974 (1951).

Both reports carried the same opening videotape of scores of pedestrians walking on a busy city street. Then the camera zoomed in on one woman, Linda Duncan, as she stood on a corner. Duncan turned and looked at the camera. She was clearly recognizable. On the 6 p.m. news there was no narration during the opening footage. The camera focused on the plaintiff Duncan and then the tape cut to a picture of the reporter, who was standing on the street, and said, "For the twenty million Americans who have herpes, it's not a cure." The remainder of the story followed. But for the 11 p.m. news, the reporter's opening statement was read by the news anchor as viewers watched the opening videotape, including the close-up of Linda Duncan. A defense motion to dismiss the privacy and defamation actions was granted as it related to the 6 p.m. newscast. The court said there was not a sufficient connection between pictures of the plaintiff and the reporter's statement. But the court denied a summary judgment relating to the 11 p.m. broadcast. "The coalescing of the camera action, plaintiff's action (turning toward the camera), and the position of the passerby caused plaintiff to be the focal point on the screen. The juxtaposition of this film and commentary concerning twenty million Americans with herpes is sufficient to support an inference that indeed the plaintiff was a victim," the court ruled. A jury should decide whether the connection was strong enough.[57]

Courts recognize that the reasonable juror is capable of distinguishing between the use of an unrelated photograph with a story that creates a false impression and one that doesn't. When the newspaper El Diario Juarez ran a story about an immigration officer who let truckloads of illegal immigrants come into the country, and who took money from drug traffickers in exchange for not checking trucks for drugs, it ran a photo of another officer, Christopher Houseman, to illustrate the report. The photo showed Houseman, who was not involved in the illegal activity, working a border checkpoint in uniform, with a police dog. There was a bridge in the background. The story about the suspect agent was datelined McAllen, Texas, and named a crossing bridge used by the agents. The picture of Houseman showed him working in El Paso, Texas, alongside a different bridge. The Texas Court of Appeals ruled the false-light claim filed by Houseman would not stand because a reasonable reader would recognize that the plaintiff was working in El Paso, not McAllen, and could not be the officer charged with illegal activity.

Sometimes an error simply occurs, and there is little anyone can do about it. A newspaper in Oklahoma published an article concerning the death of a former local schoolteacher who had been convicted of murder and who was reportedly mentally ill. But the photo used to accompany the story was that of Frenche Colbert, who lived in Phoenix, Ariz. Colbert's picture had been sent to the newspaper years earlier when he graduated from law school. Somehow, his photo got mixed up with that of the schoolteacher. There is no question that this publication put Colbert in a false light.[58] In such cases the fault requirement is a strong defense.

A simple precaution will protect publishers and broadcasters against many false-light suits. Refrain from using unrelated photos to illustrate stories and articles. When a story is published in the employee magazine about worker carelessness as a prime cause of industrial accidents, control the impulse to pull from the files a random picture of one of the employees working on the assembly line. That employee could contend that the story and photo suggest she is careless. Similarly, don't use old photos of kids hanging around the parking lot at a local

57. *Duncan* v. *WJLA-TV,* 10 M.L.R. 1395 (1984).
58. *Colbert* v. *World Publishing,* 747 P. 2d 286 (1987).

park to illustrate a news story on neighborhood complaints about drug dealing in the park. Juxtaposing the wrong pictures with the wrong words could give viewers the impression that one of these kids is selling or using drugs.

HIGHLY OFFENSIVE MATERIAL

Before a plaintiff can win a false-light case, the court must be convinced that the material that is false is highly offensive to a reasonable person. Although the records contain a handful of cases where nonoffensive material was the basis for a successful false-light suit,[59] these cases are old and should not be regarded as authoritative today. Typical of modern decisions is the case of *Cibenko* v. *Worth Publishers*. The plaintiff was a New York–New Jersey Port Authority police officer whose photograph appeared in a college sociology text. In a section of the book titled "Selecting the Criminals," the picture depicted a white police officer (Cibenko) in a public place apparently prodding a sleeping black man with his nightstick. The caption for the picture stated:

> The social status of the offender seems to be the most significant determinant of whether a person will be arrested and convicted for an offense and of the kind of penalty that will be applied. In this picture a police officer is preventing a black male from falling asleep in a public place. Would the officer be likely to do the same if the "offender" were a well-dressed, middle-aged white person?

Officer Cibenko claimed the photograph and caption made him appear to be a racist, and this portrayal was false. A U.S. District Court in New Jersey disagreed and ruled that there was no offensive meaning attached to the photograph and caption, especially not a highly offensive meaning.[60] A U.S. District Court in Maine dismissed a suit by a man who had fallen out of the hatch of a small airplane, but managed to cling to the door rails until the pilot made an emergency landing. An article in National Enquirer embellished the story somewhat, adding material on what the plaintiff had thought about as he clung to the airplane. The reporter had never communicated with the accident victim and therefore could not have known what went through his mind. The court ruled that the description of physical sensations and predictable fears, though possibly exaggerated or maybe even fanciful, was not offensive to a reasonable person.[61]

THE FAULT REQUIREMENT

Since 1967, plaintiffs in false-light suits have been required to carry a fault requirement much like the one applied in libel cases. The case in which this fault requirement was applied to invasion of privacy was the first mass media invasion-of-privacy suit ever heard by the U.S. Supreme Court.[62] In the early 1950s the James Hill family was held captive in their home for nearly 24 hours by three escaped convicts. The fugitives were captured by police shortly after

---

59. See *Molony* v. *Boy Comics Publishers,* 65 N.Y.S. 173 (1948); and *Spahn* v. *Julian Messner, Inc.,* 18 N.Y. 2d 324 (1966).
60. *Cibenko* v. *Worth Publishers,* 510 F. Supp. 761 (1981).
61. *Dempsey* v. *National Enquirer Inc.,* 687 F. Supp. 692 (1988).
62. *Time, Inc.* v. *Hill,* 385 U.S. 374 (1967).

THEATER

BANK ROBBERS HOLD FAMILY IN WHITEMARSH PRISONERS;

ACTUAL EVENT, as reported in newspaper, took place in isolated house about 10 miles from Philadelphia. There three convicts from

Lewisburg penitentiary held family of James Hill as prisoners while they hid from manhunt. All three convicts were later captured.

TRUE CRIME INSPIRES TENSE PLAY

The ordeal of a family trapped by convicts gives Broadway a new thriller, 'The Desperate Hours'

Life Magazine © 1955 Time Inc. Reprinted with permission. Photo © Cornell Capa/Magnum Photos.

FIGURE 8.1

Life magazine published this article about the James Hill family, which led the family to sue for invasion of privacy.

leaving the Hill home. The incident became a widely publicized story. At about the same time there were other similar hostage-takings in other parts of the United States. Author Joseph Hayes wrote a fictional account, a novel about such an occurrence called "The Desperate Hours," which focused on a fictional four-member Hilliard family that was held hostage by three escaped convicts. The book was made into a movie and a play. Before the play "The Desperate Hours" opened on Broadway, Life magazine published a feature story about the drama, stating that the play was a reenactment of the ordeal suffered by the James Hill family (see Figure 8.1). The actors were even taken to the home in which the Hills had lived (now vacant) and were photographed at the scene of the original captivity.

James Hill sued for invasion of privacy. He complained that the magazine had used his family's name for trade purposes and that the story put the family in a false light. "The Desperate Hours" did follow the basic outline of the Hill family ordeal, but it contained many differences. The fictional Hilliard family, for example, suffered far more physical and verbal indignities at the hands of the convicts than did the Hill family.

The family won money damages in the New York state courts,[63] but the Supreme Court of the United States vacated the lower-court rulings and sent the case back for yet another trial. The Hill family gave up at this point, and no subsequent trial was held.

63. *Hill v. Hayes,* 207 N.Y.S. 2d 901 (1960), 18 App. Div. 2d 485 (1963).

Justice William Brennan, in a 5-4 ruling, declared that the family's name and photographs had not been used for trade purposes. Brennan reminded all concerned that informative material published in newspapers and magazines is not published for purposes of trade (see pages 254–256), even though these publications generally are considered profit-making businesses.

Turning to the false-light action, Brennan applied the same First Amendment standards he had developed in the *New York Times* v. *Sullivan* libel suit to this category of invasion-of-privacy litigation (see pages 168–170). "We hold that the constitutional protections for speech and press preclude the application of the New York [privacy] statute to redress false reports of matters of public interest in the absence of proof that the defendant published the report with knowledge of its falsity or in reckless disregard of the truth."[64]

The *Time* v. *Hill* case was decided in 1967, three years after the *Sullivan* ruling. But since 1967 the high court has substantially modified the fault requirement in libel cases. In 1974 in *Gertz* v. *Welch* the court reiterated that so-called public persons must prove actual malice to maintain a successful libel action, but added that private persons must also prove fault—at least negligence.[65] Did the high court intend that this two-part fault standard be applied to false-light invasion-of-privacy cases as well? The Supreme Court had an occasion to answer this question shortly after its ruling in *Gertz* but declined to do so. In *Cantrell* v. *Forest City Publishing Co.*,[66] a false-light invasion-of-privacy case, the high court concluded that there was sufficient evidence to show that the defendant newspaper had acted with reckless disregard for the truth. Because the defendant could prove actual malice in this case, the court said it did not have to consider whether a private-person plaintiff would have to prove only negligence to sustain the fault requirement in a false-light privacy action. "This case presents no occasion to consider whether a state may constitutionally apply a more relaxed standard of liability for a publisher or broadcaster of false statements injurious to a private individual under a false-light theory of invasion of privacy or whether the constitutional standard announced in *Time, Inc.* v. *Hill* applies to all false light cases," wrote Justice Stewart for the court.

Whether the Gertz *variable-fault standard is applicable to false-light cases remains an open question.*

Whether the *Gertz* variable-fault standard is applicable to false-light cases remains an open question. Most authorities tend to think that the rule of *Time, Inc.* v. *Hill*—that all plaintiffs are required to show actual malice, knowledge of falsity or reckless disregard of the truth—will stand as the law in most jurisdictions. Several factors prompt this conclusion. The Supreme Court could have changed the rules in the *Cantrell* case, but did not. The high court could have modified the *Time, Inc.* v. *Hill* rule in *Gertz*, but did not. Finally, a statement that is not defamatory is likely to be far less damaging to a plaintiff—the less harm, higher fault requirement. Some courts have taken a different point of view and ruled that private-person false-light plaintiffs must prove only negligence.[67] But most courts that have considered the matter have ruled that all false-light plaintiffs must show actual malice to recover.[68]

---

64. *Time, Inc.* v. *Hill,* 385 U.S. 374 (1967).
65. 418 U.S. 323 (1974).
66. 419 U.S. 245 (1974).
67. See *Wood* v. *Hustler,* 736 F. 2d 1084 (1984); and *Crump* v. *Beckley Newspapers,* 370 S.E. 2d 70 (1984).
68. See *Dodrill* v. *Arkansas Democrat Co.,* 5 M.L.R. 1090 (1979); *McCall* v. *Courier-Journal and Louisville Times Co.,* 4 M.L.R. 2337 (1979), aff'd 6 M.L.R. 1112 (1980); *Goodrich* v. *Waterbury Republican-American Inc.,* 448 A. 2d 1317 (1987); *Colbert* v. *World Publishing Co.,* 747 P. 2d 286 (1987); *Ross* v. *Fox Television Stations Inc.,* 34 M.L.R. 1567 (2006); *Welling* v. *Weinfeld,* 113 Ohio St. 3d 464 (2007); and *Meyerkord* v. *Zipatoni Co.,* 276 S.W. 3d 319 (2008).

Before the discussion of the right of privacy comes to an end, a few points should be reiterated. First, remember that only people have the right of privacy. Corporations, businesses and governments do not enjoy the legal right of privacy as such. Second, it is impossible to civilly libel a dead person, but a few state privacy statutes make it possible for an heir to maintain an action for invasion of privacy.

Although privacy law is not as well charted as libel law, and although there are fewer privacy cases, suits for invasion of privacy are a growing menace to journalists. If journalists stick to the job of responsibly reporting the news, they may rest assured that the chance for a successful privacy suit is slim.

SUMMARY

It is an invasion of privacy to publish false information that places an individual into what is called a false light. However, this false information must be considered offensive to a reasonable person. Also, the plaintiff must prove that the information was published negligently, with knowledge of its falsity, or with reckless disregard for the truth.

One common source of false-light privacy suits is any drama that adds fictional material to an otherwise true story. The use of fictional rather than real names in such a drama will normally preclude a successful invasion-of-privacy suit. The coincidental use of a real name in a novel or stage play will not stand as a cause of action for invasion of privacy. Most false-light cases, however, result from the publication of false information about a person in a news or feature story. Pictures of people who are not involved in the stories that the pictures are used to illustrate frequently provide false-light privacy suits.

BIBLIOGRAPHY

Andrews, Edmund. "European Law Aims to Protect Privacy of Data." *The New York Times,* 26 October 1998, A1.

Burns, John F. "British Judge Rules Tabloid Report Tying Grand Prix Boss to 'Orgy' Violated Privacy." *The New York Times,* 25 July 2008, A6.

Kalven, Harry Jr. "Privacy in Tort Law—Were Warren and Brandeis Wrong?" *Law and Contemporary Problems* 31 (1966): 326.

Marcus, Paul, and Tara L. McMahon. "Limiting Disclosure of Rape Victims' Identities." *Southern California Law Review* 64 (1991): 1019.

Pember, Don R. "The Burgeoning Scope of Access Privacy and the Portent for a Free Press." *Iowa Law Review* 64 (1979): 1155.

———. *Privacy and the Press.* Seattle: University of Washington Press, 1972.

Pember, Don R., and Dwight L. Teeter. "Privacy and the Press Since *Time* v. *Hill.*" *Washington Law Review* 50 (1974): 57.

Pilgrim, Tim A. "Docudramas and False Light Invasion of Privacy." *Communications and the Law,* June 1988, 3.

Prosser, William L. "Privacy." *California Law Review* 48 (1960): 383.

Shukousky, Paul. "High School Students Sue Over Articles on Sex Lives." *Seattle Post-Intelligencer,* 13 November 2008, B3.

Warren, Samuel D., and Louis D. Brandeis. "The Right to Privacy." *Harvard Law Review* 4 (1890): 220.

Wyatt, Robert O. *Free Expression and the American Public.* Murfreesboro: Middle Tennessee State University, 1991.

CHAPTER 9

Gathering Information

RECORDS AND MEETINGS

This chapter focuses on how the law affects the efforts of reporters and ordinary citizens to gather information about what is going on in the nation and their communities. Until about 20 years ago the text focused on federal and state statutes that either permit or limit the gathering of information from government records or from meetings of government agencies. Today the law regarding news gathering is also focused on efforts by the government and others to stop the press from collecting data about a wide range of people and activities. Both topics are covered here. Additional material on access to the judicial process and judicial records is presented in Chapter 12.

Information is the lifeblood of American journalism and American politics. Until the mid-20th century there were few significant rules that defined the rights of citizens, including journalists, to gain access to the information generated and kept by the government. Reporters developed sophisticated but informal schemes with news sources in government to get the material they needed. The average citizen was shut out.

Since the 1950s state and federal governments have passed laws defining public access to records and meetings. If there was a "Golden Age of Access" to information it was likely in the 1970s and early 1980s. Since then there has been a growing government resistance to public (especially press) access to such materials—a resistance exacerbated by the events of Sept. 11, 2001.

Obama declared a new era of open government.

President Barack Obama vowed to change this shortly after taking office. He declared a new era of open government and asserted that when it comes to Freedom of Information Act (FOIA) requests to government agencies, there should be a clear presumption in favor of disclosure and that, in turn, disclosure should be timely.[1] Making good on that promise, the U.S. Attorney's Office in New York City released a letter in March 2009 acknowledging that the Central Intelligence Agency had destroyed, during the administration of George W. Bush, 92 videotapes of terrorist interrogations when it was faced with an ACLU FOIA request. That same month the Justice Department released to the ACLU nine secret legal memorandums relating to the Bush administration's surveillance and national security efforts immediately following Sept. 11, 2001. And in April 2009, after a protracted battle, the Justice Department released to the ACLU four more secret memos from the Bush administration's Office of Legal Counsel, each written between 2002 and 2005 and relating to techniques used to interrogate terrorism suspects.

But the Obama administration was not always forthcoming with documents. President Obama in May 2009 reneged on an earlier promise to release to the ACLU more than 40 photographs depicting the abusive treatment of detainees in Iraq and Afghanistan by U.S. personnel. The originally scheduled release was made in response to a FOIA lawsuit, filed in 2004, after a federal appellate court ruled in favor of the ACLU in *ACLU* v. *Department of Defense*, 543 F. 3d 59 (2d Cir. 2008). Obama, however, said he was going to fight that decision and not release the photos because he claimed they would inflame anti-American opinion and put U.S. troops in greater danger. In June 2009 the 2nd U.S. Circuit Court of Appeals allowed Obama to keep the photographs secret until the Supreme Court could hear the case and determine whether, as he

---

1. Memorandum for the Heads of Executive Departments and Agencies, Freedom of Information Act, Jan. 21, 2009, available online at http://www.whitehouse.gov/the_press_office/FreedomofInformationAct.

claimed, their release would create a grave risk of inciting violence and riots against American and coalition forces. The Senate gave support to Obama on the detainee-abuse photos, when it passed a bill in June 2009 that would allow the president to withhold them. This wasn't the only early instance where Obama violated his pledge of government transparency, as his administration (via the Department of Homeland Security and Secret Service) refused in 2009 to release White House visitor and guest logs. Similarly, the Secret Service declined to disclose to the Washington-based group Citizens for Responsibility and Ethics the list of health-care-industry executives who visited the White House to meet with Obama. Those records might reveal those trying to influence Obama's efforts to reshape health care.

Access to government information today is denied in many ways, from secret docketing of cases so the public doesn't even know they exist to the use of the states' secret privilege to withhold documents or testimony that allegedly could jeopardize national security (see pages 82–83). In 2006 The New York Times exposed a seven-year-old program under which government intelligence agencies removed from public access at the National Archives in Washington, D.C., "thousands of historical documents that were available for years, including some already published by the State Department and others photocopied years ago by private historians."[2] In brief, the federal government was reclassifying as confidential and secret more than 55,000 previously declassified pages from its document repository. Elsewhere, the government classified as "top secret" information about detainees in the CIA's secret prison program in Europe in 2006.[3] The nonprofit National Security Archive at George Washington University reported in 2006 that government classification of "sensitive but unclassified" information is another problematic area, noting that "unlike classified records or ordinary agency records subject to FOIA, there is no monitoring of or reporting on the use or impact of protective sensitive unclassified information markings. Nor is there a procedure for the public to challenge protective markings."[4]

Keeping and maintaining secrets is expensive. In its "Secrecy Report Card 2008," an organization called OpenTheGovernment.org found that "the government spent $195 maintaining the secrets already on the books for every one dollar the government spent declassifying documents in 2007, a 5 percent increase in one year. At the same time, fewer pages were declassified than in 2006."[5]

Finally, access to information sometimes is denied by the incredibly lengthy delays of government agencies in responding to requests for records. For instance, the National Security Archive reported in July 2007 that five different federal government agencies had FOIA requests that had been pending for 15 or more years, including six requests that were made back in the 1980s. A recent example illustrates the problem: In January 2009, reporter Mark Schleifstein of the Times-Picayune in New Orleans was still waiting for reports he requested in October 2005 from the Federal Emergency Management Agency (FEMA) regarding the type and amount of help needed after Hurricane Katrina hit southeastern Louisiana in August that year.[6] As Schleifstein put it, "almost all government bureaucrats—city, state and federal—hate public records laws and usually break them. Through some mysterious process, they come to believe they, rather than you, own the public records."

Keeping and maintaining secrets is expensive.

2. Shane, "U.S. Reclassifies Many Documents."
3. Shane, "Detainees' Access to Lawyers."
4. *Pseudo-Secrets,* i.
5. *Secrecy Report Card 2008*, OpenTheGovernment.org, available online at http://www.openthegovernment.org/otg/SecrecyReportCard08.pdf.
6. Schleifstein, "Broken Records; Three Years Later, FEMA Still Giving Out Excuses, Not Documents."

*But rights and liberties
are grounded in the
law.*

Journalists and citizen activists are often forced to go to court to try to assert rights they believe have been abridged by government restrictions on access to information. But rights and liberties are grounded in the law. When someone goes to court and asks for something, the first thing the judge will say is "Show me the law." So if journalists hope to use the law for assistance, they must find support in one of those sources of the law discussed in Chapter 1.

NEWS GATHERING AND THE LAW

In order for journalists to gather news, they must have access to information. While information to courts, trials and judicial proceedings is discussed in Chapter 12, there are three primary sources of law to which journalists might look to find a legal right of access to information such as documents, records, meetings and venues. Those sources of law are

- Common law
- Constitutional law (the First Amendment to the U.S. Constitution)
- Statutory law (both state and federal statutes)

Despite the tradition of open government both in this country and in Great Britain, common law provides only bare access to government documents and to meetings of public agencies. Secrecy in England had a direct impact on how colonial legislatures conducted their business. The Constitutional Convention of 1787 in Philadelphia was conducted in secret. The public and the press had almost immediate access to sessions in the U.S. House of Representatives, but it was not until 1794 that spectators and reporters were allowed into the Senate chamber. Although today access is guaranteed to nearly all sessions of Congress, much (maybe even most) congressional business is conducted by committees that frequently meet in secret.

Common-law precedents exist that open certain public records to inspection by members of the public, but distinct limitations have been placed on this common-law right. For example, under common law a person seeking access to a record normally must have an "interest" in that record. Most often this interest must relate to some kind of litigation in which the person who seeks the record is a participant. Also, only those records "required to be kept" by state law are subject to even such limited disclosure under common law. Many important records kept by the government are not "required to be kept" by law. Hence, common law must be found wanting as an aid in the process of news gathering.

THE CONSTITUTION AND NEWS GATHERING

Does the U.S. Constitution provide any assistance to citizens who seek to scrutinize government records or attend meetings of government bodies? Surprisingly the First Amendment plays a rather insignificant role in defining the rights of citizens and journalists in the news-gathering process. The amendment was drafted in an age when news gathering was not a primary function of the press. The congressional records of the drafting and adoption of the First Amendment fail to support the notion that the protection of the news-gathering process was to be included within the scope of freedom of the press. The First Amendment was seen as a means by which the public could confront its government, not necessarily report on its activities.[7]

The Supreme Court has explored the nexus between freedom of expression and news gathering. In a non-press-related case in 1964, the high court ruled that the constitutional right to speak and publish does not carry with it the unrestrained right to gather information.[8] Eight years later Justice Byron White, speaking for three other members of the court, said: "Nor is it suggested that news gathering does not qualify for First Amendment protection; without some protection for seeking out the news, freedom of the press could be eviscerated."[9] Many First Amendment lawyers regard this statement as a fountain from which a constitutionally based right to gather news springs, but others disagree. White's statement was dictum in a case that involved the right of journalists to refuse to reveal the names of confidential news sources (see Chapter 10). And White said he didn't see any connection at all between news gathering and a reporter's right to protect the name of a news source. The sentence was hardly a ringing endorsement of a First Amendment right of access to information. These comments are as far as the high court has gone in dealing with this issue in an abstract or theoretical way.

"Without some protection for seeking out the news, freedom of the press could be eviscerated."

The high court has been asked on three occasions whether the First Amendment guarantees a journalist the unobstructed right to gather news in a prison. In each case the court said no. In *Pell* v. *Procunier,*[10] reporters in California attempted to interview specific inmates at California prisons. In *Saxbe* v. *Washington Post,*[11] reporters from that newspaper sought to interview specific inmates at federal prisons at Lewisburg, Pa., and Danbury, Conn. In both instances the press was barred from conducting the interviews. The U.S. Bureau of Prisons rule, which is similar to the California regulation, states:

> Press representatives will not be permitted to interview individual inmates.
> This rule shall apply even where the inmate requests or seeks an interview.

At issue was not access to the prison system. The press could tour and photograph prison facilities, conduct brief conversations with randomly encountered inmates and correspond with inmates through the mails. In addition, the federal rules had been interpreted to permit journalists to conduct lengthy interviews with randomly selected groups of inmates. In fact, a reporter in the Washington Post case did go to Lewisburg and interview a group of prisoners.

The argument of the press in both cases was that to ban interviews with specific inmates abridged the First Amendment protection afforded the news-gathering activity of a free press. The Supreme Court disagreed in a 5-4 decision in both cases. Justice Stewart wrote in the majority opinion that the press already had substantial access to the prisons and that there was no evidence that prison officials were hiding things from reporters. Stewart rejected the notion that the First Amendment gave newspeople a special right of access to the prisons. "Newsmen have no constitutional right of access to prisons or their inmates beyond that afforded the general

"Newsmen have no constitutional right of access to prisons or their inmates beyond that afforded the general public."

---

7. See Rourke, *Secrecy and Publicity;* and Padover, *The Complete Madison.*
8. *Zemel* v. *Rusk,* 381 U.S. 1 (1964).
9. *Branzburg* v. *Hayes,* 408 U.S. 665 (1972).
10. 417 U.S. 817 (1974).
11. 417 U.S. 843 (1974).

public," the justice wrote.[12] Since members of the general public have no right to interview specific prisoners, the denial of this right to the press does not infringe on the First Amendment.

The high court did not disagree with the findings of the district court in the *Saxbe* case that face-to-face interviews with specific inmates are essential to accurate and effective reporting about prisoners and prisons. What the court seemed to say was that while the First Amendment guarantees freedom of expression, it does not guarantee effective and accurate reporting.

In 1978 the high court split along similar lines on a case involving press access to a county jail.[13] An inmate at the Santa Rita County, Calif., jail committed suicide in 1975. Following the death and a report by a psychiatrist that jail conditions were bad, KQED television sought permission to inspect and take pictures in the jail. Sheriff Houchins announced that the media could certainly participate in one of the six tours of the jail facility given to the public each year. However, the tours did not visit the disciplinary cells nor the portion of the jail in which the suicide had taken place. No cameras or tape recorders were allowed, but photographs of some parts of the jail were supplied by the sheriff's office.

Reporters at KQED took a jail tour, but were not happy at the limits placed on them. Sheriff Houchins contended that unregulated visits through the jail by the press would infringe on the inmates' right of privacy, could create jail celebrities out of inmates that would in turn cause problems for jailers, and would disrupt jail operations. Houchins noted that reporters did have access to inmates—they could visit individual prisoners, could visit with inmates awaiting trial, could talk by telephone with inmates, could write letters to prisoners and so forth. But KQED argued that it had a constitutionally protected right to gather news and challenged the limits.

"Neither the First Amendment nor the Fourteenth Amendment mandates a right of access to government information or sources of information within the government's control."

Chief Justice Warren Burger wrote the opinion for the court in the 4-3 decision. "Neither the First Amendment nor the Fourteenth Amendment mandates a right of access to government information or sources of information within the government's control," Burger asserted. The chief justice seemed troubled by the argument of KQED that only through access to the jail could the press perform its public responsibility.

> Unarticulated but implicit in the assertion that the media access to jail is essential for an informed public debate on jail conditions is the assumption that the media personnel are the best qualified persons for the task of discovering malfeasance in public institutions. . . . The media are not a substitute for or an adjunct of government. . . . We must not confuse the role of the media with that of government.[14]

In June 2009 the 2nd U.S. Circuit Court of Appeals held in *Hammer* v. *Ashcroft,* 570 F. 3d 798 (2009), that a rule banning in-person meetings between reporters and prisoners held in the special confinement unit (mostly comprised of death-row inmates) at the federal prison in Terre Haute, Ind., was permissible and did not violate prisoners' rights. Prisoners in other units, however, were allowed in-person interviews with the press. In upholding the rule, the appellate court observed that the inmates in the special confinement unit were not denied all

---

12. *Pell* v. *Procunier,* 417 U.S. 817 (1974).
13. *Houchins* v. *KQED,* 438 U.S. 1 (1978).
14. Ibid.

access to the press, as they were allowed to use telephones and U.S. Mail to communicate with reporters. The court found that a reasonable justification for the rule against face-to-face interviews with death-row inmates was the danger that such interviews, when televised, would turn the inmates into celebrities. The government did not want people to become celebrities by committing crimes, such as Oklahoma City bomber Timothy McVeigh who was held at Terre Haute before being executed. The government also feared that celebrity prisoners will create envy and jealousy among the prison population, leading to possible disturbances.

In 1980 in a case that many commentators hailed as the beginning of a general constitutionally guaranteed "right to know," the Supreme Court ruled that the First Amendment does establish for all citizens the right to attend criminal trials.[15] (See Chapter 12 for a full discussion of this case.) But while Chief Justice Burger's opinion was quite explicit regarding the First Amendment and attendance at criminal trials, it was obscure regarding the larger constitutional right to gather news in other contexts. And the high court has done little in the past two decades to clarify its position on this question. Although it has decided a number of right-of-access cases since *Richmond Newspapers,*[16] the Supreme Court has never explicitly recognized this right outside of judicial proceedings.

The lower federal and state courts tend to mirror the rulings by the Supreme Court that reject the notion of a First Amendment right of access to information and meetings. There are, however, significant exceptions:

- In 2008 a federal district court reiterated the findings of other courts that "exit polling, which involves a discussion of governmental affairs and politics as well as the media's right to gather news, is protected by the First Amendment."[17] The court noted that while content-based regulations on exit polling are impermissible, content-neutral time, place and manner regulations (see Chapter 3) may be okay depending upon how far away the media are kept from the polls.

- When the White House staff tried to exclude camera crews with CNN from the pool of network television photographers who cover the president, a U.S. District Court forbade the discriminatory action, noting that the First Amendment includes a "right of access to news and information concerning the operations and activities of government."[18]

- A U.S. District Court in Ohio ruled in 1988 that the press and the public have a qualified First Amendment right of access to the legislative process—in this case a city council meeting. The court said there was always a First Amendment presumption in favor of open government meetings, a presumption that can only be overcome by a formal showing of a need for privacy and confidentiality.[19]

---

15. *Richmond Newspapers v. Virginia,* 448 U.S. 555 (1980).
16. See, for example, *Press-Enterprise Co.* v. *Riverside Superior Court,* 464 U.S. 501 (1984).
17. *American Broadcasting Companies, Inc.* v. *Ritchie,* 36 M.L.R. 2601 (D. Minn. 2008). See also *CBS, Inc.* v. *Smith,* 681 F. Supp. 794 (S.D. Fla. 1988) (holding that it is "clear that the conduct of exit polling and journalistic interviews are protected by the First Amendment guarantees of free speech and free press"); and *Daily Herald Co.* v. *Munro,* 838 F. 2d 380 (9th Cir. 1988) (holding that exit polling is "speech that is protected, on several levels, by the First Amendment").
18. *CNN* v. *ABC,* 518 F. Supp. 1238 (1981).
19. *WJW* v. *Cleveland,* 686 F. Supp. 177 (1988).

▪ Finally, in 2002 the 9th U.S. Circuit Court of Appeals held that the public enjoys "a First Amendment right of access to view executions from the moment the condemned is escorted into the execution chamber."[20] This right of access, the appellate court wrote, includes the right to watch so-called initial procedures, including the forcible restraint of the condemned and the fitting of that person "with the apparatus of death." The court reasoned, in part, that "informed public debate is the main purpose for granting a right of access to governmental proceedings."

Unfortunately decisions like these stand in stark contrast to a larger body of case law that denies this proposition. For instance, a federal court in Arkansas in 2008 disagreed with the 9th Circuit's ruling described above regarding a First Amendment right of public access to witness executions. In rejecting the existence of such a right, U.S. District Judge Susan Webber Wright wrote in *Arkansas Times* v. *Norris* that "the Supreme Court has never recognized a First Amendment right of access to executions," and added that of all the federal appellate courts, only the 9th Circuit has held that the First Amendment includes a right of public access to executions.[21] In reaching her anti-access conclusion, Judge Webber Wright observed that "in contrast to the unbroken, uncontradicted history of access to criminal trials, in the 1830s, executions in the United States became private events and moved from the public square to inside prison walls." Other courts have denied a First Amendment right of access in similar situations.

In 2004 the 8th U.S. Circuit Court of Appeals held in *Rice* v. *Kempker* that "the First Amendment does not protect the use of video cameras or any other cameras or, for that matter, audio recorders in the execution chamber."[22] In this case, a religious-based group in Missouri called New Life Evangelistic Center wanted to videotape the execution of a convicted murderer, Daniel Basile, in a Missouri correctional facility, and it asserted a First Amendment right of public access. The organization contended that allowing viewers to see the horror of a man put to death would convince people that capital punishment is wrong and thus would help end capital punishment in Missouri and in the United States. The appellate court, however, reasoned that "neither the public nor the media has a First Amendment right to videotape, photograph, or make audio recordings of government proceedings that are by law open to the public." Most courts have refused to recognize the First Amendment as a means to gain access to government records, government meetings or government facilities. A key point that must be remembered regarding these rulings: In virtually all the instances noted in which a court has ruled that the First Amendment does provide a means of gaining access to a meeting or a record, the court has emphasized that this right belongs to both the press and the public. Reporters are not given any special rights in this regard, only those rights that all citizens enjoy.

"Neither the public nor the media has a First Amendment right to videotape, photograph, or make audio recordings of government proceedings that are by law open to the public."

Access to Government Officials: A Right to Interview?

Each example described so far involved a question of First Amendment access to either a place, such as a government-run prison, or to a proceeding like a government meeting or an execution. But what happens when a reporter simply wants access to speak with a person—namely, a

---

20. *California First Amendment Coalition* v. *Woodford,* 299 F. 3d 868 (2002).
21. 36 M.L.R. 1405 (E.D. Ark. 2008).
22. *Rice* v. *Kempker,* 374 F. 3d 675 (2004).

government official such as a mayor or a governor—and that official has issued a "no-comment policy" and refuses to speak with specific members of the press? Is there, in other words, a First Amendment right of access for the media to conduct one-on-one interviews with government officials such that the officials cannot refuse to speak with the news media?

The answer appears to be no. In 2006 the 4th U.S. Circuit Court of Appeals held that then Maryland Gov. Robert L. Ehrlich Jr. did not violate the First Amendment rights of two Baltimore Sun reporters when he issued a directive denying them interview access. In *Baltimore Sun* v. *Ehrlich*,[23] the paper claimed the no-access directive was in retaliation for what the governor believed was negative coverage and commentary by Sun journalists David Nitkin and Michael Olesker. The appellate court, however, held that "no actionable retaliation claim arises when a government official denies a reporter access to discretionarily afforded information or refuses to answer questions." It reasoned that the governor's response to the Sun's coverage "is a pervasive feature of journalism and of journalists' interaction with government. Having access to relatively less information than other reporters on account of one's reporting is so commonplace that to allow the Sun to proceed on its retaliation claim addressing that condition would 'plant the seed of a constitutional case' in 'virtually every' interchange between public official and press." The appellate court added that "in the ongoing intercourse of government and press, a reporter endures only *de minimis* [minimal] inconvenience when a government official denies the reporter access to discretionary information or refuses to answer the reporter's questions because the official disagrees with the substance or manner of the reporter's previous expression in reporting."

This ruling agrees with the 2005 federal district court decision in *Youngstown Publishing Co.* v. *McKelvey*.[24] In this case, a judge held that a no-comment policy issued in 2003 by George McKelvey, then the mayor of Youngstown, Ohio, that directed city employees not to speak with reporters from a bimonthly newspaper called the Business Journal did not violate the First Amendment. The judge concluded "the right of access sought by the *Business Journal* is to information not otherwise available to the public, and, therefore, is a privileged right of access above that of the general public to which no constitutional right of access applies. The no-comment policy does not impede the *Business Journal* from engaging in a constitutionally protected activity, and Plaintiffs cannot establish this element of their First Amendment retaliation claim." Although the paper appealed to the 6th Circuit, the appellate court dismissed the case in June 2006 as moot because a new mayor had taken office and withdrawn McKelvey's edict to various city officials instructing them not to speak to reporters from the Business Journal. In brief, the new mayor's rescission of the no-comment policy meant there no longer was a case to hear.[25]

In 2007, however, in a slightly different scenario, a federal judge held in *Citicasters Co.* v. *Finkbeiner* that the mayor of Toledo, Ohio, could not exclude a specific radio reporter from attending the mayor's press conferences that are open generally to all journalists.[26] Judge

23. 437 F. 3d 410 (4th Cir. 2006). The governor's order provided in relevant part that "effective *immediately,* [author's emphasis], no one in the Executive Department or Agencies is to speak with David Nitkin or Michael Olesker until further notice. Do not return calls or comply with any requests. The Governor's Press Office feels that currently both are failing to objectively report on any issue dealing with the Ehrlich-Steele Administration."
24. 2005 U.S. Dist. LEXIS 9476 (N.D. Ohio 2005).
25. 34 M.L.R. 2036 (6th Cir. 2006).
26. Permanent Injunction, *Citicasters Co.* v. *Finkbeiner*, Case No. 07-CV-00117 (N.D. Ohio 2007).

James G. Carr reasoned that a press conference is a public event, in contrast to the cases of *Baltimore Sun* v. *Ehrlich* and *Youngstown Publishing Co.* v. *McKelvey* in which reporters were denied private interview access and/or direct comments to their questions. The mayor's office unsuccessfully argued that the radio personality who was denied access was not a news reporter but was an entertainer.

Viewed collectively, then, this trio of cases suggests that while government officials can refuse to grant one-on-one interview access to specific reporters and can refuse to give comments to specific members of the news media, they cannot selectively deny access to specific reporters from public press conferences that are open to all members of the news media.

The First Amendment Protection of News Gathering

Plaintiffs' attorneys now are suing not just for how news is reported, *but increasingly for how news is* gathered.

As it grows harder for plaintiffs to win libel suits against the media (actual malice is tough for public officials and public figures to prove), plaintiffs' attorneys now are suing not just for how news is *reported,* but increasingly for how news is *gathered.* The First Amendment generally provides no special protection for journalists or exemption from generally applicable laws when they gather news. Arguments that the constitutional protection of a free press allows journalists to bend or break criminal and civil laws when gathering news typically are rejected by courts.

"It is well settled that the First Amendment does not grant the press automatic relief from laws of general application."

In 1998, for example, a U.S. District Court in Maryland refused to dismiss charges of transporting and receiving child pornography against a freelance journalist who attempted to block the prosecution by arguing that he was gathering news, not child pornography. Lawrence Matthews said that law enforcement officials were too zealous in their prosecution of Internet users and that the news stories resulting from his investigation would reveal this overly aggressive official action. His work was in the public interest, he said. But the court was not moved. "It is well settled that the First Amendment does not grant the press automatic relief from laws of general application," Judge Williams said. "If law enforcement officials are doing something improper in their investigations the court does not understand how the defendant would uncover malfeasance by receiving and disseminating the materials himself."[27] In 2000 the 4th U.S. Circuit Court of Appeals affirmed Judge Williams' decision and rejected Matthews' assertion that the First Amendment entitled him to assert a legitimate-journalistic-purpose defense to conviction under federal child pornography laws.[28] It also rejected the friend-of-the-court argument of the Reporters Committee for Freedom of the Press that there should be a more general journalistic news-gathering exemption from those laws. The appellate court cited with approval the Supreme Court's opinion in *Branzburg* v. *Hayes* for the proposition that the First Amendment does not provide "a license on either the reporter or his news sources to violate valid criminal laws."[29]

Most reporters don't violate criminal statutes, as Matthews was charged with doing, to investigate how the police enforce those statutes. But reporters do break other laws. An overview of some of these kinds of situations will demonstrate that the courts are no more tolerant of these actions.

27. *U.S.* v. *Matthews,* 11 F. Supp. 2d 656 (1998). Matthews was sentenced to 18 months in prison.
28. *U.S.* v. *Matthews,* 209 F. 3d 338 (2000), cert. den., 531 U.S. 910 (2000).
29. 408 U.S. 665, 691 (1972).

Trespass   In 2009 a West Virginia judge held that two photojournalists did not have a First Amendment–based right to be on the property of Massey Energy Company to shoot pictures of a group of protesters complaining about so-called mountaintop removal mining. The two were given trespass citations. More disturbingly, in August 2008 during the Democratic convention in Denver, ABC news producer Asa Eslocker was arrested and charged with trespassing while standing on a public sidewalk (a place where he had the right to be) and taking photographs of Democratic senators and VIP donors leaving a private meeting at a hotel (the charge ultimately was dropped by the Denver city attorney). Every year, it seems, journalists run afoul of the law on trespass charges, some of which are no doubt legitimate and others which appear to be trumped up by law enforcement officials in deliberate efforts to censor the press. **Trespass** is an intentional, unauthorized (i.e., without consent) entry onto land that is occupied or possessed by another. While consent is a defense to a claim of trespass, journalists who exceed the scope of consent by taking actions in abuse of the authorized entry or by going into places beyond where they have permission may be held liable.

Reporters may face both civil liability and criminal prosecution when they trespass. It is important for journalists to remember, as one federal appellate court wrote in 1995, that "there is no journalists' privilege to trespass."[30] What's more, reporters don't have the right to trespass on private property or even government-owned property.

A recent case illustrates the dangers of criminal trespass. Reporter Bryon Wells of the East Valley Tribune near Phoenix, Ariz., sought to interview a recently fired local police officer named Daniel Lovelace. Lovelace had been involved in a fatal shooting and was charged, at the time, with second-degree murder. Wells went through a closed but unlocked gate, posted with a "no trespassing" sign, and entered Lovelace's fenced property. The reporter walked to the front door, rang the bell and was told by the woman who answered, Lovelace's wife, to leave. Wells apparently left peacefully, but in 2004 a judge upheld Wells' conviction for misdemeanor criminal trespass—he was fined $300 and sentenced to a year of probation—based on the incident.[31] In upholding a ruling by a lower-court judge, Judge Michael D. Jones wrote that "reporters who are in violation of a criminal trespass statute are not exempt from prosecution simply because they are exercising a First Amendment right." The Arizona criminal trespass law at issue provides: "A person commits criminal trespass in the first degree by knowingly . . . entering or remaining unlawfully in a fenced residential yard."[32]

Not all reporters who enter private property uninvited are necessarily trespassing. Whether or not the owner or occupant of the property asks the reporter to leave is a critical factor. A woman who permitted a CBS television crew to accompany a crisis intervention team that entered her home was later unable to maintain that the visit had been a trespass, a court ruled.[33] Also, the public is invited to visit some kinds of private property, and the press is a part of the public. ABC sent a camera crew to secretly film eye examinations being given to patients at an optical business. The exams were being administered in the portion of the business that was open to customers who wandered in seeking information, medication or other services. The 7th U.S. Circuit Court of Appeals rejected a trespass action brought by the

Reporters may face both civil liability and criminal prosecution when they trespass.

30. *Desnick* v. *American Broadcasting Companies, Inc.,* 44 F. 3d 1345, 1351 (1995).
31. "Judge Upholds Reporter's Trespassing Conviction," *Arizona* v. *Wells,* 2004 WL 1925617 (Ariz. Super. 2004).
32. Arizona Revised Statute § 13-1504 (2004).
33. *Baugh* v. *CBS, Inc.,* 828 F. Supp. 745 (1993).

owners of the property, saying that there was no invasion in this case of any of the interests that the tort of trespass is designed to protect, namely the use and enjoyment of one's property without interference. The offices were open to anyone who sought ophthalmologic services offered by the business. The activity in the office was not disrupted; there was no invasion of anyone's private space.[34]

Even when the media are found civilly liable for trespass, they may not always be responsible under trespass law for so-called publication damages—monetary losses that flow from the actual publication or broadcast of footage. In a case involving a different cause of action—intrusion into seclusion—the operators of a medical laboratory filed a trespass complaint against ABC for the broadcast of a report that included footage obtained by ABC employees when they trespassed into certain areas of the laboratory.[35] The report, however, contained only 52 seconds of relatively innocuous videotape obtained during the trespass itself. The 9th U.S. Circuit Court of Appeals held that the plaintiff "fails to identify any damages flowing specifically from this 52-second videotape clip" and concluded that "the alleged trespass was not the legal cause of the publication damages that Medical Lab seeks." The real damage, the appellate court reasoned, was caused by other information broadcast by ABC that was obtained without trespassing. It thus refused to award the plaintiff damages under trespass law for the broadcast.

Is it a trespass to photograph or film a person from above his or her home or other private property using a helicopter to get the desired images?

Is it a trespass to photograph or film a person from above his or her home or other private property using a helicopter to get the desired images? It all depends on how high the chopper passes. Television newsmagazines often try to capture images of celebrity weddings using aerial shots taken from hovering helicopters. In a slightly different twist, a news helicopter hovered for 10 minutes above the home of Gail Bevers to obtain footage for a story about the poor condition of rental properties. Bevers, who was "scared to death" by the helicopter, sued for trespass. In 2002 a Texas appellate court hearing her case observed that "one of the key facts in ascertaining whether a flight through airspace constitutes a trespass is the altitude of the aircraft."[36] The court noted that while "landowners have no right to exclude overflights above their property because airspace is part of the public domain," flights that are within the "immediate reaches of the airspace next to the land" and that also interfere substantially with the use and enjoyment of that land may constitute a trespass. In Bevers' case, the court concluded "a single ten-minute hover over her property at 300 to 400 feet does not, as a matter of law, rise to the level of 'substantial interference' with the use and enjoyment of the underlying land." The appellate court thus affirmed summary judgment for the media defendants.

What if the reporter accompanies government officials, police or firefighters onto the property? Can these government agents give permission for the press to illegally enter private property? The simple answer is no. And the courts have ruled that not only are reporters potentially liable for damages in such a case, but the law officers themselves may be at risk for bringing reporters along.

In 1999 the Supreme Court of the United States unanimously ruled that when law enforcement officers permit reporters to accompany them when they enter private homes to conduct

34. *Desnick* v. *American Broadcasting Companies, Inc.,* 44 F. 3d 1345 (1995).
35. *Medical Laboratory Management Consultants* v. *American Broadcasting Companies, Inc.,* 306 F. 3d 808 (2002).
36. *Bevers* v. *Gaylord Broadcasting Co.,* 30 M.L.R. 2586, 2590 (2002).

searches or arrests, the officers violate "the right of residential privacy at the core of the Fourth Amendment." Two cases found their way to the high court. The first, *Wilson* v. *Layne,* resulted when members of a joint federal and local law enforcement task force invited a Washington Post reporter and photographer to accompany them when they arrested fugitives in Rockville, Md., just outside the nation's capital. The other case, *Hanlon* v. *Berger,* involved agents of the U.S. Fish and Wildlife Service who invited reporters and photographers from CNN to accompany them as they searched the property of a Montana rancher for evidence that the property owner was illegally poisoning wildlife. The issue the Supreme Court focused upon was whether the government agents who brought the journalists onto the private property could be held responsible for civil rights violations; in other words, could the property owners sue the government agents for violating their Fourth Amendment rights against an illegal search? The government agents attempted to justify the invitations by arguing that such close-up coverage of their action will assist the public in understanding law enforcement problems and help the police in getting more public cooperation. "Surely the possibility of good public relations for the police is simply not enough, standing alone, to justify the ride-along intrusion into a private home," Chief Justice William Rehnquist wrote for the court. The chief justice quoted an almost 400-year-old British court ruling in supporting the high court's decision: "The house of everyone is to him as his castle and fortress, as well for his defence [*sic*] against injury and violence, for his repose." But because the law concerning media ride-alongs had not been developed when these arrests took place, the high court ruled that it would be unfair to subject the police officers in this case to money damages for their behavior. The officers could not have clearly foreseen that what they did would be a violation of the Constitution.[37]

> *"Surely the possibility of good public relations for the police is simply not enough, standing alone, to justify the ride-along intrusion into a private home."*

In this instance the court did not rule on the matter of the liability of reporters and photographers who enter private premises with the permission of police. The *Berger* case was remanded to the 9th U.S. Circuit Court of Appeals in light of the high-court ruling regarding the liability of the police.[38] In an earlier decision, the Court of Appeals had ruled that, because of the extremely close cooperation between the journalists and the government agents who searched the Montana ranch, the television reporters and producers were actually "state actors" or "joint actors" with the wildlife agents and could be subject to the same kind of Fourth Amendment action brought against the federal officers.[39] After the Supreme Court decision, the appellate court ruled that the journalists did not enjoy the kind of qualified immunity that had shielded the government agents in the *Wilson* case, reinstated Berger's Fourth Amendment claim against the reporters, and also reversed a lower court's dismissal of claims for trespass and the intentional infliction of emotional distress against the media defendants.[40] In 2001 Paul Berger finally reached a confidential settlement agreement with CNN, bringing the case to a close for an undisclosed amount of cash.[41]

In 2008, a federal judge treated the cast and crew of the news show Dateline NBC as government actors when they worked closely with law enforcement officials in the staging

37. *Wilson* v. *Layne,* 526 U.S. 603 (1999).
38. *Hanlon* v. *Berger,* 526 U.S. 808 (1999).
39. *Berger* v. *Hanlon,* 129 Г. 3d 505 (1997).
40. *Berger* v. *Hanlon,* 188 F. 3d 1155 (1999). The rancher and his wife were absolved of all felony charges, but the search was nevertheless broadcast 10 different times by CNN.
41. "CNN, Federal Government Settle Suit with Montana Rancher."

and filming of an episode of Dateline's "To Catch a Predator," a now-cancelled series that involved sting operations to catch alleged sexual predators preying on minors via the Internet.[42] U.S. District Judge Denny Chin observed:

> In producing "To Catch A Predator," Dateline provides equipment, money, services, and other things of value to local police departments. In return, local law enforcement agrees to participate in the show, permits Dateline to videotape arrests in "dramatically-staged scenarios," provides Dateline with confidential data, and permits [NBC correspondent Chris] Hansen to interview suspects even before detectives interview them.

Reporters who want to enter private property need the permission of the occupant or the owner of the property.

Reporters who want to enter private property need the permission of the occupant or the owner of the property. Police and firefighters are unable to give the press this permission. Reporters who are sent to cover demonstrations or protests that may stray onto nonpublic areas are advised to meet with the police beforehand and explain what they will be doing. They should carry full press credentials and obey all legitimate police orders. Reporters need to be careful not to interfere with police or have a verbal confrontation with officers who are attempting crowd control. Tensions run high, and the police often fear losing control of the situation. For instance, a photographer for The Daily Collegian, the student newspaper at Pennsylvania State University, was arrested in October 2008 and charged with misdemeanor counts of failure to disperse and disorderly conduct while he was on assignment taking photographs of a riot in downtown State College, Pennsylvania, after the Nittany Lions' football win over Ohio State. Local police asserted that Michael Felletter helped incite the riot, contending that his taking photographs would excite the crowd and encourage destructive behavior. In July 2009, Judge David E. Grine dismissed the charges against Felletter, writing in *Commonwealth* v. *Felletter* that police testimony made it clear "that rioters were becoming more disorderly around Defendant's camera. That, however, is not Defendant's fault, and is the responsibility of those who were at the riot and actually acting disorderly." There was no word on how much taxpayer money was wasted by the prosecution on the case that targeted a student journalist who was just doing his job. There are myriad catchall laws in most cities and states, laws like interfering with an officer in the execution of his or her duty, that might be the basis for an arrest even if a trespass is not involved (see pages 318–319). When applied to the press, these laws might be unconstitutional,[43] but such a ruling will not be made until weeks or months after the journalist has been arrested.

Harassment   In 1996 a federal judge in Pennsylvania took the extraordinary action of enjoining the news-gathering activities of two reporters who worked for the television infotainment program "Inside Edition." Reporters Paul Lewis and Stephen Wilson were preparing a story on the high salaries paid to corporate executives at U.S. HealthCare while the company was imposing severe cost cutting on patients. The story focused on Leonard Abramson, board chair, and Abramson's daughter and son-in-law, Nancy and Richard Wolfson, who also worked at U.S. HealthCare. The Wolfsons argued that the reporters used ambush interviews, shotgun microphones and other electronic equipment to harass them and invade their privacy after they rejected requests for on-camera interviews. The reporters went so far, the

42. *Conradt* v. *NBC Universal, Inc.*, 536 F. Supp. 2d 380 (S.D. N.Y. 2008).
43. *City of Houston* v. *Hill,* 482 U.S. 451 (1987).

couple said, as to follow their daughter to school and to follow the entire family when they took a vacation in Florida. The Wolfsons sued the reporters for tortious stalking, harassment, trespass and invasion of privacy–intrusion upon seclusion, and asked the judge to stop the reporters from using the intrusive news-gathering techniques until a jury trial was held. The judge thought the Wolfsons would prevail in their lawsuit against the reporters. He said that through their unreasonable surveilling, hounding and following, the two news gatherers had effectively rendered the family captive in their own home. The judge entered a preliminary injunction that barred Lewis and Wilson from any conduct, with or without the use of cameras, that invades the Wolfsons' privacy, actions including but not limited to harassing, hounding, following, intruding, frightening, terrorizing or ambushing the family.[44] In January 1997, the parties reached a settlement and the judge dissolved the preliminary injunction he had issued against "Inside Edition."

Swarming paparazzi that block streets and sidewalks and drive dangerously while aggressively hounding celebrities like Lindsay Lohan, Paris Hilton and Britney Spears are such a problem in Los Angeles that nearby municipalities in 2008 formed a task force and considered passing laws that would provide a personal-safety zone around celebrities. Such floating buffer zones, however, are of questionable constitutional validity and would be difficult to enforce. In addition, as Los Angeles Police Chief William Bratton has stated, there is no need for additional statutes, as laws against trespassing, jaywalking, reckless driving and battery (if a photographer touches a celebrity) already are on the books that can be used against these intruders.[45] Chapter 7 discusses a California statute passed shortly after the death of Princess Diana.

Floating buffer zones, however, are of questionable constitutional validity.

Fraud   Fraud is a knowingly false statement of a material or significant fact that is communicated with the intent to induce the plaintiff to rely on that statement and that does, in fact, induce the plaintiff to reasonably rely upon it to the plaintiff's harm or injury. Typically we think of sellers of goods as engaging in fraud when they lie to buyers about the quality of those goods. But can journalists be held liable for fraud when they try to obtain information by telling a lie? Imagine this scenario. A newspaper editor hears well-founded rumors that a local retail business is cheating its customers. To check out this story, two newspaper reporters apply for jobs at the business to take a look at what goes on inside. The pair use false names, fake work histories, and tell the business owners they are looking for work. They do not reveal they are newspaper reporters and will be spying on the other workers at the business. Are the reporters' activities legal? In 1996 a jury in North Carolina decided that ABC television journalists had committed fraud and an assortment of other legal wrongs when they lied about their backgrounds and intentions in order to get jobs at a supermarket chain the network was investigating for potential health code violations. A damage award of $5 million was later reduced to all but nothing ($2) when a U.S. Court of Appeals ruled that the behavior of the two journalists did not meet the strict legal standard for fraud required by North Carolina statutes.[46] But this high-profile case, which generated considerably more news coverage than

---

44. *Wolfson* v. *Lewis,* 924 F. Supp. 1413 (1996).
45. Orlov, "Privacy: Celebrities Make Their Case for Cracking Down on Aggressive Paparazzi."
46. *Food Lion Inc.* v. *Capital Cities/ABC,* 194 F. 3d 505 (1999); see also Barringer, "Appeals Court Rejects Damages."

the original ABC broadcast about the supermarket chain, brought into sharp focus the issue of reporters pretending to be people they are not in order to secretly gather news. In a different state with a different statute the fraud conviction might have been sustained. Indeed, in Minnesota just a year later, WCCO television and one of its reporters were found guilty of both fraud and trespass in a situation that mirrored the ABC case. In this instance the reporter lied about her background and her reportorial intentions when she applied for a position as a volunteer at a care facility for people with mental retardation. She secretly videotaped activities at the facility and portions of the tape were later telecast.[47]

An issue closely related to fraud is impersonation by journalists of government officials in order to obtain information. Such impersonation is prohibited by both federal and state law and the First Amendment provides no defense. For instance, journalist Avi Lidgi was sentenced in April 2002 to one-year probation and 60 hours of community service by a federal court for posing as both a federal prosecutor and a federal judge's aide in order to obtain secret legal documents in an espionage case in Cleveland, Ohio.[48] The 27-year-old journalist agreed to plead guilty to one count of impersonating a federal official after a grand jury had indicted him on three counts and he faced up to nine years in prison.

Failure to Obey Lawful Orders   Police and fire officials at the scene of disasters, accidents and fires frequently restrict the access of the press and public to the site. Reporters must respect these rules or face charges of disorderly conduct or worse. For instance, a reporter for the Fayetteville Observer, Robert Boyer, was convicted in 2005 of failing to leave a crime scene and sentenced to 60 hours of community service.[49] The case arose after Boyer went to the scene of a homicide in a neighborhood of Fayetteville, N.C. After reportedly refusing to cooperate after being asked and ordered by police six different times to move back from the crime scene, Boyer was arrested and charged with the misdemeanor offense of resisting, delaying or obstructing an officer. Boyer unsuccessfully argued to the district court judge that the local police broke department policy by failing to use crime-scene tape to block public access to the dead-end street where the crime occurred. The police, instead, stationed an officer, along with his car, on the street to tell others it was a crime scene. The lesson here is this: Journalists must be careful not only to notice and obey the location of crime-scene tape but also to obey the lawful commands and orders of the police when no tape is present.

In May 2009, reporter Diane Bukowski of the Michigan Citizen was convicted on felony charges of obstructing police after she allegedly crossed a taped-off crime scene to take photographs. Bukowski claimed she was targeted for arrest because she had previously reported on brutality by the local police.

The First Amendment thus does not give the press special rights of access to disaster scenes or protect reporters from arrest and disorderly conduct charges when they fail to obey lawful commands of police at accident scenes. But at least three states—California, Ohio and Oregon—have statutes that carve out some (although not complete) protection for journalists gathering news in certain situations. California, for example, allows "duly authorized" members

---

47. *Special Force Ministries* v. *WCCO Television*, 584 N.W. 2d 789 (1998).
48. "Journalist Gets Probation."
49. Boyer appealed his conviction, and in April 2005 the local district attorney's office agreed to dismiss the case in exchange for Boyer's written apology to the police chief. "N.C. Reporter Apologizes; Charge Dismissed."

of "any news service, newspaper, or radio or television station or network" to enter areas closed by law enforcement due to a "flood, storm, fire, earthquake, explosion, accident or other disaster,"[50] while Oregon provides journalists with "reasonable access" to search and rescue areas.[51]

Grand juries work behind closed doors, and courts are very sensitive when anyone attempts to elicit information from the jurors about what has taken place. Any attempt to induce grand jurors to reveal secret testimony can surely be punished by the courts.

Taping and Recording   Many other laws may directly affect news gathering. And the First Amendment does not offer a shield to reporters who violate these, either. For example, in most states and the District of Columbia, a reporter can secretly record a conversation or interview with a news source. These are known as one-party consent states, since only one party to the conversation (the journalist taping it) needs to know it is being recorded. While 38 states and the District of Columbia fall into this journalist-friendly, one-party consent category, a dozen states require reporters to obtain permission from all parties in a conversation before recording (all-party consent states).[52] These laws prohibit anyone from secretly recording a conversation face-to-face, on the telephone or almost anywhere. For instance, California Penal Code Section 632 provides that a crime is committed by anyone (including a journalist) who

> intentionally and *without the consent of all parties* [emphasis added] to a confidential communication, by means of any electronic amplifying or recording device, eavesdrops upon or records the confidential communication, whether the communication is carried on among the parties in the presence of one another or by means of a telegraph, telephone, or other device, except a radio.

California courts have held that a "confidential communication" is one in which a party to the conversation has an objectively reasonable expectation that it is not being overheard or recorded.[53] A violation occurs at the moment the recording is made, *regardless* of whether the material recorded is later published or aired.

What law applies if a person calling from a one-party consent state records a conversation with a recipient who lives in an all-party consent state? In 2006, the Supreme Court of California held in *Kearney* v. *Salomon Smith Barney* that California's all-party consent statute applied and controlled when a caller from Georgia (a one-party consent state) secretly recorded a conversation with a California resident.[54] Maryland also holds that its all-party consent law controls when out-of-state callers record conversations.[55] Journalists calling into all-party consent states are wise to get permission before taping.

Nearly half the states and the federal government have laws prohibiting eavesdropping. A growing number of states also have statutes that prohibit secretly taking a video recording or still photograph of a person in a location where he or she has a reasonable expectation of privacy. These laws target video voyeurs, but they impact journalists and legitimate photographers.

---

50. California Penal Code § 409.5 (2007). See also Ohio Revised Code Annotated § 2917.13 (2006).
51. Oregon Revised Statute § 401.570 (2006).
52. The 12 all-party consent states are California, Connecticut, Florida, Illinois, Maryland, Massachusetts, Michigan, Montana, Nevada, New Hampshire, Pennsylvania and Washington.
53. *Flanagan* v. *Flanagan,* 41 P. 3d 575 (2002).
54. 39 Cal. 4th 95 (2006).
55. *Perry* v. *Maryland,* 357 Md. 37 (Md. Ct. App. 1999).

Anyone who hopes to practice journalism without violating the law needs to know the laws in his or her particular state that relate to news gathering. There are subtle differences among the state laws, and the statutes change from time to time. Awareness of the law is the best protection a reporter can have. A good resource on taping can be found online at the Reporters Committee for Freedom of the Press Web site at http://www.rcfp.org/taping.

SUMMARY

Gaining access to government-held information is a major problem for journalists and citizens alike. The law is not always helpful. Common law offers little assistance to people attempting to inspect government records. The U.S. Constitution was drafted when news gathering was not the central role of the press. There is little evidence that the right to gather news was intended to be guaranteed by the First Amendment. Federal courts have suggested that news and information gathering is entitled to some protection under the U.S. Constitution, but they have been stingy in granting such protection. The U.S. Supreme Court has limited the rights of reporters to gather information at prisons and jails to the same rights enjoyed by other citizens. Lower courts have found broader, albeit qualified, constitutional rights of access. Courts have not permitted, however, the use of the First Amendment to immunize reporters from legal consequences that result when the law is broken while news is being gathered. Many plaintiffs find it is easier to sue the press for how the news has been gathered than for libel or invasion of privacy. Suits for trespass, fraud, misrepresentation, failure to obey lawful orders and other causes of action are common.

THE FREEDOM OF INFORMATION ACT

Neither common law nor the Constitution has provided the clear and well-defined right of access to government information that most citizens believe is needed. Beginning in the early 1950s, there were concerted efforts by press and citizen lobbying groups to pass statutes that guarantee to public and press alike the right to inspect records and other information held by the government and to attend meetings held by public agencies. These laws now exist in almost every state. In addition, there are federal open-records and open-meetings laws. Let us look at the federal legislation first.

In 1966, after many years of hearings, testimony and work, Congress adopted the **Freedom of Information Act (FOIA)**, which was ostensibly designed to open up records and files long closed to public inspection. The documentary evidence left by Congress relating to the passage of this measure leaves little doubt that the purpose of this bill was to establish a general philosophy of the fullest possible disclosure of government-held records. The Senate Report's Purpose of the Bill section quotes James Madison:

> Knowledge will forever govern ignorance, and a people who mean to be their own governors, must arm themselves with the power knowledge gives. A popular government without popular information or the means of acquiring it, is but a prologue to a farce or a tragedy or perhaps both.[56]

Both the public and the press have accepted this philosophy.

56. U.S. Senate, *Clarifying and Protecting,* 2–3.

FOIA, now more than 40 years old, is a critical tool for journalists. Examples of the recent successful use of FOIA requests include:

■ The production in 2008 by the National Archives of Hillary Rodham Clinton's daily calendars showing her activities when she was first lady after a FOIA request was made by Judicial Watch, a conservative public interest group, nearly two years earlier.

■ The release in August 2009 to Bloomberg News by the Federal Reserve of records identifying the companies in the Fed's 11 emergency lending programs that were set up during the 2008–2009 financial crisis to prop up failing banks. The Manhattan Chief U.S. District Judge rejected the Fed's argument that the loan records weren't covered by FOIA because their disclosure would harm borrowers' competitive positions and lead to a possible run on the banks (i.e., people withdrawing all of their money because the bank is failing).

■ The release in 2007 of FBI files showing that former Chief Justice William Rehnquist, who served on the nation's high court from 1971 until his death in 2005, "took a powerful sedative during his first decade on the Supreme Court and grew so dependent on it that he became delusional and tried to escape from a hospital in his pajamas when he stopped taking the drug in 1981."[57]

FOIA fights for documents often are lengthy and expensive, even if they ultimately prove successful. For instance, a federal judge in 2008 found that the National Nuclear Security Administration (NNSA) had "engaged in a continuing pattern and practice of unlawful delay in responding" to FOIA requests dating back to 2004 for documents relating to radioactive waste and contamination from nuclear weapons production buried in a waste site at Sandia National Laboratories in Albuquerque, N.M.[58] Under FOIA rules, government agencies must answer requests for documents within 20 days after they are received. Judge Robert S. Brack wrote that "in light of the Kafkaesque review process adopted by [NNSA], it is not surprising that the delay in this case stretched many months beyond the statutorily-prescribed time frame." He blasted the agency's FOIA response process as "exceedingly complex," "labyrinthine" and certain to ensure delays.

Government agencies must answer requests for documents within 20 days after they are received.

A University of California, Irvine, professor named Jonathan Wiener gained access in late 2004 to the last 10 pages of an approximately 300-page file the FBI kept on the late Beatles member John Lennon.[59] The FBI maintained files on what it considered to be anti-government activists of the era, and from 1971 to 1972 it gathered data on Lennon, such as memos describing his donations to a group that planned to demonstrate at the 1972 Republican National Convention. Wiener filed his original FOIA request with the FBI back in 1983, and he received 248 pages from the file on Lennon 14 years later in 1997. In 2004 a federal judge ordered the FBI to release the last 10 pages to Wiener, but the government vowed to fight in the 9th U.S. Circuit Court of Appeals. Finally, in December 2006 after a federal mediator brokered a settlement, the 10 pages were released, prompting Wiener to wryly remark, "I doubt that Tony Blair's

---

57. Cooperman, "Sedative Withdrawal Made Rehnquist Delusional."
58. Memorandum Opinion and Order, *Citizen Action* v. *Department of Energy*, Case No. 06-0726 (Mar. 31, 2008).
59. Yi, "Professor Wins Release of Last FBI Data on Beatle."

government will launch a military strike on the U.S. in retaliation for the release of these documents. Today, we can see that the national security claims that the FBI has been making for 25 years were absurd from the beginning."[60]

MILLIONS OF REQUESTS MADE, MILLIONS OF DOLLARS SPENT

How many FOIA requests are made each year? The answer is literally millions and millions. According to the Office of Information and Privacy at the U.S. Department of Justice, the total number of FOIA requests received by all 15 federal departments and 77 federal agencies during fiscal year 2007 was 21,758,651. That was 346,080 more requests received than during fiscal year 2006.

What did it cost to process those requests in fiscal year 2007? The total cost of FOIA-related activities for all federal departments and agencies, as reported in annual FOIA reports, was an estimated $369,431,500. Of that whopping sum, more than $16 million was spent on costs related to litigation, while less than $11 million was recouped by the government in FOIA processing costs.

APPLYING THE LAW

The usefulness of any freedom of information act depends in no small part on the way the government chooses to interpret and apply it. Some observers said that George W. Bush had a greater penchant for secrecy than any recent president.

The terrorist attacks in New York and Washington, D.C., and the subsequent move to tighten homeland security had an immediate impact on the application of the federal freedom of information law. In October 2001 then Attorney General John Ashcroft ordered all agencies covered by the law to review more closely which documents they release under the law. The attorney general's policy permits agencies to withhold information on any "sound legal basis" and to carefully consider threats to national security and law enforcement effectiveness. In addition, government agencies began after Sept. 11, 2001, to remove information from their official Web sites, sites that are accessible to any Internet user. The kinds of data expunged included the location and operating status of nuclear power plants, maps of the nation's transportation infrastructure and information about chemicals used at industrial sites.

Upon taking office in January 2009, President Barack Obama issued a memorandum suggesting his administration would bring new openness to government and, in particular, to how it responds to FOIA requests. He declared:

> The Freedom of Information Act should be administered with a clear presumption: In the face of doubt, openness prevails. The Government should not keep information confidential merely because public officials might be embarrassed by disclosure, because errors and failures might be revealed, or because of speculative or abstract fears. Nondisclosure should

---

60. Weinstein, "FBI to Release Last of Its John Lennon Files."

> never be based on an effort to protect the personal interests of Government
> officials at the expense of those they are supposed to serve. In responding
> to requests under the FOIA, executive branch agencies (agencies) should
> act promptly and in a spirit of cooperation, recognizing that such agencies
> are servants of the public.[61]

Despite such rhetoric of transparency, secrecy still continued under the Obama administration. For instance, The New York Times filed a lawsuit in March 2009 after the U.S. Department of Treasury and the Federal Reserve repeatedly failed to meet deadlines in responding to FOIA requests for records relating to how taxpayer dollars were being spent under the federal government's $700 billion Troubled Asset Relief Program (TARP). Similarly, Fox Business News, which successfully sued the government under FOIA for TARP information in February 2009, received thousands of heavily redacted documents (documents in which words were blacked-out so as not to be read).

A blow to access advocates came when President George W. Bush signed into law the Homeland Security Act of 2002.[62] One of the most controversial provisions of this law is known as the Critical Information Infrastructure Act. It makes exempt from FOIA, as well as state and local disclosure laws, so-called critical infrastructure information that is voluntarily submitted to the federal government—specifically, to the Department of Homeland Security (DHS)—by private people and, more notably, business entities. What is the problem with this? As the San Francisco Chronicle opined in an editorial, the law "allows private parties to hide information about 'critical infrastructure'—including concerns about health and safety—simply by submitting the data voluntarily to the new department. The information could apply to privately operated power plants, bridges, dams, ports or chemical plants."[63] The new law also keeps private the name of the person or entity submitting the information.

The result, as Sen. Patrick Leahy (D-Vt.) observed, is the "most severe weakening of the Freedom of Information Act in its 36-year history" and "a big-business wish-list gussied up in security garb." In particular, the act encourages businesses to submit information concerning critical infrastructure information—defined broadly to include "information not customarily in the public domain and related to the security of critical infrastructure or protected systems"—not only by making that information exempt from FOIA and state disclosure laws but also by granting those companies immunity from "any civil action arising under Federal or State law if such information is submitted in good faith." It creates criminal penalties for anyone who discloses the submitted information. The potential for abuse is clear: Companies

---

61. Memorandum for the Heads of Executive Departments and Agencies, Freedom of Information Act, Office of the President, Jan. 21, 2009, available online at http://www.whitehouse.gov/the_press_office/ FreedomofInformationAct.

U.S. Attorney General Eric Holder issued a memorandum in March 2009 calling for openness when interpreting FOIA and encouraging "agencies to make discretionary disclosures of information. An agency should not withhold records merely because it can demonstrate, as a technical matter, that the records fall within the scope of a FOIA exemption." Memorandum for Heads of Executive Departments and Agencies, the Freedom of Information Act, Office of the Attorney General, Mar. 19, 2009, available online at http:// www.usdoj.gov/ag/foia-memo-march2009.pdf.

62. Public Law No. 107–296.

63. Editorial, "Reinforce Anti-Secrecy Law," A24.

may file information with the government to keep it out of the hands of the press and to shield themselves from lawsuits arising from wrongdoing that information otherwise exposes.

High-level policy decisions are not the only reason freedom of information laws often fail to work as they were intended. For whatever reason, most government bureaucrats at all levels find it extremely difficult to share the records they hold with the nation's citizens. Consequently, bizarre stories emerge as agencies try to block access to records that by all accounts should be made public. When former Associated Press correspondent Terry Anderson asked the FBI for access to material in his personal files that related to Arab terrorists who had held him hostage in Lebanon for six years, the agency refused, claiming that releasing the records would violate the terrorists' right of privacy. Public ridicule forced Attorney General Janet Reno to reverse the FBI on this point, but she still denied Anderson's request, citing national security reasons. The fact of the matter is that no administration since the Freedom of Information Act was adopted more than 40 years ago has truly invested sufficient time and energy to make it work the way it was envisioned. Only the dogged efforts of private citizens, scholars and journalists have occasionally broken down the walls between the bureaucracy and the citizenry it is supposed to serve.

ONCE DENIED, TWICE TRIED: DUPLICATIVE FOIA REQUESTS BY DIFFERENT PEOPLE

Imagine that Mr. Anderson makes a FOIA request for specific records from a government agency and the agency denies the request. Then, after suing the agency for the records, Mr. Anderson's request is rejected by a federal judge. Now Mr. Schement, who has no legal relationship to Mr. Anderson and who did not control, finance or otherwise participate in Mr. Anderson's unsuccessful lawsuit for the records, files his own separate FOIA request seeking the same documents from the same agency. Is Mr. Schement's request automatically precluded and denied because Mr. Anderson lost an earlier court battle for the same records? No, according to a 2008 U.S. Supreme Court ruling.[64] The outcome of the earlier lawsuit does not bar a repetitive request by a different person who has no legal relationship with the party who litigated the first case and who did not control or participate in that earlier suit. In allowing for such duplicative requests by independent people, the Supreme Court wrote that "our decisions emphasize the fundamental nature of the general rule that a litigant is not bound by a judgment to which she was not a party."

FOIA AND ELECTRONIC COMMUNICATION

By 2000 the vast majority of government records were created, transported and stored electronically. As computer technology replaced paper records, agencies within the federal government balked at allowing access to these electronic records. Most bureaucrats seemed to

---

64. *Taylor v. Sturgell*, 128 S. Ct. 2161 (2008).

hold the opinion that the electronic records were a special class of data, outside the range of FOIA and off limits to the public.[65] Officials argued that if they had to perform even simple computer programming to retrieve the information sought by the requester, the information fell outside the broad mandate of disclosure of FOIA. This mind-set was not confined to the lower echelons of the administration. High officials in both the first Bush and the Clinton administrations fought efforts by the National Security Archive to force the government to save electronic messages (e-mail) sent by computer. Officials in the Bush administration sought to erase from computer files all records of communications among officials during the eight years of the Reagan presidency. The case was still in the courts when Clinton was inaugurated in 1993 and his administration continued to argue the position taken by the Bush administration that the government had a right to dispose of this information as it saw fit. The U.S. Court of Appeals for the District of Columbia Circuit rejected this argument in August 1993, ruling that the government must preserve electronic messages and memos under the same standards that have always been applied to paper communications.[66]

In 1996 Congress finally adopted an amendment to the Freedom of Information Act that requires government agencies to apply the same standards of disclosure to electronic records that they have always applied to paper documents. This includes all e-mail correspondence as well as letters or notes. The Electronic Freedom of Information Act, as codified at 5 U.S.C. § 552 and known as e-FOIA, also establishes priorities that the agencies must apply when faced with multiple requests for computer searches for records. Top priority goes to FOIA requests in which a delay would threaten the life or safety of an individual. Next in line comes the news media and others in the business of disseminating information to the public. The new law also requires agencies to publish an online index of the documents they have and to make a reasonable attempt to provide documents in the requested format, that is, on tapes, diskettes, paper and so on. The law does not, however, define electronic information, instead leaving this important question to federal agencies and the courts.

In 2007 the National Security Archive at George Washington University issued a bad-news report finding that only about one in five federal agencies (21 percent) posted on the Web all four categories of records that e-FOIA specifically requires agencies to post. (The four required categories are opinions/orders of the agency, statements of the agency's policies, the agency's staff manuals and frequently requested records from the agency.) The archive also reported that only 36 percent of agencies provided the required indexes of records on their Web sites.[67] In addition, a scant 26 percent of federal agencies provided online forms for submitting FOIA requests. In brief, more than a decade after e-FOIA became law, it was not working.

REFORMING FOIA: THE OPEN GOVERNMENT ACT OF 2007

In December 2007 President Bush signed the first major amendments to FOIA in many years. The Openness Promotes Effectiveness in Our National Government Act

---

65. Morrissey, "FOIA Foiled?" 29.
66. *Armstrong* v. *Executive Office of the President,* 1 F. 3d 1274 (D.C. Cir. 1993).
67. National Security Archive, "File Not Found," available online at http://www.gwu.edu/~nsarchiv/NSAEBB/NSAEBB216/index.htm.

of 2007 (OPEN Government Act) did not alter the nine FOIA exemptions described in this chapter. Instead, it made several reforms designed to expedite processing of FOIA requests; help requesters more easily obtain better information about the status of their requests; and hold federal agencies more accountable if they fail to timely respond to requests. Specific changes included

- requiring government agencies to assign a tracking number for each FOIA request that will take more than 10 days to process and to establish a phone number or an Internet site to help requesters check the status of their requests.

- penalizing agencies that fail to timely comply with the 20-day window in which to respond to a FOIA request by not allowing those agencies to charge any search and duplication fees related to that request unless there are "unusual or exceptional circumstances" that justify the delay.

- allowing recovery of attorney fees and litigation costs to FOIA requesters who substantially prevail in FOIA lawsuits against government agencies if the requester either wins a court order for the records sought or if the government agency, in the midst of the lawsuit, voluntarily decides to stop fighting the request and to provide the records. In June 2009, the U.S. Court of Appeals for the D.C. Circuit held in *Summers* v. *Department of Justice* that the OPEN Government Act of 2007 does not apply retroactively when it comes to awarding attorney fees and litigation costs to prevailing plaintiffs challenging a FOIA denial.

- creating the Office of Government Information Services (OGIS) to serve as an ombudsperson and to mediate FOIA disputes as a nonexclusive alternative to litigation, including issuing advisory opinions if mediation does not resolve a dispute. The OGIS also is charged with both reviewing compliance by government agencies with FOIA's rules and making recommendations to Congress and the president on how to improve FOIA. A battle over the location of OGIS ensued in 2008, with Congress wanting it located at the National Archives and Records Administration (as the legislation called for) and President Bush wanting it housed at the Justice Department (a location some thought would jeopardize the independence of OGIS). In early 2009, however, President Barack Obama submitted his proposed 2010 budget, calling for $1 million to help fund OGIS and to locate it in the National Archives as originally intended. Miriam Nisbet was hired in 2009 to head OGIS, becoming the first person to fill the role of FOIA ombudsperson at the National Archives and Records Administration. She previously headed UNESCO's information society division in France.

In addition to these highlights, other reforms brought about by the OPEN Government Act of 2007 are described later in this chapter.

AGENCY RECORDS

The broad outlines of the federal Freedom of Information Act, the nine areas of exempted information, and suggested ways in which a journalist or citizen can use the law are sketched out in the next few pages. One can write an open-records law in two basic ways. The first way is to declare that the following kinds of records are to be accessible for public inspection and then list the kinds of records that are open. The second way is to proclaim that all government records are open for public inspection except the following kinds of records and then list the exceptions. Congress approved the second kind of law in 1966, and it went into effect in 1967. The law has been amended several times, with substantial changes being enacted in 1974, 1976, 1986 and 1996, as well as in 2002 with the adoption of the Homeland Security Act (page 323), which directly affects FOIA. FOIA was most recently amended in 2007 when, as noted in the preceding box, President Bush signed into law the OPEN Government Act of 2007.

What Is an Agency?

The U.S. Freedom of Information Act gives any person access to all the records kept by all federal agencies, unless the information falls into one of nine categories of exempted material. An agency has been defined under the law as

> any executive department, military department, government corporation, government-controlled corporation or other establishment in the executive branch of government (including the executive office of the president), or any independent regulatory agency.

The law governs records held by agencies in the executive branch of government and all the independent regulatory agencies like the **Federal Trade Commission (FTC),** the Federal Aviation Agency, the Nuclear Regulatory Commission, the Social Security Administration and the Securities and Exchange Commission. The law does not cover records held by Congress or the federal courts. Some agencies associated with the executive branch of government also fall outside the purview of the law. In 1985 the U.S. Court of Appeals for the District of Columbia Circuit ruled that the Council of Economic Advisors, which works closely with the president on economic matters, is not covered by the law because it exists solely to advise and assist the president and makes no policy on its own. The agency has no regulatory power; it cannot issue rules or regulations. Although FOIA does govern some operations in the executive office of the president, the law does not reach "the president's immediate personal staff or units in the executive office whose *sole function* is to advise and assist the president," the court ruled.[68]

A couple of quasi-governmental entities raise interesting questions as to whether they are agencies subject to FOIA. The Smithsonian Institution in Washington, D.C., for instance, is not a government agency and is not subject to FOIA, even though the vast majority of its budget comes from taxpayer dollars. After financial scandals and spending problems rocked the museum, however, a bill was introduced in Congress in 2008 to make it a government agency. To address these concerns and to fend off legislation, the Smithsonian responded in November 2008 by holding what The New York Times described as its "first public board

The law does not cover records held by Congress or the federal courts.

68. *Rushforth v. Council of Economic Advisors,* 762 F. 2d 1038 (1985).

meeting in its 162-year history . . . as part of its new commitment to openness and account-ability."[69] The Smithsonian also formally adopted in January 2009 a new policy, patterned after FOIA, to allow for the disclosure of more records.

In contrast to the Smithsonian, the U.S. Postal Service is considered a government agency and features its own FOIA Web site at http://www.usps.com/foia. Although Amtrak (the National Railroad Passenger Corporation) is a private corporation operated for profit and is not technically a government agency, it too is subject to FOIA, under provisions of the Rail Passenger Service Act. On the other hand, the Corporation for Public Broadcasting, a private, nonprofit corporation that was created by Congress in 1967, is not subject to FOIA.

What Is a Record?

Congress did not specify the physical characteristics of a record in the Freedom of Information Act. Certainly records are paper documents, e-mail and other computer-generated material.[70] But the term "record" also includes films, tapes and even three-dimensional objects such as evidence in a criminal prosecution. The FOIA statute provides that a record includes information "maintained by an agency in any format, including an electronic format." Importantly, the OPEN Government Act of 2007 expanded the description of a record to also include information "maintained for an agency by an entity under government contract." This change is key: It means that records held by outside private contractors working for the government are subject to FOIA requests.

Records held by outside private contractors working for the government are subject to FOIA requests.

What Is an Agency Record?

"Agency" has been defined under the law; so has "record." What is an agency record? It is not, unfortunately, simply a combination of the definition of these two terms. In this case the whole, the term "agency record," involves a good deal more than the sum of its parts. Courts have established the following definition of an agency record:

If the record is either created or obtained by an agency, and the record is under agency control at the time of the FOIA request, it is very likely an agency record.

If the agency has created the document but does not possess or control it, it is not an agency record.

If the agency merely possesses the document but has not created it, it might be an agency record, or it might not. If the agency came into possession of the document as a part of its official duties, it is probably an agency record. If it just happens to have the document, it is probably not an agency record.

In 2009 U.S. District Judge Royce C. Lamberth held that White House visitor logs are public records subject to FOIA since they are under the legal "control" of a government agency, U.S. Department of Homeland Security (DHS), even if they are transferred to the

---

69. Pogrebin, "At Public Board Meeting, Smithsonian Practices New Openness."
70. *Long* v. *IRS,* 596 F. 2d 362 (1979).

White House or the Office of the Vice President and destroyed or deleted from DHS' internal files.[71] The Secret Service, which actually creates the records, is a division of DHS. Judge Lamberth also concluded that the logs do not fall within the scope of the presidential communications privilege and thus are not shielded from disclosure by FOIA Exemption 5 (see pages 333–335). In an earlier ruling in the same case,[72] he articulated four factors relevant in determining if an agency exercises sufficient "control" over a document to render it an "agency record":

1. The intent of the document's creator to retain or relinquish control over the records.

2. The ability of the agency to use and dispose of the record as it sees fit.

3. The extent to which agency personnel have read or relied upon the document.

4. The degree to which the document was integrated into the agency's record system or files.

FOIA EXEMPTIONS

A document or tape or file that has been determined to be an agency record accessible via the Freedom of Information Act may still be withheld from public inspection if it properly falls into one of the nine categories of exempted material. Please note, federal agencies *are not required* to withhold documents from disclosure simply because they are included in an exempted category.[73] The law simply says they may withhold such material. The nine exemptions outlined in the following pages are fairly specific, yet not specific enough to be free from substantial judicial interpretation. How a judge defines a word or phrase in these exemptions can result in a significant change in the meaning of the law and can lead to either expanded public access or, more likely in recent years, substantially reduced public access. We will examine each exemption separately, try to outline its meaning, and briefly explore case law that illuminates how the exemption is applied. It is important to remember that in light of the war on terror it is likely that many of these exemptions will be viewed even more broadly by government agencies and the courts.

Which of the following exemptions are used most by government agencies and departments? According to the Office of Information and Privacy at the U.S. Department of Justice, Exemption 6 (personal privacy) was the single exemption cited most often in fiscal year 2007. However, when all of the subsections under Exemption 7 (law enforcement purposes) are counted together, the total for Exemption 7 far exceeded that of Exemption 6. But the exemptions themselves are not the only reasons requests are denied. In particular, 64 of all federal departments and agencies cited "no records" as the most often used reason for nondisclosure in fiscal year 2007. Under the OPEN Government Act of 2007, when a government agency

Federal agencies are not required *to withhold documents from disclosure simply because they are included in an exempted category.*

---

71. *Citizens for Responsibility and Ethics in Washington* v. *U.S. Department of Homeland Security*, 2009 WL 50149 (D.D.C. Jan. 9, 2009). Another recent opinion related to White House visitor logs is *Judicial Watch, Inc.* v. *U.S. Secret Service*, 579 F. Supp. 2d 182 (D.D.C. 2008).

72. *Citizens for Responsibility and Ethics in Washington* v. *U.S. Department of Homeland Security*, 527 F. Supp. 2d 76 (D.D.C. 2007).

73. See *Chrysler Corp.* v. *Brown,* 441 U.S. 281 (1979).

deletes or redacts part of the material provided to a requester, it must indicate directly "on the released portion of the record" the amount of information deleted, as well as "the exemption under which the deletion is made."

EXEMPTIONS TO DISCLOSURE UNDER THE FREEDOM OF INFORMATION ACT

1. National security matters
2. Housekeeping materials
3. Material exempted by statute
4. Trade secrets
5. Working papers/lawyer–client privileged materials
6. Personal privacy files
7. Law enforcement records
8. Financial institution materials
9. Geological data

National Security

Exemption 1: Matters specifically authorized under criteria established by an executive order to be kept secret in the interest of national defense or foreign policy and in fact properly classified pursuant to such an executive order. This exemption deals with a wide range of materials, but primarily with information related to national security and national defense, intelligence gathering and foreign relations. The system has a three-tier classification. Material, the release of which could reasonably be expected to damage national security, is classified as "confidential," the lowest level of classification. The "secret" classification is used to shield material that if disclosed could be expected to cause serious damage to national security. "Top secret," the highest level of classification, is reserved for material that if revealed could be expected to cause exceptionally grave damage to national security.[74]

Although government agencies have the burden to justify nondisclosure under any FOIA exemption, courts applying Exemption 1 give substantial deference and weight to agency affidavits implicating national security. In fact, they rule in favor of the government on Exemption 1 if an agency's affidavits (1) describe justifications for nondisclosure in reasonably specific detail; (2) demonstrate the information withheld logically falls within the claimed exemption; and (3) are not contradicted by evidence in the record or by evidence of agency bad faith. Applying this test in 2006, a federal judge held that the Department of Defense was protected under Exemption 1 from disclosing photographs of past and present detainees at the U.S. facility at Guantanamo Bay, Cuba. Among other things, the judge accepted the government's claim that public disclosure of the photos "would both increase the risk of retaliation against the detainees

---

74. Executive Order No. 12958, 3 C.F.R. 333 (1996).

and their families and exacerbate the detainees' fears of reprisal, thus reducing the likelihood that detainees would cooperate in intelligence-gathering efforts."[75]

Housekeeping Practices

Exemption 2: Matters related solely to the internal personnel rules and practices of an agency. Exemption 2 shields two types of records from disclosure. First, it protects agencies from the burden of producing records about internal agency workings that are trivial and of no public interest. Such trivial administrative data include employee work schedules, coffee break rules, personnel parking lot assignments and sick leave policies. As the Supreme Court wrote in 1976, Exemption 2 "relieve[s] agencies of the burden of assembling and maintaining for public inspection matter in which the public could not reasonably be expected to have an interest."[76]

Second, Exemption 2 safeguards predominantly internal documents, the disclosure of which may significantly risk the circumvention of a legal requirement such as agency regulations or statutes. Put differently, these risk-of-circumvention documents are predominantly internal but relate to matters of a more substantial nature. For instance, in 2006 a federal judge ruled against a FOIA request by the Los Angeles Times seeking records of the names of private security contractors (private groups hired to provide security for the U.S. government, construction contractors and others in Iraq) that filed Serious Incident Reports (SIRs) with the U.S. military. SIRs document private security contractors' involvement in or observation of life-threatening events, including hostile interactions with insurgents. Citing Exemption 2, the judge initially found that "SIRs are compiled for predominantly internal purposes: to provide intelligence information to the military." He then held that releasing the names of security contractors "would risk circumvention of the law and the military's efforts to establish stability for reconstruction efforts in Iraq."[77] Specifically, the judge cited favorably a government affidavit that claimed "releasing contractor names would enable insurgent forces to conduct unlawful activities and avoid detection by identifying specific responses and locations with specific contractors and focusing on those believed to be more vulnerable."

The Justice Department claims that, since Sept. 11, 2001, Exemption 2 has "fundamental importance to homeland security." It contends that broad new categories of homeland-security-related information fall under Exemption 2 such as information that could reveal identity of informants and "unclassified but sensitive" materials such as those revealing "critical infrastructure."[78]

Statutory Exemption

Exemption 3: Matters specifically exempted from disclosure by statute (other than section 552b of this title) provided that such statute (a) requires that the matters be withheld from the public in such a manner as to leave no discretion on the issue, or

---

75. *Associated Press* v. *U.S. Department of Defense,* 462 F. Supp. 2d 573 (S.D. N.Y. 2006).
76. *Air Force* v. *Rose,* 425 U.S. 352, 369–70 (1976).
77. *Los Angeles Times* v. *Department of Army,* 442 F. Supp. 2d 880 (C.D. Cal. 2006).
78. "U.S. Department of Justice, Freedom of Information Act Guide & Privacy Act Overview," available online at http://www.usdoj.gov/oip/exemption2.htm#initial.

(b) establishes particular criteria for withholding or refers to particular types of matters to be withheld. This exemption is designed to protect from disclosure information required or permitted to be kept secret by scores of other federal laws. A wide range of records fall under this exemption, including Census Bureau records, public utility information, trade secrets, patent applications, tax returns, bank records, veterans benefits and documents held by both the CIA and the National Security Agency.

Courts generally ask three questions when determining whether Exemption 3 applies to a specific record or document:

1. Is there a specific statute that authorizes or requires the withholding of information?
2. Does the statute designate specific kinds of information or outline specific criteria for information that may be withheld?
3. Does the record or information that is sought fall within the categories of information that may be withheld?

If all three questions are answered yes, disclosure can be legally denied.

The CIA has managed to use this exemption to almost completely shield its operations from public scrutiny.

Via congressional action and numerous court rulings the CIA has managed to use this exemption to almost completely shield its operations from public scrutiny. In 1984 Congress voted to exempt all CIA operational files from release under the Freedom of Information Act. In 1985 the Supreme Court ruled that records relating to CIA-funded research from 1952 to 1966 at 80 universities to study the effects of mind-altering substances on humans were off-limits to public inspection. A lawyer named John Sims wanted to see the names of the schools and the individuals who had participated in the research projects. The agency argued that the names were exempt from disclosure because, under a 1947 law, the names of intelligence sources cannot be disclosed by the CIA. The Supreme Court agreed and ruled that the director of the spy agency had broad authority under the 1947 National Security Act to protect all sources of information, confidential or not.[79]

An appellate court held the Bureau of Alcohol, Tobacco, Firearms and Explosives did not need to produce, per Exemption 3, to the City of Chicago records held in ATF databases about the sale and recovery of firearms. The court held that provisions in a 2005 federal appropriations act specifying the ATF's firearm databases were "immune from legal process" and "not . . . subject to subpoena or other discovery in any civil action" and were intended "to cut off access to the databases for any reason not related to law enforcement." Chicago wanted the records not for law enforcement but to help in a civil action it filed against gun makers and dealers for creating a public nuisance.[80]

Trade Secrets

Exemption 4: Trade secrets and commercial or financial information obtained from any person and privileged or confidential. Two kinds of information are exempt from disclosure under this exemption—trade secrets and financial or commercial information. The trade secret exemption has not been heavily litigated. In 1983 the U.S. Court of Appeals for the District

---

79. *Sims* v. *CIA,* 471 U.S. 159 (1985). Sims today is a constitutional law professor at the University of the Pacific McGeorge School of Law in Sacramento, Calif.
80. *City of Chicago* v. *U.S. Department of Treasury,* 423 F. 3d 777 (7th Cir. 2005).

of Columbia Circuit fashioned a definition of a trade secret that considerably narrowed the exemption. In litigation initiated by Ralph Nader's Public Citizen Health Research Group, the court said a trade secret is "an unpatented, commercially valuable plan, appliance, formula, or process which is used for the making, preparing, compounding, treating, or processing of articles or materials which are trade commodities, and that can be said to be the end product of either innovation or substantial effort."[81]

The "commercial or financial information" part of Exemption 4 applies not only to records that reveal basic commercial operations or relate to the income-producing aspects of a business, but also more broadly to situations "when the provider of the information has a commercial interest in the information submitted to the agency."[82] For example, a federal appellate court held that a nonprofit organization's reports submitted to the federal Nuclear Regulatory Commission that described the operations of its members' nuclear power plants contained commercial information.[83] The court found that the "commercial fortunes" of the organization's member utilities "could be materially affected by the disclosure of health and safety problems experienced during the operation of nuclear power facilities."

Working Papers/Discovery

Exemption 5: Interagency and intra-agency memorandums and letters which would not be available by law to a party other than an agency in litigation with the agency. This exemption shields two kinds of materials from disclosure. The first are best described as working papers: studies, reports, memoranda and other sorts of documents that are prepared and circulated to assist government personnel make a final report, an agency policy or a decision of some kind. For Exemption 5 to apply to such documents used in the decision-making processes of an agency, the documents typically must be (1) pre-decisional (used before a decision is made by the agency); and (2) deliberative (the documents must play a direct part in the deliberative process of making recommendations and decisions). This section of the law also exempts from disclosure communications between an agency and its attorney, material that is traditionally protected by the attorney-client privilege. (In any lawsuit, communications between an attorney and a client are private.)

Sometimes documents generated to help formulate a policy become the basis for that policy and are noted or discussed in the final decision or policy statement. The Supreme Court ruled in 1975 that Exemption 5 cannot be used to shield such documents. Once the decision has been made, the court said, public disclosure of these materials cannot damage the decision-making process.[84]

The second part of the exemption protects from public disclosure material that would not normally be open to inspection in a civil legal proceeding. There is something called the discovery process that is a part of all litigation. Through discovery one party is able to gain access to evidence, testimony and other kinds of material possessed by the other party. But some kinds of material are not accessible through this discovery process. When a private person consults

---

81. *Public Citizen Health Research Group* v. *Food and Drug Administration,* 704 F. 2d 1280 (1983).
82. *Baker & Hostetler LLP* v. *U.S. Department of Commerce,* 473 F. 3d 312 (D.C. Cir. 2006).
83. *Critical Mass Energy Project* v. *Nuclear Regulatory Commission,* 830 F. 2d 278 (D.C. Cir. 1987).
84. *NLRB* v. *Sears, Roebuck and Company,* 421 U.S. 132 (1973).

an attorney and discusses matters relevant to a lawsuit, what is said during those conversations is confidential. The attorney cannot be forced to reveal the substance of the conversation. Similarly, most documents that pass between the client and the attorney are considered confidential or privileged. Thus, in addition to attorney-client privileged communications, documents considered the "work product" of an attorney (those prepared by an attorney in the course of litigation or in contemplation of litigation that is reasonably regarded as inevitable under the circumstances) are generally exempt. This part of Exemption 5 shields the same kinds of conversations and materials that are generated between a federal agency and its attorneys.

In 2001 the Supreme Court limited the scope of Exemption 5 when it said communication between a group of Native-American tribes and the Bureau of Indian Affairs, a government agency that represents the United States in the nation's relationships with the tribes, was not covered by Exemption 5. The issue focused on a dispute about the allocation of water from the Klamath River Basin in Oregon and northern California. A group of irrigators filed a series of FOIA requests to see copies of correspondence between the tribes and the BIA regarding water issues. The government rejected the request, claiming that because of the special relationship between the tribes and the BIA, the records should be protected under Exemption 5 in much the same way that correspondence between lawyers and clients is protected. The Supreme Court, in a unanimous ruling, rejected this argument. Justice David Souter wrote for the court that although there are surely exceptions to the general rule of public disclosure mandated by the Freedom of Information Act, these exceptions are to be applied narrowly. "All of this boils down to requesting that we read an 'Indian trust' exemption into the statute, a reading that is out of the question," Souter wrote. The court also rejected the notion that the communication between the tribes and the BIA was comparable to communication between an agency and an outside consultant, material that is sometimes regarded as interagency or intra-agency memoranda.[85]

Exemption 5 also includes an **executive privilege** doctrine related to the president, including a presidential communications privilege.[86] Details are complex, but three points are key. First, these privileges are not absolute. Second, while the "Executive Office of the President" is an agency subject to FOIA, the "Office of the President" (the president's immediate key advisers, such as the chief of staff and White House counsel, who have significant responsibility for investigating and formulating presidential advice) is not subject to FOIA. Finally, as an appellate court observed in 2004, the confines of the presidential communications privilege are construed narrowly, balancing a president's need for confidentiality and frank advice with the obligations of open government.[87]

President Richard Nixon tried to argue that access to the infamous White House tapes that played a critical role in the Watergate scandal should be protected by an absolute executive privilege. The Supreme Court ruled that the absolute privilege was developed to protect military and diplomatic secrets. A qualified privilege might be applicable in other situations, but in those cases the need for confidentiality must be balanced against other values. In this case, the need for the tapes in a criminal investigation outweighed the need for secrecy, the court said.[88]

---

85. *Department of the Interior* v. *Klamath Water Users,* 532 U.S. 1 (2001).
86. See *Judicial Watch, Inc.* v. *Department of Justice,* 365 F. 3d 1108 (D.C. Cir. 2004).
87. Ibid.
88. *U.S.* v. *Nixon,* 418 U.S. 683 (1974).

In 2008, a federal court held that Exemption 5's presidential communications privilege protected from disclosure 68 pages of e-mails sent between officials in the White House and the Department of Justice relating to the controversial termination and dismissal of several U.S. attorneys while Alberto Gonzales was attorney general.[89] The Justice Department claimed the e-mails pertained "to matters such as responding to an upcoming Congressional hearing, formulating official responses to inquiries from outside the Executive Branch, suggesting a plan of action for the appointment of a U.S. Attorney or conferring on issues arising from such appointments, recommending revisions to documents, and planning for the hiring of new Department personnel." Such decision-making materials were protected because the presidential communications privilege sweeps up both final and postdecisional materials, as well as predeliberative ones, and it extends to the president's immediate advisers and documents not actually reviewed by the president.

Personal Privacy

Exemption 6: Personnel and medical files and similar files the disclosure of which would constitute a clearly unwarranted invasion of privacy. This exemption shields "personnel and medical files and similar files." Personnel files and medical files are fairly easy to identify. Courts have had more of a problem determining the nature of a "similar file." The key consideration is not the kind of file at issue, but the kind of information in the file that is the object of the FOIA request. An individual's medical and personnel files contain highly personal information about an individual. A file is a "similar file" if it contains this same kind of personal information.[90] Not every file that contains personal information will be considered a similar file. "The test is not merely whether the information is in some sense personal," a U.S. Court of Appeals ruled, "but whether it is of the same magnitude—as highly personal in nature—as contained in personnel or medical records."[91]

In the late 1980s The New York Times sought access to the voice communications tape recorded aboard the space shuttle Challenger just before it exploded in January 1987. The National Aeronautics and Space Administration argued that the tape was shielded from disclosure because it contained personal information similar to that contained in personnel and medical files. Both the U.S. District Court[92] and a panel of judges on the U.S. Court of Appeals[93] ruled that the tape contained nothing as personal as material in personnel or medical files. But the government petitioned for a rehearing of the case by the full membership of the appellate court, and in a 6-5 ruling the appellate court overturned the earlier decisions. "While the taped words do not contain information about the personal lives of the astronauts, disclosure of the file would reveal the sound and inflection of the crew's voices during the last seconds of their lives," the court said. The information recorded through the capture of a person's voice is distinct and is in addition to the information contained in the words themselves, the six judges noted.[94]

89. *Democratic National Committee* v. *Department of Justice*, 539 F. Supp. 2d 363 (D.D.C. 2008).
90. *State Department* v. *Washington Post*, 456 U.S. 595 (1982).
91. *Kurzon* v. *Health and Human Services*, 649 F. 2d 65 (1981).
92. *New York Times* v. *NASA*, 679 F. Supp. 33 (1987).
93. *New York Times* v. *NASA*, 852 F. 2d 602 (1988).
94. *New York Times* v. *NASA*, 970 F. 2d 1002 (1990).

A ruling that a file is a medical or personnel or similar file does not automatically bar the release of data in the file. Establishing that the information or material sought is the kind of information protected by Exemption 6 is just the first step. The court must then determine that

1. the release of this information will constitute an invasion of personal privacy, *and*
2. this invasion of personal privacy is clearly unwarranted.

The Supreme Court made it clear in 1976 that exemption is not intended to preclude every incidental invasion of privacy, but rather "only such disclosures as constitute clearly unwarranted invasions of personal privacy."[95] The government normally carries the burden of proof that the release of the information will amount to an unwarranted invasion of privacy. But this burden is not a terribly heavy one. For example, a U.S. District Court accepted government arguments that the release of the voice communications tape-recorded aboard the space shuttle Challenger would be an unwarranted invasion of privacy.[96] The ruling was made despite the fact that a printed transcript of the tape had been previously released.

In 2008 a federal appellate court held that the privacy interests protected by Exemption 6 outweighed any public interest in releasing to the Associated Press (AP) petitions sent by John Walker Lindh, the so-called American Taliban, to the Office of the Pardon Attorney seeking to reduce his 20-year prison sentence after he pled guilty to aiding the Taliban in Afghanistan.[97] In describing the privacy interests at stake, the appellate court noted that "a Petition for Commutation of Sentence requires the applicant to provide his name, social security number, date and place of birth, criminal record, conviction information, information about any post-conviction relief sought, a detailed account of the circumstances surrounding the offense, and a detailed explanation of the reasons clemency should be granted." The court then had to address "whether Lindh's privacy interest outweighs any public interest that would be served by disclosure of the documents." Observing that the AP had presented no evidence to refute a Justice Department filing asserting that Lindh's petition had nothing to do with any alleged government misconduct, the appellate court concluded that the "AP has failed to demonstrate that disclosure of Lindh's petition would serve a cognizable public purpose such that it may not be withheld." The court also observed that the privacy concerns in Exemption 7(c), discussed later in this chapter, would prevent the disclosure of Lindh's petitions.

In 2009 the 2nd U.S. Circuit Court of Appeals held that Exemption 6 allowed the Department of Defense to redact, from two personal letters sent via the Red Cross by family members of detainees held at Guantanamo Bay to their loved ones, the names and addresses of the detainees' family members.[98] The families' letters had been submitted by the detainees at their Administrative Review Board hearings, where they testified against the Taliban. The appellate court initially determined the letters, which were requested by the AP, constituted "similar files" within the meaning of Exemption 6, reasoning that the term "has a broad meaning and encompasses the government's records on an individual which can be identified as applying to that individual." It then held that "disclosing the family members' names and addresses to the AP, and consequently to the public at large, involves a measurable privacy

---

95. *Department of the Air Force* v. *Rose,* 425 U.S. 352 (1976).
96. *New York Times* v. *NASA,* 782 F. Supp. 628 (1991).
97. *Associated Press* v. *Department of Justice*, 549 F. 3d 62 (2d Cir. 2008).
98. *Associated Press* v. *Department of Defense*, 554 F. 3d 274 (2d Cir. 2009).

interest because the information that would be revealed by disclosure is the type of information that a person would ordinarily not wish to make known about himself or herself." The court reasoned that "the names and addresses of the family members, if disclosed, would reveal that particular persons are relatives of certain detainees held at Guantanamo Bay" and "would also reveal that the family members are relatives of certain Guantanamo Bay detainees who testified about the Taliban." The government claimed that this, in turn, could jeopardize the physical safety of the family members, who might be retaliated against by the Taliban. Next, the court balanced this privacy interest against what it called "FOIA's basic purpose of opening agency action to the light of public scrutiny," remarking that "whether Exemption 6 applies requires balancing an individual's right to privacy against the preservation of FOIA's basic purpose of opening agency action to the light of public scrutiny." The AP claimed the family members' identifying information was necessary to see whether the Department of Defense properly followed up on claims of mistaken identity by the detainees. The court, however, ruled in favor of the Department of Defense and concluded that "disclosing names and addresses of the family members would constitute a clearly unwarranted invasion of the family members' privacy interest because such disclosure would not shed any light on DOD's action in connection with the detainees' claims at issue here."

Law Enforcement

Exemption 7: Records or information compiled for law enforcement purposes, but only to the extent that the production of such law enforcement records or information (a) could reasonably be expected to interfere with enforcement proceedings, (b) would deprive a person of a right to a fair trial or an impartial adjudication, (c) could reasonably be expected to constitute an unwarranted invasion of personal privacy, (d) could reasonably be expected to disclose the identity of a confidential source, including a state, local or foreign agency or authority or any private institution which furnished information on a confidential basis, and, in the case of a record or information compiled by criminal law enforcement authority in the course of a criminal investigation or by an agency conducting a lawful national security intelligence investigation, information furnished by confidential source, (e) would disclose techniques and procedures for law enforcement investigations or prosecutions, or would disclose guidelines for law enforcement investigations or prosecutions if such disclosure could reasonably be expected to risk circumvention of the law, or (f) could reasonably be expected to endanger the life or physical safety of any individual.

Exemption 7 provides an agency a broad exception to the general rule of access. Like Exemption 6, Exemption 7 requires a two-tiered test in its application. The first tier or question (what lawyers and judges often call the threshold question) is this: Was the information or record sought compiled for law enforcement purposes?

If the government is unable to show that the records were compiled for law enforcement purposes, the exemption does not apply. But the courts are generally willing to grant the government wide latitude in applying this test. The key question is whether the information is being used for law enforcement purposes when the response to the FOIA inquiry is sent to the person seeking the data.

Law enforcement agencies, however, are not given carte blanche discretion to designate any record they choose as one gathered for law enforcement purposes. Seth Rosenfeld sued the Department of Justice and the FBI to gain access to records of FBI investigations of faculty, students and journalists at the University of California in the early 1960s when the so-called Free Speech Movement challenged the university administration's regulations barring political activities on campus. The federal agencies argued that the material had been gathered for the purpose of examining whether the student movement had been captured from within by communists. The U.S. Court of Appeals for the 9th Circuit agreed that although some of the material sought by Rosenfeld had indeed been gathered for legitimate law enforcement purposes, other records were gathered long after the need for such an investigation ceased to exist. The law enforcement purpose argument was only a pretext, the court said, invoked to pursue routine monitoring of many individuals and to shield the harassment of the political opponents of the FBI.[99]

Information compiled for law enforcement purposes may still be accessible under the Freedom of Information Act. The court next must determine whether the release of the material would result in one of the six consequences outlined in *a* through *f* in the exemption; for example, would the release of the information be expected to interfere with law enforcement proceedings or deprive a person of a right to a fair trial?

Congress amended Exemption 7 in 1986 and gave federal law enforcement agencies far broader authority to refuse FOIA requests. Courts have read the exemption in an expansive manner, giving the FBI, the Secret Service, the Drug Enforcement Administration and other federal police agencies even more legal excuses to deny access to information they possess. For example, in 1989 the Supreme Court agreed that the release of computerized arrest records (often called "rap sheets") held by the FBI could reasonably be expected to constitute an unwarranted invasion of personal privacy. The rap sheets contain information indicating arrests, indictments, acquittals, convictions and sentences on about 24 million people in the nation. Some of this material is highly sensitive, but much of it has been publicized previously when individuals were being processed by the criminal justice system. In addition, all of these data are available from state and local law enforcement agencies across the nation. The FBI has simply put together all the bits and pieces of data about an individual held by various police agencies into a single, computerized file.

CBS reporter Robert Schnake sought such information from the FBI on Charles Medico. The agency denied the request, citing the personal privacy factor in Exemption 7. A U.S. District Court supported the agency, saying the material sought by Schnake would be personal to Medico. But the U.S. Court of Appeals for the District of Columbia Circuit reversed this decision, noting that the government cannot assert a privacy interest in records it holds when the records are already available from state and local authorities.[100] The Supreme Court reversed this ruling in a 9-0 decision. The privacy interest in a rap sheet is substantial, wrote Justice John Paul Stevens for the court. "The substantial character of that interest is affected by the fact that in today's society the computer can accumulate and store information that would have otherwise surely been forgotten long before a person attains the age of 80, when the F.B.I.'s rap sheets are discarded," Stevens added. Federal computers, he said, make easily available information that would be difficult to obtain by other means. "Plainly there is a vast difference between the public records that might be found after a diligent search of courthouse

99. *Rosenfeld* v. *U.S. Department of Justice,* 57 F. 3d 803 (1995).
100. *Reporters Committee for Freedom of the Press* v. *Justice Department,* 816 F. 2d 730 (1987).

files, county archives, and local police stations throughout the county and a computerized summary located in a single clearinghouse of information," Stevens noted.[101]

The U.S. Supreme Court held in 2004 in *National Archives & Records Administration* v. *Favish* that Exemption 7(c) prevented the release to Allan Favish of certain death-scene photographs of Vincent Foster Jr., deputy counsel to President Bill Clinton.[102] Favish wanted the photos because he questioned the government's finding that Foster's death was a suicide; he believed the government's investigations of Foster's death were "grossly incomplete and untrustworthy" (Favish's beliefs are found on his Web site at http://www.allanfavish.com/foster.htm). Foster's family members, however, objected to the release of the photos. They contended their own personal privacy interests would be harmed by such release, and thus they argued the photos were shielded by Exemption 7(c) to secure what the Supreme Court called "their own refuge from a sensation-seeking culture for their own peace of mind and tranquility."

Exemption 7(c) prevented the release to Allan Favish of certain death-scene photographs.

In ruling for Foster's immediate relatives, the high court initially held that Exemption 7(c) permits surviving family members to assert their own privacy rights against public intrusions when it comes to death-scene images of their immediate relatives. The court then turned to whether the release of the photos would be an unwarranted intrusion on the privacy rights of those family members. Justice Anthony Kennedy wrote for the court:

> Where there is a privacy interest protected by Exemption 7(c) and the public interest being asserted is to show that responsible officials acted negligently or otherwise improperly in the performance of their duties, the requester must establish more than a bare suspicion in order to obtain disclosure. Rather, the requester [Favish] must produce evidence that would warrant a belief by a reasonable person that the alleged Government impropriety might have occurred.

The court concluded Allan Favish had not met this burden, finding that he had "not produced any evidence that would warrant a belief by a reasonable person that the alleged Government impropriety might have occurred to put the balance into play."

The *Favish* opinion ranks as an important victory for privacy rights advocates and a blow to access supporters, including journalists. A statutory right to privacy now has been extended to protect the privacy interests of surviving family members of a deceased individual. Recall from Chapter 7 that "only people enjoy protection for their right to privacy". After the *Favish* opinion, and in the very limited but important context of FOIA actions, this now means that the relatives of dead people enjoy protection for their right to privacy in some circumstances. It is important to note the limitations of the decision in *Favish*. In particular, the Supreme Court did not create a general "survivor right of privacy" for purposes of other contexts or tort-based privacy lawsuits (see Chapters 7 and 8). Rather, the court engaged in the very precise and limited practice of statutory construction when it interpreted the meaning of a single statutory FOIA exemption, namely 7(c). As attorneys might put it, the holding in the *Favish* opinion was "narrow."

The narrowness of the *Favish* conclusion is suggested by a federal court's 2005 decision in *Showler* v. *Harper's Magazine* involving a father who claimed that an open-casket

---

101. *Justice Department* v. *Reporters Committee,* 109 S. Ct. 1486 (1989).
102. 541 U.S. 157 (2004).

© AP/Wide World Photos

photograph of his deceased son taken at a public funeral and published in a magazine violated the father's right of privacy.[103] The judge in *Showler* found *Favish* distinguishable because the photo in the open casket was "taken at a public, newsworthy event. The scene documented in the photograph was the same scene the funeral attendees observed." In 2007 an appellate court upheld the dismissal of the father's lawsuit in *Showler,* noting that "*Favish* is inapplicable to this analysis because it relies on a statutory privacy right under the FOIA, not a cause of action for invasion of privacy."[104]

Financial Records

Exemption 8: Matters contained in or related to examination, operating, or condition reports prepared by, on behalf of, or for the use of any agency responsible for the regulation and supervision of financial institutions. This is a little-used exemption that is designed to prevent the disclosure of sensitive financial reports or audits that, if made public, might undermine the public confidence in banks, trust companies, investment banking firms and other financial institutions.

---

103. 34 M.L.R. 2524 (E.D. Okla. 2005).
104. *Showler* v. *Harper's Magazine Foundation,* 35 M.L.R. 1577 (10th Cir. 2007).

In 2007 a federal court held that the U.S. Securities and Exchange Commission had successfully asserted Exemption 8 to withhold documents relating to an SEC investigation of Charles Schwab Corporation and Nucor Corporation.[105] The court initially found that the "purpose underlying Exemption 8 is to ensure financial institutions' security" and that "Congress also enacted Exemption 8 to promote communication between banks and regulating agencies." It then held that Exemption 8 protected the requested documents because they "were produced in connection with an ongoing SEC examination or investigation and provide insight into the information and entities the SEC attorneys were examining and investigating."

Geological Data

Exemption 9: Geological and geophysical information and data, including maps concerning wells. People who drill oil and gas wells provide considerable information about these wells to the government. This exemption prevents speculators and other drillers from gaining access to this valuable information.

HANDLING FOIA REQUESTS

Filing a FOIA request is a relatively simple matter. For instance, the Reporters Committee for Freedom of the Press has an online request letter generator on its Web site at http://www.rcfp.org/foi_letter/generate.php. Government agencies also provide extensive online information about filing FOIA requests. For example, the U.S. Department of Justice maintains a link on its Web site at http://www.usdoj.gov/oip/index.html devoted to the Freedom of Information Act.

Government departments must answer requests for records and documents within 20 business days. A journalist can, however, ask for an "expedited review" if there is an urgent need for the information. A requester is entitled to an expedited review if he or she is a person primarily engaged in disseminating information and there is an urgency to inform the public about an actual or alleged governmental activity. If an appeal is filed after a denial, the agency has only 20 days to rule on the appeal. Each agency must publish quarterly, or more frequently, an index of the documents and records it keeps.

Government departments must answer requests for records and documents within 20 business days.

Agencies are required to report to Congress each year and must include in the report a list of the materials to which access was granted and to which access was denied and the costs incurred. The OPEN Government Act of 2007 also requires that, in addition to reporting the median number of days required to process requests, government agencies provide the "average number of days for the agency to respond to a request beginning on the date on which the request was received by the agency, the median number of days for the agency to respond to such requests, and the range in number of days for the agency to respond to such requests." In addition, in a way of shaming foot-dragging agencies into compliance, government agencies

---

105. *Gavin* v. *Securities and Exchange Commission*, 2007 U.S. Dist. LEXIS 62252 (D. Minn. Aug. 23, 2007). The SEC has successfully asserted Exemption 8 in other matters. See *Bloomberg* v. *Securities and Exchange Commission*, 357 F. Supp. 2d 156 (D.D.C. 2004) (holding the interests behind Exemption 8 "would undeniably be served by exempting documents summarizing a meeting at which financial institutions were encouraged to engage in a candid assessment of industry problems and discussions regarding potential self-regulatory responses").

must now report their 10 oldest pending requests. If a citizen or a reporter has to go to court to get the agency to release materials and the agency loses the case, the agency may be assessed the cost of the complainant's legal fees and court costs. FOIA allows a court to award reasonable attorney fees to a plaintiff who has "substantially prevailed" in a FOIA lawsuit against a government agency, although a court is not required to grant such fees. In other words, even if a plaintiff is eligible to obtain attorney fees, he or she may not be entitled to them. In determining if a prevailing plaintiff is entitled to them, courts often consider and weigh four factors: (1) the public benefit derived from the case (will, for instance, the released information help the public in making vital political choices?); (2) the commercial benefit to the plaintiff (did the plaintiff sell a profitable book based upon the information he or she obtained?); (3) the nature of the plaintiff's interest in the records (does the plaintiff have personal motive or profit motive?); and (4) the reasonableness of the agency's withholding (did the agency have a reasonable basis in law for denying the request?). Finally, agency personnel are now personally responsible for granting or denying access, a requirement federal agencies object to strenuously. An employee of an agency who denies a request for information must be identified to the person who seeks the material, and if the access is denied in an arbitrary or capricious manner, the employee can be disciplined by the Civil Service Commission.

There is no initial fee to file a FOIA request, but agencies may charge reasonable fees for searching, copying and reviewing files, depending on the particular category into which a FOIA requester falls. FOIA divides requesters into three groups for fee purposes:

1. **Commercial Requesters:** Charged for search time, processing time (costs incurred during initial review of a record to see if it must be disclosed under FOIA) and duplicating.
2. **Educational Institutions, Non-Commercial Scientific Institutions and Representatives of the News Media:** Charged only for duplicating (first 100 pages free).
3. **All Other Requesters:** Charged for search time (after two free hours) and duplicating (first 100 pages free).

Anyone who seeks a fee waiver under FOIA must show that the disclosure of the information is "in the public interest because it is likely to contribute significantly to public understanding of the operations or activities of the government and is not primarily in the commercial interest of the requester." Significantly, the OPEN Government Act of 2007 broadened the definition of a "representative of the news media" exempt from document search fees to include a freelance journalist working for a news media entity "if the journalist can demonstrate a solid basis for expecting publication through that entity, whether or not the journalist is actually employed by the entity." In addition, the act made it clear that "as methods of news delivery evolve (for example, the adoption of the electronic dissemination of newspapers through telecommunications services), such alternative media shall be considered to be news-media entities."

Under an executive order signed by President George W. Bush in 2005, each federal agency must maintain a "FOIA Requester Service Center" that requesters may contact to speak with a FOIA public liaison in order to check on the status of their FOIA requests and to receive information about an agency's response. Are the FOIA service centers and liaisons useful? A 2008 report, issued by the National Security Archive (NSA), tested the centers and liaisons at different government agencies and found the experiences were generally "positive" and that "the new customer service system has made it easier to follow up on requests."[106] The report determined that of the 53 service centers called by the NSA to check on the status of a request, 44 provided "at least basic information on the pending FOIA request," such as where the request stood in the processing queue, while all 53 agencies called were able to confirm that the request in question was received. The report noted, however, that whether the public will actually use the centers remains to be seen. The OPEN Government Act of 2007 discussed earlier turned the establishment of FOIA public liaisons under Bush's executive order into statutory law that requires each government agency to have one or more such public liaisons that are "responsible for assisting in reducing delays, increasing transparency and understanding of the status of requests and assisting in the resolution of disputes."

The Freedom of Information Act is not difficult to use. Both the Student Press Law Center and the Reporters Committee for Freedom of the Press offer free automated open-records request letters. The fill-in-the-blank format is easy to complete before printing it out on a computer. The online services of the SPLC can be accessed through http://www.splc.org. The Reporters Committee for Freedom of the Press has an excellent "Federal Open Government Guide" that was updated in 2009 and is available online at http://www.rcfp.org/fogg.

This part of Chapter 9 provided an overview of the federal Freedom of Information Act. Five excellent online resources—the first four of which are private organizations, while the final two are government agencies—related to FOIA that supply more details and information are:

- **National Security Archive, George Washington University:**
  http://www.gwu.edu/~nsarchiv/nsa/foia.html
- **National Freedom of Information Center**
  http://www.nfoic.org
- **Public Citizen Freedom of Information Clearinghouse**
  http://www.citizen.org/litigation/free%5Finfo
- **RCFP Federal Open Government Guide**
  http://www.rcfp.org/fogg
- **U.S. Department of Justice, FOIA Information Center:**
  http://www.usdoj.gov/oip/index.html
- **Federal Communications Commission (FCC) FOIA Center:**
  http://www.fcc.gov/foia

TIPS ON HOW TO GET RECORDS

Many old journalistic hands argue that formal FOIA requests should be a last resort. Jack Briggs, former editor of the Tri-City (Wash.) Herald, advises reporters to do the following:

- Ask informally for documents—a formal FOIA request often takes much longer.
- Look to public court records for information that takes longer to get through a FOIA request.

---

106. *Knight Open Government Survey 2008*, 4–5, available online at http://www.gwu.edu/~nsarchiv/NSAEBB/NSAEBB246/eo_audit.pdf.

> ■ Cultivate trusted sources within federal agencies.
>
> ■ Follow up FOIA requests with telephone calls.
>
> ■ Don't kick and scream, unless kicking and screaming is justified. And don't forget to occasionally praise the FOIA officer who helps you.

FEDERAL OPEN-MEETINGS LAW

In 1976 Congress passed and the president signed into law the **Government in Sunshine Act,** the **federal open-meetings law.** The statute affects approximately 50 federal boards, commissions and agencies "headed by a collegial body composed of two or more individual members, a majority of whom are appointed to such position by the president with the advice and consent of the Senate." Importantly for media law students, this includes the Federal Communications Commission, and meetings of three or more of the five FCC commissioners must be open to the public. Ironically, the Government in Sunshine Act has been criticized by some as actually promoting secrecy at the FCC, with many of the real discussions and debates happening in closed-door meetings between two commissioners or in meetings between legal assistants and liaisons for the commissioners. These public bodies are required to conduct their business meetings in public. Notice of public meetings must be given one week in advance, and the agencies are required to keep careful records of what occurs at closed meetings. The law also prohibits informal communication between officials of an agency and representatives of companies and other interested persons with whom the agency does business unless this communication is recorded and made part of the public record.

Courts have strictly interpreted the requirement that the law applies only to bodies whose members are appointed by the president.

Courts have strictly interpreted the requirement that the law applies only to bodies whose members are appointed by the president. In 1981 the U.S. Court of Appeals for the District of Columbia Circuit ruled that the Government in Sunshine Act did not govern meetings of the Chrysler Loan Guarantee Board, a body created by Congress to oversee federal loan guarantees for the financially troubled automaker. People who served on the board were not actually named by the president, but served because they held other federal offices (i.e., secretary of the treasury, comptroller general, chair of the Federal Reserve). "If Congress had wanted to subject the board to the provisions of the Sunshine Act, it could have so provided when the board was established," the court noted.[107] A board or agency must also have some independent authority to act or take action before the law applies. A U.S. Court of Appeals ruled that the law does not apply to the president's Council of Economic Advisors. The sole function of the CEA is to advise and assist the president, the court said. It has no regulatory power. It cannot fund projects, even though it may appraise them. It has no function, save advising and assisting the president. Hence, it is not subject to either the FOIA or the Government in Sunshine Act.[108] Even agencies or commissions that fall under the aegis of the law may meet behind closed doors. The 1976 law lists 10 conditions or exemptions under which closed meetings might be held. The first nine of

---

107. *Symons* v. *Chrysler Corporation Loan Guarantee Board,* 670 F. 2d 238 (1981).
108. *Rushforth* v. *Council of Economic Advisors,* 762 F. 2d 1038 (1985).

these exemptions mirror the exemptions in the Freedom of Information Act. The 10th exemption focuses on situations in which the agency is participating in arbitration or is in the process of adjudicating or otherwise disposing of a case.

This exemption was used to block access to a meeting of the Nuclear Regulatory Commission. The NRC was discussing the reopening of the nuclear power plant at Three Mile Island in Pennsylvania. The federal district court ruled that this meeting would likely focus on the final adjudication of the federal action involving the nuclear reactor and hence could be closed to press and public.[109]

SUMMARY

Statutes provide public access to both federal records and meetings held by federal agencies. The federal records law, the Freedom of Information Act, makes public all records including electronic records and e-mail held by agencies within the executive branch of government and the independent regulatory commissions. Courts have given a broad meaning to the term "record" but have ruled that an agency must normally create and possess such a record before it becomes subject to FOIA. Nine categories of information are excluded from the provisions of the law. These include exemptions for national security, agency working papers, highly personal information and law enforcement files. Agencies must publish indexes of the records they hold and must permit copying of these materials. It is important to follow specific procedures when making a FOIA request to see certain records or documents.

The Government in Sunshine Act is the federal open-meetings law. This law reaches about 50 agencies in the executive branch and the regulatory commissions. Members of these organizations are not permitted to hold secret meetings unless they will discuss material that falls into one of 10 categories. These categories mirror the FOIA exemptions but also include a provision that permits closed-door meetings to discuss attempts to arbitrate or adjudicate certain cases or problems.

STATE LAWS ON MEETINGS AND RECORDS

It is not as easy to talk about access at the state level as it is at the federal level, because the discussion involves hundreds of different statutes. (Most states have multiple laws dealing with access to meetings, access to records and other access situations.) The following pages provide at best a few generalizations. Harold Cross made some of the most astute generalizations in 1953 in his pioneering book "The People's Right to Know."[110] Cross was really the first scholar to present a comprehensive report on access problems. In his book he listed four issues, or questions, common to every case of access:

1. Is the particular record or proceeding public? Many records and meetings kept or conducted by public officers in public offices are not really public at all. Much of the work of the police, though they are public officers and work in public buildings, is not open to public scrutiny.

109. *Philadelphia Newspapers* v. *Nuclear Regulatory Commission,* 9 M.L.R. 1843 (1983).
110. Cross, *The People's Right to Know.*

2. Is public material public in the sense that records are open to public inspection and sessions are open to public attendance? Hearings in juvenile courts are considered public hearings for purposes of the law, but they are often not open to the public.

3. Who can view the records and who can attend the meetings open to the public? Many records, for example, might be open to specific segments of the public, but not to all segments. Automobile accident reports by police departments are open to insurance company adjusters and lawyers, but such records are not usually open to the general public.

4. When records and meetings are open to the general public and the press, will the courts provide legal remedy for citizens and reporters if access is denied?

The last question is probably not as important today as it was when Cross wrote his book in 1953, for at that time access to many public records and meetings in the states was based on common law. Today this fact is no longer true. Access to meetings and records is nearly always governed by statute, and these statutes usually, but not always, provide a remedy for citizens who are denied access. This provision is more widespread in open-meetings laws, which tend to be more efficient in providing access, than in open-records laws, which are still weak and vague in many jurisdictions.

STATE OPEN-MEETINGS LAWS

All 50 states have statutes that mandate open meetings, and these laws range from good to awful. The need for **open-meetings laws** is obvious. There never was a solid common-law right to attend the meetings of public bodies, and as noted earlier, the constitutional provisions regarding freedom of expression have proved inadequate with regard to access.

It is difficult to make generalizations about these 50 different state laws. In 2006 the Reporters Committee for Freedom of the Press published the fifth edition of its "Open Government Guide," which it describes as "a complete compendium of information on every state's open records and open meetings laws. Each state's section is arranged according to a standard outline, making it easy to compare laws in various states." This helpful guide for all journalists is found on the Web at http://www.rcfp.org/ogg.

One of the most important aspects of any open-meetings law is the strong sanctions that may be imposed on government officials who fail to follow the mandate of the law. Laws that provide for substantial personal fines against these individuals are generally more desirable than laws that impose only small fines or no penalties at all. Another important part of an open-meetings law is the legislative declaration at the beginning of the law. A clear, strong statement in favor of open access to meetings of government bodies can persuade a judge trying to interpret the law to side with the advocates of access rather than with the government. For example, in the state of Washington the open-meetings law begins as follows:

> The legislature finds and declares that all . . . public agencies of this state and subdivisions thereof exist to aid in the conduct of the people's business. It is the intent of this chapter that their actions be taken openly and that their deliberations be conducted openly.

State open-meetings laws are normally written in one of two ways. Some laws declare that all meetings are open, except the following. Meetings that are closed are then listed. Other state laws simply list the agencies that must hold open meetings. The Congress of the United States is clearly excluded from the provisions of the federal open-meetings law. State legislatures are generally excluded from the provisions of their state open-meetings laws as well. But the issue is not quite as clear-cut as the situation at the federal level. Some state open-meetings laws do in fact cover some kinds of legislative proceedings. State open-meetings laws routinely do not include meetings of parole and pardon boards, of law enforcement agencies, of military agencies like the National Guard, of medical agencies like hospital boards, and so forth.

A good open-meetings law will specifically define a meeting by giving the number of members of the board or commission who must be present to constitute a public meeting (a quorum? at least two? etc.), by stating that all deliberative stages of the decision-making process are considered meetings and must be open to the public, and by stating that social gatherings and chance encounters are not considered meetings and are therefore excluded from the provisions of the law. Some laws are not this specific and merely refer to all meetings, all regular or special meetings, all formal meetings, or whatever. As noted earlier, courts are still struggling to determine whether so-called e-meetings, communication by group members via the computer, constitute a meeting under the law.

Most open-meetings laws provide for closed meetings, or **executive sessions,** in certain kinds of cases. Meetings at which personnel problems are discussed are an obvious example. A public airing of a teacher's personal problems could be an unwarranted invasion of privacy. The discussion of real estate transactions is another obvious example. All but 13 state open-meetings laws contain a provision that no final action can be taken at an executive session, that the board or commission must reconvene in public before a final determination can be made on any issue.

When a presiding officer of a governmental body announces at a meeting that the body is going into executive session, a reporter at the meeting should make certain of the following items:

1. The presiding officer has specified what topics will be discussed during the closed session, or why the executive session has been called.
2. A reporter who believes that a meeting is being closed improperly should formally object. He or she should ask members of the body specifically which provision in the law they are using to go into closed session. It is not inappropriate to ask for a vote of the body to make certain the required simple majority (or two-thirds majority in some states) approves of the closed session.
3. The reporter should also ask what time the closed session will end, so he or she can attend a reconvened public session.

Most open-meetings statutes require not only that meetings be open to the public, but also that the public be notified of both regular and special meetings far enough in advance that they can attend if they wish. Time requirements vary, but normally a special meeting cannot be held without an announcement a day or two in advance.

Virtually all laws provide some kind of injunctive or other civil remedy if the law is violated; almost half the statutes provide for criminal penalties if the statute is knowingly violated. In many states any action taken at a meeting that was not public, but should have been public, is null and void. The action must be taken again at a proper meeting. Most laws provide fines and short jail terms for public officers who knowingly violate the law, but prosecution is rare.

What should a reporter do when asked to leave a meeting that he or she believes should be open to the press and public? First, find out who has denied you access to the meeting and ask for the legal basis of this denial. Never leave a meeting voluntarily; but if ordered to leave, do so and contact your editor immediately. Resistance is not advised, for criminal charges may be filed against you. Whereas open-meetings laws provide a good means of access to proceedings, the reporter possesses what is probably a more powerful weapon—the power of publicity. Public officials don't like stories about secret meetings. If an agency abuses its right to meet in executive session, describe these meetings as they really are—secret sessions. A photo essay showing a meeting room door open, closing and closed, accompanied by a caption citing appropriate parts of the open-meetings law, will often get a reporter back into a proceeding faster than a court action.

Whereas open-meetings laws provide a good means of access to proceedings, the reporter possesses what is probably a more powerful weapon—the power of publicity.

OPEN-MEETINGS TIPS FOR REPORTERS

- Ask for the legal basis for closure.
- Find out who is asking that the meeting be closed and why.
- Never leave a meeting voluntarily, but don't resist being escorted out the door.
- Call your editor immediately.
- Use publicity as well as the law to gain access.

STATE OPEN-RECORDS LAWS

Every state in the union also has some kind of **open-records law.** The access laws either follow the federal formula—all records are open except the following—or list the kinds of records that the public does have a right to inspect.

The scope and reach of state open-records laws, which sometimes are known as public-records laws or state freedom-of-information laws, will vary from state to state. It is important to know what the law is in your state. Excellent online resources relating to state open-records laws include:

- **Reporters Committee for Freedom of the Press, Open Government Guide**
  http://www.rcfp.org/ogg
- **National Freedom of Information Coalition, State FOI Laws**
  http://www.nfoic.org/state-foi-laws

In addition, there are many organizations across the country that concentrate primarily on the open-records laws of a specific state. Some of these organizations, which include both privately funded groups and government entities, have created helpful handbooks for journalists summarizing the open-records statutes and open-meetings laws in a given state. The organizations listed below are merely examples of such groups for different states:

- **California: The First Amendment Project**
  http://www.thefirstamendment.org
- **Connecticut: Freedom of Information Commission**
  http://www.state.ct.us/foi
- **Florida: First Amendment Foundation & The Brechner Center**
  http://www.floridafaf.org
  http://brechner.org

- **New York: Committee on Open Government**
  http://www.dos.state.ny.us/coog/coogwww.html
- **Pennsylvania: Pennsylvania Freedom of Information Coalition**
  http://www.pafoic.org
- **Texas: Freedom of Information Foundation of Texas**
  http://www.foift.org

It is important to check your state's records laws on a constant basis, as they often are amended. For instance, Pennsylvania adopted a new Right to Know Act that took effect on January 1, 2009, and created a presumption of openness for most records kept by local and state government agencies.

Most state laws permit inspection of records by any person, but a few limit access to public records to citizens of the state. The reason people want to see a record is normally considered immaterial when determining whether they can gain access to the record. The freedom of information laws provide access to records held by public agencies in the state, and normally these statutes provide a broad definition of these agencies. Normally included are state offices, departments, divisions, bureaus, boards and commissions. Records kept by local government agencies (cities, counties, villages) are also included, as are those kept by school districts, public utilities and municipal corporations. In some states these laws also apply to records held by the governor.[111] These state laws do not normally govern records kept by courts or the legislature. Frequently these branches of government have established their own policies regarding access to records. State laws follow either a liberal or conservative definition of a public record. *All records possessed by an agency* are deemed to be public records in those states with liberal definitions of a public record. But some state laws are more conservative and provide access only to those *records that are required to be kept by law.*

Most state laws permit inspection of records by any person.

The validity of state open-records laws that include a "citizens-only" provision is highly doubtful today. In 2006 a federal appellate court in *Lee* v. *Minner*[112] held that Delaware's Freedom of Information Act—which applied only to Delaware residents and restricted non-Delaware citizens' rights to access, inspect and copy public documents—was unconstitutional. The 3rd U.S. Circuit Court of Appeals reasoned that Delaware's law violated the U.S. Constitution's privileges and immunities clause that holds that a state may not discriminate against noncitizens with respect to any protected right unless the state has a substantial reason for its discriminatory policy. Delaware had claimed that its citizens-only limitation allowed it to define its own "political community," but the appellate court held that "there is no nexus between the State's purported objective and its practice of prohibiting noncitizens from obtaining public records."

R U A RECORD? 4 HOW LONG? TEXT MESSAGES, E-MAILS & PUBLIC RECORDS

Are text messages made by public officials on government-owned phones and handheld devices public records under state open-records laws? That's an issue with which courts now are grappling. Courts in Michigan faced it in 2008 when Detroit

---

111. Bush, "Access to Governors' Records," 135.
112. 458 F. 3d 194 (3d Cir. 2006).

newspapers used that state's freedom of information law to request incriminating text messages made by Kwame Kilpatrick, the disgraced former mayor of Detroit. A Michigan court ordered Kilpatrick to produce more sexually explicit text messages between himself and his former chief of staff, Christine Beatty. The produced text messages also revealed a secret agreement to hide the existence of text messages that demonstrated Kilpatrick and Beatty lied during a police whistle-blower lawsuit.

Most states treat e-mail messages made on government computers and sent or received in the conduct of public business as public records; for instance, Florida defines public records to include "data processing software or other material, *regardless of physical form [emphasis added]*." In 2009, a judge in Carson City, Nev., ordered that state's governor, Jim Gibbons, to produce six e-mails to the Reno Gazette-Journal under Nevada's open-records law, but also held that more than 90 other e-mails were either personal or privileged and thus not subject to disclosure. A New Jersey appellate court held in 2009 that e-mails sent between Gov. Jon Corzine and Carla Katz, a labor union president with whom Corzine once had a close personal relationship, were public records under New Jersey's Open Public Records Act.[113] It observed that the e-mails "were received and sent in the course of the governor's official business." But the appellate court also concluded they were protected from disclosure by the governor's "executive privilege" protecting the confidentiality of sensitive communications pertaining to the executive function (the theory is that such a privilege enhances the effectiveness of the decision-making and investigatory duties of the executive).

In 2009 a battle was being fought in West Virginia over e-mails sent between Elliott Maynard, a former justice on that state's highest court, and Donald Blankenship, the head of Massey Energy. Judges in West Virginia are subject to that state's open-records law, and e-mails there are treated as records (West Virginia defines publicly available records as "any writing containing information relating to the conduct of the public's business, prepared, owned and retained by a public body"). The Associated Press sought the e-mails to determine if there may have been an improper relationship between Maynard and Blankenship that could have influenced Maynard's decision in a case that Blankenship's company had pending before the West Virginia courts.

State laws often are silent, however, on how long employees must retain e-mails, and it sometimes is up to state attorneys general to issue opinions on the matter. A 50-state survey by the AP in 2008 on government e-mail retention "found a wide variety of laws and practices, with the vast majority of states officially treating e-mail like printed documents. But most of the states with e-mail laws allow officials to choose which ones to turn over in Freedom of Information requests and to decide on their own when e-mail records are deleted."[114] The issue is contentious. In 2008, for example, a number of news organizations in North Carolina, along with the Raleigh News & Observer, sued that state's governor, Mike Easley, "over his administration's deletion of e-mail, which they say violates the state's Public Records Law."[115] In January 2009 outgoing Missouri Gov.

---

113. *Wilson* v. *Brown*, 962 A. 2d 1122 (N.J. Super. A.D. 2009). In March 2009 the New Jersey Supreme Court declined to hear the case, thus making final the earlier 2009 appellate court ruling.
114. *Associated Press*, "E-mail Public Documents Get Erased, Disappear."
115. Eisley, "N&O Sues Easley Over Records Law."

Matt Blunt reached a court-approved settlement requiring him to turn over thousands of e-mails to investigators in a case centering on whether Blunt wrongfully deleted other e-mails in violation of Missouri's open-records law.[116] Missouri's law considers e-mails to be public records, but Blunt disputed whether his office had to retain the e-mails and he admitted no wrongdoing in the settlement.

All state freedom of information laws provide exemptions to disclosure. Agencies *may* withhold material that falls under an exemption in some states; agencies *must* withhold this information in other states. Six common exemptions to the state open-records laws are the following:

1. Information classified as confidential by state or federal law
2. Law enforcement and investigatory information
3. Trade secrets and commercial information
4. Preliminary departmental memorandums (working papers)
5. Personal privacy information
6. Information relating to litigation against a public body

Can state and local governments copyright certain records?

Can state and local governments copyright certain records they create and maintain in order to stop their widespread distribution under freedom of information laws? That issue arose in South Carolina in 2008 when the state's highest court in *Seago* v. *Horry County* considered whether further dissemination of public documents obtained pursuant to the South Carolina Freedom of Information Act "may be restricted where the government entity claims the information is copyright-protected under the federal copyright law."[117] The dispute centered on a company that collected electronic mapping data, including digital photographic maps, from various government entities (in this case, Horry County) and then charged customers a fee for accessing such data on its Web site. Horry County had copyrighted parts of its mapping data. In ruling in favor of the county, the Supreme Court of South Carolina held that "while public information must be granted pursuant to FOIA, a public entity may restrict further commercial distribution of the information pursuant to a copyright."

Obtaining copies of state records can sometimes be an expensive proposition. For instance, in 2008 the sheriff of Shiawassee County, Mich., charged a local newspaper, the Argus-Press, $10 for a letter the sheriff sent denying a request for documents under Michigan's freedom of information law.[118] That's correct—a charge of $10 *not* to obtain copies of any actual records, but for a missive responding to a request and denying access. When records are produced, the charges may be steep. For example, in 2008 the Missouri Department of Revenue was ordered by a state judge to stop charging $7 for copies of an individual's driver license and motor vehicle records. The judge held that the figure, which was $1.25 before being raised in May 2008 to $7 under the guise of covering costs for a new computer system for storing the records operated by a private company, violated Missouri's open-records law, which limits charges to only actual

---

116. Messenger, "Judge OKs Deal on Blunt E-Mails."
117. 663 S.E. 2d 38 (S.C. 2008).
118. Adams, "FOIA Denial Called into Question."

copying costs plus staff time spent in retrieving documents.[119] Also in 2008, a Kansas blogger named Bob Weeks was told it would cost $1,350 to obtain four days' worth of e-mails sent and received by Kansas Gov. Kathleen Sebelius and her staff. The whopping sum was based on a 25-cent-per-page copying fee, plus the cost of having "to pay a lawyer in the governor's office $27 an hour, for 50 hours, to read the e-mails to make sure they [weren't] exempt from disclosure."[120] An appellate court in New Jersey in 2008 upheld a "special service charge" of more than $1,800 meted out to a freelance journalist for a request under New Jersey's Open Public Records Act, which allows for "reasonable" charges to be made when production of records involves an "extraordinary expenditure of time and effort."[121]

Journalists in 2008 wanted to review Alaska Gov. Sarah Palin's e-mail correspondence.

When journalists in 2008 wanted to review Alaska Gov. Sarah Palin's e-mail correspondence with other state employees when Palin was running for vice president, they were told that Alaska charges about $960 per each e-mail account searched. The figure was derived by multiplying 13 hours of labor by the approximately $74 hourly charge for a technology employee to gather and review the e-mails. A search through the e-mails of all 16,000 or so state employees thus would cost about $15 million.

When states fail to comply with their own open-records laws, however, they too can pay a high price. In 2008, for example, a judge in Pennsylvania ordered the Pennsylvania Higher Education Assistance Agency (PHEAA) to pay legal fees totaling nearly $50,000 to attorneys for the Associated Press, Patriot News in Harrisburg and WTAE-TV in Pittsburgh who sought records "in an effort to determine how PHEAA spent nearly $900,000, starting in 2000, at seven board retreats at resorts."[122] The records that PHEAA sought to suppress ultimately "showed payments for $100 facials, a $95-a-person buffet, $175 for falconry lessons and a $491 limousine ride to shopping outlets." To make matters worse, PHEAA spent nearly $400,000 of taxpayers' money in its unsuccessful effort to suppress the records in question.

Across the country, King County, Wash., paid $225,000 in 2009 to settle a lawsuit brought by a conservative blogger who had requested a list of the names of the people in that county who voted in the 2004 gubernatorial elections. The blogger, Stefan Sharkansky, sought the names to show possible fraud and illegal vote counting that could have impacted the tightly contested race that year for Washington governor between Chris Gregoire and Dino Rossi. King County failed for more than two years to complete the request.

THE PRIVATIZATION OF PUBLIC GOVERNMENT

One of the challenges facing the press today results from the trend of private companies taking over what has been traditionally regarded as government business. For-profit and nonprofit organizations are replacing the government in operating public schools, jails and prisons, state

---

119. *Associated Press*, "Mo. Judge Blocks $7 Fee for Driver's License Records." Missouri later scaled back the charge to $ 3.82 per record, but in April 2009 Cole County Circuit Judge Richard Callahan declared that price too steep under Missouri's open-records law. Information about Missouri's laws regarding open records and open meetings can be found online at the Web site of the Missouri attorney general at http://ago.mo.gov/sunshinelaw/sunshinelaw.htm.
120. Lefler, "Open-Records Requests Can Spell High Fees."
121. *Fisher* v. *Division of Law*, 946 A. 2d 53 (N.J. 2008).
122. Eshelman, "PHEAA Told to Pay Legal Fees for Media."

and local welfare agencies, and many other state services. These private agencies are not generally regarded to have the same responsibilities as public agencies to maintain open records or hold meetings in public. For instance, in October 2006 the Ohio Supreme Court held in *Oriana House, Inc.* v. *Montgomery* that a private corporation called Oriana House, which contracted with Summit County, Ohio, to operate its alternative jail sentencing and rehabilitation programs, was not the "functional equivalent" of a government agency and thus was not subject to the Ohio Public Records Act.[123] By a 4-3 decision, Ohio's high court found Oriana House exempt, even though Oriana House performed duties historically left to government agencies and despite the fact that it received all of Summit County's funds for running community-based correctional facilities and programs. The majority emphasized, instead, the fact there was "no evidence . . . that any government entity controls the day-to-day operations of Oriana House" and that Oriana House was "created as a private, nonprofit corporation. It was not established by a government entity." Sadly for journalists and access advocates, the majority concluded that "a private business does not open its records to public scrutiny merely by performing services on behalf of the state or a municipal government. It ought to be difficult for someone to compel a private entity to adhere to the dictates of the Public Records Act." The Ohio Supreme Court applied the same functional-equivalency test later in December 2006 in *Repository* v. *Nova Behavioral Health, Inc.* and reached the same unfortunate, access-denied conclusion, holding that a private, nonprofit corporation that supplies, under contract, mental health services for Stark County, Ohio, was not subject to the state's Public Records Act despite receiving 92 percent of its money from the largely taxpayer-funded Stark County Community Mental Health Board.[124] In ruling against a request for records from Nova Behavioral Health made by the Canton Repository newspaper, the 4-3 majority opinion reasoned that "the provision of mental-health services generally is not a historically or uniquely governmental function. Nova's operations were independent of government. The Stark County CMHB did not make decisions for or control or direct the day-to-day operations of Nova." The dissent, in contrast, wrote that "[a] private entity that receives the level of public funding that Nova received should not be permitted to keep the public from knowing how it has managed its public responsibilities."

Although the two Ohio rulings are not access friendly, some courts have held differently in similar scenarios. For instance, a judge in Tennessee ruled in 2008 that a private prison company was the functional equivalent of a government agency and thus was subject to Tennessee's open-records law.[125] The judge found it significant that the state's constitution makes prison maintenance a state function. The private company, Corrections Corporation of America, operates more than a half-dozen detention facilities in Tennessee. In August 2009 the Tennessee Court of Appeals upheld the decision. It observed that the state could not delegate away to a private entity its responsibilities. The Supreme Court of Wisconsin held in 2008 that municipalities may not avoid liability under Wisconsin's open-records law by contracting with an independent contractor assessor for the collection and custody of its property assessment records, and by then directing any requester of those records to such an assessor.[126]

---

123. 854 N.E. 2d 193 (Ohio 2006).
124. 859 N.E. 2d 936 (Ohio 2006).
125. *Associated Press,* "Judge: Private Prison Company Must Produce Records."
126. *Wiredata, Inc.* v. *Village of Sussex,* 751 N.W. 2d 736 (Wisc. 2008).

But problems still persist when government entities find creative ways to use private contractors to avoid having their records produced. In 2008 a private search firm was used to find a new chancellor for the University of Arkansas for Medical Sciences.[127] To circumvent that state's freedom of information laws, the search firm was officially hired not by the university, but by the University of Arkansas Foundation Inc., a privately funded group not subject to the Arkansas Freedom of Information Act.

SUMMARY

All states have laws that govern access to public meetings and public records. Good state open-meetings laws have strong legislative declarations in support of public meetings, specifically define a public meeting by listing the number of members who must gather to constitute a meeting, and declare void all actions taken during a meeting that was improperly closed to the public. Most laws provide for closed sessions to discuss such matters as personnel actions, real estate transactions and litigation.

State open-records laws tend to mirror the federal law. Both state and local agencies are governed by the laws, which apply to most governmental bodies except the legislature and the courts. Most state laws govern all records kept by these agencies, but a few are applicable only to records that are required to be kept by law. Exemptions to state open-records laws include material specifically excluded by other statutes, law enforcement investigatory information, working papers and highly personal information. Most laws provide for access to the judicial system in case a request for data is rejected, but both New York and Connecticut have established commissions to act as arbiters in these matters, and Florida has adopted a constitutional amendment that governs access throughout state government. A major concern facing both journalists and the public today is the growing use of private businesses to carry out governmental functions.

LAWS THAT RESTRICT ACCESS TO INFORMATION

All three were adopted in the name of protecting the right to privacy.

Just as there are laws that provide for public access to government-held documents, there are laws that specifically preclude access to government-held information. There are provisions in scores of federal laws alone that limit the right of access. Tax statutes, espionage laws, legislation on atomic energy and dozens of other kinds of laws are filled with limitations on the dissemination of information (e.g., personal information on taxes, national security questions and matters relating to nuclear weapons). But in addition to these kinds of laws, the federal government has adopted in the past four decades at least three rather broad sets of regulations regarding information held by the government. All three were adopted in the name of protecting the right to privacy. While these regulations cannot be considered here in a comprehensive sense, people who gather information for a living need to be aware of their implications.

---

127. Heard, "UAMS to Keep Search Private; Foundation Hires Recruitment Firm."

SCHOOL RECORDS

The Family Educational Rights and Privacy Act (FERPA), adopted in 1974 and also known as the Buckley Amendment, is a federal law designed to safeguard the privacy of students' "education records."[128] It applies to all levels of schools (grade schools, high schools and universities) that receive funds under any program administered by the U.S. Department of Education. FERPA, in brief, affects

▮ *who can access education records* (defined as records "directly related to a student" that are "maintained by an educational agency or institution"); and

▮ *what information a school may or may not disclose* without the permission of either a student or parent.

The most recent amendments to its regulations interpreting FERPA took effect in January 2009. What follows is an overview of the law.

Under FERPA, parents can inspect their child's education records until their child turns 18 or attends a school beyond the high school level. Thus, in general, parents cannot access education records of their college-attending child, unless their child grants them written permission. Exceptions, however, permit disclosure to a student's parents without consent if (1) the student is a dependent for federal tax purposes; (2) there is a health or safety emergency involving the student; or (3) if the student is under 21 and violated a law or policy concerning use or possession of alcohol or controlled substances.

FERPA impacts journalists covering colleges and universities because it generally prohibits such institutions from disclosing a student's education records, without that student's prior consent, if the records contain "personally identifiable information." Such information includes a student's name, address, date and place of birth, Social Security and student identification numbers, as well as (under the regulations that took effect in 2009) any "other information that . . . is linked or linkable to a specific student that would allow a reasonable person in the school community, who does not have personal knowledge of the relevant circumstances, to identify the student with reasonable certainty." Any and all such personally identifiable information, when located in a student's education records (for instance, a transcript or discipline report), would need to be redacted (blacked out or removed) before the records could be disclosed without permission. The names and addresses of a student's parents (including mother's maiden name) and family members also cannot be disclosed without permission.

FERPA impacts journalists covering colleges and universities.

On the other hand, FERPA allows disclosure without consent of so-called directory information (a student's name, major, address and telephone number, for instance) that might be listed in an online or hard-copy student directory. However, colleges must tell students about directory information and give them a chance to request its nondisclosure; in brief, students must have notice and opportunity to opt out of the disclosure.

In a portion of FERPA that is critical for student journalists reporting on campus crime, FERPA states that education records do *not* include "records maintained by a law enforcement unit of the educational agency or institution that were created by that law enforcement unit for the purpose of law enforcement." In other words, incident reports, arrest reports, parking

128. 20 U.S.C. § 1232g (2009). The Department of Education maintains a Web site devoted to FERPA, available at http://www.ed.gov/policy/gen/guid/fpco/ferpa/index.html.

tickets and other documents made by campus or university police are not "education records" covered by FERPA and thus they may be obtained without a student's permission.

In 2009, students at the Daily Texan, the newspaper at the University of Texas at Austin, were doing battle with university administrators over access to e-mails between student government officials allegedly relating to fraud, with the university asserting that FERPA prevented their disclosure because the e-mails revealed students' names. Such situations, sadly, are not rare.

Universities commonly invoke and misuse FERPA to hide information about their athletic programs.

A comprehensive May 2009 study and report by the Columbus Dispatch called "Secrecy 101" revealed that many universities commonly invoke and misuse FERPA to hide information about their athletic programs, student-athletes and even boosters. Some universities—Nebraska, Nevada and West Virginia, for example—used FERPA to refuse to release any and all documents to the Columbus Dispatch relating to NCAA violations, citing student privacy concerns.

In 2002 the U.S. Supreme Court issued a 7-2 opinion interpreting the Family Educational Rights and Privacy Act that could help the media obtain campus crime reports and records by reducing universities' worries about being sued for violating the law. In particular, the court held that FERPA does not give students the personal right to sue their schools for releasing personal material covered by that statute.[129] The remedy for violation, the court held, is not an individual lawsuit but, as noted previously, solely the loss to schools of federal funds.

HEALTH AND MEDICAL RECORDS

In 2003 a new set of privacy rules and regulations went into effect that limit the ability of journalists to obtain information about patients in hospitals and in the custody of other health care providers. The rules, officially known as the Federal Standards for Privacy of Individually Identifiable Health Information, were enacted pursuant to the Health Insurance Portability and Accountability Act of 1996, which is commonly known by the acronym HIPAA (see page 278). The Seattle Times wrote that "for the news media, HIPAA rules will mean that in the event of a shooting, car crash or other newsworthy event, hospitals will disclose no information unless a reporter knows the patient's name. In the past, reporters could ascertain a patient's condition in those situations without a name."[130] In a special white paper called "The Lost Stories," Jennifer LaFleur of the Reporters Committee for Freedom of the Press (RCFP) observed that "under HIPAA, hospitals may release only the name and one-word status of the patient—but only if the patient has agreed to have his or her name released and then only if the reporter has the individual's full name."[131] LaFleur added that many "journalists around the country report that police and fire departments have cited HIPAA for not disclosing accident information."

It is important to note that police and fire departments, along with other law enforcement agencies, are *not* entities covered by HIPAA. Thus HIPAA does not give the police the power or the right to keep secret information in their reports and logs about accident or shooting victims. The entities covered by HIPAA, in contrast, are health plans, health care clearinghouses and health care providers.

The Department of Health and Human Services maintains a Web site devoted to HIPAA and its privacy provisions. It is located at http://www.hhs.gov/ocr/privacy/index.html and

129. *Gonzaga University* v. *Doe,* 536 U.S. 273 (2002).
130. Ostrom, "Privacy Rules to Limit Word on Patients."
131. LaFleur, "The Lost Stories."

journalists seeking information from health care providers should be familiar with its myriad relevant terms and provisions. One very important statement for journalists on that Web site relates to the relationship between HIPAA and state open-records laws. It can be found on a link for frequently asked questions about state public records laws. In particular, the Web site provides that "if a state agency is not a 'covered entity' . . . it is not required to comply with the HIPAA Privacy Rule and, thus, any disclosure of information by the state agency pursuant to its state public records law would not be subject to the Privacy Rule." This makes it clear that police and fire departments, which are not covered entities, cannot hide behind HIPAA to keep information secret that is otherwise open under a state law.

In an important decision related to this last matter, the attorney general for Kentucky, Greg Stumbo, handed journalists a victory when he issued an opinion in August 2004 declaring that HIPAA does not apply in that state to the names of injured people mentioned in police reports.[132] Parsed differently, police in Kentucky cannot use HIPAA to withhold their incident reports mentioning injured people who were taken to health care providers.

Does HIPAA trump or supersede state laws governing open records and document disclosure? The good news—so far—is that the answer is no in the two states that have addressed the issue. A Texas appellate court ruled in favor of the Austin American-Statesman newspaper in 2006 and held that the Texas Public Information Act is not pre-empted by HIPAA, thus allowing disclosure under the state act of information about allegations and investigations of abuse in state facilities for people who are mentally challenged, as well as the names of facilities in which the alleged incidents occurred.[133] Similarly, the Ohio Supreme Court ruled in 2006 in favor of the Cincinnati Enquirer, holding that HIPAA does not supersede disclosure requirements under Ohio's Public Records Act.[134] The decision allowed the Enquirer to obtain copies of notices from the Cincinnati Health Department of property owners cited for lead-paint contamination violations.

In another early development of the law related to HIPAA as it affects the news media, a federal judge in Colorado ruled in 2004 that HIPAA does not create a private cause of action for hospitals and medical care providers to sue news entities that publish medical records.[135] In that case, the Rocky Mountain News had obtained and published material contained in a hospital's secret peer review report, and the hospital sued the newspaper alleging that its use of the report violated HIPAA. Judge Walker D. Miller dismissed the lawsuit, however. He reasoned that "federal courts have consistently refused to find a private right of action under HIPAA" and observed that both the language and structure of HIPAA do not provide for a private cause of action.

Seemingly inappropriate stretches of HIPAA still occur. In 2008 a Nebraska judge cited HIPAA when denying a historical society's request for records identifying 957 people buried in graves marked only by numbers at a psychiatric institution's cemetery in Hastings, Neb., from the 1880s through the late 1950s. The records are held by the Hastings Regional Center, a health care provider. Although the burial records in question obviously related to individuals deceased for many decades and despite the general legal maxim that an individual's right to privacy dies

132. "Medical Privacy Law Does Not Apply."
133. *Abbott* v. *Texas Department of Mental Health & Mental Retardation,* 212 S.W. 3d 648 (Tex. Ct. App. 2006).
134. *Cincinnati Enquirer* v. *Daniels,* 844 N.E. 2d 1181 (Ohio 2006).
135. *University of Colorado Hospital Authority* v. *Denver Publishing Co.,* 32 M.L.R. 2251 (D. Colo. 2004).

with the individual, Adams County District Judge Terri Harder nonetheless found the records constituted "individually identifiable health information" protected from disclosure by HIPAA and that their release "would reveal that the individual[s] [were] institutionalized for a mental illness or for a condition serious enough to require institutionalization."[136] The Adams County Historical Society appealed and the Nebraska Supreme Court agreed to hear the case, with oral argument occurring in 2009. The Reporters Committee for Freedom of the Press, along with several other news media organizations, filed a friend-of-the-court brief in 2009 urging Nebraska's high court to reverse Judge Harder's ruling and to release the names of the deceased.[137]

In May 2009, however, the Nebraska Supreme Court reversed the lower court's decision and allowed access to the names. It wrote that "although HIPAA prevents the release of individually identifiable medical information, it also provides for release of information when required by state law. Nebraska's public records statutes require that medical records be kept confidential, but exempt birth and death records from that requirement. Our privacy laws also apply to medical records and patient histories, but not to records of deaths. The records sought by ACHS are records of deaths and therefore are public records."

THE FEDERAL PRIVACY LAW

The **Privacy Act** of 1974 has two basic thrusts. First, it attempts to check the misuse of personal data obtained by the federal government, the quantity of which has, of course, reached staggering proportions. Second, the law is intended to provide access for individuals to records about themselves that are held by federal agencies. The first objective of the law could be the more troublesome to the press.

The act requires that each federal agency limit the collection of information to that which is relevant and necessary, to collect information directly from the subject concerned when possible, and to allow individuals to review and amend their personal records and information. Also, under the act agencies are forbidden from disclosing what is called "a personally identifiable record" without the written consent of the individual to whom the record pertains. Since this section of the law is seemingly contradictory to the spirit of the federal FOIA, Congress was forced to clarify the responsibilities of federal agencies with regard to the law. A provision was added to the Privacy Act that declares that records required to be disclosed under FOIA are not subject to the provisions of the Privacy Act and consequently cannot be withheld from inspection. To the government official with control of information, however, neither the Privacy Act nor FOIA is unambiguous.

One federal appellate court recently summed up the tension between FOIA and the Privacy Act, writing that "the net effect of the interaction between the two statutes is that where the FOIA requires disclosure, the Privacy Act will not stand in its way, but where the FOIA would permit withholding under an exemption, the Privacy Act makes such withholding mandatory upon the agency."[138]

The Privacy Act is best known to journalists today as the law under which government scientists Wen Ho Lee and Steven Hatfill sued the government for leaking allegedly

---

136. *Associated Press*, "Judge Says Regional Center Burial Records Can Remain Sealed."
137. Brief of Amici Curiae, *Nebraska* v. *Kinyoun*, Case No. A-08-339 (filed Jan. 8, 2009).
138. *News-Press* v. *Department of Homeland Security*, 489 F. 3d 1173, 1189 (11th Cir. 2007).

defamatory, confidential information about them to members of the news media.[139] Both Lee and Hatfill, the former falsely accused of espionage on behalf of China and the latter falsely accused of sending Anthrax-laced letters to members of Congress and the media shortly after Sept. 11, 2001, sought subpoenas against journalists to compel them to testify and to reveal the names of their confidential government sources who leaked to them information that was protected under the Privacy Act. The Privacy Act provides a private right of action against a government agency when records pertaining to an individual have been improperly disclosed by that agency.

CRIMINAL HISTORY PRIVACY LAWS

In accordance with the broad scope of the Omnibus Crime Control and Safe Streets Act of 1968, the federal Law Enforcement Assistance Administration, an agency created by the Nixon administration to help local police forces fight crime, sought to develop a national computerized record-keeping system. The system that was established permits any police department in the nation to have access to the records of virtually all other police departments.

Congressional concern about the misuse of this record system led to limitations on access to the data. Police records have always contained a considerable amount of information that is erroneous, out-of-date or private. The centralized record-keeping system presents a problem referred to by some writers as the "dossier effect." The contrast between these computerized and centrally maintained records immediately accessible across the country and those police records of the past was sharp and immediately evident: Fragmented, original-source records kept by a single police agency for a limited geographical area were not readily accessible because of their bulk and associated indexing problems. Hence, federal policy mandated that states, if they wish to participate in the national record-keeping system, adopt rules that, among other things, limit the dissemination of some criminal history nonconviction data.

The "Code of Federal Regulations" ("Criminal Justice Information Systems") defines nonconviction data as

> arrest information without disposition if an interval of one year has elapsed from the date of arrest and no active prosecution of the charge is pending, or information disclosing that the police have elected not to refer a matter to a prosecutor, or that a prosecutor has elected not to commence criminal proceedings, or that proceedings have been indefinitely postponed, as well as all acquittals and all dismissals.

As a result of the state laws, press access to criminal history records kept by the police has been virtually eliminated unless data sought are pertinent to an incident for which a person is currently being processed by the criminal justice system, are conviction records, or are original records of entry, such as arrest records, that are maintained chronologically and are accessible only on that basis. Reporters can also obtain information about arrests not resulting in conviction, however, if they are aware of the specific dates of the arrests. It is hard to determine whether these laws have substantially affected the press's ability to report on the

---

139. See *Lee* v. *Department of Justice*, 401 F. Supp. 2d 123 (D.D.C. 2005); and *Hatfill* v. *Gonzales*, 505 F. Supp. 2d 33 (D.D.C. 2007).

criminal justice system. A good police reporter usually can gain access to information he or she wants to see. Nevertheless, potential problems are apparent. One commentator noted:

> On the one hand, the uncontrolled dissemination and publication of certain criminal history records can adversely affect the individual himself. On the other hand, the public and the press must have access to basic records of official action if they are to effectively scrutinize and evaluate the operations of the police, the prosecuting agencies, and the courts.[140]

The ability to achieve that scrutiny is important. For example, it is possible to envision a situation in which a prosecutor is accused of favoring friends or certain ethnic or racial groups when deciding whether to prosecute arrested persons. Without access to arrest records that can be compared with prosecution records, such a charge would be difficult to investigate. People within the criminal justice system could gain access to the needed records, but history indicates that they must be prodded before they take action. And, of course, prodding is the function of the press.

STATE STATUTES THAT LIMIT ACCESS TO INFORMATION

All states have statutes that limit access to information that would otherwise be available under a freedom of information law.

All states have statutes that limit access to information that would otherwise be available under a freedom of information law. Washington, for example, has more than 100 different laws that govern the access to particular information. Some of these state statutes are aimed at blocking access to trade secrets; others limit access to information submitted to the state in compliance with environmental laws. In 2001, in direct response to the racetrack death of driver Dale Earnhardt at the Daytona 500 and the subsequent request for autopsy photographs by the Orlando Sentinel and other newspapers, the Florida legislature passed a bill that was signed into law that makes confidential and exempt from that state's public records act photographs and videotapes of autopsies.[141] The newspapers had sought access to the photographs to determine the reasons for Earnhardt's death and, in particular, whether a particular safety device might have saved his life. In 2002 a Florida appellate court upheld the constitutionality of that statute and its retroactive application, and the Supreme Court of Florida declined to hear the case in July 2003, letting the appellate court decision stand.[142] Finally, in December 2003, the U.S. Supreme Court declined to hear the case.[143]

SUICIDE PHOTOS AND THE D.C. MADAM: PRIVACY CONCERNS VERSUS OPEN RECORDS IN FLORIDA

Privacy and images of the dead were at issue once again in Florida in 2008 when requests by the St. Petersburg Times under the state's public records law were made to obtain photos of the "D.C. Madam," Deborah Jeane Palfrey, taken by local police

---

140. Higgins, "Press and Criminal Record Privacy," 509.
141. Florida Statute § 406.135 (2001).
142. *Campus Communications, Inc.* v. *Earnhardt,* 821 So. 2d 388 (2002). The Supreme Court of Florida's decision not to hear the case came in a close 4-3 vote.
143. *Campus Communications, Inc.* v. *Earnhardt,* 124 S. Ct. 821 (2003).

shortly after her suicide near her mother's home in Tarpon Springs, Fla. Palfrey's mother, Blanche Palfrey, claimed that publication of the death-scene images of her daughter, who was convicted earlier that year of running a prostitution ring once used by U.S. Senator David Vitter of Louisiana, would violate her own privacy and cause her emotional distress. Her attorney cited the same statute that arose from the Dale Earnhardt case, claiming that suicide photographs were akin to autopsy photos. In August 2008 Judge Linda R. Allen rejected this argument but nonetheless issued a ruling that struck a balance between privacy and the public's right to know—she allowed the photos to be viewed and seen at the Tarpon Springs Police Department, but not to be duplicated or reproduced.

Divorce is another area where some states adopt statutes limiting public access to certain records. For instance, in 2006 a California appellate court in *Burkle* v. *Burkle* struck down a state statute that allowed a party in a divorce case, upon request to a judge, to have sealed in their entirety any and all court documents referencing in any way the financial assets and liabilities of the parties getting divorced.[144] Although the court acknowledged privacy interests of divorcing parties in financial information (including the possibility of identity theft), it nonetheless found that "the First Amendment provides a right of access to court records in divorce proceedings" and held the statute was overbroad and not narrowly tailored to protect privacy interests. In particular, the statute mandated a judge to automatically seal in their entirety court pleadings relating to financial information even if they just briefly mentioned that information, rather than providing the judge with discretion to redact only those specific parts of the documents relating to financial information that actually could harm privacy interests. Courts in other states have struck down similar laws—sometimes based on a First Amendment right of access, sometimes based on a state constitutional right of access.[145]

In 2009, when Jon and Kate Gosselin, stars of the reality series "Jon & Kate Plus 8," filed for divorce, they did so in Montgomery County, Pa. (rather than their own Berks County), where divorce filings are automatically sealed from public view. It apparently was one of the few things in their lives they didn't want publicly exploited.

Jon and Kate Gosselin filed for divorce where filings are secret.

THE ABUSIVE RECORD REQUESTER: NEW EFFORTS BY STATES TO STOP EXCESSIVE REQUESTS

In 2009 Assembly Bill 520 was introduced in California that would allow state court judges there to issue protective orders limiting the number and scope of requests a person may make under the California Public Records Act if judges determine that

---

144. 135 Cal. App. 4th 1045 (2006). The California Supreme Court declined to hear the case. *Burkle* v. *Burkle,* 2006 Cal. LEXIS 5955 (2006).
145. See *Associated Press* v. *New Hampshire,* 153 N.H. 120 (2005), which held unconstitutional a New Hampshire law limiting access to divorce records that abrogated "entirely the public right of access to a class of court records," and emphasized that "the New Hampshire Constitution creates a public right of access to court records."

the requestors have sought records for "an improper purpose" such as harassment of a public agency or its employees. The state of Washington passed a law in 2009 that allows state government agencies to obtain injunctions preventing prisoners in that state from obtaining records if the requests are made to harass or intimidate the agencies or its employees or if the requests might assist criminal activity. Other states either are considering or have considered similar measures to stop abusive record requests.

SUMMARY

All the states and the federal government have laws that specifically exclude certain kinds of information from the public scrutiny. Some of these exclusions were noted in the discussion of Exemption 3 of the Freedom of Information Act. Today, the right to privacy has been erected as a substantial barrier to access to information held by government agencies. The federal government has adopted a law protecting the privacy of student records. Congress passed a federal privacy law, which often conflicts with the provisions of FOIA. The federal government has also insisted that states pass statutes that control access to criminal history records. Much privacy legislation has been passed by the states themselves, and today the right to privacy is being used frequently to block access to public records.

BIBLIOGRAPHY

Adams, Dominic. "FOIA Denial Called into Question." *Argus-Press*, 25 August 2008, A1.

Associated Press. "E-Mail Public Documents Get Erased, Disappear." 14 July 2008.

——— "Judge: Private Prison Company Must Produce Records." 29 July 2008.

——— "Judge Says Regional Center Burial Records Can Remain Sealed." 16 February 2008.

——— "Mo. Judge Blocks $7 Fee for Driver's License Records." 31 May 2008.

Barringer, Felicity. "Appeals Court Rejects Damages Against ABC in Food Lion Case." *The New York Times,* 21 October 1999, A1.

Beesley, Susan L., and Theresa Glover. "Developments Under the Freedom of Information Act, 1986." *Duke Law Journal* (1987): 521.

Boule, Margie. "No-Fly List Clips Singer, But Parent Who Abducts Kids Glides." *Oregonian,* 30 September 2004, E01.

Burns, Robert. "Document: Bin Laden Evaded U.S. Forces." *Associated Press,* 22 March 2005.

The Bush Administration and the News Media. Washington, D.C.: Reporters Committee for Freedom of the Press, 1992.

Bush, Ellen M. "Access to Governors' Records: State Statutes and the Use of Executive Privilege." *Journalism Quarterly* 71 (1994): 135.

The Clinton Administration and the News Media. Washington, D.C.: Reporters Committee for Freedom of the Press, 1996.

Clymer, Adam. "Government Openness at Issue as Bush Holds on to Records." *The New York Times,* 3 January 2003, A1.

"CNN, Federal Government Settle Suit with Montana Rancher." *Associated Press,* 5 June 2001.

Cooperman, Alan. "Sedative Withdrawal Made Rehnquist Delusional in' 81." *Washington Post,* 5 January 2007, A1.

Cross, Harold. *The People's Right to Know.* New York: Columbia University Press, 1953.

Denniston, Lyle. "Reagan Legacy: Law Against Leaks." *Washington Journalism Review,* December 1988, 10.

Dobbs, Michael. "Records Counter a Critic of Kerry." *Washington Post,* 19 April 2004.

Editorial. "Reinforce Anti-Secrecy Law." *San Francisco Chronicle,* 4 April 2003, A24.

Editorial. "Turn Over the Logs, Mr. Bush." *Hartford Courant,* 16 January 2007, A8.

Eilperin, Juliet. "Bush Appointee Said to Reject Advice on Endangered Species." *Washington Post,* 30 October 2006, A3.

Eisely, Matthew. "N&O Sues Easley Over Records Law." *News & Observer,* 15 April 2008, A1.

Eshelman, Nancy. "PHEAA Told to Pay Legal Fees for Media." *Patriot News,* 12 February 2008, A1.

Fought, Barbara C. "Privatization Threatens Access." *Quill,* September 1997, 8.

Greenhouse, Linda. "Police Violate Privacy in Home Raids with Journalists." *The New York Times,* 25 May 1999, A25.

Grossman, Andrea. "Editor Awarded Almost $67,000 in Attorney Fees." *Reporters Committee for Freedom of the Press,* 24 January 2007, http://www.rcfp.org/news/2007/0124-foi-editor.html.

Halstuk, Martin. "In Review: The Threat to Freedom of Information." *Columbia Journalism Review,* January-February 2002, 8.

Hayes, Michael J. "Whatever Happened to 'The Right to Know'? Access to Government-Controlled Information Since *Richmond Newspapers.*" *Virginia Law Review* 73 (1987): 111.

Heard, Kenneth. "UAMS to Keep Search Private; Foundation Hires Recruitment Firm." *Arkansas Democrat-Gazette,* 4 September 2008, A1.

Higgins, Steven. "Press and Criminal Record Privacy." *St. Louis University Law Journal* 20 (1977): 509.

Homefront Confidential: How the War on Terrorism Affects Access to Information and the Public's Right to Know. 6th ed. Arlington, Va: Reporters Committee for Freedom of the Press, 2005.

How to Use the Federal FOI Act. 8th ed. Arlington, Va.: FOI Service Center, 1998.

"Journalist Gets Probation for Posing as Federal Official." *Plain Dealer,* 13 April 2002, B2.

"Judge Upholds Reporter's Trespassing Conviction." *Associated Press,* 6 July 2004.

Kaplan, Carl S. "Judge Says Recording of Electronic Chats Is Legal." *Cyber Law Journal,* 14 January 2000.

Kirtley, Jane E., ed. *The First Amendment Handbook.* Washington, D.C.: Reporters Committee for Freedom of the Press, 1986.

Knight Open Government Survey 2008. Washington, D.C.: National Security Archive at George Washington University, 2008.

LaFleur, Jennifer. *The Lost Stories: How a Steady Stream of Laws, Regulations and Judicial Decisions Have Eroded Reporting on Important Issues.* Arlington, Va.: Reporters Committee for Freedom of the Press, 2003.

Lefler, Dion. "Open-Records Requests Can Spell High Fees." *Wichita Eagle,* 9 March 2008, A1.

Lewis, Neil. "White House Holds Up Release of Reagan-Era Documents." *The Oregonian,* 9 June 2001, A10.

Lundstrom, Margie, "The Privacy Boogeyman Runs Amok as Public Records Are Sealed." *Sacramento Bee,* 5 March 2005, A3.

Marwick, Christine M., ed. *Litigation Under the Amended Freedom of Information Act.* 2nd ed. Washington, D.C.: American Civil Liberties Union and Freedom of Information Clearing House, 1976.

"Medical Privacy Law Does Not Apply." *Associated Press,* 28 August 2004.

Meier, Barry. "Jury Says ABC Owes Damages of $5.5 Million." *The New York Times,* 23 January 1997, A1.

Messenger, Tony. "Judge OKs Deal on Blunt E-Mails." *St. Louis Post-Dispatch*, 6 January 2009, B2.

Middleton, Kent. "Journalists, Trespass, and Officials: Closing the Door on *Florida Publishing Co.* v. *Fletcher.*" *Pepperdine Law Review* 16 (1989): 259.

Mifflin, Laurie. "Judge Slashes $5.5 Million Award to Grocery Chain for ABC Report." *The New York Times,* 30 August 1997, A1.

Morrissey, David H. "FOIA Foiled?" *Presstime,* March 1995, 29.

"N.C. Reporter Apologizes; Charge Dismissed." *Associated Press,* 28 April 2005.

Orlov, Rick, and Kerry Cavanaugh. "Privacy: Celebrities Make Their Case for Cracking Down on Aggressive Paparazzi." *Los Angeles Daily News*, 1 August 2008, A1.

Ostrom, Carol M. "Privacy Rules to Limit Word on Patients." *The Seattle Times,*13 April 2003, B1.

Padover, Saul, ed. *The Complete Madison.* New York: Harper & Row, 1953.

Pember, Don R. "The Burgeoning Scope of 'Access Privacy' and the Portent for a Free Press." *Iowa Law Review* 64 (1979): 1155.

Pogrebin, Robin. "At Public Board Meeting, Smithsonian Practices New Openness." *The New York Times*, 18 November 2008, A13.

Pseudo-Secrets: A Freedom of Information Audit of the U.S. Government's Policies on Sensitive Unclassified Information. Washington, D.C.: National Security Archive, George Washington University, March 2006.

"Rancher at Center of Lawsuit Over Televised Raid Dies." *Associated Press,* 17 April 2003.

Riechmann, Deb. "Congress Fears Nuclear Secrets May Slip Out in Old Documents." *Seattle Post-Intelligencer,* 25 August 1999, A5.

Ritter, Bob. *New Technology and the First Amendment.* Greencastle, Ind.: SPJ Reports, 1993.

Rourke, Francis. *Secrecy and Publicity.* Baltimore: Johns Hopkins University Press, 1961.

Schiesel, Seth. "Jury Finds NBC Negligent in 'Dateline' Report." *The New York Times,* 9 July 1998, A19.

Schleifstein, Mark. "Broken Records; Three Years Later, FEMA Still Giving Out Excuses, Not Documents." *Times-Picayune*, 25 January 2009, Metro 5.

Schulz, David A. "Troubling Ruling Restricts News Gathering." *Editor & Publisher,* 29 June 1996, 5.

Secrecy Report Card 2006. Washington, D.C.: OpenTheGovernment.org, 2006.

Secrecy Report Card 2007. Washington, D.C.: OpenTheGovernment.org, 2007.

Secrecy Report Card 2008. Washington, D.C.: OpenTheGovernment.org, 2008.

Shane, Scott. "Detainees' Access to Lawyers Is Security Risk, C.I.A. Says." *The New York Times,* 5 November 2006, A29.

———. "U.S. Reclassifies Many Documents in Secret Review." *The New York Times,* 21 February 2006, A1.

Sherer, Michael D. "Free-Lance Photojournalists and the Law." *Communications and the Law* 10 (1988): 39.

Stewart, Potter. "Or of the Press." *Hastings Law Journal* 26 (1975): 631.

U.S. Senate. *Clarifying and Protecting Right of Public to Information.* 89th Cong., 1st Sess., 1965, S. Rept. 813.

Weiner, Tim. "Lawmaker Tells of High Cost of Data Secrecy." *The New York Times,* 28 June 1996, A9.

———. "U.S. Plans Secrecy Overhaul to Open Millions of Records." *The New York Times,* 18 March 1994, A1.

Weinstein, Henry. "FBI to Release Last of Its John Lennon Files." *Los Angeles Times,* 20 December 2006, B1.

Wicklein, John. "FOIA Foiled." *American Journalism Review,* April 1996, 36.

Yi, Daniel. "Professor Wins Release of Last FBI Data on Beatle." *Los Angeles Times,* 1 October 2004.

CHAPTER 10

Protection of News Sources/Contempt Power

The lifeblood of journalism is information. Each day reporters gather information. It is not uncommon for people outside the news-gathering business to want the information gathered by journalists. Sometimes they merely seek copies of what has already appeared in print or over the airwaves. Sometimes they want more: information that has not been published; photos or video that have not been broadcast; the names of people who provided information to the journalists. Judges, grand juries and even legislative committees all have the power to issue subpoenas to try to force reporters to reveal this information. The first part of this chapter explores exactly how much protection the law provides to reporters who refuse to cooperate when they are presented with subpoenas and how the actions of the journalist ultimately affect what we all read, see and hear.

Anyone who refuses to submit to a court order can be punished with a citation for contempt of court, a swift judicial ruling in which the target can find himself or herself in jail in a matter of hours. This occurred several times in recent years when journalists went to jail for refusing to reveal either their confidential sources or their unpublished information.

JOURNALISTS, JAIL AND CONFIDENTIAL SOURCES

The following are some harsh occupational hazards of which aspiring journalists must be aware:

1. If you refuse to reveal, after having been subpoenaed to do so, the name of a confidential source to a grand jury investigating a potential criminal law violation, then you can be held in contempt of court, ordered to go to jail and forced to pay (along with your newspaper, TV station or Web site employer) an often steep monetary fine. For instance, former New York Times reporter Judith Miller spent 85 days in a Virginia detention facility in 2005 after she refused to reveal the identity of the confidential source who leaked to her the name of Valerie Plame as a covert CIA operative.

2. If you refuse to turn over your notes, photographs or videotapes after having been ordered to do so by a judge in a criminal or civil law proceeding, then you might be held in contempt, ordered to go to jail and forced to pay (along with your newspaper, TV station or Web site employer) an often steep monetary fine. For example, freelance blogger Josh Wolf spent a record-setting 226 days in jail in 2006 and 2007 after he refused, in the face of a subpoena, to turn over unaired videotape he made of a demonstration in San Francisco that damaged a police car.

3. If you breach a promise of confidentiality given to a source by revealing and disclosing that source's name in court, to a grand jury or simply by publishing it in the pages of your newspaper or on its Web site, then you can be sued by that source in a civil law proceeding for monetary damages on a theory known as promissory estoppel.

If you breach a promise of confidentiality given to a source by revealing and disclosing that source's name in court, to a grand jury or simply by publishing it in the pages of your newspaper or on its Web site, then you can be sued.

Journalists who refuse either to comply with subpoenas and court orders to reveal the identity of confidential sources or to turn in court their notes, photographs and videotapes are forced to turn for possible protection either to legislatively created shield laws or to judicially adopted First Amendment (and sometimes common-law) privileges to try to ward off contempt orders, jail sentences and monetary fines. As this chapter makes clear, however, the mere existence of a shield law in your state or the recognition of a court-created First Amendment privilege does not guarantee that you will get off the legal hook. Fewer than 40 states had adopted shield laws by the start of 2010, with the scope of those laws varying significantly in terms of (1) who is protected, (2) what is protected, and (3) when material is protected. What is more, the U.S. Supreme Court has held that there is no First Amendment privilege for a journalist to refuse to testify before a grand jury proceeding. In civil and criminal proceedings (as compared to grand jury proceedings), lower federal appellate courts and some state courts have recognized First Amendment–based privileges, but these judicially created privileges are not absolute and may be overcome.

So why are journalists subject to subpoenas, requests for information and court orders? There are several answers to that question.

Most journalists are highly efficient information gatherers. Some information that journalism gather is not included in the newspaper stories or television reports they prepare. Sometimes the source of a story doesn't want to be named and asks the reporter to promise not to reveal his or her identity. The obvious example here is the Watergate source known only as Deep Throat until he finally came forward in 2005 to reveal his identity as W. Mark Felt. Felt died in December 2008 at age 95 as the most famous confidential source in modern American journalism history. But reporters are not only efficient gatherers, they are excellent record keepers as well. Unreported material is often retained in notebooks and computer memories, or on videotape and audiotape. For some people this undisclosed information is important, even vital. Law enforcement officials frequently want to know what a criminal suspect told a journalist during an interview—only parts of which have been published or broadcast. Libel plaintiffs often need to know the identity of the sources used by reporters in preparation of a story in order to try to prove the story was untrue or fabricated or published with malice. Video recordings of a violent demonstration are often useful to police who seek to identify those who incited the violence or committed criminal acts. Hence, reporters are often asked to reveal information they have gathered but chosen not to publish or broadcast. Most of the time journalists comply with such requests. At times, however, they refuse. When this happens, those interested in obtaining this information often get a court order or **subpoena** to force the journalist to reveal the name of the news source or to disclose the confidential information. Or government agents may get a **warrant** to search a newsroom or a reporter's home to find the information they want.

In our society the press is supposed to represent a neutral entity as it gathers and publishes news and information. When the government or anyone else intrudes into the newsroom or the reporter's notebook, it compromises this neutrality. A news source who normally trusts journalists may choose not to cooperate with a reporter if government agents can learn the source's name by threatening the reporter with a court order. Television news crews will hardly be welcome at protest rallies if the demonstrators know that the government will use the film to identify and prosecute the protesters. The effectiveness of the reporter as an information gatherer may be seriously compromised if government agents or civil and criminal litigants can force journalists to reveal information they choose not to disclose. Society also may ultimately suffer because the flow of information to the public may be reduced.

So why are journalists subject to subpoenas, requests for information and court orders? There are several answers to that question.

In our society the press is supposed to represent a neutral entity as it gathers and publishes news and information.

NEWS AND NEWS SOURCES

If news and information are the lifeblood of the press, then news sources are one of the important wells from which that lifeblood springs. Many journalists are often no better than the sources they can cultivate. News sources come in all shapes and sizes. Occasionally their willingness to cooperate with a reporter is dependent on assurances from the journalist that their identity will not be revealed. Why would a news source wish to remain anonymous? There are many reasons. Often the source of a story about criminal activities has participated

*Why would a news
source wish to remain
anonymous? There are
many reasons.*

in criminal activities and has no desire to publicize this fact. Frequently the source of a story about government mismanagement or dishonesty is an employee of that government agency, and revelation of his or her identity as a whistle-blower could result in loss of the job for informing the press of the errors made by the employee's superiors. Some people simply do not want to get involved in all the hassle that frequently results when an explosive story is published; by remaining anonymous they can remain out of the limelight.

Journalists have always used confidential sources and obtained information that government officials sought to uncover. The earliest reported case of a journalist's refusal to disclose his sources of information took place in 1848 when a reporter for the New York Herald refused to reveal to the U.S. Senate the name of the person who had given him a secret copy of the treaty the United States was negotiating to end the Mexican-American War. He was held in contempt of the Senate and jailed. A U.S. Court of Appeals denied the journalist's petition for release.[1] But the issue of journalists protecting the identity of a confidential source surfaced infrequently in the next 120 years. In fact, from 1911 to 1968 only 17 cases involving a reporter's confidential sources were reported, according to an article in the California Law Review.[2]

There is little mystery as to why the requests to journalists to reveal the names of sources or share confidential information with authorities escalated at the end of the 1960s and into the 1970s. The nation went through a period of great social upheaval, and the press played a significant role in documenting the confrontations between blacks and whites, between war protesters and police, between the mainstream culture and the nascent counterculture. The press was often privy to information that government officials wanted and thought they needed. The confidential relationship between a journalist and a news source often sparks the interest of authorities who are seeking to discover who leaked confidential information to the press. Leaks, apparently from the office of independent counsel Kenneth Starr, facilitated much of the early reporting about the Clinton-Lewinsky affair. Stopping such "leaks" is given a high priority by others in government. Members of the U.S. Senate grilled reporters Nina Totenberg of National Public Radio and Timothy Phelps of Newsday in early 1992 to try to get them to reveal the names of confidential informants who leaked to them a statement made by law professor Anita Hill during the Senate confirmation hearings for Judge Clarence Thomas. Thomas was being considered for an appointment to the U.S. Supreme Court at the time, and Hill charged the jurist with sexual harassment. The pair of reporters were threatened with subpoenas and possible contempt charges for failing to cooperate. But leadership in the Senate finally abandoned the quest for the information, letting Totenberg and Phelps off the hook.

A LEAKY FEDERAL GOVERNMENT? 2008 FIGHTS OVER CONFIDENTIAL GOVERNMENT SOURCES

As noted earlier, New York Times reporter Judith Miller spent 85 days confined in a Virginia detention facility in 2005 for refusing to reveal to a federal grand jury the name of the government source who leaked to her the identity of covert CIA operative

1. *Ex parte Nugent,* 16 Fed. Cas. 471 (1848).
2. "The Newsman's Privilege," 1198.

Valerie Plame. Less known is that several journalists are subpoenaed every year in federal court to disclose the identity of federal officials who allegedly leak to them confidential information. Consider three cases from 2008:

- Washington Times reporter Bill Gertz was subpoenaed by a federal judge in California to reveal the identity of confidential government sources he used when writing a 2006 story about a federal investigation of a Chinese espionage ring and its alleged efforts to steal U.S. Navy technology. In the May 16, 2006, story at issue, Gertz identified his sources as "senior justice department officials" who agreed to speak with him "on the condition of anonymity." In July 2008 U.S. District Court Judge Cormac J. Carney ruled in favor of Gertz, holding he could not be compelled to testify and reasoning that "the freedom of the press is a paramount interest" and that "it is undeniable that Mr. Gertz was performing a vital public service" by reporting on the espionage matter. After the judge's ruling in his favor on First Amendment grounds, Gertz remarked that "the identity of these confidential news sources must be protected if our press freedoms, fundamental to the effective functioning of our democratic system, are to endure. Efforts by government to compel reporters to disclose news sources must be resisted."[3]

- New York Times and Pulitzer Prize-winning reporter James Risen was subpoenaed in 2008 to reveal to a federal grand jury the identity of government sources he used for a chapter in his 2006 book "State of War" that describes the Central Intelligence Agency's alleged efforts to spy on Iran's nuclear program. While Risen was fighting the subpoena in 2008, the government got a hold of his telephone records in a back-door effort to identify his government sources by looking at the numbers Risen had called.

- Detroit Free Press reporter David Ashenfelter was fighting a subpoena in both 2008 and 2009 to compel him to reveal the names of U.S. Department of Justice officials who leaked to him confidential information regarding an internal investigation into possible ethics violations committed by former Assistant U.S. Attorney Richard Convertino. This battle is described in more detail later in this chapter.

A journalist served with a subpoena has few options. The reporter or news organization can cooperate with those who seek the information and reveal what it is they want to know. This cooperation could damage the reporter-source relationship or threaten the image of independence fostered by most news media. The journalist can seek to have the subpoena withdrawn or attack the order in court and hope to have it quashed. Going to court can be

---

3. Ramstack, "Judge Upholds Reporter's Right to Protect Sources."

expensive and is time-consuming. If in the end the journalist refuses to cooperate, he or she will likely be held in contempt of court. A fine and a jail sentence usually follow. So the choice for the journalist is not an easy one.

But the choice for society is difficult as well. The interests that are involved in this dilemma are basic to our system of government and political values. On one hand, it is clearly the obligation of every citizen to cooperate with the government and testify before the proper authorities. This concept was so well established by the early 18th century that it had become a maxim. John Henry Wigmore, in his classic treatise on evidence, cites the concept thus: "The public has a right to everyman's evidence."[4] The Sixth Amendment to the U.S. Constitution guarantees the right to have witnesses and to compel them to testify in our behalf. And surely this right is a valuable one, both to society and to the individual seeking to prove his or her innocence of charges of wrongdoing. The Supreme Court in 1919 wrote on the duties and rights of witnesses:

The Sixth Amendment to the U.S. Constitution guarantees the right to have witnesses and to compel them to testify in our behalf.

> [I]t is clearly recognized that the giving of testimony and the attendance upon court or grand jury in order to testify are public duties which everyone within the jurisdiction of the government is bound to perform upon being properly summoned, . . . the personal sacrifice involved is a part of the necessary contribution to the public welfare.[5]

But society benefits from information provided by the news media. When a reporter is forced to break a promise of confidentiality or is used as an arm of law enforcement investigators, it harms this flow of information. People who know things, often important things, simply won't give this information to journalists for fear of being exposed if the reporter is squeezed for the information. The fragile reporter-source relationship may be damaged.

TIPS FOR REPORTERS ON PROMISING CONFIDENTIALITY

Here are some suggestions that were given by newspaper attorney David Utevsky to reporters and writers at a seminar in Seattle.

- Do not routinely promise confidentiality as a standard interview technique.
- Avoid giving an absolute promise of confidentiality. Try to persuade the source to agree that you may reveal his or her name if you are subpoenaed.
- Do not rely exclusively on information from a confidential source. Get corroboration from a nonconfidential source or documents.
- Consider whether others (police, attorneys, etc.) will want to know the identity of the source before publishing or broadcasting the material. Will you be the only source of this information, or can they get it elsewhere?

---

4. Wigmore, *Anglo-American System of Evidence.*
5. *Blair* v. *U.S.,* 250 U.S. 273 (1919).

> ▮ Consider whether you can use the information without disclosing
> that it was obtained from a confidential source.
>
> Reporters should always consult with a supervisor or editor before promising
> anonymity to a source; if a legal action results the journalist will have to rely on the
> news outlet to assist in defending the action.

As more and more reporters were called on to cooperate with legal authorities during the last 40 years, the courts and state legislatures were asked to fashion protection for both the legal system and the press. What was needed were rules that required the reporter to share valuable information with the parties that needed it, but only in those rare circumstances when severe harm might result without this cooperation. These rules are called the reporter's privilege. Such a privilege is not a novelty in the law. A variation of this privilege is given to doctors, lawyers, members of the clergy and even accountants in some instances. The reporter's privilege that emerged in the past three decades is hardly a nice, neat, legal proposition. The source of the privilege varies from jurisdiction to jurisdiction. In some places its genesis is in the U.S. or state constitution; in other places it flows from the common law or state statute. The scope of the privilege also varies from jurisdiction to jurisdiction. A reporter in Michigan may be legally immune from a certain kind of subpoena, whereas her counterpart in Ohio may not enjoy the same immunity. What follows is a general outline of the broad provisions of the privilege, focusing especially on the rights that spring from the First Amendment. To be safe a journalist should know the specific law in his or her own state. An excellent online resource for the rules of each state that is prepared by the Reporters Committee for Freedom of the Press is called "The Reporter's Privilege." It can be found on the RCFP Web site, http://www.rcfp.org/privilege, and is billed by that organization as "a complete compendium of information on the reporter's privilege—the right not to be compelled to testify or disclose sources and information in court—in each state and federal circuit."

The reporter's privilege that emerged during the past three decades is hardly a nice, neat, legal proposition.

THE FAILURE TO KEEP A PROMISE

Many journalists are reluctant to reveal the names of their sources because they think it would be unethical or would diminish their ability to use the source at some point in the future. About 20 years ago reporters discovered another reason to protect the identity of a source: They could be sued if they broke their promise of confidentiality.

In 1991 a five-justice majority of the U.S. Supreme Court held in *Cohen* v. *Cowles Media, Inc.*[6] that the First Amendment does not bar and does not prevent a lawsuit against a journalist who breaches a promise of confidentiality to a source when the source suffers direct harm from reliance on the breached promise. In this case, a Republican political operative named Dan Cohen was given a promise of anonymity by reporters from two Minnesota papers in return for information Cohen would supply about a rival candidate for public office. The information Cohen gave turned out to be both old and insignificant, and the newspapers'

6. 501 U.S. 663 (1991).

editors decided the real story was not the information Cohen supplied but, instead, Cohen's own tactics in spreading dirt under the cloak of anonymity about a rival candidate. The two newspapers thus decided to reveal Cohen's name, a move that cost Cohen his job when his employer read his name and then fired him.

Upholding Cohen's right to sue the papers for their breached confidentiality promise under a legal theory called promissory estoppel, the majority held that "the First Amendment does not confer on the press a constitutional right to disregard promises that would otherwise be enforced under state law." The majority found the case was controlled by a "well-established line of decisions holding that generally applicable laws do not offend the First Amendment simply because their enforcement against the press has incidental effects on its ability to gather and report the news." This language is important for journalists to remember when gathering news: They cannot break general laws and then try to claim a First Amendment exemption from them. Recall this same maxim from the discussion in Chapter 9 of the Lawrence Matthews case involving child pornography (see page 312).

Promissory estoppel is an old Anglo-American legal rule that was promulgated to prevent injustice when someone fails to keep a promise that he or she has made, a promise that by itself does not add up to an enforceable contract, but a promise someone else has relied on. To prevail in an action for promissory estoppel the plaintiff is usually required to show

1. *that the defendant made a clear and definite promise to the plaintiff;*
2. *that the defendant intended to induce the plaintiff's reliance on that promise;*
3. *that the plaintiff, in fact, reasonably relied on that promise to his or her detriment and harm; and*
4. *that the promise must be enforced by the court in the interests of justice to the plaintiff.*

Imagine a journalist tries to convince a lab technician at a chemical company to reveal specific information that proves that her employer is polluting a nearby stream. She is reluctant; she fears she will be fired if her cooperation with the reporter is discovered. But the reporter presses her and clearly promises that he will never, under any circumstance, reveal her name if she gives him the information. The story is published. The employee is subsequently fired after the reporter provides her name to a state legislative committee investigating the pollution. She then could bring an action for promissory estoppel.

In the immediate wake of the *Cohen* ruling another lawsuit began in Minnesota in which a woman named Jill Ruzicka sued Glamour magazine. The periodical published an article on therapist-patient sexual abuse that included an interview with Ruzicka, who had previously sued both her therapist and the state agency whose job it was to regulate such practitioners. Ruzicka agreed to be interviewed on the condition that she not be identified. She wasn't named in the article, but she argued that the reporter's description of her story made her identity obvious to most readers. The case made several stops in federal courts[7] before the 8th U.S. Circuit Court of Appeals ordered a lower court to hold a trial. The appellate judges said that the promise to shield Ruzicka's identity was definite enough under state law to support an action for promissory estoppel. The court said that because the magazine editors had added

---

7. *Ruzicka* v. *Conde Nast Publications, Inc.,* 939 F. 2d 578 (1991), 774 F. Supp. 303 (1992).

identifying details to the description of Ruzicka after she had approved the original draft of the article, a jury could find that the magazine had failed to keep its promise not to disclose the plaintiff's identity.[8]

Perhaps the most significant recent opinion in this area was handed down in 2005 by the 6th U.S. Circuit Court of Appeals in a case called *Ventura* v. *Cincinnati Enquirer.*[9] Plaintiff George G. Ventura sued the newspaper and its publisher, the Gannett Co., for causes of action including breach of contract and promissory estoppel. Ventura claimed that Enquirer reporters disclosed his identity as a confidential news source to a grand jury investigating the illegal news-gathering actions of one of the paper's reporters, Michael Gallagher. Specifically, Ventura had entered into an agreement in 1997 with Gallagher, who was then working on an exposé of Chiquita Brands International, Inc. Ventura, an attorney, had worked as legal counsel for the massive firm best known for its bananas, but he had left under what the appellate court described as "less than amicable circumstances." Ventura thus agreed to give Gallagher, under a promise of confidentiality, private passwords and secret access codes to Chiquita's internal voice-mail systems. Gallagher then used the passwords and codes to illegally invade the Chiquita voice-mail system—conduct for which Gallagher was both fired by the Enquirer and subpoenaed to testify before a grand jury. It was during this testimony that Gallagher provided to the grand jury tape recordings of telephone conversations he had with Ventura regarding Chiquita's voice-mail system. The recordings supplied by Gallagher led, in part, to the indictment of Ventura on multiple counts of attempted unauthorized access to a computer system. Ventura, however, sought civil redress from Gallagher, the Enquirer and Gannett, claiming the disclosure of the tapes to the grand jury violated his confidentiality agreement with Gallagher. Ventura, however, would lose his civil lawsuit.

In sustaining the trial court's grant of summary judgment in favor of the Enquirer and against Ventura on causes of action breach of contract and promissory estoppel, the 6th Circuit found that "Ohio public policy precludes enforcement of agreements to conceal a crime where, as here, the plaintiff [Ventura] is effectively urging the court to enforce an agreement he reached with a co-conspirator [Gallagher] to withhold evidence of plaintiff's crimes." The appellate court determined that "that public policy precludes the plaintiff from enforcing any promise by Gallagher to conceal the plaintiff's criminal activity." Put differently, the 6th Circuit recognized an absolute privilege or immunity for Gallagher to give up Ventura's name without facing civil liability because such a privilege "will encourage the reporting of criminal activity by removing any threat of reprisal in the form of civil liability. This, in turn, will aid in the proper investigation of criminal activity and the prosecution of those responsible for the crime."

TIPS FOR REPORTERS WHEN CONFRONTED WITH A SOURCE WHO DEMANDS CONFIDENTIALITY

1. Assume the interview is on the record unless the subject seeks anonymity.

---

8. *Ruzicka* v. *Conde Nast Publications, Inc.*, 999 F. 2d 1319 (1993).
9. 396 F. 3d 784 (6th Cir. 2005).

2. Realize that there is no obligation to grant anonymity for information that has already been provided.

3. Before making any promise to a source, try to find something out about the information and where it comes from.

4. Talk with an editor or news director before making any promises to a source.

5. Keep any promise made to a source simple and easy to fulfill, and be certain both you and the source completely understand the conditions to which you have agreed.

6. Record any promise you make to a source.

7. Avoid adding material to a story that a source has already approved, or try to avoid promising the source that he or she has story approval.

What does all of this mean? If—and that's a very big if—other courts adopt the logic of the 6th U.S. Circuit Court of Appeals, the outcome in *Ventura* v. *Cincinnati Enquirer* suggests that reporters may be free to breach agreements of confidentiality to sources, without fear of civil liability, but only if they are revealing the names of the sources to a prosecutor in a grand jury setting. The 6th Circuit's decision examined the public policy of only one state—Ohio—and reporters should not assume the holding will be stretched to other jurisdictions.

CONSTITUTIONAL PROTECTION OF NEWS SOURCES

In 1972 the Supreme Court of the United States ruled, in a 5-4 decision, that there was no privilege under the First Amendment for journalists to refuse to reveal the names of confidential sources or other information when called to testify before a grand jury.[10] This ruling is the last word the nation's high court has spoken on the subject. Federal appellate courts in 2005 and 2006 upheld this aging precedent from *Branzburg* v. *Hayes* in cases involving journalists—Judith Miller of The New York Times and freelance video blogger Joshua Wolf—jailed for refusing to comply with grand jury subpoenas.[11] At the same time, however, most federal courts have limited the *Branzburg* ruling to apply only to grand jury settings, and they have created, either under First Amendment or common-law principles, qualified (limited) protection for journalists not to testify in other, non-grand-jury settings. The following describes how it got to this point, starting with the *Branzburg* case and ruling.

The Supreme Court consolidated three similar cases in *Branzburg* to consider whether the First Amendment privileged journalists not to testify before grand juries about confidential information. One case involved Paul Branzburg, a reporter for the Louisville Courier-Journal.

10. *Branzburg* v. *Hayes,* 408 U.S. 665 (1972).
11. *In re Grand Jury Subpoena: Judith Miller,* 397 F. 3d 964 (D.C. Cir. 2005); and *In re Grand Jury Subpoena: Joshua Wolf,* 35 M.L.R. 1207 (9th Cir. 2006).

Branzburg was called to testify in 1971 about drug use in Kentucky after he wrote two stories about drugs and drug dealers in the area. In the second case, Paul Pappas, a television reporter for a Massachusetts television station, was called before a grand jury to relate what he had seen and heard when he spent three hours at a Black Panther headquarters in July 1970. Finally, New York Times reporter Earl Caldwell was subpoenaed to appear before a grand jury investigating the activities of the Black Panthers in Oakland, Calif. Caldwell, a black man, had gained the confidence of the leaders of the militant group and had consistently written illuminating stories about the Panthers that demonstrated an astute awareness of their activities. The decisions in the three cases are referred to collectively as the *Branzburg* ruling.

The Supreme Court fractured into three groups in deciding this case. Four justices, led by Byron White, who wrote the court's opinion, ruled that there was no First Amendment privilege for reporters called to testify before a grand jury. White said that although the court was sensitive to First Amendment considerations, the case did not present any such considerations. There were no prior restraints, no limitations on what the press might publish, and no order for the press to publish information it did not wish to. No penalty for publishing certain content was imposed. White wrote:

> The use of confidential sources by the press is not forbidden or restricted. . . .
>
> The sole issue before us is the obligation of reporters to respond to grand jury subpoenas as other citizens do and answer questions relevant to an investigation into the commission of crime. Citizens generally are not constitutionally immune from grand jury subpoenas; and neither the First Amendment nor other constitutional provisions protect the average citizen from the disclosing to a grand jury information that he has received in confidence.[12]

Reporters are no better than average citizens, White concluded.

The four dissenters differed sharply with the other justices. Justice William O. Douglas took the view that the First Amendment provides the press with an absolute and unqualified privilege. In any circumstance, under any condition, the reporter should be able to shield the identity of a confidential source. Justices Potter Stewart, William Brennan and Thurgood Marshall were unwilling to go as far as Douglas and instead proposed that reporters should be protected by a privilege that is qualified, not absolute. These three dissenters argued that the reporter should be able to protect the identity of the confidential source unless the government can show the following:

1. That there is a probable cause to believe that the reporter has information that is clearly relevant to a specific violation of the law
2. That the information sought cannot be obtained by alternative means less destructive of First Amendment rights
3. That the state has a compelling and overriding interest in the information

When the government cannot fulfill all three requirements, Justice Stewart wrote for the dissenters, the journalist should not be forced to testify.

---

12. *Branzburg* v. *Hayes,* 408 U.S. 665 (1972).

Justice Lewis Powell provided the fifth vote needed for the court to reject the notion of a constitutional privilege for reporters. But whereas Powell voted with those who could find no privilege in the First Amendment, his brief concurring opinion seemed to support the opposite proposition. "The Court does not hold that newsmen, subpoenaed to testify before a grand jury, are without constitutional rights with respect to the gathering of news or in safeguarding their sources," he wrote. No harassment of reporters will be allowed, and a balance must be struck between freedom of the press and the obligation of all citizens to give relevant testimony. "In short, the courts will be available to newsmen under circumstances where legitimate First Amendment interests require protection," Powell wrote. Two years later, in a footnote in another case, *Saxbe* v. *Washington Post,*[13] Powell emphasized that the high court's ruling in *Branzburg* was an extremely narrow one and that reporters were not without First Amendment rights to protect the identity of their sources.

LOWER-COURT RULINGS

Most lower federal courts have treated the high court's decision in Branzburg *as the very narrow ruling that Justice Powell said it was in 1974.*

Most lower federal courts have treated the high court's decision in *Branzburg* as the very narrow ruling that Justice Powell said it was in 1974. The *Branzburg* ruling focused on a reporter's responsibility to testify before a grand jury. And that is generally how the lower courts have applied the precedent, granting reporters a qualified right to refuse testimony in other kinds of circumstances. Note the language from the 3rd U.S. Circuit Court of Appeals in a 1979 ruling, which characterized *Branzburg* in this fashion:

> There (in *Branzburg*), the Supreme Court decided that a journalist does not have an absolute privilege under the First Amendment to refuse to appear and testify before a grand jury to answer questions relevant to an investigation of the commission of a crime. No Supreme Court case since that decision has extended the holding beyond that which was necessary to vindicate the public interest in law enforcement and ensuing effective grand jury proceedings.[14]

Not all the U.S. Courts of Appeals have looked at *Branzburg* in such an expansive manner. In 1998 a panel of judges in the 5th Circuit wrote:

> Although some courts have taken from Justice Powell's concurrence a mandate to construct a broad, qualified news reporters' privilege in criminal cases, we decline to do so. Justice Powell's separate writing only emphasizes that at a certain point, the First Amendment must protect the press from government intrusion.[15]

The court went on to require a television station to surrender the unaired portions of a videotape interview with a man accused of arson.

Ten of 12 of the U.S. appeals courts have ruled that the First Amendment provides at least limited protection for reporters who are asked to testify or produce photos or other mate-

---

13. 417 U.S. 843 (1974).
14. *Riley* v. *Chester,* 612 F. 2d 708 (1979).
15. *U.S.* v. *Smith,* 135 F. 2d 363 (1998); see also *WTHR-TV* v. *Cline,* 693 N.E. 2d 1 (1998).

rials at hearings other than grand jury proceedings.* The 6th U.S. Circuit Court of Appeals (Kentucky, Michigan, Ohio and Tennessee) rejected this notion in 1987. "Because we conclude that acceptance of the position . . . would be tantamount to our substituting, as a holding in *Branzburg,* the dissent written by Justice Stewart, we must reject that position. . . . That portion of Justice Powell's opinion certainly does not warrant rewriting the majority opinion to grant a First Amendment testimonial privilege to news reporters," the court ruled.[16]

The 6th Circuit's refusal to recognize a qualified First Amendment privilege for reporters proved pivotal more than two decades later in 2008. That's when a federal judge in Michigan (a state in the 6th Circuit) ordered David Ashenfelter, a Pulitzer Prize-winning reporter for the Detroit Free Press, to reveal the identity of anonymous Justice Department officials he used as sources for a negative story four years earlier about Richard Convertino, then an assistant U.S. attorney. Convertino later filed a civil lawsuit against the Justice Department for allegedly violating the federal Privacy Act (see Chapter 9) by leaking confidential and harmful information about him from his personnel file. To determine the identity of the unnamed leakers within the Justice Department, Convertino subpoenaed Ashenfelter, who refused to reveal his sources. In ruling against Ashenfelter in August 2008, Judge Robert Cleland wrote that "the Sixth Circuit has explicitly declined to recognize a qualified First Amendment privilege for reporters," and he pointed out the need for disclosure, writing that "Convertino cannot sustain his burden of proof on the Privacy Act claim without identifying Ashenfelter's source."[17] In October that year, Ashenfelter failed to show up at a deposition where he would have been questioned about his sources—a brazen move that typically triggers contempt proceedings. In November 2008 Judge Cleland once again denied Ashenfelter's request for a protective order and told him to appear at the deposition. Ashenfelter then tried a new and somewhat novel tactic to keep silent at a December 2008 deposition: He repeatedly invoked his right against self-incrimination protected by the Fifth Amendment to the U.S. Constitution (that right might be relevant to the extent that Convertino had suggested that Ashenfelter conspired with, protected and abetted the Justice Department leakers by refusing to reveal their identities when they broke federal laws by revealing the investigation of Convertino).

In February 2009 Ashenfelter was ordered to reappear for a deposition in April and to either answer Convertino's questions about the Justice Department sources or to provide evidence of the specific criminal charge underlying his Fifth Amendment objection. Judge Cleland also allowed Ashenfelter to submit a sealed affidavit prior to the deposition to explain the grounds for the Fifth Amendment objection. The battle continued until the April 21, 2009, deposition, during which Judge Cleland ruled in favor of Ashenfelter when he asserted his Fifth Amendment right against self-incrimination after Convertino's attorney asked Ashenfelter to

Judge Cleland ruled in favor of Ashenfelter when he asserted his Fifth Amendment right against self-incrimination.

*The 5th U.S. Circuit Court of Appeals is included among the 10 because, despite the 1998 ruling in *U.S.* v. *Smith,* judges in the circuit have ruled that a privilege exists at least for civil suits. (See, for example, *Miller* v. *Transamerican Press, Inc.,* 621 F. 2d 721 [1980].) The 1998 decision did not reject these earlier rulings, but argued that because a criminal case was at issue, a different standard should apply.

16. *Storer Communications* v. *Giovan,* 810 F. 2d 580 (1987).
17. *Convertino* v. *U.S. Department of Justice,* 2008 WL 4104347 (E.D. Mich. Aug. 28, 2008). See also *Convertino* v. *U.S. Department of Justice,* 2008 WL 4998369 (E.D. Mich. Nov. 21, 2008); *Convertino* v. *U.S. Department of Justice,* Order and Order Denying Non-Party Respondent's Emergency Order, Case No. 07-CV-13842 (E.D. Mich. Mar. 31, 2009).

reveal the names of his sources. That ruling, which kept Ashenfelter from going to jail, was hailed by many observers as a victory for freedom of the press, even though it rested on the Fifth Amendment and not the First Amendment.

That did not end the legal battle, however, as Convertino subpoenaed the Detroit Free Press (for whom Ashenfelter works) for information regarding all stories the newspaper had published about him. The newspaper fought back in court in June 2009, calling that request a "fishing expedition," a legal metaphor suggesting that Convertino was casting the net of his subpoena too far and wide.

Guided by Judge Richard Posner, the 7th Circuit Court of Appeals in *McKevitt* v. *Pallasch*[18] refused to recognize a reporter's privilege and, instead, held that "courts should simply make sure that a subpoena . . . directed to the media . . . is reasonable in the circumstances, which is the general criterion for judicial review of subpoenas." While the ultimate impact of this decision is yet unclear, one thing definitely is certain: It represents a substantial rethinking of the *Branzburg* decision by an extremely well-respected jurist. As of November 2009, 37 states had enacted a statutory protection called a **shield law** that offers reporters some (although not usually absolute) protection against being forced to reveal the identity of confidential sources. Figure 10.1 shown later in this chapter shows a map indicating which states have shield laws. Appellate courts in all of the remaining 13 states, except for Wyoming, have recognized various kinds of constitutional and/or common-law testimonial privileges for reporters.

The constitutional privilege has considerable elasticity.

The constitutional privilege has considerable elasticity. Its successful application depends on several factors. What kind of proceeding is involved? The privilege is more readily granted to a journalist involved in a civil suit than to one called to testify before a grand jury. What kind of material is sought? A journalist is more likely to be protected by the privilege when the name of a confidential source is sought than when courts are seeking testimony about information that is not confidential or about events actually witnessed by the reporter. Finally, testimonial privilege derived by both federal and state courts through the Constitution or the common law is qualified by the various tests that courts have developed, tests that usually mirror the one outlined by Justice Stewart in *Branzburg*. Is the information important? Is it clearly relevant to the proceedings? Is there somewhere else to get the information? It is important to remember that without a binding Supreme Court ruling, the lower federal and state courts have been permitted to fashion their own rules; and there is distinct variance from state to state, federal circuit to federal circuit. Look to the court precedents in your region as the final authority in this matter.

Civil Cases

Courts are most likely to recognize the right of a journalist to refuse to testify in a civil action.

A reporter could be called to testify in three different kinds of court proceedings: a civil lawsuit, a criminal case or a grand jury. Courts are most likely to recognize the right of a journalist to refuse to testify in a civil action, and least likely to recognize this right if the reporter is called before a grand jury. Recognition of the privilege in civil cases came only a year after the *Branzburg* ruling, when a U.S. District Court in Washington, D.C., quashed a subpoena issued to reporters from a variety of newspapers and magazines who were thought to have materials obtained during their coverage of the Watergate break-in. The materials were sought

18. 339 F. 3d 530 (7th Cir. 2003).

by members of the Democratic National Committee who were suing to win damages from some of the Watergate burglars.[19] The court said that reporters had at least a qualified privilege under the First Amendment to refuse to answer such questions or provide such material. Four years later the 10th U.S. Circuit Court of Appeals ruled that filmmaker Arthur Hirsch could not be forced to reveal confidential information he had obtained in connection with a civil suit by the estate of Karen Silkwood against the Kerr-McGee Corporation.[20] Silkwood died mysteriously in an auto accident after she threatened to expose improper safety conditions at the nuclear facility at which she worked. Hirsch was preparing a documentary film on Karen Silkwood's life and death.

In a typical civil suit, the court will ask three questions when deciding whether to force the reporter to testify:

In a typical civil suit, the court will ask three questions.

1. Has the person seeking the information from the reporter—normally the plaintiff—shown that this information is of *certain relevance* in the case? It must be related to the matter before the court.

2. Does this information go to the heart of the issue before the court? That is, is it critical to the outcome of the case?

3. Can the person who wants the information show the court that there is no other source for this information?

If all three questions are answered yes, the chances are good that the court will require the reporter to reveal the confidential information. How rigorously the judge applies this test often depends on the reporter's relationship to the lawsuit. If the reporter is not a party to the lawsuit but merely has information that may be of value to one or both parties, a judge typically applies the test very rigorously and normally the journalist will not be required to testify. But that is not always the case. In 1996 a federal judge in Connecticut ruled that a reporter had to testify in a securities case as to whether one of the defendants had actually made the statements that were attributed to him in a newspaper article written by the reporter.[21] The judge ruled that the testimony sought was directly relevant to the case and was unavailable from another source. The court also noted that it was not seeking information about a confidential source. If the reporter is a party in the lawsuit, either as a plaintiff or a defendant, courts are less willing to let the journalist off the hook. In these instances it is more likely, but still not common, for the court to require the reporter to cooperate.

In August 2007, in Dr. Steven Hatfill's civil lawsuit against the federal government for leaking to journalists his name as the possible perpetrator who mailed anthrax-laced letters in 2001, a federal judge ordered six nonparty journalists to reveal the names of their confidential FBI and Justice Department sources that leaked Hatfill's name.[22] Although recognizing that the journalists had a qualified First Amendment–based privilege not to testify, U.S. District Court Judge Reggie B. Walton reasoned that the privilege had been overcome by Hatfill because "the actual identity of the sources will be important and quite possibly essential" to

---

19. *Democratic National Committee* v. *McCord,* 356 F. Supp. 1394 (1973).
20. *Silkwood* v. *Kerr-McGee,* 563 F. 2d 433 (1977).
21. *SEC* v. *Seahawk Deep Ocean Technology, Inc.,* 166 F.R.D. 268 (1996).
22. *Hatfill* v. *Gonzales,* 505 F. Supp. 2d 33 (D.D.C. 2007).

his lawsuit and because Hatfill "has exhausted all reasonable alternatives for acquiring the sources of the leaked information."

Although three of the journalists caught a break when their sources voluntarily released them from their promises of confidentiality, the Hatfill saga continued in 2008 when former USA Today reporter Toni Locy, as described later in this chapter, was held in contempt of court by Judge Walton and ordered to personally pay up to $5,000 a day until she revealed to Hatfill the name of her source.[23] Judge Walton prohibited Locy from accepting reimbursement from USA Today to satisfy the monetary sanction, although an appellate court quickly stayed the fines until it could hear the matter in full,[24] and it later dismissed the matter as moot after Hatfill settled his case with the government for more than $5 million.[25]

Reporters far more commonly find themselves as defendants in lawsuits, typically a libel suit. Oftentimes the plaintiff seeks to know about sources the reporter used to prepare the libelous story, or where and how the reporter got information for the libelous story. Whether the court will force the reporter to testify in such instances usually depends on several factors, all of which are related to the three-part test outlined earlier. A plaintiff will often be required to show that the information held by the reporter goes to the very heart of the lawsuit. For example, the plaintiff may have to show that he or she cannot possibly prove negligence or actual malice (see Chapter 5 to refresh your memory on these matters) without information from the reporter.[26] Or, the court will require that the plaintiff show that the libel claim actually has merit, that it is not simply an attempt to harass the defendant.[27] Finally, the court will usually require the plaintiff to show that there is no other source for this information, that the plaintiff has exhausted all other potential means of gaining this information. In 1979 the U.S. Supreme Court ruled that it was not an infringement of the reporters' First Amendment rights for the defendant to ask reporters what they were thinking about as they prepared the libelous story.[28] Such questions may or may not involve confidential sources.

The reporter who refuses to obey a court order and give the plaintiff critical information in a libel suit surely faces a **contempt of court** charge and potentially a fine and a jail sentence. But that is not all. In a few cases when a reporter has refused to reveal his or her source for a libelous story, the court has ruled as a matter of law that no source for the story exists.[29] This declaration effectively strips away the libel defense for a newspaper or broadcasting station. In effect, the judge is saying that the reporter made up the story. This is not a common occurrence, but it certainly is a frightening one.

For instance, in the case of *Ayash* v. *Dana-Farber Cancer Institute*[30] the Supreme Judicial Court of Massachusetts in 2005 affirmed a default judgment against The Boston Globe in a libel suit because the newspaper failed to disclose confidential sources. In this lawsuit Dr. Lois J.

---

23. *Hatfill* v. *Mukasey,* 539 F. Supp. 2d 96 (D.D.C. 2008).
24. *Hatfill* v. *Mukasey,* 2008 U.S. App. LEXIS 5755 (D.C. Cir. Mar. 11, 2008).
25. *Hatfill* v. *Mukasey,* Order, No. 08-5049 (D.C. Cir. Nov. 17, 2008).
26. *Cervantes* v. *Time,* 446 F. 2d 986 (1972).
27. *Senear* v. *Daily Journal-American,* 641 P. 2d 1180 (1982).
28. *Herbert* v. *Lando,* 441 U.S. 153 (1979).
29. See *Downing* v. *Monitor Publishing,* 415 A. 2d 683 (1980); and *Sierra Life* v. *Magic Valley Newspapers,* 623 P. 2d 103 (1980).
30. 822 N.E. 2d 667; 33 M.L.R. 1513 (Mass. 2005).

Ayash of the Dana-Farber Cancer Institute alleged that The Globe published a series of scathing and inaccurate articles in 1995 written by reporter Richard A. Knox about Ayash's treatment of several patients who allegedly were given overdoses of a highly toxic chemotherapy drug, thereby destroying the doctor's reputation. One article even ran under the blunt (and, if false, defamatory) headline "Doctor's Orders Killed Cancer Patient" (remember from Chapter 4 and the description from the case involving Kato Kaelin that, if false, headlines can form the basis for a libel suit). During the discovery stage of the litigation, Ayash sought the identities of sources consulted by Knox before writing articles that were subsequently published in The Globe and that formed, at least in part, the basis of the doctor's lawsuit. At the trial court level, The Globe had refused to provide information that would lead to the identities of Knox's confidential sources, despite a court order to disclose their identities. Massachusetts is one of 13 states that does not have a shield law giving some protection to reporters against disclosure of confidential information (see pages 397–401). A judgment of civil contempt was entered by the trial court judge against The Globe and Knox and, in turn, the judge awarded a pretrial judgment against them. A jury was allowed to determine damages and it meted out a whopping $2.1 million award to Ayash.

In affirming both the default judgment and the damage award, the Massachusetts high court noted that "the Globe defendants had no special constitutional or statutory testimonial privilege, based on their status as a newspaper publisher or reporter, that would justify their refusal to obey the orders." It agreed with the trial court judge's determination that "the plaintiff's need for the requested information outweighed the public interest in the protection of the free flow of information to the press." The Massachusetts high court's decision affirming the award sparked renewed discussion in that state's legislature in 2005 about the need to join the majority of states and adopt a shield law to protect reporters such as Richard Knox from making the uncomfortable choice between either breaching promises of confidentiality to their sources or facing entry of default judgments with potentially devastating jury awards.

Finally, the 9th U.S. Circuit Court of Appeals handed down an important ruling in 1993 when it extended the reporter's privilege in a civil suit to the authors of books as well. Typically the privilege has been granted to so-called working journalists, salaried employees of newspapers, magazines and broadcasting stations. Freelance writers like book authors were often denied the protection. The court ruled that a book author clearly had a right to invoke the First Amendment privilege.[31] "The journalist's privilege is designed to protect investigative reporting regardless of the medium used to report the news to the public," Judge Norris wrote.

Criminal Cases

Courts have granted the First Amendment privilege to reporters quite freely in civil actions in part, at least, because there is no competing constitutional right involved. In a criminal case, however, the privilege for the reporter must be balanced against the Sixth Amendment right of the defendant to compel testimony on his or her behalf. Consequently, it is somewhat less likely that a court will permit a reporter to refuse to answer questions about the identity of a confidential source or other confidential information. Courts most often apply slight variations of the Stewart test from the *Branzburg* case (see pages 376–378) to determine whether the journalist will be compelled to testify.

In a criminal case, the privilege for the reporter must be balanced against the Sixth Amendment right of the defendant to compel testimony on his or her behalf.

31. *Shoen* v. *Shoen,* 5 F. 3d 1289 (1993).

In *U.S.* v. *Burke,* for example, the defendant was indicted for conspiracy in connection with a basketball point-shaving scheme at Boston College and attempted to impeach the testimony of the prosecution's chief witness, a reputed underworld figure. The defendant asked the court to subpoena the unpublished notes and drafts of Sports Illustrated reporter Douglas Looney, who had interviewed the witness. The U.S. Court of Appeals for the 2nd Circuit quashed the subpoena, noting that a court may order reporters to reveal confidential sources only when the information is (1) highly material and relevant, (2) necessary or critical to the defense, and (3) unobtainable from other sources.[32]

In 1984 the Washington state Supreme Court ruled that an Everett (Wash.) Herald reporter did not have to reveal the names of several confidential sources he had used to prepare an article about alleged cult activities at an 80-acre farm near rural Snohomish, Wash. The owner of the farm, Theodore Rinaldo, had been convicted of statutory rape, assault, coercion and intimidating a witness. A year after his conviction, several persons who had testified on Rinaldo's behalf at his trial stepped forward and admitted they had committed perjury. It was during his second trial for tampering with witnesses and other offenses that Rinaldo tried to force reporter Gary Larson to reveal the names of persons who gave the reporter information for six articles that had brought the activities at the farm to the attention of local authorities. Justice James Dolliver, speaking for the court, ruled that Rinaldo would have to show that the information was necessary or critical to his defense and that he had made a reasonable effort to get the material by other means. He could not make such a showing, and the subpoena was quashed.[33]

More recently, the First Amendment privilege came into play in a high-profile criminal case involving John Phillip Walker Lindh, the so-called American Taliban who was indicted in February 2002 after he allegedly joined certain terrorist organizations in Afghanistan to fight against American forces. Robert Young Pelton, a freelance journalist who was covering the military conflict in Afghanistan on behalf of CNN, had interviewed Lindh after Lindh was captured by U.S. troops in November 2001. Attorneys for Lindh subpoenaed Pelton to testify about the interview at a hearing on various motions they had filed to suppress evidence in the case against their client. Pelton moved to quash the subpoena on the ground that he had a First Amendment privilege against disclosure of information obtained during the news-gathering process in Afghanistan. In July 2002, however, Pelton's motion to quash was denied by a federal district court judge in Alexandria, Va.[34] The judge held that the First Amendment privilege grounded in Justice Powell's concurrence in *Branzburg* applies only "where the journalist produces some evidence of confidentiality or governmental harassment." Pelton conceded that there was no confidentiality of sources involved—Lindh was the source—and thus the judge held that "he cannot invoke any First Amendment privilege on the basis of confidentiality of sources or government harassment." Pelton, however, raised another argument that was also rejected by the court—"that the special circumstance of his role as a war correspondent in Afghanistan is a sufficient factor to trigger application of the privilege." The judge called this a "novel claim," found absolutely no case law precedent to support it, and thus denied Pelton's motion to quash the subpoena. Ultimately, Lindh pleaded guilty just three days after

32. *U.S.* v. *Burke,* 700 F. 2d 70 (1983).
33. *State* v. *Rinaldo,* 684 P. 2d 608 (1984).
34. *U.S.* v. *Lindh*, 210 F. Supp. 2d 780 (E.D. Va. 2002).

the judge's decision to two charges of aiding the Taliban and carrying explosives and therefore Pelton never was forced to testify.

Grand Jury Proceedings

Although the qualified privilege for reporters to refuse to reveal the identities of confidential sources in civil and criminal actions has been recognized by most lower federal courts and state supreme courts that have considered the question, these same courts have routinely refused to extend the First Amendment privilege to grand jury proceedings. This refusal is true even though the grand jury's power to force disclosure is not constitutionally guaranteed, as is the criminal defendant's right to compel a witness to testify. The obvious explanation for this reluctance on the part of judges is that the single U.S. Supreme Court precedent on the question focused on grand jury testimony and in that case, *Branzburg* v. *Hayes,*[35] the high court ruled that no privilege existed.

For example, in 2001, the 5th U.S. Circuit Court of Appeals rejected an appeal from a freelance writer named Vanessa Leggett who refused to turn over research materials to a federal grand jury in Houston. Leggett was trying to write a book about a 1997 murder that was being investigated by the Justice Department. Texas then had no shield law to protect reporters although it now does (see pages 397–401), but there was considerable doubt Leggett would have qualified for protection under the law in any case since she was a freelancer, not a staff reporter for a publication. The appellate court rejected her effort to invoke the constitutional privilege. The court said while the privilege under the First Amendment may protect a journalist's confidential sources in civil cases, its applicability is diminished in criminal cases and it reaches its nadir or lowest point in grand jury proceedings. "The public's interest in law enforcement proceedings always outweighs the media interests," the court ruled.[36] The Supreme Court declined in 2002 to hear Leggett's case.

What happens when the individual requesting the information is a special prosecutor rather than a grand jury? The 1st U.S. Circuit Court of Appeals squarely addressed this question in 2004 when it handed down its decision in *In re Special Proceedings.*[37] The appellate court, in a blow to journalists, held that "*Branzburg* governs in this case even though we are dealing with a special prosecutor rather than a grand jury," adding that "the considerations bearing on privilege are the same in both cases." The court thus refused to extend a reporter's privilege when confidential information is requested by a special prosecutor.

The case transpired in the context of an FBI investigation, called "Operation Plunder Dome," into governmental corruption in Providence, R.I. The investigation was successful, as it sent several city officials, including former Mayor Vincent "Buddy" Cianci, to prison. The First Amendment dispute involved efforts to obtain the name of a source that leaked to James Taricani, a veteran television reporter covering "Operation Plunder Dome," a copy of a secret surveillance videotape of an FBI informant handing an envelope that allegedly contained a $1,000 cash bribe to a Providence city official named Frank E. Corrente. Corrente was later convicted of bribery.

Taricani's station, the Providence NBC-affiliate WJAR-TV, aired a portion of the secret tape, and a federal judge appointed a special prosecutor to determine who leaked it to Taricani. When Taricani refused to give up his confidential source, he was hit by the judge

---

35. 408 U.S. 665 (1972).
36. *In re Grand Jury Subpoenas,* 29 M.L.R. 2301 (2001).
37. 373 F. 3d 37 (1st Cir. 2004).

Investigative broadcast journalist Jim Taricani was sentenced to six months of home confinement in late 2004 for refusing to divulge the identity of a confidential source.

© AP/Wide World Photos

with civil contempt and a $1,000-a-day fine. In holding that the opinion in *Branzburg,* which rejected a testimonial privilege in grand jury proceedings, also controlled cases involving special prosecutors, the 1st U.S. Circuit Court of Appeals affirmed the district court judge's civil contempt finding against Taricani. It wrote that "there is no doubt that the request to Taricani was for information highly relevant to a good faith criminal investigation" and that "reasonable efforts were made to obtain the information elsewhere." Importantly, the appellate court cited somewhat favorably Judge Posner's 2003 opinion in the *McKevitt* case (see page 380) that was skeptical of the *Branzburg* opinion offering any protection to journalists beyond what ordinary relevance and reasonableness requirements would demand.

With the appellate court decision going against Taricani, the district court began assessing the $1,000-a-day fine against the reporter in August 2004. By early November of 2004, Taricani still had not revealed his source and, in the process, he had racked up (and paid) fines of about $85,000. Recognizing the civil fine was not forcing Taricani to give up his confidential source, U.S. District Court Judge Ernest Torres then ordered Taricani tried for criminal contempt unless the reporter gave up his source. In taking this step, the judge suspended the $1,000 fine because the case was now about *criminal* contempt, not a *civil* penalty. Judge Torres soon found Taricani guilty of criminal contempt, prompting the Emmy Award-winning journalist to proclaim, "When I became a reporter 30 years ago, I never imagined that I would be put on trial and face the prospect of going to jail simply for doing my job."[38]

In December 2004, shortly before Taricani was to be sentenced for his criminal contempt conviction, an attorney named Joseph Bevilacqua Jr. came forward and admitted under oath that he was Taricani's source for the videotape. Bevilacqua had represented one of the city officials, Joseph Pannone, convicted in the corruption scandal in Providence that Taricani was investigating. Bevilacqua's admission, however, did not negate the criminal contempt

38. Belluck, "Reporter Is Found Guilty."

conviction of journalist Taricani. On December 9, 2004, the 55-year-old Taricani was sentenced to six months of home confinement. Judge Torres chose home confinement rather than prison because of health concerns about Taricani. The judge stated from the bench, "Except for his health and history of a good record, all of the factors call for a meaningful prison sentence."[39] During his confinement, Tariacani could leave his home only for medical treatments.

Taricani ultimately was released from home confinement in April 2005 upon recommendation from his probation officer, about two months earlier than originally scheduled. Despite the early release, the case of Jim Taricani represents a very low mark in recent years in terms of the legal protection that journalists have—or don't have—in protecting their sources. Had it not been for his fragile health, Taricani would have landed in jail for protecting his source rather than getting home confinement.

ANONYMITY AND THE INTERNET

An interesting problem related to the matter of reporters protecting the identity of their sources is whether or not the parties in a lawsuit can force online service providers (OSPs) to reveal the names of people who post anonymous messages on the Web. In 2009, for instance, fashion model and former Vogue cover girl Liskula Cohen filed a motion against Google and Blogger.com to compel them in a defamation suit to reveal the identity of the person who anonymously posted comments on a blog calling her a skank, a ho and "other defamatory statements concerning her appearance, hygiene and sexual conduct."[40] In August 2009 Judge Joan A. Madden ruled in favor of Cohen and held that Google and/or its Blogger.com subsidiary had to reveal to the former model the identity of the anonymous blogger (via the IP and e-mail address) who posted the defamatory comments about her at http://skanksnyc.blogspot.com. Cohen then discovered the blogger was a female acquaintance she knew from parties and restaurants. Also in 2009 a Texas judge ordered a Web site called Topix.com to reveal the identities of more than 170 people who posted anonymous and allegedly defamatory comments about the defendants in a sexual assault case. The defendants were acquitted in the assault case and then filed a civil libel suit against the anonymous posters who accused them of criminal wrongdoing and other tawdry deeds.[41]

The problem gained widespread media attention in 2008 when a now-defunct Web site called JuicyCampus.com, which boasted the motto "Always Anonymous . . . Always Juicy" and later "C'mon. Give Us the Juice," became known for allowing college students to anonymously post gossip about fellow students that was sometimes offensive, homophobic and/or defamatory.[42] Or imagine that someone creates a fake MySpace profile about you that says defamatory things and you want to unmask its creator. Can you find out who posted it?

39. Belluck, "Reporter Who Shielded Source."
40. Gregorian, "Model Snared in Ugly Web."
41. See "Texas Judge Orders 178 Anonymous 'John Does' Who Posted on Topix Be Revealed," available online at http://www.citmedialaw.org/blog/2009/texas-judge-orders-178-anonymous-john-does-who-posted-topix-be-revealed.
42. JuicyCampus likely would have been protected from liability for defamatory statements created and posted by others under Section 230 of the Communications Decency Act, which shields online service providers and interactive computer services from liability for content created and posted by third parties (see Chapter 4 regarding libel on the Internet). People who posted defamatory comments on JuicyCampus, however, were not shielded from liability. At least two states in 2008 investigated whether JuicyCampus was engaging in possible fraud by failing to follow its own terms-of-use agreement by allowing defamatory messages to be posted. In February 2009 JuicyCampus was shut down by its founder, Matt Ivester, who denied the closure related to potential legal liability problems but rather was based on economic and advertising issues.

The answer is yes, sometimes, if certain steps are met. State courts across the country are grappling with the issue of anonymous postings and when to allow those harmed by them to force the OSP or host in question to disclose the poster's identity. In particular, they are attempting to accommodate competing interests, namely the judicially recognized First Amendment right to engage in anonymous speech (see Chapter 3 regarding prior restraints and protests) versus compensating those harmed by anonymous Internet speech that is defamatory or otherwise unlawful, such as the disclosure of proprietary information like trade secrets. The First Amendment right to engage in anonymous speech is not absolute; it may be overcome in some situations. Determining when, however, is tricky. As a California appellate court wrote in 2008 in a case involving allegedly defamatory postings on a Yahoo! message board and in which the plaintiff sought the identity of the poster of those comments, "the proper focus . . . should be on providing an injured party a means of redress without compromising the legitimate right of the Internet user to communicate freely with others."[43] A New Jersey appellate court ruled that a subpoena to ascertain the identity of anonymous Internet posters in a libel case should not be issued unless the plaintiff could first make a prima facie case for libel.[44] The court outlined a four-part test it said lower courts should follow that is known as the *Dendrite* test:

> The plaintiff must first make an effort to notify the anonymous poster that he or she is the subject of an application for disclosure.
>
> The plaintiff must identify and set forth the allegedly defamatory statements.
>
> The plaintiff must provide sufficient evidence to support each element of the cause of action, including the harm that has allegedly been incurred.
>
> The court must then balance the defendant's right to anonymous speech under the First Amendment (see page 120) against the strength of the plaintiff's case and the necessity of disclosure to allow the plaintiff to proceed properly.

In the New Jersey case the unidentified posters were named as defendants in the lawsuit. A federal court in Washington state fashioned a somewhat similar rule in a suit in which the anonymous posters were not a party in the lawsuit. It said the subpoena would not be issued unless the information sought went to a core claim made by the plaintiff or the defense, the information was directly or materially relevant to the case, and the party seeking the identities had demonstrated that the information was unavailable from other sources.[45] This test from the Washington case of *Doe* v. *2TheMart.com* was adopted in 2008 by a federal judge in a Pennsylvania case in which plaintiff Brenda Enterline sought the identity of anonymous posters who commented on a story, posted on the Web site of the Pocono Record, about Enterline's sexual harassment lawsuit against a local medical center.[46] As in *2TheMart.com*, the anonymous posters were not defendants in the plaintiff's lawsuit, but rather were people who Enterline thought had information that could help her win that lawsuit. U.S. District Judge A. Richard Caputo ruled against Enterline and in favor of the Pocono Record, reasoning that identity of the anonymous posters, although "directly and materially related to the

---

43. *Krinsky* v. *Doe 6*, 159 Cal. App. 4th 1154, 1167 (Cal. Ct. App. 2008).
44. *Dendrite International Inc.* v. *Doe,* 775 A. 2d 756 (N.J. Super. Ct. 2001).
45. *Doe* v. *2TheMart.com Inc.,* 140 F. Supp. 2d 1088 (W.D. Wash. 2001).
46. *Enterline* v. *Pocono Medical Center*, 37 M.L.R. 1057 (M.D. Pa. 2008).

Plaintiff's core claims of sexual harassment and retaliation," wasn't necessary for her to pursue her claims against the hospital. Judge Caputo wrote that "that much of the information [Enterline] hopes to uncover after learning the identities of commentators on the newspaper's website is information that will be obtained through normal, anticipated forms of discovery, including depositions of Enterline's co-workers." In brief, there were alternative ways of obtaining information to help her lawsuit against the hospital that did "not encroach on the First Amendment rights of the anonymous commentators." The Pocono Record, in brief, did not have to give up its posters' identities.

In a 2005 libel opinion called *Doe* v. *Cahill* based on statements posted on a Web log (a "blog"), the Supreme Court of Delaware held that "the summary judgment standard is the appropriate test by which to strike the balance between a defamation plaintiff's right to protect his reputation and a defendant's right to exercise free speech anonymously."[47] What does this mean? The court called it a "modified" two-part version of the *Dendrite* test. In particular, the plaintiff must (1) make reasonable efforts to notify the defendant (the anonymous poster) that he is the subject of a subpoena or application for an order of disclosure; and (2) provide sufficient evidence to support and sustain each and every element of the plaintiff's cause of action versus the defendant (in this case, defamation) against a motion for **summary judgment** (see glossary).

The *Cahill* summary judgment test from Delaware was adopted in 2006 by a federal judge in Arizona when a plaintiff, hotel chain Best Western, sought the identities of defendants who posted anonymous messages on an Internet site that allegedly harmed Best Western. The court found this test appropriate for balancing "a First Amendment right to anonymous Internet speech" (see page 120 regarding anonymous speech) with the recognition that "the right to speak anonymously is not absolute" and Best Western's "need for discovery to redress alleged wrongs."[48]

In late 2007 an Arizona appellate court in *Mobilisa, Inc.* v. *Doe*[49] adopted a variation of the *Dendrite* test when it held that in order to compel discovery of an anonymous Internet poster's identity, the requesting party must show three things:

1. The anonymous poster was given adequate notice and a reasonable opportunity to respond to the discovery request (the requesting party, in other words, must make efforts to notify the anonymous poster, via the same medium used by the anonymous poster to send or post the contested message, and give the anonymous party a reasonable chance to respond to such notice);

2. The requesting party's cause of action against the anonymous poster is strong enough to survive a motion for summary judgment on the elements of the claim, not dependent upon knowing the identity of the anonymous poster; and

3. Balancing the parties' competing interests and needs (the need for the information versus the right to speak anonymously) favors disclosure.

---

47. *Doe* v. *Cahill,* 884 A. 2d 451 (Del. 2005).
48. *Best Western International, Inc.* v. *Doe,* 2006 U.S. Dist. LEXIS 56014 (D. Ariz. 2006). Other courts, however, have questioned the *Cahill* summary judgment standard in defamation cases involving anonymous Internet postings. See *McMann* v. *Doe,* 460 F. Supp. 2d 259 (D. Mass. 2006).
49. 170 P. 3d 712 (Ariz. Ct. App. 2007).

The bottom line is that although courts in many states had not yet addressed the issue by the end of 2009, most of those that did were adopting, in some variation or another, either the *Dendrite* or *Cahill* test. For instance, the Court of Appeals of Maryland (the highest court in that state) adopted a five-part variation of *Dendrite* in February 2009 in *Independent Newspapers, Inc.* v. *Brodie*. In August 2009 the U.S. Court of Appeals for the District of Columbia in *Solers, Inc.* v. *Doe* adopted a modified version of the *Cahill* test.

Importantly, each of these cases was a civil lawsuit. The situation differs in criminal cases, where federal courts consistently conclude that Internet subscribers have no right of privacy under the Fourth Amendment safeguard against unreasonable searches with respect to identifying information on file with their OSPs. Some state constitutions, however, recently have been held to include such a privacy expectation in criminal cases when the government subpoenas an OSP for identifying records of a person who uses an anonymous screen name (OSP address).[50]

NONCONFIDENTIAL INFORMATION AND WAIVER OF THE PRIVILEGE

While U.S. courts have been willing to permit journalists to protect confidential sources and confidential information, most have been far more reluctant to protect reporters when nonconfidential information is at issue. And most subpoenas issued today to journalists are to gain access to nonconfidential information.

Typical is a ruling by the 5th U.S. Circuit Court of Appeals that said that reporters do not enjoy any privilege, qualified or otherwise, not to disclose nonconfidential information in a criminal case.[51] This ruling seems to be in line with previous court rulings. A U.S. District Court ruled in 1990 that a journalist who witnessed a beating of a criminal suspect by police had to testify on behalf of the injured party. "This court knows of no authority to support the proposition that such personal observations are privileged simply because the eyewitness is a journalist," the judge ruled.[52]

Photographers have been forced to surrender photos they have taken of building fires,[53] industrial accidents,[54] fatal auto accidents[55] or even of an individual who has filed a personal injury lawsuit against an insurance company.[56] The press has generally been unable to convince judges that it has an important interest at stake when it refuses to cooperate with those who seek nonconfidential information.

This sentiment certainly was true in 2006 when the 9th U.S. Circuit Court of Appeals denied First Amendment protection for Joshua Wolf, who videotaped a protest demonstration and refused to turn over the tape to government authorities. The appellate court wrote that "[t]he taped

50. See *New Jersey v. Reid,* 914 A. 2d 310 (N.J. 2007), which holds that a criminal defendant has an expectation of privacy under the New Jersey Constitution regarding identifying information held by an OSP, and adding that "the right to privacy of New Jersey citizens under our State Constitution has been expanded to areas not afforded such protection under the Fourth Amendment."

51. *U.S.* v. *Smith,* 135 F. 3d 963 (1998).

52. *Dillon* v. *San Francisco,* 748 F. Supp. 722 (1990).

53. *Marketos* v. *American Employers Insurance Co.,* 460 N.W. 2d 272 (1990).

54. *Stickels* v. *General Rental Co., Inc.,* 750 F. Supp. 729 (1990).

55. *Idaho* v. *Salsbury,* 924 P. 2d 208 (1996).

56. *Weathers* v. *American Family Mutual Insurance Co.,* 17 M.L.R. 1534 (1990).

activities occurred entirely in public and did not occur in response to Wolf's prompting, whether by questions or recording. He simply videotaped what people did in a public place. Wolf does not claim that he filmed anything confidential nor that he promised anyone anonymity or confidentiality. Therefore, this case does not raise the usual concerns in cases involving journalists."[57]

Even when federal courts have recognized a qualified privilege to protect nonconfidential information, the scope of the privilege has been very limited. For instance, the 2nd U.S. Circuit Court of Appeals, which includes New York, Connecticut and Vermont, in 1998 "recognized a qualified privilege for nonconfidential press information," but noted that "where nonconfidential information is at stake, the showing needed to overcome the journalists' privilege is less demanding than for material acquired in confidence."[58]

Reporters must worry about another aspect of the privilege, the problem that through some action they may actually waive their right to refuse to testify. A case in Washington, D.C., focuses on this dilemma. Six police officers brought a $9 million lawsuit against the city and top police officials. They were disciplined by the police department after a botched 1986 drug operation that failed to net the hundreds of arrests expected. In the wake of the failed raid, Washington Post reporter Linda Wheeler revealed in a newspaper story that the Post had obtained secret plans for the raid. The six officers who were disciplined argued that leaks from high-level police officials, not from them, caused the raid to fail. And they subpoenaed Wheeler to find out where she got the plans for the operation.

Reporters must worry about another aspect of the privilege, the problem that through some action they may actually waive their right to refuse to testify.

The reporter refused to identify her source and was found in contempt of court. The court said that any privilege a reporter might enjoy in such an instance was waived when, in 1986, she told her husband and another man, both officers in the U.S. Park Police, the name of her confidential source. "A reporter cannot choose in 1986 to disclose her source to others . . . and then choose in 1991—as a witness in a judicial proceeding—not to make this same disclosure," wrote Judge Richard A. Levie. The District of Columbia Court of Appeals upheld this ruling.[59]

Wheeler was excused from testifying in the summer of 1991 when a mistrial was declared in the lawsuit, but a retrial was scheduled. The reporter's husband, to whom she had revealed the identity of her source, was forced to testify before the hearing was adjourned. "This could become a very effective harassment technique," said Jane Kirtley, who was then executive director of the Reporters Committee for Freedom of the Press. She suggested that a judge or attorney might say, "Well, journalists, I recognize you're covered by a shield law or a reporter's privilege, but I'm just going to bring in your spouse, your kid, your parents, your dog, anybody who's around, and see what they know."

The question of waiving a reporter-source privilege also arises in the context of state statutory shield laws addressed later in this chapter. Two recent cases involving a discussion of the

57. *In re Grand Jury Subpoena: Joshua Wolf,* 35 M.L.R. 1207 (9th Cir. 2006).
58. *Gonzales* v. *National Broadcasting Co., Inc.,* 186 F. 3d 102 (2d Cir. 1998). A few other federal appellate courts have recognized the existence of a qualified privilege to protect information in a reporter's possession that comes from a nonconfidential source. See. *U.S.* v. *LaRouche Campaign,* 841 F. 2d 1176 (1st Cir. 1988); and *Mark* v. *Shoen,* 48 F. 3d 412 (9th Cir. 1995), which held that "where information sought is not confidential, a civil litigant is entitled to requested discovery notwithstanding a valid assertion of the journalist's privilege by a nonparty only upon a showing that the requested material is: (1) unavailable despite exhaustion of all reasonable alternative sources; (2) noncumulative; and (3) clearly relevant to an important issue in the case."
59. *Wheeler* v. *Goulart,* 18 M.L.R. 2296 (1990); and *Goulart* v. *Barry,* 18 M. L.R. 2056 (1991).

possible waiver of such statutory privileges for journalists are *Flores* v. *Cooper Tire and Rubber Co.*[60] and *McGarry* v. *University of San Diego.*[61]

There is really no bright line marking when and how a reporter may in fact waive the privilege. The law is too diffuse for such a generalization. But reporters who have promised confidentiality should keep the information completely confidential.

WHO IS A JOURNALIST?

An emerging problem relating to the constitutionally based journalist's privilege is, Who is a journalist?[62] When the privilege was developed in the 1970s and 1980s the definition of a journalist was relatively clear: A journalist was someone who gathered news for a news medium. In the 21st century, with the growth of interactive computer communication and 900 number information services, virtually anyone can report the news, or what he or she might refer to as the news. Should anyone who uses the Internet or a 900 telephone number to spread information be regarded as a journalist for purposes of the law? This issue has not been resolved, but at least one court has attempted to solve the dilemma.

Mark Madden is an irrepressible professional-wrestling commentator who "broadcast" his commentary via 900-number telephone calls. His commentaries were usually sarcastic, sometimes fanciful and always provocative. To listen to these messages callers paid $1.69 per minute. World Championship Wrestling (WCW) owns the line and paid Madden $350 per week to operate it.[63] During a commentary Madden reported that the World Wrestling Federation (WWF), the archrival of the WCW, was in serious financial difficulty. WCW and WWF were suing each other, claiming unfair competition. Madden was subpoenaed to testify about the sources for his report on WWF's financial difficulties. Madden raised the First Amendment privilege, claiming he was a journalist entitled to constitutional protection. A U.S. District Court agreed in 1997,[64] but the U.S. Court of Appeals overturned the lower-court decision in July 1998. The appellate judges said that Madden was an entertainer disseminating hype, not news.

In ruling that Madden was not a journalist, the three-judge panel from the 3rd U.S. Circuit Court of Appeals defined a journalist (for purposes of application of the privilege) in this fashion: A journalist is one

- who engages in investigative reporting;
- who gathers news; and
- who possesses the intent at the beginning of the news-gathering process to disseminate this news to the public.[65]

Since this ruling other cases have been reported. A U.S. District Court in the District of Columbia has ruled that cyberjournalist/rumor-monger Matt Drudge was protected by the constitutional journalistic privilege in the libel suit brought against him by Sydney Blumenthal[66]. But a federal

---

60. 178 P. 3d 1176 (Ariz. 2008) (involving Arizona's shield law).

61. 154 Cal. App. 4th 97 (Cal. 2007) (involving California's shield law).

62. Calvert, "And You Call Yourself a Journalist?"

63. Glaberson, "Wrestling Insults."

64. *Titan Sports Inc.* v. *Turner Broadcasting Systems Inc.*, 967 F. Supp. 142 (1997).

65. *In re Madden*, 151 F. 3d 125 (1998).

66. *Blumenthal* v. *Drudge*, 186 F.R.D. 236 (1999).

court ruled in 1999 that a cyberscribe in Colorado who maintained a Web site offering information about the University of Colorado athletic programs did not have a constitutional right to be given the same privileges that school officials accord to other "accredited members of the news media." Theodore Smith was not a journalist.[67] These cases are just the opening chapters of what is surely to be a long saga regarding who is and who is not a journalist.

Indeed, in 2003 the 2nd U.S. Circuit Court of Appeals jumped into the fray and denied journalistic status to a financial ratings agency called Fitch, Inc., which had sought to quash a subpoena under New York's shield law.[68] Although not addressing the constitutional journalistic privilege, the federal appellate court nonetheless considered whether the New York shield law, which protects journalists from contempt for refusing to comply with a nonparty subpoena when the subpoena seeks to discover information conveyed to a journalist in confidence, included protection for a financial ratings company. New York's law defines a professional journalist as "one who, for gain or livelihood, is engaged in gathering, preparing, collecting, writing, editing, filming, taping or photographing of news intended for a newspaper, magazine, news agency, . . . or other professional medium or agency which has as one of its regular functions the processing and researching of news intended for dissemination to the public." Fitch contended that it fits this definition because "it conducts research, fact-gathering, and analytical activity that is directed towards matters of general public concern, just like any journalist, and notes that it makes its information available on its web site to the general public." The appellate court rejected this argument, reasoning in part that "Fitch only 'reports on' specific transactions for which it has been hired. Unlike a business newspaper or magazine, which would cover any transactions deemed newsworthy, Fitch only 'covers' its own clients. We believe this practice weighs against treating Fitch like a journalist." The appellate court did, however, leave some breathing room for future cases and debate when it wrote, "we conclude that the district court did not abuse its discretion in finding that Fitch was not entitled to assert the journalist's privilege for the information at issue. For the sake of clarity, we note that we are not deciding the general status of a credit rating agency like Fitch under New York's Shield Law: Whether Fitch, or one of its rivals, could ever be entitled to assert the newsgathering privilege is a question we leave for another day."

One of the newest and most intriguing issues involving the question of who is a journalist, for purposes of both state shield laws (see pages 397–401) and the First Amendment journalistic privilege protection, centers on the status of so-called bloggers—individuals who keep and maintain Web logs (blogs). In 2006 a California appellate court concluded in *O'Grady* v. *Superior Court*[69] that the publishers of two Web sites—O'Grady's PowerPage[70] and Apple Insider[71]—carrying information about Apple computers and other Apple products were entitled to protection under both California's shield law as well as the First Amendment and state constitution. Apple had subpoenaed the operators of both Web sites in order to find out who leaked to them Apple's secret plans to release a particular computer device. The Web

---

67. *Smith* v. *Plati*, D. Colo., No. 99-K-491, 7/22/99.
68. *In re Fitch, Inc., & American Savings Bank, FSB,* v. *UBS Painewebber, Inc.,* 330 F. 3d 104 (2003).
69. 139 Cal. App. 4th 1423 (2006).
70. The site can be found online at http://www.powerpage.org.
71. The site can be found online at http://www.appleinsider.com.

site operators argued they were acting as publishers, editors and reporters in posting the information on their sites and thus did not need to reveal the names of their sources.

By their terms, both the California shield law and state constitution protect "a publisher, editor, reporter or other person connected with or employed upon a newspaper, magazine or other periodical publication" from disclosing sources of information.[72] Notice how the precise language includes newspapers and magazines but is silent about Web sites and digital media. In holding, however, that this language protected the Web operators of PowerPage and Apple Insider, the appellate court wrote that these sites "came into possession of, and conveyed to their readers, information those readers would find of considerable interest" and noted that "in no relevant respect do they appear to differ from a reporter or editor for a traditional business-oriented periodical who solicits or otherwise comes into possession of confidential internal information about a company." The court added that the Web sites differed from traditional news periodicals "only in their tendency, which flows directly from the advanced technology they employ, to continuously update their content." Turning to the First Amendment claim of protection, the court found "no sustainable basis to distinguish [the Web site operators] from the reporters, editors, and publishers who provide news to the public through traditional print and broadcast media," adding that they "gather, select, and prepare, for purposes of publication to a mass audience, information about current events of interest and concern to that audience." Whether courts in other states will take such a pro-journalist, pro-blogger approach remains to be sorted out.

TELEPHONE RECORDS

The names of confidential news sources, reporters' notes, news film and photographs are not the only records that have been sought by government agents and attorneys through the use of a subpoena. In particular, reporters' telephone records provide a trail of numbers that could reveal the identity of confidential sources.

HOLD THAT CALL! DANGEROUS DIALING FOR JOURNALISTS

In 2008, when the Justice Department was trying to determine the identity of government officials who allegedly leaked information about military intelligence issues to New York Times reporter James Risen, several former government employees were called before a federal grand jury and shown their telephone records documenting their calls with Risen. Because telephone records, including those of reporters and sources, can be subpoenaed by the government and may provide a trail to a confidential source, the executive director of the Reporters Committee for Freedom of the Press, Lucy Dalglish, gave this piece of sage advice to investigative reporters in April 2008: "Do your reporting the old fashioned way—meet your sources on a park bench."[73] She urged reporters investigating potentially sensitive topics not to use either their home or office phones when contacting confidential sources. In brief, don't leave

---

72. California Evidence Code § 1070 (2007); and California Constitution, Article I, § 2.
73. Shenon, "Leak Inquiry Said to Focus on Calls with Times."

a paper trail! This wise advice took on greater urgency in August 2008 when then FBI Director Robert S. Mueller III issued a formal apology to editors at The New York Times and Washington Post for secretly and improperly obtaining four years earlier the phone records of reporters for those papers working in Indonesia. The FBI covertly obtained the records in 2004 as part of a terrorism investigation by using so-called exigent letters that are designed to request toll-billing records from phone companies in emergency situations without going through the normal legal hoops.

In 2006 a federal appellate court in *New York Times Co.* v. *Gonzales*[74] considered a federal grand jury subpoena seeking 11 days' worth of telephone records of two New York Times reporters who had investigated a secret government plan to freeze the assets of two Islamic charities that allegedly funded terrorism. The subpoenas were served on the telephone service providers of The Times as part of an investigation to find out who leaked and disclosed without authorization to the reporters the government's plans. The good news for The Times' reporters was that the appellate court initially held that "whatever rights a newspaper or reporter has to refuse disclosure in response to a subpoena extends to the newspaper's or reporter's telephone records in the possession of a third party provider." The court reasoned that "the telephone is an essential tool of modern journalism and plays an integral role in the collection of information by reporters," and thus "any common law or First Amendment protection that protects the reporters also protects their third party telephone records sought by the government."

But the bad news was that the appellate court also held that whatever common-law privilege might protect reporters in such cases, it is a qualified (limited) privilege overcome on the facts of this case by the need of the government. The appellate court wrote:

> The government has a compelling interest in maintaining the secrecy of imminent asset freezes or searches lest the targets be informed and spirit away those assets or incriminating evidence. At stake in the present investigation, therefore, is not only the important principle of secrecy regarding imminent law enforcement actions but also a set of facts—informing the targets of those impending actions—that may constitute a serious obstruction of justice.

In ordering the review of the phone records, the court added that the reporters "are the only witnesses—other than the source(s)—available to identify the conversations in question and to describe the circumstances of the leaks," and that "the reporters' actions are central to (and probably caused) the grand jury's investigation. Their evidence as to the relationship of their source(s) and the leaks themselves . . . is critical to the present investigation." The court also flatly rejected the newspaper's argument that the First Amendment protected the reporters, reasoning that the Supreme Court's precedent from *Branzburg* v. *Hayes* (see pages 376–378) controlled (it too was a grand jury setting) and did not provide any privilege against grand jury subpoenas. The Supreme Court in November 2006 refused to disturb the appellate court's decision against The New York Times.[75]

---

74. 459 F. 3d 160 (2d Cir. 2006).
75. *New York Times Co.* v. *Gonzales,* 127 S. Ct. 721 (2006).

Nearly two decades before, a different appellate court also had dealt a blow to journalists in *Reporters Committee for Freedom of the Press* v. *American Telephone & Telegraph Co.*[76] The *Reporters Committee* case, as the appellate court in *New York Times* v. *Gonzales* interpreted it 18 years later, "suggested that journalists have no more First Amendment rights in their toll-call records in the hands of third parties than they have in records of third party airlines, hotels, or taxicabs."

SUMMARY

In recent years more and more reporters have been called to testify in legal proceedings. Often they are asked to reveal confidential information to aid police in criminal investigations, to assist in the defense of a criminal defendant, or to help a libel plaintiff establish negligence or actual malice. Failure to comply with a court order can result in a citation for contempt of court. The Supreme Court of the United States ruled in 1972 that reporters were like all other citizens: They did not enjoy a First Amendment privilege that permitted them to refuse to testify before a grand jury. Despite this high-court ruling, the lower federal courts and state courts have fashioned a constitutional, common-law privilege that often protects a journalist who has been subpoenaed to testify at a legal hearing. The privilege is qualified. In many instances a court will not require a journalist to testify unless the person seeking the information held by the journalist can demonstrate that the reporter has information that is relevant to the hearing, that there is a compelling need for the disclosure of this information, and that there are no alternative sources for this information.

Courts tend to apply this three-part test differently in different types of legal proceedings. Journalists are most likely to escape being forced to testify in a civil suit, especially if the reporter is not a party to the suit in some way. Reporters are more likely to be forced to testify in a criminal case, but there are numerous examples of reporters being granted a qualified privilege to escape such testimony as well. Reporters called to testify before a grand jury, however, usually are required to honor the subpoena. More and more courts are seeking journalists' testimony regarding nonconfidential information, and the law is of substantially less protective value in these cases. A U.S. Court of appeals has ruled that the records of toll telephone calls made by journalists may also be subpoenaed to further legitimate law enforcement proceedings.

LEGISLATIVE AND EXECUTIVE PROTECTION OF NEWS SOURCES

By November 2009 all states except Wyoming provided some form of legally recognized protection, albeit in varying degrees and forms, for journalists seeking to preserve confidentiality of sources and/or information. In particular, 37 states had shield laws protecting reporters,

---

76. 593 F. 2d 1030 (D.C. Cir. 1978).

while other states recognized a judicially created privilege rooted in one or more of three sources—the First Amendment, a state constitution or the common law. It is important to note that a state with a statutory shield law may also recognize a judicially created privilege, so a reporter in a given state may have two possible avenues of protection.

As of October 2009, however, there was no federal statutory shield law to protect reporters who are hauled before federal courts and federal grand juries. But efforts to enact such a measure were under way in Congress that year with the Free Flow of Information Act of 2009. It would provide a qualified privilege (a privilege that is not absolute or complete) for journalists to keep sources confidential in federal proceedings; the privilege would not apply in certain circumstances, most notably when the identity of the source is necessary either to prevent or to identify a perpetrator of an act of terrorism against the United States or its allies or other significant and specified harm to national security. President Barack Obama supported a proposal for a federal shield law during the 2008 presidential campaign, and the Free Flow of Information Act of 2009 actually stood a decent chance of becoming law. Momentum for a federal shield law grew in 2009 when Attorney General Eric Holder testified in front of the U.S. Senate Judiciary Committee that he would support such legislation, provided that it did not jeopardize national security and that his office could continue to prosecute individuals leaking such national security information.

SHIELD LAWS

In 1896 Maryland became the first state to grant journalists a limited privilege to refuse to testify in legal proceedings. In May 2009 Texas became the 37th state to adopt a shield law (see Figure 10.1). The year before, Maine and Hawaii became the 35th and 36th states, respectively, to adopt shield laws. The District of Columbia also has such a law. Shield laws are statutes, adopted by state legislative bodies, except in the case of Utah, in which that state's high court in early 2008 approved and adopted a reporter's shield rule (Utah Rule of Evidence 509) governing all court proceedings in that state (Utah was the 34th state to adopt a shield law). The Utah rule was proposed and advocated by several journalism groups. There often is substantial variance from state to state in both the scope of protection and the definitions used in these shield laws (there is, for example, no uniform definition across the states in terms of who constitutes a journalist or reporter protected under these laws).

In 1896 Maryland became the first state to grant journalists a limited privilege to refuse to testify in legal proceedings.

These laws, in more or less limited terms, outline the reporter's privilege that has been established by the state. The statutes generally establish who can use the privilege (i.e., who is a reporter?), the kinds of information the privilege protects (i.e., confidential and nonconfidential; sources only or sources and information), and any qualifications that might accrue (i.e., the privilege is waived through voluntary disclosure of other parts of the material; instances when disclosure is mandated).

For example, the Alabama shield law provides the following:

> No person engaged in, connected with, or employed on any newspaper, radio broadcasting station or television station, while engaged in a news gathering capacity shall be compelled to disclose, in any legal proceeding or trial, before any court or before a grand jury of any court, before the presiding officers of any tribunal or his agent or agents, or before any committee of the legislature, or elsewhere, the sources of any information

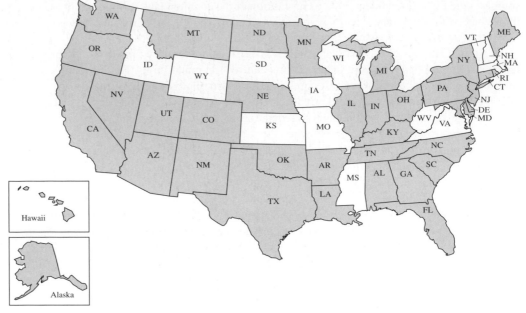

SHADED STATES HAVE SHIELD LAWS

FIGURE 10.1

As of November 2009, 37 states plus the District of Columbia had some form of a shield law.

Source: Agents of Discovery, 2009

procured or obtained by him and published in the newspaper, broadcast by any broadcasting station, or televised by any television station on which he is engaged, connected with or employed.[77]

The precise language of state shield laws is very important in determining both who and what they will and will not cover or protect. This was illustrated in 2005 in the case of *Price* v. *Time, Inc.* in which the 11th U.S. Circuit Court of Appeals held that Alabama's shield law, quoted immediately above in this section, did not apply to the magazine Sports Illustrated. Engaging in the process of statutory construction (see page 9), the appellate court held that the Alabama statute's phrase "newspaper, radio broadcasting station or television station" did not cover magazines like Sports Illustrated. In reaching this conclusion, the appellate court followed the plain meaning rule—it gave the statutory words their ordinary meaning and did not impart its own views on the legislative language. The 11th Circuit wrote that "it seems to us plain and apparent that in common usage 'newspaper' does not mean 'newspaper and magazine.'"

Despite such possible limitations (another big issue today is whether bloggers are protected by a given shield law), they can be useful. Consider three examples of the successful use of shield laws in 2008:

---

77. Alabama Code, 12-21-142 (2003).

■ Pennsylvania's shield law was used by 15 journalists, working for several newspapers and the Associated Press, to quash subpoenas requesting their phone records and notes, as well as calling on them to testify, regarding their sources for possibly leaked information about a grand jury investigation that led to the indictment of a casino operator. Pennsylvania's shield law provides, in relevant part, that a journalist cannot "be required to disclose the source of any information . . . in any legal proceeding, trial or investigation before any government unit."[78]

■ The Minnesota Supreme Court refused to reverse a lower appellate court's determination that the state's shield law, called the Minnesota Free Flow of Information Act, protected journalists at a Mankato newspaper from being forced to give a prosecutor unpublished notes taken during a telephone interview with a shooter while in the midst of a standoff with law enforcement officials. The Minnesota shield law protects, in relevant part, journalists from being compelled "to disclose any unpublished information" obtained while on the job, including "notes, memoranda, recording tapes, film or other reportorial data," unless the individual seeking the information proves "there is a compelling and overriding interest requiring the disclosure of the information where the disclosure is necessary to prevent injustice."[79] Although the notes in the Mankato case related to an incident in which both the shooter and officers were shot (the shooter later committed suicide and thus could not be prosecuted), the appellate court concluded that the prosecutor had not demonstrated that their discovery was necessary to prevent injustice from occurring.

■ The Pennsylvania Supreme Court held in September 2008 that Pennsylvania's shield law "prohibits the compelled disclosure of a confidential source's identity, or any information which could expose the source's identity," even in the context of a civil defamation case against a newspaper in which the plaintiffs alleged that the journalists and confidential source were direct participants in the criminal disclosure of grand jury proceedings.[80] The Pennsylvania high court, citing the "unambiguous language" of the state's shield law, held that it provides for "absolute protection of a source's identity." The court added that "the news media have a right to report news, regardless of how the information was received."[81]

---

78. 42 Pennsylvania Consolidated Statutes Annotated § 5942 (2008).

79. Minnesota Statutes Annotated §§ 595.021–595.024. See *In re Death Investigation of Skjervold*, 742 N.W. 2d 686 (Minn. Ct. App. 2007), rev. den. Mar. 18, 2008 (unpublished opinion).

80. *Castellani* v. *Scranton Times*, 956 A. 2d 937 (Pa. 2008). The Pennsylvania shield law provides that "no person engaged on, connected with, or employed by any newspaper of general circulation or any press association or any radio or television station, or any magazine of general circulation, for the purpose of gathering, procuring, compiling, editing or publishing news, shall be required to disclose *the source of any information* procured or obtained by such person, *in any legal proceeding*, trial or investigation *before any government unit* [emphasis added]." 42 Pennsylvania Consolidated Statutes Annotated § 5942 (2008).

81. The Pennsylvania Supreme Court, however, hedged this absolutist language in a footnote in *Castellani*, writing that it was not considering a case in which the state was seeking "a reporter's evidence concerning the source of a grand jury leak in a criminal investigation or prosecution of that leak." The court remarked that such an issue "is not before us and we save its consideration for another day. Put another way, we need not determine whether there is any situation where the absolute language of the shield law would have to yield to a competing, constitutional value."

Many other cases could be cited to show how shield laws have protected journalists, but these laws have problems as well. Not the least of these problems is that many judges don't like shield laws. They believe the laws unfairly impinge on judicial discretion, denying judges the authority to compel testimony when it is needed in a lawsuit. Hence, in many instances the laws are interpreted very narrowly. Judges follow the letter of the law, but not the spirit of the legislation. For example, the California Supreme Court ruled that whereas a reporter could not be held in contempt for refusing to produce unpublished photos he had taken of an automobile accident, he might still be subject to other sanctions, such as money damages, for failing to comply with the order. The state shield law protects a reporter only from a contempt citation.[82] The New York shield law failed to protect NBC when it was ordered to provide video outtakes of a protest demonstration staged in early 1998 by thousands of construction workers. The trial judge ruled that the government—which wanted to use the videotape to identify workers so they could be prosecuted—had demonstrated that the material was highly relevant and unavailable from other sources.[83] This showing defeated the protection of the shield law.

In 2009 a New Jersey Superior Court judge held that that state's shield law did not protect a blogger, who was being sued for defamation, from revealing her sources for online allegations she posted on the Oprano.com forum about the operators of a computer software company called Too Much Media LLC. The blogger, Shellee Hale, claimed to be reporting on the company and in the process of writing an article about it, but she had no connection to any legitimate news publication, as Judge Louis Locascio noted. He suggested in his opinion that Hale was "doing little more than shouting from atop a digital soapbox."

Also in 2009 a Texas judge held that the then recently adopted shield law in that state protected the Abilene Reporter-News from being forced to disclose the identity of people who posted anonymous comments in response to the newspaper's online stories about a particular murder case. The defendant charged with that murder claimed he needed the names to help him obtain a fair trial under the Sixth Amendment.

Shield laws suffer from other deficiencies as well. Here are some of the problems:

- Few of the laws give a protection that exceeds, or is even equal to, that given by the constitutional privilege.
- The laws in most of the states are significantly qualified. For example, the laws in Alaska, Louisiana, New Mexico and North Dakota can be overcome by a mere judicial determination that justice or public policy requires the privilege to yield to some other interest.[84]
- In some states the reporter waives the privilege upon disclosure of any portion of the confidential matter.[85]
- In other states the shield law will not apply unless there was an understanding of confidentiality between the reporter and the source.[86]
- State shield laws often exclude freelance writers, book authors and cable television operators, as well as bloggers.

---

82. *The New York Times* v. *Santa Barbara Superior Court,* 796 P. 2d 811 (1990).
83. *In re Grand Jury Subpoenas,* 27 M.L.R. 1723 (1998).
84. *Confidential Sources and Information.*
85. *In re Schuman,* 537 A. 2d 297 (1988).
86. *Outlet Communications, Inc.* v. *Rhode Island,* 588 A. 2d 1050 (1991).

▮ Shield laws rarely cover what a reporter witnesses, only what a reporter has been told or given.[87] For instance, an appellate court in Maryland held in May 2003 that that state's shield law did not protect reporters from complying with administrative subpoenas seeking their testimony at police department administrative hearings when those reporters personally observed and witnessed the relevant event about which their testimony was sought.[88]

An appellate court in 2008 expansively interpreted New York's shield law, holding that it protects authors of nonfiction books about matters of public interest from disclosing their confidential sources.[89] The interpretation was expansive because New York's shield law does not specifically identify either the medium of books or the authors of books within its definition of protected "professional journalists." New York's shield law, by its terms, defines professional journalists as people who write, gather or edit "news intended for [a] newspaper, magazine, news agency, press association or wire service or *other professional medium or agency which has as one of its regular functions the processing and researching of news intended for dissemination to the public* [emphasis added]."[90] The appellate court concluded that authors of nonfiction books about matters of public interest are "news"[91] and fall within the italicized portion of this language, even if the book in question—in this case, one about Donald Trump called "TrumpNation"—is entertaining and written in "a breezy, irreverent style."

In 2008 a new question arose about the scope of state shield laws in the digital age: Do shield laws protect newspapers from revealing the identities of people who anonymously post allegedly defamatory comments on newspapers' Web sites regarding online stories they read? The issue is hot, as many papers allow readers to anonymously post comments about online stories, and sometimes those anonymous comments defame individuals described in the online stories. The newspapers, of course, know the IP addresses of the anonymous posters on their Web sites. Judges in Florida, Montana and Oregon ruled in 2008 that the shield laws in those three states were drafted broadly enough to protect newspapers there from giving up the IP addresses of people who anonymously post on newspapers' Web sites, at least when the comments relate to the articles that spawned the postings.[92] Whether shield laws in other states will be interpreted so broadly as to prevent the disclosure of the identity of such third-party, newspaper-Web site posters remains to be seen.

The perfect shield law would likely be preferable to the First Amendment privilege; but the perfect shield law does not exist. Hence, even in those states that have a shield law, reporters frequently end up relying on the constitutional privilege.

---

87. *Delaney* v. *Superior Court,* 249 Cal. Rptr. 60 (1988); and *Minnesota* v. *Knutson,* 523 N.W. 2d 909 (1994).

88. *Prince George's County, Maryland* v. *Hartley,* 31 M.L.R. 1679 (2003).

89. *Trump* v. *O'Brien,* 958 A. 2d 85 (N.J. 2008). The appellate court was in New Jersey, but it had to interpret New York's shield law given the connections of both the plaintiff and defendant to New York state.

90. New York Civil Rights Law § 79-h(a)(6) (2008).

91. New York's shield law defines "news" as information "concerning local, national or worldwide events or other matters of public concern or public interest or affecting the public welfare." New York Civil Rights Law § 79-h(a)(8) (2008).

92. Order, *Beal* v. *Calobrisi*, Case No. 08-Ca-1075 (Fla. Cir. Ct. Okaloosa County Oct. 9, 2008), available online at http://www.newsroomlawblog.com/uploads/file/Beal_v__Calobrisi.pdf; and Associated Press, "Judge: Shield Law Protects Anonymous Commentators."

FEDERAL GUIDELINES

As a kind of corollary to a shield law, the Department of Justice has adopted rules that define when and how a federal prosecuting attorney can obtain a subpoena against a working reporter.[93] Here is a summary of the guidelines:

I. **The Department of Justice must attempt to strike a balance between the public's interest in the free dissemination of ideas and information and the public interest in effective law enforcement when determining whether to seek a subpoena for a journalist's confidential information.**

II. **All reasonable attempts should be made to obtain the information from alternative sources before considering issuing a subpoena to a member of the news media.**

III. **Negotiations with the news media to gain the information sought shall be pursued in all cases in which a subpoena to a member of the news media is contemplated.**

IV. **If the negotiations fail (if the reporter won't provide the material voluntarily), the attorney general must approve the subpoena based on the following guidelines:**

   a. There must be sufficient evidence of a crime from a nonpress source. The department does not approve of using reporters as springboards for investigation.

   b. The information the reporter has must be essential to a successful investigation—not peripheral or speculative.

   c. The government must have unsuccessfully attempted to get the information from an alternative, nonpress source.

   d. Great caution must be exercised with respect to subpoenas for unpublished information or where confidentiality is alleged.

   e. Even subpoenas for published information must be treated with care, because reporters have encountered harassment on the grounds that information collected will be available to the government.

   f. The subpoena must be directed to specific information.

TELEPHONE RECORDS

Rules 1 through 3 in the guidelines just listed apply as well when federal agents seek to subpoena the toll telephone records of members of the media. If the negotiations to get the records fail, the agents must seek permission from the attorney general to issue the subpoena. In such a case the following guidelines apply:

1. There should be reasonable grounds to believe that a crime has been committed and that the information sought is essential to the successful investigation of that crime.

2. The subpoena should be directed at only relevant information regarding a limited subject matter and should cover a limited period of time.

93. See 28 C.F.R. § 50.10.

3. The government should have pursued all reasonable alternative means before seeking the subpoena.

4. Reporters must be given timely notice that the government intends to issue a subpoena.

5. Information obtained through the subpoena must be closely guarded so that unauthorized persons cannot gain access to it.

NEWSROOM SEARCHES

Is a newsroom or a journalist's home protected by the First Amendment from a search by the police or federal agents? The Supreme Court of the United States refused to extend the First Amendment in such a manner in 1978.[94] Since then, however, Congress and many state legislatures have provided qualified legislative protection for premises where news and scholarship are produced. The lawsuit that resulted in the Supreme Court ruling stemmed from the political turmoil of the early 1970s, a period that generated many of the previously discussed cases regarding reporters' sources.

Is a newsroom or a journalist's home protected by the First Amendment from a search by the police or federal agents?

In April 1971 police were asked to remove student demonstrators who were occupying the administrative offices of Stanford University Hospital. When police entered the west end of the building, demonstrators poured out of the east end, and during the ensuing melee outside the building, several police officers were hurt, two seriously. The battle between the police and the students was photographed by a student, and the following day pictures of the incident were published in the Stanford Daily student newspaper. In an effort to discover which students had attacked the injured police officers, law enforcement officials from Santa Clara County secured a warrant for a search of the Daily's newsroom, hoping to find more pictures taken by the student photographer. There was no allegation that any member of the Daily staff was involved in the attack or other unlawful acts. No evidence was discovered during the thorough search.

This type of search is known as an innocent third-party search, or simply a third-party search. Police search the premises or a room for evidence relating to a crime even though there is no reason to suspect that the owner of the premises or the occupant of the room is involved in the crime that is being investigated. Such searches are not uncommon, but in the lawsuit that followed, the student newspaper argued that this kind of search threatened the freedom of the press and should not be permitted unless police officials first obtain a subpoena—which is more difficult for police to get than a simple search warrant is. The subpoena process would also provide the press with notice prior to the search and allow editors and reporters to challenge the issuance of the subpoena.

This type of search is known as an innocent third-party search.

The newspaper argued that the unannounced third-party search of a newsroom seriously threatened the ability of the press to gather, analyze and disseminate news. The searches could be physically disruptive for a craft in which meeting deadlines is essential. Confidential sources—fearful that some evidence that would reveal their identity might surface in such a search—would refuse to cooperate with reporters. Reporters would be deterred from keeping notes and tapes if such material could be seized in a search. All of this, and more, could have a chilling effect on the press, lawyers for the newspaper argued.

94. *Zurcher v. Stanford Daily,* 436 U.S. 547 (1978).

The Supreme Court, in a 5-3 ruling, disagreed with the newspaper. Justice Byron White ruled that the problem was essentially a Fourth Amendment question (i.e., was the search permissible under the Fourth Amendment?), not a First Amendment question, and that under existing law a warrant may be issued to search any property if there is reason to believe that evidence of a crime will be found. "The Fourth Amendment has itself struck the balance between privacy and public need and there is no occasion or justification for a court to revise the Amendment and strike a new balance," White wrote. The associate justice conceded that "where the materials sought to be seized may be protected by the First Amendment, the requirements of the Fourth Amendment must be applied with 'scrupulous exactitude.'" He added, "Where presumptively protected materials are sought to be seized, the warrant requirement should be administered to leave as little as possible to the discretion of the officer in the field." But Justice White rejected the notion that such unannounced searches are a threat to the freedom of the press, arguing that the framers of the Constitution were certainly aware of the struggle between the press and the Crown in the 17th and 18th centuries, when the general search warrant was a serious problem for the press. Yet the framers did not forbid the use of search warrants where the press was involved, White asserted. They obviously believed the protections of the Fourth Amendment would sufficiently protect the press.[95]

Newsroom searches by the police, a rarity in the decades before the *Zurcher* case, suddenly became a common occurrence. Journalists sought legislative relief from this onslaught and Congress responded by adopting the Privacy Protection Act of 1980.[96] The law limits the way law officers and government agents can search for or seize materials that are in the hands of persons working for the mass media or persons who expect to publicly disseminate the material in some other manner (e.g., public speech). The statute designates two categories of material that are protected: work products and documentary materials. The law says a work product "encompasses the material whose very creation arises out of a purpose to convey information to the public." In layperson's language, work products are reporters' notes, undeveloped film, outtakes and so forth. Documentary materials are described as "materials upon which information is formally recorded," such as government reports, manuscripts and the like. Congress based the statute on the commerce clause in the U.S. Constitution in order to extend the reach of the law to include state and local agencies as well as federal law enforcement personnel. To obtain either work products or documentary materials, law enforcement agencies must obtain a subpoena; a search warrant will not do. There are, however, exceptions to the rule. A law enforcement agency may conduct a warranted search of a newsroom to find work products in either of the following two situations:

1. When there is a probable cause to believe that the person possessing such materials has committed or is committing a criminal offense to which the materials will relate.

2. Where there is reason to believe that the immediate seizure of such materials is necessary to prevent the death of or serious harm to a person.

95. *Zurcher v. Stanford Daily,* 436 U.S. 547 (1978).
96. See 42 U.S.C §§ 2000aa–2000aa-12.

A search warrant may be used instead of a subpoena to obtain documentary materials if either of the two conditions just listed is met or in either of these two situations:

1. There is reason to believe that the giving of notice pursuant to gaining a subpoena would result in the destruction, alteration, or concealment of such materials.

2. That such materials have not been provided in response to a court order directing compliance with a subpoena, all other legal remedies have been exhausted, and there is reason to believe that further delay in gaining the material would threaten the interests of justice.

In most instances, then, law enforcement personnel will be forced to seek a subpoena to gain access to information kept in a newsroom or a reporter's home.

HOW TO RESPOND TO A SUBPOENA

What should a reporter do if he or she is subpoenaed? First, try to avoid the problem altogether. Don't give a promise of confidentiality to a source without first carefully considering whether such a promise is actually needed to get the story. Discuss the matter with an editor or the news director before agreeing to keep the name of a source confidential. Also, don't talk, even informally, with people outside the newspaper about stories in which confidential information or sources are involved. Such discussions may be ruled to constitute a waiver of the privilege you seek to assert at a later date.

What should a reporter do if he or she is subpoenaed?

But if a subpoena should arrive, the first thing to remember is that the police are not coming to your door to arrest you. The subpoena is simply an order that you have been called to appear at some type of proceeding or supply certain documents. So don't panic. Tell your editor or news director immediately. Ask to talk with your news organization's legal counsel. Don't attempt to avoid being served with the subpoena. While a reporter is under no obligation to make the job easier for the person serving the subpoena, resistance to this service may result in the subpoena being abandoned and a search warrant issued in its place. Don't ever accept a subpoena for someone else.

Ask to talk with your news organization's legal counsel.

If the subpoena requests only published material, or video that has previously been broadcast, the newspaper or broadcasting station may simply provide this material without dispute. Journalists should be familiar with their news organization's policy on retaining notes, tapes, first drafts and so on. If there is no policy, it is worthwhile to ask management to consider adopting one. Once the subpoena has been served, the material sought is considered official evidence, and if it is destroyed to avoid having to produce it, the reporter very likely will be held in contempt of court. So once you have been served, begin gathering the material together in case you have to surrender it at some later time.

If you believe that the material or names of sources should be withheld, and your news organization disagrees, it is in your interest to hire your own attorney to represent you. The company attorney is working for the company, not you. Finally, remember that the odds of being forced to give up the material or names are low. The law is, for the most part, on your side these days.

SUMMARY   State legislatures and the federal government have adopted statutes and rules that offer some protection to journalists who hold confidential information sought by government agents and other individuals. Thirty-seven states have adopted shield laws, which provide a qualified privilege for reporters to refuse to testify in legal proceedings. Although these statutes can be helpful, they are not without problems. There is a lack of consistency among the state shield laws. These laws have definitional problems that permit courts to construe them very narrowly. The laws usually protect only what someone tells a reporter, not what a reporter personally sees or hears. Often courts see the statutes as legislative interference with judicial prerogatives and interpret the laws in the least useful manner.

The Department of Justice has adopted rules that govern when and how federal agents may subpoena journalists, records possessed by journalists and journalists' telephone toll records. The rules require federal agents to strike a balance between the public's interest in the free flow of information and effective law enforcement.

Congress passed the Privacy Protection Act of 1980 in response to a ruling by the U.S. Supreme Court that the First Amendment does not ban searches of newsrooms or reporters' homes. This act requires federal, state and local police agencies who seek a journalist's work products or other documentary materials to get a subpoena for these materials rather than seize them under the authority of a search warrant. The statute does provide exceptions to these rules. For example, premises may be searched and materials seized under a search warrant if police believe the reporter has committed a crime, if there is reason to believe someone will be harmed if the materials are not seized, or if police fear the materials might be destroyed if a subpoena is sought.

THE CONTEMPT POWER

Those who work in the mass media and run afoul of judicial orders or the commands of legislative committees can quickly feel the sharp sting of a contempt citation. Reporters who refuse to respond to a subpoena, editors who criticize a judge, newspapers that refuse to pay a libel or invasion-of-privacy judgment, all of these and more can be held in contempt. For example, former USA Today reporter Toni Locy was held in contempt by a federal judge in 2008 and fined $5,000 per day after she did not reveal her sources for stories connecting scientist Steven J. Hatfill to a series of Anthrax-laced letters sent in late 2001.[97] Under the contempt ruling, the fines added up for every day that Locy refused to give up her sources' identity, and Locy was personally liable for paying the fines (the contempt order precluded her from accepting reimbursement from her employer or others to satisfy the monetary sanction). Hatfill had sued the federal government under the Privacy Act (see Chapter 9), claiming his privacy was violated by government employees who deliberately leaked his name to certain journalists as a person of interest in the investigation into who sent the letters. Hatfill subpoenaed Locy, as well as a number of other journalists, seeking to find out who their government sources were. Locy

97. *Hatfill* v. *Mukasey*, 539 F. Supp. 2d 96 (D.D.C. 2008). An appellate court stayed the contempt fine while the case was on appeal. *Hatfill* v. *Mukasey*, 2008 U.S. App. LEXIS 5755 (D.C. Cir. Mar. 11, 2008).

refused to reveal her sources, claiming she couldn't remember them. United States District Judge Reggie B. Walton rejected Locy's argument that her refusal to disclose the identity of her sources was sanctioned by either the First Amendment or a common-law privilege she requested that Walton recognize. Locy escaped paying a steep contempt fine, however, when the government agreed later in 2008 to pay Hatfill $5.8 million to settle his case before an appellate court could rule on the merits of Hatfill's efforts to force Locy to testify. In November 2008 a three-judge panel of the U.S. Circuit Court of Appeals for the District of Columbia vacated Judge Walton's contempt order and dismissed the case as moot due to the settlement. Judge Walton then issued a one-page order in February 2009 accepting the appellate court's ruling and vacating his own earlier contempt decision. Despite the settlement and tossing out of the contempt order, however, Hatfill still wanted Locy to pay his hefty legal fees sustained during the period of time when she refused to give up her sources.

In another high-profile case in 2004, U.S. District Judge Thomas Penfield Jackson held five different reporters in contempt of court.[98] Why? Because they refused to comply with an earlier order he had issued requiring them to reveal the identity of the confidential sources they used in reporting on the espionage investigation of Dr. Wen Ho Lee, a former Los Alamos nuclear scientist who was later cleared of all but one of the 59 charges against him.[99] In August 2004 Judge Jackson ordered each reporter, including journalists from such prestigious papers as the Los Angeles Times and The New York Times, to pay a fine of $500 a day until the reporter complied with the earlier order seeking the identity of the sources. Lee sought the names as part of a lawsuit he filed against the federal government. In June 2005 a unanimous three-judge panel of the U.S. Court of Appeals for the District of Columbia in *Lee* v. *Department of Justice* upheld the contempt charges and the $500-a-day fines issued by Judge Jackson against four of five reporters Lee had subpoenaed and deposed. In November 2005 a fifth reporter—Walter Pincus of the Washington Post—was held in civil contempt in the *Lee* case for refusing to reveal a confidential source.

KINDS OF CONTEMPT

Varieties of contempt are recognized through common law, and efforts have been made to label these varieties. But these efforts have been unsatisfactory; there is frequently disagreement among courts about what kinds of behavior constitute what kinds of contempt. No attempt will be made to resolve these discrepancies in this book. It is sufficient to note that judges use the contempt power for two purposes:

A court can use the contempt power to protect the rights of a litigant in a legal dispute. A reporter who refuses to reveal the name of a source critical to the defense of a person charged with larceny could endanger the person's right to a fair trial. The contempt power can be used to force the reporter to testify. Similarly, a broadcasting station that refuses to pay the plaintiff a judgment after losing a libel case endangers the right of the injured party to repair his or her reputation. Again, the contempt power can be used to force the broadcaster to pay the judgment.

---

98. *Lee* v. *U.S. Department of Justice,* 327 F. Supp. 2d 26 (D.D.C. Aug. 18, 2004).
99. Jurkowitz, "Reporters Found in Contempt."

The contempt power can be used to vindicate the law, the authority of the court or the power of the judge. A defendant who refuses to stop talking during a trial or an attorney who continually ignores judicial warnings against talking to reporters about the merits of the case can be punished with a contempt citation. So can a writer who carelessly and aggressively criticizes a court ruling in a newspaper editorial.

Judges who use the contempt power to protect the rights of litigants usually impose an indeterminate sentence against the target of the contempt. That is, a judge can jail a reporter until he or she is willing to reveal the name of the critical source. Or the court can fine the broadcaster a specific amount each day until the civil judgment is paid. The punishment is used to coerce the target of the citation to take some action.

Judges who use the contempt power to vindicate the law, the authority of the court or the power of the judge will generally impose a determinate sentence—that is, a specific fine ($25,000) or jail sentence (30 days in jail). Here the sentence is strictly punishment; no coercion is implied.

Contempt and the Press

The contempt power is broad and touches all manner of persons who run afoul of a judge. Journalists are among those at jeopardy. What kinds of situations are most likely to result in contempt problems for the press? To list a few:

1. Failure to pay a judgment in a libel or invasion-of-privacy case.
2. Failure to obey a court order. The judge rules that no photos may be taken in the courtroom, or orders reporters not to publish stories about certain aspects of a case. If these orders are disobeyed, a contempt citation may result.
3. Refusal of a journalist to disclose the identity of a source or to testify in court or before a grand jury.
4. Critical commentary about the court. This might be an editorial critical of the court or a cartoon mocking the judge. Contempt citations have been issued to punish the press in such cases.
5. Tampering with a jury. A reporter tries to talk with jurors during a trial, asking questions about their views on the defendant's innocence or guilt.

These situations are some of the more common ways that members of the press might become involved in a contempt problem, although the list is by no means exhaustive.

COLLATERAL BAR RULE

When a journalist violates a court order, a contempt citation is probably forthcoming. But what if the court order appears to be illegal or unconstitutional on its face? Can a journalist still be held in contempt of court for violating such an order? The answer to that important question is maybe, for there is no clear resolution of this matter at present. The legal concept involved is called the **collateral bar rule,** a rule that requires that all court orders, even those that appear to be unconstitutional and are later deemed to be unconstitutional by an appellate court, must still be obeyed until they are overturned. The collateral bar rule states that a person who violates a court order cannot collaterally challenge the order's constitutionality as a defense to the contempt charge. Instead, that person must obey the order and hope to get it overturned on appeal. While this rule has been rarely invoked against the press, a U.S. Court of Appeals ruling from 1972 stands as a stark reminder of its meaning. In that case reporters Gibbs Adams and Larry Dickinson of the Baton Rouge (La.) Morning Advocate and State Times ignored what they believed was an unconstitutional court order forbidding them from publishing information about what took place in an open federal court hearing. The pair, who were each fined $300, appealed the order and the 5th U.S. Circuit Court of Appeals ruled that the trial judge's actions were clearly unconstitutional. At the same time, the court upheld the contempt citations, ruling that a person may not, with impunity, violate a court order that later turns out to be invalid.[100]

While this rule, sometimes called the *Dickinson rule,* seems grossly unfair, there is a logic to it. The court system would cease to operate as it does if people had a choice of whether or not to obey a court order. Without the power to coerce behavior, judges would be unable to discharge their duties and responsibilities, and courts would become mere boards of arbitration that issue advisory opinions. The judge who wrote the opinion in the *Dickinson* case probably spoke for many jurists when he wrote, "Newsmen are citizens too. They too may sometimes have to wait."[101]

Only one important collateral bar case involving the press has occurred since this 1972 ruling. In this case a federal judge in Rhode Island found the Providence Journal and its editor, Charles Hauser, in contempt of court for violating the judge's order forbidding the publication of any information that had been obtained by the government from an illegal FBI wiretap.[102] The 1st U.S. Circuit Court of Appeals ruled that the trial judge's order was transparently invalid and could not serve as a basis for a contempt citation. The appellate court added, however, that in the future publishers and broadcasters should first try to get an appellate review before violating a court order.[103] With the 5th Circuit and the 1st Circuit somewhat in disagreement about this matter, the Supreme Court agreed to hear an appeal. But after reading briefs and hearing arguments, the members of the high court dismissed the appeal because the special prosecutor who handled the appeal for the government had failed to obtain proper authorization from the Solicitor General of the United States to petition for a writ of certiorari.[104] At the federal level, then, the issue remains unresolved. But courts in Washington and Illinois have flatly rejected the rationale of the *Dickinson* case,[105] and courts in Arizona,[106] California,[107] Massachusetts[108] and Alabama[109] have considered the matter but have issued ambiguous rulings.

While this rule, sometimes called the Dickinson rule, *seems grossly unfair, there is a logic to it.*

---

100. *U.S.* v. *Dickinson,* 465 F. 2d 496 (1972).

101. Ibid.

102. *In re Providence Journal,* 630 F. Supp. 993 (1986).

103. *In re Providence Journal,* 820 F. 2d 1354 (1987).

104. *U.S.* v. *Providence Journal,* 108 S. Ct. 1502 (1998).

105. *State ex rel Superior Court* v. *Sperry,* 483 P. 2d 609 (1971); and *Cooper* v. *Rockford Newspapers,* 365 N.E. 2d 746 (1977).

106. *Phoenix Newspapers* v. *Superior Court,* 418 P. 2d 594 (1966); and *State* v. *Chavez,* 601 P. 2d 301 (1979).

107. *In re Berry,* 493 P. 2d 273 (1968).

108. *Fitchburg* v. *707 Main Corp.,* 343 N.E. 2d 149 (1976).

109. *Ex parte Purvis,* 382 So. 2d 512 (1980).

SUMMARY   The power of a judge to punish for contempt of court is a remnant of the power of English royalty. Today, courts have broad powers to punish people who offend the court, interfere with legal proceedings or disobey court orders. Contempt is used both to protect the rights of private persons who are litigating matters in the courts and to punish a wrong committed against the court itself.

Some limits have been placed on the contempt power. Legislatures often restrict the kinds of sentences judges may impose for contempt or require a jury trial before a contempt conviction. The Supreme Court has ruled that before criticism of a court may be punished by contempt, it must be shown that the criticism created a clear and present danger of the likelihood of interference with the administration of justice. In some jurisdictions appellate courts have ruled that people must obey even unconstitutional contempt orders (the *Dickinson* rule).

BIBLIOGRAPHY

Agents of Discovery. Washington, D.C.: Reporters Committee for Freedom of the Press, 2003.

Alexander, Laurence B., and Leah Cooper. "Words That Shield: A Textual Analysis of the Journalist's Privilege." *Newspaper Research Journal* 18 (1997): 51.

Associated Press. "Judge: Shield Law Protects Anonymous Commentators." 4 September 2008.

Barringer, Felicity. "Justice Department in Rare Move, Obtains a Reporter's Phone Records." *The New York Times,* 29 August 2001, A18.

Belluck, Pam. "Reporter Is Found Guilty for Refusal to Name Source." *The New York Times,* 19 November 2004, A24.

———. "Reporter Who Shielded Source Will Serve Sentence at Home." *The New York Times,* 10 December 2004, A28.

Berger, Robert G. "The 'No Source' Presumption: The Harshest Remedy." *American University Law Review* 36 (1987): 603.

Broder, John M. "From Grand Jury Leaks Comes a Clash of Rights." *The New York Times,* 15 January 2005, A8.

Calvert, Clay. "And You Call Yourself a Journalist? Wrestling With a Definition of 'Journalist' in the Law." *Dickinson Law Review* 103 (1999): 411.

Confidential Sources and Information. Washington, D.C.: Reporters Committee for Freedom of the Press, 1993.

Fost, Dan. "Bay Judge Weighs Rights of Bloggers." *San Francisco Chronicle,* 8 March 2005, A1.

Frazer, Douglas H. "The Newsperson's Privilege in Grand Jury Proceedings: An Argument for Uniform Recognition and Application." *Journal of Criminal Law and Criminology* 75 (1984): 413.

Glaberson, William. "Wrestling Insults Fuel Free Speech Case." *The New York Times,* 24 October 1998, A10.

Gregorian, Dareh. "Model Snared in Ugly Web." *New York Post*, 6 January 2009, 7.

Jurkowitz, Mark. "Reporters Found in Contempt in Nuclear Case." *The Boston Globe,* 19 August 2004, A3.

Kase, Kathryn. "When a Promise Is Not a Promise: The Legal Consequences for Journalists Who Break Promises of Confidentiality to Sources." *Hastings Communications and Entertainment Law Journal* 12 (1990): 565.

Langley, Monica, and Lee Levine. "*Branzburg* Revisited: Confidential Sources and First Amendment Values." *George Washington Law Review* 57 (1988): 13.

Liptak, Adam. "Reporter from Time Is Held in Contempt in C.I.A. Leak Case." *The New York Times,* 10 August 2004, A1.

Malheiro, Sharon K. "The Journalist's Reportorial Privilege—What Does It Protect and What Are Its Limits?" *Drake Law Review* 38 (1988–89): 79.

Mullen, Lawrence J. "Developments in the News Media Privilege: The Qualified Constitutional Approach Becoming Common Law." *Maine Law Review* 33 (1981): 401.

"The Newsman's Privilege: Government Investigations, Criminal Prosecutions, and Private Litigation." *California Law Review* 58 (1970): 1198.

Parrell, Mark J. "Press/Confidential Source Relations: Protecting Sources and the First Amendment." *Communications and the Law* 47, March 1993.

Ramstack, Tom. "Judge Upholds Reporter's Right to Protect Sources." *Washington Times*, 25 July 2008, A1.

Shenon, Philip. "Leak Inquiry Said to Focus on Calls with Times." *The New York Times*, 12 April 2008, A16.

Tucker, Neely. "Wen Ho Lee Reporters Held in Contempt." *Washington Post,* 19 August 2004, A02.

Utevsky, David. "Protection of Sources and Unpublished Information." Paper presented at the meeting of Washington Volunteer Lawyers for the Arts, Seattle, Wash., 27 January 1989.

Wigmore, John H. *A Treatise on the Anglo-American System of Evidence in Trials at Common Law.* 2nd ed. Boston: Little, Brown, 1934.

CHAPTER 11

Free Press–Fair Trial

TRIAL-LEVEL REMEDIES AND RESTRICTIVE ORDERS

Legal problems frequently arise as the press and the criminal justice system intersect in our society. These problems are usually cast as the result of two seemingly conflicting constitutional rights: the right to a free press guaranteed by the First Amendment, and the right to a fair trial guaranteed by the Sixth Amendment. If the press publishes and broadcasts anything it chooses about a crime or a criminal suspect, isn't it possible readers and viewers will make up their minds about the guilt or innocence of the accused? And if they do, won't the members of the jury (who are also readers and viewers) approach the case with prejudice either for or against the defendant? What will happen to the guarantee of a fair trial? But if the court moves to restrict this publicity by the mass media to protect the integrity of the trial process, won't this interfere with the rights of the press? What about the First Amendment? We explore these issues in this chapter and in Chapter 12. Included is a discussion of the kinds of publicity that may damage the right to a fair trial, and the various schemes adopted by the courts to try to minimize the impact of this publicity or restrict the flow of this kind of information.

PREJUDICIAL CRIME REPORTING

Americans' fascination with news about crime is not a recent fetish. Indeed, the people of this nation have always found stories about crime and criminals alluring. In the 19th century, hangings were public spectacles with a carnival-like atmosphere and were usually well attended. Today so-called true crime and mystery novels are among the most popular print genres, and dramas about crime and criminals usually rank among the most popular TV shows. (See the various episodes of "Law and Order" and "CSI," and their multiple offspring, for example.)

The news media, especially television news, are also saturated with stories about crime and the administration of criminal justice. Many television news producers salivate at the prospect of yet another celebrity trial—be it Robert Blake, Kobe Bryant, Michael Jackson, Martha Stewart or whoever. It is hard to judge whether there are more stories about crime in a particular news medium today, say in the Chicago Tribune or on WCCO-TV in Minneapolis, or whether it just seems that way because there are so many more mass media covering crime. Five hundred or so print and broadcast reporters were on hand for the first day of the Michael Jackson trial in California in early 2005. That is clearly more than cover most institutions of the federal government, major political events, or even more important trials like the prosecution of the executives of Enron, a case in which there were millions of victims of the company's fraudulent operations. And in vying for the short attention span of most Americans, many members of the press have few qualms about reporting stories that go beyond the facts of a case to include rumors, their own opinions about guilt or innocence, and speculations by the scores of so-called experts who dwell just beyond the boundaries of the actual courthouse proceedings.

This quasi–news reporting of crime and the criminal justice system is at the heart of the long-standing matter that journalists and lawyers alike call the free press–fair trial controversy. This controversy—like the news coverage of crime—also dates to the early years of the republic. Many lawyers and judges argue that it is extremely difficult or even impossible for a defendant to get a fair trial—a right guaranteed by the Sixth Amendment—when important segments of the press have already decided the individual is guilty. This kind of publicity, they say, will surely influence members of the community who will ultimately sit on the jury that decides the defendant's guilt or innocence. Reporters and editors argue that the influence of the press is seriously exaggerated in such arguments, and regardless, the First Amendment protects the press from government interference, even if it occasionally acts irresponsibly.

No one claims that all reporting about crime or criminals is a problem. While the heavy emphasis by the press on reporting crime is regarded as misplaced by most observers, even the severest critics agree that most stories are straightforward and fair. But potential problems arise in those instances when the press saturates a community with stories about a particular crime or criminal defendant—the killing of Matthew Shepard in Wyoming and JonBenet Ramsey in Colorado; the Washington, D.C., sniper shootings; the Laci Peterson murder; the sexual assault charges against Kobe Bryant; or the child molestation allegations against Michael Jackson. What kind of news creates the greatest danger of prejudice? Here is a list of some of the more common kinds of stories that critics say can endanger the defendant's rights:

1. **Confessions or stories about the confession that a defendant is said to have made, which include even alluding to the fact that there may be a confession.** The Fifth Amendment says that a person does not have to testify against himself or herself.

John Mark Karr lied to police when he confessed to killing JonBenet Ramsey.

© AP/Wide World Photos

Sometimes confessions that are made are later retracted. The Associated Press reported in June 2001 that a man who spent 22 years in prison in Florida after he confessed to six murders and a rape was released when DNA evidence indicated he didn't commit the crimes. The man, who had the mental capacity of an 8-year-old, confessed to the crimes to please the detectives, whom he regarded as his buddies, lawyers said.[1] In 2006 John Mark Karr confessed to killing 6-year-old JonBenet Ramsey in 1996. Only after he was extradited from Thailand did authorities conclude the confession was a lie.

2. **Stories about the defendant's performance on a test, such as a polygraph, lie detector or similar device, and about the defendant's refusal to take such a test.** Many kinds of so-called scientific or forensic evidence, which may help police identify a suspect, are not admissible as evidence at a trial, often because they are not completely reliable. Even DNA evidence is not always 100 percent conclusive if the DNA materials were not properly gathered or processed.

1. Farrington, "DNA Indicates Confessions."

3. **Stories about the defendant's past criminal record or that describe the defendant as a former convict.** This information is not permitted at the trial. It may seem entirely logical to some people that when someone has committed 99 robberies and is again arrested for robbery, the accused probably did commit the crime. As a matter of fact, past behavior is immaterial in the current trial for robbery. The state must prove that the defendant committed *this* robbery.

4. **Stories that question the credibility of witnesses and that contain the personal feelings of witnesses about prosecutors, police, victims or even judges.**

5. **Stories about the defendant's character** (he or she hates children and dogs), **associates** (he or she hangs around with known syndicate mobsters) **and personality** (he or she attacks people on the slightest provocation).

6. **Stories that tend to inflame the public mood against the defendant.** Such stories include editorial campaigns that demand the arrest of a suspect before sufficient evidence has been collected; person-on-the-street interviews concerning the guilt of the defendant or the kind of punishment that should be meted out after the accused is convicted; televised debates about the evidence of the guilt or innocence of the defendant. All these kinds of stories put the jury in the hot seat as well as circulate vast quantities of misinformation.

7. **Stories that are published or broadcast before a trial that suggest, imply or flatly declare that the defendant is guilty.** Months before Scott Peterson went on trial in 2004 for the murder of his wife and unborn child, many people in the mass media, espcially television commentators, opined that he was guilty of the crime. That the jury ultimately agreed is immaterial. Even a person who is ultimately convicted is guaranteed a fair trial.

IMPACT ON JURORS

That intensive press coverage of a criminal case *might* jeopardize the rights of the defendant is generally assumed. But whether it *will* in fact harm the defendant's Sixth Amendment rights remains more of an open question. There are those who argue vigorously that any publicity can result in a jury biased for or against the defendant. And many of these true believers don't stop with criticism of the news media. In the spring of 2005 U.S. News and World Report magazine published a long story on how the popular drama "C.S.I." (and its various clones), a program about crime scene investigators, was influencing jury verdicts across the nation. Some prosecutors argued that many jurors who regularly watched the program were demanding scientific evidence, including positive DNA test results, before they were willing to convict. Some defense attorneys argued the opposite side, claiming that the television programs portrayed forensic or scientific evidence as being unambiguous and more certain than it really is. The problem with both sets of assertions is that there was, at that time, simply no evidence to support them. The advocates could point to only a handful of cases in which they said they believed the jury made the incorrect decision, and then blamed it on the television show.

In fact, there is a serious lack of evidence that even intensive press coverage of a particular case can have a negative impact on the defendant. For nearly 60 years social scientists have attempted to prove or disprove this assumption with less than great success. The law prohibits the use of real jurors in actual trials as subjects for this research. Consequently, researchers have tried to generate other means to gather the data that is needed. Some have attempted to replicate a trial in an experimental setting. Others have used survey research methods to poll members of a community about what they know and think about highly publicized criminal cases in the area. Neither technique has provided totally satisfactory results. Complicating the resolution of this problem is the fact that many social scientists are beginning to believe that people tend to remember far less about what they read or watch on television or blogs than has been traditionally assumed. Social scientists, then, have failed to firmly establish the validity of the assumption that prejudicial publicity will seriously damage the defendant's fair trial rights.

Some people familiar with the controversy have expressed reservations about this traditional assumption. After a substantial study, University of Wisconsin researcher Robert E. Drechsel concluded that "the evidence also indicates that the magnitude of the fair trial–free press issue may be overblown. Most trial judges and other judicial sources do not seem to perceive frequent major problems with prejudicial publicity."[2] And the judges on at least two U.S. appeals courts have expressed a similar sentiment. "Pretrial publicity does not, however, lead in every criminal case to an unfair trial," noted judges on the 9th U.S. Circuit Court of Appeals in 1988.[3] Judges on the 4th U.S. Circuit Court of Appeals said that "it verges upon insult to depict all potential jurors as nothing more than malleable and mindless creations of pre-trial publicity." They added, "There is somewhat of a tendency to frequently overestimate the extent of the public's awareness of news."[4]

The next issue to focus on is the jury itself. Just what is an impartial juror?

"Most trial judges and other judicial sources do not seem to perceive frequent major problems with prejudicial publicity."

THE LAW AND PREJUDICIAL NEWS

The definition of an impartial juror used by the courts in the United States is more than 200 years old and stems from a ruling in 1807 by Chief Justice John Marshall in the trial of the former U.S. vice president Aaron Burr for treason. Charges that the jurors were biased were made at the trial. Marshall proclaimed that an impartial juror was one free from the dominant influence of knowledge acquired outside the courtroom, free from strong and deep impressions that close the mind. "Light impressions," Marshall wrote, "which may fairly be supposed to yield to the testimony that may be offered, which leave the mind open to a fair consideration of that testimony, constitute no sufficient objection to a juror."[5]

In the last 55 years the U.S. Supreme Court has fashioned other tests to guide trial judges and appellate courts, tests constructed on Chief Justice John Marshall's words. The high court has decided several cases relating to pretrial publicity, but three decisions stand out. The first stemmed from a series of brutal killings in Indiana. Leslie Irvin was arrested in connection with a series of six murders. Statements that Irvin had confessed to all six killings received widespread publicity. At the trial, of 430 persons called as potential jurors, 375 told the judge that they believed Irvin was guilty. Of the 12 jurors finally selected, eight told the court they thought he was guilty before the trial started. The Supreme Court overturned Irvin's murder conviction, noting that in this case, in which so many persons so many times admitted prejudice, statements of impartiality could be given little weight.[6]

---

2. Drechsel, "Media-Judiciary Relations," 1.
3. *Seattle Times* v. *U.S. District Court,* 845 F. 2d 1243 (1988).
4. *The Washington Post Co.* v. *Hughes,* 923 F. 2d 324 (1991).
5. *U.S.* v. *Burr,* 24 Fed. Cas. 49 No. 14692 (1807).
6. *Irvin* v. *Dowd,* 366 U.S. 717 (1961).

Fourteen years later surfer Jack Murphy, nicknamed "Murph the Surf," appealed his conviction for robbery and assault, arguing he had been denied a fair trial because of pretrial publicity. Murphy was involved in the theft of millions of dollars in jewels (including the fabled Star of India sapphire) from New York City's Museum of National History. He claimed the jury had been prejudiced by the massive publicity about the burglary as well as stories about his previous criminal record and other shady exploits. The Supreme Court disagreed. Only 20 of the 78 potential jurors who were questioned told the Florida trial judge they believed Murphy was guilty. The high court said that this ratio was not comparable to the evidence of hostility or overwhelming prejudice toward the defendant that was found in the *Irvin* case. The Constitution requires that the defendant have a "panel of impartial, indifferent jurors," ruled Justice Thurgood Marshall; "they need not, however, be totally ignorant of the facts and issues involved."[7] It is sufficient that a juror can lay aside his or her impressions and personal opinions and render a considered opinion based on the evidence presented in court. Many people see this 1975 ruling in *Murphy* v. *Florida* as rejecting the often-asserted principle that publicity about a criminal case automatically results in bias toward the defendant.

The high court re-emphasized this point nine years later in the case of *Patton* v. *Yount*.[8] In this ruling the court said that "the relevant question is not whether the community remembered the case, but whether the jurors at Yount's trial had such a fixed opinion that they could not judge impartially the guilt of the defendant."

WHAT IS AN IMPARTIAL JUROR?

An impartial juror is one whose mind is free from the dominant influence of knowledge acquired outside the courtroom, free from strong and deep impressions that close the mind. *U.S.* v. *Burr,* **1807.**

"The constitution requires that the defendant have a panel of impartial, indifferent jurors. They need not, however, be totally ignorant of the facts and issues involved." *Murphy* v. *Florida,* **1975.**

"The relevant question is not whether the people in the community remember the case, but whether the jurors had such a fixed opinion they could not judge impartially the guilt of the defendant." *Patton* v. *Yount,* **1984.**

On the basis of these rulings and others, two important generalizations emerge. The high court is willing to permit jury service by a person who possesses knowledge or has opinions about a case, so long as

1. the knowledge or opinions are not so closely held that they cannot reasonably be put aside in the face of evidence; and
2. the publicity surrounding the case is not so widespread and prejudicial as to render a potential juror's assurances of impartiality as unbelievable.[9]

---

7. *Murphy* v. *Florida,* 421 U.S. 784 (1975).
8. 467 U.S. 1025 (1984).
9. See Minow and Cate, "Who Is an Impartial Juror?" 631.

SUMMARY

The First Amendment to the U.S. Constitution guarantees freedom of the press; the Sixth Amendment guarantees every criminal defendant a fair trial. Many people believe these two amendments are in conflict because, often, publicity about a criminal case can prejudice a community against a defendant and make it impossible to find a fair and impartial jury in the case. The kinds of publicity that can be most damaging to a defendant include material about confessions or alleged confessions, stories about a past criminal record, statements about the defendant's character, comments about the defendant's performance on scientific tests or refusal to take such tests, and statements made before a trial suggesting the defendant's guilt.

Social science has not yet proved that such publicity does in fact create prejudice or that people cannot set aside their beliefs about a case and render a verdict based on the facts presented at the trial. An impartial juror is not required to be free of all knowledge or impressions about a case; the juror must be free of deep impressions and beliefs that will not yield to the evidence that is presented in court during the trial.

TRADITIONAL JUDICIAL REMEDIES

For more than 200 years American judges have had tools at their disposal to try to mitigate or lessen the impact that pretrial publicity might have on a trial. These tools range from carefully examining potential jurors about their knowledge of the case, to moving the trial, to delaying a hearing while publicity abates. As a last resort a criminal conviction can be reversed if there is evidence that the trial was tainted by publicity.* But this last resort is costly because it usually involves a retrial, resulting in added expense and inconvenience for all parties involved. These traditional judicial tools, sometimes called trial-level remedies, permit the court to reduce the impact of the publicity on the trial without inhibiting the press in any way.

As a last resort a criminal conviction can be reversed if there is evidence that the trial was tainted by publicity.

TRIAL-LEVEL REMEDIES FOR PRETRIAL PUBLICITY

1. Voir dire
2. Change of venue
3. Change of veniremen
4. Continuance
5. Admonition
6. Sequestration

VOIR DIRE

Before prospective jurors finally make it to the jury box, they are questioned by the attorneys in the case and oftentimes the judge. These interviews are designed to protect the judicial process from jurors who have already made up their minds about the case or who have strong biases toward one

* For example, a Kansas judge declared a mistrial in a 2008 rape case when a local newspaper published a story that possibly violated the fair-trial rights of the defendant. See http://www.repf.org/newsitems/index.php?i=6902.

party or the other. In a process called **voir dire** (to "tell the truth" in its original French meaning), each prospective juror is questioned prior to being impaneled in an effort to discover bias. Pretrial publicity is only one source of juror prejudice. If the prospective juror is the mother of a police officer, she is likely to be biased if the defendant is on trial for shooting a police officer. Perhaps the juror is a business associate of the defendant. Possibly the juror says she doesn't believe in psychology or psychiatry, and the defendant intends to use an insanity defense.

When a pool of potential jurors (called the venire) is assembled, a preliminary screening may take place through the use of a written questionnaire. After this initial screening both sides in the case then question the remaining members of the venire, and either side can ask the court to excuse a potential juror. This procedure is called challenging a juror. There are two kinds of challenges: **challenges for cause** and **peremptory challenges.** To challenge a juror for cause, an attorney must convince the court that there is a good reason for this person not to sit on the jury. Deep-seated prejudice is one good reason. Being an acquaintance of one of the parties in the case is also a good reason. Any reason can be used to challenge a potential juror. All the attorney must do is to convince the judge that the reason is proper. In the 2007 trial of Lewis "Scooter" Libby, former chief of staff for Vice President Dick Cheney, the judge allowed defense attorneys to challenge for cause any potential jurors who said they did not trust the Bush administration, or opposed its policies. There is no limit on the number of challenges for cause that both prosecutor and defense attorney may exercise.

A peremptory challenge is somewhat different. This challenge can be exercised without cause, and the judge has no power to refuse such a challenge.* There is a limit, however, on the number of such challenges that may be exercised. Sometimes there are as few as two or three and sometimes as many as 10 or 20, depending on the case, the kind of crime involved, the state statute and sometimes the judge. This kind of challenge is reserved for use against people whom the defense or the prosecution does not want on the jury but whom the judge refuses to excuse for cause. An attorney may have an intuitive hunch about a potential juror and want that person eliminated from the final panel. Or the juror's social or ethnic background may suggest a problem to the attorney.

To select jury members for the typical criminal trial, attorneys rely on the answers to the questions they ask potential jurors and on their intuition. In the occasional high-profile trial it is not uncommon for attorneys on both sides to undertake a far deeper scrutiny of the panel of potential jurors. For example, for the trial in the spring of 2001 of a former Ku Klux Klansman accused of murdering four young black girls when he bombed a Birmingham, Ala., church in 1963, the prosecution organized focus groups and polled nearly 500 residents of the Birmingham area to help them understand racial attitudes in the community. Government attorneys used the information they got from this research to help them select a jury, a jury of eight whites and four blacks, which later deliberated for just over two hours before bringing

---

*In 1986 the Supreme Court tried to place limits on the use of peremptory challenges to exclude people from a jury solely on the basis of their race (see *Batson* v. *Kentucky,* 476 U.S. 29 [1986]). But this ruling failed to live up to its promise, according to many defense attorneys, who argue that the use of peremptory challenges to remove black jurors continues. The high court tried again in 2008 when it reversed a conviction of a black man, who had been on death row for 12 years, because the prosecutor in the trial had used improper tactics to pick an all-white jury (see *Snyder* v. *Louisiana*, No. 06-10119). The court has also indicated it is concerned about excluding potential jurors solely because of their gender in some cases (e.g., excluding women from juries in rape trials).

in a conviction.[10] Before Martha Stewart went to trial in early 2004 for obstruction of justice and securities fraud, her lawyers and advisers used polling and focus groups to try to uncover the kind of person who might make a favorable juror in her case.

Is voir dire a good way to screen prejudiced jurors? The vast majority of trial judges who are asked this question say they believe the question-and-answer process is either highly effective or moderately effective in screening out biased jurors.[11] Most lawyers say they agree that voir dire can be effective, to a point. Still, it is difficult to argue with critics who say that voir dire uncovers only the prejudice that the prospective juror is aware of or is not too embarrassed to admit. Biased jurors can lie when questioned about their biases. They may not even know their mind is made up about the guilt or innocence of the defendant. And the prejudices may have nothing to do with pretrial news coverage of the crime. Potential jurors may be prejudiced against defendants because of their race, the kind of work they do or the neighborhood in which they live.

Good lawyers walk a fine line in selecting jurors. A defense attorney certainly doesn't want a juror who knows all about the case and has already made up his or her mind regarding a defendant's guilt. On the other hand, a juror who doesn't know anything about a widely publicized case might be just as bad. Mark Twain once facetiously suggested that "ignoramuses alone could mete out unsullied justice."* Few attorneys want the jury box filled with ignoramuses. The feelings of most good attorneys are reflected in remarks made by U.S. Attorney Jay B. Stephens, who suggested that the best jurors are intelligent jurors who listen to the evidence, who evaluate the evidence and who do not go off on extraneous kinds of issues. "That purpose is served, I think, by informed jurors, by jurors who are an integral part of the community, who participate in the community, who are aware of what is going on in the community and who stay informed."[12]

CHANGE OF VENUE

A serious crime that has been heavily publicized in one community might have received scant press coverage in another community in the state. The court can, in order to impanel a jury of citizens who know much less about the case, move the trial to the second community. This change of location of the trial is called a **change of venue.** If this relocation of the trial is ordered, all the participants in the trial—the prosecutor, defense attorney, judge, defendant, witnesses and others—go to this new location for the trial. The jury is selected from citizens in the new community. In 2003, for example, the trials of the snipers who terrorized the Washington, D.C., suburbs were moved a considerable distance from communites where the crimes were committed. And the trial of Scott Peterson for killing his pregnant wife was moved 50 miles from his hometown of Modesto, Calif., the following year.

A trial in a state court can be moved to any other venue in the same state. A federal case can be moved to any other federal court, although keeping the trial as close as possible to the site of the crime is considered desirable. The federal trial in 1997 of the defendants charged with bombing of the federal building in Oklahoma City was moved to Denver, a city in the adjacent state of Colorado. In that case the move out of state rather than to another city in

---

*Mark Twain, *Roughing It* (New York: New American Library Edition, 1962).
10. Sack, "Research Guided Jury Selection."
11. Bush, *Free Press and Fair Trial.*
12. U.S. Senate Subcommittee, *Federal Jury Selection,* 581.

Oklahoma was prompted by the need to find courtroom facilities that could accommodate a trial of that magnitude.

Change of venue is costly. Witnesses, attorneys and others must be transported and housed and fed while the trial takes place in a distant city. The defendant must surrender the constitutional right to a trial in the district in which the crime was committed. Publicity about the case could appear in the media located in the community in which the trial is scheduled to be held, defeating the purpose of the change of venue. Often the effectiveness of the change of venue depends on how far the trial is moved from the city in which the crime was committed. A trial judge in Washington state who was concerned about newspaper coverage of a local murder case granted a change of venue. But he moved the trial to an adjoining county, the only other county in the state in which the "offending" newspaper had significant circulation. The move accomplished very little, and the judge ultimately was forced to close portions of the proceedings to the press.[13] While a change of venue can reduce the risk of prejudicial publicity influencing a jury, other equally problematic factors may be introduced into the trial. The difference in the ethnic and racial composition of one community as opposed to another could possibly change the outcome of a trial. When the 1992 trial of four white police officers accused of beating Rodney King, a black man, was moved to the largely white distant suburbs of Los Angeles in a change of venue, three of the officers were acquitted of the charges and the jury failed to reach a verdict regarding the fourth officer. This despite the fact that the beating was captured on videotape by a bystander. The officers' federal trial for violation of King's civil rights was held in the city of Los Angeles with a racially mixed jury, and all the officers were convicted.

In some states it is possible for the defense to seek a **change of veniremen** rather than a change of venue. Instead of moving the trial to another city, the court imports a jury panel from a distant community. In the summer of 2004 a federal judge in Alabama agreed to a plan to try Eric Rudolph, who was accused of planting a bomb outside an abortion clinic in Birmingham, in Birmingham, but ruled that the jurors in the trial would be picked from communities in the northern part of the state instead of the three-county area surrounding that city. Rudolph later pleaded guilty to the crime. When this procedure is employed it usually means that the judge and attorneys visit the distant communities and select a jury panel, then transport the jurors to the community in which the trial will be held. This procedure costs the state less money, since all it must do is pay the expenses of the jurors for the duration of the trial.

Often the effectiveness of the change of venue depends on how far the trial is moved from the city in which the crime was committed.

CONTINUANCE

When a trial is continued, or a **continuance** is granted, the trial is delayed. By postponing a trial for weeks or even months, a judge expects that the people in the community will forget at least some of what has been written or broadcast about the case, and that expectation is probably legitimate. However, before a trial may be postponed, the defendant must sacrifice his or her right to a speedy trial, something guaranteed under the Constitution. Because the courtrooms in America are clogged, there are few truly speedy trials today, but a continuance delays a trial even longer. The defendant may spend this additional time in jail if bail has not been posted. It is also possible, even likely, that when the trial is finally set to begin, publicity about the case will reappear in the mass media.

13. *Federated Publications* v. *Kurtz,* 94 Wash. 2d 51 (1980).

But a continuance is a perfect solution in some cases. One judge told of how, just as he was scheduled to begin hearing a medical malpractice suit on a Monday morning, the Sunday paper, quite innocently, carried a long feature story on the skyrocketing costs of physicians' malpractice insurance because of the large malpractice judgments handed down in courts. The article pointed out that physicians passed the additional insurance charges along to patients. The story was widely read. Jurors, who also pay doctors' bills, might hesitate to award a judgment to an injured patient knowing that it would raise insurance rates and ultimately cost patients more. The judge therefore continued the case for two months to let the story fade from the public mind.

ADMONITION TO THE JURY

Once a jury is impaneled, its members are instructed by the judge to render their verdict in the case solely on the basis of the evidence presented in the courtroom. Judges say they believe that most jurors take this **admonition** quite seriously. Jurors are also warned not to read newspaper stories or watch television broadcasts about the case while the trial is being held. Often jurors are excused from the courtroom while the trial judge hears arguments from the attorneys or even testimony from witnesses. In such instances the court usually wants to determine whether certain evidence is admissible in the case before the evidence is presented to the jury. The press may publish or broadcast reports about this evidence, whether or not it is admitted in the case. It would accomplish very little to keep such evidence from the jury during the trial if jurors could watch news stories about it during the evening television newscasts.

The following admonition, which is one used by King County, Wash., superior court judges, is typical:

> Do not discuss this case or any criminal case or any criminal matter among yourselves or with anyone else. Do not permit anyone to discuss such subjects with you or in your presence. . . . Do not read, view, or listen to any report in a newspaper, radio, or television on the subject of this trial or any other criminal trial. Do not permit anyone to read about or comment on this trial or any criminal trial to you or in your presence.

Evidence gathered in the last century revealed that most jurors pay close attention to these instructions. In the single major study in which real jury deliberations were examined to determine the impact of mass media publicity in trials, researchers found that jurors listen carefully to and follow the cautionary instructions given to them by judges. Again, the notion rooted deeply in American jurisprudence is that the jurors should decide the case solely on the evidence presented in court. The facts presented to the jury have been subjected to scrutiny and challenge from both sides in the case and have been ruled admissible by the judge.

However, technology has reared its head in the 21st century and this safeguard is being tested as never before. More and more judges are noting that jurors are using Blackberrys, iPhones and other personal communication devices to gather information on their own during a trial, and to communicate with people outside the trial. As New York Times reporter John Schwartz noted recently, jurors using these small devices can look up the name of a defendant on the Web, examine the site of a crime using Google Maps, tell their friends what is happening in the jury room and find out many other details about a case that aren't brought before the court by the attorneys. Mistrials are becoming more common because of this extrajudicial activity by jurors. In Arkansas, a building products company asked a court to overturn a

$12.6 million judgment because a juror allegedly used Twitter to send updates during the civil trial. In Pennsylvania, lawyers for a former state senator charged with corruption demanded a mistrial because a juror posted updates on the case on Twitter and Facebook. More and more judges are now warning jurors against such practices in their standard admonitions. Some courts are beginning to restrict the use of personal communication devices by jurors in the courthouse, and in some instances jurors are required to surrender such devices until the trial is completed, Schwartz reported. But the practice is far from being completely controlled.[14]

SEQUESTRATION OF THE JURY

Once a jury is selected, or impaneled, the problem of pretrial publicity diminishes. But other problems emerge. It is not uncommon for jurors to be removed from the courtroom during a trial while attorneys make arguments about the admissibility of evidence or the possible testimony of a witness. Except in extraordinary cases the public and press remain in the courtroom during these episodes, and what is discussed can and likely will be reported in newspapers and on television. Or prejudicial information may be generated by people outside the courtroom during the trial and, again, be reported by the news media. In some instances the aforementioned admonition to the jurors may be considered insufficient to shield them from this publicity, and so the members of the panel are isolated from outsiders during the trial. They are not allowed to go home each evening but are housed in a hotel. They eat their meals together, relax together, go to and from the courthouse together. Telephone calls and e-mail (if permitted) are screened by court personnel. Newspapers and television news broadcasts are also screened for stories about the trial. This process is called **sequestration of the jury** and is mandatory in some states for trials that last longer than a day, unless both the state and the defense agree to waive the procedure. In a few other states sequestration of the jury is required in all death penalty cases. In most jurisdictions, however, the jurors are isolated only if the judge specifically orders it.

Sequestration of the jury can have serious drawbacks for the state, the jurors and the criminal justice system. It costs the state a lot of money to house and feed the jurors. New York reportedly spent $2.5 million a year putting up jurors overnight until mandatory sequestration was abandoned in 2001.[15] It cost jurors both time and money. Staying in a hotel and eating in restaurants for two or three days may be considered a lark by some people, but the trials in which jurors are sequestered often last weeks or even months. Lives are seriously disrupted, and few jurors can afford a loss of income over such a prolonged period of time. In extremely long trials, some jury members suffering hardships will ask to be excused before the trial is completed. And many attorneys fear the criminal justice system may be compromised as well. Sequestration may keep jurors free from unwanted prejudicial publicity about the case, but could generate a prejudice in jurors of a different kind, a prejudice against one party or the other for keeping them away from family and friends for an extended period. Defense attorneys express this fear most often, saying they believe jurors will blame the defendant for their hardships. But it was reported after the 1995 O.J. Simpson criminal trial that some jurors, who were sequestered for almost as long as Simpson was jailed, said they empathized with the defendant because of this.[16] The jurors in the second O.J. trial, the civil suit in which he was found guilty, were not sequestered.

14. Bush, *Free Press and Fair Trial;* and Schwartz, "As Jurors Turn to Google."
15. Sengupta, "New York State."
16. Labaton, "Lessons of Simpson Case."

SUMMARY

Trial courts have many ways to compensate for the prejudicial pretrial publicity in a criminal case. Each citizen is questioned by the attorneys and the judge before being accepted as a juror. During this voir dire examination, questions can be asked of the potential jurors about the kinds of information they already know about the case. People who have already made up their minds about the defendant's guilt or innocence can be excluded from the jury.

Courts have the power to move a trial to a distant county to find a jury that has not been exposed to the publicity about the case that has been generated by local mass media. While such a change of venue can be costly, it can also be an effective means of compensating for sensational publicity about a case.

A trial can be delayed until the publicity about the case dies down. The defendant must waive the right to a speedy trial, but, except in highly sensational cases, granting a continuance in a trial can thwart the impact of the massive publicity often generated in the wake of a serious crime.

Jurors are always admonished by the judge to base their decision on the facts presented in court and not to read or view any news stories about the case while they are on the jury. There is evidence that they take these warnings quite seriously.

In important cases it is always possible to seclude, or sequester, the jury after it is chosen to shield it from publicity about the trial.

RESTRICTIVE ORDERS TO CONTROL PUBLICITY

Judges have been trying for many, many years to compensate for prejudicial pretrial publicity using the remedies outlined in the previous section. Some jurists and lawyers feel that these schemes are badly out-of-date. The mass media—especially cable TV channels and Internet blogs and other sites—have become far more ubiquitous in the past two decades. It costs the state more money to try a defendant when there is a change of venue or when an extensive voir dire is needed. These remedies don't always work, it is contended. There is a better solution to the problem: The court should control the kind and amount of information that is published or broadcast about the case. If this is done, it won't be necessary later on to compensate for any prejudicial publicity.

The Supreme Court gave trial judges guidance in adopting ways to limit the publication and broadcast of prejudicial information in a 1966 decision involving one of the most highly publicized criminal trials of the 20th century: the prosecution of Dr. Sam Sheppard for the murder of his pregnant wife, Marilyn. Mrs. Sheppard was killed early in the morning on July 4, 1954. Her husband, Sam, claimed she was bludgeoned to death by an intruder who attacked her in her bedroom as she slept. From the very beginning of the investigation local police thought Sheppard was the killer. The case, which had all the elements of a good murder mystery, caught the fancy of the nation's press and was front-page news in all parts of the country. After three weeks of intense publicity, Sheppard was arrested and charged with murder. Publicity increased during the preliminary examination and trial, and few were surprised when the wealthy osteopath was convicted. Twelve years later, after several appeals had been denied, the U.S. Supreme Court reversed Sam

Headlines like these in the Cleveland Press pressured police to move against Sam Sheppard in 1954.

Quit Stalling and Bring Him In!

CELEBREZZE SAYS BAY MAYOR IS PROTECTING MURDER SUSPECT

Special thanks to Cleveland State University Library

Sheppard's conviction, ruling that he had been denied a fair trial because of pretrial and trial publicity about the case.[17]

The Supreme Court was critical of the press coverage of the case, noting that bedlam often reigned both before and during the trial. And while Justice Tom Clark did not excuse the journalists for their excesses, his sharpest criticism was aimed at the trial judge for allowing things to get so far out of hand. Clark said Judge Blythin and the other officers of the courts should have done more to control the use of the courtroom by the press; to control the release of information to the press by lawyers and police officers; and to even proscribe extrajudicial statements by lawyers, witnesses or other trial participants that divulged prejudicial matters.[18] The Supreme Court made it quite clear that it would hold the trial judge responsible for ensuring that the defendant's rights were not jeopardized by prejudicial press publicity.

What the high court suggested, albeit obliquely, was that judges use court orders (called **restrictive orders**) to control the behavior of the participants in the trial. Limit what they can say, when they can say it, and to whom they speak. If no prejudicial information is given to reporters, it cannot be published or broadcast. And that will go a long way in protecting the rights of the accused. The American Bar Association made a similar proposal two years later. Within a short time restrictive orders became a popular way for judges to control the amount and kind of publicity about a pending criminal trial. But the judges went a step further than the high court proposed in 1966. Some orders were aimed not only at the participants in trials, but at the press as well. Some courts issued restrictive orders (or what journalists called

---

17. *Sheppard* v. *Maxwell,* 384 U.S. 333 (1966). Sheppard was retried by the state of Ohio after the Supreme Court ruling. He was acquitted in this second trial. But his life was in ruins, and he died several years later of a liver disease. And yes, this case was the inspiration for both the television series and the movie called "The Fugitive."

18. *Sheppard* v. *Maxwell,* 384 U.S. 333 (1966).

gag orders) to the press, forbidding the publication or broadcast of specific kinds of information, or even barring journalists from commenting on some aspects of a pending trial. This latter kind of order raised distinct and troubling First Amendment questions, for however the orders were structured, or whatever they were called, they amounted to the baldest form of prior censorship.

As we consider these restrictive orders in the following pages remember that they fall into two distinct categories:

- Orders that are aimed directly at the press, limiting what can be published or broadcast
- Orders that are aimed at the participants in the trial, limiting what they can tell the public and reporters about the pending legal matters

RESTRICTIVE ORDERS AIMED AT THE PRESS

There is no such thing as a typical restrictive order; in fact, that is one of the virtues seen in them by judges. Each order can be fashioned to fit the case at hand. They are often quite comprehensive. Orders aimed at the press usually limit the press coverage of certain specific details about a case; a defendant's confession or prior criminal record, for example. Orders aimed at the participants in a trial are usually much broader, forbidding comments by attorneys, witnesses and others about any aspect of the case. In 1975 another sensational murder case began, one that would ultimately bring the issue of pretrial publicity and gag orders before the Supreme Court.

Erwin Simants was arrested and charged in North Platte, Neb., with the murder of all six members of the Henry Kellie family. Like the *Sheppard* case, the arrest of Simants caught the eye of the national news media, and local judge Hugh Stuart had his hands full with scores of reporters from around the state and the nation. Stuart responded by issuing a restrictive order barring the publication or broadcast of a wide range of information that he said would be prejudicial to Simants. The order was later modified by the Nebraska Supreme Court to prohibit only the reporting of the existence and nature of any confessions or admissions Simants might have made to police or any third party and any other information "strongly implicative" of the accused. The order was to stand in effect until a jury was chosen.

The press in the state appealed the publication ban to the U.S. Supreme Court, and in June 1976 the high court ruled that Judge Stuart's order was an unconstitutional prior restraint on the press. All nine members of the court agreed that Judge Stuart's court order was a violation of the First Amendment. But is such a restrictive order aimed at the press a violation of the First Amendment in every case? This is where the high court split. Four justices—Potter Stewart, William Brennan, Thurgood Marshall and John Paul Stevens—said that this kind of restrictive order would never be permissible. Four other justices—Warren Burger, Harry Blackmun, William Rehnquist and Lewis Powell—said that such orders may be permissible in extraordinary circumstances. And the ninth justice—Byron White—said there was really no need in this case to decide whether this kind of restrictive order might be permissible in extreme cases, but concurred with Chief Justice Burger's opinion that became the court's opinion.

The chief justice wrote that a restrictive order levied against the press might be permissible where the "gravity of the evil, discounted by its improbability, justifies such an invasion of free speech as is necessary to avoid the danger."[19] Burger then outlined a three-part test to be used to evaluate whether a restrictive order that limited the press would pass First Amendment scrutiny. He said that such an order could be constitutionally justified only if these conditions are met:

1. Intense and pervasive publicity concerning the case is certain.
2. No other alternative measure might mitigate the effects of the pretrial publicity.
3. The restrictive order will in fact effectively prevent prejudicial material from reaching potential jurors.

Prior restraint is the exception, not the rule, Chief Justice Burger wrote. There must be a clear and present danger to the defendant's rights before such a restrictive order can be constitutionally permitted, he said. In Simants' case, Burger said, while there was heavy publicity about the matter, there was no evidence that Judge Stuart had considered the efficacy of other remedies to compensate for this publicity. Also, the small community was filled with rumors about Simants and what he had told the police. Burger expressed serious doubts whether the restrictive order would have in fact kept prejudicial information out of public hands.

NEBRASKA PRESS ASSOCIATION TEST FOR RESTRICTIVE ORDERS AIMED AT THE PRESS

1. There must be intense and pervasive publicity about the case.
2. No other alternative measure might mitigate the effects of the pretrial publicity.
3. The restrictive order will in fact effectively prevent prejudicial publicity from reaching potential jurors.

Please note, the Supreme Court did not declare restrictive orders aimed only at *trial participants* to be unconstitutional. This issue was not raised in the trial, but it was and still is assumed that courts have much broader power to limit what attorneys, police and other trial participants can say about a case out of court. "Guidelines on Fair Trial/Free Press," issued by the United States Judicial Conference, for example, specifically recommends that federal courts adopt rules that limit public discussion of criminal cases by attorneys and court personnel and suggests that courts issue special rules in sensational criminal cases to bar extrajudicial comments by all trial participants. But, in light of the ruling in *Nebraska Press Association* v. *Stuart,* the guidelines state:

> No rule of court or judicial order should be promulgated by a United States district court which would prohibit representatives of the news media from broadcasting or publishing any information in their possession relating to a criminal case.

19. *Nebraska Press Association* v. *Stuart,* 427 U.S. 539 (1976).

In both 1978 and 1979 the Supreme Court issued opinions in cases that had the effect of reinforcing the rule from the *Nebraska Press Association* decision; that is, restrictions on what the press may publish are to be tolerated only in very rare circumstances. In 1978 the high court prohibited the state of Virginia from punishing the Virginian Pilot newspaper for publishing an accurate story regarding the confidential proceedings of a state judicial review commission.[20] A Virginia state statute authorized the commission to hear complaints of a judge's disability or misconduct, and because of the sensitive nature of such hearings, the Virginia law closed the proceedings to the public and the press. The state argued that confidentiality was necessary to encourage the filing of complaints and the testimony of witnesses, to protect the judge from the injury that might result from the publication of unwarranted or unexamined charges, and to maintain confidence in the judiciary that might be undermined by the publication of groundless charges. Although acknowledging the desirability of confidentiality, the Supreme Court nevertheless ruled against the state. Chief Justice Burger, writing for a unanimous court, stated that the "publication Virginia seeks to punish under its statute lies near the core of the First Amendment, and the Commonwealth's interests advanced by the imposition of criminal sanctions are insufficient to justify the actual and potential encroachments on freedom of speech and of the press." The court did acknowledge that the state commission could certainly meet in secret and that its reports and materials could be kept confidential. But while the press has no right to gain access to such information, once it possesses the information, it cannot be punished for its publication. In this sense the court followed the *Nebraska Press Association* rule limiting restraints placed on the press's right to publish.

In 1979 the high court declared unconstitutional a West Virginia statute that made it a crime for a newspaper to publish, without the written approval of the juvenile court, the name of a youth charged as a juvenile offender.[21] Again Chief Justice Burger wrote the opinion for the court and stressed the fact that once the press has legally obtained truthful information, it may publish this information. In this case two Charleston, W.Va., newspapers published the name of a 14-year-old boy who was arrested for the shooting death of a 15-year-old student. Reporters for the newspapers got the name from people who had witnessed the shooting. "If the information is lawfully obtained," the chief justice wrote, "the state may not punish its publication except when necessary to further an interest more substantial than is present here."

"If the information is lawfully obtained, the state may not punish its publication except when necessary to further an interest more substantial than is present here."

The number of restrictive orders aimed at the press has dwindled substantially during the past three decades as a result of these three rulings. Most trial judges won't even bother to issue an order when it is requested.

Typical is the response of a U.S. District Court judge in New York state during the trial of a state legislator charged with failing to report $225,000 in income on his federal tax return and with lying to federal agents. The defendant asked the court to enjoin the press and the government prosecutors from issuing or publishing press releases, mug shots, and photos and video taken during his so called perp walk into the courthouse. The judge agreed there had been considerable publicity about the case, and that pictures of the defendant in handcuffs might interfere with his fair trial rights. But the judge pointed out there were seven million

20. *Landmark Communications* v. *Virginia,* 435 U.S. 829 (1978).
21. *Smith* v. *Daily Mail Publishing Co.,* 443 U.S. 97 (1979).

people in the federal court district and trial was not scheduled to start for six months. Surely with a jury pool this large, and by using a comprehensive voir dire, an impartial jury could be seated, the judge said. Request for the restrictive order was denied.[22]

When a trial court does issue such an order, it is typically overturned on appeal. For example, the Florida District Court of Appeals in 2005 voided a court order issued by a judge during a sensational murder trial in an effort to protect the privacy of the jurors and the defendant's fair trial rights. The defendant was tried and was subsequently convicted of abducting, raping and killing an 11-year-old girl and was sentenced to death. The court ordered all trial participants to refer to the jurors by number during the proceeding, forbid the press from publishing the names and addresses of jurors, no matter how they got this information, and barred journalists from publishing photographs of jurors' faces. The appellate court ruled the prior restraint did not satisfy the requirements of the *Nebraska Press Association* test. The court acknowledged there was extensive and intense press coverage of the case, but said that the judge failed to consider alternatives to the prior censorship. The court also said the order was too broad. There was no time limit on the ban on photography, and it applied to locations outside the courthouse.[23]

The Supreme Court of Mississippi in December 1998 threw out both a contempt citation and a gag order in a case involving the publication of material relating to a defendant's juvenile record.[24] The juvenile record was discussed by the prosecutor at an open sentencing hearing in an effort to convince the judge to impose a maximum sentence on a defendant who had been convicted of manslaughter. The judge told the reporter, Cynthia Jeffries of the Delta Democrat Times, not to include any material about the juvenile record in her story. Three days after the hearing the newspaper carried a story containing this information. Jeffries was arrested and brought before the judge, who found her in contempt for violating the order and sentenced her to three days in jail. The state's high court said the judge's action was improper in two ways. First, the judge treated this situation as a direct contempt—a contempt committed in the presence of the court when in fact the contempt was committed outside the courtroom as the article was published. Jeffries should have had the benefit of procedural safeguards that accompany charges of an indirect or constructive contempt, the court ruled. Second, the court order regarding the juvenile record was invalid. The judge did not even consider the *Nebraska Press Association* test, the court ruled. The order should not have been issued had that test been applied, since it would not have been effective in protecting the defendant's rights. The courtroom was full of other people during the hearing, all of whom heard the same information the newspaper published. Also, the court could have used other means to avoid the problem in the first place, such as having the discussion about the juvenile record in the judge's chambers, away from the open courtroom.

The Arkansas Supreme Court in 2006 struck down a restrictive order issued against the press that forbid the press from publishing testimony given at a public hearing by the mayor of West Helena, Ark. City council members had brought a suit against the mayor when the executive tried to get rid of the chief of police. Mayor Johnny Weaver had filed a complaint with the Judicial Discipline and Disability Commission against the judge in the case, claiming the jurist was guilty of misconduct. At a pretrial hearing the mayor outlined his complaints

22. *U.S.* v. *Corbin*, 37 M.L.R. 1840 (2009).
23. *Sarasota Herald-Tribune* v. *State*, 924 So. 2d 8 (2005).
24. *Jeffries* v. *Mississippi*, 724 So. 2d 897 (1998).

against the judge. The judge then closed the hearing and prohibited any reporting of the mayor's testimony because, he said, charges like these made to the Judicial Commission are normally confidential at this stage of the process, and the charges could damage the judge's reputation and even undermine public confidence in the judicial system. The state high court said that the restrictive order issued by the court could have the same effect of undermining public confidence in the court, the issue of who was to be the city's police chief was of great interest, and none of the concerns raised by the trial judge were sufficient to overcome the presumption against prior restraint.[25]

Finally, in 2005 the 2nd U.S. Court of Appeals ruled that a trial judge's fear of a mistrial was not a sufficient reason to issue an order barring the press from revealing the names of the jurors in a trial of a former bank executive for obstructing a federal stock investigation. The appellate court noted that the jurors' names had been announced in open court, and that the record simply did not show that reporting these names would impair the defendant's right to a fair trial. Also, the trial judge had not even considered whether a viable alternative to the gag order might prevent the harm the judge assumed would result if the names were published, the court said.[26]

Are gag orders against the press ever affirmed by appellate courts? If there is good reason, such an order may be sustained. During the pretrial proceedings in the Kobe Bryant rape trial an electronic transcript of an in-camera (nonpublic) hearing that would have revealed the rape victim's identity was accidentally disseminated to seven media outlets. The trial court issued an order barring the press from disseminating the information contained in this document. The Colorado Supreme Court upheld the trial court's order. While the court noted the U.S. Supreme Court rulings on permitting the publication of rape victims' identities (see pages 281–282), it also noted Justice Marshall's statement that the state courts were not completely without the power to shield the identity of the victim of a sexual assault if such shielding were needed to protect an interest of the highest order, in this case the mandate of the Colorado rape shield statute.[27] Of course the rape charges against the NBA star were subsequently dropped.

RESTRICTIVE ORDERS AIMED AT TRIAL PARTICIPANTS

While the law regarding restrictive orders aimed at the press is generally clear and has evolved swiftly since 1976, the law regarding restrictive orders barring participants from speaking or publishing about a case is less distinct and is still developing. The theory behind gagging the participants in the trial is simple: If attorneys, police officers, witnesses and others are forbidden from speaking about the case, reporters will be denied access to a considerable amount of material that might very well be prejudicial. Stories will not be written or broadcast, and potential jurors will not see or hear such information.

Gag orders aimed at the trial participants are not common, nor are they unusual, especially in high-profile cases involving celebrities or other high-visibility defendants. The judge in the 2005 Michael Jackson child molestation trial barred attorneys from discussing the case outside the courtroom. Lawyers, witnesses and police officers were barred from discussing

25. *Helena Daily World* v. *Simes,* 34 M.L.R. 1329 (2006).
26. *U.S.* v. *Quattrone,* 402 F. 3d 304 (2005).
27. *Colorado* v. *Bryant,* 94 P. 3d 624 (2004).

the case against Scott Peterson for the murder of his wife and unborn child. These orders are often quite comprehensive. When the federal government prosecuted Richard Scrushy, the former corporate chairman and CEO of HealthSouth, a giant HMO, the case generated substantial publicity. A federal judge in Alabama issued a broad-based restrictive order to block extrajudicial statements by parties and the attorneys.[28] The order said:

- No extrajudicial statements until the final verdict by any participant, including witnesses, concerning
  1. materials provided in discovery in preparation for the case;
  2. character, credibility, reputation or criminal record of a party or witness, or the expected testimony of a party or witness;
  3. matters that counsel should know would be inadmissible at the trial, and would create a substantial risk of prejudicing a trial jury; and
  4. with the exception of Scrushy personally, any opinions as to the defendant's guilt or innocence.
- Participants must remove from their existing Web pages extrajudicial comments, allegations of prosecutorial misconduct and information discovered in the course of criminal discovery.
- Counsel for parties must avoid commenting in court papers that are not filed under seal on evidence that is irrelevant to legal matters involved in the case.
- All court personnel must not disclose any information relating to the case that is not part of the public record.

For many years trial judges were generally free to issue restrictive orders aimed at participants with little justification. In recent years, however, appellate courts are applying stricter rules that courts must follow.

- The California Court of Appeals ruled in 2007 that a gag order prohibiting all parties in a criminal trial from disseminating items of tangible evidence such as autopsy reports, crime scene photos, crime scene diagrams and other similar items to the public or press was invalid. The trial court had no evidence to support the order, the court said, relying on mere speculation as to probable harm.[29]
- The North Carolina Court of Appeals ruled in 2007 that a gag order, which forbade the parties in a civil suit and their attorneys from communicating with the news media regarding litigation, was unconstitutional. The trial court did not enter findings of fact that a clear threat existed to the fairness of the trial, and did not consider less restrictive alternatives the court said.[30]
- And in 2008 the Nevada Supreme Court ruled that a gag order preventing all parties and their attorneys from disclosing any documents or discussing any portion of a case involving child support payments following a divorce proceeding violated both the U.S. and the Nevada constitutions.[31]

---

28. *U.S.* v. *Scrushy,* 32 M.L.R. 1814 (2004).
29. *Dixon* v. *Superior Court*, 36 M.L.R. 1505 (2007).
30. *Beaufort County Board of Education* v. *Beaufort County Board of Commissioners*, 645 S.E. 2d 857 (2007).
31. *Johnson* v. *Eighth Judicial District Court*, 182 P. 3d 194 (2008).

Even when a restrictive order is justified, trial judges must be careful about the manner in which they shape the order. When a judge in New York barred all parties from discussing *any* aspect of a criminal case, and threatened potential violators with a substantial fine, the 2nd U.S. Circuit Court of Appeals ruled that the order was inappropriate, even if needed. "The limitations on attorney speech should be not broader than necessary to protect the integrity of the judicial system and the defendant's right to a fair trial. The court said this order was too broad, and there was no determination that an alternative to this kind of blanket order would not work as well.[32] And the Ohio Court of Appeals ruled that a restrictive order that said "All parties to this action are hereby restrained from issueing any public comments about the pending status of this litigation" was not specific enough to block a litigant from writing a letter to a newspaper responding to an accusation published in the newspaper against his character. Barring comments about pending litigation did not cover comments made by the litigant in the newspaper, the court said.[33]

Finally, in a highly unusual case from New York, a trial court rejected a request for a gag order against a witness in a racketeering case, a witness who just happened to be a member of the media. John A. Gotti Jr. was indicted for racketeering and other offenses that were related to the attempted murder in 1992 of Curtis Sliwa, the man who founded the Guardian Angels, a community-based anti-crime group. For years Sliwa insisted that Gotti ordered him killed, and he said so repeatedly on a talk radio program he aired on WABC-AM. The show has a large listenership. Gotti asked the court to bar Sliwa from making such extrajudicial statements, or talking in any way about the merits of the case since he would almost certainly be a witness at Gotti's trial. The court agreed that the comments could be prejudicial, but said a restrictive order would be less effective than a thorough voir dire and strong jury instructions. The court said it hoped that Sliwa would respect Gotti's right to a fair trial and refrain from making prejudicial comments on the radio, but that a gag order was a last resort it was not willing to impose at that time.[34]

Lawyers specifically may be barred under court rules or codes of conduct from making extrajudicial comments on a case, whether or not a restrictive order has been issued. The U.S. Supreme Court made that clear in a 1991 ruling that focused on an alleged violation of general court rules that applied to attorneys. A lawyer named Dominic Gentile, who represented a client charged with taking money and drugs from a safety deposit box rented by undercover police agents, held a press conference in which he claimed that police were using his client as a scapegoat. Gentile said his client was innocent, that a police officer was the likely thief who took the money and drugs, and described some of the witnesses for the prosecution in the case as drug dealers. Gentile's client was acquitted, but the Nevada Supreme Court ruled that the attorney's comments at the press conference violated a court rule that limits what an attorney can say about a pending case. The rule prohibited attorneys in a criminal case from making prejudicial statements about the character, credibility, reputation or criminal record of a party, suspect or witness. The rule did provide a so-called safe haven for lawyers who were permitted to "elaborate the general nature" of the defense.

32. *U.S. v. Salameh,* 992 F. 2d 445 (1993).
33. *In re Contempt of Richard Scaldini,* 2008 Ohio 6154 (2008).
34. *U.S. v. Gotti,* 33 M.L.R. 1083 (2004).

The Supreme Court ruled by a 5-4 vote that states may prohibit out-of-court statements by attorneys if these statements have a substantial likelihood of materially prejudicing the proceeding.[35] But the court also ruled by the same 5-4 margin that the Nevada rule prohibiting extrajudicial comments by attorneys was a violation of Gentile's constitutional rights because it was too vague. The so-called safe-haven provisions contained terms that were so imprecise that they failed to give fair notice of what is permitted and what is forbidden, which could lead to discriminatory enforcement of the rule. What the court said, then, was that rules like these are permissible limits on free speech so long as they spell out specifically what can and cannot be said.

It is common following the completion of a lawsuit for attorneys to talk with jurors to discover what factors led to the verdict the jurors reached. Today in highly publicized trials, reporters also want to talk with the jurors. It is not uncommon today for tabloid television programs and tabloid newspapers to offer jurors large sums of money if they will talk on the record about their deliberations. Many people believe such juror interviews are detrimental to the legal system. "It is now assumed that jurors must deliberate in secret so that they may communicate freely with one another, secure in the knowledge that what they say will not be passed along to others," noted Yale law professor Abraham S. Goldstein.[36]

It is not uncommon today for tabloid television programs and tabloid newspapers to offer jurors large sums of money if they will talk on the record about their deliberations.

A judge can certainly bar a juror from speaking with reporters while the trial is in progress or before the jury deliberations are completed. But once a jury has completed its work and is dismissed by the judge, the law becomes considerably murkier. Judges raise several concerns relating to the jury. One is to protect the jurors from harassment by the press. The pushing and shoving to get an interview can sometimes get intense. Another is to protect the sanctity of the deliberations. There are as many as 12 people on a jury. If one member speaks with reporters, it often reveals the actions and comments of other members of the panel. Finally, there are cases where subsequent trials of other defendants may involve the same crime, and juror comments about their deliberations could have an impact on these forthcoming hearings. And there is always the potential of a retrial following an appeal by the defendant who was found guilty by the jurors. In New Jersey in 2002 a jury was unable to reach a verdict in the trial of a former rabbi who was charged with killing his wife. The trial was extensively covered by the press and was televised by Court TV. Following the first trial the court forbade the press from contacting or attempting to interview the jurors. The New Jersey Supreme Court affirmed this order, ruling that interviews with jurors might reveal insights into the juror deliberative process, including the reaction to evidence presented in the trial. This would give the prosecution an advantage at the retrial, the court said.[37]

Courts have tried a variety of schemes to limit press communications with jurors following trials. Some judges have tried to solve this problem by denying the press and the public access to the names and addresses of the jurors (see page 455). Courts have gone so far as to shield all identifying information about the jurors, such as names, addresses, professions, ages and so on. The members of such an anonymous jury are referred to only by number. For example, before the so-called Unabomber, Ted Kaczynski, pleaded guilty in 1996 to sending bombs to people via the mail, all identifying information about the 12 jurors and six alternates

---

35. *Gentile* v. *Nevada State Bar,* 111 S. Ct. 2770 (1991).
36. Goldstein, "Jury Secrecy and the Media," 295.
37. *State* v. *Neulander,* 30 M.L.R. 2281 (2002).

selected to hear his case was confidential. Anonymous juries were also used in both Oklahoma City bombing prosecutions and in the trials of the Branch Davidian survivors, Oliver North and the World Trade Center bombers. First Amendment advocates note that the anonymous jury, once a rarity, seems to be becoming far more commonplace today.[38] But others note that this kind of jury was typically used in the past with very high-profile trials, and the nation has simply experienced a great many more such trials in recent years. (See page 455 for discussion on access to juror identities.)

Other judges have issued restrictive orders barring the news media from questioning jurors about their deliberations. These efforts have had mixed results. As a general rule, orders prohibiting media access to jurors for an unlimited duration are unconstitutional. But general rules are hard to fashion because of the significant differences that often exist among trials. In November 1997 the 5th U.S. Circuit Court of Appeals upheld such an order in a high-profile racketeering trial. Trial judge Sarah Vance told jurors they could not be interviewed "by anyone concerning the deliberations of the jury" unless she issued an order permitting it. The appellate court said the order was justified, considering the intense media scrutiny of the trial. The U.S. Supreme Court refused to review the decision.[39]

In another case, however, the Texas Court of Appeals invalidated a trial court's order that barred jurors from talking with the press. A highly publicized civil case involving an explosion at a Texas City oil refinery ended with a settlement after 10 days of testimony. But other litigants were also suing the oil company for damages based on the same explosion, so the court forbade jurors telling reporters how they would have decided the case if the trial had been completed. The court said it was concerned about interfering with the rights of the other parties in future trials. The appellate court said the trial court did not show that the judicial process would be irreparably harmed without the gag order, and there was nothing in the record to show that the court considered less restrictive means, such as a change of venue. Also, the trial court's conclusion that an extensive voir dire of future jurors (from a pool of 1,200) would be inconvenient was insufficient.[40]

Some judges have only limited discretion in this matter. For example, "The Handbook for Jurors," published by the U. S. Judicial Conference, specifically says that it should be up to each juror to decide whether he or she talks with the press following a trial. Some appellate courts have not permitted trial judges to ban such interviews. The 9th U.S. Circuit Court of Appeals struck down a lower-court order that prohibited anyone from interviewing jurors after a trial. The order was issued by the trial court to minimize harassment of jurors, according to the trial judge, but the Court of Appeals ruled that not all jurors might regard media interviews as harassment.[41] The Kentucky Supreme Court in 2000 overturned a trial court's order forbidding anyone to initiate contact with a juror even after the trial was completed. The order was needed, the trial judge said, to ensure jurors' personal safety and privacy. The state high court said the order was too broad. If a former juror doesn't want to talk with a reporter, he or she should refuse the interview. If the reporter persists, the former juror can complain to authorities about harassment or intimidation. He or she can even

38. Kirtley, *The Privacy Paradox.*
39. *U.S.* v. *Cleveland,* 128 F. 3d 267 (1997).
40. *In re Hearst Newspapers Partnership LP,* 241 S.W. 3d 190 (2007).
41. *U.S.* v. *Sherman,* 581 F. 2d 1358 (1978).

institute a civil suit against the reporter. But the court order barring anyone from contacting the former jurors after the trial went far beyond the court's jurisdiction, which ended when the trial ended.[42]

Finally, the U.S. Supreme Court ruled in 1990 that a Florida statute prohibiting witnesses who testified before a grand jury from revealing what they had said, even after the grand jury's term had expired, was unconstitutional.[43] Proceedings before grand juries are ultrasecret. Nothing but the true bill, or **indictment,** issued by a grand jury is a part of the public record. A reporter was working on a story when he uncovered information the prosecutor believed the grand jury should hear. The reporter was subpoenaed and testified before the grand jury. After he had given his testimony, he sought to write a news story about his investigation as well as his experiences before the grand jury. But the statute blocked his effort, so he sued in U.S. District Court to have the law declared to be unconstitutional. Ultimately, the Supreme Court did just that.

Chief Justice William Rehnquist wrote that traditionally courts have taken very seriously the need for secrecy in grand jury proceedings. But, he said, "we have recognized that the invocation of grand jury interests is not some talisman that dissolves all constitutional protections." In this case, the chief justice said, the situation involved a reporter's right to divulge information of which he was in possession before he testified before the grand jury, not information he had gained as a result of his participation in the grand jury proceeding. Citing the ruling in *Smith* v. *Daily Mail Publishing Co.*[44] (see page 429), Rehnquist said the state could not punish a journalist for publishing information that he or she had legally obtained. While important interests were at stake in maintaining a veil around the activities of a grand jury, these interests in this case were insufficient to outweigh the First Amendment interests.

Restrictive orders that bar the press from publishing information about a criminal case have ceased to be a serious problem for journalists. Orders that limit what trial participants can say remain a nuisance, however, and probably do not serve the judicial system as well as many observers might imagine. Rumors tend to thrive in an atmosphere in which the release of accurate information is stifled. It would be better perhaps to provide journalists determined to publish something about a case with accurate and truthful statements rather than push them to report what is ground out by a rumor mill.

SUMMARY   In some instances trial courts have attempted to limit the publication of prejudicial information about a case by issuing court orders restricting what the press may publish or what the trial participants may publicly say about a case. These restrictive orders grew out of a famous U.S. Supreme Court decision in the mid-1960s that ruled a trial judge is responsible for controlling the publicity about a case.

In 1976 the Supreme Court ruled that the press may not be prohibited from publishing information it has legally obtained about a criminal case unless these conditions are met:

---

42. *Cape Publications Inc.* v. *Braden,* 39 S.W. 3d 823 (2001).
43. *Butterworth* v. *Smith,* 110 S. Ct. 1376 (1990).
44. *Smith* v. *Daily Mail Publishing Co.,* 443 U.S. 97 (1979).

1. Intense and pervasive publicity about the case is certain.
2. No other reasonable alternative is likely to mitigate the effects of the pretrial publicity.
3. The restrictive order will prevent prejudicial material from reaching the jurors.

In two subsequent rulings the high court reaffirmed its 1976 decision that confidential information legally obtained by the press may be published. These cases involved the name of a juvenile suspect in a murder case and the names of judges whose conduct had been reviewed by a confidential state judicial commission.

Although judges may still limit what trial participants say publicly about a case, even these restrictive orders have come under constitutional scrutiny in recent years.

BIBLIOGRAPHY

Bush, Chilton R., ed. *Free Press and Fair Trial: Some Dimensions of the Problem.* Athens: University of Georgia Press, 1971.

Drechsel, Robert E. "An Alternative View of Media-Judiciary Relations: What the Non-Legal Evidence Suggests about the Fair Trial–Free Press Issue." *Hofstra Law Review* 18 (1989): 1.

Farrington, Brendan. "DNA Indicates Confessions Were False." *Seattle Post-Intelligencer,* 16 June 2001, A3.

Friendly, Alfred, and Ronald Goldfarb. *Crime and Publicity.* New York: Random House, Vintage Books, 1968.

Goldstein, Abraham S. "Jury Secrecy and the Media: The Problem of the Postverdict Interview." *University of Illinois Law Review,* no. 295 (1993).

Kirtley, Jane, ed. *The Privacy Paradox.* Arlington, Va.: Reporters Committee for Freedom of the Press, 1998.

Labaton, Stephen. "Lessons of Simpson Case Are Reshaping the Law." *The New York Times,* 6 October 1995, A1.

Minow, Newton, and Fred Cate. "Who Is an Impartial Juror in an Age of Mass Media?" *American University Law Review* 40 (1991): 631.

Pember, Don R. "Does Pretrial Publicity Really Hurt?" *Columbia Journalism Review,* September/October 1984, 16.

Sack, Kevin. "Research Guided Jury Selection in Bombing Trial." *The New York Times,* 3 May 2001, A12.

Schwartz, John. "As Jurors Turn to Google and Twitter, Mistrials Are Popping Up." *The New York Times,* 18 March 2009, A1.

Sengupta, Somini. "New York State Ends the Mandatory Sequestration of Jurors." *The New York Times,* 31 May 2001, A20.

U.S. Senate Subcommittee on Improvement in Judicial Machinery of the Senate Judiciary Committee. *Hearings on Federal Jury Selection.* 90th Cong., 1st Sess., 1967, 581.

CHAPTER 12

Free Press–Fair Trial

CLOSED JUDICIAL PROCEEDINGS

Faced with Supreme Court rulings that blocked the use of restrictive orders to stop press coverage of the criminal justice system, judges in the 1980s began to close judicial proceedings to deny to reporters information that may be prejudicial to the defendant's fair trial rights. The press challenged these closures, and as with the restrictive orders, appellate courts found that such closures usually violated the First Amendment. This issue, as well as a discussion of the right to take photographic and electronic recording equipment into the courtroom and voluntary press guidelines, is the focus of this chapter.

CLOSED PROCEEDINGS AND SEALED DOCUMENTS

News coverage of crime, criminals and trials has long been a staple of the American press. A century ago the police reporter, not the political correspondent nor the journalist who covers the government, was the top dog at most newspapers. Tension between the press and the judicial system has also existed for a long time. But as the 21st century unfolds, many observers have suggested that the circumstances that foster this tension have substantially increased. Why?

- The size and reach of the mass media has increased dramatically in the past quarter century. Crime news not only continues to fill newspapers, magazines and the traditional broadcast media, but also is an important part of cable television channels, the growing number of tabloid publications and the Internet. The threat of damaging the rights of the defendant has increased.

■ The war on terror and the government's legal response to it has resulted in growing secrecy at all levels of the legal system, from apprehension of suspected terrorists, through their incarceration in special facilities, to secret trials. Reporters and many civil libertarians want greater access to these processes; government officials have resisted these calls for openness.

■ A growing number of litigants who are brought to court for a variety of reasons seek to shield their activities by asking courts to seal records and close hearings, and too many courts are willing to accede to these requests. Again, public scrutiny of the judicial process suffers as a result.

■ The intense public fascination with celebrities, sports figures, musicians, movie stars and others also includes a morbid curiosity about individuals charged with crime. Some of these individuals, like Michael Jackson and Kobe Bryant, were already famous before their brushes with the law. Others, like fertilizer salesman Scott Peterson, are simply ordinary men or women who by their actions are thrust into the sharp glare of the public spotlight. Publicity in these cases often saturates the nation.

Judges who are severely limited by appellate courts in their ability to block what the press prints or broadcasts about a case sought other means to put controls on pretrial publicity. They began instead to limit public and press access to judicial proceedings and documents. In a series of rulings the Supreme Court curbed this power as well, but not quite as neatly as it had done with restrictive orders aimed at the press. The issue is far from being resolved and the closure of hearings and documents continues today, at an increasing rate, in the eyes of some observers.

This chapter explores the issue of access to the justice system. The Supreme Court first attempted to resolve the growing tendency to close hearings and seal documents in 1980. Two other decisions followed in the middle of the decade. Today a judge who is asked to close a judicial hearing or seal court documents faces a considerable hurdle if he or she agrees to bar the press and the public from the proceeding or deny access to documents. An outline of the judicial test that establishes this hurdle follows, along with an examination of how this test has been applied in a variety of situations.

OPEN COURTS AND THE CONSTITUTION

In 1980 the U.S. Supreme Court ruled 7-1 (Justice Lewis Powell took no part in this case) that there was a right under both common law and the First Amendment to the U.S. Constitution for the public and the press to attend a criminal trial.[1] Six years later the high court extended this right of access to other judicial proceedings and records. In its ruling in this case, *Press-Enterprise* v. *Riverside Superior Court,*[2] the justices fashioned a rather complicated test that a judge must apply before he or she can constitutionally close off access to the judicial process.

1. *Richmond Newspapers* v. *Virginia,* 448 U.S. 555 (1980).
2. 478 U.S. 1 (1986).

The first thing a judge must determine if the closure issue arises is whether the proceeding or document is what the law regards as presumptively open or closed. A hearing that is presumptively open, for example, is one that is normally open to the public and the press. To determine whether the proceeding or document is presumptively open or not, the judge must ask a couple of questions:

1. **whether this kind of hearing (or document, if access to a court record is involved) has traditionally and historically been open to the press and public, or**

2. **whether public and press access to this hearing will play a positive role in the functioning of the judicial process.**

While the question of the presumptiveness of access seems simple enough (Was the hearing or record traditionally open? Will access play a positive role in the functioning of the judicial process?), sometimes it is not. For example, in 2007 a U.S. District Court in Illinois ruled that there was no presumptive access to the names and addresses of jurors in a criminal trial because this information had not been historically or traditionally accessible, and access to this information was not tied to the proper functioning of the judicial process.[3] Twenty months later the 3rd U.S. Court of Appeals ruled in just the opposite way, saying that these names had been historically accessible. In an earlier era, the court said, when communities were small, everyone generally knew the names of jurors in a criminal trial. And for nearly a millennium before the 1970s, the withholding of jurors' names was "very rare."[4] If the court determines that this kind of hearing has traditionally been open, *or* that allowing the press and the public to attend the hearing will have a positive impact on the judicial process, then he or she must declare the hearing to be presumptively open. Then it is up to those seeking to close the hearing, the defendant or the state, to convince the court that there is a good reason to close it. In doing this, the advocates of closure must

1. **advance an overriding interest that is likely to be harmed if the proceeding remains open or the court permits access to the court document.** Examples of such interests include the right to a fair trial for the defendant, or protection of a witness's privacy. Then the advocate of closure must

2. **prove to the court that if the hearing or document is open to the press and public, there is a *substantial probability* that this interest will be harmed,** that the jury will be prejudiced or the privacy of the witness will be invaded, for example.

The words "substantial probability" are important; this is a high threshold for the advocate of closure to meet. A showing that there is a "chance" or even a "likelihood" of harm is insufficient to support a motion for closure.

If the advocate of closure proves that there is a substantial probability that such harm may occur, then the judge must

3. **consider whether there are reasonable alternatives to closure that might solve the problem.** Perhaps a thorough voir dire or change of venue would reduce the

---

3. *United States* v. *Black*, 483 F. Supp. 2d 618 (2007).
4. *United States* v. *Wecht*, 3d Cir., No. 07-4767, 8/1/08.

probability of prejudice. Closure of the hearing or the sealing of the document should be the last option, not the first option, considered by the court.

If there are no viable alternatives, then it is the responsibility of the judge to

4. **narrowly tailor the closure so there is an absolute minimum of interference with the rights of the press and public to attend the hearing or see the document.** A pretrial hearing on evidence might include many issues beyond the single issue that could harm the defendant. The court must close only that portion of the hearing dealing with the single issue. Or the court must exclude the press and public from only that portion of a witness's testimony that might cause embarrassment or humiliation, not the entire testimony.

Finally, the trial judge must

5. **make evidentiary findings to support this decision and prepare a thorough factual record relating to the closure order, a record that can be evaluated by an appellate court.** This final element is important. Appellate courts want to be certain that the trial judge thoughtfully and carefully considered options other than closure as a solution to the problem. The Georgia Supreme Court voided an order closing the pretrial phase of a sensational murder trial because the judge had stated simply that alternatives to closure were considered and found to be insufficient. "A closure order must fully articulate the alternatives to closure and the reasons why the alternatives would not protect the movant's [the party seeking closure] rights," the court ruled.[5]

And in 2005 the Illinois Court of Appeals rejected a trial court's order blocking public and media access to certain pretrial hearings and records. The court issued the order because, it said, media access to the material, which included inadmissible evidence, would "tend" to create "more than a potential problem." The appellate court said the judge failed to cite any facts to support his fears of potential problems. There must be a specific finding based on fact showing a substantial probability of harm. Also, the trial judge failed to consider alernatives to closure.[6]

This *Press-Enterprise* test applies to documents as well as to hearings, and a decision by the 10th U.S. Circuit Court of Appeals is instructive in how the test is applied. Journalists covering the trials of Timothy McVeigh and Terry L. Nichols, who were charged with bombing the federal building in Oklahoma City, sought access to documents relating to the proceedings. They sought redacted (censored) portions of Nichols' motion to suppress certain evidence and exhibits, notes made by an FBI agent who initially interviewed Nichols, and redacted portions of McVeigh's and Nichols' motions for separate trials. The court said that while suppression motions are traditionally open, access has not been historically extended to evidence ruled inadmissible, and in this case only the inadmissible material has been sealed. Access to raw notes, such as those written by the FBI agent, is not supported by either tradition or logic because it would provide exposure to hearsay and other unsupported and inadmissible matter. Finally, the court said it would assume, because of traditional practice, that there is a right of

5. *Rockdale Citizen Publishing Co. v. Georgia*, 463 S.E. 2d 864 (1995).
6. *People v. LaGrone*, 838 N.E. 2d 142 (2005).

access to some portions of the documents relating to separate trials. With regard to the latter set of documents, the court said release of the material could endanger both defendants' right to a fair trial since these papers contained candid material needed by the court to assess whether separate trials were necessary. The appellate court said it would not second-guess this decision, since the trial judge had made adequate findings to support the closure order.[7]

OPEN AND CLOSED TRIALS

With guidance from the Supreme Court, lower courts have applied the rules in the *Press-Enterprise* test to a wide variety of hearings and documents. Most of the cases expanding the open-access provisions have resulted from newspapers and broadcasting stations challenging court rulings to close the proceedings. But fewer and fewer access challenges are occurring today because the press is not raising this issue. Why? Partly because many of the small, medium and even some large media organizations are suffering financially, and don't have the resources to mount expensive litigation. As one media analyst described it, many in the press have shifted their emphasis from pursuing First Amendment principles to survival. And some large companies that have bought up hundreds of family-owned media operations in the past three decades as business ventures don't share the journalistic commitment to open government.*

Judges have an exceedingly difficult time closing off access to traditional criminal trials. The Supreme Court spoke unambiguously about such hearings in the 1980 ruling, *Richmond Newspapers* v. *Virginia.*[8] The case stemmed from a state court ruling in a Virginia trial.

In March 1976 John Stevenson was indicted for murder. He was tried and convicted of second-degree murder, but his conviction was reversed. A second trial ended in a mistrial when a juror asked to be excused in the midst of the hearing. A third trial also resulted in a mistrial because a prospective juror told other prospective jurors about Stevenson's earlier conviction on the same charges. This exchange was not revealed until after the trial had started. As proceedings were about to begin for the fourth time in late 1978, the defense asked that the trial be closed. The prosecution did not object and the court closed the trial. Richmond newspapers protested the closure to no avail. An appeal came before the U.S. Supreme Court in February 1980.

Chief Justice Burger wrote the court's opinion, noting that "through its evolution the trial has been open to all who cared to observe." A presumption of open hearings is the very nature of a criminal trial under our system of justice, the chief justice added. Although there is no specific provision in the Bill of Rights or the Constitution to support the open trial, the expressly guaranteed freedoms in the First Amendment "share a common core purpose of assuring freedom of communication on matters relating to the functioning of government," Burger wrote. "In guaranteeing freedoms such as those of speech and press the First Amendment can be read as protecting the right of everyone to attend trials so as to give meaning to those explicit guarantees," he added. The First Amendment, then, the chief justice noted,

The First Amendment, then, the chief justice noted, prohibits the government from summarily closing courtroom doors, which had been open to the public at the time that amendment was adopted.

---

*See Adam Liptak's report in *The New York Times*, "Shrinking Newsrooms Wage Fewer Battles for Public Access to Courtrooms," for a fuller discussion of this issue.

7. *U.S.* v. *McVeigh,* 119 F. 3d 806 (1997).

8. 448 U.S. 555 (1980).

PRESS-ENTERPRISE TEST FOR THE CLOSURE OF PRESUMPTIVELY OPEN JUDICIAL PROCEEDINGS AND DOCUMENTS

1. The party seeking closure, the defendant or the government or sometimes both, must advance an overriding interest that is likely to be harmed if the proceeding or document is open.

2. Whoever seeks the closure must demonstrate that there is a "substantial probability" that this interest will be harmed if the proceeding or document remains open.

3. The trial court must consider reasonable alternatives to closure.

4. If the judge decides that closure is the only reasonable solution, the closure must be narrowly tailored to restrict no more access than is absolutely necessary.

5. The trial court must make adequate findings to support the closure decision.

---

prohibits the government from summarily closing courtroom doors, which had been open to the public at the time that amendment was adopted.

But the chief justice refused to see the First Amendment as an absolute bar to closed trials. He noted that in some circumstances, which he explicitly declined to define at that time, a trial judge could bar the public and the press from a trial in the interest of the fair administration of justice. But, while the court did not outline such circumstances, it was clear from both the tone and the language of the chief justice's opinion that in his mind such circumstances would indeed be unusual. Justices White, Stevens, Brennan, Marshall, Stewart and Blackmun all concurred with the chief justice in five separate opinions. All but Stewart went further in guaranteeing access to trials than did Chief Justice Burger. Justice Rehnquist dissented.

The Supreme Court has not yet ruled that civil trials are open to the press and public, but lower federal and state courts have made such rulings. In 1984 the U.S. Court of Appeals for the 3rd Circuit ruled that civil proceedings are also presumptively open to the public and the press. In *Publicker Industries* v. *Cohen*,[9] a lawsuit involving a corporate proxy fight, the court noted that a "survey of authorities identifies as features of the civil justice system many of those attributes of the criminal justice system on which the Supreme Court relied in holding that the First Amendment guarantees to the public and to the press the right of access to criminal trials." The right is not absolute, the court said, but absent a clear showing that closing the trial serves an important governmental interest and that closing the trial is the only way to serve this interest, the civil proceeding should be open. In 1999 the California Supreme Court became the first state high court to make the same ruling, that the press and the public have a constitutional right of access to a civil proceeding.[10]

There are, of course, exceptions to the rule that trials are open to the press and the public. Here are a few examples.

---

9. 733 F. 2d 1059 (1984).
10. *NBC Subsidiary (KNBC-TV Inc.)* v. *Superior Court,* 980 P. 2d 337 (1999).

Juvenile Hearings. Traditionally, judicial hearings involving juveniles have been closed to the press and the public. Protecting both the victim and the accused is the common rationale that supports this policy. The victims are often juveniles as well, and the attempt to rehabilitate a juvenile offender is an underlying tenet of juvenile justice. Rehabilitation efforts might be much more difficult if the community is informed about the offender.

However, policies regarding the juvenile justice process have changed over the past two decades. Access to these proceedings is not commonplace, but not unusual either. There are at least a couple of reasons for this. First, many states have classified juvenile proceedings into two groups: those in which a juvenile is charged with a crime, and those in which the juvenile is the subject of a hearing related to child abuse, parental neglect, family reconciliation, dependency or some other similar concern. The law in many of the states that have instituted this two-tier system has made the first category of hearing (a criminal hearing) presumptively open to the press and the public, and the second kind of hearing (the kind concerned with social problems) presumptively closed. But at least a dozen states now regard this second kind of hearing presumptively open as well. In many instances juvenile court judges allow reporters to attend these hearings to get a sense of the problems with which the court is dealing, but grant access only if the journalists agree to refrain from identifying the parties in any story they publish or broadcast. Juvenile crime has taken on far more serious proportions in the past quarter century, and this is the second reason for increased openness. Whereas petty theft and assault were about the only charges placed against juveniles 50 years ago, robbery, rape and even murder charges are not uncommon today. Public concern has forced increased scrutiny of the juvenile justice process.

Despite the trend toward more access to juvenile hearings, the law is inconsistent from state to state, and case to case. The Ohio Supreme Court ruled in 2006 that in that state, juvenile proceedings are neither presumed open nor closed. The decision must be made by the court on a case-by-case basis, considering whether access to the proceeding could harm the child, whether this harm outweighs the benefits of public access and whether there are reasonable alternatives to closure.[11] Furthermore the 3rd U.S. Court of Appeals ruled in 1994 that the federal Juvenile Delinquency Act, a statute that governs the treatment of those under the age of 18 who are charged with violating the law, does not require that federal juvenile proceedings be open or closed. Rather, courts must make rulings regarding this issue on a case-by-case basis, balancing the interests of all parties involved.[12]

Here is a sampling of court decisions on juvenile hearings.

- The New Mexico Supreme Court ruled in 2001 that the press did not have an unqualified right of access to child abuse and neglect proceedings, especially if the identities of the parties were likely to become public.[13]
- The New York Family Court ruled in 2006 that the privacy interests of a sibling of a 7-year-old who was beaten to death by her parents outweighed the public's interest to be privy to the workings of the court.[14]

---

11. *State ex rel Plain Dealer Publishing Co.* v. *Floyd,* 34 M.L.R. 2325 (2006).
12. *U.S.* v. *A. D.,* 28 F. 3d 1353 (1994); see also *U.S.* v. *Three Juveniles,* 61 F. 2d 86 (1995).
13. *Albuquerque Journal* v. *Jewell,* 18 P. 3d 334 (2001).
14. *In re S/B/B/R Children,* 34 M.L.R. 2147 (2006).

■ The Vermont Supreme Court ruled more than 25 years ago that a judge could close a proceeding to consider the legal status of a 15-year-old boy who was accused of murdering one girl and assaulting another. Publicity is often seen as a reward for hard-core juvenile offenders, the court said.[15]

■ But in 2005 the Missouri Supreme Court ruled that the proceeding in which a juvenile was to be tried for a killing should be open because the charge would be first-degree murder if an adult were being tried for the same crime.[16]

■ And in 2007 the Ohio Supreme Court ruled that a juvenile judge erred when he barred a photographer from photographing a 15-year-old defendant during a public court hearing. The defendant was accused of aggravated murder and robbery. The judge made the decision without holding a hearing on the need for his order when the boy's parents objected to the photography. The state high court ruled that during the hearing, a judge who denies access must find substantial evidence that the media's presence could harm the defendant or endanger the proceedings fairness, that the harm outweighs the public benefit, and that no alternatives to barring the media are available.[17]

Journalists and others concerned with reporting on juvenile proceedings should acquaint themselves with the law on this topic in their states or court district. Judges within a state may have varying interpretations of what is often ambiguous law. But for now and the foreseeable future, juvenile hearings remain an exception to the rule that criminal trials are normally open to the press and public.

Victim and Witness Protection. The Supreme Court has ruled that it is permissible for a state to attempt to protect the victim of a sexual assault by permitting the closing of a trial during the victim's testimony. Laws exist in many states that provide for such closure. But these laws can permit the court only to close the proceeding during the testimony; they cannot require that such a closure take place. A Massachusetts statute required closure of a trial during the testimony of a juvenile sex offense victim. The U.S. Supreme Court ruled that the law was unconstitutional. Justice William Brennan agreed that the state has a strong interest in protecting the victim in this kind of a case. The law was nevertheless flawed, he said, because it *required* closure of the proceeding. "As compelling as that interest is, it does not justify a mandatory closure rule, for it is clear that the circumstances of the particular case may affect the significance of the [state] interest," Brennan wrote. Under the statute, the trial judge is not permitted to allow testimony in open court, even if the victim desires it, the jurist noted.[18] A 1992 Washington state law that required courts to ensure that the identities of juvenile victims of sexual assault were not disclosed was ruled unconstitutional as well, since it would have required trial judges to close the courtroom during such hearings.[19] But in 2008 a U.S. District Court in Idaho closed the courtroom during the testimony of a 12-year-old girl during a

---

15. *In re J. S.,* 438 A. 2d 1125 (1981).

16. *State ex rel St. Louis Post-Dispatch LLC* v. *Garvey,* 179 S.W. 3d 899 (2005).

17. *State ex rel Dispatch Printing Co.* v. *Geer,* 114 Ohio St. 3d 511 (2007); see also *Chicago Tribune Co.* v. *Mauffray,* 996 So. 2d 1273 (2008).

18. *Globe Newspapers* v. *Superior Court,* 457 U.S. 596 (1982).

19. *Allied Daily Newspapers* v. *Eikenberry,* 848 P. 2d 1258 (1993).

capital sentencing hearing regarding her suffering at the hands of a convicted sex offender and murderer. The defendant had killed several of the girl's family members, kidnapped her and her brother and then killed her brother. The judge ruled that there was a "compelling interest" in protecting the well-being of the surviving victim from embarrassment and psychological harm that outweighed the media's First Amendment right of access to that portion of the criminal judicial proceeding. Transcripts of the girl's testimony were provided to the press and public later.[20]

Appellate courts usually permit the closure of those portions of a trial during which an undercover police officer testifies. The Appellate Division of the New York Supreme Court ruled in 1997 that a trial court acted properly when it closed the courtroom during the testimony of undercover officers because these police officers continued to work ongoing investigations in the specific area in which the defendant was arrested and they said they feared for their safety if the courtroom remained open during their testimony.[21] But such closure is not automatic. In a 1993 case the state's high court ruled that it was improper for a trial judge to close the court during an undercover officer's testimony based only on the showing that this officer continued to operate undercover in "the Bronx area." The Bronx encompasses 41 square miles and includes 2.1 million people, the court said. Closing a trial based on this interest would in effect require automatic closure every time any undercover officer testified.[22]

Ever since the terrorist attacks on Sept. 11, 2001, and the initiation of fighting in Iraq and Afghanistan, the U.S. government has been faced with the dilemma of what to do with the hundreds of prisoners detained as suspected terrorists, associates of terrorists, enemy combatants and so on. How should these people be brought to justice? What kind of trials—if any—should be held? What constitutional rights, if any, do these detainees have? What courts have jurisdiction to hear cases involving these individuals? These questions, and others, had not been completely resolved by late 2009, more than eight years after the beginning of the so-called war on terror.

Linked to these questions is another issue. Should whatever judicial process is chosen be open to the press and public, like a normal criminal trial? Officials in the administration of President George W. Bush were adamant that any kind of public court hearing could pose a serious threat to national security. Government lawyers advanced what has been called the "mosaic theory" to support their arguments. This theory holds that any information, seemingly innocuous bits of data, that is revealed at a public hearing can be assimilated by other terrorists and help them understand the direction of the government's investigations, thereby compromising the nation's safety. Civil libertarians and others, however, have argued that public trials are fundamental to American law, and everyone—from suspected mass murderers to accused extortionists to alleged terrorists or enemy combatants—has a right to a public hearing.

To describe these issues as complicated is a serious understatement. The military, Congress, all levels of the federal courts, including the Supreme Court, and officials at the White House are all players in this matter. There is hope that the Obama administration will work to

---

20. *In re Spokesman-Review,* D. Idaho, No. MC 08-6420-5-EJL, 8/5/08. *United States* v. *Duncan,* No. 07-023-N-EJS, 8/5/08.
21. *New York* v. *Rivera,* 656 N.Y.S. 2d 884 (1997); see also *Ayala* v. *Speckard,* 131 F. 3d 62 (1997).
22. *New York* v. *Martinez,* 82 N.Y. 2d 436 (1993).

resolve questions about what kind of judicial proceedings will be held, if any, but there are no guarantees. In May of 2009, spokespersons at the Obama White House said the administration would prosecute some of the detainees in a military commission–style hearing, but would grant more rights to the accused. The best we can do in this chapter is to briefly outline what is known now, and not speculate about what may lie ahead.

Traditional Military Courts.   Press and public access to military courts is generally open under both military law (Rules for Courts Martial 806 [b]) and the First Amendment.[23] There are exceptions. For example, when classified information is introduced at trial, closure will be permitted if the order is narrowly tailored—that is, no more of the hearing is closed than is necessary to protect the government's interest barring access to the classified material. But according to a report issued by the Reporters Committee for Freedom of the Press in August of 2008, public and press access to and information about both pretrial hearings and courts-martial of men and women in uniform has been routinely denied in recent years. The study showed that the military has refused in about half the cases to provide any information about the pretrial hearing, declined to disclose courts-martial schedules and docketing information for both pretrials and courts-martial, and even withheld basic details such as the defendant's name and the criminal charge at issue.[24]

Military Tribunals or Commissions.   In the wake of the terrorist attacks of Sept. 11, 2001, President Bush signed an order allowing special military tribunals or commissions to try those individuals suspected of terrorist activities. The commissions were to be used to determine the fate of the scores of people who had been detained in the wake of the attacks and were imprisoned primarily at a military facility at Guantanamo Bay, Cuba. The Supreme Court ruled in June of 2006 that the commissions were illegal, saying the president did not have the authority to establish these tribunals, and that they violated provisions of both the Uniform Code of Military Justice and the Geneva Conventions.[25] Nine months later Congress enacted a new law re-establishing the commissions in a modified form. There had been at least two commission trials at Guantanamo at the time this was written. The most publicized was the trial and conviction of Salim Hamdan, who was found guilty of supporting terrorism because he was a former driver for Osama bin Laden. The hearing was ostensibly open, but most neutral observers said it was open in name only. No one could attend the sessions without military orders. The few journalists who did manage to attend were accompanied at all times by military escorts, who stood guard even outside the latrine. There were secret court filings and closed sessions.[26] Whether or not this pattern of pseudo openness will continue with a new administration in power that has promised more transparency in government remains to be seen.

Secret Proceedings in Federal Courts.   The government detained an Algerian who was in the United States on a student visa because of his alleged contact with three of the Sept. 11 hijackers. All proceedings, including the court proceedings involving the South Florida resident, were conducted in secret. The records in the case were closed. There was no public

23. Cys and Mar, "Media Access to the New Special Tribunals."
24. http://www.rcfp.org/newsitems/index.php?!=6914.
25. *Hamdan* v. *Rumsfeld,* 126 S. Ct. 2749 (2006).
26. Glaberson, William, "A Conviction, But a System Still on Trial."

record that the case even existed until a clerk made a docketing error. This was a straightforward habeas corpus hearing (a hearing in which the government must justify its reason for the detention of any person), a kind of hearing that has traditionally been open. The detainee's appeal to the 11th U.S. Court of Appeals was publicly docketed, but entire pages of the public record are blank. Kamel Bellahouel lost his case and was eventually deported. The U.S. Supreme Court denied certiorari.

SUMMARY

American courtrooms traditionally have been open to the press and the public, but in the wake of the rejection of restrictive orders as a means to control publicity, some judges attempted to resolve this problem by closing off access to judicial proceedings and records. In the 1980s the Supreme Court fashioned a legal test, the *Press-Enterprise* test, for judges to use to determine if access to hearings and documents could be limited without violating the First Amendment. Since that time courts have ruled that both criminal and civil trials must generally remain open. Exceptions have been granted for closure during the testimony of crime victims and some witnesses, and some juvenile proceedings. The question of whether military commission hearings used to try individuals suspected of terrorist activities will be open remains an open question.

CLOSURE OF OTHER HEARINGS

To laypeople, the judicial process generally means trials. But a surprisingly large percentage of the process takes place in hearings that are not trials, hearings that often resolve many of the issues formerly decided at trials. The growth of the wide array of especially pretrial hearings is the result of court decisions in the 1960s that substantially expanded defendants' rights in criminal cases, major changes in the way in which the criminal justice system works and attempts by members of the judiciary to work more closely with people who staff the penal institutions and social service agencies.

There are evidentiary or suppression hearings, pretrial detention hearings, plea hearings, presentence and postsentence hearings and so on. Many of these hearings take place long before the trial begins, weeks before the jury is even selected. Some focus on information that may be highly prejudicial to the defendant. At an evidentiary hearing, for example, the court may rule that a key piece of evidence, such as a weapon, is inadmissible at the trial because it was improperly seized by the police. The fact that the defendant had a weapon is certainly prejudicial. If this fact is publicized, some argue, it won't matter that the evidence is barred from trial because the members of the community, the jurors, will already know a weapon exists. Or the state may believe that the publicity about certain kinds of evidence may adversely affect the future prosecution of other defendants.

Since 1986 American courts have ruled that a wide range of judicial proceedings are presumptively open to the press and public. The Supreme Court has specifically ruled that both pretrial evidentiary hearings[27] (such as a hearing to consider motions to suppress evidence) and

Since 1986 American courts have ruled that a wide range of judicial proceedings are presumptively open to the press and public.

27. *Press-Enterprise* v. *Riverside Superior Court*, 478 U.S. 1 (1986).

voir dire proceedings[28] are presumptively open. These rulings apply to all courts, everywhere. Before such hearings can be closed the trial judge must apply the rigid requirements of the *Press-Enterprise* test. This presents a high hurdle for a proponent of closure to cross. For example, a New Jersey trial judge closed a post-verdict jury voir dire to explore possible juror misconduct in a civil case. The judge said he wanted to talk with jurors about possible inappropriate behavior by one member of the jury. When the order was challenged, the appellate court agreed that there was no evidence that such hearings had been traditionally open. However, "Having the public observe the hearing would certainly discourage perjury and provide the public with evidence that juror actions are not unchecked," the court said. The hearing was presumptively open, and the judge failed to provide reasons to support closure, the court ruled.[29]

In South Carolina a trial judge closed the pretrial suppression hearing in a highly publicized murder case. The defendant was accused of killing his girlfriend with a shotgun in a grocery store. A hostage situation resulted, and this was covered on live television. Nearly 40 newspaper stories were published about the case. The judge said he was concerned about racial issues related to the case, and what he called the hot-button issue of domestic violence. The South Carolina Supreme Court rejected the closure order. "Though those concerns were no doubt genuine, closing the courtroom could not possibly have alleviated them," the court ruled. Closing the hearing had no impact at all on the ability of the press to continue to disseminate news about the case. Even assuming a substantial probability that pretrial publicity would be prejudicial to the defendant, closing the pretrial hearing could not have prevented that prejudice, the court said, noting that a thorough voir dire was the preferred method to protect the defendant's rights.[30]

Other rulings on open hearings have come from U.S. Courts of Appeals and state appellate courts. Consequently, these rulings don't apply as broadly; they may, in fact, be confined to a single federal jurisdiction or a state. It is fair to say, however, that in most situations the following kinds of proceedings are regarded as open and can be closed only by a strong showing of the substantial probability of harm to some other compelling interest:

- Pretrial detention hearings
- Bail hearings
- Plea hearings
- Voir dire proceedings
- Sentencing hearings
- Attorney disciplinary hearings

But because a kind of hearing is presumptively open doesn't mean it will always be open. Voir dire hearings offer a good example. Most of the time they are open. Lawyers for TV personality Martha Stewart sought closure of the examination of prospective jurors because of the intense media interest in the case and fears that potential jurors would be reluctant to tell the truth when questioned in front of the press. The trial court agreed, but the ruling was reversed by the 2nd U.S. Court of Appeals. The appellate judges noted that the media interest in the case had not resulted in disruption of the proceedings or disclosure of

---

28. *Press-Enterprise* v. *Riverside Superior Court,* 464 U.S. 501 (1984).
29. *Barber* v. *Shop-Rite of Englewood & Associates Inc.,* 923 A. 2d 286 (2007).
30. *Ex parte Hearst-Argyle Television Inc.,* 34 M.L.R. 1833 (2006).

information the court had barred the press from revealing. Also, the judges said they refused to believe that jurors would be less likely to be candid if they testified in front of the press. "It is difficult to conceive of a potential juror who would be willing to reveal a bias against the defendants in their presence, but not in the presence of reporters," the court said.[31] In 2004 the Washington state Supreme Court overturned a first-degree murder conviction because the trial court violated the defendant's right to a public trial when it barred the public—including the defendant's family—from the voir dire proceeding because the courtroom was too small. The judge also failed to apply the *Press-Enterprise* test, the court noted.[32]

In other cases, the appellate courts have permitted closure of the jury selection process in order to protect the identity of the jurors,[33] or to ensure getting frank and candid responses from potential jurors.[34] In Detroit in 2003 the trial judge closed several phases of the voir dire during the trial of four men charged with conspiracy in relation to the Sept. 11, 2001, terrorist attacks. The judge said he issued the order to protect the privacy rights of the jurors, to shield them from undue harassment by the press and others. He said he was also concerned that press coverage of the voir dire could influence the responses given by the potential jury members.[35]

Some courts use other strategies to deal with potential or real juror problems. The U.S. Court of Appeals for the 5th Circuit ruled that it was permissible for a trial judge to question two jurors privately in his chambers about possible misconduct. This ruling came during the second trial of Edwin Edwards, who was then between his terms as governor of Louisiana. The first trial ended in a mistrial. During the second trial a juror reported to the marshal that another juror had remarked, "Did you know the last jury got paid for voting acquittal?" The judge questioned both jurors in chambers about the matter. He said he did so to keep the matter away from other jurors. The same thing happened a few days later and the judge responded in the same fashion. After the trial ended, the press sought a transcript and received an edited version with the jurors' names and other details stricken from the record. The court of appeals supported the judge. It noted that historically such questioning of jurors has been conducted in private. In addition, opening up such a hearing could be extremely harmful in this case, turning what the court called a "tempest in a teapot" into a mistrial. The court also supported the judge's decision to edit the transcript in order to protect the jurors from embarrassment.[36]

But there are some kinds of proceedings that the courts have said are not presumptively open and generally remain closed to public scrutiny. The 6th U.S. Circuit Court of Appeals ruled that the press and public do not enjoy a presumptive right of access to what is called a summary jury trial, a rather unusual judicial proceeding sometimes used in civil cases. The **summary jury trial** is a device used by courts to attempt to get the parties in the case to settle their dispute before going to a full-blown jury trial. In such a case the attorneys present much-abbreviated arguments to jurors. There are no witnesses called, and objections to evidence or other matters are strongly discouraged. After hearing the arguments, the jurors

31. *ABC Inc.* v. *Stewart,* 360 F. 3d 90 (2004).
32. *In re Personal Restraint Petition of Orange,* 32 M.L.R. 2569 (2004).
33. Liptak, "Nameless Juries on the Rise."
34. *In re South Carolina Press Association,* 946 F. 2d 1037 (1991).
35. *U.S.* v. *Koubriti,* 252 F. Supp. 2d 424 (2003).
36. *U.S.* v. *Edwards,* 823 F. 2d 111 (1987).

issue an informal verdict that can then be used to settle the case. For example, if plaintiff Jones loses the verdict in the summary jury trial, she may be more willing to settle the case without a normal trial. The court said that there was no First Amendment right of access to such proceedings because such a right was not historically recognized and that permitting access might actually work against the purpose of the summary trial, that is, the settlement of the dispute.[37]

Grand jury proceedings are secret—and always have been. This is not an issue the press has disputed, but in two recent instances sensitive grand jury materials have been leaked to the press, much to the distress of defense lawyers, who argue that the release of this material violates the rights of defendants and can taint potential jurors. In December 2004 the San Francisco Chronicle published parts of federal grand jury testimony that suggested several major-league baseball players had used steroids. The following month both ABC News and a Web site called thesmokinggun.com carried substantial excerpts from grand jury proceedings in the Michael Jackson child molestation case. Under California law grand jury transcripts are usually made public before the start of a trial, but in this case the judge had barred the release of the material because of the intense media coverage of the case. No penalties were exacted against the press in these cases,[38] but the mass media walk on very thin legal ice when they publish secret material generated by a grand jury hearing. The First Amendment provides little protection in such a case. (See pages 376–386 to see how the First Amendment rarely protects journalists who refuse to reveal the names of sources of such grand jury materials.) Rules that preserve the secrecy of grand jury proceedings apply equally to proceedings ancillary to grand jury proceedings.

Finally, there is a dispute among the courts today whether deportation hearings should be open or closed. The press generally ignored such hearings until the government began to deport Middle Eastern aliens who they said were in some way connected to terrorist activities. These hearings then became news, and questions began to arise whether they should be open or closed. Two U.S. Courts of Appeal have split on whether press and public access should be permitted. In a case from Michigan, the 6th U.S. Court of Appeals ruled that because the proceedings exhibited substantial, quasi-judicial characteristics, they should be treated like criminal trials and were presumptively open.[39] The court said the hearings had been traditionally open to the public, and the openness plays a significant, positive role, ensuring fairness and preventing mistakes. Thus, any order to close a hearing is governed by the requirements of the *Press-Enterprise* test and must be narrowly tailored. But the 3rd U.S. Court of Appeals, in a case from New Jersey, ruled just the opposite, that deportation hearings are not presumptively open.[40] The court said the deportation hearing process had been codified by Congress and never explicitly contained a guarantee of access. Many hearings have been closed and must be closed, the court said, because they are often held in places that are inaccessible to the public, such as prisons. In addition, the court said, the harm that opening such hearings could do outweighs the potential positive impact of permitting public and press access. The court agreed with the government that an open hearing could reveal government sources and

37. *Cincinnati Gas and Electric Co.* v. *General Electric,* 854 F. 2d 900 (1988).
38. Broder, "From Grand Jury Leaks."
39. *Detroit Free Press* v. *Ashcroft,* 30 M.L.R. 2313 (2002).
40. *North Jersey Media Group Inc.* v. *Ashcroft,* 308 F. 3d 198 (2002).

methods of investigation, could assist members of terrorist cells that are still operating and could damage the privacy interests of the detainees. The ruling in this case was appealed by a group of New Jersey newspapers that challenged the blanket policy of closing the hearings, arguing the government should have to justify the closings on a case-by-case basis. The Supreme Court rejected the appeal so the law remains unsettled.

ACCESSIBLE AND INACCESSIBLE DOCUMENTS

While a wide range of documents have been ruled presumptively open and hence potentially accessible by the press and public, sealing court records is a growing problem. Courts will agree to seal records to help the litigants avoid embarrassment, to encourage them to settle disputes and for a variety of other reasons. In the summer of 2008 the Tulsa World newspaper reported that records in more than 2,000 court cases in Oklahoma were sealed between 2003 and 2007. These included divorce documents, wrongful death settlements and even name changes.[41] The problem has become so serious in some jurisdictions that in 2007, the state of Nevada created a committee to draft new rules governing the preservation, public access and sealing of civil court records.[42]

Any party in a proceeding can ask that the records be sealed, but judges are supposed to apply the rules of the *Press-Enterprise* test (see pages 441–442) to determine whether such closure of records is permissible. Over the past two decades a wide range of documents have been ruled to be presumptively open.

Evidence Introduced in Open Court. Evidence that is introduced in open court is generally accessible. The Florida Court of Appeals ruled in 2005 that crime scene photos, crime scene videotapes and autopsy photos that were admitted into evidence in open court could be inspected by members of the press to determine whether the verbal descriptions of these materials provided by a witness were accurate. The court acknowledged the pictures were distressing to the family and friends of the victim, but that open justice was paramount in this case.[43] The 4th U.S. Court of Appeals ruled in 2006 that documentary evidence that was shown to the jury in open court in the trial of accused terrorist Zacarias Moussaoui should be accessible by the press.[44] However, a federal district court ruled in the same case that an audiotape of the Cockpit Voice Recorder of Flight 93 that crashed in Pennsylvania on Sept. 11, 2001, that was played for the jury should not be released to the press and public. Privacy rights of the victims and concerns of family members outweighed the right of the public to have access to the tape. A written transcript of the tape was made available, however.[45]

Court Docket Sheet. The 2nd U.S. Court of Appeals ruled in 2004 that there is a qualified First Amendment right to inspect these sheets that provide an index to judicial proceedings and documents.[46]

---

41. http://www.rcfp.org/newsitems/index.php?!=6907.
42. *In re Creation of a Committee to Review the Preservation, Access and Sealing of Court Records,* 36 M.L.R. 1253 (2007).
43. *Sarasota Herald-Tribune v. State,* 924 So. 2d 8 (2005).
44. *In re Associated Press,* 34 M.L.R. 1449 (2006).
45. *United States v. Moussaoui,* 34 M.L.R. 1546 (2006).
46. *Hartford Courant v. Pellegrino,* 371 F. 3d 49 (2004).

Documents Filed in Pretrial Proceedings. The 9th U.S. Court of Appeals ruled that pretrial proceedings are open and "there is no reason to distinguish between pretrial proceedings and the documents filed in regard to them."[47]

Presentencing and Postsentencing Reports. The U.S. Court of Appeals for the 9th Circuit ruled that unless a judge could demonstrate a compelling need to keep such records sealed, they should be open for public inspection.[48] But this isn't always the rule. In 2001 a federal court in Pennsylvania sealed a presentencing report on a former state senator who had pleaded guilty to charges of corruption. The court cited the defendant's right to privacy and the court's need for confidentiality to support its ruling.[49]

Plea Agreements. These are written agreements between a prosecutor and a defendant in which the accused agrees to plead guilty, usually to a lesser charge than originally filed.

Information, Indictments, Search Warrants and Supporting Affidavits, Evidence and Other Materials Related to Sentencing. The first four items all relate to materials generated in charging a suspect with a crime, or gathering material needed for prosecution. Sentencing materials may go beyond these kinds of documents and include items that are not admissible as evidence in determining an individual's guilt or innocence. A U.S. District Court in North Carolina ruled in 2005 that search warrant affidavits used during the course of an investigation of an FBI special agent accused of receiving gifts from a witness should be accessible. Any negative publicity before the trial could be addressed through voir dire, the court said.[50] And a federal court in the District of Columbia ruled in 2008 that there is a First Amendment right of access to search warrant materials after an investigation has concluded.[51]

But judges are often willing to draw a line if they feel that public interest will be harmed if some kinds of material are made public. A federal court in New York ruled in 2001 that while the press could have access to letters sent to the clerk of courts about a defendant who was about to be sentenced, similar letters that were sent to the court itself and used by the judge in the sentencing process were off-limits. The judge ruled that the people who sent those letters had an expectation of privacy about their comments, and there was a need for uninhibited commentary on the sentencing issue, something that might be deterred if citizens thought their ideas and opinions would be made public.[52] The Kentucky Supreme Court ruled in 2002 that a trial court could permanently seal some of the allegations of sexual abuse that were made against Roman Catholic priests in the diocese. The trial court said these particular allegations were a sham, immaterial, redundant and "scandalous." The state high court said it was difficult to see how access to such allegations would further the public's understanding of the judicial process and agreed that release of this material could cause irreparable harm to the diocese.[53]

---

47. *A.P.* v. *U.S. District Court,* 705 F. 2d 1143 (1983).
48. *U.S.* v. *Schlette,* 685 F. 2d 1574 (1988); *United States* v. *Langston,* 37 M.L.R. 1411 (2008).
49. *United States* v. *Loeper,* 132 F. Supp. 2d 337 (2001).
50. *U.S.* v. *Blowers,* 34 M.L.R. 1235 (2005).
51. *In re Application of the New York Times Co. for Access to Certain Sealed Court Records,* D.D.C., No. 08-00576 (RCL), 11/17/08.
52. *U.S.* v. *Lawrence,* 29 M.L.R. 2294 (2001).
53. *Roman Catholic Diocese of Lexington* v. *Noble,* 92 S.W. 3d 724 (2002).

Juror Records. Access to information about jurors has become a sensitive issue during the past 15 to 20 years. As activity in the criminal courts has increased and fewer Americans seem willing to serve as jurors, judges have become increasingly protective of those citizens who are willing to perform this important public duty. In most trials the names and addresses of jurors are regarded as public records, open to inspection by the press and the public. But in some cases, judges have refused to reveal the names and addresses of the jurors, even after the trial has concluded. (And sometimes when the information is public, the courts have tried to bar the press from revealing this information in the mass media. See pages 434–435.) Reasons cited for shielding the identities of jurors range from protecting them from outside pressure during a trial, to protecting them from harassment by the press and others after a trial, to concerns about their safety if unpopular verdicts are handed down.

The appellate courts seem to be of two minds on whether such denial of access is permitted under the common law or the Constitution. The 3rd and 4th U.S. Court of Appeals, the Michigan Court of Appeals and the Pennsylvania Supreme Court have all ruled that there is at least a qualified right of access to these records.[54] The qualifications usually revolve around when and how the information is disseminated. The North Dakota Supreme Court ruled in 2008 that juror information was a public record, even if the trial court had promised jurors that the information they had provided on extensive jury questionnaires would be protected.[55] However, the 5th U.S. Court of Appeals, the Oregon Supreme Court and the Massachusetts Supreme Judicial Court have ruled that juror information is not necessarily accessible.[56]

Publishing the names and addresses of jurors, whether permitted or not, is a decision that journalists have to study closely as an ethical issue. The knee-jerk reaction—"if we can get it, we'll publish it"—is inappropriate. In the wake of the first Rodney King trial in southern California in which the officers accused of the beating were exonerated, rioting broke out on the streets of Los Angeles by people protesting the verdict. One newspaper still published jurors' names, something that could have jeopardized the safety of each of these citizens. Key questions need to be asked: What is the purpose of publishing these names? Will publishing the names enlighten readers and viewers in an important way? Or will this action jeopardize the jurors' privacy or even safety? Responsible editors and broadcasters will take the high road.

At least one federal court has also ruled that the notes sent by members of the jury to the judge seeking instructions on matters of law or evidentiary questions are off-limits as well. The judge denied a request by a newspaper to see such records in a complicated case against five defendants that produced 90 separate verdicts. The sanctity of jury deliberations outweighed any First Amendment considerations, the court said. "Just as there is no right of access to the jury's deliberations while they are deliberating . . . there is no right of access to problems which the jurors perceived were preventing them from deliberating," the court ruled.[57]

---

54. *In re Baltimore Sun*, 14 M.L.R. 2378 (1998); *People* v. *Mitchell*, 592 N.W. 2d 798 (1999); *Commonwealth* v. *Long*, 922 A. 2d 892 (2007); and *United States* v. *Wecht*, 3rd Cir. No. 07-4767, 8/1/08.
55. *Forum Communications Co.* v. *Paulson*, 36 M.L.R. 1929 (2008).
56. *U.S.* v. *Edwards*, 823 F. 2d 111 (1987); *Jury Service Resource Center* v. *Muniz*, 34 M.L.R. 1727 (2006); and *Commonwealth* v. *Silva*, 864 N.E. 2d 1 (2007).
57. *United States* v. *Kemp*, 366 F. Supp. 2d 255 (2005).

Out-of-Court Settlements. There are some areas in which public and press access to court documents is routinely denied. Civil lawsuits often end with an out-of-court settlement; that is, both parties agree to a settlement without completing the trial. In the past, cases involving defective tires on Ford Explorers, the dangers of silicone breast implants, exploding cigarette lighters and defective television receivers were all settled out of court, and the terms and nature of the settlements were shrouded under confidentiality orders. Oftentimes judges play an important role in generating such settlements. These settlement agreements have tradition-ally been considered a private matter between the parties in the lawsuit.[58] Today more and more of these agreements contain provisions that the terms of the settlement are to remain confidential. Defendants often seek confidentiality to avoid the disclosure of sensitive or potentially damaging information. Plaintiffs are willing to agree to confidentiality in order to obtain a higher amount of money in the settlement. Therefore, the sealing of out-of-court settlements has become somewhat commonplace. At first glance there seems little difficulty with such sealed agreements; after all, these are private agreements between private parties. But the public interest can be harmed in some instances. The confidential settlement of a mal-practice suit against a doctor, for example, will provide compensation to the injured patient. But such a settlement denies other patients knowledge of the doctor's wrongdoing. If an auto manufacturer obtains a confidential settlement with a customer who was injured because of a faulty part in the car, other owners of the same vehicle may not be warned of the danger.

Journalists are increasingly seeking access to such sealed agreements. Their quest for information is somewhat compromised by the fact that newspapers and broadcasting stations sometimes will seek the confidential settlement of a libel or invasion-of-privacy action. Most judges have not been receptive to the arguments that the press and public should have access to sealed agreements. Many jurists believe that the secrecy clause in these agreements encourages the settlement of lawsuits, and with courts in America as crowded as they are, judges favor anything that will reduce their caseload.* In 1986 the 3rd U.S. Circuit Court of Appeals ruled that there is a right of public access to sealed settle-ment agreements, the first important court to make such a ruling.[59] Since then a few other courts have ordered that such agreements be open for inspection.[60] As a rule, however, these agreements remain beyond the reach of even First Amendment arguments. Reporters who expose the terms of such secret settlements can face severe consequences. A court clerk mistakenly gave reporter Kirsten Mitchell a file containing the details of a secret settlement between Conoco Inc. and residents of a mobile home park who alleged that Conoco had contaminated their water supply. When the Wilmington (N.C.) Morning Star published a story about the settlement, the court held both the reporter and the newspaper in contempt. They were jointly fined $500,000.[61]

Many jurists believe that the secrecy clause in these agreements encourages the settlement of lawsuits, and with courts in America as crowded as they are, judges favor anything that will reduce their caseload.

---

*In 1995 the Judicial Conference of the United States, a policy-making body for the federal courts, rejected a proposal that would have made the sealing of records almost automatic in civil cases.

58. See Bechamps, "Sealed Out-of-Court Settlements," 117.

59. *Bank of America* v. *Hotel Rittenhouse Assoc.,* 800 F. 2d 339 (1986).

60. See *EEOC* v. *The Erection Co.,* 900 F. 2d 168 (1990); *Pansy* v. *Stroudsburg,* 22 F. 3d 772 (1994); *Des Moines School District* v. *Des Moines Register and Tribune Co.,* 487 N.W. 2d 667 (1992); and *CLB* v. *PHC,* 36 M.L.R. 1990 (2008).

61. *Ashcraft* v. *Conoco Inc.,* 26 M.L.R. 1620 (1998).

Protective Court Orders. Other documents normally closed to inspection are records provided by litigants to the opposing party in a lawsuit that are covered by a protective court order. During the discovery process, both sides in a legal dispute are permitted to explore the records and witnesses and other material held by the opposing party. The court can assist in this process by first compelling disclosure of the information, and second, by issuing an order forbidding the parties from revealing the information to outside parties. A recent case in Pennsylvania provides a good example of what can happen.

An officer in the Pennsylvania State Police Department filed a civil action against several employees of the state police claiming that they retaliated against him for speaking out about what he regarded as faulty radar speed-detection devices used by the state police. Through the discovery process he obtained documents relating to those devices and his lawyer gave some of them to the press. The defendants in the case got a protective order from the court to prevent further disclosure of these documents to the press. The trial court justified the order by citing broad allegations that disclosure of the material would result in serious harm. The 3rd U.S. Court of Appeals vacated the order, ruling that there was simply no good cause for it to be entered. The court outlined a seven-part test that should have been applied by the trial judge. The criteria in the test included questions about whether disclosure could violate privacy interests or cause serious embarrassment, whether the purpose in seeking the protected information was legitimate and whether the case involved issues important to the public. The district court had ruled the release of the material to the press could prejudice potential jurors. "This is exactly the type of broad, unsubstantiated allegation of harm that does not support a showing of good cause," the court said. The case involved both public officials and issues important to the public. "Disturbingly, some courts routinely sign orders which contain confidentiality clauses without considering the propriety of such orders on the countervailing public interests which are sacrificed by the order," the court added.[62]

Sadly, this case is not typical. In 1984 the Supreme Court ruled that protective orders like the one just discussed are not the classic kind of prior restraint that requires "exacting First Amendment scrutiny."[63] This decision has given broad leeway for judges to routinely issue such orders.

National Security. The nation's fight against terrorism and terrorist acts has resulted in many instances of closed court records. In early 2007 The New York Times reported that the Bush administration was employing extraordinary secrecy in defending civil lawsuits filed against the National Security Agency because of its highly classified domestic surveillance program. "Plaintiffs and judges' clerks cannot see its secret filings. Judges have to make appointments to review them and are not allowed to keep copies," the newspaper reported.[64]

The case of accused terrorist Zacarias Moussaoui provides an example of the access difficulties presented by such cases. In this instance, the government not only sought to deny access to certain portions of the proceedings, it also successfully convinced the judge to seal most of the court records. The questions focused on whether Moussaoui, a French citizen, could have access to captured Al Qaeda witnesses who he contended would help him prove

62. *Shingara* v. *Skiles,* 420 F. 3d 301 (2005).
63. *Seattle Times Co.* v. *Rhinehart,* 104 S. Ct. 2199 (1984).
64. Liptak, "Secrecy at Issue."

his innocence. In August 2002 Judge Leonie Brinkema sealed many of the proceedings when the government contended that Moussaoui could use the material he placed in the record to secretly communicate with co-conspirators or sympathizers with coded messages. At the time, Moussaoui, who was ostensibly defending himself, was filing great numbers of highly inflammatory pleadings. Judge Brinkema modified her order a month later and said materials would be unsealed 10 days after they were filed, giving the government time to challenge the release of individual documents.[65] In April 2003 several news organizations went to court to try to gain access to these materials.[66] The following day the judge announced that she had serious doubts whether the government could actually prosecute Moussaoui in a civilian court "under the shroud of secrecy under which it seeks to proceed."[67] The case, then, might have to be moved to a military tribunal, in which secrecy would be more readily tolerated (see page 448). Moussaoui abruptly pleaded guilty in April 2005 to charges of conspiracy and the access issues became moot.

The qualified First Amendment right of access to judicial proceedings and documents has gone a long way to block attempts by courts to keep the public and the press out of the courtroom. Many trial judges, however, still see closure as a simple solution to the problem of publicity about a criminal case. And often the motion for closure is made totally unexpectedly. What should a reporter do when faced with such a problem? Here are some tips for journalists from "The First Amendment Handbook" prepared by the Reporters Committee for Freedom of the Press.

■ If you know your news organization will send an attorney to court to argue against closure, ask if you may speak with the judge for a moment.

■ Inform the judge that your news organization objects to the closure and would like an opportunity to argue against it. Ask for a brief recess so the attorney can come to court. If you know the name of the attorney, give his or her name to the judge. This information will bolster your credibility. Ask that your objection to the closure be made a part of the record.

■ If the judge won't let you speak and orders you to leave, leave. If you refuse, you could be arrested and cited for contempt of court.

■ When you leave the courtroom, write a short note to the judge explaining that your news organization wants to oppose the closure and that you will contact your editor or lawyer immediately. Give the note to a court officer and call your superiors.

TIPS FOR REPORTERS WHEN JUDICIAL HEARING IS CLOSED

■ Call the editor immediately to get a lawyer on the job.

■ Make a formal objection to closure.

■ Ask the judge to delay the closure until the lawyer arrives.

---

65. *United States* v. *Moussaoui,* 31 M.L.R. 1574 (2002).
66. Shenon, "News Groups Want Terror Case Files."
67. Shenon, "Judge Critical of Secrecy."

ACCESS AND THE BROADCAST JOURNALIST

Access to the judicial process for the broadcast journalist involves two issues that normally don't concern reporters in the print media.

■ Is it possible to obtain copies of evidence contained on audio- or videotape, and then air these tapes?

■ It is possible to broadcast or telecast the entire judicial proceeding?

Two Supreme Court rulings initially loomed as major stumbling blocks for broadcast journalists: a 1965 ruling (*Estes* v. *Texas*[68])that generally supported the ban on the telecast or broadcast of judicial proceedings, and a 1978 ruling (*Nixon* v. *Warner Communications*[69]) in which the high court refused to recognize the right of the journalists to make copies of audiotaped evidence for broadcast on the news. *Estes* will be discussed shortly. The second case involved tapes made by President Richard Nixon at the White House that were used as evidence in many of the Watergate trials of the 1970s. Broadcasters wanted to make copies of these tapes and play them for radio listeners and television viewers. The Supreme Court agreed that there is a generally recognized right of access to inspect evidentiary records in a case but said that this right was not an absolute right. "The decision as to access is one best left to the sound discretion of the trial court, a discretion to be exercised in light of the relevant facts and circumstances of the particular case," the court ruled. Courts have come a long way in granting press access to judicial evidence since 1978. But because the Nixon case focused specifically on the broadcast of taped evidence, those judges who wish to resist the broadcasters' efforts to use taped evidence in their newscasts have a fairly strong precedent on their side.[70] This section first focuses on gaining access to audio- or videotape evidence, then, the recording or televising of judicial proceedings.

Access to Evidence

Courts consider a variety of factors when considering a request to permit the broadcast of audio- or videotape evidence.

■ **Was the material introduced into evidence in open court, or have written transcripts of the material been provided?** If the answer is yes to either question it is more likely, but by no means certain, that the court will agree to the request. In one of the earliest cases involving such a request TV journalists sought to broadcast videotapes of an FBI sting operation that involved members of the U.S. House of Representatives and Senate. The tapes had been played to the jury in open court, and several of the defendants were convicted. The trial judge refused the request, saying that if the tapes were televised, it would be difficult to later empanel a jury should an appellate court order a retrial. The U.S. Court of Appeals reversed the decision, stating that the trial court must keep in mind the nation's strong tradition of access to judicial proceedings when

Access to the judicial process for the broadcast journalist involves two issues that normally don't concern reporters in the print media.

68. 381 U.S. 532 (1965).
69. 434 U.S. 591 (1978).
70. See, for example, *Group W Television Inc.* v. *Maryland,* 626 A. 2d 1032 (1993).

it balanced the competing interests. And in balancing these interests, "the court must give appropriate weight and consideration to the presumption—however gauged—in favor of public access to judicial records." The appellate court admitted a retrial might be a problem, but the tapes contained only admissible evidence that had been introduced in open court.[71] If the material has not or will not be introduced into evidence, chances of airing it are slim. In the highly publicized trial of John Hinckley, who was accused of trying to assassinate President Ronald Reagan, the television networks sought to televise the videotaped deposition of actress Jodie Foster, but the tape was never admitted into evidence. It was simply a statement from a witness; it just happened to be videotaped. The request was refused.[72] (Hinckley, who was found innocent by reason of insanity, was apparently infatuated with Foster and this fantasy played a part in his motivation to shoot the president.)

■ **Could broadcast of the material prejudice the fair trial rights of the defendant?** The Maryland Court of Special Appeals affirmed a lower-court ruling barring the broadcast of home videotape that was introduced as evidence in a murder trial. Pictured in the videotape were two men who were charged with the murder of the victim. The defendants were being tried separately and the trial judge barred the telecast of the videotape until the trial of the second defendant was concluded. The fair trial rights of the second defendant took precedence over any common law or First Amendment right to gain access to and then broadcast the evidence, the court said[73] Eight years later, however, the 2nd U.S. Court of Appeals ruled it was permissible for the broadcast media to air tapes presented as evidence by the government at a pretrial detention hearing. Defendants argued that the broadcast of the tapes could endanger their fair trial rights, but the appellate court said these concerns could be addressed by a thorough voir dire, or even a change of venue.[74]

■ **What people are on the audio- or videotape?** Tapes of defendants or police officers are more likely to be released than tapes of victims or witnesses. Jodie Foster was an innocent third party who was inadvertently pulled into the Hinckley case. A U.S. District Court in Minnesota rejected requests from broadcasters for permission to air videotapes of a hostage recorded by her kidnapper. The court said airing the tape would cause severe hardship for the woman, and would not serve a useful public purpose.[75]

■ **Will airing the tape result in serving a public purpose?** Will it help members of the community understand the workings of the court, or law enforcement operations or important aspects of a trial? A court is more likely to permit the airing of so-called electronic evidence if it accomplishes a useful public purpose, as opposed to simply titillating listeners and viewers.

71. *In re Application of NBC,* 653 F. 2d 609 (1981).
72. *In re Application of ABC,* 537 F. Supp. 1168 (1982).
73. *Group W Television Inc.* v. *Maryland,* 626 A. 2d 1032 (1993).
74. *United States* v. *Graham,* 257 F. 3d 143 (2001).
75. *In re Application of KSTP,* 504 F. Supp. 360 (1980).

RECORDING AND TELEVISING JUDICIAL PROCEEDINGS

In 1976, only about 35 years ago, cameras and other recording equipment were barred from courtrooms in all but two states, Texas and Colorado. Today, such equipment is permitted in at least some courtrooms in all 50 states.* Mississippi and South Dakota became the final two states to join in this massive reversal of the older rules. The rules vary from state to state and are often complex. Here is a brief overview of some of the kinds of variations that exist:

- In nearly all states cameras and/or recording equipment are permitted in both trial and appellate courts. In a handful of states recording is permitted only in appellate courts. But these state rules tend to be fluid and change from time to time. For example, both Indiana and Delaware were experimenting in 2009 with permitting cameras at some trial proceedings, in addition to appellate hearings. The best source for information regarding what is permitted in an individual state is the Web site maintained by the Radio-Television News Directors Association, http://www.rtnda.org.
- In some states the right to use this equipment in a courtroom is presumed. In other states broadcasters and photographers must first get the permission of the judge or justices or even the parties. But in either case, a judge can bar electronic equipment if there is sufficient reason.
- In some instances parties involved in the legal proceeding must agree before they can be photographed. But their refusal to be photographed cannot totally block cameras from recording the rest of the participants or the proceedings in general.
- Jurors cannot be photographed in some states.

This swift reversal of the rules regarding the use of cameras in the courtroom climaxed a 40-year struggle by the press for relaxation of prohibitions that were instituted in the 1930s. At that time the press had conducted itself in an outrageous fashion in covering the trial of Bruno Hauptmann, who in 1934 was charged with kidnapping the baby of Charles and Anne Lindbergh. The trial judge, who had great difficulty in controlling the press, ordered that no pictures be taken during the court sessions. But photographers equipped with large, bulky, flash-equipped cameras moved freely about the courtroom and took pictures whenever there was a recess, a delay or a pause in the trial. As a result of this episode, the American Bar Association adopted rules prohibiting the use of cameras and other electronic equipment in courtrooms. The rules, known as Canon 35, were adopted in most states and were followed in practice in those states that did not officially adopt the rules.[76]

At that time the press had conducted itself in an outrageous fashion in covering the trial of Bruno Hauptmann, who in 1934 was charged with kidnapping the baby of Charles and Anne Lindbergh.

Photographic technology changed dramatically in the 1940s and 1950s. The size of cameras shrunk and high-speed film made it possible to take pictures indoors without flash equipment. In addition, broadcast journalism took on new importance. News photographers and broadcasters began to put pressure on the American Bar Association and the courts to change the policies limiting photographic coverage of the judicial process. But a Supreme

*In some state and federal courtrooms judges are permitting bloggers and microbloggers, who are sitting in the courtroom (but not jurors) to stream constant updates about what is happening in the courtroom during the trial, so long as the tweets and other text messages are sent in a way that does not result in a distraction in the courtroom. See Weiss, "Judge Explains Why."
76. White, "Cameras in the Courtroom."

Court ruling in 1965 temporarily took the steam out of this movement. In an appeal from a highly sensational criminal trial in Texas that involved not murder, kidnapping or rape but a huge financial swindle involving fertilizer tanks, the high court ruled that photography and broadcasting equipment simply created too many impediments to a fair trial. The pretrial hearing of Billie Sol Estes had been televised, and still photographers were permitted throughout the trial. There was disruption at the pretrial hearing when 12 camera operators crowded into the tiny courtroom, where cables and wire snaked across the floor. Microphones were everywhere and most observers agreed that the press caused a significant distraction during the hearing. Things were better at the trial, but the damage had been done. The high court reversed the conviction because, it said, Estes had been denied a fair trial because of the presence of the cameras and recorders. "While maximum freedom must be allowed the press in carrying out this important function [informing the public] in a democratic society, its exercise must necessarily be subject to the maintenance of absolute fairness in the judicial process," Justice Tom Clark wrote for the court.[77]

Experimentation with cameras in the courtroom continued. Telecasting equipment improved. Journalists demonstrated to judges that they could act responsibly if they were permitted access to courtrooms with their cameras and recorders. More and more states began to permit telecasts and broadcasts of criminal and civil trials as well as of the oral arguments at appellate hearings. In the early 1980s two former Miami police officers challenged the new rules in Florida that permitted cameras in the courtroom. They argued that television coverage of their trial in and of itself had deprived them of a fair trial. The Florida Supreme Court rejected their contention, and the U.S. Supreme Court agreed to hear the case. In a unanimous decision the high court ruled that the mere presence of cameras in the courtroom or simply televising or broadcasting portions of a trial does not in and of itself cause prejudice to the defendant or interfere with the right to a fair trial.[78] Chief Justice Burger wrote that at present "no one has been able to present empirical data sufficient to establish that the mere presence of the broadcast media inherently has an adverse effect on that [trial] process." It is true the presence of such equipment in the courtroom or the broadcast of a trial could endanger the defendant's right to a fair trial. But, Burger said, "an absolute constitutional ban on broadcast coverage of trials cannot be justified simply because there is a danger that, in some cases, prejudicial broadcast accounts of pretrial and trial events may impair the ability of jurors to decide the issue of guilt or innocence uninfluenced by extraneous matter." The chief justice said that in order to block the use of cameras and recorders at a trial, a defendant must demonstrate to the court how the trial will be adversely affected by the presence of this equipment. To overturn a conviction at a trial that has been televised, the defendant will need to show that the recording and photography equipment actually made a substantial difference in some material aspect of the trial. Proof that the jurors were aware of the cameras or that the presence of television cameras "told" jurors this was a big trial will not be sufficient to demonstrate prejudice, Burger wrote.

State Courts. Since the 1981 high-court ruling, state courts have developed their own standards to assess complaints of prejudice from defendants who do not want their trials televised,

77. *Estes* v. *Texas,* 381 U.S. 532 (1965).
78. *Chandler* v. *Florida,* 449 U.S. 560 (1981).

or who allege after a conviction that their rights were violated. In Florida, for example, the state Supreme Court has ruled that the trial court must hold an evidentiary hearing if a defendant or other participant protests the television coverage. Before cameras and recorders may be excluded, there must be a finding that the electronic coverage of the trial would have an important "qualitatively different effect" on the trial than would other types of coverage.[79] In 2005 the Mississippi Supreme Court ruled that a trial court could not bar a television station from televising a sentencing hearing unless the court could justify closing the proceeding to all mass media.[80] And the Georgia Supreme Court ruled in the same year that a trial court must cite a specific factual basis to deny a newspaper's request to take still photographs at a murder trial. Speculation regarding potential harm was not sufficient.[81]

State rules on the admission of cameras to the courtroom vary. In some states cameras will not be permitted unless various key trial participants agree. In more states the cameras are allowed on the discretion of the judge. If a participant objects to the admission of cameras to the courtroom, the press must honor this objection and refrain from photographing or recording this individual. And judges can and do require cameras to be turned off during the presentation of certain kinds of evidence, such as gory crime scene photos. Most states have adopted guidelines that establish the number of still and motion picture cameras permitted in the courtroom at any one time. Rules often specify where the cameras may be placed, require that all pictures be taken with available light and even set standards of dress for photographers and technicians. The press must often be willing to share the fruits of the photography through pooling agreements, since most states have guidelines limiting movement and placement of cameras to when the court is in recess only.

Federal Courts. The U.S. Judicial Conference, a policy-making body for the federal courts, has largely rejected the notion that cameras should be permitted in federal courtrooms. In rare instances cameras are permitted in appellate courtrooms, but only if acceptable to the judges in a particular circuit (notably the 2nd and 9th Circuits at this time). Legislation has been introduced in Congress that would give federal judges the discretion to permit cameras in their courtrooms, but it has failed to pass each time. Some federal trial judges have tried to look past the policies and rules of the Judicial Conference, to local court rules that they say are different. For example, in January 2009 a U.S. District Court in Massachusetts announced it would permit the gavel-to-gavel webcasting of a hearing in a file-sharing copyright case. The judge said local court rules permitted such coverage, despite the rulings by the U.S. Judicial Conference. Three months later the 1st U.S. Court of Appeals reversed the order permitting the webcasting, saying the trial court had exceeded its discretion.[82,83]

Executions. Courts have barred the televising of executions in the United States, most recently in the summer of 2004 when the 8th U.S. Court of Appeals ruled that there was no

79. *Florida* v. *Palm Beach Newspapers,* 395 So. 2d 544 (1981).
80. *In re WBLT Inc.,* 905 So. 2d 1196 (2005).
81. *Morris Communications LLC* v. *Griffin,* 33 M.L.R. 2394 (2005).
82. *In re Zyprexa Product Liability Litigation,* 36 M.L.R. 1575 (2008); *E*Trade Financial Corp* v. *Deutsche Bank AG,* 36 M.L.R. 2494 (2008); and *Capitol Records, Inc.* v. *Alaujan,* No. 03 cv 11661-NG 1/14/09.
83. *In re Sony BMG Music Entertainment,* 564 F. 3d 1 (2009).

First Amendment right to videotape an execution. The decision upheld a Missouri corrections department policy barring all cameras and recording devices from execution chambers.[84] Similar decisions have been rendered for the past 15 years.[85]

Broadcasters have also failed in their attempts to get cameras and other recording equipment into the jury room. In November 2002 a trial judge in Houston said he would allow the PBS documentary series "Frontline" to film the jury deliberations in a death penalty case. The 17-year-old defendant and his mother agreed to the filming, as did the young man's attorney. "If the State of Texas wants to execute a 17-year-old, the whole world should be watching to make sure it is done right," attorney Ricardo Rodriquez said. But the state argued against the filming, claiming the process would turn the deliberations into a "Survivor"-style reality program. Scholars who study juries tended to agree, calling the comparison with the popular TV program correct. "Conscripting citizens for a reality television program strikes me as a bad idea," Shari Diamond, a law professor at Northwest University told New York Times reporter Adam Liptak.[86] "It involves jurors in signing on for a national public performance. The potential for that having a distorting effect on their work is palpable," she added.

Three months later the Texas Criminal Court of Appeals, the state's highest criminal appeals court, rejected the judge's plan. The court cited a state statute that said, "No person shall be permitted to be with a jury while it is deliberating." This prohibits the taping, the court said, adding that it believed that the filming would introduce "outside influence and pressure" on the jury.[87]

Some state courts have on occasion permitted the filming of jury deliberations in criminal cases. The taping of jury deliberations in civil cases for research or educational purposes has also taken place.[88] But as a general rule, cameras and audio recording equipment are barred from the jury room, and it is unlikely that this prohibition will change anytime soon.

SUMMARY

The right of access to pretrial proceedings and documents is qualified. The presumption that these hearings are open can be overcome only by a showing that there is an overriding interest that must be protected, that there is a "substantial probability" that an open hearing will damage this right, that the closure is narrowly tailored to deny access to no more of the hearing than is necessary to protect this interest, that the court has considered reasonable alternatives to closure, that closure of the hearing would in fact protect the interest that has been raised, and that the trial judge has articulated findings—which may be reviewed by an appellate court—that support these four points.

Broadcast journalists are given somewhat less access when they seek to obtain copies of audio- or videotaped evidence or seek to record or televise a judicial proceeding. Access

84. *Rice* v. *Kempker,* 374 F. 3d 675 (2004).
85. See *KQED, Inc.* v. *Vasquez,* 18 M.L.R. 2323 (1991). See also *Campbell* v. *Blodgett,* 982 F. 2d 1356 (1993); *California First Amendment Coalition* v. *Calderon,* 130 F. 3d 976 (1998); and *Entertainment Network Inc.* v. *Lappin,* 134 F. Supp. 2d 1002 (2001).
86. Liptak, "Inviting TV into Jury Room."
87. *State ex rel Rosenthal* v. *Poe,* Tex. Crim. App. No. 74, 515, 2/13/03.
88. Liptak, "Inviting TV into Jury Room."

to the taped evidence is developing through a case-by-case approach, and courts have granted journalists increasing rights to make copies of this material for later broadcast. Cameras and recording devices are now permitted in courts in all but two states and the District of Columbia. The Supreme Court has ruled that the mere presence of such devices does not in and of itself prejudice a defendant's right to a fair trial. The federal courts have generally refused to permit cameras in the courtroom. Cameras are barred from executions, and the filming of jury deliberations is generally prohibited.

BENCH-BAR-PRESS GUIDELINES

Both restrictive orders and the closure of court proceedings are admittedly effective ways of stopping publicity from reaching the hands of potential jurors, but they are equally dangerous in a representative democracy where information about how well government is operating is fundamental to the success of the political system. The bench, the bar and the press in many states have found that cooperation, restraint and mutual trust can be equally effective in protecting the rights of a defendant, while at the same time far less damaging to rights of the people.

Judges, lawyers and journalists have tried to reach a common understanding of the problems of pretrial news coverage and have offered suggestions as to how most of these problems might be resolved. These suggestions are usually offered in the form of guidelines or recommendations to the press and to participants in the criminal justice system. **Bench-bar-press guidelines** normally suggest to law enforcement officers that certain kinds of information about a criminal suspect and a crime can be released and published with little danger of harm to the trial process. The guidelines also suggest to journalists that the publication of certain kinds of information about a case (see the list of damaging kinds of statements on pages 414–416) can be harmful to the defendant's chances for a fair trial without providing the public with useful or important information. The guidelines are often presented in a very brief form; at other times they encompass several pages of text.

Bench-bar-press guidelines have existed in some states for more than 50 years. In some communities these guidelines work very well in managing the problems surrounding the free press–fair trial dilemma. A spirit of cooperation exists between press, courts, attorneys and law enforcement personnel. In such communities it is rare to find a restrictive order or a closed courtroom. But most communities and states have found it takes considerable effort to make the guidelines work. Drafting the guidelines is only the first step. If, after agreement is reached on the recommendations, the bench, the bar and the press go their separate ways, the guidelines usually fail as a means of resolving the free press–fair trial problems.

A good deal of space has been devoted to the free press–fair trial problem because it is an important issue and because it continues to be a problem. Within both the press and the law, sharp divisions regarding solution of the problem remain. Many years ago, during a battle over a free press–fair trial issue in one southern state, the national office of the American Civil Liberties Union filed an amicus curiae (friend of the court) brief supporting a free and unfettered press, while the state chapter of the same civil liberties group filed a brief in favor of the court's position supporting a fair trial.

Most communities and states have found it takes considerable effort to make the guidelines work.

465

Crime, especially violent crime, has become the focus of many segments of the American press. Television news is especially afflicted by this trend. But serious reporting on the criminal justice system remains in short supply, despite the importance to society of the tasks undertaken by the police, the prosecutors and the courts. Many years ago, in "Crime and Publicity," Alfred Friendly and Ronald Goldfarb wrote:

> To shackle the press is to curtail the public watch over the administration of criminal justice. . . . The press serves at the gatehouse of justice. Additionally, it serves in the manorhouse itself, and all along the complicated route to it from the police station and the streets, to the purlieus of the prosecutor's office, to the courtroom corridors where the pressures mount and the deals are made.[89]

The two authors also point out that we do not want a press that is more or less free, just as we should not tolerate trials that are almost fair. "And to complicate the issue," they note, "it is evident that a free press is one of society's principal guarantors of fair trials, while fair trials provide a major assurance of the press's freedom."

Reporters dealing with the courts and the court system must be extremely sensitive to these issues. They should not be blinded to the sensitive mechanisms that operate in the courts to provide justice and fairness as they clamor for news. At the same time they should not let the authoritarian aspects of the judicial system block their efforts to provide the information essential to the functioning of democracy.

SUMMARY

In some states the press, attorneys and judges have agreed to try to solve the problems surrounding the free press–fair trial controversy through voluntary bench-bar-press agreements. Such agreements usually contain suggestions to all parties as to what information should and should not be publicized about criminal cases. When the guidelines work, there is usually a cooperative, rather than a combative, spirit among the members of the press, the judiciary and the bar. These guidelines often reduce or eliminate the need for restrictive orders or closed hearings.

BIBLIOGRAPHY

Bechamps, Anne T. "Sealed Out-of-Court Settlements: When Does the Public Have a Right to Know?" *Notre Dame Law Review* 66 (1990): 117.

Broder, John M. "From Grand Jury Leaks Comes a Clash of Rights." *The New York Times,* 15 January 2005, A8.

Bush, Chilton R., ed. *Free Press and Fair Trial: Some Dimensions of the Problem.* Athens: University of Georgia Press, 1971.

Cys, Richard L., and Andrew M. Mar. "Media Access to the New Special Tribunals: Lessons Learned from History and the Military Courts." *First Amendment Law Letter,* Winter 2002, 1.

89. Friendly and Goldfarb, *Crime and Publicity.*

Friendly, Alfred, and Ronald Goldfarb. *Crime and Publicity.* New York: Random House, Vintage Books, 1968.

Glaberson, William. "A Conviction, But a System Still on Trial." *The New York Times*, 10 August 2008, 20.

Liptak, Adam. "Inviting TV into Jury Room in Capital Case." *The New York Times,* 11 November 2002, A1.

———. "Secrecy at Issue in Suits Opposing Domestic Spying." *The New York Times,* 26 January 2007, A1.

———. "Shrinking Newsrooms Wage Fewer Battles for Public Access to Courtrooms." *The New York Times*, 1 September 2009, A10.

Shenon, Philip. "Judge Critical of Secrecy in Terror Case Prosecution." *The New York Times,* 5 April 2003, B13.

———. "News Groups Want Terror Case Files." *The New York Times,* 4 April 2003, B13.

Weiss, Debra Cassens. "Judge Explains Why He Allowed Reporter to Live Blog Federal Criminal Trial." *ABA Journal Law News Now*, 16 January 2009.

White, Frank W. "Cameras in the Courtroom: A U.S. Survey." *Journalism Monographs* 60 (1979).

CHAPTER 13

Regulation of Obscene and Other Erotic Material

In June 2008 a jury in Tampa convicted Paul Little, a long-time Southern California adult movie producer known as Max Hardcore, on multiple counts of transporting obscene material via the Internet and U.S. mail. That October he was sentenced to 46 months in prison, and a judge denied his motion to remain free while the case was being appealed. One must understand that Little did not sell his sexually explicit DVDs to either a minor or an unsuspecting adult; rather, he was ensnared by federal officials who knowingly downloaded and ordered his material (and not from Little himself even, but from a third-party distributor to whom he had sold it). The federal government scored another victory in an obscenity case when the individual defendants, Robert Zicari and Janet Romano, pleaded guilty in March 2009 to a felony charge of conspiracy to distribute obscene material through the mails and over the Internet in a long-running case called *United States* v. *Extreme Associates*. In July 2009 Zicari and Romano were both sentenced to one year plus one day in federal prison. These were just two of several federal obscenity prosecutions in 2008 and 2009 against adult movie producers and their companies, such as veteran John Stagliano and his Evil Angel business. Although adult entertainment was conservatively estimated by the Adult Video News trade publication in 2008 to be a $12-billion-a-year industry in the United States with mainstream popularity (more than 12,000 adult DVD titles were produced in 2008, and veteran adult stars like Ron Jeremy and Jenna Jameson today are pop-cultural icons), sexually explicit content is loathed and reviled by many. It is criticized by both religious conservatives and anti-pornography feminists.

Sexual speech that meets a three-part test for obscenity falls outside First Amendment protection.

In addition, sexual speech that meets a three-part test for obscenity falls outside First Amendment protection. This chapter examines contemporary U.S. obscenity law, including the definition of obscenity, as well as government efforts to regulate sexually explicit content on the Web and the zoning of sexually oriented businesses. As becomes clear, sexual content is the battleground where fervent fights for freedom of expression are fought today.

THE LAW OF OBSCENITY

An "intractable problem"—that's how U.S. Supreme Court Justice John Harlan described regulation of sexually explicit speech in 1966.[1] Sadly, it remains equally problematic today, despite two important facts:

1. The nation's high court made it clear more than 50 years ago in *Roth* v. *United States*[2] that a narrow category of sexually explicit speech called "obscenity" is not protected by the First Amendment freedoms of speech and press.
2. The Supreme Court articulated in 1973 in *Miller* v. *California*[3] a test still used by all courts for determining when speech is obscene.

Problems exist today for many reasons. First, the *Miller* obscenity test (see pages 474–478) leaves much flexibility and wiggle room for interpretation in its actual application by judges and juries. The test also embraces the use of contemporary community standards

---

1. *A Book Named "John Cleland's Memoirs of a Woman of Pleasure"* v. *Massachusetts,* 383 U.S. 413, 455 (1966) (Harlan, J., dissenting).
2. 354 U.S. 476 (1957).
3. 413 U.S. 15 (1973).

that vary from state to state, leading to the anomalous result that any given adult DVD might be protected by the First Amendment in one state but not in another.

Second, technologies like the Web and cell phones, as well as cable and satellite television services such as video-on-demand and pay-per-view movies, have made adult content readily accessible. In brief, the genie is out of the bottle. That's good news for consenting adults who want to view it in the privacy of their homes where no one else in the community needs to see or be offended by it,[4] but it is unfortunate news for parents of minors, as young children may come across it (either intentionally or unexpectedly) with greater ease. Third, some people feel that speech considered obscene under *Miller* nonetheless deserves First Amendment protection. Not only is sexually explicit content an incredibly popular form of entertainment enjoyed by many adults, but evidence is inconsistent and conflicting about whether viewing it really causes harm.

Feminist legal scholars like Catharine MacKinnon claim pornography objectifies women and represents "the power of men over women, expressed through unequal sex, sanctioned both through and prior to state power."[5] Others feel equally as strongly, coming from a conservative, religious-based perspective, that pornography harms family values, erodes marriages and leads to addiction that destroys users' lives. Although the arguments of both anti-porn feminists and religious conservatives certainly deserve study, it must be emphasized that the term "pornography" is not the same thing as obscenity. In fact, while obscenity has a legal definition under the *Miller* test, the term "pornography" is without legal significance in the United States and instead is commonly used (and misused) as a catch-all term by laypeople to describe anything sexually explicit they find offensive or believe is harmful. Beyond this, many women in the adult industry today such as Stormy Daniels and Jenna Jameson are highly successful businesspeople working in one of the very few industries in which women typically make twice as much money as men. This is not to say that exploitation does not exist in the adult industry (as it does in almost any industry), but simply to recognize that Daniels, Jameson and their ilk contradict the notion that all sexual content necessarily harms women. In 2009 Daniels even launched an exploratory committee as she considered running in 2010 for the U.S. Senate seat held by Louisiana's David Vitter, who in 2007 was identified as a client of a prostitution service in Washington, D.C.

Fourth, there is the question of the inefficient use of scarce government monetary resources in prosecuting obscenity cases today when the content involves adults who freely consented to take part in the activities shown. Many people feel there are greater problems to worry about, such as child pornography—a distinct category of sexually explicit speech that, like obscenity, is not protected by the First Amendment (see pages 480–482)—and terrorism and global warming. Despite the absence of federal obscenity prosecutions under the administration of former President Bill Clinton (Clinton's Justice Department focused instead on child pornography and cyber stalkers), the Bush administration launched several high-profile

© *AP/Wide World Photos*

Stormy Daniels, a leading adult film star, had recent crossover appearances in the comedy "The 40-Year-Old Virgin" and the cable series "Dirt."

4. The argument that obscenity laws violate an adult's constitutional right to privacy—not simply the First Amendment protection of speech—to watch sexual content in the privacy of his or her home was made successfully in 2005 before a federal court in Pittsburgh, Pa., in *United States* v. *Extreme Associates, Inc.,* 352 F. Supp. 2d 578 (W.D. Pa. 2005). The decision, however, was reversed by an appellate court, and the Supreme Court refused to hear the case, thus sending it back to a trial court. *United States* v. *Extreme Associates, Inc.,* 431 F. 3d 150 (3d Cir. 2005), cert. den., 126 S. Ct. 2048 (2006).
5. MacKinnon, *Only Words,* 40.

> ## COMMON TERMS
>
> ***Obscenity***—A narrow class of material defined by the Supreme Court in the *Miller* test. Material that is obscene is not protected by the First Amendment. Obscene material is sometimes referred to as hard-core pornography.
>
> ***Indecent Material***—Material that may be sexually graphic; often referred to as adult material or sexually explicit material. This material is protected under the First Amendment. However, such material may be barred in works available to children (variable obscenity laws) and in over-the-air (as opposed to cable or satellite-generated) radio and television broadcasts. (See Chapter 16 for a full discussion of broadcast indecency.)
>
> ***Pornography***—This term has no legal significance but is often used by laypeople and politicians to describe anything from real obscenity to material such as a passionate love scene that is simply offensive to the viewer. The overuse (and misuse) of this imprecise term tends to add more confusion to an already muddled legal landscape.

obscenity prosecutions of adult content producers. Whether the Obama administration opts to vigorously target adult content remains to be seen.

Finally, there is the problem of dealing with sexually explicit content that may not quite rise to the level of obscenity under *Miller* (in other words, it may not be quite as "bad" as obscenity), but that nonetheless is sexual and is broadcast over the nation's television and radio airwaves. As Chapter 16 discusses, the Federal Communications Commission restricts such nonobscene sexual content if it satisfies the FCC's definition of indecency (another legal definition that, like obscenity under the *Miller* test, is extremely problematic in its real-world application).

EARLY OBSCENITY LAW

The first obscenity prosecution in the United States occurred in 1815, when Jesse Sharpless was fined for exhibiting a painting of a man "in an imprudent posture with a woman." There are on record earlier convictions for offenses tied to obscenity; these were prosecutions under common law for crimes against God, not for merely displaying erotic pictures. In 1821 Peter Holmes was convicted for publishing an erotically enhanced version of John Cleland's *Memoirs of a Woman of Pleasure.*

As the 19th century progressed, obscenity laws and prosecutions became more common, ebbing and flowing with major reform movements in the 1820s and 1830s and in the wake of the Civil War. The first federal obscenity statute, a customs law regulating the importation of obscene articles, was adopted in 1842. The most comprehensive federal statute adopted during the century became law in 1873. Known as the Comstock Act because of the intense pressure applied on Congress by Anthony Comstock, the law declared that all obscene books, pamphlets, pictures and other materials were nonmailable. No definition of obscenity was provided by Congress, however. The Comstock law, as amended, remains the federal law today.

Federal agencies such as the Bureau of Customs and the Post Office were the nation's most vigilant obscenity fighters during the late 19th and first half of the 20th centuries. These agencies banned, burned and confiscated huge amounts of erotic materials, including religious objects, pieces of art, books (including some of the best written during that era), magazines (including science and diving publications) and a wide array of material on birth control. When the motion picture industry began to grow in the early part of this century, local and state censors went after films that they believed to be obscene as well. The courts, especially the federal courts, became inundated with obscenity prosecutions and appeals. The U.S. Supreme Court seemed especially drawn to such litigation. Between 1957 and 1977, for example, the high court heard arguments in almost 90 obscenity cases and wrote opinions in nearly 40 of those cases. The remainder were decided by memoranda orders (see page 21 for a definition of this term).

DEFINING OBSCENITY

Outlawing obscenity is one thing; defining it is something else. When American courts, in the wake of the adoption of the Comstock Act in 1873, first began considering what is and what is not obscenity they borrowed a British definition called the *Hicklin* rule.[6] Under this rule a work is obscene if **it has a tendency to deprave and corrupt those whose minds are open to such immoral influences and into whose hands it might fall.** If something might influence the mind of a child, it was regarded as obscene for everyone, under this definition. In addition, if any part of the work, regardless of how small, met this definition, the entire work was regarded as obscene. This very broad and loose definition made it possible for both federal and state authorities to wage an aggressive and highly successful war against erotic materials in the first half of the 20th century.

In 1957 the Supreme Court abandoned the *Hicklin* rule, declaring that because of this rule American adults were permitted to read or watch only what was fit for children. "Surely this is to burn the house, to roast the pig," Justice Felix Frankfurter noted.[7] In abandoning the *Hicklin* rule, the high court was forced to fashion a new definition of obscenity, beginning with the case of *Roth* v. *U.S.*[8] in 1957. Over the next nine years, in a variety of obscenity rulings, what was called the *Roth-Memoirs* test was developed by the Supreme Court.[9] The test had three parts.

First, the dominant theme of the material taken as a whole must appeal to prurient interest in sex.

Second, a court must find that the material is patently offensive because it affronts contemporary community standards relating to the description or representation of sexual matters.

Third, before something can be found to be obscene, it must be utterly without redeeming social value.

While this entire test was far narrower than the *Hicklin* rule, it was the third part of the test that continually bedeviled government prosecutors. If a work had even the slightest social value, it could not be deemed to be obscene.

---

6. *Regina* v. *Hicklin,* L.R. 3 Q.B. 360 (1868).
7. *Butler* v. *Michigan,* 352 U.S. 380 (1957).
8. 354 U.S. 476 (1957).
9. See *Manual Enterprises, Inc.* v. *J. Edward Day,* 370 U.S. 478 (1962); *Jacobellis* v. *Ohio,* 378 U.S. 184 (1964); and *Memoirs of a Woman of Pleasure* v. *Massachusetts,* 383 U.S. 413 (1966).

SUMMARY   Prosecutions for obscenity did not occur in this nation until the early 19th century. In the 1820s and 1830s, many states adopted their first obscenity laws. The first federal law was passed in 1842. The government actively prosecuted obscenity in the wake of the Civil War, and in 1873 Congress adopted a strict new obscenity law. Obscenity was defined as being anything that had a tendency to deprave and corrupt those whose minds might be open to such immoral influences and into whose hands it might happen to fall. This rule, called the *Hicklin* rule, meant that if any part of a book or other work had the tendency to deprave or corrupt any person (such as a child or overly sensitive individual) who might happen to see the work, the material was obscene and no person could buy it or see it. This definition facilitated government censorship of a wide range of materials.

In the 1950s and early 1960s, the Supreme Court adopted a new three-part definition or test for obscenity, the *Roth-Memoirs* test.

CONTEMPORARY OBSCENITY LAW

President Lyndon Johnson appointed a commission in 1967 to study the regulation of obscenity. Two years later a majority of the members of this blue-ribbon panel issued a report recommending the repeal of all laws that restricted the use of erotic materials by consenting adults.[10] But this was 1969 and Johnson was no longer president. Richard Nixon sat in the White House and rejected the report. He vowed never to relax in the fight against obscenity, rejecting the commission's conclusion that the regular viewing or reading of obscenity produced no harmful effects in normal adults. By 1973, when the case of *Miller* v. *California* [11] was decided, a more conservative Supreme Court had its chance to redefine obscenity. This new test is the one courts must use today.

THE *MILLER* TEST

Marvin Miller was convicted of violating the California Penal Code for sending five unsolicited brochures to a restaurant in Newport Beach. The brochures, which advertised four erotic books and one film, contained pictures and drawings of men and women engaging in a variety of sexual activities. The recipient of the mailing complained to police, and Miller was prosecuted by state authorities.

In *Miller,* for the first time since 1957, a majority of the Supreme Court reached agreement on a definition of obscenity. Chief Justice Warren Burger and four other members of the high court agreed that material is obscene if the following standards are met:

In Miller, *for the first time since 1957, a majority of the Supreme Court reached agreement on a definition of obscenity.*

1. **An average person, applying contemporary local community standards, finds that the work, taken as a whole, appeals to prurient interest.**
2. **The work depicts in a patently offensive way sexual conduct specifically defined by applicable state law.**
3. **The work in question lacks serious literary, artistic, political or scientific value.**

10. *Report of the Commission on Obscenity and Pornography.*
11. 413 U.S. 15 (1973).

The implications and ambiguities in these three elements create the need for fuller explanation. As a result of the *Miller* ruling and subsequent obscenity decisions handed down by the court since 1973, some guidelines have emerged.

An Average Person

The first element of the *Miller* test asks if an average person, applying contemporary community standards, would find that the work, taken as a whole, appeals to prurient interest. It is the trier of fact who will make this determination. This can be the trial judge, but more commonly it is the jury. The Supreme Court expects the trier of fact to rely on knowledge of the standards of the residents of the community to decide whether the work appeals to a prurient interest. The juror is not supposed to use his or her own standards in this decision. The Supreme Court noted in 1974:

> This Court has emphasized on more than one occasion that a principal concern in requiring that a judgment be made on the basis of contemporary community standards is to assure that the material is judged neither on the basis of each juror's personal opinion nor by its effect on a particular sensitive or insensitive person or group.[12]

Note the last phrase in this quote. The court expects the standards of an average person to be applied in making this critical determination. In California a trial judge told jurors to consider the effect of the material on all the members of the community, including children and highly sensitive persons. The Supreme Court ruled that these jury instructions were faulty.[13] "Children are not to be included for these purposes as part of the 'community,'" wrote Chief Justice Burger. However, instructing the jury to consider the impact of the material on sensitive or insensitive persons is permissible, so long as these persons are looked on as part of the entire community. "The community includes all adults who comprise it, and a jury can consider them all in determining relevant community standards," Burger wrote.

Prurient interest has been defined by courts to mean a shameful or morbid interest in nudity, sex or excretion. Two things are key here. First, in determining if material appeals to a prurient interest, the work must be taken as a whole (a single scene from a DVD cannot be considered in isolation or standing alone; all of the contents of the DVD must be viewed in the aggregate). Second, the definition of prurient interest focuses only on nudity, sex and excretion; it has nothing to do with violence. Thus obscenity law deals only with sexually oriented content, not violent stories or violent images.

Prurient interest has been defined by courts to mean a shameful or morbid interest in nudity, sex or excretion.

Community Standards

The definition of community standards is a key to the first part of the *Miller* test. Chief Justice Burger made it clear in the *Miller* decision that local standards were to be applied. In most jurisdictions the term "local standards" has been translated to mean "state standards." All communities within the same state share the same standards. The question of applicable community standards becomes an important factor in cases that involve the shipment of erotic

---

12. *Hamling* v. *United States,* 418 U.S. 87 (1974).
13. *Pinkus* v. *U.S.,* 436 U.S. 293 (1978).

material over long distances within the United States and in cases involving the importation of sexually explicit material from outside the United States.

In prosecutions initiated by the U.S. Postal Service, the government is free to choose the venue in which to try the case. This might be the city from which the material was sent; it might be the city in which it was received; or it might be any city through which the material passed during its transit. For example, a trial involving a magazine sent from Boston to Dallas might be held in Boston, Dallas or anywhere in between. So Massachusetts standards might apply at the trial, or Texas standards, or even Pennsylvania or Kentucky standards if the publication passed through or over those states during its shipment. This government practice is called "venue shopping," or selecting a site where a conviction is most easily obtained. A postmaster in Oregon asked a postmaster in Wyoming to solicit (using a false name) erotic material distributed by an Oregon man. After the defendant sent material to Wyoming he was tried using Wyoming standards, not Oregon standards. The record shows that the defendant had never resided in, traveled through or had any previous business contact in Wyoming. The 10th U.S. Circuit Court of Appeals upheld the conviction, noting that under the existing law "federal enforcement officers . . . are free to shop for venue from which juries with the most restrictive views are likely to be impanelled."[14] When imported erotic material is seized, the standards of the state in which the material is seized are applied at trial.

When imported erotic material is seized, the standards of the state in which the material is seized are applied at trial.

Courts are permitting the government to select the venue for prosecution.

The growth of the Internet, which is a global communication system, has generated numerous difficulties in the application of the concept of local or even state standards. It is one thing to shut down a bookstore in Dallas or prosecute a distributor in Minneapolis. But a Web site operator in Seattle can reach users in all parts of the world in a matter of seconds. Whose community standards should apply? The standard where the sender lives, or any of the various standards where the receivers live?

What is taking place is that courts are permitting the government to select the venue for prosecution, as they have done in the past with material shipped by the Postal Service. For instance, the federal government in 2003 successfully gained both jurisdiction and an obscenity indictment in Pittsburgh, Pa., to prosecute a Southern California–based adult content producer, Extreme Associates, Inc., and its California proprietors, Rob Black and Lizzie Borden. How did the case wind up in Pennsylvania? A postal inspector in Pittsburgh accessed and registered as a member of Extreme Associates' Web site and then viewed movie clips on the site and ordered videos from it. The case was brought in Pittsburgh largely because its community standards are more conservative than those of Southern California, where the adult video industry is headquartered.

How does one prove what contemporary community standards are when it comes to sexually explicit content? It is not easy. First, it is for the jury (or the judge if there is no jury) to decide what the community standards are. Jurors must speculate about what other adults in their community would accept and tolerate. Most people, of course, don't talk with their neighbors about what, if any, adult DVDs they watch or which adult magazines they buy. Imagine, then, the difficulty in guessing what the standard is in a city with hundreds of thousands of people or a state with millions. Second, the government is not required to present any evidence about community standards. An obscenity defendant, however, may put on evidence of what the community standards allegedly are. One way to try to demonstrate this

14. *U.S.* v. *Blucher,* 581 F. 2d 244 (1978).

is a "comparables" argument. In particular, a defense attorney will demonstrate that sexually explicit material that is exactly comparable to that being targeted for prosecution is freely sold at stores in the community and, by extension, the community tolerates the material being prosecuted. Thus, if Barely Legal magazine is prosecuted in a community but comparable magazines that also focus on young women are freely sold, this would be relevant for determining the community's tolerance of the content in Barely Legal. Today, including in the 2008 prosecution of Paul Little noted at the start of the chapter, defense attorneys are using in-court, search-engine demonstrations to prove either that many people in the community regularly search online for sexually explicit content exactly like that being prosecuted or to show that there are places online (and thus within their virtual community) where they can purchase material similar to that being prosecuted. Such Internet searches using the likes of Google and Yahoo! may provide accurate measures of the type of content people are willing to view in privacy and at home.

One way to try to demonstrate this is a "comparables" argument.

Patent Offensiveness

The second element of the *Miller* test says that a work is obscene if it depicts in a patently offensive way sexual conduct specifically defined by applicable state law. Patent offensiveness is also to be judged by the trier of fact, using contemporary community standards. But the Supreme Court has put limits on this judgment, ruling that only what it calls hard-core sexual material meets the patently offensive standard. Georgia courts ruled that the motion picture "Carnal Knowledge," an R-rated film starring Jack Nicholson and Candice Bergen, was patently offensive. The Supreme Court reversed this ruling, saying that the Georgia courts misunderstood this second part of the *Miller* test.[15] Material that was patently offensive, Justice Rehnquist wrote, included "representations or descriptions of ultimate sexual acts, normal or perverted, actual or simulated" and "representations or descriptions of masturbation, excretory functions, and lewd exhibition of genitals." Rehnquist acknowledged that this catalog of descriptions was not exhaustive, but that only material like this qualifies as patently offensive material. The second part of the *Miller* test was "intended to fix substantive constitutional limitations . . . on the type of material . . . subject to a determination of obscenity," he added.

State laws are supposed to define the kinds of material or conduct that are prohibited as obscene. Many state obscenity statutes contain Rehnquist's descriptions as their definition of obscenity. Other state laws are less precise. The Supreme Court has even given its approval to state laws that contain no descriptive phrases so long as the state supreme court has construed (or interpreted) the law to prohibit only the narrowly defined kind of material outlined by Justice Rehnquist.[16]

State laws are supposed to define the kinds of material or conduct that are prohibited as obscene.

Serious Value

To be obscene a work must lack serious literary, artistic, political or scientific value. While not as broad as the "utterly without redeeming social value" element in the *Roth-Memoirs* test, this third criterion in the *Miller* test nevertheless acts as a brake on judges and juries eager to convict on the basis of the first two parts of the test. The judge is supposed to play a

15. *Jenkins* v. *Georgia*, 418 U.S. 153 (1974).
16. *Ward* v. *Illinois*, 431 U.S. 767 (1977).

pronounced role in deciding whether a work has serious value. The serious value element is not judged by the tastes or standards of the average person. The test is not whether an ordinary person in the community would find serious literary, artistic, political or scientific value, but whether a reasonable person *could* find such value in the material.[17] Jurors are supposed to determine whether a reasonable person would see a serious value in the work. Both the state and the defense will frequently introduce expert testimony to try to "educate" the jury on the relative merit of the material in question.

For instance, when the Cincinnati Contemporary Arts Center was prosecuted for obscenity in 1990 for a display of photographs by Robert Mapplethorpe (some photos featured homoerotic and sadomasochistic images), defense attorney Lou Sirkin used experts from the art world (museum directors/curators) to testify before the jury about the serious artistic value of the photos. The testimony was pivotal in gaining an acquittal for the museum.[18] Today, when adult DVDs and videos are prosecuted as obscene, defense attorneys often call sex therapists and experts from places like the Kinsey Institute for Research in Sex, Gender and Reproduction to describe how the content is used by normal couples to stimulate their own sex lives, learn about different sexual practices and open up discussion about their sexual habits. In other words, adult DVDs and videos can have educational value. Such was the case in 2000 when a jury of 12 women near St. Louis, Mo., found two adult videos featuring anal, oral and vaginal sex among women and between men and women were not obscene after hearing testimony from sex therapist Dr. Mark F. Schwartz of the Masters and Johnson clinic.[19]

THE *MILLER* TEST

1. An average person, applying contemporary local community standards, finds that the work, taken as a whole, appeals to prurient interest.
2. The work depicts in a patently offensive way sexual conduct specifically defined by applicable state law.
3. The work in question lacks serious literary, artistic, political or scientific value.

OTHER STANDARDS

The three-part test developed in *Miller* v. *California* is the legal test for obscenity in the United States today. But the Supreme Court, lower courts and other elements of the government have with varying degrees of success attempted to raise additional standards by which to judge erotic material. Here is a brief outline of some of these standards.

Variable Obscenity

The Supreme Court has ruled it is permissible for states to adopt what are known as **variable obscenity statutes.** Material that may be legally distributed and sold to adults

17. *Pope* v. *Illinois,* 481 U.S. 497 (1987).
18. Wilkerson, "Obscenity Jurors Were Pulled 2 Ways."
19. Munz, "Jury Finds Explicit Videos From Store Are Not Obscene."

may be banned for distribution or sale to juveniles, usually anyone under the age of 18. Variable obscenity means a state can have two standards for obscenity, one for adults and one for minors. This concept emerged from *Ginsberg* v. *New York* in 1968.[20] In *Ginsberg* the Supreme Court ruled that the First Amendment did not bar New York state from prosecuting the owner of a Long Island luncheonette who sold four so-called girlie magazines to a 16-year-old boy. The magazines, which contained female nudity, could have been legally sold to an adult. Justice Brennan said the state could maintain one definition of obscenity for adults and another for juveniles because the Supreme Court recognized the important state interest in protecting the welfare of children. But even variable obscenity statutes are not without constitutional limits. In 1975 the Supreme Court struck down such a law in *Erznoznik* v. *City of Jacksonville*[21] because the definition of material that could not be distributed to juveniles was not specific enough. A city ordinance barred drive-in theaters from showing films in which either female breasts or buttocks were exposed if the theater screen was visible from the street. The ordinance was justified as a means of protecting young people from exposure to such material. "Only in relatively narrow and well-defined circumstances may government bar dissemination of protected material to children," Justice Lewis Powell wrote. Banning the exhibition of nudity is simply not narrow enough; only materials that have significant erotic appeal to juveniles may be suppressed under such a statute, he added. A simple ban on all nudity, regardless of context, justification or other factors, violates the First Amendment.

Although states and cities may adopt variable obscenity laws, these regulations cannot in any way interfere with the flow of constitutionally protected material to adults. One permissible way of striking the balance between allowing adults to see sexual content but shielding minors from it is the use of so-called blinder racks (opaque covers) where magazines are sold. Blinder racks cover up all but the very top part of magazines, thus allowing adults to view the magazines' titles but covering up the sexual images below them that minors should not see. Ordinances that require the use of blinder racks to cover up the lower two-thirds of magazines are perfectly legal. Another permissible way of striking the balance is to require a store that rents or sells adult DVDs to segregate those DVDs into a separate section of the store that only adults can enter.

Ordinances that require the use of blinder racks are perfectly legal.

The tricky issue is how to define the material that minors cannot purchase. The material is not obscene under *Miller* (adults thus can purchase it), but any definition cannot be drafted so broadly as to prohibit the sale of all images of nudity to minors (that would sweep up biology textbooks). Many states use the phrase "harmful to minors" to describe sexual material that is permissible for adults to purchase but that minors may not buy. These definitions often are tweaked or modified versions of the *Miller* test. For instance, Florida uses the term "harmful to minors" and defines it as any image "depicting nudity, sexual conduct, or sexual excitement when it: (a) predominantly appeals to a prurient, shameful, or morbid interest; (b) is patently offensive to prevailing standards in the adult community as a whole with respect to what is suitable material or conduct for minors; and (c) taken as a whole, is without serious literary, artistic, political, or scientific value for minors."[22]

20. 390 U.S. 51 (1968).
21. 422 U.S. 205 (1975).
22. Florida Statute § 847.001 (2008).

Child Pornography

The production, distribution and possession of child pornography is not protected by the First Amendment.

The production, distribution and possession of child pornography is not protected by the First Amendment. Federal statutes outlaw images of minors—people under age 18—engaged in "sexually explicit conduct," including sexual intercourse, bestiality and masturbation, as well as images depicting a "lascivious exhibition of the genitals or pubic area."[23] Laws against child pornography are justified by both the physical and emotional harm minors incur during its creation, as well as by the fact that the images are a permanent record of participation and exploitation that could haunt the children when they grow up if discovered by others.

It is important to note that the kind of material outlawed does not have to meet the test of obscenity outlined in the *Miller* ruling. In other words, images of minors engaged in sexually explicit conduct do not need to rise to the level of obscenity under *Miller* in order for them to constitute child pornography—an illegal product—and fall outside the scope of First Amendment protection. An Ohio statute banned the possession of any depiction of a minor in a state of nudity who is not the person's child or ward. This statute would have, for example, barred grandparents from possessing nude baby pictures of their grandchildren. The Ohio Supreme Court narrowed the meaning of the language of the statute, ruling it could bar only "depictions of nudity involving a lewd exhibition or graphic focus on a minor's genitals." The U.S. Supreme Court gave its approval to such an interpretation.[24]

In 1996 Congress adopted an amendment to the original federal child pornography law that barred the sale and distribution of any images that "appear" to depict minors performing sexually explicit acts. Under this statute child pornography is defined to include not only actual images (photos, videotapes, films) of children but also computer-generated images and other pictures that are generated by electronic, mechanical or other means in which "such visual depiction is, or appears to be, a minor engaging in sexually explicit conduct." Whereas the original child pornography laws were justified as a means to protect children from being exploited, the 1996 Child Pornography Prevention Act (CPPA) was justified as a means to protect children from pedophiles and child molesters, people whose criminal behavior may be stimulated by such images. The law specifically stated that no prosecution can be maintained if the material was produced by adults and was not advertised, promoted, described or presented in such a way as to suggest children were in fact depicted in the images. In 2002 the Supreme Court ruled that important segments of the law violated the First Amendment. Justice Anthony Kennedy wrote that the CPPA "prohibits speech that records no crime and creates no victims by its production." Instead, he said, "the statute prohibits the visual depiction of an idea—that of teenagers engaging in sexual activity—that is a fact of modern society and has been a theme in art and literature throughout the ages." The court also ruled that the justification for the law was insufficient since Congress failed to produce any evidence of more than a remote connection between speech that might encourage thoughts or impulses and any resulting child abuse. "The mere tendency of speech to encourage unlawful acts is not a sufficient reason for banning it," Kennedy added.[25]

---

23. 18 U.S.C. § 2256 (2007).
24. *Osborne* v. *Ohio*, 495 U.S. 103 (1990).
25. *Ashcroft* v. *Free Speech Coalition*, 535 U.S. 234 (2002).

After the Supreme Court struck down the CPPA, Congress passed the PRO-TECT Act (short for Prosecutorial Remedies and Other Tools to End the Exploitation of Children Today Act of 2003) which was, in part, aimed at curbing the promotion (or "pandering") of child pornography. By its terms, the PROTECT Act prohibits a person from knowingly advertising, promoting or soliciting material "in a manner that reflects the belief, or that is intended to cause another to believe" that the advertised material is child pornography involving real minors, even if the underlying material does not, in fact, include real minors or is otherwise completely innocuous. In 2008 the U.S. Supreme Court in *United States* v. *Williams* upheld the PROTECT Act, concluding that it was neither overbroad nor vague (see pages 10–11 discussing the vagueness and overbreadth doctrines) and finding that a crime is committed under the act "only when the speaker believes or intends the listener to believe that the subject of the proposed transaction depicts *real* [author's emphasis] children."[26] Writing the majority opinion, Justice Antonin Scalia made it clear the high court was not overruling its 2002 decision in *Ashcroft* v. *Free Speech Coalition* involving the CPPA. "Simulated child pornography will be as available as ever, so long as it is offered and sought as such, and not as real child pornography," Scalia wrote. Although one can be convicted under the PROTECT Act even if the advertised material is not real child pornography, Scalia interpreted the act as requiring, for conviction, "that the defendant hold, and make a statement that reflects, the belief that the material is child pornography; or that he communicate in a manner intended to cause another so to believe." In what situations, then, does the PRO-TECT Act apply? Scalia observed that "an Internet user who solicits child pornography from an undercover agent violates the statute, even if the officer possesses no child pornography. Likewise, a person who advertises virtual child pornography as depicting actual children also falls within the reach of the statute."

In an interesting twist on the U.S. Supreme Court's 2002 ruling involving the CPPA and "virtual" child pornography, the Ohio Supreme Court in 2007 in *Ohio* v. *Tooley* upheld a state statute prohibiting blended or "morphed" images that digitally combine and graft separate photos of actual adults and real children in order to create the appearance of sexual acts.[27] In brief, under the Ohio statute, prosecutors in that state must still prove beyond a reasonable doubt (the standard of proof in a criminal case) that a real child is pictured in the morphed photograph in order to gain a conviction while, consistent with the U.S. Supreme Court's ruling in the *Free Speech Coalition* case involving the CPPA described earlier, images that involve only computer-generated and completely fictitious images of children remain protected under the First Amendment. The Ohio Supreme Court thus drew a critical distinction between

- *virtual child pornography* (images that are either entirely computer-generated or that are created using only adults) protected by the First Amendment; and
- *morphed child pornography* (images that are created by altering a real child's image to make it appear that the child is engaged in some type of sexual activity) not protected by the First Amendment.

---

26. 128 S.Ct. 1830 (2008).
27. 872 N.E. 2d 894 (Ohio 2007), cert. den., 128 S. Ct. 912 (2008).

In 2008 the U.S. Supreme Court chose not to disturb the Ohio Supreme Court's ruling in *Tooley* when it denied the defendant's petition for a writ of certiorari in the case.

Children as Child Pornographers and Sexting

What happens when a child is a child pornographer?

A new issue regarding child pornography involves minors who create their own sexual content and then post the images on online social networks or trade them via cell phones, the latter process known as "sexting." In other words, what happens when a child is a child pornographer? In 2009 six students at Greensburg Salem High School in Pennsylvania faced child pornography charges based on nude and seminude photos that some girls at the school took of themselves and then sent to their male schoolmates' cell phones. The girls, who were 14 and 15 years old, were charged with manufacturing and disseminating child pornography, while the boys who received them were charged with possession. Similarly, a 14-year-old girl from New Jersey was arrested and faced child pornography charges in 2009 after she posted about 30 nude and explicit photographs of herself on MySpace. In 2008 a 17-year-old boy from LaCrosse, Wis., faced felony child pornography charges after he posted on his MySpace page nude photos of a 16-year-old female. Ironically, the alleged victim in the case testified that she took the photos and sent them by e-mail to the defendant. Although nudity by itself generally does not amount to child pornography (there must either be a depiction of sexually explicit conduct or a lascivious exhibition of the genitals or pubic area to constitute child pornography), minors who take, possess or distribute sexually explicit photos of other minors (and themselves) are not exempt from child pornography statutes.

Obscenity and Women

Some feminist scholars assert that sexually explicit content subordinates women to men.

Some feminist scholars assert that sexually explicit content subordinates women to men; objectifies and exploits women as sex objects for men's pleasure; and leads to violence.[28] In 1984 Indianapolis adopted a statute, based on such arguments, banning "pornography"—not obscenity. It defined pornography as "the graphic sexually explicit subordination of women, whether in pictures or in words" that also includes such things as women being presented "as sexual objects who enjoy pain or humiliation" or "as sexual objects for domination, conquest, violation, exploitation, possession, or use, or through postures or positions of servility or submission or display." In 1985 an appellate court declared the law unconstitutional in *American Booksellers Association, Inc.* v. *Hudnut*,[29] noting it went far beyond regulating obscenity under the *Miller* test. The court found the statute constituted viewpoint-based discrimination (see page 94) on speech. It wrote that, under the statute, "speech that 'subordinates' women and also, for example . . . presents women in 'positions of servility or submission or display' is forbidden, no matter how great the literary or political value of the work taken as a whole. [Conversely,] speech that portrays women in positions of equality is lawful, no matter how graphic the sexual content. This is thought control. It establishes an 'approved' view of women." The decision ended adoption of similar laws in the United States.

28. See MacKinnon, *Only Words;* and Stark and Whisnant, *Not for Sale.*
29. 771 F. 2d 323 (7th Cir. 1985).

The *Miller* test is used today by American courts to determine whether something is obscene. It has three parts. Material is obscene under the following conditions:

SUMMARY

1. An average person, applying contemporary local community standards, finds that the work, taken as a whole, appeals to prurient interest. This requires the fact finder to apply local (usually state) standards rather than a national standard.
2. The work depicts in a patently offensive way sexual conduct specifically defined by applicable state law. Again, the fact finder in the case determines patent offensiveness, based on local community standards. But the Supreme Court has ruled that only so-called hard-core pornography can be found to be patently offensive. Also, either the legislature or the state Supreme Court must specifically define the kind of offensive material that may be declared to be obscene.
3. The material lacks serious literary, artistic, political or scientific value.

The Supreme Court has ruled that states may use a broader definition of obscenity when they attempt to block the sale or distribution of erotic material to children or when they attempt to stop the exploitation of children who are forced to engage in sexual conduct by filmmakers. But such laws must be careful so as not to unconstitutionally ban legal material as well. Laws aimed at stopping the use of children in preparing sexually explicit material have also been permitted by the high court.

CONTROLLING OBSCENITY

For more than a century, the typical manner in which the state has attempted to control obscenity has been through a criminal prosecution. Such lawsuits are complicated, and to be successful in these cases, prosecutors must follow carefully prescribed paths in deciding whether material is obscene, in collecting and seizing evidence and in making arrests. Often people charged with exhibiting or selling obscene materials seek to plea-bargain with the state to reduce the charge. Booksellers, theater owners and other merchants who deal in sexually explicit materials often do not want to fight the government in an obscenity prosecution. They are not in the business to crusade for the First Amendment. Their goal is to stay out of jail and to return to selling books or showing movies. If the state can be convinced to reduce the obscenity charge in exchange for a guilty plea, the defendant can often get by with paying a fine instead of going to jail and be back in business within a few days of the arrest. Prosecutors seem amenable to such plea bargaining because, as one noted, "our business is to stop public distribution of certain obscene materials, not put people in jail."

If a case goes to trial, the judge and the jury must determine whether the material sold or exhibited is obscene. The fact finder in the trial—the jury, or the judge if there is not a jury—determines Parts 1 and 2 of the *Miller* test, prurient appeal and patent offensiveness. A jury can also rule on the serious value of a work, but since this determination is normally regarded as a matter of law, a judge plays a far greater role in this determination.

In addition to determining whether the material is obscene, jurors are also called on to answer the question of whether the defendant was knowledgeable about the contents of what was being sold, distributed or published. This is called *scienter,* or guilty knowledge. In a 1959 case, *Smith* v. *California,*[30] the U.S. Supreme Court ruled that before a person can be convicted for selling obscene books or magazines or whatever, the state has to prove that the seller was aware of the contents of this material. "If the bookseller is criminally liable without knowledge of the contents … he will tend to restrict the books he sells to those he has inspected; and thus the state will have imposed a restriction upon the distribution of constitutionally protected as well as obscene literature," Justice Brennan wrote.

But what exactly must the state prove under the scienter requirement? Does the government have to produce evidence that the seller of the erotic material knew that it was obscene, but sold it anyway? No. The high court has ruled that it is sufficient that the government prove that the defendant had a general knowledge of the contents of the material, that a movie contains sadistic scenes, for example.[31] In the mid-1990s the prosecutor of Whatcom County, Wash., brought obscenity charges against two persons who operated a newsstand in the city of Bellingham for selling a publication called Answer Me! a magazine devoted to the discussion of rape. The newsstand operators insisted that the contents of the magazine, though sexually graphic, were nevertheless a satire. The prosecutor disagreed. But in the end that issue proved to be irrelevant. The jury acquitted the couple because, jurors said, the state had failed to prove that the newsstand operators were aware of the contents of the publication. There was insufficient evidence of scienter, or guilty knowledge.[32]

The criminal prosecution of obscenity in any community depends on whether the local prosecutor wants to be aggressive in this area of the law. Some prosecutors are militant foes of erotic material and continually prosecute purveyors of adult material. A great many more, however, find obscenity prosecutions far less important than the murder, rape, assault, robbery and burglary cases that deluge their offices. At the same time, the citizens of some communities are far more tolerant of adult material than their counterparts in other regions.

In addition to simple criminal statutes banning the production, sale and distribution of obscene material, the government uses other means to stop the flow of such material. Some communities have tried to use what are called civil nuisance laws in this effort. These are laws that define the sale or distribution of obscenity as a public nuisance. Obscenity is defined by the three-part *Miller* test. Prosecutors can bring a nuisance suit against an adult bookstore or an adult theater, much as they can bring a nuisance action against a factory that is generating too much noise or a home owner who is running a commercial auto repair operation out of his garage. A judge will first rule on whether the material that is being sold or distributed is in fact obscene. If the court finds that it is, an injunction will be issued ordering the defendant to stop such sale or distribution—to abate the nuisance.

Statutes originally aimed at fighting organized crime are also used to curb the manufacture and flow of obscenity.

Statutes originally aimed at fighting organized crime are also used to curb the manufacture and flow of obscenity. These statutes are called RICO laws, in reference to the 1970 federal Racketeering Influence and Corrupt Organizations Act. The purpose of this statute was to eradicate organized crime in the United States by establishing new penal provisions and enhanced remedies to deal with the unlawful activities of organized crime. About 30 states have joined the federal government in adopting RICO laws. These statutes provide

30. 361 U.S. 147 (1959).
31. *Hamling* v. *United States,* 418 U.S. 87 (1974).
32. Sheehan and Buller, "Jury Acquits."

significantly stiffer penalties—up to 20 years in jail and a large fine—for violating the provisions of the law, and they also permit the government to seek forfeiture of any profits and proceeds derived from the illegal activity.[33] To win convictions under the RICO laws the government must show that there has been a pattern of illegal activities, which is generally defined as two or more illegal acts. The Supreme Court has permitted the government to use these laws in prosecuting those who generate and distribute pornography. Constitutional challenges have been raised to the seizure of assets of booksellers and distributors, confiscations that involve not only obscene material but nonobscene books and magazines and films as well. But the Supreme Court rejected the argument that such seizures constitute prior restraints or unconstitutional censorship, and called the forfeitures criminal punishments.[34]

POSTAL CENSORSHIP

No government agency is more diligent in policing obscenity in the United States than the U.S. Postal Service. It was, for instance, a postal inspector who purchased five DVDs and had them delivered to a post office box in Tampa that resulted in the 2008 obscenity conviction of California-based Paul Little described at the start of the chapter. The post office has been on the job for more than a century. In 1878 the U.S. Supreme Court ruled that the use of mail in the United States is a privilege, not a right.[35] This ruling has given the Postal Service substantial power to control the content of the mail. Although the government cannot legally tamper with first-class mail, it is still illegal to send obscenity through the mail regardless of how it is delivered. Magazine sellers, book distributors and others who use other postal classifications (second class, fourth class) to ship their goods face even more serious problems. Postal inspectors also police the Internet.

The 1873 Comstock Act (see page 472) provides the basic authority for the U.S. Postal Service to regulate the flow of erotic material in the mail. But many other laws are also applicable. For example, postal patrons who have received unwanted solicitations for what they define as obscene material can request the Postal Service to inform the mailer that they no longer wish to receive such material. Once this notice is sent by the Postal Service to the mailer, any subsequent mailing to that particular patron is a violation of the law. Because the mail patron decides whether the material is obscene, this law can affect a broad range of solicitations. The Supreme Court upheld the constitutionality of this law, Section 3008 of Title 39 of the U.S. Code, in a 1970 ruling.[36] Chief Justice Burger wrote: "It seems to us that a mailer's right to communicate must stop at the mailbox of an unreceptive addressee."

Section 3010 of Title 39 of the U.S. Code permits a mail patron to block the delivery of sexually oriented advertising, even if he or she has never received such a mailing.

FILM CENSORSHIP

Censorship of motion pictures by cities and states is an infrequent occurrence today. This is due largely to two facts: (1) so-called adult theaters have become virtually extinct in the Internet age, and (2) most commercial theaters don't show movies rated NC-17. As recently as the

Censorship of motion pictures by cities and states is an infrequent occurrence today.

33. Bunker, Gates and Splichal, "RICO and Obscenity Prosecutions," 692.
34. *Alexander* v. *U.S.,* 509 U.S. 544 (1993).
35. *Ex parte Jackson,* 96 U.S. 727 (1878).
36. *Rowan* v. *Post Office,* 397 U.S. 728 (1970).

mid-1960s, however, there were active censorship boards in nearly 50 American cities. The application of a voluntary film rating system by the Motion Picture Association of America (G, PG, PG-13, R and NC-17) has satisfied the concerns of most people worried about the content of the movies.

Motion pictures were not granted First Amendment protection until 1952.[37] During the 1960s and 1970s courts scrutinized several local film censorship ordinances and established rigid guidelines to force local communities to conform to First Amendment principles.[38] Generally, censorship boards and the courts must make prompt rulings on whether a film may be exhibited, and the government bears the burden of proving that a film is not protected by the First Amendment.

Adult video stores still face attacks in some towns.

Video dealers are not bound by the MPAA rating code, and often stock films that would only be exhibited in so-called X-rated movie houses. The constitutional rules that limit censoring movies in theaters apply in no small measure to video sales and rentals as well. Adult video stores still face attacks in some towns. For instance, a jury of four men and three women in Staunton, Va., convicted Rick Krial, owner of an adult store called After Hours Video, of a misdemeanor in 2008 for selling a DVD the jury deemed obscene. The obscene DVD, "City Girls Extreme Gangbang," featured multiple-partner sex acts (a second video was determined by the jury not to be obscene). The state-court case arose after undercover police officers purchased several DVDs shortly after the store opened in October 2007. Staunton is not an isolated incident. In December 2008 Loren Jay Adams of Indianapolis was sentenced to 33 months in federal prison after being convicted earlier that year by a jury of six obscenity counts after he and his company, Hard2Find Videos, shipped and distributed obscene films from Indiana to West Virginia through the U.S. mail. In November 2008 in Widener, Ark., the owners of two Adult World stores were charged with promoting and selling obscene materials.

SUMMARY Postal censorship has historically been an important means used by the U.S. government to control the flow of obscene material in the United States, including material on the Internet. Today the Postal Service is less aggressive and permits postal patrons themselves to block the delivery of solicitations for adult materials and other obscene publications. Communities may also censor films before they are shown, or limit video and DVD rentals, so long as the community follows strict procedures laid down by the U.S. Supreme Court.

REGULATION OF NONOBSCENE EROTIC MATERIAL

Battles over obscenity have gone on for more than a century. But as the Supreme Court narrowed its definition of legal obscenity during the past 50 years, more and more pressure has been applied by advocacy groups and even some government agencies to stop the flow of nonobscene, adult material that would probably have been considered legally obscene half

37. *Burstyn* v. *Wilson,* 343 U.S. 495 (1952).
38. See, for example, *Freedman* v. *Maryland,* 380 U.S. 51 (1965); *Interstate Circuit* v. *Dallas,* 390 U.S. 676 (1968); and *Star* v. *Preller,* 419 U.S. 956 (1974).

a century ago, but is protected by the First Amendment today. In fact, in many respects, this has become the primary battleground in the fight over the distribution and exhibition of adult, sexually explicit material. Magazines like Penthouse and Playboy, rap music, homoerotic art exhibits, adult videos and sexually oriented sites on the Internet are among a wide variety of mass media targeted for control and even censorship in various parts of the nation. Although this material is certainly offensive to some people, it generally enjoys the full protection of the First Amendment because it does not qualify as obscenity under the *Miller* test. Here is an outline of some of these legal skirmishes.

SEXUALLY ORIENTED BUSINESSES

Sexually oriented businesses (SOBs)—strip clubs, adult video stores and adult theaters—are subject to two types of local laws:

1 *Zoning regulations*
2. *Expressive conduct regulations*

To the extent speech products (DVDs, videos and magazines) sold in these establishments are not obscene under the *Miller* test,[39] and to the extent that the U.S. Supreme Court has held that nude dancing "is expressive conduct that is entitled to some quantum of protection under the First Amendment,"[40] the zoning of SOBs and the regulation of activities inside them raise constitutional issues of free expression. In fact, federal and state courts hear at least a dozen challenges each year to these laws.

When cities zone SOBs, they use one of two approaches—clustering the businesses into a single area (called a red-light district or combat zone), or dispersing them across the community, usually to remote industrial areas away from schools and most residential areas. These zoning tactics are OK if certain criteria are met. For instance, the Supreme Court in *Renton* v. *Playtime Theatres, Inc.* upheld a municipal ordinance in Washington state prohibiting adult theaters from locating within 1,000 feet of any residential zone, family dwelling, church, park or school.[41] The high court allows such zoning laws and subjects them to a relatively relaxed form of judicial scrutiny if they are designed to decrease and reduce so-called *secondary effects* of SOBs. Secondary effects of SOBs are problems that may go on outside an SOB such as increased crime rates, decreased property values and decreased quality of life. If a municipality proves that it is targeting such negative secondary effects ostensibly caused

When cities zone SOBs, they use one of two approaches.

39. Although hard to believe, a few states today consider sex toys like vibrators to be "obscene" sexual devices and thus outlaw their sale and distribution. For example, the 11th U.S. Circuit Court of Appeals in 2007 upheld an Alabama statute that prohibits the commercial distribution of devices "primarily for the stimulation of human genital organs." *Williams* v. *Morgan,* 478 F. 3d 1316 (11th Cir. 2007), cert. den., 128 S. Ct. 77 (2007). The 11th Circuit found that protecting "public morality" was a sufficient reason to justify and uphold the Alabama law. In 2008, however, the 5th U.S. Circuit Court of Appeals struck down a similar Texas statute that made it a crime to promote, sell, give or lend a sexual device unless done so "for a bona fide medical" purpose. *Reliable Consultants* v. *Earle,* 517 F. 3d 738 (5th Cir. 2008). The 5th Circuit, citing the U.S. Supreme Court's 2003 ruling in *Lawrence* v. *Texas* (see page 5), rejected Texas' public morality justification and found, instead, that the statute "impermissibly burdens the individual's substantive due process right to engage in private intimate conduct of his or her choosing."
40. *City of Erie* v. *Pap's A.M.,* 529 U.S. 277 (2000).
41. 475 U.S. 41 (1986).

by SOBs and, conversely, is not targeting the actual speech inside the SOB, then the ordinance is considered content neutral and the municipality simply must prove that the zoning law

1. serves a substantial government interest, and
2. does not completely ban all SOBs in the municipality and unreasonably limit alternative avenues of communications.

Notice how this approximates the intermediate scrutiny standard of review for content-neutral time, place and manner regulations (see pages 110–113). In applying this test, courts generally give vast deference to municipalities. While municipalities are required to rely on some pre-enactment evidence of negative secondary effects that "must fairly support the municipality's rationale for its ordinance,"[42] this often is not a burdensome task. For instance, they are not required to conduct their own studies about negative secondary effects in their communities and they are not required to submit empirical data of alleged harms caused by SOBs. As one federal district court put it in 2008, "the burden is not heavy" and municipalities may rely on any evidence "reasonably believed to be relevant," but there must be something "more than unwritten 'common sense' rationales to trigger the secondary effects exception" and the municipality must, either in the zoning bill itself or in its legislative history, make "more than passing reference as to the secondary effects of adult establishments to establish that those effects are the predominant concern of the municipality."[43] Another federal court wrote in 2008 that "a municipality's legislative record need not be based on empirical data or constitute a scientific study" and "it may rely on anecdotal evidence in determining any potential secondary effects."[44] The bottom line is that a municipality's burden is lax and it doesn't have to conduct its own original studies (it can rely on studies from similar municipalities), as long as it actually relies on some evidence that it reasonably believes is relevant and that fairly supports its regulations.

Although owners of SOBs may counter such evidence and have done so successfully in some recent cases as courts grow more skeptical of alleged secondary effects,[45] this is a time-consuming and expensive task in terms of hiring expert witnesses and commissioning their own studies, and the evidence SOBs produce must cast direct doubt on that offered by the municipality.

When it comes to proving a substantial interest, courts usually find with no hesitation that municipalities have a substantial interest in curbing the secondary effects associated with adult entertainment establishments. In 2006, however, a federal court issued a restraining order against a Duluth, Minn., ordinance that limited the hours of operation of SOBs. The court noted

---

42. *City of Los Angeles* v. *Alameda Books, Inc.,* 535 U.S. 425, 438 (2002).

43. *Chicago Joe's Tea Room, LLC* v. *Village of Broadview,* 2008 U.S. Dist. LEXIS 84762 (N.D. Ill. Sept. 11, 2008).

44. *Regensberger* v. *City of Waterbury,* 2008 U.S. Dist. LEXIS 65142 (D. Conn. Aug. 25, 2008).

45. See *Daytona Grand, Inc.* v. *City of Daytona Beach,* 2006 U.S. Dist. LEXIS 41164 (M.D. Fla. 2006), which struck down an ordinance prohibiting nude dancing in clubs that sell alcohol after the clubs introduced expert testimony and evidence refuting the municipality's claim of a link between secondary effects and the combination of drinking alcohol and viewing nude entertainment. Even this victory for an SOB was short-lived, however, as a federal appellate court in June 2007 reversed the district court's decision and held that the SOB's experts "failed to cast direct doubt on all of the evidence" that the City of Daytona Beach had relied on to show secondary effects. *Daytona Grand, Inc.* v. *City of Daytona Beach,* 490 F. 3d 860 (11th Cir. 2007).

that Duluth "presented no legislative history indicating that the hours of operation restriction is necessary to combat adverse secondary effects," and concluded that the plaintiff-SOB was "likely to succeed on its claim that the statute was not designed to promote the substantial governmental interest of combating negative secondary effects."[46]

On the requirement of not completely banning all SOBs and not unreasonably limiting the space in the community in which they can be located, courts are clear that the land available for SOBs does not need to be the most commercially favorable and that there does not, in fact, need to be much space available. For instance, the ordinance of Renton, Wash., was upheld by the Supreme Court even though it left open just 5 percent (520 acres) of all land for SOB use. However, a municipality cannot enact a zoning law that provides for fewer available locations than there are presently operating SOBs in the municipality, and an SOB forced to move by a new zoning law must have ample opportunity for relocation.[47]

In addition to zoning SOBs, many municipalities enact laws affecting the expressive conduct that takes place inside these businesses. As noted earlier, nude dancing is considered speech by the U.S. Supreme Court, yet it and other courts have allowed cities to adopt minimal clothing requirements (G-strings, thongs and pasties) since these interfere in a very minor way with the erotic message conveyed by dancing. As the Supreme Court stated in 2000 in upholding an Erie, Pa., ban on public nudity against a lawsuit filed by a nude dancing establishment, "any effect [of wearing G-strings and pasties] on the overall expression is *de minimis*."[48] Municipalities also are allowed to adopt reasonable rules designed to prevent sexual conduct and contact such as lap dances between dancers and patrons. Typical efforts include:

- Minimum distance requirements between dancers and patrons
- Stage height requirements
- Railing requirements around stages
- Rules against direct tipping
- Minimum levels of lighting
- Rules prohibiting doors and partitions on booths and VIP rooms

Like zoning regulations, these restrictions affecting expressive conduct inside SOBs are subject to intermediate scrutiny review if they target negative secondary effects on public health and safety such as the spread of sexually transmitted diseases, lewdness and public indecency. Assuming that the authority to regulate SOBs rests with the government entity that is trying to regulate them, all the government needs to prove is that the regulations

1. serve a substantial government interest unrelated to the content of speech, and
2. are narrowly tailored (not substantially broader than necessary) to serve the interest.

---

46. *Northshor Experience, Inc.* v. *City of Duluth,* 442 F. Supp. 2d 713 (D. Minn. 2006).

47. *Fly Fish, Inc.* v. *City of Cocoa Beach,* 337 F. 3d 1301 (11th Cir. 2003).

48. *City of Erie* v. *Pap's A.M.,* 529 U.S. 277, 294 (2000). Appellate courts have since noted that statutes requiring dancers to wear more than just G-strings, thongs and pasties may actually infringe too much on speech rights. *Peek-a-Boo Lounge* v. *Manatee County,* 337 F. 3d 1251 (11th Cir. 2003) held that a statute requiring clothing that covers "one-third of the buttocks" and "one-fourth of the female breast" area "effectively redraw[s] the boundary between nudity and non-nudity, thereby prohibiting erotic dancers from wearing the amount of body covering the [Supreme] Court found to be consistent with the First Amendment."

In 2008 the 6th U.S. Circuit Court of Appeals applied this intermediate scrutiny standard and upheld a Kenton County, Ky., ordinance that requires dancers to stay at least five feet away from areas of an SOB occupied by customers for at least one hour after they perform seminude on stage.[49] This postperformance, anti-commingling ordinance was aimed at reducing the secondary effect of prostitution, which Kenton County contended sometimes arises in SOBs when performers sit down next to customers immediately after dancing and ask the customers to buy them "conversation drinks" that, in turn, sometimes lead to sex acts. Observing that the ordinance "restricts only those dancers performing on a particular night and restricts them only for an hour after their performances," the appellate court reasoned that Kenton County "has targeted contact between adult entertainers and customers that created a risk of prostitution. It has done so in a manner that substantially preserves the ability of those affected to communicate with each other, although in a less physical way than they could previously. We thus conclude that the provision satisfies intermediate scrutiny."

Does a regulation banning the sale of alcohol on the premises of an establishment where nudity is permitted violate the First Amendment? The answer is no, at least according to a 2008 split opinion by the 6th U.S. Circuit Court of Appeals that upheld an Ohio Liquor Control Commission rule.[50] In upholding such a separation of nudity from alcohol regulation, the two-judge majority found that the rule was intended to protect against the supposed negative secondary effects that result from combining nude dancing and alcohol. The majority also determined that the rule has only "a minimal impact on the marketplace of ideas because persons desiring to perform mainstream works of art involving nudity and sexual activity may do so in an establishment that is not licensed to sell liquor. In the alternative, they may perform their works in an establishment licensed to sell liquor if they wear clothing or pasties and a G-string and avoid sexual conduct or sexual contact." The dissenting judge found the law overbroad for two reasons: (1) its scope is not limited to sexually oriented businesses but instead sweeps up any place with a liquor license, such as comedy clubs, concert halls and playhouses; and (2) nudity is not confined to nude dancing, but includes, by way of example, "the buttocks of the dancing murderesses in [the play] *Chicago*" and "the rebellious nudity of the performers in *Hair* depicting the counter-culture of the 1960s."

ATTACKS ON THE ARTS AND POPULAR CULTURE

Beyond sexually explicit magazines, DVDs and Web sites, other forms of American popular culture often are challenged, both in court and by advocacy groups, for sexual content. For instance, in 2008 the manager of an Abercrombie & Fitch store located in a Virginia Beach shopping mall was cited by local police on a misdemeanor obscenity charge for an in-store display of two large photos of scantily dressed young models, including one that displayed a shirtless man's upper buttocks and the other that included a woman's partially bare breast. Although the photos initially were confiscated by police, the obscenity charge was later dropped. Adams Township, Pa., attempted to ban a pole-dancing exercise and fitness studio in 2008, claiming it was a sexually oriented business like those discussed earlier in this chapter; the

---

49. *729, Inc.* v. *Kenton County Fiscal Court*, 515 F. 3d 485 (6th Cir. 2008).
50. *J.L. Spoons, Inc.* v. *Dragani*, 538 F. 3d 379 (2008). The Ohio rule provides that an establishment holding a liquor permit may not knowingly or willfully allow nudity or sexual activity on its premises.

municipality relented and allowed Stephanie Babines to open her "Oh My You're Gorgeous" studio after the ACLU filed a federal lawsuit on her behalf and she promised to not allow any sexually explicit activities. The rap group 2 Live Crew's "As Nasty As They Wanna Be" recording was declared obscene by a judge in 1990,[51] and the Cincinnati Contemporary Arts Center was unsuccessfully prosecuted for obscenity that same year for a display of photographs by Robert Mapplethorpe (see page 478). In 1999 New York City Mayor Rudy Giuliani withheld funds already appropriated to the Brooklyn Museum after it opened a temporary exhibit the mayor called "sick" and "disgusting."[52] And when the National Endowment for the Arts doles out money today to artists, it is required under federal law to take "into consideration general standards of decency."[53]

Proving that censorship is no laughing matter, the late comedian Lenny Bruce was twice convicted of obscenity in 1964: once for a stand-up performance in Chicago[54] and once for a profane routine in New York City's Greenwich Village.[55] Showing how "contemporary community standards" (the phrase used in the *Miller* obscenity test) change, comedians today often "work blue," using the same words as Bruce but with little fear of obscenity prosecution. The 2005 movie "The Aristocrats" featuring multiple comedians telling "the dirtiest joke ever told" (it involves graphic descriptions of incest, bestiality and bodily excretions) is rented at video stores across the nation.

To help parents and to ward off possible government attacks on their content, the recording industry voluntarily labels its music with parental advisory stickers while the video game industry voluntarily uses a detailed set of ratings and content descriptors that the self-regulatory Entertainment Software Rating Board (ESRB) enforces. Sadly, these voluntary efforts to inform the public about content are used against both industries. For example, some chains do not sell video games rated AO (Adults Only) by the ESRB,[56] and many stores pulled "Grand Theft Auto: San Andreas" off their shelves when the game was found in 2005 to have a hidden sex scene. These actions by businesses, of course, do not raise First Amendment issues because the First Amendment only protects speech against government censorship. Nonetheless, this nongovernmental corporate censorship of speech, which is somewhat akin to community censorship (see pages 35–37), is troubling. People running a business that engages in such censorship may personally object to the messages in question or, from an economic standpoint, may fear boycotts by consumers and some religious groups if they sell the products.

The late comedian Lenny Bruce was twice convicted of obscenity in 1964.

---

51. *Skyywulker Records, Inc.* v. *Navarro,* 739 F. Supp. 578 (S.D. Fla. 1990). The conviction was thrown out by a federal appellate court because the local sheriff "submitted no evidence to contradict the [expert] testimony [put on by 2 Live Crew] that the work had artistic value." *Luke Records* v. *Navarro,* 960 F. 2d 134 (11th Cir. 1992).

52. A federal judge held the mayor's defunding of the museum violated the First Amendment, noting that the museum cannot be penalized "because of the perceived viewpoint of the works in the exhibit" and adding there was no language in the lease or contract between the City of New York and the museum "that gives the Mayor or the City the right to veto works chosen for exhibition by the Museum."*Brooklyn Institute of Arts and Sciences* v. *City of New York,* 64 F. Supp. 2d 184 (E.D. N.Y. 1999).

53. 20 U.S.C. § 954 (2007).

54. See *Illinois* v. *Bruce,* 202 N.E. 2d 497 (Ill. 1964) (reversing the conviction).

55. Thirty-nine years later, in 2003, then New York Gov. George Pitaki formally pardoned Bruce, far too late for the comedian who died of a drug overdose in 1966.

56. Johnson, "We've Been Robbed, Gamers Complain."

EROTIC MATERIALS IN CYBERSPACE

Beginning in 1996 Congress passed a series of three federal statutes designed to control what Americans could see on the Internet. It should be noted that the transmission of obscene material over the Internet is clearly banned by federal law. Statutes that make it a crime to transport obscene material in interstate commerce, whether in a truck or car, via the U.S. Postal Service or UPS, or by television transmission or satellite relay, also bar the movement of such material over the Internet, even through e-mail.[57] Transmission of child pornography via computers is also banned under federal law.

The statutes adopted by Congress focused on nonobscene, adult-oriented, sexually explicit material—material that is protected by the First Amendment. The laws included:

- 1996 Communications Decency Act
- 1998 Child Online Protection Act
- 2001 Children's Internet Protection Act

What follows is a brief summary of these regulations, as well as the court rulings that focused on the laws.

The Communications Decency Act

The Communications Decency Act (CDA) was one part of a massive law that restructured telecommunication regulations. Among other things, the act made it a crime to transmit indecent material or allow indecent material to be transmitted over public computer networks to which minors have access. Fines of $250,000 and a jail sentence of five years were possible for those convicted of violating this measure. The law defined indecency as "any comment, request, suggestion, proposal, image or other communication that, in context, depicts or describes in terms patently offensive as measured by contemporary community standards, sexual or excretory activities or organs."

In 1997 in *Reno* v. *ACLU*[58] the U.S. Supreme Court held unconstitutional the CDA's provisions protecting minors from "indecent" and "patently offensive" Internet communications. Initially observing that Internet-conveyed speech deserves the same full First Amendment protection as speech transmitted in print (see pages 128–130), Justice John Paul Stevens wrote for the majority that the statute "places an unacceptably heavy burden on protected speech" and, by going far beyond restricting obscene speech under *Miller*, "threatens to torch a large segment of the Internet community." The court did not attack the congressional goal of protecting minors from potentially harmful materials, but it criticized, on grounds of both void for vagueness and overbreadth (see pages 10–11 discussing these doctrines), the terms and language used in the CDA to carry out that goal. Not only were the terms "indecent" and "patently offensive" lacking precise definition, but the court held that the CDA, in attempting "to deny minors access to potentially harmful speech . . . effectively suppresses a large amount of speech that adults have a constitutional right to receive and to address to one another." Stevens noted that whereas the *Miller* obscenity test protects speech with serious literary, artistic, political or scientific value, the CDA lacked such a saving provision to protect socially redeeming speech that may be sexually explicit.

57. 18 U.S.C. § 1465.
58. 521 U.S. 844 (1997).

The CDA thus could stop discussion of sexually frank but legitimate topics such as birth control practices, homosexuality and the consequences of rape.

The Child Online Protection Act

The following year Congress tried again when it adopted the Child Online Protection Act (COPA). The statute prohibits commercial Web sites from knowingly transmitting to minors (people under 17 years of age) material that is harmful to minors. Harmful material was defined as material that, with respect to minors, is specifically created to appeal to prurient interests, that graphically depicts lewd or sexual behavior, and that lacks serious literary, artistic or scientific value. The law requires jurors to apply "contemporary community standards" when assessing material. A fine of $50,000 and a six-month jail sentence may be imposed for each violation. But the law includes provisions that bar any prosecution of a Web site operator who has restricted access to the site to those with credit cards, debit accounts, adult access codes or adult personal ID numbers. The idea of this provision is that only adults would have access to one of these items, and therefore the site operator could honestly believe he or she is communicating with an adult, not a minor.

In 2004, after the case bounced around the federal courts for five years, the U.S. Supreme Court upheld on First Amendment grounds a lower-court preliminary injunction against enforcement of COPA in *Ashcroft* v. *ACLU*.[59] Examining COPA as a content-based restriction on speech subject to strict scrutiny review (see page 60), the high court noted that the government must prove that COPA restricts no more speech than is necessary to achieve the goal of making the Internet safe for minors. As part of this task, the government must show that any less restrictive alternatives proposed by the ACLU and the other plaintiffs would not be as effective as COPA in serving its goal. Anthony Kennedy wrote for the five-justice majority that Internet filters that parents can purchase "are less restrictive than COPA. They impose selective restrictions on speech at the receiving end, not universal restrictions at the source." What's more, Kennedy noted that, in contrast to COPA, "promoting the use of filters does not condemn as criminal any category of speech, and so the potential chilling effect is eliminated, or at least much diminished." He added that filters "may well be more effective than COPA." Concluding that the government had not yet demonstrated that COPA is the least restrictive alternative available to protect minors, the majority sustained the preliminary injunction preventing enforcement of COPA and remanded the case for a trial on the merits.

In late 2006, the government was back in federal court in Pennsylvania trying to resuscitate COPA, with the case now called *ACLU* v. *Gonzales* (because Alberto Gonzales replaced John Ashcroft as attorney general). But in March 2007, U.S. District Court Judge Lowell A. Reed Jr. again rebuffed the government, issuing a permanent injunction against the enforcement of COPA and holding, among other things, that COPA is "not narrowly tailored to Congress' compelling interest" in protecting minors and that "COPA is impermissibly vague and overbroad" (see pages 10–11 discussing the void for vagueness and overbreadth doctrines).[60]

Amazingly, the federal government did not give up on COPA; it went back to court in 2008 (a full decade after COPA became law) to ask the 3rd U.S. Circuit Court of Appeals in

59. 542 U.S. 656 (2004).
60. *ACLU* v. *Gonzales,* 478 F. Supp. 2d 775 (E.D. Pa. 2007).

Philadelphia to overturn Judge Reed's March 2007 ruling that had permanently enjoined the measure. Predictably, the 3rd Circuit in July 2008 affirmed Reed's injunction and concluded that "COPA cannot withstand a strict scrutiny, vagueness, or overbreadth analysis and thus is unconstitutional."[61] The appellate court extolled the virtues of filtering software rather than government regulation, writing that "filters and the Government's promotion of filters are more effective than COPA." The case finally came to a close in January 2009 when the U.S. Supreme Court denied the government's petition for a writ of certiorari to revisit the 3rd Circuit's opinion. The bottom line? After more than a decade of litigation, the COPA never took effect and the First Amendment triumphed.

After more than a decade of litigation, the COPA never took effect.

The Children's Internet Protection Act

Congress made its third attempt at limiting access to the Internet in 2001 when it adopted the Children's Internet Protection Act (CIPA). The law requires public libraries to install anti-pornography filters on all their computers that provide Internet access in order to continue to receive federal funding (so-called e-rate funds) that subsidizes their Internet access. About 14 million Americans access the Web via library computers. The federal government provides about $200 million each year to pay for this access.

One problem with filters is they "overblock" and screen out innocent material and important information on topics such safe sex, rape, breast cancer and sexually transmitted diseases. Some libraries today thus maintain two sets of computers—some with filters that minors must use (a children's section), and some without filters that adults may use (an adult section). Alternatively, public libraries in Houston, Tex., have filters on all computers, but adults may request the filter be disabled before their own computer sessions.[62] Other libraries choose not to filter sexually explicit online content at all, a fact exposed in 2006 in Connecticut when a registered sex offender "was caught looking at child pornography on a computer at the main branch of the Hartford Public Library."[63] The public library system in Howard County, Md., was the only one in the state in 2006 without a filtering program, although it had a policy that prohibited viewing obscene or pornographic Web sites.[64]

In 2003 the U.S. Supreme Court upheld CIPA in *United States* v. *American Library Association* against a challenge that the act violated the First Amendment rights of adult library patrons to receive speech.[65] The court made clear that adults must be allowed, upon request, to have blocked sites unblocked and/or to have filtering software disabled during their sessions. This balances adults' rights to receive information with the interest in shielding minors from sexual expression. As Justice Kennedy wrote in concurrence, "[I]f, on the request of an adult user, a librarian will unblock filtered material or disable the Internet software filter without significant delay, there is little to this case."

Current Issues Online: The "Dot XXX" Domain

In 2007 the Internet Corporation for Assigned Names and Numbers (ICANN) rejected a proposal that ostensibly would have shielded minors from sexual content while online: the creation and

61. *ACLU* v. *Mukasey,* 534 F. 3d 181 (3d Cir. 2008), cert. den., 2009 U.S. LEXIS 598 (Jan. 21, 2009).
62. Levine and Radcliffe, "Texas AG: Children Need to Be Protected."
63. Brown, "Sex Convict Charged Again."
64. DeFord, "Libraries Rethink Unrestricted Web."
65. 539 U.S. 194 (2003).

adoption of a ".xxx" domain (akin to the ".com" or ".edu" domains) for sexually explicit Web sites. Under this now-defeated proposal, a virtual red-light district would have been created on the Web, with sexually explicit sites required to use a ".xxx" suffix instead of the typical ".com" designation. The adult industry did not support the proposal, in part because it would have created a virtual ghetto of nonobscene, First Amendment–protected speech on the Web. The adult industry suggested that a better solution was a ".kids" suffix where children and parents could find kid-friendly sites. In a letter to ICANN representatives, Hustler magazine publisher Larry Flynt called the ".xxx" proposal "an inherently dangerous idea with no real purpose," noting that it could easily become a government "tool of censorship" and adding that "alternative methods" can protect children online from exposure to sexual content.[66]

In 2008 ICANN approved a move introducing and allowing for new top-level domain names that possibly would permit (although not require) the use of a ".xxx" domain by sexually explicit Web sites. The U.S. Department of Commerce objected to the plan. Under the new system, however, offensive names would be subject to an objection-based process based upon notions of public morality and order.

A final point is important: One must not confuse the problem of stopping sexual predators in cyberspace who prey on minors with the very different issue of shielding minors from sexually explicit images of adults. The former issue does not raise any First Amendment speech concerns, but the latter certainly does.

SUMMARY

Significant efforts are made to control nonobscene sexual expression. Many cities zone sexually oriented businesses (SOBs) and impose regulations on the sexual expression that is nude dancing inside SOBs. Museums, musicians and comedians all have faced the wrath of government officials for sexual content. The movie, music and video game industries have responded with voluntary ratings or warnings designed to help inform parents and to stop further government censorship. The Internet is a key battleground for censorship of sexually explicit conduct, as evidenced by three major congressional efforts to regulate it since 1996: the Communications Decency Act, the Child Online Protection Act and the Children's Internet Protection Act.

BIBLIOGRAPHY

Above the Law: The Justice Department's War against the First Amendment. Medford, N.Y.: The American Civil Liberties Union, 1991.

Attorney General's Commission on Pornography. *Final Report.* Washington, D.C.: U.S. Department of Justice, 1986.

Blakely, C. "Is One Woman's Sexuality Another Woman's Pornography?" *Ms.,* April 1985, 37.

Brown, Tina. "Sex Convict Charged Again." *Hartford Courant,* 25 October 2006, B1.

Bunker, Matthew D., Paul H. Gates Jr., and Sigman L. Splichal. "RICO and Obscenity Prosecutions: Racketeering Laws Threaten Free Expression." *Journalism Quarterly* 70 (1993): 692.

"Court Upholds Conviction in Child Pornography Case." *The New York Times,* 12 June 1994, 16.

DeFord, Susan. "Libraries Rethink Unrestricted Web." *Washington Post,* 6 July 2006.

66. Flynt, "Dear ICANN Representatives."

de Grazia, Edward. *Girls Lean Back Everywhere: The Law of Obscenity and the Assault on Genius.* New York: Random House, 1992.

"The First Amendment Under Fire from the Left." *The New York Times,* 13 March 1994, 40.

Flynt, Larry. "Dear ICANN Representatives." Letter, April 2006, available online at http://www.freespeechcoalition.com/images/HustlerXXXLetter.jpg.

Garber, Marjorie. "Maximum Exposure." *The New York Times,* 3 December 1993, 15.

Golden, Tim. "Court Bars Decency Standards in Awarding of U.S. Arts Grants." *The New York Times,* 6 November 1996, A10.

Greenhouse, Linda. "Decency Act Fails." *The New York Times,* 27 June 1997, A1.

———. "Justices Give Reprieve to an Internet Pornography Statute." *The New York Times,* 14 May 2002, A17.

———. "Justices Uphold Decency Test in Awarding Arts Grants, Backing Subjective Judgments." *The New York Times,* 26 June 1998, A17.

Hayes, Michael. "Store Busted in Oklahoma, Porn Confiscated." Free Speech Coalition Web Site, 9 May 2006, http://www.freespeechcoalition.com/FSCView.asp?coid=243.

Johnson, Paul H. "We've Been Robbed, Gamers Complain." *Bergen County Record,* 23 July 2005, A1.

Levine, Samantha, and Jennifer Radcliffe. "Texas AG: Children Need to Be Protected from Net Predators." *Houston Chronicle,* 12 July 2006, A4.

MacKinnon, Catharine A. *Only Words.* Cambridge, Mass.: Harvard University Press, 1993.

Mendels, Pamela. "Child Pornography Issue Raised in Budget." *The New York Times,* 3 October 1996, A11.

———. "Setback for a Law Shielding Minors From Smut Web Sites." *The New York Times,* 2 February 1999, A10.

Munz, Michele. "Jury Finds Explicit Videos From Store Are Not Obscene." *St. LouisPost-Dispatch,* 27 October 2000, 1.

"Pennsylvania: Child-Pornography Ruling." *The New York Times,* 8 March 2003, A15.

"Pornography." *Ms.,* January/February 1994, 32.

Report of the Commission on Obscenity and Pornography. New York: Bantam Books, 1978.

Schwartz, John. "Internet Filters Block Many Useful Sites, Study Finds." *The New York Times,* 12 November 2002, A27.

Sheehan, Kathy, and Helen Buller. "Jury Acquits Newsstand Operators." *The Bellingham Herald,* 2 February 1996, A1.

Stark, Christine, and Rebecca Whisnant. *Not for Sale: Feminists Resisting Prostitution and Pornography.* North Melbourne, Australia: Spinifex Press, 2004.

Stein, Ronald M. "Regulation of Adult Businesses Through Zoning after *Renton.*" *Pacific Law Journal* 18 (1987): 351.

Stern, Ronald M. "Sex, Lies, and Prior Restraints: 'Sexually Oriented Business'—The New Obscenity." *University of Detroit Law Review* 68 (1991): 253.

Strossen, Nadine. *Defending Pornography, Free Speech, Sex, and the Fight for Women's Rights.* New York: Scribner, 1994.

Wilkerson, Isabel. "Obscenity Jurors Were Pulled 2 Ways." *The New York Times,* 10 October 1990, A12.

CHAPTER 14

Copyright

The law of copyright is almost 500 years old. British King Henry VIII issued the first royal grant of printing privilege, the forerunner of copyright law, in 1518. American copyright law springs from the U.S. Constitution and protects a wide variety of intellectual creations. While case law today still focuses on the rights of authors and artists who generate traditional creative compositions like books, photographs and poetry, the courtroom battles also involve the protection of motion pictures, videotapes, databases, e-books and CDs.

IMMATERIAL PROPERTY LAW

Copyright is an area of the law that deals with intangible property—property that a person cannot touch or hold or lock away for safekeeping. This concept is sometimes confusing to people; how can the law protect something you can't hold or touch? Consider that new paperback novel you just purchased at the bookstore. You own that book; you can do with it what you wish. After you read it you can sell it, donate it to Goodwill, give it to a friend to read or tear out the pages and use them to start a campfire. But you don't own the arrangement of the words in that book; whoever holds the copyright, the book publisher or author, owns that part of the book. Hence, you can't reprint the book or copy long sections of it without permission. That book consists of two pieces of property: the physical or material book, and the words and artwork printed on the pages. At first glance, to the uninitiated, immaterial property law seems both esoteric and, well, a bit dull when compared with the law regulating students' rights of free speech, the distribution of adult material or using celebrities names or images without their permission in advertising. But as mass-mediated entertainment has grown as a part of our culture and our commerce, issues relating to immaterial property rights have become somewhat more complicated and a lot more interesting to those outside the legal system.

For example, who owns sports coverage? Do newspapers and magazines and television and radio stations and bloggers and others who publish (in the broadest sense) anything and everything about professional athletes and their teams own the rights to this coverage? Do the athletes own the rights to their images and accomplishments? Or do professional team owners control the rights to the pictures and stories about their businesses and their employees? This is complicated. Take, for example, a mythical major league baseball team, the Nashville Knights. The Knights have certainly assigned the rights to broadcast their games to a radio, a television station or a cable channel. So these broadcasters own some rights, and the Knights don't want to jeopardize these lucrative contracts by giving free coverage rights to others. Then the Knights have their own Web site, and Major League Baseball has its own Internet arm, which generated about $400 million in 2008. Those are revenue sources that might be diminished if the team and baseball generally cannot limit to some extent the content in the mainstream mass media.* Reporters who cover the team expect to have access to players;

---

*Officials in some university sports conferences like the Southeastern Conference have issued rules barring fans from distributing photos or videos taken at games or team practices with camera phones or video recorders. They claim the distribution of these images online exploits the athletes, and could undermine the schools' own Web sites, causing financial harm. See Benson and Arango, "With Bloggers in the Bleachers."

when the Knights limit interviews or photo coverage so they can have exclusive reports on their own Web site, the members of the press raise freedom of the press issues. Well, the Knights are willing to work with the reporters from established newspapers or magazines or broadcast stations. But the teams expect these journalists to be disciplined and follow rules established for their behavior, both in the clubhouse and elsewhere (whom the reporters can talk to and what they can talk about). But recently a large influx of bloggers have emerged, individuals who also want access to players and the clubhouse, cybernet journalists who may or may not be willing to play by the established rules. So what is the team to do? Who owns the rights to the players and the games? Questions like this are emerging rapidly, and involve elements of immaterial property law.[1]

There are many subsections of the law of immaterial property. This chapter primarily focuses on copyright law, but first examines the law as it relates to patents, trademarks and plagiarism.

PATENTS

Patent protection has served for many decades as an important element in the technological development of the nation. Without patent law it's doubtful that this society would have enjoyed the fruits of geniuses like Thomas Edison, Alexander Graham Bell and the Wright brothers. The Constitution has given Congress the right to promote the sciences and the useful arts by protecting the rights of inventors. Hence, as author James Gleick wrote in The New York Times Magazine, the patent office is charged with the enforcement of a Faustian bargain: "Inventors give up their secrets, publishing them for all to see and absorb, and in exchange they get 20-year government-sanctioned monopolies on their technologies."[2]

There are at least three different kinds of patent protections. One variety protects inventions that have utility, such as a machine or a process. A typewriter can be patented; so can a specific way of reducing the hiss or noise on an audiotape. Patent law also protects designs— the appearance of an article of manufacture. The design of a piece of furniture or a tire tread or a belt buckle can be patented. A variety of patents protect plants, but only those kinds that can be reproduced asexually through means other than seeds, like cuttings or grafting. Patent rights do not exist until the patent is issued by the U.S. government. Hence, the famous abbreviation on many items, "pat. pending," which means the patent has been applied for and is pending.

TRADEMARKS

A trademark is any word, symbol or device—or combination of the three—that differentiates an individual's or company's goods and services from the products or services of competitors. The trademark on a particular item assures the buyer that he or she is getting the real item and protects the manufacturer or service provider from the unfair business practices of others. The function of trademark law is to stop confusion in the marketplace, to clearly identify the products and services created by specific businesses. Popsicles, Q-Tips, Jell-O, Super Glue,

---

1. For a more complete discussion of this issue see Arango's "Who owns sports coverage."
2. Gleick, "Patently Absurd."

Velcro, Walkman and thousands of other brand names are protected by trademark. Anyone can manufacture and sell a portable or pocket-size cassette tape player, but only Sony can call its player a Walkman. But it is possible to get trademark protection for more than simply a trade name. The hourglass shape of the classic Coca-Cola bottle is a registered mark. So is the art deco spire of the Chrysler Building in New York and the neoclassic facade of the New York Stock Exchange Building in the same city. The design of the back pocket of Levi's jeans is a trademark, and between 2001 and 2006 Levi Strauss filed almost 100 lawsuits against companies like Fossil and Jones Apparel, claiming they had infringed on this trademark in designing the pockets on their jeans. In 2006 the University of Alabama brought a trademark infringement suit against artist and Alabama alumnus Daniel A. Moore. Moore has made a career out of painting scenes of important moments in Alabama football history. Some of this artwork is in museums. The university claimed that Moore's paintings, reproduced in prints and on merchandise, violate the school's trademark, including the famous crimson and white color scheme.

The U.S. Olympic Committee (USOC) threatened legal action against a park ranger in the Olympic National Park in the state of Washington when he published a 56-page "Best of the Olympic Peninsula" travel guide. The USOC contends it has the exclusive right to use and control the use of the word "Olympic."

In 2005 a man named Leo Stoller claimed he had trademarked the word "stealth" and attempted to block Columbia Pictures from using the word as the title of a movie about elite U.S. Navy aviators. Legal experts pointed out that trademark law doesn't give someone exclusive rights in words, only the right to prevent consumer confusion. But Stoller continued to send out cease-and-desist letters anyway, according to an article in The New York Times.[3] Slogans such as "Don't Leave Home Without It" and "Just Do It" are registered trademarks. A generic term, one that is widely used by businesses and individuals, cannot be protected as a trademark, even if someone tries to register it. In 2004 the 4th U.S. Court of Appeals ruled that the publisher of Freebies Magazine could not claim trademark protection for the term "freebie" because it was a generic term that was in scores of dictionaries and used in hundreds of publications, advertisements and Web sites. The defendant in the case was using the term within its normal definition, a slang word for something that was given or received without charge.[4] Some telephone numbers can be protected as trademarks (e.g., 1-800-FLOWERS). In 1985 a federal court overruled a decision by the Patent and Trademark Office and granted trademark registration to a color for the first time. The Owens-Corning Fiberglas Corporation won protection for the color pink, the hue of its popular home insulation. The company showed the court it was the only manufacturer to use the color pink on insulation, it had been selling this pink product since 1956, the color pink was a basic part of its advertising and marketing strategy for the product, and that consumers, questioned in a sample survey, recognized the color pink as identifying a specific brand. In 1995 the Supreme Court reinforced this concept when it ruled unanimously that the Qualitex Company, which since the 1950s used a particular shade of green-gold on the pads it makes for use on dry-cleaning presses, can register that color as a trademark.

3. Dunlap, "What Next?"; and Moynihan. "He Says He Owns."

4. *Retail Services Inc.* v. *Freebies Publishing,* 4th Cir., No. 03-1272, 4/13/04.

This area of the law also provides protection for what are called service marks for businesses such as Holiday Inn and McDonald's and certification marks for goods and services, such as Dolby for cassette decks and Real cheese for food products. Finally, what are called collective marks identify and protect members of organizations, such as the National Association of Realtors. There is also protection for something called trade dress, the way a product is packaged. Merriam-Webster, which published the Webster's Ninth New Collegiate Dictionary, collected more than $4 million in damages in 1991 when it successfully sued Random House for trademark infringement. When Random House published its Webster's College Dictionary it copied the look of the Merriam-Webster volume. The color, the design of the dust jacket and the placement of the word "Webster's" on the spine of the book were all intended to fool potential customers, the plaintiffs argued. The jury agreed. Once registered, a trademark must be renewed after five years. Renewal is then required at 10-year intervals. But as long as it is properly renewed, a trademark can be maintained indefinitely. Some of the earliest American trademarks still in use date to the 18th and 19th centuries. Colgate dates to 1806; Gordon's (Gin) was first used in 1769. Chiquita bananas were first sold in 1876; Kodak cameras and film, 1886; and Tabasco pepper sauce, 1868.

THE FOUR MAIN FUNCTIONS OF TRADEMARKS AND SERVICE MARKS

- They identify one seller's goods and distinguish them from goods sold by others.
- They signify that all goods bearing the trademark or service mark come from a single source.
- They signify that all goods bearing the mark are of an equal level of quality.
- They serve as a prime instrument in advertising and selling goods.

While personal ownership of a trademark may exist perpetually, the ownership of a trademark or trade name can also be lost. The Ford Motor Company in 2003 wanted to name one of its automobiles "Futura," a name it had used from 1959 to 1962 and in the late 1970s and early 1980s. But when it stopped using the name, Pep Boys, an auto parts retail chain, registered the name as a trademark. Pep Boys went to court to block Ford, and a federal court ruled in 2004 that the company had abandoned the trademark when it stopped using the name some 20 years earlier. Failure to use a name for as little as three years can constitute abandonment. It is also possible that trademark protection can be lost if the owner of the mark allows others to use the mark in a generic way. For example, if the makers of Super Glue (a trade name) adhesive failed to try to stop other adhesive makers from referring to their products as super glues, the trademark protection could be lost. These generic words—nylon, dry ice, escalator, toasted corn flakes, raisin bran, aspirin, lanolin, mimeograph, cellophane, linoleum, shredded wheat, zipper, yo-yo and brassiere—were all at one time registered trademarks that slipped away from owners who failed to protect these names. And as trade names become more commonly used, there is a tendency for them to slip into a generic term. In July of 2006

While personal ownership of a trademark may exist perpetually, the ownership of a trademark or trade name can also be lost.

the owners of the search engine Google were thrilled to note that the word "google" was included in the new edition of Merriam-Webster's Collegiate Dictionary, the term going from a nonentity to common usage in less than eight years. But they were less thrilled to note that a great many people were using the term as a verb, without the capital letter *G*. ("John googled 'downtown car dealers' to find a used Honda.") What they want people to write or broadcast is that "John used the Google search engine to find a Honda at a downtown car dealer." Angry letters, threats of lawsuits, even legal action must be initiated to stop others from illegally using the name or phrase or mark. This responsibility falls on the owner of the mark; no government agency polices such misbehavior. Simple innocent infractions rarely cause serious problems for the offender. Calculated trademark infringement can be costly. In 2009 a federal court in Seattle awarded a $3.2 million judgment to Experience Hendrix and Authentic Hendrix, two firms that own and license Jimi Hendrix's likeness and music. The defendant, Electric Hendrix Spirits, advertised its Electric Hendrix Vodka as being "inspired by the innovative spirit of legendary musician Jimi Hendrix," which was a trademark infringement, the court said.[5]

Trademark law is designed to reduce the likelihood of confusion in the marketplace. But courts have ruled that a parody of a trademarked item is not necessarily an infringement because it would not generate such confusion. Hence, when Haute Diggity Dog's toys marketed its "Chewy Vuiton" dog toys, it did not infringe on the trademark of luggage and fashion designer Louis Vuitton. "The furry little 'Chewy Vuiton' imitation, as something to be chewed by a dog, pokes fun at the elegance and expensiveness of a LOUIS VUITTON handbag, which must not be chewed by a dog," the 4th U.S. Court of Appeals ruled in 2007.[6]

For many years U.S. trademark law forbade only the use of a registered trademark or trade name on a product that was similar to the product produced by the owner of the trademark or trade name. A competitor to Sony could not call its portable cassette player a Walkman, but the manufacturer of exercise equipment could call its treadmill a Walkman. In January 1996 Congress, following the lead of the legislatures in 27 states, added more muscle to trademark protection when it adopted the Federal Dilution Trademark Act. This law gives the owners of trademarks and trade names legal recourse against anyone who uses the same or similar trademarks on even dissimilar products. In other words, in the past Maytag could block the use of its trademark and name only on home appliances made by its competitors. Under the new law Maytag could block the use of its name and registered trademark on an automobile or a camera as well. And Sony could stop the exercise equipment manufacturer from calling its treadmill a Walkman. Supporters of this new legislation argued that any use of another's name or mark weakened or diluted its value and distinctiveness, even in the absence of confusion as to the source of the goods. This law does not apply to the use of a registered name or mark in news reports or news commentary, or in parody, satire or other such forms of expression.

The new law was controversial when adopted because, opponents argued, "trademark dilution" was too elusive a concept. What is dilution of a trademark? Trademark infringement requires proof of consumer confusion and is not easy to prove. The new law is supposed to give trademark holders the ability to sue for behavior that falls short of actual infringement. Recently the Supreme Court attempted, with limited success, to resolve some of this confusion

---

5. "Hendrix Inspired Vodka."
6. *Louis Vuitton Malletier S.A.* v. *Haute Diggity Dog LLC*, 507 F. 3d 252 (2007).

in a case involving a national retailer and a small entrepreneur. In 1998 Victor Moseley of Elizabethtown, Ky., opened Victor's Little Secret, a small shop in a strip mall that sells sex toys, lingerie and novelty items. Subsequently the owners of Victoria's Secret, the catalog and retail seller of lingerie and women's clothing, sued under the new law, claiming the store's name was causing dilution of the distinctive quality of their famous brand. The Supreme Court ruled in the spring of 2003 that Victoria's Secret did not have to prove actual economic harm from the appropriation of its name in its lawsuit against Moseley, but the company must show some kind of current harm (as opposed to future harm), such as a loss of its distinctive identity or a blurring of its image. But the court did not specifically outline what factors might be considered in proving such a case. The court said it would not be enough to show a mental association between the two trademarks, that consumers think of one when they see the other. It would have to be shown that consumers had a different impression of the Victoria's Secret trademark because of the competitor's branding. Justice John Paul Stevens added that it would not be enough to show only that a trademark's image had been tarnished.[7] The case was sent back to the lower court for resolution of the matter.

To establish a trademark the applicant must submit a registration application to the Patent and Trademark Office in Washington, D.C. Before submitting the application a search should first be undertaken to determine whether someone else has already registered the trademark. This search can be done at the Patent and Trademark Office Library in Arlington, Va., or at about 60 regional sites (libraries) around the nation, or through the U.S. Trademark Electronic Search Systems via the Internet. A registration fee of $325 if you file online, or $375 if you file with paper, must accompany the application. Although it is not mandatory to precede the application with a search, it is advisable. If the examiner discovers in his or her search that the mark has been previously registered, the application fee is forfeited. Anyone who claims the right to a trademark can use the™ designation with the mark to alert the public to the claim. It is not necessary to have a registration or even a pending application to use this designation. Under the law, it is the person who first uses the mark, not the person who first registers the mark, who holds the rights to the symbol or word or phrase.*

Not all trademark infringement cases end in court. When a rock band called the Postal Service put out an album in 2003 called "Give Up" on a Seattle-based independent label called Sub Pop Records, they received a cease-and-desist letter from the real Postal Service informing them that Postal Service was a registered trademark of the United States Postal Service. But 15 months later the USPS sent the band members another letter, giving them permission to use the name if they would agree to promote the use of the mail. Subsequent copies of the album and any follow-up work would have to carry a notice about the trademark. The Postal Service agreed to sell the band's CD on its Web site, potentially earning some money. The band may be asked to do some commercials for the post office and also agreed to perform at a national Postal Service executive conference.[8] And just think, no judges got involved.

---

*A booklet titled *Basic Facts About Trademarks* is available online at http://www.uspto.gov. Contact the Trademark Assistance Center at 1-800-986-9199 for a hard copy.

7. *Moseley* v. *V. Secret Catalogue, Inc.,* 537 U.S. 418 (2003). See also Greenhouse, "Ruling on *Victor* vs. *Victoria*."

8. Sisario, "Postal Service Tale."

PLAGIARISM

Editors at The New York Times expressed embarrassment and shock in May 2003 when they revealed that one of their reporters, Jayson Blair, was guilty of fabrication and plagiarism in his reporting for the venerable newspaper. Plagiarism occurs when a writer takes the ideas, thoughts or words from another and passes them off as his or her own. The notion of taking credit for the work of another is a key element in plagiarism. While the mass media is certainly not rife with plagiarism, it is probably more common than many people suspect, especially editors. One of the most disturbing revelations about the Jayson Blair case was that so few of the subjects he wrote about complained to the newspaper about his stories. They said they just assumed reporters make things up. Most cases of plagiarism that are uncovered are usually resolved outside the legal system. The plagiarist is humiliated and often fired from his or her job. The publicity damages his or her reputation. A plagiarist may lose future book contracts or assignments. When instances of plagiarism reach the courts they are generally litigated as copyright cases. But copyright infringement and plagiarism are different acts with some potential overlap, as noted by New York University professor Siva Vaidhyanathan. "One may infringe upon a copyright with plagiarizing, and one may plagiarize—use ideas without attribution—without breaking the law. Plagiarism is an ethical concept. Copyright is a legal one."[9] Allegations of plagiarism and/or copyright infringement are commonly made these days and affect all aspects of society. Some recent examples demonstrate this:

Film. In recent years charges of plagiarism or copyright infringement have been made against the producers of numerous films, including "Twister," "Amistad," "The Last Samurai," "Broken Flowers," "Wedding Crashers," "Diary of a Mad Housewife," "Syriana," "Disturbia," and "The Curious Case of Benjamin Button." None of these allegations were proven.

Books. Prominent authors Stephen E. Ambrose ("The Wild Blue") and Doris Kearns Goodwin ("The Fitzgeralds and the Kennedys") were both accused of plagiarism and admitted they had used borrowed passages in their books.

Journalism. In 1995 the Columbia Journalism Review reported that plagiarism had occurred in 20 of the nation's leading newspapers and magazines.[10] Since that report many other instances have been revealed, such as the Jayson Blair case, noted previously.

Even government officials get caught up in the web. In 2008 Tim Goeglein, a Bush White House liaison to social and religious conservatives, resigned after admitting he had repeatedly plagiarized from other writers in columns he wrote for his hometown newspaper.[11] Later that same year, Michael E. O'Neill, former chief counsel to the U.S. Senate Judiciary Committee, who was nominated to be a Federal District Court judge by President Bush, was accused of plagiarism in an article he wrote for the Supreme Court Economic Review. The Senate did not confirm his nomination.[12]

Most plagiarists aren't sinister or evil people. Few books or movies or plays or stories or songs are completely new or original; most creative people in one way or another borrow

9. Vaidhyanathan, "Copyright Jungle."
10. Lieberman, "Plagiarize."
11. Stolberg, "Bush Aide Resigns."
12. Liptak, "Copying Issue Raises Hurdle."

© Warner Brothers/Courtesy Everett Collection

The producers of the film "Syriana" (including executive producer George Clooney who starred in the film as well) were sued by a French screenwriter who claimed they had copied a screenplay she had written.

from their predecessors or colleagues. But there are ways to pay this debt, through acknowledgment or other means, that credit the author whose work is being used. Use of such material with intent to deceive is clearly morally wrong, and the law makes passing off the work of another as one's own work illegal as well.

Copyright law protects "all works of authorship fixed in a tangible medium of expression." This description includes writings, photographs, paintings, music, drama and other similar works. Ideas are usually protected by the law relating to patents or contracts. Copyright does not protect ideas, but the specific expression of those ideas. Trademark protection is based on marketplace use; patents and copyright are statutory creations. Trademark protection can last forever; copyright and patent protection is limited by law. The remainder of this chapter focuses exclusively on copyright. People who work in the mass media do not need to become copyright attorneys to avoid lawsuits in the 21st century. But news writers, broadcasters, advertising copywriters and public relations specialists and especially people who prepare material for the Web should know both how to protect their own work from theft and how to avoid illegally taking the work of someone else.

ROOTS OF THE LAW

Copyright protection was unneeded until the development of mechanical printing. The time and effort it took to hand-copy a manuscript made the theft of such work both tedious and unprofitable. But the printing press gave thieves the ability to reproduce multiple copies of a work relatively quickly and cheaply, and this capability changed things dramatically. Each subsequent technological development has put new stress and strain on copyright law. The development of motion pictures and the broadcast media, recorded music, audio- and then videotape, photocopying, and most recently interactive computer-mediated communication have all required modifications or new interpretations in the law as the government has sought to protect the right to literary property.

The British were the first to attempt such protection. Copyright law developed in England in the 16th century as the government sanctioned and supported the grant of printing privileges to certain master printers in exchange for their loyalty and assistance in ferreting out anti-government writers and publishers. But the rights of authors, as opposed to printers, were not protected until the early 18th century when the British Parliament passed the nation's first copyright law. The law gave the legal claim of ownership of a piece of literary property to the person who created the work or to a person who acquired the rights to the work from the author. The statute was a recognition by the Crown that in order to encourage the creation of books, plays and art, the creators of these works had to be assured that they would be rewarded for their labor. That is the real logic behind copyright law, the fostering of the creative spirit. If a dramatist knew, for example, that as soon as her play was published she would lose control of the work because others could freely copy it, there would be little stimulation for the creation of plays. The muses of creativity are strong, but there must be some reward to pay the piper.

That is the real logic behind copyright law, the fostering of the creative spirit.

British copyright law was applied in the colonies until American independence. American copyright law derives directly from the U.S. Constitution. In Article I, Section 8, of that document lies the basic authority for modern United States copyright law:

> The Congress shall have Power . . . To promote the Progress of Science and useful Arts, by securing for limited Times to Authors and Inventors the exclusive Right to their respective Writings and Discoveries.

This provision gives Congress the power to legislate on both copyright and patent. The Congress did just that in 1790 by adopting a statute similar to British law. The law gave authors who were U.S. citizens the right to protect their books, maps and charts for a total of 28 years—a 14-year original grant plus a 14-year renewal. In 1802 the law was amended to include prints as well as books, maps and charts. In 1831 the period of protection was expanded by 14 years. The original grant became 28 years with a 14-year renewal. Also, musical compositions were granted protection. Protection for photography, works of fine art and translations were added later in the 19th century.

A major revision of the law was enacted in 1909, and our current law was adopted in 1976. The 1976 federal law pre-empted virtually all state laws regarding the protection of writing, music and works of art. Hence, copyright law is essentially federal law and is governed by the federal statute and by court decisions interpreting this statute. In 1988 Congress finally approved U.S. participation in the 102-year-old Berne Convention, the world's pre-eminent international copyright treaty. The United States had been hesitant in the past to join the treaty because of significant differences between United States and international law, but after the 1976 revision of U.S. copyright law, the differences were minimal. American media companies, eager to expand their international business, sought to improve trade relations and strengthen U.S. influence on matters relating to international copyright law and therefore put pressure on the government to join the convention.

WHAT MAY BE COPYRIGHTED

The law of copyright gives to the author, or the owner of the copyright, the sole and exclusive right to reproduce the copyrighted work in any form for any reason. There are actually six exclusive rights recognized under the law:

- **The right of reproduction of the work**
- **The right of preparation of derivative works**
- **The right of public distribution of the work**
- **The right of public performance of the work**
- **The right of public display of the work**
- **The right of public digital performance of a sound recording**

These rights are fairly clear with regard to traditional mass media. If Bogus Publishing prints 1,000 copies of a copyrighted Stephen King novel and distributes them to bookstores, this is a violation of King's exclusive distribution rights under the law. But the rights are less clear when it comes to computers and the Internet. Is storing a copyrighted document on a hard disk or a diskette or even in the computer's RAM a violation of the exclusive right to reproduce a copyrighted item? Probably, the courts seem to indicate. Does transmitting a copyrighted work via the Internet constitute a public performance of the work? Most likely. The courts are just now sorting out these questions. Several lower courts have ruled that it can be an infringement of copyright to download material off the Internet for unauthorized use or upload copyrighted material onto a Web site or bulletin board without the permission of the copyright holder.[13] A federal court in Texas ruled in December 1997 that an online service provider that provided subscribers unauthorized copies of copyrighted images infringed on the copyright holder's rights of reproduction, distribution and display and was liable for direct copyright infringement. The provider argued that it was merely a conduit between the subscription service that scanned the photos into the system and the subscribers who downloaded them. The defendant said that all it sold was access to the subscription service, not images. The court disagreed, ruling that "Webbworld didn't sell access—it sold images."[14] However, under a federal statute adopted in 1998 an online service provider that acts as merely a *conduit* during the infringement of copyrighted works will not be held liable for the illegal act in most instances (see page 538). A U.S. District Court in Nevada ruled in 1999 that scanning a copyrighted photo into a computer for graphic manipulation and insertion into a new work constitutes a copyright infringement. The court said that digitizing any copyrighted material may support an infringement finding—even if it has only the briefest existence in a computer's memory.

Before a copyrighted work may be printed, broadcast, dramatized or translated, the consent of the copyright owner must first be obtained. The law grants this individual exclusive monopoly over the use of that material. To quote the statute specifically, copyright extends to "original works of authorship fixed in any tangible medium of expression." Congress has defined *fixed in a tangible medium* as that work that is "sufficiently permanent or stable to permit it to be perceived, reproduced, or otherwise communicated for a period of more than a transitory duration." Under these standards such items as newspaper stories or entire

13. See, for example, *Playboy Enterprises, Inc. v. Starware Publishers Corp.,* 900 F. Supp. 433 (1995).
14. *Playboy Enterprises, Inc. v. Webbworld Inc.,* D.C.N. Texas Civil No. 3196-CV-3222-H, 12/11/97.

newspapers, magazine articles, advertisements and almost anything else created for the mass media can be copyrighted. Material that is created in digital form and stored or transmitted electronically via computer diskettes or CD-ROM can also be protected by copyright. Extemporaneous performances and speeches, and improvised sketches are examples of materials that are not fixed in a tangible medium and are not protected by the federal copyright statute. But this lack of protection does not mean that someone can film or record a performer's act, for example, without the performer's permission. A federal law criminalizes the unauthorized recording of a live musical performance.[15] This action would also be forbidden by other laws, such as the right to publicity (see Chapter 7) and common-law copyright.*

The federal statute lists a wide variety of items that can be copyrighted, but this list is only illustrative. It includes the following:

1. Literary works (including computer software)
2. Musical works, including any accompanying words
3. Dramatic works, including any accompanying music
4. Pantomimes and choreographic works
5. Pictorial, graphic and sculptural works
6. Motion pictures and other audiovisual works
7. Sound recordings

Copyright law is equally specific about what cannot be copyrighted:

1. Trivial materials cannot be copyrighted. Such things as titles, slogans and minor variations on works in the public domain are not protected by the law of literary property. (But these items might be protected by other laws, such as unfair competition, for example.)
2. Ideas are not copyrightable. The law protects the literary or dramatic expression of an idea, such as a script, but does not protect the idea itself. "This long established principle is easier to state than to apply," notes law professor David E. Shipley. It is often difficult to separate expression from the ideas being expressed.

*Under the 1909 law the United States had two kinds of copyright protection: common-law copyright and statutory copyright. Much as it did in 18th-century England, common law protected any work that had not been published. Common-law protection was automatic; that is, the work was protected from the point of its creation. And it lasted forever—or until the work was published. In order to protect published works, the author, photographer or composer had to register the book or picture or song with the U.S. government and place a copyright notice on the work. The 1976 statute does away with common-law copyright for all practical purposes. The only kinds of works protected by common law are works like extemporaneous speeches and sketches that have not been fixed in a tangible medium. They are still protected from the point of their creation by common-law copyright. Once they are written down, recorded, filmed or fixed in a tangible medium in any way, they come under the protection of the new law.

15. *United States* v. *Moghadam,* 11th Cir., No. 98-2180, 5/19/99.

3. Facts cannot be copyrighted. "The world is round" is a fact. An author cannot claim that statement as his or her own and protect it through copyright.

4. Utilitarian goods—things that exist to produce other things—are not protected by copyright law, according to William Strong in "The Copyright Book." A lamp is a utilitarian object that exists to produce light. One cannot copyright the basic design of a lamp. But the design of any element that can be identified separately from the useful article can be copyrighted, according to Strong. The design of a Tiffany lamp can be copyrighted. The unique aspects of a Tiffany lamp have nothing to do with the utilitarian purpose of producing light; these aspects are purely decorative.

5. Methods, systems, and mathematical principles, formulas, and equations cannot be copyrighted. But a description, an explanation or an illustration of an idea or system can be copyrighted. In such an instance the law is protecting the particular literary or pictorial form in which an author chooses to express herself or himself, not the idea or plan or method itself. For example, an individual writes and publishes a book in which she outlines a new mathematical formula. Although the book itself may be protected by copyright, the formula cannot be, and others may use it freely. In other words, the copyright on an article or a book does not preclude the public from making use of what the book teaches.

Can all books and other creative works be copyrighted? No. The law specifically says that only "original" works can be copyrighted. What is an original work? In interpreting this term in the 1909 law, courts ruled that the word "original" means that the work must owe its origin to the author. In 1973 a court reporter (an employee of the court who transcribes the proceedings) attempted to claim copyright over a transcript he had made of some of the proceedings during the investigation of the death of Mary Jo Kopechne. This young woman drowned when a car in which she was riding and driven by Sen. Edward Kennedy went off a bridge and into a creek near Chappaquiddick, Mass. In *Lipman* v. *Commonwealth*,[16] a federal judge ruled that the transcript could not be copyrighted. "Since transcription is by very definition a verbatim recording of other persons' statements, there can be no originality in the reporter's product."

In 1985 an organization called Production Contractors Inc., or PCI, tried to block Chicago television station WGN from televising a Christmas parade on Thanksgiving Sunday. PCI, which put on the parade, sold the exclusive right to televise it to another station, WLS. The plaintiff claimed the parade was copyrighted, and WGN would be in violation of the law by televising it. A federal district court disagreed and ruled that a Christmas parade is not something that can be copyrighted; it is a common idea, not an event of original authorship.[17] A group of women in San Francisco molded the elements of erotic entertainment—strip tease, pole dancing, lap dancing—into a fitness routine and copyrighted it. Whether this copyright will hold up in court if it is challenged remains to be seen. While the individual exercises are clearly not original, the women argue that the arrangement of them into a fitness routine is, and they should be able to stop others from imitating the workout.[18]

16. 475 F. 2d 565 (1973).
17. *Production Contractors* v. *WGN Continental Broadcasting*, 622 F. Supp. 1500 (1985).
18. Oberthur, "Pole Dancing Copyright."

The work must be original. Must it be of high quality or be new or novel? The answer to both questions is no. Even common and mundane works are copyrightable. Courts have consistently ruled that it is not the function of the legal system to act as literary or art critic when applying copyright law. In 1903 Justice Oliver Wendell Holmes wrote in *Bleistein* v. *Donaldson Lithographing Co.,* "It would be a dangerous undertaking for persons trained only to the law to constitute themselves final judges of the worth of pictorial illustrations, outside of the narrowest and most obvious limits."[19] Even the least pretentious picture can be an original, Holmes noted in reference to the posters involved in this case.

The 9th U.S. Circuit Court of Appeals echoed this statement in 1992 when it ruled that raw, unedited video footage of news events was sufficiently original to be protected by copyright.[20] The case involved the Los Angeles News Service and Audio Video Reporting Service. LANS records live news events on video and then sells the unedited but copyrighted footage to television stations. The TV stations take the raw footage, edit it any way they want, and use it in newscasts. Audio Video Reporting Services videotapes newscasts and then sells clips of the newscasts to interested parties. A businesswoman who has been interviewed for a news story, for example, may want to buy a copy of the story from Audio Video. Or the parents of children featured in a news story on a school project might want to have a copy of that story.

LANS sued Audio Video, claiming that in selling these video clips, which were taken from the copyrighted raw footage LANS had provided to local television stations, Audio Video was infringing on the copyright LANS held on the videotape. Audio Video attempted to defend the suits on several bases, including the argument that raw, unedited videotape was not sufficiently original to be protected by copyright; all the photographer did was switch on the camera and point it at the news event. No creativity or intellectual input was required. The Court of Appeals disagreed, noting that there were several creative decisions involved in producing a photograph. The photographer must select the subject, the background, the perspective, consider the lighting and the action and so on. The "requisite level of creativity [to qualify as an original work] is extremely low; even a slight amount will suffice," the court said. Likewise, novelty is not important to copyright: The author does not have to be the first person to say something in order to copyright it. "All that is needed to satisfy both the Constitution and the statute is that the 'author' contributed something more than a merely trivial variation, something recognizably his own," one court ruled.[21]

COPYRIGHT AND FACTS

Facts cannot be copyrighted. That the film "Slumdog Millionaire" won the Oscar in 2009, or that John Kennedy was killed in November 1963, or that George Washington was the nation's first president are all facts. No one can claim ownership of these facts; anyone can publish or broadcast them. But this simple concept can get a bit more complicated when someone works

19. 188 U.S. 239 (1903).
20. *Los Angeles News Service* v. *Tullo,* 973 F. 2d 791 (1992).
21. *Amsterdam* v. *Triangle Publishing Co.,* 189 F. 2d 104 (1951).

diligently to collect a set of facts and then seeks to copyright his or her work. This section focuses on three such areas: databases, news events and research findings.

Telephone Books and Databases

Long before the birth of the computer, most homes contained relatively sophisticated databases. These are called telephone directories—a listing of phone company customers' names, addresses and telephone numbers. In 1991 the Supreme Court decided a seemingly innocuous case involving copyright protection for a white-pages telephone book—by any measure a collection of thousands of facts. But the ruling would have a profound impact on other kinds of databases and generate problems that have not yet been completely resolved.

The case involved a small, rural telephone company (Rural Telephone Service) that issued a standard white-pages directory of its customers' names, addresses and phone numbers, and a company (Feist Publications) that publishes regional telephone directories, which include the names, addresses and phone numbers of the customers of numerous small telephone companies. Feist asked Rural for permission to include the names of its customers in a directory, but Rural said no. Feist used the information anyway and Rural sued for copyright infringement. Feist argued that a telephone directory contains only facts, which can't be copyrighted. Rural disagreed and argued that the phone book was a collection of facts that can be copyrighted. It also raised a second argument, what some call "the sweat of the brow" doctrine. This is a legal proposition previously recognized by some courts that asserts that even though facts are not copyrightable, someone who invests substantial time and energy in amassing these facts deserves a reward for the hard work. Collecting the information that goes into a telephone directory takes time and energy, and copyright law should protect the results of this effort, Rural argued.

In a unanimous decision the Supreme Court rejected both arguments. With regard to the latter, Justice Sandra Day O'Connor said the sweat-of-the-brow doctrine was a bogus argument. Quoting former justice William Brennan, she said, "The primary objective of copyright law is not to reward the labor of authors, but to promote the process of science and the arts." O'Connor said that some compilations of facts can be protected by copyright. The key to determining whether protection is merited is whether there is *some novelty or originality in the manner in which the facts are organized or selected or coordinated.* An alphabetical listing of names—the organization of the Rural directory and indeed all white pages—is not novel enough to generate copyright protection for the directory.[22]

"The primary objective of copyright law is not to reward the labor of authors, but to promote the process of science and the arts."

In a pre-digital era, this ruling would have little impact. But in the computer age, the creation of alphabetically ordered lists of facts, which are also called databases, is one of the fastest and most profitable uses for CD-ROM computer software and interactive Web sites. Because of the *Feist* ruling, only those databases in which factual items are organized or selected or coordinated in some *novel* or *artful manner* will be protected by copyright law. Even a massive alphabetical listing of all the certified public accountants in New York state

22. *Feist Publications, Inc.* v. *Rural Telephone Service Co., Inc.,* 111 S. Ct. 1282 (1991).

or the names of all the massage parlors in California fails to meet the test laid down by the high court.[23]

Many states have misappropriation laws (see pages 514–515) that may be used to bar database piracy. Congress, under pressure from the owners of large, commercial databases, has tried several times to pass legislation to protect these collections of facts. But in every case the legislators have run into roadblocks. Organizations outside the database industry, notably libraries and some technology companies, have opposed such legislation, claiming that such laws would allow some companies to monopolize facts, and this would hamper research projects. And there of course is the constitutional issue. The Supreme Court ruled that the so-called sweat-of-the-brow doctrine was constitutionally invalid in 1991, and this doctrine is at the heart of such legislation. There was no resolution of this issue by late 2009.

News Events

When the news is reported correctly it is basically an account of facts. Can a news account be copyrighted? Can one journalist claim the exclusive right to report on a story? Suppose a TV reporter gets an exclusive interview with a reclusive public figure and then broadcasts the copyrighted interview on the evening news. Does the law of copyright prevent other journalists from relating the substance of what was revealed in that interview? The answer is no. Other stations cannot replay the same interview. Newspapers cannot publish a transcript of the interview. But both broadcast and print journalists can tell their viewers and readers what the public figure said in the interview. Copyright law doesn't even require the competitors to credit the TV journalist for the interview. Failing to give proper credit to the TV journalist who got the interview is grossly unethical but happens all too often. Charges of plagiarism might be made.

Copyright law protects the expression of the story—the way it is told, the style and manner in which the facts are presented—but not the facts in the story. For many writers this concept is a difficult one to understand and to accept. After all, if one reporter works hard to uncover a story, shouldn't he or she have the exclusive right to tell that story? This argument again reflects the sweat-of-the-brow doctrine that has been rejected by the Supreme Court. Shouldn't hard work be rewarded? In this case the law is clear: Hard work must be its own reward. Copyright protects only the way a story is told, not the facts in the story.

Research Findings and History

Gene Miller, a Pulitzer Prize-winning reporter for the Miami Herald, wrote a book titled "83 Hours Till Dawn," an account of the widely publicized kidnapping of Barbara Mackle. Miller said he had spent more than 2,500 hours on the book, and many aspects of the kidnapping

---

23. The same year the *Feist* case was decided the 2nd U.S. Circuit Court of Appeals ruled that the creator of a directory of businesses in New York City had demonstrated novelty by arranging and selecting the businesses to be included in the directory in a creative fashion. See *Key Publications, Inc.* v. *Chinatown Today*, 945 F. 2d 509 (1991). And in 1997 the 7th U.S. Circuit Court of Appeals ruled that a taxonomy (a way of describing items in a body of knowledge or practice) of dental procedures was a creative work, far different from a simple compilation. *American Dental Association* v. *Delta Dental Plan Association*, CA 7,No. 96-4140, 9/30/97. See also *Warren Publishing Co.* v. *Microdos Data Corp.*, CA 11 en banc, No. 93-8474, 6/10/97.

case were uncovered by the journalist and reported only in his book. Universal Studios wanted to film a dramatization of the 1971 incident but was unable to come to terms with Miller on payment for the rights. The studio produced the so-called docudrama anyway, and Miller sued for infringement of copyright. The similarities between Miller's book and the Universal script were striking—even some of the errors Miller had made in preparing the book were found in the film. But Universal argued that it was simply telling a story of a news event, and as such the research that Miller had done in digging out the facts regarding the story was not protected by copyright law. A U.S. District Court agreed with Miller's contention. "The court views the labor and expense of the research involved in the obtaining of those uncopyrightable facts to be intellectually distinct from those facts, and more similar to the expression of the facts than the facts themselves," the court said. The judge ruled that it was necessary to reward the effort and ingenuity involved in giving expression to a fact.[24] But the U.S. Court of Appeals for the 5th Circuit reversed the lower-court ruling. "The valuable distinction in copyright law between facts and the expression of facts cannot be maintained if research is held to be copyrightable. There is no rational basis for distinguishing between facts and the research involved in obtaining the facts," the court said. To hold research copyrightable, the court said, is no more or less than to hold that the facts discovered as a result of research are entitled to copyright protection.[25] The court added: "A fact does not originate with the author of a book describing the fact. Neither does it originate with the one who 'discovers' the fact. The discoverer merely finds and records. He may not claim that the facts are 'original' with him, although there may be originality and hence authorship in the manner of reporting, i.e. the 'expression' of the facts."

The 7th U.S. Circuit Court of Appeals handed down a similar ruling in a case involving the infamous John Dillinger, a prolific bank robber who became the subject of a widely publicized search by local police and the FBI during the 1930s. Most historians believe that Dillinger was killed on July 22, 1934, when he was shot by government agents who ensnared him in an ambush as he left the Biograph movie theater in Chicago. Jay Robert Nash has written at least two books that dispute this conclusion. Nash argues that Dillinger learned about the ambush and sent a look-alike to the theater instead. The FBI, embarrassed that its setup failed, kept quiet. Dillinger retired from a life of crime and lived the rest of his life on the West Coast.

A 1984 episode of the CBS television series "Simon and Simon" involved a story that suggested that Dillinger was still alive, living in California. Nash sued the network, claiming copyright infringement. The officials at the network admitted that they had seen Nash's books and said they had used some of his ideas. But, they argued, Nash claimed to be writing history, and history is a collection of facts. Such material cannot be copyrighted. The court agreed. The network might be liable if Nash portrayed his work as a novel, as fiction. But he didn't. "The inventor of Sherlock Holmes controls that character's fate while the copyright lasts; the first person to conclude that Dillinger survives does not get his dibs on the history," Judge Easterbrook wrote. Nash's rights lie in his expression, not in the naked truth.[26]

The dichotomy between historical fact and fiction that is fundamental to American copyright law likely would have doomed any lawsuit filed in the United States by the

---

24. *Miller* v. *Universal City Studios,* 460 F. Supp. 984 (1978).
25. *Miller* v. *Universal City Studios,* 650 F. 2d 1365 (1981).
26. *Nash* v. *CBS,* 899 F. 2d 1537 (1990).

authors of the book "Holy Blood, Holy Grail" against Dan Brown and Random House, the author and publisher of "The Da Vinci Code." Michael Baigent and Richard Leigh said they spent 10 years doing research before they published their book that argues, essentially, that Jesus was married, Mary Magdalene was his wife, they had children, and the descendents of the children are still around. Baigent and Leigh also asserted that factions within the Roman Catholic Church have, for centuries, attempted to cover up these historical facts. Along came Dan Brown, who in 2003 wrote a fictional thriller (which just happened to sell 40 million hardback copies) that suggests the same story. Brown admitted he owed a debt to the Baigent/Leigh book, which was published in 1982, but he denied he infringed upon its copyright. The plaintiffs filed their infringement lawsuit in the United Kingdom, where the fact/fiction distinction is not as widely accepted. "What makes this case so interesting is that there is little clarity [in Great Britain] over the extent to which an author can use another person's research for either background or a direct influence on a book," noted British copyright attorney Antony Gold. Baigent and Leigh argued that Brown had stolen the central theme of their historical account, but lost the case when a London court ruled that they had failed to prove this point because they could not accurately state what that central theme was.[27]

MISAPPROPRIATION

Although this chapter focuses on copyright, an ancillary area of the law needs to be briefly mentioned, as it too guards against the theft of intangible property. **Misappropriation,** or **unfair competition,** is sometimes invoked as an additional legal remedy in suits for copyright infringement. Unlike copyright, which springs largely from federal statute today, misappropriation remains largely a creature of common law. One of the most important media-oriented misappropriation cases was decided by the Supreme Court more than 80 years ago and stemmed from a dispute between the Associated Press (AP) and the International News Service (INS), a rival press association owned by William Randolph Hearst.

AP charged that INS pirated its news, saying that INS officials bribed AP employees to gain access to news before it was sent to AP member newspapers. The press agency also charged that the Hearst wire service copied news from bulletin boards and early editions of newspapers that carried AP dispatches. Sometimes INS editors rewrote the news, and other times they sent the news out on the wire just as it had been written by AP reporters. Copyright was not the question, because AP did not copyright its material. The agency said it could not copyright all its dispatches because there were too many and they had to be transmitted too fast. INS argued that because the material was not copyrighted, it was in the public domain and could be used by anyone.

Justice Mahlon Pitney wrote the opinion in the 7-1 decision. He said there can be no property right in the news itself, the events, the happenings, which are publici juris, the common property of all, the history of the day. However, the jurist went on to say:

---

27. Lyall, "Idea for 'Da Vinci Code'"; and Lattman, "English Copyright Lawsuit." In 2006 the 2nd U.S. Court of Appeals affirmed a lower-court ruling granting a summary judgment to Brown in an infringement action brought by Lewis Perdue, who claimed "The Da Vinci Code" contained material stolen from two novels he had written. The court said Brown's book was not substantially similar to either "The Da Vinci Legacy" or "Daughter of God."

> Although we may and do assume that neither party [AP or INS] has any remaining property interest as against the public in uncopyrighted matter after the moment of its first publication, it by no means follows that there is no remaining property interest in it as between themselves.[28]

Pitney said there was a distinct difference between taking the news collected by AP and publishing it for use by readers and taking the news and transmitting that news for commercial use, in competition with the plaintiff. This action is unfair competition, he said—interference with the business of the AP precisely at the point where profit is to be reaped.

In 1963 a Pennsylvania broadcasting station was found guilty of pirating the news from a local newspaper and reading it over the air as if it were the fruits of its own news-gathering efforts. In 1994 the Reading (Pa.) Eagle Co., which publishes the morning Times and the afternoon Eagle, sued another Pennsylvania radio station, WIOV in Reading, charging copyright infringement, misappropriation and unfair competition. The publisher claimed the station was lifting its news stories and sought $50,000 in damages. In 2009 the AP brought suit for misappropriation against All Headline News Corp. The defendant employs people to search the Internet for news stories for republication—sometimes after rewriting the text, but often using the entire story without any editing. The AP claimed that many of its stories were republished as being originated by All Headline News. The suit was settled after the defendant admitted many instances of improperly using the AP's content and agreed to pay damages.[29]

The law of misappropriation is intended to stop

- **a person trying to pass off his or her work as the work of someone else, and**
- **a person trying to pass off the work of someone else as his or her own work.**

Imagine that a new magazine is published with the title News-Week. The cover design mirrors that of Newsweek. The design and title would be an attempt to confuse readers and pass off the new magazine as the well-established original, a publisher trying to pass off his or her work as the work of someone else. Or imagine a daily newspaper reporter picking up a story that was published in a small weekly paper, rewriting the story and then passing it off as his or her original reporting. Such an action would be trying to pass off the work done by someone else as the daily reporter's own work.

The critical legal issue in an unfair competition or misappropriation suit is whether there is a *likelihood* that an appreciable number of ordinarily prudent purchasers will be misled, or simply confused, as to the source of the goods in question.

DURATION OF COPYRIGHT PROTECTION

The length of time that a copyright will protect a given work depends on when the work was created. The major revision of the copyright law in 1976 included a significant extension of the duration of copyright protection. In 1998 Congress adopted the Sonny Bono Copyright

---

28. *Associated Press* v. *International News Service*, 248 U.S. 215 (1919).
29. *Pottstown Daily News Publishing* v. *Pottstown Broadcasting*, 192 A. 2d 657 (1963); Shepard, "Does Radio News Rip Off Newspapers?" 15; *Associated Press* v. *All Headline News Corp.*, 608 F. Supp. 2d 454 (2009) and http://www.rcfp.org/newsitems/index.php?i=10914.

Extension Act, adding 20 more years to the protection of a copyrighted work. Any work created after January 1, 1978, will be protected for the life of the creator, plus 70 years. This rule allows creators to enjoy the fruits of their labor until death and then allows the heirs to profit from the work of their fathers, mothers, sisters or brothers for an additional length of time. After 70 years the work goes into what is called public domain. At that point it may be copied by any person for any reason without the payment of royalty to the original owner. The copyright on a work created by two or more authors extends through the life of the last author to die plus 70 years. What is called a "work for hire" is protected for 95 years after publication. Works for hire include books written by an author for a publisher, which then holds the copyright. Also included are most motion pictures, sound recordings, television programs and so on that are created through a collaborative effort.* Works created before 1978 when the 1976 law went into effect are protected for a total of 95 years from the date of the original copyright.

HOW LONG DOES COPYRIGHT PROTECTION LAST?

Works Created After January 1, 1978
The life of the creator plus 70 years.

Works Created by More Than One Person
The life of the last living creator plus 70 years.

Works for Hire
Ninety-five years after publication.

Works Created Before January 1, 1978
Ninety-five years.

The 1998 statute that extended copyright protection for an additional 20 years was challenged by critics who saw the law as a means of protecting large corporate copyright holders, who lobbied Congress vigorously for the extension, not individual creators. Some critics derisively referred to the law as the Disney Copyright Extension, since without a change in the law many of Walt Disney's cartoon characters would have fallen into the public domain. The legal challenge rested on the constitutional language that authorized Congress to protect the works of authors and inventors for a "limited time." Challengers said they did not object to the new duration of protection—the life of the creator plus 70 years; they instead said applying this extension retroactively to works already protected by copyright law violated the reasoning behind copyright law—which is to stimulate the

*The U.S. Copyright Office has available information regarding all matters relating to copyright law, including duration of protection (http://www.copyright.gov/).

creation of new works. Extending existing copyrights would not promote new creativity, they argued. In addition, a duration that is virtually perpetual, they said, violates the notion of "limited time." In 2003 the Supreme Court upheld the congressional action. Justice Ruth Bader Ginsburg said that the extension—the most recent of many extensions enacted by Congress since 1790—was within the power of Congress. She said that while it could be argued that the extension was bad public policy, it was within the power granted to the legislators by the Constitution.[30]

SUMMARY

American copyright law derives from rules and regulations established by the British government in the 16th and 17th centuries. The contemporary basis for the protection of intangible property is contained in the U.S. Constitution, and since 1789 the nation has had numerous federal copyright statutes. The current law, adopted in 1976, gives to the author or owner of a work the sole and exclusive right to reproduce the copyrighted work in any form for any reason. The statute protects all original works of authorship fixed in any tangible medium. Included are such creations as literary works, newspaper stories, magazine articles, television programs, films and even advertisements. Trivial items, utilitarian goods, ideas and methods or systems cannot be copyrighted.

News events cannot be copyrighted, but stories or broadcasts that endeavor to describe or explain these events can be copyrighted. What is being protected is the author's style or manner of presentation of the news. Similarly, facts cannot be copyrighted, but works that relate these facts can be protected as expression. While news and facts cannot be copyrighted, anyone who attempts to present news or facts gathered by someone else as his or her own work may be guilty of breaking other laws, such as misappropriation, or unfair competition. In most cases copyrighted works are protected for the life of the author or creator plus 70 years. Different rules apply for works created before 1978 and for works made for hire.

FAIR USE

Owners of a copyright are granted almost exclusive monopoly over the use of their creations. The word "almost" must be used, for there are really four limitations on this monopoly. Three of the limitations have been discussed already. First, the work must be something that can be copyrighted. There can be no legal monopoly on the use of something that cannot be protected by the law. Second, the monopoly protects only original authorship or creation. If the creation is not original, it cannot be protected. Third, copyright protection does not last forever. At some point the protection ceases and the work falls into the public domain.

The fourth limitation on exclusive monopoly is broader than the other three, is certainly more controversial and is concerned with limited copying of copyrighted material. This is the doctrine of **fair use,** which has been defined by one court as follows:

Owners of a copyright are granted almost exclusive monopoly over the use of their creations.

---

30. *Eldred* v. *Ashcroft,* 537 U.S. 186 (2003). See also Greenhouse, "20-Year Extension."

> A rule of reason . . . to balance the author's right to compensation for his
> work, on the one hand, against the public's interest in the widest possible
> dissemination of ideas and information on the other.[31]

This doctrine, then, permits limited copying of an original creation that has been properly copyrighted and has not yet fallen into the public domain.

One hundred and thirty years ago all copying of a copyrighted work was against the law. This absolute prohibition on copying constituted a hardship for scholars, critics and teachers seeking to use small parts of copyrighted materials in their work. A judicial remedy for this problem was sought. It was argued that since the purpose of the original copyright statute was to promote art and science, the copyright law should not be administered in such a way as to frustrate artists and scientists who publish scholarly materials. In 1879 the U.S. Supreme Court ruled in *Baker* v. *Selden:*

> The very object of publishing a book on science or the useful arts is to
> communicate to the world the useful knowledge which it contains. But
> this object would be frustrated if the useful knowledge could not be used
> without incurring the guilt of piracy of the book.[32]

The doctrine of fair use emerged from the courts, and under this judicial doctrine small amounts of copying were permitted so long as the publication of the material advanced science, the arts, criticism and so forth.

In 1976 Congress included the judicial doctrine of fair use in the revision of the copyright law. Section 107 of the measure declares, "The fair use of a copyrighted work . . . for purposes such as criticism, comment, news reporting, teaching (including multiple copies for classroom use), scholarship or research is not an infringement of copyright."

In determining whether the use of a particular work is a fair use, the statute says that courts should consider the following factors:

1. **The purpose and character of the use**
2. **The nature of the copyrighted work**
3. **The amount and substantiality of the portion used in relation to the copyrighted work as a whole**
4. **The effect of the use on the potential market for or value of the copyrighted work**

Each factor on this list will be considered separately as the doctrine of fair use is explored. Interestingly, the fair-use criteria included in the statute and just listed here (1 through 4) are very close to the criteria that courts used under the old common-law fair-use doctrine. This similarity is no accident. In a report issued by committees in the House and the Senate on Section 107, the legislators said that the new law "endorses the purpose and general scope of the judicial doctrine of fair use" but did not intend that the law be frozen as it existed in 1976. "The courts must be free to adapt the doctrine to particular situations on a case-by-case basis. Section 107 is intended to restate the present judicial doctrine of fair use, not to change, narrow, or enlarge it in any way."

31. *Triangle Publications* v. *Knight-Ridder,* 626 F. 2d 1171 (1980).
32. *Baker* v. *Selden,* 101 U.S. 99 (1879).

PURPOSE AND CHARACTER OF USE

The purpose and character of the use of a work is the initial factor to be considered. A use is more likely to be considered a fair use if it is a noncommercial or nonprofit use. But simply because material is used in a commercial venture doesn't disqualify it as a fair use. The U.S. Court of Appeals for the 2nd Circuit noted that according to committee reports compiled when the new copyright law was adopted, Congress did not intend that only nonprofit educational uses of copyrighted works would qualify as fair use. The reports, said the court, are "an express recognition that . . . the commercial or nonprofit character of an activity, while not conclusive with respect to fair use, can and should be weighed along with other factors in fair-use decisions."[33]

The law lists several categories of use that may be protected by fair use. These include

- criticism and comment,
- teaching, and
- scholarship and research.

Just because a use falls into one of these categories doesn't mean a fair-use defense will automatically be successful. At the same time, uses that fall outside one of these categories may still qualify as a fair use. Here are some cases that illustrate these principles.

"The Daily Show" on Comedy Central used a video clip from a public access television show, "The Sandra Kane Blew Comedy Show," to introduce a segment called Public Excess. The segment features examples of public access television. Sandra Kane, a comedienne and former stripper, sings, dances and tells jokes on her show while wearing little or no clothing. She sued for copyright infringement, but the federal court said the use of the clip by Jon Stewart on "The Daily Show" was a fair use because it was used for critical purposes. "In presenting plaintiff's clip, defendant sought to critically examine the quality of plaintiff's public access television show," the court ruled.[34] And the 2nd U.S. Court of Appeals ruled that when an operator of two Web sites that are used to criticize cults and other groups accused of mind control quoted long segments of a manual used at executive training seminars it was a fair use because he used the segments to support his criticism of the company that conducted the seminars.[35]

But a federal court in California rejected a fair-use argument made by the operator of an Internet bulletin board who posted complete copyrighted articles from the Los Angeles Times and the Washington Post on the site so people could comment on the news and criticize the manner in which the news stories were reported. The court noted that adding commentary to a verbatim copy of a copyrighted work does not automatically protect it as a fair use. The court issued an injunction barring future postings and assessed $1 million in damages against the defendant.[36] How do you explain the seemingly opposite rulings? Surely the concepts "comment" and "criticism" are elusive and subject to interpretation. But a more obvious explanation involves the amount of copyrighted material used in these three

---

33. *Maxtone-Graham v. Burtchaell,* 803 F. 2d 1253 (1986).
34. *Kane v. Comedy Partners,* 32 M.L.R. 1113 (2003).
35. *NXIVM Corp. v. Ross Inst.,* 2d Cir., No. 03-7952, 4/20/04.
36. *Los Angeles Times v. Free Republic,* 29 M.L.R. 1028 (2000).

instances. In the California case, the defendants used a great many copyrighted articles from the two newspapers. Significantly smaller amounts of copyrighted material were used in the other two cases.

The comment and criticism element is more aptly applied to republishing small segments of a work. A book reviewer is clearly protected when quoting even long passages from a work being evaluated. A journalist could undoubtedly publish one or two stanzas from a poem by a poet who was named the winner of a Pulitzer Prize. Yet if a poster publisher took the same two stanzas of poetry, printed them in large type on 11-by-14-inch stock, and tried to sell them for $10 each, the publisher would be guilty of an infringement of copyright. The purpose of the use in the case of the journalist was to give readers an example of the poet's work, but the poster publisher simply wanted to make a few bucks.

Copyright law has traditionally regarded the limited use of copyrighted material for educational purposes as a fair use. The teacher who makes copies of a short article from Newsweek and distributes them to class members is normally considered an innocent infringer. But more substantial copying may not receive the same protection, especially when commercial interests are involved. This issue came up in the 1990s when photocopy businesses worked with college and university faculty members to prepare so-called coursepaks. A faculty member would provide the copy center with a list of articles and book chapters for use in a class. The centers would then make photocopies of the material, loosely bind them and then sell these ad hoc anthologies to the students enrolled in the course for use as a text. Publishers and others who held the copyright on the material that was copied brought suit for infringement. The copy centers, like Kinko's, argued that these materials were being copied for educational purposes, an acceptable use under the law. The federal courts agreed that while the materials were ultimately being used for educational purposes, the copy centers were making the coursepaks for commercial reasons—something that did not qualify as a fair use.[37] In its ruling the 6th U.S. Court of Appeals noted that when the 1976 Copyright Act was approved, Congress had accepted guidelines for educational use copying that would be regarded as a fair use. The copying must

- **be brief—under 1,000 words;**
- **be spontaneous—there would be no time to get permission;**
- **not occur more than 9 times a term, with a limited number of copies from a single author;**
- **carry a copyright notice;**
- **not be a substitute for purchase of the original work and not cost the student more than the actual copying cost.**[38]

Use of small amounts of copyrighted material in a news article or broadcast is usually regarded as a fair use. But this kind of use has become more problematic in recent years with the growth of blogs and other Web-generated communication. In 2009 the Associated Press—a news cooperative owned by 1,500 daily newspapers that provides written articles and broadcast materials to thousands of news organizations—announced that it would consider seeking legal remedies to stop Web sites, bloggers and search engines like Google and Yahoo! from

---

37. *Basic Books Inc.* v. *Kinko's Graphics Corp.*, 758 F. Supp. 1552 (1991).
38. "Copying of Materials for Coursepak Does Not Constitute Fair Use, CA6 Rules," 1 E.P.L.R. 809 (1996).

using its work without first getting permission, and then sharing revenues earned by using the AP material. The news aggregators and search companies argued that such a use was a fair use, but the exact complaint raised by the AP has never been litigated. AP spokespeople said it was becoming all too common for bloggers to use direct quotations from AP stories, a use that sometimes went beyond a fair use. AP officials said it is more appropriate for the bloggers to use short summaries of the articles rather than the direct quotations from the stories. In July 2009 the AP announced it would henceforth attach software called metatags to its articles. The tags would explain what copyright rules apply to the reuse of the material, and alert the AP if and how the article is being revised. No legal action had been initiated when this chapter was prepared.[39]

On at least two occasions federal courts have ruled that a use that serves the public interest could qualify as a fair use. One case involved the use of copyrighted material in a biography of the reclusive multimillionaire Howard Hughes. A company owned by Hughes bought the rights to the copyrighted material when it discovered it was to be used in the biography, and then attempted to stop the publisher from using the material in the book. The 2nd U.S. Court of Appeals ruled that it would be contrary to the public interest to permit individuals to buy the rights of anything published about them to stop authors from using the material.[40] In another case a federal court ruled that it was in the public interest to permit the author of a book on the assassination of John F. Kennedy to use copyrighted frames of 8 mm motion picture film to illustrate his theory on the murder of the president. The film was shot by a spectator at the scene and was purchased by Time, Inc., which owned the copyright.[41] Please note, these are singularly uncommon rulings.

Today, some judges talk about "transformative uses" when they consider claims of fair use. What does this mean? If an individual takes a portion of a copyrighted work and uses it for another purpose, in other words transforms it, it is much more likely to be regarded as a fair use. For example, when ABC broadcast a television news report about how the advocates of the legalization of marijuana have changed the image of the typical user from the long-haired pot-head to a seriously ill medical patient, it used both the cover from a recent issue of Newsweek and a photo from a story in the issue to illustrate its video story. The magazine story had focused on the medical use of marijuana. The federal court said the use of the cover and the photo was a fair use because it was a transformative use.[42] The network had taken the original copyrighted art and transformed it into a story about the news coverage of a current issue.

Questions regarding so-called transformative use are likely to be an issue in a copyright lawsuit that was brewing in 2009 between the Associated Press and controversial street artist Shepard Fairey. In April of 2006, freelance photographer Mannie Garcia (working for the AP) took a picture of then Sen. Barack Obama at the National Press Club; a pensive Barack Obama looking upward, as if to the future, as one reporter described it. Using the photo as a starting point, Fairey created the now famous red, white and blue HOPE poster that became so popular during the presidential campaign. Hundreds of thousands of posters and stickers containing the poster image were sold; signed copies of the poster have been bought on

39. Hansell, "The Associated Press to Set Guidelines"; and Pérez-Peña, "A.P. Seeks to Rein" and "A.P. Seeks to Block."

40. *Rosemont* v. *Random House,* 366 F. 2d 303 (1966).

41. *Time, Inc.* v. *Bernard Geis Associates,* 239 F. Supp. 130 (1968).

42. *Morgenstein* v. *ABC Inc.,* 27 M.L.R. 1350 (1998).

eBay for thousands of dollars; and a stenciled collage version of the work has been added to the permanent collection of the National Portrait Gallery in Washington, D.C. In 2009 the AP claimed copyright infringement and said the use of the photo by Fairey required its permission. The news cooperative said it wanted credit and compensation. Attorneys for Fairey admit that the artist used the photo as a reference, but transformed it into a "stunning, abstracted and idealized visual image that created a powerful new meaning that conveys a radically different message" from the photo taken by Garcia.[43] There had been no court action on the matter when this chapter was being prepared.

Adding something to a copyrighted work can be considered a transformative use. But at least one court has ruled that removing something from such a work is not transformative. A company called Clean Flicks of Colorado was in the business of buying copies of films released on DVDs, and then editing them, taking out what the firm regarded as offensive content. These would then be sold to buyers who wanted a sanitized version of the film. A coalition of motion picture studios and film directors sued for copyright infringement. The company called its editing merely a transformative use; the court disagreed, ruling that transformative means adding something. Here the infringers added nothing, but merely deleted material from the original. Clean Flicks also argued it was not harming the filmmakers; it was simply exploiting a new market, a market not being served by Hollywood. After all, the company bought each DVD it altered before resale. But the court said the film studios have the right not to enter a market. "Whether these films should be edited in a manner that could make them acceptable to more of the public playing them on DVD in a home environment is more than merely a matter of marketing; it is a question of what audience the copyright owner wants to reach," wrote U.S. District Judge Richard Matsch.[44]

NATURE OF THE COPYRIGHTED WORK

Courts look at several considerations when applying this criterion in a copyright infringement action.

- **Is the copyrighted work still available?** Using part of a work that is out of print is far less serious than using a segment of a book that can be readily purchased at the local bookstore.
- **Is the copyrighted work what is called a consumable work?** A consumable work is something that is intended to be used just once: a workbook that accompanies a text, or a book of crossword puzzles. Consumables are usually cheaply priced and are intended to be used and then discarded. It would not be a fair use for a teacher to purchase a single copy of a biology workbook, make 30 photocopies of each page, and then pass out the photocopies for use by the students. But it would very likely be a fair use for the same teacher to make 30 copies of an article in Science magazine for class distribution.

---

43. Italie, "Compensation for Use"; and Kennedy, "Artist Sues the A.P." To complicate matters, Fairey asked a federal judge to declare he was protected from the AP infringement claim by fair use. Photographer Mannie Garcia asserted that he, not the AP, owned the copyright on the photo.
44. *Clean Flicks of Colorado* v. *Soderbergh,* 433 F. Supp. 2d 1236 (2006).

- **Is the work an informational work or a creative work?** It is more likely to be a fair use if the copying involves a work like a newspaper or newsmagazine article or an item in an encyclopedia rather than a novel or play or poem. This doesn't mean that copying an informational work is always a fair use; just that it is more likely to be.
- **Is the work published or unpublished?** Materials like manuscripts, letters and other works that have not yet been published are sometimes accessible by the public when they are stored in libraries or other places. The author's right to be the first to publish these works is regarded as a valuable right.

The question of the right of first publication came to the forefront more than 20 years ago when The Nation magazine pre-empted the publication of the late President Gerald Ford's memoirs by publishing a 2,250-word article that contained paraphrases and quotes from the unpublished manuscript. Only about 300 words in the article were legitimately protected by copyright, but these focused on the heart of the long memoir—Ford's discussion of why he chose to pardon former President Richard Nixon, who resigned in disgrace following his impeachment for his actions in the Watergate affair. (Nixon was impeached, but resigned before he was tried by the Senate.) When Ford's publisher sued for copyright infringement, The Nation claimed its use of the 300 words was a fair use. The U.S. Supreme Court disagreed. The U.S. Supreme Court rejected the fair-use claim and reversed the lower appellate court ruling. "In using generous verbatim excerpts of Mr. Ford's unpublished manuscript to lend authenticity to its account of the forthcoming memoirs, The Nation effectively arrogated to itself the right of first publication, an important marketable subsidiary right," Justice Sandra Day O'Connor wrote. The 1976 Copyright Act clearly recognizes the right of first publication for an author, O'Connor said. The scope of fair use is narrowed where unpublished works are concerned. The Senate report that accompanied the 1976 law specifically states: "The applicability of the fair-use doctrine to unpublished works is narrowly limited since, although the work is unavailable, this is the result of a deliberate choice on the part of the copyright owner. Under ordinary circumstances the copyright owner's 'right of first publication' would outweigh any needs of reproduction." Justice O'Connor concluded that "the unpublished nature of a work is a key, though not necessarily determinative, factor, tending to negate a defense of fair use."[45]

Mark Twain once noted that it is possible to get more out of a lesson than the teacher intended. A cat that sits on a hot stove will likely never sit on another hot stove, he noted. It is just as likely, he added, the cat won't sit on a cold stove either. Such was the case when some lower courts interpreted Justice O'Connor's opinion in the *Nation* decision. When judges read the sentence, "We conclude that the unpublished nature of a work is a key, *though not necessarily determinative,* [emphasis added] factor, tending to negate a defense of fair use," they ignored the italicized phrase. In a series of increasingly restrictive rulings, judges on the 2nd U.S. Circuit Court of Appeals, a court with considerable national authority, ruled that the copying of an unpublished work *can never* be a fair use.[46]

Justice O'Connor concluded that "the unpublished nature of a work is a key, though not necessarily determinative, factor, tending to negate a defense of fair use."

45. *Harper & Row Publishers* v. *Nation Enterprises,* 471 U.S. 539 (1985). A newspaper or television broadcast or Web site can surely summarize what it has learned from a copy of an unpublished memoir or book, but it cannot quote sentences, paragraphs or pages from the manuscript. This may be a fine line to some, but it is an important dividing line to the courts.
46. See *Salinger* v. *Random House,* 811 F. 2d 90 (1987); and *New Era Publications* v. *Henry Holt & Co., Inc.,* 873 F. 2d 576 (1990).

Congress resolved the issue in the autumn of 1992 when it amended the federal copyright statute. The law now states that "the fact that a work is unpublished shall not itself bar a finding of fair use," if such a finding is justified based on the application of all four fair-use criteria. This change puts the law back to where it was immediately after the ruling in *Harper & Row Publishers* v. *Nation Enterprises,* before appellate courts began to misinterpret it. It remains exceedingly dangerous, though not necessarily fatal, to publish or broadcast material that has never before been published. Such a use will likely be sustained only if the user can make a strong case under the other three fair-use criteria.

THE PORTION OR PERCENTAGE OF A WORK USED

The amount of a work used is not as important as the relative proportion of a work used. Word counts, for example, really don't mean as much as percentages. The use of 500 words from a 450-page book is far less damaging than the use of 20 words from a 40-word poem. How much of the work, in relation to the whole, was used? Courts will consider exact copying when looking at this question; but they will also often consider paraphrasing. Pirates will find little refuge in a dictionary of synonyms. For example, in the mid-1980s respected writer Ian Hamilton sought to publish a biography of reclusive novelist J.D. Salinger, the author of "Catcher in the Rye." Lacking Salinger's cooperation in the endeavor, Hamilton sought to prepare the biography by using portions of numerous unpublished letters the novelist had written to friends and acquaintances. Salinger sued for copyright infringement, claiming the contents of the letters were his literary property. To avoid the lawsuit Hamilton reworked the manuscript, deleting most phrases and sentences copied directly from the letters. But he extensively paraphrased the contents of the correspondence in place of using Salinger's actual words. The 2nd U.S. Circuit Court of Appeals ruled that this use was an infringement of copyright, not a fair use. Paraphrasing Salinger's words did not protect Hamilton. "What is protected is the manner of expression, the author's analysis or interpretation of events—the way he structures his material and marshalls facts, his choice of words and the emphasis he gives to particular developments," wrote Judge Jon O. Newman.[47] The paraphrasing was too close to Salinger's own choice of words, to his creativity. The biographer had taken the "heart of the material" from the letters. Hamilton abandoned his initial effort and instead wrote "In Search of J.D. Salinger," a book about Salinger's literary life (without the material from the letters) and his unsuccessful efforts to publish a biography of the reclusive author.

One of the toughest tasks facing a judge is measuring fair use when someone presents a parody of a copyrighted work. A parody is a critical and usually humorous effort to lampoon a creation. But in order to be a successful parody, the work must reflect the content of the original book or movie or song, not simply the style and presentation of the original creation. The question of parody was at the heart of one of the silliest legal actions in recent years when the Fox News Network tried to stop author Al Franken from calling his book, a critical evaluation of the conservative press in America, "Lies and the Lying Liars Who Tell Them: A Fair and Balanced Look at the Right." Fox claimed that it owned the rights to the phrase "fair and balanced," a slogan it uses to identify its newscasts. Franken said the book was a social commentary on the network and others, and that the use of the phrase was a parody. A federal

---

47. *Salinger* v. *Random House,* 811 F. 2d 90 (1987).

court agreed, saying the lawsuit was wholly without merit, both factually and legally. "Parody is a form of artistic expression protected by the First Amendment. The keystone to parody is imitation. Here, whether you agree with him or not in using the mark [fair and balanced], Mr. Franken is clearly mocking Fox," wrote judge Denny Chin.[48]

How much of the original work can be used? The U.S. Court of Appeals for the 9th Circuit ruled that it was a fair use for disc jockey Rick Dees to use the melody and some of the words from the first six bars of the song "When Sunny Gets Blue" in his comic parody, "When Sonny Sniffs Glue." The lyrics in the original song are: "When Sunny gets blue, her eyes get gray and cloudy, then the rain begins to fall." In Dees' version the lyrics are: "When Sonny sniffs glue, her eyes get red and bulgy, then her hair begins to fall." The court noted that "like a speech, a song is difficult to parody effectively without exact or near-exact copying. If the would-be parodist varies the music or the meter of the original substantially, it simply will not be recognizable to the general audience." It is this special need for accuracy that gives the parodist some license in these cases, the court added.[49]

In 1992 the 6th U.S. Court of Appeals ruled that a commercial parody, whether a book or a movie or a song, could never be a fair use. Such a work was commercial and could not be regarded as artistic comment or criticism, something usually protected under the fair-use doctrine.[50] The ruling, if widely accepted, would have had a devastating impact on an entire range of creative work. But the Supreme Court rejected this notion two years later in one of the most colorful copyright cases ever decided. The case focused on a rap music parody of the song "Oh, Pretty Woman," a 1964 rock/country hit written by Roy Orbison (who performed the song) and William Dees. Rapper Luther Campbell, leader and founder of the group 2 Live Crew, was rebuffed when he sought permission from the publisher of the song, Acuff-Rose Music, to record his version of "Oh, Pretty Woman." Campbell was sued by Acuff-Rose when he made the recording anyway with lyrics wildly divergent from the original. A trial court called the 2 Live Crew version a parody and rejected the suit, but the Court of Appeals reversed, ruling that a commercial parody could never be a fair use. The Supreme Court sided with the trial court and sent the case back for trial, ruling that a jury trial was needed to determine whether the parody was a fair use. "The language of the statute," wrote Justice David Souter, "makes it clear that the commercial or nonprofit educational purpose of a work is only one element of the first factor enquiry into its purpose and character. . . . Accordingly, the mere fact that a use is educational and not for profit does not insulate it from a finding of infringement, any more than the commercial character of a use bars a finding of fairness. If indeed, commerciality carried presumptive force against a finding of fairness, the presumption would swallow nearly all of the illustrative uses listed [in the statute] . . . including news reporting, comment, criticism, teaching, scholarship and research since these activities are generally conducted for profit in this country."[51]

Parody, Justice Souter said, springs from its allusion to the original. "Its art lies in the tension between a known original and its parodic twin." It is true the parody here took the opening lines and the musical signature. "But if quotation of the opening riff and the first line

---

48. *Fox News Network LLC* v. *Penguin Group (USA) Inc.,* 31 M.L.R. 2254 (2003).
49. *Fisher* v. *Dees,* 794 F. 2d 432 (1986).
50. *Campbell* v. *Acuff-Rose Music, Inc.,* 92 F. 2d 1429 (1992).
51. *Campbell* v. *Acuff-Rose Music, Inc.,* 114 S. Ct. 1164 (1994).

may be said to go to the 'heart' of the original, the heart is also what most readily conjures up the song for parody, and it is the heart at which parody takes aim. Copying does not become excessive in relation to parodic purpose merely because the portion taken was the original's heart." It was significant, Souter said, that after taking the first line, 2 Live Crew added its own lyrics. And while the bass riff was copied, other original sounds were added as well.

The ruling in the *Campbell* case failed to provide precise guidelines for parodists regarding how much original material can be used in a parody that can be defined as a fair use. Maybe such precise guidelines are impossible to fashion. But without them the matter of fair use and parody continues to bedevil the judiciary. In 2001 the trust that owns the rights to Margaret Mitchell's best-selling novel from the 1930s, "Gone with the Wind," went to court to block Houghton Mifflin from publishing what reviewers described as a parody of the work. The plaintiffs argued that author Alice Randall had infringed on the copyright of the book in her novel, "The Wind Done Gone," a retelling of Mitchell's story from the point of view of a slave who lived on the plantation that was the setting for the Civil War–era novel. The narrator of the Randall book is a half-sister to Mitchell's heroine, Scarlett O'Hara, and the daughter of Mammy, a character in the original story. The plaintiffs also accused Randall of including 15 characters from the original work in her novel as well as several scenes from "Gone with the Wind," and of using verbatim dialogue from the original work. The lawsuit was settled a year later.[52] And in 2009 a federal court blocked the publication in the United States of a book titled "60 Years Later: Coming Through the Rye," a novel written by Swedish author Fredrik Colting. The work focuses on a 76-year-old character named Mr. Ç, who is clearly an elderly version of Holden Caulfield, the protagonist of the classic coming-of-age novel, "Catcher in the Rye," by J.D. Salinger. The court ruled that the "Defendants have taken well more from 'Catcher,' in both substance and style," than is necessary to criticize Salinger and his attitudes and behaviors in this so-called critical parody.[53] Colting appealed this ruling, but no decision had been reached on the appeal by mid-September.

EFFECT OF USE ON MARKET

The effect of the use on the potential market for, or value of, the copyrighted work is the fourth criterion. While a cautionary note should be sounded against assigning relative weight to the four criteria, this final one—harm to the plaintiff—is given greater weight by most courts than any of the other three. In a congressional committee report on the 1976 law, the legislators noted that "with certain special exceptions . . . a use that supplants any part of the normal market for a copyrighted work would ordinarily be considered an infringement." In the action by Harper & Row against The Nation, Justice Sandra Day O'Connor noted that "this last factor is undoubtedly the single most important element of fair use."[54] "More important," Justice O'Connor wrote, "to negate fair use one need only show that if the challenged use should become widespread, it would adversely affect the potential market for the copyright work."

---

52. *Suntrust Bank* v. *Houghton Mifflin Company,* 268 F. 3d 1257 (2001). See also Kirkpatrick, "'Wind' Book Wins Ruling."
53. *Salinger* v. *Colting*, D.N.Y., 09-cv-5095, 7/1/09.
54. *Harper & Row Publishers* v. *Nation Enterprises,* 471 U.S. 539 (1985).

The inability of the plaintiff to demonstrate an adverse economic impact from the copying can frequently in and of itself sustain a fair-use ruling. In 1997 Warner Books published a book by Gerald Celente titled "Trends 2000: How to Prepare for and Profit from the Changes of the 21st Century." In a chapter on power generation the author criticized the nuclear power industry and used a photo that was previously included in an advertisement published by the United States Council for Energy Awareness. The photo was a picture of a dairy farmer, Louise Ihlenfeldt, and a cow standing in a field of clover framed against a blue sky. A print message accompanying the photo in the ad described the harmonious relationship between the Ihlenfeldt family and a nuclear power plant located only a mile away. The book author belittled the message in the ad and criticized the industry. When a copyright action was brought against Warner Books for using the photo without permission, the publisher argued fair use. The use was for profit, and the entire picture was used, the court noted, but ruled that the black-and-white reprint of the color photo was unlikely to have a negative impact on the market for the original. "The idea that a thriving market for photographs of Louise Ihlenfeldt and the cow (however dramatically portrayed) actually exists is dubious to say the least," the court ruled.[55] In 1998 a federal judge in Washington state threw out a nearly $700,000 jury award to author Wade Cook after a trial where Cook asserted that motivational writer and speaker Tony Robbins had copied two phrases originated by Cook. The jury decided that Robbins had used the two phrases, "meter drop" and "rolling stocks," as many as 12 times in a workbook he (Robbins) distributed at financial seminars. But Judge Jack Tanner said there was not a scintilla of evidence that the use of these phrases caused any harm at all to plaintiff Cook.[56] In 2002 a federal court in New York ruled that when Web site operator Susan Pitt created a "Dungeon Doll" based on an altered head of a Barbie doll for a story about sexual slavery and torture, the use of Barbie was a fair use chiefly because the erotic dolls were unlikely to affect the market for the original Barbies.[57] And the 2nd U.S. Court of Appeals rejected the claim of negative economic impact made by a company that argued that when the defendant used some of the plaintiff's copyrighted materials to support his criticism of the company, which conducted executive training seminars, this would seriously reduce the demand for the company's service. "If criticisms on the defendants' web sites kill the demand for plaintiff's services, that is the price that, under the First Amendment, must be paid in the open marketplace of ideas," the court said.[58] Of course, if the defendant had used the plaintiff's materials to operate competing training seminars, the case would likely have ended differently.

In evaluating economic impact the court considers not only direct impact, but also the impact that using the copyrighted material might have on some derivative creation. Imagine the hypothetical situation in which a screenwriter, Virginia Miller, uses a Stephen King novel as the basis of a screenplay she prepares. The screenplay contains a great deal of material from the book. In a copyright action King would have difficulty maintaining that Miller's screenplay, in and of itself, had a direct impact on the sale of his novel. Not many screenplays are sold on the retail market. But clearly, should Miller sell her screenplay to a motion picture producer, this action would probably deprive King of the likelihood that he could sell his own

55. *Baraban v. Time Warner Inc.*, 28 M.L.R. 2013 (2000).
56. "Jury Award for Wade Cook Overruled."
57. *Mattel Inc.* v. *P.H.*, 50 N.Y., No. 01 CIV. 1864 (LTS), 10/30/02.
58. *NXIVM Corp.* v. *Ross Inst.*, 2d Cir., No. 03-7952, 4/24/04.

screenplay based on the novel. King would lose a derivative right, the right of an author to market a creation derived from the original work.

When artist Jeff Koons was sued for copyright infringement for duplicating a copyrighted photograph in a sculpture, he argued that his work had no impact on the sale of the photograph. They were different works—even though they looked the same. But the U.S. Court of Appeals disagreed, ruling that while the two works were indeed different, Koons had deprived the photographer of the potential income he could earn by selling the right to copy the photograph to another artist who wanted to create a sculpture, an important derivative right.[59]

FACTORS TO BE CONSIDERED IN DETERMINING FAIR USE

1. The purpose and character of the use
2. The nature of the copyrighted work
3. The amount and substantiality of the portion used in relation to the copyrighted work as a whole
4. The effect of the use on the potential market for or value of the copyrighted work

---

APPLICATION OF THE CRITERIA

When a court is faced with a defendant who claims a fair use, it must apply the four criteria to the facts in the case. For example, conservative talk-show host Michael Savage brought a copyright infringement suit against the Council on American-Islamic Relations for its use of a four-minute excerpt from a two-hour copyrighted Savage broadcast in which he made statements attacking both the council and the Islamic religion. The short segment was included in a critique of Savage comments that was posted on the council's Web site. The council argued that its use was a fair use.

- **Purpose and character of the use:** The clips were used for criticism and comment of Savage's views. It was not unusual to use the audio clips to authenticate Savage's critical statements. This factor favors the defendant.
- **Nature of the copyrighted work:** While the works appear to be more informational than creative, because the hearing was held on the defendant's motion for a summary judgment based on the pleadings (see pages 206–207 for an explanation of this) the plaintiff's allegations that the material was in fact a "creative performance" must be assumed at this point, the court said. This factor therefore favors the plaintiff.
- **Amount and substantiality of the material used:** Four minutes from a two-hour broadcast was a reasonable amount for the purposes of criticizing the plaintiff's views on the topics. This factor favors the defendant.

---

59. *Rogers* v. *Koons,* 960 F. 2d 301 (1992).

■ **Effect on the market value of the original work:** If the use of the four-minute segment from the original show by the council led some potential listeners to reject Savage's subsequent programs, this might have an impact on Savage's future overall revenues. But the use of the clip in the council's critique would have no impact on the market for the original program that contained the four minutes of commentary. The plaintiff never even implied that there was any market for the copyrighted work outside its original airing. This factor favors the defendant. The use of the four minutes by the council was a fair use.[60]

SUMMARY

While the copyright statute gives the author or owner of a copyrighted work an exclusive monopoly over the use of that work, the law recognizes that in some instances other people ought to be able to copy portions of a protected work. No liability will attach to such copying if the use is what the law calls a fair use.

A court will consider four factors when determining whether a specific use is fair use:

1. What is the purpose and character of the use? Why was the material copied? Was it a commercial use or for nonprofit educational purpose? Was the use intended to further the public interest in some way?

2. What is the nature of the copyrighted work? Is it a consumable item such as a workbook, or is it a work more likely to be borrowed from, such as a newspaper or magazine article? Is the copyrighted work in print and available for sale? Has the work been previously published or is it unpublished?

3. How much of the copyrighted work was used in relation to the entire copyrighted work? Was it a small amount of a large work? Or was it a large portion of a small work?

4. What impact does the use have on the potential market or value of the copyrighted work? Has the use of the material diminished the chances for sale of the original work? Or is the use unrelated to the value or sale of the copyrighted material?

Although a court considers each of these items closely, most courts tend to give extra weight to item 4. In a close ruling the impact on the market or value of the copyrighted work often becomes the most crucial question.

COPYRIGHT PROTECTION AND INFRINGEMENT

Until 1989 when the provisions of the Berne Convention (see page 506) became applicable to American copyright law, a work would not be protected from infringement unless it contained a **copyright notice.** Failure to affix a notice meant the automatic loss of most copyright protection. Under international law, however, the affixing of a copyright notice is not required to protect a work. Once a work is created it is protected. American law now states that a

60. *Savage* v. *Council on American-Islamic Relations Inc.*, 36 M.L.R. 2089 (2008).

copyright notice "may" be placed on works that are publicly distributed. The U.S. Copyright office, however, still strongly urges creators to include notice on all their works. Copyright law protects the "innocent infringer" from liability for infringement. Someone who copies a work that does not contain a notice could claim an innocent infringement; that is, could argue that she did not realize the work she copied was actually protected by copyright. Although the absence of notice doesn't guarantee a finding of innocent infringement, putting notice on a work eliminates the possibility of an innocent infringement defense. Placing a proper notice on the work is simply prudent behavior.

COPYRIGHT NOTICE

A copyright notice should contain the word "Copyright," the abbreviation "Copr." or the symbol © (the letter *C* within a circle; the symbol ℗ is used on phonorecords). The year of publication must also be included in the notice. For periodicals the date supplied is the date of publication. For books the date is the year in which the book is first offered for sale (e.g., a book printed in November or December 2008 to go on sale January 2009 should carry a 2009 copyright). The notice must also contain the name of the copyright holder or owner. Most authorities recommend that both the word "Copyright" and the symbol © be used, since the use of the symbol is required to meet the standards of the international copyright agreements. The symbol © protects the work from piracy in most foreign countries. A copyright notice should look something like this:

> Copyright © 2010 by Jane Adams

The copyright notice can be placed anywhere that it "can be visually perceived" on all publicly distributed copies.

The copyright notice can be placed anywhere that it "can be visually perceived" on all publicly distributed copies. (The rules are different for sound recordings, which by nature cannot be visually perceived.) The Copyright Office of the Library of Congress has issued rules that implement the statutory description that the notice be visually perceptible. For example, the rules list eight different places where a copyright notice might be put in a book, including the title page, the page immediately following the title page, either side of the front cover and so forth. For photographs, a copyright notice label can be affixed to the back or front of a picture or on any mounting or framing to which the photographs are *permanently* attached.*

The law also provides that omission of the proper notice does not destroy copyright protection for the work if the notice is omitted from only a relatively small number of copies, if an effort is made within five years to correct the omission, or if the notice is omitted in violation of the copyright holder's express requirement that as a condition of publication the work carry a copyright notice.

At the same time, the law protects people who copy a work on which the copyright notice was inadvertently omitted. Such an innocent infringer incurs no liability—cannot be sued—unless this infringement continues beyond the time notice is received that the work has been copyrighted.

---

*The U.S. Copyright Office has available information regarding all matters relating to copyright law, including how to affix a proper copyright notice (http://www.copyright.gov/).

REGISTRATION

Under the law, once a work is created and fixed in a tangible medium it is protected by copyright. Putting notice on the work is not required, but strongly advised. The work is then protected for the life of the author plus 70 years. However, before a copyright holder can sue for infringement under the law, the copyrighted work must be registered with the federal government. To register a work the author or owner must do three things:

1. Fill out the proper registration form. The type of form varies, depending on the kind of work being registered. The forms are available from the Information and Publications Section, Copyright Office, Library of Congress, Washington, D.C. Registration forms for some kinds of material are available through the Internet.

2. Pay a $45 fee. (The fee is $35 for online registration.)

3. Deposit two complete copies of the work with the Copyright Office. (One complete copy is all that is required for unpublished works.)

The statute gives an author or owner 90 days to register a work. What happens if the work is still not registered after 90 days and an infringement takes place? The owner can still register the work and bring suit. But a successful plaintiff in such a suit cannot win statutory damages (see page 545) or win compensation for attorney fees. It is best to get into the habit of registering a work as soon as it is published or broadcast. Courts are of at least two minds regarding when a work is officially registered. Some courts have said a work is not registered— prohibiting a court from exercising jurisdiction in a case—until a certificate of registration is actually issued by the Copyright Office.[61] Other courts have ruled that official registration begins once the registration application has been mailed to the Copyright Office.[62]

INFRINGEMENT

Litigating intellectual property lawsuits has become a burgeoning cottage industry in the United States as the Muses of the creators of books, films, songs, articles and photos are seemingly unable to keep up with the insatiable appetite of the mass media for new products. A careful newspaper reader will routinely see references to new infringement actions. Most of these lawsuits don't amount to much, but they all play havoc with film producers, book publishers and others. In the spring of 2001 a woman named Nancy Stouffer sued author J.K. Rowling and the publishers of the celebrated Harry Potter books. Stouffer claimed that much earlier she had published a series of books about a bespectacled boy named Larry Potter, books that feature a set of characters called "muggles." For the uninitiated, muggles are also characters in the Harry Potter stories. Stouffer's attorneys claimed that Rowling had pirated the term, and because the Harry Potter books are so popular, the market for Stouffer's muggle merchandise dried up.[63] In September 2002 a federal judge rejected the infringement claim, saying he found only minimal similarities between the Harry Potter books and books written

61. See *Goebel* v. *Manis,* 39 F. Supp. 2d 1318 (1999), for example.

62. *Denenberg* v. *Berman,* D. Neb. No. 4: 02CV7, 7/23/02; and *Well-Made Toy Mfg. Corp.* v. *Goffa Intern Corp.,* 210 F. Supp. 2d 147 (2002), for example.

63. Kirkpatrick, "Harry Potter."

by Stouffer. In addition, the court found that the plaintiff had submitted fraudulent claims and lied in testimony.[64]

People who believe their exclusive right to control the use of a copyrighted work has been violated will sue for infringement. The federal copyright statute does not actually define infringement. The law simply states that anyone who violates any of the "exclusive rights" of the copyright holder is guilty of an infringement of copyright. Courts that litigate copyright cases seem to focus most often on three criteria to determine whether a particular use is an infringement (see following boxed text). A brief outline of each of these three points follows.

- Is the copyright on the plaintiff's work valid? While this inquiry will look at matters such as the proper registration of the work, the heart of this examination is to determine whether the copyrighted work is an original work that can be protected by copyright.
- Did the defendant have access to the plaintiff's work prior to the alleged infringement?
- Are the two works the same or substantially similar?

Originality of the Plaintiff's Work

The copyright on the plaintiff's work must be valid before a successful infringement suit can be maintained. As has been previously noted, a work that is not original cannot be protected by copyright. When a work is initially copyrighted there is no government assessment of whether it is original and can be legitimately copyrighted. The question of originality arises only if a lawsuit ensues. A central question, then, in many infringement suits is whether the plaintiff's work is original, or if the plaintiff is attempting to bring suit on the basis of the theft of material that cannot be legally copyrighted because it lacks originality or novelty.

History, for example, exists for all to use in a book or a story. Margaret Alexander brought an infringement suit against Alex Haley, claiming that he had copied portions of her novel "Jubilee" and her pamphlet "How I Wrote Jubilee" when he wrote and published his successful novel "Roots" in 1976. But the court noted that most of what Alexander claimed Haley had stolen was history—the story of the slave culture in the United States—or material in the public domain, such as folktales about early American black culture. "Where common sources exist for the alleged similarities, or the material that is similar is not original with the plaintiff, there is no infringement," the court ruled.[65]

Courts have also ruled that what are called "scènes à faire" are also uncopyrightable. These are situations and incidents in a story that flow naturally from the basic plot premise. Take, for example, the concept of a dinosaur zoo, which is not copyrightable. Elements like electrified fences, automated tours, dinosaur nurseries, uniformed workers are scènes à faire that flow from the basic premise of a dinosaur zoo—and these can't be protected by copyright either.

---

64. "In a Plagiarism Case."
65. *Alexander* v. *Haley,* 460 F. Supp. 40 (1978).

An NBC employee sued the network, arguing that he had originally proposed the concept for the highly successful "Bill Cosby Show" in 1980, some four years before the television program premiered. At that time NBC said it was not interested in the idea, the plaintiff said. But the court said that there was really nothing original in the concept proposed by plaintiff Hwesu Murray or in the Cosby show itself, for that matter. It merely combined two ideas that had been circulating for years: a family situation comedy, and the casting of blacks in nonstereotypical roles. The portrayal of a nonstereotypical black family in a half-hour show was a breakthrough in television broadcasting, the court noted, comparing the Cosby program with shows like "The Jeffersons," "Good Times," "Diff'rent Strokes" and "Sanford and Son," all of which featured blacks in fairly stereotypical roles. But the fact that such a show had never before been broadcast does not necessarily mean that the idea for the program itself was novel. "Whereas here, an idea consists in essence of nothing more than a variation on a basic theme—in this case the family situation comedy—novelty cannot be found."[66]

Access

The second dimension of an infringement suit is access: The plaintiff must convince the court that the defendant had access to the copyrighted work. An opportunity to copy has to exist. If plaintiffs cannot prove that the so-called literary pirate had a chance to see and read the work, they are hard-pressed to prove piracy. As Judge Learned Hand once wrote:

> If by some magic a man who had never known it were to compose anew Keats's, "Ode on a Grecian Urn," he would be an 'author' and if he copyrighted it, others might not copy that poem, though they might of course copy Keats's.[67]

Translating Hand's reference to John Keats' early 19th-century poem into contemporary terms, consider this hypothetical situation. A young woman, who has lived all her life on a deserted island, with no exposure to outside influences, manages to write and then publish an exact duplicate of John Grisham's novel "The Last Juror." Grisham would be hard-pressed to win a copyright infringement case because he would be unable to show that the young writer had access to his work. Obviously, such a scenario is unlikely to occur. But it makes the point. The plaintiff must prove not simply that the two works are the same, but that the defendant stole his work. To do that there must be proof that the defendant had access to the stolen work.

In 1998 Marion Leon Bea sued Home Box Office (HBO), claiming it had infringed on his script for a film called "N and Out" when it made the HBO motion picture "First Time Felon." The similarities between the two scripts were thin, the court noted. But what killed the suit was the plaintiff's inability to prove that HBO had access to his script before "First Time Felon" was produced.[68] Failure to prove that the defendant had access to a copyrighted book was also fatal to a lawsuit brought by Sonya Jason against the writers and producers of the 1978 film "Coming Home." Defendants Jane Fonda and others stated that their film was conceived in the late 1960s, that a first draft of the screenplay was completed by late 1973 and was revised in 1977. Jason's book, "Concomitant Soldier," was first printed in April 1974. Only

There must be proof that the defendant had access to the stolen work.

---

66. *Murray* v. *NBC,* 844 F. 2d 988 (1988).
67. *Sheldon* v. *Metro-Goldwyn-Mayer Pictures,* 81 F. 2d 49 (1939).
68. *Bea* v. *Home Box Office,* 26 M.L.R. 2373 (1998).

1,100 copies were printed. About 500 copies were sold in New Jersey, 100 were sold through the plaintiff's church, 200 copies were returned to the printer because they were defective, and the remaining copies were sold in Southern California. Jason claimed that a copy of the book might have been given to Nancy Dowd, a screenwriter for the film, but there was no evidence that Dowd or anyone else connected with the film had seen the book. Jason was able to prove only that several hundred copies of "Concomitant Soldier" were sold in Southern California where Fonda, Dowd and others associated with the film lived and worked. "That level of availability creates no more than a 'bare possibility' that defendants may have had access to plaintiff's book," the court said. "In and of itself, such a bare possibility is insufficient to create a genuine issue of whether defendants copied plaintiff's book."[69]

Copying and Substantial Similarity

The final factor a court will consider is whether the defendant copied the plaintiff's work. In some cases evidences of such copying is irrefutable. The defendant has dubbed copies of a DVD or CD, or has reprinted a short story or a song lyric, or simply used too much of the defendant's work in his or her work. In one of the most celebrated copyright disputes of the past decade, Harry Potter author J.K. Rowling sued the publisher of "The Harry Potter Lexicon" for copyright infringement. The lexicon stemmed from a Web site of the same name, the creation of a 50-year-old middle school librarian (and huge fan of the Potter books) named Stephen Jan Vander Ark. There are scores of Web sites and chat rooms devoted to the book series, and Rowling has supported most of them. But when RDR books announced plans to publish the lexicon—a kind of guidebook to the Potter stories—Rowling brought suit against the publisher. The plaintiffs in the case argued that the lexicon merely "compiles and repackages Ms. Rowling's fictional facts derived wholesale from the Harry Potter works without adding any new creativity, insight or criticism." RDR argued that the book provided a significant amount of original analysis and commentary concerning everything—the characters, relationships among them, the meaning of literary allusions, and so on.[70] The U.S. District Court in New York agreed with Rowling in September 2008, ruling that the works were substantially similar. There was too much of Rowling's work in the lexicon.[71] RDR announced that it would appeal the ruling.[72]

In other instances it is a bit more complicated. A photo looks a lot like a copyrighted picture, for example. In these cases judges must often take on the role of art critic to flesh out the differences between two seemingly identical works. In 1993 Random House commissioned Jack Leigh to photograph the Bird Girl statue in the Bonaventure Cemetery in Savannah, Ga., to use on the cover of a novel it was publishing called "Midnight in the Garden of Good and Evil." The book was successful and the photo became famous. When Warner Brothers made the book into a film, it wanted to use a similar photo in its advertising for the motion picture. But the owner of the statue, which had become famous because of the

---

69. *Jason* v. *Fonda,* 526 F. Supp. 774 (1981).
70. Rich, "Rowling to Testify."
71. Eligon, "Judge Rules for Rowling."
72. "Appeal Is Filed."

Leigh photo, had removed the object from the cemetery. With the statue owner's permission, the film studio had a replica crafted, took it to the cemetery, and had it photographed for promotion of the movie. When the movie came out, Leigh sued for copyright infringement. Warner Brothers had not used Leigh's picture, but it had generated a photo that was remarkably similar to the original. Judges at the 11th U.S. Circuit Court of Appeals had to analyze the similarities and differences between the two. There was a difference in the contrast of the lighting; the statue was smaller and more distant in the Warner Brothers photo; the movie poster picture had a green/orange tint; and there was a Celtic cross on the new statue. But both photos were taken from the same low angle; hanging Spanish moss bordered both photos; the statue was in the center of both pictures; the light source is from above in both shots; and the remainder of the cemetery is obscured. In this case the court ruled that there were sufficient similarities to preclude a summary judgment for Warner Brothers and sent the case back for a jury trial.[73]

More often than not, however, direct or literal copying is not an issue. In these cases the defendant is not accused of taking a particular line or segment of a work, but of appropriating "the fundamental essence or structure of the work." There must be more than minor similarities between the two works; they must be *substantially similar.* But this is another instance in which it is easier to state a rule than to apply it. How can you determine whether two works are substantially similar? Courts use a variety of tests to determine substantial similarity, but virtually all the tests focus on two aspects of the work. The courts will first ask whether the general idea or general theme of the works is the same. If the general idea of the two works is not similar, there is no infringement. Daryl Murphy filmed a documentary about the tenants residing in Chicago Housing Authority Projects. The motion picture included interviews with people who lived or had lived in the projects, and video of scenery, buildings, family gatherings and so on. Nine months later the television cartoon series "PJs" aired. It was also set in an urban housing project. Murphy sued the producers of the program, including comedian Eddie Murphy, for infringement of copyright. The federal district court ruled that the two creations were not substantially similar. The plaintiff's film is a documentary about the lives of real people living in the projects. "PJs" is a cartoon comedy. The documentary consists of disconnected series of interviews with real people. The cartoon is fiction and has a plot line in each episode. The look and feel of the two are entirely different.[74]

If the general idea in the two works is substantially similar, the court must then take a second step and look to see how the idea or concept is expressed in the works. How is the theme carried out? Some recent cases make this point. Tommy Pino sued Viacom Inc. for infringement because, he said, the defendant's reality TV show, "Pros vs. Joes," was similar to a program he proposed in a script treatment and a screenplay he submitted to a variety of agents and TV networks—including CBS, which is owned by Viacom. Both the program and Pino's proposal focused on a sports reality show featuring contests between professional athletes and amateurs. The federal court acknowledged the similarity, but the manner in which the program and the proposal developed the idea was substantially different. The plots were different, the dialogue was different, the mood was different, and the setting and pace were different. Outside of a few stock elements and the general idea, the two were not

---

73. *Leigh* v. *Warner Brothers Inc.,* 212 F. 3d 1210 (2000).
74. *Murphy* v. *Murphy*, 35 M.L.R. 1716 (2007).

substantially similar.[75] A federal court in California reached the same conclusion when E.W. Scripps Co., which owned the Food Network, was sued for infringement by an individual who claimed the Rachel Ray program, "Inside Dish," infringed on his proposal for a celebrity chef cooking show called 'Showbiz Chef." The concept behind the two shows, a talk show that features celebrity chefs as guests, was similar, but these elements cannot be protected by copyright. There was no similarity in the way the basic elements were carried out. The plots were different (the plaintiff's program had no discernable plot), the dialogue was not the same, the mood and the setting were dissimilar ("Showbiz Chef" was to be telecast from a celebrity's home, whereas the Rachel Ray show was taped at a studio), the sequence of events in the shows was not the same. No reasonable jury could conclude the shows were substantially similar, the court said.[76]

Gwen O'Donnell sued Time Warner Entertainment for infringement claiming the HBO series "Six Feet Under" was a copy of a story she had drafted in the late 1990s called "The Funk Parlor." O'Donnell's story traces the lives of people who run a small, family-owned funeral parlor in Connecticut. The HBO series is also set in a funeral parlor, but in Los Angeles. Both O'Donnell's screenplay and "Six Feet Under" commence with the death of a father and the return of a prodigal son. But the U.S. Court of Appeals ruled that was about the only similarity between the two. The death of the father in "The Funk Parlor" sets the stage for a series of additional murders. The characters, moods, themes, pace, dialogue and sequence of events is different in "Six Feet Under," the court said. "'The Funk Parlor,' a murder mystery, is driven by a series of murders, which catalyze the salvation of the business. The use of death in 'Six Feet Under' is quite different; there, death provides the focal point for exploring relationships and existential meaning," the court said. The works are not substantially similar.[77]

It is not easy to prove infringement of copyright; yet surprisingly, a large number of suits are settled each year in favor of plaintiffs. Most of these cases are settled out of court. In such instances the obvious theft of the material would generally appall an honest person. An individual who works to be creative in fashioning a story or a play or a piece of art usually has little to fear. The best and simplest way to avoid a suit for infringement is simply to do your own work, to be original.

COPYRIGHT INFRINGEMENT AND THE INTERNET

The law regulating mass media has had to adapt to changes in media technology many times in the past 219 years. When the nation's first copyright law was adopted, printed material comprised the mass media. But since then, the law has been forced to cope with photography, radio, motion pictures, sound recordings, television, audio- and videotaping, photocopying, computer programs, CD-ROM and so on. But no technology has challenged the law to the extent the Internet has. By its very nature the new medium lends itself to the theft of the work of others. As one legal expert noted, digitized information can be copied quickly, easily and cheaply, and the copy is every bit as good as the original. Once the information is copied, it can be easily distributed via the Web to receivers who can make their own copies of

75. *Pino* v. *Viacom Inc.*, 36 M.L.R. 1678 (2008).
76. *Zella* v. *E.W. Scripps Co.*, 36 M.L.R. 1353 (2007); See also *Rosenfeld* v. *Twentieth Century Fox Film Corp.*, 37 M.L.R. 1348 (2009).
77. *Funky Films Inc.* v. *Time Warner Entertainment Co.*, 34 M.L.R. 2345 (2006).

the material and further distribute it: an almost endless chain. Copyright issues involving computer-generated communication are commonplace today. Stories regarding lawsuits appear almost daily in the press. "Google settles over book copyrights," "Labels Win Suit Against Song Sharer" and "Blogger Arrested for Leaking Songs from Unreleased Guns N' Roses Album" are just three examples of recent headlines. And the owner of the copyright can be left out completely. Publishers and authors sued Google in 2009 after it announced a plan to scan all the books in the world; those in the public domain and those protected by copyright. The online giant settled the lawsuit by promising to charge customers who read the books, and share the revenues with the copyright holders. The copyright holder will also get a flat fee for the initial scanning, or can opt out of the scanning system.[78]

The ease of copying and distribution is only one problem. Many Internet users apparently don't believe that other people's works should enjoy copyright protection. When cartoonist Gary Larson pleaded with Web users to stop duplicating his "The Far Side" cartoons on the Internet, a substantial number of users replied that they would not cease the practice. "All this copyright infringement enforcing ticks me off," one user responded. "What is the Net for if we can't view a Far Side cartoon, or listen to a sound file from the Simpsons," the user asked rhetorically. There have always been people who disdained the notion that a writer or photographer should be able to protect his or her own work. But until the Internet, all that most of these people could do was steal it for themselves: illegally dub a CD or a movie, photocopy a series of short stories. Now it is possible for an individual not only to make the illegal copy, but to distribute it to 100,000 of his or her close friends in a matter of seconds.

The courts have been applying traditional copyright law to these new problems with some success. And some jurists say the application of existing law is all that is required to solve the problems. "New technologies—from television, to video cassette recorders, to digitized transmissions—have all been made to fit within the overall scheme of copyright law and to serve the ends to which copyright was intended to promote," wrote U.S. District Judge Leonie Brinkema. "The Internet is no exception."[79] Other observers say they believe that new laws are needed.

Digital Millennium Copyright Act

An international group, the World Intellectual Property Organization, framed new copyright rules in two treaties in the mid-1990s that give copyright protection to the owners of digitized works. The treaties also provide for the fair-use defense in cyberspace.[80] The United States agreed to abide by these new rules in adopting the Digital Millennium Copyright Act (DMCA) in 1998. But this law went beyond the WIPO treaties and also prevents the circumvention of technological measures that control access to copyrighted works—so-called encryption codes—and outlaws the manufacture, importation or sale of devices used to circumvent such protections. In the summer of 2001, a 27-year-old Russian cryptographer

---

78. Johnson-Laird, "Exploring the Information Superhighway"; and Cohen, "A Google Search."
79. *Religious Technology Center* v. *Lerma,* 24 M.L.R. 2473 (1996).
80. Schiesel, "Global Agreement Reached."

named Dmitry Sklyarov was arrested in Las Vegas after giving a presentation to a convention of computer hackers on ways to decrypt the software used to protect electronic books. Six months later the government agreed to defer the prosecution of Sklyarov in return for his promise to testify against his employer, Elcomsoft, a Russian software company. A basic question in this case and others that spring from this section of the 1998 act is this: *Can the government make it a crime to manufacture and sell a device that can be used to circumvent copyright protection if that device can be used for other, legal purposes as well?* In 1984 the Supreme Court was asked that question about another technological invention, the videocassette recorder (VCR). Hollywood television production companies sought to stop the sale of the new device in the United States because it could be used to make copies of the copyrighted programs broadcast on television. At that time the Supreme Court ruled that even though some people may use the device illegally, there were numerous legal purposes for the VCR as well. The manufacturer of the machine could not be held liable for those who used the device illegally.[81] But times have changed, people in the entertainment industry argue. Copying protected material has become too easy and can be done too rapidly for rights holders to catch up with the illegal users. It is time to ban the devices. This is a basic legal issue in any case to determine whether software or hardware violates the DMCA. Does the machine or the program that permits illegal activity have functions that are clearly legal as well? Federal courts have upheld the constitutionality of the DMCA.[82] The 2nd U.S. Court of Appeals agreed that computer code is protected by the First Amendment but said a narrowly drawn statute—like the DMCA—would not violate the Constitution. But the issue is far from resolved, as more litigation enters the halls of justice. The law carries criminal penalties, a possible $500,000 fine and a five-year jail sentence. The 1998 law also imposes a compulsory licensing and royalty scheme for the transmission of music on the Internet similar to the scheme used to collect royalties for music broadcast on radio or television and exempts Internet service providers (ISPs) from copyright liability for simply transmitting copyrighted material users have put on the Internet.

This last provision may soon get a serious court test because of YouTube, the video-sharing Web site owned by Google. YouTube, a free online site (the company makes its money by carrying advertising), was founded in 2005 and allows anyone to upload and download video footage. The site carries hundreds of thousands of video clips, many of them copyrighted material. In 2007, Viacom, the parent company of MTV and Comedy Central, demanded that YouTube remove more than 100,000 clips of video the company says it owns. Viacom also demanded that YouTube begin automatically filtering out material that is obviously copyrighted. After making the demand, Viacom filed a $1 billion copyright infringement suit against Google. YouTube began removing material owned by Viacom while it evaluated the merits of the lawsuit. Other companies like NBC Universal, the Walt Disney Company and News Corporation were also negotiating with the site, asking that YouTube either remove copyrighted material, or begin paying a licensing fee for the use of the material. YouTube contends that as long as it removes copyrighted material when asked to, it is immune from legal liability because of the DMCA. A federal court may have to make that decision. John G.

81. *Sony Corp.* v. *Universal City Studios, Inc.,* 464 U.S. 417 (1984).
82. *Universal City Studios, Inc.* v. *Corley,* 2d Cir., No. 00-9185, 11/28/01. See also *Felten* v. *Recording Industry Association of America,* D.N.J., No. CV-01-2669 (GEB), 11/27/01.

Paltrey Jr., the executive director of the Berkman Center for Internet and Society at Harvard Law School, told The New York Times in 2007 that while YouTube may be able to use this defense, "I don't think the law is entirely clear." And if the company loses the argument, the damages could be astronomically high, he added.[83]

This lawsuit was proceeding as this chapter was prepared. In July of 2008 a federal judge ordered YouTube to give Viacom data outlining what viewers were watching which videos. This order involved a staggering amount of data, since in April alone 82 million people in the United States watched 4.1 billion video clips on the site, according to one source. While the lawsuit simmered, YouTube began to remove video clips that had been prepared by amateurs that contained copyrighted material, such as music. A spokesperson for the Warner Music Group, one of the plaintiffs in the suit against YouTube, said that the popular site generates revenues from content posted by fans, which typically requires licenses from rights holders. The music company makes YouTube aware of videos containing its copyrighted content, and then the YouTube ID tool takes down the unlicensed tracks, regardless of whether they are professionally made music videos or amateur material. An example of one of the items removed was a video of a high school sophomore who recorded herself playing the piano and singing "Winter Wonderland," a copyrighted song.[84]

File Sharing

File sharing, or the ability of computer users to move files from one computer to another or a great many other computers, caused some of the most perplexing and widely publicized copyright problems during the past decade. But by late 2009 file sharing had ceased to be a primary issue in copyright litigation; not because the questions had been resolved, but because this was a problem that appeared to be intractable. Every time a legal solution was fashioned, new technology allowed file sharers to bypass the legal limits put in place. At some point, leaders of especially the recording industry concluded that there was little more they could do to stop the widespread sharing of music. As someone said, the genie was out of the bottle.

The theft of recorded music via the Internet wasn't a serious problem until the late 1990s because it took too long to download a song. But the development of inexpensive data compression technology solved this problem, and the introduction of MP3 players, which brought this technology within reach of music lovers, resulted in the dramatic growth of illegal music file sharing. The music industry tried to block the manufacture and sale of the MP3 players, but the courts ruled they were simply space shifters, not audio recording devices. "The player merely makes copies in order to render portable . . . files that already reside in a user's hard drive," the court said, comparing the new device to a home video recorder, which the Supreme Court had ruled was legal.[85]

File-sharing services like Napster, StreamCast Networks, Grokster and many others began to spring up, facilitating the free transfer of copyrighted music, giving music fans access to recorded music without having to purchase a CD. One by one these services were

83. Fabrikant and Hansell, "Viacom Tells YouTube."
84. Helft, "Google Told to Turn Over"; and Arango, "Rights Clash on YouTube."
85. *Recording Industry Association of America* v. *Diamond Multimedia Systems,* 9th Cir., No. 98-56727, 6/15/99.

sued for abetting copyright infringement, and for the most part, the courts supported the recording industry in its attempts to stop the piracy.[86]* But the litigation was costly, time-consuming and did not end the problems generated by file sharing, as new, slightly different services sprang up. The industry then began to attack the file sharers themselves, individuals who used the peer-to-peer music sharing systems. From 2003 to the end of 2008 the Recording Industry of America (RIAA), the trade group representing the recording industry, sued about 35,000 people for swapping songs online. Judgments or settlements averaged about $3,500 in these cases—hardly worth the cost of the lawsuit.[87]

While this was happening Apple introduced the iPod and later the iPhone, two new devices for downloading music. Coupled with iTunes and other Web sites where music could be legally purchased, access to legal downloads became relatively commonplace. The recording companies made deals with Apple (and other device makers like Microsoft which introduced the Zune) to provide access to their recorded music and waived their digital copyrights for a small per-song fee. Songs generally cost 99 cents, with the label getting 70 cents and Apple (or whomever) getting the rest. By 2009 Apple was the nation's largest marketer of recorded music. These developments substantially reduced the illegal file-sharing problem, with the legitimate sale of digital music tracks rising for the first time in years. At the end of 2008 the RIAA announced it would cease suing individual file sharers, and instead work with Internet service providers to cut abusers' access if they ignore repeated warnings.

By the time this chapter is published new technology will undoubtedly be on the market that could change the music-sharing equation in even other ways. In early 2009 many experts were predicting that the future of music buying is over mobile phones, not buying individual songs but by paying a monthly subscription to hear a vast database of music.[88] Stay tuned for further developments.

FILM AND TELEVISION

Both the film and television industries—in many cases the same companies produce products for both—face problems similar to those experienced by the recording industry. At a time when DVD sales are shrinking, network television audiences are getting smaller, and theater attendance is barely holding even, the video industry is losing billions of dollars ($7.1 billion in 2005) to piracy. Illegal downloading of movies has been a problem for several years. In April of 2009 a television comedian joked that during the previous weekend one million people had watched the movie "X-Men Origins: Wolverine." "Of course," he noted, "the film doesn't open until May 1." There were even some published reviews of the pirated film.

---

*In 2009 a Swedish court convicted four men for their involvement in an Internet file-sharing service, the Pirate Bay, of violating copyright laws.

86. *APM Records Inc.* v. *Napster Inc.,* 239 F. 3d 1004 (2001); *Metro-Goldwyn-Mayer Studios Inc.* v. *Grokster Ltd.,* 125 S. Ct. 2264 (2005).

87. Nakashima, "Music Industry Desists." In 2009, however, a jury decided that a Boston University graduate student who admitted to downloading more than 800 songs from the Internet should pay damages totaling $675,000.

88. Arango, "Despite iTunes Accord."

While downloading was the piracy method of choice, more recently the industry has had to face a new threat—streaming technology that makes TV shows and films instantly available. SurfTheChannel.com, a Swedish site, provides users with links to several sites in China and other countries that use the streaming technology to allow viewers instant access to the pirated copies. What SurfTheChannel does is legal, their spokespersons argue, because the pirated content isn't on SurfTheChannel's network. But others argue that anyone linking users to copyrighted content knows or should know that what he or she is doing is illegal.

The use of camcorders in theaters accounts for most piracy, but many video products are stolen or copied during the production process. To combat the problem, many studios are releasing both older and new TV shows for free viewing online. And contrary to previous practice, many major feature films are being released on the same day worldwide, not on staggered dates. The industry believes most people would rather pay to see a high-quality copy of a film, so long as they can see it as soon as it is released for commercial distribution.[89]

POLITICS AND COPYRIGHT

The 2008 political campaign was the first to highlight the fact that candidates are increasingly using the Internet to spread their political messages. But candidates are discovering that some copyright holders are using provisions in the 1998 Digital Millennium Copyright Act (DMCA) to block (one observer described it as censoring) their messages. The law states that a Web carrier cannot be held liable for transmitting copyrighted material without the permission of the owner so long as it quickly removes that material when informed by the copyright owner that it is infringing on the copyright. (See pages 537–539.) The DMCA requires immediate removal; there is no time for a hearing on whether the use may be a fair use. That would come later, if it comes at all.

During the election campaign, Fox News ordered John McCain to stop using a clip of him taken from a Fox-moderated political debate. The Warner Music Group demanded that YouTube remove an amateur video attacking Barack Obama that included music owned by the Warner Music Group. Less than three weeks before the 2008 election network news organizations told YouTube to remove McCain commercials that included snippets of their copyrighted news broadcasts.[90] Some authorities, like Stanford law professor Lawrence Lessig, have argued that in the instances just recounted and others, the use would surely qualify as a fair use. But there is no time to get such a court ruling during a hectic, fast-moving political campaign. Lessig argues that the DMCA should be amended to make it clear it was not intended to be used as it has been during the campaign, but only to protect copyright holders who might suffer serious economic harm if the material is not removed from the transmitting site.[91]

Sen. McCain's run-in with copyright law during the campaign didn't stop with issues regarding the DMCA. He was sued by singer-songwriter Jackson Browne who claimed McCain's campaign used his song "Running on Empty" in a commercial without permission. Browne supported Obama in the campaign. A U.S. District Court in February 2009 rejected McCain's motion for a summary judgment and set a date for a jury trial. But the lawsuit was

89. Fixmer, "Surfing Pirates."
90. Hansell, "McCain in Fight."
91. Lessig, "Copyright and Politics."

settled when the Republican Party and McCain apologized to Browne, and pledged to respect all musicians' copyrights in the future. In April of 2009 another popular singer-songwriter, Don Henley, a founding member of The Eagles, sued Charles DeVore, a Republican candidate for the U.S. Senate in California, for copyright infringement for using two of his songs, "The Boys of Summer" and "All She Wants to Do Is Dance," in campaign videos.[92]

The file-sharing dilemma is a scenario that is still playing out. And the law of copyright is rife with other problems related to the Internet as well. The uploading, distribution and downloading of copyrighted photographs is a serious matter—especially from publications like Playboy where the photos (as well as the serious articles and essays) entice most people to buy the magazine.[93] The question of whether ISPs are liable for infringement when they act as a passive conduit for photos posted by their customers is an emerging issue, with at least one court ruling that the ISPs were not liable under the federal copyright law.[94]

SUMMARY

To protect the copyright of a work, the author or owner should give proper notice and register the work with the government. A proper copyright notice looks like this:

Copyright © 2010 by Jane Adams (use the symbol ℗ for phonorecords)

Notice must be placed where it can be visually perceived. To gain the full benefits of the law, a work must be registered with the Copyright Office in the Library of Congress as well. The proper registration form along with $45 and two complete copies of the work must be sent to the Register of Copyrights. (The fee is $35 for online registration.)

When a plaintiff sues for infringement of copyright, the court will consider three important criteria. First, is the plaintiff's work original? If the plaintiff has attempted to copyright material that legitimately belongs in the public domain, the plaintiff cannot sue for infringement of copyright. Second, did the defendant have access to the plaintiff's work? There must be some evidence that the defendant viewed or heard the copyrighted work before the alleged infringement took place. Finally, is there evidence that the defendant actually copied the plaintiff's work? If no such evidence exists, are the two works substantially similar? In examining this last issue, the court seeks to determine whether the ideas in the two works are similar. If the general idea of the two works is similar, is the expression of these ideas similar as well? Problems of copyright infringement via the Internet are just beginning to be litigated, with both traditional copyright law and new statutes being applied by the courts.

Litigation on the breadth and meaning of the Digital Millennium Copyright Act is just beginning, while the recording industry's battle with peer-to-peer file sharers appears to be coming to an end. The film and TV industries, however, are facing new challenges with video pirates.

92. "Jackson Browne"; and "Don Henley Sues."
93. *Playboy Enterprises, Inc.* v. *Starware Publishers Corp.,* 900 F. Supp. 433 (1995); and *Playboy Enterprises, Inc.* v. *George Frena,* 839 F. Supp. 1552 (1993).
94. *CoStar Group Inc.* v. *LoopNet Inc.,* 4th Cir., No. 03-1911, 6/21/04.

FREELANCING AND COPYRIGHT

What rights does a freelance journalist, author or photographer hold with regard to stories or pictures that are sold to publishers? The writer or photographer is the creator of the work; he or she owns the story or the photograph. Consequently, as many rights as such freelancers choose to relinquish can be sold or given to a publisher. Beginning writers and photographers often do not have much choice but to follow the policy of the book or magazine publisher. Authors whose works are in demand, however, can retain most rights to the material for their future benefit. Most publishers have established policies on exactly what rights they purchase when they decide to buy a story or photograph or drawing. The annual edition of "The Writer's Market" is the best reference guide for the freelancer. The boxed text lists some of the rights that publishers might buy.

1. *All rights:* The creator sells complete ownership of the story or photograph.

2. *First serial rights:* The buyer has the right to use the piece of writing or picture for the first time in a periodical published anywhere in the world. But the publisher can use it only once, and then the creator can sell it to someone else.

3. *First North American serial rights:* The rights are the same as those provided in number 2, except the publisher buys the right to publish the material first in North America, not anywhere in the world.

4. *Simultaneous rights:* The publisher buys the right to print the material at the same time other periodicals print the material. All the publishers, however, must be aware that simultaneous publication will occur.

5. *One-time rights:* The publisher purchases the right to use a piece just one time, and there is no guarantee that it has not been published elsewhere first.

It is a common practice for publishers to buy all rights to a story or photograph but to agree to reassign the rights to the creator after publication. In such cases the burden of initiating the reassignment rests with the writer or photographer, who must request reassignment immediately following publication. The publisher signs a transfer of rights to the creator, and the creator should record this transfer of rights with the Copyright Office within two or three weeks. When this transaction has taken place, the creator can then resell the material.

The sale of subsidiary or additional rights to publishers by freelance writers has become far more complicated and more serious with the technological developments of the past decade. The growth of huge databases on CD-ROM and in computer memories accessible through the Internet has magnified the consequences for both the writers and photographers and the publishers. There is considerable money to be made on all sides. Six writers who sold work to The New York Times, Newsday, Sports Illustrated and other publications objected when these publications sold the contents of the newspapers and magazines to the Mead Corp., which operates the LexisNexis database, and to University Microfilms, which produces The New York Times on disc. The writers argued they deserved at least a royalty payment. But a U.S. District Court ruled in favor of publishers in a lawsuit initiated by the freelance writers. U.S. copyright law, the court said, gave the owners of a collective work (like a newspaper or magazine) the right to reproduce and distribute any "revision" of that collective work without the permission of the contributors to that work. So when a freelance writer sold an article to a newspaper, the writer was also in effect giving the publisher of the paper the right to resell the article for inclusion on a CD-ROM or a database.[95] Two years later the 2nd U.S. Circuit Court of Appeals disagreed. The judges said that while a newspaper or magazine publisher did have the right to sell a revised edition of such a publication, the law was intended to apply to later editions of the newspaper or reissues of the magazine. Databases and CD-ROMs are not revised editions of the original publications. Databases contain many articles, the court noted, that may be retrieved according to criteria unrelated to the particular edition of the magazine or newspaper in which the articles first appear.[96] In June 2001 the Supreme Court sustained the appellate court ruling. Justice Ruth Bader Ginsburg, who wrote the opinion in the 7-2 ruling, said that publishers' "encompassing construction" of their republication rights was simply unacceptable. The massive databases, which include many published issues, "no more constitutes a revision of each constituent edition than a 400-page novel quoting a sonnet in passing would represent a revision of that poem," the justice wrote. Electronic databases are not simply modern versions of old-fashioned microfilm records, she added.[97]

But the *Tasini* ruling did not answer all questions regarding subsequent use of a free-lancer's material. After the U.S. Court of Appeals ruling in *Tasini,* but three months before the Supreme Court ruling, the 11th U.S. Court of Appeals ruled that the National Geographic Society (NGS) had infringed on a group of freelance photographers' copyrights when it published their work in a 30-disc CD-ROM version ("The Complete National Geographic") of the magazine. This electronic version contained every page of every issue published since 1888, so it was essentially like a huge bound volume of all the magazines. The NGS argued that it was simply republishing the original issues, a revision that is permitted under the law. The court disagreed, noting that the electronic edition contained some material not included in the original issues, notably some animated sequences and special interactive software. This was a new work, and violated the copyright of the photographers.[98]

But more than two years later a U.S. District Court ruled in an opposite fashion in a case involving the same NGS CD-ROM disc set in a lawsuit brought by a different set of freelance photographers. The court said the 11th Circuit had misread the law, which was clarified by the Supreme Court's *Tasini* decision. So long as an individual's work (the photographer's pictures) appears in its original context in the new version, it qualifies as a permissible reproduction or revision of a collective work. What distinguishes a revision from an entirely different work is the manner in which the freelancers' work is presented to the

95. *Tasini* v. *The New York Times,* 972 F. Supp. 804 (1997).
96. *Tasini* v. *The New York Times,* 192 F. 3d 356 (1999).
97. *New York Times Co.* v. *Tasini,* 121 S. Ct. 2381 (2001). In 2006 the Canadian Supreme Court adopted a rule for freelancers similar to the holding in this case.
98. *Greenberg* v. *National Geographic Society,* 244 F. 3d 1267 (2001).

user, the court said. In this case, the CD-ROM contains exactly the same pages as appeared in the original print editions of the magazine. The addition of the software, the animated opening sequence and music does not fundamentally change the manner in which the work is presented.[99] The 2nd U.S. Court of Appeals affirmed this decision in March 2005.[100] In 2007 the 11th U.S. Court of Appeals reversed its 2001 ruling and labeled the CD-ROM collection of National Geographic a priviledged revision of the print publication that does not infringe on the freelance photographers copyrights in the photos originally published in the print edition. The key question, the court said, was whether the original context of the collective work has been preserved in the revision. In this case it was.[101] What this means for freelancers seems to be this: As long as the photographer's or writer's work is not altered, and appears in its original context in the new version on CD-ROM, DVD, or online, the use is permissible and does not infringe on their copyright—even if other elements are added to the revised version.

Finally, a federal court in New York ruled in 2001 that the basic rights granted by an author to a publisher that include the right to publish a work in book form do not include the right to publish the work as an interactive e-book. A separate agreement would be needed to permit the publication of the electronic version of the work. The case was decided under state contract law rather than federal copyright law, but the ruling is regarded as being generally applicable in other jurisdictions. The 2nd U.S. Court of Appeals affirmed this ruling in 2002.[102]

Now, more than ever, writers and photographers should be careful in spelling out the exact rights being offered to a publisher. This clarification should be done in the original query letter offering the material or in the cover letter that accompanies the final product. Contracts should be read carefully, and beginners should be wary of statements included on payment checks. It is not uncommon for a publisher to include a statement on a royalty check to the effect that "the endorsement of this check constitutes a grant of reprint rights to the publisher." In order to cash the check, the writer must agree to grant the reprint rights. In such cases writers should quickly notify the publisher that such an agreement is unacceptable and demand immediate payment for the single use of the story. Other pitfalls too numerous to mention await the inexperienced freelancer. The best advice is to understand exactly what you are doing at all times during the negotiation of rights. Take nothing for granted; just because you are honest and ethical does not mean everyone else is. And if questions come up, consult a qualified attorney. Legal advice is costly, but it can save a writer or photographer money in the long run.

DAMAGES

Plaintiffs in a copyright suit can ask the court to assess the defendant for any damage they have suffered, plus the profits made by the infringer from pirating the protected work. Damages can be a little bit or a lot. In each case the plaintiff must prove to the court the amount of the loss or the amount of the defendant's profit. But, rather than prove actual damage, the plaintiff can ask the court to assess what are called statutory damages, or damage amounts prescribed by

99. *Faulkner* v. *National Geographic Society,* 294 F. Supp. 2d 523 (2003).
100. *Faulkner* v. *Mindscape Inc.,* 402 F. 3d 304 (2005).
101. *Greenberg* v. *National Geographic Society* 488 F. 3d 1331 (2007); aff'd 11th Cir. en banc., No. 05-16964 (2008).
102. *Random House Inc.* v. *Rosetta Books LLC,* 150 F. Supp. 2d 613 (2001), aff'd 2d Cir., No. 01-7912, 3/8/02.

the statute. The smallest statutory award is $750, although in the case of an innocent infringement, the court may use its discretion and lower the damage amount. The highest statutory award is $30,000. However, if the plaintiff can prove that the infringement was committed willfully and repeatedly, the maximum damage award can be as much as $150,000.

In addition, the courts have other powers in a copyright suit. A judge can restrain a defendant from continued infringement, can impound the material that contains the infringement and can order the destruction of these works. Impoundment and destruction are rare today. A defendant might also be charged with a criminal offense in a copyright infringement case. If the defendant infringed on a copyright "willfully and for purposes of commercial advantage or private financial gain," he or she could be fined and jailed for not more than one year.

The law of copyright is not difficult to understand and should not be a threat to most creative people in the mass media. The law simply says to do your own work and don't steal from the work of others. Some authorities argue that copyright is an infringement on freedom of the press. In a small way it probably is. Nevertheless most writers, authors and reporters—people who most often take advantage of freedom of the press—support copyright laws that protect their rights to property that they create. Judge Jerome Frank once attempted to explain this apparent contradiction by arguing that we are adept at concealing from ourselves the fact that we maintain and support "side by side as it were, beliefs which are inherently incompatible." Frank suggested that we keep these separate antagonistic beliefs in separate "logic-tight compartments."

The courts have recognized the needs of society as well as the needs of authors and have hence allowed considerable latitude for copying material that serves some public function. Because of this attitude, copyright law has little, or should have little, impact on the information-oriented mass media.

BIBLIOGRAPHY

"Appeal Is Filed in Potter Lexicon Case." *The New York Times*, 15 November 2008, B2.

Arango, Tim. "Despite iTunes Accord, Music Labels Still Fret." *The New York Times*, 2 February 2008, B1.

———. "Who Owns Sports Coverage." *The New York Times*, 21 April 2009, C1.

Benson, Ken, and Tim Arango. "With Bloggers in the Bleachers, Leagues See a Threat to Profits." *The New York Times*, 20 August 2009, A1.

———. "Rights Clash on YouTube." *The New York Times*, 3 March 2008, B1.

Cohen, Naomi. "A Google Search of a Distinctly Retro Kind." *The New York Times*, 4 March 2009, C1.

"Don Henley Sues Senate Candidate Over Song Use." CNN, 18 April 2009.

Dunlap, David W. "What Next? A Fee for Looking?" *The New York Times,* 22 August 1998, B1.

Eligon, John. "Judge Rules for Rowling Against Writer of Lexicon." *The New York Times*, 9 September 2008, C1.

Fabrikant, Geraldine, and Saul Hansell. "Viacom Tells YouTube: Hands Off." *The New York Times,* 3 February 2007, B1.

Ginsburg, Jane C. "No Sweat? Copyright and Other Protection of Works of Information After *Feist* v. *Rural Telephone*." *Columbia Law Review* 92 (1992): 339.

Gleick, James. "Patently Absurd." *The New York Times Magazine,* 12 March 2000, 44.

Greenhouse, Linda. "Ruling on *Victor* vs. *Victoria* Offers Split Victory of Sorts." *The New York Times,* 5 March 2003, A16.

———. "20-Year Extension of Existing Copyrights Is Upheld." *The New York Times,* 16 January 2003, A22.

Hansell, Saul. "The Associated Press to Set Guidelines for Using Its Articles." *The New York Times*, 16 June 2008. C7.

———. "McCain in Fight Over YouTube." *The New York Times*, 20 October 2008, B8.

Helfand, Michael T. "When Mickey Mouse Is as Strong as Superman: The Convergence of Intellectual Property Laws to Protect Fictional Literary and Pictorial Characters." *Stanford Law Review* 44 (1992): 623.

Helft, Miguel. "Google Told to Turn Over User Data of YouTube. "*The New York Times,* 4 July 2008, C1.

"Hendrix Inspired VodKa." *The New York Times,* 19 February 2009, B2.

Italie, Hillel. "Compensation for Use of Copyright Obama Image Sought by AP." *The Seattle Post-Intelligencer,* 5 February 2009, A4.

"In a Plagiarism Case, Harry Potter Wins the Day." *The New York Times,* 19 September 2002, C5.

"Jackson Browne Versus John McCain." *The New York Times*, 25 February 2009, C2.

Johnson-Laird, Andy. "Exploring the Information Superhighway: The Good, the Bad, and the Ugly." Paper presented at the Electronic Information Law Institute meeting, San Francisco, March 2–3, 1995.

"Jury Award for Wade Cook Overruled." *Seattle Post-Intelligencer,* 18 December 1998, E4.

Kaplan, Benjamin, and Ralph S. Brown Jr. *Cases on Copyright.* 2nd ed. Mineola, N.Y.: Foundation Press, 1974.

Kaplan, Carl S. "In Court's View, MP3 Player Is Just a 'Space Shifter.'" *The New York Times* on the Web, 9 July 1999.

Kennedy, Randy. "Artist Sues the A.P. Over Obama Image." *The New York Times*, 10 February 2009, C1.

Kirkpatrick, David. "Court Halts Book Based on 'Gone With the Wind.'" *The New York Times,* 21 April 2001, A1.

———. "Harry Potter and the Court Battle over Creativity." *The New York Times,* 1 April 2001, A1.

———. "'Wind' Book Wins Ruling in U.S. Court." *The New York Times,* 26 May 2001, B1.

Kramer, David H. "Who Can Use Yesterday's News? Video Monitoring and the Fair Use Doctrine." *The Georgetown Law Journal* 81 (1993): 2345.

Lattman, Peter. "English Copyright Lawsuit Against 'The Da Vinci Code' Kicks Off in London." *The Wall Street Journal Online,* 26 February 2006.

Lee, Jennifer. "U.S. Arrests Russian Cryptographer as Copyright Violator." *The New York Times,* 18 July 2001, C8.

Lessig, Lawrence. "Copyright and Politics Don't Mix." *The New York Times,* 21 October 2008, A25.

Lieberman, Trudy. "Plagiarize, Plagiarize, Plagiarize." *Columbia Journalism Review,* July/August 1995, 21.

Liptak, Adam. "Copying Issue Raises Hurdle for Bush Pick." *The New York Times,* 4 July 2008, A1.

Lyall, Sarah. "Idea for 'Da Vinci Code' Was Not Stolen, Judge Says." *The New York Times,* 8 April 2006, A15.

Moynihan, Colin. "He Says He Owns the Word 'Stealth.'" *The New York Times,* 4 July 2005, C5.

Muchnick, Irvin. "Protecting Writers' Rights Online." *Macworld,* July 1996, 236.

"A New Suit Against Online Music Sites." *The New York Times,* 4 October 2001, C4.

Nakashima, Ryan. "Music Industry Desists From Suing Swappers." *The Seattle Post-Intelligencer,* 20 December 2008, B2.

Oberthur, Anna. "Pole Dancing Copyright Is Another Test for IP Laws." *Daily Journal,* 14 February 2006.

Pérez-Peña, Richard. "A.P. Seeks to Block Unpaid Use of Content." *The New York Times,* 24 July 2009, B3.

———. "A.P. Seeks to Rein in Sites Using Its Content." *The New York Times,* 6 April 2009, B1.

Rich, Motoko. "Rowling to Testify in Trial Over Potter Lexicon." *The New York Times,* 14 April 2008, B1.

Richtel, Matt, and Sara Robinson. "Ear Training: A Digital Music Primer." *The New York Times,* 19 July 1999, C6.

Robinson, Sara. "3 Copyright Lawsuits Test Limits of New Digital Media." *The New York Times,* 24 January 2000, C8.

Schiesel, Seth. "Global Agreement Reached to Widen Law on Copyright." *The New York Times,* 21 December 1996, A1.

Shannon, Victoria. "Internet Leaves Music Labels Singing Blues." *Seattle Post-Intelligencer,* 26 January 2007, C2.

Shepard, Alicia. "Does Radio News Rip Off Newspapers?" *American Journalism Review,* September 1994, 15.

Sisario, Ben. "Postal Service Tale: Indie Rock, Snail Mail and Trademark Law." *The New York Times,* 6 November 2004, A1.

Sorkin, Andrew Ross. "Software Bullet Is Sought to Kill Musical Piracy." *The New York Times,* 4 May 2003, A1.

Stolberg, Sheryl G. "Bush Aide Resigns Over Plagiarism in Columns He Wrote." *The New York Times,* 1 March 2008, A9.

Strong, William. *The Copyright Book.* Cambridge, Mass.: MIT Press, 1981.

Tatum, Kevin. "Demonstration on Internet Piracy of Copyright Properties Reinforces the Need for Legislation." *Journal of Copyright Information,* May 1996, 6.

"Trademarks and the Press." *American Journalism Review,* October 1993, 43.

Vaidhyanathan, Siva. "Copyright Jungle." *Columbia Journalism Review,* September–October 2006, 42.

Whitley, Angus. "Legal Downloads Soar in iPod World." *Seattle Post-Intelligencer,* 20 January 2005, C1.

Yen, Alfred C. "When Authors Won't Sell: Parody, Fair Use, and Efficiency in Copyright Law." *University of Colorado Law Review* 62 (1991): 79.

CHAPTER 15

Regulation of Advertising

Advertising, as a form of expression subject to legal regulation and potential First Amendment protection, is the dominant cultural icon of our time. It also is a huge business. In 2009 a 30-second commercial on the Super Bowl on NBC reportedly went for as much as $3 million. More than $10 billion alone was spent on online search ads in the United States in 2008, as well as more than $5 billion on online display ads. A single company—Procter & Gamble, the largest advertiser in the nation—spent $3.2 billion on advertising in 2008. For the 2008 Olympics in Beijing, NBC collected a whopping total of more than $1 billion in advertising revenue, with a single 30-second commercial spot during the swimming events costing up to $750,000. And while the economic woes of 2008 led to predictions of about an 8 percent drop in overall ad spending in 2009 in the United States to slightly more than $156 billion (spending on newspaper, magazine and radio ads was anticipated to decrease the most), advertising remains a ubiquitous part of our culture. Advertising dollars make possible most of the media content that we consume; were it not for ads, network television and daily newspapers would not exist. Advertising is, then, a very important form of speech.

Advertising messages are regulated by the government; in fact, advertising is probably the most heavily regulated form of modern speech and press. Laws at every level—federal, state and local—control what businesses and institutions may claim about their products and services. This chapter is an outline of the most common kinds of regulations that affect advertising; it is not comprehensive. Thousands of laws regulate advertising. People who work in advertising, especially copywriters, need a comprehensive understanding of the law and should use this material only as a starting point.

ADVERTISING AND THE FIRST AMENDMENT

Although hard to believe, it was not until 1975 that the U.S. Supreme Court first explicitly held that "commercial advertising enjoys a degree of First Amendment protection," reasoning at the time in *Bigelow* v. *Virginia* that "the relationship of speech to the marketplace of products or of services does not make it valueless in the marketplace of ideas"[1] (see page 44 regarding the marketplace of ideas). Yet the court also was clear in *Bigelow* that advertising is "subject to reasonable regulation." Since then, the high court and lower courts have developed a **commercial speech doctrine** articulating just how much First Amendment protection advertising receives and the criteria the government must satisfy to permissibly regulate it. The doctrine evolved in a series of cases in the five years after *Bigelow*.

- In 1976 the Supreme Court ruled that a Virginia statute that forbade the advertising of the price of prescription drugs violated the First Amendment.[2]
- In 1977 the high court invalidated a township ordinance in New Jersey that banned the placement of "for sale" and "sold" signs on front lawns. Township authorities said the law was needed because such signs contributed to panic selling by white homeowners who feared that property values would decline because the township was becoming populated by black families. The Supreme Court rejected this argument and ruled that the placement of such signs was protected by the First Amendment.[3]

1. 421 U.S. 809, 826 (1975).
2. *Virginia State Board of Pharmacy* v. *Virginia Citizens Consumer Council, Inc.,* 425 U.S. 748 (1976).
3. *Linmark Associates* v. *Township of Willingboro,* 431 U.S. 85 (1977).

■ In the 1980 case of *Central Hudson Gas & Electric Corp.* v. *Public Service Commission*—known today simply as *Central Hudson*—the Supreme Court held unconstitutional a New York regulation that completely banned promotional ads by electric utility companies.[4]

Not all decisions involving advertising and freedom of expression resulted in First Amendment victories. The Supreme Court allowed the Commonwealth of Puerto Rico to prohibit the owners of legal gambling casinos to advertise these establishments to the local population, the people of Puerto Rico.[5] (Commonwealth officials said the gambling casinos were for the tourists who came to the island.) In addition, the high court has granted states fairly extensive authority to regulate advertising for professional services by individuals like doctors, lawyers, dentists and others. For instance, the Supreme Court in 2006 upheld the Florida Bar's reprimand of two attorneys who used a pit bull logo and the number 1-800-PIT-BULL in their firm's advertisements.[6]

COMMERCIAL SPEECH DOCTRINE

The First Amendment does not protect either false or misleading ads or ads for unlawful goods or services.

Government may regulate truthful advertising for legal goods and services if the following conditions are met:

    a.   There is a substantial state interest to justify the regulation.

    b.   There is evidence that the regulation directly advances this interest.

    c.   There is a reasonable fit between the state interest and the government regulation.

COMMERCIAL SPEECH DOCTRINE

Although truthful advertising for lawful goods or services receives some First Amendment protection, the extent and scope of that protection is more limited when compared with political speech. While political speech is at the top of a First Amendment hierarchy of expression and while speech that fits the Supreme Court's definition of obscenity falls completely without any First Amendment protection (see Chapter 13), commercial speech lies somewhere in between.[7]

Determining what constitutes commercial speech, however, is not easy. Courts still wrestle with this threshold issue, often defining it as expression that either

■ *is related solely to the economic interests of the speaker and its audience,* or

■ *proposes a commercial transaction.*

---

4. 447 U.S. 557 (1980).

5. *Posadas de Puerto Rico Assoc.* v. *Tourism Co.,* 478 U.S. 328 (1986). However, the high court rejected the rationale of this ruling in 1996.

6. *Florida Bar* v. *Pape,* 918 So. 2d 240 (Fla. 2005), cert. den., *Pape* v. *Florida Bar,* 126 S. Ct. 1632 (2006).

7. Although the First Amendment gives limited protection to commercial speech, the Oregon Supreme Court has ruled that the Oregon Constitution gives it full protection. *Outdoor Media Dimensions, Inc.* v. *Department of Transportation,* 132 P. 3d 5 (Ore. 2006).

In some cases it is not easy to distinguish political speech from commercial speech, as courts recently have observed.[8] But the difference is critical because it is much easier for the government to justify a law regulating commercial speech under the *Central Hudson* test (as the commercial speech doctrine sometimes is known) than it is to regulate political speech under the strict scrutiny standard. In cases involving speech transpiring in the context of promotional materials and activities (a doctor, for instance, giving a talk or seminar about a new drug), courts sometimes weigh three factors to help determine if it is commercial: (1) whether the expression is an advertisement, (2) whether it refers to a specific product, and (3) whether the speaker has an economic motivation for speaking.[9]

Whereas commercial speech typically receives limited First Amendment protection, two types of commercial speech receive no protection whatsoever:

Two types of commercial speech receive no protection whatsoever.

■ **The government may ban advertising that is false, misleading or deceptive.** Much of the rest of this chapter is devoted to defining and explaining such regulation.

■ **The government may ban advertising for unlawful goods and services.** This broad exception to the protection of the First Amendment was established primarily to permit the government to bar discriminatory employment advertising. It is illegal for an employer to discriminate on the basis of race or religion or ancestry or even gender when hiring employees. Help-wanted ads that offer employment to "whites" or "men only" or whatever are also illegal.[10]

Even truthful advertising for legal goods and services can be regulated, provided that the government can satisfy the three requirements outlined here.

■ **The government must assert a substantial state interest to justify the regulation.** States that seek to limit advertising by doctors and lawyers will argue that the public is not sophisticated enough to evaluate many claims that might be made by these professionals, and even perfectly truthful claims could be deceptive. Protecting the public from such deception is a substantial state interest.[11] In 2006 a federal appellate court held that the Village of Glendale, Ohio, had substantial interests in promoting both traffic safety and community aesthetics that justified an ordinance prohibiting the display of for-sale signs on cars parked on public streets.[12]

8. See, e.g., *Bellsouth Telecommunications, Inc.* v. *Farris*, 542 F. 3d 499 (6th Cir. 2008) (involving a law that prohibited telecommunications companies from stating separately on their customers' bills a new tax imposed by Kentucky, observing that this law "facilitates keeping consumers (and voters) in the dark about the tax and its impact on their wallets," and providing that it is "difficult to pin down where the political nature of these speech restrictions ends and the commercial nature of the restrictions begins").
9. *United States* v. *Caronia,* 576 F. Supp. 2d 385, 396 (E.D. N.Y. 2008).
10. *Pittsburgh Press Co.* v. *Pittsburgh Commission on Human Relations,* 413 U.S. 376 (1973).
11. *Bates and Van O'Steen* v. *Arizona,* 433 U.S. 350 (1977).
12. *Pagan* v. *Fruchey,* 453 F. 3d 784 (6th Cir. 2006). This opinion was later vacated in 2006 when a petition for a rehearing en banc was granted. *Pagan* v. *Fruchey,* 453 F. 3d 785 (6th Cir. 2006), and in June 2007, by a narrow 8-7 vote, the appellate court reversed and declared that the Village of Glendale had failed to produce evidence sufficient to justify the ordinance. *Pagan* v. *Fruchey,* 492 F. 3d 766 (6th Cir. 2007). Importantly, however, that decision did not question the substantiality of the municipality's interests in both traffic safety and aesthetics.

■ **Next, the government must demonstrate that the ban on advertising it has instituted will directly advance the interest outlined in the previous paragraph.** Think of the interest as a kind of goal the state is seeking to reach. Will the ban on advertising help the state reach this goal? On this element, mere speculation and conjecture that a law directly advances the government's interests and alleviates the alleged harms in a material way won't cut it. Rather, as a federal appellate court wrote in 2009, "we independently evaluate [the government's] assertion that the advertising restrictions advance the state's interest, and we rely on the valid sources of history, consensus, and common sense."[13] A Baltimore ordinance that banned outdoor advertising for alcoholic beverages in areas in which children walk to school or neighborhoods in which children play was ruled permissible because it directly and materially advanced the city's interest in promoting the welfare and temperance of minors.[14]

■ **Finally, the state must show that there is a "reasonable fit" between the state interest being asserted and the government regulation.** A reasonable fit means the regulation must be narrowly tailored to achieve the desired objective, but it doesn't have to be the least restrictive means available. In 2006 a federal appellate court held that a Missouri law banning, within one mile of highways, billboard ads for sexually oriented businesses (regardless of the words or images on the billboards) was not narrowly tailored to meet the state's substantial interest in eliminating secondary effects of adult businesses (see page 487 regarding secondary effects).[15] Missouri believed that by eliminating billboard ads, fewer people would visit sexually oriented businesses, thus forcing closure due to lack of customers. Although the court found evidence the law would directly advance this substantial interest, it held the law was not narrowly tailored because it "threatens criminal prosecution for the mere inclusion of the name or address of an affected business" and thus bans "an intolerable amount of truthful speech about lawful conduct." Importantly, the court added that Missouri failed to show that "a more limited speech regulation would not have adequately served the state's interest."

A reasonable fit means the regulation must be narrowly tailored to achieve the desired objective, but it doesn't have to be the least restrictive means available.

In 2009 a judge entered a preliminary injunction (see Chapter 1 on equity law) in *Abilene Retail No. 30, Inc.* v. *Six* that stopped Kansas from enforcing a similar law targeting ads and billboards for sexually oriented businesses (see Chapter 13 regarding restrictions on sexually oriented businesses) along that state's highways. In ruling against the statute, U.S. District Judge Julie Robinson wrote that it "broadly sweeps [up] any speech that is 'for' a sexually-oriented business, whether or not that speech is obscene or relates to the sale of constitutionally protected products such as books and magazines." In other words, there was not a reasonable fit. Kansas Attorney General Steve Six announced in August 2009 that he would not appeal the decision. That same month, a judge in South Carolina in *Carolina Pride, Inc.* v.

13. *WV Association of Club Owners & Fraternal Services, Inc.* v. *Musgrave,* 2009 U.S. App. LEXIS 545 (4th Cir. 2009).

14. *Anheuser-Busch Inc.* v. *Schmoke,* 101 F. 3d 325 (1996).

15. *Passions Video, Inc.* v. *Nixon,* 458 F. 3d 837 (8th Cir. 2006), petition for rehearing denied, 2006 U.S. App. LEXIS 24092 (2006).

McMaster issued a permanent injunction against a similar ordinance in that state that prohibited billboards for sexually oriented businesses within one mile of public roads. This lawsuit, like the one in Kansas, was filed by the owner of a Lion's Den Adult Superstore that had several highway billboards. In striking down the South Carolina statute, U.S. District Judge Cameron McGowan noted how it was not narrowly tailored because it prohibited any and all billboards advertising adult businesses, regardless of the billboards' content or the legality of the businesses advertised.

Recent cases illustrate the application of the commercial speech doctrine. In 2006 the 9th U.S. Circuit Court of Appeals held in *Ballen* v. *City of Redmond* that a local law prohibiting most outdoor portable signs—reader boards, signs on trailers, sandwich boards and so on—except for real estate and political signs and several other exemptions, was unconstitutional and did not survive review under the commercial speech doctrine.[16] The dispute involved the owner of a bagel store who hired a person to stand on a sidewalk wearing a sign reading "Fresh Bagels—Now Open." The city of Redmond complained this violated its outdoor portable sign ordinance. The owner sued, claiming the law violated his First Amendment right to advertise his business.

Applying the commercial speech doctrine, the appellate court first found no dispute that the bagel sign related to a lawful activity and was not misleading, thus making it subject to First Amendment protection. The court then found that the city's interests in its anti-portable sign ordinance of promoting vehicular and pedestrian safety and preserving community aesthetics were substantial. Assuming these goals were directly advanced by the ban on most outdoor portable signs, the appellate court nonetheless struck down the law on the final part of the commercial speech doctrine because there was not a reasonable fit between the ordinance's restrictions and the city's goals. Noting the law exempted real estate signs, the court held this undermined the city's interests:

> Ubiquitous real estate signs, which can turn an inviting sidewalk into an obstacle course challenging even the most dextrous hurdler, are an even greater threat to vehicular and pedestrian safety and community aesthetics than the presence of a single employee holding an innocuous sign that reads: "Fresh Bagels—Now Open." The city has protected outdoor signage displayed by the powerful real estate industry from an ordinance that unfairly restricts the First Amendment rights of, among others, a lone bagel shop owner.

The fit between the means and ends thus was not reasonable as it discriminated unfairly based on the content of signs, protecting some signs (real estate signs) that were just as harmful to its alleged aesthetic and safety interests as unprotected signs (the walking bagel ad). The court also noted that narrower alternatives less intrusive on free speech rights could have been used to advance the city's interests, such as content-neutral time, place and manner restrictions on all commercial signs (see pages 110–113 regarding time, place and manner regulations).

In 1995 the Supreme Court struck down a federal rule that forbade brewers from listing the alcohol content on labels attached to bottles and cans of beer and malt liquor. The

---

16. 466 F. 3d 736 (9th Cir. 2006).

government justified the rule by arguing that it sought to discourage young drinkers from buying a particular beer or malt liquor simply because it had the highest alcohol content. The government's interest in reducing the amount of alcohol consumed by young people is a laudable goal, a unanimous Supreme Court said, but added that there is really no evidence this rule advances that goal. There was no government ban on the disclosure of the alcohol content in advertising for these brews, Justice Clarence Thomas wrote. Nor were there limits on the words a brewer could use to describe these products. "To be sure," Thomas wrote, "the Government's interest in combating strength wars is a valid goal. But the irrationality of this unique and puzzling framework ensures that the labeling ban will fail to achieve that end."[17]

In 1996 the Supreme Court ruled that a Rhode Island statute that barred liquor stores from advertising the price of distilled spirits ran afoul of the First Amendment. The state attempted to justify the law by arguing that the ban on advertising reduced competition in the sale of liquor, which resulted in higher liquor prices that in turn led to reduced consumption. But in his principal opinion for the badly splintered Supreme Court, Justice John Paul Stevens referred to the state's assertions that the ban would significantly reduce liquor consumption as speculation and conjecture. The justice added that raising liquor prices through taxation would have the same impact. Justice Stevens wrote, "The First Amendment directs us to be especially skeptical of regulations that seek to keep people in the dark for what the government perceives to be their own good."[18]

In 2001 the Supreme Court ruled that a Massachusetts law that banned both outdoor ads and point-of-sale ads for smokeless tobacco products and cigars within 1,000 feet of public playgrounds and schools was unconstitutional.[19] The high court conceded that the state had a substantial interest in reducing the use of such products by youngsters. A majority also agreed that there was substantial evidence that tobacco sellers had boosted the sale of these products by targeting young males in their advertising. But the rule went too far; it was not a reasonable fit. Coupled with pre-existing zoning laws in the state, the rule constitutes a complete ban on the communication of truthful information about smokeless tobacco products and cigars to adult consumers, Justice Sandra Day O'Connor wrote. The law also fails to distinguish among the types of signs with respect to their appeal to children as opposed to adults, or even their size. The law is simply not tailored narrowly enough to advance the state's declared interest without impeding protected speech as well.

In 2009 the 9th U.S. Circuit Court of Appeals considered whether Los Angeles violated the First Amendment by prohibiting most off-site commercial advertising (off-premises billboards, for instance) while simultaneously contracting itself with a private party to permit the sale of such ads at its city-owned transit stops.[20] Los Angeles asserted traffic safety and aesthetics concerns in adopting the law. The 9th Circuit applied the commercial speech doctrine and *Central Hudson* test. Initially, there was no dispute that off-site advertising generally merits some level of First Amendment protection as long as it is neither misleading nor related to an unlawful activity. The question then became whether Los Angeles could nonetheless regulate it. There was no disagreement that traffic safety and aesthetics constituted well-established substantial government

17. *Rubin* v. *Coors Brewing Co.,* 514 U.S. 476 (1995).
18. *44 Liquormart, Inc.* v. *Rhode Island,* 517 U.S. 484 (1996).
19. *Lorillard Tobacco Co.* v. *Reilly,* 533 U.S. 525 (2001).
20. *Metro Lights, LLC* v. *City of Los Angeles,* 551 F. 3d 898 (9th Cir. 2009).

interests under *Central Hudson*. The case thus boiled down to the final two parts of *Central Hudson*—whether Los Angeles' law directly advanced its interests in safety and aesthetics, and whether the law was narrowly tailored in serving those goals. The 9th Circuit found as powerful precedent (see pages 3–5 regarding precedent) the U.S. Supreme Court's 1981 ruling in *Metromedia, Inc.* v. *City of San Diego*.[21] The high court there had upheld parts of a very similar San Diego law that banned off-site commercial billboards, but not on-site commercial signs, unless the off-site signs fell into one of 12 exemptions, including "government signs" and "signs located at public bus stops." In *Metromedia*, the Supreme Court gave huge deference to the judgment of local lawmakers on the questions of whether the off-site commercial billboard ban directly advanced interests in safety and aesthetics and whether there was a reasonable fit between the means and those interests. It made no difference to the Supreme Court that San Diego's law valued some types of commercial speech (on-site signs) more than other types of commercial speech (off-site billboards); the high court accepted that off-site advertising presented a more acute problem than on-site ads simply because of the former's "periodically changing content." The Supreme Court also rejected the argument that San Diego "denigrate[d] its interest in traffic safety and beauty and defeat[ed] its own case by permitting onsite advertising and other specified signs." Instead, it simply found that a ban on *some* (but not all) off-site signs advanced traffic safety and aesthetics concerns more than does a ban on *none*. Following such vastly deferential logic, the 9th Circuit in *Metro Lights* ruled in favor of Los Angeles, reasoning:

> Los Angeles essentially argues that the proliferation of offsite advertising by numerous and disparate private parties creates more distracting ugliness than a single, controlled series of advertisements on city property over which the City wields contractual supervision. If periodically changing content was sufficient for San Diego to disfavor offsite signs in general, then we must accept that uncontrolled and incoherent proliferation is sufficient for Los Angeles to disfavor offsite signs away from transit stops.

One other dimension of the relationship between the First Amendment and advertising needs to be briefly explored. Is it a violation of the First Amendment for a newspaper, magazine or broadcasting station to refuse to carry an advertisement? No. The long-standing legal doctrine is that the First Amendment is not even implicated; such a situation is one private entity, the mass medium, refusing to do business with another private entity.* In 1996 a U.S. District Court extended this doctrine to the Internet when it ruled that a private company called Cyber Promotions had no right under the First Amendment to e-mail unsolicited promotional advertisements to America Online subscribers. The court ruled that although the Internet provides the opportunity to disseminate vast amounts of information, the Internet does not have at the present time the means to police the dissemination of that information. "We therefore find that . . . the private online service has a right to prevent unsolicited e-mail solicitations from reaching its subscribers over the Internet," Judge Weiner wrote.[22]

---

*Broadcasters do have certain obligations related to carrying political advertising. See Chapter 16. In addition, if the publication is not privately owned but rather is published by a government entity, such as a state university's alumni magazine, there may be some situations in which advertisements cannot be rejected. See *Rutgers 1000 Alumni Council* v. *Rutgers,* 803 A. 2d 679 (2002).

21. 453 U.S. 490 (1981).

22. *Cyber Promotions, Inc.* v. *America Online, Inc.,* 1 E.P.L.R. 756 (1996), 24 M.L.R. 2505 (1996).

COMPELLED ADVERTISING SUBSIDIES AND GOVERNMENT SPEECH

Almost anyone who has watched television advertisements during the past decade or so is familiar with trademarked slogans such as "Beef. It's What's for Dinner" and "Got Milk?" The former phrase played a pivotal role in a case decided by the U.S. Supreme Court in 2005. The case did not involve the just-discussed commercial speech from *Central Hudson* but, instead, addressed "whether a federal program that finances generic advertising to promote an agricultural product violates the First Amendment."[23] In particular, *Johanns* v. *Livestock Marketing Association* centered on a federal statute and related order adopted in the 1980s under which the U.S. secretary of agriculture imposes a $1-per-head assessment, known as a checkoff, on all sales of cattle in the United States. Although $1 taken alone may seem small for each sale, the program has collected more than $1 billion since 1988. A large portion of that money, under the federal Beef Promotion and Research Act, has gone to finance generic advertising for the beef industry, including the "Beef. It's What's for Dinner" campaign.

Although that slogan at first may seem to benefit the entire beef and cattle industry, a number of cattle producers objected to it because, as the Supreme Court put it, "the advertising promotes beef as a generic commodity, which, they contended, impedes their efforts to promote the superiority of, *inter alia,* American beef, grain-fed beef, or certified Angus or Hereford beef." In other words, the Livestock Marketing Association and the other plaintiff in the case objected to the fact that they were compelled to subsidize speech—the generic beef advertising campaign—to which they objected. They would, instead, rather spend their own money on distinctive advertising for a particular niche or premium variety of beef, such as organically fed. The plaintiffs thus alleged a violation of their First Amendment right not to be compelled to fund speech—an unenumerated right to remain silent, as it were—with which they disagreed.

A First Amendment right not to be compelled by the government to speak has been recognized by the Supreme Court in some situations. For instance, in the seminal 1943 opinion in *West Virginia Board of Education* v. *Barnette,* the court held that children in public schools could not be forced or compelled to recite the Pledge of Allegiance or salute the American flag.[24] The students had a right, in other words, to not speak. The majority of the court in *Livestock Marketing Association,* however, distinguished that case and others like it on the ground that the beef situation was a compelled-subsidy case—not a true compelled-speech case—and, more important, the advertising campaign itself represented "government speech," not speech by a private person against his or her wishes. Writing for a six-justice majority, Justice Antonin Scalia wrote that "the message set out in the beef promotions is from beginning to end the message established by the Federal Government" and that the secretary of agriculture "exercises final approval authority over every word used in every promotional campaign." The majority concluded that while "citizens may challenge compelled support of private speech" they "have no First Amendment right not to fund government speech." To illustrate his point, Scalia noted that a person may not opt out of paying income taxes just

A First Amendment right not to be compelled by the government to speak has been recognized by the Supreme Court in some situations.

---

23. *Johanns* v. *Livestock Marketing Association,* 544 U.S. 550 (2005).
24. 319 U.S. 624 (1943).

because he or she doesn't agree with how the government is spending the money. In brief, the majority of the court concluded that the beef advertising is the government's own speech and, as such, does not raise First Amendment problems. The court thus ruled in favor of the federal beef promotion program and its compelled subsidization of advertising to which some cattle ranchers and farmers object.

SUMMARY   American advertising is regulated by laws adopted by all levels of government. People who work in advertising must be aware of such rules as well as all other regulations (libel, invasion of privacy, obscenity) that restrict the content and flow of printed and broadcast material. Since the mid-1970s commercial advertising has been given the qualified protection of the First Amendment because much advertising contains information that is valuable to consumers. The government may prohibit advertising (1) that promotes an unlawful activity or (2) that is misleading or untruthful. The state may also regulate truthful advertising for lawful activities and goods if it can prove (1) there is a substantial state interest to justify the regulation, (2) that such regulation directly advances this interest, and (3) that there is a reasonable fit between the interest asserted and the governmental regulation. Advertising by professionals such as attorneys and physicians may be regulated in a more restrictive fashion.

THE REGULATION OF ADVERTISING

The regulation of deceptive or untruthful advertising is a large and difficult task policed by the advertising industry itself, the mass media and various governmental agencies. Let's briefly examine the current process of regulation.

SELF-REGULATION

Newspapers, magazines, broadcasting stations, online service providers and other mass media all have rules that more or less regulate the kind of advertising they will carry. These guidelines spring from a variety of concerns. Sometimes the owner of the medium thinks the product that is being advertised is offensive, like NC-17 or adult movies, or condoms. Other times the ads themselves might be regarded as tasteless, like an advertisement for clothing in which the models are scantily dressed or posed erotically. It is not uncommon that an advertisement is rejected because of economic interests. A television station won't advertise a sporting event that will be telecast on a competing channel. Ads that promote illegal goods and services, that contain claims that appear to be deceptive or are not substantiated, or that unfairly trash a competitor's products might also be rejected. For instance, in late 2004 CBS, NBC and ABC stopped running certain television ads produced for the Miller Brewing Co. that poked fun at rival Anheuser-Busch's top-selling product, Budweiser, and that allegedly made unsubstantiated claims about taste tests comparing Miller Genuine Draft and Miller Lite with Budweiser and Bud Light.[25] CBS found the three Miller ads to be "unduly disparaging." Remember, a mass medium is permitted to reject any content it chooses, with or without a reason.

25. Daykin, "Networks Blow Whistle on Ads"; and Cancelada, "CBS and NBC Will Stop Running Some Miller Ads."

There are two key divisions of the Better Business Bureau's National Advertising Review Council that provide both advice to advertisers and out-of-court methods for resolving disputes about advertisements. They are:

There are two key divisions of the Better Business Bureau's National Advertising Review Council.

▪ **National Advertising Division (NAD):** This organization, a self-regulatory forum for the advertising industry, reviews national advertising for truthfulness and accuracy, and it provides a form of alternative dispute resolution for companies that is cheaper than litigation. For instance, in April 2009 NAD recommended that battery manufacturer Duracell modify or discontinue certain advertising claims for its Coppertop batteries after they were challenged by rival Energizer, maker of e2 Lithium batteries. NAD also found in 2009 that Wal-Mart provided reasonable support for its "Unbeatable Prices" advertising claim, which included a price-matching disclosure statement ("We'll match the price of any local competitor's printed ad for an identical product. See manager for restrictions"). NAD recommended, however, that Wal-Mart make its disclosures substantially clearer and more conspicuous in its printed and broadcast advertising and on its in-store signage. NAD also suggested that Wal-Mart stop making a separate claim that "you could save on average over $700 a year" if you bought certain items there, compared to other grocery stores. Learn more about NAD at its Web site at http://www.nadreview.org.

▪ **Child Advertising Review Unit (CARU):** This agency describes itself as the children's arm of the advertising industry's self-regulation program, and it evaluates child-directed advertising and promotional material in all media to advance truthfulness, accuracy and consistency with its "Self-Regulatory Guidelines for Children's Advertising" and relevant laws. Some of its activities today include reviewing companies' Web sites that target children for their compliance with the Children's Online Privacy Protection Act (see pages 575–576). Learn more about CARU at its Web site at http://www.caru.org. In addition, the guidelines for children's advertising are located at http://www.caru.org/guidelines/index.aspx.

With the economy tanking in 2008, NAD was busy dealing with more comparison-ad disputes. The Wall Street Journal reported in October 2008 that NAD was "fielding many more complaints from marketers who believe they are the victim of misleading comparison ads."[26] In particular, NAD reportedly had 15 advertisers in August 2008 alone "challenge competitive ads that rivals had begun using—compared with six challenges in August 2007." As the Journal put it, "as the economy gets ugly, marketers are getting nasty too" by "stepping up their so-called attack ads, calling out rivals by name, comparing products and poking fun at competitors." Sometimes, of course, companies choose not to use NAD but instead to file lawsuits, as was the case in 2009 when PepsiCo Inc. sued Coca-Cola Co. regarding an ad for Coke's Powerade ION-4 sports drink that favorably compared it to PepsiCo's Gatorade (see pages 560–563 regarding lawsuits by competitors). The PepsiCo complaint claimed "there is no evidence, scientific or otherwise, that Powerade Ion-4 functions better than Gatorade as a sports drink." Likewise, FedEx sued UPS in 2009 over a national TV ad run by UPS claiming

"As the economy gets ugly, marketers are getting nasty too."

---

26. Vranica, "And in This Corner. . . . Marketers Take Some Jabs."

it was ranked the most-reliable package shipping company, and UPS stopped running the ad in response to the lawsuit. Such lawsuits by competitors are discussed in the next section of this chapter.

If an advertiser disagrees with a NAD or CARU decision, it can appeal to the **National Advertising Review Board (NARB).** Its Web site is found at http://www.narbreview.org.

LAWSUITS BY COMPETITORS AND CONSUMERS

Using mouthwash is just as effective as flossing when it comes to fighting tooth and gum decay. Pfizer Inc. made that claim in a massive multimedia advertising campaign launched in June 2004 called "The Big Bang" on behalf of its well-known Listerine brand mouthwash. One television commercial asserted, "Listerine's as effective as floss at fighting plaque and gingivitis. Clinical studies prove it." But a subsidiary of Johnson & Johnson that manufactures dental floss contended the assertion on behalf of Listerine was false and deceptive, and it sued Pfizer in federal court under the federal Lanham Act, saying the campaign constituted an unfair threat against sales of dental floss. In 2005 a federal court in New York ruled in favor of Johnson & Johnson, holding that "Pfizer's implicit message that Listerine can replace floss is false and misleading."[27] U.S. District Court Judge Denny Chin issued an injunction that ordered Pfizer to stop its campaign. Chin wrote, "I find that Pfizer's advertisements do send the message, implicitly, that Listerine is a replacement for floss—that the benefits of flossing may be obtained by rinsing with Listerine, and that, in particular, those consumers who do not have the time or desire to floss can switch to Listerine instead." Pfizer, in fact, had to spend $2 million in 2005 to deploy about 4,000 workers across the United States to place stickers on Listerine bottles that were sitting on store shelves in order to cover up its claim and to remove tags carrying the claim that were hung around bottlenecks of the mouthwash.

Lawsuits for false advertising claims were relatively rare until the last quarter of the 20th century. With the rapid growth of comparative advertising (in which the advertised product is compared to a competitor's product), more and more advertisers have taken competitors to court over what they claim is deceptive and false advertising.

A recent example of a competitor-versus-competitor lawsuit, based on alleged false advertising and filed under the federal Lanham Act, is *Schick Manufacturing* v. *Gillette Co.*[28] The case pitted the two shaving-razor giants against each other. The plaintiff, Schick, contended that Gillette made false claims in 2004 about the prowess of the Gillette M3 Power razor system on television commercials and that, in turn, those misleading ads hurt the sales of Schick's own Quattro razor. The M3 includes a battery-powered feature that causes the razor to oscillate. One aspect of the Gillette M3 commercial to which Schick objected included an animated representation of the purported effect of the M3 Power razor on hair. In particular, as the court noted, "the animation, which lasts approximately 1.8 seconds, shows many hairs growing at a significant rate, many by as much as four times the original length." Schick believed this illustration showed a false amount of extension of the beard allegedly generated by the M3. The court ruled in favor of Schick, rejecting Gillette's creative yet unsuccessful argument that animated exaggeration does not constitute falsity. U.S. District

27. *McNeil-PPC, Inc.* v. *Pfizer, Inc.,* 351 F. Supp. 2d 226 (S.D. N.Y. 2005).
28. 372 F. Supp. 2d 273 (D. Conn. 2005).

Court Judge Janet C. Hall wrote that "a defendant cannot argue that a television advertisement is 'approximately' correct or, alternatively, simply a representation in order to excuse a television ad or segment thereof that is literally false." She concluded that while "a cartoon will not exactly depict a real-life situation, . . . a party may not distort an inherent quality of its product in either graphics or animation. Gillette acknowledges that the magnitude of beard hair extension in the animation is false. The court finds, therefore, that any claims with respect to changes in angle and the animated portion of Gillette's current advertisement are literally false." This is an important lesson for all undergraduates majoring in advertising to understand—be careful not to exaggerate claims, either in words or in images, such as commercial animation. Each can be deemed false in a court of law.

This lawsuit was filed under provisions of the federal Lanham Act, which was adopted more than 60 years ago by Congress to stop unfair competition in the marketplace. Section 43(a) creates a legal cause of action for false advertising. The statute, set forth at 15 U.S.C. § 1125, provides that a person who generates "any false designation of origin, false or misleading description of fact, or false or misleading representation of fact, which . . . in commercial advertising or promotion, misrepresents the nature, characteristics, qualities, or geographic origin of his or another person's goods, services, or commercial activities" is liable for civil damages. As originally written, the law prevented only one advertiser from making false statements about his or her own goods ("The new Escalade will get 60 miles to the gallon in city driving"). But Congress amended the act in 1989, and now the law also prohibits an advertiser from making false claims about a competitor's product as well ("The new Escalade will get 26 miles per gallon in city driving, while the Dodge Neon gets only 5 miles to the gallon"). This provision of the Lanham Act was seldom used by advertisers until the 1970s. Between 1946 and 1968 the courts heard fewer than 30 false advertising cases.[29] Several developments propelled the growth of Lanham Act false advertising activity:

- Comparative advertising, in which an advertiser not only promotes his or her own goods but tends to disparage the product made by a competitor, became more common. Television networks had arbitrarily refused to air such commercials until urged to do so by the Federal Trade Commission, which suggested that such advertising would enhance the competitive nature of the marketplace.

- Advertising, as a part of the marketing mix for all products, took on more importance in the past 50 years. Sellers invested huge sums in building product images and establishing product claims. Attempts by competitors to undermine or dilute these images or claims were regarded more seriously than in the past.

- It became somewhat easier for plaintiffs to win Lanham Act false advertising suits.[30] The test of false advertising, for years a complex configuration of criteria, was reduced to basically three parts:

  1. What message, either explicitly or implicitly, does the ad convey?
  2. Is this message false or misleading?
  3. Does this message injure the plaintiff?

29. Pompeo, "To Tell the Truth," 565.
30. Singdahlsen, "The Risk of Chill," 339.

■ The size of damage awards skyrocketed. Plaintiffs in Lanham Act cases had traditionally sought only to stop the competitor's advertising claims. It was easier to block a competitor's claims than to win damages, because in order to gain a monetary award the plaintiff had to show specific monetary loss, something that is often difficult to do given the nebulous nature of advertising claims and the forces that motivate a consumer to buy a specific brand of a product. But courts began to ease this standard at about the same time that they began to increase the size of damage awards.[31] Not only is it now possible for plaintiffs to win actual damages and court costs from the defendant, but they can also tap into any profit made by the competitor through the use of a bogus advertising campaign. On top of this, the judge can double or triple the damage award in cases of especially flagrant falsity.

In summary, competitor-versus-competitor lawsuits are now common. In 2006, for example, Time Warner Cable sued rival DIRECTV Group, accusing it of running "blatantly false" newspaper ads to lure customers to its football programming, while Coca-Cola agreed to stop airing one TV advertisement and to modify another for its Powerade Option sports drink after being sued by Pepsi, owner of the rival drink Gatorade, for making allegedly false and unsubstantiated claims of superiority.

Consumers, as opposed to competitors, have a much more difficult time in maintaining an action for false advertising.

Consumers, as opposed to competitors, have a much more difficult time in maintaining an action for false advertising. Part of the reason for this is that the Lanham Act's rules against false advertising, which are designed to remedy unfair competition, generally allow only economic competitors to sue. It is very difficult for noncompetitors to gain standing to sue for false advertising under the Lanham Act. This was vividly illustrated in 2002 when a federal district court rejected tennis player Anna Kournikova's motion for a preliminary injunction based on a Lanham Act claim for false advertising against Penthouse magazine after it had published photos of a woman sunbathing topless whom it falsely represented on its cover and on its inside pages as Kournikova.[32] The June 2002 issue of Penthouse proclaimed on its cover in bold capital letters, "EXCLUSIVE ANNA KOURNIKOVA CAUGHT CLOSE UP ON NUDE BEACH." The photos inside, however, were not of the Russian-born tennis player, who is known more for her beauty than for her on-court prowess. Kournikova sued the company that publishes Penthouse magazine, General Media Communications, Inc., on several causes of action, one of which was false advertising under the Lanham Act. But the court, while calling the magazine's conduct "reprehensible," rejected the claim for a preliminary injunction, writing that "Kournikova cannot seriously argue that she is a competitor of Penthouse in any meaningful sense. Although Penthouse and Kournikova may be competing

---

31. See *PPX Enterprises* v. *Audiofidelity Enterprises,* 818 F. 2d 266 (1987); and *U-Haul International* v. *Jartran, Inc.,* 793 F. 2d 1034 (1986).

32. *Kournikova* v. *General Media Communications, Inc.,* 2002 U.S. Dist. LEXIS 25810 (2002), aff'd 51 Fed. Appx. 739 (9th Cir. 2002). In May 2003 the same judge reheard Kournikova's Lanham Act claim for false advertising, but this time on the defendant's motion for summary judgment. Judge Gary Allen Fees now found that while Kournikova may actually be a competitor with *Penthouse* in the "entertainment business" by selling sexually appealing products like her 2003 calendar, she once again had presented no evidence of competitive injury. The judge thus granted *Penthouse*'s motion for summary judgment on the false advertising Lanham Act claim. Once again, Kournikova lost, something she is now accustomed to both on court and in court. *Kournikova* v. *General Media Communications, Inc.,* 278 F. Supp. 2d 111 (2003).

for the use of Kournikova's name and identity, this is not sufficient to constitute a 'competitive injury' for standing under a false advertising claim." There is no common-law tort for deceptive advertising. As George and Peter Rosden point out in their massive compendium "The Law of Advertising," historically, common-law courts have not been receptive to protecting consumers. "During the most formative period of common law," they write, "only a few goods in the marketplace were manufactured products so that the buyer was in an excellent position to judge for himself goods offered to him."[33] The basic slogan in those days was caveat emptor, or buyer beware.

Recently some consumer class-action lawsuits have netted huge settlements. In 2006 a $10.5 million settlement was reached in a case claiming that ubiquitous psychologist and general know-it-all "Dr. Phil" McGraw made false and misleading claims for "Shape Up!" diet supplements (Dr. Phil did not admit liability and denied wrongdoing under the settlement).[34]

Recently some consumer class-action lawsuits have netted huge settlements.

STATE AND LOCAL LAWS

State regulation of advertising predates federal regulation by several years. This fact is not surprising when you consider that at the time the public became interested in advertising regulation—around the turn of the century—the federal government was a minuscule creature relative to its present size. Harry Nims, a New York lawyer, drafted a model law called the **Printers' Ink statute** (it was Printers' Ink magazine that urged passage of the law) in 1911. Most states today have such laws. In addition, many states have what are called unfair and deceptive acts and practices statutes, which give consumers the right to seek a judicial remedy in false advertising cases. These acts are often called "Little FTC Acts," and the guidelines developed by the FTC in applying federal advertising law (discussed shortly) are used by the state courts in administering these state regulations.[35] In addition, many local governments have consumer protection laws that apply broadly to false advertising.

In 2008, in an action brought by New York Attorney General Andrew Cuomo under New York's consumer protection laws, Judge Joseph C. Teresi ruled that Texas-based computer maker Dell, Inc. had repeatedly engaged in "misleading, deceptive and unlawful business conduct, including false and deceptive advertising of financing promotions and the terms of warranties, fraudulent, misleading and deceptive practices in credit financing and failure to provide warranty service and rebates."[36] The judge also ruled against Dell Financial Services. In a press release after the victory, Cuomo proclaimed that "for too long at Dell the promise of customer service was a bait and switch that left thousands of people paying for essentially no service at all. We have won an important victory that will force Dell to live up to its responsibilities and pay back its customers for profits that were pocketed but not deserved."[37]

33. Rosden and Rosden, *The Law of Advertising.*
34. Selvin, "'Dr. Phil' Diet Pill Maker Settles Suit."
35. Kertz and Ohanian, "Recent Trends," 603.
36. Decision and Order, *New York v. Dell, Inc.*, RJI No. 01-07-089339 (N.Y. Sup. Ct. Albany County, May 25, 2008).
37. Press release, "Attorney General's Office Wins Major Suit Against Dell," May 27, 2008, available online at http://www.oag.state.ny.us/media_center/2008/may/may27a_08.html.

FEDERAL REGULATION

A variety of federal agencies are empowered to enforce consumer protection laws. The Federal Trade Commission (FTC) is the primary agent of the government, but clearly not the only agent. Beginning in the 1990s the Food and Drug Administration (FDA) began an aggressive campaign against a variety of companies to force them to change their labeling and promotional practices.

The FDA issued a warning letter in 2009 to General Mills.

For instance, the FDA issued a warning letter in 2009 to General Mills, asserting that certain labeling claims about the ability of Cheerios Toasted Whole Grain Oat Cereal to reduce cholesterol ("You can Lower Your Cholesterol 4% in 6 weeks") meant that the cereal was being promoted by General Mills to treat conditions that would subject it to regulation as a drug. How could a breakfast cereal possibly be classified as an unapproved new drug? Because, according to the FDA, some of the claims on the boxes for the cereal suggest that it is intended for use in the prevention, mitigation, and treatment of hypercholesterolemia and coronary heart disease. The FDA's warning letter did not mean that the cereal was dangerous, but instead that it may not be being marketed properly with the above claim without an approved new-drug application. The FDA also criticized certain assertions made on the official Web site for the cereal (http://www.wholegrainnation.com), alleging the claims were misbranding the cereal and making unauthorized health assertions. General Mills contested the FDA's allegations.

The FTC was created by Congress in 1914 to police unfair methods of business competition. The agency was to make certain that Company A did not engage in practices that gave it an unfair advantage over its competitor, Company B. Of course, an unfair advantage may be gained through the use of false or misleading advertising. As originally conceived, the FTC was not supposed to worry about the impact of advertising on consumers, only competitors. During the 1920s, however, the FTC substantially enlarged its mission in an effort to try to protect consumers as well. This effort was suddenly stopped in 1931 when the Supreme Court ruled that the FTC had illegally enlarged its jurisdiction and that it could only attempt to regulate advertising that unfairly affected the advertiser's competitor.[38]

In 1938 Congress adopted the Wheeler-Lea Amendment to the Trade Commission Act, which gave the FTC the power to proceed against all unfair and deceptive acts or practices in commerce, regardless of whether they affect competition. Since that time the commission has developed into one of the nation's largest independent regulatory agencies. In addition to policing false advertising, the FTC is charged with enforcing the nation's antitrust laws and several federal statutes such as the Truth in Lending Law and the Fair Credit Reporting Act. The five members of the commission are appointed by the president and confirmed by the Senate for a term of seven years. No more than three of the commissioners can be from the same political party. A chairperson, one of the five commissioners, is appointed by the president. Although the agency is located in Washington, D.C., it has 11 regional offices throughout the nation.

The history of the agency reveals that it has often been swept by the political winds of the time. For years it was known as the "Little Gray Lady on Pennsylvania Avenue" because of its timid performance. During the late 1960s and 1970s, in an era of consumer concern, the

---

38. *FTC* v. *Raladam,* 283 U.S. 643 (1931).

FTC showed new muscle and attacked some of the nation's largest advertisers, such as Coca-Cola and ITT Continental Baking. In the 1980s the FTC reflected the spirit of deregulation that ran throughout Washington, D.C., as Ronald Reagan entered the White House.

In the 1990s the agency renewed its aggressive efforts, instituting false advertising actions against several national advertisers, including Kraft General Foods, and bringing charges against a group of companies that were using program-length TV ads called infomercials to sell a variety of goods and services, including diet plans and treatments for cellulite buildup and baldness. The agency also brought a complaint against the tobacco industry that ultimately ended the career of Joe Camel and other cigarette advertising designed to appeal to children.

On the antitrust front, the FTC was active in recent years. For instance, it intervened in 2009 in the proposed multi-billion-dollar acquisition by Dow Chemical Co. of rival chemical manufacturer Rohm & Haas Co., claiming a merger would violate antitrust laws. Dow settled with the FTC, agreeing both to sell off certain assets to an FTC-approved acquirer were it to buy Rohm & Haas and to put procedures in place to ensure it would not have access to competitively sensitive nonpublic information regarding any businesses it would acquire from its rival. In 2008 the FTC moved to stop a merger between the makers of popular seasoning salts. The FTC claimed that a proposed takeover by spice giant McCormick & Co., which did about $2.7 billion in sales in 2006 and produces Season-All products, of both the Lawry's and Adolph's seasoning salt brands would be anti-competitive and likely lead to higher prices. The FTC alleged that the U.S. market for branded seasoning salt is highly concentrated, with McCormick's Season-All and Lawry's products comprising most of the $100 million in annual sales. Also in 2008 the FTC filed a complaint alleging that French beverage giant Pernod Ricard's proposed $9 billion acquisition of Swedish company Vin & Sprit (V&S) would violate U.S. antitrust laws by effectively combining the two most popular brands of "super-premium" vodka in the United States, Absolut (made by V&S) and Stolichnaya (distributed by Pernod Ricard). The FTC argued that if Pernod Ricard owned Absolut while also distributing Stolichnaya, it could profitably raise the price of either brand. The FTC ultimately secured an agreement from Pernod Ricard that it would stop distributing Stolichnaya.

On the antitrust front, the FTC was active in recent years.

Telemarketing

The FTC initiated in 2003 one of its most popular and well-used programs—the National Do Not Call Registry that allows people to block the calls of telemarketers. The registry, however, would also prove controversial. In particular, several telemarketing agencies filed lawsuits in 2003 against the FTC, alleging that it was beyond the scope of the FTC's jurisdiction to adopt the National Do Not Call Registry and claiming that the registry violated the First Amendment right of free speech of advertisers who use telemarketing.

In 2004 the U.S. Court of Appeals for the 10th Circuit upheld the National Do Not Call Registry in *Mainstream Marketing Services, Inc.* v. *Federal Trade Commission.*[39] In concluding that the registry did not violate the First Amendment free speech rights of telemarketers,

---

39. 358 F. 3d 1228 (2004), cert. den., 543 U.S. 812 (2004).

the appellate court applied the commercial speech doctrine and *Central Hudson* test (see pages 551–556). In a unanimous opinion, the appellate court wrote that

> the government has asserted substantial interests to be served by the do-not-call registry (privacy and consumer protection), the do-not-call registry will directly advance those interests by banning a substantial amount of unwanted telemarketing calls, and the regulation is narrowly tailored because its opt-in feature ensures that it does not restrict any speech directed at a willing listener. In other words, the do-not-call registry bears a reasonable fit with the purposes the government sought to advance. Therefore, it is consistent with the limits the First Amendment imposes on laws restricting commercial speech.

The FTC contended that the registry, which is a list containing the personal telephone numbers of telephone subscribers who have voluntarily indicated that they do not wish to receive unsolicited calls from commercial telemarketers, was necessary to reduce both intrusions upon consumer privacy in the home and the risk of fraudulent or abusive solicitations from telemarketers. The government had specifically limited the reach of the National Do Not Call Registry, which already had more than 50 million phone numbers by the time the appellate court issued its February 2004 opinion, only to telemarketing calls made by or on behalf of sellers of goods or services, and not to charitable or political fund-raising calls. The telemarketers, however, argued that the exemptions for political and charitable calls made the statute "underinclusive"—that to effectively serve the interests of protecting privacy and preventing fraud, the registry should also apply to political and charitable solicitations, not just to commercial sales calls. The appellate court, however, rejected the underinclusiveness argument, writing that "First Amendment challenges based on underinclusiveness face an uphill battle in the commercial speech context. As a general rule, the First Amendment does not require that the government regulate all aspects of a problem before it can make progress on any front." In other words, the government could focus its attention with the registry only on the problems caused by commercial sales calls without having to also sweep up and control problems caused by political and charitable calls.

The decision marked a victory for privacy advocates but can be seen as a blow to the free speech rights of telemarketers.

The decision marked a victory for privacy advocates but can be seen as a blow to the free speech rights of telemarketers. The U.S. Supreme Court turned back a challenge to the appellate court's ruling, thus bringing an end (at least for the time being) to telemarketers' efforts to invoke free speech arguments to have the popular ban on unwanted phone solicitations declared unconstitutional. In addition to the national registry, courts have upheld state do-not-call registries, paying favorable attention to the voluntary "opt-in" nature of the state laws (in other words, the registries apply only to individuals who sign up for them, rather than automatically applying to everyone).[40]

In 2008 President George W. Bush signed legislation under which numbers placed on the list remain on it permanently unless consumers specifically request a number's removal by

---

40. *National Coalition of Prayer, Inc.* v. *Carter,* 455 F. 3d 783 (7th Cir. 2006), which upheld Indiana's do-not-call list that allows Indiana telephone customers to add themselves to the list, and wrote that "the state's interest in protecting residents' right not to endure unwanted speech in their own homes outweighs any First Amendment interests"; and *Fraternal Order of Police* v. *Stenehjem,* 431 F. 3d 591 (8th Cir. 2005), which upheld North Dakota's do-not-call registry as a statute that "significantly furthers the state's interest in residential privacy."

calling 1-888-382-1222. The law originally required consumers to re-register their numbers every five years to remain on the registry. By October 2008, there were more than 172 million phone numbers registered on the do-not-call list.

To access the registry to learn the numbers they cannot call, telemarketers pay a fee. For instance, to access the registry in fiscal year 2009, telemarketers paid either $54 for each area code of data accessed or $14,850 for access to every area code in the registry, whichever figure was less. Telemarketers could access the first five area codes of data at no charge, and certain exempt organizations could access all data for free. Fees increase annually at the rate of change of the consumer price index.

There is an "established business relationship" (EBR) exception to the do-not-call provisions that allows a company to call a consumer with whom it has such a relationship, even if the consumer's number is on the registry. An EBR exists when a consumer has purchased, rented or leased the company's goods or services within 18 months preceding a telemarketing call.

There is an "established business relationship" (EBR) exception to the do-not-call provisions.

Finally, under the FTC's rules, telemarketers cannot call a person between the hours of 9:00 p.m. and 8:00 a.m. unless the person has given prior consent to such late-night, early-morning calls. Learn more about the Do Not Call Registry by visiting the FTC's Web site at http://www.ftc.gov/donotcall. Rules governing the conduct of telemarketers are found at http://www.ftc.gov/bcp/edu/microsites/donotcall/businfo.html.

The FTC, with the help of the Department of Justice, actively enforces the do-not-call rules. In 2009, for instance, it obtained federal court orders requiring two groups of vacation and timeshare companies (Westgate Resorts, Ltd. and All In One Vacation Club, LLC) to pay a total of almost $1.2 million for violating the rules. The FTC contended the companies called consumers whose phone numbers were on the Do Not Call Registry without having obtained their express written agreement or having an EBR.

In an even larger action, DIRECTV and Comcast Corp. agreed in 2009 to pay a total of $3.21 million to settle separate FTC charges that they violated certain do-not-call provisions, including charges that they or their telemarketers called consumers who specifically had told the companies not to call them again. The settlement marked the second time that DIRECTV had violated the rules, as it already had paid out $5.3 million as part of a 2005 federal court order.

In August 2009 the FTC banned so-called robocalls (those annoying prerecorded commercial telemarketing calls to consumers) unless the telemarketing company has obtained written permission from a consumer to receive such calls. Sellers and telemarketers that transmit such messages to consumers that haven't granted permission to accept them face penalties of up to $16,000 per call.

In August 2009, the FTC banned so-called robocalls.

REGULATING JUNK E-MAIL AND SPAM

One of the most pervasive and annoying forms of advertising today is on the Internet. Almost everyone who uses electronic mail has received unsolicited commercial advertising known as "spam." Without a filter or other form of protection on one's computer or e-mail system, spam can clutter an online mailbox. What's more, spam frequently takes the form of sexually explicit advertisements that may be both unwanted by, and offensive to, its recipients. On the other hand, to the extent that spam pertains to a lawful product and is neither false nor deceptive, it constitutes commercial speech protected by the

First Amendment. Spam also represents an economically efficient and inexpensive way of marketing one's product or service.

To address the negative aspects of spam, Congress passed and President George W. Bush signed into law in 2003 the CAN-SPAM Act.[41] The act's title represents a tortured acronym for a bill officially called the "Controlling the Assault of Non-Solicited Pornography and Marketing Act of 2003." It applies to "commercial electronic mail messages" that have as their "primary purpose" the "commercial advertisement or promotion of a commercial product or service."

In an excellent article on the CAN-SPAM Act,[42] attorneys Glenn B. Manishin and Stephanie A. Joyce identify five specific components of the law:

1. **False/Misleading Messages:** Commercial e-mail messages that include "materially false or misleading" header information or deceptive subject lines are prohibited.

2. **Functioning Return Address and Opt-Out Mechanism:** All commercial e-mail messages must contain either a functioning return address or an Internet-based reply "opt-out" mechanism for at least 30 days after transmission of a message.

3. **10-Day Prohibition Period:** Spam senders are barred from transmitting commercial e-mail messages to any recipient after 10 business days following the exercise by the recipient of his or her right to opt out of future commercial e-mail messages.

4. **Disclosure Requirements:** All commercial e-mail messages must disclose three specific items of content: (a) a clear and conspicuous identification of the message as an "advertisement or solicitation," (b) a notice of the "opt-out" mechanism, and (c) a "valid physical postal address." All commercial e-mail "that includes sexually oriented material" must also include a warning label on the subject line. To implement this provision, the FTC in May 2004 adopted a rule requiring spammers who send sexually oriented material to include the warning "SEXUALLY-EXPLICIT:" in the e-mail subject line or face fines for violations of federal law.[43] In addition, the matter in the spam e-mail message that is initially viewable when it is opened cannot include any sexually oriented material.

5. **Aggravated Violations:** The act proscribes as "aggravated violations," warranting additional civil and commercial penalties, (a) e-mail "harvesting" or the knowing use of harvested addresses, (b) the automated creation of multiple e-mail accounts used for commercial e-mail, and (c) the use of unauthorized relays for commercial e-mail messages.

In 2008 the FTC clarified that the "valid physical postal address" that must be disclosed by the sender of commercial e-mail messages can be either a registered post office box or a private mailbox established under U.S. Postal Service regulations. In addition, the FTC in 2008 made it clear that the "opt-out" mechanism used by a commercial sender cannot require a recipient to take any steps other than sending a reply e-mail message or visiting a single Internet Web page to opt out of receiving future e-mail from that sender.

41. 15 U.S.C. § 7701 et seq. (2004).
42. Manishin and Joyce, "Current Spam Law & Policy."
43. 16 C.F.R. 316 (2004).

The CAN-SPAM Act does not provide for a private legal cause of action or remedy for spam recipients. Instead, the FTC enforces the law. For instance, the FTC in 2008 obtained a record $2.9 million settlement from online advertiser ValueClick, Inc. for sending, among other things, deceptively labeled e-mail messages offering free gifts and merchandise. In brief, the FTC claimed the subject lines or headers were materially misleading and designed to drive consumers to the company's Web sites where they "were led through a maze of expensive and burdensome third-party offers—including car loans and satellite television subscriptions—which they were required to 'participate in' at their own expense, in order to receive the promised 'free' merchandise."[44] Also in 2008, the FTC obtained a court-ordered settlement against ATM Global Systems, Inc., which operates a number of sexually explicit Web sites, including a dating service called SexyFriendSearch.com.[45] The FTC contended that ATM and its operators violated the CAN-SPAM Act by sending spam with false or misleading header information, failing to include an opt-out mechanism and failing to include a valid postal address. ATM allegedly used several affiliated Web sites, who were paid commissions for referrals to SexyFriendsSearch.com who signed up as members, to send spam with lurid subject lines that contained hyperlinks to ATM's Web sites. The settlement barred ATM from engaging in future violations of CAN-SPAM Act, required ATM to establish an effective monitoring program for its affiliates and imposed a $75,000 civil penalty.

The CAN-SPAM Act does not provide for a private legal cause of action.

Perhaps the biggest spam victory ever for the FTC came in October 2008. That's when it obtained a temporary restraining order from a federal judge stopping the spamming practices of the individuals and companies that operated the HerbalKing international spam network. HerbalKing was the worst and largest spam gang for much of 2007 and 2008, according to the Spamhaus Project, an organization that tracks spammers and works with law enforcement to identify and pursue them worldwide.[46] The FTC claimed the network, allegedly under the leadership of Lance Atkinson, a New Zealand citizen living in Australia, and Jody Smith of Texas, sold prescription drugs and bogus male-enhancement products while making false and misleading claims about them. It purportedly "recruited spammers around the world to send billions of spam messages directing consumers to Web sites operated by an affiliate program called 'Affking.' By using false header information to hide the origin of the messages, failing to provide an opt-out link, and failing to list a physical postal address, the defendants violated the CAN-SPAM."[47]

Perhaps the biggest spam victory ever for the FTC came in October 2008.

In 2007 the federal government gained its first in-court criminal conviction before a jury under CAN-SPAM when Jeffrey Brett Goodin of Azusa, Calif., was found guilty of "phishing" for financial information when he sent thousands of e-mails that falsely appeared to be from America Online's Billing Department to AOL subscribers. Later in 2007, Jeffrey A. Kilbride of Venice, Calif., and James R. Schaffer of Paradise Valley, Ariz., were each sentenced

---

44. Press release, "ValueClick to Pay $2.9 Million to Settle FTC Charges," March 17, 2008, available online at http://www.ftc.gov/opa/2008/03/vc.shtm.
45. Press release, "FTC Halts Illegal Spam Operation; Adult Site Violated CAN-SPAM Act," May 6, 2008, available online at http://www.ftc.gov/opa/2008/05/atmglobal.shtm.
46. The Spamhaus Project can be found online at http://www.spamhaus.org.
47. Press release, "FTC Shuts Down, Freezes Assets of Vast International Spam E-Mail Network," Oct. 14, 2008, available online at http://www.ftc.gov/opa/2008/10/herbalkings.shtm.

to more than five years in federal prison after a jury convicted them on eight counts, including violating the CAN-SPAM Act by sending spam messages using falsified headers and domain names. The charges related to running an international pornographic spamming business that grossed more than $1 million. More recently, in 2008 so-called Spam King Robert Soloway of Seattle, Wash., was sentenced to nearly four years in prison for violating the CAN-SPAM Act "by falsifying the header information in his e-mail messages. The program he used automatically substituted the e-mail recipient's name for that of Soloway's, making it appear that the recipient had sent a message to himself or herself or used bogus addresses in the from field."[48]

Some states have their own statutes targeting such e-mails.

In addition to the federal CAN-SPAM Act, some states have their own statutes targeting such e-mails. In September 2008, however, Virginia's law restricting unsolicited bulk e-mails was declared unconstitutional by that state's highest court, thus allowing a notorious spammer named Jeremy Jaynes, who was convicted under it, to go free (Jaynes sent more than 10,000 spam in 24 hours on at least three occasions).[49] The Virginia Supreme Court concluded the law was "unconstitutionally overbroad . . . because it prohibits the anonymous transmission of all unsolicited bulk e-mails including those containing political, religious or other speech protected by the First Amendment to the United States Constitution" (see page 11 regarding the overbreadth doctrine). The problem with Virginia's law, in brief, was that it was not limited in scope to only commercial or fraudulent e-mails. In describing the importance of protecting anonymous noncommercial e-mails with political content, the Virginia Supreme Court cited as precedent the U.S. Supreme Court's ruling in *McIntyre* v. *Ohio Elections Commission* (see page 120). The Virginia decision does not impact the federal CAN-SPAM Act, and the U.S. Supreme Court declined in March 2009 to review the Virginia Supreme Court's ruling.

In addition to tackling the problem of spam, the federal government is increasingly involved in taking on another new and pesky form of advertising—unsolicited commercial facsimile messages. President George W. Bush signed into law the Junk Fax Prevention Act of 2005, which revises the Telephone Consumer Protection Act of 1991. Specifically, the Junk Fax Prevention Act of 2005 bans unsolicited advertisement faxes unless there is an "established business relationship" between the sender and recipient, known as an EBR exemption. If an EBR exists, then express consent of the fax recipient is not needed before a commercial fax may be sent, provided that the fax number was voluntarily given by the recipient. In 2008 the FCC clarified that facsimile numbers compiled on behalf of a fax sender are presumed to be voluntarily available for public distribution if they are obtained from the recipient's own directory, advertisement or Internet site. The Junk Fax Prevention Act of 2005 also imposes an opt-out provision requirement somewhat akin to that in the CAN-SPAM Act. In particular, the first page or cover sheet of all unsolicited fax ads must include a cost-free, opt-out provision allowing the recipient to be removed from the distribution list. The Federal Communications Commission is charged with investigating complaints and enforcing the new law. The FCC maintains a Web site with information about fax advertising regulations at http://www.fcc.gov/cgb/consumerfacts/unwantedfaxes.html.

48. Shukovsky, "'Spam King' Gets Nearly 4 Years in Prison."
49. *Jaynes* v. *Virginia*, 666 S.E. 2d 303 (Va. 2008).

SUMMARY

Self-regulation by the advertising industry has increased in recent years, especially with the growth of comparative advertising. The National Advertising Division and the Child Advertising Review Unit, divisions within the Better Business Bureau, are the primary agents for this self-regulation. Such regulation is geared toward satisfying the interests of advertisers rather than consumers, however. There has also been a rapid increase in lawsuits brought by advertisers against one another under Section 43(a) of the Lanham Act. An advertiser seeking redress under this federal law can seek to stop the misleading practice and/or win money damages. Again, this law provides little relief for consumers. Laws banning false advertising exist at both the state and local levels, but tend to be applied half-heartedly. The Federal Trade Commission remains the nation's most potent weapon against false or misleading advertising.

FEDERAL TRADE COMMISSION

One of the FTC's most important responsibilities is to ensure that Americans are not victimized by unfair, misleading or deceptive advertising. Through custom and practice, the agency has defined advertising as any action, method or device intended to draw the attention of the public to merchandise, to services, to people and to organizations. Trading stamps, contests, freebies, premiums and even product labels are included in this definition, in addition to the more common categories of product and service advertising. At times a business has challenged the FTC by arguing that its particular exposition is not an advertisement but an essay or a statement of business philosophy. Rarely have these challenges been successful. Normally, what the FTC says in an advertisement is considered to be an advertisement for purposes of regulation.[50]

Normally, what the FTC says in an advertisement is considered to be an advertisement for purposes of regulation.

Does the FTC regulate all advertising? Legally, no, it cannot. But practically, it can regulate almost all advertising. Because the agency was created under the authority of Congress to regulate interstate commerce, products or services must be sold in interstate commerce or the advertising medium must be somehow affected by interstate commerce before the FTC can intervene. Although many products and services are sold locally only, nearly every conceivable advertising medium is somehow affected by or affects interstate commerce. All broadcasting stations are considered to affect interstate commerce. Most newspapers ship at

---

50. The courts are not quite this consistent in defining advertising. Judges in both New York and California were asked recently whether statements taken from the text of a book and reprinted on promotional blurbs on the cover of the book were ads for the book or part of the text of the book. The publication involved was the *Beardstown Ladies' Common-Sense Investment Guide,* a volume that contained highly exaggerated claims for the success of a particular investing scheme. All sides agreed that the false claims in the book were fully protected by the First Amendment, but the plaintiffs in both cases argued that when the claims were reprinted on the cover of the book (and the outside of a videotape cassette box) they were advertising or commercial speech and did not enjoy the full protection of the First Amendment. The court in California said the comments were commercial speech and not fully protected. The court in New York came to the opposite conclusion. See *Keimer* v. *Buena Vista Books,* 89 Cal. Rptr. 2d 781 (1999); and *Lacoff* v. *Buena Vista Publishing Inc.,* 705 N.Y.S. 2d 183 (2000).

least a few copies across state lines. Even when a newspaper is not mailed across state lines, it is very likely that some of the news in the newspaper comes across state lines or that the paper on which the news is printed, the ink and type used to print the news, or parts of the printing machinery travel across state lines.

Importantly today, the FTC's prohibition against unfair or deceptive advertising and fraudulent marketing in any medium includes the Internet. The FTC in 2007 received more than 42,000 fraud complaints regarding Internet services and more than 24,000 fraud complaints regarding Internet auctions. The FTC maintains an entire Web site devoted to Internet fraud at http://www.onguardonline.gov. In 2009 the FTC issued a set of principles to encourage and guide industry self-regulation in the area of online behavioral advertising, which tracks a person's online activities in order to deliver advertising tailored to his or her interests. The practice of online behavioral advertising raises clear privacy concerns, as advertisers collect data via cookies about people, including the Web sites they visit and the search commands they enter. The report, "Self-Regulatory Principles for Online Behavioral Advertising," has guidelines regarding data capture, retention and dissemination, and can be found online at http://www.ftc.gov/os/2009/02/P085400behavadreport.pdf.

The FTC's rules against deceptive advertising break down into two critical components.

In a nutshell, the FTC's rules against deceptive advertising break down into two critical components:

1. Advertising must be truthful and not misleading, with misleading ads sweeping up those in which relevant information is omitted, those that imply something that's not true and those in which any disclaimers or disclosures are not clear and not prominent enough for reasonable consumers to see, hear and understand them.

2. All claims made in advertisements must be substantiated such that, before disseminating an ad, advertisers must have a reasonable basis for any and all express and/or implied product claims, with claims relating to health and safety coming under even closer FTC scrutiny that typically requires proof by competent and reliable scientific evidence.

Undergraduate advertising majors thus are well advised when they enter the profession to remember a few simple things: Ads must tell the truth, not mislead (either by sins of omission or sins of express or implied misrepresentation) and be backed up with prior substantiation.

In the actual implementation and application of the two critical components of the FTC's rules against deceptive advertising, three key considerations emerge that are set forth in the following box and then described in greater detail.

FTC DEFINITION OF FALSE OR DECEPTIVE ADVERTISING

1. There must be a representation, omission or practice that is likely to mislead the consumer.
2. The act or practice must be considered from the perspective of a consumer who is acting reasonably.
3. The representation, omission or practice must be material.

FALSE ADVERTISING DEFINED

1. **There must be a representation, omission or practice that is likely to mislead the consumer.** The commission considers the entire advertisement as well as all other elements of a transaction when making this determination. As one federal court observed in 2008, "when assessing the meaning and representations conveyed by an advertisement, the court must look to the advertisement's overall, net impression rather than the literal truth or falsity of the words in the advertisement."[51] The same court noted that an ad's meaning "may be resolved by the terms of the advertisement itself or by evidence of what consumers interpreted the advertisement to convey." It also is important to remember that an ad may mislead because it omits material information.

   The court must look to the advertisement's overall, net impression.

2. **The act or practice must be considered from the perspective of a consumer who is acting reasonably.** The test is whether the consumer's interpretation or reaction is reasonable. When advertisements or sales practices are targeted to a specific audience, such as those aimed at children or people who are elderly or terminally ill, they will be viewed from the perspective of a reasonable member of that group. Also, advertising aimed at a special vocational group, such as physicians, will be evaluated from the perspective of a reasonable member of that group. A well-educated physician might be better able to understand a complicated pharmaceutical ad than the average individual can.

   The advertiser is not responsible for every interpretation or behavior by a consumer. The law is not designed to protect the foolish or the "feeble minded," the commission has noted. "Some people, because of ignorance or incomprehension, may be misled by even a scrupulously honest claim," one commissioner noted. "Perhaps a few misguided souls believe, for example, that all Danish pastry is made in Denmark. Is it therefore an actionable deception to advertise Danish pastry when it is made in this country? Of course not," the commissioner noted.[52] When an advertisement conveys more than one meaning to a reasonable consumer, one of which is false, the seller is liable for the misleading interpretation. Here is a classic example: "Jones Garage will put a new motor in your car for only $350." What does this claim mean? One meaning is that the garage will sell you a new motor and install it for only $350. But an equally reasonable meaning is that for only $350 the garage will install a motor that you already own. If the second meaning is intended, the seller may very well be held responsible for the first meaning—which was not intended—as well.

   The commission evaluates the entire advertisement when examining it for misrepresentation. Accurate information in the text may not remedy a false headline, because a reasonable consumer may only glance at the headline. If a television announcer proclaims that a watch is 100 percent waterproof, the advertiser cannot qualify this claim in a long printed message in small type that crawls across the bottom of the TV screen while the announcer tries to sell the product.[53] Nissan Motor Corporation agreed to stop its "Nissan Challenge" promotional advertising

   Accurate information in the text may not remedy a false headline.

51. *FTC v. National Urological Group,* 2008 U.S. Dist. LEXIS 44145 (N.D. Ga. June 4, 2008).
52. *In re Kirchner,* 63 F.T.C. 1282 (1963), aff'd 337 F. 2d 751 (1964).
53. *Giant Food, Inc.* v. *FTC,* 322 F. 2d 977 (1963).

campaign. On its face the advertising said that Nissan would give consumers $100 if they bought a Honda Accord or Toyota Camry after test-driving a Nissan Stanza. But in order to get the $100 consumers had to meet several conditions, which were not prominently noted in the advertising. Consumers had to actually buy a Honda or Toyota, take delivery of it, and submit proof of purchase to Nissan within seven days of the test drive—but not on the same day as the test drive.[54] Similarly, an advertiser cannot correct a misrepresentation in an advertisement with point-of-sale information. A seller cannot advertise a vacuum cleaner as having a 100 percent money-back guarantee and then expect to qualify that claim in a tag that is attached to the product as it is displayed for sale in a store. Qualifying disclosures must be legible and understandable, the FTC has ruled.

Qualifying disclosures must be legible and understandable, the FTC has ruled.

"The commission generally will not bring advertising cases based on subjective claims (taste, feel, appearance, smell)," according to the 1983 guidelines. The agency says it believes the typical reasonable consumer does not take such claims seriously and thus they are unlikely to be deceptive. Such claims are referred to as **puffery** and include representations that a store sells "the most fashionable shoes in town" or a cola drink is "the most refreshing drink around."

Finally, the commission has stated that when consumers can easily evaluate the product or service, when it is inexpensive, and when it is frequently purchased, the commission scrutinizes the advertisement or representation in a less critical manner. "There is little incentive for sellers to misrepresent ... in these circumstances since they normally would seek to encourage repeat purchases," a 1983 statement proclaims.

3. **The representation, omission or practice must be material.** A material misrepresentation or practice is one that is likely to affect a consumer's choice of a product. In other words, according to the commission policy statement, "it is information that is important to the consumer." The FTC considers certain categories of information to be more important than others when deciding whether a claim is material. Express claims as to the attributes of a product are always considered material. Advertising claims that significantly involve health and safety are usually presumed to be material. Information pertaining to the "central characteristics of the product or service" is usually considered to be material. Information has also been found to be material where it concerns the purpose, efficacy or cost of the product or service. Claims about durability, performance, warranties or quality have also been considered material.

Demonstrations or mock-ups often become the subject of FTC inquiries, and the question of materiality is often raised. For many years a shaving cream manufacturer claimed that its product was so good that it could be used to shave sandpaper. In a TV demonstration, Rapid Shave was spread on sandpaper and then, a few moments later, the sand was shaved off. The demonstration was phony. What the demonstrator shaved was not sandpaper, but sand sprinkled on glass. The FTC argued that this advertisement was deceptive and that the claim that Rapid Shave could be used to shave sandpaper was a material representation. The Supreme Court agreed, despite the plea from Colgate-Palmolive that the product really

---

54. "Nissan Unit Will Pull Ads."

could shave sandpaper if it was left on the paper long enough, but because the sand and the paper were the same color, a TV demonstration did not work. Hence the company had to use sand on glass.[55] The FTC found that two demonstrations used to advertise an immersion-style kitchen mixer in a 30-minute infomercial called "Amazing Discoveries: Magic Wand" were phony and hence misleading. The advertiser used a pineapple with the center core removed and precrushed to create the impression that Magic Wand could crush a whole fresh pineapple. The marketers also claimed Magic Wand would whip up skim milk, but they actually used a commercial dairy topping in their demonstration, the FTC said.[56]

But not all mock-ups or fake demonstrations are necessarily deceptive. Only those that are used to support a material product claim must be restricted. For example, plastic ice cubes may be substituted for the real thing in an advertisement for a soft drink because no claim about the quality of the ice cubes is involved.

MEANS TO POLICE DECEPTIVE ADVERTISING

In dealing with false advertising, the FTC's greatest enemy is the time needed to bring an action against an advertiser. Since advertising campaigns are ephemeral, the FTC often has difficulty in catching up with the advertiser before the short-lived campaign has been replaced with something else. But if time is the greatest enemy, publicity is the FTC's strongest ally. Advertisers don't like the publicity that accompanies a charge of false advertising. Bad publicity can cost a company millions of dollars. In addition, consumer reaction to the charges often results in lost sales as well.

In addition to the informal sanction of publicity, the FTC has a wide range of remedies to deal with advertising. Let's briefly look at this arsenal.

FTC TOOLS OR REMEDIES TO STOP FALSE ADVERTISING

- Guides and the Child Online Privacy Protection Act
- Voluntary compliance
- Consent agreement
- Litigated orders
- Substantiation
- Corrective advertising
- Injunctions
- Trade regulation rules

Guides and the Child Online Privacy Protection Act

The FTC issues industry guides for a variety of products, services and marketing practices. These guides are policy statements that alert businesses to what the agency believes

---

55. *FTC v. Colgate-Palmolive Co.*, 380 U.S. 374 (1965).
56. Tewkesbury, "FTC Restricts Claims."

are permissible advertising claims or practices. Hundreds of such guides have been issued, including a guide on when the word "free" can and cannot be used in advertising, and guides for advertising private vocational schools, home study courses and environmental claims. The FTC's Guides, Reports and Policy Statements are found online at two links:

- http://www.ftc.gov/bcp/menus/resources/guidance/adv.shtm
- http://www.ftc.gov/bcp/menus/resources/guidance.shtm

In July 1997 the FTC issued a statement that laid down principles by which it would evaluate the propriety of information collection and endorsement practices on Web sites used by children. The statement says, for example, that it is deceptive for a Web site operator to represent that the personally identifiable information it collects from a child will be used for one purpose if the information will really be used for another purpose. The guide also says it is improper for Web site operators to collect personally identifiable information about children and sell or disclose this information to third parties without the consent of the parents. In 1998 those guidelines were transformed into law after Congress passed the Children's Online Privacy Protection Act (COPPA), which the FTC now actively enforces as the "COPPA Rule" to protect the privacy of children online. The FTC maintains a Web site with details about COPPA at http://www.ftc.gov/bcp/conline/edcams/coppa/intro.htm. One must understand that COPPA applies to Web sites directed at children and that collect personal information from them. Under COPPA, a child-directed site must include a link, situated in a clear and prominent place, to the site's privacy policy that must explain what types of personal information are collected, how that information is collected and how the Web site will use it. The privacy policy also must tell the visitor whether the site gives the personal information to anyone else.

The FTC vigorously enforces COPPA. In December 2008 Sony BMG Music Entertainment agreed to pay $1 million as part of a settlement to resolve Federal Trade Commission charges it violated COPPA and the FTC's rules implementing COPPA.[57] The FTC alleged that, through its music fan Web sites, Sony BMG improperly collected, maintained and disclosed personal information from thousands of children under the age of 13, without their parents' consent. The civil penalty paid by Sony BMG matched the largest penalty ever in a COPPA case.

The FTC's guides don't have the force of law; in other words, a business that violates a provision of a guide is not automatically guilty of false advertising. The FTC usually requires an advertiser to substantiate claims that go beyond those permitted by the guides or may even bring a false advertising action against the business. The guides are of great benefit, however, to honest advertisers who seek to stay within the boundaries of what is allowable under the law.

COPPA applies to Web sites directed at children and that collect personal information from them.

Voluntary Compliance

Industry guides apply only to prospective advertising campaigns, events that have not yet occurred. The next remedy on the ladder is voluntary compliance and is used for advertising campaigns that are over or nearly over. Imagine that a company is nearing the end of an advertising campaign in which it has advertised that its mouthwash can prevent a consumer from getting a common cold. The FTC believes that the claim is deceptive. If the advertiser has had a good record in the past and if the offense is not too great, the company can voluntarily

57. Press release, "Sony BMG Settles Charges Its Music Fan Websites Violated the Children's Online Privacy Protection Act," Dec. 11, 2008, available online at http://www.ftc.gov/opa/2008/12/sonymusic.shtm.

agree to terminate the advertisement and never use the claim again. In doing this, the advertiser makes no admission and the agency no determination that the claim is deceptive. There is just an agreement not to repeat that particular claim in future advertising campaigns. Such an agreement saves the advertiser considerable legal hassle, publicity and money, all especially desirable since the advertising campaign is over or almost over. This remedy is infrequently used.

Consent Agreement

The most commonly used FTC remedy is the consent agreement, or **consent order or decree.** This is a written agreement between the commission and the advertiser in which the advertiser agrees to refrain from making specific product claims in future advertising. The advertiser admits no wrongdoing by signing such an order, so there is no liability involved. The consent agreement is merely a promise not to do something in the future. Sometimes the misleading statements are minor errors, but other times they represent a major attempt at deception. In 2009 Kellogg entered into a consent agreement with the FTC to settle charges that ads touting a breakfast of Frosted Mini-Wheats as "clinically shown to improve kids' attentiveness by nearly 20%" were false and violated federal law. The settlement bars deceptive or misleading cognitive health claims for Kellogg's breakfast foods and snack foods and prohibits it from misrepresenting any tests or studies. In 2008 the makers of the popular Airborne Effervescent Health Formula, a tablet marketed as a cold prevention and treatment remedy, agreed to pay millions of dollars to settle FTC charges that it did not have competent and reliable scientific evidence to support its advertising claims. The settlement prohibits Airborne Health, Inc. and Victoria Knight-McDowell, the former schoolteacher who invented Airborne, from making false and unsubstantiated cold prevention, germ-fighting and efficacy claims. The FTC determined "there is no credible evidence that Airborne products, taken as directed, will reduce the severity or duration of colds, or provide any tangible benefit for people who are exposed to germs in crowded places" such as airplanes, offices or schools.[58] Airborne was the top-selling immune support dietary supplement in 2008. In December 2008 the attorneys general of 32 states reached a separate $7 million settlement with Airborne Health, Inc. in which the company made no admission of any wrongdoing. Here are some other examples of recent consent agreement settlements:

Airborne Effervescent Health Formula . . . agreed to pay millions of dollars to settle FTC charges

- ▋ In 2006, the makers of three skin gels—Tummy Flattening Gel, Cutting Gel and Dermalin APg—that claimed in television and magazine ads to melt away fat wherever applied, agreed to not make unsubstantiated claims that either they or any substantially similar products cause weight or fat loss.[59]
- ▋ In 2005, Tropicana Products, Inc. agreed to stop making claims, unless they can be substantiated in the future by reliable scientific evidence, that drinking two to three glasses each day of its "Healthy Heart" orange juice would produce dramatic effects on blood pressure and cholesterol and thereby reduce the risk of heart disease and stroke.[60]

58. Press release, "Makers of Airborne Settle FTC Charges of Deceptive Advertising; Agreement Brings Total Settlement Funds to $30 Million," Aug. 14, 2008, available online at http://www.ftc.gov/opa/2008/08/airborne.shtm.

59. Press release, "Major Weight-Loss Marketers Pay $3 Million," May 11, 2006, available online at http://www.ftc.gov/opa/2006/05/basicresearch.htm.

60. Press release, "FTC Puts the Squeeze on Tropicana's Orange Juice Claims," available online at http://www.ftc.gov/opa/2005/06/tropicana.htm.

Considerable pressure is placed on the advertiser to agree to a consent order. Refusing to sign the agreement will result in litigation and publicity. The publicity can do more harm to the advertiser than a monetary fine. Also, the time factor works in the advertiser's favor. Typically the advertising campaign is already over.

What happens to an advertiser who signs a consent decree, then violates the provisions of the decree? In 1997 Mazda Motors of America signed an agreement to disclose far more clearly in its advertising important terms and conditions it imposed in leasing automobiles, including the up-front costs and the number, amount and timing of scheduled lease payments. While the company did improve disclosure in its advertising, it still spent too much time and space highlighting low monthly payments and insufficient time and space outlining the total lease cost, the government said. In October 1999 the FTC, working in conjunction with 24 states, levied a $5.25 million fine against the automaker for failing to follow the stipulations it agreed to in the consent decree.[61]

Litigated Order

Sometimes an advertiser doesn't want to sign a consent agreement. It may believe that the advertising claim is truthful or may simply want to hold off any FTC ban on certain kinds of product claims. In this case the commission can issue an order, usually called a **litigated order,** to stop the particular advertising claim. Staff attorneys at the FTC will issue a complaint against the advertiser, and a hearing will be held before an administrative law judge. The judge can uphold the complaint or reject it. In either case, the losing side can appeal to the federal trade commissioners for a final ruling. If the advertiser loses this final appeal before the commissioners, he or she can appeal the litigated order in federal court. Failure to abide by the provisions of a litigated order can result in the advertiser facing a severe civil penalty, as much as $10,000 per day. In the long-running (11 years) Geritol case, for example, the commission issued an order in 1965 prohibiting the J.B. Williams Company from implying in its advertising for Geritol that its product could be helpful to people who complained that they were tired and run-down.[62] The commission contended that medical evidence demonstrated that Geritol, a vitamin-and-iron tonic, helps only a small percentage of people who are tired and that in most people tiredness is a symptom of ailments for which Geritol has no therapeutic value. The J.B. Williams Co. violated the cease and desist order (at least, that is what the commission alleged) and in 1973 was fined more than $800,000. A court of appeals threw out the fine in 1974 and sent the case back to district court for a jury trial, which the advertisers had been denied the first time around.[63] The jury was to decide whether the Geritol advertisements did in fact violate the cease and desist order. At a second hearing in 1976, the FTC won a $280,000 judgment against the patent medicine manufacturer.

In 2006 a company called Sunny Health Nutrition Technology & Products, Inc. paid $375,000 to settle FTC charges that it made false and unsubstantiated claims for a dietary

---

61. "Mazda Gets Hit with $5.25 Million in Fines."
62. *J.B. Williams* v. *FTC,* 381 F. 2d 884 (1967).
63. *U.S.* v. *Williams Co.,* 498 F. 2d 414 (1974).

supplement called HeightMax, including claims that HeightMax causes users to grow an additional two to three inches in six months and that it increases lean body mass and reduces body fat in users ages 12 to 25.[64] Fans of "Napoleon Dynamite" may laugh here, recalling Uncle Rico's marketing of a fictitious herbal product called Bust Must Plus to rapidly enhance breast size.

Fans of "Napoleon Dynamite" may laugh here.

In 2004 Chief Administrative Law Judge Stephen J. McGuire ordered the marketers of a device called the Ab Force belt to stop making claims that it caused or promoted weight, inches, and fat loss; caused or promoted well-defined abdominal muscles; or was an effective alternative to regular exercise.[65] The gizmo, which was marketed on infomercials by a New Jersey–based operation called Telebrands Corporation, is an electronic muscle stimulation (EMS) device that causes the muscles to contract involuntarily. Judge McGuire concluded that the Ab Force advertisements were "likely to mislead consumers, acting reasonably under the circumstances, in a material respect."

Substantiation

Advertising **substantiation** has been an important part of the FTC regulatory scheme since 1972. The basis of the program is simple: The commission asks advertisers to substantiate claims made in their advertisements. The FTC does not presume that the claims are false or misleading. The advertiser is simply asked to prove the claims are truthful. The substantiation process today involves panels of experts who scrutinize advertisements and target for documentation those claims that seem most suspect. The most recent commission policy statement on substantiation was issued in 1984. Under this policy, express substantiation claims, such as "doctors recommend" and "specific tests prove," require the level of proof advertised. Otherwise, advertisers will be expected to have at least a "reasonable basis" for claims in their advertising, wrote attorney Thomas J. McGrew in the Los Angeles Daily Journal.[66] The degree of substantiation that will be deemed reasonable varies with "the type of claim, the product, the consequences of a false claim, the benefits of a truthful claim, the cost of developing substantiation . . . and the amount of substantiation experts in the field believe is reasonable," the policy statement said. Claims for health-related products like dietary supplements and weight-loss pills require substantiation, before the claims are made, by what the FTC calls "competent and reliable scientific evidence."

Corrective Advertising

Corrective advertising is a highly controversial scheme based on the premise that to merely stop an advertisement is in some instances insufficient. If the advertising campaign is successful and long running, a residue of misleading information remains in the mind of the public after the offensive advertisements have been removed. Under the corrective advertising scheme,

---

64. Press release, "FTC Targets Bogus Claims for Pill Advertised to Make Kids Taller," Nov. 28, 2006, available online at http://www.ftc.gov/opa/2006/11/heightmax.htm.
65. *In re Telebrands Corp.,* Initial Decision, Docket No. 9313 (Sept. 15, 2004).
66. McGrew, "Advertising Law."

the FTC forces the advertiser to inform the public that in the past it has not been honest or has been misleading. One commentator called the scheme "commercial hara-kiri."

The corrective advertising sanction was first used by the FTC in 1971 and was applied frequently during the heady consumer protection years of the 1970s. The agency has never outlined a hard-and-fast policy regarding when corrective advertising will be used. In response to a request from the Institute for Public Representation for such a policy statement, the FTC said corrective advertising may be applied:

> If a deceptive advertisement has played a substantial role in creating or reinforcing in the public's mind a false and material belief which lives on after the false advertising ceases, there is clear and continuing injury to competition, and to the consuming public as consumers continue to make purchasing decisions based on the false belief.

Since the early 1980s the corrective advertising sanction has been used sparingly by the agency. But it does still exist as a policy choice. In May 1999 the FTC ordered a giant pharmaceutical company, Novartis A.G., to run advertising correcting earlier statements that called its Doan's back-pain relievers superior to other analgesics. The agency said the company must spend $8 million on advertising messages that include the words, "Although Doan's is an effective pain reliever, there is no evidence that Doan's is more effective than other pain relievers for back pain." The company must make similar disclosures on its packaging for one year.[67]

Injunctions

Attorneys for the FTC can seek these restraining orders in federal court.

When Congress passed the Trans-Alaska Pipeline Authorization Act in 1973, attached to that piece of legislation was a bill that authorized the FTC to seek an injunction to stop advertisements that it believed violated the law. Attorneys for the FTC can seek these restraining orders in federal court. An injunction is clearly a drastic remedy and one that the agency has said it will not use often. Spokespersons for the FTC have said that the agency will use the power only in those instances in which the advertising can cause harm, in those cases that contain a clear law violation, and in those cases in which there is no prospect that the advertising practice will end soon.

In September 2004 the FTC reached a massive settlement, including a permanent injunction, in federal court with Kevin Trudeau, a prolific marketer who had either appeared in or produced hundreds of infomercials. The settlement enjoined Trudeau from appearing in, producing or disseminating future infomercials that advertise any type of product, service, or program to the public, except for truthful infomercials for informational publications.[68] Trudeau agreed to these prohibitions and to pay the FTC $2 million to settle charges that he falsely claimed that a coral calcium product called Coral Calcium Supreme can cure cancer and other serious diseases and that a purported analgesic called Biotape can permanently cure or relieve severe pain. In nationally televised infomercials, Trudeau had advertised that Coral Calcium Supreme, a dietary supplement purportedly made from Japanese marine

---

67. "Novartis Is Ordered to Fix Doan's Ads."
68. *FTC* v. *Trudeau,* Stipulated Final Order for Permanent Injunction and Settlement of Claims for Monetary Relief, Case Nos. 03 C-3904 and 98-C-016 (N.D. Ill. 2004).

coral, provided the same amount of bio-available calcium as two gallons of milk, could be absorbed into the body faster than ordinary calcium, and could cure illnesses such as cancer and heart disease. In another infomercial, Trudeau asserted that Biotape, an adhesive strip, provided permanent relief from severe pain, including debilitating back pain and pain from arthritis. Lydia Parnes, acting director of the FTC's Bureau of Consumer Protection, said the permanent injunction "is meant to shut down an infomercial empire that has misled American consumers for years. Other habitual false advertisers should take a lesson; mend your ways or face serious consequences."

To no one's surprise, a federal judge in November 2007 found Trudeau in contempt for violating the 2004 permanent injunction by misrepresenting, during yet more infomercials, the content of his book, "The Weight Loss Cure 'They' Don't Want You to Know About."[69] Trudeau repeatedly claimed during the infomercials, which were staged to look like interviews conducted by a talk-show host with Trudeau about his book, that his diet was "easy." In fact, as U.S. District Judge Robert W. Gettleman pointed out in an opinion that called Trudeau both "one heck of a salesman" and "an ex-felon" (he had two felony convictions in the 1990s related to bad checks and credit card fraud), the diet's regimen was very complex and difficult. Gettleman wrote:

To no one's surprise, a federal judge in November 2007 found Trudeau in contempt.

> Nowhere in the infomercials does Trudeau make any mention of the colonics, the organ "cleanses," the requirement of walking a mile a day outdoors, the need to only [eat] 100% organic foods, or the specified supplements and food products. He also fails to mention that the diet requires fifteen colonics in a 30-day period and a 500-calorie per day limit necessitating a physician's supervision.

In August 2008 Judge Gettleman rejected Trudeau's motion for reconsideration of the 2007 contempt finding, once again determining the infomercials violated the terms of the 2004 injunction.[70] Gettleman noted that "the language of that injunction could not be clearer: Trudeau was allowed to make infomercials in connection with the advertising or promotion of publications provided that he 'must not misrepresent the content of the book.'" As punishment for violating the 2004 injunction, the judge found against Trudeau "in the sum of $5,173,000, representing a conservative estimate of the royalties Trudeau realized from the sale of the Weight Loss Book through the offending infomercials." Gettleman also banned Trudeau for three years from producing, broadcasting or participating in the production or broadcast of any infomercials for products, including books, in which Trudeau has any interest. Just a few months later, in November 2008, Gettleman amended the judgment (upon the urging by the FTC) against Trudeau to a whopping $37,616,161—the approximate amount consumers paid in response to Trudeau's deceptive infomercials.[71]

Trade Regulation Rules

In January 1975 President Ford signed the Magnuson-Moss Warranty–Federal Trade Commission Improvement Act, the most significant piece of trade regulation legislation since

69. *FTC* v. *Trudeau,* 2007 U.S. Dist. LEXIS 85214 (N.D. Ill. Nov. 16, 2007).
70. *FTC* v. *Trudeau,* 2008 U.S. Dist. LEXIS 59675 (N.D. Ill. Aug. 7, 2008).
71. Supplemental Order & Judgment, *FTC* v. *Trudeau,* Case No. 03 C-3904 (N.D. Ill. Nov. 4, 2008).

the Wheeler-Lea Amendment in 1938. The new law did many things, but basically it greatly enlarged both the power and the jurisdiction of the FTC. Until the bill was signed, the FTC was limited to dealing with unfair and deceptive practices that were "in commerce." The new law expanded the jurisdiction to practices "affecting commerce." The change of a single word gave the FTC broad new areas to regulate. The law also gave the agency important new power.

Three sections of the act expanded the remedies the FTC can use against deceptive advertising. First, the agency was given the power to issue trade regulation rules defining and outlawing unfair and deceptive acts or practices. The importance of this power alone cannot be overestimated. In the past the agency had to pursue deceptive advertisements one at a time. Imagine, for example, that four or five different breakfast cereals all advertise that they are good for children because they contain nine times the recommended daily allowance of vitamins and minerals. Medical experts argue that any vitamins in excess of 100 percent of the recommended daily allowance are useless; therefore, these advertisements are probably deceptive or misleading. In the past the FTC would have had to issue a complaint against each advertiser and in each case prove that the statement was a violation of the law. Under the new rules, the agency can issue a trade regulation rule—as it had done for nutritional claims—that declares that claims of product superiority based on excessive dosage of vitamins and minerals are false and misleading. If advertisers make such claims, they are in violation of the law. All the commission must prove is that the advertiser had actual knowledge of the trade regulation rule, or "knowledge fairly implied from the objective circumstances."

The advantages of the **trade regulation rules (TRRs)** are numerous. They speed up and simplify the process of enforcement. Advertisers can still litigate the question, challenge the trade regulation rule, seek an appeal in court and so forth. In most cases they probably will not go to that expense. Trade regulation rules have had a great deterrent effect, as they comprehensively delimit what constitutes an illegal practice. In the past, after the commission issued a cease and desist order, businesses frequently attempted to undertake practices that fell just outside the narrow boundaries of the order. The TRRs are much broader and make it much harder for advertisers to skirt the limitations. Finally, via TRRs the FTC is able to deal with problems more evenhandedly. An entire industry can be treated similarly, and just one or two businesses are not picked out for complaint.

The second aspect of the law that improved FTC remedies allowed the FTC to seek civil penalties against anyone who knowingly violates the provisions of a litigated order, even if that person was not originally the subject of the order. To wit: Chemical company A sells a spray paint that is toxic if used in a closed area, but the product is advertised as being completely harmless. The FTC moves against the company and issues a cease and desist order stating that in the future the firm must not advertise the product as being completely harmless. Chemical company B also sells a spray paint that has the same toxicity and is advertised the same way. If it can be shown that company B was aware of the provisions of the order against company A and continued to advertise its product as being completely safe, B can be fined up to $10,000 per day for violating the order, even though the order is not directed against B.

The third section of the law gave the FTC the right to sue in federal court on behalf of consumers victimized by practices that are in violation of a cease and desist order or by practices that are in violation of a TRR, a right that the agency has been reluctant to use.

SUMMARY

The Federal Trade Commission has the power to regulate virtually all advertising that is deceptive or misleading. To be deceptive an advertisement must contain a representation, omission or practice that is likely to mislead the consumer; the advertisement or practice must be considered from the perspective of a reasonable consumer; and the representation, omission or practice must be material. The FTC has many remedies to regulate deceptive or untruthful advertising:

1. Guides or advisory opinions that attempt to outline in advance what advertisers may say about a product
2. Voluntary agreements by advertisers to terminate a deceptive advertisement
3. Consent agreements or consent orders signed by advertisers promising to terminate a deceptive advertisement
4. Litigated orders to advertisers to terminate a particular advertising claim, failure to comply with which can result in severe penalty
5. Substantiation of advertisements, in which the advertiser must prove all claims made in an advertisement
6. Corrective advertising, in which an advertiser must admit in future advertisements that past advertisements have been incorrect
7. Injunctive power to immediately halt advertising campaigns that could cause harm to consumers
8. Trade regulation rules that can be issued to regulate advertising throughout an entire industry

THE REGULATORY PROCESS

To understand the importance of the regulatory process, students should be familiar with procedures followed in a deceptive advertising case, be aware of the kinds of advertising that can be considered deceptive, and be familiar with the defenses to a charge of deceptive advertising.

PROCEDURES

The FTC does not attempt to scrutinize every advertisement that is published or broadcast. Most cases come to the attention of the agency from letters written by either consumers or competitors. Today, an individual can file a complaint online from the FTC's Web site at http://www.ftc.gov. When a complaint is received, FTC staff attorneys examine it to see if it has merit. If they can find none, the case ends. If the staff members believe there is a provable violation, then a proposed complaint, a proposed consent agreement, and a memorandum are prepared for the commissioners. The commissioners then vote on whether to issue a complaint.

If the commissioners agree that the advertisement is in violation of the law, the advertiser is notified and given the opportunity to either sign the consent agreement that has been drafted or negotiate with the agency for a more favorable order. At this point one of three things can happen:

1. The advertiser can agree to sign the agreement, and the commissioners vote to accept this agreement. If this happens the order is published and made final in 60 days.
2. The advertiser can agree to sign the agreement, but the commissioners reject it.
3. The advertiser can refuse to sign the agreement.

If either of the latter two events occurs, a complaint is issued against the advertiser, and a hearing is scheduled before an administrative law judge. The judge works within the FTC and officiates at these hearings. The hearing is a lot like a trial, only more informal. If the judge believes that there is substantial evidence that the advertisement violates the law, he or she will issue an order telling the advertiser to stop this illegal practice (this is the litigated order). The judge also has the authority to dismiss the case. At this point either side can appeal to the commissioners to overturn the ruling of the judge.

If the commissioners agree that the advertisement is not misleading or deceptive, the case ends. But if the commissioners support an administrative law judge's ruling against an advertiser, the order becomes law after it is finalized by an appellate court. The advertiser may appeal this decision in a federal court.

There are only a handful of reasons that a judge can use to overturn the commission decision.

It is difficult for courts to reverse an FTC ruling. There are only a handful of reasons that a judge can use to overturn the commission decision. The case goes to an appeals court, and there is no new finding of fact: What the FTC says is fact, is fact. The following are all instances in which a court can overturn an FTC ruling: (1) "convincing evidence" that the agency made an error in the proceedings; (2) no evidence to support the commission's findings; (3) violation of the Constitution—for example, the agency did not provide due process of law; (4) the action goes beyond the agency's powers; (5) facts relied on in making the ruling are not supported by sufficient evidence; and (6) arbitrary or capricious acts by the commission. An appeal of an adverse ruling by a circuit court can be taken to the Supreme Court, but only if certiorari is granted.

SPECIAL CASES OF DECEPTIVE ADVERTISING

A few special problems regarding deceptive advertising deserve special mention before we leave this topic.

TESTIMONIALS

Pfizer, Inc. cancelled commercials for its Lipitor cholesterol pill.

All TV viewers have seen famous athletes and celebrities, as well as experts and ordinary consumers, on commercials making claims about products they supposedly use or in which they otherwise believe. The issue of truth and deception in such ads gained both public and congressional attention in 2008 when Pfizer, Inc. cancelled commercials for its Lipitor cholesterol pill that featured Robert Jarvik, an artificial heart pioneer. As the Los Angeles Times reported, "the ads conveyed the impression that Jarvik was imparting medical advice, although in reality he's not licensed to practice medicine. They also used a body double to depict Jarvik robustly rowing across a mountain lake."[72] USA Today noted that although "Jarvik graduated from medical school, he's not licensed to practice medicine or to write prescriptions. He doesn't see patients. He was a consultant to Lipitor-maker Pfizer, under contract for $1.35 million. And he didn't start taking Lipitor until a month after he started doing the ads."[73] Congress held hearings on the matter.

The FTC enforces rules regarding endorsements of products and services by consumers, celebrities, experts and organizations. It defines an endorsement as any advertising message (including things such as verbal statements, demonstrations and depictions of the name of an individual or the name or seal of an organization) that consumers likely are to believe reflects the opinions, beliefs, findings or experiences of a party other than the sponsoring advertiser.[74] Under the FTC's rules, several key points emerge that must be understood by advertising students:

- Endorsements must reflect the honest opinions, findings, beliefs or experiences of the endorser and may not contain any representations that would be deceptive or could not be substantiated if made directly by the advertiser.[75]
- An advertiser may use an endorsement of an expert or celebrity only as long as it has good reason to believe that the endorser continues to subscribe to the views presented.[76]
- If an ad represents that an endorser uses the product, then the endorser must have been a bona fide user of it at the time the endorsement was given and, in addition, the advertiser may continue to run the ad only so long as it has good reason to believe that the endorser remains a user of the product.
- Ads presenting endorsements by individuals who are represented, either directly or by implication, to be "actual consumers" must use actual consumers, in both the audio and video, or else they must clearly and conspicuously disclose that the people in such ads are not actual consumers of the advertised product.[77]
- If an ad represents, either directly or by implication, that the endorser is an expert, then the endorser's qualifications must in fact give him or her the expertise that he or she is represented as possessing with respect to the endorsement.[78]

In 2007 the FTC requested public comment on its "Guides Concerning the Use of Endorsements and Testimonials in Advertising," which are available online at http://www.ftc. gov/bcp/guides/endorse.htm and which had not been revised since 1980. In November 2008, in response to feedback, the FTC proposed several minor revisions to its guides, including, among others, clarification that when determining whether statements in an ad constitute an endorsement, it does not matter whether the statements made by an endorser are identical to

72. Lazarus, "Drug Ads a Test of Doctors' Patience."
73. Editorial, "Can You Believe What You See on TV? Ask Your Doctor."
74. 16 C.F.R. § 255.0 (2008).
75. 16 C.F.R. § 255.1 (2008).
76. Ibid.
77. 16 C.F.R. § 255.2 (2008).
78. 16 C.F.R. § 255.3 (2008).

or different than those made by the sponsoring advertiser. One significant proposed change by the FTC in November 2008 was to amend its guides to make explicit

> two principles that the Commission's law enforcement activities have already made clear. The first is that advertisers are subject to liability for false or unsubstantiated statements made through endorsements, or for failing to disclose material connections between themselves and their endorsers. The second is that endorsers may also be subject to liability for their statements.[79]

The most controversial proposed change, primarily affecting companies that advertise products, pills and diets designed to reduce weight, relates to commercials in which a real person (an endorser) claims to have lost a huge sum of weight ("I lost 40 pounds in just two weeks") and the advertiser runs a so-called disclaimer of typicality at the bottom of the commercial stating something like "Individual Results May Vary" or "Results Not Typical." Under the proposed new guides, such disclaimers indicating that the results of the endorser are unusual or out of the ordinary would not be enough to protect the advertiser from potential liability. Instead, the FTC's guides would be revised such that testimonials that do not depict typical consumer experiences should be accompanied by a clear and conspicuous disclosure of the results consumers can generally expect to achieve from the advertised product or program. In other words, commercials should make clear what the typical results are (and, of course, have prior substantiation for such claims); merely stating that the results of the endorser are not typical will not cut it.

The FTC sought public comment on the proposed changes in its guides on endorsements and testimonial through the end of January 2009. That feedback was then considered by the FTC, which adopted most of the changes later that year.

BAIT-AND-SWITCH ADVERTISING

The FTC prohibits **bait-and-switch advertising,** which it defines as "an alluring but insincere offer to sell a product or service which the advertiser in truth does not intend or want to sell. Its purpose is to switch consumers from buying the advertised merchandise, in order to sell something else, usually at a higher price or on a basis more advantageous to the advertiser."[80] The FTC's rules state, among other things, the following:

- No ad containing an offer to sell a product should be published if the offer is not a bona fide effort to sell that product.[81]
- Advertisers cannot engage in practices that discourage purchase of advertised merchandise as part of a bait scheme to sell other merchandise, such as refusing to show or sell the product offered in accordance with the terms of the offer.[82]

---

79. Notice of Proposed Changes to the Guides and Request For Public Comments, *16 C.F.R. Part 255: Guides Concerning the Use of Endorsements and Testimonials in Advertising,* November 2008, available online at http://www.ftc.gov/os/2008/11/P034520endorsementguides.pdf.
80. 16 C.F.R. § 238.0 (2008).
81. 16 C.F.R. § 238.1 (2008).
82. 16 C.F.R. § 238.3 (2008).

Bait-and-switch advertising is not the same as loss-leader advertising, legal in many places, in which a merchant offers to sell one item at below cost (the leader) in order to get customers into the store in the hope that they will then buy additional merchandise at regular cost. Supermarkets use this scheme and so do other retail outlets. Those states that outlawed this practice did so because of pressure from small merchants who cannot afford to sell anything at a loss and do not want to be put at a marketing disadvantage with high-volume sellers.

DEFENSES

The basic defense against any false advertising complaint is truth—that is, proving that a product does what the advertiser claims it does, that it is made where the advertiser says it is made, or that it is as beneficial as it is advertised to be. Although the burden is on the government to disprove the advertiser's claim, it is always helpful for an advertiser to offer proof to substantiate advertising copy.

Another angle that advertisers can pursue is to attack a different aspect of the government's case rather than try to prove the statement true. For example, an advertiser can argue that the deceptive statement is not material to the advertisement as a whole (that is, it will not influence the purchasing decision) or that the advertisement does not imply what the government thinks it implies. For example, to say, as Dry Ban did, that a deodorant "goes on dry" does not mean that it is dry when it is applied, merely that its application is drier than that of other antiperspirants.

ADVERTISING AGENCY/PUBLISHER LIABILITY

If you go to work at an advertising agency, you must understand that your agency may be held liable if it is an active participant in preparing a deceptive advertisement or if it knows or should know that an ad is either false or lacks substantiation. In fact, the FTC makes it clear that an agency has "a duty to ascertain the existence of substantiation for the claims which it makes."[83]

A new issue is the potential liability for Web sites such as Craigslist and Roommates. com for posting ads by other individuals who make statements that violate federal or state laws. In 2008 the 7th U.S. Circuit Court of Appeals held that Craigslist was protected from liability by Section 230 of the Communications Decency Act (CDA) (see pages 147–148) after it posted rental ads with discriminatory statements such as "no minorities" and "no children" that violate the federal Fair Housing Act.[84] The Fair Housing Act is regularly enforced against print newspapers that run such discriminatory ads. The 7th Circuit, however, held that Craigslist was protected by Section 230 of the CDA, which generally shields online service providers from liability when they are mere conduits (rather than publishers or speakers) for information posted by third parties. The appellate court reasoned that Craigslist "is not the author of the ads and could not be treated as the 'speaker' of the posters' words." But another 2008 opinion, this one before the 9th U.S. Circuit Court of Appeals and involving

A new issue is the potential liability for Web sites such as Craigslist.

83. *Bristol-Myers Co.,* 102 F.T.C. 21, 366 (1983).
84. *Chicago Lawyers' Committee* v. *Craigslist, Inc.,* 519 F. 3d 666 (7th Cir. 2008).

Roommates.com, reached the opposite conclusion. It held that an online roommate-matching service was not immune to liability under Section 230 of the CDA for posting information by others that violated the Fair Housing Act and California housing discrimination laws.[85] The problem for Roommates.com was that it solicited specific content from users and forced them to use pull-down menus with questions featuring specific answer options in which they could express illegal and discriminatory views. As Judge Alex Kozinski wrote for the majority of the 9th Circuit:

> Roommate both elicits the allegedly illegal content and makes aggressive use of it in conducting its business. Roommate does not merely provide a framework that could be utilized for proper or improper purposes; rather, Roommate's work in developing the discriminatory questions, discriminatory answers and discriminatory search mechanism is directly related to the alleged illegality of the site.

In brief, Roommates.com was more akin to a publisher or speaker rather a mere conduit for the information that it posts. Craigslist, in contrast, did not solicit any content but merely provided a forum for ads.

SUMMARY Complaints against advertisers are prepared by the FTC staff and approved by a vote of the commission. Administrative law judges can hold hearings, which are somewhat like trials, to determine whether the FTC charges are valid. A U.S. Court of Appeals can review all commission orders. Advertisers need to take special care when dealing with testimonials and endorsements. The law outlaws bait-and-switch advertising, in which customers are lured to a store with promises of low prices but then are pushed by salespeople to buy more expensive products. Although ad agencies and publishers/broadcasters are generally not held liable in cases of false or harmful advertising, there are signs that the law is changing.

BIBLIOGRAPHY

"A Positive Agenda for Consumers: The FTC Year in Review." Federal Trade Commission, April 2003.

Cancelada, Gregory. "CBS and NBC Will Stop Running Some Miller Ads After Complaint by A-B." *St. Louis Post-Dispatch,* 18 December 2004, B03.

Cushman, John Jr. "Judge Rules F.D.A. Has Right to Curb Tobacco as Drug." *The New York Times,* 26 April 1997, A1.

Davidson, Paul. "Feds Say Telemarketer Violated No-Call Rules." *USA Today,* 1 September 2004, 3B.

Daykin, Tom. "Networks Blow Whistle on Ads." *Milwaukee Journal Sentinel,* 6 January 2005, D3.

85. *Fair Housing Council of San Fernando Valley* v. *Roommates.com, LLC,* 521 F. 3d 1157 (9th Cir. 2008).

DeVore, P. Cameron. "Commercial Speech: 1988." Remarks to Communications Law 1988 Practicing Law Institute, New York City, 10 November 1988.

———. "Supreme Court Boots Commercial Speech." *First Amendment Law Letter,* Fall 1990, 5.

Editorial, "Can You Believe What You See on TV? Ask Your Doctor." *USA Today*, 15 May 2008, 10A.

"Election Ad Law Struck Down." *The Washington Newspaper,* July 1998, 1.

Greenhouse, Linda. "Justices Strike Down Ban on Casino Gambling Ads." *The New York Times,* 15 June 1999, A1.

Howard, John A., and James Hulbert. *A Staff Report to the Federal Trade Commission.* Washington, D.C.: Federal Trade Commission, 1974.

Kogan, Jay S. "Celebrity Endorsement: Recognition of a Duty." *John Marshall Law Review* 21 (1987): 47.

Labaton, Stephen. "The Regulatory Signals Shift." *The New York Times,* 6 June 2001, C1.

Lazarus, David. "Drug Ads a Test of Doctors' Patience." *Los Angeles Times,* 14 May 2008, C1.

Manishin, Glenn B., and Stephanie A. Joyce. "Current Spam Law & Policy: An Overview and Update." *Computer & Internet Lawyer,* September 2004, 1.

Mann, Charles C., and Mark L. Plummer. "The Big Headache." *The Atlantic Monthly,* October 1988, 39.

"Mazda Gets Hit with $5.25 Million in Fines." *Seattle Post-Intelligencer,* 1 October 1999, B2.

McGrew, Thomas J. "Advertising Law: Inactive FTC, Activism in Courts." *Los Angeles Daily Journal,* 17 January 1985.

Morris, Brian. "Consumer Standing to Sue for False and Misleading Advertising under Section 43(a) of the Lanham Trademark Act." *Memphis State University Law Review* 17 (1987): 417.

"A Nissan Unit Will Pull Ads." *The New York Times,* 10 March 1993.

"Novartis Is Ordered to Fix Doan's Ads." *The New York Times,* 28 May 1999, C16.

Pompeo, Paul E. "To Tell the Truth: Comparative Advertising and Lanham Act Section 43(a)." *Catholic University Law Review* 36 (1987): 565.

Rohde, David. "Sweepstakes in Agreement to Reimburse New Yorkers." *The New York Times,* 25 August 1998, A16.

Rohrer, Daniel M., ed. *Mass Media, Freedom of Speech, and Advertising.* Dubuque, Iowa: Kendall/Hunt, 1979.

Rosden, George E., and Peter E. Rosden. *The Law of Advertising.* New York: Matthew Bender, 1986.

Savage, David G. "Supreme Court Upholds Fees for Beef Ads." *Los Angeles Times,* 24 May 2005, A12.

Selvin, Molly. "'Dr. Phil' Diet Pill Maker Settles Suit." *Los Angeles Times,* 26 September 2006, C8.

Shukovsky, Paul. "'Spam King' Gets Nearly 4 Years in Prison." *Seattle Post-Intelligencer,* 23 July 2008, A1.

Singdahlsen, Jeffrey P. "The Risk of Chill: A Cost of the Standards Governing the Regulation of False Advertising under Section 43(a) of the Lanham Act." *Virginia Law Review* 77 (1991): 339.

Tepper, Maury. "False Advertising Claims and the Revision of the Lanham Act: A Step in Which Direction?" *Cincinnati Law Review* 59 (1991): 957.

Tewkesbury, Don. "FTC Restricts Claims by Infomercial Producers." *Seattle Post-Intelligencer,* 8 July 1993.

Vranica, Suzanne. "And in This Corner. . . . Marketers Take Some Jabs." *Wall Street Journal*, 2 October 2008, B6.

Waltzer, Garrett J. "Monetary Relief for False Advertising Claims Arising Under Section 43(a) of the Lanham Act." *UCLA Law Review* 34 (1987): 953.

Weber, Matthew G. "Media Liability for Publication of Advertising: When to Kill the Messenger." *Denver University Law Review* 68 (1991): 57.

"2004 Weight-Loss Advertising Survey: A Report from the Staff of the Federal Trade Commission." Federal Trade Commission, April 2005.

CHAPTER 16

Telecommunications Regulation

Volumes of federal rules govern the operation of telecommunications in the United States. A substantial number of them focus on technical rules; for example, regulations on the height of broadcast towers or the power of transmitters. In this chapter we focus on two other kinds of rules: those that govern who can own and operate telecommunications facilities and those that regulate content carried over these facilities. Both sets of rules implicate the First Amendment, and there is a wealth of material in this edition on the regulation of "indecent" broadcast content.

A PROLOGUE TO THE PRESENT

In the area of telecommunications regulation the past is an important prologue to the present. The past three decades witnessed a revolution in the governance of broadcasting and cablecasting, a revolution not yet over. These changes are highly controversial. Many people who have lived through them say the very soul of broadcasting has been irrevocably harmed. Other people, many of whom work in the industry, argue that the changes were long overdue. The changes were wrought by Congress and the Federal Communications Commission, under pressure from both the telecommunications industry and the federal courts. They are the result of a fundamental change in the way the industry is viewed, as less of a publicly oriented entity designed to serve society and more of a private business whose primary responsibilities lie with its customers (primarily advertisers) and its stockholders. An incremental but substantial redefinition of the meaning of the First Amendment spurred these developments. To understand telecommunications regulations today it is necessary to spend a few paragraphs discussing the development of both the telecommunications industry and the government rules that shaped it.

HISTORY OF REGULATION

The electromagnetic spectrum . . . through which radio signals travel is a finite medium.

The regulation of telecommunications in the United States dates from 1910, shortly after radio was developed. Congress passed a law that required all U.S. passenger ships to have a radio. Two years later the federal legislature adopted the **Radio Act of 1912,** which required that all radio transmitters be licensed by the federal government and that radio operators be licensed by the government as well. In the 1920s radio grew far faster than most observers had thought possible. There were millions of listeners and far too many stations. The electromagnetic spectrum, or the airwaves, through which radio signals travel is a finite medium. As a modern freeway can hold only so many vehicles, the airwaves can hold only so many radio signals. Too many cars on the highway cause accidents and gridlock. Too many radio signals meeting in the spectrum cause similar chaos. Signals overlap and block each other. To listeners the result is gibberish. Near the end of the 1920s a reluctant Congress was forced to act once again; it adopted the **Radio Act of 1927,** a comprehensive set of rules aimed at creating order from the problem caused by too many people trying to broadcast radio signals at the same time. The new law governed who could and could not broadcast, and when they could broadcast. But it focused on the content of radio programs as well. Both the licensing and the content regulations implicated the First Amendment. Radio broadcasting surely amounted to speech and press, rights guaranteed under the Bill of Rights. Surprisingly, the issue hardly arose.

The 1927 statute was substantially amended and revised seven years later when Congress adopted the **Federal Communications Act** in 1934. This law remains as the base for all telecommunications regulation today. It expanded the earlier statute to include telephones and the telegraph as well as radio. And it provided for the appointment of the Federal Communications Commission, or FCC, to regulate all these telecommunications media—the same FCC that years later is the bane of Eminem and Howard Stern's existence.

THE CHANGING PHILOSOPHY OF BROADCAST REGULATION

Although debate over First Amendment protection of broadcasting was never truly joined, a philosophy that justified a substantial regulation of broadcasting nevertheless existed, anchored by two seemingly immutable propositions. First, the broadcast spectrum is a limited transmission pathway. Not all who want to transmit radio signals can do so. The notion that there are a finite number of frequencies on which to broadcast and, in turn, that there are more people who want to broadcast than there are available frequencies is known as **spectrum scarcity.** Second, while private individuals might own the transmitters, the towers, the microphones and all the other paraphernalia that allow radio signals to be transmitted, the American people own the transmission path, the radio spectrum, through which the signals travel to the listener's radio set. As such, those who *use* the spectrum are bound to serve the needs of those who *own* the spectrum. So somebody had to decide who, among all those who sought to broadcast, should have that privilege. Rules were also needed to ensure that broadcasters met the needs of the spectrum owners. That is when the government stepped in, deciding who could and who could not broadcast, and establishing rules to ensure that those who did broadcast met their responsibilities to the people. The government called these responsibilities "meeting the public interest, convenience or necessity," or PICON, an acronym that became the code word to justify all the rules relating to broadcasting. And within PICON's critical concept of "public interest," the FCC traditionally has identified three major policy objectives that allegedly lead to its promotion:

The broadcast spectrum is a limited transmission pathway. Not all who want to transmit radio signals can do so.

PICON [is the] acronym that became the code word to justify all the rules relating to broadcasting.

- Competition
- Diversity
- Localism

Broadcasters who fulfilled the public interest mandate were permitted to use the airwaves to reap power and wealth; those who did not were punished by fines or loss of the privilege of broadcasting. Both Congress and the Federal Communications Commission fashioned a wide range of rules to ensure the fidelity of broadcasters between the late 1920s and the 1960s. Some of the issues that were dealt with were

- who could and could not broadcast, and how long a broadcast license could be held without being renewed;
- the number of broadcast properties and other media properties, like newspapers, a single individual or company could own;
- the responsibility of broadcasters to try to divine the needs and interests of the public they served;

■ rules that required license holders to broadcast information about important community issues and to make certain that all sides of these issues were represented in the broadcasts;

■ rules that ensured that political candidates would have access to radio and television stations to communicate with the voters; and

■ rules that limited the number of commercial minutes that could be contained in each broadcast hour.

The thrust of these rules was simple. It was thought that the broadcast industry could best serve the nation if as many different individuals as possible owned the limited number of broadcast stations and if those who were permitted to broadcast provided a broad range of material to entertain, educate and inform the listeners and viewers. The government, primarily the FCC, would ensure that these rules were followed.

But the two propositions that provided the underpinning for this regulatory philosophy turned out to be less immutable than first imagined, and the rationale for regulation began to unravel. True, the broadcast spectrum is limited. But new media forms, like cable television and the Internet, promised new pathways with unlimited transmission space. The notion that broadcasters must serve the public interest began to erode under pressure from the new economic liberalism that grew in the last 25 years of the 20th century. The idea of serving the interests of the market as opposed to serving the needs of the public developed as a dominant theme in the industry. The large corporations that owned much of the telecommunications media argued that giving listeners and viewers what they wanted to hear and watch made more sense than giving them what the government thought they should hear and see. It was also more lucrative for station owners. So capitalism and market-driven theories were in; paternalism and PICON were put on the back burner. There became a heated battle over the meaning of the term "public interest" in the PICON acronym that still exists today. Is the public interest

The notion that broadcasters must serve the public interest began to erode . . . in the last 25 years of the 20th century.

■ whatever the public *wants* (whatever the public is interested in watching)?

■ whatever the public *needs* (even if it is not interested in watching it)?

In addition, didn't the First Amendment bar just the sort of meddling that the government was undertaking with its myriad regulations? Ultimately the regulators, courts and even Congress bought into these ideas.

The incremental application of this new philosophy resulted in a general dismantling of broadcast regulations. These changes occurred over the past 35 years. A recent significant shift transpired in December 2007 when the FCC narrowly approved the relaxation of a long-standing ban against a single company owning both a newspaper and a television station in the same city or market.[1] The new cross-ownership rule now allows a company to own one newspaper and one television station in the same city if (1) the city is in one of the 20 largest media markets, (2) the television station is not ranked among the top four stations in the market, and (3) at least eight independent "major media voices" remain in the market. A major media voice includes full-power commercial and noncommercial TV stations and major newspapers. The 2007 change was so controversial that the U.S. Senate in 2008 adopted a "resolution of

1. Although the outright ban on cross-ownership of a newspaper and television station in the same city had existed since 1975, the FCC had granted several waivers to companies allowing for cross-ownership on a case-by-case basis.

disapproval" against it. The change also was challenged in federal court, with all challenges ultimately consolidated and transferred in late 2008 to the same panel of the 3rd U.S. Circuit Court of Appeals that ruled in 2004 in the *Prometheus Radio Project* case described in the next section. On the other hand, some businesses wanted the rule relaxed even more. Rupert Murdoch's News Corp. sought an FCC waiver in April 2008 that would allow it to continue to own two newspapers (the Wall Street Journal and New York Post) and two TV stations in New York City, at the same time it was trying to purchase a third newspaper there, Newsday (Murdoch later withdrew his Newsday bid).

Prior to the December 2007 change in the cross-ownership rule, the FCC had modified other long-standing rules affecting ownership, including controversial efforts in 2003 at relaxing ownership rules that were rebuffed by a federal appellate court. Those 2003 efforts are described in the next section on the *Prometheus Radio Project* case. Rules regarding the number of radio and/or television stations a single broadcaster could own, rules limiting the ownership of a newspaper and broadcasting property in the same city by a single individual, and rules limiting the number of customers a multiple-system cable operator could serve were all relaxed. The length of time a broadcast license can be held without being renewed was substantially lengthened. Details about most of the modified rules are outlined in subsequent sections of this chapter, but a great many regulations have simply been abandoned. Included were the following:

- Rules that restricted the major television networks from owning and syndicating television programs
- Rules that required broadcasters to formally ascertain the needs and interests of listeners and viewers so they could devise programming that best served these needs
- Rules that required broadcasters to report all sides of important public controversies in their community, the so-called fairness doctrine
- Rules that indirectly limited the number of commercial minutes that could be broadcast every hour
- Rules that barred one individual from owning both a radio and television station in one of the top 50 markets
- Rules that limited the rates a cable television provider could charge subscribers
- Rules that prohibited a television station from owning a cable system and a television station in the same market, or vice versa
- Rules that prohibited a television network from owning another television network
- Rules that required television stations to provide free reply time for opponents of political candidates endorsed by the station, and for people whose reputation or integrity was attacked by someone using the station
- Rules that prohibit a cable television system from carrying the signal of any broadcast station if the system owns a broadcast station in the same local market

THE *PROMETHEUS* DECISION AND SUBSEQUENT FALLOUT

The FCC's 2003 attempt to loosen up ownership restrictions met with stiff judicial resistance when the new rules were challenged in 2004 before the 3rd U.S. Circuit Court of Appeals by a number of citizen-activist groups. The aftershocks of the opinion are still felt today.

The case *Prometheus Radio Project* v. *FCC*[2] affirmed the power of the FCC to regulate media ownership. But, more important, it also held that "the Commission has not sufficiently justified its particular chosen numerical limits for local television ownership, local radio ownership, and cross-ownership of media within local markets." For instance, the appellate court held that while the FCC has the authority and power to repeal its ban that prohibits common ownership of a full-service television broadcast station and a daily public newspaper in the same media community (known as the television/newspaper cross-ownership rule), the numerical limits that the FCC adopted in its place in 2003 on matters such as cross-ownership of newspapers, radio stations and television stations (see page 601) were not sufficiently justified by the FCC. The two-judge majority of the 3rd Circuit wrote:

> We have identified several provisions in which the Commission [FCC] falls short of its obligation to justify its decisions to retain, repeal, or modify its media ownership regulations with reasoned analysis. The Commission's derivation of new Cross-Media Limits, and its modification of the numerical limits on both television and radio station ownership in local markets, all have the same essential flaw: an unjustified assumption that media outlets of the same type make an equal contribution to diversity and competition in local markets.

The appellate court then instructed the FCC either to come up with additional justifications for its efforts to relax media ownership rules or to modify them. Until that time, the appellate court continued to stay the enforcement of the new rules (to put them on hold, as it were)—it previously had issued an emergency order in September 2003 preventing the FCC from enforcing the rules. As Bill Carter wrote in The New York Times, "frustration was the dominant emotion among media company executives" when they read the decision because "they will be stymied for some time in trying to take advantage of the relaxed FCC rules."[3] The now enjoined 2003 rules, for instance, would have allowed a media conglomerate to own a daily newspaper, three TV stations, eight radio stations and a cable system in the same city.

The *Prometheus Radio Project* decision, however, did leave intact the 39 percent "national audience reach" limit (see page 601) on television ownership adopted by Congress in 2004, thus allowing Viacom and News Corp., both of which already owned enough stations in 2004 to reach that cap, not to have to worry about selling off or divesting themselves of any stations. The term "national audience reach" is defined as the total number of television households reached by a single entity's stations, with UHF stations attributed with only 50 percent of the television households reached (known as a "50 percent UHF discount"). In addition to this 39 percent rule for national audience reach remaining in effect in the realm of television, there continues to be no limit on the total number of radio stations that a single entity/licensee can own on a national basis.

In 2005 the U.S. Supreme Court declined, without comment, to review the 3rd Circuit's opinion in *Prometheus Radio Project*. This meant that the 2003 changes enjoined by the 3rd Circuit would stay enjoined and thus not go into effect. Concomitantly, the more restrictive ownership provisions that existed prior to 2003 (such as the television/newspaper cross-ownership rule that generally bans a company from owning both a commercial broadcast station and a daily

---

2. 373 F. 3d 372 (3d Cir. 2004), cert. den., 125 S. Ct. 2904 (2005).
3. Carter, "Media Ruling Merely Irritates Big Owners."

paper in the same city) will control, by and large, mass media transactions until the FCC develops either better justifications for its 2003 changes or proposes new rules.

In February 2008 the FCC released a massive report and order on its broadcast ownership rules (see page 601 setting forth the FCC's multiple ownership rules). The report, which the FCC had adopted two months earlier, also addressed the concerns of the 3rd Circuit in *Prometheus Radio Project*. The bottom line from the 2008 report and order is that the FCC generally left intact most of its ownership rules but, importantly, it modified the newspaper/broadcast cross-ownership rule that, since 1975, had banned cross-ownership by a single entity of a daily newspaper and a television or radio broadcast station operating in the same local market. As described earlier, the new rule allows for cross-ownership of one newspaper and one radio station or TV station in top 20 markets if certain conditions are met (see page 594). The change quickly was challenged in federal court and two of the five FCC commissioners (the two Democrats at the time) objected to it. All lawsuits challenging the change were consolidated and moved in late 2008 before the same panel of the 3rd U.S. Circuit Court of Appeals that had rejected in *Prometheus Radio Project* the FCC's 2003 efforts to loosen up its ownership rules. In relaxing the cross-ownership rule, the FCC wrote in its 2008 report:

> By modestly loosening the 32-year prohibition on newspaper/broadcast cross-ownership, our approach balances the concerns of many commenters that we not permit excessive consolidation with concerns of other commenters that we afford some relief to assure continued diversity and investment in local news programming. We believe that the decisions we adopt today serve our public interest goals, appropriately take account of the current media marketplace, and comply with our statutory responsibilities.[4]

SUMMARY

Radio, the original electronic medium, was regulated almost from its inception. But until 1927 the regulation was minimal and failed to control the growing number of competitive broadcasters in a way that served the needs of the listeners. Congress passed comprehensive broadcasting rules in 1927, rules based on the assumption that because broadcasters used a valuable public resource, the radio spectrum or airwaves, they should be required to serve the public interest. This philosophy engendered the growth of broadcast regulation until the 1980s, when a competing philosophy constructed on free market economic theory began to dominate Congress and the government regulatory agencies. Under the new scheme, traditional market forces are seen as the best regulator of any industry. In the past 30 years, broadcasting and the telecommunications industry have seen a period of substantial deregulation, although the 2004 appellate court decision in *Prometheus Radio Project* v. *FCC* may have put a halt to that, at least when it comes to ownership issues.

---

4. *In re 2006 Quadrennial Regulatory Review*, Report and Order and Order on Reconsideration, FCC 07-216 (adopted Dec. 18, 2007; released Feb. 4, 2008), available online at http://hraunfoss.fcc.gov/edocs_public/attachmatch/FCC-07-216A1.pdf.

BASIC BROADCAST REGULATION

FEDERAL COMMUNICATIONS COMMISSION

The 1934 Federal Communications Act provided that a seven-member **Federal Communications Commission (FCC)** regulate the broadcast industry. In 1982 Congress reduced the size of the commission to five members. Members of the FCC are appointed by the president, with the approval of the Senate, to serve a five-year term. One member is selected by the president to be chairperson. No more than a simple majority of the commission (three members) can be from the same political party. In early 2009, President Barack Obama nominated attorney and media executive Julius Genachowski to be the new chairperson of the FCC, replacing the Bush-appointed Republican chair Kevin Martin. The U.S. Senate confirmed Genachowski's appointment in June 2009. The Harvard Law School–educated Genachowski previously worked at the FCC during the administration of Bill Clinton as a legal adviser to then FCC chair Reed Hundt. Some anticipated that Genachowski's guidance will lead the FCC to increasingly focus on high-tech, Internet-based issues affecting broadband use and access, such as net neutrality (see pages 130–132).

President Barack Obama nominated . . . Julius Genachowski to be the new chairperson of the FCC.

Like all administrative agencies, the FCC is guided by broad congressional mandate—in this case the Federal Communications Act. The agency has the power to make rules and regulations within the broad framework of the act, and these regulations carry the force of the law. With regard to some matters, the 1934 law is very specific. For example, Section 315—the equal opportunity provision (or equal time rule)—details regulations concerning the use of the broadcast media by political candidates. But in other areas, Congress was eloquently vague. The mandate that broadcasters operate their stations in "the public interest, convenience or necessity" can mean almost anything a person wants it to mean.

The FCC has been criticized for being too political, too opaque in its decision-making processes and too often influenced by the interests of major businesses and telecommunications companies rather than by the magic concept of the public interest. On this latter point, some have said derisively that the initials *FCC* actually stand for "Forever Captured by Corporations," a reference to the notion of "industry capture" in which an agency's agenda and decisions are heavily influenced, if not controlled, by the interests of media industries. Other critics have blamed the FCC for not focusing enough on new innovations and new communications technologies and, instead, reacting to problems as they arise. These critics suggest that *FCC* stands for "From Crisis to Crisis."

Powers

States, counties and cities have no regulatory power over broadcasting stations.

Congress approved the 1934 law under the authority of the commerce clause of the U.S. Constitution. States, counties and cities have no regulatory power over broadcasting stations. The federal government has *pre-empted* the law in this area (state and local authorities have retained some jurisdiction to regulate cable television and other telecommunication industries such as common carriers). Under the 1927 act, the question had arisen whether this clause meant that the federal government lacked power to regulate broadcasters whose signals did not cross state lines, stations that were not engaged in interstate commerce. In 1933 in *FRC* v. *Nelson Brothers,*[5] the U.S. Supreme Court ruled that state lines did not divide radio waves

5. 289 U.S. 266 (1933).

and that national regulation of broadcasting was not only appropriate but also essential to the efficient use of radio facilities.

Some communications businesses—telephone and telegraph companies, for example—have been designated common carriers by the government. A common carrier must do business with any customer who wishes to use its service. Broadcasting stations are not common carriers. They may refuse to do business with whomever they please. In addition, the commission lacks the power to set rates for the sale of broadcasting time. Broadcasting is founded on the basis of free competition among holders of broadcast licenses.

Broadcasting stations are not common carriers.

The act makes it clear that although broadcasters may freely compete, they in no way assume ownership of a frequency or wavelength by virtue of using it for three years or for 300 years. When a license is granted, the broadcaster must sign a form in which any claim to the perpetual use of a particular frequency is waived.

Censorship Powers

Technically, the FCC lacks the power to censor broadcasters. Section 326 of the act states:

> Nothing in this act shall be understood or construed to give the commission the power of censorship over radio communications or signals transmitted by any radio station, or condition shall be promulgated or fixed by the commission which shall interfere with the right of free speech by means of radio communication.

In some instances the prohibition against censorship is applied literally, but the FCC can punish a broadcaster through a fine (called a forfeiture) or the refusal to renew a license if the broadcaster carries programming that in some way violates the law. The Supreme Court adopted this understanding of Section 326 in 1978 when it affirmed the agency's censure of radio station WBAI in New York for airing a monologue by comedian George Carlin that contained what the FCC said was indecent language.[6] Most people would call this censorship. Section 326, then, has limited meaning and is of limited value to broadcasters.

The commission has broad-ranging powers in dealing with American broadcasters. (These include the power to regulate the activities of the American broadcast networks. See *National Broadcasting Co.* v. *U.S.*)[7] Section 303 of the act outlines some of the basic responsibilities of the agency, which include classification of stations, determination of the power and technical facilities licensees must use, and specification of hours during the day and night that stations can broadcast. The FCC also regulates the location of stations, the area each station can serve, the assignment of frequency or wavelength, and even the designation of call letters. There are not many things that broadcasters can do without first seeking the approval or consent of the FCC.

Perhaps nothing better illustrates the sheer power of the FCC than the following example: In 2009 the FCC oversaw the massive switch and conversion of TV broadcasters in the United States from analog signals to digital signals. The move was originally slated for February that year, but later was changed to June 2009 after Congress passed the DTV Delay Act which extended the deadline for full-power TV stations to complete their transition to

6. *FCC* v. *Pacifica Foundation,* 438 U.S. 726 (1978).
7. 319 U.S. 190 (1943).

all-digital broadcasting. The FCC allowed some stations to transition before that June deadline, provided public interest concerns were met.

The key powers held by the FCC, however, focus on licensing, renewal of licenses and the authority to regulate programming and program content. It is toward these powers that primary consideration is directed in the remainder of this chapter.

LICENSING

Licensing broadcasters is one of the most important functions of the FCC. In addition to getting a license for a new station, the broadcaster must also seek FCC approval for most operational changes, such as increasing power, changing the antenna height or location, selling the station, transferring ownership and so forth. Broadcasting licenses are granted to radio and television stations for eight years.

Licenses are granted to radio and television stations for eight years.

The FCC's Media Bureau is responsible for licensing radio and television broadcast services in the United States. As of January 1, 2009, the FCC had issued more than 29,800 total licenses for all forms of broadcast stations, ranging from AM and FM radio stations (both commercial and educational) to UHF and VHF television stations (including both commercial and educational) to low-power TV and radio stations. There were, for example, 4,786 AM radio stations and 6,427 commercial FM stations at the start of 2009. Unauthorized and unlicensed stations, often known as pirate radio stations, still exist today. They are subject to a variety of enforcement actions by the FCC's Enforcement Bureau, including the seizure of equipment, imposition of monetary fines, ineligibility to hold any FCC license and criminal penalties.

An applicant for a broadcast license may seek a license to operate a new station or an existing station that he or she wishes to purchase. In either case the process is extremely complicated. Attorneys familiar with FCC rules guide the applicant throughout the process. Someone seeking a license for a new station, more and more a rarity as the broadcast spectrum is being filled up, must first obtain what is called a construction permit. Obtaining this permit is actually the biggest hurdle. If the permit is granted, if construction of the station conforms to technical requirements, and if the work is completed within the time specified by the permit, the license is routinely issued.

The prospective licensee must meet several qualifications:

1. The applicant must be a citizen of the United States. Companies with less than 25 percent foreign ownership also qualify.*

2. The applicant must have sufficient funds to build and operate the station for at least three months without earning any advertising revenue.

3. The applicant must either possess or be able to hire people who possess the technical qualifications to operate a broadcasting station.

4. The applicant must be honest and open in dealing with the commission and must have good character. Making fraudulent statements on the application can doom the applicant to failure. The character matter relates to violation of FCC rules and regulations as well as felony convictions of the owners or managers.

*The FCC in 1995 granted Rupert Murdoch, owner of the Fox Network and eight television stations, a waiver of this rule. Although Murdoch is a naturalized U.S. citizen, News Corp., Murdoch's parent company, which owns a 99 percent share in the broadcast properties, is an Australian company.

Multiple Ownership Rules

The government has always placed a cap on the number of broadcast properties any single individual or company could own. As recently as 1984 that number was 21—seven TV, seven AM radio and seven FM radio stations. The rule represented classical libertarian First Amendment theory; that is, the more voices that are capable of speaking in the marketplace, the more likely truth will be discovered. These rules have been whittled away in the past quarter century under pressure from the industry and from Congress. In addition, the federal courts ruled that unless the government could show specifically how these rules served the public interest, they would have to be abandoned. Simply arguing that a diversity of broadcast voices was better for the nation could not carry the day.

In 2009 some of the key federal rules in effect related to ownership issues included:

- **Television/newspaper cross-ownership ban:** This rule, which was modified in December 2007, generally prohibits common ownership of a full-service broadcast station (television or radio) and a daily newspaper, unless a daily newspaper seeks to combine with a radio station in a top 20 market or a daily newspaper seeks to combine with a television station in a top 20 market, provided the TV station is not ranked among the top four stations in the market and that at least eight independent major media voices remain in the market. As noted, a major media voice includes full-power commercial and noncommercial TV stations and major newspapers.[8]
- **National television ownership rule:** A single entity may own any number of television stations on a nationwide basis as long as the station group collectively reaches no more than 39 percent of the total national TV viewing audience.
- **National radio ownership rule:** There is no limit on the number of radio stations nationally that a single entity like Clear Channel can own. (In 2007 Texas-based Clear Channel operated more than 1,100 radio stations that reached more than 110 million listeners every week in all 50 states.)
- **Local television ownership limit:** A single entity may own two TV stations in the same local market (known as a "designated market area" or "DMA" in FCC lingo) if (1) the contours of the stations do not overlap; or (2) at least one of the two stations is not ranked among the top four stations in terms of audience share and at least eight independently owned and operating commercial or noncommercial full-power broadcast television stations would remain in the market after the combination of the two jointly owned stations.
- **Local radio ownership limit:** The limits are based on a sliding scale related to the size of the local market. In general, one entity may own (a) up to five commercial radio stations, not more than three of which are in the same service (i.e., AM or

---

8. Although there is a presumption against waiving the cross-ownership rule, the FCC applies four factors when reviewing any proposed combination: (1) the extent to which cross-ownership will serve to increase the amount of local news disseminated through the affected media outlets in the combination; (2) whether each affected media outlet in the combination will exercise its own independent news judgment; (3) the level of concentration in the market area; and (4) the financial condition of the newspaper or broadcast station, and if the newspaper or broadcast station is in financial distress, the owner's commitment to invest significantly in newsroom operations.

FM), in a market with 14 or fewer radio stations; (b) up to six commercial radio stations, not more than four of which are in the same service, in a market with between 15 and 29 radio stations; (c) up to seven commercial radio stations, not more than four of which are in the same service, in a radio market with between 30 and 44 (inclusive) radio stations; and (d) up to eight commercial radio stations, not more than five of which are in the same service, in a radio market with 45 or more radio stations.

▪ **Dual network ban:** Common ownership of multiple broadcast networks generally is permitted, with the exception that mergers are prohibited between or among the "top four" networks (ABC, CBS, Fox and NBC).

The government has also attempted to ensure racial and gender diversity in the ownership of telecommunications properties. From time to time, the FCC has instituted numerous programs to try to make it easier for blacks, Hispanics and other ethnic minorities as well as women to own radio and television stations and hold jobs in broadcasting. The courts have viewed such efforts with suspicion for the most part. The Supreme Court in 1990 upheld the constitutionality of these preferential programs, with Justice William Brennan writing that the federal government has the power to devise what he called "benign race conscious" measures to the extent they serve important governmental objectives. Enhancing diversity in broadcast ownership was an important governmental objective, Brennan said.[9] But by 1995 many affirmative action programs in the United States were under attack. Not surprisingly, the high court reversed its earlier stance in a 1995 ruling and said that government set-aside programs that benefited minorities were illegal.[10] In the fall of 2002 the FCC tried once again to increase racial diversity in broadcasting with a new set of rules that in effect required intensive recruiting for vacancies within a station and longer-term recruitment initiatives by broadcasters designed to inform all members of the community about employment opportunities in broadcasting. Substantial record-keeping requirements were included. These records are scrutinized by the government during the licensing and relicensing processes, but the new system appeared to many observers to be less "coercive" than the previous attempts. Data on minority ownership can be found on the FCC's Web site at http://www.fcc.gov/ownership/data.html.

Often more than one applicant seeks a single broadcast license. In the past the FCC used an elaborate formula that contained a variety of criteria to determine which applicant deserved to get the license. But in 1993 a federal court ruled that this so-called comparative-hearing process was capricious and arbitrary and had little relevance to whether the operation of a broadcasting station by a particular license applicant would serve the public interest.[11] While the FCC struggled to develop new criteria for its hearing process, Congress stepped in and told the agency that in the future it should award the license to the qualified applicant who was willing to pay the most money for it to the current owner. In other words, the agency should use an auction system. That is the way in which most licenses that are contested are awarded today.

---

9. *Metro Broadcasting, Inc.* v. *FCC,* 497 U.S. 547 (1990).
10. *Adarand Constructors, Inc.* v. *Pena*, 515 U.S. 200 (1995).
11. *Bechtel* v. *Federal Communications Commission,* 10 F. 3d 875 (1993).

A licensee doesn't have to pay the government for the license, but it must pay an annual licensing fee to hold the license. The fee is based on whether the license is for a television or radio station, and the size of the market served by the station.

License Renewal

Broadcasting licenses must be renewed every eight years. The current renewal process is certainly not automatic, but it is very close. Unless the license holder has seriously fouled up in the preceding eight years, the FCC will not even consider other applicants for the license. Congress has instructed the FCC to renew a broadcaster's license as long as

The current renewal process is certainly not automatic, but it is very close.

1. the station has served the public interest, convenience and necessity;
2. the licensee has not committed any *serious* violations of the Communications Act or commission rules and regulations; and
3. the licensee has not committed any other violations of the Communications Act or the rules and regulations of the commission that, taken together, would constitute a pattern of abuse.

The act specifically states that the commission cannot even consider whether the public interest might be better served by granting the license to someone other than the license holder. If the commission determines that the license holder has in fact failed to meet the requirements listed here, the license renewal must be denied. Only after the renewal is denied can the commission consider other applicants for the license.

Only after the renewal is denied can the commission consider other applicants for the license.

What kinds of law violations is the FCC sensitive about? Stations that broadcast fraudulent advertising have been denied the renewal of their licenses.[12] The renewal of a license for a station that was used solely to promote the causes of its owner was denied.[13] If a station does not adequately supervise the programming it carries, its license may not be renewed.[14] Today, most nonrenewals result from the applicant lying on the renewal application. Federal courts have ruled that denial of a license renewal does not violate the First Amendment. Acknowledging that a First Amendment issue might arise when a licensee is stripped of the power to broadcast, the U.S. Court of Appeals for the District of Columbia Circuit nevertheless ruled nearly 80 years ago:

> This does not mean that the government, through agencies established by Congress, may not refuse a renewal of license to one who has abused it to broadcast defamatory or untrue matter. In that case there is not a denial of freedom of speech, but merely the application of the regulatory power of Congress in a field within the scope of its legislative authority.[15]

The previous year another U.S. Court of Appeals judge had ruled that the commission had a perfect right to look at past programming practices of a renewal applicant to determine whether the license should be renewed.

---

12. *May Seed and Nursery,* 2 F.C.C. 559 (1936).
13. *Young People's Association for the Propagation of the Gospel,* 6 F.C.C. 178 (1936).
14. *Cosmopolitan Broadcasting Corp.,* 59 F.C.C. 2d 558 (1976).
15. *Trinity Methodist Church, South v. FRC,* 62 F. 2d 650 (1932).

THE UNLICENSED USE OF WHITE SPACES: FILLING IN EMPTY SPECTRUM

The FCC in late 2008 adopted rules that allow sophisticated new wireless and mobile devices to operate without a license on previously unused portions of the broadcast television spectrum known as "white spaces." These are the spaces that fall in between TV channels and previously were used by older technologies such as wireless microphones worn by on-stage performers and football referees and coaches. The new rules continue to allow wireless microphones to use the white spaces, but now also permit new devices that transmit broadband data to use the spaces, provided those devices do not interfere with TV channels or wireless microphones (the latter situation would give new meaning to a referee calling interference). The new devices are subject both to equipment certification by the FCC's laboratory and removal from the market if they cause harmful interference.

The Public's Role

Although it is rare, a renewal applicant can also face a challenge from listeners and viewers. In particular, either a formal petition to deny or an informal objection to a radio or television license renewal application may be filed with the FCC after the filing of the license renewal application by a station. The last day for filing a petition to deny is one month before the license expiration date. The FCC provides details about the renewal process, including the filing of petitions to deny renewals and informal objections, on its Web site at http://www.fcc.gov/mb/video/renewal.html. Stations are required to maintain public inspection files that must be available for public review at any time during regular business hours and made available for printing or machine reproduction upon request made in person. Further information on public inspection files can be found on the FCC's Web site at http://www.fcc.gov/eb/broadcast/pif.html.

SUMMARY

The five-member Federal Communications Commission was established to regulate the broadcasting industry. The agency has the responsibility to supervise all over-the-air broadcasting, as well as any other electronic communication that has an impact on over-the-air communications. Although the FCC is forbidden by law from censoring the content of broadcast programming, the agency nevertheless has considerable control over what is broadcast by radio and television. By licensing and relicensing broadcasting stations, the FCC can ensure that broadcasters meet certain standards, including programming standards.

Broadcast stations are licensed for eight years. To gain a license to broadcast, an applicant must meet several important criteria established by Congress and the FCC. When two or more people seek the same license, the FCC uses an auction process to select who will get the license. The auction replaces a comparative hearing process that was based on applicant merit. This latter process was costly and time-consuming, and courts ruled that at least one criterion used in the process was unenforceable. Listeners and viewers can challenge a renewal. Public participation in this process is relatively rare, and recent rule changes have made it even harder for citizens to mount an effective license challenge.

REGULATION OF PROGRAM CONTENT

SANCTIONS

Failure to abide by programming rules can cost a broadcast license at renewal time. But this sanction is rarely imposed by the FCC. The agency has a wide range of other kinds of sanctions, however, which are frequently levied against those who transgress the regulations (see boxed text).

FCC REMEDIES AGAINST BROADCASTERS FOR CONTENT VIOLATIONS

1. Issue a warning notice.
2. Impose a monetary fine (a "forfeiture"; an increasingly common remedy).
3. Place conditions on renewal of a broadcast license.
4. Revoke a broadcaster's license entirely (very rarely used).

Broadcasters have myriad programming responsibilities that range from the very broad, such as serving the public interest in the community in which it is licensed, to the very small, such as airing a proper station break at prescribed times of the day or night. Like the rules related to licensing, rules related to program content are also evolving quickly in this new century. The FCC itself has made changes, but oftentimes it has been the courts that have insisted on the abandonment or modification of rules. Rules related to the broadcast of information and advertising of lotteries were deemed unconstitutional by the U.S. Supreme Court,[16] as noted in Chapter 15.

Can the FCC control a broadcast station's format as part of its regulation of programming content? For many years the FCC resisted efforts by citizens' groups to force the agency to get involved when a radio station dropped one kind of music format—classical, for example—and adopted another format, such as rock. But listeners went to federal court, and the FCC was ordered in 1970 to *review* a format change by a station when the abandonment of a unique format produced community protests.[17] The U.S. Court of Appeals for the District of Columbia Circuit went one step further in 1974 and ordered the FCC to *hold a hearing* whenever a unique format was being abandoned by a radio station and people in the community objected.[18] A unique format would be one that no other station in the market used. The loss of this format would deny the citizens in the community access to a particular kind of music or programming. Normally it has been supporters of classical music who have protested when a local station drops the classical format. But in Seattle in 1981, New Wave rock fans mounted a protest when the community's only (at that time) New Wave music station abandoned that format. Despite the earlier court rulings, the FCC continued to argue through the late 1970s

Can the FCC control a broadcast station's format as part of its regulation of programming content?

---

16. *Greater New Orleans Broadcasting Association v. United States,* 119 S. Ct. 1923 (1999).
17. *Citizens' Committee to Preserve the Voice of the Arts in Atlanta v. FCC,* 436 F. 2d 263 (1970).
18. *Citizens' Committee to Save WEFM v. FCC,* 506 F. 2d 246 (1974).

that the marketplace should determine the broadcaster's format; the government should not get involved. And in 1981 the Supreme Court of the United States supported the agency and overturned a lower federal court decision calling for a hearing on a format change. Justice Byron White, writing for the majority, stated, "We decline to overturn the commission's policy statement which prefers reliance on market forces to its own attempt to oversee format changes at the behest of disaffected listeners." Justice White warned the agency, however, to be alert to the consequences of its policies and stand ready to change its rules if necessary to serve the public interest more fully.[19]

REGULATION OF CHILDREN'S PROGRAMMING

There are two key aspects to the FCC's regulation of children's television programming:

1. Limitations on commercials during programming targeting children
2. Requirements regarding educational programming that must be carried

The FCC also bars what it calls "program-length commercials" targeting children.

With regard to limits on commercials, the FCC mandates that in an hour-long program aired primarily for an audience of children 12 years old and younger, advertisements must not exceed 10.5 minutes on the weekends and 12 minutes during the week. The commercial time limits, however, are not applicable to noncommercial educational stations that are prohibited from airing commercials. The FCC also bars what it calls "program-length commercials" targeting children. What does this term mean? When an advertisement for a product is aired in a program associated with that product, the entire program is counted as commercial time. An example is a cartoon program that airs a commercial for the dolls of its characters during the program broadcast. Children's programs must also be separated by either buffers or substantial pauses from commercials to help minors distinguish between shows and ads.

In terms of educational programming, the FCC today, under guidelines it adopted in 1996 to comply with the Children's Television Act of 1990, mandates that broadcasters carry a minimum of three hours per week (averaged over a six-month period in order to provide broadcasters with scheduling flexibility) of "core educational programming." Such programming must be specifically designed to serve the educational and informational needs of children ages 16 years and under. It must be

- at least 30 minutes long;
- aired between 7:00 a.m. and 10:00 p.m.; and
- a regularly scheduled weekly program not pre-empted more than 10 percent of the time.

In 2007, Univision Communications, the largest Spanish-language broadcaster in the United States, agreed to pay $24 million in light of allegations that some Univision stations failed to comply with the FCC's three-hour, core-educational children's programming requirements. In particular, it was alleged that Univision, in an attempt to satisfy these obligations, had instead aired Spanish-language telenovelas that were not specifically created for children and that did not serve a significant educational purpose.[20]

19. *FCC* v. *WNCN Listeners Guild,* 101 S. Ct. 1266 (1981).
20. *In re Shareholders of Univision Communications Inc.,* Memorandum Opinion and Order, FCC 07-24 (March 27, 2007).

Complete and current information on children's television programming rules and requirements can be found on the FCC's Web site at http://www.fcc.gov/cgb/consumerfacts/childtv.html.

In a very different effort to protect children when watching television, the FCC in 2009 implemented the Child Safe Viewing Act of 2007, which was adopted December 2008 and directed the FCC to initiate a proceeding to examine "the existence and availability of advanced blocking technologies that are compatible with various communications devices or platforms." In particular, the proceeding was designed to examine blocking technologies that (1) may be appropriate across a wide variety of distribution platforms and devices; (2) can filter language based upon information in closed captioning; (3) can operate independently of preassigned ratings; and (4) may be effective in enhancing a parent's ability to protect his or her child from indecent or objectionable programming, as determined by the parent. Such technologies would be in addition to or otherwise enhance the V-chip that has been installed on all TV sets with screens of 13 inches or larger sold in the United States since 2000. As described later in this chapter, the V-chip works in conjunction with the TV Parental Guidelines that include both age- and content-based ratings for television programs (see page 618).

Change may be coming to the FCC's regulation of television programming for kids. In July 2009, then newly appointed FCC chairperson Julius Genachowski testified before the U.S. Senate Committee on Commerce, Science and Technology during a hearing called "Rethinking the Children's Television Act for a Digital Media Age." Emphasizing a number of changes that have occurred in the media environment since the Children's Television Act was passed in 1990, Genachowski stated that he wanted to explore several issues, including the quantity and quality of current educational programming; parental ability to find educational programming and other useful information; the capability of new digital technologies to better inform parental choices; the current state of advertising on children's programming, as well as other programming with children in the audience; and an assessment of concerns and opportunities presented by the digital media world. Genachowski also announced that he had directed the FCC staff to conduct an inquiry into how the FCC can best protect children and empower parents in the digital age. At the same hearing, U.S. Senator Jay Rockefeller of West Virginia said he would introduce a bill designed to safeguard minors from violent content and other supposedly harmful matter.

OBSCENE, INDECENT AND PROFANE MATERIAL

During a public rally in late 2008 celebrating the Philadelphia Phillies World Series triumph that year, second baseman Chase Utley exuberantly dropped the proverbial "f-bomb," going out live on at least five broadcast television stations and one radio station to a combined audience of more than 800,000 people. The FCC shortly thereafter received more than two dozen complaints from viewers and listeners, each asking it to take action against the stations that aired the unscripted but offending language. Does the FCC have the authority and power to fine broadcasters for such speech? During NBC's broadcast of the 2009 Golden Globe awards, movie director Darren Aronofsky was shown giving the middle-finger gesture. The FCC soon received multiple complaints. Should NBC be fined for broadcasting the unscripted and offensive hand gesture? These issues are addressed in this section.

Chase Utley exuberantly dropped the proverbial "f-bomb."

The sale, distribution or publication of obscenity is illegal by virtue of myriad federal, state and local laws. Obscenity is not protected by the First Amendment, as noted in Chapter 13. Similarly, the broadcast of obscenity over television or radio is illegal under the Federal Communications Act. But federal law also makes it illegal to broadcast what is called indecent material via radio and over-the-air television (cable is treated differently and will be discussed later in the chapter). The courts have defined obscenity. The struggle to find a workable definition for indecency has been much more difficult.

The broadcast of obscenity over the airwaves has never been a serious problem. Indecency was not a problem either, until more recent times. In television the issue first reached national prominence in 1975 when ABC, CBS and NBC, with the cooperation of the National Association of Broadcasters and the FCC, instituted what they called "the family hour" in prime time.[21] Stations that subscribed to programming policies established by the NAB, and most of them did, were told to set aside the hours from 7 to 9 each evening for family viewing; programs with sexual overtones and excessive violence were taboo in this period. The result was a few months of silly self-censorship (e.g., the word "virgin" was cut from one program, and performers on programs starring Cher and Cloris Leachman were recostumed in a more modest fashion) before a federal court ruled that the constraints constituted a violation of the First Amendment because they had been motivated by the FCC.[22]

Until recently, over-the-air television, as opposed to cable channels like HBO or MTV which are governed by far more relaxed standards (see page 633), rarely generated indecency complaints because it sought to appeal to a large, heterogeneous audience. Radio stations, on the other hand, were more brazen and frequently subject to fines for broadcasting indecent material. But TV broadcasters began to push vigorously at the legal boundaries in recent years. When CBS telecast a salacious Super Bowl halftime show in 2004 that included a very fleeting glimpse of singer Janet Jackson's breast, it ignited a firestorm of criticism that included angry congressional hearings. Mea culpas by industry officials did little to quiet the anger, and many observers agreed that the government would take some action to reduce the sexual openness on the small screen. Action against the Super Bowl broadcast came in September 2004 (see page 612). Congress showed its resolve in 2006 to punish indecent broadcasts when it increased tenfold the maximum fine the FCC can mete out against a station for a single instance of indecent or profane content, raising the amount from $32,500 to a whopping $325,000. Signed into law by then President George W. Bush, the dramatic increase may make broadcasters think twice before airing potentially indecent content. Many broadcasters responded in 2004 after the Janet Jackson incident to the political pressures placed by Congress and the FCC by engaging in self-censorship—NBC, for example, eliminated "a glimpse of an 80-year-old patient's breast" from an episode of "ER,"[23] and several ABC affiliates in November 2004 chose not to carry the network's showing of Steven Spielberg's movie "Saving Private Ryan" because of its coarse language and intense violence[24]—and quickly settling

---

21. Cowan, *See No Evil.*
22. *Writers Guild* v. *FCC,* 423 F. Supp. 1064 (1976). A U.S. Court of Appeals later overturned the lower-court ruling on the grounds that the U.S. District Court lacked jurisdiction in the case, that the issue should have first gone to the FCC for resolution. See *Writers Guild* v. *ABC,* 609 F. 2d 355 (1979). The networks made no effort to re-establish the policy.
23. Collins, "The Decency Debate."
24. Huff, "Fear Over 'Private' Parts."

A fleeting glimpse of Janet Jackson's right breast during the 2004 Super Bowl halftime show sparked an FCC crackdown on broadcast indecency. Jackson is shown here with singer Justin Timberlake.

Source: © AP/Wide World Photos

indecency actions for massive amounts of money. For instance, Clear Channel Communications, the nation's largest radio chain with approximately 1,100 stations, paid the FCC a record $1.75 million to settle a slew of pending indecency complaints filed by listeners against its stations, as well as $800,000 in outstanding fines, based on broadcasts by Howard Stern and other radio personalities. Stern would later announce in 2004 that he was leaving broadcast radio and escaping the reach of both the FCC's fines and Clear Channel's self-censorship by moving in 2006 to Sirius Satellite Radio. Satellite radio currently is not subject to the FCC's indecency regulations.

Satellite radio currently is not subject to the FCC's indecency regulations.

In 2008 the FCC earned the dubious distinction of winning a "Lifetime Muzzle Award" presented by the Thomas Jefferson Center for the Protection of Free Expression. The center, which posted the announcement on its Web site at http://www.tjcenter.org/muzzles/muzzle-archive-2008/#item12, gave the award to the FCC for what it called "years of applying inconsistent (if not arbitrary) standards in determining what is 'indecent' on broadcast airwaves—regardless of the political party in control of the Congress or the White House." The center added that the FCC's current crackdown on indecency, including the use of isolated and fleeting expletives during broadcasts, "is but the most recent in a long series of transgressions."

How did it come to this point? It began about three decades ago with a case called *FCC* v. *Pacifica Foundation*. The Supreme Court ruled in 1978 that it was not a violation of the

First Amendment to bar indecency during certain times of the day from the airwaves. The high court upheld an FCC ruling that radio station WBAI in New York City had violated the law when it broadcast during the afternoon a recorded monologue by comedian George Carlin.[25] The monologue, called "Seven Dirty Words," was broadcast on the listener-supported station during a long discussion on the English language. The FCC said it was impermissible to broadcast "language that describes in terms patently offensive as measured by contemporary community standards for the broadcast medium, sexual or excretory activities and organs, *at times when there is a reasonable risk children may be in the audience* [emphasis added]." The agency said it was unlikely children would be listening or watching after 10 p.m. and before 6 a.m., and it later designated this eight-hour block of time a safe harbor for the broadcast of adult material.

In the years following this high court ruling the FCC refined its policies on indecent broadcasts. It was consistently challenged in court, but generally the agency's policy weathered these challenges.[26] Then in 2001 the commission published a new and fairly comprehensive policy statement relating to the broadcast of indecent matter.[27]

The commission's definition of indecency remains the standard: language or material that, in context, depicts or describes, in terms patently offensive as measured by contemporary community standards for the broadcast medium, sexual or excretory activities or organs.

Before finding a broadcast indecent, the FCC must make two determinations.

Before finding a broadcast indecent, the FCC must make two determinations. First, the material must fall within the subject matter scope of indecency; that is, it must depict or describe sexual or excretory activities. Second, it must be patently offensive as measured by contemporary community standards for the broadcast medium. The standards are not local and do not encompass any particular geographic area. "Rather, the standard is that of an average broadcast viewer or listener," the policy statement said.

Notice that speech must relate to sexual or excretory activities or organs in order for it to fall within the FCC's definition of indecency. Thus, when radio host Don Imus in 2007 referred to members of the Rutgers women's basketball team as "nappy-headed hos," the language did not fall within the scope of indecency. The language certainly was racist, offensive and disagreeable, but it did not depict sexual or excretory organs and activities. The firing of Imus by CBS Radio thus was an act of community censorship (see page 35)—in this case, corporate censorship—rather than government censorship.

Although this definition of indecency and the two-step determination process remains intact today, the commission issued a controversial order in March 2004 that radically changed how the FCC interprets and applies its own standards. In particular, the FCC ruled that the use of the phrase "this is really, really fucking brilliant" by Bono, lead singer for the Irish rock group U2, during an acceptance speech at the 2003 Golden Globe Awards television program and broadcast by NBC outside the FCC's safe-harbor time period, constituted "material in violation of the applicable indecency and profanity prohibitions."[28] The decision

25. *FCC* v. *Pacifica Foundation,* 438 U.S. 726 (1978).
26. *Action for Children's Television* v. *F.C.C.,* 58 F. 3d 654 (1995); *Action for Children's Television* v. *F.C.C.,* U.S. Sup. Ct. No. 95-520, cert. den.; and *Pacifica Foundation* v. *F.C.C.,* U.S. S. Ct. No. 95-509, cert. den.
27. *In re Industry Guidelines on the Commission's Case Law Interpreting 18 U.S.C. §1464 and Enforcement Policies Regarding Broadcast Indecency,* FCC, File No. EB-00-1H-0089, April 6, 2001.
28. *In re Complaints Against Various Broadcast Licensees Regarding Their Airing of the "Golden Globe Award" Program,* Memorandum Opinion and Order, File No. EB-03-IH-0110 (March 18, 2004).

stunned many legal observers. Why? Because Bono's use of the word "fucking" was both isolated and fleeting—it was not repeated or dwelled upon, a factor that traditionally is important for the FCC in determining whether or not speech is patently offensive—and because it was not used in a sexual sense, but rather as a modifier for emphasis of how "brilliant" it was that U2 had won for Best Original Song. Furthermore, officials at NBC had no advance knowledge that Bono was going to use the expletive in question, and the network was able to "bleep" the language for its West Coast airing of the program (the program was aired live to the East Coast).

Bono's use of the word "fucking" was both isolated and fleeting.

Despite these facts, the FCC concluded that Bono's language, as used in context, was both indecent and profane. As to why the program was indecent, the FCC began its analysis by rearticulating its two-step process for indecency determinations, writing that "indecency findings involve at least two fundamental determinations. First, the material alleged to be indecent must fall within the subject matter scope of our indecency definition; that is, the material must describe or depict sexual or excretory organs or activities. . . . Second, the broadcast must be patently offensive as measured by contemporary community standards for the broadcast medium."

With respect to the first step, the FCC found that "given the core meaning of the 'F-Word,' any use of that word or a variation, in any context, inherently has a sexual connotation, and therefore falls within the first prong of our indecency definition." Turning to the second step of its indecency analysis—whether the broadcast of Bono's speech was patently offensive under contemporary community standards for the television medium—the FCC wrote:

> The "F-Word" is one of the most vulgar, graphic and explicit descriptions of sexual activity in the English language. Its use invariably invokes a coarse sexual image. The use of the "F-Word" here, on a nationally telecast awards ceremony, was shocking and gratuitous. In this regard, NBC does not claim that there was any political, scientific or other independent value of use of the word here, or any other factors to mitigate its offensiveness.

The FCC thus concluded that the Golden Globes broadcast was indecent. Importantly, the commission suggested that NBC could have prevented the entire problem, writing that the network "and other licensees could have easily avoided the indecency violation here by delaying the broadcast for a period of time sufficient for them to effectively bleep the offending word." The FCC then added a new element to its indecency calculus, holding that the "ease with which broadcasters today can block even fleeting words in a live broadcast is an element in our decision to act upon a single and gratuitous use of a vulgar expletive." In addition, the commission wrote that "the mere fact that specific words or phrases are not sustained or repeated does not mandate a finding that material that is otherwise patently offensive to the broadcast medium is not indecent." What's more, the commission held that it made no difference whatsoever that NBC did not intend for the offensive language to occur.

The FCC did much more, however, than just hold the broadcast to be indecent; it also concluded that the broadcast was profane. Federal law provides: "Whoever utters any obscene, indecent, or *profane language* by means of radio communication shall be fined under this title or imprisoned not more than two years, or both."[29] Prior to the dispute over Bono's language

The FCC did much more, however, than just hold the broadcast to be indecent; it also concluded that the broadcast was profane.

29. 18 U.S.C. § 1464 (2004).

during the Golden Globes ceremony, however, the FCC narrowly had limited the statutory meaning of the term "profane language" to "blasphemy or divine imprecation." It completely reversed course, however, in March 2004 and concluded that Bono's acceptance speech was profane. The FCC wrote:

> Broadcasters are on notice that the Commission in the future will not limit its definition of profane speech to only those words and phrases that contain an element of blasphemy or divine imprecation, but, depending on the context, will also consider under the definition of "profanity" the "F-Word" and those words (or variants thereof) that are as highly offensive as the"F-Word," to the extent such language is broadcast between 6 a.m. and 10 p.m. We will analyze other potentially profane words or phrases on a case-by-case basis.

The FCC in 2009 defined profane language.

In summary, the FCC's 2004 opinion regarding Bono's speech was an aggressive new approach by the commission to clean up language on the public airwaves. The FCC not only concluded that Bono's speech was indecent, but it also opened up a second avenue of attack, under the guise of profane language, for regulating broadcast content. The FCC in 2009 defined profane language as language that is "so grossly offensive to members of the public who actually hear it as to amount to a nuisance." In a separate statement to the FCC's opinion, then FCC chair Michael C. Powell wrote, "This sends a signal to the industry that the gratuitous use of such vulgar language on broadcast television will not be tolerated."

In September 2004 the FCC once again vigorously applied its indecency standard when it released a Notice of Apparent Liability (NAL) for a whopping aggregate sum of $550,000 against various television licensees concerning their February 1, 2004, broadcast of the Super Bowl XXXVIII halftime show.[30] The amount was, at the time, the largest indecency fine ever levied against a television broadcaster, namely CBS affiliates. The FCC focused its inquiry on Janet Jackson and Justin Timberlake's performance of the song "Rock Your Body." The raunchy duet infamously concluded with Timberlake's removal of a portion of Jackson's leather bustier, briefly exposing her breast to the camera, at the precise moment when Timberlake finished the song's lecherous last lyric, "gonna have you naked by the end of this song."

The FCC initially set forth three factors that it often considers to determine patent offensiveness.

The FCC applied its two-step indecency analysis to this performance, considering first whether the broadcast described or depicted sexual or excretory organs or activities, and then, second, whether it was patently offensive as measured by contemporary community standards for the broadcast medium. The first step was easily satisfied, as the FCC wrote that the broadcast culminated in on-camera partial nudity with Jackson's exposed breast, thus constituting a depiction of a sexual organ. As to the second step—whether the broadcast was patently offensive—the FCC initially set forth three factors that it often considers to determine patent offensiveness:

1. The explicitness or graphic nature of the description
2. Whether the material dwells on or repeats at length descriptions of sexual or excretory organs or activities
3. Whether the material is used to shock, titillate or pander

---

30. *In re Complaints Against Various Television Licensees Concerning Their February 1, 2004, Broadcast of the Super Bowl XXXVIII Halftime Show,* Notice of Apparent Liability for Forfeiture, File No. EB-04-IH-0011 (Sept. 22, 2004).

Applying these three factors in a totality-of-the-circumstances approach in which they are weighed and balanced with each other, the FCC concluded that the broadcast was indeed patently offensive. It initially found that the videotape of the performance "leaves no doubt that the Jackson/Timberlake segment is both explicit and graphic. The joint performance by Ms. Jackson and Mr. Timberlake culminated in Mr. Timberlake pulling off part of Ms. Jackson's bustier and exposing her bare breast. CBS admits that the CBS Network Stations broadcast this material, including the image of Ms. Jackson's bared breast." The FCC then reasoned that the "nudity here was designed to pander to, titillate and shock the viewing audience. The fact that the exposure of Ms. Jackson's breast was brief is thus not dispositive." In determining the amount of the fine to mete out, the FCC wrote:

> Officials of CBS [the broadcast network for the Super Bowl] and MTV [which produced the halftime show] did have prior knowledge of, indeed were intricately involved in the planning process for, and tacitly approved, the sexually provocative nature of the Jackson/Timberlake segment. Moreover, they extensively promoted this aspect of the broadcast in a manner designed to pander, titillate and shock. Viacom [owner of both CBS and MTV] made a calculated and deliberate decision to air the Jackson/Timberlake segment containing material that would shock Super Bowl viewers, and to accurately promote it as such.

The Super Bowl decision did not mark the end of the FCC's crackdown on broadcast indecency in 2004. In fact, less than one month later, the commission issued a proposed fine totaling more than $1.18 million—more than double the amount of the Super Bowl fine, and a new record-level fine for indecency on a television program—against 169 Fox Television Network stations for airing an April 2003 episode of a reality-based program called "Married by America." The episode included scenes in which party-goers licked whipped cream from strippers' bodies in a sexually suggestive manner. Although the program electronically obscured any nudity, the FCC nonetheless held that the broadcast was indecent, in part because it believed that "the sexual nature of the scenes is inescapable, as the strippers attempt to lure party-goers into sexually compromising positions."[31] The FCC added that "merely obscuring (or 'pixilating') sexual organs does not necessarily remove a broadcast from our indecency analysis." It wrote that "although the nudity was pixilated, even a child would have known that the strippers were topless and that sexual activity was being shown."

While the FCC began its vigorous new approach to both indecency and profanity in 2004 with decisions affecting the Golden Globes, the Super Bowl and "Married by America," one thing did not change: the so-called safe harbor time period when such content is protected from the FCC's regulation. The safe-harbor period today remains in effect from 10 p.m. to 6 a.m.—an eight-hour window during which both indecent and profane language may be broadcast. Obscene speech, however, falls completely outside the scope of First Amendment protection (see Chapter 13) and is not protected at any time of day. In other words, there is no safe-harbor period for obscenity on the public airwaves.

The safe-harbor period today remains in effect from 10 p.m. to 6 a.m.

31. *In re Complaints Against Various Licensees Regarding Their Broadcast of the Fox Television Network Program "Married by America" on April 7, 2003,* Notice of Apparent Liability for Forfeiture, File No. EB-03-IH-0162 (Oct. 12, 2004).

The bottom line from the indecency bloodbath of 2004 was that the FCC issued a record annual total of 12 Notices of Apparent Liability for Monetary Forfeiture—nine directed at radio shows and three targeting television programs—and proposed more than $7.9 million in fines.* That dollar amount is a whopping increase from the paltry $48,000 in FCC-proposed fines from 2000 against a total of only seven radio programs and none targeting television content.

Did the FCC continue to expand its aggressive approach to indecency in 2005? The answer is no.

The FCC rejected a complaint in 2005 filed by the American Family Association that claimed that an ABC broadcast of the award-winning World War II movie "Saving Private Ryan" was both indecent and profane.[32] The film's dialogue contains a number of expletives that are repeated over and over, including variations of the same word ("fuck") that landed Bono and NBC in trouble. Although the FCC once again found that this word has an inherently sexual meaning, it nonetheless found that, as used in the context of the movie "Saving Private Ryan," it was not patently offensive. The FCC wrote:

> We do not find indecent every depiction or description of sexual or excretory organs or activities. Rather . . . we find material indecent only if it is patently offensive based on an examination of the material's explicit or graphic nature, whether it is dwelled upon or repeated, and whether it appears to pander or is intended to titillate or shock the audience. In connection with the third factor, we consider whether the material has any social, scientific or artistic value, as finding that material has such value may militate against finding that it was intended to pander, titillate or shock.

Applying this approach to the ABC broadcast of "Saving Private Ryan," the FCC found that, although the language was repeated and dwelled upon, "the complained-of material, in context, is not pandering and is not used to titillate or shock." This factor was key to its decision. The commission added that the language in question "is integral to the film's objective of conveying the horrors of war through the eyes of these soldiers, ordinary Americans placed in extraordinary situations. Deleting all of such language or inserting milder language . . . would have altered the nature of the artistic work and diminished the power, realism and immediacy of the film experience for viewers." The FCC's opinion rejecting the indecency and profanity complaints against the movie thus represents a major victory for the First Amendment rights of both broadcasters and their audiences—in particular the audience's right to receive and view important films.

---

*In addition to the amount of the 12 notices of apparent liability issued for 2004, this figure includes (1) $952,500 from a consent decree settlement over indecency allegations with radio giant Clear Channel; (2) $258,000 from a consent decree settlement over indecency allegations against Emmis radio; and (3) $3,059,580 from a consent decree settlement over indecency allegations with Viacom.

32. *In re Complaints Against Various Television Licensees Regarding Their Broadcast on November 11, 2004, of the ABC Television Network's Presentation of the Film "Saving Private Ryan,"* Memorandum Opinion and Order, File No. EB-04-IH-0589 (Feb. 28, 2005).

Although 2005 saw the FCC issue zero notices of apparent liability against broadcasters for indecent or profane content, the commission was back at it again in 2006. The FCC that year upheld its decision (and the $550,000 fine), against an appeal by CBS, that the 2004 Super Bowl halftime show featuring Janet Jackson was indecent. Perhaps more significantly, the FCC issued a record Notice of Apparent Liability of more than $3.6 million in March 2006 against CBS affiliates in the Central and Mountain time zones for airing an episode of "Without a Trace" outside the safe-harbor zone that featured "material graphically depicting teenage boys and girls participating in a sexual orgy."[33] Although the episode never showed any actual nudity or real sex, the FCC reasoned that the material

> does depict male and female teenagers in various stages of undress. The scene also includes at least three shots depicting intercourse, two between couples and one "group sex" shot. In the culminating shot of the scene, the witness exclaims to the others in the party that the victim is a "porn star." The action briefly returns to the present . . . as the victim is shown wearing bra and panties, straddled on top of one male character, while two other male characters kiss her breast near the bra strap. The lower portion of the panties is shaded, but she is shown moving up and down while the male teenager thrusts his hips into her crotch.

With this is mind, the FCC noted that "the material is particularly egregious because it focuses on sex among children," and it reasoned that "the complained-of material is pandering, titillating and shocking to the audience. The explicit and lengthy nature of the depictions of sexual activity, including apparent intercourse, goes well beyond what the story line could reasonably be said to require." The FCC thus seemed to go beyond the scope of its authority to take on the role of producer and director, somehow knowing what scripts, plots and story lines are required to convey a message. The commission added that the content in question was "portrayed in such a manner that a child watching the program could easily discern that the teenagers shown in the scene were engaging in sexual activities, including apparent intercourse."

In 2007 the FCC's efforts to penalize the fleeting, one-time use of expletives like that in the case described earlier involving Bono were dealt a judicial setback. In particular, the 2nd U.S. Circuit Court of Appeals held in June 2007 in a case called *Fox Television Stations* v. *FCC* that the FCC's decision to punish fleeting expletives as indecent was arbitrary and capricious. The appellate court thus vacated the FCC's policy of punishing such speech as indecent and profane, and it ordered the FCC to go back to better justify its decision to penalize fleeting expletives.

In 2008 the 3rd U.S. Circuit Court of Appeals dealt another very similar blow to the FCC. In particular, the 3rd Circuit ruled in *CBS Corporation* v. *FCC*[34] that when the FCC

---

33. *In re Complaints Against Various Television Licensees Concerning Their Dec. 31, 2004, Broadcast of the Program "Without a Trace,"* Notice of Apparent Liability for Forfeiture, File No. EB-05-IH-0035 (Mar. 15, 2006).
34. 535 F. 3d 167 (3d Cir. 2008).

held CBS liable for a monetary penalty for the Super Bowl halftime show incident involving Janet Jackson, "the FCC arbitrarily and capriciously departed from its prior policy excepting fleeting broadcast material from the scope of actionable indecency." In other words, the FCC had not offered what the appellate court termed "a reasoned explanation for its policy departure" to suddenly go after broadcasts of fleeting words and images that are allegedly indecent (in this case, the less-than-one-second glimpse of Jackson's breast).

The U.S. Supreme Court agreed to hear the FCC's appeal of the 2nd Circuit's 2007 ruling against the commission's punishment of fleeting expletives, with oral argument taking place before the high court in *FCC* v. *Fox Television Stations* in November 2008. The underlying facts of the *Fox Television Stations* case involved two separate broadcasts with brief and unscripted expletives. In one instance, singer Cher uttered the following remark during an acceptance speech for an award at the Billboard Music Awards: "I've had unbelievable support in my life and I've worked really hard. I've had great people to work with. Oh, yeah, you know what? I've also had critics for the last 40 years saying that I was on my way out every year. Right. So fuck 'em. I still have a job and they don't." The other situation also occurred during an awards show when Nicole Richie, commenting to Paris Hilton about the hardships encountered during the filming of their reality TV show "The Simple Life," stated: "Why do they even call it 'The Simple Life?' Have you ever tried to get cow shit out of a Prada purse? It's not so fucking simple." The narrow issue the Supreme Court had to consider was whether the 2nd Circuit erred in striking down the FCC's determination that the broadcast of vulgar expletives may violate federal restrictions against indecent broadcasts when the expletives in question are isolated and not repeated. It was the first time the Supreme Court had heard a case involving the FCC's power over indecent broadcasts since its 1978 ruling in the George Carlin case of *FCC* v. *Pacifica Foundation* described earlier in this chapter.

In April 2009 a divided Supreme Court in *FCC* v. *Fox Television Stations, Inc.* narrowly upheld the FCC's decision to punish isolated and fleeting expletives and, in doing so, it reversed the 2nd Circuit's ruling. In reaching this decision, however, the majority of the high court avoided the First Amendment free speech issue and, instead, considered only whether the FCC's recent decision to punish broadcasters for fleeting expletives (after years of having not done so) was arbitrary or capricious. Under the federal Administrative Procedure Act, a government agency's change in policy can be declared invalid if the change was arbitrary and capricious. Writing for a majority of the Supreme Court, Justice Antonin Scalia held that the APA standard required the FCC to show that "there are good reasons for the new policy" and that the FCC "believes it to be better" than the old policy of not punishing broadcasters for such fleeting expletives. Scalia wrote that the FCC's "reasons for expanding the scope of its enforcement activity were entirely rational," pointing out that "it is surely rational (if not inescapable) to believe that a safe harbor for single words would likely lead to more widespread use of the offensive language." Scalia added that "the fact that technological advances have made it easier for broadcasters to bleep out offending words further supports the Commission's stepped-up enforcement policy." The bottom line is that the FCC's policy was left intact as a matter of administrative law, not constitutional law.

In light of its ruling in the *Fox Television Stations* case, the U.S. Supreme Court in May 2009 vacated the 3rd Circuit's opinion in *CBS Corporation* v. *FCC* in which, as noted earlier, the 3rd Circuit had thrown out a $550,000 fine issued by the FCC against CBS for the Janet Jackson halftime performance during the 2004 Super Bowl. The 3rd Circuit had declared the

FCC's crackdown on isolated and fleeting images of sexual or excretory images arbitrary and capricious under the Administrative Procedure Act. The Supreme Court wrote that it was remanding the case back to the 3rd Circuit "for further consideration in light of *FCC v. Fox Television Stations*."

A final thought on the subject of broadcast indecency is important here before moving on to the topic of broadcast violence (note, by the way, that the FCC's definition of indecency has *nothing* to do with violence, but only sex and excretory organs and activities). In particular, there is a lesson to be learned from the FCC's crackdown in 2004, and that lesson is this: One cannot overestimate the power of a small but very vocal and well-organized minority to influence the decisions of the FCC. According to official documents on the FCC's Web site (http://www.fcc.gov), the commission received only 111 total complaints in 2000 about allegedly indecent content and a slightly higher 346 complaints in 2001. But then, at that point, the numbers ratchet up significantly and dramatically, first to 13,922 in 2002, then to 202,032 in 2003, and, finally, to a whopping 1,405,419 complaints regarding allegedly indecent content in 2004. Why the sudden increase? Was the general public simply fed up with broadcast content? It turns out that in 2003 and 2004, more than 98 percent of those complaints (excluding ones filed about the Super Bowl halftime show in 2004) were filed by just one single organization: the Parents Television Council (PTC). There was not, in other words, some massive outpouring of complaints from the general populace, but rather from one group with an agenda of censorship. In contrast, there was not a similar uprising of "free speech" organizations against either the PTC or the FCC. A secondary lesson, then, is this: One must fight for free speech rights and not take them for granted, lest minority interests like the PTC silence what the majority of the public want to watch.

One cannot overestimate the power of a small but very vocal and well-organized minority to influence the decisions of the FCC.

What, then, does it take for a group like the PTC or an individual to file a complaint with the FCC alleging that particular broadcast material is indecent? Three things are required by the FCC before it will investigate a viewer's or listener's complaint. In particular, so-called complainants must provide the FCC with

Three things are required by the FCC before it will investigate a viewer's or listener's complaint.

1. the date and time of the broadcast in question;
2. the call sign and letters of the station that aired the content; and
3. a significant excerpt of the program.

The first requirement is important because, if the broadcast occurred during the safe-harbor period of 10:00 p.m. to 6:00 a.m., then any complaint for indecent content or profane language will be dismissed. That eight-hour window is when indecent and profane content (although not obscene speech) is protected from the FCC's wrath.

The second requirement is important because the FCC must know the particular station—the particular broadcast licensee—that carried the content. That station will, in turn, be named and investigated by the FCC.

Finally, the third requirement—that a significant excerpt of the program be provided to the FCC by the complainant—can be satisfied in several different ways. For instance, the complaining viewer may provide a full or partial tape or transcript of not only *what* was said but the *context* in which it was said. It is not enough for the complainant simply to state that "there was a broadcast involving sexual dialogue." That won't cut it. More details showing what was actually said (the precise language used or images shown) and the context in which it was said are key. Today it is easy for a group like the PTC to file a complaint online. The FCC accepts e-mail complaints online at fccinfo@fcc.gov.

VIOLENCE ON TELEVISION

The first thing to note in starting this section is that violent content is not included in the FCC's definition of indecency discussed in the last section. Broadcast indecency currently focuses only on sexual or excretory organs or activities, *not* on violent images or story lines. Parsed differently and more bluntly, violence and sex simply are not the same thing in the FCC's regulatory universe.

Violence and sex simply are not the same thing in the FCC's regulatory universe.

Congress added new rules to the broad array of broadcast regulations when it adopted legislation in the Telecommunications Act of 1996 to regulate violence on television. The law required the manufacturers of television sets to include a microchip—nicknamed the V-chip—in television receivers manufactured after January 1, 2000. Sets with screens smaller than 13 inches are exempt from the regulation. This chip, along with a programming rating system imposed on broadcasters, permits viewers to block out violent television programming. The V-chip is activated by a signal contained in each television broadcast. The signal tells the receiver that a program with a certain rating is being transmitted. If the receiver is programmed to reject such a broadcast, reception of the show will be blocked. Two years after the law was passed, the broadcast industry, children's advocacy groups, the motion picture industry and the FCC agreed on a rating system. The ratings appear in the corner of the TV screen for the first 15 seconds of a program. They also are included in many magazine and newspaper listings for programs. Ratings are given to all TV programs except news, sports and unedited movies on premium cable channels. There are six possible ratings: TV-Y; TV-7; TV-G; TV-PG; TV-14; and TV-MA. Descriptions of each are available at the FCC's Web site at http://www.fcc.gov/cgb/consumerfacts/vchip.html. In addition to the ratings, there are content descriptors designated by letters, including *V* (violence); *S* (sexual situations); *L* (language); and *D* (suggestive dialogue).

Most over-the-air and cable broadcasters have adopted the system. A few have not. But the industry's acceptance of the V-chip ratings seems far more enthusiastic than that of television set owners. A 2004 survey by the Kaiser Family Foundation found that "just 24% of parents used TV ratings often and only 15% used the V-chip."[35]

In 2007 the FCC issued a massive report in which it asked Congress to give it the power to regulate "excessively violent programming" on both broadcast and cable television, such as time-channeling such content away from hours when children are likely to be watching TV. If Congress were to pass such a law giving the FCC power to regulate TV violence, not only would it mark a radical shift from its traditional approach of not censoring violent content, but the law would certainly be challenged in court on First Amendment grounds. In particular, defining "violent" content would be very difficult and subject to a void for vagueness challenge. In addition, a law targeting violent programming would be a content-based law subject to the strict scrutiny standard of judicial review. By October 2009, however, the FCC still lacked the authority to regulate violent programming. But look for Senator Jay Rockefeller to propose such legislation in the near future.

35. Puzzanghera, "A Campaign to Head Off New Decency Rules."

SUMMARY

The FCC has broad control over the content of broadcast programming. To enforce this control, the agency has a wide variety of sanctions, which include letters of reprimand, fine or forfeiture, and nonrenewal or revocation of broadcast licenses. Content regulations involve a wide range of broadcast programming. In the broadest sense, the broadcaster must program to meet the needs of the community. But programming rules also involve simple regulations, such as the requirement to present station identification at various times of the broadcast day.

The FCC has chosen not to attempt to control the selection of format by a broadcaster. Citizens groups have urged the FCC to hold hearings when a radio station drops one program format and adopts a new one. In the early 1970s federal courts supported these citizen protests, but in 1981 the U.S. Supreme Court ruled that the government need not get involved when a broadcaster decides to switch from one format to another. In the mid-1980s the FCC attempted to remove rules dictating programming standards for children's broadcasting. Congress resisted these changes and forced the agency to reinstate rules regarding both the number of commercial minutes permitted per hour in children's programming and minimum service standards for the younger viewers.

Federal law prohibits the broadcast of any obscene or indecent material. In 1978 the Supreme Court ruled that a radio or television station could be punished for broadcasting material that is not obscene but merely indecent. The court based its ruling on the premise that children might be present during the broadcast. In 2004 the FCC began an all-out crackdown on indecent content. In 1996 Congress mandated that microchip circuitry be added to new television sets that would allow parents to block programs rated as violent. In 2007 the FCC asked Congress to give it power to regulate violent content, much like it regulates indecent content.

REGULATION OF POLITICAL PROGRAMMING

The guarantees of freedom of speech and freedom of the press were added to the Constitution in large measure to protect political debate in the nation from government interference. In recent years the courts and the FCC have voided two important content regulations that were related in many instances to political discussion, the Fairness Doctrine and rules that focused on personal attacks and political editorials. The Fairness Doctrine, generated by the FCC in the late 1940s, stipulated that all broadcasters had a responsibility to provide coverage of important public issues that arose in their communities. In providing such coverage the broadcasters had the additional obligation of ensuring that all significant viewpoints on these issues were represented. In the late 1980s the FCC said it would no longer enforce the Fairness Doctrine and a U.S. Court of Appeals subsequently ruled that the agency was within its rights to abandon the doctrine.[36] The personal attack rules stipulated that when broadcasters air what amounts to a personal attack on an individual or group, they must also notify the target of the broadcast attack and offer free time for the target to reply. The rules on political editorials were similar. If a broadcaster endorsed a candidate for political office, the opposing candidate

36. *Syracuse Peace Council* v. *FCC,* 867 F. 2d 654 (1989). See also *Arkansas AFL-CIO* v. *FCC,* 11 F. 3d 1430 (1993).

had to be notified about the endorsement and given an opportunity to respond. In October 2000 a U.S. Court of Appeals ordered the FCC to repeal these rules because of, among other reasons, First Amendment concerns.[37] Other rules remain, however.

The FCC stopped enforcing the Fairness Doctrine in 1987.

Although the FCC stopped enforcing the Fairness Doctrine in 1987, there were concerns among many Republicans and, in particular, conservative radio talk-show hosts that it would be resurrected by President Barack Obama and a Democratic-controlled Congress. Calling it the "Hush Rush" doctrine because the Fairness Doctrine ostensibly would require a radio station playing three hours of programming by conservative Rush Limbaugh each day to also put on three hours of programming by a liberal talk-show host in order to balance out viewpoints and thus be fair to all sides, Republicans introduced several "pre-emptive strike" bills, such as the Broadcaster Freedom Act of 2009, in both the U.S. Senate and House of Representatives in early 2009 that would prevent the FCC from adopting and enforcing the Fairness Doctrine. President Obama, however, stated in February 2009 that he opposed any move to resurrect the Fairness Doctrine. In July 2009 the Rules Committee of the House of Representatives blocked a Republican move to pass a bill that would have prevented the FCC from reviving the Fairness Doctrine.

The FCC has a Web page (http://www.fcc.gov/mb/policy/political/candrule.htm) devoted exclusively to statutes and rules on candidate appearances and candidate advertising. What follows is a discussion of two of those rules: the candidate access rule and the equal opportunity/equal time rule.

CANDIDATE ACCESS RULE

Broadcasters cannot completely block candidates for *federal* office from buying airtime on the station to promote their candidacies because of the existence of the **candidate access rule. Section 312**(a)(7) of the Federal Communications Act, adopted in 1971 by Congress, states that a broadcast license can be revoked for willful and repeated failure "to allow reasonable access to or to permit the purchase of reasonable amounts of time for the use of a broadcasting station by a legally qualified candidate for federal elective office on behalf of his candidacy." This statute applies only to candidates for federal office: presidents and vice presidents and U.S. senators and representatives.

Federal courts have provided important interpretations of this statute. Two cases stemmed from the 1980 presidential election campaign. The Carter-Mondale presidential committee sought to buy 30 minutes of time on all three networks in early December 1979 for President Jimmy Carter to announce that he would be a candidate for re-election and to present a film outlining Carter's record as president. The request was made in October 1979. NBC refused. ABC said it could not reach a decision on the question. CBS offered two five-minute segments, one at 10:55 p.m. and one during the day. Privately, all three networks were fearful of breaking into their prime-time entertainment schedules for a political broadcast. But publicly, the broadcasters argued that the political campaign had not yet started; it was too early to begin to carry political programming (the election was scheduled for November 1980).

---

37. *Radio-Television News Directors Association* v. *FCC*, 229 F. 3d 269 (2000).

The FCC ruled against the networks, the U.S. Court of Appeals for the District of Columbia Circuit ruled against the networks, and the U.S. Supreme Court ruled against the networks. The high court ruled in its 6-3 decision that a broadcaster could not institute an across-the-board policy rejecting all requests from federal candidates for airtime.[38] Chief Justice Burger wrote that once a political campaign begins, a broadcaster must give reasonable and good faith attention to access requests from legally qualified candidates.

> Such requests must be considered on an individualized basis, and broadcasters are required to tailor their responses to accommodate, as much as reasonably possible, a candidate's stated purpose in seeking air time. In responding to access requests, however, broadcasters may also give weight to such factors as the amount of time previously sold to the candidate, the disruptive impact on regular programming, and the likelihood of requests for time by rival candidates under the equal opportunities provision of Section 315(a). These considerations may not be invoked as pretexts for denying access; to justify a negative response, broadcasters must cite a realistic danger of substantial program disruption—perhaps caused by insufficient notice to allow adjustments in the schedule—or of an excessive number of equal time requests.

Burger added that broadcasters must explain their reasons for refusing airtime or making limited counteroffers so the FCC can review these decisions if needed. Each of the networks had argued, however, that the 1980 presidential campaign had not really started. After all, the time period sought by Carter was 11 months prior to the election. In this case the networks should not be bound by Section 312, they asserted. The majority of the Supreme Court rejected this argument, noting the following evidence that the campaign had started:

1. Ten Republican candidates and two Democratic candidates had announced they were running for president.

2. The selection of delegates to the national political conventions had started in many states.

3. Many candidates were making speeches in an effort to raise money.

4. The Iowa caucuses to select convention delegates were scheduled for January, one month after the broadcast time sought by Carter.

5. Newspapers had been covering the national political campaign for at least two months.

Burger rejected the notion that Section 312 created a right of access to the media. None is created by this decision, he added. But a licensed broadcaster is "granted the free and exclusive use of a limited and valuable part of the public domain; when he accepts that franchise, it is burdened by enforceable public obligations."[39]

The Supreme Court's ruling means that a broadcaster cannot adopt an across-the-board policy of rejecting all requests for airtime. Each request must be considered individually and can be rejected only if the broadcaster can demonstrate good cause.

The Supreme Court's ruling means that a broadcaster cannot adopt an across-the-board policy of rejecting all requests for airtime.

38. *CBS* v. *FCC,* 453 U.S. 567 (1981).
39. Ibid.

Section 312 implies that the candidate can seek to buy time on a station or ask for free time. Does this mean a broadcast station must *give* a candidate for federal office free time if fulfilling such a request would not interfere substantially with the broadcast schedule or would not prompt requests for equal time from other candidates? The U.S. Court of Appeals for the District of Columbia Circuit answered no when that question was asked. Broadcasters may meet the demands of Section 312 by either giving the candidate free time or making time available for purchase, the court said.[40]

In September 1999 the FCC reversed a decision it had made five years earlier and ruled that federal candidates who seek to buy broadcasting time cannot be limited to buying only 30- and 60-second spots. In 1994 the FCC had ruled that broadcasters could refuse to sell the longer spots. The 1999 ruling did not specify a length of time the candidates could buy, but the agency did note that five-minute spots might be better for the candidates.

Supporters of Section 312 see it as a means to permit candidates for federal office to use the important broadcast communication channels in this nation to talk to prospective voters. Opponents say Section 312 is government interference in broadcasters' operation of their business, and it can cause severe financial hardship if programming schedules are disrupted to facilitate political broadcasts.

When Congress adopted Section 312 in 1971, it also specified the highest rates that a broadcaster can charge a candidate for federal office for using station facilities. The general rule is that 45 days before a primary election and 60 days before a general election, the charge to a candidate cannot exceed the lowest rate the station charges its local advertisers for that particular time slot. At other times the rate must be "comparable" to what the station charges other advertisers. These rules contain other considerable details that are important but are too involved to outline here. Students who intend to enter broadcast sales should closely study Section 312(a)(7) of 47 United States Code.

Although Section 312 applies only to candidates for federal office, a station that routinely denied candidates for state and local office reasonable access to communicate with voters would undoubtedly be sanctioned by the government. The FCC has interpreted Section 307 of the Communications Act, which outlines a licensee's public interest responsibilities, to bar any station from denying any candidate reasonable access simply to avoid obligations under the equal opportunity rules, which will be outlined next.

EQUAL OPPORTUNITY/EQUAL TIME RULE

Section 315 of the Communications Act outlines what are called the equal opportunity or **equal time rules.** These rules have been a part of the law since it was passed in 1934, although this section was substantially amended in 1959. The rules are quite simple. If a broadcasting station permits one legally qualified candidate for any elective public office to use its facilities, it must afford an equal opportunity for all other legally qualified candidates for the same office.

What does equal opportunity mean? It means equal time, equal facilities and comparable costs. If John Smith buys one-half hour of television time on station WKTL to campaign for the office of mayor, other legally qualified candidates for that office must be allowed to

---

40. *Kennedy for President Committee* v. *FCC,* 636 F. 2d 417 (1980).

purchase one-half hour of time as well. If Smith is able to use the station's equipment to pre-record his talk, other candidates must have the same opportunity. If the station charges Smith $100 for the one-half hour of time, the station must charge his opponents $100.

The station does not have to solicit appearances by the other candidates; it merely must give them the opportunity to use the facilities if they request such use within one week of Smith's appearance. Finally, Section 315 does not provide a right of access to any candidate to use a station's facilities. Section 315 applies only if the station first chooses to permit one candidate to appear on the station. However, remember the earlier discussion about requirements that exist under Section 312 and the general public interest standards that govern station operation.

Section 315 specifically bars the station from censoring material in broadcasts made by political candidates, and the courts interpret this provision quite strictly.

Use of the Airwaves

Under Section 315 if one candidate gets the use of a broadcast facility, his or her opponents get to use the facility as well. What is a "use" under the law? Any presentation or appearance that features a candidate's voice or image is regarded as a "use" by the FCC. It is not a use if, for example, in a political advertisement an announcer simply recites the candidate's record or his or her position on an issue. Similarly, it is not a use if the candidate's voice or image is used by an opponent in one of his or her ads. But short of these exceptions most other appearances count, including appearances on TV entertainment programs like a situation comedy, and even appearances in televised feature films. In 2003 the scheduled appearance by Mayor John F. Street of Philadelphia on the CBS drama "Hack" was canceled by the network when it was learned that Street was in a campaign for re-election. The network said the appearance might trigger provisions of Section 315 and force the Philadelphia CBS affiliate to give his opponents equal television exposure.[41] And when Arnold Schwarzenegger became a candidate for governor in the 2003 California recall election, television stations in that state were forced to stop showing his movies, or face requests from the 134 other candidates on the ballot for equal time.

In 2008 during the Democratic primary race for a state representative position in Massachusetts, candidate Brian Ashe was granted 20 free commercial spots, each 30 seconds long, and four 15-second commercial spots by a radio station in Springfield, Mass.[42] Why? Because his opponent, Kateri B. Walsh, had continued to host a radio program on that same station after she announced her candidacy. The station, WHYN-AM 560 radio, also agreed not to continue to carry Walsh's show as long as she remained a candidate.

In 1959 Congress amended Section 315 and carved out four rather broad exceptions to the meaning of the term "use." Since 1959 the FCC has liberally interpreted these exceptions to broaden them even more. The following appearances by a candidate do not constitute a use under the law. That is, an opponent cannot use one of these appearances as a justification for equal time from the station.

41. "Pennsylvania: Mayor Cut from TV Show."
42. Goonan, "Brian Ashe, Candidate for 2nd Hampden District, Says He Has Reached Accord with Radio Station Over Opponent's Program."

> **APPEARANCES BY A POLITICAL CANDIDATE THAT ARE NOT GOVERNED BY EQUAL OPPORTUNITY RULE**
>
> ▮ Appearance in a bona fide newscast
>
> ▮ Appearance in a bona fide news interview
>
> ▮ Appearance in the spot news coverage of a bona fide news event
>
> ▮ Incidental appearance in a news documentary

The FCC has ruled that "Entertainment Tonight" constitutes a bona fide newscast.

1. **The appearance by a candidate in a bona fide or legitimate newscast does not constitute use of the facility in the eyes of the law.** Section 315 will not be triggered. This exemption is expansive. The FCC has ruled that "Entertainment Tonight" constitutes a bona fide newscast and that appearances by legally qualified candidates for public office on "Access Hollywood" should be accorded the bona fide newscast exemption from the equal opportunity provision. The FCC's principal consideration is whether the program reports news of some area of current events in a manner similar to more traditional newscasts, and it declines to evaluate the relative quality or significance of the topics and stories selected for newscast coverage. The FCC ruled that an appearance in a news clip broadcast as a part of the program "McLaughlin Group" constitutes an appearance in a newscast.[43] But a candidate appearance during the panel discussion part of the program would not fall under the newscast exemption. If the newscaster or reporter who reads the news is a candidate for public office, this exemption does not apply to that candidacy.

2. **The appearance of a candidate in a bona fide news interview does not constitute a use.** The FCC has defined a bona fide news interview program as one that is regularly scheduled, within the journalistic control of the producers, and is produced as a newsworthy and good faith journalistic exercise, not an attempt to advance a particular candidacy. This exemption is quite broad. The FCC concluded that an October 2006 interview by Jay Leno on "The Tonight Show" with California Gov. Arnold Schwarzenegger—then running for re-election—was a bona fide news interview, noting that "the fact that many interviews on the program concern entertainment is irrelevant" and adding that Leno's lack of journalistic credentials was not controlling.[44] The FCC has held that interviews conducted on the "Sally Jessy Raphael Show," "Jerry Springer," "Politically Incorrect" and "Howard Stern" also fall within the bona fide news interview exemption.

3. **The appearance of a candidate in the spot news coverage of a bona fide news event is not use.** When candidate Smith is interviewed at the scene of a warehouse fire about the problems of arson in the city, this is not use in terms of Section 315. Political conventions are considered bona fide news events; therefore an appearance by a candidate at the convention can be broadcast without invoking Section 315.

4. **The appearance of a candidate in a news documentary is not a use if the appearance is incidental to the presentation of the subject of the program.**

43. *Telecommunications Research and Action Center v. FCC,* 26 F. 3d 185 (1994).
44. *In re Equal Opportunities Complaint Filed by Angelides for Governor Campaign Against 11 California Stations,* DA 06-2098 (Oct. 26, 2006).

Imagine that during a 2012 election campaign for a U.S. Senate seat from Washington, a Seattle television station broadcasts a documentary on the 1991 Persian Gulf War and the role played by a particular U.S. Air Force unit that before the war was stationed at an air base in the state. One segment focuses on the wartime experiences of Luis Sanchez, a fighter pilot who was shot down over Iraq during the war but managed to elude the enemy for 10 days before reaching safety in Saudi Arabia. Sanchez is a candidate for the Senate seat. Would his appearance in this documentary trigger Section 315? Would the TV station be required to give time to his opponent? No. Because Sanchez's appearance focuses exclusively on his experiences during the war and not his political candidacy, his appearance in the documentary is regarded as an incidental appearance.

Debates between political candidates are considered bona fide news events, and the broadcast of these events will not initiate use of Section 315. This is true even if the broadcaster sponsors the debate.

In 1996 the major television networks gave free time to Bill Clinton and Bob Dole to air their statements about major issues in the campaign. CBS and NBC did this within the scope of their evening newscasts and were not required to give time to other presidential candidates. ABC, PBS and Fox aired the short statements at other times, and the FCC declared that such telecasts were on-the-spot coverage of bona fide news events and exempted the three networks from obligations under Section 315.

Press conferences held by political candidates are also normally considered bona fide news events and are exempt from the provisions of Section 315. The FCC considers three criteria to determine if a candidate's press conference is exempt from the equal opportunity provision. They are:

1. Whether the conference is broadcast live
2. Whether, in the good faith determination of the broadcaster, it is a bona fide news event
3. Whether there is evidence of broadcaster favoritism or bias toward a candidate

Legally Qualified Candidates

The FCC has attempted to define who is and who is not a legally qualified candidate as precisely as possible (see boxed text).

A LEGALLY QUALIFIED CANDIDATE IS ANY PERSON

■ who publicly announces that he or she is a candidate for nomination or election to any local, county, state or federal office, *and*

■ who meets the qualifications prescribed by law for that office, *and*

■ who qualifies for a place on the ballot or is eligible to be voted for by sticker or write-in methods, *and*

■ who was duly nominated by a political party that is commonly known and regarded as such or makes a substantial showing that he or she is a bona fide candidate.

In primary elections, Section 315 applies to intraparty elections, not interparty elections.

In primary elections, Section 315 applies to intraparty elections, not interparty elections. In a primary election Democrats run against Democrats, Republicans run against Republicans, Libertarians run against Libertarians. If there is an appearance by a Democrat, the other Democratic candidates for the same office must be afforded an equal opportunity. The station does not have to give Republicans or Libertarians or even independents the opportunity to make an appearance. During general elections, Section 315 applies across party lines since at this point all candidates are running against each other for the same office.

Whereas only an appearance by the candidate himself or herself can trigger Section 315, appearances by supporters of the candidate trigger another regulation called the **Zapple Rule.** This rule was formulated by the FCC in response to a letter from Nicholas Zapple, who was a staff member on the Senate Subcommittee on Communications. This rule states that if a broadcaster permits the supporter of a candidate to make an appearance on the station, then the station must provide an equal opportunity for an appearance by supporters of other legally qualified candidates for the same office. In the FCC's 1972 "Report Regarding the Handling of Political Broadcasts," the agency outlined the Zapple Rule in this way:

> The commission held in "Zapple" that when a licensee sells time to supporters or spokesmen of a candidate during an election campaign who urge the candidate's election, discuss the campaign issues, or criticize an opponent then the licensee must afford comparable time to the spokesmen for an opponent. Known as the quasi-equal opportunity or political party corollary to the fairness doctrine, the "Zapple" doctrine is based on the equal opportunity requirement of Section 315 of the Communications Act; accordingly, free reply time need not be afforded to respond to a paid program.

Two last points need to be made about Section 315. First, since broadcasters are not permitted to censor the remarks of a political candidate, they are immune from libel suits based on those remarks. In 1959 the Supreme Court ruled that because stations cannot control what candidates say over the air, they should not be held responsible for the remarks. The candidate, however, can still be sued.[45] Second, ballot issues like school bond levies, initiatives and referendums do not fall under Section 315. Do these rules apply to the Internet? No Supreme Court or federal appellate court ruling has focused specifically on that question. But clearly, since the Supreme Court ruled in 1997[46] that communication on the Internet enjoys the same First Amendment protection as communication in the printed press, it would seem highly improbable that the candidate access rule, the equal opportunity rule or any broadcast regulation could be applied to the Internet.

SUMMARY

Several rules govern political broadcasts carried by radio and television broadcasters. Section 312 of the Federal Communications Act states that broadcasters cannot have an across-the-board policy rejecting all paid and nonpaid appearances by candidates for federal office. A candidate's request must be evaluated and can be rejected only if it could cause serious disruption of program schedules or might prompt an excessive number of equal time requests.

45. *Farmers Educational and Cooperative Union of America* v. *WDAY,* 360 U.S. 525 (1959).
46. *Reno* v. *American Civil Liberties Union,* 117 S. Ct. 2329 (1997).

Although this rule applies only to requests from candidates for federal office, the government's mandate that broadcasters operate their stations in the public interest may very well include similar standards for the treatment by broadcasters of requests for access to airtime from state and local candidates.

Section 315 states that if a broadcaster provides one candidate for office with the opportunity to use a station's broadcast facilities, all other legally qualified candidates for the same office must be given the same opportunity. The use of the station's facilities includes all appearances on the station with the exception of the following:

1. Bona fide newscasts
2. Bona fide news interviews
3. Spot news coverage
4. Incidental appearance in a news documentary

Candidate press conferences and debates between candidates are considered spot news events. During primary elections, Section 315 applies only to candidates from the same political party running against each other to win the party's nomination to run in the general election.

NEWS AND PUBLIC AFFAIRS

While the FCC has been quite willing to impose content regulations on entertainment programming, the agency has purposely steered away from making similar rules regarding broadcast news. The violence ratings do not apply to television news, for example. The agency reinforced this position in 1998 when it rejected a petition to strip four Denver television station licenses on the grounds that the news programs on the stations are heavily saturated with violent content. A group called Media Watch asked the FCC to deny the station's license renewals because the news programming contained "toxic" levels of television violence, which in turn leads to "fear, disrespect, imitative behavior, desensitization and increased violent behavior." The agency responded by saying that "journalistic or editorial discretion in the presentation of news and public information is the core concept of the First Amendment free press guarantee."[47]

Although the FCC takes action when it has documented evidence that a station has engaged in deliberate distortion of the news, the agency generally defers to the judgment of broadcasters, due to First Amendment free press concerns. As the FCC provided in 2009 on its Web page titled Complaints About Broadcast Journalism:

> As public trustees, broadcasters may not intentionally distort the news. Broadcasters are responsible for deciding what their stations present to the public. The FCC has stated publicly that "rigging or slanting the news is a most heinous act against the public interest." The FCC does act to

Broadcasters may not intentionally distort the news.

47. Brooke, "FCC Supports TV News."

protect the public interest where it has received documented evidence of such rigging or slanting. This kind of evidence could include testimony, in writing or otherwise, from "insiders" or persons who have direct personal knowledge of an intentional falsification of the news. Of particular concern would be evidence about orders from station management to falsify the news. In the absence of such documented evidence, the FCC has stressed that it cannot intervene.[48]

The FCC enforces a separate provision that targets news hoaxes.

In addition to taking action against deliberate and documented news distortions, the FCC enforces a separate provision that targets news hoaxes. In particular, the FCC prohibits broadcast licensees from broadcasting false information concerning crimes and catastrophes if three things exist:

1. the licensee knows the information is false;
2. it is foreseeable that broadcast of the information will cause substantial public harm; and
3. broadcast of the information does in fact directly cause substantial public harm.

VIDEO NEWS RELEASES, SPONSORSHIP IDENTIFICATION AND THE FCC

Video news releases (VNRs) are the broadcast equivalent of written press releases that masquerade as news but, in reality, are created by public relations firms or government agencies. They often involve video clips that feature a person who appears to be a reporter covering a real story, when in fact the person is an actor, or they come with a script that can be read as a voice-over by a local news anchor. Groups like the Center for Media and Democracy[49] claim that VNRs, which are virtually indistinguishable today from real news clips, amount to fake news and press release journalism, especially when local television stations run them unedited as if they really were news and fail to disclose their origin. Several federal government agencies under the administration of George W. Bush used VNRs to convey their messages.

VNRs raise obvious ethical issues for the broadcast news stations that air them because they blur the line between objective news content and commercials or propaganda. But VNRs also raise legal issues of sponsorship identification that the FCC addresses. In particular, the FCC in August 2006 launched a major investigation of 77 broadcast licensees to determine whether the sources of the VNRs they aired were properly disclosed to viewers during news broadcasts. This followed on the heels of a Public Notice issued by the FCC in 2005 under which the agency made it clear that "whenever broadcast stations and cable operators air VNRs, licensees and operators generally must clearly disclose to members of their audiences the nature, source and sponsorship of the material that they are viewing. We will take appropriate enforcement action against entities that do not comply with these rules."[50] The FCC can impose monetary fines of $32,500 per violation when a station fails to label a VNR.

48. "*FCC Consumer Facts: Complaints About Broadcast Journalism,*" available online at http://www.fcc.gov/cgb/consumerfacts/journalism.html.
49. The Web site for this organization is available online at http://www.prwatch.org.
50. Public notice, Media Bureau Docket No. 05-171, FCC 05-84, April 13, 2005.

The Radio-Television News Directors Association (RTNDA) strenuously objected to the FCC crackdown on the use of VNRs, citing First Amendment concerns about government intrusion into broadcast newsrooms and interference editorial judgment. As attorneys for the RTNDA contended in an October 2006 letter to the FCC, "determining the content of a newscast, including when and how to identify sources, is at the very heart of the responsibilities of electronic journalists, and these decisions must remain far removed from government involvement or supervision. The government would not dream of inserting itself into a print newsroom to dictate or otherwise oversee how newspaper editors utilize press releases."[51] The RTNDA also asserted that the FCC's sponsorship-identification rules[52] apply not to VNRs but to issues of so-called payola that typically arise when radio stations or their employees receive actual monetary compensation or gifts in return for airing specific songs. For instance, in 2007 four companies—CBS Radio, Citadel Broadcasting, Clear Channel and Entercom Communications—agreed to pay a combined $12.5 million to close investigations into possible violations of the FCC's payola rules, thus resolving allegations that the broadcasters may have accepted cash or other valuable consideration from record labels in exchange for airplay of artists from those labels, without disclosing those arrangements.[53] In the case of VNRs, however, typically there is no payment; the VNRs are offered free-of-charge to stations with no express or implied promise made to air the footage.

But the fact that no money directly changes hands when a VNR is aired may not always get a station off the legal hook. In September 2007 the FCC issued a notice of apparent liability against Comcast for transmitting, without providing sponsorship identification, on its CN8 channel in Philadelphia a VNR for a product called "Nelson's Rescue Sleep" as part of a daily segment on a show called "Art Fennell Reports" that focuses on consumer issues. The FCC stated in that case that it would enforce its rules regarding sponsorship identification, even if there is no payment made between the VNR company and the station, if there is "too much focus on a product or brand name in the programming."[54] Later that same month, the FCC went after Comcast for another four VNRs aired on the same channel and program.

The sponsorship-identification rules were called into play in two very different contexts in 2008. First, the FCC released a Notice of Inquiry seeking comments by broadcasters and the public regarding trends in embedded advertising (also known as product placement and product integration) and potential changes to the sponsorship-identification rules to address such covert ads. The practice of product placement was increasing on broadcast TV, with many brands popping up prominently (and for a price) in shows, because people use digital video recorders to skip regular commercials. The FCC ultimately may crack down on embedded ads, although it surely will face intense lobbying by advertisers and broadcasters against tighter regulation. Second, acting in response to complaints lodged by Congress, the FCC investigated whether several military analysts who appeared on newscasts to address the war in Iraq failed to disclose ties to the Pentagon or White House that may have created conflicts of interests and bias such that they were motivated to promote the military's agenda. Some

The FCC ultimately may crack down on embedded ads

51. Letter from Kathleen A. Kirby, counsel for the RTNDA, to Marlene H. Dortch, secretary of the FCC, Oct. 5, 2006, available online at http://www.rtnda.org/foi/vnr_filling.pdf.
52. 47 U.S.C. §§ 317, 508; 47 C.F.R. §§ 73.1212, 76.1615.
53. Press release, "Broadcasters Pay $12.5 Million to Resolve Possible 'Payola' Violations," April 13, 2007, FCC Web site, available online at http://hraunfoss.fcc.gov/edocs_public/attachmatch/DOC-272304A1.pdf.
54. *In re Comcast Corp.*, Notice of Apparent Liability for Forfeiture, File No. EB-06-IH-3723 (Sept. 21, 2007).

people suspected the military analysts were embedded by the government in newscasts to plant favorable comments about the war rather than to give objective viewpoints.

THE FIRST AMENDMENT

Broadcasting stations are not common carriers; that is, they have the right to refuse to do business with anyone they choose. During 1969 and 1970 two groups, the Democratic National Committee and a Washington, D.C., organization known as Business Executives Movement for Peace, sought to buy time from television stations and networks to solicit funds for their protest of the Vietnam War and to voice their objections to the way the war was being waged by the government. Broadcasters rebuffed these groups on the grounds that airing such controversial advertisements and programming would evoke the fairness doctrine, and they would then be obligated to ensure that all sides of the controversy were aired. Such action was a nuisance and could be costly. The broadcasters told the Democratic committee and the business executives that one of their basic policies was not to sell time to any individual or group seeking to set forth views on controversial issues.

When this policy was challenged before the FCC, the commission sided with the broadcasters, noting that it was up to each individual licensee to determine how best to fulfill fairness doctrine obligations. But the U.S. Court of Appeals for the District of Columbia Circuit reversed the FCC ruling, stating that the right of the public to receive information is deeply rooted in the First Amendment. A ban on editorial advertising, the court ruled, "leaves a paternalistic structure in which licensees and bureaucrats decide what issues are important, whether to fully cover them, and the format, time and style of coverage." This kind of system, the court ruled, is inimical to the First Amendment.[55]

> It may unsettle some of us to see an antiwar message or a political party message in the accustomed place of a soap or beer commercial. . . . We must not equate what is habitual with what is right or what is constitutional. A society already so saturated with commercialism can well afford another outlet for speech on public issues. All that we may lose is some of our apathy.

The victory of the business organization and the Democrats was short-lived, for by a 7-2 vote, the U.S. Supreme Court overturned the appellate court ruling. Stations have an absolute right to refuse to sell time for advertising dealing with political campaigns and controversial issues, the court ruled. To give the FCC the power over such advertising runs the risk of enlarging government control over the content of broadcast discussion of public issues.

In response to the argument that by permitting broadcasters to refuse such advertising, we place in their hands the power to decide what the people shall see or hear on important public issues, Justice Burger wrote:

"For better or worse, editing is what editors are for."

> For better or worse, editing is what editors are for; and editing is the selection and choice of material. That editors—newspaper or broadcast—can and do abuse this power is beyond doubt, but that is no reason to deny the discretion Congress provided. Calculated risks of abuse are taken in order to preserve high values.[56]

55. *In re Business Executives Movement for Peace v. FCC,* 450 F. 2d 642 (1971).
56. *CBS v. Democratic National Committee,* 412 U.S. 94 (1973).

The court was badly fractured on this case, and Justices Brennan and Marshall dissented. Only two other justices—Stewart and Rehnquist—joined the chief justice in his opinion. The remainder joined in overturning the appeals court ruling, but for their own reasons.

Finally, the high court used the First Amendment to strike down a congressional statute forbidding all noncommercial educational broadcasting stations that receive money from the Corporation for Public Broadcasting from editorializing on any subject at all.[57] The ban on all editorials by every station that receives CPB funds was too broad and far exceeded what is necessary to protect against the risk of governmental interference or to prevent the public from assuming that editorials by public broadcasting stations represent the official views of government.

The government exercises limited control over the content of public affairs broadcasts. The FCC has thus far rejected all complaints that television news coverage was slanted or staged and has made it difficult for those who seek to pursue this cause with the agency. The Supreme Court has given broadcasters the right to determine whether to air specific editorial advertising and has struck down a statute that forbade public broadcasting stations from telecasting editorial opinions.

SUMMARY

REGULATION OF NEW TECHNOLOGY

Over-the-air broadcasting has been the primary focus of government attempts to regulate the electronic communications media, but as new technologies have emerged, the Federal Communications Commission and the Congress have moved to pass rules to govern their operation as well. Cable television has been the subject of numerous FCC rule-making efforts and two comprehensive federal statutes. Rules regulating low-power television, multipoint distribution services, satellite master antenna television and direct satellite broadcasting have also been promulgated. The deregulatory waves that have swept away many broadcast rules have also hit cable regulation. In 2001 a federal court ordered the FCC to reconsider and justify rules that limited both the size and program content of cable systems. Congress had given the FCC the authority to limit the number of cable subscribers one multiple system operator could reach— 30 percent of all cable subscribers—and to prevent a cable operator, like AOL Time Warner for example, from filling the cable package it offered subscribers with programs created only by its affiliated companies. Only 40 percent of the programming could be produced by affiliated companies. The U.S. Court of Appeals ruled that both rules implicated the First Amendment and could be sustained only if it was shown they advanced important government interests unrelated to the suppression of speech and did not impact or limit more speech than necessary to further those interests. The court said in imposing the rules that the FCC had not adequately justified the need for the 30 percent cap on subscribers or the 40 percent cap on programming.[58]

---

57. *FCC* v. *League of Women Voters,* 468 U.S. 912 (1984).
58. Labaton and Fabrikant, "U.S. Court Ruling Lets Cable Giants." See also *Time Warner Entertainment Co.* v. *FCC,* 240 F. 3d 1126 (2001).

SATELLITE RADIO

Just as air-conditioning once was a fancy option on the automobile that now is taken for granted by many buyers, today a prized new option on a car or SUV is a satellite radio—something that likely will become a standard vehicle feature in the not-so-distant future. Satellite radio stands in contrast to the free, over-the-air terrestrial radio to which we are accustomed. Sirius Satellite Radio, helped by the well-publicized $500 million signing of talk-show host and self-proclaimed "King of All Media" Howard Stern, claimed more than six million subscribers by the start of 2007, while rival XM Satellite Radio had slightly more than 7.63 million subscribers at that time.[59]

Howard Stern's switch to satellite radio is important for media law students to understand. While free, over-the-air radio broadcasting is subject to the FCC's rules governing indecency and profanity discussed earlier in this chapter, satellite radio is—at least at the time this book went to press—exempt from similar content-based rules. Thus shock jocks like Howard Stern on Sirius and the rival duo of Opie & Anthony on XM can freely use profanity and expletives at any time of the day on satellite radio with no need to fear the wrath of the FCC. Whereas some in Congress want to change this situation so that the FCC can police satellite radio content just as it now does broadcast indecency, in the meantime there is the slight potential that satellite radio will develop into a verbal gutter, so to speak, where profane content thrives. This is not likely to be the case, however, because satellite radio companies typically offer subscribers well over 100 diverse and largely commercial-free channels. What's more, the content sweeps up far more than shock jocks.

Although the FCC does not yet control indecent content on either satellite radio or cable television, it does regulate other aspects of the relatively new medium of satellite radio. For example, Sirius, which was founded in 1990 (two years before XM), had to apply to the FCC to launch its three current satellites that were operating by 2000. The FCC also regulates power levels and emissions from satellite radio devices and modulators, as well as the land antennas that transmit signals from satellites used by Sirius and XM to local devices.

The FCC approved by a 3-2 vote the merger of Sirius and XM.

In July 2008, with both companies struggling financially, the FCC approved by a 3-2 vote the merger of Sirius and XM (the new company is Sirius XM Radio Inc.), with all three Republican commissioners voting for it and the two Democrats voting against it. At the time, XM had approximately 9.6 million subscribers, while Sirius boasted 8.9 million. The newly merged company anticipated saving about $400 million in 2009. FCC approval came only after the two companies agreed to pay almost $20 million in combined fines for using some ground-based repeaters (signal towers) for their satellite signals that were not authorized by the FCC and for selling receiving devices that exceeded FCC-established power limits and thus interfered with reception of FM radio signals (indeed, Howard Stern's program on Sirius had bled onto National Public Radio's FM signal in some cases!). In addition, the combined companies agreed to cap prices on some services for three years after the merger and to set aside a portion of their channels (4 percent of the full-time audio channels on the Sirius platform and 4 percent of the full-time channels on the XM platform) for minority-owned entities. They also agreed to offer new packages of programs, including two á la carte options. In brief,

---

59. Semuels, "Sirius Gives Stern, Agent $83-million Stock Bonus."

the FCC used the merger review as an opportunity to impose burdens on and extract concessions from the new company. The Justice Department in March 2008 declared the merger would not violate antitrust laws.

Whether the cost-saving synergies created by the merger ultimately benefit the public interest—the critical concept for FCC regulation (see page 594)—or whether the new monopoly harms consumers remains to be seen. Initial signs weren't good, as the new company's stock price tumbled sharply in the months immediately following the merger, and it faced massive debt payments and more predicted losses in 2009. In early 2009, with Sirius XM teetering on the verge of bankruptcy, Liberty Media agreed to loan the faltering company $530 million in exchange for a 40 percent stake of it.

INTERNET

In April 2009 the FCC began the process of developing a national broadband plan designed to ensure that every American has access to broadband capability. The move came as part of the massive federal stimulus package, known as the American Recovery and Reinvestment Act of 2009, in which Congress charged the FCC with creating a national broadband plan by February 17, 2010. The first step in that process involved the FCC soliciting public input from all stakeholders, including consumers; industry; large and small businesses; nonprofits; the community of individuals with disabilities; governments at the federal, state, local and tribal levels; and all other interested parties. The plan eventually would impact Internet providers, cable companies and telephone companies. The FCC in October 2009 adopted new network neutrality principles on the Internet (see pages 130–132).

CABLE TELEVISION

Cable television first appeared in the 1940s. It was called community antenna television (CATV). In rural communities where television reception was poor because of distance or topography, entrepreneurs installed large antennas on hilltops to receive the incoming television signals and then transmitted these signals (for a small price) to local homeowners via coaxial cable. The FCC first asserted its jurisdiction of cable or CATV in the early 1960s. But the agency had to move tenuously at first because its right to regulate cable television was not clearly established. Cable is not broadcast; signals travel through wires, not the airwaves. There is no scarcity of spectrum space, that important factor that justifies government regulation of broadcasting. Cable is not a common carrier, as are telephone and telegraph. The FCC authority to regulate these point-to-point services does not establish its right to regulate cable. It took more than 20 years, with the adoption of the Cable Communications Policy Act of 1984, before FCC jurisdiction over cable was firmly established.

FEDERAL LEGISLATION REGULATING CABLE TELEVISION

Two federal laws provide the foundation of the regulation of cable television. The first measure, the comprehensive Cable Communications Policy Act of 1984, was a cable-friendly measure designed to foster the orderly growth of this new medium. Cable flourished under this law. By the 1990s nearly all American homes had access to cable television, and more than 60 percent of all Americans received their television via cable. But viewers, and then

Viewers complained about escalating cable rates among other things.

members of Congress, became angry at many heavy-handed policies adopted by the cable industry using the freedom it had been granted under the 1984 legislation. Viewers complained about escalating cable rates among other things. In 1992 Congress adopted the Cable Television Consumer Protection and Competition Act, a decidedly not cable-friendly measure that imposed rate regulations on most cable systems, directed the FCC to develop mandatory service standards for cable television, and greatly strengthened the competitive position of local, over-the-air television stations vis-à-vis cable. The 1984 law remains the basic regulatory measure. Its most important provisions are outlined on the following pages. It will be noted where the 1992 law has modified this legislation.

In December 2007 the FCC narrowly voted to retain its 30 percent cap on cable ownership. This rule, known as a horizontal ownership limit, sets the maximum number of subscribers that a single cable operator may serve at 30 percent of households nationwide. The 30 percent limit, which was first established in 1993 and then modified in 1999, was challenged in federal court by Time Warner in 2001. The court determined that the FCC lacked a sufficient evidentiary basis for the 30 percent cap, and it sent the rule back to the FCC to further justify its existence. In justifying the 30 percent cap in 2007, the FCC contended the limit was necessary to ensure that no single cable operator would create a barrier to a video programming network's entry into the market or cause a video programming network to exit the market simply by declining to carry the network. But in August 2009, the U.S. Court of Appeals for the District of Columbia struck down the FCC's 30 percent cap limiting the number of U.S. cable subscribers that any one cable company can have. The court held the FCC's decision to adopt the 30 percent figure was "arbitrary and capricious."

The decision in *Comcast Corp.* v. *FCC* forces the FCC to go back to the drawing board to either better support its 30 percent subscriber cap or to develop a different plan altogether. In a cursory, two-sentence response to the ruling, FCC Chair Julius Genachowski said his staff was "reviewing the court's decision with respect to the limit previously adopted and the Commission will take this decision fully into account in future action."

The Cable Communications Policy Act of 1984 (hereafter Cable Act) was adopted after decades of crazy-quilt regulation at the federal, state and local levels. The act was needed because some state and local governments were attempting to assert increased control over an industry that had become increasingly national in scope. In the summer of 1988, in a decision regarding the right of the FCC to establish certain technical standards for cable television, the Supreme Court read the new Cable Act in an expansive fashion, giving the FCC assurances that its regulation of the medium would be supported under the law.[60]

Purpose of the Law

The purposes of this legislation are enumerated in Section 601 of the Cable Act itself. They are as follows:

1. To establish a national policy concerning cable communications
2. To establish franchise procedures and standards that encourage the growth and development of cable systems and that ensure that cable systems are responsive to the needs and interests of the local community

60. *New York City* v. *FCC,* 486 U.S. 57 (1988).

3. To establish guidelines for the exercise of federal, state and local authority with respect to the regulation of cable systems

4. To ensure and encourage that cable communications provide the widest possible diversity of information sources and services to the public

5. To establish a process that protects cable operators against unfair denials of renewal by franchising authorities and that provides for an orderly process for consideration of renewal proposals

Jurisdiction and Franchises

The federal government has jurisdiction to regulate cable television, but has given local governments the power to impose a variety of obligations on cable operators. The local government is what is called the "franchising authority"; it is given the power to grant the cable system the right to operate in a particular area. This right is contained in a franchise agreement, which gives the cable operator the right to serve customers in a particular area in exchange for the promise to provide certain standards of service. Until about 20 years ago, this was an exclusive right. This means that only a single operator served a particular community. Cable companies often had to bid against one another to win this exclusive right. These exclusive agreements were challenged on constitutional grounds, but the Supreme Court did not outlaw their use.[61] Congress did, however, in 1992. Economics, even more than government policy, makes it unlikely that more than a single operator will serve the cable customers in a community. The cost of wiring a community is simply prohibitive without the promise of exclusivity. If, as some predict, the day comes when a single wire carries all telephone, television and Internet traffic in a community, and the use of that wire is open to anyone who seeks to send a signal, competition for cable customers within a city or even a neighborhood may become a reality.

The 1984 statute speaks of "services" and "facilities and equipment." "Services" generally means programming. "Facilities and equipment" refers to hardware of the system and the physical capabilities of the system, such as channel capacity, two-way or one-way, and so on. Local governments are generally barred from establishing requirements for service or programming but are given a wide latitude to establish standards for equipment and facilities. The local government can insist that a cable operator provide broad categories of programming to meet the needs of children, different ethnic groups, or others and can insist that the cable operator provide public access channels for citizens to use.

Rate regulation has consistently been a bone of contention between cable operators and government regulatory bodies, both federal and local. The 1984 and 1992 cable laws gave the FCC substantial power to control what cable companies charge their customers. The 1996 Telecommunications Act reversed this policy and immediately abolished the FCC's power to regulate the rates for small cable systems and ordered the agency to phase out rate regulation for larger systems by March 1999. The marketplace model was the justification for this change in policy, and supporters of deregulation argued that the delivery of television programming through telephone lines and by direct broadcast satellite (DBS) would force cable operators

---

61. *Los Angeles* v. *Preferred Communications,* 476 U.S. 488 (1986).

to keep their rates competitive. But the competition to cable did not develop.[62] The telephone companies lost interest in carrying television programming when they discovered they could make more money providing homeowners and businesses with hookups to the Internet. And television viewers resisted direct broadcast satellite services because these providers were not permitted to transmit programming from local television stations. In 1999 Congress changed the law and required DBS operators whose systems carried even one local channel to carry all the local channels.[63] The satellite operators didn't like this, but their challenge of the law on First Amendment grounds failed.[64] The change actually spurred the growth of DBS home receiving systems, but this seemed to have little impact on higher-than-ever cable rates in most communities.

Must-Carry Rules

Historically the government required all cable operators to retransmit the signals of all local television stations. These requirements were called the "must-carry rules" and were instituted to protect local broadcasters. By the 1980s, when cable networks proliferated, many cable operators found the rules to be onerous because they required operators to carry local over-the-air stations in preference to the more attractive (and lucrative for them) cable networks. Despite the so-called lack of scarcity in cable at the time, most systems were limited to 36 channels. The must-carry rules were challenged, and in 1985 a U.S. Court of Appeals ruled them to be a violation of the First Amendment.[65] By forcing a cable operator to carry a local station, the government denied the cable operator his or her First Amendment rights to communicate some other kind of programming. In other words, the court saw the must-carry rules as a content-based regulation. Attempts by the government to recast the rules failed to win court approval.[66] The 1992 cable law attempted to strengthen the position of the local broadcaster and contained substantially modified must-carry rules. Under this law the local broadcaster could either insist that the cable operator retransmit the station's signal to subscribers or forbid the cable operator from retransmitting the signal unless he or she paid what is called a retransmission fee. The application of the must-carry provisions varied with the channel capacity of the cable system. Small systems with less than 12 channels, for example, had to carry only three local commercial stations and one noncommercial station. Larger cable systems had to carry most or all local stations. Independent local stations with limited popularity insisted on cable carriage; popular network-affiliated stations often sought the retransmission fee.

Congress justified the new rules with the argument that 60 percent of Americans receive their television signals via cable. The heart of the American broadcasting system has consistently been local broadcasting. If cable operators are free to refuse to carry local broadcasters on their cable systems, this action could cause serious harm to the local stations. Cable operators said this fear was groundless, that it would be imprudent of them to drop the retransmission of popular local stations. But many local stations are not that popular, the broadcasters

62. Gomery, "Cable TV Rates"; and Labaton, "Cable Rates Rising."
63. The Satellite Home Viewer Improvement Act of 1999; see also Clausing, "Satellite TV Is Poised."
64. *Satellite Broadcasting and Communications Association* v. *Federal Communications Commission,* 275F. 3d 337 (2001).
65. *Quincy Cable* v. *FCC,* 768 F. 2d 1434 (1985).
66. *Century Communications* v. *FCC,* 835 F. 2d 292 (1987).

said, and the cable operator earns substantially more revenue by carrying a cable channel than by retransmitting a local broadcast signal. Many of the less popular over-the-air channels could be abandoned and ultimately die.

Turner Broadcasting, which owned several cable channels that might be displaced by the addition of local channels to the limited cable mix, challenged the new rules and a protracted legal battle ensued.[67] In two separate decisions the Supreme Court ultimately approved the new rules. Opponents of the rules challenged them on the grounds that by forcing a cable operator to carry one channel rather than another, the government was imposing decisions regarding the content of cable television on a system operator and that this content regulation violated the First Amendment. Justice Anthony Kennedy agreed that the rules do impact content because they determine who is allowed to speak in a given cable market. "But they do so based only upon the manner in which the speakers transmit their messages to viewers, not upon the messages they carry," he said.[68] The justification for the rules—the protection of local over-the-air broadcasting, the promotion of a diversity of programming sources, and the maintenance of fair competition in the TV market—is sufficient, the court said, inasmuch as in the end the rules are content neutral.[69] The issue of carrying local signals has receded with the growth of the capacity of most cable systems, yet the competition among cable channels to gain access to cable systems is as heated as ever.

Programming and Freedom of Expression

The FCC has imposed on cable systems that originate programming many of the same content rules that govern over-the-air television. The equal time rules, the "lowest unit rate" rule for political advertising, the candidate access rules, the sponsor identification rule and many others apply to cable-originated programs. Federal rules prohibit the broadcast of obscenity on over-the-air television; similar rules apply to cable. The FCC has also ruled that over-the-air broadcasters must limit their broadcast of indecent material to those hours when children are not likely to be in the television viewing audience, between 10 p.m. and 6 a.m. (see page 613). But Congress and the courts have, in the past, given cable television operators far greater leeway in the broadcast of indecency. Federal courts, for example, have consistently struck down attempts by the states to bar cable companies from transmitting indecent or adult programming but denied cable operators any right to censor programming.[70] The 1984 Cable Act required that every cable operator provide, on request from a subscriber, a lock box device that permits the subscriber to block out the reception of specific channels. The 1992 law contained hastily drafted provisions that *permitted* cable operators to prohibit indecent programming on the commercial leased-access channels and on the public access channels available to government and public schools. If the operator decided to permit indecent programming on the commercially leased channels, these signals had to be scrambled and subscribers could only view these channels by requesting access in writing 30 days in advance of the viewing.

---

67. *Turner Broadcasting System, Inc.* v. *FCC,* 819 F. Supp. 32 (1993).
68. *Turner Broadcasting System, Inc.* v. *FCC,* 114 S. Ct. 2445 (1994).
69. *Turner Broadcasting System, Inc.* v. *FCC,* 117 S. Ct. 1174 (1997).
70. See, for example, *Home Box Office* v. *Wilkinson,* 531 F. Supp. 987 (1982); and *Jones* v. *Wilkinson,* 800 F. 2d 989 (1986), aff'd 480 U.S. 926 (1987).

In 1993 these provisions were declared to be unconstitutional by the U.S. Court of Appeals for the District of Columbia Circuit because they restricted speech protected by the First Amendment.[71] But two years later the full court sitting en banc reversed this earlier ruling. Then the court ruled that the provisions that *permitted* the cable operator to ban indecent programming from the access channels didn't involve any action by the government. The censorship is the result of an action by the cable system operator, a private party. Hence there were no First Amendment implications to these provisions.[72] In June 1996 a badly splintered Supreme Court voided some of these new cable rules but sustained other portions of the law. The court sustained the portion of the law that allowed the cable operator to ban patently offensive programming from the leased-access channels but struck down the regulation that required cable operators to scramble such programming and force subscribers to ask for access in writing. This latter rule limited what subscribers could see and constituted an invasion of their privacy by forcing them to acknowledge in writing that they wanted to see such programming, the court said. At the same time, the high court struck down that portion of the law that gave cable operators the right to ban indecent programming from the government access channels. The court said there was no history of problems of the transmission of indecency on such channels and indicated a concern that conservative cable operators might try to control the kind of programming telecast on public access channels, traditionally the haven of nonprofit organizations who seek to communicate with the larger audience.[73]

In December 1998 a special three-judge panel of the U.S. District Court for Delaware struck down Section 505 of the 1996 Communications Decency Act, which required the distributors of adult programming over cable television to completely scramble both the video and audio signals, regardless of whether customers requested the programming to be scrambled. The law was aimed at protecting children from what is called "signal bleed," or incomplete scrambling. When signal bleed occurs, viewers can see and hear portions of the scrambled program. Programming distributors who could not fulfill this obligation were told to confine the transmission of this adult programming to the hours between 10 p.m. and 6 a.m. Playboy Entertainment challenged the provision, arguing that cable operators who could not afford the expensive scrambling technology would simply stop carrying this kind of programming rather than risk violating the law. The court ruled that while the government had a legitimate interest in attempting to shield young people from the adult programming, Section 505 was not the least restrictive means to fulfill this interest. The court said another provision in the CDA, which requires cable operators to supply blocking devices to subscribers who want them to screen out such channels, accomplishes the same goal without substantially interfering with the program distributors' First Amendment rights.[74] Two years later the Supreme Court affirmed the lower-court decision by a 5-4 vote. Justice Anthony Kennedy wrote that because signal-scrambling technology is imperfect, the "only reasonable way for a substantial number of cable operators to comply with the letter of §505 is to 'time channel,' which silences protected speech for two-thirds of the day in every home in a cable service area, regardless of the presence

71. *Alliance for Community Media* v. *FCC,* 10 F. 3d 812 (1993).
72. *Alliance for Community Media* v. *FCC,* 56 F. 3d 105 (1995).
73. *Denver Area Educational Telecommunications Consortium Inc.* v. *FCC; Alliance for Community Media* v. *FCC,* 1 E.P.L.R. 331 (1996); and Greenhouse, "High Court Splits," A1.
74. *Playboy Entertainment Group, Inc.* v. *U.S.,* 30 F. Supp. 2d 702 (1998).

or likely presence of children or the wishes of the viewer." This requirement is a significant restriction on First Amendment protected speech, he wrote. The capacity required in cable systems to allow subscribers to block unwanted channels is a far narrower and less restrictive alternative that would still serve the government's interest.[75]

The Cable Act has established that third parties—that is, people other than the cable operator or the local government—must have access to the cable system. Several means are provided for such access. The local franchising authorities are permitted to require that the cable operator provide public access and government and educational access channels. A public access channel is set aside for free public use on a nondiscriminatory, first-come, first-served basis. Neither the cable operator nor the government can censor what appears on such a channel. The franchising authority can prescribe limited (content-neutral) time, place and manner rules for the public access channel, such as deciding that the access channel will give each user 30 minutes of time or that they must sign up three days before the date they wish to use the channel. But these are about the only limits. The government and educational channels are used either by schools or to broadcast public hearings or city council meetings. These channels are to be programmed as the government sees fit.

Commercial access channels must also be provided by the cable operator. The law provides that a certain number of channels must be set aside for use by "unaffiliated programmers" at reasonable rates. The cable operator cannot control the content of these programs. The number of channels that must be set aside for commercial access depends on the number of activated channels in the cable system. An activated channel is one that is being used or is available for use. The cable operator can set the price and conditions of use for these channels, so long as they are "reasonable." Costs cannot have anything to do with content; that is, a cable operator cannot charge someone who puts on a conservative talk show $100 per hour and someone who puts on a liberal talk show $500. However, the cable operator can set different rates for different categories of program; for example, news programs cost $50 per hour, movies $100 per hour.

Commercial access channels must also be provided by the cable operator.

SUMMARY

The power of the FCC to regulate cable television was a clouded issue for many years. Slowly but surely, the commission, with the permission of the courts, moved to regulate this new technology. In 1984 both the Supreme Court and Congress gave the FCC what seemed to be clear jurisdiction to set broad rules for governing cable television. But a subsequent Court of Appeals ruling has cast some doubt on all government regulation of cable.

The Cable Communications Policy Act of 1984 is a comprehensive measure setting policies and standards for the regulation of cable television. The 1992 Cable Television Consumer Protection and Competition Act made some modifications in the earlier law. Local governments are given the primary responsibility under this measure to regulate the cable systems in their communities. They may issue franchises, collect franchise fees and renew franchises. The Cable Act also provides for the inclusion of public, government and commercial access channels.

75. *United States* v. *Playboy Entertainment Group, Inc.*, 529 U.S. 803 (2000); the FCC repealed these rules in November 2001.

BIBLIOGRAPHY

Ahrens, Frank. "FCC's New Standards-Bearer." *Washington Post,* 17 March 2005, E01.
———. "Powell Calls Rejection of Media Rules a Disappointment." *Washington Post,* 29 June 2004, E01.
———. "Radio Giant in Record Indecency Settlement." *Washington Post,* 9 June 2004, A1.

Andrews, Edmund. "Court Upholds a Ban on 'Indecent' Broadcast Programming." *The New York Times,* 1 July 1995, A9.

Barstow, David, and Robin Stein. "Under Bush, a New Age of Prepackaged News." *The New York Times,* 13 March 2005, A1.

Bernstein, Andrew A. "Access to Cable, Natural Monopoly, and the First Amendment." *Columbia Law Review* 86 (1986): 1663.

Blair, Jayson. "FCC Approves One Owner for New York Area TV Stations." *The New York Times,* 26 July 2001, C18.

Brooke, James. "The FCC Supports TV News as Free Speech." *The New York Times,* 3 May 1998, A13.

Brown, Rhonda. "Ad Hoc Access: The Regulation of Editorial Advertising on Television and Radio." *Yale Law and Policy Review* 6 (1998): 449.

Carter, Bill. "Media Ruling Merely Irritates Big Owners." *The New York Times,* 25 June 2004, C1.

Clausing, Jeri. "Satellite TV Is Poised for New Growth." *The New York Times,* 26 November 1999, C1.

Collins, Scott. "The Decency Debate; Pulled Into a Very Wide Net: Unusual Suspects Have Joined the Censor's Target List, Making for Strange Bedfellows (Wait Can We Say That?)." *Los Angeles Times,* 28 March 2004, E26.

Cowan, Geoffrey. *See No Evil.* New York: Simon & Schuster, 1979.

Creech, Kenneth C. *Electronic Media Law and Regulation.* Boston: Focal Press, 1993.

Cys, Richard L., "Broadcaster License Auctions: A Replacement for Comparative Hearings." *WSAB Bulletin,* January 1998, 4.

"FCC Repeals Network Rule." *The New York Times,* 20 April 2001, C13.

Fogarty, Joseph R., and Marcia Spielholz. "FCC Cable Jurisdiction: From Zero to Plenary in Twenty-Five Years." *Federal Communications Law Journal* 37 (1979): 361.

Gomery, Douglas. "Cable TV Rates: Not a Pretty Picture." *American Journalism Review,* July/August 1998, 66.

Goonan, Peter. "Brian Ashe, Candidate for 2nd Hampden District, Says He Has Reached Accord with Radio Station Over Opponent's Program." *The Republican* (Springfield, Mass.), 11 September 2008, B1.

Greenhouse, Linda. "High Court Splits on Indecency Law Cable TV." *The New York Times,* 29 June 1996, A1.

Huff, Richard. "Fear Over 'Private' Parts." *Daily News* (New York), 11 November 2004, 111.

Kirtley, Jane. "Second Guessing News Judgment." *American Journalism Review,* October 1998, 86.

Labaton, Stephen. "Cable Rates Rising as Industry Nears End of Regulation." *The New York Times,* 3 March 1999, A1.

———. "Media Companies Succeed in Easing Ownership Limits." *The New York Times,* 16 April 2001, A1.

———, and Geraldine Fabrikant. "U.S. Court Ruling Lets Cable Giants Widen Their Reach." *The New York Times,* 31 March 2001, A1.

Lee, Jennifer. "Bill to Raise Indecency Fines Is Reintroduced." *The New York Times,* 9 October 2004, C3.

Levi, Lili. "The Hard Case of Broadcast Indecency." *New York University Review of Law and Social Change* 20 (1992–93): 49.

Maynard, John. "FCC Is Asked to Revoke the Licenses of Two D.C. Stations." *Washington Post,* 2 September 2004, C7.

McChesney, Robert W. "Battle for U.S. Airwaves, 1928–1935." *Journal of Communication* 40 (Autumn 1990): 29.

Myerson, Michael. "The Cable Communications Policy Act of 1984: A Balancing Act on the Coaxial Wires." *Georgia Law Review* 19 (1985): 543.

Miflin, Lawrie. "Revisions in TV Ratings Called Imminent." *The New York Times,* 16 June 1997, B1.

———. "TV Ratings Accord Comes Under Fire from Both Flanks." *The New York Times,* 11 July 1997, A1.

Pember, Don R. *Mass Media in America.* 6th ed. New York: Macmillan, 1992.

"Pennsylvania: Mayor Cut from TV Show." *The New York Times,* 8 April 2003, A17.

Poling, Travis. "Clear Channel Puts Indecency Issue Behind." *San Antonio Express-News,* 10 June 2004, 1E.

Powe, Lucas A. *American Broadcasting and the First Amendment.* Berkeley: University of California Press, 1982.

Puzzanghera, Jim. "A Campaign to Head Off New Decency Rules." *Los Angeles Times,* 26 July 2006, C3.

Rutenberg, Jim. "Few Parents Use the V-Chip, a Survey Shows." *The New York Times,* 25 July 2001, B1.

Semuels, Alana. "Sirius Gives Stern, Agent $83-million Stock Bonus." *Los Angeles Times,* 10 January 2007, C1.

Siklos, Richard. "Broadcast Radio Is Scrambling to Regain Its Groove." *The New York Times,* 15 September 2006, C1.

Triplett, William. "Orgs Seek FCC Review of Bush Vids." *Daily Variety,* 22 March 2005, 6.

Tuohy, Lynne, and John M. Moran. "Judge Orders Tribune to Sell WTXX-TV." Hartford Courant, 22 March 2005, B7.

GLOSSARY

A

absolute privilege An immunity from libel suits granted to government officials and others based on remarks uttered or written as part of their official duties.

absolutist theory The proposition that the First Amendment is an absolute, and that government may adopt no laws whatsoever that abridge freedom of expression.

actual damages Damages awarded to a plaintiff in a lawsuit based on proof of actual harm to the plaintiff.

actual malice A fault standard in libel law: knowledge before publication that the libelous material was false or reckless disregard of the truth or falsity of the libelous matter.

administrative agency An agency, created and funded by Congress, whose members are appointed by the president and whose function is to administer specific legislation, such as law regulating broadcasting and advertising.

admonition to a jury Instructions from a judge to a trial jury to avoid talking to other people about the trial they are hearing and to avoid news broadcasts and newspaper or magazine stories that discuss the case or issues in the case.

Alien and Sedition Acts of 1798 Laws adopted by the Federalist Congress aimed at stopping criticism of the national government by Republican or Jeffersonian editors and politicians.

amici curiae "Friends of the court"; people who have no specific legal stake in a lawsuit but are allowed to appear on behalf of one of the parties in a case.

answer A document often filed by a defendant in response to a civil complaint that denies allegations and factual assertions.

appellant The party who initiates or takes the appeal of a case from one court to another.

appellate court A court that has both original and appellate jurisdiction; a court to which cases are removed for an appeal.

appellee The person in a case against whom the appeal is taken; that is, the party in the suit who is not making the appeal.

appropriation In the law of privacy, use of a person's name or likeness without consent for advertising or trade purposes.

arraignment The first official court appearance made by a criminal defendant at which he or she is formally charged with an offense and called on to plead guilty or not guilty to the charges contained in the state's indictment or information.

B

bait-and-switch advertising An illegal advertising strategy in which the seller baits customers by an advertisement with a low-priced model of a product but then switches customers who seek to buy the product to a much higher-priced model by telling them that the cheaper model does not work well or is no longer in stock.

bench-bar-press guidelines Informal agreements among lawyers, judges, police officials and journalists about what should and should not be published or broadcast about a criminal suspect or criminal case before a trial is held.

bond; bonding A large sum of money given by a publisher to a government to be held to ensure good behavior. Should the publisher violate a government rule, the bond is forfeited to the government, and the newspaper or magazine cannot be published again until a new bond is posted.

C

California Plan See *Missouri Plan*.

candidate access rule Section 312 of the Federal Communications Act, which forbids a broadcaster from instituting an across-the-board policy that denies all candidates for federal office the opportunity to use the station to further a political campaign.

case reporter A book containing a chronological collection of the opinions rendered by a particular court for cases that were decided by the court.

challenge for cause The request by a litigant in a criminal or civil case that a juror be dismissed for a specific reason.

change of veniremen Drawing a jury from a distant community in order to find jurors who have heard little or nothing about a criminal case or criminal defendant.

change of venue Moving a trial to a distant community in order to find jurors who have not read or viewed prejudicial publicity about the defendant.

Child Advertising Review Unit (CARU) The children's branch of the advertising industry's self-regulation program that evaluates child-directed advertising and promotional material in all media in order to advance truthfulness and accuracy and to protect minors' online privacy while visiting advertisers' Web sites.

citation The reference to a legal opinion contained in a case reporter that gives the name, volume number and page number where the opinion can be found. The year the opinion was rendered is also included in the citation.

civil complaint A written statement of the plaintiff's legal grievance, which normally initiates a civil suit.

Classified Information Procedures Act (CIPA) This federal law gives procedures for courts to apply in determining whether to protect and seal classified information that could jeopardize national security from unnecessary public disclosure at any stage of a criminal trial.

collateral bar rule A rule that bars someone who violates a court order from trying to defend this action by arguing that the court order was unconstitutional.

commercial speech doctrine The legal doctrine that states that truthful advertising for products and services that are not illegal is normally protected by the First Amendment to the U.S. Constitution.

common law Principles and rules of law that derive their authority not from legislation but from community usage and custom.

concurring opinion A written opinion by an appellate judge or justice in which the author agrees with the decision of the court but normally states reasons different from those in the court opinion as the basis for his or her decision.

consent A defense in both libel and invasion of privacy cases that provides that individuals who agree to the publication of a libelous story or the appropriation of their name cannot then maintain a lawsuit based on the libel or the appropriation.

consent order or decree A document in which an individual agrees to terminate a specific behavior, such as an advertising campaign, or to refrain from a specific action, such as making a certain advertising claim.

constitution A written outline of the organization of a government that provides for both the rights and responsibilities of various branches of the government and the limits of the power of the government.

contempt of court An act of disobedience or disrespect to a judge, which may be punished by a fine or jail sentence.

continuance The delay of a trial or hearing; that is, the trial is postponed.

copyright That body of law that protects the works created by writers, painters, photographers, performing artists, inventors and others who create intangible property.

copyright notice The words "Copyright © 2010 by Don R. Pember," for example, which indicate to a user that a work is copyrighted by the author or creator.

corrective advertising Rules established by the Federal Trade Commission that require an advertiser to correct the false impressions left by deceptive advertising in a certain percentage of future advertisements.

court's opinion The official opinion of an appellate court that states the reasons or rationale for a decision.

criminal libel A libel against the state, against the dead, or against a large, ill-defined group (such as a race) in which the state prosecutes the libel on behalf of the injured parties.

criminal prosecution; criminal action A legal action brought by the state against an individual or group of individuals for violating state criminal laws.

criminal syndicalism laws Laws that outlaw advocacy, planning or processes aimed at establishing the control over industry by workers or trade unions.

D

damages Money awarded to the winning party in a civil lawsuit.

defamation Any communication that holds a person up to contempt, hatred, ridicule or scorn and lowers the reputation of the individual defamed.

defendant The person against whom relief or recovery is sought in a civil lawsuit; the individual against whom a state criminal action is brought.

demurrer An allegation made by the defendant in a lawsuit that even if the facts as stated by the plaintiff are true, they do not state a sufficient cause for action.

de novo "New or fresh." In some instances a court of general jurisdiction will hear an appeal from a case from a lower court and simply retry the case. This is a de novo hearing.

dicta Remarks in a court opinion that do not speak directly to the legal point in question.

direct appeal The statutorily granted right of an aggrieved party to carry the appeal of a case to the U.S. Supreme Court. The high court can deny this right if the appeal lacks a substantial federal question.

dissenting opinion A written opinion by a judge or justice who disagrees with the appellate court's decision in a case.

E

en banc; sitting en banc A French term to describe all or most of the justices or judges of an appellate court sitting together to hear a case. This situation is the opposite of the more typical situation in which a small group (called a panel) of judges or justices in a particular court hears a case.

equal time rules Section 315 of the Federal Communications Act, which states that when broadcasters permit a legally qualified candidate for elective office to use their broadcasting facilities, all other legally qualified candidates for the same elective office must be given similar opportunity.

equity A system of jurisprudence, distinct from common law, in which courts are empowered to decide cases on the basis of equity or fairness and are not bound by the rigid precedents that often exist in common law.

Espionage Act A law adopted by Congress in 1917 that outlawed criticism of the U.S. government and its participation in World War I in Europe.

executive privilege An asserted common-law privilege of the president and other executives to keep presidential papers, records and other documents secret, even from Congress.

executive session A popular euphemism for a closed meeting held by a government body such as a city council or school board.

F

fair comment A libel defense that protects the publication of libelous opinion that focuses on the public activities of a person acting in a public sphere.

fair use A provision of the copyright law that permits a limited amount of copying of material that has been properly copyrighted.

false light That portion of privacy law that prohibits all publications or broadcasts that falsely portray an individual in an offensive manner.

Federal Communications Act The law, adopted in 1934, that is the foundation for the regulation of broadcasting in the United States.

Federal Communications Commission (FCC) A five-member body appointed by the president whose function is to administer the federal broadcasting and communications laws.

federal open-meetings law (Government in Sunshine Act) A federal law that requires approximately 50 federal agencies and bureaus to hold all their meetings in public, unless a subject under discussion is included within one of the 10 exemptions contained in the statute.

Federal Trade Commission (FTC) A five-member body appointed by the president whose function is to administer the federal laws relating to advertising, antitrust and many other business matters.

fighting words doctrine A legal doctrine that permits prior censorship of words that create a clear and present danger of inciting an audience to disorder or violence.

FOIA See *Freedom of Information Act*.

Freedom of Information Act (FOIA) A federal law that mandates that all the records created and kept by federal agencies in the executive branch of government must be open for public inspection and copying, except those records that fall into one of nine exempted categories listed in the statute.

FTC See *Federal Trade Commission*.

G

gag order A restrictive court order that prohibits all or some participants in a trial from speaking about a case or that stops publications and broadcasting stations from reporting on certain aspects of a case.

Government in Sunshine Act See *federal open-meetings law*.

grand jury A jury whose function is to determine whether sufficient evidence exists to issue an indictment or true bill charging an individual or individuals with a crime and to take such persons to trial. It is called a grand jury because it has more members than a petit, or trial, jury.

H

heckler's veto A situation that occurs when the audience's negative, adverse and sometimes violent reaction to the message conveyed by a peaceful speaker is allowed to control and silence the speaker. The duty, instead, should be on the government to protect the speaker rather than to allow a "veto" of the speech by the audience.

I

identification As used in a libel suit, the requirement that the plaintiff prove that at least one person believes that the subject of the libelous remarks is the plaintiff and not some other person.

impeachment A criminal proceeding against a public officer that is started by written "articles of impeachment" and followed by a trial. The House of Representatives, for example, can issue articles of impeachment against the president, who is then tried by the Senate.

indictment A written accusation issued by a grand jury charging that an individual or individuals have committed a specific crime and should be taken to trial.

information A written accusation issued by a public officer rather than by a grand jury charging that an individual or individuals have committed a specific crime and should be taken to trial.

intermediate scrutiny The standard of judicial review for content-neutral laws, such as time, place and manner regulations, that requires the government to prove that the regulation is content neutral; justified by a substantial interest; not a complete ban on communication; and narrowly tailored.

intrusion An invasion of privacy committed when one individual intrudes upon or invades the solitude of another individual.

invasion of privacy A civil tort that emerged in the early 20th century and contains four distinct categories of legal wrongs: appropriation, intrusion, publication of private facts and false light.

J

judgment of the court The final ruling of a court, which determines the outcome of a lawsuit. It is different from the verdict, which is the decision of the jury in a trial.

judicial decree A judgment of a court of equity; a declaration of the court announcing the legal consequences of the facts found to be true by the court.

judicial instructions A statement (often written) made by a judge to the members of a jury informing them about the law (as distinguished from the facts) in a case.

judicial review The power of a court to declare void and unenforceable any statute, rule or executive order that conflicts with an appropriate state constitution or the federal constitution.

jury A group of men and women called together in a trial court to determine the facts in a civil or criminal lawsuit. It is sometimes called a petit jury to distinguish it from a grand jury.

jury nullification The controversial power of a jury, despite its sworn duty under oath to apply a law as interpreted and instructed by a judge, to instead ignore (and thereby to "nullify") a law and decide a case according to its own conscience and sensibilities or, as the U.S. Supreme Court once put it, the ability of a jury to acquit "in the teeth of both law and facts."

L

legal brief; brief Written legal argument presented to the court by one or both parties in a lawsuit.

libel Published or broadcast communication that lowers the reputation of an individual by holding him or her up to contempt, ridicule or scorn.

licensing process The process by which a government gives a publisher or a broadcaster prior permission to print a newspaper or operate a broadcasting station. Revocation of a license can be used as punishment for failing to comply with the law or the wishes of the government. Licensing of the printed press in the United States ended in the 1720s.

litigant A party in a lawsuit; a participant in litigation.

litigated order An order issued by a government agency, like the FTC, requiring that a particular practice, such as a certain advertisement, be stopped.

M

memorandum order The announcement by an appellate court of a decision in a case that does not include a written opinion containing the rationale or reasons for the ruling.

misappropriation Taking what belongs to someone else and using it unfairly for one's own gain; for example, attempting to pass off a novel as part of a popular series of novels written and published by someone else. It is often called unfair competition.

Missouri Plan A system used in some states by which judges are appointed to the bench initially and then must stand for re-election on a ballot that permits citizens to vote to retain or not retain the judge.

N

National Advertising Division (NAD) Part of the Council of Better Business Bureaus, this industry organization evaluates and rules on the truthfulness of advertising claims. Complaints are normally brought to the NAD by competing advertisers.

National Advertising Review Board (NARB) The appeals body of a two-tier system created by the advertising community in 1971 for self-regulation that works closely with the National Advertising Division, the investigative body, in affiliation with the Better Business Bureau.

negligence A fault standard in libel and other tort law. Negligent behavior is normally described as an act or action that a reasonably prudent person or a reasonable individual would not have committed. In libel law, courts often measure negligence by asking whether the allegedly libelous material was the work of a person who exercised reasonable care in preparation of the story.

neutral reportage An emerging libel defense or privilege that states that it is permissible to publish or broadcast an accurate account of information about a public figure from a reliable source even when the reporter doubts the truth of the libelous assertion. The defense is not widely accepted.

nonjusticiable matter An issue that is inappropriate for a court to decide because the jurists lack the knowledge to make the ruling, because another branch of government has the responsibility to answer such questions, or because a court order in the matter would not likely be enforceable or enforced.

O

open-meetings laws State and federal statutes that require that certain meetings of public

agencies—normally in the executive branch of government—be open to the public and the press.

open-records laws State and federal statutes that require that certain records of public agencies—normally in the executive branch of government—be open for inspection and copying by the public and the press.

opinion The written statement issued by a court that explains the reasons for a judgment and states the rule of law in the case.

oral argument An oral presentation made to a judge or justices in which the litigants argue the merits of their case.

original jurisdiction Jurisdiction in the first instance, as distinguished from appellate jurisdiction. A court exercising original jurisdiction determines both the facts and the law in the case; courts exercising appellate jurisdiction may rule only on the law and the sufficiency of the facts as determined by a trial court.

overbreadth doctrine A statute or regulation will be declared unconstitutional if it sweeps up and bans a substantial amount of protected speech in the process of targeting unprotected speech; in other words, the doctrine prohibits the government from banning unprotected speech if a substantial amount of protected speech is prohibited or chilled in the same process.

P

per curiam opinion An unsigned court opinion. The author of the opinion is not known outside the court.

peremptory challenge A challenge without stated cause to remove a juror from a panel. Litigants are given a small number of such challenges in a lawsuit.

petitioner One who petitions a court to take an action; someone who starts a lawsuit, or carries an appeal to a higher court (appellant). This person is the opposite of a respondent, one who responds to a petition.

plaintiff An individual who initiates a civil lawsuit.

pleadings The written statements of the parties in a lawsuit that contain their allegations, denials and defenses.

plurality opinion A Supreme Court opinion in which five justices cannot agree on a single majority opinion—there is no opinion of the court—but that is joined by more justices than any other opinion in the case.

precedent An established rule of law set by a previous case. Courts should follow precedent when it is advisable and possible.

presumed damages Damages a plaintiff can get without proof of injury or harm.

pretrial hearing A meeting prior to a criminal trial at which attorneys for the state and for the defense make arguments before a judge on evidentiary questions—for example, whether a confession made by the defendant should be admitted as evidence at the trial. This type of hearing is sometimes called a suppression hearing.

Printers' Ink statute A model law drafted in 1911 to control false or misleading advertising. Most states adopted some version of this model in the early 20th century. Such laws are largely ineffective because they are not normally enforced.

prior restraint Prepublication censorship that forbids publication or broadcast of certain objectionable material, as opposed to punishment of a perpetrator after the material has been published or broadcast.

Privacy Act A federal statute that forbids the disclosure of specific material held by federal agencies on the grounds that its release could invade the privacy of the subject of the report or document.

public figure The designation for a plaintiff in a libel suit who has voluntarily entered a public controversy in an effort to influence public opinion in order to generate a resolution of the issue.

public official The designation of a plaintiff in a libel suit who is an elected public officer or is an appointed public officer who has or appears to have considerable responsibility for or control over the conduct of governmental affairs.

publication In libel law, exposing an allegedly libelous statement to one person in addition to the subject of the libel.

publication of private information In privacy law, publicizing embarrassing private information about an individual that is not of legitimate public concern. More than one person must see or hear this information.

puffery Often expansive hyperbole about a product that does not contain factual claims of merit. Normally, puffery is permitted by the law (e.g., "This is the best-looking automobile on the market today").

punitive damages Money damages awarded to a plaintiff in a lawsuit aimed not to compensate for harm to the injured party but to punish the defendant for his or her illegal conduct.

Q

qualified privilege In libel law, the privilege of the reporter (or any person) to publish a fair and accurate report of the proceedings of a public meeting or public document and be immune from lawsuit for the publication of libel uttered at the meeting or contained in the document.

R

Radio Act of 1912 The first federal broadcast law, which imposed only minimal regulation on the fledgling broadcast industry. Radio operators were required to have a license under this statute.

Radio Act of 1927 The first comprehensive national broadcast law, which provided the basic framework for the regulation of broadcast that was later adopted in the Federal Communications Act of 1934.

respondent The person who responds to a petition placed before a court by another person; the opposite of the petitioner. At the appellate level, the respondent is often called the appellee.

restrictive order A court order limiting the discussion of the facts in a criminal case both by participants in the case and by the press. See also *gag order*.

retraction In libel law, a statement published or broadcast that attempts to retract or correct previously published or broadcast libelous matter. A timely retraction will usually mitigate damages, and in some states that have retraction laws, plaintiffs must seek a retraction before beginning a lawsuit or they lose the opportunity to collect anything but special damages.

right of publicity An offshoot of privacy law that protects the right of persons to capitalize on their fame or notoriety for commercial or advertising purposes.

right of reply A little-used libel defense that declares as immune from a lawsuit a libelous remark made against an individual in reply to a previously published libelous remark made by that individual.

rule of four At least four justices of the U.S. Supreme Court must agree to hear a case before a petition for a writ of certiorari will be granted.

S

scienter Guilty knowledge. In many criminal prosecutions, the state must prove that the accused was aware of the nature of his or her behavior. In an obscenity case, for example, the state must normally show that the defendant was aware of the contents of the book he or she sold.

secret dockets The practice by some courts of keeping private and out of the view of both reporters and the general public the names and docket numbers of cases, thus keeping secret the very existence of the cases themselves.

Section 312 See *candidate access rule*.

Section 315 See *equal time rules*.

Sedition Act of 1918 An amendment to the Espionage Act adopted in the midst of World War I that severely limited criticism of the government and criticism of U.S. participation in the European war.

seditious libel Libeling the government; criticizing the government or government officers. It is sometimes called sedition.

sequestration of the jury Separating the jury from the community during a trial. Usually a jury is lodged at a hotel and members are required to eat together. In general, sequestration means to keep jurors away from other people. Exposure to news reports is also screened to shield jurors from information about the trial.

shield laws State statutes that permit reporters in some circumstances to shield the name of a confidential news source when questioned by a grand jury or in another legal forum.

single mistake rule In libel law, a rule that states that it is not libelous to accuse a professional person or businessperson of making a single mistake (e.g., "Dr. Pat Jones incorrectly diagnosed the patient's illness").

sitting en banc See *en banc*.

slander Oral defamation.

Smith Act A federal law adopted in 1940 that makes it illegal to advocate the violent overthrow of the government.

special damages Damages that can be awarded to a plaintiff in a lawsuit upon proof of specific monetary loss.

spectrum scarcity The notion, in the realm of the FCC's regulation of over-the-air broadcasting, that there are a finite number of frequencies on which to broadcast and that, in turn, there are more people who want to broadcast than there are available frequencies.

stare decisis "Let the decision stand." This concept is the operating principle in the common-law system and requires that judges follow precedent case law when making judgments.

state secrets privilege An executive branch privilege, often asserted during wartime, that allows the government to block a lawsuit if any information disclosed during it would adversely affect national security. Under this doctrine, the United States may prevent disclosure of information during a judicial proceeding if there is a "reasonable danger" the disclosure would expose military matters that, in the interest of national security, should not be divulged.

statute of limitations A law that requires that a legal action must begin within a specified period of time (usually one to three years for a civil case) after the legal wrong was committed.

statutes Laws adopted by legislative bodies.

statutory construction The process undertaken by courts to interpret or construe the meaning of statutes.

strict scrutiny The standard of judicial review for content-based statutes, requiring the government to prove that it has a compelling interest (an interest of the highest order) in regulating the speech at issue and that the means of serving that interest are narrowly tailored such that no more speech is restricted than is necessary to serve the allegedly compelling interest.

subpoena A court document that requires a witness to appear and testify or to produce documents or papers pertinent to a pending controversy.

substantiation A Federal Trade Commission rule that requires an advertiser to prove the truth of advertising claims made about a product or service.

summary judgment A judgment granted to a party in a lawsuit when the pleadings and other materials in the case disclose no material issue of fact between the parties, making it possible for the case to be decided on the basis of the law by the court. A summary judgment avoids a costly jury trial.

summary jury trial An abbreviated jury trial where jurors hear arguments but no witnesses are called and little evidence is presented. The jurors can issue an informal verdict, which can be used as the basis for a settlement of the case, thus avoiding a full-blown and costly trial.

survival statute A statute that permits an heir to continue to maintain a lawsuit if the plaintiff died after the suit was filed but before it was resolved.

symbolic speech doctrine The two-part judicial test used to determine when conduct rises to the level of "speech" within the meaning of the First Amendment. The person engaging in the conduct must intend to convey a particularized message with his or her conduct and there must be a substantial likelihood, under the circumstances in which the conduct takes place, that some members of the audience will understand the meaning that was intended.

T

time, place and manner restrictions or rules Rules, when justified by a substantial government interest, that can regulate the time, place and manner of speaking or publishing and the distribution of printed material.

tort A civil wrong not based on a contract, against the person or property of another. Typical torts are libel, invasion of privacy, trespass and assault.

trade libel Product disparagement, and not considered true libel; disparaging a product as opposed to the manufacturer or maker of the product.

trade regulation rules (TRRs) Rules adopted by the Federal Trade Commission that prohibit specific advertising claims about an entire class of products. For example, makers of fruit drinks that contain less than 10 percent fruit juice cannot advertise these products as fruit juice.

trespass Unlawful entry on another person's land or property.

trial court Normally the first court to hear a lawsuit. This court is the forum in which the facts are determined and the law is initially applied, as opposed to an appellate court, to which decisions are appealed.

U

unfair competition See *misappropriation*.

V

variable obscenity statutes A Supreme Court doctrine that permits states to prohibit the sale, distribution or exhibition of certain kinds of nonobscene matter to children, so long as these laws do not interfere with the accessibility of this material to adults.

verdict The decision of a trial jury based on the instructions given to it by the judge.

viewpoint-based discrimination The worst form of content-based regulation that exists when the government censors or regulates one particular viewpoint or side on a given topic or issue but does not censor or regulate another viewpoint or side on the same topic or issue. For instance, if the government censored pro-life speech on the topic of abortion but did not censor pro-choice speech on the topic of abortion, that would constitute viewpoint-based discrimination. Viewpoint-based discrimination by the government on speech is always unconstitutional.

void for vagueness doctrine A statute or regulation is unconstitutional if it is so vague that a person of reasonable and ordinary intelligence would not know, from looking at its terms, what speech is allowed and what speech is prohibited.

voir dire A preliminary examination the court makes of people chosen to serve as jurors in a trial. People can be challenged for cause or on the basis of a peremptory challenge by either side in the legal dispute.

W

warrant A written order, signed by a judge or magistrate, that may take many varieties, such as a search warrant that allows a law enforcement officer to search for and seize property or possessions that constitute evidence of the commission of a crime.

writ of certiorari A writ by which an appellant seeks the review of a case by the U.S. Supreme Court. When the writ is granted, the court will order the lower court to send up the record of the case for review.

Z

Zapple Rule A corollary to the equal time rules that states that when the supporters of a legally qualified candidate are given time on a radio or television broadcast, the supporters of all other legally qualified candidates for the same office must also be given equal opportunity.

TABLE OF CASES

INDEX

Page numbers followed by *n* indicate footnotes and page numbers in **boldface** indicate terms of Glossary.